SUPPLEMENTS

Teaching and Learning Supplements are a special part of this book. Each supplement is customer driven, user friendly, and fully integrated. No other financial statement analysis book offers instructors a greater wealth of instructional and learning resources.

- *Online Learning Center:* http://www.mhhe.com/subramanyam10e
- *Instructor's Solutions Manual*—on Online Learning Center
- *Test Bank*—on Online Learning Center
- *Chapter Lecture Slides*—PowerPoint version; on Online Learning Center
- *Case Material*—Primis custom case selection: www.mhhe.com/primis
- Financial Accounting Video Library Volumes 1 through 4: ISBN: 0-07-237616-3 EAN-978-0-07-237616-6

- *Prerequisite Skills Development: MBA Survival Kit CD,* ISBN: 0-07-304454-7 EAN-978-0-07-304454-5 *Essentials of Finance with Accounting CD,* ISBN: 0-07-256472-5 EAN-978-0-07-256472-3
- *Financial Shenanigans (casebook),* ISBN: 0-07-138626-2 EAN-978-0-07-138626-5
- *Customer Service*—1-800-338-3987

ORGANIZATION AND FOCUS

Financial statement analysis is part of the broader task of business analysis. Chapters 1 and 2 provide an overview and describe this broader task, including industry and strategy analysis. Chapters 3, 4, 5, and 6 focus on accounting analysis and the necessary adjustments to financial statements. Chapters 7, 8, 9, 10, and 11 focus on financial analysis, including prospective analysis. The following diagram reflects this organization and focus:

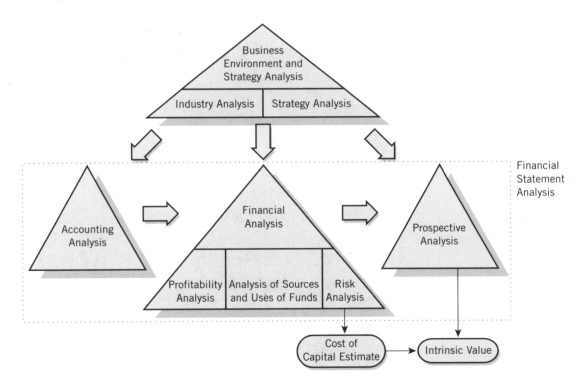

FINANCIAL
STATEMENT
ANALYSIS

TENTH EDITION

K. R. SUBRAMANYAM
University of Southern California

JOHN J. WILD
University of Wisconsin at Madison

McGraw-Hill Irwin

Boston   Burr Ridge, IL   Dubuque, IA   New York   San Francisco   St. Louis
Bangkok   Bogotá   Caracas   Kuala Lumpur   Lisbon   London   Madrid   Mexico City
Milan   Montreal   New Delhi   Santiago   Seoul   Singapore   Sydney   Taipei   Toronto

 **McGraw-Hill Irwin**

FINANCIAL STATEMENT ANALYSIS

Published by McGraw-Hill/Irwin, a business unit of The McGraw-Hill Companies, Inc., 1221 Avenue of the Americas, New York, NY, 10020. Copyright © 2009, 2007, 2004, 2001, 1998, 1993, 1989, 1983, 1978, 1974 by The McGraw-Hill Companies, Inc. All rights reserved. No part of this publication may be reproduced or distributed in any form or by any means, or stored in a database or retrieval system, without the prior written consent of The McGraw-Hill Companies, Inc., including, but not limited to, in any network or other electronic storage or transmission, or broadcast for distance learning.

Some ancillaries, including electronic and print components, may not be available to customers outside the United States.

This book is printed on acid-free paper.

2 3 4 5 6 7 8 9 0 QPD/QPD 0 9 8

ISBN   978-0-07-337943-2
MHID   0-07-337943-3

Editorial director: *Stewart Mattson*
Executive editor: *Richard T. Hercher, Jr.*
Editorial assistant: *Christina Lane*
Associate marketing manager: *Dean Karampelas*
Managing editor: *Lori Koetters*
Senior production supervisor: *Debra R. Sylvester*
Design coordinator: *Joanne Mennemeier*
Lead media project manager: *Cathy L. Tepper*
Cover design: *JoAnne Schopler*
Cover image: *Getty images*
Typeface: *10/12 Caslon Book BE*
Compositor: *ICC Macmillan Inc.*
Printer: *Quebecor World Dubuque Inc.*

Library of Congress Cataloging-in-Publication Data

Subramanyam, K. R.
    Financial statement analysis/K. R. Subramanyam, John J. Wild. – 10th ed.
        p. cm.
    Wild's name appears first on earlier editions.
    Includes index.
    ISBN-13: 978-0-07-337943-2 (alk. paper)
    ISBN-10: 0-07-337943-3 (alk. paper)
        1. Financial statements. I. Wild, John J. II. Title.
HF5681.B2W4963 2009
657'.3–dc22

                                                                2008008981

www.mhhe.com

DEDICATION

To my wife Jayasree, son Sujay, and our parents

—K. R. S.

To my wife Gail and children Kimberly, Jonathan, Stephanie, and Trevor

—J. J. W.

Welcome to the tenth edition of *Financial Statement Analysis*. This book is the product of extensive market surveys, chapter reviews, and correspondence with instructors and students. We are delighted that an overwhelming number of instructors, students, practitioners, and organizations agree with our approach to analysis of financial statements. This book forges a unique path in financial statement analysis, one that responds to the requests and demands of modern-day analysts. From the outset, a main goal in writing this book has been to respond to these needs by providing the most progressive, accessible, current, and user-driven textbook in the field. We are pleased that the book's reception in the United States and across the world has exceeded expectations.

Analysis of financial statements is exciting and dynamic. This book reveals keys to effective analysis to give readers a competitive advantage in an increasingly competitive marketplace. We know financial statements are relevant to the decisions of many individuals including investors, creditors, consultants, managers, auditors, directors, analysts, regulators, and employees. This book equips these individuals with the analytical skills necessary to succeed in business. Yet, experience in teaching this material tells us that to engage readers we must demonstrate the relevance of analysis. This book continually demonstrates that relevance with applications to real world companies. The book aims to benefit a broad readership, ranging from those with a simple curiosity in financial markets to those with years of experience in accounting and finance.

ORGANIZATION AND CONTENT

This book's organization accommodates different teaching styles. While the book is comprehensive, its layout allows instructors to choose topics and depth of coverage as desired. Readers are told in Chapter 1 how the book's topics are related to each other and how they fit within the broad discipline of financial statement analysis. The book is organized into three parts:

1. Analysis Overview

2. Accounting Analysis

3. Financial Analysis

ANALYSIS OVERVIEW

Chapters 1 and 2 are an overview of financial statement analysis. We introduce financial statement analysis as an integral part of the broader framework of business analysis. We examine the role of financial statement analysis in different types of business analysis such as equity analysis and credit analysis. We emphasize the understanding of business activities–planning, financing, investing, and operating. We describe the strategies underlying business activities and their effects on financial statements. We also emphasize the importance of accrual accounting for analysis and the relevance of conducting accounting analysis to make appropriate adjustments to financial statements before embarking on financial analysis. We apply several popular tools and techniques in analyzing and interpreting financial statements. An important and unique feature is our use of Colgate's annual report as a means to immediately engage readers and to instill relevance. The chapters are as follows:

- *Chapter 1.* We begin the analysis of financial statements by considering their relevance to business decisions. This leads to a focus on users, including what they need and how analysis serves them. We describe business activities and how they are reflected in financial statements. We also discuss both debt and equity valuation.

- *Chapter 2.* This chapter explains the nature and purpose of financial accounting and reporting, including the broader environment under which financial statements are prepared and used. We highlight the importance of accrual accounting in comparison to cash accounting. We also introduce the concept of income and discuss issues relating to fair value accounting. The importance and limitations of accounting data for analysis purposes are described along with the significance of conducting accounting analysis for financial analysis.

ACCOUNTING ANALYSIS

To aid in accounting analysis, Chapters 3 through 6 explain and analyze the accounting measurement and reporting practices underlying financial statements. We organize this analysis around financing (liabilities and equity), investing (assets), and operating (income) activities. We show how operating activities are outcomes of changes in investing and financing activities. We provide insights into income determination and asset and liability measurement. Most important, we discuss procedures and clues for the analysis and adjustment of financial statements to enhance their economic content for meaningful financial analysis. The four chapters are:

- *Chapter 3.* Chapter 3 begins the detailed analysis of the numbers reflecting financing activities. It explains how those numbers are the raw material for financial analysis. Our focus is on explaining, analyzing, interpreting, and adjusting those reported numbers to better reflect financing activities. Crucial topics include leases, pensions, off-balance-sheet financing, and shareholders' equity.

- *Chapter 4.* This chapter extends the analysis to investing activities. We show how to analyze and adjust (as necessary) numbers that reflect assets such as receivables, inventories, property, equipment, and intangibles. We explain what those numbers reveal about financial position and performance, including future performance.

- *Chapter 5.* Chapter 5 extends the analysis to special intercompany investing activities. We analyze intercorporate investments, including equity method investments and investments in derivative securities, and business combinations. Also, in an appendix we examine international investments and their reporting implications for financial statements.

- *Chapter 6.* This chapter focuses on analysis of operating activities and income. We discuss the concept and measurement of income as distinct from cash flows. We analyze accrual measures in yielding net income. Understanding recognition methods of both revenues and expenses is stressed. We analyze and adjust the income statement and its components, including topics such as restructuring charges, asset impairments, employee stock options, and accounting for income taxes.

FINANCIAL ANALYSIS

Chapters 7 through 11 examine the processes and methods of financial analysis (including prospective analysis). We stress the objectives of different users and describe analytical tools and techniques to meet those objectives. The means of analysis range from computation of ratio and cash flow measures to earnings prediction and equity valuation. We apply analysis tools that enable one to reconstruct the economic reality embedded in financial statements. We demonstrate how analysis tools and techniques enhance users' decisions–including company valuation and lending decisions. We show how financial statement analysis reduces uncertainty and increases confidence in business decisions. This section consists of five chapters and a Comprehensive Case:

- *Chapter 7.* This chapter begins our study of the application and interpretation of financial analysis tools. We analyze cash flow measures for insights into all business activities, with special emphasis on operating activities. Attention is directed at company and industry conditions when analyzing cash flows.

- *Chapter 8.* Chapter 8 emphasizes return on invested capital and explains variations in its measurement. Attention is directed at return on net operating assets and return on equity. We disaggregate both return measures and describe their relevance. We pay special attention to disaggregation of return on equity into operating and nonoperating components, as well as differences in margins and turnover across industries.

- *Chapter 9.* We describe forecasting and pro forma analysis of financial statements. We present forecasting of the balance sheet, income statement, and statement of cash flows with a detailed example. We then provide an example to link prospective analysis to equity valuation.

- *Chapter 10.* This chapter focuses on credit analysis, both liquidity and solvency. We first present analysis tools to assess liquidity–including accounting-based ratios, turnover, and operating activity measures. Then, we focus on capital structure and its implications for solvency. We analyze the importance of financial leverage and its effects on risk and return. Analytical adjustments are explained for tests of liquidity and solvency. We describe earnings-coverage measures and their interpretation.

- *Chapter 11.* The final chapter emphasizes earnings-based analysis and equity valuation. The earnings-based analysis focuses on earnings quality, earnings persistence, and earning power. Attention is directed at techniques for measuring and applying these concepts. Discussion of equity valuation focuses on forecasting accounting numbers and estimating company value.

- *Comprehensive Case.* This case is a comprehensive analysis of financial statements and related notes. We describe steps in analyzing the statements and the essential attributes of an analysis report. Our analysis is organized around key components of financial statement analysis: cash analysis, return on invested capital, asset utilization, operating performance, profitability, forecasting, liquidity, capital structure, and solvency.

KEY CHANGES IN THIS EDITION

Many readers provided useful suggestions through chapter reviews, surveys, and correspondence. We made the following changes in response to these suggestions:

- **Colgate Replaces Dell as a Featured Company.** Colgate provides a stable consumer products company to illustrate the analysis; it is also used to explain many business practices and is of interest to a broad audience. Campbell Soup is retained as another company for illustrations and assignments.

- **Discussion on Fair Value Accounting (Chapter 2).** The large-scale adoption of fair value accounting is one of the most significant events in the history of accounting. Fair value accounting will fundamentally change the way we analyze the financial statements. Chapter 2 provides a conceptual introduction to fair value accounting by incorporating some of the material from the recent standards on fair value accounting. The discussion also covers analysis implications of fair value accounting.

- **Discussion on Concept of Income (Chapter 2).** The discussion on income concepts has been streamlined and moved to Chapter 2. Covering income concepts in the overview part of the text will provide a nice framework to understand accounting analysis issues covered in Chapters 3 to 6.

- **Expanded Discussion of Accrual Accounting (Chapter 2).** Accrual accounting is the cornerstone of financial statement analysis. This edition includes further discussion to aid students in their analysis and interpretation of company fundamentals.

- **Streamlining and updating discussion on postretirement benefits (Chapter 3).** A revised Chapter 3 further streamlines the discussion relating to pensions and other postretirement employee benefits (OPEBs). In particular, the discussion in the chapter has been considerably shortened to give an overview of pension and OPEB accounting. A detailed discussion of pension accounting mechanics with the help of an integrated illustration is now provided separately in an appendix. The discussion has also been updated so as to incorporate the recent changes to pension and OPEB accounting with its analysis implications.

- **Equity Carve-Outs Included (Chapter 3).** Equity carve-outs, spin-offs, and split-offs have increased in frequency as companies seek to unlock shareholder value. Chapter 3 includes a new section to introduce the accounting for and interpretation of them.

- **Investments in Marketable and Derivative Securities (Chapter 5).** This edition consolidates all securities investments in one chapter. The discussion has been updated to incorporate some of the latest fair value–based standards. The analysis of foreign currency disclosures is streamlined and placed in an appendix to Chapter 5.

- **Fair Value Option (Chapter 5).** Companies are now allowed the option of measuring financial assets and liabilities on a fair value basis. Chapter 5 now includes a separate section regarding the fair value option with its analysis implications.

- **Employee Stock Options Updated (Chapter 6).** The discussion on employee stock options has been streamlined and updated to incorporate the latest accounting pronouncements.

- **Income Tax Accounting Streamlined (Chapter 6).** The discussion on income tax accounting and analysis has been thoroughly rewritten and streamlined.

- **Comprehensive Case Expanded to Include a Revised Disaggregation of Return on Equity.** Analysis framework in Chapter 8 is extended to the comprehensive case to reinforce the importance of the operating and nonoperating distinction for financial statement analysis.

- **EOC Material Streamlined and Updated.** End-of-chapter material has been streamlined and updated to reflect changes to the text.

- **Book Is Focused and Practical.** The authors continue to emphasize a streamlined and concise book with an abundance of practical applications and directions for analysis.

INNOVATIVE PEDAGOGY

We believe people learn best when provided with motivation and structure. The pedagogical features of this book facilitate those learning goals. Features include:

- **Analysis Feature.** An article featuring an actual company launches each chapter to highlight the relevance of that chapter's materials. In-chapter analysis is performed on that company. Experience shows readers are motivated to learn when their interests are piqued.

- **Analysis Objectives.** Chapters open with key analysis objectives that highlight important chapter goals.

- **Analysis Linkages.** Linkages launch each chapter to establish bridges between topics and concepts in prior, current, and upcoming chapters. This roadmap–titled *A Look Back, A Look at This Chapter,* and *A Look Ahead*–provides structure for learning.

- **Analysis Preview.** A preview kicks off each chapter by describing its content and importance.

- **Analysis Viewpoint.** Multiple role-playing scenarios in each chapter are a unique feature that show the relevance of financial statement analysis to a wide assortment of decision makers.

- **Analysis Excerpt.** Numerous excerpts from practice–including annual report disclosures, newspaper clippings, and press releases–illustrate key points and topics. Excerpts reinforce the relevance of the analysis and engage the reader.

- **Analysis Research.** Multiple, short boxes in each chapter discuss current research relevant to the analysis and interpretation of financial statements.

- **Analysis Annotations.** Each chapter includes marginal annotations. These are aimed at relevant, interesting, and topical happenings from business that bear on financial statement analysis.

- **Analysis Feedback.** End-of-chapter assignments include numerous traditional and innovative assignments augmented by several cases that draw on actual financial statements such as those from American Airlines, Best Buy, Campbell Soup, Cendant, Citicorp, Coca-Cola, Colgate, Delta Airlines, Kimberly-Clark, Kodak, Marsh Supermarkets, Merck, Microsoft, Newmont Mining, Philip Morris, Quaker Oats, Sears, TYCO, Toys "R" Us, United Airlines, Walt Disney, and Wal-Mart. Assignments are of four types: *Questions, Exercises, Problems,* and *Cases.* Each assignment is titled to reflect its purpose–many require critical thinking, communication skills, interpretation, and decision making. This book stands out in both its diversity and number of end-of-chapter assignments. Key check figures are selectively printed in the margins.

- **Analysis Focus Companies.** Entire financial statements of two companies–Colgate and Campbell Soup–are reproduced in the book and used in numerous assignments. Experience shows that frequent use of annual reports heightens interest and learning. These reports include notes and other financial information.

TARGET AUDIENCE

This best-selling book is targeted to readers of all business-related fields. Students and professionals alike find the book beneficial in their careers as they are rewarded with an understanding of both the techniques of analysis and the expertise to apply them. Rewards also include the skills to successfully recognize business opportunities and the knowledge to capitalize on them.

The book accommodates courses extending over one quarter, one semester, or two quarters. It is suitable for a wide range of courses focusing on analysis of financial statements, including upper-level "capstone" courses. The book is used at both the undergraduate and graduate levels, as well as in professional programs. It is the book of choice in modern financial statement analysis education.

SUPPLEMENT PACKAGE

This book is supported by a wide array of supplements aimed at the needs of both students and instructors of financial statement analysis. They include:

- **Book Website.** [http://www.mhhe.com/subramanyam10e] The Web is increasingly important for financial statement analysis. This book has its own dedicated Online Learning Center, which is an excellent starting point for analysis resources. The site includes links to key websites as well as support materials for both instructors and students.

- **Instructor's Solutions Manual.** An Instructor's Solutions Manual contains complete solutions for assignments. It is carefully prepared, reviewed, and checked for accuracy. The Manual contains chapter summaries, analysis objectives, and other helpful materials. It has transition notes to instructors for ease in moving from the ninth to the tenth edition. It is available on the Online Learning Center.

- **Test Bank.** The Test Bank contains a variety of test materials with varying levels of difficulty. All materials are carefully reviewed for consistency with the book and thoroughly examined for accuracy. It is available on the Online Learning Center.

- **Chapter Lecture Slides.** A set of PowerPoint slides is available for each chapter. They can be used to augment the instructor's lecture materials or as an aid to students in supplementing in-class lectures. It is available on the Online Learning Center.

- **Casebook Support.** Some instructors augment the book with additional case materials. While practical illustrations and case materials are abundant in the text, more are available. These include (1) *Primis* custom case selection [www.mhhe.com/primis] and (2) *Financial Shenanigans*–ISBN: 978-0-07-138626-5(0-07-138626-2).

- **Financial Accounting Video Library.** The Financial Accounting Video Library includes short, action-oriented videos for lively classroom discussion of topics, including disclosure practices, accounting quality, the role of International Accounting Standards, and the impact of regulators. (ISBN 978-0-07-237616-6[0-07-237616-3])

- **Prerequisite Skills Development.** There are materials to aid readers in understanding basic accounting and finance concepts: (1) *MBA Survival Kit–Accounting Interactive CD*–ISBN: 978-0-07-304454-5(0-07-304454-7), and (2) *Essentials of Finance with Accounting Review CD*–ISBN: 978-0-07-256472-3(0-07-256472-5).

- **Customer Service.** 1-800-338-3987 or access http://www.mhhe.com

ACKNOWLEDGMENTS

We are thankful for the encouragement, suggestions, and counsel provided by many instructors, professionals, and students in writing this book. It has been a team effort and we recognize the contributions of all these individuals. They include the following professionals who read portions of this book in various forms:

Kenneth Alterman
(Standard & Poor's)

Michael Ashton
(Ashton Analytics)

Clyde Bartter
(Portfolio Advisory Co.)

Laurie Dodge
(Interbrand Corp.)

Vincent C. Fung
(PricewaterhouseCoopers)

Hyman C. Grossman
(Standard & Poor's)

Richard Huff
(Standard & Poor's)

Michael A. Hyland
(First Boston Corp.)

Robert J. Mebus
(Standard & Poor's)

Robert Mednick
(Arthur Andersen)

William C. Norby
(Financial Analyst)

David Norr
(First Manhattan Corp.)

Thornton L. O'Glove
(Quality of Earnings Report)

Paul Rosenfield
(AICPA)

George B. Sharp
(CITIBANK)

Fred Spindel
(PricewaterhouseCoopers)

Frances Stone
(Merrill Lynch & Co.)

Jon A. Stroble
(Jon A. Stroble & Associates)

Jack L. Treynor
(Treynor-Arbit Associates)

Neil Weiss
(Jon A. Stroble & Associates)

Gerald White
(Grace & White, Inc.)

We also want to recognize the following instructors and colleagues who provided valuable comments and suggestions for this edition and past editions of the book:

Rashad Abdel-Khalik
(University of Illinois)

M. J. Abdolmohammadi
(Bentley College)

Robert N. Anthony
(Harvard University)

Hector R. Anton
(New York University)

Terry Arndt
(Central Michigan University)

Florence Atiase
(University of Texas at Austin)

Dick Baker
(Northern Illinois University)

Steven Balsam
(Temple University)

Mark Bauman
(University of Northern Iowa)

William T. Baxter
(CUNY–Baruch)

William Belski
(Virginia Tech)

Martin Benis
(CUNY–Baruch)

Shyam Bhandari
(Bradley University)

Fred Bien
(Franklin University)

John S. Bildersee
(New York University)

Linda Bowen
(University of North Carolina–Chapel Hill)

Vince Brenner
(Louisiana State University)

Abraham J. Briloff
(CUNY–Baruch)

Gary Bulmash
(American University)

Joseph Bylinski
(University of North Carolina)

Douglas Carmichael
(CUNY–Baruch)

Benny R. Copeland
(University of North Texas)

Harry Davis
(CUNY–Baruch)

Peter Lloyd Davis
(CUNY–Baruch)

Wallace N. Davidson III
(University of North Texas)

Timothy P. Dimond
(Northern Illinois University)

Peter Easton
(University of Notre Dame)

James M. Emig
(Villanova University)

Calvin Engler
(Iona College)

Karen Foust
(Tulane University)

Thomas J. Frecka
(University of Notre Dame)

WaQar I. Ghani
(Saint Joseph's University)

Don Giacomino
(Marquette University)

Edwin Grossnickle
(Western Michigan University)

Peter M. Gutman
(CUNY–Baruch)

J. Larry Hagler
(East Carolina University)

James William Harden
(University of North Carolina at Greensboro)

Frank Heflin
(Purdue University)

Steven L. Henning
(Southern Methodist University)

Yong-Ha Hyon
(Temple University)

Henry Jaenicke
(Drexel University)

Keith Jakob
(University of Montana)

Kenneth H. Johnson
(Georgia Southern University)

Janet Kimbrell
(Oklahoma State University)

Jo Koehn
(Central Missouri State)

Homer Kripke
(New York University)

Linda Lange
(Regis University)

Russ Langer

Barbara Leonard
(Loyola University, Chicago)

Steven Lillien
(CUNY–Baruch)

Ralph Lim
(Sacred Heart University)

Thomas Lopez
(Georgia State University)

Mostafa Maksy
(Northeastern Illinois University)

Brenda Mallouk
(University of Toronto)

Ann Martin
(University of Colorado–Denver)

Martin Mellman
(Hofstra University)

Krishnagopal Menon
(Boston University)

William G. Mister
(Colorado State University)

Stephen Moehrle
(University of Missouri–St. Louis)

Belinda Mucklow
(University of Wisconsin)

Sia Nassiripour
(William Paterson University)

Hugo Nurnberg
(CUNY-Baruch)

Per Olsson
(Duke University)

Paruchara Pacharn
(SUNY–Buffalo)

Zoe-Vonna Palmrose
(University of Southern California)

Stephen Penman
(Columbia University)

Marlene Plumlee
(University of Utah)

Sirapat Polwitoon
(Susquehanna University)

Tom Porter
(NERA Economic Consulting)

Eric Press
(Temple University)

Chris Prestigiacomo
(University of Missouri at Columbia)

Larry Prober
(Rider University)

William Ruland
(CUNY–Baruch)

Stanley C. W. Salvary
(Canisius College)

Phil Shane
(University of Colorado at Boulder)

Don Shannon
(DePaul University)

Ken Shaw
(University of Missouri)

Lenny Soffer
(University of Illinois–Chicago)

Pamela Stuerke
(University of Rhode Island)

Karen Taranto
(George Washington University)

Gary Taylor
(University of Alabama)

Rebecca Todd
(Boston University)

Bob Trezevant
(University of Southern California)

John M. Trussel
(Penn State University at Harrisburg)

Joseph Weintrop
(CUNY–Baruch)

Jerrold Weiss
(Lehman College)

J. Scott Whisenant
(University of Houston)

Kenneth L. Wild
(University of London)

Richard F. Williams
(Wright State University)

Philip Wolitzer
(Marymount Manhattan College)

Christine V. Zavgren

Stephen Zeff
(Rice University)

We acknowledge permission to use materials adapted from examinations of the Association for Investment Management and Research (AIMR) and the American Institute of Certified Public Accountants (AICPA). Also, we are fortunate to work with an outstanding team of McGraw-Hill/Irwin professionals, extending from editorial to marketing to sales.

Special thanks go to our families for their patience, understanding, and inspiration in completing this book, and we dedicate the book to them.

K. R. Subramanyam
John J. Wild

As a team, K. R. Subramanyam and John Wild provide a blend of skills uniquely suited to writing a financial statement analysis and valuation textbook. They combine award-winning teaching and research with a broad view of accounting and analysis gained through years of professional and teaching experiences.

K. **R. Subramanyam** is the KPMG Foundation Professor of Accounting at the Marshall School of Business, University of Southern California. He received his MBA from the Indian Institute of Management and his PhD from the University of Wisconsin. Prior to obtaining his PhD, he worked as an international management consultant and as a financial planner for General Foods.

Professor Subramanyam has taught courses in financial statement analysis, financial accounting, and managerial accounting at both the graduate and undergraduate levels. He is a highly regarded teacher, recognized for his commitment and creativity in business education. His course in financial statement analysis is one of the most popular courses in the Marshall School of Business. Professor Subramanyam is a National Talent Scholar, a member of Beta Alpha Psi, and a Deloitte and Touche National Fellow. For many years he was a Leventhal Research Fellow at the Marshall School of Business. Professor Subramanyam is actively involved in several national and international organizations, such as the American Accounting Association. He has served these organizations in several capacities, including as a member of the Committee to Identify Seminal Contributions to Accounting and as program coordinator for national conferences.

Professor Subramanyam's research interests span a wide range, including financial accounting standards, the economic effects of financial statements, implications of earnings management, financial statement analysis and valuation, financial regulation and auditing issues. Professor Subramanyam is a prolific and highly cited author. His articles appear in leading academic journals such as *The Accounting Review, Journal of Accounting and Economics, Journal of Accounting Research, Contemporary Accounting Research, Review of Accounting Studies, Journal of Accounting and Public Policy,* and *Journal of Business Finance and Accounting.* Professor Subramanyam has won both national and international research awards, including the *Notable Contribution to the Auditing Literature* from the American Accounting Association. Professor Subramanyam serves on the editorial boards of *The Accounting Review, Contemporary Accounting Research* and *Auditing: A Journal of Practice and Theory.*

Professor Subramanyam's work has also had wide impact outside the academe. For example, his work on auditor independence was prominently featured in congressional testimony. In addition, his research has been widely covered by the international media that includes, among others, *The Wall Street Journal, The Economist, BusinessWeek, Barrons, Los Angeles Times, Chicago Tribune, Boston Globe, Sydney Morning Herald, The Atlanta Journal-Constitution, Orange County Register, Bloomberg.com,* and *Reuters.*

John **J. Wild** is professor of accounting and the Robert and Monica Beyer Distinguished Professor at the University of Wisconsin at Madison. He previously held appointments at Michigan State University and the University of Manchester in England. He received his BBA, MS, and PhD from the University of Wisconsin.

Professor Wild teaches courses in accounting and analysis at both the undergraduate and graduate levels. He has received the Mabel W. Chipman Excellence-in-Teaching Award, the Departmental Excellence-in-Teaching Award, and the Teaching Excellence Award from the 2003 and the 2005 MBA graduation classes at the University of Wisconsin. He also received the Beta Alpha Psi and Salmonson Excellence-in-Teaching Award from Michigan State University. Professor Wild is a past KPMG Peat Marwick National Fellow and is a prior recipient of fellowships from the American Accounting Association and the Ernst & Young Foundation.

Professor Wild is an active member of the American Accounting Association and its sections. He has served on several committees of these organizations, including the Outstanding Accounting Educator Award, Wildman Award, National Program Advisory, Publications, and Research Committees. Professor Wild is author of the best-selling book, *Financial Accounting*, published by McGraw-Hill/Irwin. His many research articles on financial accounting and analysis appear in *The Accounting Review, Journal of Accounting Research, Journal of Accounting and Economics, Contemporary Accounting Research, Journal of Accounting, Auditing & Finance, Journal of Accounting and Public Policy, Journal of Business Finance and Accounting, Auditing: A Journal of Theory and Practice,* and other accounting and business periodicals. He is past associate editor of *Contemporary Accounting Research* and has served on editorial boards of several respected journals, including *The Accounting Review* and the *Journal of Accounting and Public Policy.*

CONTENTS IN BRIEF

CONTENTS

FINANCIAL
STATEMENT
ANALYSIS

1

OVERVIEW OF FINANCIAL STATEMENT ANALYSIS

A LOOK AT THIS CHAPTER •

We begin our analysis of financial statements by considering its relevance in the broader context of business analysis. We use Colgate Palmolive Co. as an example to help us illustrate the importance of assessing financial performance in light of industry and economic conditions. This leads us to focus on financial statement users, their information needs, and how financial statement analysis addresses those needs. We describe major types of business activities and how they are reflected in financial statements. A preliminary financial analysis illustrates these important concepts.

A LOOK AHEAD >

Chapter 2 describes the financial reporting environment and the information included in financial statements. Chapters 3 through 6 deal with accounting analysis, which is the task of analyzing, adjusting, and interpreting accounting numbers that make up financial statements. Chapters 7 through 11 focus on mastering the tools of financial statement analysis and valuation. A comprehensive financial statement analysis follows Chapter 11.

ANALYSIS OBJECTIVES

- Explain business analysis and its relation to financial statement analysis.

- Identify and discuss different types of business analysis.

- Describe component analyses that constitute business analysis.

- Explain business activities and their relation to financial statements.

- Describe the purpose of each financial statement and linkages between them.

- Identify the relevant analysis information beyond financial statements.

- Analyze and interpret financial statements as a preview to more detailed analyses.

- Apply several basic financial statement analysis techniques.

- Define and formulate some basic valuation models.

- Explain the purpose of financial statement analysis in an efficient market.

Something to Smile About?

NEW YORK, NY–Colgate has been creating smiles the world over for the past 200 years. However, the smiles are not limited to users of its immensely popular toothpaste. Colgate's financial and stock price performance during the past decade has given plenty for its shareholders to smile about. Stock price has more than doubled over this period, generating average returns for Colgate's stockholders to the tune of about 12.5% per year, almost double that on the S&P 500 over a comparable period. Earnings have doubled even though shareholder capital actually declined, indicating that the earnings growth has been fueled by improving productivity with which Colgate uses its capital.

One of the world's oldest corporations, Colgate today is a truly global company, with a presence in almost 200 countries and sales revenues of above $12 billion. Its brand name–most famously associated with its toothpaste–is one of the oldest and best recognized brands in the world. In fact, the brand has been so successful that "Colgate" has become a generic word for toothpaste in many countries, spawning imitations over which the company has been engaged in bitter legal disputes.

Colgate leverages the popularity of its brand as well as its international presence and implements a business strategy that focuses on attaining market leadership in certain key product categories and markets where its strengths lie. For example, Colgate controls almost a third of the world's toothpaste market where it has been gaining market share in the recent past! Such market leadership allows it pricing power in the viciously competitive consumer products' markets. A total consumer orientation, constant innovation, and relentless quest for improving cost efficiencies have been Colgate's hallmarks to success.

Another key feature in Colgate's strategy has been its extremely generous dividend policy; over the past 10 years Colgate has paid out almost $11 billion to its shareholders through cash dividends and stock buybacks, which is significantly more than the money it has raised from its shareholder's in its entire history! Colgate's dividend policy reflects its management philosophy of staying focused on generating superior shareholder returns rather than pursuing a strategy of misguided growth. Small, in Colgate's case, has certainly been beautiful!

Source: Company's 10 Ks.

PREVIEW OF CHAPTER 1

Financial statement analysis is an integral and important part of the broader field of business analysis. **Business analysis** is the process of evaluating a company's economic prospects and risks. This includes analyzing a company's business environment, its strategies, and its financial position and performance. Business analysis is useful in a wide range of business decisions such as whether to invest in equity or in debt securities, whether to extend credit through short- or long-term

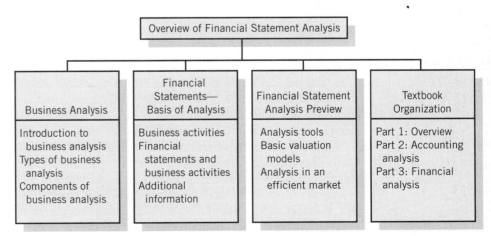

loans, how to value a business in an initial public offering (IPO), and how to evaluate restructurings including mergers, acquisitions, and divestitures. **Financial statement analysis** is the application of analytical tools and techniques to general-purpose financial statements and related data to derive estimates and inferences useful in business analysis. Financial statement analysis reduces reliance on hunches, guesses, and intuition for business decisions. It decreases the uncertainty of business analysis. It does not lessen the need for expert judgment but, instead, provides a systematic and effective basis for business analysis. This chapter describes business analysis and the role of financial statement analysis. The chapter also introduces financial statements and explains how they reflect underlying business activities. We introduce several tools and techniques of financial statement analysis and apply them in a preliminary analysis of Colgate. We also show how business analysis helps us understand Colgate's prospects and the role of business environment and strategy for financial statement analysis.

........BUSINESS ANALYSIS

This section explains business analysis, describes its practical applications, identifies separate analyses that make up business analysis, and shows how it all fits in with financial statement analysis.

Introduction to Business Analysis

Financial statement analysis is part of business analysis. Business analysis is the evaluation of a company's prospects and risks for the purpose of making business decisions. These business decisions extend to equity and debt valuation, credit risk assessment, earnings predictions, audit testing, compensation negotiations, and countless other decisions. Business analysis aids in making informed decisions by helping structure the decision task through an evaluation of a company's business environment, its strategies, and its financial position and performance.

To illustrate what business analysis entails we turn to Colgate. Much financial information about Colgate–including its financial statements, explanatory notes, and selected news about its past performance–is communicated in its *annual report* reproduced in Appendix A near the end of this book. The annual report also provides qualitative information about the Colgate's strategies and future plans, typically in the Management Discussion and Analysis, or MD&A, section.

An initial step in business analysis is to evaluate a company's business environment and strategies. We begin by studying Colgate's business activities and learn that it is a leading global consumer products company. Colgate has several internationally well-known brands that are primarily in the oral, personal, and home care markets. The company has brands in markets as varied as dental care, soaps and cosmetics, household cleaning products, and pet care and nutrition. The other remarkable feature of Colgate is its comprehensive global presence. More than 70% of Colgate's revenues are derived from international operations. The company operates in 200 countries around the world, with equal presence in every major continent! Exhibit 1.1 identifies Colgate's operating divisions.

Colgate's strengths are the popularity of its brands and the highly diversified nature of its operations. These strengths, together with the static nature of demand for consumer products, give rise to Colgate's financial stability, thereby reducing risk for its equity and debt investors. For example, Colgate's stock price weathered the bear market of 2000–2002, when the S&P 500 shed almost half its value (see Exhibit 1.2). The static nature of demand in the consumer products' markets, however, is a double-edged

Colgate's Operating Divisions: Oral, Personal, and Home Care   *Exhibit 1.1*

	($ MILLION)		
	Net Sales	Operating Profit	Total Assets
North America*	$ 2,591	$ 550	$2,006
Latin America	3,020	873	2,344
Europe/South Pacific	2,952	681	2,484
Greater/South Pacific	2,006	279	1,505
Total oral, personal, home care	$10,569	$2,383	$8,339
Pet nutrition†	$ 1,669	$ 448	$ 647
Total operating divisions	$12,238	$2,831	$8,986
Corporate	N/A	($ 670)	$ 152
Total for company	$12,238	$2,161	$9,138

*North America net sales in the United States for oral, personal, and home care were $2,211, $2,124, and $2,000 in 2006, 2005, and 2004, respectively.

†Net sales in the United States for pet nutrition were $898, $818, and $781 in 2006, 2005, and 2004, respectively.

Colgate Stock Price Growth versus S&P Growth   *Exhibit 1.2*

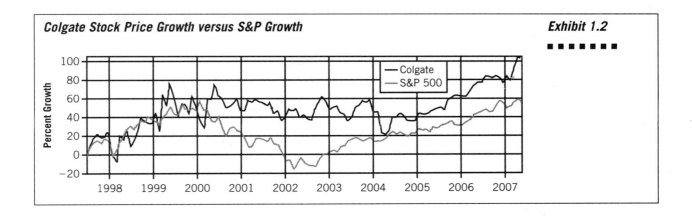

sword: while reducing sales volatility, it also fosters fierce competition for market share. Colgate has been able to thrive in this competitive environment by following a carefully defined business strategy that develops and increases market leadership positions in certain key product categories and markets that are consistent with the company's core strengths and competencies and through relentless innovation. For example, the company uses its valuable consumer insights to develop successful new products regionally, which are then rolled out on a global basis. Colgate also focuses on areas of the world where economic development and increasing consumer spending provides opportunities for growth. Despite these strategic overtures, Colgate's profit margins are continuously squeezed by competition. The company was thus forced to initiate a major restructuring program in 2004 to reduce costs by trimming its workforce by 12% and shedding several unprofitable product lines.

Colgate's brand leadership together with its international diversification and sensible business strategies have enabled it to become one of the most successful consumer products' companies in the world. In 2006, Colgate earned $1.35 billion on sales revenues of more than $12 billion. Its operating profit margin was in excess of 10% of sales, which translates to a return on assets of above 15%, suggesting that Colgate is fairly profitable. Colgate's small equity base, however, leverages its return on equity in 2006 to a spectacular 98%, one of the highest of all publicly traded companies. The stock market has richly rewarded Colgate's excellent financial performance and low risk: the company's price-to-earnings and its price-to-book ratios are, respectively, 26 and 23, and its stock price has doubled during the past 10 years.

In our previous discussion, we reference a number of financial performance measures, such as operating profit margins, return on assets, and return on equity. We also refer to certain valuation ratios such as price-to-earnings and price-to-book, which appear to measure how the stock market rewards Colgate's performance. Financial statements provide a rich and reliable source of information for such financial analysis. The statements reveal how a company obtains its resources (financing), where and how those resources are deployed (investing), and how effectively those resources are deployed (operating profitability). Many individuals and organizations use financial statements to improve business decisions. Investors and creditors use them to assess company prospects for investing and lending decisions. Boards of directors, as investor representatives, use them to monitor managers' decisions and actions. Employees and unions use financial statements in labor negotiations. Suppliers use financial statements in setting credit terms. Investment advisors and information intermediaries use financial statements in making buy-sell recommendations and in credit rating. Investment bankers use financial statements in determining company value in an IPO, merger, or acquisition.

To show how financial statement information helps in business analysis, let's turn to the data in Exhibit 1.3. These data reveal that over the past 10 years, Colgate's earnings

---

Exhibit 1.3   **Colgate's Summary Financial Data (in billions, except per share data)**

	2006	2005	2004	2003	2002	2001	2000	1999	1998	1997	1996
Net sales	$12.24	$11.40	$10.58	$9.90	$9.29	$9.08	$9.00	$8.80	$8.66	$8.79	$8.49
Gross profit	7.21	6.62	6.15	5.75	5.35	5.11	5.00	4.84	4.62	4.56	4.52
Operating income	1.46	1.44	1.41	1.51	1.39	1.28	1.19	1.09	0.99	0.90	0.80
Net income	1.35	1.35	1.33	1.42	1.29	1.15	1.06	0.94	0.85	0.74	0.64
Restructuring charge (after tax)	0.29	0.15	0.06	0.04							
Total assets	9.14	8.51	8.67	7.48	7.09	6.99	7.25	7.42	7.69	7.54	7.90
Total liabilities	7.73	7.16	7.43	6.59	6.74	6.14	5.78	5.59	5.60	5.36	5.89
Long-term debt	2.72	2.92	3.09	2.68	3.21	2.81	2.54	2.24	2.30	2.34	2.79
Shareholders' equity	1.41	1.35	1.25	0.89	0.35	0.85	1.47	1.83	2.09	2.18	2.03
Treasury stock at cost	8.07	7.58	6.97	6.50	6.15	5.20	4.04	3.06	2.33	1.68	1.47
Basic earnings per share	2.61	2.54	2.45	2.60	2.33	2.02	1.81	1.57	1.40	1.22	1.05
Cash dividends per share	1.25	1.11	0.96	0.90	0.72	0.68	0.63	0.59	0.55	0.53	0.47
Closing stock price	65.24	54.85	51.16	50.05	52.43	57.75	64.55	65.00	46.44	36.75	23.06
Shares outstanding (billions)	0.51	0.52	0.53	0.53	0.54	0.55	0.57	0.58	0.59	0.59	0.59

increased by 111%. This earnings growth was driven by both a 44% increase in revenues and an increase of approximately 30% in operating profit margin. Thus, Colgate has grown earnings rapidly, despite modest growth in revenues, through increased margins arising from cost reduction. Colgate pays generous dividends: over the past 10 years it has paid more than $4 billion in cash dividends and almost $7 billion through stock repurchases (see movement in treasury stock). Therefore, Colgate has returned around $11 billion to its shareholders over the past 10 years, which comprises most of its earnings during this period. By paying out most of its earnings, Colgate has been able to maintain a small equity base–shareholder's equity actually *decreased* over this period. All this makes Colgate's earnings growth story even more compelling: the company has grown earnings without increasing its invested capital. Its return on equity has consequently exploded from 35% in 1997 to 98% in 2006. One downside of maintaining a small equity base is Colgate's high leverage–for example, the company's ratio of total liabilities to equity is above 5. However, the extremely stable nature of Colgate's financial performance affords such structuring of the balance sheet to leverage returns for its equity shareholders.

Further examination of Exhibit 1.3 reveals that much of Colgate's earnings growth over the past decade has occurred primarily in the first seven years. The most recent three years' performance has been fairly lackluster. After dropping slightly in 2004, earnings have since remained stagnant and Colgate has been able to achieve modest growth in earnings per share over this period only by reducing its equity base. However, this earnings stagnation is partly because of costs related to Colgate's restructuring program that commenced in 2004; earnings grew 12% over the last three years after removing the costs related to restructuring activities.

Is the summary financial information sufficient to use as a basis for deciding whether or not to invest in Colgate's stock or in making other business decisions? The answer is clearly no. To make informed business decisions, it is important to evaluate Colgate's business activities in a more systematic and complete manner. For example, equity investors desire answers to the following types of questions before deciding to buy, hold, or sell Colgate stock:

- What are Colgate's future business prospects? Are Colgate's markets expected to grow? What are Colgate's competitive strengths and weaknesses? What strategic initiatives has Colgate taken, or does it plan to take, in response to business opportunities and threats?
- What is Colgate's earnings potential? What is its recent earnings performance? How sustainable are current earnings? What are the "drivers" of Colgate's profitability? What estimates can be made about earnings growth?
- What is Colgate's current financial condition? What risks and rewards does Colgate's financing structure portray? Are Colgate's earnings vulnerable to variability? Does Colgate possess the financial strength to overcome a period of poor profitability?
- How does Colgate compare with its competitors, both domestically and globally?
- What is a reasonable price for Colgate's stock?

Creditors and lenders also desire answers to important questions before entering into lending agreements with Colgate. Their questions include the following:

- What are Colgate's business plans and prospects? What are Colgate's needs for future financing?

FALLING STAR
Regulators slapped a fine on Merrill Lynch and banned one of its star analysts from the securities industry for life for privately questioning a telecom stock while he publicly boosted it.

- What are Colgate's likely sources for payment of interest and principal? How much cushion does Colgate have in its earnings and cash flows to pay interest and principal?
- What is the likelihood Colgate will be unable to meet its financial obligations? How volatile are Colgate's earnings and cash flows? Does Colgate have the financial strength to pay its commitments in a period of poor profitability?

Answers to these and other questions about company prospects and risks require analysis of both qualitative information about a company's business plans and quantitative information about its financial position and performance. Proper analysis and interpretation of information is crucial to good business analysis. This is the role of financial statement analysis. Through it, an analyst will better understand and interpret both qualitative and quantitative financial information so that reliable inferences are drawn about company prospects and risks.

Types of Business Analysis

Financial statement analysis is an important and integral part of business analysis. The goal of business analysis is to improve business decisions by evaluating available information about a company's financial situation, its management, its plans and strategies, and its business environment. Business analysis is applied in many forms and is an important part of the decisions of security analysts, investment advisors, fund managers, investment bankers, credit raters, corporate bankers, and individual investors. This section considers major types of business analysis.

Credit Analysis

Creditors lend funds to a company in return for a promise of repayment with interest. This type of financing is temporary since creditors expect repayment of their funds with interest. Creditors lend funds in many forms and for a variety of purposes. **Trade** (or operating) **creditors** deliver goods or services to a company and expect payment within a reasonable period, often determined by industry norms. Most trade credit is short term, ranging from 30 to 60 days, with cash discounts often granted for early payment. Trade creditors do not usually receive (explicit) interest for an extension of credit. Instead, trade creditors earn a return from the profit margins on the business transacted. **Nontrade creditors** (or debtholders) provide financing to a company in return for a promise, usually in writing, of repayment with interest (explicit or implicit) on specific future dates. This type of financing can be either short or long term and arises in a variety of transactions.

In pure credit financing, an important element is the fixed nature of benefits to creditors. That is, should a company prosper, creditors' benefits are limited to the debt contract's rate of interest or to the profit margins on goods or services delivered. However, creditors bear the *risk of default*. This means a creditor's interest and principal are jeopardized when a borrower encounters financial difficulties. This asymmetric relation of a creditor's risk and return has a major impact on the creditor's perspective, including the manner and objectives of credit analysis.

Credit analysis is the evaluation of the creditworthiness of a company. *Creditworthiness* is the ability of a company to honor its credit obligations. Stated differently, it is the ability of a company to pay its bills. Accordingly, the main focus of credit analysis is on risk, not profitability. Variability in profits, especially the sensitivity of profits to downturns in business, is more important than profit levels. Profit levels are important only to the extent they reflect the margin of safety for a company in meeting its obligations.

Credit analysis focuses on downside risk instead of upside potential. This includes analysis of both liquidity and solvency. **Liquidity** is a company's ability to raise cash in the short term to meet its obligations. Liquidity depends on a company's cash flows and the makeup of its current assets and current liabilities. **Solvency** is a company's long-run viability and ability to pay long-term obligations. It depends on both a company's long-term profitability and its capital (financing) structure.

The tools of credit analysis and their criteria for evaluation vary with the term (maturity), type, and purpose of the debt contract. With short-term credit, creditors are concerned with current financial conditions, cash flows, and the liquidity of current assets. With long-term credit, including bond valuation, creditors require more detailed and forward-looking analysis. Long-term credit analysis includes projections of cash flows and evaluation of extended profitability (also called *sustainable earning power*). Extended profitability is a main source of assurance of a company's ability to meet long-term interest and principal payments.

Equity Analysis

Equity investors provide funds to a company in return for the risks and rewards of ownership. Equity investors are major providers of company financing. Equity financing, also called *equity* or *share capital,* offers a cushion or safeguard for all other forms of financing that are senior to it. This means equity investors are entitled to the distributions of a company's assets only after the claims of all other senior claimants are met, including interest and preferred dividends. As a result, equity investors are said to hold a *residual interest.* This implies equity investors are the first to absorb losses when a company liquidates, although their losses are usually limited to the amount invested. However, when a company prospers, equity investors share in the gains with unlimited upside potential. Thus, unlike credit analysis, equity analysis is symmetric in that it must assess both downside risks and upside potential. Because equity investors are affected by all aspects of a company's financial condition and performance, their analysis needs are among the most demanding and comprehensive of all users.

Individuals who apply active investment strategies primarily use technical analysis, fundamental analysis, or a combination. **Technical analysis,** or charting, searches for patterns in the price or volume history of a stock to predict future price movements. **Fundamental analysis,** which is more widely accepted and applied, is the process of determining the value of a company by analyzing and interpreting key factors for the economy, the industry, and the company. A main part of fundamental analysis is evaluation of a company's financial position and performance.

A major goal of fundamental analysis is to determine intrinsic value, also called *fundamental value.* **Intrinsic value** is the value of a company (or its stock) determined through fundamental analysis without reference to its market value (or stock price). While a company's market value can equal or approximate its intrinsic value, this is not necessary. An investor's strategy with fundamental analysis is straightforward: buy when a stock's intrinsic value exceeds its market value, sell when a stock's market value exceeds its intrinsic value, and hold when a stock's intrinsic value approximates its market value.

To determine intrinsic value, an analyst must forecast a company's earnings or cash flows and determine its risk. This is achieved through a comprehensive, in-depth analysis of a company's business prospects and its financial statements. Once a company's future profitability and risk are estimated, the analyst uses a valuation model to convert these estimates into a measure of intrinsic value. Intrinsic value is used in many contexts, including equity investment and stock selection, initial public offerings, private placements of equity, mergers and acquisitions, and the purchase/sale of companies without traded securities.

Other Uses of Business Analysis

Business analysis and financial statement analysis are important in a number of other contexts.

- **Managers.** Analysis of financial statements can provide managers with clues to strategic changes in operating, investing, and financing activities. Managers also analyze the businesses and financial statements of competing companies to evaluate a competitor's profitability and risk. Such analysis allows for *interfirm comparisons,* both to evaluate relative strengths and weaknesses and to *benchmark* performance.

- **Mergers, acquisitions, and divestitures.** Business analysis is performed whenever a company restructures its operations, through mergers, acquisitions, divestitures, and spin-offs. Investment bankers need to identify potential targets and determine their values, and security analysts need to determine whether and how much additional value is created by the merger for both the acquiring and the target companies.

- **Financial management.** Managers must evaluate the impact of financing decisions and dividend policy on company value. Business analysis helps assess the impact of financing decisions on both future profitability and risk.

- **Directors.** As elected representatives of the shareholders, directors are responsible for protecting the shareholders' interests by vigilantly overseeing the company's activities. Both business analysis and financial statement analysis aid directors in fulfilling their oversight responsibilities.

- **Regulators.** The Internal Revenue Service applies tools of financial statement analysis to audit tax returns and check the reasonableness of reported amounts.

- **Labor unions.** Techniques of financial statement analysis are useful to labor unions in collective bargaining negotiations.

- **Customers.** Analysis techniques are used to determine the profitability (or staying power) of suppliers along with estimating the suppliers' profits from their mutual transactions.

Components of Business Analysis

Business analysis encompasses several interrelated processes. Exhibit 1.4 identifies these processes in the context of estimating company value—one of the many important applications of business analysis. Company value, or intrinsic value, is estimated using a valuation model. Inputs to the valuation model include estimates of future payoffs (prospective cash flows or earnings) and the cost of capital. The process of forecasting future payoffs is called *prospective analysis.* To accurately forecast future payoffs, it is important to evaluate both the company's business prospects and its financial statements. Evaluation of business prospects is a major goal of *business environment and strategy analysis.* A company's financial status is assessed from its financial statements using

Component Processes of Business Analysis   *Exhibit 1.4*

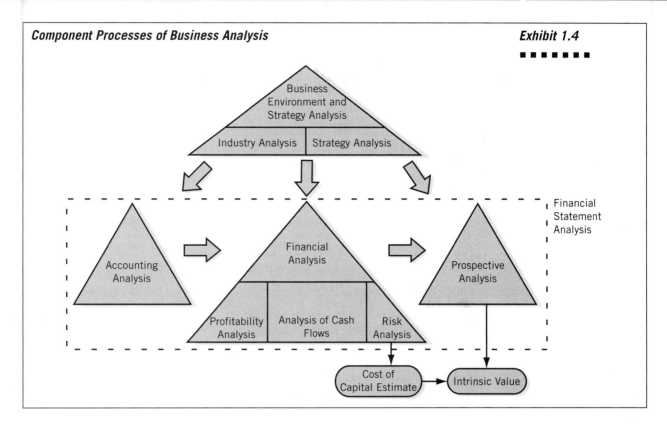

financial analysis. In turn, the quality of financial analysis depends on the reliability and economic content of the financial statements. This requires *accounting analysis* of financial statements. Financial statement analysis involves all of these component processes—accounting, financial, and prospective analyses. This section discusses each of these component processes in the context of business analysis.

Business Environment and Strategy Analysis

Analysis of a company's future prospects is one of the most important aims of business analysis. It also is a subjective and complex task. To effectively accomplish this task we must adopt an interdisciplinary perspective. This includes attention to analysis of the business environment and strategy. Analysis of the business environment seeks to identify and assess a company's economic and industry circumstances. This includes analysis of its product, labor, and capital markets within its economic and regulatory setting. Analysis of business strategy seeks to identify and assess a company's competitive strengths and weaknesses along with its opportunities and threats.

Business environment and strategy analysis consists of two parts—industry analysis and strategy analysis. **Industry analysis** is the usual first step since the prospects and structure of its industry largely drive a company's profitability. Industry analysis is often done using the framework proposed by Porter (1980, 1985) or value chain analysis. Under this framework, an industry is viewed as a collection of competitors that jockey for bargaining power with consumers and suppliers and that actively compete among

BENCHMARKING
The Web offers benchmarking info to help with analysis of business environment and strategy:

www.apqc.org
www.benchnet.com
www.bmpcoe.org

themselves and face threats from new entrants and substitute products. Industry analysis must assess both the industry prospects and the degree of actual and potential competition facing a company. **Strategy analysis** is the evaluation of both a company's business decisions and its success at establishing a competitive advantage. This includes assessing a company's expected strategic responses to its business environment and the impact of these responses on its future success and growth. Strategy analysis requires scrutiny of a company's competitive strategy for its product mix and cost structure.

Business environment and strategy analysis requires knowledge of both economic and industry forces. It also requires knowledge of strategic management, business policy, production, logistics management, marketing, and managerial economics. Because of its broad, multidisciplinary nature, it is beyond the scope of this book to cover all of these areas in the context of business environment and strategy analysis and how they relate to financial statements. Still, this analysis is necessary for meaningful business decisions and is implicit, if not explicit, in all analyses in this book.

Accounting Analysis

Accounting analysis is a process of evaluating the extent to which a company's accounting reflects economic reality. This is done by studying a company's transactions and events, assessing the effects of its accounting policies on financial statements, and adjusting the statements to both better reflect the underlying economics and make them more amenable to analysis. Financial statements are the primary source of information for financial analysis. This means the quality of financial analysis depends on the reliability of financial statements that in turn depends on the quality of accounting analysis. Accounting analysis is especially important for comparative analysis.

We must remember that accounting is a process involving judgment guided by fundamental principles. While accounting principles are governed by standards, the complexity of business transactions and events makes it impossible to adopt a uniform set of accounting rules for all companies and all time periods. Moreover, most accounting standards evolve as part of a political process to satisfy the needs of diverse individuals and their sometimes conflicting interests. These individuals include *users* such as investors, creditors, and analysts; *preparers* such as corporations, partnerships, and proprietorships; *regulators* such as the Securities and Exchange Commission and the Financial Accounting Standards Board; and still others such as auditors, lawyers, and educators. Accordingly, accounting standards sometimes fail to meet the needs of specific individuals. Another factor potentially impeding the reliability of financial statements is error from accounting estimates that can yield incomplete or imprecise information.

These accounting limitations affect the usefulness of financial statements and can yield at least two problems in analysis. First, lack of uniformity in accounting leads to comparability problems. **Comparability problems** arise when different companies adopt different accounting for similar transactions or events. Comparability problems also arise when a company changes its accounting across time, leading to difficulties with temporal comparability.

Second, discretion and imprecision in accounting can distort financial statement information. **Accounting distortions** are deviations of accounting information from the underlying economics. These distortions occur in at least three forms. (1) Managerial estimates can be subject to honest errors or omissions. This *estimation error* is a major cause of accounting distortions. (2) Managers might use their discretion in accounting to manipulate or window-dress financial statements. This *earnings management* can cause accounting distortions. (3) Accounting standards can give rise to accounting distortions from a failure to capture economic reality. These three types of accounting distortions create accounting risk in financial statement analysis. **Accounting risk** is the uncertainty in financial statement analysis due to accounting distortions. A major goal of accounting analysis is to evaluate and reduce accounting risk and to improve the economic content of financial statements, including their comparability. Meeting this goal usually requires restatement and reclassification of financial statements to improve their economic content and comparability. The type and extent of adjustments depend on the analysis. For example, adjustments for equity analysis can differ from those for credit analysis.

Accounting analysis includes evaluation of a company's *earnings quality* or, more broadly, its accounting quality. Evaluation of earnings quality requires analysis of factors such as a company's business, its accounting policies, the quantity and quality of information disclosed, the performance and reputation of management, and the opportunities and incentives for earnings management. Accounting analysis also includes evaluation of earnings persistence, sometimes called *sustainable earning power.* We explain analysis of both earnings quality and persistence in Chapters 2 and 11.

Accounting analysis is often the least understood, appreciated, and effectively applied process in business analysis. Part of the reason might be that accounting analysis requires accounting knowledge. Analysts that lack this knowledge have a tendency to brush accounting analysis under the rug and take financial statements as reported. This is a dangerous practice because accounting analysis is crucial to any successful business or financial analysis. Chapters 3–6 of this book are devoted to accounting analysis.

Financial Analysis

Financial analysis is the use of financial statements to analyze a company's financial position and performance, and to assess future financial performance. Several questions can help focus financial analysis. One set of questions is future oriented. For example, does a company have the resources to succeed and grow? Does it have resources to invest in new projects? What are its sources of profitability? What is the company's future earning power? A second set involves questions that assess a company's track record and its ability to deliver on expected financial performance. For example, how strong is the company's financial position? How profitable is the company? Did earnings meet analyst forecasts? This includes an analysis of why a company might have fallen short of (or exceeded) expectations.

Financial analysis consists of three broad areas–profitability analysis, risk analysis, and analysis of sources and uses of funds. **Profitability analysis** is the evaluation of a company's return on investment. It focuses on a company's sources and levels of profits and involves identifying and measuring the impact of various profitability drivers. It also includes evaluation of the two major sources of profitability–margins (the portion of sales not offset by costs) and turnover (capital utilization). Profitability analysis also focuses on reasons for changes in profitability and the sustainability of earnings. The topic is discussed in detail in Chapter 8. **Risk analysis** is the evaluation of a company's ability to meet its commitments. Risk analysis involves assessing the solvency and liquidity of a company along with its earnings variability. Because risk is of foremost concern to creditors, risk analysis is often discussed in the context of credit analysis. Still, risk analysis is important to equity analysis, both to evaluate the reliability and sustainability of company performance and to estimate a company's cost of capital. We explain risk analysis along with credit analysis in Chapter 10. Analysis of cash flows is the evaluation of how a company is obtaining and deploying its funds. This analysis provides insights into a company's future financing implications. For example, a company that funds new projects from internally generated cash (profits) is likely to achieve better future performance than a company that either borrows heavily to finance its projects or, worse, borrows to meet current losses. We explain analysis of cash flows in Chapter 7.

Prospective Analysis

Prospective analysis is the forecasting of future payoffs–typically earnings, cash flows, or both. This analysis draws on accounting analysis, financial analysis, and business environment and strategy analysis. The output of prospective analysis is a set of expected future payoffs used to estimate company value.

While quantitative tools help improve forecast accuracy, prospective analysis remains a relatively subjective process. This is why prospective analysis is sometimes referred to as an art, not a science. Still, there are many tools we can draw on to help enhance this analysis. We explain prospective analysis in detail in Chapter 9.

Valuation

Valuation is a main objective of many types of business analysis. Valuation refers to the process of converting forecasts of future payoffs into an estimate of company value. To determine company value, an analyst must select a valuation model and must also estimate the company's cost of capital. While most valuation models require forecasts of future payoffs, there are certain ad hoc approaches that use current financial information. We examine valuation in a preliminary manner later in this chapter and again in Chapter 11.

Financial Statement Analysis and Business Analysis

■ ■ ■ ■ ■ ■ ■
KNOW-NOTHING CEOs
The know-nothing defense of CEOs such as MCI's Bernie Ebbers was shattered by novel legal moves. Investigators proved that CEOs knew the internal picture was materially different than the external picture presented to shareholders.

Exhibit 1.4 and its discussion emphasizes that financial statement analysis is a collection of analytical processes that are part of business analysis. These separate processes share a common bond in that they all use financial statement information, to varying degrees, for analysis purposes. While financial statements do contain information on a company's business plans, analysis of a company's business environment and strategy is sometimes viewed outside of conventional financial statement analysis. Also, prospective analysis pushes the frontier of conventional financial statement analysis. Yet most agree that an important part of financial statement analysis is analyzing a company's business environment and strategy. Most also agree that valuation, which requires forecasts, is part of financial statement analysis. Therefore, financial statement analysis should be, and is, viewed as an important and integral part of business analysis and all of its component analyses. At the same time, it is important to understand the scope of financial statement analysis. Specifically, this book focuses on financial statement analysis and not on aspects of business analysis apart from those involving analysis of financial statements.

FINANCIAL STATEMENTS— BASIS OF ANALYSIS
Business Activities

A company pursues a number of activities in a desire to provide a salable product or service and to yield a satisfactory return on investment. Its financial statements and related disclosures inform us about the four major activities of the company: planning, financing, investing, and operating. It is important to understand each of these major business activities before we can effectively analyze a company's financial statements.

Planning Activities

A company exists to implement specific goals and objectives. For example, Colgate aspires to remain a powerful force in oral, personal, and home care products. A company's goals and objectives are captured in a **business plan** that describes the company's purpose, strategy, and tactics for its activities. A business plan assists managers in focusing their efforts and identifying expected opportunities and obstacles. Insight into the business plan considerably aids our analysis of a company's current and future prospects and is part of the analysis of business environment and strategy. We look for information on company objectives and tactics, market demands, competitive analysis, sales strategies (pricing, promotion, distribution), management performance, and financial projections. Information of this type, in varying forms, is often revealed in financial statements. It is also available through less formal means such as press releases, industry publications, analysts' newsletters, and the financial press.

Two important sources of information on a company's business plan are the Letter to Shareholders (or Chairperson's Letter) and Management's Discussion and Analysis (MD&A). Colgate, in the Business Strategy section of its 10-K filing with the SEC (its annual report), discusses various business opportunities and plans as reproduced here:

ANALYSIS EXCERPT

Executive Overview. Colgate-Palmolive Company seeks to deliver strong, consistent business results and superior shareholder returns by providing consumers, on a global basis, with products that make their lives healthier and more enjoyable. To this end, the Company is tightly focused on two product segments: Oral, Personal, and Home Care; and Pet Nutrition.

The Company competes in more than 200 countries and territories worldwide, with established businesses in all regions contributing to the Company's sales and profitability. This geographic diversity and balance helps to reduce the Company's exposure to business and other risks in any one country or part of the world.

To achieve its financial objectives, the Company focuses the organization on initiatives to drive growth and to fund growth. The Company seeks to capture significant opportunities for growth by identifying and meeting consumer needs within its core categories, in particular by deploying valuable consumer and shopper insights in the development of successful new products regionally which are then rolled out on a global basis. Growth opportunities are enhanced in those areas of the world in which economic development and rising consumer incomes expand the size and number of markets for the Company's products.

The investments needed to fund this growth are developed through continuous, corporate-wide initiatives to lower costs and increase effective asset utilization. The Company also continues to prioritize its investments toward its higher-margin businesses, specifically Oral Care, Personal Care, and Pet Nutrition.

Additional discussion appears in the Management's Discussion and Analysis section of Colgate's annual report. These two sources are excellent starting points in constructing a company's business plan and in performing a business environment and strategy analysis.

It is important to stress that business planning is not cast in stone and is fraught with uncertainty. Can Colgate be certain of the future of consumer and business computing needs? Can Colgate be certain its raw material costs will not increase? Can Colgate be sure how competitors will react? These and other questions add risk to our analysis. While all actions involve risk, some actions involve more risk than others. Financial statement analysis helps us estimate the degree of risk, or uncertainty, and yields more informed and better decisions. While information taken from financial statements does not provide irrefutable answers, it does help us to gauge the soundness of a company's business opportunities and strategies and to better understand its financing, investing, and operating activities.

Financing Activities

A company requires financing to carry out its business plan. Colgate needs financing for purchasing raw materials for production, paying its employees, acquiring complementary companies and technologies, and for research and development. **Financing activities** refer to methods that companies use to raise the money to pay for these needs. Because of their magnitude and their potential for determining the success or failure of a venture, companies take care in acquiring and managing financial resources.

There are two main sources of external financing–equity investors (also called owners or shareholders) and creditors (lenders). Decisions concerning the composition of financing activities depend on conditions existing in financial markets. Financial markets are potential sources of financing. In looking to financial markets, a company considers several issues, including the amount of financing necessary, sources of financing (owners or creditors), timing of repayment, and structure of financing agreements. Decisions on these issues determine a company's organizational structure, affect its growth, influence its exposure to risk, and determine the power of outsiders in business decisions. The chart in the margin shows the makeup of total financing for selected companies.

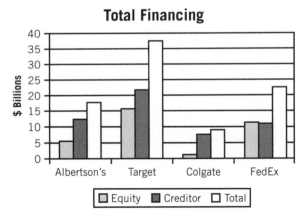

Total Financing

Equity investors are a major source of financing. Colgate's balance sheet shows it raised $1.95 billion by issuing stock to equity investors. Investors provide financing in a desire for a return on their investment, after considering both expected return and risk. **Return** is the equity investor's share of company earnings in the form of either earnings distribution or earnings reinvestment. **Earnings distribution** is the payment of dividends to shareholders. Dividends can be paid directly in the form of cash or stock dividend, or indirectly through stock repurchase. **Dividend payout** refers to the proportion of earnings distributed. It is often expressed as a ratio or a percentage of net earnings. **Earnings reinvestment** (or earnings retention) refers to retaining earnings within the company for use in its business; this is also called *internal financing*. Earnings reinvestment is often measured by a retention ratio. The **earnings retention ratio,** reflecting the proportion of earnings retained, is defined as one less the dividend payout ratio.

Equity financing can be in cash or any asset or service contributed to a company in exchange for equity shares. Private offerings of shares usually involve selling shares to one or more individuals or organizations. Public offerings involve selling shares to the public. There are significant costs with public offerings of shares, including government regulatory filings, stock exchange listing requirements, and brokerage fees to selling agents. The main benefit of public offerings of shares is the potential to raise substantial funds for business activities. Many corporations offer their shares for trading on organized exchanges like the New York, Tokyo, Singapore, and London stock markets. Colgate's common stock trades on NYSE under the symbol CL. The chart in the margin above shows the makeup of equity financing for selected companies. Negative amounts of contributed capital for Colgate indicate that repurchases of common stock (called treasury stock) have exceeded capital contributions.

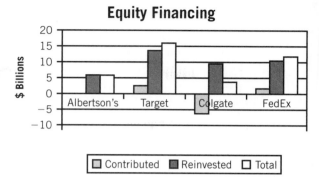

Companies also obtain financing from creditors. Creditors are of two types: (1) debt creditors, who directly lend money to the company, and (2) operating creditors, to whom the company owes money as part of its operations. Debt financing often occurs through loans or through issuance of securities such as bonds. Debt financers include organizations like banks, savings and loans, and other financial or nonfinancial institutions. Operating creditors include suppliers, employees, the government, and any other entity to whom the company owes money. Even employees who are paid periodically, say weekly or monthly, are implicitly providing a form of credit financing until they are paid for their efforts. Colgate's balance sheet shows total creditor financing of $7.73 billion, which is about 85% of its total financing. Of this amount, around $3.67 billion is debt financing, while the remaining $4.06 billion is operating creditor financing.

Creditor financing is different from equity financing in that an agreement, or contract, is usually established that requires repayment of the loan with interest at specific dates. While interest is not always expressly stated in these contracts, it is always implicit. Loan periods are variable and depend on the desires of both creditors and companies. Loans can be as long as 50 years or more, or as short as a week or less.

Like equity investors, creditors are concerned with return and risk. Unlike equity investors, creditors' returns are usually specified in loan contracts. For example, a 20-year, 10%, fixed-rate loan means that creditors receive a 10% annual return on their investment for 20 years. Colgate's long-term loans are due from 2007 to 2011 and carry different interest rates. The returns of equity investors are not guaranteed and depend on the level of future earnings. Risk for creditors is the possibility a business will default in repaying its loans and interest. In this situation, creditors might not receive their money due, and bankruptcy or other legal remedies could ensue. Such remedies impose costs on creditors.

SCAM SOURCING

According to regulators, the five most common ways investors get duped are (1) unlicensed securities dealers, (2) unscrupulous stockbrokers, (3) research analyst conflicts, (4) fraudulent promissory notes, and (5) prime bank schemes.

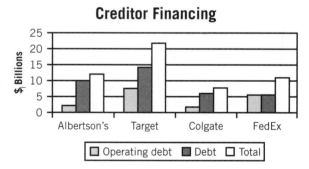

ANALYSIS VIEWPOINT   ***. . . YOU ARE THE CREDITOR***

Colgate requests a $500 million loan from your bank. How does the composition of Colgate's financing sources (creditor and equity) affect your loan decision? Do you have any reluctance making the loan to Colgate given its current financing composition? *[Note: Solutions to Viewpoints are at the end of each chapter.]*

Investing Activities

Investing activities refer to a company's acquisition and maintenance of investments for purposes of selling products and providing services, and for the purpose of investing excess cash. Investments in land, buildings, equipment, legal rights (patents, licenses, copyrights), inventories, human capital (managers and employees), information systems, and similar assets are for the purpose of conducting the company's business operations. Such assets are called **operating assets.** Also, companies often temporarily or permanently invest excess cash in securities such as other companies' equity stock, corporate and government bonds, and money market funds. Such assets are called **financial assets.** Colgate's balance sheet shows its 2006 investment, or asset, base is $9.14 billion, of which $7.13 billion is in operating assets and the rest is in financial assets. The chart in the margin shows the operating and financial assets of selected companies.

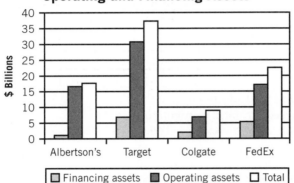

Operating and Financing Assets

Information on both financing and investing activities assists us in evaluating business performance. Note the value of investments always equals the value of financing obtained. Any excess financing not invested is simply reported as cash (or some other noncash asset). Companies differ in the amount and composition of their investments. Many companies demand huge investments in acquiring, developing, and selling their products, while others require little investment. Size of investment does not necessarily determine company success. It is the efficiency and effectiveness with which a company carries out its operations that determine earnings and returns to owners.

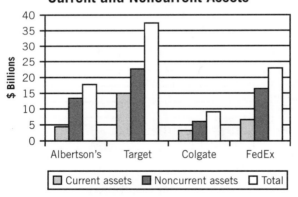

Current and Noncurrent Assets

Investing decisions involve several factors such as type of investment necessary (including technological and labor intensity), amount required, acquisition timing, asset location, and contractual agreement (purchase, rent, and lease). Like financing activities, decisions on investing activities determine a company's organizational structure (centralized or decentralized), affect growth, and influence riskiness of operations. Investments in short-term assets are called **current assets.** These assets are expected to be converted to cash in the short term. Investments in long-term assets are called **noncurrent assets.** Colgate invests $3.30 billion in current assts (36% of total assets) and $2.70 billion in plant and machinery (30% of total assets). Its remaining assets include other long-term assets and intangibles.

Operating Activities

One of the more important areas in analyzing a company is operating activities. **Operating activities** represent the "carrying out" of the business plan given its financing and investing activities. Operating activities involve at least five possible components: research and development, procurement, production, marketing, and administration. A proper mix of the components of operating activities depends on the type of business, its plans, and its input and output markets. Management decides on the most efficient and effective mix for the company's competitive advantage.

Operating activities are a company's primary source of earnings. Earnings reflect a company's success in buying from input markets and selling in output markets. How well a company does in devising business plans and strategies, and deciding the mix of operating activities, determines its success or failure. Analysis of earnings figures, and their component parts, reflects a company's success in efficiently and effectively managing business activities.

Revenues, Expenses, and Income

Colgate earned $1.383 billion in 2006. This number by itself is not very meaningful. Instead, it must be compared with the level of investment used to generate these earnings. Colgate's return on beginning-of-year total assets of $8.51 billion is 15.9% ($1.353 billion/$8.510 billion)–a superior return by any standard, and especially so when considering the highly competitive nature of the consumer products industry.

Financial Statements Reflect Business Activities

At the end of a period–typically a quarter or a year–financial statements are prepared to report on financing and investing activities at that point in time, and to summarize operating activities for the preceding period. This is the role of financial statements and the object of analysis. It is important to recognize that financial statements report on financing and investing activities at a point in time, whereas they report on operating activities for a period of time.

Balance Sheet

The **accounting equation** (also called the balance sheet identity) is the basis of the accounting system: Assets = Liabilities + Equity. The left-hand side of this equation relates to the resources controlled by a company, or **assets.** These resources are investments that are expected to generate future earnings through operating activities. To engage in operating activities, a company needs financing to fund them. The right-hand side of this equation identifies funding sources. **Liabilities** are funding from creditors and represent obligations of a company or, alternatively, claims of creditors on assets. **Equity** (or shareholders' equity) is the total of (1) funding invested or contributed by owners (contributed capital) and (2) accumulated earnings in excess of distributions to owners (retained earnings) since

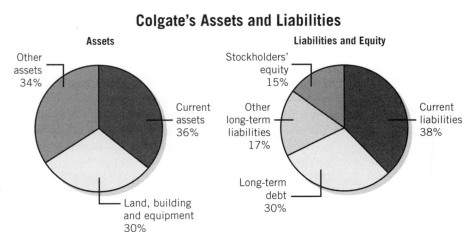

inception of the company. From the owners', or shareholders', point of view, equity represents their claim on company assets. A slightly different way to describe the accounting equation is in terms of sources and uses of funds. That is, the right-hand side represents sources of funds (either from creditors or shareholders, or internally generated) and the left-hand side represents uses of funds.

Assets and liabilities are separated into current and noncurrent amounts. **Current assets** are expected to be converted to cash or used in operations within one year or the operating cycle, whichever is longer. **Current liabilities** are obligations the company is expected to settle within one year or the operating cycle, whichever is longer. The difference between current assets and current liabilities is called **working capital.**

It is revealing to rewrite the accounting equation in terms of business activities–namely, investing and financing activities: Total investing = Total financing; or alternatively: Total investing = Creditor financing + Owner financing.

Remember the accounting equation is a balance sheet identity reflecting a *point* in time. Operating activities arise over a *period* of time and are not reflected in this identity. However, operating activities can affect both sides of this equation. That is, if a company is profitable, both investing (assets) and financing (equity) levels increase. Similarly, when a company is unprofitable, both investing and financing decline.

The balance sheet of Colgate is reproduced in Exhibit 1.5. Colgate's total investments (assets) on December 31, 2006, are $9.14 billion. Of this amount, creditor financing totals $7.73 billion, while the remaining $1.41 billion represents claims of shareholders.

Income Statement

An income statement measures a company's financial performance between balance sheet dates. It is a representation of the operating activities of a company. The income statement provides details of revenues, expenses, gains, and losses of a company for a time period. The bottom line, **earnings** (also called *net income*), indicates the profitability of the company. Earnings reflects the return to equity holders for the period under consideration, while the line items of the statement detail how earnings are determined. Earnings approximate the increase (or decrease) in equity before considering distributions to and contributions from equity holders. For income to exactly measure change in equity, we need a slightly different definition of income, called *comprehensive income,* which we discuss in the section on links between financial statements later in this chapter.

The income statement includes several other indicators of profitability. **Gross profit** (also called *gross margin*) is the difference between sales and cost of sales (also called *cost of goods sold*). It indicates the extent to which a company is able to cover costs of its products. This indicator is not especially relevant for service and technology companies where production costs are a small part of total costs. **Earnings from operations** refers to the difference between sales and all operating costs and expenses. It usually excludes financing costs (interest) and taxes. **Earnings before taxes,** as the name implies, represents earnings from continuing operations before the provision for income tax. **Earnings from continuing operations** is the income from a company's continuing business after interest and taxes. It is also called *earnings before extraordinary items and discontinued operations*. We discuss these alternative earnings definitions in Chapter 6.

Earnings are determined using the **accrual basis** of accounting. Under accrual accounting, revenues are recognized when a company sells goods or renders services,

Colgate's Consolidated Balance Sheets

Exhibit 1.5

As of December 31,	2006	2005
Assets		
Current Assets		
Cash and cash equivalents	$ 489.5	$ 340.7
Receivables (net of allowances of $46.4 and $41.7, respectively)	1,523.2	1,309.4
Inventories	1,008.4	855.8
Other current assets	279.9	251.2
Total current assets	3,301.0	2,757.1
Property, plant and equipment, net	2,696.1	2,544.1
Goodwill, net	2,081.8	1,845.7
Other intangible assets, net	831.1	783.2
Other assets	228.0	577.0
Total assets	$ 9,138.0	$ 8,507.1
Liabilities and Shareholders' Equity		
Current Liabilities		
Notes and loans payable	$ 174.1	$ 171.5
Current portion of long-term debt	776.7	356.7
Accounts payable	1,039.7	876.1
Accrued income taxes	161.5	215.5
Other accruals	1,317.1	1,123.2
Total current liabilities	3,469.1	2,743.0
Long-term debt	2,720.4	2,918.0
Deferred income taxes	309.9	554.7
Other liabilities	1,227.7	941.3
Total liabilities	7,727.1	7,157.0
Commitments and contingent liabilities	—	—
Shareholders' Equity		
Preference stock	222.7	253.7
Common stock, $1 par value (1,000,000,000 shares authorized,		
732,853,180 shares issued)	732.9	732.9
Additional paid-in capital	1,218.1	1,064.4
Retained earnings	9,643.7	8,968.1
Accumulated other comprehensive income	(2,081.2)	(1,804.7)
	9,736.2	9,214.4
Unearned compensation	(251.4)	(283.3)
Treasury stock, at cost	(8,073.9)	(7,581.0)
Total shareholders' equity	1,410.9	1,350.1
Total liabilities and shareholders' equity	$ 9,138.0	$ 8,507.1

regardless of when it receives cash. Similarly, expenses are matched to these recognized revenues, regardless of when it pays cash. The income statement of Colgate, titled consolidated statement of income, for the preceding three years is shown in Exhibit 1.6. Colgate's 2006 revenues totaled $12.238 billion. Of this amount, $10.885 billion are costs of operations and other expenses, yielding net income of $1.353 billion. Colgate's

Exhibit 1.6

Colgate's Consolidated Statements of Income

For the years ended December 31,	2006	2005	2004
Net sales	$12,237.7	$11,396.9	$10,584.2
Cost of sales	5,536.1	5,191.9	4,747.2
Gross profit	6,701.6	6,205.0	5,837.0
Selling, general and administrative expenses	4,355.2	3,920.8	3,624.6
Other (income) expense, net	185.9	69.2	90.3
Operating profit	2,160.5	2,215.0	2,122.1
Interest expense, net	158.7	136.0	119.7
Income before income taxes	2,001.8	2,079.0	2,002.4
Provision for income taxes	648.4	727.6	675.3
Net income	$ 1,353.4	$ 1,351.4	$ 1,327.1
Earnings per common share, basic	$ 2.57	$ 2.54	$ 2.45
Earnings per common share, diluted	$ 2.46	$ 2.43	$ 2.33

earnings have been stagnant during these three years despite a healthy increase in revenues, suggesting that the company is still struggling to keep its costs under control.

Statement of Shareholders' Equity

The statements of retained earnings, comprehensive income and changes in capital accounts are often called the statements of changes in shareholders' equity. (In this section, we will use the title statement of changes in shareholders' equity). This statement is useful in identifying reasons for changes in equity holders' claims on the assets of a company. Colgate's statement of changes in shareholders' equity for the most recent year is shown in Exhibit 1.7. During this period, shareholders' equity changes were due mainly to the issuing stock (mainly related to employee stock options), repurchasing stock (treasury shares) and reinvesting earnings. Colgate details these changes under five columns: Common Shares, Additional Paid-in Capital, Treasury Stock, Retained Earnings, and Accumulated Other Comprehensive Income (Loss). Common Shares and Additional Paid-In Capital together represent Contributed Capital and are often collectively called *share capital* (many analysts also net Treasury Stock in the computation of share capital). The change in Colgate's retained earnings is especially important because this account links consecutive balance sheets through the income statement. For example, consider Colgate's collective retained earnings increase from $8.968 billion in 2005 to $9.643 billion in 2006. This increase of $0.675 billion is explained by net earnings of $1.353 billion minus dividends of $0.678 billion. Because dividends almost always are distributed from retained earnings, the retained earnings balance often represents an upper limit on the amount of potential dividend distributions.

Colgate includes a separate column for comprehensive income. Comprehensive income is a measure of the ultimate "bottom line" income, that is, changes to shareholder's equity excluding transactions involving exchanges with shareholders. Colgate's 2006 comprehensive income is $1.458 billion. In addition to net income, comprehensive income includes certain adjustments classified as other comprehensive income. The two

Colgate's Consolidated Statements of Retained Earnings, Comprehensive Income, and Changes in Capital Accounts

Exhibit 1.7
■ ■ ■ ■ ■ ■ ■

	Common Shares		Additional Paid-in Capital	Treasury Shares		Retained Earnings	Accumulated Other Compre-hensive Income	Compre-hensive Income
	Shares	Amount		Shares	Amount			
Balance, December 31, 2005	516,170,957	$732.9	$1,064.4	216,682,223	$(7,581.0)	$8,968.1	$(1,804.7)	
Net income						1,353.4		$1,353.4
Other comprehensive income:								
Cumulative translation								
adjustment							89.1	89.1
Adjustment to initially apply								
SFAS 158, net of taxes							(380.7)	
Minimum Pension liability								
adjustment, net of tax							19.2	19.2
Other							(4.1)	(4.1)
Total comprehensive income								$1,457.6
Dividends declared:								
Series B Convertible								
Preference Stock,								
net of taxes						(28.7)		
Common stock						(649.1)		
Stock-based compensation								
expense			116.9					
Shares issued for stock options ...	7,095,538		107.7	(7,095,538)	227.7			
Treasury stock acquired	(14,982,242)			14,982,242	(884.7)			
Other	4,374,334		(70.9)	(4,374,334)	164.1			
Balance, December 31, 2006	512,658,587	$732.9	$1,218.1	220,194,593	$(8,073.9)	$9,643.7	$(2,081.2)	

major adjustments included in comprehensive income are the cumulative (foreign currency) translation adjustment ($0.089 billion) and the minimum pension liability adjustment ($0.019 billion). The largest constituent of other comprehensive income, however, is adjustment for the initial application of *SFAS 158*–a new pension standard that became applicable only in 2006–to the tune of $0.381. This amount is not included in comprehensive income for the year. Also the cumulative total of the other comprehensive income adjustments are shown under the column "accumulated other comprehensive income". All items–including the effect of *SFAS 158* application–affect the change in accumulated comprehensive income, from $1.805 billion in 2005 to $2.081 billion in 2006. While most companies show accumulated comprehensive income as a separate line item within shareholder's equity, conceptually it is just part of a company's retained earnings. We discuss comprehensive income in detail in Chapter 6.

The third heading in the statement of shareholders' equity shows details of treasury stock. Treasury stock is discussed in Chapter 3. For now, it is sufficient to view the treasury stock amount as the difference between cash paid for share repurchases and the proceeds from reselling those shares. The treasury stock amount reduces equity. Colgate's treasury stock at the end of 2006 is more than $8 billion, which is above 80% of its shareholder's equity (before treasury stock) of $9.485 billion. Much of the treasury stock amount is attributable to stock repurchases—in 2006 alone Colgate repurchased $0.885 billion of its stock. Colgate's treasury share amount largely explains its small equity base.

Statement of Cash Flows

Earnings do not typically equal net cash flows, except over the life of a company. Because accrual accounting yields numbers different from cash flow accounting, and we know that cash flows are important in business decisions, there is a need for reporting on cash inflows and outflows. For example, analyses involving reconstruction and interpretation of business transactions often require the statement of cash flows. Also, certain valuation models use cash flows. The statement of cash flows reports cash inflows and outflows separately for a company's operating, investing, and financing activities over a period of time.

Colgate's statement of cash flows is reproduced in Exhibit 1.8. Colgate's 2006 cash balance increases by $0.149 billion, from $0.341 billion to $0.490 billion. Of this increase in net cash, Colgate's operating activities provided $1.822 billion, its investing activities used $0.620 billion, and its financing activities used $1.059 billion.

Links between Financial Statements

Financial statements are linked at points in time and across time. These links are portrayed in Exhibit 1.9 using Colgate's financial statements. Colgate began 2006 with the investing and financing amounts reported in the balance sheet on the left side of Exhibit 1.9. Its investments in assets, comprising both cash ($0.341 billion) and noncash assets ($8.166 billion), total $8.507 billion. These investments are financed by both creditors ($7.157 billion) and equity investors ($1.350), the latter comprising preference and equity share capital ($2.051 billion) and retained earnings ($6.880 billion, which includes accumulated comprehensive income and other items) less treasury stock ($7.581 million). Colgate's operating activities are shown in the middle column of Exhibit 1.9. The statement of cash flows explains how operating, investing, and financing activities increase Colgate's cash balance from $0.341 billion at the beginning of the year to $0.490 billion at year end. This end-of-year cash amount is reported in the year-end balance sheet on the right side of Exhibit 1.9. Colgate's net income of $1.353 billion, computed as revenues less cost of sales and expenses, is reported in the income statement. Net income less dividends paid explain movement in retained earnings reported in the statement of shareholder's equity. In addition, movement in accumulated comprehensive income is explained by other comprehensive income during the year. Finally, movement in treasury stock arises both from issue and repurchase of treasury stock.

To recap, Colgate's balance sheet is a listing of its investing and financing activities at a *point in time*. The three statements that report on (1) cash flows, (2) income, and (3) shareholders' equity, explain changes (typically from operating activities) over a *period of time* for Colgate's investing and financing activities. Every transaction captured in these three latter statements impacts the balance sheet. Examples are (1) revenues and expenses affecting earnings and their subsequent reporting in retained earnings, (2) cash transactions in the statement of cash flows that are summarized in the cash balance on the balance sheet, and (3) all revenue and expense accounts that affect one or more balance sheet accounts. In sum, financial statements are linked by design: the period-of-time statements (income statement, statement of cash flows, and statement of shareholders' equity) explain point-in-time balance sheets. This is known as the *articulation* of financial statements.

Colgate's Consolidated Statements of Cash Flows

Exhibit 1.8

■ ■ ■ ■ ■ ■ ■

For the years ended December 31,	2006	2005	2004
Operating Activities			
Net income	$ 1,353.4	$ 1,351.4	$ 1,327.1
Adjustments to reconcile net income to net cash provided by operations:			
Restructuring, net of cash	145.4	111.6	38.3
Depreciation and amortization	328.7	329.3	327.8
Gain before tax on sale of noncore product lines	(46.5)	(147.9)	(26.7)
Stock-based compensation expense	116.9	41.1	29.3
Cash effects of changes in:			
Receivables	(116.0)	(24.1)	(5.6)
Inventories	(118.5)	(46.8)	(76.1)
Accounts payable and other accruals	149.9	152.7	80.1
Other noncurrent assets and liabilities	8.2	17.1	60.1
Net cash provided by operations	1,821.5	1,784.4	1,754.3
Investing Activities			
Capital expenditures	(476.4)	(389.2)	(348.1)
Payment for acquisitions, net of cash acquired	(200.0)	(38.5)	(800.7)
Sale of noncore product lines	55.0	215.6	37.0
Purchases of marketable securities and investments	(1.2)	(20.0)	(127.7)
Proceeds from sales of marketable securities and investments	—	10.0	147.3
Other	2.2	1.4	1.8
Net cash used in investing activities	(620.4)	(220.7)	(1,090.4)
Financing Activities			
Principal payments on debt	(1,332.0)	(2,100.3)	(753.9)
Proceeds from issuance of debt	1,471.1	2,021.9	1,246.5
Payments to outside investors	—	(89.7)	—
Dividends paid	(677.8)	(607.2)	(536.2)
Purchases of treasury shares	(884.7)	(796.2)	(637.9)
Proceeds from exercise of stock options and excess tax benefits	364.4	47.1	70.4
Net cash used in financing activities	(1,059.0)	(1,524.4)	(611.1)
Effect of exchange rate changes on cash and cash equivalents	6.7	(18.2)	1.5
Net increase in cash and cash equivalents	148.8	21.1	54.3
Cash and cash equivalents at beginning of year	340.7	319.6	265.3
Cash and cash equivalents at end of year	$ 489.5	$ 340.7	$ 319.6
Supplemental Cash Flow Information			
Income taxes paid	$ 647.9	$ 584.3	$ 593.8
Interest paid	168.3	149.9	123.2
Principal payments on ESOP debt, guaranteed by the Company	45.0	37.0	29.8

ANALYSIS VIEWPOINT   ***. . . YOU ARE THE INVESTOR***

You are considering buying Colgate stock. As part of your preliminary review of Colgate, you examine its financial statements. What information are you attempting to obtain from each of these statements to aid in your decision?

Exhibit 1.9   ***Financial Statement Links—Colgate***

■ ■ ■ ■ ■ ■ ■

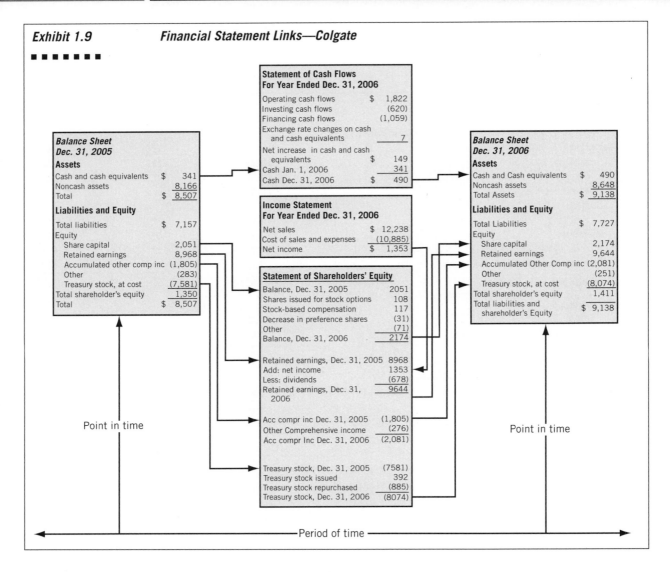

Additional Information

Financial statements are not the sole output of a financial reporting system. Additional information about a company is also communicated. A thorough financial statement analysis involves examining this additional information.

- **Management's Discussion and Analysis (MD&A).** Companies with publicly traded debt and equity securities are required by the Securities and Exchange Commission to file a Management's Discussion and Analysis (MD&A). Management must highlight any favorable or unfavorable trends and identify significant events and uncertainties that affect a company's liquidity, capital resources, and results of operations. They must also disclose prospective information involving material events and uncertainties known to cause reported financial information to be less indicative of future operating activities or financial condition. The MD&A for Colgate shown in Appendix A includes a year-by-year analysis along with an evaluation of its liquidity and capital resources by business activities.

- **Management Report.** The purposes of this report are to reinforce: (1) senior management's responsibilities for the company's financial and internal control system and (2) the shared roles of management, directors, and the auditor in preparing financial statements. Colgate's report, titled Report of Management, discusses its policies and procedures to enhance the reliability of its financial records. Its report also highlights the role of its audit committee of the board of directors in providing added assurance for the reliability of financial statements.

- **Auditor Report.** An external auditor is an independent certified public accountant hired by management to provide an opinion on whether or not the company's financial statements are prepared in conformity with generally accepted accounting principles. Financial statement analysis requires a review of the auditor's report to ascertain whether the company received an unqualified opinion. Anything less than an unqualified opinion increases the risk of analysis. Colgate's Report of Independent Accountants, prepared by PricewaterhouseCoopers, is reproduced in Appendix A. Colgate received an unqualified opinion. We discuss audit reports in Appendix 2A.

- **Explanatory Notes.** Explanatory notes that accompany financial reports play an integral part in financial statement analysis. Notes are a means of communicating additional information regarding items included or excluded from the body of the statements. The technical nature of notes creates a need for a certain level of accounting knowledge on the part of financial statement analysts. Explanatory notes include information on: (1) accounting principles and methods employed, (2) detailed disclosures regarding individual financial statement items, (3) commitments and contingencies, (4) business combinations, (5) transactions with related parties, (6) stock option plans, (7) legal proceedings, and (8) significant customers. The notes for Colgate follow its financial statements in Appendix A.

- **Supplementary Information.** Supplemental schedules to the financial statement notes include information on: (1) business segment data, (2) export sales, (3) marketable securities, (4) valuation accounts, (5) short-term borrowings, and (6) quarterly financial data. Several supplemental schedules appear in the annual report of Colgate. An example is the information on segment operations included as note 14 in Colgate's annual report.

- **Proxy Statements.** Shareholder votes are solicited for the election of directors and for corporate actions such as mergers, acquisitions, and authorization of securities. A **proxy** is a means whereby a shareholder authorizes another person to act for him or her at a meeting of shareholders. A **proxy statement** contains information necessary for shareholders in voting on matters for which the proxy is solicited. Proxy statements contain a wealth of information regarding a company including the identity of shareholders owning 5% or more of outstanding shares, biographical information on the board of directors, compensation arrangements with officers and directors, employee benefit plans, and certain transactions with officers and directors. Proxy statements are not typically part of the annual report.

DOUBLE TROUBLE
PricewaterhouseCoopers earned $13 million from audit fees and $18 million from tax fees it charged to scandal-ridden Tyco International Ltd. in 2001. The Sarbanes-Oxley Act now limits the consulting work that may be performed by a company's auditors.

GREEN REPORT CARD
About one-half of the 250 largest global companies produce corporate responsibility reports.

·······FINANCIAL STATEMENT ANALYSIS PREVIEW

A variety of tools designed to fit specific needs are available to help users analyze financial statements. In this section, we introduce some basic tools of financial analysis and apply them to Colgate's annual report. Specifically, we apply comparative financial statement analysis, common-size financial statement analysis, and ratio analysis. We also briefly describe cash flow analysis. This preview to financial analysis is mainly limited to some common analysis tools, especially as pertaining to ratio analysis. Later chapters describe more advanced, state-of-the-art techniques, including accounting analysis, that considerably enhance financial statement analysis. This section concludes with an introduction to valuation models.

Analysis Tools

This section gives preliminary exposure to five important sets of tools for financial analysis:

1. Comparative financial statement analysis
2. Common-size financial statement analysis
3. Ratio analysis
4. Cash flow analysis
5. Valuation

Comparative Financial Statement Analysis

Individuals conduct **comparative financial statement analysis** by reviewing consecutive balance sheets, income statements, or statements of cash flows from period to period. This usually involves a review of changes in individual account balances on a year-to-year or multiyear basis. The most important information often revealed from comparative financial statement analysis is trend. A comparison of statements over several periods can reveal the direction, speed, and extent of a trend. Comparative analysis also compares trends in related items. For example, a year-to-year 10% sales increase accompanied by a 20% increase in freight-out costs requires investigation and explanation. Similarly, a 15% increase in accounts receivable along with a sales increase of only 5% calls for investigation. In both cases we look for reasons behind differences in these interrelated rates and any implications for our analysis. Comparative financial statement analysis also is referred to as *horizontal analysis* given the left-right (or right-left) analysis of account balances as we review comparative statements. Two techniques of comparative analysis are especially popular: year-to-year change analysis and index-number trend analysis.

Year-to-Year Change Analysis.   Comparing financial statements over relatively short time periods—two to three years—is usually performed with analysis of year-to-year changes in individual accounts. A year-to-year change analysis for short time periods is manageable and understandable. It has the advantage of presenting changes in absolute dollar amounts as well as in percentages. Change analyses in both amounts and percentages are relevant since different dollar bases in computing percentage changes can yield large changes inconsistent with their actual importance. For example, a 50% change from a base amount of $1,000 is usually less significant than the same percentage change from a base of $100,000. Reference to dollar amounts is necessary to retain a proper perspective and to make valid inferences on the relative importance of changes.

Computation of year-to-year changes is straightforward. Still, a few rules should be noted. When a negative amount appears in the base and a positive amount in the next period (or vice versa), we cannot compute a meaningful percentage change. Also, when there is no amount for the base period, no percentage change is computable. Similarly, when the base period amount is small, a percentage change can be computed but the number must be interpreted with caution. This is because it can signal a large change merely because of the small base amount used in computing the change. Also, when an

Complications in comparative analysis and how we confront them are depicted in the following five cases:

ILLUSTRATION 1.1

			CHANGE ANALYSIS	
Item (in millions)	Period 1	Period 2	Amount	Percent
Net income (loss)	$(4,500)	$1,500	$ 6,000	—
Tax expense	2,000	(1,000)	(3,000)	—
Cash	10	2,010	2,000	20,000%
Notes payable	—	8,000	8,000	—
Notes receivable	10,000	—	(10,000)	(100%)

item has a value in the base period and none in the next period, the decrease is 100%. These points are underscored in Illustration 1.1.

Comparative financial statement analysis typically reports both the cumulative total for the period under analysis and the average (or median) for the period. Comparing yearly amounts with an average, or median, computed over a number of periods helps highlight unusual fluctuations.

Exhibit 1.10 shows a year-to-year comparative analysis using Colgate's income statements. This analysis reveals several items of note. First, net sales increased by 7.38% but cost of goods sold increased by only 6.63%, therefore increasing Colgate's gross profit by 8.01%, which is higher than its revenue increase. Overall, this suggests that Colgate has been able to control its production costs and therefore increase its profit margin on sale. Selling, general, and administrative expenses increased by 11.07%. In its MD&A section, Colgate attributes this increase to higher levels of advertising, charges related to the company's restructuring program, and incremental stock-based compensation expense recognized as a result of adopting the new accounting standard, *SFAS 123R*. Colgate's R&D declined slightly since 2004, partially attributable to the company's

Colgate's Comparative Income Statements

Exhibit 1.10

	($ MILLION)			
	2006	2005	Change	% Change
Net sales	$12,238	$11,397	$841	7.38%
Cost of sales	5,536	5,192	344	6.63
Gross profit	6,702	6,205	497	8.01
Selling, general, and administrative expenses . .	4,355	3,921	434	11.07
Other expense, net	186	69	117	169.57
Operating profit	2,161	2,215	(54)	−2.44
Interest expense, net	159	136	23	16.91
Income before income taxes	2,002	2,079	(77)	−3.70
Provision for income taxes	648	728	(80)	−10.99
Net income	$ 1,354	$ 1,351	$ 3	0.22

strategy of outsourcing a portion of its R&D activities. Pretax income decreased by 3.70%, but tax expense decreased by 10.99%, thereby increasing net income by 0.22%. Colgate reports that the increased tax expense is primarily the result of a tax incentive provided by the American Jobs Creation Act of 2004, which allowed the company the incremental repatriation of $780 million of foreign earnings, as well as the lower effective tax rate on charges incurred in connection with the company's 2004 restructuring program. In sum, Colgate is performing well in a tough competitive environment.

Index-Number Trend Analysis.   Using year-to-year change analysis to compare financial statements that cover more than two or three periods is sometimes cumbersome. A useful tool for long-term trend comparisons is *index-number trend analysis*. Analyzing data using index-number trend analysis requires choosing a base period, for all items, with a preselected index number usually set to 100. Because the base period is a frame of reference for all comparisons, it is best to choose a normal year with regard to business conditions. As with computing year-to-year percentage changes, certain changes, like those from negative amounts to positive amounts, cannot be expressed by means of index numbers.

When using index numbers, we compute percentage changes by reference to the base period as shown in Illustration 1.2.

ILLUSTRATION 1.2

■ ■ ■ ■ ■ ■ ■

CenTech's cash balance (in thousands) at December 31, Year 1 (the base period), is $12,000. Its cash balance at December 31, Year 2, is $18,000. Using 100 as the index number for Year 1, the index number for Year 2 equals 150 and is computed as:

$$\frac{\text{Current year balance}}{\text{Base year balance}} \times 100 = \frac{\$18,000}{\$12,000} \times 100 = 150$$

The cash balance of CenTech at December 31, Year 3, is $9,000. The index for Year 3 is 75 and is computed as:

$$\frac{\$9,000}{\$12,000} \times 100 = 75$$

The change in cash balance between Year 1 and Year 2 for this illustration is 50% (150 − 100), and is easily inferred from the index numbers. However, the change from Year 2 to Year 3 is not 75% (150 − 75), as a direct comparison might suggest. Instead, it is 50%, computed as $9,000/$18,000. This involves computing the Year 2 to Year 3 change by reference to the Year 2 balance. The percentage change is, however, computable using index numbers only. For example, in computing this change, we take 75/150 = 0.50, or a change of 50%.

For index-number trend analysis, we need not analyze every item in financial statements. Instead, we want to focus on significant items. We also must exercise care in using index-number trend comparisons where changes might be due to economy or industry factors. Moreover, interpretation of percentage changes, including those using index-number trend series, must be made with an awareness of potentially inconsistent applications of accounting principles over time. When possible, we adjust for these inconsistencies. Also, the longer the time period for comparison, the more distortive are effects of any price-level changes. One outcome of trend analysis is its power to convey insight into managers' philosophies, policies, and motivations. The more diverse the environments constituting the period of analysis, the better is our picture of how managers deal with adversity and take advantage of opportunities.

Results of index-number trend analysis on selected financial statement items for Colgate are reported in Exhibit 1.11. Sales have been steadily increasing since 2002 but followed by a slower increase in operating expenses.

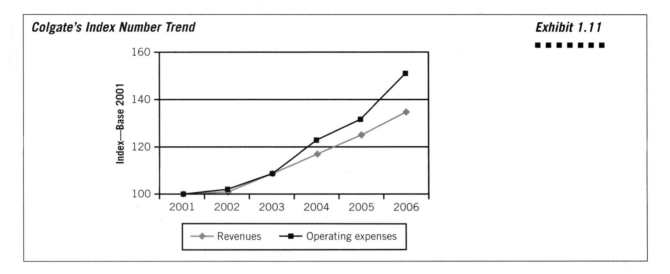

Colgate's Index Number Trend   *Exhibit 1.11*

Common-Size Financial Statement Analysis

Financial statement analysis can benefit from knowing what proportion of a group or subgroup is made up of a particular account. Specifically, in analyzing a balance sheet, it is common to express total assets (or liabilities plus equity) as 100%. Then, accounts within these groupings are expressed as a percentage of their respective total. In analyzing an income statement, sales are often set at 100% with the remaining income statement accounts expressed as a percentage of sales. Because the sum of individual accounts within groups is 100%, this analysis is said to yield **common-size financial statements.** This procedure also is called *vertical analysis* given the up-down (or down-up) evaluation of accounts in common-size statements. Common-size financial statement analysis is useful in understanding the internal makeup of financial statements. For example, in analyzing a balance sheet, a common-size analysis stresses two factors:

1. Sources of financing–including the distribution of financing across current liabilities, noncurrent liabilities, and equity.
2. Composition of assets–including amounts for individual current and noncurrent assets.

Common-size analysis of a balance sheet is often extended to examine the accounts that make up specific subgroups. For example, in assessing liquidity of current assets, it is often important to know what proportion of current assets is composed of inventories, and not simply what proportion inventories are of total assets. Common-size analysis of an income statement is equally important. An income statement readily lends itself to common-size analysis, where each item is related to a key amount such as sales.

To varying degrees, sales impact nearly all expenses, and it is useful to know what percentage of sales is represented by each expense item. An exception is income taxes, which is related to pre-tax income and not sales.

Temporal (time) comparisons of a company's common-size statements are useful in revealing any proportionate changes in accounts within groups of assets, liabilities, expenses, and other categories. Still, we must exercise care in interpreting changes and trends as shown in Illustration 1.3.

ILLUSTRATION 1.3

■ ■ ■ ■ ■ ■ ■

The recent three years' account balances for both Patents and Total Assets of Meade Co. are:

	2006	2005	2004
Patents	$ 50,000	$ 50,000	$ 50,000
Total assets	$1,000,000	$750,000	$500,000
Patents/Total assets	5%	6.67%	10%

While the dollar amount for patents remains unchanged for this period, increases in total assets progressively reduce patents as a percentage of total assets. Since this percent varies with both the change in the absolute dollar amount of an item and the change in the total balance for its category, interpretation of common-size analysis requires examination of both the amounts for the accounts under analysis and the bases for their computations.

Common-size statements are especially useful for intercompany comparisons because financial statements of different companies are recast in common-size format. Comparisons of a company's common-size statements with those of competitors, or with industry averages, can highlight differences in account makeup and distribution. Reasons for such differences should be explored and understood. One key limitation of common-size statements for intercompany analysis is their failure to reflect the relative sizes of the companies under analysis. A comparison of selected accounts using common-size statements along with industry statistics is part of the comprehensive case following Chapter 11.

Colgate's common-size income statements are shown in Exhibit 1.12. In 2006, Colgate earned around 11 cents per dollar of sales, in contrast to almost 14 cents in 2002, a drop of 3 cents per dollar of sales. *Prima facie,* this is not a good sign because it suggests the inability of the company to pass its costs on to its customers. Further analysis shows the following. Income tax provision decreased by more than 1% of sales in 2006; a large part of this decrease is due to changes in tax laws. Therefore, on a pretax basis the picture is worse: between 2002 and 2006 Colgate's income before taxes dropped by 3.7% of revenues, from 20.1% to 16.4%. What accounts for this decrease? First, Colgate's cost of sales has remained roughly proportional to sales revenue since 2002, resulting in a stable gross profit margin. This is a remarkable achievement, considering the significant increase over this period in the prices of several commodities that are raw materials for Colgate's products. Therefore, Colgate's cost of production has remained under control. Second, SG&A expenses, as a proportion of sales revenue, have been increasing steadily by almost 3% since 2002. In addition, other expenses have gone up by 1% of sales since 2002, with much of the increase occurring in 2006. Together, these two items explain the decrease in income before taxes. While some of this increase is attributable to increasing advertising and marketing costs to combat increasing competition, much of this increase in both SG&A and other

Colgate's Common-Size Income Statements   *Exhibit 1.12*

Common size	2006	2005	2004	2003	2002
Net revenue	100.0	100.0	100.0	100.0	100.0
Cost of sales	45.2	45.6	44.9	45.0	45.4
Gross profit	54.8	54.4	55.1	55.0	54.6
Selling, general, and administrative expenses	35.6	34.4	34.2	33.3	32.6
Other (income) expense, net	1.5	0.6	0.9	(0.2)	0.2
Operating profit	17.7	19.4	20.0	21.9	21.7
Interest expense, net	1.3	1.2	1.1	1.3	1.5
Income before income taxes	16.4	18.2	18.9	20.6	20.1
Provision for income taxes	5.3	6.4	6.4	6.3	6.3
Net income	11.1	11.9	12.5	14.4	13.9

expenses is attributable to costs related to Colgate's 2004 restructuring program (see Appendix A for details), which accounts for about 3% of revenues on a pretax basis. If we exclude restructuring costs, Colgate's net income in 2006 is 13% of revenues, which is only marginally lower than that in 2002.

Common-size analysis of Colgate's balance sheets is in Exhibit 1.13. Because Colgate is a manufacturing company, PP&E constitutes almost 30% of its total assets. The share of PP&E has dropped from around 35% in 2002, partly because of depreciation of aging assets and because of increasing outsourcing of its manufacturing operations. Intangible assets and goodwill account for 31.9% of its assets, indicating significant acquisitions in the past. In comparison, 36% of Colgate's assets are current, up from 31.4% in 2002. While receivables are the largest component of current assets, much of the increase in current assets is explained by increases in cash and in inventory. Current liabilities are 38.4% of assets, which is larger than its current assets. This does not bode well for Colgate's liquidity. Current portion of long-term debt constitutes 8.5% of its current liabilities. Colgate's operating working capital (operating current assets less operating current assets) is 3% of its assets, suggesting that Colgate has not tied up much money in its working capital. A lion's share of Colgate's financing is debt: total liabilities are almost 85% of assets, of which more than 38% is long-term debt (including current portion). Colgate's shareholder's equity makes interesting reading. Just 21% of Colgate's assets have been financed by equity share capital, retained earnings (net of accumulated comprehensive income) are 83% of assets and a whopping 88% of its assets are treasury stock, which suggests significant stock repurchases. Because of the significant stock repurchase activity, Colgate's share of net equity financing is just 15% of assets. For most companies, such a small share of equity financing may be cause for concern, but in Colgate's case it just reflects its generous payout to shareholders.

Ratio Analysis

Ratio analysis is among the most popular and widely used tools of financial analysis. Yet its role is often misunderstood and, consequently, its importance often overrated. A ratio expresses a mathematical relation between two quantities. A ratio of 200 to 100 is expressed as 2:1, or simply 2. While computation of a ratio is a simple arithmetic

Exhibit 1.13

■ ■ ■ ■ ■ ■ ■

Colgate's Common-Size Balance Sheets

	2006	2005	2004	2003	2002
Assets					
Current assets					
Cash and cash equivalents	5.4	4.0	3.7	3.6	2.4
Receivables, net	16.7	15.4	15.2	16.3	16.2
Inventories	11.0	10.1	9.7	9.3	9.5
Other current assets	3.1	3.0	2.9	3.9	3.4
Total current assets	36.1	32.4	31.6	33.4	31.4
Property, plant, and equipment, net	29.5	29.9	30.5	34.0	35.2
Goodwill, net	22.8	21.7	21.8	17.4	16.7
Other intangible assets, net	9.1	9.2	9.6	8.0	8.6
Other assets	2.5	6.8	6.5	7.3	8.1
Total assets	100.0	100.0	100.0	100.0	100.0
Liabilities and Shareholders' Equity					
Current liabilities					
Notes and loans payable	1.9	2.0	1.5	1.4	1.3
Current portion of long-term debt	8.5	4.2	5.2	4.2	4.2
Accounts payable	11.4	10.3	10.0	10.1	10.3
Accrued income taxes	1.8	2.5	1.8	2.5	1.7
Other accruals	14.4	13.2	13.0	14.6	12.8
Total current liabilities	38.4	32.2	31.5	32.7	30.3
Long-term debt	29.8	34.3	35.6	35.9	45.3
Deferred income taxes	3.4	6.5	5.9	6.1	6.9
Other liabilities	13.4	9.9	12.7	13.4	12.5
Total liabilities	84.6	84.1	85.6	88.3	95.1
Shareholders' Equity					
Preferred stock	2.4	3.0	3.2	3.9	4.6
Common stock	8.0	8.6	8.5	9.8	10.3
Additional paid-in capital	13.3	12.5	12.6	15.1	16.0
Retained earnings	105.5	105.4	94.8	99.4	91.8
Accumulated other comprehensive income	(22.8)	(21.2)	(20.8)	(25.0)	(26.3)
Unearned compensation	(2.8)	(3.3)	(3.5)	(4.4)	(4.8)
Treasury stock, at cost	(88.4)	(89.1)	(80.3)	(86.9)	(86.8)
Total shareholders' equity	15.4	15.9	14.4	11.7	4.9
Total liabilities and shareholders' equity	100.0	100.0	100.0	100.0	100.0

operation, its interpretation is more complex. To be meaningful, a ratio must refer to an economically important relation. For example, there is a direct and crucial relation between an item's sales price and its cost. Accordingly, the ratio of cost of goods sold to sales is important. In contrast, there is no obvious relation between freight costs and the balance of marketable securities. The example in Illustration 1.4 highlights this point.

Consider interpreting the ratio of gasoline consumption to miles driven, referred to as miles per gallon (mpg). On the basis of the ratio of gas consumption to miles driven, person X claims to have the superior performer, that is, 28 mpg compared to person Y's 20 mpg. Is person X's vehicle superior in minimizing gas consumption? To answer that question there are several factors affecting gas consumption that require analysis before we can properly interpret these results and identify the superior performer. These factors include: (1) weight load, (2) type of terrain, (3) city or highway driving, (4) grade of fuel, and (5) travel speed. Numerous as the factors influencing gas consumption are, evaluating a gas consumption ratio is a simpler analysis than evaluating financial statement ratios. This is because of the interrelations in business variables and the complexity of factors affecting them.

We must remember that ratios are tools to provide us with insights into underlying conditions. They are one of the starting points of analysis, not an end point. Ratios, properly interpreted, identify areas requiring further investigation. Analysis of a ratio can reveal important relations and bases of comparison in uncovering conditions and trends difficult to detect by inspecting the individual components that make up the ratio. Still, like other analysis tools, ratios often are most useful when they are future oriented. This means we often adjust the factors affecting a ratio for their probable future trend and magnitude. We also must assess factors potentially influencing future ratios. Therefore, the usefulness of ratios depends on our skillful application and interpretation of them, and these are the most challenging aspects of ratio analysis.

Factors Affecting Ratios.   Beyond the internal operating activities that affect a company's ratios, we must be aware of the effects of economic events, industry factors, management policies, and accounting methods. Our discussion of accounting analysis later in the book highlights the influence of these factors on the measurements underlying ratios. Any limitations in accounting measurements impact the effectiveness of ratios.

Prior to computing ratios, or similar measures like trend indices or percent relations, we use accounting analysis to make sure the numbers underlying ratio computations are appropriate. For example, when inventories are valued using LIFO (see Chapter 4) and prices are increasing, the current ratio is understated because LIFO inventories (the numerator) are understated. Similarly, certain lease liabilities are often unrecorded and disclosed in notes only (see Chapter 3). We usually want to recognize lease liabilities when computing ratios like debt to equity. We also need to remember that the usefulness of ratios depends on the reliability of the numbers. When a company's internal accounting controls or other governance and monitoring mechanisms are less reliable in generating credible figures, the resulting ratios are equally less reliable.

Ratio Interpretation.   Ratios must be interpreted with care because factors affecting the numerator can correlate with those affecting the denominator. For instance, companies can improve the ratio of operating expenses to sales by reducing costs that stimulate sales (such as advertising). However, reducing these types of costs is likely to yield long-term declines in sales or market share. Thus, a seemingly short-term improvement in profitability can damage a company's future prospects. We must interpret such changes appropriately. Many ratios have important variables in common with other ratios. Accordingly, it is not necessary to compute all possible ratios to analyze a situation. Ratios, like most techniques in financial analysis, are not relevant in isolation. Instead, they are usefully interpreted in comparison with (1) prior ratios, (2) predetermined standards, and (3) ratios of competitors. Finally, the variability of a ratio across time is often as important as its trend.

Illustration of Ratio Analysis. We can compute numerous ratios using a company's financial statements. Some ratios have general application in financial analysis, while others are unique to specific circumstances or industries. This section presents ratio analysis as applied to three important areas of financial statement analysis:

1. **Credit (Risk) Analysis**
   a. **Liquidity.** To evaluate the ability to meet short-term obligations.
   b. **Capital structure and solvency.** To assess the ability to meet long-term obligations.
2. **Profitability Analysis**
   a. **Return on investment.** To assess financial rewards to the suppliers of equity and debt financing.
   b. **Operating performance.** To evaluate profit margins from operating activities.
   c. **Asset utilization.** To assess effectiveness and intensity of assets in generating sales, also called *turnover.*
3. **Valuation**
   a. To estimate the intrinsic value of a company (stock).

Exhibit 1.14 reports results for selected ratios having applicability to most companies. A more complete listing of ratios is located on the book's inside cover. Data used in this illustration are from Colgate's annual report in Appendix A, although most ratios can be computed from informations in the financial statements presented in Exhibits 1.5 through 1.8.

Exhibit 1.14

■ ■ ■ ■ ■ ■ ■

Financial Statement Ratios for Colgate (2006)

Liquidity

$$\text{Current ratio} = \frac{\text{Current assets}}{\text{Current liabilities}} = \frac{\$3,301.0}{\$3,469.1} = 0.95$$

$$\text{Acid-test ratio} = \frac{\text{Cash and cash equivalents} + \text{Marketable securities} + \text{Accounts receivable}}{\text{Current liabilities}}$$

$$= \frac{\$489.5 + \$1,523.2}{\$3,469.1} = 0.58$$

$$\text{Collection period} = \frac{\text{Average accounts receivable}}{\text{Sales}/360} = \frac{(\$1,523.2 + \$1,309.4)/2}{12,237.7/360} = 41.66 \text{ days}$$

$$\text{Days to sell inventory} = \frac{\text{Average inventory}}{\text{Cost of sales}/360} = \frac{(\$1,008.4 + \$855.8)/2}{\$5,536.1/360} = 60.61 \text{ days}$$

Capital Structure and Solvency

$$\text{Total debt to equity} = \frac{\text{Total liabilities}}{\text{Shareholder's equity}} = \frac{\$7,727.1}{\$1,410.9} = 5.48$$

$$\text{Long-term debt to equity} = \frac{\text{Long-term liabilities}}{\text{Shareholders' equity}} = \frac{\$4,258.0}{\$1,410.9} = 3.02$$

$$\text{Times interest earned} = \frac{\text{Income before income taxes and interest expense}}{\text{Interest expense}} = \frac{\$2,001.8 + \$158.7}{\$158.7} = 13.61$$

(continued)

Financial Statement Ratios for Colgate *(concluded)*

■ ■ ■ ■ ■ ■ ■ ■

Return on Investment

$$\text{Return on assets} = \frac{\text{Net income} + \text{interest expense} \times (1 - \text{Tax rate})}{\text{Average total assets}}$$

$$= \frac{\$1,353.4 + \$158.7(1 - 0.35)}{(\$9,138.0 + \$8,507.1)/2} = 16.51\%$$

$$\text{Return on common equity} = \frac{\text{Net income}}{\text{Average shareholders' equity}} = \frac{\$1,353.4}{(\$1,410.9 + \$1,350.1)/2} = 98.04\%$$

1380.5

Operating Performance

$$\text{Gross profit margin} = \frac{\text{Sales} - \text{Cost of sales}}{\text{Sales}} = \frac{\$12,237.7 - \$5,536.1}{\$12,237.7} = 54.76\%$$

$$\text{Operating profit margin (pretax)} = \frac{\text{Income from operations}}{\text{Sales}} = \frac{\$2,160.5}{\$12,237.7} = 17.65\%$$

$$\text{Net profit margin} = \frac{\text{Net income}}{\text{Sales}} = \frac{\$1,353.4}{\$12,237.7} = 11.01\%$$

Asset Utilization

$$\text{Cash turnover} = \frac{\text{Sales}}{\text{Average cash and equivalents}} = \frac{\$12,237.7}{(\$489.5 + \$340.7)/2} = 29.48$$

$$\text{Accounts receivable turnover} = \frac{\text{Sales}}{\text{Average accounts receivable}} = \frac{\$12,237.7}{(\$1,523.2 + \$1,309.4)/2} = 8.64$$

$$\text{Inventory turnover} = \frac{\text{Cost of sales}}{\text{Average inventory}} = \frac{\$5,536.1}{(\$1,008.4 + \$855.8)/2} = 5.94$$

$$\text{Working capital turnover} = \frac{\text{Sales}}{\text{Average working capital}} = \frac{\$12,237.7}{[(\$3,301.0 - \$3,469.1) + (\$2,757.1 - \$2,743.0)]/2} = -158.93$$

$$\text{PPE turnover} = \frac{\text{Sales}}{\text{Average PPE}} = \frac{\$12,237.7}{(\$2,696.1 + \$2,544.1)/2} = 4.67$$

$$\text{Total asset turnover} = \frac{\text{Sales}}{\text{Average total assets}} = \frac{\$12,237.7}{(\$9,138.0 + \$8,507.1)/2} = 1.39$$

Market Measures

$$\text{Price-to-earnings} = \frac{\text{Market price per share}}{\text{Earnings per share}} = \frac{\$65.24}{\$2.57} = 25.39$$

$$\text{Earnings yield} = \frac{\text{Earnings per share}}{\text{Market price per share}} = \frac{\$2.57}{\$65.24} = 3.94\%$$

$$\text{Dividend yield} = \frac{\text{Cash dividends per share}}{\text{Market price per share}} = \frac{\$1.25}{\$65.24} = 1.92\%$$

$$\text{Dividend payout rate} = \frac{\text{Cash dividends per share}}{\text{Earnings per share}} = \frac{\$1.25}{\$2.57} = 48.64\%$$

$$\text{Price-to-book} = \frac{\text{Market price per share}}{\text{Book value per share}} = \frac{\$65.24}{\$2.81} = 23.22$$

Credit Analysis. First, we focus on *liquidity*. Liquidity refers to the ability of an enterprise to meet its short-term financial obligations. An important liquidity ratio is the *current ratio*, which measures current assets available to satisfy current liabilities. Colgate's current ratio of 0.95 implies there are 95 cents of current assets available to meet each $1 of currently maturing obligations. A more stringent test of short-term liquidity, based on the *acid-test ratio*, uses only the most liquid current assets: cash, short-term investments, and accounts receivable. Colgate has 58 cents of such liquid assets to cover each $1 of current liabilities. Both these ratios suggest that Colgate's liquidity situation is cause for concern. Still, we need more information to draw definite conclusions about liquidity. The length of time needed for conversion of receivables and inventories to cash also provides useful information regarding liquidity. Colgate's *collection period* for receivables is approximately 42 days, and its *days to sell inventory* is 61. Neither of these indicates any liquidity problems. However, these measures are more useful when compared over time (i.e., changes in these measures are more informative about liquidity problems than levels). Overall, our brief analysis of liquidity suggests that while Colgate's composition of current assets and current liabilities are cause for concern, its receivables and inventory periods coupled with its excellent cash flow from operations (see later discussion) indicate that there is not much cause for concern.

Analysis of Solvency. Solvency refers to the ability of an enterprise to meet its long-term financial obligations. To assess Colgate's long-term financing structure and credit risk, we examine its *capital structure and solvency*. Its *total debt-to-equity ratio* of 5.48 indicates that for each $1 of equity financing, $5.48 of financing is provided by creditors. Its *long-term debt-to-equity ratio* is 3.02, revealing $3.02 of long-term debt financing to each $1 of equity. Both these ratios are extremely high for a manufacturing company; such high ratios are more typical for a financial institution! On their own, they do raise concerns about Colgate's ability to service its debt and remain solvent in the long run. However, these ratios do not consider Colgate's excellent profitability. Another ratio that also considers profitability in addition to capital structure is the *times interest earned ratio* (or *interest coverage ratio*), which is the ratio of a company's earnings before interest to its interest payment. Colgate's 2006 earnings are 13.61 times its fixed (interest) commitments. This ratio indicates that Colgate will have no problem meeting its fixed-charge commitments. In sum, given Colgate's high (and stable) profitability, its solvency risk is low.

Profitability Analysis. We begin by assessing different aspects of return on investment. Colgate's *return on assets* of 16.51% implies that a $1 asset investment generates 16.51 cents of annual earnings prior to subtracting after-tax interest. Equity holders are especially interested in management's performance based on equity financing, so we also look at the return on equity. Colgate's *return on common equity* (or more commonly termed as *return on equity*) of 98.04% suggests it earns 98.04 cents annually for each $1 of equity investment. Both of these ratios are significantly higher than the average for publicly traded companies of approximately 7% and 12%, respectively. Colgate's return on equity, in particular, is probably one of the highest among U.S. companies.

    Another part of profitability analysis is evaluation of *operating performance*. This is done by examining ratios that typically link income statement line items to sales. These ratios are often referred to as *profit margins*, for example, gross profit margin (or more concisely gross margin). These ratios are comparable to results from common-size income statement analysis. The operating performance ratios for Colgate in Exhibit 1.14

■ ■ ■ ■ ■ ■ ■

DEBT TRIGGER

GM's bloated pension obligations and poor earnings resulted in a downgrade of its $300 billion in debt. This reflects a higher probability of default. Debt-rating downgrades usually result in higher interest rates for the borrower and can trigger bond default.

reflect a remarkable operating performance in the face of a highly competitive environment. Colgate's *gross profit margin* of 54.7% reflects its inherent ability to sell well above its cost of production, despite the intensely competitive consumer products' markets. Its pre-tax *operating profit margin* of 17.65% and *net profit margin* of 11.01% is well above average for U.S. companies. In sum, Colgate's pricing power and superior control of production costs make it a very profitable company.

Asset utilization analysis is closely linked with profitability analysis. Asset utilization ratios, which relate sales to different asset categories, are important determinants of return on investment. These ratios for Colgate indicate above average performance. For example, Colgate's total asset turnover of 1.39 is higher than the average for all publicly traded companies in the United States. Also Colgate's working capital turnover is negative, because its current assets are below its current liabilities. This indicates that Colgate has not invested in working capital.

Valuation.   Exhibit 1.14 also includes five valuation measures. Colgate's price-to-earnings ratio of 25.39 and price-to-book of 23.22 are high and reflect the market's favorable perception of Colgate as a solid performer. Colgate's dividend payout rate of 48.64% is high, indicating that Colgate chooses to pay out a large proportion of its profits.

Ratio analysis yields many valuable insights as is apparent from our preliminary analysis of Colgate. We must, however, keep in mind that these computations are based on numbers reported in Colgate's financial statements. We stress in this book that our ability to draw useful insights and make valid intercompany comparisons is enhanced by our adjustments to reported numbers prior to their inclusion in these analyses. We also must keep in mind that ratio analysis is only one part of financial analysis. An analyst must dig deeper to understand the underlying factors driving ratios and to effectively integrate different ratios to evaluate a company's financial position and performance.

Cash Flow Analysis

Cash flow analysis is primarily used as a tool to evaluate the sources and uses of funds. Cash flow analysis provides insights into how a company is obtaining its financing and deploying its resources. It also is used in cash flow forecasting and as part of liquidity analysis.

Colgate's statement of cash flows reproduced in Exhibit 1.8 is a useful starting point for cash flow analysis. Colgate generated $1.822 billion from operating activities. It then used $620 million for investing activities, primarily for capital expenditure and payment for acquisitions. Colgate also paid $1.332 million for debt retirement, which it financed by issuing fresh debt to the tune of $1.471 billion. The remaining cash flow was primarily returned to its shareholders, in the form of common dividends ($0.678 billion) and repurchase of common stock ($0.885 billion). Overall, Colgate's financing activities resulted in a net cash outflow to the tune of $1.059 million. After accounting for foreign currency exchange rate fluctuations, Colgate's cash flow increased by $148 million during 2006.

This preliminary analysis shows that Colgate generated copious cash flows from its operations. After using some of it for capital expenditure and acquisitions, the rest of the generated cash was paid back to shareholders through dividends and stock repurchases. While this simple analysis of the statement of cash flows conveys much information about the sources and uses of funds at Colgate, it is important to analyze cash flows in more detail for a more thorough investigation of Colgate's business and financial activities. We return to cash flow analysis in Chapters 7 and 9.

Valuation Models

■ ■ ■ ■ ■ ■ ■
IPO MISDEALS
Investment banking institutions have recently been investigated for allegedly allocating hot-selling IPO shares to favored executives to cut more investment-banking deals instead of selling them to the highest bidders.

Valuation is an important outcome of many types of business and financial statement analysis. **Valuation** normally refers to estimating the intrinsic value of a company or its stock. The basis of valuation is **present value theory.** This theory states the value of a debt or equity security (or for that matter, any asset) is equal to the sum of all expected future payoffs from the security that are discounted to the present at an appropriate *discount rate*. Present value theory uses the concept of *time value of money*—it simply states an entity prefers present consumption more than future consumption. Accordingly, to value a security an investor needs two pieces of information: (1) expected future payoffs over the life of the security and (2) a discount rate. For example, future payoffs from bonds are principal and interest payments. Future payoffs from stocks are dividends and capital appreciation. The discount rate in the case of a bond is the prevailing interest rate (or more precisely, the *yield to maturity*), while in the case of a stock it is the risk-adjusted *cost of capital* (also called the *expected rate of return*).

This section begins with a discussion of valuation techniques as applied to debt securities. Because of its simplicity, debt valuation provides an ideal setting to grasp key valuation concepts. We then conclude this section with a discussion of equity valuation.

Debt Valuation

The value of a security is equal to the present value of its future payoffs discounted at an appropriate rate. The future payoffs from a debt security are its interest and principal payments. A bond contract precisely specifies its future payoffs along with the investment horizon. The value of a bond at time t, or B_t, is computed using the following formula:

$$B_t = \frac{I_{t+1}}{(1+r)^1} + \frac{I_{t+2}}{(1+r)^2} + \frac{I_{t+3}}{(1+r)^3} + \cdots + \frac{I_{t+n}}{(1+r)^n} + \frac{F}{(1+r)^n}$$

■ ■ ■ ■ ■ ■ ■
MUTUAL FUNDS
The mutual-fund industry has more than $6 trillion in equity, bond, and money-market funds.

where I_{t+n} is the interest payment in period $t + n$, F is the principal payment (usually the debt's face value), and r is the investor's required interest rate, or yield to maturity. When valuing bonds, we determine the expected (or desired) yield based on factors such as current interest rates, expected inflation, and risk of default. Illustration 1.5 offers an example of debt valuation.

ILLUSTRATION 1.5
■ ■ ■ ■ ■ ■ ■

On January 1, Year 1, a company issues $100 of eight-year bonds with a year-end interest (coupon) payment of 8% per annum. On January 1, Year 6, we are asked to compute the value of this bond when the yield to maturity on these bonds is 6% per annum.

Solution: These bonds will be redeemed on December 31, Year 8. This means the remaining term to maturity is three years. Each year-end interest payment on these bonds is $8, computed as 8% × $100, and the end of Year 8 principal payment is $100. The value of these bonds as of January 1, Year 6, is computed as:

$$\$8/(1.06) + \$8/(1.06)^2 + \$8/(1.06)^3 + \$100/(1.06)^3 = \$105.35$$

Equity Valuation

Basis of Equity Valuation. The basis of equity valuation, like debt valuation, is the present value of future payoffs discounted at an appropriate rate. Equity valuation, however, is more complex than debt valuation. This is because, with a bond, the future payoffs are specified. With equity, the investor has no claim on predetermined payoffs. Instead, the equity investor looks for two main (uncertain) payoffs–dividend payments and capital appreciation. Capital appreciation denotes change in equity value, which in turn is determined by future dividends, so we can simplify this task to state that the value of an equity security at time t, or V_t, equals the sum of the present values of all future expected dividends:

$$V_t = \frac{E(D_{t+1})}{(1+k)^1} + \frac{E(D_{t+2})}{(1+k)^2} + \frac{E(D_{t+3})}{(1+k)^3} + \cdots$$

where D_{t+n} is the dividend in period $t + n$, and k is the cost of capital. This model is called the **dividend discount model.** This equity valuation formula is in terms of *expected* dividends rather than *actual* dividends. We use expectations instead of actual dividends because, unlike interest and principal repayments in the case of a bond, future dividends are neither specified nor determinable with certainty. This means our analysis must use forecasts of future dividends to get an estimate of value.

Alternatively, we might define value as the present value of future cash flows. This definition is problematic for at least two reasons. First, the term *cash flows* is vague. There are many different types of cash flows: operating cash flows, investing cash flows, financing cash flows, and net cash flows (change in cash balance). Hence, which type of cash flows should one use? Second, while we can rewrite the equity valuation formula in terms of one type of cash flows, called *free cash flows*, it is incorrect to define value in terms of cash flows. This is because dividends are the actual payoffs to equity investors and, therefore, the only appropriate valuation attribute. Any other formula is merely a derived form of this fundamental formula. While the free cash flow formula is technically exact, it is simply one derived formula from among several. One can also derive an exact valuation formula using accounting variables independent of cash flows.

Practical Considerations in Valuation. The dividend discount model faces practical obstacles. One main problem is that of infinite horizon. Practical valuation techniques must compute value using a finite forecast horizon. However, forecasting dividends is difficult in a finite horizon. This is because dividend payments are discretionary, and different companies adopt different dividend payment policies. For example, some companies prefer to pay out a large portion of earnings as dividends, while other companies choose to reinvest earnings. This means actual dividend payouts are not indicative of company value except in the very long run. The result is that valuation models often replace dividends with earnings or cash flows. This section introduces two such valuation models–the free cash flow model and the residual income model.

The **free cash flow to equity model** computes equity value at time t by replacing expected dividends with expected free cash flows to equity:

$$V_t = \frac{E(FCFE_{t+1})}{(1+k)^1} + \frac{E(FCFE_{t+2})}{(1+k)^2} + \frac{E(FCFE_{t+3})}{(1+k)^3} + \cdots$$

where $FCFE_{t+n}$ is free cash flow to equity in period $t + n$, and k is cost of capital. *Free cash flows to equity* are defined as cash flows from operations less capital expenditures plus increases (minus decreases) in debt. They are cash flows that are free to be paid to equity investors and, therefore, are an appropriate measure of equity investors' payoffs.

Free cash flows also can be defined for the *entire* firm. Specifically, free cash flows to the firm (or simply *free cash flows*) equal operating cash flows (adjusted for interest expense and revenue) less investments in operating assets. Then, the value of the entire firm equals the discounted expected future free cash flows using the weighted average cost of capital. (Note, the value of equity equals the value of the entire firm less the value of debt.)

The **residual income model** computes value using accounting variables. It defines equity value at time t as the sum of current book value and the present value of all future expected residual income:

$$V_t = BV_t + \frac{E(RI_{t+1})}{(1+k)^1} + \frac{E(RI_{t+2})}{(1+k)^2} + \frac{E(RI_{t+3})}{(1+k)^3} + \cdots$$

where BV_t is book value at the end of period t, RI_{t+n} is residual income in period $t + n$, and k is cost of capital. **Residual income** at time t is defined as comprehensive net income minus a charge on beginning book value, that is, $RI_t = NI_t - (k \times BV_{t-1})$.

While both of these models overcome some problems in using dividends, they still are defined in terms of an infinite horizon. To derive value using a finite horizon (say, 5 or 10 years), we must replace the present value of future dividends beyond a particular future date by an estimate of **continuing value** (also called **terminal value**). Unlike forecasts of payoffs for the finite period that often are derived using detailed prospective analysis, a forecast of continuing value is usually based on simplifying assumptions for growth in payoffs. While forecasting continuing value often is a source of much error, its estimation is required in equity valuation.

Note that all three models–dividend discount, free cash flow to equity, and residual income–are identical and exact in an infinite horizon. Therefore, choosing a valuation model is based on practical considerations in a finite horizon setting. Moreover, an important criterion is to choose a valuation model least dependent on continuing value. While the free cash flow to equity and dividend discount models work well under certain circumstances in finite horizons, the residual income model usually outperforms both. Illustration 1.6 shows the mechanics of applying the dividend discount model, the free cash to equity model, and the residual income model. Still, a complete understanding of these valuation models, the implications of finite horizons, and the practical considerations of alternative models is beyond the scope of this chapter. We return to these issues in Chapter 11.

ILLUSTRATION 1.6

∎∎∎∎∎∎∎

At the end of year 2004, Pitbull Co. owns 51% of the equity of Labrador, an entirely equity-financed company. By agreement with Labrador's shareholders, Pitbull agrees to acquire the remaining 49% of Labrador shares at the end of year 2009 at a price of $25 per share. Labrador also agrees to maintain annual cash dividends at $1 per share through 2009. An analyst makes the following projections for Labrador:

(in $ per share)	2004	2005	2006	2007	2008	2009
Dividends	—	$1.00	$1.00	$1.00	$1.00	$1.00
Operating cash flows	—	1.25	1.50	1.50	2.00	2.25
Capital expenditures	—	—	—	1.00	1.00	—
Increase (decrease) in long-term debt	—	(0.25)	(0.50)	0.50	—	(1.25)
Net income	—	1.20	1.30	1.40	1.50	1.65
Book value	$5.00	—	—	—	—	—

At this same time (end of year 2004), we wish to compute the intrinsic value of the remaining 49% of Labrador's shares using the alternative valuation models (assume a cost of capital of 10%).

Solution: Since Pitbull will acquire Labrador at the end of 2009 for $25 per share, the terminal value is set–this spares us the task of estimating continuing (or terminal) value. Using the **dividend discount model,** we determine intrinsic value at the end of year 2004 as:

$$\text{Intrinsic value} = \frac{\$1}{(1.1)^1} + \frac{\$1}{(1.1)^2} + \frac{\$1}{(1.1)^3} + \frac{\$1}{(1.1)^4} + \frac{\$1}{(1.1)^5} + \frac{\$25}{(1.1)^5} = 19.31$$

Next, to apply the free cash flow to equity model, we compute the following amounts for Labrador:

(in $ per share)	2005	2006	2007	2008	2009
Operating cash flows*	$1.25	$1.50	$1.50	$2.00	$2.25
− Capital expenditures*	—	—	(1.00)	(1.00)	—
+/− Debt increase (decrease)	(0.25)	(0.50)	0.50	—	(1.25)
= Free cash flow to equity	$1.00	$1.00	$1.00	$1.00	$1.00

*Amounts taken from analyst's projections.

The excess cash flows not needed for the payment of dividends are used to reduce long-term debt. The free cash flows to equity, then, are the cash flows available to pay the dividend requirement of $1. Then, using the free cash flows to equity model, we determine the value of the firm as:

$$\text{FCFE value} = \frac{\$1}{(1.1)^1} + \frac{\$1}{(1.1)^2} + \frac{\$1}{(1.1)^3} + \frac{\$1}{(1.1)^4} + \frac{\$1}{(1.1)^5} + \frac{\$25}{(1.1)^5} = 19.31$$

The free cash flows to equity model values the cash flows generated by the firm, whether or not paid out as dividends.

Finally, to apply the residual income model, we compute the following amounts for Labrador:

(in $ per share)	2005	2006	2007	2008	2009
Net income*	$1.20	$1.30	$1.40	$1.50	$ 1.65
− Capital charge (10% of beg. book value*)	(0.50)	(0.52)	(0.55)	(0.59)	(0.64)
= Residual income	$0.70	$0.78	$0.85	$0.91	$ 1.01
+ Gain on sale of equity to Pitbull (terminal value)					$17.95[†]

*Amounts taken from analyst's projections.
[†]$25 − $7.05.

Using the **residual income model,** we compute intrinsic value at the end of year 2004 as:

$$\text{Intrinsic value} = \$5.00 + \frac{\$0.70}{(1.1)^1} + \frac{\$0.78}{(1.1)^2} + \frac{\$0.85}{(1.1)^3} + \frac{\$0.91}{(1.1)^4} + \frac{\$1.01}{(1.1)^5} + \frac{\$17.95}{(1.1)^5} = \$19.31$$

All three models yield the same intrinsic value.

Analysis in an Efficient Market

Market Efficiency

■ ■ ■ ■ ■ ■ ■
**BEATING THE
(FOOTBALL) ODDS**
An article in *Journal of Business* looks at the efficiency of the pro football-betting market. Efficiency tests are applied to movements in point spreads. Results show it's possible to make some money by adopting a contrarian strategy— that is, waiting till the last minute and then betting against point-spread shifts. But such a strategy is only marginally profitable after accounting for the casinos' fee. That is, the football-betting market appears inefficient, but not enough for investors to capitalize on its inefficiencies.

The **efficient market hypothesis,** or EMH for short, deals with the reaction of market prices to financial and other information. There are three common forms of EMH. The *weak form* EMH asserts that prices reflect fully the information contained in historical price movements. The *semistrong form* EMH asserts that prices reflect fully all publicly available information. The *strong form* EMH asserts that prices reflect *all* information including inside information. There is considerable research on EMH. Early evidence so strongly supported both weak and semistrong form EMH that efficiency of capital markets became a generally accepted hypothesis. More recent research, however, questions the generality of EMH. A number of stock price anomalies have been uncovered suggesting investors can earn excess returns using simple trading strategies. Nevertheless, as a first approximation, current stock price is a reasonable estimate of company value.

Market Efficiency Implications for Analysis

EMH assumes the existence of competent and well-informed analysts using tools of analysis like those described in this book. It also assumes analysts are continually evaluating and acting on the stream of information entering the marketplace. Extreme proponents of EMH claim that if all information is instantly reflected in prices, attempts to reap consistent rewards through financial statement analysis is futile. This extreme position presents a paradox. On one hand, financial statement analysts are assumed capable of keeping markets efficient, yet these same analysts are assumed as unable to earn excess returns from their efforts. Moreover, if analysts presume their efforts in this regard are futile, the efficiency of the market ceases.

Several factors might explain this apparent paradox. Foremost among them is that EMH is built on aggregate, rather than individual, investor behavior. Focusing on aggregate behavior highlights average performance and ignores or masks individual performance based on ability, determination, and ingenuity, as well as superior individual timing in acting on information. Most believe that relevant information travels fast, encouraged by the magnitude of the financial stakes. Most also believe markets are rapid processors of information. Indeed, we contend the speed and efficiency of the market are evidence of analysts at work, motivated by personal rewards.

EMH's alleged implication regarding the futility of financial statement analysis fails to recognize an essential difference between information and its proper interpretation. That is, even if all information available at a given point in time is incorporated in price, this price does not necessarily reflect value. A security can be under- or overvalued, depending on the extent of an incorrect interpretation or faulty evaluation of available information by the aggregate market. Market efficiency depends not only on availability of information but also on its correct interpretation. Financial statement analysis is complex and demanding. The spectrum of financial statement users varies from an institutional analyst who concentrates on but a few companies in one industry to an unsophisticated chaser of rumors. All act on information, but surely not with the same insight and competence. A competent analysis of information entering the marketplace requires a sound analytical knowledge base and an information mosaic—one to fit new information to aid in evaluation and interpretation of a company's financial position and performance. Not all individuals possess the ability and determination to expend

Analysis Research
■■■■■■■
IS THE STOCK MARKET EFFICIENT?

The efficient markets hypothesis (EMH) has driven many investment strategies for the past three decades. While Wall Street has not embraced EMH as wholeheartedly as the academic community, it has won many converts. While no one maintains that markets are *strong form* efficient, there is a wealth of evidence suggesting that the stock markets (at least in the United States) are both *weak form* and *semistrong form* efficient. That is, stock prices are serially uncorrelated—meaning there are no predictable patterns in prices. Stock markets seemingly respond rapidly to information, such as earnings announcements and dividend changes. The markets also seem to filter information, making it difficult to fool the market with cosmetic accounting changes. For example, the markets seem to understand the implications of alternative accounting choices, such as LIFO and FIFO. Probably the strongest evidence in favor of market efficiency is the dismal performance of investment managers. A majority of investment funds underperform market indexes such as the S&P 500. Moreover, even those managers who outperform the indexes show little consistency over time. Further evidence that Wall Street has embraced EMH is the popularity of

buy-and-hold (which assumes you can't time the market) and *indexing* (which assumes you can't identify winning stocks) strategies.

Still, there is growing evidence suggesting the market is not as efficient as presumed. This evidence on market efficiency, called *anomalies* by EMH believers, began surfacing in the past decade. Consider some of the more intriguing bits of evidence. First, stock markets exhibit some *weak form inefficiency*. For example, the market exhibits systematic "calendar" patterns. The well-known *January effect*, where stock prices (especially those of small companies) increase abnormally in the month of January, is the best known example. Another example is that the average return on the Dow Jones Industrial Average for the six months from November through April is more than four times the return for the other six-month period. Still another is that stock returns show patterns based on the day of the week—Monday is the worst day, while Wednesday and Friday are best. Second, there is evidence of *semistrong form inefficiency*. The P/E anomaly and the price-to-book effects—where stocks with low price-to-earnings or price-to-book ratios outperform those with high

ratios—suggest the potential of value-based strategies to beat the market. Also, there are a number of accounting-based market anomalies. The best known is the post-earnings announcement drift, where stock prices of companies with good (bad) earnings news continue to drift upward (downward) for months after the earnings announcements. Recent evidence also suggests that managers might be able to "fool" the market with accrual manipulations—a strategy of buying stocks with low accruals and selling stocks with high accruals beats the market. Furthermore, evidence suggests the residual income valuation model can identify over- and undervalued stocks (as well as over- and undervaluation of the market as a whole). Evidence also suggests that investment strategies using analysts' consensus ratings can beat the market.

These findings of market inefficiency give rise to an alternative paradigm, called *behavioral finance*, suggesting that markets are prone to irrationalities and emotion. While the proliferation of evidence suggesting inefficiency does not necessarily imply that markets are irrational and chaotic, it does suggest that blind faith in market efficiency is misplaced.

the efforts and resources to create an information mosaic. Also, timing is crucial in the market.

Movement of new information, and its proper interpretation, flows from the well-informed and proficient segment of users to less-informed and inefficient users. This is consistent with a gradual pattern of processing new information. Resources necessary for competent analysis of a company are considerable and imply that certain market segments are more efficient than others. Securities markets for larger companies are more efficient (informed) because of a greater following by analysts due to potential rewards from information search and analysis compared to following smaller, less-prominent companies. Extreme proponents of EMH must take care in making sweeping generalizations. In the annual report of Berkshire Hathaway, its chairman and famed investor

■■■■■■■
SELLING SHORT
A short-seller sells shares that are borrowed, either from an institutional investor or from a retail brokerage firm, and then hopes to replace the borrowed shares at a lower price, pocketing the difference.

Warren Buffett expresses amazement that EMH is still embraced by some scholars and analysts. This, Buffett maintains, is because by observing correctly that the market is frequently efficient, they conclude incorrectly it is *always* efficient. Buffett declares, "the difference between these propositions is night and day."

Analysis Research
■ ■ ■ ■ ■ ■

TITANIC EFFICIENCY

If the market's reaction to the sinking of the *Titanic* in 1912 is any guide, investors were pretty sharp even in the pre-"efficient market" era. The *Titanic* was owned by White Star Line, a subsidiary of

International Mercantile Marine (IMM) that was traded on the NYSE. The ship cost $7.5 million and was insured by Lloyd's for $5 million, so the net loss to IMM was about $2.5 million. The two-day

market-adjusted returns on IMM's stock (covering the day the news of the tragedy broke and the day after) reflect a decline of $2.6 million in the value of IMM—uncannily close to the $2.5 million actual net loss.

Source: BusinessWeek (1998)

■ ■ ■ ■ ■ ■ ■ ■ BOOK ORGANIZATION

This book is organized into 11 chapters in three parts, see Exhibit 1.15. Part I, covering Chapters 1–2, introduces financial statement analysis. Chapter 1 examines business analysis and provides a preview of selected financial statement analysis techniques. Chapter 2 focuses on financial accounting–its objectives and its primary characteristics. It also explains the importance of accrual accounting, its superiority over cash flow accounting, and provides an overview of accounting analysis. Part II, covering

Exhibit 1.15   *Organization of the Book*
■ ■ ■ ■ ■ ■

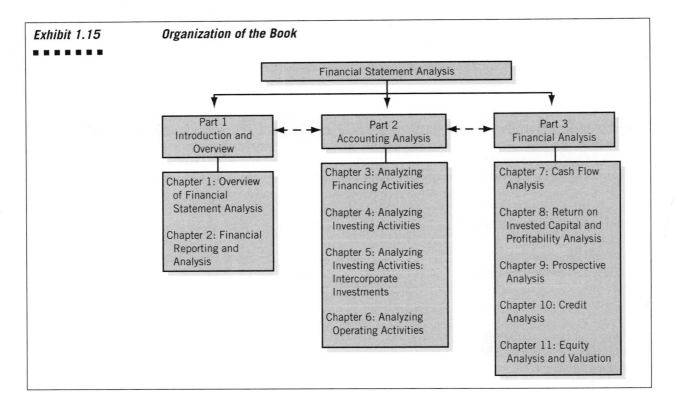

Chapters 3–6, emphasizes accounting analysis. It describes accounting analysis for financing, investing, and operating activities. Part III, covering Chapters 7–11, focuses on financial analysis. Chapter 7 explains the analysis of cash flows, while Chapter 8 describes profitability analysis. Chapter 9 discusses forecasting and pro forma analysis, and Chapters 10–11 highlight two major applications of financial statement analysis—credit analysis and equity analysis.

The book concludes with a comprehensive case analysis of the financial statements of Campbell Soup Company. We apply and interpret many of the analysis techniques described in the book using this case. Appendix A reproduces annual report excerpts from two companies that are often referred to in the book: Colgate and Campbell Soup. Throughout this book, the relation of new material to topics covered in earlier chapters is described to reinforce how the material fits together in an integrated structure for financial statement analysis.

GUIDANCE ANSWERS TO ANALYSIS VIEWPOINTS

CREDITOR A creditor (or banker) is concerned about Colgate's ability to satisfy its loan obligations. Interest and principal payments must be paid, whereas dividends to owners (shareholders) are optional. Colgate has $5.48 of creditor financing for every dollar of equity financing. Moreover, more than half of the creditor financing is interest bearing debt. Prima facie, therefore there is some concern about Colgate's ability to pay interest and principal. However, Colgate's superior profitability suggests that such a concern is unwarranted: Colgate's earnings before interest and taxes are $2.15 billion, which is more than 13 times its interest bill of $158 million. Additionally Colgate's income over the past ten years has been very stable, which makes it more likely that Colgate will be able to meet interest and principal payments on its debt.

INVESTOR As a potential investor, your review of financial statements focuses on Colgate's ability to create and sustain net income. Each of the statements is important in this review. The income statement is especially important as it reveals management's current and past success in creating and sustaining income. The cash flow statement is important in assessing management's ability to meet cash payments and the company's cash availability. The balance sheet shows the asset base from which future income is generated, and it reports on liabilities and their due dates.

QUESTIONS

1–1. Describe business analysis and identify its objectives.

1–2. Explain the claim: *Financial statement analysis is an integral part of business analysis.*

1–3. Describe the different types of business analysis. Identify the category of users of financial statements that applies to each different type of business analysis.

1–4. What are the main differences between credit analysis and equity analysis? How do these impact the financial statement information that is important for each type of analysis?

1–5. What is fundamental analysis? What is its main objective?

1–6. What are the various component processes in business analysis? Explain with reference to equity analysis.

1–7. Describe the importance of accounting analysis for financial analysis.

1–8. Describe financial statement analysis and identify its objectives.

1–9. Identify at least five different internal and external users of financial statements.

1–10. Identify and discuss the four major activities of a business enterprise.

1–11. Explain how financial statements reflect the business activities of a company.

1–12. Identify and discuss the four primary financial statements of a business.

1–13. Explain why financial statements are important to the decision-making process in financial analysis. Also, identify and discuss some of their limitations for analysis purposes.

1–14. Identify at least seven additional sources of financial reporting information (beyond financial statements) that are useful for analysis.

1–15. Identify and discuss at least two areas of financial analysis.

1–16. Identify and describe at least four categories of financial analysis tools.

1–17. Comparative analysis is an important tool in financial analysis.
    a. Explain the usefulness of comparative financial statement analysis.
    b. Describe how financial statement comparisons are effectively made.
    c. Discuss the necessary precautions an analyst should take in performing comparative analysis.

1–18. Is past trend a good predictor of future trend? Justify your response.

1–19. Compare the "absolute amount of change" with the percent change as an indicator of change. Which is better for analysis?

1–20. Identify conditions that prevent computation of a valid percent change. Provide an example.

1–21. Describe criteria in selecting a base year for index-number trend analysis.

1–22. Explain what useful information is derived from index-number trend analysis.

1–23. Common-size analysis is an important tool in financial analysis.
    a. Describe a common-size financial statement. Explain how one is prepared.
    b. Explain what a common-size financial statement report communicates about a company.

1–24. What is a necessary condition for usefulness of a ratio of financial numbers? Explain.

1–25. Identify and describe limitations of ratio analysis.

1–26. Ratio analysis is an important tool in financial analysis. Identify at least four ratios using:
    a. Balance sheet data exclusively.
    b. Income statement data exclusively.
    c. Both balance sheet and income statement data.

1–27. Identify four specialized financial analysis tools.

1–28. What is meant by "time value of money"? Explain the role of this concept in valuation.

1–29. Explain the claim: *While we theoretically use the effective interest rate to compute a bond's present value, in practice it is the other way around.*

1–30. What is amiss with the claim: *The value of a stock is the discounted value of expected future cash flows?*

1–31. Identify and describe a technique to compute equity value only using accounting variables.

1–32. Explain how the efficient market hypothesis (EMH) depicts the reaction of market prices to financial and other data.

1–33. Discuss implications of the efficient market hypothesis (EMH) for financial statement analysis.

EXERCISES

EXERCISE 1–1

Discretion in Comparative Financial Statement Analysis

The preparation and analysis of comparative balance sheets and income statements are commonly applied tools of financial statement analysis and interpretation.

Required:

a. Discuss the inherent limitations of analyzing and interpreting financial statements for a single year. Include in your discussion the extent that these limitations are overcome by use of comparative financial statements computed over more than one year.

b. A year-to-year analysis of comparative balance sheets and income statements is a useful analysis tool. Still, without proper care, such analysis can be misleading. Discuss factors or conditions that contribute to such a possibility. How can additional information and supplementary data (beyond financial statements) help prevent this possibility?

Express the following income statement information in common-size percents and assess whether this company's situation is favorable or unfavorable.

EXERCISE 1–2
Computing Common-Size Percents

HARBISON CORPORATION
Comparative Income Statement
For Years Ended December 31, 2006 and 2005

	2006	2005
Sales	$720,000	$535,000
Cost of goods sold	475,200	280,340
Gross profit	244,800	254,660
Operating expenses	151,200	103,790
Net income	$ 93,600	$150,870

Mixon Company's year-end balance sheets show the following:

EXERCISE 1–3
Evaluating Short-Term Liquidity

	2006	2005	2004
Cash	$ 30,800	$ 35,625	$ 36,800
Accounts receivable, net	88,500	62,500	49,200
Merchandise inventory	111,500	82,500	53,000
Prepaid expenses	9,700	9,375	4,000
Plant assets, net	277,500	255,000	229,500
Total assets	$518,000	$445,000	$372,500
Accounts payable	$128,900	$ 75,250	$ 49,250
Long-term notes payable secured by mortgages on plant assets	97,500	102,500	82,500
Common stock, $10 par value	162,500	162,500	162,500
Retained earnings	129,100	104,750	78,250
Total liabilities and equity	$518,000	$445,000	$372,500

Required:

Compare the year-end short-term liquidity position of this company at the end of 2006, 2005, and 2004 by computing the: (*a*) current ratio and (*b*) acid-test ratio. Comment on the ratio results.

Refer to Mixon Company's balance sheets in Exercise 1–3. Express the balance sheets in common-size percents. Round to the nearest one-tenth of a percent.

EXERCISE 1–4
Common-Size Percents

EXERCISE 1–5
Evaluating Short-Term Liquidity

Refer to the information in Exercise 1–3 about Mixon Company. The company's income statements for the years ended December 31, 2006 and 2005 show the following:

	2006	2005
Sales	$672,500	$530,000
Cost of goods sold $410,225		$344,500
Other operating expenses 208,550		133,980
Interest expense 11,100		12,300
Income taxes 8,525		7,845
Total costs and expenses	(638,400)	(498,625)
Net income	$ 34,100	$ 31,375
Earnings per share	$ 2.10	$ 1.93

Required:

For the years ended December 31, 2006 and 2005, assume all sales are on credit and then compute the following: (*a*) collection period, (*b*) accounts receivable turnover, (*c*) inventory turnover, and (*d*) days' sales in inventory. Comment on the changes in the ratios from 2005 to 2006.

EXERCISE 1–6
Evaluating Risk and Capital Structure

Refer to the information in Exercises 1–3 and 1–5 about Mixon Company. Compare the long-term risk and capital structure positions of the company at the end of 2006 and 2005 by computing the following ratios: (*a*) total debt ratio and (*b*) times interest earned. Comment on these ratio results.

EXERCISE 1–7
Evaluating Efficiency and Profitability

Refer to the financial statements of Mixon Company in Exercises 1–3 and 1–5. Evaluate the efficiency and profitability of the company by computing the following: (*a*) net profit margin, (*b*) total asset turnover, and (*c*) return on total assets. Comment on these ratio results.

EXERCISE 1–8
Evaluating Profitability

Refer to the financial statements of Mixon Company in Exercises 1–3 and 1–5. The following additional information about the company is known:

Common stock market price, December 31, 2006 ...... $15.00
Common stock market price, December 31, 2005 ...... 14.00
Annual cash dividends per share in 2006 .... 0.60
Annual cash dividends per share in 2005 .... 0.30

To help evaluate the profitability of the company, compute the following for 2006 and 2005: (*a*) return on common stockholders' equity, (*b*) price-earnings ratio on December 31, and (*c*) dividend yield.

EXERCISE 1–9
Determining Income Effects from Common-Size and Trend Percents

Common-size and trend percents for JBC Company's sales, cost of goods sold, and expenses follow:

	COMMON-SIZE PERCENTS			TREND PERCENTS		
	2006	2005	2004	2006	2005	2004
Sales	100.0%	100.0%	100.0%	104.4%	103.2%	100.0%
Cost of goods sold	62.4	60.9	58.1	112.1	108.2	100.0
Expenses	14.3	13.8	14.1	105.9	101.0	100.0

Determine whether net income increased, decreased, or remained unchanged in this three-year period.

Huff Company and Mesa Company are similar firms that operate in the same industry. The following information is available:

EXERCISE 1–10
Analyzing Short-Term Financial Conditions

	HUFF			MESA		
	2006	**2005**	**2004**	**2006**	**2005**	**2004**
Current ratio	1.6	1.7	2.0	3.1	2.6	1.8
Acid-test ratio	0.9	1.0	1.1	2.7	2.4	1.5
Accounts receivable turnover	29.5	24.2	28.2	15.4	14.2	15.0
Inventory turnover	23.2	20.9	16.1	13.5	12.0	11.6
Working capital	$60,000	$48,000	$42,000	$121,000	$93,000	$68,000

Write a one-half page report comparing Huff and Mesa using the available information. Your discussion should include their ability to meet current obligations and to use current assets efficiently.

Compute index-number trend percents for the following accounts, using Year 1 as the base year. State whether the situation as revealed by the trends appears to be favorable or unfavorable.

EXERCISE 1–11
Computing Trend Percents

	Year 5	**Year 4**	**Year 3**	**Year 2**	**Year 1**
Sales	$283,880	$271,800	$253,680	$235,560	$151,000
Cost of goods sold	129,200	123,080	116,280	107,440	68,000
Accounts receivable	19,100	18,300	17,400	16,200	10,000

Compute the percent of increase or decrease for each of the following account balances:

EXERCISE 1–12
Computing Percent Changes

	Year 2	**Year 1**
Short-term investments	$217,800	$165,000
Accounts receivable	42,120	48,000
Notes payable	57,000	0

Compute the present value for each of the following bonds:

EXERCISE 1–13
Debt Valuation (annual interest)

a. Priced at the end of its fifth year, a 10-year bond with a face value of $100 and a contract (coupon) rate of 10% per annum (payable at the end of each year) with an effective (required) interest rate of 14% per annum.

b. Priced at the beginning of its 10th year, a 14-year bond with a face value of $1,000 and a contract (coupon) rate of 8% per annum (payable at the end of each year) with an effective (required) interest rate of 6% per annum.

c. What is the answer to *b* if bond interest is payable in equal semiannual amounts?

On January 1, Year 1, you are considering the purchase of $10,000 of Colin Company's 8% bonds. The bonds are due in 10 years, with interest payable semiannually on June 30 and effective December 31. Based on your analysis of Colin, you determine that a 6% (required) interest rate is appropriate.

EXERCISE 1–14
Valuation of Bonds (semiannual interest)

Required:

a. Compute the price you will pay for the bonds using the present value model (round the answer to the nearest dollar).

b. Recompute the price in *a* if your required rate of return is 10%.

c. Describe risk and explain how it is reflected in your required rate of return.

EXERCISE 1–15
Residual Income
Equity Valuation

On January 1, Year 1, you are considering the purchase of Nico Enterprises' common stock. Based on your analysis of Nico Enterprises, you determine the following:

1. Book value at January 1, Year 1, is $50 per share.
2. Predicted net income per share for Year 1 through Year 5 is $8, $11, $20, $40, and $30, respectively.
3. For Year 6 and continuing for all years after, predicted residual income is $0.
4. Nico is not expected to pay dividends.
5. Required rate of return (cost of capital) is 20%.

Required:

Determine the purchase price per share of Nico Enterprises' common stock as of January 1, Year 1, using the residual income valuation model (round your answer to the nearest cent). Comment on the strengths and limitations of this model for investment decisions.

PROBLEMS

PROBLEM 1–1
Analyzing Efficiency
and Financial Leverage

Kampa Company and Arbor Company are similar firms that operate in the same industry. Arbor began operations in 2001 and Kampa in 1995. In 2006, both companies pay 7% interest on their debt to creditors. The following additional information is available:

	KAMPA COMPANY			ARBOR COMPANY		
	2006	2005	2004	2006	2005	2004
Total asset turnover	3.0	2.7	2.9	1.6	1.4	1.1
Return on total assets	8.9%	9.5%	8.7%	5.8%	5.5%	5.2%
Profit margin	2.3%	2.4%	2.2%	2.7%	2.9%	2.8%
Sales	$400,000	$370,000	$386,000	$200,000	$160,000	$100,000

Write a one-half page report comparing Kampa and Arbor using the available information. Your discussion should include their ability to use assets efficiently to produce profits. Also comment on their success in employing financial leverage in 2006.

PROBLEM 1–2
Calculation and Analysis
of Trend Percents

Selected comparative financial statements of Cohorn Company follow:

COHORN COMPANY
Comparative Income Statement ($000)
For Years Ended December 31, 2000–2006

	2006	2005	2004	2003	2002	2001	2000
Sales	$1,594	$1,396	$1,270	$1,164	$1,086	$1,010	$828
Cost of goods sold	1,146	932	802	702	652	610	486
Gross profit	448	464	468	462	434	400	342
Operating expenses	340	266	244	180	156	154	128
Net income	$ 108	$ 198	$ 224	$ 282	$ 278	$ 246	$214

COHORN COMPANY
Comparative Balance Sheet ($000)
December 31, 2000–2006

	2006	2005	2004	2003	2002	2001	2000
Assets							
Cash	$ 68	$ 88	$ 92	$ 94	$ 98	$ 96	$ 99
Accounts receivable, net	480	504	456	350	308	292	206
Merchandise inventory	1,738	1,264	1,104	932	836	710	515
Other current assets	46	42	24	44	38	38	19
Long-term investments	0	0	0	136	136	136	136
Plant and equipment, net	2,120	2,114	1,852	1,044	1,078	960	825
Total assets	$4,452	$4,012	$3,528	$2,600	$2,494	$2,232	$1,800
Liabilities and Equity							
Current liabilities	$1,120	$ 942	$ 618	$ 514	$ 446	$ 422	$ 272
Long-term liabilities	1,194	1,040	1,012	470	480	520	390
Common stock	1,000	1,000	1,000	840	840	640	640
Other contributed capital	250	250	250	180	180	160	160
Retained earnings	888	780	648	596	548	490	338
Total liabilities and equ	$4,452	$4,012	$3,528	$2,600	$2,494	$2,232	$1,800

Required:

a. Compute trend percents for the individual items of both statements using 2000 as the base year.

b. Analyze and comment on the financial statements and trend percents from part a.

CHECK
2006, total assets
trend, 247.3%

Perform a comparative analysis of Eastman Corporation by completing the analysis below. Describe and comment on any significant findings in your comparative analysis.

PROBLEM 1–3
Comparative Income Statement Analysis

EASTMAN CORPORATION
Income Statement ($ millions)
For Years Ended December 31

	Year 6	Year 5	Year 4	Cumulative Amount	Average Annual Amount
Net sales .... $		$3,490	$2,860	$	$
Cost of goods sold	3,210				2,610
Gross profit	3,670	680	1,050		1,800
Operating expenses					
Income before taxes	2,740	215	105		
Net income	$1,485	$ 145	$ 58		

CHECK
Average net income, $563

Compute increases (decreases) in percents for both Years 6 and 7 by entering all the missing data in the table below. Analyze and interpret any significant results revealed from this trend analysis.

PROBLEM 1–4
Index-Number Trend Analysis

Statement Item	YEAR 7		YEAR 6		YEAR 5
	Index No.	Change in Percent	Index No.	Change in Percent	Index No.
Net sales	_____	29%	100	____%	90
Cost of goods sold	139	____	100	____	85
Gross profit	126	____	100	____	80
Operating expenses	_____	20	100	____	65
Income before tax	_____	14	100	____	70
Net income	129	____	100	____	75

CHECK
Year 6 net income
percent, 33.3%

PROBLEM 1–5

Understanding Financial
Statement Relations:
Balance Sheet
Construction

Assume you are an analyst evaluating Mesco Company. The following data are available in your financial analysis (unless otherwise indicated, all data are as of December 31, Year 5):

Retained earnings, December 31, Year 4	$98,000	Days' sales in receivables	18 days
Gross profit margin ratio	25%	Shareholders' equity to total debt	4 to 1
Acid-test ratio	2.5 to 1	Sales (all on credit)	$920,000
Noncurrent assets	$280,000	Common stock: $15 par value; 10,000 shares issued
Days' sales in inventory	45 days	and outstanding; issued at $21 per share

Required:

Using these data, construct the December 31, Year 5, balance sheet for your analysis. Operating expenses (excluding taxes and cost of goods sold for Year 5) are $180,000. The tax rate is 40%. Assume a 360-day year in ratio computations. No cash dividends are paid in either Year 4 or Year 5. Current assets consist of cash, accounts receivable, and inventories.

CHECK
Total assets, $422,500

PROBLEM 1–6

Understanding Financial
Statement Relations:
Balance Sheet
Construction

You are an analyst reviewing Foxx Company. The following data are available for your financial analysis (unless otherwise indicated, all data are as of December 31, Year 2):

Current ratio	2	Days' sales in inventory	36 days
Accounts receivable turnover	16	Gross profit margin ratio	50%
Beginning accounts receivable	$50,000	Expenses (excluding cost of goods sold) ...	$450,000
Return on end-of-year common equity ...	20%	Total debt to equity ratio	1
Sales (all on credit)	$1,000,000	Noncurrent assets	$300,000

Required:

Using these data, construct the December 31, Year 2, balance sheet for your analysis. Current assets consist of cash, accounts receivable, and inventory. Balance sheet classifications include cash, accounts receivable, inventory, total noncurrent assets, total current assets, total current liabilities, total noncurrent liabilities, and equity.

CHECK
Total assets, $500,000

PROBLEM 1–7

Understanding Financial
Statement Relations:
Dividend and Balance
Sheet Construction

You are planning to analyze Voltek Company's December 31, Year 6, balance sheet. The following information is available:

1. Beginning and ending balances are identical for both accounts receivable and inventory.
2. Net income is $1,300.
3. Times interest earned is 5 (income taxes are zero). Company has 5% bonds outstanding and issued at par.
4. Net profit margin is 10%. Gross profit margin is 30%. Inventory turnover is 5.
5. Days' sales in receivables is 72 days.
6. Sales to end-of-year working capital is 4. Current ratio is 1.5.
7. Acid-test ratio is 1.0 (excludes prepaid expenses).
8. Plant and equipment (net) is $6,000. It is one-third depreciated.
9. Dividends paid on 8% nonparticipating preferred stock are $40. There is no change in common shares outstanding during Year 6. Preferred shares were issued two years ago at par.

10. Earnings per common share are $3.75.

11. Common stock has a $5 par value and was issued at par.

12. Retained earnings at January 1, Year 6, are $350.

Required:

a. Given the information available, prepare this company's balance sheet as of December 31, Year 6 (include the following account classifications: cash, accounts receivable, inventory, prepaid expenses, plant and equipment (net), current liabilities, bonds payable, and stockholders' equity).

b. Determine the amount of dividends paid on common stock in Year 6.

CHECK
Total assets, $15,750

The balance sheet and income statement for Chico Electronics are reproduced below (tax rate is 40%).

PROBLEM 1–8
Financial Statement Ratio Analysis

CHICO ELECTRONICS
Balance Sheet ($ thousands)
As of December 31

	Year 4	Year 5
Assets		
Current assets		
Cash	$ 683	$ 325
Accounts receivable	1,490	3,599
Inventories	1,415	2,423
Prepaid expenses	15	13
Total current assets	3,603	6,360
Property, plant and equipment, net	1,066	1,541
Other assets	123	157
Total assets	$4,792	$8,058
Liabilities and Shareholders' Equity		
Current liabilities		
Notes payable to bank	$ —	$ 875
Current portion of long-term debt	38	116
Accounts payable	485	933
Estimated income tax liability	588	472
Accrued expenses	576	586
Customer advance payments	34	963
Total current liabilities	1,721	3,945
Long-term debt	122	179
Other liabilities	81	131
Total liabilities	1,924	4,255
Shareholders' equity		
Common stock, $1.00 par value; 1,000,000 shares authorized;		
550,000 and 829,000 outstanding, respectively	550	829
Preferred stock, Series A 10%; $25 par value; 25,000 authorized;		
20,000 and 18,000 outstanding, respectively	500	450
Additional paid-in capital	450	575
Retained earnings	1,368	1,949
Total shareholders' equity	2,868	3,803
Total liabilities and shareholders' equity	$4,792	$8,058

CHICO ELECTRONICS
Income Statement ($ thousands)
For Years Ending December 31

	Year 4	Year 5
Net sales	$7,570	$12,065
Other income, net	261	345
Total revenues	7,831	12,410
Cost of goods sold	4,850	8,048
General, administrative, and		
marketing expense	1,531	2,025
Interest expense	22	78
Total costs and expenses	6,403	10,151
Net income before tax	1,428	2,259
Income tax	628	994
Net income	$ 800	$ 1,265

Required:

Compute and interpret the following financial ratios of the company for Year 5:

a. Acid-test ratio.

b. Return on assets.

CHECK
(*d*) EPS, $1.77

c. Return on common equity.

d. Earnings per share.

e. Gross profit margin ratio.

f. Times interest earned.

g. Days to sell inventory.

h. Long-term debt to equity ratio.

i. Total debt to equity.

j. Sales to end-of-year working capital.

(CFA Adapted)

PROBLEM 1–9

*Financial Statement
Ratio Computation and
Interpretation*

As a consultant to MCR Company, you are told it is considering the acquisition of Lakeland Corporation. MCR Company requests that you prepare certain financial statistics and analysis for Year 5 and Year 4 using Lakeland's financial statements that follow:

LAKELAND CORPORATION
Balance Sheet
December 31, Year 5 and Year 4

	Year 5	Year 4
Assets		
Current assets		
Cash	$ 1,610,000	$ 1,387,000
Marketable securities	510,000	—
Accounts receivable, less allowance for bad debts		
Year 5, $125,000; Year 4, $110,000	4,075,000	3,669,000
Inventories, at lower of cost or market	7,250,000	7,050,000
Prepaid expenses	125,000	218,000
Total current assets	13,570,000	12,324,000
Plant and equipment, at cost		
Land and buildings	13,500,000	13,500,000
Machinery and equipment	9,250,000	8,520,000
Total plant and equipment	22,750,000	22,020,000
Less: Accumulated depreciation	13,470,000	12,549,000
Total plant and equipment—net	9,280,000	9,471,000
Long-term receivables	250,000	250,000
Deferred charges	25,000	75,000
Total assets	$23,125,000	$22,120,000
Liabilities and Shareholders' Equity		
Current liabilities		
Accounts payable	$ 2,950,000	$ 3,426,000
Accrued expenses	1,575,000	1,644,000
Federal taxes payable	875,000	750,000
Current maturities on long-term debt	500,000	500,000
Total current liabilities	5,900,000	6,320,000
Other liabilities		
5% sinking fund debentures, due January 1,		
Year 16 ($500,000 redeemable annually)	5,000,000	5,500,000
Deferred taxes on income, due to depreciation	350,000	210,000
Total other liabilities	5,350,000	5,710,000
Shareholders' equity		
Preferred stock, $1 cumulative, $20 par, preference		
on liquidation $100 per share (authorized: 100,000 shares;		
issued and outstanding: 50,000 shares)	1,000,000	1,000,000
Common stock, $1 par (authorized: 900,000 shares;		
issued and outstanding: Year 5, 550,000 shares;		
Year 4, 500,000 shares)	550,000	500,000
Capital in excess of par value on common stock	3,075,000	625,000
Retained earnings	7,250,000	7,965,000
Total shareholders' equity	11,875,000	10,090,000
Total liabilities and shareholders' equity	$23,125,000	$22,120,000

LAKELAND CORPORATION
Statement of Income and Retained Earnings
For Years Ended December 31, Year 5 and Year 4

	Year 5	Year 4
Revenues		
Net sales	$48,400,000	$41,700,000
Royalties	70,000	25,000
Interest	30,000	—
Total revenues	$48,500,000	$41,725,000
Costs and expenses		
Cost of sales	$31,460,000	$29,190,000
Selling, general, and administrative	12,090,000	8,785,000
Interest on 5% sinking fund debentures	275,000	300,000
Provision for Federal income taxes	2,315,000	1,695,000
Total costs and expenses	$46,140,000	$39,970,000
Net income	$ 2,360,000	$ 1,755,000
Retained earnings, beginning of year	7,965,000	6,760,000
Subtotal	$10,325,000	$ 8,515,000
Dividends paid		
Preferred stock, $1.00 per share in cash	50,000	50,000
Common stock		
Cash—$1.00 per share	525,000	500,000
Stock—(10%)—50,000 shares at		
market value of $50 per share	2,500,000	—
Total dividends paid	$ 3,075,000	$ 550,000
Retained earnings, end of year	$ 7,250,000	$ 7,965,000

Additional Information:

1. Inventory at January 1, Year 4, is $6,850,000.

2. Market prices of common stock at December 31, Year 5 and Year 4, are $73.50 and $47.75, respectively.

3. Cash dividends for both preferred and common stock are declared and paid in June and December of each year. The stock dividend on common stock is declared and distributed in August of Year 5.

4. Plant and equipment disposals during Year 5 and Year 4 are $375,000 and $425,000, respectively. Related accumulated depreciation is $215,000 in Year 5 and $335,000 in Year 4. At December 31, Year 3, the plant and equipment asset balance is $21,470,000, and its related accumulated depreciation is $11,650,000.

Required:

Compute the following financial ratios and figures for both Year 5 and Year 4. Identify and discuss any significant year-to-year changes.

At December 31:

a. Current ratio.

b. Acid-test ratio.

c. Book value per common share.

For year ended December 31:

d. Gross profit margin ratio.

e. Days to sell inventory.

f. Times interest earned.

g. Common stock price-to-earnings ratio (end-of-year value).

h. Gross capital expenditures.

CHECK

(g) Year 5 PE, 17.5

(AICPA Adapted)

Selected ratios for three different companies that operate in three different industries (merchandising, pharmaceuticals, utilities) are reported in the table below:

PROBLEM 1–10

Identifying Industries from Financial Statement Data

Ratio	Co. A	Co. B	Co. C
Gross profit margin ratio	18%	53%	n.a.
Net profit margin ratio	2%	14%	8%
Research and development to sales	0%	17%	0.1%
Advertising to sales	7%	4%	0.1%
Interest expense to sales	1%	1%	15%
Return on assets	11%	12%	7%
Accounts receivable turnover	95 times	5 times	11 times
Inventory turnover	9 times	3 times	n.a.
Long-term debt to equity	64%	45%	89%

n.a. = not applicable

Required:

Identify the industry that each of the companies, A, B, and C, operate in. Give at least two reasons supporting each of your selections.

The Tristar Mutual Fund manager is considering an investment in the stock of Best Computer and asks for your opinion regarding the company. Best Computer is a computer hardware sales and service company. Approximately 50% of the company's revenues come from the sale of computer hardware. The rest of the company's revenues come from hardware service and repair contracts. Below are financial ratios for Best Computer and comparative ratios for Best Computer's industry. The ratios for Best Computer are computed using information from its financial statements.

PROBLEM 1–11

Ratio Interpretation– Industry Comparisons

	Best Computer	Industry Average
Liquidity ratios		
Current ratio	3.45	3.10
Acid-test ratio	2.58	1.85
Collection period	42.19	36.60
Days to sell inventory	18.38	18.29
Capital structure and solvency		
Total debt to equity	0.674	0.690
Long-term debt to equity	0.368	0.400
Times interest earned	9.20	9.89
Return on investment		
Return on assets	31.4%	30.0%
Return on common equity	52.6%	50.0%

	Best Computer	Industry Average
Operating performance		
Gross profit margin	36.0%	34.3%
Operating profit margin	16.7%	15.9%
Pre-tax profit margin	14.9%	14.45%
Net profit margin	8.2%	8.0%
Asset utilization		
Cash turnover	40.8	38.9
Accounts receivable turnover	6.90	8.15
Sales to inventory	29.9	28.7
Working capital turnover	8.50	9.71
Fixed asset turnover	15.30	15.55
Total assets turnover	3.94	3.99
Market measures		
Price-to-earnings ratio	27.8	29.0
Earnings yield	8.1%	7.9%
Dividend yield	0%	0.5%
Dividend payout rate	0%	2%
Price-to-book	8.8	9.0

Required:

a. Interpret the ratios of Best Computer and draw inferences about the company's financial performance and financial condition—ignore the industry ratios.

b. Repeat the analysis in (*a*) with full knowledge of the industry ratios.

CHECK

Acct. recble., Above norm

c. Indicate which ratios you consider to deviate from industry norms. For each Best Computer ratio that deviates from industry norms, suggest two possible explanations.

PROBLEM 1–12
Equity Valuation

Ace Co. is to be taken over by Beta Ltd. at the end of year 2007. Beta agrees to pay the shareholders of Ace the book value per share at the time of the takeover. A reliable analyst makes the following projections for Ace (assume cost of capital is 10% per annum):

($ per share)	2002	2003	2004	2005	2006	2007
Dividends	—	$1.00	$1.00	$1.00	$1.00	$1.00
Operating cash flows	—	2.00	1.50	1.00	0.75	0.50
Capital expenditures	—	—	—	1.00	1.00	—
Debt increase (decrease)	—	(1.00)	(0.50)	1.00	1.25	0.50
Net income	—	1.45	1.10	0.60	0.25	(0.10)
Book value	9.00	9.45	9.55	9.15	8.40	7.30

CHECK

(*b*) Value using RI, $8.32

Required:

a. Estimate Ace Co.'s value per share at the end of year 2002 using the dividend discount model.

b. Estimate Ace Co.'s value per share at the end of year 2002 using the residual income model.

c. Attempt to estimate the value of Ace Co. at the end of year 2002 using the free cash flow to equity model.

CASES

CASE 1–1

Comparative Analysis: Return on Invested Capital

Key comparative figures ($ millions) for both **NIKE** and **Reebok** follow:

**NIKE
Reebok**

Key Figures	NIKE	Reebok
Financing (liabilities + equity)	$5,397.4	$1,756.1
Net income (profit)	399.6	135.1
Revenues (sales)	9,553.1	3,637.4

Required:

a. What is the total amount of assets invested in (*a*) NIKE and (*b*) Reebok?

b. What is the return on investment for (*a*) NIKE and (*b*) Reebok? NIKE's beginning assets equal $5,361.2 (in millions) and Reebok's beginning assets equal $1,786.2 (in millions).

c. How much are expenses for (*a*) NIKE and (*b*) Reebok?

d. Is return on investment satisfactory for (*a*) NIKE and (*b*) Reebok [assume competitors average a 4% return]?

e. What can you conclude about NIKE and Reebok from these computations?

CHECK
Nike ROI, 7.4%

CASE 1–2

Comparative Analysis: Comparison of Balance Sheet and Income Statement

Key comparative figures ($ millions) for both **NIKE** and **Reebok** follow:

**NIKE
Reebok**

Key Figures	NIKE	Reebok	Key Figures	NIKE	Reebok
Cash and equivalents	$ 108.6	$ 209.8	Income taxes	$ 253.4	$ 12.5
Accounts receivable	1,674.4	561.7	Revenues (Nike)	9,553.1	—
Inventories	1,396.6	563.7	Net sales (Reebok)	—	3,643.6
Retained earnings	3,043.4	1,145.3	Total assets	5,397.4	1,756.1
Costs of sales	6,065.5	2,294.0			

Required:

a. Compute common-size percents for both companies using the data provided.

b. Which company incurs a higher percent of their revenues (net sales) in income taxes?

c. Which company retains a higher portion of cumulative net income in the company?

d. Which company has a higher gross margin ratio on sales?

e. Which company holds a higher percent of its total assets as inventory?

CASE 1–3

Comparative Analysis: Credit and Equity Analysis

Two companies competing in the same industry are being evaluated by a bank that can lend money to only one of them. Summary information from the financial statements of the two companies follows:

	Datatech Company	Sigma Company		Datatech Company	Sigma Company
Data from the current year-end balance sheet:			**Data from the current year's income statement:**		
Assets			Sales	$660,000	$780,200
Cash	$ 18,500	$ 33,000	Cost of goods sold	485,100	532,500
Accounts receivable, net	36,400	56,400	Interest expense	6,900	11,000
Notes receivable (trade)	8,100	6,200	Income tax expense	12,800	19,300
Merchandise inventory	83,440	131,500	Net income	67,770	105,000
Prepaid expenses	4,000	5,950	Basic earnings per share	1.94	2.56
Plant and equipment, net	284,000	303,400			
Total assets	$434,440	$536,450			

	Datatech Company	Sigma Company		Datatech Company	Sigma Company
			Beginning-of-year data:		
Liabilities and Stockholders' Equity			Accounts receivable, net	$ 28,800	$ 53,200
Current liabilities	$ 60,340	$ 92,300	Notes receivable (trade)	0	0
Long-term notes payable	79,800	100,000	Merchandise inventory	54,600	106,400
Common stock, $5 par value ...	175,000	205,000	Total assets	388,000	372,500
Retained earnings	119,300	139,150	Common stock, $5 par value ...	175,000	205,000
Total liabilities and equity	$434,440	$536,450	Retained earnings	94,300	90,600

Required:

CHECK
Accounts receivable
turnover, Sigma, 13.5 times

a. Compute the current ratio, acid-test ratio, accounts (including notes) receivable turnover, inventory turnover, days' sales in inventory, and days' sales in receivables for both companies. Identify the company that you consider to be the better short-term credit risk and explain why.

b. Compute the net profit margin, total asset turnover, return on total assets, and return on common stockholders' equity for both companies. Assuming that each company paid cash dividends of $1.50 per share and each company's stock can be purchased at $25 per share, compute their price-earnings ratios and dividend yields. Identify which company's stock you would recommend as the better investment and explain why.

CASE 1–4

Business Decisions
Using Financial Ratios

Jose Sanchez owns and operates Western Gear, a small merchandiser in outdoor recreational equipment. You are hired to review the three most recent years of operations for Western Gear. Your financial statement analysis reveals the following results:

	2006	2005	2004
Sales index-number trend	137.0	125.0	100.0
Selling expenses to net sales	9.8%	13.7%	15.3%
Sales to plant assets	3.5 to 1	3.3 to 1	3.0 to 1
Current ratio	2.6 to 1	2.4 to 1	2.1 to 1
Acid-test ratio	0.8 to 1	1.1 to 1	1.2 to 1
Merchandise inventory turnover	7.5 times	8.7 times	9.9 times
Accounts receivable turnover	6.7 times	7.4 times	8.2 times
Total asset turnover	2.6 times	2.6 times	3.0 times
Return on total assets	8.8%	9.4%	10.1%
Return on owner's equity	9.75%	11.50%	12.25%
Net profit margin	3.3%	3.5%	3.7%

Required:

Use these data to answer each of the following questions with explanations:

a. Is it becoming easier for the company to meet its current debts on time and to take advantage of cash discounts?

b. Is the company collecting its accounts receivable more rapidly over time?

c. Is the company's investment in accounts receivable decreasing?

d. Are dollars invested in inventory increasing?

CHECK
Plant assets are increasing

e. Is the company's investment in plant assets increasing?

f. Is the owner's investment becoming more profitable?

g. Is the company using its assets efficiently?

h. Did the dollar amount of selling expenses decrease during the three-year period?

Refer to **Campbell Soup Company's** financial statements in Appendix A.

Campbell Soup Company

CASE 1–5

Financial Statement Ratio Computation

Required:

Compute the following ratios for Year 11.

Liquidity ratios:
 a. Current ratio
 b. Acid-test ratio
 c. Days to sell inventory
 d. Collection period
Capital structure and solvency ratios:
 e. Total debt to total equity
 f. Long-term debt to equity
 g. Times interest earned
Return on investment ratios:
 h. Return on total assets
 i. Return on common equity
Operating performance ratios:
 j. Gross profit margin ratio
 k. Operating profit margin ratio
 l. Pretax profit margin ratio
 m. Net profit margin ratio

Asset utilization ratios:*
 n. Cash turnover
 o. Accounts receivable turnover
 p. Inventory turnover
 q. Working capital turnover
 r. Fixed assets turnover
 s. Total assets turnover
Market measures (Campbell's stock price per share is $46.73 for Year 11):
 t. Price-to-earnings ratio
 u. Earnings yield
 v. Dividend yield
 w. Dividend payout rate
 x. Price-to-book ratio

* For simplicity in computing utilization ratios, use end-of-year values and not average values.

Explain and interpret the major business activities–namely, planning, financing, investing, and operating. Aim your report at a general audience such as shareholders and employees. Include concrete examples for each of the business activities.

CASE 1–6

Describe and Interpret Business Activities

As controller of Tallman Company, you are responsible for keeping the board of directors informed about the company's financial activities. At the recent board meeting, you presented the following financial data:

CASE 1–7

Ethics Challenge

	2006	2005	2004		2006	2005	2004
Sales trend percent	147.0%	135.0%	100.0%	Accounts receivable turnover	7.0 times	7.7 times	8.5 times
Selling expenses to net sales	10.1%	14.0%	15.6%	Total asset turnover	2.9 times	2.9 times	3.3 times
Sales to plant assets	3.8 to 1	3.6 to 1	3.3 to 1	Return on total assets	9.1%	9.7%	10.4%
Current ratio	2.9 to 1	2.7 to 1	2.4 to 1	Return on stockholders' equity	9.75%	11.50%	12.25%
Acid-test ratio	1.1 to 1	1.4 to 1	1.5 to 1	Profit margin	3.6%	3.8%	4.0%
Merchandise inventory turnover	7.8 times	9.0 times	10.2 times				

After the meeting, the company's CEO held a press conference with analysts in which she mentions the following ratios:

	2006	2005	2004		2006	2005	2004
Sales trend percent	147.0%	135.0%	100.0%	Sales to plant assets	3.8 to 1	3.6 to 1	3.3 to 1
Selling expenses to net sales	10.1%	14.0%	15.6%	Current ratio	2.9 to 1	2.7 to 1	2.4 to 1

Required:

a. Why do you think the CEO decided to report these 4 ratios instead of the 11 ratios that you prepared?

b. Comment on the possible consequences of the CEO's reporting decision.

CASE 1–8

Comparative Analysis

Colgate and Kimberly-Clark

Kimberly-Clark is a household products company that produces and sells various paper products under popular brand names such as Kleenex and Scott. In many respects, Kimberly-Clark is similar to Colgate: both are mature and profitable consumer products' companies that are of similar size. Therefore, Kimberly-Clark is a good company to compare Colgate's financial performance with. Refer to select financial information about Colgate over the 1996–2006 period reproduced in Exhibit 1.3. The table below provides identical information relating to Kimberly-Clark over the same period.

KIMBERLY-CLARK SUMMARY FINANCIAL DATA

(In billions, except per share data)	2006	2005	2004	2003	2002	2001	2000	1999	1998	1997	1996
Net sales	16.75	15.90	15.08	14.35	13.57	14.52	13.98	13.01	12.30	12.55	13.15
Gross profit	6.36	6.12	5.91	5.66	5.55	6.71	6.38	6.00	5.25	5.30	5.47
Operating income (after tax)	1.65	1.70	1.91	1.81	1.80	1.75	1.96	1.82	1.24	1.02	1.53
Net income	1.50	1.57	1.80	1.69	1.67	1.61	1.80	1.67	1.10	0.90	1.40
Restructuring charge (after tax)	0.35	0.17									
Net income before restructuring	1.84	1.74	1.80	1.69	1.67	1.61	1.80	1.67	1.10	0.90	1.40
Operating income before restructuring	2.00	1.86	1.91	1.81	1.80	1.75	1.96	1.82	1.24	1.02	1.53
Total assets	17.07	16.30	17.02	16.78	15.59	15.01	14.48	12.82	11.69	11.27	11.85
Total liabilities	10.97	10.75	10.39	10.01	9.94	9.36	8.71	7.72	7.66	7.14	7.36
Long-term debt	2.28	2.59	2.30	2.73	2.84	2.42	2.00	1.93	2.07	1.80	1.74
Shareholders' equity	6.10	5.56	6.63	6.77	5.65	5.65	5.77	5.09	4.03	4.13	4.48
Treasury stock at cost	1.39	6.38	5.05	3.82	3.35	2.75	1.97	1.42	1.45	0.62	0.21
Basic earnings per share	3.27	3.30	3.64	3.34	3.24	3.04	3.34	3.11	2.00	1.62	2.49
Cash dividends per share	1.97	1.85	1.64	1.37	1.21	1.14	1.09	1.03	1.02	0.96	0.92
Closing stock price	67.95	59.65	65.81	59.09	47.47	59.80	70.69	65.44	54.50	49.31	47.63
Shares outstanding (billions)	0.46	0.46	0.48	0.50	0.51	0.52	0.53	0.54	0.54	0.56	0.56

Required:

Conduct a detailed comparative analysis of Colgate and Kimberly-Clark's financial performance over the 1997–2006 period.

Specifically:

a. Conduct an index-number trend analysis separately for every item reported in the table (e.g., net sales, gross profit, etc.). Use 1996 as the base year (i.e., set 1996 numbers equal to 100).

b. Calculate the following ratios for every year for each company: return on investment (return on assets, return on common equity), operating performance (gross profit margin, operating profit margin), asset utilization (total asset turnover), capital structure (total debt to equity, long-term debt to equity), dividend payout rate, and market measures (price-to-earnings, price-to-book).

c. Conduct an index-number trend analysis separately for every one of the ratios that you computed in (b). Once again use 1996 as the base year.

d. For analysis in (a), (b), and (c) that involves net income or operating income, it is important to also examine these numbers after removing the costs relating to restructuring activities. The table calculates net income and operating income after adding the pretax cost of restructuring (e.g., net income before restructuring). Similarly determine net income and operating income before restructuring for Colgate using the data in Exhibit 1.3. Then compute all trends and ratios using these adjusted income numbers in addition to those using the reported numbers.

e. Finally, we need to determine the stock price performance of the two companies over this period. To do that, we need to determine cum-dividend return. Cum-dividend return is the return on a stock including cash dividends. Colgate's cum-dividend return over this period is 12.5% compared to 5.9% for Kimberly-Clark. For advanced analysis that uses finance techniques, verify these numbers. Those who don't want to do this advanced analysis can merely use the cum-dividend returns' numbers provided above. (Hint: This is advanced analysis that covers material from finance outside the scope of this chapter and should be attempted only by those who are conversant with finance techniques. Cum-dividend return is determined by the following formula: Cum-dividend return for a year = [(Closing stock price + Dividend paid during the year)/Opening stock price] −1. For example, Kimberly-Clark's cum-dividend return in 1997 is [(49.31 + 0.96)/47.63] −1 = 5.5%. Using this formula, determine the cum-dividend return for each company for every year. Then determine the compounded per-year return over the entire period).

f. Examine all of the previous analyses and provide a commentary that compares the performance of Colgate and Kimberly-Clark over the 1997–2006 period.

Note: This case involves extensive data analysis and should be done using Excel (or similar software). To facilitate the analysis in Excel, the data in Exhibit 1.3 and in the table above are available in Excel format and can be downloaded from the book's website.

2

FINANCIAL REPORTING AND ANALYSIS

A LOOK BACK `<`

We began our study of financial statement analysis with an overview in Chapter 1. We saw how financial statements reflect business activities—financing, investing, and operating. We also performed a preliminary analysis of Dell.

A LOOK AT THIS CHAPTER `•`

This chapter focuses on financial reporting and its analysis. We describe the financial reporting environment, including the principles underlying accounting. The advantages and disadvantages of accrual versus cash flow measures are discussed. We also explain the need for accounting analysis and introduce its techniques.

A LOOK AHEAD `>`

Chapters 3 through 6 of this book are devoted to accounting analysis. Chapter 3 focuses on financing activities. Chapters 4 and 5 extend this to investing activities. Each of these chapters describes adjustments of accounting numbers that are useful for financial statement analysis.

ANALYSIS OBJECTIVES

• Explain the financial reporting and analysis environment.

• Identify what constitutes generally accepted accounting principles (GAAP).

• Describe the objectives of financial accounting; identify qualities of accounting information and principles and conventions that determine accounting rules.

• Describe the relevance of accounting information to business analysis and valuation, and identify its limitations.

• Explain the importance of accrual accounting and its strengths and limitations.

• Understand economic concepts of income, and distinguish it from cash flows and reported income; learn to make adjustments to reported income to meet analysis objectives.

• Explain fair value accounting and its differences from the historical cost model; identify the merits and demerits of fair value accounting and its implications for analysis.

• Describe the need for and techniques of accounting analysis.

• Explain the relevance of auditing and the audit report (opinion) for financial statement analysis (Appendix 2A).

• Analyze and measure earnings quality and its determinants (Appendix 2B).

Cash Is King . . . without Clothes

Bentonville, AR–There is a children's fable about the king who was deceived into believing he wore clothes made of special fabric when in actuality he was naked. All of his subjects were afraid to tell him and, instead, praised the king on his magnificent clothes. All, that is, except a child who dared to speak the truth. The king was quick to recognize the reality of the child's words and, eventually, rewarded him handsomely.

Cash is the king–without clothes (accruals)–in this children's fable. Experts know cash alone is incomplete, but many too often mindlessly act as if it is sufficient. Just as the dressing of robes, crown, and staff better reflects the reality of the king, so does the dressing of accruals better reflect the reality of a company's financial position and performance.

Yet, we too often witness the naive use of accruals. Accounting analysis overcomes this failing. As with the king, if the clothes of accruals fail to reflect reality, the aim of accounting analysis is to adjust those clothes to better reflect reality.

> **. . . cash and accruals play supporting roles . . .**

The upshot is that neither cash nor accruals is king. Instead, both cash and accruals play supporting roles, where adjusted or recasted information from accounting and financial analyses plays the lead role. As in the fable, recognition of this reality is richly rewarded.

This chapter takes data from two retailers, Kmart and Wal-Mart, to explore the relative importance of cash and accruals in explaining stock prices. Findings show the power of accrual income in explaining stock prices.

We also link the relative explanatory power of cash and income to a company's life cycle. This linkage highlights different roles that each play at different times. This knowledge provides an advantage in analyzing information for business decisions.

We must learn from the king in the fable and not be deceived into believing cash or income is an all-encompassing, idyllic measure of financial performance. Otherwise, we are destined to be caught with our pants down.

PREVIEW OF CHAPTER 2

Chapter 1 introduced financial statements and discussed their importance for business analysis. Financial statements are the products of a financial reporting process governed by accounting rules and standards, managerial incentives, and enforcement and monitoring mechanisms. It is important for us to understand the financial reporting environment along with the objectives and concepts underlying the accounting information presented in financial statements. This knowledge enables us to better infer the reality of a company's financial position and performance. In this chapter we discuss the concepts underlying financial reporting, with special emphasis on accounting rules. We begin by describing the financial reporting environment. Then we discuss the purpose of financial reporting–its objectives and how these objectives determine both the quality of the accounting information and the principles and conventions that underlie accounting rules. We also examine the relevance of accounting information for business analysis and valuation, and we identify limitations of accounting information. We conclude with a discussion of accruals–the cornerstone of modern accounting. This includes an appraisal of accrual accounting in comparison with cash flow accounting and the implications for financial statement analysis.

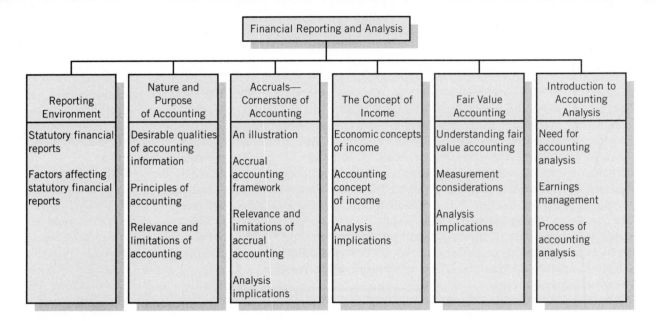

Statutory financial reports–primarily the financial statements–are the most important product of the financial reporting environment. Information in financial statements is judged relative to (1) the information needs of financial statement users and (2) alternative sources of information such as economic and industry data, analyst reports, and voluntary disclosures by managers. It is important to understand the factors that affect the nature and content of financial reports to appreciate the financial accounting information reported in them. The primary factors are *accounting rules* (GAAP), *manager motivations, monitoring and enforcement mechanisms, regulators, industry practices,* and *other information sources.* We examine these and other components of the financial reporting environment in this section.

Statutory Financial Reports

Statutory financial reports are the most important part of the financial reporting process. While we are familiar with financial statements–especially the annual report–there are other important statutory financial reports that an analyst needs to review. We examine three categories of these reports in this section: financial statements, earnings announcements, and other statutory reports.

Financial Statements

We described the components of an annual report in Chapter 1. Strictly speaking, the annual report is not a statutory document. It often serves to publicize a company's products, services, and achievements to its shareholders and others. The statutory equivalent to the annual report is the **Form 10-K,** which public companies must file with the SEC. The annual report includes most of the information in the Form 10-K. Still, because the Form 10-K usually contains relevant information beyond that in the annual report, it is good practice to regularly procure a copy of it. Both current and past Form 10-Ks–as well as other regulatory filings–are downloadable from EDGAR at the SEC website [**www.sec.gov**].

Companies are also required to file a **Form 10-Q** quarterly with the SEC to report selected financial information. It is important to refer to Form 10-Q for *timely* information.

Unfortunately, most companies release very condensed quarterly information, which limits its value. When analyzing quarterly information, we need to recognize two crucial factors:

1. **Seasonality.** When examining trends, we must consider effects of *seasonality*. For example, retail companies make much of their revenues and profits in the fourth quarter of the calendar year. This means analysts often make comparisons with the same quarter of the prior year.
2. **Year-end adjustments.** Companies often make adjustments (for example, inventory write-offs) in the final quarter. Many of these adjustments relate to the entire year. This renders quarterly information less reliable for analysis purposes.

Earnings Announcements

Annual and quarterly financial statements are made available to the public only after the financial statements are prepared and audited. This time lag usually spans one to six weeks. Yet, companies almost always release key summary information to the public earlier through an **earnings announcement.** An earnings announcement is made available to traders on the stock exchange through the broad tape and is often reported in the financial press such as *The Wall Street Journal.* Earnings announcements provide key summary information about company position and performance for both quarterly and annual periods.

While financial statements provide detailed information that is useful in analysis, research shows that much of the immediate stock price reaction to quarterly financial information (at least earnings) occurs on the day of the earnings announcement instead of when the full financial statements are released. This means an investor is unlikely to profit by using summary information that was previously released. The detailed information in financial statements can be analyzed to provide insights about a company's performance and future prospects that are not available from summary information in earnings announcements.

Recently, companies have focused investors' attention on **pro forma earnings** in their earnings announcements. Beginning with GAAP income from continuing operations (excluding discontinued operations, extraordinary items, and changes in accounting principle), the additional transitory items (most notably, restructuring charges) remaining in income from continuing operations are now routinely excluded in computing pro forma income. In addition, companies are also excluding expenses arising from acquisitions, compensation expense in the form of stock options, income (losses) from equity method investees, research and development expenditures, and others. Companies view the objective of this reformulation as providing the analyst community with an earnings figure closer to "core" earnings, purged of transitory and nonoperating charges, which should have the highest relevance for determining stock price.

Significant differences between GAAP and pro forma earnings are not uncommon. For example, for the first three quarters of 2001, the 100 companies that make up the NASDAQ 100 reported $82.3 billion in combined *losses* to the Securities and Exchange Commission (SEC). For the same period, these companies reported $19.1 billion in combined *profits* to shareholders via headline, "pro forma" earnings reports–a difference of $101.4 billion or more than $1 billion per company. (Source: John J. May, SmartStock Investor.com, January 21, 2002)

It is generally acknowledged that additional disclosures by management can help investors understand the core drivers of shareholder value. These provide insight into the way companies analyze themselves and can be useful in identifying trends and predicting future operating results. The general effect of pro forma earnings is purportedly to eliminate transitory items to enhance year-to-year comparability. Although this might

■ ■ ■ ■ ■ ■ ■
AUDIT PRESS
A survey of CFOs found that auditors challenged the company's financial results in less than 40% of audits. Of the CFOs challenged, most refused to back down—specifically, 25% persuaded the auditor to agree to the practice in question, and 32% convinced the auditor that the results were immaterial. Only 43% made changes to win the auditor's approval.

■ ■ ■ ■ ■ ■ ■
EARLY BIRDS
More companies are issuing a warning or *earnings preannouncement* to avoid nasty negative surprises when they report bad-news earnings.

be justified on the basis that the resulting earnings have greater predictive ability, important information has been lost in the process. Accounting is beneficial in reporting how effective management has been in its stewardship of invested capital. Asset write-offs, liability accruals, and other charges that are eliminated in this process may reflect the outcomes of poor investment decisions or poor management of corporate invested capital. Investors should not blindly eliminate the information contained in nonrecurring, or "noncore," items by focusing solely on pro forma earnings. A systematic definition of operating earnings and a standard income statement format might offer helpful clarification, but it should not be a substitute for the due diligence and thorough examination of the footnotes that constitute comprehensive financial statement analysis.

Other Statutory Reports

Beyond the financial statements, companies must file other reports with the SEC. Some of the more important reports are the **proxy statement,** which must be sent along with the notice of the annual shareholders' meeting; **Form 8-K,** which must be filed to report unusual circumstances such as an auditor change; and the **prospectus,** which must accompany an application for an equity offering. Exhibit 2.1 lists many of the key statutory reports and their content.

Exhibit 2.1	**Key SEC Filings**		
■■■■■■■	Title	Description	Important Contents from Analysis Perspective
	Form 10-K	Annual report	Audited annual financial statements and management discussion and analysis.
	Form 10-Q	Quarterly report	Quarterly financial statements and management discussion and analysis.
	Form 20-F	Registration statement or annual report by foreign issuers	Reconciliation of reports using non-U.S. GAAP to one using U.S. GAAP.
	Form 8-K	Current report	Report filed within 15 days of the following events: (1) change in management control; (2) acquisition or disposition of major assets; (3) bankruptcy or receivership; (4) auditor change; (5) director resignation.
	Regulation 14-A	Proxy statement	Details of board of directors, managerial ownership, managerial remuneration, and employee stock options.
		Prospectus	Audited financial statements, information about proposed project or share issue.

Factors Affecting Statutory Financial Reports

The main component of financial statements (and many other statutory reports) is financial accounting information. While much of financial accounting information is determined by GAAP, other determinants are preparers (managers) and the monitoring and enforcement mechanisms that ensure its quality and integrity.

Generally Accepted Accounting Principles (GAAP)

Financial statements are prepared in accordance with **GAAP,** which are the rules and guidelines of financial accounting. These rules determine measurement and recognition policies such as how assets are measured, when liabilities are incurred, when revenues and gains are recognized, and when expenses and losses are incurred. They also dictate what information must be provided in the notes. Knowledge of these accounting principles is essential for effective financial statement analysis.

GAAP Defined.   GAAP are a collection of standards, pronouncements, opinions, interpretations, and practice guidelines. Various professional and quasistatutory bodies such as the Financial Accounting Standards Board (FASB), the SEC, and the American Institute of Certified Public Accountants (AICPA) set GAAP. From an analysis viewpoint, the most important types of accounting rules and guidelines are:

- *Statements of Financial Accounting Standards (SFAS).*
- *APB Opinions.*
- *Accounting Research Bulletins (ARB).*
- *AICPA pronouncements.* The AICPA issues guidelines for certain topics yet to be addressed by the FASB in its *Statements of Position (SOP)* or for those involving industry-specific matters in its *Industry Audit and Accounting Guidelines.*
- *EITF Bulletins. EITF Bulletins* are issued by the FASB's Emerging Issues Task Force.
- Industry practices.

Setting Accounting Standards.   Standard setting in the United States (unlike many other nations) is mainly the responsibility of the private sector, with close ties to the accounting profession. The FASB currently serves as the standard-setting body in accounting. It consists of seven full-time paid members, who represent various *interest groups* such as investors, managers, accountants, and analysts. Before issuing a standard, the FASB issues, in most cases, a discussion memorandum for public comment. Written comments are filed with the board, and oral comments can be voiced at public hearings that generally precede the issuance of an *Exposure Draft* of the proposed standard. After further exposure and comment, the FASB usually issues a final version of an *SFAS*. It also sometimes issues interpretations of pronouncements.

Standard setting by the FASB is a political process, with increasing participation by financial statement users. From an analysis viewpoint, this political process often results in standards that are compromise solutions that fall short of requiring the most relevant information. Controversy surrounding executive stock options (ESOs) is a case in point. Even after the FASB voted to include the cost of ESOs in reported earnings, fierce lobbying by Silicon Valley companies forced the FASB to retreat. It eventually issued a watered-down standard *(SFAS 123)* that failed to require companies to recognize the cost of options in earnings. Instead, companies were allowed to bury this expense in notes to the financial statements. A decade later, in the post-Enron period as legislators pressed for more transparency in financial reporting, the ESO issue was raised once again and the FASB finally passed a standard requiring recognition of ESO expenses in the income statement.

Role of the Securities and Exchange Commission.   The SEC is an independent, quasi-judicial government agency that administers the Securities Acts of 1933 and 1934. These acts pertain to disclosures related to public security offerings. The SEC plays a crucial role both in regulating information disclosure by companies with publicly traded securities and in monitoring and enforcing compliance with accepted practices.

The SEC can override, modify, or introduce accounting reporting and disclosure requirements. It can be viewed as the final authority on financial reporting. However, the SEC respects the accounting profession and understands the difficulties in developing accepted accounting standards. Consequently, it has rarely used its regulatory authority, but has become increasingly aggressive in modifying FASB standards. Current public attitudes toward, and confidence in, financial reporting in large part

FASB RAP

The rap on FASB from business includes (1) too many costly rule changes, (2) unrealistic and confusing rules, (3) bias toward investors, not companies, and (4) resistance to global standards.

CHIEF PAY

The annual salary of an FASB member exceeds $500,000.

SHAME ON SEC

In his firm's proxy, Warren Buffett writes: "The SEC should be shamed by the fact that they have long let themselves be muscled by business executives."

determine the SEC involvement in accounting practice. SEC involvement is also affected by the aggressiveness of its chief accountant.

International Financial Reporting Standards. International Financial Reporting Standards (IFRS) are formulated by the International Accounting Standards Board (IASB), which is a body representing accountants and other interested parties from different countries. While the IFRS are currently not applicable in the United States—for example, foreign companies listed on U.S. exchanges need to reconcile IFRS-based numbers with U.S. GAAP—there is mounting pressure on the SEC to accept these standards in one form or another. We need to be aware of the growing influence of the IFRS outside the United States.

The FASB is currently involved in a joint project with the IASB—called the "convergence" project—that aims to eventually eliminate all differences between the two sets of standards. Considerable progress has been achieved to date in this direction.

Managers

Primary responsibility for fair and accurate financial reporting rests with managers. Managers have ultimate control over the integrity of the accounting system and the financial records that make up financial statements. Recognizing this fact, the Sarbanes-Oxley Act of 2002 requires the CEO to personally certify the accuracy and the veracity of the financial statements.

We know judgment is necessary in determining financial statement numbers. While accounting standards reduce subjectivity and arbitrariness in these judgments, they do not eliminate it. The exercise of managerial judgment arises both because accounting standards often allow managers to choose among alternative accounting methods and because of the estimation involved in arriving at accounting numbers.

Judgment in financial accounting involves *managerial discretion*. Ideally, this discretion improves the economic content of accounting numbers by allowing managers to exercise their skilled judgment and to communicate their private information through their accounting choices and estimates. For example, a manager could decrease the allowance for bad debts based on inside information such as the improved financial status of a major customer. Still, in practice, too many managers abuse this discretion to manage earnings and window-dress financial statements. This *earnings management* can reduce the economic content of financial statements and can reduce confidence in the reporting process. Identifying earnings management and making proper adjustments to reported numbers are important tasks in financial statement analysis.

Managers also can indirectly affect financial reports through their collective influence on the standard-setting process. Managers are a powerful force in determining accounting standards. Managers also provide a balancing force to the demands of users in standard setting. While users focus on the benefits of a new standard or disclosure, managers focus on its costs. Typically, managers oppose a standard that: (1) decreases reported earnings; (2) increases earnings volatility; or (3) discloses competitive information about segments, products, or plans.

Monitoring and Enforcement Mechanisms

Monitoring and enforcement mechanisms ensure the reliability and integrity of financial reports. Some of these, such as the SEC, are set by fiat. Other mechanisms, such as auditing, evolve over time. The importance of these mechanisms for the credibility and survival of financial reporting cannot be overemphasized.

■ ■ ■ ■ ■ ■
RISKY MANAGERS
An executive-search firm conducted profiles of more than 1,400 managers of large companies. The results indicated that one out of eight execs can be termed *high risk*—they believe the rules do not apply to them, lack concern for others, and rarely possess feelings of guilt.

■ ■ ■ ■ ■ ■
HOT SEAT
It's been a difficult period for auditor PricewaterhouseCoopers and its clients—some examples: Tyco International Ltd.'s CEO Dennis Kozlowski and CFO Mark Swartz allegedly looted millions from the company. Software maker MicroStrategy settled an SEC suit alleging it had violated accounting rules and overstated its results. Telecom giant Lucent Technologies has been under scrutiny for its accounting practices.

Auditors.   External auditing is an important mechanism to help ensure the quality and reliability of financial statements. All public companies' financial statements must be audited by an independent certified public accountant (CPA). The product of an audit is the auditor's report, which is an integral part of financial statements. The centerpiece of an audit report is the **audit opinion.** An auditor can (1) issue a clean opinion, (2) issue one or more types of qualified opinions, or (3) disclaim expressing any opinion.

ANALYSIS VIEWPOINT   ***. . . YOU ARE THE AUDITOR***

Your audit firm accepts a new audit engagement. How can you use financial statement analysis in the audit of this new client?

Corporate Governance.   Another important monitor of financial reports is corporate governance mechanisms within a company. Financial statements need approval by a company's *board of directors.* Many companies appoint an *audit committee*–a subcommittee of the board–to oversee the financial reporting process. An audit committee is appointed by the board and is represented by both managers and outsiders. Audit committees are often entrusted with wide-ranging powers and responsibilities relating to many aspects of the reporting process. This includes oversight of accounting methods, internal control procedures, and internal audits. Many believe that an independent and powerful audit committee is a crucial corporate governance feature that contributes substantially to the quality of financial reports. Most companies also perform *internal audits,* which are another defense against fraud and misrepresentation of financial records.

Securities and Exchange Commission.   The SEC plays an active role in monitoring and enforcing accounting standards. All public companies must file audited financial statements (10-Ks and 10-Qs) with the SEC. The SEC staff checks these reports to ensure compliance with statutory requirements, including adherence to accounting standards. The SEC has brought enforcement actions against hundreds of companies over the years for accounting violations. These violations range from misinterpretation of standards to outright fraud and falsification of accounts. Enforcement actions against companies and their managers range from restatement of financial statements to fines and imprisonment. Recently, the SEC has been actively attempting to curb earnings management.

Litigation.   Another important monitor of managers (and auditors) is the threat of litigation. The amount of damages relating to accounting irregularities paid by companies, managers, and auditors in the past decade is estimated in the billions of dollars. The threat of litigation influences managers to adopt more responsible reporting practices both for statutory and voluntary disclosures.

■ ■ ■ ■ ■ ■ ■
TWISTED BOARDS
Some boards don't get it. After all the recent concern with corporate governance, the board of Conseco—the financial services giant—gave an $8 million bonus to CEO Gary Wendt even though he presided over only one profitable quarter in the previous two years.

■ ■ ■ ■ ■ ■ ■
TOP BOARDS
Attributes of a good board include:
Independence—CEO cronies are out. Eliminate insiders and cross-directorships.
Quality—Meetings include real, open debate. Appoint directors familiar with managers and the business.
Accountability—Directors hold stakes in the company and are willing to challenge the CEO.

ANALYSIS VIEWPOINT   ***. . . YOU ARE THE DIRECTOR***

You are named a director of a major company. Your lawyer warns you about litigation risk and the need to constantly monitor both management and the financial health of the company. How can financial statement analysis assist you in performing your director duties?

Alternative Information Sources

Financial statements have long been regarded as a major source of information for users. However, financial statements increasingly compete with alternative sources of information. One major source of alternative information is analysts' forecasts and recommendations. Another source is economic, industry, and company-specific news. With continued development of the Internet, information availability for investors will increase. In this section we discuss some of the major alternative information sources: (1) economy, industry, and company news; (2) voluntary disclosures; and (3) information intermediaries (analysts).

Economic, Industry, and Company Information.   Investors use economic and industry information to update company forecasts. Examples of macroeconomic news that affects the entire stock market include data on economic growth, employment, foreign trade, interest rates, and currency exchanges. The effects of economic information vary across industries and companies based on the perceived exposure of an industry's or a company's profits and risks to that news. Investors also respond to industry news such as commodity price changes, industry sales data, changes in competitive position, and government regulation. Moreover, company-specific information impacts user behavior—examples are news of acquisitions, divestitures, management changes, and auditor changes.

Voluntary Disclosure.   Voluntary disclosure by managers is an increasingly important source of information. One important catalyst for voluntary disclosure is the Safe Harbor Rules. Those rules provide legal protection against genuine mistakes by managers who make voluntary disclosures.

There are several motivations for voluntary disclosure. Probably the most important motivation is *legal liability*. Managers who voluntarily disclose important news, especially of an adverse nature, have a lower probability of being sued by investors. Another motivation is that of *expectations adjustment*. It suggests managers have incentives to disclose information when they believe the market's expectations are sufficiently different from their own. Still another motivation is that of *signaling*, where managers are said to disclose good news to increase their company's stock price. A more recent motivation advanced for voluntary disclosures is the intent to *manage expectations*. Specifically, managers are said to manage market expectations of company performance so that they can regularly "beat" market expectations.

Information Intermediaries.   Information intermediaries, or analysts, play an important and unique role in financial reporting. On one hand, they represent a sophisticated and active group of users. On the other hand, they constitute the single most important source of alternative information. As such, standard setters usually respond to analysts' demands as well as the threat they pose as a competing source of information.

Information intermediaries represent an industry involved in collecting, processing, interpreting, and disseminating information about the financial prospects of companies. This industry includes security analysts, investment newsletters, investment advisers, and debt raters. Security analysts constitute the largest segment of information intermediaries, which include both buy-side analysts and sell-side analysts. Buy-side analysts are usually employed by investment companies or pension funds such as *TIAA-CREF, Vanguard,* or *Fidelity.* These analysts do their analysis for in-house use. Sell-side analysts provide analysis and recommendations to the public for a fee, for example *Value Line* and *Standard & Poors,* or privately to their clients, for example, analysts at *Salomon Smith*

Barney and *Charles Schwab.* In short, sell-side analysts' reports are used by outsiders while buy-side analysts' reports are used internally. Another large component of information intermediaries includes investment newsletters such as *Dow Theory Forecasts* and *Smart Money.* Credit rating agencies such as Moody's also are information intermediaries whose services are aimed at credit agencies.

Information intermediaries are not directly involved in making investment and credit decisions. Instead, their objective is to provide information useful for those decisions. Their outputs, or products, are forecasts, recommendations, and research reports. Their inputs are financial statements, voluntary disclosures, and economic, industry, and company news. Information intermediaries create value by processing and synthesizing raw and diverse information about a company and output it in a form useful for business decisions. They are viewed as performing one or more of at least four functions:

1. **Information gathering.** This involves researching and gathering information about companies that is not readily available.
2. **Information interpretation.** A crucial task of an intermediary is the interpretation of information in an economically meaningful manner.
3. **Prospective analysis.** This is the final and most visible task of an information intermediary—involving both business analysis and financial statement analysis. The output includes earnings and cash flow forecasts.
4. **Recommendation.** Analysts also often make specific recommendations, such as buy/hold/sell recommendations for stocks and bonds.

By providing timely information that is often of a prospective nature and readily amenable to investment decision making, investment intermediaries perform an important service. Arguably, the growth of information intermediaries has reduced the importance of financial statements to capital markets. Still, information intermediaries depend significantly on financial statements, while at the same time they view financial statements as a competing information source.

■ ■ ■ ■ ■ ■ ■
PHONY INFO
Regulators allege that Merrill Lynch and Citigroup's Smith Barney issued upbeat research to win investment-banking clients. Also under investigation were CSFB and Morgan Stanley.

■ ■ ■ ■ ■ ■ ■
EARNINGS SEER
According to a recent study, 1,025 of 6,000 companies beat analysts' earnings forecasts in at least 9 of the past 12 quarters.

NATURE AND PURPOSE OF FINANCIAL ACCOUNTING

In this section we discuss the desirable qualities, principles, and conventions underlying financial accounting. With this insight, we can evaluate the strengths and weaknesses of accounting and its relevance to effective analysis and decision making.

Desirable Qualities of Accounting Information

Relevance is the capacity of information to affect a decision and is the first of two primary qualities of accounting information. This implies that *timeliness* is a desirable characteristic of accounting information. Interim (quarterly) financial reports are largely motivated by timeliness.

Reliability is a second important quality of financial information. For information to be reliable it must be verifiable, representationally faithful, and neutral. *Verifiability* means the information is confirmable. *Representational faithfulness* means the information reflects reality, and *neutrality* means it is truthful and unbiased.

Accounting information often demands a trade-off between relevance and reliability. For example, reporting forecasts increase relevance but reduce reliability. Also, while analysts' forecasts are relevant, they are less reliable than actual figures based on historical data. Standard setters often struggle with this trade-off.

Comparability and consistency are secondary qualities of accounting information. *Comparability* implies that information is measured in a similar manner across companies. *Consistency* implies the same method is used for similar transactions across time. Both comparability and consistency are required for information to be relevant and reliable.

Important Principles of Accounting

The desirable qualities of accounting information serve as conceptual criteria for accounting principles. Skillful use of accounting numbers for financial analysis requires an understanding of the accounting framework underlying their computation. This includes the principles governing measurement of assets, liabilities, equity, revenues, expenses, gains, and losses.

Accrual Accounting

Modern accounting adopts the accrual basis over the more primitive cash flow basis. Under accrual accounting, revenues are recognized when earned and expenses when incurred, regardless of the receipt or payment of cash. The accrual basis is arguably the most important, but also controversial, feature of modern accounting. We focus on accrual accounting later in this chapter.

Historical Cost and Fair Value

Traditionally, accounting has used the *historical cost* concept for measuring and recording the value of assets and liabilities. Historical costs are values from actual transactions that have occurred in the past, so historical cost accounting is also referred to as *transactions-based* accounting. The advantage of historical cost accounting is that the value of an asset determined through arm's-length bargaining is usually fair and objective. However, when asset (or liability) values subsequently change, continuing to record value at the historical cost—that is, at the value at which the asset was originally purchased—impairs the usefulness of the financial statements, in particular the balance sheet.

Recognizing the limitations of historical cost accounting, standard setters are increasingly moving to an alternative form of recording asset (or liability) values based on the concept of *fair value*. Broadly, fair values are estimates of the *current* economic value of an asset or liability. If a market exists for the asset, it is the current market value of the asset. Fair value accounting is currently being used to record the value of many financial assets, such as marketable securities. However, the FASB has recognized the conceptual superiority of the fair value concept and has, in principle, decided to eventually move to a model where all asset and liability values are recorded at fair value. For the purposes of analysis, it is crucially important to understand the exact nature of fair value accounting, its current status and where it is heading, and also its advantages and limitations both for credit and equity analysis. Acknowledging its importance, we devote an entire section to fair value accounting later in this chapter.

Materiality

Materiality, according to the FASB, is "the magnitude of an omission or misstatement of accounting information that, in the light of surrounding circumstances, makes it possible that the judgment of a reasonable person relying on the information would be changed or influenced by the omission or misstatement." One problem with materiality is a concern that some preparers of financial statements and their auditors use it to avoid unwanted disclosures. This is compounded by the fact there is no set criteria guiding either the preparer or user of information in distinguishing between material and nonmaterial items.

Conservatism

Conservatism involves reporting the least optimistic view when faced with uncertainty in measurement. The most common occurrence of this concept is that gains are not recognized until they are realized (for example, appreciation in the value of land) whereas losses are recognized immediately. Conservatism reduces both the reliability and relevance of accounting information in at least two ways. First, conservatism understates both net assets and net income. A second point is that conservatism results in selectively delayed recognition of good news in financial statements, while immediately recognizing bad news. Conservatism has important implications for analysis. If the purpose of analysis is equity valuation, it is important to estimate the conservative bias in financial reports and make suitable adjustments so that net assets and net income are better measured. In the case of credit analysis, conservatism provides an additional margin of safety. Conservatism also is a determinant of earnings quality. While conservative financial statements reduce earnings quality, many users (such as Warren Buffett) view conservative accounting as a sign of superior earnings quality. This apparent contradiction is explained by conservative accounting reflecting on the responsibility, dependability, and credibility of management.

Academic research distinguishes between two types of conservatism. *Unconditional conservatism* is a form of conservative accounting that is applied across the board in a consistent manner. It leads to a perpetual understatement of asset values. An example of unconditional conservatism is the accounting for R&D: R&D expenditures are written off when incurred, regardless of their economic potential. Because of this, the net assets of R&D-intensive companies are always understated. *Conditional conservatism* refers to the adage of "recognize all losses immediately but recognize gains only after they are realized." Examples of conditional conservatism are writing down assets—such as PP&E or goodwill—when there has been an economic impairment in their value, that is, reduction in their future cash-flow potential. In contrast, if the future cash flow potential of these assets increases, accountants do not immediately write up their values—the financial statements only gradually reflect the increased cash flow potential over time as and when the cash flows are realized. Of the two forms of conservative accounting, unconditional conservatism is clearly more valuable to an analyst—especially a credit analyst—because it conveys timely information about adverse changes in the company's underlying economic situation.

Relevance and Limitations of Accounting
Relevance of Financial Accounting Information

Accounting for business activities is imperfect and has limitations. It is easy to focus on these imperfections and limitations. However, there is no comparable substitute. Financial accounting is and remains the only relevant and reliable system for recording, classifying, and summarizing business activities. Improvement rests with refinements in this time-tested system. It is incumbent on anyone who desires to perform effective financial

TIMING
Recording revenues early inflates short-run sales and earnings. Industries such as software sales and services, where service contracts and upgrades can stretch revenue out for years, are especially vulnerable to manipulation.

Analysis Research
■■■■■■■

ACCOUNTING INFORMATION
AND STOCK PRICES

Do summary accounting numbers such as earnings (net income) explain a company's stock prices and returns? The answer is yes. Evidence from research shows a definite link between the type of *news* or *surprise* conveyed in earnings and a company's stock returns. Good earnings news (positive surprise) is accompanied by positive stock returns, whereas bad earnings news (negative surprise) is associated with negative returns. The more good or bad the earnings news (i.e., the greater the magnitude of the earnings surprise), the greater is the accompanying stock price reactions.

A substantial portion of the stock returns associated with earnings news occurs prior to the earnings announcement, indicating that the stock market is able to infer much of the earnings news well before it is announced. This evidence suggests that accounting information, to a large extent, plays a *feedback role* wherein it confirms prior beliefs of the market. Interestingly, stock returns after the earnings announcement also appear to be associated with the earnings news. This phenomenon, called the *post-earnings announcement drift,* is arguably a form of stock market inefficiency and is exploited by several *momentum* based investing strategies.

Research shows us that many factors influence the relationship between accounting earnings and stock prices. These include company factors such as risk, size, leverage, and variability that decrease the influence of earnings on stock prices, and factors such as earnings growth and persistence that increase their impact. Our analysis must recognize those influences that impact the relevance of accounting numbers for security analysis.

Research also shows the importance of earnings information to the market has declined over time, especially in the past two decades. Some of the suggested reasons for this decline are increased reporting of losses, increased magnitude of one-time charges and other special items, and increased importance of R&D and intangible assets. However, research reveals that while the ability of earnings to explain prices has declined over time, this has been offset to a large extent by the increasing importance of book value.

analysis to understand accounting, its terminology, and its practices, including its imperfections and limitations.

Exactly how relevant is financial accounting information for analysis? One way to answer this question is to examine how well financial accounting numbers reflect or explain stock prices. Exhibit 2.2 tracks the ability of earnings and book value to explain stock prices, both separately and in combination, for a large cross-section of companies over a recent 40-year period. The exhibit shows that earnings and book value (combined) are able to explain between 50% and 75% of stock price behavior (except for the late 1990s period—the dot-com bubble—when the explanatory power was quite

Exhibit 2.2
■■■■■■■   **Relation between Accounting Numbers and Stock Prices***

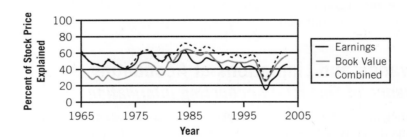

*Graphs depict the R-squared from a regression of stock price on earnings per share and/or book value for all firms available on the Industrial, Full Coverage, and Research Compustat databases.

low). This occurs even though the analysis stacks the deck against accounting numbers in several ways. First, we do not control for many other factors that affect stock prices such as interest rates. Second, we consider only two summary numbers—arguably the two most important—from the wealth of information available in financial statements. Finally, we impose an identical relation between accounting numbers and stock prices across all companies—that is, we do not consider differences across companies such as industry effects and expected growth rates.

Exhibit 2.2 does not establish causation. That is, we cannot establish the extent to which accounting numbers directly determine stock prices. This is because of the presence of alternative information such as analyst forecasts and economic statistics used in setting stock prices. Still, recall that one element of the relevance of accounting information is feedback value for revising or confirming investor beliefs. At a minimum, this analysis supports the feedback value of accounting information by revealing the strong link between accounting numbers and stock prices.

Limitations of Financial Statement Information

Analyst forecasts, reports, and recommendations along with other alternative information sources are a major competitor for accounting information. What are the advantages offered by these alternative sources? We can identify at least three:

1. **Timeliness.** Financial statements are prepared as often as every quarter and are typically released from three to six weeks after the quarter-end. In contrast, analysts update their forecasts and recommendations on a nearly real-time basis—as soon as information about the company is available to them. Other alternative information sources, such as economic, industry, or company news, are also readily available in many forms including via the Internet.
2. **Frequency.** Closely linked to timeliness is frequency. Financial statements are prepared periodically, typically each quarter. However, alternative information sources, including analysts' reports, are released to the market whenever business events demand their revision.
3. **Forward-looking.** Alternative information sources, particularly analysts' reports and forecasts, use much forward-looking information. Financial statements contain limited forecasts. Further, historical-cost-based accounting (and conservatism) usually yields *recognition lags,* where certain business activities are recorded at a lag. To illustrate, consider a company that signs a long-term contract with a customer. An analyst will estimate the impact of this contract on future earnings and firm value as soon as news about the signing is available. Financial statements only recognize this contract in future periods when the goods or services are delivered.

Despite these drawbacks, financial statements continue to be an important source of information to financial markets.

········ ACCRUALS—CORNERSTONE OF ACCOUNTING

Financial statements are primarily prepared on an accrual basis. Supporters strongly believe that accrual accounting is superior to cash accounting, both for measuring performance and financial condition. *Statement of Financial Accounting Concepts No. 1* states that "information about enterprise earnings based on accrual accounting generally provides a better indication of enterprises' present and continuing ability to generate cash flows than information limited to the financial aspects of cash receipts and payments."

Accrual accounting invokes a similarly strong response from its detractors. For detractors, accrual accounting is a medley of complex and imperfect rules that obscure the purpose of financial statements–providing information about cash flows and cash-generating capacity. For extreme critics, accrual accounting is a diversion, a red herring, that undermines the process of information dissemination. These critics claim the purpose of financial analysis is to remove the veil of accrual accounting and get to the underlying cash flows. They are troubled by the intricacy of accruals and their susceptibility to manipulation by managers.

This section presents a critical evaluation of accrual accounting. We discuss the relevance and importance of accruals, their drawbacks and limitations, and the implications of the accruals-versus-cash-flow debate for financial statement analysis. Our aim is not to take sides in this debate. We believe that cash flows and accruals serve different purposes and that both are important for financial analysis. Yet, we caution against a disregard of accruals. It is crucial for an analyst to understand accrual accounting for effective financial analysis.

Accrual Accounting—An Illustration

We explain accrual accounting, and its differences from cash accounting, with an illustration. Assume you decide to sell printed T-shirts for $10 each. Your research suggests you can buy plain T-shirts for $5 apiece. Printing would entail a front-end, fixed fee of $100 for the screen and another $0.75 per printed T-shirt. Your initial advertisement yields orders for 100 T-shirts. You then invest $700 in the venture, purchase plain T-shirts and the screen, and get the T-shirts printed (suppliers require you pay for all expenses in cash). By the end of your first week in business, all T-shirts are ready for sale. Customers with orders totaling 50 T-shirts pick up their T-shirts in that first week. But, of the 50 T-shirts picked up, only 25 are paid for in cash. For the other 25, you agree to accept payment next week. To evaluate the financial performance of your venture, you prepare cash accounting records at the end of this first week.

Statement of Cash Flows			Balance Sheet (Cash Basis)	
Receipts			**Assets**	
T-shirt sales		$250	Cash	$275
Payments				
T-shirt purchases	$500			
Screen purchase	100		**Equity**	
Printing charges	75		Beginning equity	$700
Total payments		(675)	Less net cash outflow	(425)
Net cash outflow		$(425)	Total equity	$275

The cash accounting records indicate you lost money. This surprises you. Yet, your cash balance confirms the $425 cash loss. That is, you began with $700 and now have $275 cash–obviously, a net cash outflow of $425 occurred. Consequently, you reassess your decision to pursue this venture. Namely, you had estimated cost per T-shirt as (assuming sales of 100 T-shirts): $5 for plain T-shirt, $1 for the screen, and $0.75 cents for printing. This yields your total cost of $6.75 per T-shirt. At a price of $10, you expected a profit of $3.25 per T-shirt. Yet your accounts indicate you lost money.

How can this be? After further analysis, you find the following problems with the cash basis income statement and balance sheet:

1. You have not recognized any revenues from the 25 shirts that have been sold on account (e.g., for which you have an account receivable).
2. You have treated all of the T-shirts purchased as an expense. Shouldn't this cost be matched with the revenues those T-shirts will produce when they are sold?
3. Likewise, you have treated all of the screen purchase and the T-shirt printing charges as an expense. Shouldn't this cost be matched ratably with the revenues that the screen will help generate when those revenues are recognized?

Taking these factors into consideration reveals that you have actually made a profit of $162.50 in your first week:

Income Statement			Balance Sheet (Accrual Basis)	
Revenues			**Assets**	
T-shirt sales		$500.00	Cash	$275.00
			T-shirt inventory	337.50
			Receivables	250.00
Expenses			Total assets	$862.50
T-shirt costs	$250.00			
Screen depreciation	50.00		**Equity**	
Printing charges	37.50		Beginning equity	$700.00
Total expenses		(337.50)	Add net income	162.50
Net income		$162.50	Total equity	$862.50

Your revenues now reflect all the T-shirt sales, even those for which payment has not yet been made. In addition, since only one-half of the T-shirts have been sold, only the cost of making the T-shirts sold is reflected as an expense, including the $250 of fabric costs, $37.50 of printing costs, and $50 of the cost of the screen (even that may be too high a percentage if we expect the screen to produce more than 100 T-shirts). Given the profit we have recognized, equity also increases, suggesting that you could eventually take away more than what you invested in the venture.

Both the accrual income statement and balance sheet make more sense to you than recording under cash accounting. Nevertheless, you feel uncertain about the accrual numbers. They are less concrete than cash flows–that is, they depend on assumptions. For example, you assumed that everyone who bought a T-shirt on credit is eventually going to pay for them. If some customers don't pay, then your net income (and balance sheet numbers) will change. Another assumption is that unsold T-shirts in inventory are worth their cost. What is the basis for this assumption? If you can't sell them, they are probably worthless. But if you sell them, they are worth $10 apiece. While the $6.75 cost per T-shirt seems a reasonable compromise, you still are uncertain about this number's reliability. Yet overall, while the accrual numbers are more "soft," they make more sense than cash flows.

Accrual Accounting Framework
Accrual Concept

An appealing feature about cash flows is simplicity. Cash flows are easy to understand and straightforward to compute. There also is something tangible and certain about cash flows. They seem like the real thing–not the creation of accounting methods. But unfortunately, when it comes to measuring cash-generating capacity of a company, cash flows are of limited use.

Most business transactions are on credit. Further, companies invest billions of dollars in inventories and long-term assets, the benefits of which occur over many future periods. In these scenarios, cash flow accounting (no matter how reliable it is) fails to provide a relevant picture of a company's financial condition and performance.

Accrual accounting aims to inform users about the consequences of business activities for a company's future cash flows as soon as possible with a reasonable level of certainty. This is achieved by recognizing revenue earned and expenses incurred, regardless of whether or not cash flows occur contemporaneously. This separation of revenue and expense recognition from cash flows is facilitated with *accrual adjustments,* which adjust cash inflows and cash outflows to yield revenues and expenses. Accrual adjustments are recorded after making reasonable assumptions and estimates, without materially sacrificing the reliability of accounting information. Accordingly, judgment is a key part of accrual accounting, and rules and institutional mechanisms exist to ensure reliability.

The next section begins by defining the exact relationship between accruals and cash flows. We show that accrual and cash accounting differ primarily because of timing differences in recognizing cash flow consequences of business activities and events. We then explain the accrual process of revenue and expense recognition and discuss two types of accruals, short term and long term.

Accruals and Cash Flows.   To explore the relation between accruals and cash flows to the firm, it is important to recognize alternative types of cash flows. *Operating cash flow* refers to cash from a company's ongoing operating activities. *Free cash flow* to the firm reflects the added effects of investments and divestments in operating assets. The appeal of the free cash flow to the firm concept is that it represents cash that is free to be paid to both debt and equity holders. *Free cash flow to equity,* which we introduced in Chapter 1, adds changes in the firm's debt levels to free cash flow to the firm and, thereby, yields the cash flows that are available for equity holders. When economists refer to cash flow, they are usually referring to one of these free cash flow definitions, a convention we adopt in this book. Bottom line cash flow is *net cash flow,* the change in the cash account balance (note, cash includes cash equivalents for all these definitions).

Strictly defined, *accruals* are the sum of accounting adjustments that make net income different from net cash flow. These adjustments include those that affect income when there is no cash flow impact (e.g., credit sales) and those that isolate cash flow effects from income (e.g., asset purchases). Because of double entry, accruals affect the balance sheet by either increasing or decreasing asset or liability accounts by an equal amount. Namely, an accrual that increases (decreases) income will also either increase (decrease) an asset or decrease (increase) a liability.

What is included in accruals depends on the definition of cash flow. The most common meaning of accruals is accounting adjustments that convert operating cash flow to net income. This yields the following identity: **Net income = Operating cash flow + Accruals.** Under this definition, accruals are of two types: short-term accruals, which are related to working capital items, and long-term accruals, such as depreciation and amortization. We discuss these two types of accruals later in this chapter. Note that this definition of accruals does not include accruals that arise through the process of capitalization of costs related to property, plant, and equipment (PP&E) as long-term assets.

Accrual Accounting Reduces Timing and Matching Problems.   The difference between accrual accounting and cash accounting is one of timing and matching. Accrual accounting overcomes both the timing and the matching problems that are inherent in cash accounting. *Timing* problems refer to cash flows that do not occur contemporaneously with the business activities yielding the cash flows. For example, a sale occurs in the first quarter, but cash from the sale arrives in the second quarter. *Matching* problems refer to cash inflows and cash outflows that occur from a business activity but are not matched in time with each other, such as fees received from consulting that are not linked in time to wages paid to consultants working on the project.

Timing and matching problems with cash flows arise for at least two reasons. First, our credit economy necessitates that transactions, more often than not, do not involve immediate transfer of cash. Credit transactions reduce the ability of cash flows to track business activities in a timely manner. Second, costs often are incurred before their benefits are realized, especially when costs involve investments in plant and equipment. Thus, measuring costs when cash outflows occur often fails to reflect financial condition and performance.

Note that over the life of a company, cash flows and accrual income are equal. This is because once all business activities are concluded, the timing and matching problems are resolved. Yet, as economist John Maynard Keynes once remarked, "In the long run we are all dead." This is meant to stress the importance of measuring financial condition and performance in the short run, typically at periodic points over the life of a company. The shorter these intervals, the more evident are the limitations of cash flow accounting.

Accrual Process—Revenue Recognition and Expense Matching.   Accrual accounting is comprised of two fundamental principles, revenue recognition and expense matching, which guide companies on when to recognize revenues and expenses:

1. **Revenue recognition.** Revenues are recognized when both earned and either realized or realizable. Revenues are *earned* when the company delivers its products or services. This means the company has carried out its part of the deal. Revenues are *realized* when cash is acquired for products or services delivered. Revenues are *realizable* when the company receives an asset for products or services delivered (often receivables) that is convertible to cash. Deciding when revenues are recognized is sometimes difficult. While revenues are usually recognized at point-of-sale (when delivered), they also can be recognized, depending on the circumstances, when a product or service is being readied, when it is complete, or when cash is received. We further discuss revenue recognition in Chapter 6.

2. **Expense matching.** Accrual accounting dictates that expenses are matched with their corresponding revenues. This matching process is different for two major types of expenses. Expenses that arise in production of a product or service, called *product costs*, are recognized when the product or service is delivered. All product costs remain on the balance sheet as inventory until the products are sold, at which time they are transferred into the income statement as *cost of goods sold* (COGS). The other type of expenses is called *period costs*. Some period costs relate to marketing the product or service and are matched with revenues when the revenues to which they relate are recognized. Other period costs, such as administrative expenses, do not directly relate to production or sale of products or services. They are expensed in the period they occur, which is not necessarily when cash outflows occur. We further discuss matching criteria in Chapter 6.

Short- and Long-Term Accruals.   *Short-term accruals* refer to short-term timing differences between income and cash flow. These accruals generate working capital items in the balance sheet (current assets and current liabilities) and are also called *working*

■ ■ ■ ■ ■ ■ ■

SALES SCAM
McKesson HBOC's stock price fell by nearly half when it admitted more than $44 million in recorded revenues were not, in fact, realized. One warning sign: Operating cash flow fell early and well below earnings.

capital accruals. Short-term accruals arise primarily from inventories and credit transactions that give rise to all types of receivables and payables such as trade debtors and creditors, prepaid expenses, and advances received. *Long-term accruals* arise from capitalization. Asset *capitalization* is the process of deferring costs incurred in the current period whose benefits are expected in future periods. This process generates long-term assets such as plant, machinery, and goodwill. Costs of these assets are allocated over their benefit periods and make up a large part of long-term accruals—we provide further discussion in Chapter 4. Accounting for long-term accruals is more complex and subjective than that for short-term accruals (with the possible exception of inventories). Cash flow implications of short-term accruals are more direct and readily determinable. Accordingly, analysis research finds short-term accruals more useful in company valuation. (see Dechow, 1994)

Relevance and Limitations of Accrual Accounting

This section gives a critical appraisal of the effects accrual accounting has on financial statements. We then discuss the conceptual and empirical strengths and weaknesses of accrual accounting relative to cash accounting for measuring performance and predicting future cash flows.

Relevance of Accrual Accounting

Conceptual Relevance of Accrual Accounting.   The conceptual superiority of accrual accounting over cash flows arises because the accrual-based income statement (and balance sheet) is more relevant for measuring a company's present and future cash-generating capacity. Both short-term and long-term accruals are important for the relevance of income vis-à-vis cash flows as described here:

- **Relevance of short-term accruals.** Short-term accruals improve the relevance of accounting by helping record revenues when earned and expenses when incurred. These accruals yield an income number that better reflects profitability and also creates current assets and current liabilities that provide useful information about financial condition.
- **Relevance of long-term accruals.** To see the import of long-term accruals, note that free cash flow to the firm is computed by subtracting investments in long-term operating assets from operating cash flow. Such investments pose problems for free cash flow. First, these investments are usually large and occur infrequently. This induces volatility in free cash flow. Second, free cash flow treats capital growth and capital replacement synonymously. Investments in new projects often bode well for a company and the market usually reacts positively to such capital expenditures. Yet all capital expenditures reduce free cash flow. This problem with free cash flow is evident from typical patterns of operating and investing cash flows, and their sum, free cash flows to the firm, over a company's life cycle as shown in Exhibit 2.3. Investing cash flows are negative until late maturity, and these outflows dominate operating cash inflows during most of the growth phase. This means free cash flow tends to be negative until the company's business matures. In late maturity and decline, a company divests its assets, generating positive investing cash flows and, hence, positive free cash flow. This means free cash flow is negative in the growth stage but positive in the decline stage, sending a *reverse* message about a company's prospects. Operating cash flows are not affected by operating investments as they ignore them.

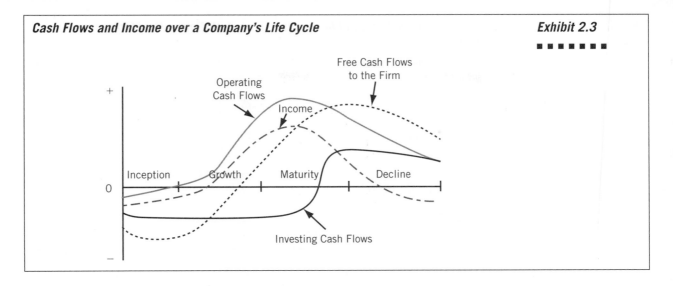

Cash Flows and Income over a Company's Life Cycle

Exhibit 2.3

Accrual accounting overcomes these limitations in free cash flow by capitalizing investments in long-term assets and allocating their costs over future benefit periods. This process of capitalization and allocation improves the relevance of income both by reducing its volatility and by matching costs of long-term investments to their benefits. The superiority of accruals in providing relevant information about a company's financial performance and condition, and for predicting future cash flows, is explained as follows:

- **Financial performance.** Revenue recognition and expense matching yields an income number superior to cash flows for evaluating financial performance. Revenue recognition ensures all revenues earned in a period are accounted for. Matching ensures that only expenses attributable to revenues earned in a period are recorded.
- **Financial condition.** Accrual accounting produces a balance sheet that more accurately reflects the level of resources available to the company to generate future cash flows.
- **Predicting future cash flows.** Accrual income is a superior predictor of future cash flows than are current cash flows for at least two reasons. First, through revenue recognition, it reflects future cash flow consequences. For example, a credit sale today forecasts cash to be received from the customer in the future. Second, accrual accounting better aligns inflows and outflows over time through the matching process. This means income is a more stable and dependable predictor of cash flows.

Empirical Relevance of Accrual Accounting.   Critics of accrual accounting decry its lower reliability and prefer reliable cash flows. Supporters assert the added relevance of accrual accounting compensates for lower reliability. They also point to institutional mechanisms, such as GAAP and auditing, that ensure at least a minimum acceptable reliability. To see whether accrual accounting works, let's examine how well accrual income and cash flows measure a company's financial performance.

To examine this question, consider these two retailers, Wal-Mart and Kmart. Exhibit 2.4 shows split-adjusted per-share stock price, net income, and free cash flow numbers for both companies over the 10-year period 1989–1998. Wal-Mart and Kmart

SALES WATCH
If accounts receivables are rising faster than sales, special scrutiny is warranted.

CASH WATCH
A company posting strong income growth but negative or low operating cash flow warrants special scrutiny.

Exhibit 2.4

■■■■■■■

Comparison of Stock Price, Net Income, and Free Cash Flow—Wal-Mart and Kmart

Fiscal year	1989	1990	1991	1992	1993	1994	1995	1996	1997	1998
Wal-Mart										
Stock price	4.22	5.33	8.25	13.47	16.28	13.25	11.44	10.19	11.87	19.91
Net income	0.18	0.24	0.28	0.35	0.44	0.51	0.58	0.60	0.67	0.78
Free cash flow	0.04	(0.01)	(0.05)	(0.17)	(0.48)	(0.50)	(0.19)	(0.21)	0.84	0.60
Kmart										
Stock price	18.94	16.62	15.50	24.50	23.25	19.63	13.63	5.88	11.13	11.00
Net income	2.00	0.81	1.89	2.02	2.07	(2.13)	0.64	(1.24)	(0.45)	0.51
Free cash flow	1.76	(2.26)	0.20	(0.47)	(2.15)	1.29	2.71	0.48	0.61	1.35

All figures are split-adjusted dollars per share from Compustat.

present an interesting contrast for this period. Wal-Mart is a growth company that has seen its market capitalization grow fivefold in this period. Kmart is arguably in decline and has experienced a 60 percent fall in market capitalization from 1994 to 1998. Since 1994, Kmart has struggled to restructure and focus its business, mainly through divesting unprofitable divisions.

Wal-Mart's income pattern is striking–the company's net income per share has grown fourfold in these 10 years, with a minimum growth of 10 percent each year. This growth pattern in net income is consistent with Wal-Mart's underlying business performance as reflected in its stock price. In contrast, Kmart's net income per share peaked in 1993 and has declined since. The net income pattern reflects the underlying economics of Kmart's business, especially the reversal of fortunes since 1994.

Unlike net income, free cash flow is not informative about either company's activities. Wal-Mart's free cash flow is markedly negative between 1990 and 1996, a period when its market capitalization doubled. From 1997, however, its free cash flow increased. The free cash flow of Kmart reveals an even more perverse relation between its performance and stock prices. Kmart's free cash flow is negative in three out of four years from 1990 to 1993, a period in which Kmart's stock increased almost 50%. However, since 1994, Kmart's free cash flow is consistently positive, while its market capitalization decreased 60%. Free cash flow appears to be a reverse indicator of performance: when free cash flow is negative, Kmart is profitable and growing; but when free cash flow turns positive, Kmart is in decline or growth is slowing.

What drives the reverse relation between free cash flow and performance for both Wal-Mart and Kmart? For an answer we need to look back at Exhibit 2.3 and the related discussion on cash flow patterns over a company's life cycle. Wal-Mart is probably nearing the end of its growth cycle and is entering maturity. Until recently, it generated negative free cash flow as it consistently spent more cash on growth than it was earning from operations. Wal-Mart's free cash flow surged in recent years both because its growth cooled and because its earlier investments are now yielding operating cash flows. Notice that Wal-Mart's cash flow patterns are consistent with the life-cycle model for a company transitioning from growth to maturity. In contrast, Kmart is probably in decline. As predicted by the life-cycle model. Kmart's investing cash flows since 1994 are positive, reflecting its downsizing as it sells assets. Cash flows generated from Kmart's divestments yield large positive free cash flow, even though its operating cash flows decline during this period.

To appreciate the limitation of free cash flow and the power of accrual income to measure financial performance, try to predict the performance of both Wal-Mart and Kmart using the pattern in net income and free cash flow for this period. For Wal-Mart, free cash flow portrays a dismal company–one that, until recently, bled cash. On the other hand, Wal-Mart's net income series shows a picture of consistent growth and profitability. Turning to Kmart, free cash flow reveals a marked upturn in business with positive free cash flow since 1994. Yet, Kmart's net income series suggests looming financial difficulties for the past five years. Which measure, accrual income or free cash flow, better reflects reality? Which measure would have been more useful to you as an equity investor in predicting stock prices? To answer these questions, compare these performance measures to the companies' actual stock prices over this period. This comparison shows the power of net income in tracking stock prices relative to free cash flow.

While this example is dated and Kmart is no longer a retail company, this example adequately serves to illustrate the advantages of accrual-based income numbers.

One case does not make a rule. Could the Kmart and Wal-Mart cases be unique in that free cash flow is otherwise superior to net income as a value indicator? To pursue this question, let's look at the relation between alternative income and cash flow measures with stock prices for a large sample of firms for a recent 10-year period. This evidence is shown in Exhibit 2.5. Here we see measures of R-squared that reflect the ability of performance measures in explaining stock prices. Note that both income measures (NI and NIBX) are better than either operating cash flow (OCF) or free cash flow (FCF) in explaining stock prices. Also, net cash flow (change in cash balance) is entirely uninformative.

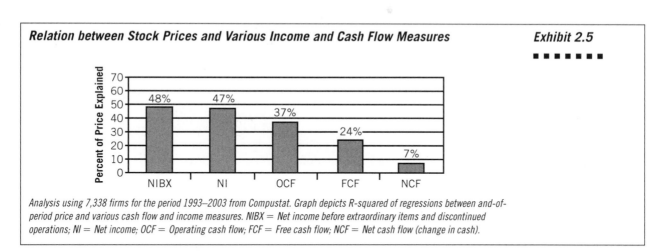

Relation between Stock Prices and Various Income and Cash Flow Measures　　　　**Exhibit 2.5**

Analysis using 7,338 firms for the period 1993–2003 from Compustat. Graph depicts R-squared of regressions between and-of-period price and various cash flow and income measures. NIBX = Net income before extraordinary items and discontinued operations; NI = Net income; OCF = Operating cash flow; FCF = Free cash flow; NCF = Net cash flow (change in cash).

A main difference between accrual accounting and cash flow accounting is timeliness in recognizing business activities. Accrual income recognizes the effects of most business activities in a more timely manner. For evidence of this, let's look at the relation between stock returns, net income, and operating cash flow over different time horizons. If we assume stock prices impound the effects of business activities in a timely manner, then the relation between stock returns and alternative performance measures reflects on the timeliness of these measures. Exhibit 2.6 shows evidence of the ability of net income and operating cash flow to explain stock returns over quarterly, annual, and four-year horizons. Net income dominates operating cash flows over all horizons.

Exhibit 2.6

■ ■ ■ ■ ■ ■ ■

Relation between Stock Returns and Both Net Income (NI) and Operating Cash Flow (OCF) for Different Time Horizons

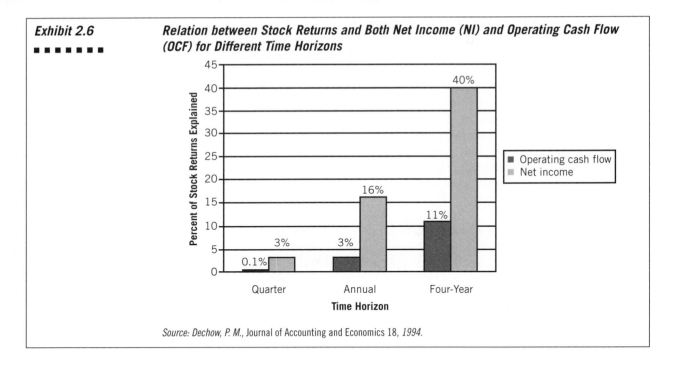

Source: Dechow, P. M., Journal of Accounting and Economics 18, *1994.*

While net income's timeliness is less impressive for shorter horizons, its superiority over operating cash flow is maintained. Operating cash flow's ability to explain stock returns over short horizons (quarterly and annual) is especially poor. This evidence supports the notion that accrual income reflects the effects of business activities in a more timely manner than do cash flows.

Analysis Implications of Accrual Accounting

Accrual accounting is ingrained in modern business. Wall Street focuses on accrual income, not cash flows. We know that accrual accounting is superior to cash accounting in measuring performance and financial condition, and in forecasting future cash flows. Still, accrual accounting has limitations. Consequently, should accrual accounting numbers always be used in business analysis and valuation, or should they sometimes be abandoned in favor of hard cash flows? If accrual accounting is used, how does one deal with its limitations? What is the role of cash flows in a world of accrual accounting? This section provides some answers to these questions. We begin with the myths and truths of both accrual and cash accounting. Then, we discuss the role of accruals and cash flows in financial statement analysis.

Myths and Truths about Accruals and Cash Flows

Several assertions exist regarding accruals and cash flows–both positive and negative. It is important for an analyst to know which assertions are true and which are not.

Accruals and Cash Flows—Myths.   There are several myths and misconceptions about accrual accounting, income, and cash flow:

- Myth: *Because company value depends on future cash flows, only current cash flows are relevant for valuation.* Even if we accept that company value depends only on future cash flows, there is no reason to necessarily link current cash flows with future cash flows. We already showed that current income is a better predictor of future cash flows than is current cash flow. We also showed that income better explains stock prices than does cash flow.

- Myth: *All cash flows are value relevant.* Many types of cash flows do not affect company value–for example, cash collected from customers on account. Also, certain types of cash flows are negatively related to company value–for example, capital expenditures reduce free cash flow but usually increase company value. Exhibit 2.7 provides additional examples.

Effects of Transactions on Income, Free Cash Flow, and Company Value   **Exhibit 2.7**

Transaction	Income Effect	Free Cash Flow Effect	Company Value Effect (Present Value of Future Dividends)
Sales on credit	Increase	Nil	Increase
Cash collections on credit sales	Nil	Increase	Nil
Inventory markdowns	Decrease	Nil	Decrease
Change depreciation from straight-line to declining balance	Decrease	Nil	Nil
Cash purchase of plant asset	Nil	Decrease	Nil*

*If the plant asset produces a return on investment in excess of the cost of capital it will increase company value.

- Myth: *All accrual accounting adjustments are value irrelevant.* It is true that "cosmetic" accounting adjustments such as alternative accounting methods for the same underlying business activity do not yield different valuations. However, not all accounting adjustments are cosmetic. A main goal of accrual accounting is to make adjustments for transactions that have future cash flow implications, even when no cash inflows or cash outflows occur contemporaneously–an example is a credit sale as shown in Exhibit 2.7.
- Myth: *Cash flows cannot be manipulated.* Not only is this statement false, it is probably easier to manipulate cash flow than to manipulate income. For example, cash flows can be increased by delaying either capital expenditures or the payment of expenses, or by accelerating cash collections from customers.
- Myth: *All income is manipulated.* Some managers do manage income, and the frequency of this practice may be increasing. However, SEC enforcement actions targeted at fraudulent financial reporting and restatements of previously issued financial statements affect a small percentage of publicly traded companies.
- Myth: *It is impossible to consistently manage income upward in the long run.* Some users assert it is impossible to manage income upward year after year because accounting rules dictate that accruals eventually reverse–that is, accrual accounting and cash accounting coincide in the long run. Still, most companies can aggressively manage income upward for several years at a time. Further, a growth company can manage income upward for an even longer period because current period upward adjustments likely exceed the reversal of smaller adjustments from prior years. Also, some companies take a "big bath" when they experience a bad period to recognize delayed expenses or aggressively record future expenses. This enables a company to more

Analysis Research
■ ■ ■ ■ ■ ■ ■

RELATIVE PERFORMANCE OF CASH FLOWS AND ACCRUALS

The relative ability of cash flows and accruals in providing value-relevant information is the focus of much research. One line of research addresses this issue by examining the relative ability of cash flows and accruals in explaining stock returns, under the assumption that stock price is the best indicator of a company's intrinsic value. Evidence reveals that both operating cash flows and accruals provide incremental value-relevant information. Yet, net income (which is the sum of accruals and operating cash flows) is superior to operating cash flows in explaining stock returns. The superiority of income is especially evident for short horizons; recall that the difference between income and cash flows is mainly timing and, thus, over long horizons—say, five or more years—income and operating cash flows tend to converge. Operating cash flows tend to perform poorly

for companies where the timing and matching problems of cash flows are more pronounced.

The use of stock price as an indicator of intrinsic value is questioned by recent evidence that the market might be attaching more weight than warranted to the accrual component of income, possibly because of a *fixation* on bottom line income. This evidence indicates that operating cash flows are more persistent than accruals and that the market overestimates the ability of accruals to predict future profitability. That is, abnormal returns can be earned from a strategy of buying stocks of companies with the lowest accruals and shorting those with the highest accruals.

Research also shows income is superior to operating cash flow in predicting future income. However, evidence relating to the relative ability of income and operating cash

flow in predicting future cash flow is mixed. While operating cash flow is superior to income in predicting operating cash flow, especially over the short run, both income and operating cash flow are useful in this task. This research also reveals the usefulness of investing and financing cash flows for prediction purposes.

In sum, while the preponderance of research shows the superiority of accruals over cash flows in providing value-relevant information, *both* accruals and cash flows are incrementally useful. This suggests that accruals income and cash flow should be viewed as complements rather than substitutes. Research also shows that the relative importance of accruals and cash flows depends on characteristics such as industry membership, operating cycle, and the point in a company's life cycle.

easily manage income upward in future periods because of fewer reversals from prior accruals.

Accruals and Cash Flows—Truths. Logic and evidence point to several notable truths about accrual accounting, income, and cash flow:

- Truth: *Accrual accounting (income) is more relevant than cash flow.* Both conceptually and practically, accrual income is more relevant than cash flow in measuring financial condition and performance and in valuation. Note this statement does not challenge the obvious relevance of *future* cash flows. Instead, it points out that *current* cash flow is less relevant than current income.
- Truth: *Cash flows are more reliable than accruals.* This statement is true and it suggests cash flows can and do play an important complementary role with accruals. However, extreme statements, such as "cash flows cannot be manipulated," are untrue. When analyzing cash flows, we also must remember they are more volatile than income.
- Truth: *Accrual accounting numbers are subject to accounting distortions.* The existence of alternative accounting methods along with earnings management reduces both comparability and consistency of accrual accounting numbers. Also, arbitrary accounting rules and estimation errors can yield accounting distortions. A financial analysis or valuation that ignores these facts, and accounting adjustments, is likely

to produce erroneous results. For example, a valuation method that simply uses price-to-earnings ratios computed using reported income is less effective.

- Truth: *Company value can be determined by using accrual accounting numbers.* Some individuals wrongly state that value is determined *only* on the basis of discounted cash flows. Chapter 1 showed that we also can determine value as the sum of current book value and discounted future residual income.

Should We Forsake Accruals for Cash Flows?

Some advocate abandoning valuation models based on accrual income in favor of a cash flow model. Often underlying this position is an attitude that accrual accounting is unscientific and irrelevant. Cash, as they say, is king. Yet, this is an attitude of extremism.

We know accrual accounting is imperfect, and that arbitrary rules, estimation errors, and earnings management distort its usefulness. We also know that accrual accounting is better than cash flows in many respects—it is conceptually superior and works practically. Consequently, abandoning accrual accounting because of its limitations and focusing only on cash flows, is throwing the baby out with the bath water. There is an enormous amount of valuable information in accrual accounting numbers.

This book takes a constructive view toward accrual accounting. That is, despite its quirks, it is useful and important for financial analysis. Our approach to analysis is to be aware of the limitations in accrual accounting and to evaluate and adjust reported numbers in financial statements through a process of accounting analysis. By this process an analyst is able to exploit the richness of accrual accounting and, at the same time, reduce its distortions and limitations. Cash flows also are important for analysis. They provide a reliability check on accrual accounting—income that consistently deviates from cash flows is usually of lower quality. Also, as we note in Chapter 1, analysis of the sources and uses of funds (or cash flows) is crucial for effective financial analysis.

·······CONCEPT OF INCOME

The previous section explained accrual accounting and its superiority to cash-basis accounting. Crucial to accrual accounting is the concept of income and its distinction from cash flow. **Income** (also referred to as **earnings** or **profit**) summarizes, in financial terms, the net effects of a business's operations during a given time period. It is the most demanded piece of company information by the financial markets. Determining and explaining a business's income for a period is the main purpose of the income statement. Conceptually, income purports to provide both a measure of the change in stockholders' wealth during a period and an estimate of a business's current profitability, that is, the extent to which the business is able to cover its costs of operations and earn a return for its shareholders. Understanding this dual role of income is important for analysis. In particular the latter role of income, that is, indicator of firm profitability, is of crucial importance to an analyst because it aids in estimating the future earning potential of the business, which arguably is one of the most important tasks in business analysis.

Accounting, or *reported,* income is different from *economic* income. This is because accountants use different criteria to determine income. To illustrate this point, consider a company with $100,000 in cash. This company uses the $100,000 to buy a condominium, which it rents out for $12,000 per year. At the end of the first year the company still owns the condo, which is valued at $125,000. Let's begin our analysis by determining various cash flow measures. Free cash flow for the year is $(88,000), while operating cash flow is $12,000. Does either of these measures indicate how much the shareholders earned during the period? No. For that we need to determine income. First, let us compute *economic income.* Economic income measures the change in shareholders' wealth during a period. Obviously the $12,000 in rental income increased shareholders' wealth. In addition, the condo appreciated by $25,000 during the year, which also increased shareholders' wealth. Therefore, economic income for the year is $37,000 (rental income, $12,000, plus holding gain, $25,000). *Accounting income,* which is based on accrual accounting, depends on the depreciation policy for the condominium. Namely, if the condominium's useful life is 50 years and its salvage value is $75,000, then yearly straight-line depreciation for the year is $500 [computed as ($100,000 − $75,000)/50 years]. This yields an accounting income of $11,500 (rental income of $12,000 less $500 depreciation) for the year. This illustration shows that economic income differs from accounting income, and both differ from the cash flow measures.

We might also notice that the $37,000 economic income is probably not sustainable. That is, we can't count on a 25% annual appreciation in the condominium's value year after year. This implies the economic income of $37,000 is less useful for forecasting future earnings. Accounting income of $11,500–at least in this case–is probably closer to *permanent* or *sustainable* income, which would help us estimate future earnings. However, while the $25,000 holding gain cannot be sustained, note that it is not entirely useless for forecasting future income; if the $25,000 increase in the condo value is permanent (i.e., the condominium value is not expected to immediately revert back to $100,000), then it is reasonable to assume that returns from owning the condo (i.e., rental income) might increase in the future.

Understanding alternative income concepts and relating these concepts to accounting income is helpful in business analysis. A major task in financial statement analysis is evaluating and making necessary adjustments to income to improve its ability to reflect business performance and forecast future earnings. In this section, we discuss alternative concepts of income, in particular, permanent income and economic income. Then, we discuss accounting income, relate it to the alternative income concepts, and describe the analysis implications.

Economic Concepts of Income

Economic Income

Economic income is typically determined as cash flow during the period plus the change in the present value of expected future cash flows, typically represented by the change in the market value of the business's net assets. Under this definition, income includes both realized (cash flow) and unrealized (holding gain or loss) components. This concept of income is similar to how we measure the return on a security or a portfolio of securities–that is, return includes both dividends and capital appreciation. Economic income measures *change* in shareholder value. As such, economic income is useful when the objective of analysis is determining the exact return to the shareholder for the period. In a sense, economic income is the bottom-line indicator of company performance–measuring the financial effects of all events for the period in a comprehensive manner. However, because of its comprehensive nature, economic income includes both recurring and nonrecurring components and is therefore less useful for forecasting future earnings potential.

Permanent Income

Permanent income (also called *sustainable income* or *recurring income*) is the stable average income that a business is expected to earn over its life, given the current state of its business conditions. Permanent income reflects a long-term focus. Because of this, permanent income is conceptually similar to *sustainable earning power,* which is an important concept for both equity valuation and credit analysis. Benjamin Graham, the mentor of investing guru Warren Buffett and the father of fundamental analysis, maintained that the single most important indicator of a company's value is its sustainable earning power. Unlike economic income, which measures *change* in company value, permanent income is directly proportional to company value. In particular, for a going concern, company value can be expressed by dividing permanent income by the cost of capital. Because of this relation, determining a company's permanent income is a major quest for many analysts. However, although permanent income has a long-term connotation, it can change whenever the long-term earnings prospects of a company are altered.

Operating Income

An alternative concept is that of **operating income,** which refers to income that arises from a company's operating activities. Finance text books often refer to this income measure as *net operating profit after tax* (NOPAT). The key feature of operating income is that it excludes all expenses (or income) that arises from the business's *financing activities* (i.e., the treasury function), such interest expense and investment income, which collectively are called **nonoperating income.** Operating income is an important concept in valuation its importance arises from the goal of corporate finance to separate the operating activities of the business from the financing (or treasury) activities. Conceptually, operating income is a distinctly different concept to that of permanent income; operating income may include certain nonrecurring components such as restructuring charges, while recurring components such as interest expense are excluded from operating income.

Accounting Concept of Income

Accounting income (or **reported income**) is based on the concept of accrual accounting. While accounting income does reflect aspects of both economic income and permanent income, it does not purport to measure either income concept. Also, accounting income suffers from measurement problems that reduce its ability to reflect economic reality. Consequently, a major task in financial statement analysis is adjusting accounting income to better reflect alternative economic concepts of income. This section describes the process by which accountants determine income. It then discusses analysis implications, including conceptual approaches to adjusting income for analysis purposes.

Revenue Recognition and Matching

A main purpose of accrual accounting is income measurement. The two major processes in income measurement are revenue recognition and expense matching.

Revenue recognition is the starting point of income measurement. The two necessary conditions for recognition are that revenues must be:

- **Realized or realizable.** For revenue to be recognized, a company should have received cash or a reliable commitment to remit cash, such as a valid receivable.
- **Earned.** The company must have completed all of its obligations to the buyer; that is, the earning process must be complete.

Once revenues are recognized, related costs are *matched* with recognized revenues to yield income. Note that an expense is incurred when the related economic event occurs, not necessarily when the cash outflow occurs.

Accounting versus Economic Income

Conceptually, accrual accounting converts cash flow to a measure of income. Recall that economic income differs from cash flow because it includes not only current cash flows but also changes in the present value of future cash flows. Similarly, recall that accrual accounting attempts to obtain an income measure that considers not only current cash flow but also future cash flow implications of current transactions. For example, accrual accounting recognizes future cash flows of credit sales by reporting revenue when the sale is consummated and before cash is received. In some respects, therefore, there is some similarity between accounting measures of income and economic income. However, accounting income does not purport to measure either economic or permanent income. Rather, it is based on a set of rules that have evolved over a long period of time to cater to several, often conflicting, objectives. It is a product of the financial reporting environment that involves accounting standards, enforcement mechanisms, and managers' incentives. It is governed by accounting rules, many of which are economically appealing and some of which are not. These rules often require estimates, giving rise to differential treatment of similar economic transactions and allowing opportunities for managers to window-dress numbers for personal gain. For all these reasons, accounting income can diverge from economic income concepts.

Some reasons accounting income differs from economic income include:

- **Alternative income concepts.** The concept of economic income is very different from the concept of permanent income. Accounting standard setters are faced with a dilemma involving which concept to emphasize. While this problem is partially resolved by reporting alternative measures of income (which we discuss subsequently in Chapter 6), this dilemma sometimes results in inconsistent measurement of accounting income. Some standards, for example, *SFAS 87* on pensions, adopt the permanent income concept, while other standards, for example, *SFAS 115* on marketable securities, adopt the economic income concept.
- **Historical cost.** The historical cost basis of income measurement introduces divergence between accounting and economic income. The use of historical cost affects income in two ways: (1) the current cost of sales is not reflected in the income statement, such as under the FIFO inventory method, and (2) unrealized gains and losses on are not recognized.
- **Transaction basis.** Accounting income usually reflects effects of transactions. Economic effects unaccompanied by an arm's-length transaction often are not considered. For example, purchase contracts are not recognized in the financial statements until the transactions occur.
- **Conservatism.** Conservatism results in recognizing income-decreasing events immediately, even if there is no transaction to back it up–for example, inventory

write-downs. However, the effect of an income-increasing event is delayed until realized. This creates a conservative (income decreasing) bias in accounting income.

- **Earnings management.** Earnings management causes distortions in accounting income that has little to do with economic reality. However, one form of earnings management–income smoothing–may, under some conditions, improve the ability of accounting income to reflect permanent income.

As noted earlier, accounting standards are moving away from historical cost and transaction basis toward a model of fair value accounting. This move is significant because it brings bottom-line income (called comprehensive income) closer to the concept of economic income.

Permanent, Transitory, and Value Irrelevant Components

We note that accounting income attempts to capture elements of both permanent income and economic income, but with measurement error. Accordingly, it is useful to view accounting income as consisting of three components:

1. **Permanent component.** The permanent (or *recurring*) component of accounting income is expected to persist indefinitely. It has characteristics identical to the economic concept of permanent income. For a going concern, each dollar of the permanent component is equal to $1/r$ dollar of company value, where r is the cost of capital.
2. **Transitory component.** The transitory (or *nonrecurring*) component of accounting income is not expected to recur–it is a one-time event. It has a dollar-for-dollar effect on company value. The concept of economic income includes both permanent and transitory components.
3. **Value irrelevant component.** Value irrelevant components have no economic content–they are accounting distortions. They arise from the imperfections in accounting. Value irrelevant components have zero effect on company value.

Analysis Implications

Adjusting accounting income is an important task in financial analysis. Before making any adjustments, it is necessary to specify the analysis objectives. In particular, it is important to determine whether the objective is determining economic income or permanent income of the company. This determination is crucial because economic income and permanent income differ in both nature and purpose, and accordingly, the adjustments necessary to determine each measure can differ substantially. We briefly discuss some conceptual issues relating to adjusting income in this section. Refer to Chapter 6 for a more detailed discussion of income measurement issues.

Adjustments for Permanent Income

We already noted that determining a company's permanent income (sustainable earning power) is a major quest in analysis. For this purpose, an analyst needs to first determine the permanent (or recurring) component of the current period's accounting income by identifying and appropriately excluding, or smoothing, transitory (nonrecurring) components of accounting income. For example, an analyst may exclude gain on sale of a major business segment when determining the permanent component of earnings. Such adjusted earnings are often referred to as **core earnings** by practicing analysts. Determining the current period's core earnings is useful for interpreting a company's P/E ratio. It is also useful for valuation techniques using earnings' multiples. Further, determining core earnings is also useful when forecasting earnings or cash flows by giving a meaningful "starting point" for the forecasting exercise and in helping derive assumptions used in forecasting.

However, we caution that the current period's core earnings are not always a good estimate of the company's permanent income. To represent permanent income, a company's core earnings must reflect the long-term earning power of the company. Current period's core earnings may not reflect a company's long-term earnings prospects for two reasons. First, although core earnings exclude components of income that are clearly identified as being transitory, there is no guarantee that the components included in determining core earnings are necessarily permanent in nature. This is especially true if the company's performance in the current period is unusual for any reason. For example, the company's sales and earnings in a year may be unusually low because of protracted labor unrest at its principal production facility. Second, an analyst must consider any long-term changes to the company's business conditions that are reflected in the non-recurring earnings' components. For example, a company may have written down fixed assets because of adverse business conditions in one of its divisions. Such an asset write-down is transitory and should not be included in core earnings for the period. However, the asset write-down does reflect the diminished future earnings prospects for a division of the company, and this information must be factored by the analyst when determining permanent income. These caveats notwithstanding, determining core earnings is an important first step in estimating a company's permanent income.

Adjustments for Economic Income

To adjust accounting income for determining economic income, we need to adopt an inclusive approach whereby we include all income components whether recurring or nonrecurring. One way to view economic income is the net change in shareholders' wealth that arises from nonowner sources; hence it includes everything that changes the net wealth of shareholders. When we make adjustments to obtain economic income, we need to realize the adjusted numbers are not faithful representations of economic income because we cannot determine the change in the value of fixed assets, which are recorded at historical cost. It is also more difficult to justify the need for making adjustments to determine economic income than for determining permanent income. However, economic income serves as a comprehensive measure of change in shareholder wealth and is thus useful as the bottom-line indicator of economic performance for the period.

Adjustment for Operating Income

When determining operating earnings, practicing analysts often start off with core earnings from which they exclude nonoperating income components such as interest expense. However, as we note earlier, operating earnings includes all revenue and expense components that pertain to the company's operating business, regardless of whether they are recurring or nonrecurring. Whether operating income should include or exclude nonrecurring items is a debatable point and will depend on the analysis objectives.

For the purpose of consistency, in this book we refer to operating income strictly with reference to where the income was generated, that is, the operating business activities rather than the treasury function, without regard to whether it is recurring or nonrecurring. Therefore, we shall view the operating/nonoperating and the recurring/nonrecurring dimensions for classifying income as independent or mutually exclusive.

.... FAIR VALUE ACCOUNTING

For more than 400 years, financial accounting has been primarily based on the *historical cost* model. Under the historical cost model, asset and liability values are determined on the basis of prices obtained from *actual transactions* that have occurred in the past. For example, the reported value of land on the balance sheet is based on the price at which it was originally purchased, and the reported value of finished goods inventory is typically determined by the cost of production based on the actual prices paid for inputs used. Income is determined primarily by recognizing revenue that was earned and realized during the period and matching costs with recognized revenues. Some deviations from historical costs are permitted primarily on a *conservative* basis. For example, inventories are valued using the lower-of-cost-or-market-value (LORCOM) rule.

An alternative to the historical cost model is *fair value* accounting. Under the fair value accounting model, asset and liability values are determined on the basis of their fair values (typically market prices) on the *measurement date* (i.e., approximately the date of the financial statements). For example, under this model, the reported value of land on the balance sheet would represent its market price on the date of the balance sheet, and the reported value of finished goods inventory would represent its estimated current sales price less any direct costs of selling. Income, under this model, simply represents the net change in the fair values of assets and liabilities during the period.

Accounting is slowly but inexorably moving toward the fair value accounting model. While fair value accounting has been applied on a selective basis during the past 20 years, there has recently been significant progress toward its widespread adoption. *SFAS 157* provides basic guidelines for adopting the fair value accounting model and *SFAS 159* recommends its voluntary adoption for a wide class of assets and liabilities. While the use of fair value accounting is still limited primarily to financial assets and liabilities—such as marketable securities or debt instruments—there are indications that a comprehensive adoption of fair value accounting for all assets and liabilities—including operating assets and liabilities—is possible in the future.

The adoption of fair value accounting constitutes a revolution in financial accounting. For better or worse, the adoption of fair value accounting will fundamentally alter the nature of the financial statements. It is therefore crucial for an analyst to understand how fair value accounting affects the financial statements and to appreciate its implications for financial statement analysis. Accordingly, in this section we will provide a broad conceptual discussion of fair value accounting and its implications for analysis. More detailed discussion of *SFAS 157* and *SFAS 159* along with actual disclosures under these standards will be discussed in Chapter 5.

Understanding Fair Value Accounting
An Example

To understand how fair value accounting works and how it relates to the traditional historical cost accounting model, we go back to the example with the real estate company presented in the previous section with some minor modifications. Specifically, a company starts Year 1 raising $100,000 in cash; $50,000 from issuing equity and $50,000 from issuing 6% bonds (at par). This company uses the $100,000 raised to buy a condominium

Exhibit 2.8

Historical Cost versus Fair Value Example

■ ■ ■ ■ ■ ■ ■

Balance Sheet	Year 1 (Opening)		Year 1 (Closing)		Year 2 (Closing)	
	Historical Cost	Fair Value	Historical Cost	Fair Value	Historical Cost	Fair Value
Assets						
Cash			$ 9,000	$ 9,000	$ 18,500	$ 18,500
Condominium	$100,000	$100,000	99,500	125,000	99,000	110,000
	$100,000	$100,000	$108,500	$134,000	$117,500	$128,500
Liabilities and Shareholder's Equity						
Long-term debt	$ 50,000	$ 50,000	$ 50,000	$ 48,000	$ 50,000	$ 50,500
Shareholders' equity	50,000	50,000	58,500	86,000	67,500	78,000
	$100,000	$100,000	$108,500	$134,000	$117,500	$128,500

Income Statement	Year 1		Year 2	
	Historical Cost	Fair Value	Historical Cost	Fair Value
Rental income	$12,000	$12,000	$12,500	$12,500
Depreciation	(500)		(500)	
Interest expense	(3,000)	(3,000)	(3,000)	(3,000)
Unrealized gain/loss on condo		25,000		(15,000)
Unrealized gain/loss on debt		2,000		(2,500)
Income (loss)	$ 8,500	$36,000	$ 9,000	($ 8,000)

on that day, which it rents out for $12,000 per year. At the end of Year 1, the company still owns the condo, which is valued at $125,000. Also, the market value of the bonds has fallen to $48,000. Now also assume that during Year 2, the company earns rental income of $12,500, the condo is valued at $110,000 at year-end, and the market value of the bonds has increased to $50,500. Assume the condo's useful life is 50 years and its salvage value is $75,000 at the end of that period. Also assume that rental income (interest on bonds) is received (paid) in cash on the last day of the year.

Exhibit 2.8 presents the balance sheets and income statements for this example based on the historical cost and the fair value accounting models. Obviously, balance sheets under both models are identical at the beginning of Year 1. The two models start diverging after that. At the end of Year 1, the historical cost model values the condo at $99,500, which is equal to its purchase price ($100,000) less accumulated depreciation ($500). The fair value model, on the other hand, values the condo at its market value at the end of Year 1 (i.e., its fair value) of $125,000. The cash balance at the end of Year 1 is $9,000, which is equal to the rental income received ($12,000) less interest paid on bonds ($3,000); both models report the identical amount of cash balance. Turning to the liabilities side of the balance sheet, we note that the historical cost model continues to report the bonds at the issue price of $50,000, whereas the fair value accounting model values the bonds at its current market value of $48,000.

We next turn to the income statement. Both rental income ($12,000) and interest expense ($3,000) are recognized similarly under the two alternative models. In addition, the historical cost model recognizes depreciation of $500 [$(100,000 − 75,000) ÷ 50], resulting in income during Year 1 of $8,500. The fair value model does not recognize depreciation. In contrast, this model recognizes an unrealized gain of $25,000 to record the appreciation in the condo's value during the year. In addition, the fair value model also recognizes an unrealized gain of $2,000, which is related to the decrease in the market value of the bonds. Therefore, income under the fair value accounting model for Year 1 is $36,000. Shareholders' equity at the end of Year 1 is equal to opening shareholders' equity plus income.

To understand how fair value accounting evolves over time, we also examine Year 2. Income, in year 2, under the historical cost model is $9,000; the increase of $500 over Year 1 reflects the increase in rental income. The fair value model, however, reports a loss of $8,000, arising because of unrealized losses on account of the $15,000 decline in the condo's market value and increase of $2,500 in the market value of bonds. The balance sheet under the historical cost model reports the condo at its depreciated value ($99,000) and the bonds at their par value ($50,000). The fair value model, in contrast, reports both the condo ($110,000) and the bonds ($50,500) at their current market values.

Contrasting Historical Cost and Fair Value Models

Our example shows how the balance sheet and income statements evolve over time under the historical cost and the fair value models. We see that there are considerable differences in the financial statements prepared under these models. What causes these differences? What is the underlying logic behind these two models of accounting? We list here some of the fundamental differences between the two models with the objective of answering these questions:

- **Transaction versus current valuation.** Under historical cost accounting, asset and liability values are largely determined by a business entity's actual transactions in the past; the valuation need not reflect current economic circumstances. In contrast, under the fair value model, asset or liability amounts are determined by the most current value using market assumptions; the valuation need not be based on an actual transaction. In our example, the condo is valued at the original $100,000–adjusted for wear and tear through depreciation–in the historical cost model because that is the original transacted price of the condo. In contrast, the fair value model updates the condo's value every period to reflect its current value, even though there has been no explicit transaction, i.e., sale or purchase of the condo.
- **Cost versus market based.** Historical cost valuation is primarily determined by the costs incurred by the business, while under the fair value model it is based on market valuation (or market-based assumptions). For example, finished goods inventory under the historical cost model will primarily reflect the cost of producing the goods, while under the fair value model it will reflect its net selling price, that is, the value that the market is willing to pay for the goods.
- **Alternative income approaches.** Under the historical cost model, income is determined by matching costs to recognized revenues, which have to be realized and earned. Under the fair value model, income is determined merely by the net change in fair value of assets and liabilities. The manner in which income is determined under the two models for Year 1 of our example is illustrated here:

Historical Cost Model		Fair Value Model	
Revenue (rental income)	$12,000	Change in net asset value:	
Less matched costs:		Increase in cash	$ 9,000
Depreciation	500	Increase in condo value	25,000
Interest expense	3,000	Decrease in debt value	2,000
Income	$ 8,500	Income	$36,000

The alternative approaches for income determination under the two models are extremely important for analysis. Income under historical cost accounting is a distinct construct that attempts to measure the current period's profitability, that is, ability of a business to generate revenues in excess of costs. In our example, we recognized revenue of $12,000 to which we matched the following costs: depreciation $500 (which is Year 1's share of the long-term cost of using the condo) and interest $3,000 (which is Year 1's share of the cost of financing the condo). Under this approach, asset (or liability) balances are often determined by how income is measured; for example, the depreciated value of the condo on the balance sheet is determined by the depreciation expense charged against income. In contrast, income under the fair value model is not separate from the valuation of the business's assets and liabilities; it is merely a measure of the net change in the value of assets and liabilities. For example as shown above, Year 1's fair value income of $36,000 is determined by a $9,000 increase in cash, a $25,000 increase in the condo's fair value and a $2,000 decrease in the fair value of debt. Therefore, one could argue that the income statement is superfluous under the fair value accounting model.

It is important to conceptually understand what income under the two models represents. Under the fair value model, accounting income approximates *economic income* (see earlier section for definition of economic income). Income under the historical cost model seeks to measure the *current profitability* of the business. While it may appear to approximate *permanent income* in our example, that is not necessarily the case.

Considerations in Measuring Fair Value
Defining Fair Value

Before providing the formal definition of *fair value,* let us try to understand the intuitive meaning of this term. Broadly, fair value means *market value*. The terminology of "fair value" was coined (instead of merely using "market value") because even if a primary market does not exist for an asset or liability from which market prices could be readily determined, one could still estimate its "fair value" by reference to secondary markets or through the use of valuation techniques. The idea behind fair value, however, is to get as close to market value as possible. Therefore, conceptually, fair value is no different from market value because it reflects current market participant (e.g., investor) assumptions about the present value of expected future cash inflows or outflows arising from an asset or a liability.

Formally, SFAS 157 defines fair value as *exchange price,* that is, the price that would be received from selling an asset (or paid to transfer a liability) in an orderly transaction between market participants on the measurement date. There are five aspects of this definition that needs to be noted:

- **On the measurement date.** The asset or liability's fair value is determined as of the *measurement date*–that is, the date of the balance sheet–rather than the date when the asset was originally purchased (or the liability originally assumed).
- **Hypothetical transaction.** The transaction that forms the basis of valuation is hypothetical. No actual sale of the asset (or transfer of liability) needs to occur. In other words, fair values are determined "as if" the asset were sold on the measurement date.
- **Orderly transaction.** The notion of an "orderly" transaction eliminates exchanges occurring under unusual circumstances, such as under duress. This

ensures that the fair value represents the exchange price under normal circumstances, such as the market price in an active (i.e., frequently traded) market.

- **Market-based measurement.** Fair values are *market-based* measurements, not *entity-specific* measurements. What does this mean? This means that fair value of an asset should reflect the price that market participants would pay for the asset (or demand for the liability), rather than the value generated through unique use of the asset in a specific business. To illustrate, consider a highly lucrative cab company that owns a single automobile. Because of excellent business prospects, the present value of future net receipts from the use of this automobile over its estimated life is expected to be $65,000. However, the market value of the automobile (based on its blue-book price) is just $15,000. The fair value of the automobile is $15,000 (i.e., its market-based exchange price) and not $65,000 (i.e., its entity-specific unique value).
- **Exit prices.** The fair value of an asset is the hypothetical price at which a business can *sell* the asset (exit price). It is not the price that needs to be paid to *buy* the asset (entry price). Similarly, for a liability, fair value is the price at which a business can transfer the liability to a third party, not the price it will get to assume the liability.

Hierarchy of Inputs

Note that fair value can be estimated for assets (or liabilities) even when active primary markets do not exist from which prices can be directly ascertained. Obviously fair value estimates that are not derived from direct market prices are less reliable. Realizing this, standard setters have established a hierarchy of fair value inputs (i.e., assumptions that form the basis for deriving fair value estimates). At the outset, two types of inputs are recognized: (1) *observable inputs,* where market prices are obtainable from sources independent of the reporting company—for example, from quoted market prices of traded securities, and (2) *unobservable inputs,* where fair values are determined through assumptions provided by the reporting company because the asset or liability is not traded. Observable inputs are further classified based on whether the prices are from primary or secondary markets. This gives rise to the following three-step hierarchy of inputs (see Exhibit 2.9):

- **Level 1 inputs.** These inputs are quoted prices in active markets for the exact asset or liability that is being valued, preferably available on the measurement date. These are the most reliable inputs and should be used in determining fair value whenever they are available.
- **Level 2 inputs.** These inputs are either (1) quoted prices from active markets for similar, but not identical, assets or liabilities or (2) quoted prices for identical assets or liabilities from markets that are not active (i.e., not frequently traded). Therefore, while these inputs are indeed market prices, the prices may be for assets (or liabilities) that are not identical to those being valued or the quotes may not be for current prices because of infrequent trading.
- **Level 3 inputs.** These are unobservable inputs and are used when the asset or liability is not traded or when traded substitutes cannot be identified. Level 3 inputs reflect manager's own assumptions regarding valuation, including internal data from within the company.

The hierarchy of inputs is extremely important. As the pyramid in Exhibit 2.9 suggests, Level 1 inputs must be most commonly used and Level 3 inputs must be used sparingly. Also, *SFAS 157* prescribes footnote disclosures where information about the level of inputs used for determining fair values must be reported. An analyst can use this information to evaluate the reliability of the fair value amounts recognized. Finally, it must be

Exhibit 2.9   *Hierarchy of Fair Value Inputs*

■ ■ ■ ■ ■ ■ ■

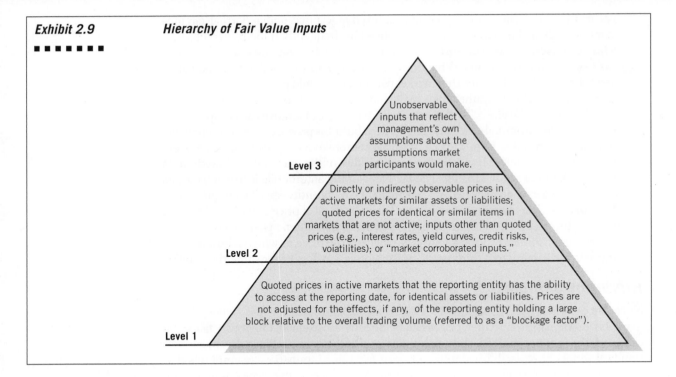

Level 3
Unobservable inputs that reflect management's own assumptions about the assumptions market participants would make.

Level 2
Directly or indirectly observable prices in active markets for similar assets or liabilities; quoted prices for identical or similar items in markets that are not active; inputs other than quoted prices (e.g., interest rates, yield curves, credit risks, voiatilities); or "market corroborated inputs."

Level 1
Quoted prices in active markets that the reporting entity has the ability to access at the reporting date, for identical assets or liabilities. Prices are not adjusted for the effects, if any, of the reporting entity holding a large block relative to the overall trading volume (referred to as a "blockage factor").

appreciated that while Level 1 and Level 2 inputs will be available for valuing financial assets and liabilities, most operating assets and liabilities may need to use Level 3 inputs.

Valuation Techniques

The appropriate valuation technique depends on the availability of input data. Once a technique is chosen, it must be used consistently, unless there is some change in circumstances that allows a more accurate determination of fair value. Three basic approaches to valuation are specified:

- **Market approach.** As the name implies, this approach directly or indirectly uses prices from actual market transactions. Sometimes, market prices may need to be transformed in some manner in determining fair value. This is approach is applicable to most of the Level 1 or Level 2 inputs.
- **Income approach.** Under this approach fair values are measured by discounting future cash flow (or earnings) expectations to the current period. Current market expectations need to be used to the extent possible in determining these discounted values. Examples of such an approach include valuing intangible assets based on expected future cash flow potential or using option pricing techniques (such as the Black-Scholes model) for valuing employee stock options.
- **Cost approach.** Cost approaches are used for determining the current replacement cost of an asset, that is, determining the cost of replacing an asset's remaining service capacity. Under this approach, fair value is determined as the current cost to a market participant (i.e., buyer) to acquire or construct a substitute asset that generates comparable utility after adjusting for technological improvements, natural wear and tear and economic obsolescence.

When determining discounted values (i.e., present values), it may be necessary to make adjustments for risk. In the case of a liability, the risk adjustment will need to consider the reporting entity's own credit risk. This will give rise to a peculiar situation, where deterioration in the creditworthiness of a company can result in a decrease in its liabilities.

Analysis Implications

The adoption of fair value accounting has significant implications for financial statement analysis. In this section, we discuss the advantages and disadvantages of fair value accounting and issues that an analyst must consider when analyzing financial statements prepared under fair value accounting. Finally, we discuss the current status of fair value accounting and future initiatives of the FASB in this direction.

Advantages and Disadvantages of Fair Value Accounting

The move toward fair value accounting has engendered intense debate. Both supporters and detractors of fair value accounting have been equally vocal in airing their views.

The major advantages of fair value accounting are as follows:

- **Reflects current information.** There is no denying that fair value accounting reflects current information regarding the value of assets and liabilities on the balance sheet. In contrast, historical cost information can be outdated, giving rise to what may be termed "hidden" assets or liabilities. For example, the assets of many manufacturing companies are seriously understated because the current market value of their real estate holdings is not reflected on the balance sheet. This is obviously the most important advantage of fair value accounting over the historical cost model. By reflecting more current information, fair value accounting is argued to be more relevant for decision making.
- **Consistent measurement criteria.** Another advantage that the standard setters stress is that fair value accounting provides the only conceptually consistent measurement criteria for assets and liabilities. At present, financial accounting follows a mish-mash of approaches that is termed the *mixed attribute model.* For example, fixed assets such as land and building are measured using historical cost, but financial assets such as marketable securities are recorded at current market prices. Even for the same item, inconsistent criteria are used because of conservatism; for example, inventory is usually valued at cost unless market value drops below cost, in which case it gets measured at market value. Under fair value accounting, it is hoped that all assets and liabilities will be measured using a consistent and conceptually appealing criterion.
- **Comparability.** Because of consistency in the manner in which assets and liabilities are measured, it is argued that fair value accounting will improve *comparability,* that is, the ability to compare financial statements of different firms.
- **No conservative bias.** Fair value accounting is expected to eliminate the conservative bias that currently exists in accounting. Eliminating conservatism is expected to improve reliability because of *neutrality,* that is, reporting information without any bias.
- **More useful for equity analysis.** One complaint of traditional accounting is that it is largely oriented to provide information useful for credit analysis. For example, the use of conservative historical costs is more designed to provide an estimate of a business's downside risk than evaluate its upside potential. Many argue that adopting the fair value model will make accounting more useful for equity analysis.

The major disadvantages of fair value accounting include the following:

- **Lower objectivity.** The major criticism against fair value accounting is that it is less reliable because it often lacks objectivity. This issue is crucially linked to the type of inputs that are used. While nobody can question the objectivity of Level 1 inputs, the same cannot be said about Level 3 inputs. Because Level 3 inputs are unobservable and based on assumptions made by managers, many fear that the extensive use of Level 3 inputs–especially for operating assets and liabilities–will lower the reliability of financial statement information.

- **Susceptibility to manipulation.** Closely linked to lower objectivity is the concern that fair value accounting would considerably increase the ability of managers to manipulate financial statements. Again, this issue is closely linked to the use of Level 3 inputs–it is more difficult to manipulate fair values when Level 1 or Level 2 inputs are used.

- **Use of Level 3 inputs.** Because Level 3 inputs are less objective, a crucial issue that will determine the reliability of fair value accounting is the extent to which Level 3 inputs will need to be used. The recent credit crisis in the United States has shown that even for financial assets or liabilities, many companies have had to resort to extensively using Level 3 inputs because of poor liquidity in the credit markets. The need to use Level 3 inputs is obviously expected to be greater for operating assets and liabilities. If Level 3 inputs are widely used, then many believe that the fair value accounting model will reduce the reliability of the financial statements.

- **Lack of conservatism.** There are many academics and practitioners who prefer conservative accounting. The two main advantages of conservatism are that (1) it naturally offsets the optimistic bias on the part of management to report higher income or higher net assets, and (2) it is important for credit analysis and debt contracting because creditors prefer financial statements that highlight downside risk. These supporters of conservative accounting are alarmed that adopting the fair value model–which purports to be unbiased–will cause financial statements to be prepared aggressively, therefore reducing its usefulness to creditors, who are one of the most important set of users of financial information.

- **Excessive income volatility.** One of the most serious concerns from adopting the fair value model is that of excessive income volatility. As we noted earlier, under the fair value accounting model income is simply the net change in value of assets and liabilities. Because assets (or liabilities) are typically large in relation to income and because fair values can change significantly across time, changes in fair values of assets can cause reported income to become excessively volatile. Much of this volatility is attributable to swings in the fair value of assets and liabilities rather than changes in the underlying profitability of the business's operations, so it is feared that income will become less useful for analysis. Standard setters are aware of this problem and have embarked on a project for changing financial statement presentation, which will consider also reporting intermediate income measures that reflect the firms operations.

Implications for Analysis

Because of the profound effect that fair value accounting will have on the financial statements, it will influence the manner in which financial statement analysis is conducted. We note some of the important issues that will need consideration when analyzing financial statements prepared under the fair value model:

- **Focus on the balance sheet.** Currently, the income statement is arguably the most important statement for analysis. In particular, equity analysts tend to pay scant attention to the balance sheet. Part of the reason for ignoring the balance sheet is that it is not particularly informative under the historical cost model. This will change with the advent of fair value accounting. The balance sheet will become an important—if not the most important—statement for analysis. In contrast, the income statement will lose some of its importance because bottom-line income will merely measure net changes in assets and liabilities. Accordingly, the focus of financial statement analysis will need to shift toward the balance sheet.

- **Restating income.** Analyzing and restating income will become an even more crucial task for the analyst. The *bottom-line income* under the fair value accounting model merely measures the net change in the fair values of assets and liabilities. This income measure is conceptually closer to economic income and is therefore less useful for analyzing current period's profitability or forecasting future earnings. An analyst needs to carefully analyze income to separate the effect of current operations from unrealized gains and losses arising from changes in fair values of assets and liabilities.

- **Analyzing use of inputs.** As noted earlier, Level 3 inputs are less reliable and more susceptible to manipulation. Therefore, a major task in financial statement analysis—when using fair value accounting information—is analyzing the levels of inputs that have been used in determining asset and liability values. In particular, it is important to identify and quantify the extent to which Level 3 inputs have been used in determining fair values. The widespread use of Level 3 inputs is an important indicator of the quality—or lack thereof—of the financial statements. Fortunately, companies are required to provide detailed footnote disclosure regarding the assumptions underlying their fair value estimates, including the type of inputs used. This information will be crucial for evaluating the quality of the financial statement information.

- **Analyzing financial liabilities.** Fair values of debt securities decline with a decrease in the creditworthiness of the borrower. This creates a counterintuitive situation with respect to the valuation of a business's financial liabilities (e.g., debt obligations). A decrease in the business's creditworthiness will result in a decrease in the fair value of the debt obligation. The decrease in fair value of the debt obligation will result in recognizing an unrealized gain, which will artificially inflate income during the period. The rationale for this accounting treatment is that when the entire balance sheet is prepared on a fair value basis, a reduction in fair value of debt is unlikely to occur without a corresponding (and probably greater) decrease in the fair value of assets. Therefore, when taken together there is unlikely to be an artificial increase in equity.

  While the explanation is logical, there is still an issue with how this accounting treatment will affect the debt equity ratio. When determining the debt equity ratio, we recommend that the *face value* of the outstanding debt should be used, rather than its fair value. This will provide a better indication of the ability of a business to meet its *fixed commitments*.

Current Status of Fair Value Adoption

In this section, we discussed conceptual issues relating to fair value accounting. Our discussions were couched under the assumption that fair value accounting was adopted for all assets and liabilities on the financial statements. While such a scenario could become reality in the future, it is important to note that fair value accounting is currently not applicable to all assets and liabilities.

At present, fair value accounting is applicable primarily to assets and liabilities that can be broadly termed as financial in nature. These include marketable securities, investments, financial instruments, and debt obligations. *SFAS 157* does not specify any new assets or liabilities that must use the fair value model. However, more recently *SFAS 159,* allows companies to *voluntarily* adopt fair value accounting for individual financial assets and obligations. We discuss these issues in more detail in Chapter 5.

In addition to financial assets and liabilities, recently assets and liabilities relating to pensions and other postretirement benefits are required to be valued on a fair value basis on the balance sheet *(SFAS 158)*. However, unrealized gains and losses arising from changes in these assets and liabilities are not recognized in net income. We discuss *SFAS 158* in detail in Chapter 3.

The FASB (and the IASB) are currently involved in examining how a more comprehensive adoption of the fair value accounting model can be undertaken, which includes using the fair value model for operating assets and liabilities. Concurrently, the FASB is considering a project that radically changes the presentation of the financial statements. These changes will have important implications for financial statement analysis.

........INTRODUCTION TO ACCOUNTING ANALYSIS

Accounting analysis is the process of evaluating the extent to which a company's accounting numbers reflect economic reality. Accounting analysis involves a number of different tasks, such as evaluating a company's accounting risk and earnings quality, estimating earning power, and making necessary adjustments to financial statements to both better reflect economic reality and assist in financial analysis.

Accounting analysis is an important precondition for effective financial analysis. This is because the quality of financial analysis, and the inferences drawn, depends on the quality of the underlying accounting information, the raw material for analysis. While accrual accounting provides insights about a company's financial performance and condition that is unavailable from cash accounting, its imperfections can distort the economic content of financial reports. Accounting analysis is the process an analyst uses to identify and assess accounting distortions in a company's financial statements. It also includes the necessary adjustments to financial statements that reduce distortions and make the statements amenable to financial analysis.

In this section, we explain the need for accounting analysis, including identifying the sources of accounting distortions. Then we discuss earnings management, its motivations and strategies, and its implications for analysis. We conclude by examining accounting analysis methods and processes.

Need for Accounting Analysis

The need for accounting analysis arises for two reasons. First, accrual accounting improves upon cash accounting by reflecting business activities in a more timely manner. But accrual accounting yields some accounting distortions that need to be identified and adjusted so accounting information better reflects business activities. Second, financial statements are prepared for a diverse set of users and information needs. This means accounting information usually requires adjustments to meet the analysis objectives of a particular user. We examine each of these factors and their implications to financial statement analysis in this section.

Accounting Distortions

Accounting distortions are deviations of reported information in financial statements from the underlying business reality. These distortions arise from the nature of accrual accounting–this includes its standards, errors in estimation, the trade-off between relevance and reliability, and the latitude in application. We separately discuss each of these sources of distortion.

Accounting Standards.   Accounting standards are sometimes responsible for distortions. At least three sources of this distortion are identifiable. First, accounting standards are the output of a political process. Different user groups lobby to protect their interests. In this process, standards sometimes fail to require the most relevant information. One example is accounting for employee stock options (ESOs).

A second source of distortion from accounting standards arises from certain accounting principles. For example, the historical cost principle can reduce the relevance of the balance sheet by not reflecting current market values of assets and liabilities. Also, the transaction basis of accounting results in inconsistent goodwill accounting wherein purchased goodwill is recorded as an asset but internally developed goodwill is not. Additionally, double entry implies that the balance sheet articulates with the income statement–meaning that many transactions affect both statements. However, an accounting rule that improves one statement often does so to the detriment of the other. For example, FIFO inventory rules ensure the inventory account in the balance sheet reflects current costs of unsold inventory. Yet, LIFO inventory rules better reflect current costs of sales in the income statement.

A third source of distortion is conservatism. For example, accountants often write down or write off the value of impaired assets, but very rarely will they write up asset values. Conservatism leads to a pessimistic bias in financial statements that is sometimes desirable for credit analysis but problematic for equity analysis.

Estimation Errors.   Accrual accounting requires forecasts and other estimates about future cash flow consequences. Use of these estimates improves the ability of accounting numbers to reflect business transactions in a timely manner. Still, these estimates yield errors that can distort the relevance of accrual accounting numbers. To illustrate, consider credit sales. Whenever goods or services are sold on credit, there is a possibility the customer will default on payment. There are two approaches to confront this uncertainty. One approach is to adopt cash accounting that records revenue only when cash is eventually collected from the customer. The other approach, followed by accrual accounting, is to record credit sales as revenue when they are earned and then make an allowance for bad debts based on collection history, customers' credit ratings, and other facts. While accrual accounting is more relevant, it is subject to distortions from errors in estimation of bad debts.

Reliability versus Relevance.   Accounting standards trade off reliability and relevance. An emphasis on reliability often precludes recognizing the effects of certain business events and transactions in financial statements until their cash flow consequences can be reasonably estimated. One example is loss contingencies. Before a loss contingency is recorded as a loss, it must be reasonably estimable. Because of this criterion, many loss contingencies are not reported in financial statements even several years after their existence is established beyond reasonable doubt. Another example of distortion due to the reliability emphasis is accounting for research and development costs. While R&D is an investment, current accounting standards require writing it off as an expense because pay-offs from R&D are less certain than payoffs from investments in, say, plant and equipment.

Earnings Management.   Earnings management is probably the most troubling outcome of accrual accounting. Use of judgment and estimation in accrual accounting allows managers to draw on their inside information and experience to enhance the usefulness of accounting numbers. However, some managers exercise this discretion to manage accounting numbers, particularly income, for personal gain, thereby reducing their quality. Earnings management occurs for several reasons, such as to increase compensation, avoid debt covenants, meet analyst forecasts, and impact stock prices. Earnings management can take two forms: (1) changing accounting methods, which is a visible form of earnings management, and (2) changing accounting estimates and policies that determine accounting numbers, which is a hidden form of earnings management. Earnings management is a reality that most users reluctantly accept as part of accrual accounting. While it is important we recognize that earnings management is not as widespread as the financial press leads us to believe, there is no doubt it hurts the credibility of accounting information. The next section includes an in-depth discussion of earnings management.

Earnings Management

Earnings management can be defined as the "purposeful intervention by management in the earnings determination process, usually to satisfy selfish objectives" (Schipper, 1989). It often involves window-dressing financial statements, especially the bottom line earnings number. Earnings management can be *cosmetic,* where managers manipulate accruals without any cash flow consequences. It also can be *real,* where managers take actions with cash flow consequences for purposes of managing earnings.

Cosmetic earnings management is a potential outcome of the latitude in applying accrual accounting. Accounting standards and monitoring mechanisms reduce this latitude. Yet, it is impossible to eliminate this latitude given the complexity and variation in business activities. Moreover, accrual accounting requires estimates and judgments. This yields some managerial discretion in determining accounting numbers. While this discretion provides an opportunity for managers to reveal a more informative picture of a company's business activities, it also allows them to window-dress financial statements and manage earnings.

Managers also take actions with cash flow consequences, often adverse, for purposes of managing earnings. For example, managers sometimes use the FIFO method of inventory valuation to report higher income even when use of the LIFO method could yield tax savings. Earnings management incentives also influence investing and financing decisions of managers. Such real earnings management is more troubling than cosmetic earnings management because it reflects business decisions that often reduce shareholder wealth.

This section focuses on cosmetic earnings management because accounting analysis can overcome many of the distortions it causes. Distortions from real earnings management usually cannot be overcome by accounting analysis alone.

Earnings Management Strategies

There are three typical strategies to earnings management. (1) Managers increase current period income. (2) Managers take a big bath by markedly reducing current period income. (3) Managers reduce earnings volatility by income smoothing. Managers sometimes apply these strategies in combination or singly at different points in time to achieve long-term earnings management objectives.

Increasing Income. One earnings management strategy is to increase a period's reported income to portray a company more favorably. It is possible to increase income in this manner over several periods. In a growth scenario, the accrual reversals are smaller than current accruals that increase income. This leads to a case where a company can report higher income from aggressive earnings management over long periods of time. Also, companies can manage earnings upward for several years and then reverse accruals all at once with a one-time charge. This one-time charge is often reported "below the line" (i.e., below the income from continuing operations line in the income statement) and, therefore, might be perceived as less relevant.

Big Bath. A "big bath strategy" involves taking as many write-offs as possible in one period. The period chosen is usually one with markedly poor performance (often in a recession when most other companies also report poor earnings) or one with unusual events such as a management change, a merger, or a restructuring. The big bath strategy also is often used in conjunction with an income-increasing strategy for other years. Because of the unusual and nonrecurring nature of a big bath, users tend to discount its financial effect. This affords an opportunity to write off all past sins and also clears the deck for future earnings increases.

Income Smoothing. Income smoothing is a common form of earnings management. Under this strategy, managers decrease or increase reported income so as to reduce its volatility. Income smoothing involves not reporting a portion of earnings in good years through creating reserves or earnings "banks," and then reporting these earnings in bad years. Many companies use this form of earnings management.

Motivations for Earnings Management

There are several reasons for managing earnings, including increasing manager compensation tied to reported earnings, increasing stock price, and lobbying for government subsidies. We identify the major incentives for earnings management in this section.

Contracting Incentives. Many contracts use accounting numbers. For example, managerial compensation contracts often include bonuses based on earnings. Typical bonus contracts have a lower and an upper bound, meaning that managers are not given a bonus if earnings fall below the lower bound and cannot earn any additional bonus when earnings exceed the upper bound. This means managers have incentives to increase or decrease earnings based on the *unmanaged* earnings level in relation to the upper and lower bounds. When unmanaged earnings are within the upper and lower bounds, managers have an incentive to increase earnings. When earnings are above the maximum bound or below the minimum bound, managers have an incentive to decrease earnings and create reserves for future bonuses. Another example of a contractual incentive is debt covenants that often are based on ratios using accounting numbers such as earnings. Since violations of debt covenants are costly for managers, they will manage earnings (usually upward) to avoid them.

Stock Price Effects. Another incentive for earnings management is the potential impact on stock price. For example, managers may increase earnings to temporarily boost company stock price for events such as a forthcoming merger or security offering, or plans to sell stock or exercise options. Managers also smooth income to lower market perceptions of risk and to decrease the cost of capital. Still another

BATH BUSTER
SEC is increasingly concerned about big-bath write-offs such as Motorola's $1.98 billion restructuring charge.

NUMBER CRUNCH
Bausch & Lomb execs say that maintaining double-digit sales and earnings growth in the 90s was all-important, creating pressures that led to unethical behavior in reporting earnings.

related incentive for earnings management is to beat market expectations. This strategy often takes the following form: managers lower market expectations through pessimistic voluntary disclosures (preannouncements) and then manage earnings upward to beat market expectations. The growing importance of momentum investors and their ability to brutally punish stocks that don't meet expectations has created increasing pressure on managers to use all available means to beat market expectations.

Other Incentives.   There are several other reasons for managing earnings. Earnings sometimes are managed downward to reduce political costs and scrutiny from government agencies such as antitrust regulators and the IRS. In addition, companies may manage earnings downward to gain favors from the government, including subsidies and protection from foreign competition. Companies also decrease earnings to combat labor union demands. Another common incentive for earnings management is a change in management. This usually results in a big bath for several reasons. First, it can be blamed on incumbent managers. Second, it signals that the new managers will make tough decisions to improve the company. Third, and probably most important, it clears the deck for future earnings increases. One of the largest big baths occurred when Louis Gerstner became CEO at IBM. Gerstner wrote off nearly $4 billion in the year he took charge. While a large part of this charge comprised expenses related to the turnaround, it also included many items that were future business expenses. Analysts estimate that the earnings increases reported by IBM in subsequent years were in large part attributed to this big bath.

Mechanics of Earnings Management

This section explains the mechanics of earnings management. Areas that offer maximum opportunities for earnings management include revenue recognition, inventory valuation, estimates of provisions such as bad debts expense and deferred taxes, and one-time charges such as restructuring and asset impairments. This section does not provide examples of every conceivable method of managing earnings. Many additional details and examples of earnings management are discussed in Chapters 3–6. In this section, we describe two major methods of earnings management—income shifting and classificatory earnings management.

▪ ▪ ▪ ▪ ▪ ▪ ▪
NIFTY SHIFTY
WorldCom execs boosted earnings by shifting (capitalizing) costs that should have been expensed to future periods.

Income Shifting.   Income shifting is the process of managing earnings by moving income from one period to another. Income shifting is achieved by accelerating or delaying the recognition of revenues or expenses. This form of earnings management usually results in a reversal of the effect in one or more future periods, often in the next period. For this reason, income shifting is most useful for income smoothing. Examples of income shifting include the following:

- Accelerating revenue recognition by persuading dealers or wholesalers to purchase excess products near the end of the fiscal year. This practice, called *channel loading*, is common in industries such as automobile manufacturing and cigarettes.
- Delaying expense recognition by capitalizing expenses and amortizing them over future periods. Examples include interest capitalization and capitalization of software development costs.

- Shifting expenses to later periods by adopting certain accounting methods. For example, adopting the FIFO method for inventory valuation (versus LIFO) and the straight-line depreciation (versus accelerated) can delay expense recognition.
- Taking large one-time charges such as asset impairments and restructuring charges on an intermittent basis. This allows companies to accelerate expense recognition and, thus, make subsequent earnings look better.

Classificatory Earnings Management.   Earnings are also managed by selectively classifying expenses (and revenues) in certain parts of the income statement. The most common form of this classificatory earnings management is to move expenses below the line, meaning report them along with unusual and nonrecurring items that usually are given less importance by analysts. Managers attempt to classify expenses in the nonrecurring parts of the income statement as these examples illustrate:

- When a company discontinues a business segment, the income from that segment must be separately reported as income (loss) from discontinued operations. This item is properly ignored in analysis because it pertains to a business unit that no longer impacts the company. But some companies load a larger portion of common costs (such as corporate overhead) to the discontinued segment, thereby increasing income for the rest of the company.
- Use of special charges such as asset impairments and restructuring charges has skyrocketed (almost 40% of companies report at least one such charge). The motivation for this practice arises from the habit of many analysts to ignore special charges because of their unusual and nonrecurring nature. By taking special charges periodically and including operating expenses in these charges, companies cause analysts to ignore a portion of operating expenses.

Analysis Implications of Earnings Management

Because earnings management distorts financial statements, identifying and making adjustments for it is an important task in financial statement analysis. Still, despite the alarming increase in earnings management, it is less widespread than presumed. The financial press likes to focus on cases of earnings management because it makes interesting reading. This gives many users the incorrect impression that earnings are managed all the time.

Before concluding a company is managing earnings, an analyst needs to check the following:

- **Incentives for earnings management.** Earnings will not be managed unless there are incentives for managing them. We have discussed some of the incentives, and an analysis should consider them.
- **Management reputation and history.** It is important to assess management reputation and integrity. Perusal of past financial statements, SEC enforcements, audit reports, auditor change history, and the financial press provides useful information for this task.
- **Consistent pattern.** The aim of earnings management is to influence a summary bottom line number such as earnings or key ratios such as the debt-to-equity or interest coverage. It is important to verify whether different components of income (or the balance sheet) are consistently managed in a certain direction. For example, if a company appears to be inflating earnings through, say, revenue recognition policies while simultaneously decreasing earnings through an inventory method change, it is less likely the company is managing earnings.

■ ■ ■ ■ ■ ■ ■

KODAK MOMENT
In the '90s, Kodak took six extraordinary write-offs totaling $4.5 billion, which is more than its net earnings for that decade.

- **Earnings management opportunities.** The nature of business activities determines the extent to which earnings can be managed. When the nature of business activities calls for considerable judgment in determining financial statement numbers, greater opportunities exist to manage earnings.

Process of Accounting Analysis

Accounting analysis involves several interrelated processes and tasks. We discuss accounting analysis under two broad areas–evaluating earnings quality and adjusting financial statements. Although separately discussed, the two tasks are interrelated and complementary. We also discuss earnings quality in more detail in Appendix 2B and adjustments to financial statements throughout Chapters 3–6.

Evaluating Earnings Quality

Earnings quality (or more precisely, accounting quality) means different things to different people. Many analysts define earnings quality as the extent of conservatism adopted by the company–a company with higher earnings quality is expected to have a higher price-to-earnings ratio than one with lower earnings quality. An alternative definition of earnings quality is in terms of accounting distortions–a company has high earnings quality if its financial statement information accurately depicts its business activities. Whatever its definition, evaluating earnings quality is an important task of accounting analysis. We briefly describe the steps in evaluating earnings quality in this section.

Steps in Evaluating Earnings Quality.   Evaluating earnings quality involves the following steps:

- **Identify and assess key accounting policies.** An important step in evaluating earnings quality is identifying key accounting policies adopted by the company. Are the policies reasonable or aggressive? Is the set of policies adopted consistent with industry norms? What impact will the accounting policies have on reported numbers in financial statements?
- **Evaluate extent of accounting flexibility.** It is important to evaluate the extent of flexibility available in preparing financial statements. The extent of accounting flexibility is greater in some industries than others. For example, the accounting for industries that have more intangible assets, greater volatility in business operations, a larger portion of its production costs incurred prior to production, and unusual revenue recognition methods requires more judgments and estimates. Generally, earnings quality is lower in such industries than in industries where the accounting is more straightforward.
- **Determine the reporting strategy.** Identify the accounting strategy adopted by the company. Is the company adopting aggressive reporting practices? Does the company have a clean audit report? Has there been a history of accounting problems? Does management have a reputation for integrity, or are they known to cut corners? It is also necessary to examine incentives for earnings management and look for consistent patterns indicative of it. Analysts need to evaluate the quality of a company's disclosures. While disclosures are not substitutes for good quality financial statements, forthcoming and detailed disclosures can mitigate weaknesses in financial statements.
- **Identify and assess red flags.** One useful step in evaluating earnings quality is to beware of red flags. Red flags are items that alert analysts to potentially more

serious problems. Some examples of red flags are:

Poor financial performance–desperate companies are prone to desperate means.

Reported earnings consistently higher than operating cash flows.

Reported pretax earnings consistently higher than taxable income.

Qualified audit report.

Auditor resignation or a nonroutine auditor change.

Unexplained or frequent changes in accounting policies.

Sudden increase in inventories in comparison to sales.

Use of mechanisms to circumvent accounting rules, such as operating leases and receivables securitization.

Frequent one-time charges and big baths.

ANALYSIS VIEWPOINT   ***. . . YOU ARE THE BOARD MEMBER***

You are a new member of the board of directors of a merchandiser. You are preparing for your first meeting with the company's independent auditor. A stockholder writes you a letter raising concerns about earnings quality. What are some questions or issues that you can raise with the auditor to address these concerns and fulfill your fiduciary responsibilities to shareholders?

Adjusting Financial Statements

The final and most involved task in accounting analysis is making appropriate adjustments to financial statements, especially the income statement and balance sheet. As discussed earlier, the need for these adjustments arises both because of distortions in the reported numbers and because of specific analysis objectives. The main emphasis of the next four chapters of this book is the proper identification and adjustment of accounting numbers. Some common adjustments to financial statements include:

- Capitalization of long-term operating leases, with adjustments to both the balance sheet and income statement.
- Recognition of ESO expense for income determination.
- Adjustments for one-time charges such as asset impairments and restructuring costs.
- Recognition of the economic (funded) status of pension and other postretirement benefit plans on the balance sheet.
- Removal of the effects of selected deferred income tax liabilities and assets from the balance sheet.

·····APPENDIX 2A: AUDITING AND FINANCIAL STATEMENT ANALYSIS

Financial statements of a company are the representations of its management, who bear the primary responsibility for the fairness of presentation and the information disclosed. Because of the importance of financial statements, there is demand for their independent verification. Public accounting meets this demand through attestation, or auditing, services. This appendix provides an overview of the relevance of auditing for our analysis. It also discusses the types of audit reports and their analysis implications.

AUDIT PROCESS

Analysts must understand what the audit opinion implies for users of financial statements and must also appreciate the limitations of the opinion and their implications for analysis of financial statements. To obtain this understanding, we must consider the standards governing auditors' behavior and the nature of audit work.

Generally Accepted Auditing Standards

Auditors typically refer to an audit made in accordance with **generally accepted auditing standards.** Audit standards are the measuring sticks assessing the quality of audit procedures. These standards are intended to ensure the auditor's responsibilities are clearly and unequivocally stated and that the degree of responsibility assumed is made clear to users.

Auditing Procedures

The basic objective of a financial statement audit is to identify errors and irregularities, which if undetected would materially affect these statements' fairness of presentation or their conformity with GAAP. To be economically feasible and justifiable, auditing aims for a reasonable level of assurance about the data under review. This means that, under a testing system, assurance is never absolute. Audit reports are subject to this inherent probability of error.

AUDIT REPORT

There is considerable debate among auditors, users, and other interested parties (courts, regulators) concerning the phrase *present fairly* in the auditor's report. Most auditors maintain that financial statements are fairly presented when they conform to accepted accounting principles and fairness is meaningful only when measured against this standard. Yet in several court cases, financial statements supposedly prepared in accordance with accounting principles were found to be misleading.

The audit report's language has been revised to narrow the gap between the responsibility auditors intend to assume and the responsibility the public believes them to assume. The language is intended to be nontechnical and to more explicitly address the responsibility the audit firm assumes, the procedures it performs, and the assurance it provides. The report indicates:

- Financial statements are audited. This is intended to be descriptive of the process.
- Financial statements are the responsibility of management and expressing an opinion on them is the auditor's responsibility. This gives users notice of responsibilities assumed by each party.
- The audit is conducted in accordance with generally accepted auditing standards and is designed to obtain reasonable assurance the financial statements are free of material misstatement.
- Auditors apply procedures to reasonably assure the financial statements are free of material misstatement, including: (1) examining on a test basis evidence supporting the amounts and disclosures in financial statements, (2) assessing accounting principles used and estimates made by management, and (3) evaluating overall financial statement presentation.

- Whether financial statements present fairly in all material respects the financial position, results of operations, and cash flows of the company for the period reported on.

Types of Audit Qualifications

There are several major types of qualifications that an auditor can express.

"Except for" Qualification

"Except for" qualifications express an opinion on the financial statements *except for* repercussions stemming from conditions that must be disclosed. They may arise from limitations in the scope of the audit that, because of circumstances beyond the auditor's control or because of restrictions imposed by the audited company, result in a failure to obtain reasonably objective and verifiable evidence. They can also arise from a lack of conformity of the financial statements to accepted accounting principles. When there are uncertainties about future events that cannot be resolved or whose effects cannot be estimated or reasonably provided for at the time an opinion is rendered, a separate paragraph is added. An example is a company with operating losses or in financial distress calling into question the company's ability to continue operating as a going concern. This paragraph refers users to the note in the financial statements providing details about the uncertainty. In cases of pervasive uncertainty that cannot be adequately measured, an auditor can, but is not required to, issue a disclaimer of opinion rather than merely call the user's attention to the uncertainty.

Companies with Uncertainties in the Audit Report

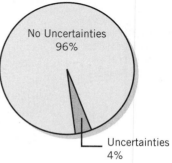

No Uncertainties 96%

Uncertainties 4%

Adverse Opinion

Auditors render adverse opinions in cases where financial statements are not prepared in accordance with accepted accounting principles, and this has a material effect on the fair presentation of the statements. An adverse opinion results generally from a situation where the audit firm is unable to convince its client to either amend the financial statements so that they reflect the auditor's estimate about the outcome of future events or adhere to accepted accounting principles. An adverse opinion must always be accompanied by the reasons for this opinion.

Disclaimer of Opinion

A disclaimer of opinion is a statement of inability to express an opinion. It must be rendered when, for whatever reason, insufficient competent evidential matter is available to the audit firm to enable it to form an opinion on the financial statements. It can arise from limitations in the scope of the audit as well as from the existence of uncertainties, the ultimate impact of which cannot be estimated. Material departures from accepted accounting principles do not justify a disclaimer of opinion. The difference between adverse opinions and disclaimers of opinion is best understood in terms of the difference existing between exceptions affecting the quality of financial statements on one hand, and those expressing uncertainties affecting the auditor's opinion on the other. For example, a situation calling for an "except for" opinion can in certain cases result in major disagreements with management requiring an adverse opinion. Finally, a disclaimer of opinion is also required if the auditor is not deemed to be "independent" in its audit of the financial statements. This lack of independence can arise, for example, if the auditor has a financial interest in the company, possibly by virtue of equity investment.

ANALYSIS IMPLICATIONS FROM AUDITING

This section describes the analysis implications related to auditing activities.

Analysis Implications of the Audit Process

Auditing is based largely on a *sampling approach* to the data and information under audit. Sample size is limited by the costs of auditing practice. Users must recognize the audit firm does not aim at, nor can ever achieve, complete certainty. Even a review of every single transaction–a process economically unjustifiable–does not achieve complete assurance.

While audited financial statements provide us some assurance about the results of the audit process, we must remember there are varying risks to our relying on audit results. These risks relate to many factors, including (1) the auditor's inability and/or unwillingness to detect fraud at the highest level and to apply necessary audit tests to this end, (2) the auditor's inability to grasp the extent of a deteriorating situation, (3) the auditor's conception of the extent of responsibilities to probe and disclose, and (4) overall audit quality. We must be aware the entire audit process is a probabilistic one subject to risks. Flawless application does not yield complete assurance and cannot ensure the auditor has elicited all the facts. This is especially the case if high-level management collusion is involved. Dependence of the auditing process on human judgment also yields varying degrees of audit quality.

Audit Risk and Its Implications

We already discussed accounting risk. Audit risk, while related, is of a different dimension and represents an equal danger to users of audited financial statements. While it is impossible for us to substitute our judgment for that of the auditor, we can use our understanding of the audit process and its limitations to make a better assessment of the degree of audit risk. The following are attributes pointing to potential areas of vulnerability:

- Growth industry or company with pressure to maintain a high market price or pursue acquisitions.
- Company in financial distress requiring financing.
- Company with high market visibility issuing frequent progress reports and earnings estimates.
- Management dominated by one or more strong-willed individuals.
- Signs of personal financial difficulties by members of management.
- Deterioration in operating performance or profitability.
- Management compensation or stock options dependent on reported earnings.
- Deterioration in liquidity or solvency.
- Capital structure too complex for the company's operations or size.
- Management compensation or stock options dependent on reported earnings.

Analysis Implications of Auditing Standards

In relying on audited financial statements, our analysis must be aware of limitations in the audit process. Moreover, we must understand what the auditor's opinion means and does not mean. The audit firm asserts it reviews the financial statements presented to it by management and ascertains whether they are in agreement with the records it audits. The audit firm also determines whether accepted principles of accounting are employed in preparing the financial statements, but does not claim to represent they are the best principles.

There are several issues that should be recognized in our analysis:

1. An auditor's knowledge of business activities underlying financial statements is not as strong as the preparer's. The audit firm knows only what it can discern on the basis of a sampling process and does not know all the facts.

2. Many financial statement items are incapable of exact measurement and the auditor merely reviews these measurements for reasonableness. Unless the auditor can show otherwise (e.g., estimating asset service lives), management's determination prevails.

3. While the audit firm is often consulted in selecting accounting principles, it is the preparer that selects and applies the principles. Auditors cannot insist on using the "best" principle any more than they can insist on a degree of disclosure above the minimum acceptable.

4. There exist limitations in the auditor's ability to audit certain areas. For example, is the audit firm able to audit the value of inventory work in progress? Can it competently evaluate the adequacy of insurance reserves? Can it estimate the value of problem loans? Can it second-guess the client's estimate of the percentage of completion of a large contract? While these questions are rarely raised in public, they present important challenges to the profession.

5. The auditor's error tolerance is higher. The auditor looks to the concept of *materiality* implying that the audit firm need not concern itself with trivial or unimportant matters. What is important or significant is a matter of judgment, and the profession has yet to precisely define the concept nor set established criteria of materiality. This yields reporting latitude.

An auditor's reference to generally accepted accounting principles in its opinion should also be understood by users of financial statements. This reference means the auditor is satisfied that principles, or standards, have authoritative support and they are applied "in all material respects." Aside from understanding the concept of materiality, our analysis must understand that the definition of what constitutes *generally accepted* is often vague and subject to latitude in interpretation and application. For example, auditing standards state "when criteria for selection among alternative accounting principles have not been established to relate accounting methods to circumstances (e.g., as in case of inventory and depreciation methods), the auditor may conclude that more than one accounting principle is appropriate in the circumstances."

Similarly ambiguous are standards relating to disclosure. While minimum standards are increasingly established in professional and SEC pronouncements, accountants do not always adhere to them. The degree to which lack of disclosure impairs fair presentation of financial statements remains subject to the auditor's judgment and discretion. There are no definite standards indicating the point where lack of disclosure is material enough to impair fairness of presentation, requiring a qualified audit report.

Analysis Implications of Auditor Opinions

When an audit firm qualifies its opinion, our analysis is faced with a problem of interpretation. That is, what is the meaning and intent of the qualification? Also, what effect does qualification have for our reliance on financial statements? The usefulness of this qualification for our analysis depends on the extent supplementary information and data enable us to assess its impact. An added dimension of confusion and difficulty of interpretation arises when the audit firm includes explanatory information in its report, merely for emphasis, without a statement of conclusions or of a qualification. We are often left wondering why the matter is emphasized and whether the auditor is attempting to express an unstated qualification or reservation.

When an audit firm is *not* satisfied with the fairness in presentation of financial statements, it issues an "except for" type of qualification, and when there are *uncertainties* that cannot be resolved, it adds explanatory language after the opinion paragraph. At some point, the size and importance of items under qualification are so large to result in an adverse opinion or disclaimer of opinion. Where is this point? At what point is a qualification no longer meaningful and an overall disclaimer of opinion necessary? Our analysis will not find any explicit guidelines in auditing standards. We must rely on the auditor's judgment with appropriate caveats.

Analysis Implications of the SEC

The SEC has moved more aggressively to monitor auditor performance and to strengthen the auditor's position in dealings with clients. Disciplinary proceedings against auditors were expanded with innovative remedies in consent decrees to include requirements for improvements in internal administration procedures, professional education, and reviews of a firm's procedures by outside professionals (peer review). In moving to strengthen the auditor's position, the SEC requires increased disclosure of the relationship between auditors and their clients, particularly in cases where changes in auditors take place. Disclosure must include details of past disagreements including those resolved to the satisfaction of the prior auditor, and note disclosure of the effects on financial statements of methods of accounting advocated by a former auditor but not followed by the client. The SEC has also moved to discourage "opinion shopping," a practice where companies allegedly canvass audit firms to gain acceptance of accounting alternatives they desire to use before hiring auditors.

This appendix shows our analysis must carefully consider the auditor's opinion and the supplementary information it refers to. While our analysis can place some reliance on the audit, we must maintain an independent and guarded view toward assurances conveyed in the auditor's report.

■ ■ ■ ■ ■ ■ ■

ACCOUNTING WATCHDOG

The new Public Company Accounting Oversight Board (PCAOB, created by the Sarbanes-Oxley Act), serves as a watchdog for wayward auditors.

.....APPENDIX 2B: EARNINGS QUALITY

Earnings quality refers to the relevance of earnings in measuring company performance. Its determinants include a company's business environment and its selection and application of accounting principles. This appendix focuses on measuring earnings quality, describing income statement and balance sheet analysis of earnings quality, and explaining how external factors impact earnings quality.

Determinants of Earnings Quality

We know earnings (income) measurement and recognition involve estimation and interpretation of business transactions and events. Our prior analysis of earnings emphasized that accounting earnings is not a unique amount but depends on the assumptions used and principles applied.

The need for estimation and interpretation in accrual accounting has led some individuals to question the reliability of *all* accrual measures. This is an extreme and unwise reaction because of the considerable wealth of relevant information communicated in accrual measures.

We know accrual accounting consists of adjusting cash flows to reflect universally accepted concepts: earned revenue and incurred expenses. What our analysis must focus on are the assumptions and principles applied, and the adjustments appropriate for our analysis objectives. We should use the information in accruals to our competitive advantage and to help us better understand current and future company performance. We must also be aware of both *accounting and audit risks* to rely on earnings. Improvements in both accounting and auditing have decreased the incidence of fraud and misinterpretation in financial statements. Nevertheless, management fraud and misrepresentation is far from eliminated, and audit failures do occur (e.g., Enron, WorldCom, and Xerox). Our analysis must always evaluate accounting and audit risk, including the character and propensities of management, in assessing earnings.

Measuring earnings quality arose out of a need to compare earnings of different companies and a desire to recognize differences in quality for valuation purposes. There is not complete agreement on what constitutes earnings quality. This section considers three factors typically identified as determinants of earnings quality and some examples of their assessment.

FRAUD ALERT
Many financial frauds are spotted by short-sellers long before regulators and the press pick them up.

1. **Accounting principles.** One determinant of earnings quality is the discretion of management in *selecting accepted accounting principles*. This discretion can be aggressive (optimistic) or conservative. The quality of conservatively determined earnings is perceived to be higher because they are less likely to overstate current and future performance expectations compared with those determined in an aggressive manner. Conservatism reduces the likelihood of earnings overstatement and retrospective changes. However, excessive conservatism, while contributing temporarily to earnings quality, reduces the reliability and relevance of earnings in the longer run. Examining the accounting principles selected can provide clues to management's propensities and attitudes.

2. **Accounting application.** Another determinant of earnings quality is management's discretion in *applying* accepted accounting principles. Management has discretion over the amount of earnings through their application of accounting principles determining revenues and expenses. Discretionary expenses like advertising, marketing, repairs, maintenance, research, and development can be *timed* to manage the level of reported earnings (or loss). Earnings reflecting timing elements unrelated to operating or business conditions can detract from earnings quality. Our analysis task is to identify the implications of management's accounting application and assess its motivations.

3. **Business risk.** A third determinant of earnings quality is the relation between earnings and business risk. It includes the effect of cyclical and other business forces on earnings level, stability, sources, and variability. For example, earnings variability is generally undesirable and its increase harms earnings quality. Higher earnings quality is linked with companies more insulated from business risk. While business risk is not primarily a result of management's discretionary actions, this risk can be lowered by skillful management strategies.

INCOME STATEMENT ANALYSIS OF EARNINGS QUALITY

Important determinants of earnings quality are management's selection and application of accounting principles. This section focuses on several important discretionary accounting expenditures to help us to assess earnings quality. *Discretionary expenditures* are outlays that management can vary across periods to conserve resources and/or influence reported earnings. For this reason, they deserve special attention in our analysis. These expenditures are often reported in the income statement or its notes, and hence, evaluation of these items is referred to as an income statement analysis of earnings quality. Two important examples are:

1. **Advertising expense.** A major portion of advertising outlays has effects beyond the current period. This yields a weak relation between advertising outlays and short-term performance. This also implies management can in certain cases cut advertising costs with no immediate effects on sales. However, long-run sales are likely to suffer. Analysis must look at year-to-year variations in advertising expenses to assess their impact on future sales and earnings quality.

2. **Research and development expense.** Research and development costs are among the most difficult expenditures in financial statements to analyze and interpret. Yet they are important, not necessarily because of their amount but because of their effect on future performance. Interestingly, research and development costs have acquired an aura of productive potential in analysis exceeding what is often warranted by experience. There exist numerous cases of successful research and development activities in areas like genetics, chemistry, electronics, photography, and biology. But for each successful project there are countless failures. These research failures represent vast sums expensed or written off without measurable benefits. Our intent is to determine the amount of current research and development costs having future benefits. These benefits are often measured by relating research and development outlays to sales growth and new product development.

Analysis of Other Discretionary Costs

There are other discretionary future-directed outlays. Examples are costs of training, selling, managerial development, and repairs and maintenance. While these costs are usually expensed in the period incurred, they often have future utility. To the extent that these costs are separately disclosed in the income statement or the notes to the financial statements, analysis should recognize their effects in assessing current earnings and future prospects.

BALANCE SHEET ANALYSIS OF EARNINGS QUALITY

Conservatism in Reported Assets

The relevance of reported asset values is linked (with few exceptions like cash, held-to maturity investments, and land) with their ultimate recognition as reported expenses. We can state this as a general proposition:

When assets are *overstated*, cumulative earnings are *overstated*.

This is true because earnings are relieved of charges necessary to bring these assets down to realizable values. Examples include the delay in recognizing impaired assets, such as obsolete inventories or unproductive plant and equipment, and the understatement of allowance for uncollectible accounts receivable. The converse is also true: when assets are *understated*, cumulative earnings are *understated*. An example is the unrecognized appreciation on an acquired business that is recorded at original purchase price.

Conservatism in Reported Provisions and Liabilities

Our analysis must be alert to the proposition relating provisions and liability values to earnings. In general,

When provisions and liabilities are *understated*, cumulative earnings are *overstated*.

This is true because earnings are relieved of charges necessary to bring the provisions or liabilities up to their market values. Examples are understatements in provisions for product warranties and environmental liabilities that yield overstatement in cumulative earnings. Conversely, an *overprovision* for current and future liabilities or losses yields an *understatement* of earnings (or overstatement of losses). An example is overestimation of severance costs of a planned restructuring.

We will describe in Chapter 6 how provisions for future costs and losses that are excessive shift the burden of costs and expenses from future income statements to the current period. Bearing in mind our propositions regarding the earnings effects from reported values of assets and liabilities, the critical analysis of these values represents an important factor in assessing earnings quality.

EXTERNAL FACTORS AND EARNINGS QUALITY

Earnings quality is affected by factors external to a company. These external factors make earnings more or less reliable. One factor is the quality of *foreign earnings*. Foreign earnings quality is affected by the difficulties and uncertainties in repatriation of funds, currency fluctuations, political and social conditions, and local customs and regulation. In certain countries, companies lack flexibility in dismissing personnel, which essentially converts labor into a fixed cost. Another factor affecting earnings quality is *regulation*. For example, the regulatory environment confronting a public utility affects its earnings quality. An unsympathetic or hostile regulatory environment can affect costs and selling prices and thereby diminish earnings quality due to increased uncertainty of future profits. Also, the stability and reliability of *earnings sources* affect earnings quality. Government defense-related revenues are dependable in times of high international tensions, but affected by political events in peacetime. *Changing price levels* affect earnings quality. When price levels are rising, "inventory profits" or understatements in expenses like depreciation lower earnings quality. Finally, because of uncertainties due to *complexities of operations,* earnings of certain conglomerates are considered of lower quality.

GUIDANCE ANSWERS TO ANALYSIS VIEWPOINTS

AUDITOR

An auditor's main objective is an expression of an opinion on the fairness of financial statements according to generally accepted accounting principles. As auditor, you desire assurance on the absence of errors and irregularities in financial statements. Financial statement analysis can help identify any errors and irregularities affecting the statements. Also, this analysis compels our auditor to understand the company's operations and its performance in light of prevailing economic and industry conditions. Application of financial statement analysis is especially useful as a preliminary audit tool, directing the auditor to areas of greatest change and unexplained performance.

DIRECTOR

As a member of a company's board of directors, you are responsible for oversight of management and the safeguarding of shareholders' interests. Accordingly, a director's interest in the company is broad and risky. To reduce risk, a director uses financial statement analysis to monitor management and assess company profitability, growth, and financial condition. Because of a director's unique position, there is near unlimited access to internal financial and other records. Analysis of financial statements assists our director in: (1) recognizing causal relationships among business activities and events, (2) helping directors focus on the company and not on a maze of financial details, and (3) encouraging proactive and not reactive measures in confronting changing financial conditions.

BOARD MEMBER

Your concern with earnings quality is to ensure earnings accurately reflect the company's return and risk characteristics. Low earnings quality implies *inflated earnings* (returns) and/or *deflated risk* not reflecting actual return or risk characteristics. Regarding inflated earnings (returns), you can ask the auditor for evidence of management's use of liberal accounting principles or applications, aggressive behavior in discretionary accruals, asset overstatements, and liability understatements. Regarding deflated risk, you can ask about earnings sources, stability, variability, and trend. Additional risk-related questions can focus on the character or propensities of management, the regulatory environment, and overall business risk.

QUESTIONS

[Superscript ^{A} $(^B)$ denotes assignments based on Appendix 2A (2B).]

2–1. Describe the U.S. financial reporting environment including the following:
   a. Forces that impact the content of statutory financial reports
   b. Rule-making bodies and regulatory agencies that formulate GAAP used in financial reports
   c. Users of financial information and what alternative sources of information are available beyond statutory financial reports
   d. Enforcement and monitoring mechanisms to improve the integrity of statutory financial reports

2–2. Why are earnings announcements made in advance of the release of financial statements? What information do they contain and how are they different from financial statements?

2–3. Describe the content and purpose of at least four financial reports that must be filed with the SEC.

2–4. What constitutes contemporary GAAP?

2–5. Explain how accounting standards are established.

2–6. Who has the main responsibility for ensuring fair and accurate financial reporting by a company?

2–7. Describe factors that bring about managerial discretion for preparing financial statements.

2–8. Describe forces that serve to limit the ability of management to manage financial statements.

2–9. Describe alternative information sources beyond statutory financial reports that are available to investors and creditors.

2–10. Describe tasks that financial intermediaries perform on behalf of financial statement users.

2–11. Explain historical cost and fair value models of accounting. What explains the move toward fair value accounting?

2–12. What is conservatism? What are its advantages?

2–13. What are the two types of conservatism? Which type of conservatism is more useful for analysis?

2–14. Describe empirical evidence showing that financial accounting information is relevant for decision making.

2–15. Describe at least four major limitations of financial statement information.

2–16. It is difficult to measure the business performance of a company in the short run using only cash flow measures because of timing and matching problems. Describe each of these problems and cite at least one example for each.

2–17. Describe the criteria necessary for a business to record revenue.

2–18. Explain when costs should be recognized as expenses.

2–19. Distinguish between short-term and long-term accruals.

2–20. Explain why cash flow measures of performance are less useful than accrual-based measures.

2–21. What factors give rise to the superiority of accrual accounting over cash accounting? Explain.

2–22. Accrual accounting information is conceptually more relevant than cash flows. Describe empirical findings that support this superiority of accrual accounting.

2–23. Accrual accounting information, cash flow information, and analysts' forecasts are information for investors. Compare and contrast each of these sources in terms of relevance and reliability.

2–24. Define income. Distinguish income from cash flow.

2–25. What are the two basic economic concepts of income? What implications do they have for analysis?

2–26. Economic income measures change in value while permanent income is proportional to value itself. Explain this statement.

2–27. Explain how accountants measure income.

2–28. Accounting income has elements of both permanent income and economic income. Explain this statement.

2–29. Distinguish between the permanent and transitory components of income. Cite an example of each, and discuss how each component affects analysis.

2–30. Define and cite an example of a value irrelevant component of income.

2–31. Determining core income is an important first step to estimating permanent income. Explain. What adjustments to net income should be made for estimating core income?

2–32. What adjustments would you make to net income to determine economic income?

2–33. Explain how accounting principles can, in certain cases, create differences between financial statement information and economic reality.

2–34. What are the key differences between the historical cost and the fair value models of accounting?

2–35. Describe what income purports to represent under the historical cost and the fair value accounting models. How is income determined under either model?

2–36. Provide a formal definition for fair value. What are the key elements of this definition?

2–37. Fair values are market-based measurements not entity-specific measurements. Explain with an example.

2–38. Explain the hierarchy of inputs used in determining fair values. The use of which level of input lowers the reliability of fair value estimates?

2–39. Which types of assets/liabilities lend themselves more easily to fair value measurements: financial or operating? Explain with reference to the hierarchy of inputs.

2–40. Describe the three basic valuation approaches for estimating fair values. Relate the valuation approaches to hierarchy of inputs.

2–41. Discuss the advantages and disadvantages of fair value accounting.

2–42. In your opinion does historical cost or fair value model generate more (a) relevant and (b) reliable accounting information? Argue your case.

2–43. What are the major issues that an analyst needs to consider when analyzing financial statements prepared under the fair value accounting model?

2–44. Explain how estimates and judgments of financial statement preparers can create differences between financial statement information and economic reality.

2–45. What is accounting analysis? Explain.

2–46. What is the process to carry out an accounting analysis?

2–47. What gives rise to accounting distortions? Explain.

2–48. Why do managers sometimes manage earnings?

2–49. What are popular earnings management strategies? Explain.

2–50. Explain what is meant by the term *earnings management* and what incentives managers have to engage in earnings management.

2–51. Describe the role that accrual accounting information and cash flow information play in your own models of company valuation.

2–52. Explain how accounting concepts and standards, and the financial statements based on them, are subject to the pervasive influence of individual judgments and incentives.

2–53. Would you be willing to pay more or less for a stock, on average, when the accounting information provided to you about the firm is unaudited? Explain.

2–54[A]. What are generally accepted auditing standards?

2–55[A]. What are auditing procedures? What are some basic objectives of a financial statement audit?

2–56[A]. What does the opinion section of the auditor's report usually cover?

2–57[A]. What are some implications to financial analysis stemming from the audit process?

2–58[A]. An auditor does not prepare financial statements but instead samples and investigates data to render a professional opinion on whether the statements are "fairly presented." List the potential implications of the auditor's responsibility to users that rely on financial statements.

2–59[A]. What does the auditor's reference to generally accepted accounting principles imply for our analysis of financial statements?

2–60[A]. What are some circumstances suggesting higher audit risk? Explain.

2–61[A]. **Citigroup** is currently audited by KPMG. Who pays KPMG for its audit of Citigroup? To whom is KPMG providing assurance regarding the fair presentation of the Citigroup financial statements? List two market forces faced by KPMG that increase the probability that the firm effectively performed an audit with the interests of financial statement users in mind.

2–62[A]. Public accounting firms are being implored to assess a company's reported earnings per share relative to the market expectation of earnings per share (e.g., consensus analysts' forecast) when establishing the level of misstatement that is considered acceptable (the materiality threshold). Explain why a 1 cent misstatement can be insignificant for one firm but significant to another otherwise comparable firm.

2–63[B]. What is meant by earnings quality? Why do users assess earnings quality? What major factors determine earnings quality?

2–64[B]. What are discretionary expenses? What is the importance of discretionary expenses for analysis of earnings quality?

2–65[B]. What is the relation between the reported value of assets and reported earnings? What is the relation between the reported values of liabilities, including provisions, and reported earnings?

2–66[B]. How does a balance sheet analysis provide a check on the validity and quality of earnings?

2–67[B]. What is the effect of external factors on earnings quality?

2–68[B]. Explain how earnings management affects earnings quality. How is earnings management distinguished from fraudulent reporting?

2–69[B]. Identify and explain three types of earnings management that can reduce earnings quality.

2–70[B]. What factors and incentives motivate companies (management) to engage in earnings management? What are the implications of these incentives for financial statement analysis?

EXERCISES

EXERCISE 2–1

Uniformity in Accounting

Some financial statement users maintain that despite its intrinsic intellectual appeal, uniformity in accounting seems unworkable in a complex modern society that relies, at least in part, on economic market forces.

Required:

a. Discuss at least three disadvantages of national or international accounting uniformity.

b. Explain whether uniformity in accounting necessarily implies comparability.

(CFA Adapted)

Announcements of good news or bad news earnings for the recently completed fiscal quarter usually create fairly small abnormal stock price changes on the day of the announcement.

Required:

a. Discuss how stock price changes over the preceding days or weeks help explain this phenomenon.

b. Discuss the types of information that the market might have received in advance of the earnings announcement.

c. How does the relatively small price reaction at the time of the earnings announcement relate to the price changes that are observed in the days or weeks prior to the announcement?

EXERCISE 2–2
Earnings Announcements and Market Reactions

Some financial statement users criticize the timeliness of annual financial statements.

Required:

a. Explain why summary information in the income statement is not new information when the annual report is issued.

b. Describe the types of information in the income statement that are new information to financial statement users when the annual report is issued.

EXERCISE 2–3
Timeliness of Financial Statements

The SEC requires companies to submit statutory financial reports on both a quarterly and an annual basis. The quarterly report is called the 10-Q.

Required:

What are two factors about quarterly financial reports that can be misleading if the analyst does not consider them when performing analysis of quarterly reports?

EXERCISE 2–4
Reliability of Quarterly Reports

The SEC requires various statutory reports from companies with publicly traded securities.

Required:

Identify which SEC report is the best place to find the following information.

a. Management's discussion of the financial results for the fiscal year.

b. Terms of the CEO's compensation and the total compensation paid to the CEO in the prior fiscal year.

c. Who is on the board of directors and are they from within or outside of the company?

d. How much are the directors paid for their services?

e. Results of operations and financial position of the company at the end of the second quarter.

f. Why a firm changed its auditors.

g. Details for the upcoming initial public offering of stock.

EXERCISE 2–5
Information in SEC Reports

Managers are responsible for ensuring fair and accurate financial reporting. Managers also have inside information that can aid their estimates of future outcomes. Yet, managers face incentives to strategically report information in their best interests.

Required:

Assume a manager of a publicly traded company is intending to recognize revenues in an inappropriate and fraudulent manner. Explain the penalty(ies) that can be imposed on a manager by the monitoring and enforcement mechanisms in place to restrict such activity.

EXERCISE 2–6
Mechanisms to Monitor Financial Reporting

EXERCISE 2–7

Incentives for
Voluntary Disclosure

There are various motivations for managers to make voluntary disclosures. Identify whether you believe managers are likely to release the following information in the form of voluntary disclosure (examine each case independently):

a. A company plans to sell an underperforming division for a substantial loss in the second quarter of next year.

b. A company is experiencing disappointing sales and, as a result, expects to report disappointing earnings at the end of this quarter.

c. A company plans to report especially strong earnings this quarter.

d. Management believes the consensus forecast of analysts is slightly higher than managers' forecasts.

e. Management strongly believes the company is undervalued at its current stock price.

EXERCISE 2–8

Financial Statement
Information versus
Analysts Forecasts

Financial statements are a major source of information about a company. Forecasts, reports, and recommendations from analysts are popular alternative sources of information.

Required:

a. Discuss the strengths of financial statement information for business decision makers.

b. Discuss the strengths of analyst forecast information for business decision makers.

c. Discuss how the two information sources in (*a*) and (*b*) are interrelated.

EXERCISE 2–9

Historical Cost versus
Fair Value

Financial statements are inexorably moving to a model where all assets and liabilities will be measured on the basis of fair value rather than historical cost.

Required:

a. Discuss the conceptual differences between historical cost and fair value.

b. Discuss the merits and demerits of the two alternative measurement models.

c. What types of assets (or liabilities) more readily lend themselves to fair value measurements? Can we visualize a scenario where all assets are measured using fair value?

d. What are the likely effects of adopting the fair value model on reported income?

EXERCISE 2–10

Accrual Accounting
versus Cash Flows

a. Identify at least two reasons why an accrual accounting income statement is more useful for analyzing business performance than a cash flow based income statement.

b. Describe what would be reported on the asset side of a cash flow based balance sheet versus the asset side of an accrual accounting balance sheet.

c. A strength of accrual accounting is its relevance for decision making. The strength of cash flow information is its reliability. Explain what makes accrual accounting more relevant and cash flows more reliable.

EXERCISE 2–11

Analyst Forecasts versus
Financial Statements

Analysts produce forecasts of accounting earnings along with other forward-looking information. This information has strengths and weaknesses versus financial statement information.

Required:

a. Discuss whether you believe analysts forecasts are more relevant for business decision making than financial statement information.

b. Discuss whether you believe analysts forecasts are more reliable than financial statement information.

Accrual accounting requires estimates of future outcomes. For example, the reserve for bad debts is a forecast of the amount of current receivables that will ultimately prove uncollectible.

Required:

Identify and explain three reasons why accounting information might deviate from the underlying economic reality. Cite examples of transactions that might give rise to each of the reasons.

EXERCISE 2–12
Accrual Accounting Measurement Error

A former Chairman of the SEC refers to hidden reserves on the balance sheet as "cookie-jar" reserves. These reserves are built up in periods when earnings are strong and drawn down to bolster earnings in periods when earnings are weak.

Required:

Reserves for (1) bad debts and (2) inventory, along with the (3) large accruals associated with restructuring charges, are transactions that sometimes yield hidden reserves.

a. For each of these transactions, explain when and how a hidden reserve is created.

b. For each of these transactions, explain when and how a hidden reserve is drawn down to boost earnings.

EXERCISE 2–13
Accounting for Hidden Reserves

In the past decade, several large "money center" banks recorded huge additions **Citicorp** to their loan loss reserve. For example, **Citicorp** recorded a one-time addition to its loan loss reserve totaling about $3 billion. These additions to loan loss reserves led to large net losses for these banks. While most analysts agree that additional reserves were warranted, many speculated the banks recorded more reserve than necessary.

Required:

a. Why might a bank choose to record more loan loss reserve than necessary?

b. Explain how overstated loan loss reserves can be used to manage earnings in future years.

EXERCISE 2–14
Banks and Hidden Reserves

PROBLEMS

Financial statement users often liken accounting standard setting to a political process. One user asserted that: *My view is that the setting of accounting standards is as much a product of political action as of flawless logic or empirical findings. Why? Because the setting of standards is a social decision. Standards place restrictions on behavior; therefore, they must be accepted by the affected parties. Acceptance may be forced or voluntary or some of both. In a democratic society, getting acceptance is an exceedingly complicated process that requires skillful marketing in a political arena.* Many parties affected by proposed standards intervene to protect their own interests while disguising their motivations as altruistic or theoretical. People often say, "If you like the answer, you'll love the theory." It is also alleged that those who are regulated by the standard-setting process have excessive influence over the regulatory process. One FASB member declared: "The business community has much greater influence than it's ever had over standard setting. I think it's unhealthy. It is the preparer community that is really being regulated in this process, and if we have those being regulated having a dominant role in the regulatory process, that's asking for major trouble."

Required:

Discuss the relevance of the accounting standard-setting process to analysis of financial statements.

PROBLEM 2–1
Financial Statement Analysis and Standard Setting

PROBLEM 2–2

Neutrality of Measurements in Financial Statements

Financial reporting has been likened to cartography:

> Information cannot be neutral–it cannot therefore be reliable–if it is selected or presented for the purpose of producing some chosen effect on human behavior. It is this quality of neutrality which makes a map reliable; and the essential nature of accounting, I believe, is cartographic. Accounting is financial mapmaking. The better the map, the more completely it represents the complex phenomena that are being mapped. We do not judge a map by the behavioral effects it produces. The distribution of natural wealth or rainfall shown on a map may lead to population shifts or changes in industrial location, which the government may like or dislike. That should be no concern of the cartographer. We judge his map by how well it represents the facts. People can then react to it as they will.

Required:

a. Explain why neutrality is such an important quality of financial statements.

b. Identify examples of the lack of neutrality in accounting reports.

PROBLEM 2–3

Analysts' Information Needs and Accounting Measurements

An editor of the *Financial Analysts Journal* reviewed an earlier edition of this book and asserted:

> Broadly speaking, accounting numbers are of two types: those that can be measured and those that have to be estimated. Investors who feel that accounting values are more real than market values should remember that, although the estimated numbers in the accounting statements often have a greater impact, singly or together, than the measured numbers, accountants' estimates are rarely based on any serious attempt by accountants at business or economic judgment.
>
> The main reason accountants shy away from precise statements of principle for the determination of asset values is that neither they nor anyone else has yet come up with principles that will consistently give values plausible enough that, if accounting statements were based on these principles, users would take them seriously.

Required:

a. Describe what is meant by measurement in accounting.

b. According to this editor, what are the kinds of measurements investors want?

c. Discuss whether the objectives of accountants and investors regarding accounting measurement are reconcilable.

PROBLEM 2–4

Standard Setting and Politics

A FASB member expressed the following view:

> Are we going to set accounting standards in the private sector or not? . . . Part of the answer depends on how the business community views accounting standards. Are they rules of conduct, designed to restrain unsocial behavior and arbitrate conflicts of economic interest? Or are they rules of measurement, designed to generalize and communicate as accurately as possible the complex results of economic events? . . . Rules of conduct call for a political process . . . Rules of measurement, on the other hand, call for a research process of observation and experimentation . . . Intellectually, the case is compelling for viewing accounting as a measurement process . . . But the history of accounting standard setting has been dominated by the other view–that accounting standards are rules of conduct. The FASB was created out of the ashes of predecessors burned up in the fires of the resulting political process.

Required:

a. Discuss your views on the difference between "rules of conduct" and "rules of measurement."

b. Explain how accounting standard setting is a political process. Identify arguments for and against viewing accounting standard setting as political.

Consider the following excerpt from the *Financial Analysts Journal:*

> Strictly speaking, the objectives of financial reporting are the objectives of society and not of accountants and auditors, as such. Similarly, society has objective law and medicine—namely, justice and health for the people—which are not necessarily the objectives of lawyers and doctors, as such, in the conduct of their respective "business."
>
> In a variety of ways, society exerts pressure on a profession to act more nearly as if it actively shared the objectives of society. Society's pressure is to be measured by the degree of accommodation on the part of the profession under pressure, and by the degree of counterpressure applied by the profession. For example, doctors accommodate society by getting better educations than otherwise and reducing incompetence in their ranks. They apply counterpressure and gain protection by forming medical associations.

PROBLEM 2–5
Accounting in Society

Required:

a. Describe ways in which society has brought pressure on accountants to better serve its needs.

b. Describe how the accounting profession has responded to these pressures. Could the profession have better responded?

A standard setter recently made a private remark that conservatism was a "barbaric relic" that violated the "neutrality" requirement of accounting information and that financial statements would be far more informative without conservatism.

PROBLEM 2–6
Conservatism

Required:

a. What is conservatism? What are the reasons why conservatism continues to be dominant in financial statements?

b. Do you agree with the observation by the standard setter?

c. As an analyst would you prefer conservative accounting? Does your answer depend on your analysis objective? For example, would you prefer conservative accounting if you were an equity analyst?

d. Many regard conservative accounting as "high-quality" accounting. Do you agree with this statement? Provide arguments for why you think conservative accounting increases or impedes accounting quality.

e. Academics refer to two forms of conservatism. What are they? Which form of conservatism do you think is more useful for an analyst?

Consider the following claim from a business observer:

PROBLEM 2–7
Financial Reporting or Financial Subterfuge

> An accountant's job is to conceal, not to reveal. An accountant is not asked to give outsiders an accurate picture of what's going on in a company. He is asked to transform the figures on a company's operations in such a way that it will be impossible to recreate the original figures.
>
> An income statement for a toy company doesn't tell how many toys of various kinds the company sold, or who the company's best customers are. The balance sheet doesn't tell how many of each kind of toy the company has in inventory, or how much is owed by each customer who is late in paying his bills.

> In general, anything that a manager uses to do his job will be of interest to some stockholders, customers, creditors, or government agencies. Managerial accounting differs from financial accounting only because the accountant has to hide some of the facts and figures managers find useful. The accountant simply has to throw out most of the facts and some of the figures that the managers use when he creates the financial statements for outsiders.
>
> The rules of accounting reflect this tension. Even if the accountant thought of himself as working only for the good of society, he would conceal certain facts in the reports he helps write. Since the accountant is actually working for the company, or even for the management of the company, he conceals many facts that outsiders would like to have revealed.

Required:

a. Discuss this observer's misgivings on the role of the accountant in financial reporting.

b. Discuss what type of omitted information the business observer is referring to.

PROBLEM 2–8
Contemporary Valuation

Equity valuations in today's market are arguably too high. Many analysts assert that price-to-earnings ratios are so high as to constitute an irrational valuation "bubble" that is bound to burst and drag valuations down. Skeptics are especially wary of the valuations for high-tech and Internet companies. Proponents of the "new paradigm" argue that the unusually high price-to-earnings ratios associated with many high-tech and Internet companies are justified because modern business is fundamentally different. In fact, many believe these companies are still, on average, undervalued. They argue that these companies have invested great sums in intangible assets that will produce large future profits. Also, research and development costs are expensed. This means they reduce income each period and are not reported as assets on the balance sheet. Consequently, earnings appear lower than normal and this yields price-to-earnings ratios that appear unreasonably high.

Required:

Assess and critique the positions of both the skeptics and proponents of this new paradigm.

PROBLEM 2–9
Income Measurement and Interpretation

In a discussion of corporate income, a user of financial statements alleges that "One of the real problems with income is that you never really know what it is. The only way you can find out is to liquidate a company and reduce everything to cash. Then you can subtract what went into the company from what came out and the result is income. Until then, income is only a product of accounting rituals."

Required:

a. Do you agree with the above statement? Explain. What problems do you foresee in measuring income in the manner described?

b. What assumptions underlie periodic measurement of income under accrual accounting? Which income approach do you think is more reasonable? Explain.

PROBLEM 2–10
Specialized Accounting Information

According to an article in *The Wall Street Journal,* a European filmmaking studio, **Polygram,** is considering funding movie production by selling securities. These securities will yield returns to investors based on the actual cash flows of the movies that are financed from the sale of these securities.

Polygram

Required:

a. What information would you suggest the filmmakers provide to investors to encourage them to invest in the production of a particular movie or movies (i.e., what information is relevant to your decision to invest in a movie)?

b. What kind of evidence can be included to support claims in the prospectus (i.e., what can maximize the reliability of the information released)?

The FASB in *SFAS No. 123,* "Accounting for Stock-Based Options," encourages (but does not require) companies to recognize compensation expense based on the fair value of stock options awarded to their employees and managers. Early drafts of this proposal *required* the recognition of the fair value of the options. But the FASB met opposition from companies and chose to only *encourage* the recognition of fair value. Recently, however, FASB has revised this standard *(SFAS 123R)* so as to require recognition of option compensation expense.

PROBLEM 2–11
Politics and Promulgation of Standards

Required:

a. Discuss the role you believe the following parties should play in the accounting standard promulgation process:

(1) FASB	(5) Companies (CEO)
(2) SEC	(6) Accounting firms
(3) AICPA	(7) Investors
(4) Congress	

b. Discuss which parties likely lobbied for the change from requiring expense recognition to only encouraging the expensing of stock options.

The following information is extracted from the annual report of **Lands' End** (in millions, except per share data):

Lands' End

PROBLEM 2–12
Relations between Income, Cash Flow, and Stock Price

Fiscal year	Year 9	Year 8	Year 7	Year 6	Year 5	Year 4
Net income	$31.2	$64.2	$ 51.0	$30.6	$36.1	$43.7
Cash from (used by) operations	74.3	(26.9)	121.8	41.4	34.5	22.4
Net cash flow	0.03	(86.5)	75.7	11.8	(16.1)	(1.2)
Free cash flow*	27.5	(74.6)	103.3	27.5	2.4	5.1
Market price per share (end of fiscal year)	32.375	39.312	28.375	14.625	16.125	24.375
Common shares outstanding	30.1	31.0	32.4	33.7	34.8	35.9

*Defined as: Cash flow from operations — Capital expenditures — Dividends.

Required:

a. Calculate and graph the following separate relations:
   (1) Net income per share (EPS) and market price per share
   (2) Cash from operations per share and market price per share
   (3) Net cash flow per share and market price per share
   (4) Free cash flow per share and market price per share

CHECK
EPS performs best

b. Which of the measures extracted from the annual report appear to best explain changes in stock price? Discuss the implications of this for stock valuation.

c. Choose another company and prepare similar graphs. Do your observations from Lands' End generalize?

PROBLEM 2–13

Earnings
Management
Strategies

The following information is taken from **Marsh**   **Marsh Supermarkets**
Supermarkets fiscal 20X7 annual report:

> During the first quarter, we made several decisions resulting in a $13 million charge to earnings. A new accounting pronouncement, *FAS 121*, required the Company to take a $7.5 million charge. *FAS 121* dictates how companies are to account for the carrying values of their assets. This rule affects all public and private companies.
>
> The magnitude of this charge created a window of opportunity to address several other issues that, in the Company's best long term interest, needed to be resolved. We amended our defined benefit retirement plan, and took significant reorganization and other special charges. These charges, including *FAS 121,* totaled almost $13 million. The result was a $7.1 million loss for the quarter and a small net loss for the year. Although these were difficult decisions because of their short term impact, they will have positive implications for years to come.

Marsh Supermarkets' net income for fiscal 20X5 and 20X6 is $8.6 million and $9.0 million, respectively.

Required:

CHECK
Big bath strategy

What earnings management strategy appears to have been used by Marsh in fiscal 20X7 in conjunction with the *FAS 121* charge (note, the $7.5 million charge from adoption of *FAS 121* is not avoidable)? Why do you think Marsh pursued this strategy?

PROBLEM 2–14

Earnings
Management
Strategies

Emerson Electric is engaged in design, manufacture, and   **Emerson Electric**
sale of a broad range of electrical, electromechanical, and electronic products and systems. The following shows Emerson's net income and net income before extraordinary items for the past 20 years (in millions):

Year	Net Income	Net Income before Extraordinary Items	Year	Net Income	Net Income before Extraordinary Items	Year	Net Income	Net Income before Extraordinary Items
Y1	$201.0	$201.0	Y8	$408.9	$408.9	Y15	$ 708.1	$ 708.1
Y2	237.7	237.7	Y9	467.2	467.2	Y16	788.5	904.4
Y3	273.3	273.3	Y10	528.8	528.8	Y17	907.7	929.0
Y4	300.1	300.1	Y11	588.0	588.0	Y18	1,018.5	1,018.5
Y5	302.9	302.9	Y12	613.2	613.2	Y19	1,121.9	1,121.9
Y6	349.2	349.2	Y13	631.9	631.9	Y20	1,228.6	1,228.6
Y7	401.1	401.1	Y14	662.9	662.9			

Emerson has achieved consistent earnings growth for more than 160 straight quarters (more than 40 years).

Required:

CHECK
Income smoothing strategy

a. What earnings strategy do you think Emerson has applied over the years to maintain its record of earnings growth?

b. Describe the extent you believe Emerson's earnings record reflects business activities, excellent management, and/or earnings management.

c. Describe how Emerson's earnings strategy is applied in good years and bad.

d. Identify years where Emerson likely built hidden reserves and the years it probably drew upon hidden reserves.

A finance textbook likens accrual accounting information to "nail soup." The recipe for nail soup includes the usual soup ingredients such as broth and noodles, but it also includes nails. This means with each spoonful of nail soup, one gets nails with broth and noodles. Accordingly, to eat the soup, one must remove the nails from each spoonful. The textbook went on to say that accountants include much valuable information in financial reports but one must remove the accounting accruals (nails) to make the information useful.

PROBLEM 2–15
Usefulness of Accrual Accounting

Required:

Critique the analogy of accrual accounting to "nail soup."

Consider the following: *While accrual accounting information is imperfect, ignoring it and making cash flows the basis of all analysis and business decisions is like throwing the baby out with the bath water.*

PROBLEM 2–16
Relevance of Accruals

Required:

a. Do you agree or disagree with this statement? Explain.

b. How does accrual accounting provide superior information to cash flows?

c. What are the imperfections of accrual accounting? Is it possible for accrual accounting to depict economic reality? Explain.

d. What is the prudent approach to analysis using accrual accounting information?

The following is an excerpt from a quarterly earnings announcement by **American Express:**

American Express

PROBLEM 2–17[B]
Earnings Quality

American Express Reports Record Quarterly Net Income of $648 Million

($ millions except per share amounts)	QUARTER ENDED SEPTEMBER 30		Percentage Inc./(Dec.)
	20X9	20X8	
Net income	$ 648	$ 574	13.0%
Net revenues	$ 4,879	$ 4,342	12.4%
Per share net income (Basic)	$ 1.45	$ 1.27	14.2%
Average common shares outstanding	446.0	451.6	(1.2%)
Return on average equity	25.3%	23.9%	

($ millions except per share amounts)	NINE MONTHS ENDED SEPTEMBER 30		Percentage Inc./(Dec.)
	20X9	20X8	
Net income	$ 1,869	$ 1,611	16.0%
Net revenues	$14,211	$12,662	12.2%
Per share net income (Basic)	$ 4.18	$ 3.53	18.4%
Average common shares outstanding	447.0	456.2	(2.0%)
Return on average equity	25.3%	23.9%	

Due to a change in accounting rules, the company is required to capitalize software costs rather than expense them as they occur. For the third quarter of 20X9, this amounted to a pre-tax benefit of $68 million (net of amortization). Also, the securitization of credit card receivables produced a gain of $55 million ($36 million after tax) in the current quarter.

Required:

Evaluate and comment on both *(a)* the earnings quality and *(b)* the relative performance of American Express in the most recent quarter relative to the same quarter of the prior fiscal year.

CASES

CASE 2–1

Analysis of Colgate's Statements

Answer the following questions using the annual report of **Colgate** in **Colgate** Appendix A.

a. Who is responsible for the preparation and integrity of Colgate's financial statements and notes? Where is this responsibility stated in the annual report?

b. In which note does Colgate report its significant accounting policies used to prepare financial statements?

c. What type of audit opinion is reported in its annual report and whose opinion is it?

d. Is any of the information in its annual report based on estimates? If so, where does Colgate discuss this?

CASE 2–2

Industry Accounting and Analysis: Historical Case

Two potential methods of accounting for the cost of oil drilling are full cost and successful efforts. Under the *full-cost method,* a drilling company capitalizes costs both for successful wells and dry holes. This means it classifies all costs as assets on its balance sheet. A company charges these costs against revenues as it extracts and sells the oil. Under the *successful-efforts method,* a company expenses the costs of dry holes as they are incurred, resulting in immediate charges against earnings. Costs of only successful wells are capitalized. Many small and midsized drilling companies use the full-cost method and, as a result, millions of dollars of drilling costs appear as assets on their balance sheets.

The SEC imposes a limit to full-cost accounting. Costs capitalized under this method cannot exceed a ceiling defined as the present value of company reserves. Capitalized costs above the ceiling are expensed. Oil companies, primarily smaller ones, have been successful in prevailing on the SEC to keep the full-cost accounting method as an alternative even though the accounting profession took a position in favor of the successful-efforts method. Because the imposition of the ceiling rule occurred during a time of relatively high oil prices, the companies accepted it, confident that it would have no practical effect on them.

With a subsequent decline in oil prices, many companies found that drilling costs carried as assets on their balance sheets exceeded the sharply lower ceilings. This meant they were faced with write-offs. Oil companies, concerned about the effect that big write-offs would have on their ability to conduct business, began a fierce lobbying effort to change SEC accounting rules so as to avoid sizable write-offs that threatened to lower their earnings as well as their equity capital. The SEC staff supported a suspension of the rules because, they maintained, oil prices could rise and because companies would still be required to disclose the difference between the market value and book value of their oil reserves. The proposal would have temporarily relaxed the rules pending the results of a study by the SEC on whether to change or rescind the ceiling test. The proposal would have suspended the requirement to use current prices when computing the ceiling amount in determining whether a write-off of reserves is required. The SEC eventually rejected the proposal that would have enabled 250 of the nation's oil and gas producing companies to postpone write-downs on the declining values of their oil and gas reserves while acknowledging that the impact of the decision could trigger defaults on bank loans. The SEC chairman said "the rules are not stretchable at a time of stress."

Tenneco Co. found a way to cope with the SEC's refusal to sanction postponement of the write-offs. It announced a switch to successful-efforts accounting along with nearly $1 billion in charges against prior years' earnings. In effect, Tenneco would take the unamortized dry-hole drilling costs currently on its balance sheet and apply them against prior years' revenues. These costs would affect prior year results only and would not show up as write-offs against currently reported income.

Required:

a. Discuss what conclusions an analyst might derive from the evolution of accounting in the oil and gas industry.

b. Explain the potential effect Tenneco's proposed change in accounting method would have on the reporting of its operating results over the years.

Canada Steel Co. produces steel casting and metal fabrications for sale to manufacturers of heavy construction machinery and agricultural equipment. Early in Year 3, the company's president sent the following memorandum to the financial vice president:

CASE 2–3^B

Earnings Quality and Accounting Changes

TO: Robert Kinkaid, Financial Vice President
FROM: Richard Johnson, President
SUBJECT: Accounting and Financial Policies

Fiscal Year 2 was a difficult year for us, and the recession is likely to continue into Year 3. While the entire industry is suffering, we might be hurting our performance unnecessarily with accounting and business policies that are not appropriate. Specifically:

(1) We depreciate most fixed assets (foundry equipment) over their estimated useful lives on the "tonnage-of-production" method. Accelerated methods and shorter lives are used for income tax purposes. A switch to straight-line for financial reporting purposes could (a) eliminate the deferred tax liability on our balance sheet, and (b) leverage our profits if business picks up in Year 4.

(2) Several years ago you convinced me to change from the FIFO to LIFO inventory method. Since inflation is now down to a 4 percent annual rate, and balance sheet strength is important in our current environment, I estimate we can increase shareholders' equity by about $2.0 million, working capital by $4.0 million, and Year 3 earnings by $0.5 million if we return to FIFO in Year 3. This adjustment is real—these profits were earned by us over the past several years and should be recognized.

(3) If we make the inventory change, our stock repurchase program can be continued. The same shareholder who sold us 50,000 shares last year at $100 per share would like to sell another 20,000 shares at the same price. However, to obtain additional bank financing, we must maintain the current ratio at 3:1 or better. It seems prudent to decrease our capitalization if return on assets is unsatisfactory and our industry is declining. Also, interest rates are lower (11 percent prime) and we can save $60,000 after taxes annually once our $3.00 per share dividend is resumed.

These actions would favorably affect our profitability and liquidity ratios as shown in the *pro forma* income statement and balance sheet data for Year 3 ($ millions).

	Year 1	Year 2	Year 3 Estimate
Net sales	$50.6	$42.3	$29.0
Net income (loss)	$ 2.0	$ (5.7)	$ 0.1
Net profit margin	4.0%	—	0.3%
Dividends	$ 0.7	$ 0.6	$ 0.0
Return on assets	7.2%	—	0.4%
Return on equity	11.3%	—	0.9%
Current assets	$17.6	$14.8	$14.5
Current liabilities	$ 6.6	$ 4.9	$ 4.5
Long-term debt	$ 2.0	$ 6.1	$ 8.1
Shareholders' equity	$17.7	$11.4	$11.5
Shares outstanding (000s)	226.8	170.5	150.5
Per common share:			
Book value	$78.05	$66.70	$76.41
Market price range	$42–$34	$65–$45	$62–$55*

*Year to date.

Please give me your reaction to my proposals as soon as possible.

Required

Assume you are Robert Kinkaid, the financial vice president. Appraise the president's rationale for each of the proposals. You should place special emphasis on how each accounting or business decision affects earnings quality. Support your response with ratio analysis.

CHECK
Sig. incr. in debt-to-equity

3

ANALYZING FINANCING ACTIVITIES

∎∎∎∎∎∎∎

A LOOK BACK `<`

Chapters 1 and 2 presented an overview of financial statement analysis and financial reporting. We showed how financial statements report on financing, investing, and operating activities. We also introduced accounting analysis and explained its importance for financial statement analysis.

A LOOK AT THIS CHAPTER `•`

This chapter describes accounting analysis of financing activities— both creditor and equity financing. Our analysis of creditor financing considers both operating liabilities and financing liabilities. Analysis of operating liabilities includes extensive study of postretirement benefits. Analysis of financing liabilities focuses on topics such as leasing and off-balance-sheet financing, along with conventional forms of debt financing. We also analyze components of equity financing and the relevance of book value.

A LOOK AHEAD `>`

Chapters 4 and 5 extend our accounting analysis to investing activities. We analyze operating assets such as current assets and property, plant, and equipment, along with investments in securities and intercorporate acquisitions. Chapter 6 analyzes operating activities.

ANALYSIS OBJECTIVES

- Identify and assess the principal characteristics of liabilities and equity.

- Analyze and interpret lease disclosures and explain their implications and the adjustments to financial statements.

- Analyze postretirement disclosures and assess their consequences for firm valuation and risk.

- Analyze contingent liability disclosures and describe their risks.

- Identify off-balance-sheet financing and its consequences to risk analysis.

- Analyze and interpret liabilities at the edge of equity.

- Explain capital stock and analyze and interpret its distinguishing features.

- Describe retained earnings and their distribution through dividends.

Post-Enron World of SPEs

Enron used a financing technique called special purpose entities (SPEs) to conceal hundreds of millions of dollars of debt from investors and to avoid recognition of losses from its investments. These entities were thinly capitalized *shell companies*. Enron utilized SPEs purchase assets at inflated prices, which allowed it to prop up earnings.

Even worse, Enron used SPEs as counterparties for hedging activities. Those SPEs issued guarantees to Enron to protect its investments from a value decline. Since the SPEs were so thinly capitalized and were managed by Enron executives, Enron was essentially insuring itself.

For the most part, SPEs have been used for decades as a legitimate financing technique and are very much in use today. Many retailers, for example, sell private label credit card receivables to an SPE that purchases them with funds raised from the sale of

> **Effects of FIN 46 on Costs and Viability of SPEs Are Yet Unclear.**

bonds to the investing public. Investors receive a quality investment and the company receives immediate cash. More generally, SPEs are an important financing tool for companies such as Target, Capital One, General Motors, Citigroup, and Dell.

However, Enron's failure and the resulting losses to investors prompted cries for stricter regulation. Congress responded with the Sarbanes-Oxley Act, and the FASB with FIN 46. FIN 46 has far-reaching effects as it requires consolidation of certain SPEs with the sponsoring company (deemed to be the "primary beneficiary"). This yields financial statements that reflect both the sponsoring company and its set of SPEs.

Abuses, such as those perpetrated by Enron, are less likely under these new accounting rules. Still, their effects on the viability and costs of SPEs as a legitimate financing tool are yet unclear.

PREVIEW OF CHAPTER 3

Business activities are financed with either liabilities or equity, or both. **Liabilities** are financing obligations that require future payment of money, services, or other assets. They are outsiders' claims against a company's present and future assets and resources. Liabilities can be either financing or operating in nature and are usually senior to those of equity holders. **Financing liabilities** are all forms of credit financing such as long-term notes and bonds, short-term borrowings, and leases. **Operating liabilities** are obligations that arise from operations such as trade creditors, and postretirement obligations. Liabilities are commonly reported as either **current** or **noncurrent**–usually based on whether the obligation is due within one year or not. **Equity** refers to claims of owners on the net assets of a company. Claims of owners are junior to creditors, meaning they are residual claims to all assets once claims of creditors are satisfied. Equity holders are exposed to the maximum risk associated with a company but also are entitled to all residual returns of a company. Certain other securities, such as convertible bonds, straddle the line separating liabilities and equity and represent a hybrid form of financing. This chapter describes these different forms of financing, how companies account and report for them, and their implications for analysis of financial statements.

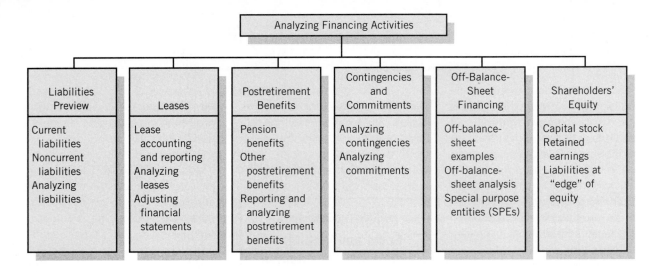

········LIABILITIES

We describe both current and noncurrent liabilities in this section. We also discuss their implications to financial statement analysis.

Current Liabilities

Current (or **short-term**) **liabilities** are obligations whose settlement requires the use of current assets or the incurrence of another current liability. The period over which companies expect to settle current liabilities is the longer of one year or the operating cycle. Conceptually, companies should record all liabilities at the present value of the cash outflow required to settle them. In practice, current liabilities are recorded at their maturity value, and not their present value, due to the short time period until their settlement.

■ ■ ■ ■ ■ ■ ■
DEBT CLASS
Improper classification of liabilities can affect key ratios in financial analysis.

Current liabilities are of two types. The first type arises from operating activities and includes taxes payable, unearned revenues, advance payments, accounts payable, and other accruals of operating expenses, such as wages payable. The second type of current liabilities arises from financing activities and includes short-term borrowings, the current portion of long-term debt, and interest payable.

Many borrowing agreements include covenants to protect creditors. In the event of default, say in the maintenance of a specified financial ratio such as the debt-to-equity ratio, the indebtedness becomes immediately due and payable. Any long-term debt in default must, therefore, be reclassified as a current liability. A violation of a noncurrent debt covenant does not require reclassification of the noncurrent liability as current provided that the lender waives the right to demand repayment for more than a year from the balance sheet date.

WR Grace (2004 10-K) provides an example of the treatment of debt for a bankrupt company:

ANALYSIS EXCERPT

Plan of Reorganization. All of the Debtors' pre-petition debt is in default due to the Filing. The accompanying Consolidated Balance Sheets reflect the classification of the Debtors' pre-petition debt within "liabilities subject to compromise."

Accounting Impact. The accompanying Consolidated Financial Statements have been prepared in accordance with Statement of Position 90-7 ("SOP 90-7"), "Financial Reporting by Entities in Reorganization Under the Bankruptcy Code." SOP 90-7 requires that financial statements of debtors-in-possession be prepared on a going concern basis, which contemplates continuity of operations, realization of assets and liquidation of liabilities in the ordinary course of business. However, as a result of the Filing, the realization of certain of the Debtors' assets and the liquidation of certain of the Debtors' liabilities are subject to significant uncertainty. Pursuant to SOP 90-7, Grace's pre-petition liabilities that are subject to compromise are required to be reported separately on the balance sheet at an estimate of the amount that will ultimately be allowed by the Bankruptcy Court. . . . Such pre-petition liabilities include fixed obligations (such as debt and contractual commitments), as well as estimates of costs related to contingent liabilities (such as asbestos-related litigation, environmental remediation, and other claims).

Noncurrent Liabilities

Noncurrent (or **long-term**) **liabilities** are obligations that mature in more than one year (or the operating cycle if longer than one year). They include loans, bonds, debentures, and notes. Noncurrent liabilities can take various forms, and their assessment and measurement requires disclosure of all restrictions and covenants. Disclosures include interest rates, maturity dates, conversion privileges, call features, and subordination provisions. They also include pledged collateral, sinking fund requirements, and revolving credit provisions. Companies must disclose defaults of any liability provisions, including those for interest and principal repayments.

A bond is a typical noncurrent liability. The bond's par (or face) value along with its coupon (contract) rate determines cash interest paid on the bond. Bond issuers some-

times sell bonds at a price either below par (at a discount) or in excess of par (at a premium). The discount or premium reflects an adjustment of the bond price to yield the market's required rate of return. A discount is amortized over the life of the bond and increases the effective interest rate paid by the borrower. Conversely, any premium is also amortized but it decreases the effective interest rate incurred.

Frequencies of Noncurrent Liabilities

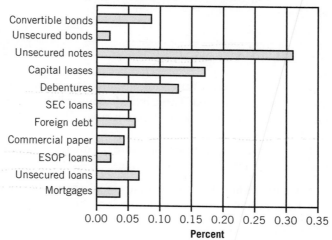

Percent

Standard setters are contemplating radical changes to the manner in which long-term debt (specifically bonds) will be reported on the balance sheet. Instead of reporting bond values at amortized cost, bonds will be reported at their respective fair values (i.e. at their market values) on the balance sheet date (see Chapter 2 for a discussion of fair value accounting). All changes in bond values will be flowed through the income statement. As a major step toward reporting financial assets and liabilities at fair value, the FASB recently issued *SFAS 159* (known as the "fair value option" standard), which allows companies to voluntarily start recognizing all or any subset of its long-term debt at fair value. It is too early to tell how this fair value option will affect the financial statements. However, Chapter 5 features a more detailed discussion of this issue.

One troubling issue that arises when long-term debt is measured at fair value is that the value of a company's reported long-term debt will *decrease* when the company's credit standing worsens (this is because decreased creditworthiness will lower the market values of bonds). This reduction in reported bond values will create *income* for the company. The justification that FASB provides for this peculiar effect is that a reduction in a company's credit standing will occur only if there is a substantial reduction in the fair value of the company's assets. This reduction in assets' fair value will cause a substantial loss during the period. Offsetting this loss through income created by decrease in fair value of debt will correctly reflect the share of losses borne by the equity and debt holders. This logic is illustrated in Illustration 3.1.

Illustration 3.1
■ ■ ■ ■ ■ ■ ■

Consider a company that has $100 million in assets funded by $50 million each of debt and equity. The company suffers a major downturn in its business during the period. Because of this, the fair value of its assets drops down to $40 million. Note that because of limited liability, equity holders cannot be liable for more than their investment in the firm of $50 million. Consequently, debt holders will have to incur a $10 million loss in value. Consequently, the market value of the company's debt drops to $40 million. The economics of this situation is correctly reflected in financial statements prepared on a fair value basis as shown below:

Opening Balance Sheet		Closing Balance Sheet		Income Statement	
Assets	$ 100	Assets	$ 40	Asset impairment loss	$ (60)
	100		40	Decrease in bond value	10
Debt	50	Debt	40	Income	$ (50)
Equity	50	Equity	0		
	$ 100		$ 40		

■ ■ ■ ■ ■ ■ ■

CONVERTIBLES

In the past decade, convertible bonds yielded about 80% of the return of stock funds but with only 65% of the price volatility.

Bond issuers offer a variety of incentives to promote the sale of bonds and reduce the interest rate required. These include convertibility features and attachments of warrants to purchase the issuer's common stock. We refer to this offer as a *convertible debt sweetener.*

Disclosure is also required for future payments on long-term borrowings and for any redeemable stock. This would include:

- Maturities and any sinking funds requirements for each of the next five years.
- Redemption requirements for each of the next five years.

Examples of disclosures for long-term liabilities are in Note 19 of the financial statements of Campbell Soup in Appendix A.

Analysis Research
■■■■■■■

ACCOUNTING-BASED
LIABILITY RESTRICTIONS

Do all bonds offer holders the same degree of security for safeguarding their investments? Are all bonds of equal risk? How might we choose among bonds with identical payment schedules and coupon rates? Analysis research on liabilities provides us with some insight into these questions. Namely, bonds are not of equal risk, and an important factor of this risk relates to restrictions, or lack thereof, in liability agreements. Creditors establish liability restrictions (or covenants) to safeguard their investments. These restrictions often limit management behavior that might harm the interests of creditors. Violating any restriction

is usually grounds for "technical default," providing creditors' legal grounds to demand immediate repayment. Liability restrictions can reduce creditors' risk exposure.

Restrictions on management behavior take many forms, including:

- Dividend distribution restrictions.
- Working capital restrictions.
- Debt-to-equity ratio restrictions.
- Seniority of asset claim restrictions.
- Acquisition and divestment restrictions.
- Liability issuance restrictions.

These restrictions limit the dilution of net assets by constraining management's ability to distribute assets

to new or continuing shareholders, or to new creditors. Details of these restrictions are often available in a liability's prospectus, a company's annual report, SEC filings, and various creditor information services (e.g., *Moody's Manuals*). Many restrictions are in the form of accounting-based constraints. For example, dividend payment restrictions are often expressed in the form of a minimum level of retained earnings that companies must maintain. This means the selection and application of accounting procedures are, therefore, potentially affected by the existence of liability restrictions.

Analyzing Liabilities

Auditors are one source of assurance in our identification and measurement of liabilities. Auditors use techniques like direct confirmation, review of board minutes, reading of contracts and agreements, and questioning of those knowledgeable about company obligations to satisfy themselves that companies record all liabilities. Another source of assurance is double-entry accounting, which requires that for every asset, resource, or cost acquired, there is a counterbalancing entry for the obligation or resource expended. However, there is *no* entry required for most commitments and contingent liabilities. In this case, our analysis often must rely on notes to financial statements and on management commentary in annual reports and related documents. We also can check on the accuracy and reasonableness of debt amounts by reconciling them to a company's disclosures for interest expense and interest paid in cash. Any significant unexplained differences require further analysis or management explanation.

When liabilities are understated, we must be aware of a likely overstatement in income due to lower or delayed expenses. The SEC censure of various companies reinforces financial statement users' concerns with full disclosure of liabilities as described here:

> **ANALYSIS EXCERPT**
>
> The SEC determined Ampex failed to fully disclose (1) its obligations to pay royalty guarantees totaling in excess of $80 million; (2) its sales of substantial amounts of prerecorded tapes that were improperly accounted for as "degaussed," or erased, to avoid payment of royalty fees; (3) income overstatements from inadequate allowances for returned tapes; and (4) multimillion dollar understatements in both its allowance for doubtful accounts receivable and its provisions for losses from royalty contracts.

We must also analyze the descriptions of liabilities along with their terms, conditions, and encumbrances. Results of this analysis can impact our assessments of both risk and return for a company. Exhibit 3.1 lists some important features we should review in an analysis of liabilities.

Exhibit 3.1
■ ■ ■ ■ ■ ■ ■

Important Features in Analyzing Liabilities

- Terms of indebtedness (such as maturity, interest rate, payment pattern, and amount).
- Restrictions on deploying resources and pursuing business activities.
- Ability and flexibility in pursuing further financing.
- Obligations for working capital, debt to equity, and other financial figures.
- Dilutive conversion features that liabilities are subject to.
- Prohibitions on disbursements such as dividends.

Minimum disclosure requirements as to debt provisions vary, but we should expect disclosure of any breaches in loan provisions that potentially limit a company's activities or increase its risk of insolvency. Accordingly, we must be alert to any explanations or qualifications in the notes or in an auditor's report such as the following from American Shipbuilding:

ANALYSIS EXCERPT

The credit agreement was amended . . . converting the facility from a revolving credit arrangement to a demand note. Under the amended agreement, the Company is required to satisfy specified financial conditions and is also required to liquidate its indebtedness to specified maximum limits . . . the Company had satisfied all these requirements except for the working capital covenant. Subsequent to that date, the Company has not maintained its compliance as to maximum indebtedness. In addition, the tangible net worth requirement was not met. . . . The Company has given notices to the agent bank of its failure to satisfy these requirements. . . . In addition to the restrictions described above, this credit facility places restrictions on the Company's ability to acquire or dispose of assets, make certain investments, enter into leases and pay dividends . . . the credit agreement disallowed the payment of dividends.

We wish to foresee problems such as these. One effective tool for this purpose is a comparative analysis of the terms of indebtedness with the *margin of safety*. Margin of safety refers to the extent to which current compliance exceeds minimum requirements.

■ ■ ■ ■ ■ ■ ■ LEASES

Leasing is a popular form of financing, especially in certain industries. A **lease** is a contractual agreement between a *lessor* (owner) and a *lessee* (user). It gives a lessee the right to use an asset, owned by the lessor, for the term of the lease. In return, the lessee makes rental payments, called *minimum lease payments* (or MLP). Lease terms obligate the lessee to make a series of payments over a specified future time period. Lease contracts can be complex, and they vary in provisions relating to the lease term, the transfer of ownership, and early termination.[1] Some leases are simply extended rental contracts, such as a two-year computer lease. Others are similar to an outright sale with a built-in financing plan, such as a 50-year lease of a building with automatic ownership transfer at the end of the lease term.

The two alternative methods for lease accounting reflect the differences in lease contracts. A lease that transfers substantially all the benefits and risks of ownership is accounted for as an asset acquisition and a liability incurrence by the lessee. Similarly, the lessor treats such a lease as a sale and financing transaction. This type of lease is called a **capital lease.** If classified as a capital lease, both the leased asset and the lease obligation are recognized on the balance sheet. All other types of leases are accounted for as **operating leases.** In the case of operating leases, the lessee (lessor) accounts for the minimum lease payment as a rental expense (revenue), and no asset or liability is recognized on the balance sheet.

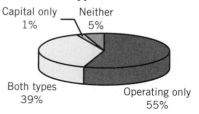

Frequencies of Different Lease Types—Lessee

- Capital only 1%
- Neither 5%
- Both types 39%
- Operating only 55%

Lessees often structure a lease so that it can be accounted for as an operating lease even when the economic characteristics of the lease are more in line with a capital lease. By doing so, a lessee is engaging in off-balance-sheet financing. *Off-balance-sheet financing* refers to the fact that neither the leased asset nor its corresponding liability are recorded on the balance sheet when a lease is accounted for as an operating lease even though many of the benefits and risks of ownership are transferred to the lessee. The decision to account for a lease as a capital or operating lease can significantly impact financial statements. Analysts must take care to examine the economic characteristics of a company's leases and recast them in their analysis of the company when necessary.

Leasing has grown in frequency and magnitude. Estimates indicate that almost one-third of plant asset financing is in the form of leasing. Leasing is the major form of financing plant assets in the retail, airline, and trucking industries. Lease financing is popular for several reasons. For one, sellers use leasing to promote sales by providing financing to buyers. Interest income from leasing is often a major source of revenue to those sellers. In turn, leasing often is a convenient means for a buyer to finance its asset purchases. Tax considerations also play a role in leasing. Namely, overall tax payments can be reduced when ownership of the leased asset rests with the party in the higher marginal tax bracket. Moreover, as described, leasing can be a source of off-balance-sheet financing. Used in this way, leasing is said to *window-dress* financial statements.

Our discussion of lease financing for the lessee begins with an explanation of the effects of lease classification on both the income statement and balance sheet. Next, we analyze lease disclosures with reference to those of Best Buy. We then provide a method for recasting operating leases as capital leases for analysis purposes when the economic characteristics support it. Our discussion also examines the impact of lease classification on financial statements and the importance of recasting leases for financial statement analysis. We limit our discussion to the analysis of leases for the lessee. Appendix 3A provides an overview of lease accounting and analysis for the lessor.

---

[1] Some leases are cancellable, but the majority of the long-term leases are noncancellable. The power of the lessee to cancel the lease is an important factor determining the economic substance of the lease. We focus discussion on noncancellable leases.

Accounting and Reporting for Leases
Lease Classification and Reporting

A lessee (the party leasing the asset) classifies and accounts for a lease as a capital lease if, at its inception, the lease meets *any* of four criteria: (1) the lease transfers ownership of the property to the lessee by the end of the lease term; (2) the lease contains an option to purchase the property at a bargain price; (3) the lease term is 75% or more of the estimated economic life of the property; or (4) the present value of the minimum lease payments (MLPs) at the beginning of the lease term is 90% or more of the fair value of the leased property. A lease can be classified as an operating lease only when *none* of these criteria are met. Companies often effectively structure leases so that they can be classified as operating leases.

When a lease is classified as a capital lease, the lessee records it (both asset and liability) at an amount equal to the present value of the minimum lease payments over the lease term (excluding *executory costs* such as insurance, maintenance, and taxes paid by the lessor that are included in the MLP). The leased asset must be depreciated in a manner consistent with the lessee's normal depreciation policy. Likewise, interest expense is accrued on the lease liability, just like any other interest-bearing liability. In accounting for an operating lease, however, the lessee charges rentals (MLPs) to expense as they are incurred; and no asset or liability is recognized on the balance sheet.

The accounting rules require that all lessees disclose, usually in notes to financial statements: (1) future minimum lease payments separately for capital leases and operating leases for each of the five succeeding years and the total amount thereafter and (2) rental expense for each period that an income statement is reported.

Accounting for Leases—An Illustration

This section compares the effects of accounting for a lease as either a capital or an operating lease. Specifically, we look at the effects on both the income statement and the balance sheet of the lessee given the following information:

- A company leases an asset on January 1, 2005–it has no other assets or liabilities.
- Estimated economic life of the leased asset is five years with an expected salvage value of zero at the end of five years. The company will depreciate this asset on a straight-line basis over its economic life.
- The lease has a fixed noncancellable term of five years with annual minimum lease payments of $2,505 paid at the end of each year.
- Interest rate on the lease is 8% per year.

We begin the analysis by preparing an amortization schedule for the leased asset as shown in Exhibit 3.2. The initial step in preparing this schedule is to determine the present (market) value of the leased asset (and the lease liability) on January 1, 2005. Using the interest tables near the end of the book, the present value is $10,000 (computed as 3.992 × $2,505). We then compute the interest and the principal amortization for each year. Interest equals the beginning-year liability multiplied by the interest rate (for year 2005 it is $10,000 × 0.08). The principal amount is equal to the total payment less interest (for year 2005 it is $2,505 − $800). The schedule reveals the interest pattern mimics that of a fixed-payment mortgage with interest decreasing over time as the principal balance decreases. Next we determine depreciation. Because this company uses straight line, the depreciation expense is $2,000 per year (computed as $10,000/5 years). We now have the necessary information to examine the effects of this lease transaction

Lease Amortization Schedule　　　　　　　　　　　　　　　　　　　　　　　　*Exhibit 3.2*

■ ■ ■ ■ ■ ■ ■ ■

Year	Beginning-Year Liability	INTEREST AND PRINCIPAL COMPONENTS OF MLP			Year-End Liability
		Interest	Principal	Total	
2005..............$10,000		$ 800	$ 1,705	$ 2,505	$8,295
2006............... 8,295		664	1,841	2,505	6,454
2007............... 6,454		517	1,988	2,505	4,466
2008............... 4,466		358	2,147	2,505	2,319
2009............... 2,319		186	2,319	2,505	0
Totals		$2,525	$10,000	$12,525	

on both the income statement and balance sheet for the two alternative lease accounting methods.

Let's first look at the effects on the income statement. When a lease is accounted for as an operating lease, the minimum lease payment is reported as a periodic rental expense. This implies a rental expense of $2,505 per year for this company. However, when a lease is accounted for as a capital lease, the company must recognize both periodic interest expense (see the amortization schedule in Exhibit 3.2) and depreciation expense ($2,000 per year in this case). Exhibit 3.3 summarizes the effects of this lease transaction on the income statement for these two alternative methods. Over the entire five-year period, total expense for both methods is identical. But, the capital lease method reports more expense in the earlier years and less expense in later years. This is due to declining interest expense over the lease term. Consequently, net income under the capital lease method is lower (higher) than under the operating lease method in the earlier (later) years of a lease.

We next examine the effects of alternative lease accounting methods on the balance sheet. First, let's consider the operating lease method. Because this company

Income Statement Effects of Alternative Lease Accounting Methods　　　　　*Exhibit 3.3*

■ ■ ■ ■ ■ ■ ■ ■

Year	OPERATING LEASE Rent Expense	CAPITAL LEASE		
		Interest Expense	Depreciation Expense	Total Expense
2005...........$ 2,505		$ 800	$ 2,000	$ 2,800
2006........... 2,505		664	2,000	2,664
2007........... 2,505		517	2,000	2,517
2008........... 2,505		358	2,000	2,358
2009........... 2,505		186	2,000	2,186
Totals..........$12,525		$2,525	$10,000	$12,525

Exhibit 3.4

■ ■ ■ ■ ■ ■ ■

Balance Sheet Effects of Capitalized Leases

Month/Day/Year	Cash	Leased Asset	Lease Liability	Equity
1/1/2005 ....$	0	$10,000	$10,000	$ 0
12/31/2005	(2,505)	8,000	8,295	(2,800)
12/31/2006	(5,010)	6,000	6,454	(5,464)
12/31/2007	(7,515)	4,000	4,466	(7,981)
12/31/2008	(10,020)	2,000	2,319	(10,339)
12/31/2009	(12,525)	0	0	(12,525)

does not have any other assets or liabilities, the balance sheet under the operating lease method shows zero assets and liabilities at the beginning of the lease. At the end of the first year, the company pays its MLP of $2,505, and cash is reduced by this amount to yield a negative balance. Equity is reduced by the same amount because the MLP is recorded as rent expense. This process continues each year until the lease expires. At the end of the lease, the cumulative amount expensed, $12,525 (as reflected in equity), is equal to the cumulative cash payment (as reflected in the negative cash balance). This amount also equals the total MLP over the lease term as seen in Exhibit 3.2.

Let's now examine the balance sheet effects under the capital lease method (see Exhibit 3.4). To begin, note the balance sheet at the end of the lease term is identical under both lease methods. This result shows that the net accounting effects under the two methods are identical by the end of the lease. Still, there are major yearly differences before the end of the lease term. Most notable, at the inception of the lease, an asset and liability equal to the present value of the lease ($10,000) is recognized under the capital lease method. At the end of the first year (and every year), the negative cash balance reflects the MLP, which is identical under both lease methods—recall that alternative accounting methods do not affect cash flows. For each year of the capital lease, the leased asset and lease liability are not equal, except at inception and termination of the lease. These differences occur because the leased asset declines by the amount of depreciation ($2,000 annually), while the lease liability declines by the amount of the principal amortization (for example, $1,705 in year 2005, per Exhibit 3.2). The decrease in equity in year 2005 is $2,800, which is the total of depreciation and interest expense for the period (see Exhibit 3.3). This process continues throughout the lease term. Note the leased asset is always lower than the lease liability during the lease term. This occurs because accumulated depreciation at any given time exceeds the cumulative principal reduction.

This illustration reveals the important impacts that alternative lease accounting methods can have on financial statements. While the operating lease method is simpler, the capital lease method is conceptually superior, both from a balance sheet and an income statement perspective. From a balance sheet perspective, capital lease accounting recognizes the benefits (assets) and obligations (liabilities) that arise from a lease transaction. In contrast, the operating lease method ignores these benefits and obligations and fully reflects these impacts only by the end of the lease term. This means the balance sheet under the operating lease method fails to reflect the lease assets and obligations of the company.

Lease Disclosures

Accounting rules require a company with capital leases to report both leased assets and lease liabilities on the balance sheet. Moreover, all companies must disclose future lease commitments for both their capital and noncancellable operating leases. These disclosures are useful for analysis purposes.

We will analyze the lease disclosures in the Best Buy Co., Inc., 2004 annual report. As of its year-end, and despite the use of leasing as a financing alternative for many of its retail locations, Best Buy reports a capital lease liability of only $16 million (versus $5.23 billion in total liabilities) on its balance sheet. As a result, only a small portion of its leased properties are recorded on the balance sheet. Exhibit 3.5 reproduces the leasing footnote from the annual report and is typical of leasing disclosures. Best Buy

---

Lease Disclosures of Best Buy   Exhibit 3.5

Lease Commitments

We lease portions of our corporate facilities and conduct the majority of our retail and distribution operations from leased locations. The leases require payment of real estate taxes, insurance and common area maintenance, in addition to rent. Most of the leases contain renewal options and escalation clauses, and certain store leases require contingent rents based on specified percentages of revenue. Other leases contain convenants related to the maintenance of financial ratios. Transaction costs associated with the sale and lease back of properties and any related gain or loss are recognized over the period of the lease agreements. Proceeds from the sale and lease back of properties are included in other current assets. Also, we lease certain equipment under noncancellable operating and capital leases. The terms of our lease agreements generally range up to 20 years.

During fiscal 2004, we entered into a capital lease agreement totaling $26 for point-of-sale equipment used in our retail stores. This lease was a noncash transaction and has been eliminated from our Consolidated Statement of Cash Flows. The composition of rental expenses for all operating leases, net of sublease rental income, during the past three fiscal years, including leases of property and equipment, was as follows:

($ millions)	2004	2003	2002
Minimum rentals	$467	$439	$366
Contingent rentals	1	1	1
Total rent expense for continuing operations	$468	$440	$367

The future minimum lease payments under our capital and operating leases, net of sublease rental income, by fiscal year (not including contingent rentals) as of February 28, 2004, are as follows ($ millions):

Fiscal Year	Capital Leases	Operating Leases
2005	$14	$ 454
2006	3	424
2007	—	391
2008	—	385
2009	—	379
Thereafter	—	2,621
Subtotal	17	
Less: imputed interest	(1)	
Present value of capital lease obligations	$16	

leases portions of its corporate offices, essentially all of its retail locations, a majority of its distribution facilities, and some of its equipment. Lease terms generally range up to 20 years. In addition to rental payments, the leases also require Best Buy to pay executory costs (real estate taxes, insurance, and maintenance). It is important to note that, in the present value computations that follow, only the minimum lease payments over the base lease term (not including renewal options), and not the executory costs, are considered.

The company classifies the vast majority of its leases as operating and provides a schedule of future lease payments in its notes to the financial statements. Best Buy will make $454 million in payments on its leases in 2005, $424 million in 2006, and so on.

Analyzing Leases

This section looks at the impact of operating versus capital leases for financial statement analysis. It gives specific guidance on how to adjust the financial statements for operating leases that should be accounted for as capital leases.

Impact of Operating Leases

While accounting standards allow alternative methods to best reflect differences in the economics underlying lease transactions, this discretion is too often misused by lessees who structure lease contracts so that they can use the operating lease method. This practice reduces the usefulness of financial statements. Moreover, because the proportion of capital leases to operating leases varies across companies, lease accounting affects our ability to compare different companies' financial statements.

Lessees' incentives to structure leases as operating leases relate to the impacts of operating leases versus capital leases on both the balance sheet and the income statement. These impacts on financial statements are summarized as follows:

- Operating leases understate liabilities by keeping lease financing off the balance sheet. Not only does this conceal liabilities from the balance sheet, it also positively impacts solvency ratios (such as debt to equity) that are often used in credit analysis.
- Operating leases understate assets. This can inflate both return on investment and asset turnover ratios.
- Operating leases delay recognition of expenses in comparison to capital leases. This means operating leases overstate income in the early term of the lease but understate income late in the lease term.
- Operating leases understate current liabilities by keeping the current portion of the principal payment off the balance sheet. This inflates the current ratio and other liquidity measures.
- Operating leases include interest with the lease rental (an operating expense). Consequently, operating leases understate both operating income and interest expense. This inflates interest coverage ratios such as times interest earned.

The ability of operating leases to positively affect key ratios used in credit and profitability analysis provides a major incentive for lessees to pursue this source of off-balance-sheet financing. Lessees also believe that classifying leases as operating leases helps them meet debt covenants and improves their prospects for additional financing.

Analysis Research
■ ■ ■ ■ ■ ■ ■

MOTIVATIONS FOR LEASING

Finance theory suggests that leases and debt are perfect substitutes. However, there is little empirical evidence supporting this *substitution hypothesis*. Indeed, evidence appears to contradict this hypothesis. Namely, companies with leases carry a higher proportion of additional debt financing than those without leases. This gives rise to the so-called leasing puzzle. Further, there is considerable variation across companies on the extent of leasing as a form of financing. What then are the motivations for leasing?

One answer relates to taxes. Ownership of an asset provides the holder with tax benefits. This suggests that the entity with the *higher* marginal tax rate would hold ownership of the asset to take advantage of

greater tax benefits. The entity with the *lower* marginal tax would lease the asset. Empirical evidence supports this tax hypothesis. Other economic factors that motivate leasing include (1) an expected use period that is less than the asset's economic life, (2) a lessor that has an advantage in reselling the asset or has market power to force buyers to lease, and (3) an asset that is not specialized to the company or is not sensitive to misuse.

Financial reporting factors also explain the popularity of leasing over other forms of debt financing. While financial accounting and tax reporting need not be identical, use of operating leases for financial reports creates unnecessary obstacles when claiming capital lease benefits

for tax purposes. This explains the choice of capital leasing for some financial reports. Still, the choice of operating leasing seems largely dictated by managers' preference for off-balance-sheet financing. Capital leasing yields deterioration in solvency ratios and creates difficulties in raising additional capital. For example, there is evidence that capital leasing increases the tightness of debt covenants and, therefore, managers try to loosen debt covenants with operating leases. While there is some evidence that private debt agreements reflect different lease accounting choices, the preponderance of the evidence suggests that creditors do not fully compensate for alternative lease accounting methods.

Because of the impacts from lease classification on financial statements and ratios, an analyst must make adjustments to financial statements prior to analysis. Many analysts convert all operating leases to capital leases. Others are more selective. We suggest reclassifying leases when necessary and caution against indiscriminate adjustments. Namely, we recommend reclassification only when the lessee's classification appears inconsistent with the economic characteristics of the lease as explained next.

Converting Operating Leases to Capital Leases

This section provides a method for converting operating leases to capital leases. The specific steps are illustrated in Exhibit 3.6 using data from Best Buy's leasing note. It must be emphasized that while this method provides reasonable estimates, it does not precisely quantify all the effects of lease reclassification for financial statements.

The first step is to assess whether or not Best Buy's classification of operating leases is reasonable. To do this, we must estimate the length of the remaining period beyond the five years disclosed in the notes–titled "Thereafter" in the Best Buy notes of Exhibit 3.5. Specifically, we divide the reported MLP for the later years by the MLP for the last year that is separately reported. For Best Buy, we divide the total MLP for the later years of $2.621 billion (for its 2004 operating leases) by the MLP reported in 2009, or $379 million, to arrive at 6.9 years beyond 2004. Adding this number to the five years already reported gives us an estimate of about 12 years for the remaining lease term. These results suggest a need for us to reclassify Best Buy's operating leases as capital leases–that is, its 12-year commitment for operating leases is too long to ignore. In

Exhibit 3.6

■■■■■■■

Determining the Present Value of Projected Operating Lease Payments and Lease Amortization ($ millions)

Year	Payment	Discount Factor	Present Value	Interest	Lease Obligation	Lease Balance
2004						$3,321
2005	$ 454	0.94518	$ 429	$193	$261	3,060
2006	424	0.89336	379	178	246	2,814
2007	391	0.84439	330	163	228	2,586
2008	385	0.79810	307	150	235	2,351
2009	379	0.75435	286	136	243	2,108
2010	379	0.71299	270	122	257	1,851
2011	379	0.67390	255	107	272	1,579
2012	379	0.63696	241	92	287	1,292
2013	379	0.60204	228	75	304	988
2014	379	0.56904	216	57	322	666
2015	379	0.53784	204	39	340	326
2016	347	0.50836	176	21	326	0
Totals	$4,654		$3,321			

particular, whenever the remaining lease period (commitments) is viewed as significant, we need to capitalize the operating leases.

To convert operating leases to capital leases, we need to estimate the present value of Best Buy's operating lease liability. The process begins with an estimate of the interest rate that we will use to discount the projected lease payments. Determining the interest rate on operating leases is challenging. For companies that report both capital and operating leases, we can estimate the implicit interest rate on the capital leases and assume operating leases have a similar interest rate. The implicit rate on capital leases can be inferred by trial and error and is equal to that interest rate that equates the projected capital lease payments with the present value of the capital leases, both of which are disclosed in the leasing footnote.

Two problems can arise when inferring the interest rate from capital lease disclosures. First, it is impossible to use this method for companies that do report capital lease details. In such a case, we need to determine the yield on the company's long-term debt or debt with a similar risk profile and then use it as a proxy for the interest rate on operating leases. A second problem can arise when the interest rates on capital and operating leases are markedly different (this can arise when operating and capital leases are entered into at different times when the interest rates are different). In this scenario, we need to adjust the capital lease interest rate to better reflect the interest rate on operating leases.

Best Buy's bond rating is BBB, which results in an effective 10-year borrowing cost of about 5.8% in 2005. For the example that follows, we use 5.8% as a discount rate to determine the present value of the projected operating lease payments. This analysis is presented in Exhibit 3.6. Lease payments for 2005–2009 are provided in the leasing footnote as required. The estimated payments after 2009 are assumed equal to the 2009 payment and continue for the next seven years with a final lease payment of $347 million in the 12th year (2016). Discounting these projected lease payments at 5.8% yields a present value of $3.321 billion. This is the amount that should be added to Best Buy's reported liabilities.

The next step in our analysis is to compute the value of the operating lease asset. Recall that the asset value of a capital lease is always lower than its corresponding liability, but how much lower is difficult to estimate because it depends on the length of the lease term, the economic life of the asset, and the lessee's depreciation policy. Consequently, for analysis of operating leases, we assume that the leased asset value is equal to the estimated liability. For Best Buy, this means both the leased asset and lease liability are estimated at $3.321 billion for 2004. We also can split the operating lease liability into its current and noncurrent components of $261 million and $3.06 billion, respectively.

Once we determine the operating lease liability and asset, we then must estimate the impact of lease reclassification on reported income. There are two expenses relating to capitalized leases—interest and depreciation. Interest expense is determined by applying the interest rate to the present value of the lease (the lease liability). For Best Buy, this is estimated at $193 million for 2005, or 5.8% of $3.321 billion (see Exhibit 3.6). Depreciation expense is determined by dividing the value of the leasehold asset by the remaining lease term. Assuming no residual value, depreciation of the $3.321 billion in leased assets on a straight-line basis over the 12-year remaining lease term yields an annual depreciation expense of $277 million. Total expense, then, is estimated at $470 million ($193 million + $277 million) for 2005, compared with $454 million in projected rent expense, an increase of $16 million pretax.

Restating Financial Statements for Lease Reclassification

Exhibit 3.7 shows the restated balance sheet and income statement for Best Buy before and after operating lease reclassification using the results in Exhibit 3.6. The operating lease reclassification has a limited effect on Best Buy's 2004 income statement. Using

---

Restated Balance Sheet after Converting Operating Leases to Capital Leases— Best Buy 2004 ($ millions)

Exhibit 3.7

Income Statement	Before	After
Sales	$24,547	$24,547
Operating expenses	23,243	23,066
Operating income before interest and taxes	1,304	1,481
Interest expense (income)	8	201
Income taxes	496	490
Income from continuing operations	800	790
Discontinued operations	(95)	(95)
Net income	$ 705	$ 695

Balance Sheet	Before	After		Before	After
Current assets	$5,724	$ 5,724	Current liabilities	$4,501	$ 4,762
Fixed assets	2,928	6,249	Long-term liabilities	729	3,789
			Stockholders' equity	3,422	3,422
Total assets	$8,652	$11,973	Total liabilities and equity	$8,652	$11,973

Exhibit 3.8

■ ■ ■ ■ ■ ■ ■

Effect of Converting Operating Leases to Capital Leases on Key Ratios—Best Buy 2004

Financial Ratios	Before	After
Current ratio...................................	1.27	1.20
Total debt to equity.........................	1.53	2.50
Long-term debt to equity...............	0.21	1.11
Net income/Ending equity..............	20.6%	20.3%
Net income/Ending assets..............	8.1%	5.8%
Times interest earned.....................	163.0	7.37

the calculations for 2005 depreciation and interest expense from Exhibit 3.6, Best Buy's 2004 income statement can be recast as follows:

- Operating expenses decrease by $177 million (elimination of $454 million rent expense reported in 2004 and addition of $277 million of depreciation expense)[2]
- Interest expense increases by $193 million (to $201 million)
- Net income decreases by $10 million [$16 million pretax $\times$ (1 − .35), the assumed marginal corporate tax rate] in 2004.

The balance sheet impact is more substantial. Total assets and total liabilities both increase markedly–by $3.321 billion at the end of 2004, which is the present value of the operating lease liability. The increase in liabilities consists of increases in both current liabilities ($261 million) and noncurrent liabilities ($3.06 billion).

Exhibit 3.8 shows selected ratios for Best Buy before and after lease reclassification. The current ratio slightly declines from 1.27 to 1.20. However, reclassification adversely affects Best Buy's solvency ratios. Total debt to equity increases by 65% to 2.50, and the long-term debt to equity ratio jumps from 0.21 to 1.11. Best Buy's interest coverage (times interest earned ratio) decreases from 163.0 (because it is recording minimal interest expense prior to the reclassification) to 7.37, but remains very strong even after the operating lease adjustment.

Return on ending equity is largely unaffected because of the small change in after-tax income (meaning equity is not markedly affected by reclassification). Profitability components, however, are significantly affected. Return on ending assets decreases from 8.1% to 5.8% due to the increase in reported assets and its consequent effect on total asset turnover. Financial leverage has increased to offset this decrease, leaving return on equity unchanged. Although ROE is unaffected, our inferences about how this return is achieved are different. Following lease capitalization, Best Buy is seen as requiring significantly more capital investment (resulting in lower turnover ratios), and is realizing its ROE as a result of a higher level of financial leverage than was apparent from its unadjusted financial statements.

---

[2] The $454 million of rent expense that is eliminated in this example is not equal to the $468 million of rent expense reported for 2004 in Best Buy's leasing footnote (Exhibit 3.5). Replacing the actual rent expense would result in a more accurate elimination of current rent expense, but would result in inequality between the rent expense that is eliminated from operating expense and the depreciation and interest components that replace it. An alternative approach is to eliminate from current operating expense the projected minimum lease payments in the lease disclosures from the prior year and to replace that amount with the projected depreciation and interest components computed as of the beginning of the year. This approach also does not eliminate the current rent expense and, instead, presumes that only the minimum lease payment (MLP) that is projected for the current year be eliminated under the assumption that the actual expense includes contingent rentals that are not relevant for analysis. Implementation of this approach requires the capitalization of the leased asset and liability for both the opening and the closing balance sheets, and, thus, requires examination of the lease footnote from both the prior and current years. All approaches have strengths and weaknesses and all rely on some estimation, not only relating to the amount of rent expense eliminated, but also with respect to the discount rate used to compute the capitalized leased asset and liability.

Analysis Research
■ ■ ■ ■ ■ ■ ■

OPERATING LEASES AND RISK

Analysis research encourages capitalizing noncancellable operating leases. The main impact of capitalizing these operating leases is an increase in the debt to equity and similar ratios with a corresponding increase in the company's risk assessment. An important question is whether off-balance-sheet operating leases actually do increase risk. Research has examined this question by assessing the effect of operating leases on *equity risk*, defined as variability in stock returns. Evidence shows that the present value of noncapitalized operating leases increases equity risk from its impact on both the debt to equity ratio and the variability of return on assets (ROA).

Analysis research also shows that only the present value of future MLPs impacts equity risk. Further, it shows that the contingent fee included in rental payments is not considered by analysts. This evidence favors the lease capitalization method adopted by accounting standards, instead of an alternative method that involves multiplying the lease rental payments by a constant.

▪▪▪▪▪▪▪POSTRETIREMENT BENEFITS

Employers often provide benefits to their employees after retirement. These **postretirement benefits** come in two forms: (1) **pension benefits,** where the employer promises monetary benefits to the employee after retirement, and (2) **other postretirement employee benefits (OPEB),** where the employer provides other (usually nonmonetary) benefits after retirement–primarily health care and life insurance. Both types of benefits pose conceptually similar challenges for accounting and analysis. Current accounting standards require that the costs of providing postretirement benefits be recognized when the employee is in active service, rather than when the benefits are actually paid. The estimated present value of accrued benefits is reported as a liability for the employer. Because of the uncertainty regarding the timing and magnitude of these benefits, postretirement costs (and liabilities) need to be estimated based on *actuarial assumptions* regarding life expectancy, employee turnover, compensation growth rates, health care costs, expected rates of return, and interest rates.

Pensions and other postretirement benefits make up a major part of many companies' liabilities. Moreover, pensions constitute a large portion of the economy's savings and investments. Current estimates are that pension plans, with assets exceeding $4 trillion cover nearly 50 million individuals. Also, pension funds control about 25% of the value of NYSE stocks, and account for nearly one-third of daily trading volume. While somewhat smaller in magnitude, OPEB, in particular health care costs, is also an important component of companies' employee costs. About one-third of U.S. workers participate in postretirement health care plans, with a total unfunded liability in the $2 trillion range. Both pension and OPEB liabilities are likely to grow because of changing demographics and increased life expectancy.

Pension plans have been in the news over the past several years. During the early part of this decade, falling interest rates and the bear market resulted in a perfect storm for pension plans, resulting in what was dubbed the "pensions crisis." The pension plans of many companies became severely underfunded, and in a number of cases (e.g., United Airlines), companies filed for bankruptcy stating that it was not possible for them to meet their pension obligations. Pension accounting (under the old standard, *SFAS 87*) was implicated in precipitating this crisis by not highlighting this problem on a timely basis. Accordingly, the FASB has reformed pension accounting and recently passed a new standard (*SFAS 158*) to, at least in part, fix the problems with pension accounting.

We first explain the accounting for pensions and other postretirement benefits separately, and then jointly discuss disclosure requirements and analysis implications.

Pension Benefits

Pension accounting requires an understanding of the economics underlying pension transactions. Consequently, we first discuss the nature of pension transactions and the economics underlying pension accounting before discussing pension accounting requirements.

Nature of Pension Obligations

Pension commitments by companies are formalized through pension plans. A **pension plan** is an agreement by the employer to provide pension benefits to the employee, and it involves three entities: the employer, who contributes to the plan; the employee, who derives benefits; and the pension fund. The **pension fund** is independent of the employer and is administered by *trustees*. The pension fund receives contributions, invests them in an appropriate manner, and disburses pension benefits to employees. This pension plan process is diagrammed in Exhibit 3.9.

Exhibit 3.9	**Elements of the Pension Process**

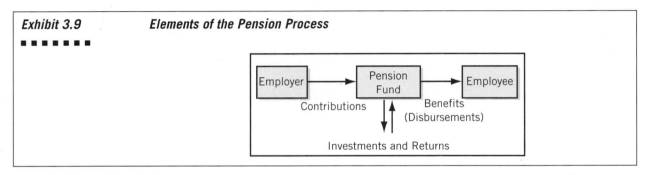

Pension plans precisely specify the benefits and the rights and responsibilities of the employer and employee. Pension plans can be divided into two basic categories. **Defined benefit** plans specify the amount of pension *benefits* that the employer promises to provide to retirees. Under defined benefit plans, the *employer* bears the risk of pension fund performance. **Defined contribution** plans specify the amount of pension *contributions* that the employer makes to the pension plan. In this case, the actual amount of pension benefits to retirees depends on the pension fund performance. Under defined contribution plans, the *employee* bears the risk of pension fund performance.

In both plans, employee benefits are usually determined through a formula linked to employee wages. Defined contribution plans *immediately* obligate the employer to pay some fixed proportion of the employees' current compensation, whereas defined benefit plans require the employer to periodically pay the employee a predetermined sum of money *after retirement* until the employee's death.

Pension payments are also affected by vesting provisions. **Vesting** is an employee's right to pension benefits regardless of whether the employee remains with the company or not. This right is usually conferred after the employee has served some minimum specified period with the employer.

Once the pension liability is determined, **funding** the expense becomes a managerial decision for defined benefit plans that is influenced by legal and tax considerations. Tax law specifies minimum funding requirements to ensure the security of retirees' benefits. It also has tax deductibility limitations for overfunded pension plans. Minimum

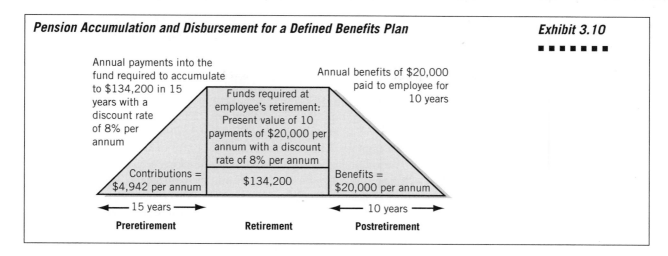

Pension Accumulation and Disbursement for a Defined Benefits Plan   *Exhibit 3.10*

funding requirements also exist under the Employee Retirement Income Security Act (ERISA). A company has the option to fund the plan exactly (by providing assets to the plan trustee that equal the pension liability) or it can overfund or underfund the plan.

We focus attention on defined benefit plans because of the challenge they pose to analysis of financial statements.[3] Exhibit 3.10 depicts the time line for a simple defined benefit plan. This case involves a single employee who is expected to retire in 15 years and is paid an annual fixed pension of $20,000 for 10 years after retirement. The discount (interest) rate is assumed to be 8% per year. We also assume the employer exactly funds the plan. While a simplification, this exhibit reflects the economics underlying defined pension plans. These plans involve current investments by the employer for future payments of benefits to the employee. The challenges for accounting are estimating the employer's pension plan liability and determining the pension expense (cost) for the period, which is different from the funding (actual contributions made) by the employer. For this purpose, accountants rely on assumptions made by specialists known as actuaries.

Economics of Pension Accounting

The challenge in accounting for defined benefit plans is that accounting estimates of liabilities and expenses need to be created for cash payments that may occur many years into the future. We will briefly discuss the underlying economic issues that affect pension accounting. Appendix 3B provides a detailed explanation of pension accounting with a comprehensive example.

Refer back to the example in Exhibit 3.10. If the employer needs to pay $20,000 per year for 10 years after retirement, he or she needs to have funds to the tune of $134,200 on the date of retirement. How do we arrive at this sum? It is the present value of $20,000 paid each year for the next 10 years at a discount (interest) rate of 8%. (Refer to Table 4 of the "Interest Tables" at the rear of this book for details of how to compute the present value of an annuity). Therefore, the employer's obligation (or liability) on the date of retirement is $134,200. We can extend this logic to determine the employer's obligation during the prior 15 years. For example, what is the employer's obligation at the start of the accumulation period, that is, 15 years before retirement? It is $42,305, which is the present value of $134,200 payable 15 years hence discounted at 8% per year. (Refer to Table 2 of the "Interest Tables" at the rear of this book for how to

---

[3] Accounting for, and analysis of, defined contribution plans is straightforward. That is, the periodic contribution by the employer is recognized as an expense in the period when it is due. There are no other liabilities of serious note.

compute present value). Therefore, the employer's liability at the start of the 15-year accumulation period is $42,305. We refer to this as the **pension obligation.**

Now consider what happens a year later. At the start of the second year (which is also the end of the first year), the employer's pension obligation has increased to $45,690, which is the present value of $134,200 due 14 years later. Note that the pension obligation has increased by $3,655 ($45,960 − $42,305) because of passage of time; we refer to this increase in the pension obligation as the **interest cost.** Meanwhile the employer has made **contributions** of $4,942 into the plan (see Exhibit 3.10). Because these contributions are invested in the capital markets, we refer to these contributed (and invested) funds as the **plan assets.** The net obligation of the employer, therefore, is $41,018, which is the difference between the pension obligation ($45,960) and the plan assets ($4,942). We refer to the net assets of the pension plan (i.e., Plan assets − Pension obligation) as the **funded status.** Because the obligation is more than the asset value, the plan is said to be *underfunded.* If the asset value exceeds the obligation, the funded status is said to be *overfunded.*

Now examine what happens yet another year later, that is, after two years of accumulation. The pension obligation is now $49,345 (present value of $134,200 payable in 13 years), resulting in interest cost for the year of $3,385. What about the employer's plan assets? Two events happen on the assets' side. First, the employer makes another contribution of $4,942. Second, the contribution made at the end of the first year earns a return of $395 (8% × $4,942). We call this return the **return on plan assets.**[4] Therefore, the plan assets at the end of the second year are equal to $10,279 ($4,942 + $4,942 + $395) and the funded status is now underfunded to the tune of $39,066 ($49,345 − $10,279). From an accounting point, it is evident that the funded status of $39,066 should appear as a liability in the balance sheet. What about the income statement effect? The net **pension cost** for the year is $2,990 (interest cost of $3,385 less return on plan assets of $395).

In reality, of course, pension plans are much more complex than that depicted in this example. For example, pension benefits payable to employees in typical defined benefit plans are proportional to the years of service that the employee puts with the employer. Because of this, the employer's obligation increases with every additional year of employee service (independent of the present value effect represented by interest cost), giving rise to another component of the pension cost called **service cost.** Service cost is the most important component of pension cost because pension costs arise only through employee service, in the absence of employee service, there is no obligation to pay pensions.

Additionally, the actuarial assumptions underlying the computation of the pension obligation–there are many, such as discount or interest rate, compensation growth rates, life expectancy, employee turnover–are subject to change, giving rise to large swings in the value of the pension obligation. These changes give rise to nonrecurring components of pension cost called **actuarial gain or loss.** To complicate matters further, pension contracts are renegotiated with employees, resulting in retroactive benefits, which give rise to another type of nonrecurring expense called **prior service cost.** Finally, it should be noted that returns on capital markets can be volatile, and therefore the actual return on plan assets can fluctuate over time. For all these reasons, the true economic pension cost can be volatile over time. As we will see later, much of the complexity in pension accounting arises from attempts to dampen volatility in the pension cost included in net income.

Finally, we need to understand how actual cash inflows and outflows from the plan affect the funded status. The major cash inflow into the plan comes through **employer**

---

[4] For simplicity, in this example we assume that the return on plan assets is equal to the discount rate. In reality, the return on plan assets can differ from the discount rate (usually the long-term return on plan assets is higher than the discount rate).

contributions, which understandably increase plan asset values. The major cash outflows from the plan are **benefit payments** to retired employees. Benefit payments reduce both plan assets (because cash has been paid from the plan assets) and the pension obligation (because part of the promised payments to the employees have been made) by exactly the same amount. Therefore, benefit payments do not affect the net funded status of the plan.

Pension Accounting Requirements

The basic framework for pension accounting under GAAP was first specified under standard *SFAS 87*. The focus of *SFAS 87* was obtaining a stable and permanent measure of pension expense. Accordingly, the pension expense included in net income—called the **net periodic pension cost**—smoothed volatile components of the pension cost (such as actuarial gains/losses, prior service cost or actual returns on plan asset) by delaying their recognition through a process of deferral and amortization. To articulate the balance sheet with the income statement, *SFAS 87* recognized merely the cumulative net periodic pension cost (termed *accrued* or *prepaid* pension cost) on the balance sheet instead of the plan's funded status. Because of this, pensions (and OPEBs) were a major source of off-balance-sheet liabilities (or assets, as the case may be). *SFAS 87* was severely criticized for this reason. Responding to criticism, the FASB recently issued *SFAS 158*, which reports the actual funded status of the pension plan on the balance sheet. The pension expense included in net income, however, remains *SFAS 87's* net periodic pension cost. The difference between the economic pension cost (which includes the volatile components) and the net periodic pension cost (which is the smoothed version specified under *SFAS 87*) is included in *other comprehensive income* for the period, which accumulates as *accumulated other comprehensive income*, which is part of shareholders' equity. Exhibit 3.11 provides an overview of current pension accounting under *SFAS 158*. However, the reader is encouraged to refer to Appendix 3B for a deeper understanding of pension accounting.

Recognized Status on the Balance Sheet.   Current pension accounting *(SFAS 158)* recognizes the funded status of the pension plans on the balance sheet. The funded status is the difference between the current market value of the pension plan assets and the pension obligation. The pension obligation definition used is the **projected benefit obligation** or PBO. The PBO is based on *estimated* employee compensation at the retirement date (rather than current compensation), which is estimated using assumptions regarding compensation growth rates. Refer to Appendix 3B for details of PBO computation. Two details need to be noted with regard to reported status on the balance sheet. First, pension assets and obligations are netted against each other (as funded status) rather than separately reported both as an asset and a corresponding liability. Second, companies do not report the funded status of pension plans as a separate line item on the balance sheet. Instead, the funded status is embedded in various assets and liabilities.

Recognized Pension Cost.   As noted earlier, the recognized pension cost included in net income (i.e., the **net periodic pension cost**) is a smoothed version of the actual economic pension cost for the period. The smoothing process, *defers* (i.e., delays recognizing) volatile, one-time items such as actuarial gains or losses and prior service cost. Also, instead of recognizing the actual return on plan assets (which can be volatile), an **expected return on plan assets**—which is an estimate of the long-term return on the plan assets—is recognized in reported pension expense. The difference between the actual and expected return is also deferred. These deferred amounts are gradually recognized in income through a process of amortization. Accordingly, the net periodic

Exhibit 3.11   ***Overview of Pension Economics and Accounting***

■ ■ ■ ■ ■ ■ ■

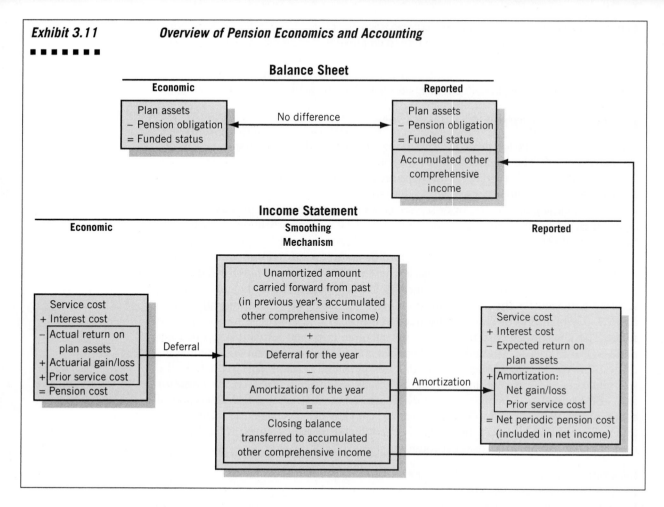

pension cost includes service cost, interest cost, expected return on plan assets and amortization of deferred items.

Articulation of Balance Sheet and Income Statement Effects.   Because all changes to the funded status (which is recognized in the balance sheet) are not included in the recognized pension cost, the balance sheet and income statement effects of pensions will not articulate. To articulate the two effects, the **net deferral** for the period (i.e., the amount deferred less the amount amortized) is included in *other comprehensive income* for the period, while the **cumulative net deferral** is included in *accumulated other comprehensive income,* which is a component of shareholders' equity. Therefore, the smoothing process adopted by current pension accounting *(SFAS 158)* allows the volatile components of pension expense to directly transfer to shareholder's equity without affecting the period's net income.

Accounting under *SFAS 87*.   The current pension rules under *SFAS 158* became operational only from late 2006 onward. Prior to that, pension accounting requirements were specified under *SFAS 87.* Because *SFAS 158* is so recent, it is important for analysts to have some idea of *SFAS 87.* The accounting treatment under *SFAS 87* and *SFAS 158* are identical but for one major difference. Like *SFAS 158, SFAS 87* also recognizes the smoothed net periodic pension cost in income. However, unlike *SFAS 158, SFAS 87* did not recognize the funded status on the balance sheet. Instead, the earlier standard merely recognizes the accumulated net periodic pension cost on the balance sheet as **accrued or**

prepaid pension cost.[5] In other words, the net deferrals that *SFAS 158* includes in accumulated other comprehensive income are altogether kept off the balance sheet under *SFAS 87*.

Other Postretirement Employee Benefits

Other postretirement employee benefits (OPEB) are certain other benefits provided by employers to retirees and their designated dependents. The primary constituent of OPEB is health care benefits. In addition, companies provide life insurance and, in rare cases, housing assistance. The underlying economics and the accounting treatment for OPEB are very similar to that for pensions–*SFAS 158* governs the accounting for both pensions and OPEB. Specifically, as with pensions, (1) OPEB costs are recognized when incurred rather than when actually paid out; (2) assets of the OPEB plan are offset against the OPEB obligation, and returns from these assets are offset against OPEB costs; and (3) actuarial gains and losses, prior service costs, and the excess of actual return over expected return on plan assets are deferred and subsequently amortized.

While OPEBs pose accounting challenges similar to those posed by pensions, there are some major differences. One difference is funding. Both because no legal requirements exist for OPEB (in contrast with ERISA requirements for pensions) and because funding them is not tax deductible (unlike pension contributions, which are), few companies specifically fund these postretirement liabilities. While companies back these obligations with assets on their balance sheets, the OPEB fund's trustees have no control over these assets. Another major difference is that OPEBs are often in the form of promised *services,* such as health care benefits, rather than monetary compensation. Accordingly, estimating these benefit obligations is especially difficult and requires a different set of actuarial assumptions. For example, trends in health care cost and the extent of Medicare usage affect estimates of health care obligations.

Other than these economic differences, OPEB accounting is directly similar to pension accounting. The balance sheet recognizes the funded status, which is the difference between the OPEB obligation and any plan assets specifically designated to meet this obligation. The OPEB obligation is called the **accumulated postretirement benefit obligation** (APBO). The OPEB cost included in net income is termed the **net periodic postretirement cost** and includes service cost, interest cost, expected return on plan assets and amortization of deferred amounts, exactly as in the case of pensions. Also, the cumulative net deferrals are included in accumulated other comprehensive income. Refer to Appendix 3B for more details regarding OPEB accounting.

Reporting of Postretirement Benefits

Reporting requirements for postretirement benefits (pensions and OPEBs) are specified in *SFAS 158*, which prescribes similar disclosure formats for both OPEBs and pension benefits. Companies rarely report as separate line items either the funded status in the balance sheet or the postretirement benefit cost in the income statement. However, the standard mandates extensive disclosures in footnotes, including details about economic and reported amounts relating to the funded status and the postretirement benefit cost, details about actuarial assumptions, and other relevant information.

Exhibit 3.12 shows excerpts from the postretirement benefits footnote in the 2006 annual report of AMR Corporation (American Airlines). AMR reports details for

■ ■ ■ ■ ■ ■ ■
HEALTH GAIN
Technology affects postretirement benefit assumptions. For example, life expectancy at birth in the Western world grew from 45 years in 1900 to over 75 years in 2000.

---

[5] *SFAS 87* does recognize an ad hoc amount in other accumulated comprehensive income called the additional minimum pension liability. However, to keep things simple, we shall ignore this element in our analysis.

Exhibit 3.12   *Excerpts from Post Retirement Benefits Footnote—AMR Corporation*

■ ■ ■ ■ ■ ■ ■

The following table provides a reconciliation of the changes in the pension and OPEB obligations and fair value of plan assets for the years ended December 31, 2006 and 2005 and a statement of funded status on those dates ($ millions):

	PENSION		OPEB	
	2006	2005	2006	2005
Change in benefit obligation:				
Benefit obligation at January 1	$11,003	$10,022	$ 3,384	$ 3,303
Service cost	399	372	78	75
Interest cost	641	611	194	197
Plan amendments (prior service cost)			(27)	
Actuarial (gains) losses	(390)	649	(212)	(12)
Benefits payments	(605)	(651)	(161)	(179)
Benefit obligation at December 31	$11,048	$11,003	$ 3,256	$ 3,384
Change in plan assets:				
Fair value of plan assets at January 1	$ 7,778	$ 7,335	$ 161	$ 151
Actual return on plan assets	1,063	779	31	11
Employer contributions	329	315	171	178
Benefits paid	(605)	(651)	(161)	(179)
Fair value of plan assets at December 31	$ 8,565	$ 7,778	$ 202	$ 161
Funded status of plan	$(2,483)	$(3,225)	$ (3,054)	$(3,223)
Less unrecognized amounts:				
Prior service cost		$ (169)		$ 60
Net gain (loss)		(2,174)		(299)
Additional minimum liability		1,381		
Amount recognized in balance sheet	$ (2,483)	$ (2,263)	$ (3,054)	$ (2,984)
Current liability	$ (8)	$ (251)	$ (187)	
Long term liability	(2,475)	(2,012)	(2,867)	$ (2,984)
	$ (2,483)	$ (2,263)	$ (3,054)	$ (2,984)
Amounts recognized in accumulated other comprehensive income (loss):				
Prior service credit (cost)	$ (153)		$ 77	
Net gain (loss)	(1,310)		(70)	
Additional minimum liability		$ (1,381)		
	$ (1,463)	$ (1,381)	$ 7	

The following table provides components of the net periodic benefit cost for the years ended December 31, 2006, 2005, and 2004 ($ millions)

	PENSION			OPEB		
	2006	2005	2004	2006	2005	2004
Service cost	$ 399	$ 372	$ 358	$ 78	$ 75	$ 75
Interest cost	641	611	567	194	197	202
Expected return on plan assets	(669)	(658)	(569)	(15)	(14)	(11)
Amortization of prior service cost	16	16	14	(10)	(10)	(10)
Amortization of net (gain) loss	80	51	57	1	2	8
Net periodic benefit cost	$ 467	$ 392	$ 427	$248	$ 250	$ 264

(continued)

Excerpts from Post Retirement Benefits Footnote—AMR Corporation *(concluded)* ■ ■ ■ ■ ■ ■ ■

	PENSION		OPEB	
	2006	**2005**	**2006**	**2005**
Weighted Average Actuarial Assumptions				
Discount rate	6.00%	5.75%	6.00%	5.75%
Compensation growth rate	3.78%	3.78%	3.78%	3.78%
Expected return on plan assets	8.75%	9.00%	8.75%	9.00%
Health care cost trend			9.00%	4.50%

	OPEB Obligation		OPEB Reported Cost	
	Increase	Decrease	Increase	Decrease
Impact of 1% change in assumed health care rate ($ million)	243	(236)	26	(24)

As of December 31, 2006, the Company's estimate of the long-term rate of return on plan assets was 8.75% based on the target asset allocation. Expected returns on longer duration bonds are based on yields to maturity of the bonds held at year-end. Expected returns on other assets are based on a combination of long-term historical returns, actual returns on plan assets achieved over the last 10 years, current and expected market conditions, and expected value to be generated through active management, currency overlay, and securities lending programs. The Company's annualized 10-year rate of return on plan assets as of December 31, 2006, was approximately 11.8%.

The Company's pension plan weighted-average asset allocations at December 31, by asset category are as follows:

	2006	**2005**	**Target**
Long-duration bonds	37%	37%	40%
U.S. stocks	30%	31%	25%
International stocks	21%	21%	20%
Emerging market stocks	6%	6%	5%
Alternative (private) investments	6%	5%	10%
	100%	100%	100%

Each asset class is actively managed and the plans' assets have produced returns, net of management fees, in excess of the expected rate of return over the last 10 years. Stocks and emerging market bonds are used to provide diversification and are expected to generate higher returns over the long-term than longer duration U.S. bonds. Public stocks are managed using a value investment approach in order to participate in the returns generated by stocks in the long-term, while reducing year-over-year volatility. Longer duration U.S. bonds are used to partially hedge the assets from declines in interest rates. Alternative (private) investments are used to provide expected returns in excess of the public markets over the long term. Additionally, the Company engages currency overlay managers in an attempt to increase returns by protecting non-U.S.-dollar denominated assets from a rise in the relative value of the U.S. dollar. The Company also participates in securities lending programs in order to generate additional income by loaning plan assets to borrowers on a fully collateralized basis.

The Company expects to contribute approximately $364 million to its defined benefit pension plans and $13 million to its OPEB plan in 2007. In addition to making contributions to its OPEB, the Company funds the majority of the benefit payments under this plan. This estimate reflects the provisions of the Pension Funding Equity Act of 2004 and the Pension Protection Act of 2006.

The following is an estimate of future benefit payments, that also reflect future service: ($ million)

	2007	**2008**	**2009**	**2010**	**2011**	**2012–2016**
Pension	$ 543	$ 584	$ 689	$ 681	$ 662	$ 3,843
OPEB	187	196	204	214	223	1,163

both pensions and OPEBs in identical formats. The note consists of five main parts: (1) an explanation of the reported position in the balance sheet, (2) details of net periodic benefit costs, (3) information regarding actuarial and other assumptions, (4) information regarding asset allocation and funding policies, and (5) expected future contributions and benefit payments. Recognize that while a single set of numbers is reported for pension and for OPEB plans, in reality these numbers are aggregations of many different plans. Also note that while the 2006 numbers are prepared in accordance with the latest pension standard *(SFAS 158)*, the 2005 numbers are presented using the earlier standard *(SFAS 87)*. We shall primarily limit our discussion to the pension plans and refer to the OPEB disclosures only occasionally.

The information regarding reported position in the balance sheet, comprises two main parts. The first part explains movement in the benefit obligation and plan assets and the determination of the funded status at the end of the year. The second part comprises details of how the pension plan's funded status is reported in the balance sheet. In 2006, AMR reports funded status of $2,483 million underfunded for pension plans. This is exactly the amount recognized in the balance sheet. In 2005, however, the amount recognized in the balance sheet of $2,263 million underfunded is different from the funded status of $3,225 million underfunded. This difference is explained by certain items that are unrecognized (i.e., kept off the balance sheet) under *SFAS 87:* cumulative net deferrals of $2,343 million, comprising $169 million prior service cost and $2,174 million net gain/loss, and an additional minimum liability of $1,381 million.[6] (Note that net (gain) loss is the sum of actuarial gains/losses and the difference between actual and expected return on plan assets that are added together and deferred collectively.) In 2006, cumulative net deferrals are reported under "amounts recognized in accumulated other comprehensive income (loss)," totaling to $1,463 million ($153 million prior service cost plus $1,310 million net gain/loss). By recognizing the cumulative net deferral in accumulated other comprehensive income, *SFAS 158* articulates the amounts on the balance sheet and income statement without having to keep items off the balance sheet as SFAS 87 did. Finally, notice that the net pension obligation is primarily included as part of long-term liabilities in the balance sheet.

The beginning and ending funded status are reconciled through explanation of changes to both the obligation and the plan assets. The change in pension obligation is explained by economic recurring and nonrecurring costs less benefits paid. In 2006, AMR's gross pension cost (Service cost + Interest cost − Actuarial gain) increased the pension obligation by $650 million. The pension obligation decreased by the amount of benefits paid ($605 million), resulting in a net increase of $45 million (from $11,003 million to $11,048 million). Turning to the plan assets, AMR's actual return on the pension assets was $1,063 million. In addition AMR contributed $329 million to the pension plan. However, $605 million of benefits were paid out, resulting in a net increase of $787 million (from $7,778 million to $8,565 million) in plan assets. The increase in the obligation of $45 million was more than offset by the increase in plan assets of $787 million, resulting in a net improvement in funded status by $742 million (from $3,225 million underfunded to $2,483 million underfunded).

The information reported for OPEBs is similar to that for pensions. The only noteworthy difference is that unlike with pensions, the OPEB plans are very significantly underfunded (plan assets of $202 million compared to an obligation of $3,256 million). Most companies do not fund the OPEB obligation because there is no legal requirement to do so.

---

[6] The additional minimum postretirement liability is an ad hoc adjustment under *SFAS 87*. Because this issue is irrelevant under the new standard *(SFAS 158)*, we shall ignore this item in our future discussion.

AMR also explains how the net periodic benefit cost (i.e., the reported cost) for both pensions and OPEBs is computed. As illustrated in Exhibit 3.11, reported pension (and OPEB) costs include recurring costs (service cost and interest cost), less the *expected* return on plan assets plus amortization of deferred nonrecurring items. In 2004, AMR's service and interest cost for pension plans are $399 million and $641 million, respectively, while its expected return on pension plan assets is $669 million. There are two amortization items: prior service cost of $16 million and net (gain) loss of $80 million. The net periodic pension (benefit) cost for 2006 is $467 million. This is the amount that is charged to the year's income, although it does not appear as a separate line item on the income statement. The periodic benefit cost for OPEBs is determined in a similar manner.

The footnote also provides a host of additional qualitative and quantitative information. We begin by examining some of the important actuarial assumptions underlying the computation of the pension and the OPEB benefit obligations and periodic benefit cost. In 2006, AMR increased its assumption regarding discount rate to 6% (from 5.75%), maintained its compensation growth assumption at 3.78%, and reduced its expected return on plan assets to 8.75% (from 9%). Finally, AMR doubled its assumption regarding health care cost trend rate to 9% in 2006 (from 4.5% in 2005). The note also provides sensitivity analysis regarding how changes in the health care cost trend assumption would affect the OPEB obligation and the reported OPEB cost. Finally, the note provides explanations for AMR's actuarial assumption choices.

The next section of the footnote provides information about AMR's plan asset allocations. AMR allocates 37% of its portfolio to bonds and 57% to equity securities, of which 27% are allocated to international markets. Finally, 6% of its assets comprise private investments. The target allocations are 40% bonds, 50% equity securities, and 10% alternative (private) investments. Therefore, the current allocation appears to overweight equity investments compared to the target allocation. AMR also provides some description of how it manages its investments and notes that its actual investment returns have exceeded expectations.

The final part of the note provides information regarding AMR's anticipated contributions and estimated benefit payments. For example, AMR expects to contribute $364 million ($13 million) to its pension (OPEB) plans in 2007. In addition, a table of anticipated benefit payments over the next 10 years is provided. AMR's anticipated benefit payments over the next 10 years is expected to be more than $7 billion for pensions and more than $2 billion for OPEBs.

Analyzing Postretirement Benefits

Analysis of postretirement benefit disclosures is an important task, both because of the magnitude of these obligations and because of the complexity of the accounting. We provide a five-step procedure for analyzing postretirement benefits: (1) determine and reconcile the reported and economic benefit cost and liability (or asset), (2) make necessary adjustments to financial statements, (3) evaluate actuarial assumptions and their effects on financial statements, (4) examine pension risk exposure, and (5) consider the cash flow implications of postretirement benefit plans.

Reconciling Economic and Reported Numbers

Exhibit 3.13 provides reconciliation between economic and reported benefit costs separately for pensions, OPEBs, and in total. The economic pension cost for AMR is an *income* of $413 million, largely because of the $1,063 million actual return on assets and the $390 million actuarial gain. In comparison, reported pension cost (included in net

Exhibit 3.13   *Reconciling Economic and Reported Numbers—AMR Corporation*

■ ■ ■ ■ ■ ■ ■

Economic and Reported Postretirement Cost–2006

$ million	PENSION Economic	PENSION Net Deferral	PENSION Reported	OPEB Economic	OPEB Net Deferral	OPEB Reported	TOTAL Economic	TOTAL Net Deferral	TOTAL Reported
Service cost	$ 399		$ 399	$ 78		$ 78	$ 477		$ 477
Interest cost	641		641	194		194	835		835
Return on plan assets	(1,063)	$ (394)	(669)	(31)	$ (16)	(15)	(1,094)	$ (410)	(684)
Actuarial (gain) loss	(390)	(390)		(212)	(212)		(602)	(602)	
Plan amendment (PSC)					(27)			(27)	
Amortization:									
Net gain/loss		(80)	80		(1)	1		(81)	81
Prior service cost		(16)	16		10	(10)		(6)	6
Total	$ (413)	$ (880)	$ 467	$ 29	$ (246)	$ 248	$ (384)	$ (1,126)	$ 715

Economic and Recognized Amounts on Balance Sheet—2006 and 2005

	2006 Pension	2006 OPEB	2006 Total	2005 Pension	2005 OPEB	2005 Total
Plan assets	$ 8,565	$ 202	$ 8,767	$ 7,778	$ 161	$ 7,939
Benefit obligation	11,048	3,256	14,304	11,003	3,384	14,387
Funded status (economic)	$ (2,483)	$ (3,054)	(5,537)	$ (3,225)	$ (3,223)	$ (6,448)
Less unrecognized:						
Net gain (loss)				(2,174)	(299)	(2,473)
Prior service cost				(169)	60	(109)
Total unrecognized				$ (2,343)	$ (239)	$ (2,582)
Additional minimum liability				1,381		1,381
Total off-balance-sheet				$ (962)	$ (239)	$ (1,201)
Amount recognized	$ (2,483)	$ (3,054)	$ (5,537)	$ (2,263)	$ (2,984)	$ (5,247)
Amount included in accumulated other comprehensive income:						
Net gain (loss)	$ (1,310)	$ (70)	$ (1,380)			
Prior service cost	(153)	77	(76)			
Total	$ (1,463)	$ 7	$ (1,456)			

Reconciling Movement in Cumulative Net Deferrals during 2006

	PENSION Net Gain/ Loss	PENSION Prior Service Cost	PENSION Total	OPEB Net Gain/ Loss	OPEB Prior Service Cost	OPEB Total	TOTAL Net Gain/ Loss	TOTAL Prior Service Cost	TOTAL Total
Opening balance	$ (2,174)	$ (169)	$ (2,343)	$ (299)	$ 60	$ (239)	$ (2,473)	$ (109)	$ (2,582)
Net deferral during 2006	864	16	880	229	17	246	1,093	33	1,126
Closing balance	$ (1,310)	$ (153)	$ (1,463)	$ (70)	$ 77	$ 7	$ (1,380)	$ (76)	$ (1,456)

income) is an *expense* of $467 million. This difference arises because the entire $390 million of actuarial gain and $394 million of the return on plan assets (specifically, the excess of actual return of $1,063 million over expected return of $669 million) are deferred. In addition, $96 million of amortization ($80 million net gain/loss and $16 million prior service cost) is included in the reported cost, resulting in a net deferral of $880 million. A similar situation prevails with respect to OPEB. Therefore, in total (pensions and OPEB together), AMR recognizes a benefit *cost* of $715 million (in net income) during 2006, even though economically it generated benefit related *income* of $384 million, because it deferred a net amount of $1,126 million. It must be noted that from 2006 onward (under the new standard, *SFAS 158*), the economic benefit income of $384 million will be recognized in *comprehensive income* and the net deferrals of $1,126 will be included in *other comprehensive income* for the year. This was not the case prior to 2006 (under *SFAS 87*).

Exhibit 3.13 next compares the net economic position (funded status) to the amount reported in the balance sheet. In 2006, AMR's funded status for pension plans was $2,483 million underfunded. These amounts are reported in the balance sheet as a net *liability*. Therefore, the amount recognized in the balance sheet is the funded status of the pension plans. This was not the case prior to 2006, where the accounting was dictated by an earlier standard, *SFAS 87*. In 2005, while AMR's pension plan's funded status was $3,225 million underfunded, the amount recognized in the balance sheet was a liability of only $2,263 million. The difference between the funded status and the amounts recognized in the balance sheet is $962 million and is made up of (1) $2,343 million of unrecognized net deferrals–$2,174 net (gain) loss and $169 million prior service cost–and (2) $1,381 offsetting additional minimum liability, which is an ad hoc adjustment. The corresponding cumulative net deferral amounts in 2006 (for pensions) total $1,463 million–$1,310 million net (gain) loss and $153 million prior service cost–and are included in accumulated comprehensive income.

In total (pensions plus OPEB), AMR's funded status of $5,537 million underfunded is reported as a liability in 2006, with cumulative net deferrals of $1,456 million reported in accumulated other comprehensive income. In contrast in 2005, only $5,247 million underfunded–out of the funded status of $6,448 million underfunded–was recognized as a liability and a total of $1,201 million was kept off the balance sheet, which included unrecognized net deferrals of $2,582 million and $1,381 additional minimum pension liability.

For 2006, we also analyze the movement in net deferrals. For brevity, we limit our discussion only to the total postretirement plans (i.e., pension plus OPEB). The opening balance of cumulative net deferrals (unrecognized in 2005) is $2,582 million, comprising $2,473 million net (gain) loss and $109 million prior service cost. Net deferrals during 2006 (refer to top panel of Exhibit 3.13 for details) were $1,126 million–$1093 million relating to net gain/loss ($410 million + $602 million + $81 million) and $33 million relating to prior service cost ($27 million + $6 million). Combining the 2006 net deferrals ($1,126 million) with the opening balance ($2,582 million), provides the 2006 net deferral closing balance of $1,456 million–$1,380 million net (gain) loss and $76 million prior service cost–which are included in accumulated other comprehensive income in the 2006 balance sheet.

Our analysis of the movement in net deferrals mirrors the effects that *SFAS 158* is expected to have on accumulated other comprehensive income. The opening and closing balances in the net deferrals would be included in accumulated comprehensive income in successive balance sheets, and the net deferral amount for the year would be included in the year's other comprehensive income. Unfortunately, because AMR adopted *SFAS 158* in 2006, the effects on accumulated comprehensive income during 2006 are complicated and cannot be readily reconciled with the movement in net deferrals.

Adjusting the Income Statement and Balance Sheet

Exhibit 3.14 illustrates the adjustments for AMR's 2006 opening and closing balance sheets and income statement from our analysis of its pension and OPEB disclosures. The use of economic benefit costs rather than reported costs results in 2006 net income that is $714 million higher, an increase of more than 300% over the reported income of $231 million. This increase in income is driven by a $1,099 million decrease in operating expenses–the difference between the economic benefit income of $384 million and reported benefit cost of $715 million–offset by an increase in the tax provision of $385 million (using a tax rate of 35%). Because the economic position (funded status) is recognized in the balance sheet in 2006 (under *SFAS 158*), no adjustments are necessary. However, the balance sheet does not reflect the funded status in 2005 (under *SFAS 87*), so we need to make adjustments. Specifically, we need to add $1,201 million–which is the net amount kept off the balance sheet–to noncurrent liabilities and adjust it to shareholders' equity.

Exhibit 3.14

■ ■ ■ ■ ■ ■ ■

Adjusting Financial Statements—AMR Corporation

	2006			2005		
$ million	Reported	Economic	Difference	Reported	Economic	Difference
Income Statement						
Operating revenues	$ 22,563	$ 22,563				
Operating expenses	(21,503)	(20,404)	$1,099			
Operating income	$ 1,060	$ 2,159				
Interest	(829)	(829)				
Tax provision		(385)	(385)			
Net income	$ 231	$ 945	$ 714			
Balance Sheet						
Assets						
Current	$ 6,902	$ 6,902		$ 6,164	$ 6,164	
Noncurrent	22,243	22,243		23,331	23,331	
Total	$ 29,145	$ 29,145		$ 29,495	$ 29,495	
Liabilities and Equity						
Current liabilities	$ 8,505	$ 8,505		$ 8,272	$ 8,272	
Noncurrent liabilities	21,246	21,246		22,653	23,854	$ 1,201
Shareholders' equity	(606)	(606)		(1,430)	(2,631)	$ (1,201)
Total	$ 29,145	$ 29,145		$ 29,495	$ 29,495	
Ratios						
Total debt to total assets	1.02	1.02		1.05	1.09	
Long-term debt to total assets	0.73	0.73		0.77	0.81	
Pretax return on assets	3.62%	7.36%				
Net income/Total assets	0.79%	3.22%				

Using net economic position (funded status) instead of the reported position (accrued pension cost) marginally increases both debt to equity ratios in 2005 (note we compute these ratios as debt over total assets because AMR's equity is negative). Also, using the economic benefit cost (income), instead of the reported benefit cost significantly increases return on assets: the pre-tax return on assets (Pretax operating income ÷ Average total assets) almost doubles from 3.62% to 7.36%, while the ratio of net income to average total assets (we are unable to compute ROE because shareholders' equity is negative) increases dramatically from 0.79% percent to 3.22% (an increase of more than 300%). Overall, recognizing the economic effects of AMR's postretirement plans in income substantially affects our evaluation of the company's financial performance.

To this point, we have examined the effects of reflecting the economic status of postretirement benefits on financial statements. Yet, an analyst must address at least three additional questions:

What postretirement benefit cost should be charged to income?

What liability should be reflected on the balance sheet, and in what format?

What are the effects of actuarial assumptions on both the income statement and the balance sheet?

We answer the first two questions in this section. The third question is addressed in the next section.

At first glance it seems that the appropriate cost to be reflected in the income statement should be the economic benefit cost. A deeper examination suggests the answer is not so obvious. Recall that reported benefit cost differs from economic cost primarily because transitory effects–such as actuarial gains and losses, prior service cost, and abnormal return on assets–are deferred and gradually amortized into reported cost through the smoothing process. The purpose of this smoothing is to obtain a more stable or permanent component of postretirement benefit cost. Accordingly, the appropriate benefit cost that should be applied for determining income depends on the objectives of the analysis. If the analyst wishes to measure permanent income (see Chapters 2 and 6), then reported cost is probably a more appropriate measure. In addition, the inclusion of nonrecurring items makes the economic benefit cost very volatile. Including this volatile economic benefit cost in net income can lead to concealing the underlying operating income of the company. For these reasons, *SFAS 158* chooses to smooth the reported benefit cost. However, if the objective of the analysis is to determine economic income, then an analyst should consider all transitory elements in income, which implies that the more useful measure of benefit cost is economic cost.

A related issue is whether benefit cost is part of operating or nonoperating income. Presumably, postretirement benefits are an integral part of employee compensation and should be classified as operating. However, further analysis reveals that not all components of these benefits are operating in nature. Certainly, service cost and related nonrecurring components such as prior service cost are operating in nature. But interest cost, return on plan assets, and related nonrecurring components, such as net gain or loss, are financing in nature and should therefore be included as part of nonoperating income.

For the second question, we turn to the balance sheet and note that the funded status reflects the true economic position of the plan and therefore is the appropriate measure of the benefit plans' net assets. Recall that the funded status is determined using the projected benefit obligation (PBO), which is determined using the expected wages of employees *at retirement*. However, an employer is legally liable for the pension obligation based on only on *current* wages. This obligation is termed the *accumulated benefit obligation* or ABO. To the extent an analyst is interested in evaluating the liquidating value of a company's net assets, a better measure of the pension liability is the ABO. Unfortunately, many companies (as in the case of AMR) do not report ABO. This means an analyst must at least concede that the pension obligation is overstated when determining liquidating value and make subjective downward adjustments to this obligation.

An analyst must also assess whether the proper balance sheet preparation is the netting of plan assets against its liabilities (as currently reported) or the separate disclosure of plan assets and plan liabilities. This issue is more than one of mere presentation. For example, if plan assets are not netted against liabilities, AMR's total debt to equity and long-term debt to equity ratios would be significantly larger. Proper presentation depends on the underlying economics of the benefit plans. One argument is that the employer's liability is only to the extent of underfunding and that the employer has no control over the benefit fund's assets, which are administered by independent trustees. This argument favors netting the fund's assets against its obligation.

It must be noted that recognizing the net economic position (funded status) on the balance sheet and the economic benefit cost in income is consistent with fair value accounting (see Chapter 2). As part of the push toward a widespread adoption of fair value accounting, the FASB is currently working on a plan to eliminate the smoothing provisions (deferral and amortization of nonrecurring items) and recognize the economic benefit cost in income within the next few years. The FASB is also considering separating the operating and nonoperating components of the pension cost and also debating whether pension assets and liabilities must be netted or reported separately.

Analysis Research
■ ■ ■ ■ ■ ■ ■   **MARKET VALUATION OF PENSIONS**

Analysis methods involve several adjustments to better reflect the economic reality of pension plans. For example, we suggest that the funded status of a plan is its "true" economic position. Also, we suggest the proper pension liability for a going concern is its PBO and that its correct balance sheet presentation is one that nets pension liabilities and plan assets as funded status. We also maintain that the net periodic pension cost (reported pension cost) is more relevant for analysis. While these assertions are reasonable, it is important to assess whether they are valid. Research attempts to address their validity by examining stock price behavior. There is evidence that the stock market views the unfunded pension obligation (i.e., the negative of the funded status) as the correct pension liability. This applies both when determining company value and when assessing systematic risk. The market also views pension assets and obligations separately as assets and liabilities of the company, rather than simply as a net amount. We also find that the market values all components of the PBO—indicating the PBO is the proper measure of the pension obligation. However, the market appears to attach more than $1 of value for every $1 of PBO. Recent research also suggests that the net periodic pension cost (i.e., the smoothed reported pension cost) is a better measure of the pension cost than the economic pension cost that includes the nonrecurring items. In fact, including the nonrecurring items in the pension cost can reduce the ability of the financial statements to reflect either the company's market value or the riskiness of its debt.

Actuarial Assumptions and Sensitivity Analysis

It is tempting to think of the net economic position (or the economic cost) of a company's benefit plans as a reliable estimate of its underlying economic fundamentals. In reality, this is not so. While the value of plan assets is based on verifiable numbers (typically market values), the benefit obligation is estimated using a number of actuarial assumptions, such as the discount rate. Moreover, the reported cost (net periodic benefit cost) is also sensitive to actuarial assumptions, such as the expected return on plan assets. Because of this sensitivity, managers may manipulate these assumptions to window-dress the financial statements. Accordingly, an important task in analysis of postretirement benefits is evaluating the reasonableness of actuarial assumptions used by the employer. This includes examining the effects of changes in assumptions on both the economic and reported numbers. Exhibit 3.15 provides a table that identifies the effects of changes in the discount rate, expected rate of return on plan assets, and compensation (and health care cost) growth on both the reported and the economic position and cost numbers. Also, the charts on the next page reflect the distribution of three key actuarial assumptions for a large sample of companies.

Effect of Actuarial Assumption Changes on Benefit Obligation and Cost

Exhibit 3.15

■ ■ ■ ■ ■ ■ ■

Assumption	Direction of Change	DIRECTION OF EFFECT ON		
		Funded Status	Economic Cost	Reported Cost
Discount rate	+	+	−	Indefinite
	−	−	+	Indefinite
Expected return	+	No effect	No effect	−
	−	No effect	No effect	+
Growth rate	+	−	+	+
	−	+	−	−

Note: Growth rate refers to both compensation and health care cost trend.

A crucial assumption is the discount rate. Changes in discount rate affect the magnitude of both the pension obligation and the economic benefit cost. A lower discount rate increases the benefit obligation and therefore reduces funded status on the balance sheet. A lower discount rate also increases the economic benefit cost during the year. The discount rate affects the reported benefit cost, although the direction of its impact is indefinite (this arises because an increase in discount rate decreases service cost but increases interest cost). While companies are supposed to determine the discount rate based on the prevailing interest rate for a corporate bond with similar risk (typically the long-term, AA-rated corporate bond), there is some latitude in its determination. Higher discount rates generally indicate more aggressive accounting practices. AMR has increased its discount rate to 6% in 2006 from 5.75% in 2005. This rate appears reasonable given the prevailing interest rates in the U.S. economy at that time. However, the increased discount rate would have reduced both AMR's benefit obligation and economic benefit cost during the year. Much of AMR's $602 million actuarial gain during 2006 is attributable to this increase in discount rate.

The expected rate of return assumption affects reported benefit cost and is a favorite tool for earnings management. The expected rate of return depends on many factors, such as the composition of the plan assets and the long-term returns on different asset classes. Higher expected rates of return indicate more aggressive accounting practices because they lower the reported benefit cost and therefore increase net income. AMR assumes an expected rate of return of 8.75% in 2006, which is slightly lower than that assumed in 2005. The direction of the change is not aggressive. However, an analyst also needs to evaluate this assumption with respect to AMR's benefit plans' asset allocations. Recall that in 2006, AMR allocated 37% of its assets to bonds and 57% to equity. Given that long-term annual returns on debt and equity in the U.S. economy are, respectively, 6% and 10%, AMR's asset allocation would imply an expected return of 8.5%, which suggests that the assumed rate is a little aggressive. However, this is not out of line with the rates assumed by most companies, as the charts reveal. Also, AMR does note that its investment performance in the past has been higher than its assumed rates of return.

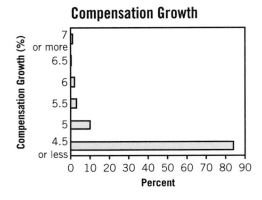
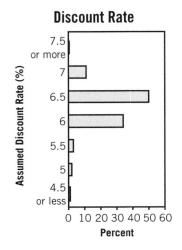
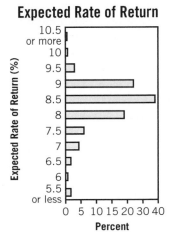

The growth rate assumption is probably of less concern than either the discount rate or the expected return assumptions. It tends to be more stable and predictable. Still, companies worry about changing compensation growth rates because they can affect labor negotiations.

Analysis Research
■ ■ ■ ■ ■ ■ ■

DO MANAGERS MANIPULATE PENSION ASSUMPTIONS?

Do managers manipulate pension assumptions to window-dress financial statements? Research reveals that managers strategically select (or adjust) pension assumptions to window-dress both the reported values on balance sheets and the funded status of pensions. Specifically, managers strategically select the discount rate to reduce the level of pension underfunding and, therefore, the debt-to-equity ratio. Also, the discount rate selected is typically slightly higher than the prevailing interest rate on securities of similar risk. This suggests an attempt to understate the pension obligation. Moreover, the discount rate and health care cost trend rates on OPEBs show evidence of underreporting of the OPEB obligation. This is especially apparent in situations where companies are close to violating debt covenants. Also, there is little relation between the expected rate of return assumption and (1) the asset composition (a higher proportion of equity should imply a higher expected rate of return) and (2) the actual fund performance. Overall, there is evidence of managerial manipulation of pension assumptions to window-dress financial statements.

Pension Risk Exposure

Pension plans can expose companies to significant risk. This risk arises to the extent to which plan assets have a different *risk profile* than the pension obligation–in particular, when changes in the market value of plan assets are not correlated with changes in the value of the pension obligation. The value of the pension obligation is sensitive to changes in the discount rate, which in turn mirrors corporate bond yields (interest rates). Therefore, changes in the pension obligation value are correlated with bond prices. Because of this, a company that invests its pension funds primarily in debt securities–such as corporate bonds–is largely protected from risk, because plan asset values will fluctuate in tandem with the value of the pension obligation. Because returns on debt are much lower than that on equity, many companies have chosen to allocate significant proportions of the plan assets to equity. Unfortunately, equity securities have different risk profiles from the pension obligation, and consequently, many companies are significantly exposed to pension risk.

Pension risk exposure became an important issue during the early 2000s in what was dubbed the "pensions crisis." Over this period, interest rates dropped sharply, which significantly increased the value of the pension obligation. However, plan assets' values decreased over a comparable period because of the bear market in stocks. This combination of factors resulted in a significant decrease in pension funding levels. Many companies' pension plans became severely underfunded, which caused some companies to default on their pension promises and even file for bankruptcy protection.

Before analyzing pension risk, we need to precisely understand what it is. Technically, we can define pension risk as the probability that a company will be unable to meet its current pension obligations. Obviously, pension risk depends on the funded status of the plan; the more underfunded the plan, the higher the pension risk. However, the funded status alone provides no information about two other factors that are critical to determining a company's pension risk: (1) *pension intensity,* that is, the size of the pension obligation (or the plan assets) in relation to the size of the company's other assets, and (2) extent to which the risk profile of the pension assets is mismatched to that of the pension obligation. An analyst needs to assess each of these two factors when evaluating a company's pension risk exposure.

Pension intensity can be measured by expressing the pension plan assets and the pension obligation separately as percentage of the company's total assets. A company with large pension assets (or obligations) relative to its total assets has greater pension risk exposure because even small percentage changes in their values can have significant effects on the company's solvency. By netting the assets with the obligation, the funded status conceals risk exposure arising from pension intensity. Because of this, some analysts argue that pension plan assets and pension obligation must be reported separately on the balance sheet.

It is more difficult to exactly measure the extent to which the risk profile of the plan assets is mismatched with that of the pension obligation. As noted earlier, a company is exposed to minimal risk if it invests its plan assets primarily in debt securities. Risk arises only when the company allocates significant proportions of its plan assets to nondebt securities such as equity or real estate. Therefore, the percentage of plan assets allocated to nondebt securities provides a good estimate of the risk arising through mismatched risk profiles.

We now evaluate the pension risk exposure of AMR Corporation. AMR's pension plan is underfunded by $2,483 million, which is 8.5% of its total assets. Its plan assets (pension obligation) are $8,565 million ($11,048 million), which translates to 29% (38%) of its total assets, suggesting fairly high pension intensity. A substantial proportion

(63%) of its plan assets are allocated to nondebt securities. Given all these factors, AMR has a high pension risk exposure.

Before concluding, we need to discuss the issue of OPEB risk exposure. Recall, there are no legal requirements to fund the OPEB obligations, so there is greater flexibility about meeting these commitments. Also, because OPEB obligations are rarely funded, the issue of matching risk profiles does not arise. However, an analyst should also evaluate both the extent of underfunding and the intensity of a company's postretirement benefit plans (i.e., pensions plus OPEBs). For AMR Corporation, the total postretirement benefit underfunding is $5,537 million (19% of total assets) and the total benefit obligation is $14,304 million (49% of total assets). This suggests that AMR Corporation has highly significant risk exposure from its postretirement plans.

ANALYSIS EXCERPT

Consumed by Postretirement Benefits

The most extreme example of postretirement benefit intensity is that of General Motors, which arguably has the largest corporate pension fund in the world. In 2006, GM's postretirement benefit obligation was a whopping $176 billion, with matching plan assets of about $130 billion, resulting in a net obligation (i.e., underfunded status) of $46 billion. Compared to around $200 billion in total assets and around $10 billion in equity unrelated to postretirement benefits, GM's postretirement benefit obligation is 87.5% of its total assets and 17.5 *times* its equity! In fact, GM's funded status reduced by almost $25 billion in 2006 because it renegotiated its OPEBs; in 2005, its net postretirement obligation was close to $70 billion. GM's reported postretirement benefit cost of $13.5 billion in 2006 was almost twice its operating loss of $7.6 billion and seven times its net loss of $1.9 billion for the year. Also, its actual return on plan assets of $17 billion was almost twice its gross profit from automotive operations! As testimony to GM's extreme postretirement benefit intensity, its entire shareholders' equity was wiped out when it began recognizing the funded status of its plans on the balance sheet in 2006. One last fact: GM paid $8 billion of pension benefits in 2006, which was 15 times as large as the cash dividend paid to its shareholders. As an analyst once quipped: General Motors is a giant pension plan that incidentally makes cars!

Cash Flow Implications of Postretirement Benefits

Cash flow implications of postretirement benefits are straightforward. That is, cash outflow is equal to the contribution made to the plan by the company. In 2006, AMR contributed $500 million to its postretirement (pension + OPEB) benefit plans (see Exhibit 3.12). The current period's cash flow number is useful neither for evaluating the profitability or the financial position of a company nor for forecasting future cash flows. This is because a company will contribute to a plan only to the extent to which it is necessary. For example, AMR made pension contributions of only $329 million in 2006, even though it paid $605 million in benefits. Companies with overfunded plans often do not need to make any contributions–for example, General Electric has made almost no contributions to its pension plan for the past 20 years. Because of this, the current year's contributions are not very informative.

However, the postretirement benefit footnote (see Exhibit 3.12) provides information that can help an analyst forecast future cash flows related to benefit plans. AMR expects to contribute $364 million into its pension plan and $200 million ($13 million contributions plus $187 million benefit payments) toward OPEBs in 2007, which suggests a combined

■ ■ ■ ■ ■ ■ ■

LABOR PAINS

In a recent 5-year period, the Labor Dept. [www.dol.gov/dol/pwba] opened 24,523 civil and 660 criminal investigations of pension plans suspected of misusing employees' money.

cash outflow of $564 million related to postretirement benefits. Estimating cash outflows beyond 2007 is complicated and will require modeling benefit plan assets and obligations.

ANALYSIS VIEWPOINT   **. . . YOU ARE THE LABOR NEGOTIATOR**

As the union negotiator on a labor contract, you request that management increase postretirement benefits to employees. Management responds with no increase in benefits but does offer a guarantee to fund a much larger portion of previously committed postretirement benefits. These funds would be dispensed to an independent trustee. You are confused since a large postretirement obligation already exists on the balance sheet. Does this benefit offer seem legitimate?

CONTINGENCIES AND COMMITMENTS
Contingencies

Contingencies are potential gains and losses whose resolution depends on one or more future events. Loss contingencies are potential claims on a company's resources and are known as **contingent liabilities.** Contingent liabilities can arise from litigation, threat of expropriation, collectibility of receivables, claims arising from product warranties or defects, guarantees of performance, tax assessments, self-insured risks, and catastrophic losses of property.

A loss contingency must meet two conditions before a company records it as a loss. First, it must be *probable* that an asset will be impaired or a liability incurred. Implicit in this condition is that it must be probable that a future event will confirm the loss. The second condition is the amount of loss must be *reasonably estimable.* Examples that usually meet these two conditions are losses from uncollectible receivables and the obligations related to product warranties. For these cases, both an estimated liability and a loss are recorded in the financial statements.

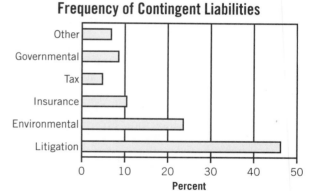

Frequency of Contingent Liabilities

If a company does not record a loss contingency because one or both of the conditions are not met, the company must disclose the contingency in the notes when there is at least a *reasonable possibility* that it will incur a loss. Such a note reports the nature of the contingency and offers an estimate of the possible loss or range of loss—or reports that such an estimate cannot be made.

Consistent with conservatism in financial reporting, companies do not recognize gain contingencies in financial statements. They can, however, disclose gain contingencies in a note if the probability of realization is high.

WARRANTIES
GE recently reported $1.3 billion in product warranty liability and $720 million in warranty expense.

Analyzing Contingent Liabilities

Reported contingent liabilities for items such as service guarantees and warranties are estimates. Our analysis of these liabilities is only as accurate as the underlying estimates, which companies often determine on the basis of prior experience or future expectations. We must exercise care in accepting management's estimates for these and other contingent liabilities. For instance, recall that Manville argued it had substantial defenses to legal claims against it due to asbestos-related lawsuits until the year it declared bankruptcy.

We also need to analyze note disclosures of all loss (and gain) contingencies. For example, note disclosure of indirect guarantees of indebtedness, such as advancing funds or covering fixed charges of another entity is important for our analysis. Note disclosure for contingencies typically includes:

- A description of the contingent liability and the degree of risk.
- The potential amount of the contingency and how participation of others is treated in determining risk exposure.
- The charges, if any, against income for the estimates of contingent losses.

Our analysis must recognize that companies sometimes underestimate or fail to recognize these liabilities.[7] One example of disclosure for a contingent liability follows:

ANALYSIS EXCERPT

There are various libel and other legal actions that have arisen in the ordinary course of business and are now pending against the Company. Such actions are usually for amounts greatly in excess of the payments, if any, that may be required to be made. It is the opinion of management after reviewing such actions with counsel that the ultimate liability which might result from such actions would not have a material adverse effect on the consolidated financial statements.

—*New York Times*

FLYER DEBT

American Airlines estimates its 2004 year-end frequent-flyer liabilities at nearly $1.4 billion.

Another example of a contingent liability involves frequent flyer mileage. Unredeemed frequent flyer mileage entitles airline passengers to billions of miles of free travel. Frequent flyer programs ensure customer loyalty and offer marketing benefits that are not cost-free. Because realization of these liabilities is probable and can be estimated, they must be recognized on the balance sheet and in the income statement.

Reserves for future losses are another type of contingency requiring our scrutiny. Conservatism in accounting calls for companies to recognize losses as they determine or foresee them. Still, companies tend, particularly in years of very poor performance, to overestimate their contingent losses. This behavior is referred to as a *big bath* and often includes recording losses from asset disposals, relocation, and plant closings. Overestimating these losses shifts future costs to the current period and can serve as a means for companies to manage or smooth income. Only in selected reports filed with the SEC are details of these loss estimates (also called *loss reserves*) sometimes disclosed, and even here there is no set requirement for detailed disclosure. Despite this, our analysis should attempt to obtain details of loss reserves by category and amount.

ECO COPS

Contingent valuation is a means of measuring environmental contingent liabilities. In this case people are surveyed and asked to assign value to environmental damage.

Two sources of useful information are (1) note disclosures in financial statements and (2) information in the Management's Discussion and Analysis section. Also, under the U.S. Internal Revenue Code, only a few categories of anticipated losses are tax deductible. Accordingly, a third source of information is analysis of deferred taxes. This analysis can reveal undisclosed provisions for future losses, because any undeductible losses should appear in the adjustments for deferred (prepaid) taxes. We also must remember that loss reserves do not alter risk exposure, have no cash flow consequences, and do not provide an alternative to insurance.

---

[7] A study found that of 126 lawsuits lost by publicly traded companies, nearly 40% were not disclosed in years preceding the loss. The implication is that companies are reluctant to disclose pending litigation, even when the risk of loss due to litigation is high.

Cigna, a property and casualty insurer, shows us how tenuous the reserve estimation process is. In a recent year, Cigna claimed it could look back on 10 years of a very stable pattern of claims (insurance reserves are designed to provide funds for claims). However, in the very next year, the incidence and severity of claims worsened. Cigna claimed that the year was an aberration and it did not increase reserves for future claims. Yet, within two years, Cigna announced a more than $1 billion charge to income to bring insurance reserves to proper levels with claims. Consequently, Cigna's reserves for these earlier years were obviously understated and its net income overstated.

The auditor's report gives us another perspective on contingencies. Still, auditors exhibit an inability to express an opinion on the outcome of contingencies. For example, the auditor's report for the years involving the Cigna case described above was unqualified. Another typical example, when they do comment on contingencies, is from the auditor's report of Harsco shown here:

■ ■ ■ ■ ■ ■ ■
DIFFERENCES
Managers and auditors often differ on whether a contingency should be recorded, disclosed, or ignored.

ANALYSIS EXCERPT

The Company is subject to the Government exercising an additional option under a certain contract. If the Government exercises this option, additional losses could be incurred by the Company. Also, the Company has filed or is in the process of filing various claims against the Government relating to certain contracts. The ultimate outcome of these matters cannot presently be determined. Accordingly, no provision for such potential additional losses or recognition of possible recovery from such claims (other than relating to the Federal Excise Tax and related claims) has been reflected in the accompanying financial statements.

Notice the intentional ambiguity of this auditor's report.

Banks especially are exposed to large contingent losses that they often underestimate or confine to note disclosure. One common example relates to losses on international loans where evidence points to impairments of assets, but banks and their auditors fail to properly disclose the impact. Another example is off-balance-sheet commitments of banks. These include such diverse commitments as standby letters of credit, municipal bond and commercial paper guarantees, currency swaps, and foreign exchange contracts. Unlike loans, these commitments are promises banks expect (but are not certain) they will not have to bear. Banks do not effectively report these commitments in financial statements. This further increases the danger of not fully identifying risk exposures of banks.

Commitments

Commitments are potential claims against a company's resources due to future performance under contract. They are not recognized in financial statements since events such as the signing of an executory contract or issuance of a purchase order is not a completed transaction. Additional examples are long-term noncancellable contracts to purchase products or services at specified prices and purchase contracts for fixed assets

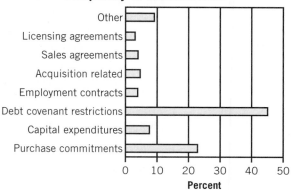

Frequency of Commitments

calling for payments during construction. An example of a commitment for Intermec Co. is shown here:

ANALYSIS EXCERPT

The Company signed a patent license agreement with its former principal supplier of hand-held laser scanning devices. This agreement provides that the Company may manufacture and sell certain laser scanning products of its own design and that the Company pay minimum royalties and purchase minimum quantities of other products from that supplier.

A lease agreement is also, in many cases, a form of commitment.

All commitments call for disclosure of important factors surrounding their obligations including the amounts, conditions, and timing. An example of how far-reaching the commitments can be is illustrated in the following note from Wells Fargo:

ANALYSIS EXCERPT

Commitments and Contingent Liabilities. In the normal course of business, there are various commitments outstanding and contingent liabilities that are properly not reflected in the accompanying financial statements. Losses, if any, resulting from these commitments are not anticipated to be material. The approximate amounts of such commitments are summarized below ($ in millions):

Standby letters of credit	$ 2,400
Commercial and similar letters of credit	400
Commitments to extend credit*	17,300
Commitments to purchase futures and forward contracts	5,000
Commitments to purchase foreign and U.S. currencies	1,500

*Excludes credit card and other revolving credit loans.

Standby letters of credit include approximately $400 million of participations purchased and are net of approximately $300 million of participations sold. Standby letters of credit are issued to cover performance obligations, including those which back financial instruments (financial guarantees).

OFF-BALANCE-SHEET FINANCING

Off-balance-sheet financing refers to the nonrecording of certain financing obligations. We have already examined transactions that fit this mold (operating leases). In addition to leases, there are other off-balance-sheet financing arrangements ranging from the simple to the highly complex. These arrangements are part of an ever-changing landscape, where as one accounting requirement is brought in to better reflect the obligations from a specific off-balance-sheet financing transaction, new and innovative means are devised to take its place.

Off-Balance-Sheet Examples

One way to finance property, plant, and equipment is to have an outside party acquire them while a company agrees to use the assets and provide funds sufficient to service the debt. Examples of these arrangements are *purchase agreements* and *through-put agreements,* where a company agrees to purchase output from or run a specified amount of goods through a processing facility, and *take-or-pay arrangements,* where a company guarantees to pay for a specified quantity of goods whether needed or not. A variation on these arrangements involves creating separate entities and then providing financing not to exceed 50% ownership—such as joint ventures or limited partnerships. Companies carry these activities as an investment and do not consolidate them with the company's financial statements. This means they are excluded from liabilities. Consider the following two practices:

ANALYSIS EXCERPT

Avis Rent-A-Car set up a separate trust to borrow money to finance the purchase of automobiles that it then leased to Avis for its rental fleet. Because the trust is separate from Avis, the debt of about $400 million is kept off the balance sheet. The chief accounting officer proclaimed: "One of the big advantages of off-balance-sheet financing is that it permits us to make other borrowings from banks for operating capital that we could not otherwise obtain." Two major competitors, Hertz and National Car Rental, bought rather than leased their rental cars.

ANALYSIS EXCERPT

Oil companies often resort to less-than-50%-owned joint ventures as a means to raise money for building and operating pipelines. While the debt service is the ultimate responsibility of the oil company, its notes simply report that the company might have to advance funds to help the pipeline joint venture meet its debt obligations if sufficient crude oil needed to generate the necessary funds is not shipped.

Also, many retailers sell receivables arising from proprietary credit cards to trusts that they establish for this purpose. The trusts raise funds for these purchases by selling bonds which are repaid from the cash collected.

Special Purpose Entities

Special purpose entities (SPE), now made infamous in the wake of Enron's bankruptcy, have been a legitimate financing mechanism for decades and are an integral part of corporate finance today. The concept is straightforward:

- An SPE is formed by the sponsoring company and is capitalized with equity investment, some of which must be from independent third parties.
- The SPE leverages this equity investment with borrowings from the credit markets and purchases earning assets from or for the sponsoring company.
- The cash flow from the earning assets is used to repay the debt and provide a return to the equity investors.

Some examples are:

- A company sells accounts receivable to the SPE. These receivables may arise, for example, from the company's proprietary credit card that it offers its customers to attempt to ensure their future patronage (e.g., the Target credit card). The company removes the receivables from its balance sheet and receives cash that can be invested in other earning assets. The SPE collateralizes bonds that it sells in the credit markets with the receivables and uses the cash to purchase additional receivables on an ongoing basis

Exhibit 3.16   *Illustration of SPE Transaction to Sell Accounts Receivable*

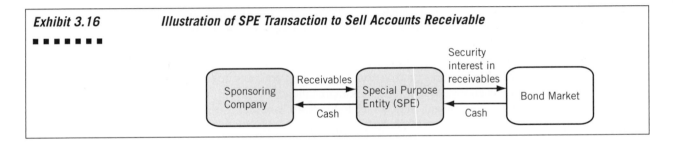

as the company's credit card portfolio grows. This process is called *securitization*. Consumer finance companies like Capital One are significant issuers of receivable-backed bonds. Exhibit 3.16 provides an illustration of the flow of funds in this use of SPEs.

- A company desires to construct a manufacturing facility. It executes a contract to purchase output from the plant. A SPE uses the contract and the property to collateralize bonds that it sells to finance the plant's construction. The company obtains the benefits of the manufacturing plant, but does not recognize either the asset or the liability on its balance sheet since executory contracts (commitments) are not recorded under GAAP and are also not considered derivatives that would require balance sheet recognition (see Chapter 5).

- A company desires to construct an office building, but does not want to record either the asset or the liability on its balance sheet. A SPE agrees to finance and construct the building and lease it to the company under an operating lease, called a synthetic lease. If structured properly, neither the leased asset nor the lease obligation are reflected on the company's balance sheet.

There are two primary reasons for the popularity of SPEs:

1. SPEs may provide a lower-cost financing alternative than borrowing from the credit markets directly. This is because the activities of the SPE are restricted and, as a result, investors purchase a well-secured cash flow stream that is not subject to the range of business risks inherent in providing capital directly to the sponsoring company.

2. Under present GAAP, so long as the SPE is properly structured, the SPE is accounted for as a separate entity, unconsolidated with the sponsoring company (see Chapter 5 for a discussion of consolidations). The company thus is able to use SPEs to achieve off-balance-sheet transactions to remove assets, liabilities, or both from its balance sheet. Because the company continues to realize the economic benefits of the transactions, operating performance ratios (like return on assets, asset turnover ratios, leverage ratios, and so on) improve significantly.

FUTURE GAAP

Regulators continue to debate the reporting standards for consolidation.

GAAP guidance relating to the accounting for SPEs and the rules for their consolidation with the sponsoring company is provided in *SFAS 140* and FIN 46R. At issue is defining when "control" of one entity over another is established, especially when the SPE does not issue common stock.

Many SPEs are not corporations and do not have stock ownership. For these entities, control is conferred via legal documents rather than stock ownership, and the typical 50% stock ownership threshold for consolidation does not apply. The FASB now classifies these SPEs as **variable interest entities** (VIEs) if either the total equity at risk is insufficient to finance its operations (usually less than 10% of assets) or the VIE lacks any one of the following: (1) the ability to make decisions, (2) the obligation to absorb losses, or (3) the right to receive returns. In this case, the VIE is consolidated with that entity that has the ability to make decisions, the obligation to absorb losses, and the right to receive returns (called the "Primary Beneficiary"). Consolidation results in the adding together of the financial statements of the Primary Beneficiary and the VIE, thus eliminating any perceived benefits resulting from off-balance-sheet treatment of the VIE.

We close our discussion of SPEs with four examples of their use.

Case of Capital One.   We begin with Capital One Financial Corporation, the consumer finance company with $53.7 billion in total assets, consisting mostly of consumer loans and credit card receivables. Capital One uses SPEs in the form of trusts to purchase portions of its consumer loan portfolio. The trusts, in turn, finance the purchase by selling bonds collateralized by the receivables.

Capital One manages nearly $80 billion in consumer loans, yet only $38 billion is reported on its balance sheet. The other $42 billion have been sold to the trust (SPE). In 2004, Capital One reported a net increase in reported consumer loans of $19 billion. It also reported cash inflows of $11 billion relating to the securitization of these loans.

Capital One is an example of a company using SPEs for a legitimate financial purpose and with full disclosure. Receivables are removed from the balance sheet only when the SPE has been properly structured with sufficient third-party equity, when Capital One has sold the assets without recourse, meaning that it is relieved of all risk of loss on the receivables, and when it has relinquished all control over the SPE (a qualifying special purpose entity). In this case, the transfer of the receivables can be recognized as a sale, with the resulting gain (loss) recognized in the income statement and the assets removed from the balance sheet.

Capital One fully discloses its off-balance-sheet financing activities so that analysts can consider their effects in the evaluation of the company's financial condition. Excerpts from the annual report of Capital One follow.

ANALYSIS EXCERPT

Off-Balance-Sheet Securitizations. The Company actively engages in off-balance-sheet securitization transactions of loans for funding purposes. The Company receives the proceeds from third-party investors for securities issued from the Company's securitization vehicles which are collateralized by transferred receivables from the Company's portfolio. Securities outstanding totaling $41.2 billion as of December 31, 2004, represent undivided interests in the pools of consumer loan receivables that are sold in underwritten offerings or in private placement transactions. The securitization of consumer loans has been a significant source of liquidity for the Company. The Company believes that it has the ability to continue to utilize off-balance-sheet securitization arrangements as a source of liquidity; however, a significant reduction or termination of the Company's off-balance-sheet securitizations could require the Company to draw down existing liquidity and/or to obtain additional funding through the issuance of secured borrowings or unsecured debt, the raising of additional deposits or the slowing of asset growth to offset or to satisfy liquidity needs.

Off-balance-sheet securitizations involve the transfer of pools of consumer loan receivables by the Company to one or more third-party trusts or qualified special purpose entities in transactions that are accounted for as sales in accordance with SFAS 140. Certain undivided interests in the pool of consumer loan receivables are sold to investors as asset-backed securities in public underwritten offerings or private placement transactions. The proceeds from off-balance-sheet securitizations are distributed

(continued)

ANALYSIS EXCERPT *(concluded)*

by the trusts to the Company as consideration for the consumer loan receivables transferred. Each new off-balance-sheet securitization results in the removal of consumer loan principal receivables equal to the sold undivided interests in the pool from the Company's consolidated balance sheet ("off-balance-sheet loans"), the recognition of certain retained residual interests and a gain on the sale. The remaining undivided interests in principal receivables of the pool, as well as the unpaid billed finance charge and fee receivables related to the Company's undivided interest in the principal receivables are retained by the Company and recorded as consumer loans on the Consolidated Balance Sheet. The amounts of the remaining undivided interests fluctuate as the accountholders make principal payments and incur new charges on the selected accounts. The amount of retained consumer loan receivables was $10.3 billion and $8.3 billion as of December 31, 2004 and 2003, respectively.

Case of eBay. eBay constructed office facilities in San Jose, California, at a total cost of $126.4 million in 2000. The property was owned by a separate entity, eBay Realty Trust, and leased to eBay. The structure of this transaction (called a "synthetic lease") was unique in that it allowed eBay to be the lessee of an operating lease for financial reporting purposes, but the owner of the property for federal tax purposes, thus allowing it to treat as deductions both the interest on the lease and the depreciation of the property. These synthetic leases became increasingly popular because they provided off-balance-sheet financing yet allowed the organization to retain all of the tax benefits of ownership.

eBay Realty Trust was formed with a nominal investment. It then agreed to construct a building for eBay, and to lease the property to eBay upon completion. Financing of the building came from lenders, with Chase Manhattan Bank serving as agent. The loan was secured by a mortgage on the property and an assignment of the lease. In addition, eBay agreed to place $126.4 million in a cash collateral account and also guaranteed the owner-lessor a minimum residual amount upon termination of the lease and sale of the property.

Synthetic leases now increasingly fall under the purview of FIN 46 and these entities are now classified as VIEs, thus requiring consolidation. eBay discusses the pending effects of the adoption of FIN 46 in its 2002 10-K and the ultimate consolidation of the VIE in its 2004 10-K, excerpts of which are provided in Exhibit 3.17. Consolidation resulted in the addition of $126.4 million of property and $122.5 million of debt to eBay's balance sheet, together with a noncontrolling interest of $3.9 million representing the investment by noncontrolling shareholders.

Case of Dell. Dell provides financing for the purchase of its computers in the form of loans and leases. Rather than provide this financing in-house, Dell entered into a joint venture (Dell Financial Services or DFS) with CIT, the consumer finance company, which provides the financing and splits the profit with Dell. By virtue of the joint venture agreement, Dell did not control this joint venture despite its 70% economic interest and, consequently, did not consolidate it in its financial statements. This entity was subsequently deemed to be a variable interest entity (VIE) under FIN 46R however, and, as a result, Dell is now required to consolidate DFS in its financial statements.

---

eBay Lease Footnotes   *Exhibit 3.17*

2002 10-K: On March 1, 2000, we entered into a five-year lease for general office facilities located in San Jose, California. This five-year lease is commonly referred to as a synthetic lease because it represents a form of off-balance-sheet financing under which an unrelated third-party funds 100% of the costs of the acquisition of the property and leases the asset to us as lessee. . . . In January 2003, the Financial Accounting Standards Board, or FASB, issued FASB Interpretation No. 46, or FIN 46, "Consolidation of Variable Interest Entities." This interpretation of Accounting Research Bulletin No. 51, "Consolidated Financial Statements," addresses consolidation by business enterprises of certain variable interest entities where there is a controlling financial interest in a variable interest entity or where the variable interest entity does not have sufficient equity at risk to finance its activities without additional subordinated financial support from other parties. . . . We expect that the adoption of FIN 46 will require us to include our San Jose facilities lease and potentially certain investments in our Consolidated Financial Statements effective July 1, 2003.

2004 10-K: In accordance with the provisions of FIN 46, "Consolidation of Variable Interest Entities," we have included our San Jose corporate headquarters lease arrangement in our consolidated financial statements effective July 1, 2003. Under this accounting standard, our balance sheet at December 31, 2003 and 2004, reflects additions for land and buildings totaling $126.4 million, lease obligations of $122.5 million and non-controlling minority interests of $3.9 million. Our consolidated statement of income for the year ended December 31, 2003, reflects the reclassification of lease payments on our San Jose corporate headquarters from operating expense to interest expense, beginning with quarters following our adoption of FIN 46 on July 1, 2003, a $5.4 million after-tax charge for cumulative depreciation for periods from lease inception through June 30, 2003, and incremental depreciation expense of approximately $400,000, net of tax, per quarter for periods after June 30, 2003. We have adopted the provisions of FIN 46 prospectively from July 1, 2003, and as a result, have not restated prior periods. The cumulative effect of the change in accounting principle arising from the adoption of FIN 46 has been reflected in net income in 2003.

Excerpts from Dell's 10-K footnote relating to Dell Financial Services are provided in Exhibit 3.18.

Interestingly, as described at the end of its footnote, Dell has renegotiated its joint venture agreement to allow it to sell finance receivables to a new "unconsolidated qualifying special purpose entity" (QSPE). QSPEs are SPEs that are structured in order to be exempt from the provisions of FIN 46R and are, therefore, not required to be consolidated. The QSPE structure requires an independent, financially solvent entity with total control over the purchased assets. The transfers are, therefore, viewed as a sale to an independent party, with a consequent removal of the assets from the balance sheet and recognition of a gain (loss) on sale. As companies begin to realize the adverse effects of consolidation under FIN 46R, many more may be establishing QSPEs as an alternative to VIEs in order to preserve off-balance-sheet treatment of the asset transfers.

Case of Enron. Our fourth example, Enron, demonstrates the misuse of special purpose entities. According to its CFO, Enron's substantial growth could not be sustained through issuing common stock because of near-term dilution and also the company could not increase its financial leverage through debt issuance for fear of jeopardizing its credit rating. As a result, the company sought to conceal massive amounts of debt and to significantly overstate its earnings with SPEs.

Enron's hedge of its investment in Rhythms NetConnections was the first of several such SPEs that the company established in order to avoid recognition of asset impairments and serves as an appropriate example of the misuse of this financial technique. Enron invested $10 million ($1.85 per share) in Rhythms in 1998. The

Exhibit 3.18

■ ■ ■ ■ ■ ■ ■

Financial Services—Dell

Dell is currently a partner in DFS, a joint venture with CIT. The joint venture allows Dell to provide its customers with various financing alternatives while CIT usually provides the financing for the transaction between DFS and the customer for certain transactions. Dell recognized revenue from the sale of products pursuant to loan and lease financing transactions of $5.6 billion, $4.5 billion, and $3.6 billion during fiscal 2005, 2004, and 2003, respectively.

Dell currently owns a 70% equity interest in DFS. During the third quarter of fiscal 2004. Dell began consolidating DFS's financial results due to the adoption of FIN 46R. FIN 46R provides that if an entity is the primary beneficiary of a Variable Interest Entity ("VIE"), the assets, liabilities, and results of operations of the VIE should be consolidated in the entity's financial statements. Based on the guidance in FIN 46R, Dell concluded that DFS is a VIE and Dell is the primary beneficiary of DFS's expected cash flows. Prior to consolidating DFS's financial results, Dell's investment in DFS was accounted for under the equity method because the company historically did not exercise control over DFS. Accordingly, the consolidation of DFS had no impact on Dell's net income or earnings per share. CIT's equity ownership in the net assets of DFS as of January 28, 2005, was $13 million, which is recorded as minority interest and included in other non-current liabilities on Dell's consolidated statement of financial position. The consolidation did not alter the partnership agreement or risk sharing arrangement between Dell and CIT.

During the third quarter of fiscal 2005, Dell and CIT executed an agreement that extended the term of the joint venture to January 29, 2010 and modified certain terms of the relationship. Prior to execution of the extension agreement, CIT provided all of the financing for transactions between DFS and the customer. The extension agreement also gives Dell the right, but not the obligation, to participate in such financings beginning in the fourth quarter of fiscal 2005. During the fourth quarter of fiscal 2005. Dell began selling certain loan and lease finance receivables to an unconsolidated qualifying special purpose entity that is wholly owned by Dell. The qualifying special purpose entity is a separate legal entity with assets and liabilities separate from those of Dell. The qualifying special purpose entity has entered into a financing arrangement with a multiseller conduit that in turn issues asset-backed debt securities to the capital markets. Transfers of financing receivables are recorded in accordance with the provisions of SFAS No. 140, *Accounting for Transfers and Servicing of Financial Assets and Extinguishment of Liabilities.* The sale of these loan and lease financing receivables did not have a material impact on Dell's consolidated financial position, results of operations, or cash flows for fiscal 2005.

following year, Rhythms went public. Enron was prohibited from selling its investment due to a prior agreement and wished to shelter its $300 million unrealized gain from potential loss.

Although the transaction is quite complicated, in essence, Enron formed an SPE and capitalized it with its own stock, covered by forward contracts to preserve the value of its investment from potential decline. The SPE, in turn, acted as the counterparty (an insurance company) to hedge Enron's investment in Rhythms and to protect the company from a possible decline in its value. If the investment declined in value, Enron, theoretically, would be able to call on the guaranty issued by the SPE to make up the loss.

If this transaction was conducted with a third party with sufficient equity of its own, Enron would have effectively hedged its investment and would not be required to report a loss if the investment declined in value. As structured, however, the SPE had no outside equity of its own and its assets consisted solely of Enron stock. The hedge was a sham. Furthermore, Enron took the position that these SPEs did not need to be consolidated in its annual report. This meant that any liabilities of the SPE would not be reflected on Enron's consolidated balance sheet.

Consolidation rules require that the SPEs be truly independent in order to avoid consolidation. That means that they should be capitalized with outside equity and effective control should remain with outside parties. Enron violated both of these

■ ■ ■ ■ ■ ■

**PARTNER
PROBLEMS**

Investment banks including CFSB and Merrill Lynch earned tens of millions of dollars helping Enron shield billions of dollars in debt by selling the company's off-balance-sheet partnerships to institutional investors.

requirements. First, in many cases Enron guaranteed the investment of its "outside" investors. That meant that the investors did not have the required risk of loss. And second, the management of the SPEs was often Enron employees with outside investors not serving in a management capacity. In the restatement of its 1997–2000 financial statements in the third quarter of 2001, Enron consolidated the SPEs. The effect was to recognize on-balance-sheet hundreds of millions of dollars of debt, to record asset impairments of approximately $1 billion, and to reduce stockholders' equity by $1.2 billion. The restatement eroded investor confidence and triggered violations of debt covenants that ultimately resulted in the bankruptcy of the company.

How much could investors have learned about these SPE activities from Enron's annual report? Exhibit 3.19 contains an excerpt from Enron's 2000 annual report, the year before its bankruptcy. The only mention of the SPEs was in a related party footnote. Enron described the hedging of its investment (merchant) portfolio and revealed that the SPEs had been capitalized with Enron common stock. It also disclosed that the managing partner of the SPE was an executive of Enron and highlighted the disclosures in a separate "Related Party" footnote. In hindsight, the disclosures proved more significant than they first appeared. Analysts are now paying much more attention to these details following the billions of dollars of losses that resulted from Enron's collapse.

Enron Related Party Transactions Footnote

Exhibit 3.19

In 2000 and 1999, Enron entered into transactions with limited partnerships (the Related Party) whose general partner's managing member is a senior officer of Enron. The limited partners of the Related Party are unrelated to Enron. Management believes that the terms of the transactions with the Related Party were reasonable compared to those which could have been negotiated with unrelated third parties.

In 2000, Enron entered into transactions with the Related Party to hedge certain merchant investments and other assets. As part of the transactions, Enron (i) contributed to newly-formed entities (the Entities) assets valued at approximately $1.2 billion, including $150 million in Enron notes payable, 3.7 million restricted shares of outstanding Enron common stock and the right to receive up to 18.0 million shares of outstanding Enron common stock in March 2003 (subject to certain conditions) and (ii) transferred to the Entities assets valued at approximately $309 million, including a $50 million note payable and an investment in an entity that indirectly holds warrants convertible into common stock of an Enron equity method investee. In return, Enron received economic interests in the Entities, $309 million in notes receivable, of which $259 million is recorded at Enron's carryover basis of zero, and a special distribution from the Entities in the form of $1.2 billion in notes receivable, subject to changes in the principal for amounts payable by Enron in connection with the execution of additional derivative instruments. Cash in these Entities of $172.6 million is invested in Enron demand notes. In addition, Enron paid $123 million to purchase share-settled options from the Entities on 21.7 million shares of Enron common stock. The Entities paid Enron $10.7 million to terminate the share-settled options on 14.6 million shares of Enron common stock outstanding. In late 2000, Enron entered into share-settled collar arrangements with the entities on 15.4 million shares of Enron common stock. Such arrangements will be accounted for as equity transactions when settled.

In 2000, Enron entered into derivative transactions with the Entities with a combined notional amount of approximately $2.1 billion to hedge certain merchant investments and other assets. Enron's notes receivable balance was reduced by $36 million as a result of premiums owed on derivative transactions. Enron recognized revenues of approximately $500 million related to the subsequent change in the market value of these derivatives, which offset market value changes of certain merchant investments and price risk management activities. In addition, Enron recognized $44.5 million and $14.1 million of interest income and interest expense, respectively, on the notes receivable from and payable to the Entities.

·······SHAREHOLDERS' EQUITY

Equity refers to owner (shareholder) financing of a company. It is viewed as reflecting the claims of owners on the net assets of the company. Holders of equity securities are typically subordinate to creditors, meaning that creditors' claims are settled first. Also, typically variation exists across equity holders on seniority for claims on net assets. Equity holders are exposed to the maximum risk associated with a company. At the same time, they have the maximum return possibilities as they are entitled to all returns once creditors are covered.

Our analysis of equity must take into account several measurement and reporting standards for shareholders' equity. Such analysis would include:

- Classifying and distinguishing among major sources of equity financing.
- Examining rights for classes of shareholders and their priorities in liquidation.
- Evaluating legal restrictions for distribution of equity.
- Reviewing contractual, legal, and other restrictions on distribution of retained earnings.
- Assessing terms and provisions of convertible securities, stock options, and other arrangements involving potential issuance of shares.

It is important for us to distinguish between liability and equity instruments given their differences in risks and returns. This is especially crucial when financial instruments have characteristics of both. Some of the more difficult questions we must confront are:

- Is a financial instrument such as mandatory redeemable preferred stock or a put option on a company's common stock–obligating a company to redeem it at a specified amount–a liability or equity instrument?
- Is a financial instrument such as a stock purchase warrant or an employee stock option–obligating a company to issue its stock at specified amounts–a liability or equity instrument?
- Is a right to issue or repurchase a company's stock at specified amounts an asset or equity instrument?
- Is a financial instrument having features of both liabilities and equity sufficiently different from both to warrant separate presentation? If yes, what are the criteria for this presentation?

The following sections help us answer these and other issues confronting our analysis of financial statements. We will return to these questions at other points in the book to further describe the analysis implications. This section first considers capital stock and then retained earnings–the two major components of equity.

Capital Stock
Reporting of Capital Stock

Reporting of capital stock includes an explanation of changes in the number of capital shares. This information is disclosed in the financial statements or related notes. The following partial list shows reasons for changes in capital stock, separated according to increases and decreases.

Sources of increases in capital stock outstanding:

- Issuances of stock.
- Conversion of debentures and preferred stock.
- Issuances pursuant to stock dividends and splits.
- Issuances of stock in acquisitions and mergers.
- Issuances pursuant to stock options and warrants exercised.

■ ■ ■ ■ ■ ■ ■
GLOBAL
Countries vary in preference given to creditors vs. shareholders; for example, Germany, France, and Japan historically give preference to shareholders.

■ ■ ■ ■ ■ ■ ■
MERGER-DADDY
The biggest-ever merger was America Online Inc.'s $166 billion, all-stock bid for Time Warner, Inc. AOL-Time Warner subsequently wrote off over $93 billion of goodwill recognized in the merger.

Sources of decreases in capital stock outstanding:

- Purchases and retirements of stock.
- Stock buybacks.
- Reverse stock splits.

Another important aspect of our analysis of capital stock is the evaluation of the options held by others that, when exercised, cause the number of shares outstanding to increase and thus dilute ownership. These options include:

- Conversion rights of debentures and preferred stock into common.
- Warrants entitling holders to exchange them for stock under specified conditions.
- Stock options with compensation and bonus plans calling for issuances of capital stock over a period of time at fixed prices—examples are qualified stock option plans and employee stock ownership plans.
- Commitments to issue capital stock—an example is merger agreements calling for additional consideration contingent on the occurrence of an event such as achieving a specific earnings level.

The importance of analyzing these disclosures is to alert us to the potential increase in the number of shares outstanding. The extent of dilution in earnings and book value per share depends on factors like the amount received or other rights given up when converting securities. We must recognize that dilution is a real cost for a company—a cost that is given little formal recognition in financial statements. We examine the impact of dilution on earnings per share in the appendix to Chapter 6.

Contributed Capital. **Contributed (or paid-in) capital** is the total financing received from shareholders in return for capital shares. Contributed capital is usually divided into two parts. One part is assigned to the par or stated value of capital shares: **common** and/or **preferred stock** (if stock is no-par, then it is assigned the total financing). The remainder is reported as **contributed** (or **paid-in**) **capital in excess of par or stated value** (also called *additional paid-in capital*). When combined, these accounts reflect the amounts paid in by shareholders for financing business activities. Other accounts in the contributed capital section of shareholders' equity arise from charges or credits from a variety of capital transactions, including (1) sale of treasury stock; (2) capital changes arising from business combinations; (3) capital donations, often shown separately as donated capital; (4) stock issuance costs and merger expenses; and (5) capitalization of retained earnings by means of stock dividends.

Treasury Stock. **Treasury stock** (or *buybacks*) are the shares of a company's stock reacquired after having been previously issued and fully paid for. Acquisition of treasury stock by a company reduces both assets and shareholders' equity. Consistent with this transaction, treasury stock is not an asset, it is a *contra-equity account* (negative equity). Treasury stock is typically recorded at *cost,* and the most common method of presentation is to deduct treasury stock cost from the total of shareholders' equity. When companies record treasury stock at par, they typically report it as a contra to (reduction of) its related class of stock.

Classification of Capital Stock

Capital stock are shares issued to equity holders in return for assets and services. There are two basic types of capital stock: preferred and common. There also are a number of different variations within each of these two classes of stock.

■ ■ ■ ■ ■ ■ ■
MERGER DISCLOSURE
New accounting rules require companies to explain in more detail why they are making an acquisition. They must tell what assets, including intangible ones such as goodwill and patents, they are getting for their money.

Preferred Stock.   **Preferred stock** is a special class of stock possessing preferences or features not enjoyed by common stock. The more typical features attached to preferred stock include:

- Dividend distribution preferences including participating and cumulative features.
- Liquidation priorities–especially important since the discrepancy between par and liquidation value of preferred stock can be substantial. For example, Johnson Controls issued preferred stock with a par value of $1 and a liquidation value of $51.20.
- Convertibility (redemption) into common stock–the SEC requires separate presentation of these shares when preferred stock possesses characteristics of debt (such as redemption requirements).
- Nonvoting rights–which can change with changes in items such as arrearages in dividends.
- Call provisions–usually protecting preferred shareholders against premature redemption (call premiums often decrease over time).

While preferred shareholders are usually senior to common shareholders, the preferred shareholders' rights to dividends are usually fixed. Yet, their dividend rights can be cumulative, meaning they are entitled to arrearages (prior years) of dividends before common shareholders receive any dividends.

Among preferred stock classes, we find a variety of preferences relating to dividend and liquidation rights. These features, and the fixed nature of their dividends, often give preferred stock the appearance of liabilities. An important distinction between preferred shareholders and creditors is that preferred stockholders are typically not entitled to demand redemption of their shares. Nevertheless, some preferred stocks possess set redemption dates that can include sinking funds–funds accumulated for expected repayment. Characteristics of preferred stock that would make them more akin to common stock include dividend participation rights, voting rights, and rights of conversion into common stock. Preferred stock often has a par value, but it need not be the amount at which it was originally issued.

Common Stock.   **Common stock** is a class of stock representing ownership interest and bearing ultimate risks and rewards of company performance. Common stock represents **residual interests**–having no preference, but reaping residual net income and absorbing net losses. Common stock can carry a par value; if not, it is usually assigned a stated value. The par value of common stock is a matter of legal and historical significance–it usually is unimportant for modern financial statement analysis.

There is sometimes more than one class of common stock for major companies. The distinctions between common stock classes typically are differences in dividend, voting, or other rights.

Analyzing Capital Stock

Items that constitute shareholders' equity usually do not have a marked effect on income determination and, as a consequence, do not seriously impact analysis of income. The more relevant information for analysis relates to the composition of capital accounts and to their applicable restrictions. Composition of equity is important because of provisions that can affect residual rights of common shares and, accordingly, the rights, risks, and returns of equity investors. Such provisions include dividend participation rights, conversion rights, and a variety of options and conditions that characterize complex securities frequently issued under merger agreements–most of which dilute common equity. It is important that we reconstruct and explain changes in these capital accounts.

Retained Earnings

Retained earnings are the earned capital of a company. The retained earnings account reflects the accumulation of undistributed earnings or losses of a company since its inception. This contrasts with the capital stock and additional paid-in capital accounts that constitute capital contributed by shareholders. Retained earnings are the primary source of dividend distributions to shareholders. While some states permit distributions to shareholders from additional paid-in capital, these distributions represent capital (not earnings) distributions.

Cash and Stock Dividends

A **cash dividend** is a distribution of cash to shareholders. It is the most common form of dividend and, once declared, is a liability of a company. Another form of dividend is the *dividend in kind,* or property dividend. These dividends are payable in the assets of a company, in goods, or in the stock of another corporation. Such dividends are valued at the market value of the assets distributed.

ANALYSIS EXCERPT

Ranchers Exploration and Development Corp. distributed a dividend in kind using gold bars. Also, Dresser Industries paid a dividend in kind with "a distribution of one INDRESCO share for every five shares of the Company's common stock."

A **stock dividend** is a distribution of a company's own shares to shareholders on a pro rata basis. It represents, in effect, a permanent capitalization of earnings. Shareholders receive additional shares in return for reallocation of retained earnings to capital accounts. Accounting for *small* (or *ordinary*) *stock dividends,* typically less than 20% to 25% of shares outstanding, requires the stock dividend be valued at its market value on the date of declaration. *Large stock dividends* (or "split-ups effected in the form of a dividend"), typically exceeding 25% of shares outstanding, require that the stock dividend be valued at the par value of shares issued. We must not be misled into attaching substantive value to stock dividends. Companies sometimes encourage such inferences for their own self-interests as shown here:

ANALYSIS EXCERPT

Wickes Companies announced a stock dividend "in lieu of the quarterly cash dividend." Its management asserted this stock "dividend continues Wickes' 88-year record of uninterrupted dividend payments."

Restrictions on Retained Earnings

Retained earnings can be restricted as to the payment of dividends as a result of contractual agreements, such as loan covenants, or by action of the board of directors. **Restrictions** (or **covenants**) **on retained earnings** are constraints or requirements on the retention of a certain retained earnings amount. An important restriction involves limitations on a company's distribution of dividends. Bond indentures and loan agreements are typical sources of these limitations. **Appropriations of retained earnings** are reclassifications of retained earnings for specific purposes. Through management action, and with board of director approval in compliance with legal requirements, companies can appropriate retained earnings. Appropriations of retained earnings recognize that the company does not intend to distribute these amounts as dividends, but rather to reserve them for a specific purpose. Neither of these restrictions sets aside cash. They only serve to notify investors that the future payment of dividends is restricted in some manner.

Spin-Offs and Split-Offs

Companies often divest subsidiaries, either in an outright sale or as a distribution to shareholders. The sale of a subsidiary is accounted for just like the sale of any other asset: a gain (loss) on the sale is recognized for the difference between the consideration received and the book value of the subsidiary investment. Distributions of subsidiary stock to shareholders can take one of two forms:

Spin-off, the distribution of subsidiary stock to shareholders as a dividend; assets (investment in subsidiary) are reduced as is retained earnings.

Split-off, the exchange of subsidiary stock owned by the company for shares in the company owned by the shareholders; assets (investment in subsidiary) are reduced and the stock received from the shareholders is treated as treasury stock.

If these transactions affect shareholders on a pro rata basis (equally), the investment in the subsidiary is distributed at book value. For non-pro rata distributions, the investment is first written up to market value, resulting in a gain on the distribution, and the market value of the investment is distributed to shareholders.

To illustrate, AT&T split off the Wireless subsidiary as a separate company via an exchange of the wireless subsidiary stock owned by AT&T for shares in AT&T owned by its shareholders. Since the exchange was a non-pro rata distribution, the shares were written up to market value prior to the exchange, resulting in a gain of $13.5 billion as reported below:

ANALYSIS EXCERPT

On July 9, 2001, AT&T completed the split-off of AT&T Wireless as a separate, independently traded company. All AT&T Wireless Group tracking stock was converted into AT&T Wireless common stock on a one-for-one basis, and 1.136 million shares of AT&T Wireless common stock held by AT&T were distributed to AT&T common shareowners on a basis of 1.609 shares of AT&T Wireless for each AT&T share outstanding. AT&T common shareowners received whole shares of AT&T Wireless common stock and cash payments for fractional shares. The IRS ruled that the transaction qualified as tax-free for AT&T and its shareowners for U.S. federal income tax purposes, with the exception of cash received for fractional shares. The split-off of AT&T Wireless resulted in a tax-free noncash gain on disposition of discontinued operations of $13.5 billion, which represented the difference between the fair value of the AT&T Wireless tracking stock at the date of the split-off and AT&T's book value of AT&T Wireless.

AT&T next spun off its Broadband subsidiary in connection with its acquisition by Comcast. The spin-off was effected as a non-pro rata distribution to shareholders and, consequently, was recorded at fair market value, resulting in a gain of $1.3 billion as reported here:

ANALYSIS EXCERPT

On November 18, 2002, AT&T spun-off AT&T Broadband, which was comprised primarily of the AT&T Broadband segment, to AT&T shareowners. The Internal Revenue Service (IRS) ruled that the transaction qualified as tax-free for AT&T and our shareowners for U.S. federal income tax purposes, with the exception of cash received for fractional shares. In connection with the non-pro rata spin-off of AT&T Broadband, AT&T wrote up the net assets of AT&T Broadband to fair value. This resulted in a noncash gain on disposition of $1.3 billion, which represented the difference between the fair value of the AT&T Broadband business at the date of the spin-off and AT&T's book value of AT&T Broadband, net of certain charges triggered by the spin-off and their related income tax effect. These charges included compensation expense due to accelerated vesting of stock options, as well as the enhancement of certain incentive plans.

In both of these cases, the transactions with AT&T shareholders were non-pro rata, meaning that different groups of AT&T shareholders were treated differently. Had these transactions been effected on a pro rata basis (all shareholders receiving their pro rata share of the distribution), the subsidiary stock would have been distributed at book value and no gain would have been recognized. Our analysis must be cognizant of these noncash, transitory gains when evaluating income.

Prior Period Adjustments

Prior period adjustments are mainly corrections for errors in prior periods' financial statements. Companies exclude them from the income statement and report them as an adjustment (net of tax) to the beginning balance of retained earnings.

ANALYSIS VIEWPOINT   *. . . YOU ARE THE SHAREHOLDER*

You own common stock in a company. This company's stock price doubled in the past 12 months, and it is currently selling at $66. Today, the company announces a 3-for-1 "stock split effected in the form of a dividend." How do you interpret this announcement?

Book Value per Share
Computation of Book Value per Share

Book value per share is the per share amount resulting from a company's liquidation at amounts reported on its balance sheet. *Book value* is conventional terminology referring to net asset value—that is, total assets reduced by claims against them. The *book value of common stock* is equal to the total assets less liabilities and claims of securities senior to common stock (such as preferred stock) at amounts reported on the balance sheet (but can also include unbooked claims of senior securities). A simple means of computing book value is to add up the common stock equity accounts and reduce this total by any senior claims not reflected in the balance sheet (including preferred stock dividend arrearages, liquidation premiums, or other asset preferences to which preferred shares are entitled).

The shareholders' equity section of Kimberly Corp. for periods ending in Years 4 and 5 is reproduced here as an example of the measurement of book value per share:

	Year 5	Year 4
Preferred stock, 7% cumulative, par value $100 (authorized 4,000,000 shares; outstanding 3,602,811 shares)	$ 360,281,100	$ 360,281,100
Common stock, par value $16.67 (authorized 90,000,000 shares; outstanding 54,138,137 shares at December 31, Year 5, and 54,129,987 shares at December 31, Year 4)	902,302,283	902,166,450
Retained earnings	2,362,279,244	2,220,298,288
Total shareholder's equity	$3,624,862,627	$3,482,745,838

Note: Preferred stock is nonparticipating and callable at 105. Dividends for Year 5 are in arrears.

Our calculation of book value per share for both common and preferred stock at the end of Year 5 follows:

	Preferred	Common	Total
Preferred stock* (at $100 par)	$360,281,100		$ 360,281,100
Dividends in arrears (7%)	25,219,677		25,219,677
Common stock		$ 902,302,283	902,302,283
Retained earnings (net of amount attributed to dividend in arrears)		2,337,059,567	2,337,059,567
Total	$385,500,777	$3,239,361,850	$3,624,862,627
Divided by number of shares outstanding	3,602,811	54,138,137	
Book value per share	$107.00	$59.84	

*The call premium does not normally enter into computation of book value per share because the call provision is at the option of the company.

Relevance of Book Value per Share

Book value plays an important role in analysis of financial statements. Applications can include the following:

- Book value, with potential adjustments, is frequently used in assessing merger terms.
- Analysis of companies composed of mainly liquid assets (finance, investment, insurance, and banking institutions) relies extensively on book values.
- Analysis of high-grade bonds and preferred stock attaches considerable importance to asset coverage.

These applications must recognize the accounting considerations entering into the computation of book value per share such as the following:

- Carrying values of assets, particularly long-lived assets like property, plant, and equipment, are usually reported at cost and can markedly differ from market values.
- Internally generated intangible assets often are not reflected in book value, nor are contingent assets with a reasonable probability of occurrence.

Also, other adjustments often are necessary. For example, if preferred stock has characteristics of debt, it is appropriate to treat it as debt at the prevailing interest rate. In short, book value is a valuable analytical tool, but we must apply it with discrimination and understanding.

Liabilities at the "Edge" of Equity

This section describes two items straddling liabilities and equity–redeemable preferred stock and minority interest.

Redeemable Preferred Stock

Analysts must be alert for equity securities (typically preferred stock) that possess mandatory redemption provisions making them more akin to debt than equity. These securities require a company to pay funds at specific dates. A true equity security does not impose such requirements. Examples of these securities, under the guise of preferred stock, exist for many companies. Tenneco's annual report refers to its preferred stock redemption provision as follows:

ANALYSIS EXCERPT

The aggregate maturities applicable to preferred stock issues outstanding at December 31, 2001, are none for 2002, $10 million for 2003, and $23 million for each of 2004, 2005, and 2006.

The SEC asserts that redeemable preferred stocks are different from conventional equity capital and should *not* be included in shareholders' equity nor combined with nonredeemable equity securities. The SEC also requires disclosure of redemption terms and five-year maturity data. Accounting standards require disclosure of redemption requirements of redeemable stock for each of the five years subsequent to the balance sheet date. Companies whose shares are not publicly traded are not subject to SEC requirements and can continue to report redeemable preferred stock as equity. Still, our analysis should treat them for what they are–an obligation to pay cash at a future date.

APPENDIX 3A: LEASE ACCOUNTING AND ANALYSIS—LESSOR

Many manufacturing companies lease their products rather then sell them outright. Examples are IBM and Caterpillar. Other companies, like General Electric, act as financial intermediaries, purchasing the assets from manufacturers and leasing them to the ultimate user. Leasing has become an important ingredient in the sales of products and is now also a significant factor in the analysis of financial statements. This appendix briefly describes the accounting and analysis of leases from the perspective of a lessor. The accounting for leases by the lessor is similar to that for lessees. With minor exceptions, the lessor categorizes the lease as operating or capital to parallel the classification by the lessee. If classified as an operating lease, the leased asset remains on the lessor's balance sheet, and the rent payments are treated as income when received. The lessor continues to record depreciation expense on the leased asset. The difference between the rent income and the depreciation expense is the lessor's profit on the lease.

If the lease is classified as capital, the lessor removes the leased asset from its balance sheet and records a receivable equal to the sum of the expected minimum lease payments. The difference between the receivable and the asset removed from the balance sheet is classified as a liability, unearned income, which is reduced and recorded as earned income periodically over the life of the lease. Two types of leases are important from the lessor's point of view:

1. **Sales-type lease.** In this case, the cost of the leased asset is different from its fair market value at the date it is leased. This situation might arise, for example, with a company like IBM that manufactures computers and leases them to its customers. In this case, accountants take the view that the asset has been sold and IBM has entered into a subsequent financing transaction with the lessee. As a result, IBM records a sale, cost of goods sold, and gross profit at the time the lease is executed. IBM, therefore, records gross profit upon the lease of the computer and lease revenue over the life of the lease equal to its unearned revenue when the lease is signed. Furthermore, since the leased asset has been removed from the balance sheet, IBM no longer records depreciation expense.

2. **Direct financing lease.** Companies like General Electric Capital Corporation engage in direct financing leases. In this case, GECC is acting like a bank. It purchases the asset from the manufacturer and leases it directly to the customer. In this case, the value of the lease (present value of the lease payments receivable) is equal to the cost of the asset purchased and no sale or gross profit is recorded. Instead, GECC recognizes lease income gradually over the life of the lease.

ANALYSIS IMPLICATIONS

The analysis implications of leasing are similar to those involving any extension of credit. Be aware of the risks inherent in any extension of credit. An analysis of the adequacy of the reserve for uncollectible lease receivables in comparison with the loss experience of the lessor is required. And second, recognize that lease receivables will be collected over a period of years and compare the average life of the lease portfolio with that of the company's liabilities. That is, it is inappropriate to finance fixed-rate leases of intermediate duration with short-term floating rate debt.

Lessors often package service contracts with leases to gain additional revenue. Under GAAP, income from the service contract must be recognized ratably over the life of the contract. In an effort to boost current period sales and profits, companies have attempted to accelerate the revenue recognition from service contracts by recording relatively more of the initial contract in the lease itself, thus increasing sales and gross profit and reducing the future payments under the service contract. Xerox is a company challenged by the SEC for this practice. Analysts must be aware of this possibility and examine carefully the relative components of lease income and service revenue mix in the company's total sales.

SALE-LEASEBACK

A **sale-leaseback** transaction involves the sale of an owned asset and execution of a lease on the same asset. Companies often use sale-leasebacks to free up cash from existing assets, primarily real estate. Generally, any profit realized on the value of the asset sold must be deferred and recognized over the life of the lease as a reduction of lease expense.

.....APPENDIX 3B: ACCOUNTING SPECIFICS FOR POSTRETIREMENT BENEFITS

ECONOMICS OF PENSION ACCOUNTING

In this section, we examine the economics underlying accounting for defined benefit pension plans. The following example is used to illustrate the discussion:

- Consider a pension plan with a single employee, J. Smith, who joined the plan exactly five years ago on January 1, 2001. Smith is due to retire on December 31, 2025, and is expected to live for 10 years after retirement.
- J. Smith's current compensation is $10,000 per annum. Actuarial estimates indicate that compensation is expected to increase by 4% per annum over the next 20 years.
- The pension plan specifies the following formula for determining the employee's pension benefit: "The annual pension is equal to one week's compensation at the time of retirement multiplied by the number of years worked under the plan." Employees vest four years after joining the plan.
- At December 31, 2005, the fair value of assets in the pension fund is $2,000. In 2006, the employer contributes $200 to the pension fund.
- Return on pension assets is 22% in 2006. The long-term return is expected to be 10% per annum.
- Discount rate is 7% per annum.

Pension Obligation

Exhibit 3B.1 explains the computation of the pension obligation, under alternative assumptions, for the J. Smith example. We first determine the pension obligation as of December 31, 2005. This computation is explained in the two columns headed "2005 Formula." We describe two alternative definitions for the pension obligation:

Determining Pension Obligations under Different Assumptions—J. Smith Example

Exhibit 3B.1

■ ■ ■ ■ ■ ■ ■

| | 2005 FORMULA | | 2006 FORMULA | ASSUMPTION CHANGE | |
	Actual	Projected	Projected	Actuarial	Plan
At December 31, 2025 (Retirement)					
Salary per year.........................	$10,000	$21,911	$21,911	$26,533	$26,533
Pension per year	962	2,107	2,528	3,061	4,592
Present value of pension...........	6,753	14,798	17,757	21,503	32,254
At December 31, 2005					
Present value of pension...........	1,745	3,824			
At December 31, 2006					
Present value of pension...........		4,091	4,910	5,946	8,919

1. **Accumulated benefit obligation (ABO)** is the actuarial present value of the future pension benefits payable to employees at retirement based on their *current* compensation and service to date. (The term *actuarial* signifies it is based on assumptions such as life expectancy and employee turnover.) This present value is equivalent to an employer's current obligation if the plan is discontinued immediately. The computation of ABO for the J. Smith example is illustrated in the column headed "Actual" in Exhibit 3B.1. Because J. Smith has been with the plan for five years, the annual pension benefit, given current compensation, is $962 (5/52 × $10,000). This pension benefit can be viewed as a fixed annuity of $962 per annum for 10 years. Given a discount rate of 7% per annum, the value of these pension benefits at retirement is $6,753 [7.0236 (from interest tables) × $962]. This means the entire stream of future pension benefits is represented by a single lump sum payment of $6,753 on December 31, 2025. The present value of this amount as of the end of 2005, or $1,745 [computed as $6,753 × 0.2584 (from interest tables)], is the accumulated benefit obligation (ABO).

2. **Projected benefit obligation (PBO)** is the actuarial estimate of future pension benefits payable to employees on retirement based on *expected future* compensation and service to date. This estimate is a more realistic estimate of the pension obligation. In our example, J. Smith's salary is expected to increase by 4% per annum. The computation of PBO for the J. Smith example is shown in the column headed "Projected" in Exhibit 3B.1. The PBO at December 31, 2005, is $3,824. The only difference between the ABO and PBO is that we consider the expected salary at retirement ($21,911) instead of Smith's current salary ($10,000) when determining periodic pension payment. Expected salary is estimated using the annual compensation growth of 4% [computed as $10,000 × $(1.04)^{20}$]. By using current salary, the ABO would understate the pension obligation.

Pension Assets and Funded Status

The market value of plan assets at December 31, 2005, in the J. Smith example is given as $2,000. While the assets' value exceeds the ABO, it is lower than the PBO. The difference between the value of the plan assets and the PBO is called the **funded status** of the plan, which represents its net economic position. A plan is said to be *overfunded* when the value of pension assets exceeds the PBO. It is *underfunded* when the value of pension assets is less than the PBO. The J. Smith plan is underfunded by $1,824 ($3,824 − $2,000).

There are various reasons for overfunding, including tax-free accumulation of funds, outstanding company performance, or better-than-expected fund investment performance. Company raiders sometimes consider overfunded pension plans as sources of funds to help finance their acquisitions. The implications of overfunded pension plans include:

- Companies can discontinue or reduce contributions to the pension fund until pension assets equal or fall below the PBO. Reduced or discontinued contributions have income statement and cash flow implications.
- Companies can withdraw excess assets. Recaptured amounts are subject to income taxes. Since companies often use pension funding as a tax shelter, reversion excise taxes are often imposed.

There also are reasons for underfunding, including poor investment performance, changes in pension rules such as granting of retroactive benefits, and inadequate contributions by the employer. However, employers are subject to certain minimum funding requirements by law.

Pension Cost

Economic pension cost (or expense) is the net cost arising from changes in net economic position (or funded status) for the period.[8] Economic pension cost includes both recurring (or normal) and nonrecurring (or abnormal) components. Any return on pension plan assets is used to offset these costs in arriving at a net economic pension cost.

Recurring pension cost consists of two components:

1. **Service cost** is the actuarial present value of the pension benefit earned by employees based on the pension benefit formula. It is the increase in the projected benefit obligation that arises when employees work another period. Service cost arises only for plans where the pension amount is based on periods of service.
2. **Interest cost** is the increase in the projected benefit obligation that arises when the pension payments are one period closer to being made. This cost arises because the PBO is the present value of the future pension benefits, which increases over time due to the *time value of money*. Interest cost is computed by multiplying beginning-period PBO by the discount rate.

These recurring costs can be explained by returning to the J. Smith example. See the column headed "Projected" under the main heading "2006 Formula" in Exhibit 3B.1. The PBO at the end of 2006 is $4,910–an increase of $1,086 from 2005 (recall PBO in 2005 was $3,824). What drives this increase? There are two factors. First, while Smith's compensation is unchanged, the pension benefit per year increases in 2006 (from $2,107 to $2,528). This increase occurs because Smith's pension in 2006, as per the formula, is based on six weeks' compensation rather than on five weeks' compensation (as in 2005). The effect of this change is determined by comparing the present values of pension benefits at December 31, 2006, using the 2005 formula versus the 2006 formula. Specifically, the present value using the 2005 formula is $4,091, which is $819 lower than the present value using the 2006 formula. This means the PBO increases by $819 in 2006 because Smith serves an additional year–hence, the term *service* cost. Next, compare the present values using the 2005 formula at the end of 2005 and 2006. The present values of identical future benefits–represented by the identical lump sum of $14,798 at the end of 2025–increases from $3,824 in 2005 to $4,091 in 2006. This $267 increase is because of the time value of money; hence, the term *interest* cost (interest cost also is computed as 7% × $3,824).

Nonrecurring pension cost, arising from events such as changes in actuarial assumptions or plan rules, consists of two components:

1. **Actuarial gain or loss** is the change in PBO that occurs when one or more actuarial assumptions are revised in estimating PBO. A revised discount rate is the most frequent source of revision as it depends on the prevailing interest rate in the economy. Other assumptions that can change are mortality rates, employee turnover, and compensation growth rates. Altering these assumptions can have major effects on PBO and, hence, on economic pension cost.
2. **Prior service cost** arises from changes in pension plan rules on PBO. Prior service cost includes retroactive pension benefits granted at the initiation of a pension plan or benefits created by plan amendments typically occurring during collective bargaining or labor negotiations. These changes are often retroactive and give credit for employees' prior services.

These nonrecurring costs are explained by returning to the J. Smith example. First, let's consider an actuarial change: Assume the actuary changes the assumption regarding

---

[8] We refer to this cost as the *economic* pension cost to distinguish it from the *reported* pension cost determined under GAAP that is discussed in the next section.

compensation growth rate from 4% to 5%. Because of this assumption change, Smith's estimated compensation at retirement increases from $21,911 to $26,533 (see column headed "Assumption Change–Actuarial" in Exhibit 3B.1). This change also increases the PBO at the end of 2006 by $1,036 (from $4,910 to $5,946), representing an actuarial loss.

Additionally, let's assume the pension formula changes to one-and-one-half weeks' compensation per year of service (instead of one week per year of service). This effect is shown in the column headed "Assumption Change–Plan" in Exhibit 3B.1. This results in the pension benefit per annum increasing by 50% from $3,061 to $4,592. This also yields a corresponding increase of $2,973 ($8,919 − $5,946) in the PBO. Because this change compensates Smith for any prior service, it represents a prior service cost.

The final component in arriving at the net economic pension cost is to adjust for the actual return on plan assets:

- **Actual return on plan assets** is the pension plan's earnings. Earnings on the plan's assets consist of: *investment income*–capital appreciation and dividend and interest received, less management fees, plus *realized and unrealized appreciation* (or minus depreciation) of other plan assets. The return on plan assets usually reduces pension cost (unless the return is negative, in which case it increases pension cost). In the J. Smith example, actual return on plan assets in 2006 is $440 (22% of $2,000).

The determination of the net economic cost is summarized at the bottom of Exhibit 3B.2 (with amounts from the J. Smith example).

Articulation of Pension Cost and Funded Status

This section explains the articulation of economic pension cost and the funded status. Articulation arises from the linkage of the balance sheet, the income statement, and the statement of cash flows that is inherent in accrual accounting. Understanding this articulation improves analysis of pension accounting.

Exhibit 3B.2 shows this articulation for the J. Smith example using T-accounts. For 2006, assume both the actuarial and the prior service cost changes are in effect. The beginning balance on the pension obligation is $3,824 (which is the PBO at the end of 2005–see Exhibit 3B.1) and the closing balance is $8,919 (which is the PBO at the end of 2006 after both actuarial and prior service cost effects). The change in the pension obligation is entirely explained by the gross pension cost. Benefits paid reduce the pension obligation, but no benefits are paid in this example.

The pension asset opening balance of $2,000 increases to $2,640 at the end of 2006. Employer's contributions ($200) and actual return on assets ($440) make up this change. Any benefits paid would decrease both pension assets and PBO equally, but again, no benefits are paid in this example. The net economic position (or funded status) is the difference between the value of pension assets and the projected benefit obligation. The net economic position deteriorates from $1,824 underfunded to $6,279 underfunded. The movement in funded status is summarized in Exhibit 3B.2.

PENSION ACCOUNTING REQUIREMENTS

A large component of the (economic) net pension cost comprises of nonrecurring items. In the J. Smith example, $4,009 (Actuarial gain/loss $1,036 + Prior service cost $2,973) out of a total net cost of $4,655 are nonrecurring. In addition the $440 return

Articulation of Net Economic Position (Funded Status) and Economic Pension Cost: J. Smith Example

Exhibit 3B.2

■ ■ ■ ■ ■ ■ ■

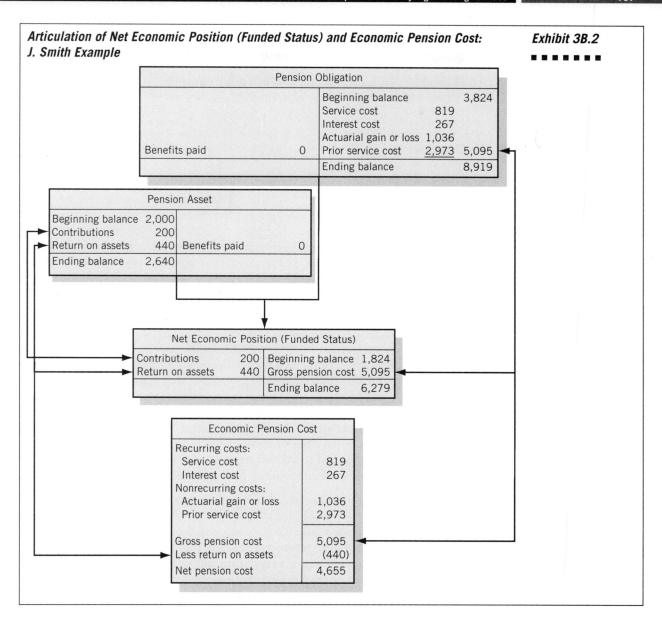

Pension Obligation		
	Beginning balance	3,824
	Service cost	819
	Interest cost	267
	Actuarial gain or loss	1,036
Benefits paid 0	Prior service cost	2,973 5,095
	Ending balance	8,919

Pension Asset			
Beginning balance	2,000		
Contributions	200		
Return on assets	440	Benefits paid	0
Ending balance	2,640		

Net Economic Position (Funded Status)			
Contributions	200	Beginning balance	1,824
Return on assets	440	Gross pension cost	5,095
		Ending balance	6,279

Economic Pension Cost	
Recurring costs:	
Service cost	819
Interest cost	267
Nonrecurring costs:	
Actuarial gain or loss	1,036
Prior service cost	2,973
Gross pension cost	5,095
Less return on assets	(440)
Net pension cost	4,655

on plan assets also includes a large nonrecurring component—one cannot expect to earn 22% return every year on pension assets! These nonrecurring components make the net pension cost extremely volatile. Realizing this problem, current pension accounting (which is specified under *SFAS 158*) creates an elaborate smoothing mechanism wherein the recognition of the volatile and nonrecurring components of the economic pension cost are delayed through deferral and subsequent amortization. The balance sheet, however, recognizes the funded status of the plan. The income statement and balance sheet effects are articulated by recognizing the difference between the economic pension cost and its smoothed counterpart (which is included in net income) in *other comprehensive income*. In the subsequent pages, we shall explain how current pension accounting operates in greater detail, using the J. Smith example.

Exhibit 3B.3   *Economic versus Reported Pension Costs—J. Smith Example*

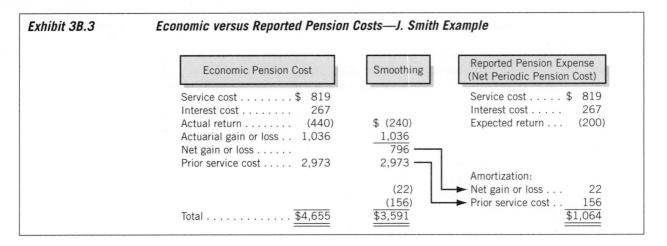

Economic Pension Cost		Smoothing	Reported Pension Expense (Net Periodic Pension Cost)	
Service cost	$ 819		Service cost	$ 819
Interest cost	267		Interest cost	267
Actual return	(440)	$ (240)	Expected return . . .	(200)
Actuarial gain or loss . .	1,036	1,036		
Net gain or loss		796		
Prior service cost	2,973	2,973		
			Amortization:	
		(22)	Net gain or loss . . .	22
		(156)	Prior service cost . .	156
Total	$4,655	$3,591		$1,064

Recognized Pension Cost

Exhibit 3B.3 compares the economic pension cost (determined based on actual fluctuations in pension assets and liabilities) with the amount that is recognized in net income (termed the **net periodic pension cost**). The actual return on plan assets has been replaced with an **expected return on plan assets.** Furthermore, the actuarial gain or loss (arising from changes in assumptions used to compute the pension liability) is not recognized in current income. Instead, it is deferred, and only a portion is recognized (via amortization). A similar treatment is accorded to prior service cost. Although the economic pension cost in this example equals $4,655, the reported pension cost is only $1,064 because a net amount of $3,591 ($3,769 deferral less $178 amortization) of pension-related expense has been deferred through the smoothing mechanism. The net deferrals of $3,591 will be charged to other comprehensive income for the year.

We review each deferral (and amortization) here in detail:

- **Expected return on plan assets.** While capital markets are volatile in the short run, long-term returns are more predictable. Pension plans invest for the long run, so it makes sense to include only the stable expected return on plan assets (rather than the volatile actual return) when computing pension cost. Accordingly, the differences between expected and actual returns are deferred. Expected return on plan assets is computed by multiplying the expected long-term rate of return on plan assets by the market value of plan assets at the beginning of the period. In the J. Smith example, expected return is $200 = 10% (expected return on plan assets) × $2,000 (opening market value of plan assets). Actual return is $440, and therefore $240 ($440 − $200) is deferred.
- **Deferral of actuarial gains and losses.** Actuarial gains and losses arise from changes in actuarial assumptions. The most common change is that relating to changes in discount rates, which are related to fluctuations in interest rates in the economy. Because actuarial gains and losses are nonrecurring in nature, they are also deferred. In the J. Smith example, actuarial loss of $1,036 is deferred.
- **Amortization of net gain or loss.** First, deferrals of actuarial gains and losses and the difference between expected and actual return are netted together as **net gain or loss.**[9] Next, this netted amount is added to any unamortized balance carried

---

[9] The logic for this netting is that these two items naturally tend to offset each other if plan funds are invested in securities that have a similar risk profile as the pension obligation.

forward from the past (i.e., net cumulative deferral less cumulative amortization at the beginning of the period) to determine the total unrecognized net gain or loss. Then, a *corridor method* is applied to determine whether, and how much of, the unrecognized net gain or loss should be amortized. The corridor is the *larger* of 10% of plan assets' value or 10% of the pension liability (PBO) at the beginning of the year. Only the *excess* of unrecognized net gain or loss above the corridor is amortized on a straight-line basis over the average remaining service period of plan employees. In the J. Smith example, the net gain or loss is $796 ($1,036 − $240); this includes only the unrecognized portion for the year because there is no carry-forward from the previous years. Opening PBO and plan asset value are $3,824 and $2,000, respectively, and so the corridor is 10% × $3,824 = $382. Therefore, the amount that qualifies for amortization is $414 ($796 − $382). The remaining service life for J. Smith is 19 years, so amortization of net gain or loss is approximately $22 ($414 ÷ 19).

- **Deferral and amortization of prior service cost.** Prior service costs are retroactive benefits that arise mainly through renegotiation of pension contracts. They pertain to many periods and are nonrecurring by nature. Accordingly, pension accounting defers and amortizes prior service cost effects over the average remaining service period of the plan employees on a straight-line basis. Such deferred recognition allows these costs of retroactive benefits to be matched against future economic benefits expected to be realized from their granting. In the J. Smith example, prior service cost is $2,973 and is amortized over 19 years at $156 per year.

Recognized Status on the Balance Sheet

Under current pension accounting rules *(SFAS 158)*, the funded status of the pension plan is recognized in the balance sheet. In the J. Smith example, therefore, the amount reported in the balance sheet will be a net liability of $6,279. Two issues need to be noted in this regard. First, companies do not report the pension liability (or asset, as the case may be) as a separate line item on the balance sheet. For example, Colgate distributes its pension liabilities among current and noncurrent liabilities and noncurrent assets (see Appendix A at the end of this book). Second, because the amount recognized in the income statement (i.e., the net periodic pension cost) includes deferrals, it will not articulate with the funded status shown on the balance sheet. The net deferrals are charged to *other comprehensive income* and will be included in the balance sheet as part of *accumulated comprehensive income,* which is part of shareholders equity. In the J. Smith example, $3,591 will be charged to other comprehensive loss for the period, and the same amount will also appear in accumulated other comprehensive loss in the balance sheet (because there is no opening balance in accumulated other comprehensive income).

For the J. Smith example, the articulation between the income statement and balance sheet is as follows:

Closing funded status in balance sheet	$6,279
Opening funded status in balance sheet	1,824
Change in funded status (increase in liability)	$4,455
Explained by:	
Decrease in retained earnings (pension expense)	$1,064
Decrease in accumulated comprehensive income	3,591
Decrease in cash (contribution)	(200)
	$ 4,455

OVERVIEW OF OPEB ACCOUNTING

OPEB accounting is currently governed by *SFAS 158*, which is the same standard that governs pension accounting. The accounting for OPEBs is directly parallel to that of pension accounting. We examine some details next.

Recognized Status on the Balance Sheet

The starting point in determining the OPEB obligation is estimating the **expected postretirement benefit obligation** (EPBO), which is the present value of future OPEB payments associated with the employees. The entire EPBO is not immediately recognized in the financial statements. Instead, the total EPBO is allocated over the employees' expected service with the company. Therefore, the obligation that is recognized in the balance sheet at a given point in time is the fraction of the EPBO that is proportional to the length of the employee's current service. This proportionate obligation, termed the **accumulated postretirement benefit obligation** (APBO), is recognized on the balance sheet. That is, the APBO is that portion of the EPBO "earned" by employee services as of a given date. The funded status of OPEBs is the difference between the APBO and the fair value of assets designated to meet this obligation (if any).

Recognized OPEB Cost

OPEB cost recognized in net income includes the following components:

- **Service cost.** The actuarial present value of benefits earned by employees during the period, that is the portion of EPBO attributable to the current year. EPBO is typically allocated to each year in the expected service period of the employees on a straight-line basis.
- **Interest cost.** The imputed growth in APBO during a period using an assumed discount rate.
- **Expected return on plan assets.** This is equal to the opening fair market value of OPEB plan assets multiplied by the long-term expected rate of return on those assets.
- **Amortization of net gain or loss.** As with pensions, actuarial gains and losses can arise when actuarial assumptions, such as the health care cost trend rates, are revised over time. The actuarial gains/losses are added to the difference between actual and expected return on plan assets, and the net amount (termed net gain or loss) is deferred. The cumulative net gain or loss is amortized on a straight-line basis over the employee's service using a similar 10% corridor as in the case of pensions.
- **Amortization of prior service cost.** Retroactive benefits' changes from plan amendments, or prior service costs, are deferred and amortized on a straight-line basis over the employee's expected remaining service period.

Articulation of Balance Sheet and Net Income

As with pensions, the smoothed net postretirement benefit cost will not articulate with changes to the funded status in the balance sheet. Again as in the case of pensions, the net deferrals during a year are included in other comprehensive income for that year and the cumulative net deferrals are included in accumulated other comprehensive income.

GUIDANCE ANSWERS TO ANALYSIS VIEWPOINTS

LABOR NEGOTIATOR

We first must realize that while postretirement benefits are recorded as liabilities on the balance sheet (and as expenses on the income statement), their funding is less than guaranteed. It is clear from management's counteroffer that this company does not fully fund postretirement benefits—note, funding is not required in accounting for these benefits. This lack of funding can yield substantial losses for employees if the company is insolvent and it cannot be forced to fund these obligations. As labor negotiator, you sometimes must trade off higher current wages for rewards such as postretirement benefits *and* a guarantee to fund those benefits. From the company's perspective, it wishes to limit recorded liabilities and its funding commitments as it depletes resources. Your task as labor's representative is to obtain both postretirement benefits and funding for those benefits. Accordingly, while you need to weigh the pros and cons of the details, management's offer should be viewed seriously as a real employee benefit.

MONEY MANAGER

Your decision involves aspects of both risk and return. From the perspective of risk, preferred stock is usually a senior claimant to the net assets of a company. This means that in the event of liquidation, preferred stock receives preference before any funds are paid to common shareholders. From the perspective of return, the decision is less clear. Your common stock return involves both cash dividends and price appreciation, while preferred stock return relates primarily to cash dividends. If recent returns are reflective of future returns, then your likely preference is for preferred stock given its equivalence in returns along with its reduced risk exposure.

SHAREHOLDER

Your interpretation of this stock split is likely positive. This derives from the 'information signal' usually embedded in this type of announcement. Also, a lower price usually makes the stock more accessible to a broader group of buyers and can reduce transaction costs in purchasing it. Yet, too low a price can create its own problems. Consequently, a split is perceived as a signal of management's expectation (forecast) that the company will perform at the same or better level into the future. We must recognize there is no tangible shareholder value in a split announcement—namely, there is no income to shareholders. However, there is transfer of an amount from retained earnings to common stock.

QUESTIONS

[Superscript $^{A(B)}$ identifies assignment material based on Appendix 3A(3B).]

3–1. Identify and describe the two major sources (as linked with business activities) of current liabilities.

3–2. Identify the major disclosure requirements for financing-related current liabilities.

3–3. Describe the conditions necessary to demonstrate the ability of a company to refinance its short-term debt on a long-term basis.

3–4. Explain how bond discounts and premiums usually arise. Describe how they are accounted for.

3–5. Both convertibility and warrants attached to debt aim at increasing the attractiveness of debt securities and lowering their interest cost. Describe how the costs of these two features affect income and equity.

3–6. Explain how the issuance of convertible debt and warrants can affect the valuation analysis conducted by current and potential stockholders.

3–7. Describe the major disclosure requirements for long-term liabilities.

3–8. Debt contracts usually place restrictions on the ability of a company to deploy resources and to pursue business activities. These are often referred to as debt covenants.
   a. Identify where information about such restrictions is found.
   b. Define margin of safety as it applies to debt contracts and describe how the margin of safety can impact assessment of the relative level of company risk.

3–9. Explain how analysis of financial statements is used to evaluate a company's liabilities, both existing and contingent.

3–10. *a.* Describe the criteria for classifying leases by a *lessee.*
      b. Prepare a summary of accounting for leases by a *lessee.*

3–11.[A] *a.* Identify the different classifications of leases by a *lessor.* Describe the criteria for classifying each lease type.
      b. Explain the accounting procedures for leases by a *lessor.*

3–12.[A] Describe the provisions concerning leases involving real estate.

3–13. Discuss the implications of lease accounting for the analysis of financial statements.

3–14.[A] When a lease is considered an operating lease for both the lessor and the lessee, describe what amounts will be found on the balance sheets of both the lessor and the lessee related to the lease obligation and the leased asset.

3–15.[A] When a lease is considered a capital lease for both the lessor and the lessee, describe what amounts will be found on the balance sheets of both the lessor and the lessee related to the lease obligation and the leased asset.

3–16. Discuss how the lessee reflects the cost of leased equipment in the income statement for (*a*) assets leased under operating leases and (*b*) assets leased under capital leases.

3–17.[A] Discuss how the lessor reflects the benefits of leasing in the income statement under (*a*) an operating lease and (*b*) a capital lease.

3–18. Companies use various financing methods to avoid reporting debt on the balance sheet. Identify and describe some of these off-balance-sheet financing methods.

3–19. Describe differences between defined benefit and defined contribution pension plans. How does the accounting differ across these two types of plans?

3–20. From a purely economic point of view define what constitutes the following: (*a*) pension obligation, (*b*) pension plan assets, (*c*) net economic position of the pension plan, and (*d*) economic pension cost.

3–21. What are the primary nonrecurring components of pension cost? Describe how current pension accounting defers and amortizes these nonrecurring components.

3–22. The pension cost included in net income is the net periodic pension cost. How does it differ from the economic pension cost? What is the rationale for recognizing the smoothed net periodic pension cost instead of the economic pension cost in income?

3–23. What does current pension accounting *(SFAS 158)* recognize in the balance sheet? How is it different from what was recognized earlier (under *SFAS 87*)?

3–24. How does current pension accounting *(SFAS 158)* articulate the net economic position (funded status) recognized in the balance sheet with the smoothed net periodic pension cost recognized in net income?

3–25. What are other postretirement employee benefits (OPEBs)? What are the major differences between pensions and OPEBs?

3–26. What are the primary categories of information disclosed in the postretirement benefit footnote?

3–27. What considerations must be kept in mind when adjusting the financial statements (balance sheet and income statement) for postretirement benefits?

3–28. What are the major actuarial assumptions underlying the postretirement benefits? Explain how a manager can manipulate these assumptions to window-dress the financial statements.

3–29. Define and describe pension risk exposure. What combination of factors precipitated the "pensions crisis" in the early 2000s? What are the three things that an analyst should check when evaluating pension risk?

3–30. What determines a company's cash flows related to pensions and OPEBs? Why are current cash outflows relating to pensions not a good predictor for future cash flows?

3–31.[B] Describe alternative measures for the pension obligation. Which measure is legally binding?

3–32.[B] Describe the "corridor method" for deferring and amortizing actuarial gains and losses and return on plan assets. What is the rationale for using this method?

3–33.[B] What is the OPEB obligation and how is it determined?

3–34. *a.* Explain a loss contingency. Provide examples.
  b. Explain the two conditions necessary before a company can record a loss contingency against income.

3–35. Define the term *big bath*. Explain when a manager would consider "taking a big bath" and how analysis of current financial position and future profitability might be adjusted if one suspects that a company has taken a big bath.

3–36. Define a commitment and provide three examples of commitments for a company.

3–37. Explain when a commitment becomes a recorded liability.

3–38. Define off-balance-sheet financing and provide three examples.

3–39. Describe the required financial statement disclosures for financial instruments with off-balance-sheet risk of loss. How might these disclosures be used to assist financial analysis?

3–40. Describe the criteria a company must meet before a transfer of receivables with recourse can be booked as a sale rather than as a loan.

3–41. Explain how off-balance-sheet financing items should be treated for financial analysis purposes.

3–42. Identify types of equity securities that are similar to debt.

3–43. Identify and describe several categories of reserves, allowances, and provisions for expenses and losses.

3–44. Explain why analysis must be alert to the accounting for future loss reserves.

3–45. Distinguish between different kinds of deferred credits on the balance sheet. Discuss how to analyze these accounts.

3–46. Identify objectives of the classifications and note disclosures associated with the equity section of the balance sheet. Explain the relevance of these disclosures to analysis of financial statements.

3–47. Identify features of preferred stock that make it similar to debt. Identify the features that make it more like common stock.

3–48. Explain the importance of disclosing the liquidation value of preferred stock, if different from par or stated value, for analysis purposes.

3–49. Explain why the accounting for small stock dividends requires that market value, rather than par value, of the shares distributed be charged against retained earnings.

3–50. Identify what items are treated as prior period adjustments.

3–51. Many companies report "minority interests in subsidiary companies" between the long-term debt and equity sections of a consolidated balance sheet; others present them as part of shareholders' equity.
  a. Describe minority interest.
  b. Indicate where on the consolidated balance sheet it best belongs. Discuss what different points of view these differing presentations represent.

EXERCISES

Refer to the financial statements of **Campbell Soup** in Appendix A.

Campbell Soup

EXERCISE 3–1
Interpreting and Analyzing Debt Disclosures

CHECK
(a) $(33.2) mil.

Required:

a. Determine the net change in long-term debt during Year 11.

b. Analyze and discuss the relative mix of debt financing for Campbell Soup. Do you think Campbell Soup has any solvency or liquidity problems? Do you think the company should have more or less debt relative to equity (or is its current financing strategy proper)? Do you think that Campbell Soup would encounter difficulty if they wanted to issue additional debt to fund an especially attractive business opportunity?

EXERCISE 3–2

Evaluating Accounting for Leases by the Lessee

On January 1, Year 8, Von Company entered into two noncancellable leases of new machines for use in its manufacturing operations. The first lease does not contain a bargain purchase option and the lease term is equal to 80% of the estimated economic life of the machine. The second lease contains a bargain purchase option and the lease term is equal to 50% of the estimated economic life of the machine.

Required:

a. Explain the justification for requiring lessees to capitalize certain long-term leases. Do not limit your discussion to the specific criteria for classifying a lease as a capital lease.

b. Describe how a lessee accounts for a capital lease at inception.

c. Explain how a lessee records each minimum lease payment for a capital lease.

d. Explain how Von should classify each of the two leases. Provide justification.

(AICPA Adapted)

EXERCISE 3–3

Distinguishing between Capital and Operating Leases

Capital leases and operating leases are two major classifications of leases.

Required:

a. Describe how a lessee accounts for a capital lease both at inception of the lease and during the first year of the lease. Assume the lease transfers ownership of the property to the lessee by the end of the lease.

b. Describe how a lessee accounts for an operating lease both at inception of the lease and during the first year of the lease. Assume the lessee makes equal monthly payments at the beginning of each month during the lease term. Describe any changes in the accounting when rental payments are not made on a straight-line basis.

Note: Do not discuss the criteria for distinguishing between capital and operating leases.

(AICPA Adapted)

EXERCISE 3–4[A]

Analyzing and Interpreting Sales-Type and Financing Leases

Sales-type leases and direct financing leases are two common types of leases from a lessor's perspective.

Required:

Compare and contrast a sales-type lease with a direct-financing lease on the following dimensions:

a. Gross investment in the lease.

b. Amortization of unearned interest income.

c. Manufacturer's or dealer's profit.

Note: Do not discuss the criteria for distinguishing between sales-type, direct financing, and operating leases.

(AICPA Adapted)

EXERCISE 3–5

Recognizing Unrecorded Liabilities for Analysis

Consider the following excerpt from an article published in **Forbes:**

Forbes

The Supersolvent No longer is it a mark of a fuddy-duddy to be free of debt. There are lots of advantages to it. One is that you always have plenty of collateral to borrow against if you do get into a jam. Another is that if a business investment goes bad, you don't have to pay interest on your mistake . . . debt-free, you don't have to worry about what happens if the prime rate goes to 12% again. You might even welcome it. You could lend out your own surplus cash at those rates.

The article went on to list 92 companies reporting no more than 5% of total capitalization in noncurrent debt on their balance sheets.

Required:

Explain how so-called debt-free companies (in the sense used by the article) can possess substantial long-term debt or other unrecorded noncurrent liabilities. Provide examples.

(CFA Adapted)

Nearly all companies confront loss contingencies of various forms.

Required:

a. Describe what conditions must be met for a loss contingency to be accrued with a charge to income.

b. Explain when disclosure is required, and what disclosures are necessary, for a loss contingency that does not meet the criteria for accrual of a charge to income.

EXERCISE 3–6

Interpreting Disclosures for Loss Contingencies

Lawsuits are one type of contingent loss, where the loss is contingent upon an adverse settlement or verdict in the case. Domestic tobacco companies are currently facing lawsuits from several states. The tobacco litigation loss contingency should be accrued if a loss is probable and can be estimated. Probable and estimable are difficult concepts that offer managers a fair degree of discretion.

Required:

a. List two reasons why the managers in this case might resist quantification and accrual of a loss liability.

b. Describe a circumstance when managers might be willing to accrue a contingent loss that they had earlier resisted accruing.

EXERCISE 3–7

Analyzing Loss Contingencies

Refer to the financial statements of **Campbell Soup** in Appendix A.

Campbell Soup

Required:

a. Identify the cause of the $101.6 million increase in shareholders' equity for Year 11.

b. Compute the average price at which treasury shares were repurchased during Year 11.

c. Compute the book value of common stock at the end of Year 11.

d. Compare the book value per share of common stock and the average price at which treasury shares were repurchased during the year (a measure of average market value per share during the year). What are some reasons why these figures are different?

EXERCISE 3–8

Analyzing Equity and Book Value

CHECK
(c) $14.12

Ownership interests in a corporation are reported both in the balance sheet under shareholders' equity and in the statement of shareholders' equity.

Required:

a. List the principal transactions and events reducing the amount of retained earnings. (Do not include appropriations of retained earnings.)

b. The shareholders' equity section of the balance sheet makes a distinction between contributed capital and retained earnings. Discuss why this distinction is important.

c. There is frequently a difference between the purchase price and sale price of treasury stock. Yet, practitioners agree that a corporation's purchase or sale of its own stock cannot result in a profit or loss to the corporation. Explain why corporations do not recognize the difference between the purchase and sale price of treasury stock as a profit or loss.

EXERCISE 3–9

Interpreting Shareholders' Equity Transactions

EXERCISE 3–10
Interpreting
Capital Stock

Capital stock is a major part of a corporation's equity. The term *capital stock* embraces both common and preferred stock.

Required:

a. Identify the basic rights inherent in ownership of common stock and explain how owners exercise them.

b. Describe preferred stock. Discuss various preferences often afforded preferred stock.

c. In the analysis and interpretation of equity securities of a corporation, it is important to understand certain terminology. Define and describe the following equity items:
   (1) Treasury stock   (2) Stock right   (3) Stock warrant

EXERCISE 3–11
Dividends and
Capital Stock

Presidential Realty Corporation   **Presidential Realty Corporation**
reports the following regarding its
distributions paid on common stock: "Cash distributions on common stock were charged to paid-in surplus because the parent company has accumulated no earnings (other than its equity in undistributed earnings of certain subsidiaries) since its formation."

Required:

a. Explain whether these cash distributions are dividends.

b. Speculate as to why Presidential Realty made such a distribution.

EXERCISE 3–12
Dividends versus
Treasury Stock

The purchase of treasury stock (commonly called stock buybacks) is being done with increasing frequency in lieu of dividend payments.

Required:

a. Explain why stock buybacks are similar to dividends from the company's viewpoint.

b. Explain why managers might prefer the purchase of treasury shares to the payment of dividends.

c. Explain why investors might prefer that firms use excess cash to purchase treasury shares rather than pay dividends.

EXERCISE 3–13
Cash Balance
Pension Plan

IBM recently announced its intention to begin offering a cash balance pension plan.   **IBM**
A cash balance pension plan is a form of defined contribution pension plan. IBM is
not alone as there is a distinct trend in favor of defined contribution pension plans.

Required:

a. Describe the ramifications for analysis of the level and variability of both earnings and cash flows for defined benefit versus defined contribution pension plans.

b. Why do you think managers prefer the defined contribution pension plan?

c. Under what circumstances would employees favor defined benefit versus defined contribution plans?

EXERCISE 3–14
Understanding
Defined Benefit
Pension Plans

Carson Company sponsors a defined benefit pension plan. The plan provides pension benefits determined by age, years of service, and compensation. Among the components included in the recognized net pension cost for a period are service cost, interest cost, and actual return on plan assets.

Required:

a. Identify at least two accounting challenges of the defined benefit pension plan. Why do these challenges arise?

b. How does Carson determine the service cost component of the net pension cost?

c. How does Carson determine the interest cost component of the net pension cost?

d. How does Carson determine the actual return on plan assets component of the net pension cost?

(AICPA Adapted)

PROBLEMS

Refer to the financial statements of **Campbell Soup Company** in Appendix A.

Campbell Soup Company

PROBLEM 3–1

Interpreting Notes Payable and Lease Disclosures

Required:

a. Campbell Soup Company has zero coupon notes payable outstanding.
   (1) Indicate the total amount due noteholders on the maturity date of these notes.
   (2) The liability for these notes is lower than the maturity value. Describe the pattern in the reported amounts for this liability in future years.
   (3) Ignoring dollar amounts, prepare the annual journal entry that Campbell Soup Company makes to record the liability for accrued interest.

b. Campbell Soup reports long-term debt on the balance sheet totaling $772.6 million. Conceptually, what does the amount $772.6 represent? Over what years will cash outflows occur as related to this debt?

c. The note on leases reports future minimum lease payments under capital leases as $28.0 million and the present value of such payments as $21.5 million. Identify which amount is actually paid in future years.

d. Identify where in the financial statements that Campbell Soup reports the payment obligation for operating leases of $71.9 million.

e. Predict what interest expense will be in Year 12 assuming no substantial change in the debt structure (Hint: Identify the substantial interest-bearing obligations of the company and multiply that balance times an appropriate estimate of the effective rate for that debt).

CHECK
(*e*) Rate is 11.53%

On January 1, Year 1, Burton Company leases equipment from Nelson Company for an annual lease rental of $10,000. The lease term is five years, and the lessor's interest rate implicit in the lease is 8%. The lessee's incremental borrowing rate is 8.25%. The useful life of the equipment is five years, and its estimated residual value equals its removal cost. Annuity tables indicate that the present value of an annual lease rental of $1 (at 8% rate) is $3.993. The fair value of leased equipment equals the present value of rentals. (Assume the lease is capitalized.)

PROBLEM 3–2

Capital Lease Implications for Financial Statements

Required:

a. Prepare accounting entries required by Burton Company for Year 1.

b. Compute and illustrate the effect on the income statement for the year ended December 31, Year 1, and for the balance sheet as of December 31, Year 1.

c. Construct a table showing payments of interest and principal made every year for the five-year lease term.

d. Construct a table showing expenses charged to the income statement for the five-year lease term if the equipment is purchased. Show a column for (1) amortization, (2) interest, and (3) total expenses.

e. Discuss the income and cash flow implications from this capital lease.

CHECK
Interest is $2,649.95
for Year 2

On January 1, Borman Company, a lessee, entered into three noncancellable leases for new equipment identified as: Lease J, Lease K, and Lease L. None of the three leases transfers ownership of the equipment to Borman at the end of the lease term. For each of the three leases, the present value at the beginning of the lease term of the minimum lease payments, excluding that portion of the payments representing executory costs such as insurance, maintenance, and taxes to be paid by the lessor, including any profit thereon, is 75% of the excess of the fair value of the equipment to the lessor at the inception of the lease over any related investment tax credit retained by the lessor and expected to be realized by the lessor. The following additional information is distinct for each lease:

PROBLEM 3–3

Explaining and Interpreting Leases

- Lease J does not contain a bargain purchase option; the lease term is equal to 80% of the estimated economic life of the equipment.
- Lease K contains a bargain purchase option; the lease term is equal to 50% of the estimated economic life of the equipment.

- Lease L does not contain a bargain purchase option; the lease term is equal to 50% of the estimated economic life of the equipment.

Required:

a. Explain how Borman Company should classify each of these three leases. Discuss the rationale for your answer.

b. Identify the amount, if any, Borman records as a liability at inception of the lease for each of the three leases.

c. Assuming that Borman makes the minimum lease payments on a straight-line basis, describe how Borman should record each minimum lease payment for each of these three leases.

d. Assess accounting practice in accurately portraying the economic reality for each lease.

(AICPA Adapted)

PROBLEM 3–4
Interpreting
Accounting
for Bonds

One means for a corporation to generate long-term financing is through issuance of noncurrent debt instruments in the form of bonds.

Required:

a. Describe how to account for proceeds from bonds issued with detachable stock purchase warrants.

b. Contrast a serial bond with a term (straight) bond.

c. Interest expense, under the generally accepted effective interest method, equals the book value of the debt (face value plus unamortized premium or minus unamortized discount) multiplied by the effective rate of the debt. Any premium or discount is amortized to zero over the life of the bond. Explain how both interest expense and the debt's book value will differ from year-to-year for debt issued at a premium versus a discount.

d. Describe how to account for and classify any gain or loss from reacquisition of a long-term bond prior to its maturity.

e. Assess accounting for bonds in the analysis of financial statements.

PROBLEM 3–5
Leases, Pensions,
and Receivables
Securitization

Westfield Capital Management Co.'s equity investment strategy is to invest in companies with low price-to-book ratios, while considering differences in solvency and asset utilization. Westfield is considering investing in the shares of either Jerry's Departmental Stores (JDS) or Miller Stores (MLS). Selected financial data for both companies follow:

SELECTED FINANCIAL DATA AS OF MARCH 31, 2006

($ millions)	JDS	MLS
Sales	$21,250	$18,500
Fixed assets	5,700	5,500
Short-term debt		1,000
Long-term debt	2,700	2,500
Equity	6,000	7,500
Outstanding shares (in millions)	250	400
Stock price ($ per share)	51.50	49.50

Required:

a. Compute each of the following ratios for both JDS and MLS:
   (1) Price-to-book ratio
   (2) Total-debt-to-equity ratio
   (3) Fixed-asset-utilization (turnover)

b. Select the company that better meets Westfield's criteria.

c. The following information is from these companies' notes as of March 31, 2006:

(1) JDS conducts a majority of its operations from leased premises. Future minimum lease payments (MLP) on noncancellable operating leases follow ($ millions):

MLP

2007............................$	259
2008............................	213
2009............................	183
2010............................	160
2011............................	155
2012 and later............	706
Total MLP........................	$1,676
Less interest...............	(676)
Present value of MLP........	$1,000
Interest rate.....................	10%

(2) MLS owns all of its property and stores.

(3) During the fiscal year ended March 31, 2006, JDS sold $800 million of its accounts receivable with recourse, all of which was outstanding at year-end.

(4) Substantially all of JDS's employees are enrolled in company-sponsored defined contribution plans. MLS sponsors a defined benefits plan for its employees. The MLS pension plan assets' fair value is $3,400 million. No pension cost is accrued on its balance sheet as of March 31, 2006 (note that MLS accounts for its pension plans under *SFAS 87*). The details of MLS's pension obligations follow:

($ millions)	ABO	PBO
Vested $1,550		$1,590
Nonvested 40		210
Total $1,590		$1,800

Compute all three ratios in part (*a*) after making necessary adjustments using the note information. Again, select the company that better meets Westfield's criteria. Comment on your decision in part (*b*) relative to the analysis here.

(CFA Adapted)

CHECK
(*c*) Price-to-Adjusted-Book, JDS = $2.15, MLS = $2.18

The U.S. government actively seeks the identification and cleanup of sites that contain hazardous materials. The Environmental Protection Agency (EPA) identifies contaminated sites under the Comprehensive Environmental Response Compensation and Liability Act (CERCLA). The government will force parties responsible for contaminating the site to pay for cleanup whenever possible. Also, companies face lawsuits for persons injured by environmental pollution. Potentially responsible parties include current and previous owners and operators of hazardous waste disposal sites, parties who arranged for disposal of hazardous materials at the site, and parties who transported the hazardous materials to the site. Potentially responsible parties should accrue a contingent environmental liability if the outcome of pending or potential action is probable to be unfavorable and a reasonable estimate of costs can be made. Amounts for environmental liabilities can be large. For example, **Exxon** paid damages totaling $5 billion for the highly publicized Exxon Valdez tanker accident. Estimates to clean up sites identified by the EPA range as high as $500 billion to $750 billion. The 'superfund' sites are sites with the highest priority for cleanup under CERCLA. Estimates to clean up these sites alone total $150 billion. The responsible parties face additional lawsuits as well and these potential losses are not included in these totals.

Exxon

PROBLEM 3–6
*Analyzing
Environmental Liability
Disclosures*

Required:

a. Discuss why environmental liabilities are especially difficult to measure.

b. Discuss how you would adjust the financial analysis of companies that are predisposed to environmental legal action but have not accrued any contingent loss amounts. For example, how might you adjust your beliefs about the financial position of Union Carbide and its competitors following the Bhopal tragedy?

c. Identify three industries that you consider as likely to face significant environmental risk. Explain.

PROBLEM 3–7

Analyzing Pension Plan Disclosures

CHECK
(b) Year 11 rate, 8.75%

Refer to the financial statements of **Campbell Soup** in Appendix A. The Note on Pension Plans and Retirement Benefits describes computation of pension expense, projected benefit obligation (PBO), and other elements of the pension plan (all amounts in millions).

Campbell Soup Company

Required:

a. Explain what the service cost of $22.1 for Year 11 represents.

b. What discount rate did the company assume for Year 11? What is the effect of Campbell's change from the discount rate used in Year 10?

c. How is the "interest on projected benefit obligation" computed?

d. Actual return on assets is $73.4. Does this item enter in its entirety as a component of pension cost? Explain.

e. Campbell shows an accumulated benefit obligation (ABO) of $714.4. What is this obligation?

f. Identify the PBO amount and explain what accounts for the difference between it and the ABO.

g. Has Campbell funded its pension expense at the end of Year 11?

PROBLEM 3–8ᴮ

Predicting Pension Expense

CHECK
Predicted expense, $463 mil.

The weighted-average discount rate used in determining General Energy Co.'s actuarial present value of its pension obligation is 8.5%, and the assumed rate of increase in future compensation is 7.5%. The expected long-term rate of return on its plan assets is 11.5%. Its pension obligation at the end of Year 6 is $2,212,000, and its accumulated benefit obligation is $479,000. Fair value of its assets is $3,238,000. The service cost for Year 6 is $586,000.

Required:

Predict General Energy Co.'s Year 7 net periodic pension expense given a 10% growth in service cost, the amortization of deferred loss over 30 years, and no change in the other assumed rates. Show calculations.

CASES

CASE 3–1

Interpreting Pension and OPEB Disclosures

Refer to Colgate's annual report in Appendix A at the end of the book and answer the following questions:

Colgate

a. What type of pension plan does Colgate have for a majority of its employees? What are the primary other postre-tirement benefits (OPEBs) that Colgate offers its employees?

b. Separately for pensions (U.S. and international) and OPEBs, answer the following questions for both 2006 and 2005:
   (1) What is the closing net economic position of the plan? Is it a net asset or net liability?
   (2) What is the closing amount reported in the balance sheet? Is it a net asset or net liability?

(3) Where in the balance sheet are the reported amounts included?

(4) For 2005, what causes the reported amounts to deviate from the net economic position?

(5) Identify the amount of accumulated benefit obligation (ABO) and the projected benefit obligation (PBO). Which amount is recognized in the balance sheet? Which is closer to Colgate's legal obligation?

(6) What is the net economic position of each plan if it is terminated?

(7) What is the closing value of plan assets? Which asset classes does Colgate invest in and what proportions?

(8) What is the reported benefit cost that is included in net income for the year? What are its components?

(9) Identify and quantify the nonrecurring amounts that are deferred during the year.

(10) What is Colgate's actual return on plan assets? How much does it recognize for the year (when determining reported benefit cost)?

(11) Identify how the reported cost is articulated with the net position included in the balance sheet. (Hint: How are the net deferrals recognized—or not recognized—on the balance sheet?) What are the differences between 2005 and 2006?

(12) What are the key actuarial assumptions that Colgate makes? Has Colgate changed any assumptions during 2006? What effects will the changes have on Colgate's economic and reported position and cost?

(13) What is Colgate's cash flow with respect to postretirement plans? What is the estimated cash flow for 2007?

Refer to Colgate's Annual Report in Appendix A at the end of the book and answer the following questions:

Colgate

CASE 3–2
Analyzing Pensions and OPEBs

a. Make necessary financial adjustments to reflect the net economic position of the pension and OPEB plans on the balance sheet and the economic benefit cost in income for 2006 and 2005. What effects do these adjustments have on the following ratios: (1) debt to equity, (2) long-term debt to equity, (3) ROE, and (4) ROA? Discuss the appropriate presentation (and recognition) of postretirement benefits on the balance sheet and in net income for different analysis objectives.

b. Evaluate the reasonableness of the key actuarial assumptions made by Colgate in 2006 and 2005. Why are the assumptions different for domestic and international pension plans? What are the effects of changes in assumptions in 2006 on the financial statements?

c. What is the nature of Colgate's risk exposure from its pension and OPEB plans? Quantify this risk, examining the extent of underfunding, pension (OPEB) intensity, and likely mismatch in the risk profiles of plan assets and obligation.

d. Examine the nature of Colgate's contributions to the benefit plans. How useful are current contributions to estimate future contributions? Is it possible to estimate Colgate's cash flows with respect to its benefit plans in 2007 and thereafter?

Refer to the annual report of **Campbell Soup** in Appendix A.

Campbell Soup

CASE 3–3
Analyzing and Interpreting Liabilities

Required:

a. Identify Campbell Soup's major categories of liabilities. Identify which of these liabilities require recognition of interest expense.

b. Reconcile activity in the long-term borrowing account for Year 11.

c. Describe the composition of Campbell Soup's long-term liabilities account using its note 19.

CASE 3–4

Analyzing and Interpreting Equity

Refer to the annual report of **Campbell Soup** in Appendix A.

Campbell Soup

Required:

a. Determine the book value per share of Campbell Soup's common stock for Year 11.

b. Identify the par value of Campbell Soup's common shares. Determine the number of common shares authorized, issued, and outstanding at the end of Year 11.

CHECK

(c) Year 11 repurchase price, $51.72

c. Determine how many common shares Campbell Soup repurchased as treasury stock for Year 11. Determine the price at which Campbell Soup repurchased the shares.

CASE 3–5

Leasing in the Airline Industry

The airline industry is one of the more volatile industries. During lean years in the early 1990s, the industry wiped out the earnings it had reported during its entire history. Pan American Airlines and Eastern Airlines ceased operations, while Continental Airlines, TWA, and US Air filed for bankruptcy protection. The industry bounced back in the mid-1990s, riding on the wings of the U.S. economic prosperity and lower energy prices. The airlines have been especially profitable since 1996, with returns on equity often in excess of 25%. The stock market has recognized the stellar growth in profitability as market capitalization of many airlines has tripled since then.

Volatility in airlines' earnings arises from a combination of demand volatility, cost structure, and competitive pricing. Air travel demand is cyclical and sensitive to the economy's performance. The cost structure of airlines is dominated by fixed costs, resulting in high operating leverage. While most airlines break even at 60% flight occupancy, deviations from this can send earnings soaring upward or downward. Also, the airline industry is price competitive. Because of their cost structure (low variable but high fixed costs), airlines tend to reduce fares to increase market share during a downturn in demand. These fare reductions often lead to price wars, which reduces average unit revenue. Hence, airfares are positively correlated with volume of demand, resulting in volatile revenues. When this revenue variability is combined with fixed costs, it yields volatile earnings.

Airline companies lease all types of assets–aircraft, airport terminal, maintenance facilities, property, and operating and office equipment. Lease terms range from less than a year to as much as 25 years. While many companies report some capital leases on the balance sheet, most companies are increasingly structuring their leases, long-term and short-term, as operating leases. The condensed balance sheets and income statements along with excerpts of lease notes from the 1998 and 1997 annual reports for **AMR (American Airlines), Delta Airlines,** and **UAL (United Airlines)** follow.

	AMR		DELTA		UAL	
	1998	**1997**	**1998**	**1997**	**1998**	**1997**
Balance Sheets ($ millions)						
Assets						
Current assets.....................................	$ 4,875	$ 4,986	$ 3,362	$ 2,867	$ 2,908	$ 2,948
Freehold assets (net)...........................	12,239	11,073	9,022	7,695	10,951	9,080
Leased assets (net)............................	2,147	2,086	299	347	2,103	1,694
Intangibles and other..........................	3,042	2,714	1,920	1,832	2,597	1,742
Total assets	$22,303	$20,859	$14,603	$12,741	$18,559	$15,464

	AMR		DELTA		UAL	
	1998	**1997**	**1998**	**1997**	**1998**	**1997**
Liabilities and equity						
Current liabilities						
Current portion of capital lease......	$ 154	$ 135	$ 63	$ 62	$ 176	$ 171
Other current liabilities..................	5,485	5,437	4,514	4,021	5,492	5,077
Long-term liabilities						
Lease liability	1,764	1,629	249	322	2,113	1,679
Long-term debt............................	2,436	2,248	1,533	1,475	2,858	2,092
Other long-term liabilities	5,766	5,194	4,046	3,698	3,848	3,493
Preferred stock			175	156	791	615
Shareholder's equity						
Contributed capital........................	3,257	3,286	3,299	2,896	3,518	2,877
Retained earnings	4,729	3,415	1,776	812	1,024	300
Treasury stock...............................	(1,288)	(485)	(1,052)	(701)	(1,261)	(840)
Total liabilities and equity.................	**$22,303**	**$20,859**	**$14,603**	**$12,741**	**$18,559**	**$15,464**
Income Statement ($ millions)						
Operating revenue..............................	$19,205	$18,184	$14,138	$13,594	$17,561	$17,378
Operating expenses............................	(16,867)	(16,277)	(12,445)	(12,063)	(16,083)	(16,119)
Operating income.............................	**2,338**	**1,907**	**1,693**	**1,531**	**1,478**	**1,259**
Other income and adjustments	198	137	141	91	133	551
Interest expense*	(372)	(420)	(197)	(216)	(361)	(291)
Income before tax.............................	**2,164**	**1,624**	**1,637**	**1,406**	**1,250**	**1,519**
Tax provision	(858)	(651)	(647)	(561)	(429)	(561)
Continuing income	**$ 1,306**	**$ 973**	**$ 990**	**$ 845**	**$ 821**	**$ 958**

Includes preference dividends.

($ millions)	AMR		DELTA		UAL	
	Capital	**Operating**	**Capital**	**Operating**	**Capital**	**Operating**
Excerpts from Lease Notes (1998)						
MLP Due						
1999..............................$	273	$ 1,012	$100	$ 950	$ 317	$ 1,320
2000............................	341	951	67	950	308	1,329
2001............................	323	949	57	940	399	1,304
2002............................	274	904	57	960	341	1,274
2003............................	191	919	48	960	242	1,305
2004............................	1,261	12,480	71	10,360	1,759	17,266
Total MLP due.....................	2,663	$17,215	400	$15,120	3,366	$23,798
Less interest......................	(745)		(88)		(1,077)	
Present value of MLP..........$1,918			$312		$2,289	

($ millions)	AMR		DELTA		UAL	
	Capital	Operating	Capital	Operating	Capital	Operating
Excerpts from Lease Notes (1997)						
MLP Due						
1998............................	$ 255	$ 1,011	$101	$ 860	$ 288	$ 1,419
1999...........................	250	985	100	860	262	1,395
2000...........................	315	935	68	840	241	1,402
2001...........................	297	931	57	830	314	1,380
2002...........................	247	887	57	850	277	1,357
2003 and after..............	1,206	13,366	118	9,780	1,321	19,562
Total MLP due...................	2,570	$18,115	501	$14,020	2,703	$26,515
Less interest.....................	(806)		(117)		(853)	
Present value of MLP.........	$1,764		$384		$1,850	

Both the capital and operating leases are noncancellable. Interest rates on the leases vary from 5% to 14%. (Assume a 35% marginal tax rate for all three companies.)

Required:

a. Compute key liquidity, solvency, and return on investment ratios for 1998 (current ratio, total debt to equity, long-term debt to equity, times interest earned, return on assets, return on equity). Comment on the financial performance, financial position, and risk of these three companies—both as a group and individually.

b. To understand the effect of high operating leverage on the volatility of airlines' earnings, prepare the following sensitivity analysis: Assume that 25% of airline costs are variable—that is, for a 1% increase (decrease) in operating revenues operating costs increase (decrease) by only 0.25%. Recast the income statement assuming operating revenues decrease by two alternative amounts: 5% and 10%. What happens to earnings at these reduced revenue levels? Also, compute key ratios at these hypothetical revenue levels. Comment on the risk of these companies' operations.

c. Why do you think the airline industry relies so heavily on leasing as a form of financing? What other financing options could airlines consider? Discuss their advantages and disadvantages versus leasing.

d. Examine the lease notes. Do you think the lease classification adopted by the companies is reasonable? Explain.

CHECK
(e) AMR restated Year 8
continuing income, $1,210

e. Reclassify all operating leases as capital leases and make necessary adjustments to both the balance sheet and income statement for 1998. [Hint: (1) Use the procedures described in the chapter. (2) Assume identical interest rates for operating and capital leases. (3) Do not attempt to articulate the income statement with the balance sheet, i.e., make balance sheet and income statement adjustments separately without "tallying" the effects on the two statements. (4) Make adjustments to the tax provision using a 35% marginal tax rate. Since all leases are accounted for as operating leases for tax purposes, converting operating leases to capital leases will create deferred tax liabilities. However, since we are not articulating the income statement with the balance sheet, the deferred tax effects on the balance sheet can be ignored.]

f. What assumptions did you make when reclassifying leases in (e)? Evaluate the reasonableness of these assumptions and suggest alternative methods you could use to improve the reliability of your analysis.

g. Repeat the ratio analysis in (a) using the restated financial statements from (e). Comment on the effect of the lease classification for the ratios and your interpretation of the companies' profitability and risk (both collectively and individually).

h. Using the results of your analysis in (g), explain the reliance of airline companies on lease financing and their lease classifications. What conclusions can you draw about the importance of accounting analysis for financial analysis in this case?

It is recommended that this case is solved using Excel. Case data in Excel format is available on the book's website.

Condensed financial statements of **General Electric,** along with note information regarding postretirement benefits, are shown here:

General Electric   CASE 3–6

Analyzing Post Retirement Benefits

INCOME STATEMENTS

($ millions)	1998	1997	1996
Revenues	$100,469	$90,840	$79,179
Cost of goods and services	(42,280)	(40,088)	(34,591)
Interest, insurance, and financing	(20,970)	(18,083)	(15,615)
Other expenses	(23,477)	(21,250)	(17,898)
Minority interest	(265)	(240)	(269)
Earnings before tax	13,477	11,179	10,806
Tax provision	(4,181)	(2,976)	(3,526)
Net earnings	$ 9,296	$ 8,203	$ 7,280

BALANCE SHEETS

	1998	1997
Assets		
Current assets	$243,662	$212,755
Plant assets	35,730	32,316
Intangible assets	23,635	19,121
Other	52,908	39,820
Total assets	$355,935	$304,012
Liabilities and Equity		
Current liabilities	$141,579	$120,667
Long-term borrowing	59,663	46,603
Other liabilities	111,538	98,621
Minority interest	4,275	3,683
Equity share capital	7,402	5,028
Retained earnings	31,478	29,410
Total liabilities and equity	$355,935	$304,012

POSTRETIREMENT BENEFITS—NOTES

($ millions)	PENSION BENEFITS			RETIREE HEALTH AND LIFE BENEFITS		
	1998	1997	1996	1998	1997	1996
Effect on Operations						
Expected return on plan assets	$ 3,024	$ 2,721	$2,587	$ 149	$ 137	$ 132
Service cost for benefits earned	(625)	(596)	(550)	(96)	(107)	(93)
Interest cost on benefit obligation	(1,749)	(1,686)	(1,593)	(319)	(299)	(272)
Prior service cost	(153)	(145)	(99)	(8)	11	31
SFAS 87 "transition gain"	154	154	154	—	—	—
Net actuarial gain recognized	365	295	210	(39)	(32)	(43)
Special early retirement cost	—	(412)	—	—	(165)	—
Post retirement benefit income/(cost)	$ 1,016	$ 331	$ 709	$ (313)	$ (455)	$(245)
Benefit Obligation (as of Dec. 31)						
Balance at January 1	$25,874	$23,251		$ 4,775	$ 3,954	
Service cost for benefits earned	625	596		96	107	
Interest cost on benefit obligation	1,749	1,686		319	299	
Participant contributions	112	120		24	21	
Plan amendments	—	136		—	369	
Actuarial loss	1,050	1,388		268	301	
Benefits paid	(1,838)	(1,715)		(475)	(441)	
Special early retirement cost	—	412		—	165	
Balance at Dec. 31	$27,572	$25,874		$ 5,007	$ 4,775	

($ millions)	PENSION BENEFITS			RETIREE HEALTH AND LIFE BENEFITS		
	1998	1997	1996	1998	1997	1996
Fair Value of Plan Assets (as of Dec. 31)						
Balance at January 1	$38,742	$33,686		$ 1,917	$ 1,682	
Actual return on plan assets............................	6,363	6,587		316	343	
Employer contributions	68	64		339	312	
Participant contributions..................................	112	120		24	21	
Benefits paid	(1,838)	(1,715)		(475)	(441)	
Balance at Dec. 31	$43,447	$38,742		$ 2,121	$ 1,917	
Prepaid Pension Asset (as of Dec. 31)						
Fair value of plan assets	$43,447	$38,742		$ 2,121	$ 1,917	
Add/deduct unrecognized balances:						
SFAS 87 transition gain	(308)	(462)		—	—	
Net actuarial gain	(9,462)	(7,538)		358	296	
Prior service cost..	850	1,003		108	116	
Benefit obligation	(27,572)	(25,874)		(5,007)	(4,775)	
Pension liability..	797	703		—	—	
Prepaid pension asset	$ 7,752	$ 6,574		$(2,420)	$(2,446)	
Actuarial Assumptions (as of Dec. 31)						
Discount rate..	6.75%	7.00%	7.50%	6.75%	7.00%	7.50%
Compensation increase	5.00	4.50	4.50	5.00	4.50	4.50
Return on assets..	9.50	9.50	9.50	9.50	9.50	9.50
Health care cost trend				7.80	7.80	8.00

Note that this postretirement data was reported under the older standard *(SFAS 87)*. The recognition of net position on the balance sheet under the current standard *(SFAS 158)* is different.

CHECK
Restated Year 8 D/E and
ROE are 6.0 and 18.29%

Required:

a. Determine the economic position of the postretirement plans for each of 1998 and 1997. Restate the balance sheets and examine the effect of reflecting the true position on key ratios (debt to equity, long-term debt to equity, return on equity).

b. What is economic pension cost for each of 1998 and 1997? Reconcile it with the reported pension expense. Determine the pension expense you would consider when determining GE's permanent income and economic income.

c. Examine how the current accounting (under *SFAS 158*) would recognize and report the provided pension and OPEB numbers. In particular, discuss how the net economic position will be featured in the balance sheet with specific reference to how the balance sheet numbers will be articulated with that recognized in the income statement (periodic net benefit cost).

d. Evaluate the key actuarial assumptions. Is there any hint of earnings management?

e. In its editorial, *Barron's* hinted GE was using pensions to manage its earnings growth:

> In 1997, pension income chipped in $331 million of GE's total earnings of $8.2 billion. In 1998, pension income accounted for $1.01 billion of the company's total earnings of $9.3 billion. Okay, let's suppose that there was no contribution to earnings in either years (these are not, in any case, actual cash additions). Minus the noncash contributions from the pension plans, GE's 1997 net was $7.9 billion; its 1998 net amounted to $8.3 billion. On this basis, the rise in earnings last year was roughly $400 million, or about 5.1%. And 5.1%, while respectable, is a good cut below the 13% the company triumphantly announced . . . GE's shares, as we observed, are selling at some 40 times last year's earnings.

Do you agree with *Barron's* editorial? In what manner, if any, might GE be managing its earnings through pensions?

f. Note the reference to cash flows in the *Barron's* editorial—"these are not, in any case, actual cash additions." Is it true that every earnings effect that does not necessarily have an equal and contemporaneous cash flow effect is tainted in some manner? Answer this question with respect to GE's pension disclosures. What are the cash flows relating to GE's postretirement plans? How useful are these cash flows for understanding the economics of postretirement benefit plans—are they more meaningful than the pension expense (income) number?

g. Evaluate GE's pension (and OPEB) risk exposure.

Much of the litigation against **Philip Morris** is related to exposure of persons to environmental tobacco smoke. This is addressed by Philip Morris in the following excerpts from its Year 8 annual report:

Philip Morris

CASE 3–7

Analysis of Contingent Liabilities–Philip Morris

Pending claims related to tobacco products generally fall within three categories: (i) smoking and health cases alleging personal injury brought on behalf of individual plaintiffs, (ii) smoking and health cases alleging personal injury and purporting to be brought on behalf of a class of individual plaintiffs, and (iii) health care cost recovery cases brought by governmental and non-governmental plaintiffs seeking reimbursement for health care expenditures allegedly caused by cigarette smoking. Governmental plaintiffs have included local, state, and certain foreign governmental entities. Non-governmental plaintiffs in these cases include union health and welfare trust funds, Blue Cross/Blue Shield groups, HMO's, hospitals, Native American tribes, taxpayers, and others. Damages claimed in some of the smoking and health class actions and health care cost recovery cases range into the billions of dollars. Plaintiffs' theories of recovery and the defenses raised in those cases are discussed below.

In recent years, there has been a substantial increase in the number of smoking and health cases being filed. As of December 31, Year 8, there were approximately 510 smoking and health cases filed and served on behalf of individual plaintiffs in the United States against PM Inc. and, in some cases, the Company, compared with approximately 375 such cases on December 31, Year 7, and 185 such cases on December 31, Year 6. Many of these cases are pending in Florida, West Virginia and New York. Fifteen of the individual cases involve allegations of various personal injuries allegedly related to exposure to environmental tobacco smoke ("ETS").

In addition, as of December 31, Year 8, there were approximately 60 smoking and health putative class actions pending in the United States against PM Inc. and, in some cases, the Company (including eight that involve allegations of various personal injuries related to exposure to ETS), compared with approximately 50 such cases on December 31, Year 7, and 20 such cases on December 31, Year 6. Most of these actions purport to constitute statewide class actions and were filed after May Year 6 when the Fifth Circuit Court of Appeals, in the *Castano* case, reversed a federal district court's certification of a purported nationwide class action on behalf of persons who were allegedly "addicted" to tobacco products.

During Year 7 and Year 8, PM Inc. and certain other United States tobacco product manufacturers entered into agreements settling the asserted and unasserted health care cost recovery and other claims of all 50 states and several commonwealths and territories of the United States. The settlements are in the process of being approved by the courts, and some of the settlements are being challenged by various third parties. As of December 31, Year 8, there were approximately 95 health care cost recovery actions pending in the United States (excluding the cases covered by the settlements), compared with approximately 105 health care cost recovery cases pending on December 31, Year 7, and 25 such cases on December 31, Year 6.

There are also a number of tobacco-related actions pending outside the United States against PMI and its affiliates and subsidiaries including, as of December 31, Year 8, approximately 27 smoking and health cases initiated by one or more individuals (Argentina (20), Brazil (1), Canada (1), Italy (1), Japan (1), Scotland (1) and Turkey (2)), and six smoking and health class actions (Brazil (2), Canada (3) and Nigeria (1)). In addition, health care cost recovery actions have been brought in Israel, the Republic of the Marshall Islands and British Columbia, Canada, and, in the United States, by the Republics of Bolivia, Guatemala, Panama and Nicaragua.

Pending and upcoming trials: As of January 22, Year 9, trials against PM Inc. and, in one case, the Company, were underway in the *Engle* smoking and health class action in Florida (discussed below) and in individual smoking and health cases in California and Tennessee. Additional cases are scheduled for trial during Year 9, including three health care cost recovery actions brought by unions in Ohio (February), Washington (September) and New York (September), and two smoking and health class actions in Illinois (August) and Alabama (August). Also, twelve individual smoking and health cases against PM Inc. and, in some cases, the Company, are currently scheduled for trial during Year 9. Trial dates, however, are subject to change.

Verdicts in individual cases: During the past three years, juries have returned verdicts for defendants in three individual smoking and health cases and in one individual ETS smoking and health case. In June Year 8, a Florida appeals court reversed a $750,000 jury verdict awarded in August Year 6 against another United States cigarette manufacturer. Plaintiff is seeking an appeal of this ruling to the Florida Supreme Court. Also in June Year 8, a Florida jury awarded the estate of a deceased smoker in a smoking and health case against another United States cigarette manufacturer $500,000 in compensatory damages, $52,000 for medical expenses and $450,000 in punitive damages. A Florida appeals court has ruled that this case was tried in the wrong venue and, accordingly, defendants are seeking to set aside the verdict and retry the case in the correct venue. In Brazil, a court in Year 7 awarded plaintiffs in a smoking and health case the Brazilian currency equivalent of $81,000, attorneys' fees and a monthly annuity of 35 years equal to two-thirds of the deceased smoker's last monthly salary. Neither the Company nor its affiliates were parties to that action.

Litigation settlements: In November Year 8, PM Inc. and certain other United States tobacco product manufacturers entered into a Master Settlement Agreement (the "MSA") with 46 states, the District of Columbia, the Commonwealth of Puerto Rico, Guam, the United States Virgin Islands, American Samoa and the Northern Marianas to settle asserted and unasserted health care cost recovery and other claims. PM Inc. and certain other United States tobacco product manufacturers had previously settled similar claims brought by Mississippi, Florida, Texas and Minnesota (together with the MSA, the "State Settlement Agreements") and an ETS smoking and health class action brought on behalf of airline attendants. The State Settlement Agreements and certain ancillary agreements are filed as exhibits to various of the Company's reports filed with the Securities and Exchange Commission, and such agreements and the ETS settlement are discussed in detail therein.

PM Inc. recorded pre-tax charges of $3,081 million and $1,457 million during Year 8 and Year 7, respectively, to accrue for its share of all fixed and determinable portions of its obligations under the tobacco settlements, as well as $300 million during Year 8 for its unconditional obligation under an agreement in principle to contribute to a tobacco growers trust fund, discussed below. As of December 31, Year 8, PM Inc. had accrued costs of its obligations under the settlements and to tobacco growers aggregating $1,359 million, payable principally before the end of the year Year 10. The settlement agreements require that the domestic tobacco industry make substantial annual payments in the following amounts (excluding future annual payments contemplated by the agreement in principle with tobacco growers discussed below), subject to adjustment for several factors, including inflation, market share and industry volume: Year 9, $4.2 billion (of which $2.7 billion related to the MSA and has already been paid by the industry); Year 10, $9.2 billion; Year 11, $9.9 billion; Year 12, $11.3 billion; Year 14 through Year 17, $8.4 billion; and thereafter, $9.4 billion. In addition, the domestic tobacco industry is required to pay settling plaintiff's attorneys' fees, subject to an annual cap of $500 million, as well as additional amounts as follows: Year 9, $450 million; Year 10, $416 million; and Year 11 through Year 12, $250 million. These payment obligations are the several and not joint obligations of each settling defendant. PM Inc.'s portion of the future adjusted payments and legal fees, which is not currently estimable, will be based on its share of domestic cigarette shipments in the year preceding that in which the payment is made. PM Inc.'s shipment share in Year 8 was approximately 50%.

The State Settlement Agreements also include provisions relating to advertising and marketing restrictions, public disclosure of certain industry documents, limitations on challenges to tobacco control and underage use laws and other provisions. As of January 22, Year 9, the MSA had been approved by courts in 41 states and in the District of Columbia, Puerto Rico, Guam, the United States Virgin Islands, American Samoa and Northern Marianas. If a jurisdiction does not obtain final judicial approval of the MSA by December 31, Year 11, the agreement will be terminated with respect to such jurisdiction.

As part of the MSA, the settling defendants committed to work cooperatively with the tobacco grower community to address concerns about the potential adverse economic impact of the MSA on that community. To that end, in January Year 9, the four major domestic tobacco product manufacturers, including PM Inc., agreed in principle to participate in the establishment of a $5.15 billion trust fund to be administered by the tobacco growing states. It is currently contemplated that the trust will be funded by industry participants over twelve years, beginning in Year 9. PM Inc. has agreed to pay $300 million into the trust in Year 9, which amount has been charged to Year 8 operating income. Subsequent annual industry payments are to be adjusted for several factors, including inflation and United States cigarette consumption, and are to be allocated based on each manufacturer's market share.

The Company believes that the State Settlement Agreements may materially adversely affect the business, volume, results of operations, cash flows or financial position of PM Inc. and the Company in future years. The degree of the adverse impact will depend, among other things, on the rates of decline in United States cigarette sales in the premium and discount segments, PM Inc.'s share of the domestic premium and discount cigarette segments, and the effect of any resulting cost advantage of manufacturers not subject to the MSA and the other State Settlement Agreements. As of January 22, Year 9, manufacturers representing almost all domestic shipments in Year 8 had agreed to become subject to the terms of the MSA.

Required:

a. Philip Morris classifies pending tobacco lawsuits against the company into three general categories. What are these three categories? What is the number of claims for each of these categories at the end of Year 8?

b. Can you determine how much liability is recorded for each of these categories as of December 31, Year 8? Explain.

c. Can you determine what amount is charged against earnings in Year 8 for contingent tobacco litigation losses? Explain.

d. Do you believe the eventual losses will exceed the losses currently recorded on the balance sheet? Explain.

e. Describe adjustments to PM's financial statements, and to an investor's financial analysis of PM, to reflect estimates of under- or overaccrued losses.

4

ANALYZING INVESTING ACTIVITIES

A LOOK BACK <

Our discussion of accounting analysis began with the analysis and interpretation of financing activities. We studied the interaction of financing activities with operating and investing activities and the importance of creditor versus equity financing.

A LOOK AT THIS CHAPTER •

Our discussion of accounting analysis extends to investing activities in this chapter. We analyze assets such as receivables, inventories, property, equipment, and intangibles. We show how these numbers reflect company performance and financing requirements, and how adjustments to these numbers can improve our analysis.

A LOOK AHEAD >

Chapter 5 extends our analysis of investing activities to intercorporate investments. Analyzing and interpreting a company's investing activities requires an understanding of the differences in accounting for various investment classes. Chapter 6 focuses on operating activities and income measurement.

ANALYSIS OBJECTIVES

- Define current assets and their relevance for analysis.

- Explain cash management and its implications for analysis.

- Analyze receivables, allowances for bad debts, and securitization.

- Interpret the effects of alternative inventory methods under varying business conditions.

- Explain the concept of long-term assets and its implications for analysis.

- Interpret valuation and cost allocation of plant assets and natural resources.

- Describe and analyze intangible assets and their disclosures.

- Analyze financial statements for unrecorded and contingent assets.

Managing Operating Assets

Dell Computer's effective inventory management is legendary. *Fortune* (2005) reports "a fundamental difference between Dell and the competition is that at Dell, every single machine is made for a specific order. The others are producing machines to match a sales forecast. The advantages that Dell derives from this model on the factory floor are tangible and enormous. For instance, industry sources say Dell now carries only four days of inventory, while IBM has 20 days and HP has 28. Obviously, low inventory frees up mountains of cash for Dell that is otherwise tied up at IBM and HP."

Dell is also effective at lean manufacturing: Again, *Fortune* (2005) reports that Dell "urges its suppliers—everyone from drive makers to Intel—to warehouse inventory as close to its factories as possible. Any cost that can be

'shared with' (read 'transferred to') those suppliers, is. (Does that remind anyone of a certain large retailer headquartered in Bentonville, Ark.?) Pay a visit to a Dell plant and you can watch workers unload a supplier's components almost right onto the assembly line." Dell uses its suppliers to reduce the

> **Effective management of operating assets is key**

amount of raw materials inventories it maintains and streamlines manufacturing to reduce the amount of work-in-process inventories that are tied up on the factory floor.

Dell conducts its operating activities with 3 to 5 times less long-term operating assets than HP and IBM. Its lower capital

investment frees up cash that is used for more productive purposes. It also reduces overhead costs, such as depreciation, insurance, and maintenance, which improves profitability.

Further, although Dell provides financing of consumer purchases, it does not carry those receivables on its balance sheet. Instead, it has worked out an arrangement with CIT, the consumer finance company, to underwrite and carry its receivables. Dell gets the sales, and CIT handles the credit for a fee.

Effective management of operating assets is key to achieving high performance. Nobody does that better than Dell. This has helped Dell produce a 42% return on its equity, which is 50% higher than IBM and nearly five times higher than HP.

PREVIEW OF CHAPTER 4

Assets are resources controlled by a company for the purpose of generating profit. They can be categorized into two groups—current and noncurrent. **Current assets** are resources readily convertible to cash within the *operating cycle* of the company. Major classes of current assets include cash, cash equivalents, receivables, inventories, and prepaid expenses. **Long-term** (or **noncurrent**) **assets** are resources expected to benefit the company for periods beyond the current period. Major long-term assets include property, plant, equipment, intangibles, investments, and deferred charges. An alternative distinction often useful for analysis is to designate assets as either financial assets or operating assets. **Financial assets** consist mainly of marketable securities and other investments in nonoperating assets. They usually are valued at fair (market) value and are expected to yield returns equal to their risk-adjusted cost of capital. **Operating assets** constitute most of a company's assets. They usually are valued at cost and are expected to yield returns in excess of the weighted-average cost of capital. This chapter discusses accounting issues involving the valuation of assets, other than intercorporate investments, and their subsequent cost allocation. We explain the implications of asset accounting for credit and profitability analysis and for equity valuation. The content and organization of this chapter follows:

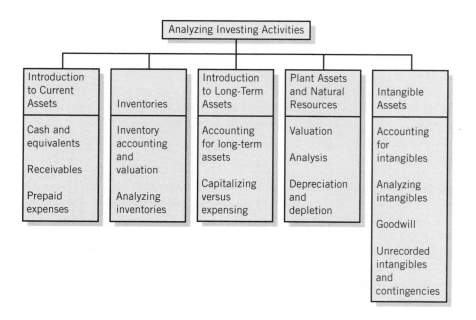

Assets relating to investments in marketable securities and equity investments in consolidated and unconsolidated affiliates, together with investments in derivative securities, are discussed in Chapter 5.

·······INTRODUCTION TO CURRENT ASSETS

Current assets include cash and other assets that are convertible to cash, usually within the operating cycle of the company. An **operating cycle,** shown in Exhibit 4.1, is the amount of time from commitment of cash for purchases until the collection of cash resulting from sales of goods or services. It is the process by which a company converts cash into short-term assets and back into cash as part of its ongoing operating activities. For a manufacturing company, this would entail purchasing raw materials, converting them to finished goods, and then selling and collecting cash from receivables. Cash represents the starting point, and the end point, of the operating cycle. The operating cycle is used to classify assets (and liabilities) as either current or noncurrent. Current assets are expected to be sold, collected, or used within one year or the operating cycle, whichever is longer.[1] Typical examples are cash, cash equivalents, short-term receivables, short-term securities, inventories, and prepaid expenses.

The excess of current assets over current liabilities is called **working capital.** Working capital is a double-edged sword–companies need working capital to effectively operate, yet working capital is costly because it must be financed and can entail other operating costs, such as credit losses on accounts receivable and storage and logistics

---

[1] Similarly, current liabilities are obligations due to be paid or settled within the longer of one year or the operating cycle.

Operating Cycle

Exhibit 4.1

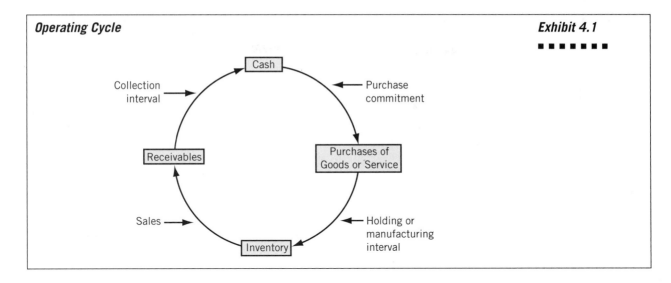

costs for inventories. Many companies attempt to improve profitability and cash flow by reducing investment in current assets through methods such as effective credit underwriting and collection of receivables, and just-in-time inventory management. In addition, companies try to finance a large portion of their current assets through current liabilities, such as accounts payable and accruals, in an attempt to reduce working capital.

Because of the impact of current assets (and current liabilities) on liquidity and profitability, analysis of current assets (and current liabilities) is very important in both credit analysis and profitability analysis. We shall discuss these issues at length later in the book. In this chapter, we limit analysis to the accounting aspects of current assets, specifically their valuation and expense treatment.

Cash and Cash Equivalents

Cash, the most liquid asset, includes currency available and funds on deposit. **Cash equivalents** are highly liquid, short-term investments that are (1) readily convertible into cash and (2) so near maturity that they have minimal risk of price changes due to interest rate movements. These investments usually carry maturities of three months or less. Examples of cash equivalents are short-term treasury bills, commercial paper, and money market funds. Cash equivalents often serve as temporary repositories of excess cash.

The concept of **liquidity** is important in financial statement analysis. By liquidity, we mean the amount of cash or cash equivalents the company has on hand and the amount of cash it can raise in a short period of time. Liquidity provides flexibility to take advantage of changing market conditions and to react to strategic actions by competitors. Liquidity also relates to the ability of a company to meet its obligations as they mature. Many companies with strong balance sheets (where there exists substantial equity capital in relation to total assets) can still run into serious difficulties because of illiquidity.

Companies differ widely in the amount of liquid assets they carry on their balance sheets. As the graphic indicates, cash and cash equivalents as a percentage of total assets ranges from 2% (Target) to 22% (Dell). These differences can result from a number of factors. In general, companies in a dynamic industry require increased liquidity to take advantage of opportunities or to react to a quickly changing competitive landscape.

GLOBAL
A company must disclose restrictions on cash for accounts located in foreign countries.

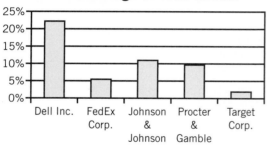

Cash and Cash Equivalents as a Percentage of Total Assets

In addition to examining the amount of liquid assets available to the company, analysts must also consider the following:

1. To the extent that cash equivalents are invested in equity securities, companies risk a reduction in liquidity should the market value of those investments decline.
2. Cash and cash equivalents are sometimes required to be maintained as compensating balances to support existing borrowing arrangements or as collateral for indebtedness. For example, eBay, Inc., was required under the terms of a lease to place $126 million out of its $400 million in cash and investment securities as collateral for the term of the lease. These investments were, therefore, not available to meet normal operating needs of the company.

Receivables

Receivables are amounts due to the company that arise from the sale of products or services, or from advances (loaning of money) to other companies. **Accounts receivable** refer to amounts due to the company that arise from sales of products and services. **Notes receivable** refer to formal written promises of indebtedness due. Certain other receivables often require separate disclosure by source, including receivables from affiliated companies, corporate officers, company directors, and employees. Companies can establish receivables without the formal billing of a debtor. For example, costs accumulated under a cost-plus-fixed-fee contract or some other types of contracts are usually recorded as receivables when earned, even though not yet billed to the customer. Also, claims for tax refunds often are classified as receivables. Receivables classified as current assets are expected to be collected within a year or the operating cycle, whichever is longer.

Valuation of Receivables

It is important to analyze receivables because of their impact on a company's asset position and income stream. These two impacts are interrelated. Experience shows that companies do not collect all receivables. While decisions about collectibility can be made at any time, collectibility of receivables as a group is best estimated on the basis of past experience, with suitable allowance for current economy, industry, and debtor conditions. The risk in this analysis is that past experience might not be an adequate predictor of future loss, or that we fail to fully account for current conditions. Losses with receivables can be substantial and affect both current assets and current and future net income.

In practice, companies report receivables at their **net realizable value**—total amount of receivables less an allowance for uncollectible accounts. Management estimates the allowance for uncollectibles based on experience, customer fortunes, economy and industry expectations, and collection policies. Uncollectible accounts are written off against the allowance (often reported as a deduction from receivables in the balance sheet), and the expected loss is included in current operating expenses. Our assessment of earnings quality is often affected by an analysis of receivables and their collectibility. Analysis must be alert to changes in the allowance account—computed relative to sales, receivables, or industry and market conditions.

Analyzing Receivables

While an unqualified opinion of an independent auditor lends assurance to the validity of receivables, our analysis must recognize the possibility of error in judgment as to their ultimate collection. We also must be alert to management's incentives in reporting higher levels of income and assets. In this respect, two important questions confront our analysis of receivables.

Collection Risk.   Most provisions for uncollectible accounts are based on past experience, although they make allowance for current and emerging economic, industry, and debtor circumstances. In practice, management likely attaches more importance to past experience—for no other reason than economic and industry conditions are difficult to predict. Our analysis must bear in mind that while a formulaic approach to calculating the provision for bad debts is convenient and practical, it reflects a mechanical judgment that yields errors. Analysis must rely on our knowledge of industry conditions to reliably assess the provision for uncollectibles.

Full information to assess *collection risk* for receivables is not usually included in financial statements. Useful information must be obtained from other sources or from the company. Analysis tools for investigating collectibility include:

- Comparing competitors' receivables as a percentage of sales with those of the company under analysis.
- Examining customer concentration—risk increases when receivables are concentrated in one or a few customers.
- Computing and investigating trends in the average collection period of receivables compared with customary credit terms for the industry.
- Determining the portion of receivables that are renewals of prior accounts or notes receivable.

An interesting case involving valuation of receivables and its importance for analysis is that of Brunswick Corp. In a past annual report, Brunswick made a "special provision for possible losses on receivables" involving a write-off of $15 million. Management asserted circumstances revealed themselves that were not apparent to management or the auditor at the end of the previous year when a substantial amount of these receivables were reported as outstanding. Management explained these write-offs as follows (dates adapted):

ANALYSIS EXCERPT

Delinquencies in bowling installment payments, primarily related to some of the large chain accounts, continued at an unsatisfactory level. Nonchain accounts, which comprise about 80% of installment receivables, are generally better paying accounts. . . . In the last quarter of 20X6, average bowling lineage per establishment fell short of the relatively low lineage of the comparable period of 20X5, resulting in an aggravation of collection problems on certain accounts. The fact that collections were lower in late 20X6 contributed to management's decision to increase reserves. After the additional provision of $15 million, total reserves for possible future losses on all receivables amounted to $66 million.

While it is impossible to precisely define the moment when collection of a receivable is sufficiently doubtful to require a provision, the relevant question is whether our analysis can warn us of an inadequate provision. In year 20X5 of the Brunswick case, our analysis should have revealed the inadequacy of the bad debt provision (reflected in the ratio of the allowance for uncollectible accounts to gross accounts receivable) in light of known industry conditions. Possibly not coincidentally, Brunswick's income peaked in 20X5–the year benefiting from the insufficient provision (the insufficient allowance for uncollectible accounts resulted in less bad debt expense and higher income).

Our analysis of current financial position and a company's ability to meet current obligations as reflected in measures like the current ratio also must recognize the importance of the operating cycle in classifying receivables as current. The operating cycle can result in installment receivables that are not collectible for several years or even decades being reported in current assets (e.g., wineries). Our analysis of current assets, and their relation to current liabilities, must recognize and adjust for these timing risks.

ANALYSIS VIEWPOINT　　　　　　　　　　　　**. . . YOU ARE THE AUDITOR**

Your client reports preliminary financial results showing a 15% growth in earnings. This growth meets earlier predictions by management. In your audit, you discover management reduced its allowance for uncollectible accounts from 5% to 2% of gross accounts receivable. Absent this change, earnings would show 9% growth. Do you have any concern about this change in estimate?

Authenticity of Receivables.　The description of receivables in financial statements or notes is usually insufficient to provide reliable clues as to whether receivables are genuine, due, and enforceable. Knowledge of industry practices and supplementary sources of information are used for added assurance. One factor affecting authenticity is the *right of merchandise return.* Customers in certain industries, like the magazine, textbook, or toy industries, enjoy a substantial right of merchandise return. Our analysis must allow for return privileges. Liberal return privileges can impair quality of receivables.

Receivables also are subject to various contingencies. Analysis can reveal whether contingencies impair the value of receivables. A note to the financial statements of O. M. Scott & Sons reveals several contingencies:

ANALYSIS EXCERPT

Accounts receivable: Accounts receivable are stated net after allowances for returns and doubtful accounts of $472,000. Accounts receivable include approximately $4,785,000 for shipments made under a deferred payment plan whereby title to the merchandise is transferred to the dealer when shipped; however, the Company retains a security interest in such merchandise until sold by the dealer. Payment to the Company is due from the dealer as the merchandise is sold at retail. The amount of receivables of this type shall at no time exceed $11 million under terms of the loan and security agreement.

Receivables like these often entail more collection risk than receivables without contingencies.

Securitization of Receivables.　Another important analysis issue arises when a company sells all or a portion of its receivables to a third party which, typically, finances the sale by selling bonds to the capital markets. The collection of those receivables provides the source for the yield on the bond. Such practice is called **securitization.** (The sale of receivables to a bank or commercial finance company is called **factoring.**) Receivables can be sold with or without recourse to a buyer (*recourse* refers to guarantee of collectibility). Sale of receivables *with recourse* does not effectively transfer risk of ownership of receivables from the seller.

Receivables can be kept off the balance sheet only when the company selling its receivables surrenders all control over the receivables to an independent buyer of sufficient financial strength. This means as long as a buyer has any type of recourse or the selling company has any degree of retained interest in the receivables, the company selling receivables has to continue to record both an asset and a compensating liability for the amount sold.

The securitization of receivables is often accomplished by establishing a special purpose entity (SPE), such as the trust in Illustration 4.1, to purchase the receivables from the company and finance the purchase via sale of bonds into the market. Capital One Financial Corporation (discussed in Chapter 3) provides an excellent example of a company securitizing a significant portion of its receivables. The consumer finance company has sold $42 billion of its $80 billion loan portfolio and acknowledges that securitization is a significant source of its financing.

ILLUSTRATION 4.1

Syntex Co. securitizes its entire receivables of $400 million with no recourse by selling the portfolio to a trust that finances the purchase by selling bonds. As a result, the receivables are removed from the balance sheet and the company receives $400 million in cash. The balance sheet and key ratios of Syntex are shown below under three alternative scenarios: (1) before securitizing the receivables; (2) after securitizing receivables with off-balance-sheet financing (as reported under GAAP); and (3) after securitizing receivables *but* reflecting the securitization as a borrowing (reflecting the analyst's adjustments). Notice how scenario 2, compared to the true economic position of scenario 3, window-dresses the balance sheet by not reporting a portion of current liabilities.

BALANCE SHEET

	Before	After	Adjusted		Before	After	Adjusted
Assets				**Liabilities**			
Cash	$ 50	$ 450	$ 450	Current liabilities	$ 400	$ 400	$ 800
Receivables	400	0	400	Noncurrent liabilities	500	500	500
Other current assets	150	150	150				
Total current assets	600	600	1,000	**Equity**	600	600	600
Noncurrent assets	900	900	900				
Total assets	$1,500	$1,500	$1,900	Total liabilities and equity	$1,500	$1,500	$1,900

KEY RATIOS

Current ratio	1.50	1.50	1.25
Total debt to equity	1.50	1.50	2.17

Sears, Roebuck and Company also has employed this technique to remove a sizable portion of its receivables from its balance sheet and provides an example of off-balance-sheet effects of securitization that have been negated under current accounting standards. The sale of receivables to a SPE only removes them from the balance sheet so long as the SPE is not required to be consolidated with the company selling the receivables. Consolidation (covered in Chapter 5) results in an adding together of the balance sheets of the company and the SPE, thus eliminating the benefits of the securitization.

The consolidation rules regarding SPEs are complicated, and if the SPEs are not properly structured, can result in consolidation of the SPE with the selling company. *SFAS 140,* "Accounting for Transfers and Servicing of Financial Assets and Extinguishments of Liabilities," and FIN 46R, "Consolidation of Variable Interest Entities," (explained in Chapter 3) established new conditions for a securitization to be accounted for as a sale of receivables and consequent removal from the balance sheet. Essentially, to avoid consolidation (which results in continued reporting of the receivables as an asset on the balance sheet), the company selling the receivables cannot have any recourse or other continuing involvement with the receivables after the sale and the purchasing company must be independent and sufficiently capitalized (usually taken to be at least 10% equity) to finance its operations without outside support. As a result of the standard, Sears now consolidates its receivable trusts, thus recognizing on its balance sheet $8 billion of previously unconsolidated credit card receivables and related borrowings. The company now accounts for the securitizations as secured borrowings.

Prepaid Expenses

Prepaid expenses are advance payments for services or goods not yet received. Examples are advance payments for rent, insurance, utilities, and property taxes. Prepaid expenses usually are classified in current assets because they reflect services due that would otherwise require use of current assets.

•••••••INVENTORIES
Inventory Accounting and Valuation

Inventories are goods held for sale as part of a company's normal business operations. With the exception of certain service organizations, inventories are essential and important assets of companies. We scrutinize inventories because they are a major component of operating assets and directly affect determination of income.

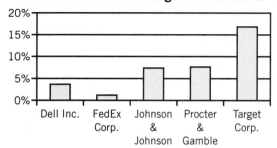

Inventories as a Percentage of Total Assets

The importance of costing methods for inventory valuation is due to their impact on net income and asset valuation. Inventory costing methods are used to allocate cost of goods available for sale (beginning inventory plus net purchases) between either cost of goods sold (an income deduction) or ending inventory (a current asset). Accordingly, assigning costs to inventory affects both income and asset measurements.

The **inventory equation** is useful in understanding inventory flows. For a merchandising company:

Beginning inventories + Net purchases − Cost of goods sold = Ending inventories

This equation highlights the flow of costs within the company. It can be expressed alternatively as shown in the graphic to the right.

The costs of inventories are initially recorded on the balance sheet. As the inventories are sold, these costs are removed from the balance sheet and flow into the income statement as cost of goods sold (COGS). Costs cannot be in two places at the same time; either they remain on the balance sheet (as a future expense) or are recognized currently in the income statement and reduce profitability to match against sales revenue.

An important concept in inventory accounting is the flow of costs. If all inventories acquired or manufactured during the period are sold, then COGS is equal to the cost of the goods purchased or manufactured. When inventories remain at the end of the accounting period, however, it is important to determine which inventories have been sold and which costs remain on the balance sheet. GAAP allows companies several options to determine the order in which costs are removed from the balance sheet and recognized as COGS in the income statement.

Cost of Goods Available for Sale
(= Beginning inventories +
Cost of inventories acquired during the period)

Ending Inventories
(balance sheet)

Cost of Goods Sold
(income statement)

Inventory Cost Flows

To illustrate the available cost-flow assumptions, assume that the following reflects the inventory records of a company:

Inventory on January 1, Year 2	40 units @ $500 each	$20,000
Inventories purchased during the year	60 units @ $600 each	36,000
Cost of goods available for sale	100 units	$56,000

Now, assume that 30 units are sold during the year at $800 each for total sales revenue of $24,000. GAAP allows companies three options in determining which costs to match against sales:

First-In, First-Out.   This method assumes that the first units purchased are the first units sold. In this case, these units are the units on hand at the beginning of the period. Under FIFO, the company's gross profit is as follows:

Sales	$24,000
COGS (30 @ $500 each)	15,000
Gross profit	$ 9,000

Also, because $15,000 of inventory cost has been removed, the remaining inventory cost to be reported on the balance sheet at the end of the period is $41,000.

Last-In, First-Out.   Under the LIFO inventory costing assumption, the last units purchased are the first to be sold. Gross profit is, therefore, computed as

Sales	$24,000
COGS (30 @ $600 each)	18,000
Gross profit	$ 6,000

And because $18,000 of inventory cost has been removed from the balance sheet and reflected in COGS, $38,000 remains on the balance sheet to be reported as inventories.

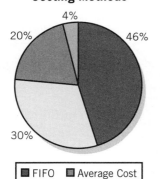

Companies Employing Various Inventory Costing Methods

- FIFO 46%
- Average Cost 4%
- LIFO 30%
- Other 20%

Average Cost. This method assumes that the units are sold without regard to the order in which they are purchased and computes COGS and ending inventories as a simple weighted average as follows:

Sales	$24,000
COGS (30 @ $560 each)	16,800
Gross profit	$ 7,200

COGS is computed as a weighted average of the total cost of goods available for sale divided by the number of units available for sale ($56,000/100 = $560). Ending units reported on the balance sheet are $39,200 (70 units × $560 per unit).

Analyzing Inventories
Inventory Costing Effects on Profitability

To summarize, the financial results of using each of the three alternative methods are:

	Beginning Inventory	Purchases	Ending Inventory	Cost of Goods Sold
FIFO	$20,000	$36,000	$41,000	$15,000
LIFO	20,000	36,000	38,000	18,000
Average cost	20,000	36,000	39,200	16,800

The income statements under the three methods, then, are as follows:

	Sales	Cost of Goods Sold	Gross Profit
FIFO	$24,000	$15,000	$9,000
LIFO	24,000	18,000	6,000
Average cost	24,000	16,800	7,200

As the examples presented here highlight, gross profit can be affected by the company's choice of its inventory costing method. *In periods of rising prices,* FIFO produces higher gross profits than LIFO because lower cost inventories are matched against sales revenues at current market prices. This is sometimes referred to as *FIFO's phantom profits* as the gross profit is actually a sum of two components: an **economic profit** and a **holding gain.** The economic profit is equal to the number of units sold multiplied by the difference between the sales price and the replacement cost of the inventories (approximated by the cost of the most recently purchased inventories):

$$\text{Economic profit} = 30 \text{ units} \times (\$800 - \$600) = \$6,000$$

The holding gain is the increase in replacement cost since the inventories were acquired and is equal to the number of units sold multiplied by the difference between the current replacement cost and the original acquisition cost:

$$\text{Holding gain} = 30 \text{ units} \times (\$600 - \$500) = \$3,000$$

Of the $9,000 in reported gross profit, $3,000 relates to the inflationary gains realized by the company on inventories it purchased some time ago at prices lower than current prices.

Holding gains are a function of the inventory turnover (e.g., how long the goods remain on the shelves) and the rate of inflation. Once a serious problem, these gains have been mitigated during the past decade due to lower inflation and management scrutiny of inventory quantities through improved manufacturing processes and better inventory controls. In countries with higher inflation rates than the United States, however, FIFO holding gains can still be an issue.

Inventory Costing Effects on the Balance Sheet

In periods of rising prices, and assuming that the company has not previously liquidated older layers of inventories, LIFO reports ending inventories at prices that can be significantly lower than replacement cost. As a result, balance sheets for LIFO companies do not accurately represent the current investment that the company has in its inventories. John Deere, for example, recently reported inventories under LIFO costing nearly $2 billion. Had these inventories been valued under FIFO, the reported amount would have been $3 billion, a 50% increase. More than $1 billion of invested capital was omitted from its balance sheet.

Analysis Research
■■■■■■■

PREDICTIONS USING INVENTORY LEVELS

Can our analysis use changes in a company's inventory levels to predict future sales and earnings? From one perspective, evidence of increased inventory can reveal management's expected increase in sales. From another, increased inventory can suggest excess inventory due to an unexpected sales decrease. Analysis research indicates we must cautiously interpret changes in inventory levels, even within industries and types of inventories.

For *manufacturing* companies, an increase in finished goods inventory is a predictor of increased sales but with decreased earnings—that is, evidence suggests companies reduce prices to dispose of undesirable inventory at lower profit margins. Periods subsequent to this increase in finished goods inventory do not appear to fully recover, meaning future sales and earnings do not rebound to previous levels. In contrast, an increase in raw materials or work-in-process inventory tends to foreshadow both increased sales and earnings that persist.

Evidence with *merchandising* companies suggests a slightly different pattern. Specifically, an increase in merchandise inventory implies future increased sales but with reduced earnings. This pattern is consistent with less demand, subsequently followed by reduced inventory prices to dispose of undesirable inventory—yielding lower profit margins.

These research insights can be useful in our analysis of inventory. Yet we must not ignore the role of inventory methods and estimates in determining inventory dollar levels. We must jointly consider these latter factors and adjust for them, in light of these research implications.

Inventory Costing Effects on Cash Flows

The increase in gross profit under FIFO also results in higher pretax income and, consequently, higher tax liability. In periods of rising prices, companies can get caught in a cash flow squeeze as they pay higher taxes and must replace the inventories sold at replacement costs higher than the original purchase costs. This can lead to liquidity problems, an issue that was particularly acute in the high inflationary period of the 1970s.

One of the reasons frequently cited for the adoption of LIFO is the reduction of tax liability in periods of rising prices. The IRS requires, however, that companies using LIFO inventory costing for tax purposes also use it for financial reporting. This is the **LIFO conformity rule.**

Companies using LIFO inventory costing are required to disclose the amount at which inventories would have been reported had the company used FIFO inventory costing. The difference between these two amounts is called the **LIFO reserve.** Analysts can use this reserve to compute the amount by which cash flow has been affected both cumulatively and for the current period by the use of LIFO. For example, John Deere reports the following in a recent annual report:

($ millions)	2004	2003
Raw materials and supplies.............	$ 589	$ 496
Work-in-process	408	388
Finished machines and parts	2,004	1,432
Total FIFO value	3,001	2,316
Less adjustment to LIFO value	1,002	950
Inventories	$1,999	$1,366

LIFO inventories are reported on the balance sheet at $1,999 million. Had the company used FIFO inventory costing, inventories would have been reported at $3,001 million. The difference of $1,002 million is the LIFO reserve. This is the amount by which inventories and pretax income have been reduced because the company adopted LIFO. Assuming a 35% tax rate, Deere has saved more than $350 million ($1,002 million $\times$ 35%) through the use of LIFO inventory costing. During 2004, the LIFO reserve increased by $52 million ($950 million to $1,002 million). For 2004, then, LIFO inventory costing decreased pretax income by $52 million and decreased taxes by $18 million ($52 million $\times$ 35% tax rate). The net decrease in income is, therefore, $34 million in that year.

Analysis Research
■ ■ ■ ■ ■ ■ ■

LIFO RESERVE AND COMPANY VALUE

What is the relation between the LIFO reserve and company value? A common assumption is that the LIFO reserve represents an unrecorded asset. Under this view, the magnitude of the LIFO reserve reflects a current value adjustment to inventory. Analysis research has investigated this issue, with interesting results.

Contrary to the "unrecorded asset theory," evidence from practice is consistent with a *negative* relation between the LIFO reserve and company market value. This implies the higher the LIFO reserve is, the lower the company value. Why this negative relation? An "economic effects theory" suggests that companies adopt LIFO if the present value of expected tax savings exceeds the costs of adoption (such as administrative costs). If we assume the present value of tax savings is related to the anticipated effect of inflation on inventory costs (a reasonable assumption), a negative relation might reflect the decline in the real value of a company due to anticipated inflation. Our analysis must therefore consider the possibility that companies using LIFO and companies using FIFO are inherently different and that adjustments using the LIFO reserve reflect this difference.

Other Issues in Inventory Valuation

LIFO Liquidations.   Companies are required to maintain each cost level as a separate inventory pool (e.g., the $20,000 and $36,000 inventory pools in our initial example). When a *reduction* in inventory quantities occurs, which can occur as a company becomes leaner or downsizes, companies dip into earlier cost layers to match against current selling prizces. For FIFO inventory costing, this does not present a significant problem as ending inventories are reported at the most recently acquired costs and earlier cost layers do not differ significantly from current cost. For LIFO inventories, however, ending inventories can be reported at much older costs that may be significantly lower or higher than current costs. In periods of rising prices, this reduction in inventory quantities, known as **LIFO liquidation,** results in an increase in gross profit that is similar to the effect of FIFO inventory costing. In periods of *declining* prices, however, the reduction of inventory quantities can lead to a *decrease* in reported gross profit as higher cost inventories are matched against current sales.

The effect of LIFO liquidation can be seen in the inventory footnote of a recent Stride Rite Corporation annual report. The company indicates that reductions in inventory quantities resulted in the sale of products carried at prior years' costs that were different from current costs. As a result of these inventory reductions, net income *increased* by $47 million and $141 million in the current and prior year, and *decreased* by $120 million two years prior, as a result of reductions in inventory quantities. Analysts need to be aware of the effects on profitability of these LIFO liquidations.

Analytical Restatement of LIFO to FIFO.   When financial statements are available using LIFO, and if LIFO is the method preferred in our analysis, the income statement requires no major adjustment since cost of goods sold approximates current cost. The LIFO method, however, leaves inventories on the balance sheet at less recent, often understated costs. This can impair the usefulness of various measures like the current ratio or inventory turnover ratio. We already showed that LIFO understates inventory values *when prices rise*. Consequently, LIFO understates the company's debt-paying ability (as measured, for example, by the current ratio), and overstates inventory turnover. To counter this we use an analytical technique for adjusting LIFO statements to approximate a pro forma situation assuming FIFO. This balance sheet adjustment is possible when a company discloses the amount by which current cost exceeds reported cost of LIFO inventories, the LIFO reserve. The following three adjustments are necessary:

(1) Inventories = Reported LIFO inventory + LIFO reserve
(2) Increase deferred tax payable by: (LIFO reserve × Tax rate)
(3) Retained earnings = Reported retained earnings + [LIFO reserve × (1 − Tax rate)]

We illustrate these adjustments to restate LIFO inventories to FIFO using Campbell Soup's financial statements from Appendix A–see Illustration 4.2.

ILLUSTRATION 4.2
■ ■ ■ ■ ■ ■ ■

Campbell's Soup Note 14 reports "adjustments of inventories to LIFO basis" (the LIFO reserve) are $89.6 million in Year 11 and $84.6 million in Year 10. To restate Year 11 LIFO inventories to a FIFO basis we use the following analytical entry (an analytical entry is an adjustment aid for purposes of accounting analysis):

Inventories[a]	89.6	
Deferred Tax Payable[b]		30.5
Retained Earnings[c]		59.1

[a]*Inventories increase by $89.6 to approximate current cost (note: a low turnover ratio can result in inventories of FIFO not reflecting current cost).*
[b]*Since inventories increase, a provision for taxes payable in the future is made, using a tax rate of 34% (from Note 9)—computed as $89.6 × 34%. The reason for tax deferral is this analytical entry reflects an accounting method different from that used for tax purposes.*
[c]*Higher ending inventories imply lower cost of goods sold and higher cumulative net income flowing into retained earnings (net of tax)—computed as $89.6 × (1 − 34%).*

Similarly, to adjust Year 10 LIFO inventories to FIFO, we use the following analytical entry:

Inventories	84.6	
Deferred Tax Payable		28.8
Retained Earnings		55.8

ILLUSTRATION 4.3

■ ■ ■ ■ ■ ■ ■

To assess the impact on Year 11 income from restatement of inventories from LIFO to FIFO for Campbell Soup, we make the following computations:

	YEAR 11		
	Under LIFO	Difference	Under FIFO
Beginning inventory	$819.8[a]	$84.6[b]	$904.4
+ Purchases (P)[c]	P	—	P
− Ending inventory	(706.7)[d]	(89.6)[b]	(796.3)
= Cost of goods sold	P + $113.1	$ (5.0)[d]	P + $108.1

[a] As reported per balance sheet, see Note 14.
[b] Per financial statement Note 14.
[c] Because purchases (P) are unaffected by using either LIFO or FIFO, purchases need not be adjusted to arrive at the effect on cost of goods sold or income. If desired, we can compute purchases for Year 11 as: $4,095.5 (cost of goods per income statement) + $706.7 (ending inventory) − $819.8 (beginning inventory) = $3,982.4.
[d] Restatement to FIFO decreases cost of goods sold by $5.0 and, therefore, increases income by $5.0 × (1 − 0.34), or $3.3 using a 34% tax rate.

We also can readily compute income statement impacts from the adjustment of LIFO inventories to FIFO inventories, see Illustration 4.3.

Illustration 4.3 shows us that the income restatement (net of tax) from LIFO to FIFO for Campbell Soup for Year 11 is $3.3. This amount is reconciled with the adjustments to retained earnings (balance sheet restatement) as implied from the analytical entries (see Illustration 4.2) for Years 10 and 11:

Year 10 Credit to Retained Earnings	−	Year 11 Credit to Retained Earnings	=	Increase in Year 11 Income
$55.8		$59.1		$3.3

Generally, when prices rise, LIFO income is less than FIFO income. However, the net effect of restatement in any given year depends on the combined effects of the change in beginning and ending inventories and other factors including liquidation of LIFO layers.

Analytical Restatement of FIFO to LIFO.   The adjustment from FIFO to LIFO, unfortunately, involves an important assumption and may, therefore, be prone to error. Remember that FIFO profits include a holding gain on beginning inventory. It is helpful to think of this gain as the beginning inventory (BI_{FIFO}) multiplied by an inflation rate for the particular lines of inventory that the firm carries. Let us call this rate r. Then, current FIFO profits include a holding gain equal to $BI \times r$. This means that cost of goods sold (FIFO) is understated by $BI_{FIFO} \times r$. Therefore, to compute LIFO cost of goods sold ($COGS_{LIFO}$), simply add $BI_{FIFO} \times r$ to $COGS_{FIFO}$ as follows:

$$COGS_{LIFO} = COGS_{FIFO} + (BI_{FIFO} \times r)$$

Note that this inflation factor, r, is not a general rate of inflation like the CPI or the producer's price index. It is an inflation index relating to the specific lines of inventory carried by the firm. To the extent that the firm carries a number of product lines, in theory, these must each be estimated separately.

Analysis Research
■ ■ ■ ■ ■ ■ ■

INVENTORY METHOD
CHOICE

Why are all firms not using LIFO? Or FIFO? Or another method? Can a company's choice of inventory method help direct our analysis of a company? Analysis research on inventory provides answers to some of these questions. Specifically, information on inventory method choice for a company can give us insights into the company and its environment.

For companies choosing LIFO, the following characteristics are common:

- Greater expected tax savings.
- Larger inventory balances.
- Less tax loss carryforwards.
- Lower variability in inventory balances.
- Less likelihood of inventory obsolescence.

- Larger in size.
- Less leveraged.
- Higher current ratios.

Accordingly, knowledge of inventory method choice can reveal information about a company's characteristics or circumstances otherwise obscured by the complexity of data or operations.

How does one estimate r? There are several possibilities. First, the analyst might use indices published by the U.S. Department of Commerce for the firm's particular industry. Second, to the extent that the firm is involved in a commodity-based business, commodity indices might be used under the assumption that other cost components of its inventory vary proportionately with that of its raw materials. Third, the analyst can examine rates of inflation for the firm's competitors. To the extent that a company carrying similar lines of products can be found that uses LIFO inventory costing, the rate of inflation can be estimated as the increase in the LIFO reserve divided by the competitor's FIFO inventories at the end of the previous year as follows:

$$r = \frac{\text{Change in LIFO reserve}}{\text{FIFO inventories from previous year-end}}$$

Inventory Costing for Manufacturing Companies and the Effect of Production Increases

The cost of inventories for manufacturing consists of three components:

1. Raw materials—the cost of the basic materials used to manufacture the product.
2. Labor—the cost of the direct labor required to transform the product to a finished state.
3. Overhead—the indirect costs incurred in the manufacturing process, such as depreciation of the manufacturing equipment, supervisory wages, and utilities.

Companies can estimate the first two components fairly accurately from design specifications and time and motion studies on the assembly line. Overhead is often the largest component of product cost and the most difficult to measure at the product level. In total, overhead must be allocated to all products produced. But which products get what portion of the total? Accountants generally subscribe to the notion that those products consuming most of the resources (e.g., requiring the most costly production machinery or the most engineering time) should be allocated most of the overhead. Inventory costing for manufacturing companies is generally covered in managerial accounting courses and is beyond the scope of this text. Analysts need to be aware, however, that overhead cost allocation is not an exact science and is highly dependent on the assumptions used.

Analysts also need to understand the effect of production levels on profitability. Overhead is allocated to all units produced. Instead of expensing these costs as period expenses, they are included in the cost of inventories and remain on the balance sheet until the inventories are sold, at which time they are reflected as cost of goods sold in the income statement. If an increase in production levels causes ending inventories to increase, more of the overhead costs remain on the balance sheet and profitability increases. Later, if inventory quantities decrease, the income statement is burdened by not only the current overhead costs, but also previous overhead costs that have been removed from inventories in the current year, thus lowering profits. Analysts need to be aware, therefore, of the effect of changing production levels on reported profits.

Lower of Cost or Market

The generally accepted principle of inventory valuation is to value at the **lower of cost or market.** This simple phrase masks the complexities and variety of alternatives to which it is subject. It can significantly affect periodic income and inventory values. The lower-of-cost-or-market rule implies that if inventory declines in market value below its cost for any reason, including obsolescence, damage, and price changes, then inventory is written down to reflect this loss. This write-down is effectively charged against revenues in the period the loss occurs. Because write-ups from cost to market are prohibited (except for recovery of losses up to the original cost), inventory is conservatively valued.

Market is defined as current replacement cost through either purchase or reproduction. However, market value must not be higher than net realizable value nor less than net realizable value reduced by a normal profit margin. The upper limit of market value, or net realizable value, reflects completion and disposal costs associated with sale of the item. The lower limit ensures that if inventory is written down from cost to market, it is written down to a figure that includes realization of a normal gross profit on subsequent sale. **Cost** is defined as the acquisition cost of inventory. It is computed using one of the accepted inventory costing methods—for example, FIFO, LIFO, or average cost. Our analysis of inventory must consider the impact of the lower-of-cost-or-market rule. When prices are rising, this rule tends to *undervalue* inventories regardless of the cost method used. This depresses the current ratio. In practice, certain companies voluntarily disclose the current cost of inventory, usually in a note.

ANALYSIS EXCERPT

Toro Company's initial venture into snowblowers was less than successful. Toro reasoned that snowblowers were a perfect complement to its lawnmower business, especially after higher than normal snowfall in recent years. Toro reacted and produced snowblowers as if snow was both a growth business and fell as reliably as grass grows. When, in its launch year, winter yielded a less than normal snowfall, both Toro and its dealers were bursting with excess inventory. Many dealers were so financially pressed that they were unable to finance lawnmower inventories for the summer season.

ANALYSIS VIEWPOINT   *. . . YOU ARE THE BUYING AGENT*

You are trying to reach agreement with a supplier on providing materials for manufacturing. To make its case for a higher price, the supplier furnishes an income statement revealing a historically low 20% gross margin. In your analysis of this statement, you discover a note stating that market value of inventory declined by $2 million this period and, therefore, ending inventory is revalued downward by that amount. Is this note relevant for your price negotiations?

INTRODUCTION TO LONG-TERM ASSETS

To this point, we have explained the analysis of current assets. The remainder of this chapter focuses on long-term assets. Long-term assets are resources that are used to generate operating revenues (or reduce operating costs) for more than one period. The most common type of long-term asset is *tangible fixed assets* such as property, plant, and equipment. Long-term assets also include *intangible assets* such as patents, trademarks, copyrights, and goodwill. This section discusses conceptual issues pertaining to long-term assets. We then separately discuss accounting and analysis issues relating to tangible assets and natural resources, intangible assets, and unrecorded assets.

Accounting for Long-Term Assets

This section explains the concept of long-term assets and the processes of capitalization, allocation, and impairment.

Capitalization, Allocation, and Impairment

The process of long-term asset accounting involves three distinct activities: capitalization, allocation, and impairment. **Capitalization** is the process of deferring a cost that is incurred in the current period, but whose benefits are expected to extend to one or more future periods. It is capitalization that creates an asset account. **Allocation** is the process of periodically expensing a deferred cost (asset) to one or more future expected benefit periods. This allocation process is called *depreciation* for tangible assets, *amortization* for intangible assets, and *depletion* for natural resources. **Impairment** is the process of writing down the book value of the asset when its expected cash flows are no longer sufficient to recover the remaining cost reported on the balance sheet. This section discusses each of these three accounting activities.

Capitalization.   A long-term asset is created through the process of capitalization. Capitalization means putting the asset on the balance sheet rather than immediately expensing its cost in the income statement. For *hard assets,* such as PPE, this process is relatively simple; the asset is recorded at its purchase price. For *soft assets* such as R&D, advertising, and wage costs, capitalization is more problematic. Although all of these costs arguably produce future benefits and, therefore, meet the test to be recorded as an asset, neither the amount of the future benefits, nor their useful life, can be reliably measured. Consequently, costs for internally developed soft assets are immediately expensed and are not recorded on the balance sheet.

One area that has been particularly troublesome for the accounting profession has been the capitalization of software development costs. GAAP differentiates between two types of costs: the cost of software developed for internal use and the cost of software that is developed for sale or lease. The cost of computer software developed for internal use should be capitalized and amortized over its expected useful life. An important factor bearing on the determination of software's useful life is expected obsolescence. Software that is developed for sale or lease to others is capitalized and amortized only after it has reached *technological feasibility.* Prior to that stage of development, the software is considered to be R&D and is expensed accordingly.

Allocation.   Allocation is the periodic assignment of asset cost to expense over its expected useful life (benefit period). Allocation of costs is called **depreciation** when applied to tangible fixed assets, **amortization** when applied to intangible assets, and **depletion** when applied to natural resources. Each refers to cost allocation. We must remember that cost allocation is a process to match asset cost with its benefits—it is not a *valuation* process. Asset carrying value (capitalized value less cumulative cost allocation) need not reflect fair value.

Three factors determine the cost allocation amount: useful life, salvage value, and allocation method. We discuss these factors shortly. However, each of these factors requires estimates—estimates that involve managerial discretion. Analysis must consider the effects of these estimates on financial statements, especially when estimates change.

Impairment.   When the expected (undiscounted) cash flows are less than the asset's carrying amount (cost less accumulated depreciation), the asset is deemed to be impaired and is written down to its fair market value (the discounted amount of expected cash flows). The effect is to reduce the carrying amount of the asset on the balance sheet and to reduce profitability by a like amount. The fair value of the asset, then, becomes the new cost and is depreciated over its remaining useful life. It is not written up if expected cash flows subsequently improve. From our analysis perspective, two distortions arise from asset impairment:

1. Conservative biases distort long-term asset valuation because assets are written down but not written up.
2. Large transitory effects from recognizing asset impairments distort net income.

Note that asset impairment is still an allocation process, not a move toward valuation. That is, an asset impairment is recorded when managers' expectations of future cash inflows from the asset fall below carrying value. This yields an immediate write-off in a desire to better match future cost allocations with future benefits.

Capitalizing versus Expensing: Financial Statement and Ratio Effects

Capitalization is an important part of accounting. It affects both financial statements and their ratios. It also contributes to the superiority of earnings over cash flow as a measure of financial performance. This section examines the effects of capitalization (and subsequent allocation) versus immediate expensing for income measurement and ratio computation.

Effects of Capitalization on Income

Capitalization has two effects on income. First, it postpones recognition of expense in the income statement. This means capitalization yields higher income in the acquisition period but lower income in subsequent periods as compared with expensing of costs. Second, capitalization yields a smoother income series. Why does immediate expensing yield a volatile income series? The answer is volatility arises because capital expenditures are often "lumpy"—occurring in spurts rather than continually—while revenues from these expenditures are earned steadily over time. In contrast, allocating asset cost over benefit periods yields an accrual income number that is a more stable and meaningful measure of company performance.

Effects of Capitalization for Return on Investment

Capitalization decreases volatility in income measures and, similarly, return on investment ratios. It affects both the numerator (income) and denominator (investment bases) of the return on investment ratios. In contrast, expensing asset costs yields a lower investment base and increases income volatility. This increased volatility in the numerator (income) is magnified by the smaller denominator (investment base), leading to more volatile and less useful return ratios. Expensing also introduces bias in income measures, as income is understated in the acquisition year and overstated in subsequent years.

Effects of Capitalization on Solvency Ratios

Under immediate expensing of asset costs, solvency ratios, such as debt to equity, reflect more poorly on a company than warranted. This occurs because the immediate expensing of costs understates equity for companies with productive assets.

Effects of Capitalization on Operating Cash Flows

When asset costs are immediately expensed, they are reported as operating cash outflows. In contrast, when asset costs are capitalized, they are reported as investing cash outflows. This means that immediate expensing of asset costs both overstates operating cash outflows and understates investing cash outflows in the acquisition year in comparison to capitalization of costs.

PLANT ASSETS AND NATURAL RESOURCES

Property, plant, and equipment (or plant assets) are noncurrent tangible assets used in the manufacturing, merchandising, or service processes to generate revenues and cash flows for *more than one period*. Accordingly, these assets have expected useful lives

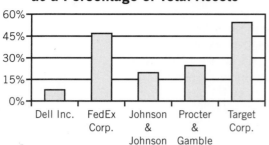

Property, Plant, and Equipment as a Percentage of Total Assets

extending over more than one period. These assets are intended for use in operating activities and are not acquired for sale in the ordinary course of business. Their value or service potential diminishes with use, and they are typically the largest of all operating assets. *Property* refers to the cost of real estate; *plant* refers to buildings and operating structures; and *equipment* refers to machinery used in operations. Property, plant, and equipment are also referred to as *PPE assets, capital assets,* and *fixed assets.*

Valuing Plant Assets and Natural Resources

This section describes the valuation of plant assets and natural resources.

Valuing Property, Plant, and Equipment

The historical cost principle is applied when valuing property, plant, and equipment. Historical cost valuation implies a company initially records an asset at its purchase cost. This cost includes any expenses necessary to bring the asset to a usable or serviceable condition and location such as freight, installation, taxes, and set-up. All costs of acquisition and preparation are capitalized in the asset's account balance. Justification for the use of historical cost primarily relates to its **objectivity.** Historical cost valuation of plant assets, if consistently applied, usually does not yield serious distortions. This section considers some special concerns that arise when valuing assets.

Valuing Natural Resources

Natural resources, also called **wasting assets,** are rights to extract or consume natural resources. Examples are purchase rights to minerals, timber, natural gas, and petroleum. Companies report natural resources at historical cost plus costs of discovery, exploration, and development. Also, there often are substantial costs subsequent to discovery of natural resources that are capitalized on the balance sheet, and are expensed only when the resource is later removed, consumed, or sold. Companies typically allocate costs of natural resources over the total units of estimated reserves available. This allocation process is called *depletion* and is discussed in Chapter 6.

Depreciation

A basic principle of income determination is that income benefiting from use of long-term assets must bear a proportionate share of their costs. Depreciation is the allocation of the costs of plant and equipment (land is not depreciated) over their useful lives. Although added back in the statement of cash flows as a noncash expense, depreciation does *not* provide funds for replacement of an asset. This is a common misconception. Funding for capital expenditures is achieved through operating cash flow and financing activities.

Rate of Depreciation

The rate of depreciation depends on two factors: useful life and allocation method.

Useful Life. The useful lives of assets vary greatly. Assumptions regarding useful lives of assets are based on economic conditions, engineering studies, experience, and information about an asset's physical and productive properties. Physical deterioration is an important factor limiting useful life, and nearly all assets are subject to it. The frequency and quality of maintenance bear on physical deterioration. Maintenance can extend useful life but cannot prolong it indefinitely. Another limiting factor is obsolescence, which impacts useful life through technological developments, consumption patterns, and economic forces. Ordinary obsolescence occurs when technological developments make an asset inefficient or uneconomical before its physical life is complete. Extraordinary obsolescence occurs when revolutionary changes occur or radical shifts in demand ensue. High-tech equipment is continually subject to rapid obsolescence. The integrity of depreciation, and that of income determination, depends on reasonably accurate estimates and timely revisions of useful lives. These estimates and revisions are ideally not influenced by management's incentives regarding timing of income recognition.

Allocation Method. Once the useful life of an asset is determined, periodic depreciation expense depends on the allocation method. Depreciation varies significantly depending on the method chosen. We consider the two most common classes of methods: straight-line and accelerated.

• **Straight-line.** The straight-line method of depreciation allocates the cost of an asset to its useful life on the basis of equal periodic charges. Exhibit 4.2 illustrates depreciation of an asset costing $110,000, with a useful life of 10 years and a salvage value of $10,000 (salvage value is the amount for which the asset is expected to be sold at the end of its useful life). Each of the 10 years is charged with one-tenth of the asset's cost less the salvage value—computed as ($110,000 − $10,000)/10 years.

Straight-Line Depreciation   *Exhibit 4.2*

End of Year	Depreciation	Accumulated Depreciation	Asset Book Value
			$110,000
1	$10,000	$ 10,000	100,000
2	10,000	20,000	90,000
⋮	⋮	⋮	⋮
9	10,000	90,000	20,000
10	10,000	100,000	10,000

The rationale for straight-line depreciation is the assumption that physical deterioration occurs uniformly over time. This assumption is likely more valid for fixed structures such as buildings than for machinery where utilization is a more important factor. The other determinant of depreciation, obsolescence, is not necessarily uniformly applicable over time. Yet in the absence of information on probable rates of depreciation, the straight-line method has the advantage of simplicity. This attribute, perhaps more than

Companies Employing Various Depreciation Methods

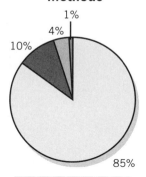

1%
4%
10%
85%

- ☐ Straight-Line
- ■ Accelerated
- ☐ Units-of-Production
- ■ Other

any other, accounts for its popularity. As the marginal graphic shows, straight-line depreciation is used by approximately 85% of publicly traded companies for financial reporting purposes (accelerated methods of depreciation are used for tax returns as we discuss below).

Our analysis must be aware of conceptual flaws with straight-line depreciation. Straight-line depreciation implicitly assumes that depreciation in early years is identical to that in later years when the asset is likely less efficient and requires increased maintenance. Another flaw with straight-line depreciation, and one of special interest for analysis, is the resulting distortion in rate of return. Namely, straight-line depreciation yields an increasing bias in the asset's rate of return pattern over time. To illustrate, assume the asset in Exhibit 4.2 yields a constant income of $20,000 per year before depreciation. Straight-line depreciation yields an increasing bias in the asset's rate of return as shown here:

End of Year	Income before Depreciation	Depreciation	Net Income	Beginning Year Book Value	Return on Book Value
1	$20,000	$10,000	$10,000	$110,000	9.1%
2	20,000	10,000	10,000	100,000	10.0
3	20,000	10,000	10,000	90,000	11.1
⋮	⋮	⋮	⋮	⋮	⋮
10	20,000	10,000	10,000	10,000	100.0

While increasing maintenance costs can decrease income before depreciation, they do not negate the overall effect of an increasing return over time. Certainly, an increasing return on an aging asset is not reflective of most businesses.

- **Accelerated.** Accelerated methods of depreciation allocate the cost of an asset to its useful life in a decreasing manner. Use of these methods is encouraged by their acceptance in the Internal Revenue Code. Their appeal for tax purposes is the acceleration of cost allocation and the subsequent deferral of taxable income. The faster an asset is written off for tax purposes, the greater the tax deferral to future periods and the more funds immediately available for operations. The conceptual support for accelerated methods is the view that decreasing depreciation charges over time compensate for (1) increasing repair and maintenance costs, (2) decreasing revenues and operating efficiency, and (3) higher uncertainty of revenues in later years of aged assets (due to obsolescence).

The two most common accelerated depreciation methods are declining balance and sum of the years' digits. The *declining-balance method* applies a constant rate to the declining asset balance (carrying value). In practice, an approximation to the exact rate of declining-charge depreciation is to use a multiple (often two times) of the straight-line rate. For example, an asset with a 10-year useful life is depreciated at a double-declining-balance rate of 20% computed as $[2 \times (\frac{1}{10})]$. The *sum-of-the-years'-digits method* applies a decreasing fraction to asset cost less salvage value. For example, an asset depreciated over a five-year period is written off by applying a fraction whose denominator is the sum of the five years' digits $(1 + 2 + 3 + 4 + 5 = 15)$ and whose numerator is the remaining life from the beginning of the period. This yields a fraction of $\frac{5}{15}$ for the first year, $\frac{4}{15}$ for the second year, progressing to $\frac{1}{15}$ in the fifth and final year.

Exhibit 4.3 illustrates these accelerated depreciation methods applied to an asset costing $110,000, with a salvage value of $10,000 and a useful life of 10 years. Because an asset is never depreciated below its salvage value, companies take care to ensure that

■ ■ ■ ■ ■ ■ ■

MACRS

U.S. tax rules use a Modified Accelerated Cost Recovery System (MACRS) for asset depreciation. MACRS assigns assets to classes where depreciable life and rate are defined.

Accelerated Depreciation　　　　　　　　　　　　　　　　　　　　　　　　　　*Exhibit 4.3*

End of Year	DEPRECIATION		CUMULATIVE DEPRECIATION	
	Double-Declining	Sum-of-the Years'-Digits	Double-Declining	Sum-of-the Years'-Digits
1	$22,000	$18,182	$ 22,000	$ 18,182
2	17,600	16,364	39,600	34,546
3	14,080	14,545	53,680	49,091
4	11,264	12,727	64,944	61,818
5	9,011	10,909	73,955	72,727
6	7,209	9,091	81,164	81,818
7	5,767	7,273	86,931	89,091
8	4,614	5,455	91,545	94,546
9	4,228*	3,636	95,773	98,182
10	4,227*	1,818	100,000	100,000

*Reverts to straight-line

declining-balance methods do not violate this. When depreciation expense using the declining-balance method falls below the straight-line rate, it is common practice to use the straight-line rate for the remaining periods.

• **Special.** Special methods of depreciation are found in certain industries like steel and heavy machinery. The most common of these methods links depreciation charges to *activity* or intensity of asset use. For example, if a machine has a useful life of 10,000 running hours, the depreciation charge varies with hours of running time rather than the period of time. It is important when using *activity methods* (also called unit-of-production methods) that the estimate of useful life be periodically reviewed to remain valid under changing conditions.

Depletion

Depletion is the allocation of the cost of natural resources on the basis of rate of extraction or production. The difference between depreciation and depletion is that depreciation usually is an allocation of the cost of a productive asset over time, while depletion is an allocation of cost based on unit exploitation of natural resources like coal, oil, minerals, or timber. Depletion depends on production–more production yields more depletion expense. To illustrate, if an ore deposit costs $5 million and contains an estimated 10 million recoverable tons, the depletion rate per ton of ore mined is $0.50. Production and sale of 100,000 tons yields a depletion charge of $50,000 and a net balance in the asset account at year-end of $4.95 million. Our analysis must be aware that, like depreciation, depletion can produce complications such as reliability, or lack thereof, of the estimate of recoverable resources. Companies must periodically review this estimate to ensure it reflects all information.

Impairment

Plant assets and natural resources are typically depreciated over their useful lives. Depreciation is based on the principle of *allocation*. That is, the cost of a long-lived asset is allocated to the various periods when it is used. The purpose of depreciation is income determination; it is a method for matching costs of long-lived assets to revenues generated from their use. It is important to note that depreciation is not a *valuation* exercise. In other words, the carrying value of a depreciated asset (i.e., the asset's cost less accumulated depreciation) is not designed to reflect the current value of that asset.

Does accounting make any attempts to reflect the current value of the asset on the balance sheet? Current accounting does so, but on a conservative basis. That is, when the depreciated amount of an asset is estimated to be higher than its current estimated value (often, its market value), then its amount on the balance sheet is written down to reflect its current value. Such a write-down (or write-off) is termed **impairment.** Current accounting rules for impairment of long-lived assets are specified under *SFAS 121* and its successor *SFAS 144*. We shall discuss impairment in detail under nonrecurring items in Chapter 6.

At present, accounting does not allow a write-up of an asset's value to reflect its current market value. However, this is expected to change as standard setters eventually move toward a comprehensive model of fair value accounting (see Chapter 2).

Analyzing Plant Assets and Natural Resources

Valuation of plant assets and natural resources emphasizes objectivity of historical cost. Unfortunately, historical costs are not especially relevant in assessing replacement values or in determining future need for operating assets. Also, they are not comparable across different companies' reports and are not particularly useful in measuring opportunity costs of disposal or in assessing alternative uses of funds. Further, in times of changing price levels, they represent a collection of expenditures reflecting different purchasing power.

Analysis Research
■ ■ ■ ■ ■ ■ ■   **WRITE-DOWN OF ASSET VALUES**

Asset write-downs are increasingly conspicuous due to their escalating number and frequency in recent years. Are these write-downs good or bad signals about current and future prospects of a company? What are the implications of these asset write-downs for financial analysis? Are write-downs relevant for security valuation? Do write-downs alter users' risk exposures? Analysis research is beginning to provide us insights into these questions.

Evidence shows that companies that previously recorded write-downs are more likely to report current and future write-downs. This result adds further complexity to our analysis and interpretation of earnings. Research also examines whether companies take advantage of the discretionary nature of asset write-downs to manage earnings toward a target figure. Evidence on this question shows management tends to time asset write-downs for a period when the company's financial performance is already low relative to competitors. While this evidence is consistent with companies loading additional charges against income in years when earnings are unfavorable (referred to as a *big bath*), it is also consistent with management taking an appropriate reduction in asset value due to decreasing earnings potential. Regardless, our analysis of a company's financial statements that include write-downs must consider their implications in light of current business conditions and company performance.

Write-up of plant assets to market is not acceptable accounting. Yet, conservatism permits a write-down if a permanent impairment in value occurs. A write-down relieves future periods of charges related to operating activities. Amerada Hess Corp. reports the following asset write-down in its annual report:

> **ANALYSIS EXCERPT**
>
> The Corporation recorded a special charge to earnings of $536,692,000 ($432,742,000 after income taxes, or $5.12 per share). The special charge consists of a $146,768,000 write-down in the book value of certain ocean-going tankers and a $389,924,000 provision for marine transportation costs in excess of market rates.

While realities of business dictate numerous uncertainties, including accounting estimation errors, our analysis demands scrutiny of such special charges. Accounting rules for impairments of long-term assets require companies to periodically review events or changes in circumstances for possible impairments. Nevertheless, companies can still defer recognition of impairments beyond the time when management first learns of them. In this case, subsequent write-downs can distort reported results. Under current rules, companies use a "recoverability test" to determine whether an impairment exists. That is, a company must estimate future net cash flows expected from the asset and its eventual disposition. If these expected net cash flows (undiscounted) are less than the asset's carrying amount, it is impaired. The impairment loss is measured as the excess of the asset's carrying value over fair value, where fair value is the market value or present value of expected future net cash flows.

Analyzing Depreciation and Depletion

Most companies use long-term productive assets in their operating activities and, in these cases, depreciation is usually a major expense. Managers make decisions involving the depreciable base, useful life, and allocation method. These decisions can yield substantially different depreciation charges. Our analysis should include information on these factors both to effectively assess earnings and to compare analysis of companies' earnings.

One focus of analysis is on any revisions of useful lives of assets. While such revisions can produce more reliable allocations of costs, our analysis must approach any revisions with concern, because such revisions are sometimes used to shift or smooth income across periods. The following General Motors revision had a major earnings impact:

> **ANALYSIS EXCERPT**
>
> The corporation revised the estimated service lives of its plants and equipment and special tools. . . . These revisions, which were based on . . . studies of actual useful lives and periods of use, recognized current estimates of service lives of the assets and had the effect of reducing . . . depreciation and amortization charges by $1,236.6 million or $2.55 per share.

In this case, GM's "studies of actual useful lives" were less than precise since three years later GM took a $2.1 billion charge to cover expenses of closing several plants and for other plants not to be closed for several years. Further analysis suggests evidence of earnings management by a newly elected chairman who explained this as "a major element in GM's long-term strategic plan to improve the competitiveness and profitability of its North American operations." That is, by charging $2.1 billion of plant costs to current earnings that otherwise would be depreciated in future periods, GM reduces future expenses and increases future income.

The quality of information in annual reports regarding allocation methods varies widely and is often less complete than disclosures in SEC filings. More detailed information typically includes the method or methods of depreciation and the range of useful lives for various asset categories. However, even this information is of limited usefulness. It is difficult to infer much from allocation methods used without quantitative information on the extent of their use and the assets affected. Basic information on ranges of useful lives and allocation methods contributes little to our analysis as evidenced in the following disclosure from Dow Chemical, which is typical:

ANALYSIS EXCERPT

Property at December 31	Estimated Useful Lives
Land	—
Land and waterway improvements	15–25 years
Buildings	5–55 years
Machinery and equipment	3–20 years
Utility and supply lines	5–20 years
Other property	3–30 years

There is usually no disclosure on the relation between depreciation rates and the size of the asset pool, nor between the rate used and the allocation method. While use of the straight-line method enables us to approximate future depreciation, accelerated methods make this approximation less reliable unless we can obtain additional information often not disclosed.

Another challenge for our analysis arises from differences in allocation methods used for financial reporting and for tax purposes. Three common possibilities are:

1. Use of straight-line for both financial reporting and tax purposes.
2. Use of straight-line for financial reporting and an accelerated method for tax. The favorable tax effect resulting from higher tax depreciation is offset in financial reports with interperiod tax allocation discussed in Chapter 6–the favorable tax effect derives from deferring tax payments, yielding cost-free use of funds.
3. Use of an accelerated method for both financial reporting and tax. This yields higher depreciation in early years, which can be extended over many years with an expanding company.

Disclosures about the impact of these differing possibilities are not always adequate. Adequate disclosures include information on depreciation charges under the alternative allocations. If a company discloses deferred taxes arising from accelerated depreciation for tax, our analysis can approximate the added depreciation due to acceleration by dividing the deferred tax amount by the current tax rate. We discuss how to use these expanded disclosures for the composition of deferred taxes in Chapter 6.

In spite of these limitations, our analysis should not ignore depreciation information, nor should it focus on income before depreciation. Note, depreciation expense derives from cash spent *in the past*–it does not require any current cash outlay. For this reason, a few analysts refer to income before depreciation as *cash flow*. This is an unfortunate oversimplification because it omits many factors constituting cash flow. It is, at best, a poor estimate because it includes only selected inflows without considering a company's commitment to outflows like plant replacement, investments, or dividends. Another misconception from this cash flow simplification is that depreciation is but a "bookkeeping expense" and is different from expenses like labor or material and, thus, can be dismissed or accorded less importance than other expenses. Our analysis must not make this mistake. One reason for this misconception is the absence of any current cash outflow. Purchasing a machine with a five-year useful life is, in effect, a prepayment for five years of services. For example, take a machine and assume a worker operates it for eight hours a day. If we contract with this worker for services over a five-year period and pay for them in advance, we would allocate this pay over five years of work. At the end of the first year, one-fifth of the pay is expensed and the remaining four-fifths of pay is an asset for a claim on future services. The similarity between the labor contract and the machine is apparent. In Year 2 of the labor contract, there is no cash outlay, but there is no doubt about the reality of labor costs. Depreciation of machinery is no different.

Analyzing depreciation requires evaluation of its adequacy. For this purpose we use measures such as the ratio of depreciation to total assets or the ratio of depreciation to other size-related factors. In addition, there are several measures relating to plant asset age that are useful in comparing depreciation policies over time and across companies, including the following:

Average total life span = Gross plant and equipment assets/Current year depreciation expense.

Average age = Accumulated depreciation/Current year depreciation expense.

Average remaining life = Net plant and equipment assets/Current year depreciation expense.

These measures provide reasonable estimates for companies using straight-line depreciation but are less useful for companies using accelerated methods. Another measure often useful in our analysis is:

$$\textit{Average total life span} = \textit{Average age} + \textit{Average remaining life}$$

Each of these measures can help us assess a company's depreciation policies and decisions over time. Average age of plant and equipment is useful in evaluating several factors including profit margins and future financing requirements. For example, capital-intensive companies with aged facilities often have profit margins not reflecting the higher costs of replacing aging assets. Similarly, the capital structures of these companies often do not reflect the financing necessary for asset replacement. Finally, when these analytical measures are used as bases of comparison across companies, care must be exercised because depreciation expense varies with the allocation method and assumptions of useful life and salvage value.

Analyzing Impairments

Three analysis issues arising with impairment are: (1) evaluating the appropriateness of the amount of the impairment, (2) evaluating the appropriateness of the timing of the impairment, and (3) analyzing the effect of the impairment on income.

Evaluating the appropriateness of the amount of impairment is the most difficult analysis task. Here are some issues that an analyst can consider. First, identify the asset class is being written down or written off. Next, measure the percentage of the asset that is being written off. Then evaluate whether the write-off amount is appropriate for the asset class. For this, footnote information detailing reasons for taking the impairment write-off can help. Also, if the write-off is occurring because of an industrywide downturn or market crash, it is useful to compare the percentages of the write-off with those taken by other companies in the industry.

Evaluating the timing of the impairment write-off is also important. It is important to note whether the company is taking timely write-offs or delaying taking write-offs.

Once again comparison with other companies in the industry can help. Also, one needs to note whether a company in bunching large write-offs in a single period as part of a "big bath" earnings management strategy.

Finally, dealing with the effects of write-offs on income is an important issue that an analyst needs to examine. We discuss this issue in detail in Chapter 6.

········INTANGIBLE ASSETS

Intangible assets are rights, privileges, and benefits of ownership or control. Two common characteristics of intangibles are high uncertainty of future benefits and lack of physical existence. Examples of important types of intangibles are shown in Exhibit 4.4. Intangible assets often (1) are inseparable from a company or its segment, (2) have indefinite benefit periods, and (3) experience large valuation changes based on competitive circumstances. Historical cost is the valuation rule for *purchased* intangibles. Still, there is an important difference between accounting for tangible and intangible assets. That is, if a company uses materials and labor in constructing a tangible asset, it capitalizes these costs and depreciates them over the benefit period. In contrast, if a company spends monies advertising a product or training a sales force—creating *internally generated* intangibles—it cannot usually capitalize these costs even when benefits for future periods are likely. Only purchased intangibles are recorded on the balance sheet. This accounting treatment is due to conservatism—presumably from increased uncertainty of realizing the benefits of intangibles such as advertising and training vis-à-vis the benefits of tangible assets such as buildings and equipment.

Exhibit 4.4	***Selected Categories of Intangible Assets***

- Goodwill
- Patents, copyrights, tradenames, and trademarks
- Leases, leaseholds, and leasehold improvements
- Exploration rights and natural resource development costs
- Special formulas, processes, technologies, and designs
- Licenses, franchises, memberships, and customer lists

Accounting for Intangibles
Identifiable Intangibles

Identifiable intangibles are intangible assets that are separately identified and linked with specific rights or privileges having limited benefit periods. Candidates are patents, trademarks, copyrights, and franchises. Companies record them at cost and amortize them over their benefit periods. The writing off to expense of the entire cost of identifiable intangibles at acquisition is prohibited.

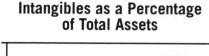

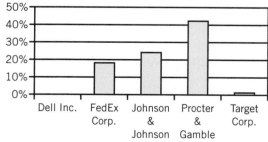

Intangibles as a Percentage of Total Assets

Unidentifiable Intangibles

Unidentifiable intangibles are assets that are either developed internally or purchased but are not identifiable and often possess indefinite benefit periods. An example is goodwill. When one company acquires another company or segment, it needs to allocate the amount paid to all identifiable assets (including identifiable intangible assets) and liabilities according to their fair market values. Any excess remaining after this allocation is allocated to an unidentifiable intangible asset called goodwill. Goodwill can be a sizable asset, but it is recorded only upon purchase of another entity or segment (internally developed goodwill is not recorded on the balance sheet). Its makeup varies considerably—it can refer to an ability to attract and retain customers or to qualities inherent in business activities such as organization, efficiency, and effectiveness. Goodwill implies earning power. Stated differently, goodwill translates into future excess earnings, where this excess is the amount above normal earnings. Excess earnings are similar to *residual income (abnormal earnings)* described in Chapter 1.

Amortization of Intangibles

When costs are capitalized for identifiable tangible and intangible assets, they must be subsequently amortized over the benefit periods for these assets. The length of a benefit period depends on the type of intangible, demand conditions, competitive circumstances, and any other legal, contractual, regulatory, or economic limitations. For example, patents are exclusive rights conveyed by governments to inventors for a specific period. Similarly, copyrights and trademarks convey exclusive rights for specific periods. Leaseholds and leasehold improvements are benefits of occupancy that are contractually set by the lease. Also, if an intangible materially declines in value (applying the recoverability test), it is written down. As discussed in Chapter 5, under current accounting standards goodwill is not amortized but is tested annually for impairment.

Analyzing Intangibles

Analysts often treat intangibles with suspicion when analyzing financial statements. Many analysts associate intangibles with riskiness. We encourage caution and understanding when evaluating intangibles. Intangibles often are one of the more valuable assets a company owns, and they can be seriously misvalued.

Analysis of goodwill reveals some interesting cases. Since goodwill is recorded only when acquired, most goodwill likely exists off the balance sheet. Yet, we know that goodwill is eventually reflected in superearnings. If superearnings are not evident, then goodwill, whether purchased or not, is of little or no value. To illustrate this point, consider the write-off of goodwill reported by Viacom.

ANALYSIS EXCERPT

As a result of the impairment test, the Company recorded an impairment charge of $18.0 billion in the fourth quarter recorded in the Company's Consolidated Statement of Operations for the year ended December 31, 2004. The $18.0 billion reflects charges to reduce the carrying value of goodwill at the Radio segment of $10.9 billion and the Outdoor segment of $7.1 billion as well as a reduction of the carrying value of intangibles of $27.8 million related to the FCC licenses at the Radio segment.

Our analysis of intangibles other than goodwill also must be alert to management's latitude in amortization. Since less amortization increases reported earnings, management might amortize intangibles over periods exceeding their benefit periods. We are probably confident in assuming any bias is in the direction of a lower rate of amortization. We can adjust these rates if armed with reliable information on intangibles' benefit periods.

In analyzing intangibles, we must be prepared to form our own estimates regarding their valuation. We must also remember that goodwill does not require amortization and that auditors have a difficult time with intangibles, especially goodwill. They particularly find it difficult to assess the continuing value of unamortized intangibles.

Our analysis must be alert to the composition, valuation, and disposition of goodwill. Goodwill is written off when the superior earning power justifying its existence disappears. Disposition, or write-off, of goodwill is frequently timed by management for a period when it has the least impact on the market.

ANALYSIS VIEWPOINT   **. . . YOU ARE THE ENVIRONMENTALIST**

You are testifying at congressional hearings demanding substantially tougher pollution standards for paper mills. The industry's spokesperson insists tougher standards cannot be afforded and continually points to an asset to liability ratio of slightly above 1.0 as indicative of financial vulnerability. You counter by arguing the existence of undervalued and unrecorded intangible assets for this industry. The spokesperson insists any intangibles are worthless apart from the company, that financial statements are fairly presented and certified by an independent auditor, and that intangible assets are irrelevant to these hearings. How do you counter the spokesperson's arguments?

Unrecorded Intangibles and Contingencies

Our discussion of assets is not complete without tackling intangible and contingent assets not recorded in a balance sheet. One important asset in this category is internally generated goodwill. In practice, expenditures toward creating goodwill are expensed when incurred. To the extent goodwill is created and is salable or generates superior earning power, a company's current income is understated due to expenses related to goodwill development. Similarly, its assets would fail to reflect this future earning power. Our analysis must recognize these cases and adjust assets and income accordingly.

Another important category of unrecorded assets relates to service or idea elements. Examples are television programs carried at amortized cost (or nothing) but continuing to yield millions of dollars in licensing fees (such as *Seinfeld, Star Trek*) and current drugs taking years to develop but whose costs were written off many years earlier. Other examples are developed brands (trade names) like Coca-Cola, McDonald's, Nike, and Kleenex. Exhibit 4.5 shows value estimates for some major brands.

Exhibit 4.5

■ ■ ■ ■ ■ ■ ■

Valuation of Brands (*Source:* Interbrand Website)

Rank 2004	Brand Value ($ millions)
1 Coca-Cola	$67,394
2 Microsoft	61,372
3 IBM	53,791
4 GE	44,111
5 Intel	33,499
6 Disney	27,113
7 McDonald's	25,001
8 Nokia	24,041
9 Toyota	22,673
10 Marlboro	22,128

GUIDANCE ANSWERS TO ANALYSIS VIEWPOINTS

AUDITOR

Yes, as an auditor you are concerned about changes in estimates, especially when those changes exactly coincide with earlier predictions from management. An auditor must be certain the estimate of uncollectible accounts is reasonable in light of current industry, economic, and customer conditions.

BUYING AGENT

Yes, a buying agent should not necessarily compensate suppliers for potentially poor purchasing decisions. The supplier's 20% reported gross margin "buries" the $2 million market adjustment in its cost of goods sold. The buyer should remove the market adjustment from cost of goods sold and place it among operating expenses in the income statement. Accordingly, the supplier's gross margin would be $2 million greater and, hence, the buyer has a legitimately stronger negotiating position for a lower price.

ENVIRONMENTALIST

This is a challenging case. On one hand, the spokesperson's claim that intangibles are irrelevant is in error—intangible assets confer substantial economic benefits to companies and often make up a major part of assets. Moreover, the spokesperson's reliance on auditors to certify the fairness of financial statements according to accepted accounting principles is misguided. Because accounting principles do not permit capitalization of internally generated intangibles, and do not require adjustment of intangibles to market values, and do not value many intangibles (human resources, customer/buyer relationships), an auditor's certification is insufficient evidence on the worth of intangibles. On the other hand, the spokesperson is correct in questioning the value of intangibles apart from the company. Absent the sale of a company or a segment, the cash inflow from intangibles is indirect—from above-normal earnings levels. Also, most lending institutions do not accept intangibles as collateral in making credit decisions. In sum, resolution of these hearings must recognize the existence of intangibles, the sometimes high degree of uncertainty regarding value and duration of intangibles, the limited worth of intangibles absent liquidation of all or part of a company, and finally the need for a "political" decision reflecting the needs of society.

QUESTIONS

4–1. Companies typically report compensating balances that are required under a loan agreement as unrestricted cash classified within current assets.
   a. For purposes of financial statement analysis, is this a useful classification? Explain.
   b. Describe how you would evaluate compensating balances.

4–2. a. Explain the concept of a company's operating cycle and its meaning.
   b. Discuss the significance of the operating cycle to classification of current versus noncurrent items in a balance sheet. Cite examples.
   c. Is the operating cycle concept useful in measuring the current debt-paying ability of a company and the liquidity of its working capital components?
   d. Describe the impact of the operating cycle concept for classification of current assets in the following industries: (1) tobacco, (2) liquor, and (3) retailing.

4–3. a. Identify the main concerns in analysis of accounts receivable.
   b. Describe information, other than that usually available in financial statements, that we should collect to assess the risk of noncollectibility of receivables.

4–4. a. What is meant by the factoring or securitization of receivables?
   b. What does selling receivables with recourse mean? What does it mean to sell them without recourse?
   c. How does selling receivables (particularly with recourse) potentially distort the balance sheet?

4–5. a. Discuss the consequences for each of the acceptable inventory methods in recording costs of inventories and in determination of income.
   b. Comment on the variation in practice regarding the inclusion of costs in inventories. Give examples of at least two sources of such cost variations.

4–6. a. Describe the importance of the level of activity on the unit cost of goods produced by a manufacturer.
   b. Allocation of overhead costs requires certain assumptions. Explain and illustrate cost allocations and their links to activity levels with an example.

4–7. Explain the major objective(s) of LIFO inventory accounting. Discuss the consequences of using LIFO in both measurement of income and the valuation of inventories for the analysis of financial statements.

4–8. Discuss current disclosures for inventory valuation methods and describe how these disclosures are useful in our analysis. Identify additional types of inventory disclosures that would be useful for analysis purposes.

4–9. Companies typically apply the lower-of-cost-or-market (LCM) method for inventory valuation.
    a. Define *cost* as it applies to inventory valuation.
    b. Define *market* as it applies to inventory valuation.
    c. Discuss the rationale behind the LCM rule.
    d. Identify arguments against the use of LCM.

4–10. Compare and contrast the effects of LIFO and FIFO inventory costing methods on earnings in an inflationary period.

4–11. Manufacturers report inventory in the form of raw materials, work-in-process, and finished goods. For each category, discuss how an increase might be viewed as a positive or a negative indicator of future performance depending on the circumstances that led to the inventory build up.

4–12. Comment on the following: Depreciation accounting is imperfect for analysis purposes.

4–13. Analysts cannot unequivocally accept the depreciation amount. One must try to estimate the age and efficiency of plant assets. It is also useful to compare depreciation, current and accumulated, with gross plant assets, and to make comparisons with similar companies. While an analyst cannot adjust earnings for depreciation with precision, an analyst doesn't require precision. Comment on these statements.

4–14. Identify analytical tools useful in evaluating deprecation expense. Explain why they are useful.

4–15. Analysts must be alert to what aspects of goodwill in their analysis of financial statements?

4–16. Explain when an expenditure should be capitalized versus when it should be expensed.

4–17. Distinguish between a "hard asset" and a "soft asset." Cite several examples.

4–18. The net income of companies that explore for natural resources can sometimes bear little relation to the asset amounts reported on the balance sheet for natural resources.
    a. Explain how the lack of a relation between income and natural resource assets can occur.
    b. Describe circumstances when a more economically sensible relation is likely to exist.

4–19. From the view of a user of financial statements, describe objections to using historical cost as the basis for valuing tangible assets.

4–20. a. Identify the basic accounting procedures governing valuation of intangible assets.
    b. Distinguish between accounting for internally developed and purchased goodwill (and intangibles).
    c. Discuss the importance of distinguishing between identifiable intangibles and unidentifiable intangibles.
    d. Explain the principles underlying amortization of intangible assets.

4–21. Describe analysis implications for goodwill in light of current accounting procedures.

4–22. Identify five types of deferred charges and describe the rationale of deferral for each.

4–23. a. Describe at least two assets not recorded on the balance sheet.
    b. Explain how an analyst evaluates unrecorded assets.

EXERCISES

EXERCISE 4–1

Analyzing Allowances for Uncollectible Receivables

On December 31, Year 1, Carme Company reports its accounts receivable from credit sales to customers. Carme Company uses the allowance method, based on credit sales, to estimate bad debts. Based on past experience, Carme fails to collect about 1% of its credit sales. Carme expects this pattern to continue.

Required:

a. Discuss the rationale for using an allowance method based on credit sales to estimate bad debts. Contrast this method with an allowance method based on the accounts receivable balance.

b. How should Carme report its allowance for bad debts account on its balance sheet at December 31, Year 1? Describe the alternatives, if any, for presentation of bad debt expense in Carme's Year 1 income statement.

c. Explain the analysis objectives when evaluating the reasonableness of Carme's allowance for bad debts.

(AICPA Adapted)

K2 Sports, a wholesaler that has been in business for two years, purchases its inventories from various suppliers. During these two years, each purchase has been at a lower price than the previous purchase. K2 uses the lower-of-(FIFO)-cost-or-market method to value its inventories. The original cost of the inventories exceeds its replacement cost, but it is below the net realizable value (also, the net realizable value less a normal profit margin is lower than replacement cost for the inventories).

EXERCISE 4–2
Assessing Inventory Cost and Market Values

Required:

a. What criteria should be used in determining costs to include in inventory?

b. Why is the lower-of-cost-or-market rule used in valuing inventory?

c. At what amount should K2 report its inventories on the balance sheet? Explain the application of the lower-of-cost-or-market rule in this situation.

d. What would be the effect on ending inventories and net income for the second year had K2 used the lower-of-(average) cost-or-market inventory method instead of the lower-of-(FIFO)-cost-or-market inventory method? Explain.

(AICPA Adapted)

Cost for inventory purposes should be determined by the inventory cost flow method best reflecting periodic income.

EXERCISE 4–3
Explaining Inventory Measurement Methods

Required:

a. Describe the inventory cost flow assumptions of (1) average-cost, (2) FIFO, and (3) LIFO.

b. Discuss management's usual reasons for using LIFO in an inflationary economy.

c. When there is evidence the value of inventory, through its disposal in the ordinary course of business, is less than cost, what is the accounting treatment? What concept justifies this treatment?

(AICPA Adapted)

Inventory and cost of goods sold figures prepared under the LIFO cost flow assumption versus the FIFO cost flow assumption can differ dramatically.

EXERCISE 4–4
Usefulness of LIFO and FIFO Inventory Disclosures

Required:

a. Would an analyst consider ending inventory asset value more useful if computed using LIFO or FIFO? Explain.

b. Would an analyst consider cost of goods sold more useful if computed using LIFO or FIFO? Explain.

c. Assume a company uses the LIFO cost flow assumption. Identify any FIFO-computed values that are useful for analysis purposes, and explain how they are determined using financial statement information.

Refer to the financial statements of **Campbell Soup Company** in Appendix A.

Campbell Soup Company

EXERCISE 4–5
Restating Inventory from LIFO to FIFO

Required:

a. Compute Year 10 cost of goods sold and gross profit under the FIFO method. (*Note:* At the end of Year 9, LIFO inventory is $816.0 million, and the excess of FIFO inventory over LIFO inventory is $88 million.)

b. Explain the potential usefulness of the LIFO to FIFO restatement in *a*.

c. Compute ending inventory under the FIFO method for both Years 10 and 11.

d. Explain why the FIFO inventory computation in *c* might be useful for analysis.

CHECK
(*c*) Year 11 FIFO Inventory, $796.3 mil.

EXERCISE 4–6
LIFO and FIFO
Financial Effects

During a period of rising inventory costs and stable output prices, describe how net income and total assets would differ depending upon whether LIFO or FIFO is applied. Explain how your answer would change if the company is experiencing declining inventory costs and stable output prices.

(CFA Adapted)

EXERCISE 4–7
Identifying Unrecorded
Assets

A balance sheet, which is intended to present fairly the financial position of a company, frequently is criticized for not reflecting all assets under the control of a company.

Required:

Cite five examples of assets that are not presently included on the balance sheet. Discuss the implications of unrecorded assets for financial statement analysis.

(CFA Adapted)

EXERCISE 4–8
Expensing versus
Capitalizing Costs

An analyst must be familiar with the determination of income. Income reported for a business entity depends on proper recognition of revenues and expenses. In certain cases, costs are recognized as expenses at the time of product sale; in other situations, guidelines are applied in capitalizing costs and recognizing them as expenses in future periods.

Required:

a. Under what circumstances is it appropriate to capitalize a cost as an asset instead of expensing it? Explain.

b. Certain expenses are assigned to specific accounting periods on the basis of systematic and rational allocation of asset cost. Explain the rationale for recognizing expenses on such a basis.

(AICPA Adapted)

EXERCISE 4–9
Analytical Measures of
Plant Assets

Refer to the financial statements of **Colgate** in Appendix A.   **Colgate**

Required:

a. Compute the following analytical measures applied to Colgate for 2006.
(1) Average total life span of plant and equipment.
(2) Average age of plant and equipment.
(3) Average remaining life of plant and equipment.

b. Discuss the importance of these ratios for analysis of Colgate.

EXERCISE 4–10
Analytical Measures of
Plant Assets

Refer to the financial statements of **Camp-bell Soup Company** in Appendix A.   **Campbell Soup Company**

Required:

CHECK
(a) (3) Year 11, 7.23 years

a. Compute the following analytical measures applied to Campbell Soup for both Years 10 and 11:
(1) Average total life span of plant and equipment.
(2) Average age of plant and equipment.
(3) Average remaining life of plant and equipment.

b. Discuss the importance of these ratios for analysis of Campbell Soup.

EXERCISE 4–11
Identifying Assets

Which of the following items are classified as assets on a typical balance sheet?

a. Depreciation.

b. CEO salary.

c. Cash.

d. Deferred income taxes.

e. Installment receivable (collectible in 3 years).

f. Capital withdrawal (dividend).

g. Inventories.

h. Prepaid expenses.

i. Deferred charges.

j. Work-in-process inventory.

k. Depreciation expense.

l. Bad debts expense.

m. Loan to officers.

n. Loan from officers.

o. Fully trained sales force.

p. Common stock of a subsidiary.

q. Trade name purchased.

r. Internally developed goodwill.

s. Franchise agreements obtained at no cost.

t. Internally developed e-commerce system.

Refer to the financial statements of **Campbell Soup Company** in Appendix A.

Campbell Soup

EXERCISE 4–12

Restating and Analyzing Inventory from LIFO to FIFO

Required:

Campbell Soup mainly uses the LIFO cost assumption in determining its cost of goods sold and inventory amounts. Compute both ending inventory and gross profit of Campbell Soup for Year 11 assuming the company uses FIFO inventory accounting.

PROBLEMS

Assume you are analyzing the financial statements of ABEX Chemicals. Your analysis raises concerns with certain accounting procedures that potentially distort its operating results.

Required:

a. Data for ABEX Corp. is reported in Case 10–5. Using the data in Exhibit I of that case, describe how ABEX's use of the FIFO method in accounting for its petrochemical inventories affects its division's operating margin for each of the following periods:
   (1) Years 5 through 7.
   (2) Years 7 through 9.

b. ABEX is considering adopting the LIFO method of accounting for its petrochemical inventories in either Year 10 or Year 11. Recommend an adoption date for LIFO and justify your choice.

(CFA Adapted)

PROBLEM 4–1

Interpreting and Restating Inventory from FIFO to LIFO

CHECK
(a) (2) FIFO increases margins

BigBook.Com uses LIFO inventory accounting. Notes to BigBook.Com's Year 9 financial statements disclose the following (it has a marginal tax rate of 35%):

PROBLEM 4–2

Restating Inventory from LIFO to FIFO

Inventories	Year 8	Year 9
Raw materials	$392,675	$369,725
Finished products	401,342	377,104
	794,017	746,829
Less LIFO reserve	(46,000)	(50,000)
	$748,017	$696,829

Required:

a. Determine the amount by which Year 9 retained earnings of BigBook.Com changes if FIFO is used.

b. Determine the amount by which Year 9 net income of BigBook.Com changes if FIFO is used for both Years 8 and 9.

c. Discuss the usefulness of LIFO to FIFO restatements in an analysis of BigBook.Com.

(AICPA Adapted)

CHECK
(b) $2,600

PROBLEM 4–3
Analysis of Inventory and Related Adjustments

Excerpts from the annual report of **Lands' End** follow ($ in thousands):   **Lands' End**

	Year 9	Year 8
Inventory................	$219,686	$241,154
Cost of sales...........	754,661	675,138
Net income	31,185	64,150
Tax rate..................	37%	37%

Note 1: If the first-in, first-out (FIFO) method of accounting for inventory had been used, inventory would have been approximately $26.9 million and $25.1 million higher than reported at Year 9 and Year 8, respectively.

Required:

a. What would ending inventory have been at Year 9 and Year 8 had FIFO been used?
b. What would net income for the year ended Year 9 have been had FIFO been used?
c. Discuss the usefulness of LIFO to FIFO restatements for analysis purposes.

PROBLEM 4–4
T-Account Analysis of Plant Assets

Refer to the financial statements of **Campbell Soup** in Appendix A.   **Campbell Soup**

Required:

a. By means of T-account analysis, explain the changes in Campbell's Property, Plant, and Equipment account for Year 11. Provide as much detail as the disclosures enable you to provide. (*Hint:* Utilize information disclosed on the Form 10-K schedule attached at the end of its annual report in Appendix A.)
b. Explain the usefulness of this type of analysis.

PROBLEM 4–5
Capitalizing versus Expensing of Costs

Trimax Solutions develops software to support e-commerce. Trimax incurs substantial computer software development costs as well as substantial research and development (R&D) costs related to other aspects of its product line. Under GAAP, if certain conditions are met, Trimax capitalizes software development costs but expenses the other R&D costs. The following information is taken from Trimax's annual reports ($ in thousands):

	1999	2000	2001	2002	2003	2004	2005	2006
R&D costs..	$ 400	$ 491	$ 216	$ 212	$ 355	$ 419	$ 401	$ 455
Net income..	312	367	388	206	55	81	167	179
Total assets (at year-end)......................	3,368	3,455	3,901	4,012	4,045	4,077	4,335	4,650
Equity (at year-end)..............................	2,212	2,460	2,612	2,809	2,889	2,915	3,146	3,312
Capitalized software costs								
Unamortized balance (at year-end)....	20	31	27	22	31	42	43	36
Amortization expense	4	7	9	12	13	15	15	14

Required:

a. Compute the total expenditures for software development costs for each year.
b. R&D costs are expensed as incurred. Compare and contrast computer software development costs with the R&D costs and discuss the rationale for expensing R&D costs but capitalizing some software development costs.
c. Based on the information provided, when do successful research efforts appear to produce income for Trimax?
d. Discuss how income and equity are affected if Trimax invests more in software development versus R&D projects (focus your response on the accounting, and not economic, implications).

e. Compute net income, return on assets, and return on equity for year 2006 while separately assuming (1) Software development costs are expensed as incurred and (2) R&D costs are capitalized and amortized using straight line over the following four years.
f. Discuss how the two accounting alternatives in *e* would affect cash flow from operations for Trimax.

Sports Biz, a profitable company, built and equipped a $2,000,000 plant brought into operation early in Year 1. Earnings of the company (before depreciation on the new plant and before income taxes) is projected at: $1,500,000 in Year 1; $2,000,000 in Year 2; $2,500,000 in Year 3; $3,000,000 in Year 4; and $3,500,000 in Year 5. The company can use straight-line, double-declining-balance, or sum-of-the-years'-digits depreciation for the new plant. Assume the plant's useful life is 10 years (with no salvage value) and an income tax rate of 50%.

PROBLEM 4–6
Alternative Depreciation Methods

Required:

Compute the separate effect that *each* of these three methods of depreciation would have on:

a. Depreciation

b. Income taxes

c. Net income

d. Cash flow (assumed equal to net income before depreciation)

(CFA Adapted)

CHECK
Year 1 net income ($000s), SL: $650, DDB: $550, SYD: $568.2

Assume that a machine costing $300,000 and having a useful life of five years (with no salvage value) generates a yearly income before depreciation and taxes of $100,000.

PROBLEM 4–7
Analyzing Depreciation for Rates of Return

Required:

Compute the annual rate of return on this machine (using the beginning-of-year book value as the base) for each of the following depreciation methods (assume a 25% tax rate):

a. Straight-line

b. Sum-of-the-years' digits

CHECK
Year 2 return, SL: 12.5%, SYD: 7.5%

Among the crucial events in accounting for property, plant, and equipment are acquisition and disposition.

PROBLEM 4–8
Property, Plant, and Equipment Accounting and Analysis

Required:

a. What expenditures should be capitalized when a company acquires equipment for cash?

b. Assume the market value of equipment acquired is not determinable by reference to a similar purchase for cash. Describe how the acquiring company should determine the capitalizable cost of equipment for each of the following separate cases when it is acquired in exchange for:
   (1) Bonds having an established market price.
   (2) Common stock not having an established market price.
   (3) Dissimilar equipment having a determinable market value.

c. Describe the factors that determine whether expenditures toward property, plant, and equipment already in use should be capitalized.

d. Describe how to account for the gain or loss on sale of property, plant, and equipment for cash.

e. Discuss the important considerations in analyzing property, plant, and equipment.

Mirage Resorts, Inc., recently completed construction of Bellagio Hotel and Casino in Las Vegas. Total cost of this project was approximately $1.6 billion. The strategy of the investors is to build a gambling environment for "high rollers." As a result, they paid a premium for property in the "high rent" district of the Las Vegas Strip and built a facility inspired by the drama and elegance of fine art. The investors are confident that if the facility attracts high volume and high stakes gaming, the net revenues will justify the $1.6 billion investment several times over. If the facility fails to attract high rollers, this investment will be a financial catastrophe. Mirage Resorts depreciates its fixed assets using the straight-line method over the estimated useful lives of the assets. Assume construction of Bellagio is completed and the facility is opened for business on January 1, Year 1. Also assume annual net income before depreciation and taxes from Bellagio is $50 million, $70 million, and $75 million for Year 1, Year 2, and Year 3, and that the tax rate is 25%.

PROBLEM 4–9
Capitalization, Depreciation, and Return on Investment

Required:

Compute the return on assets for the Bellagio segment for Year 1, Year 2, and Year 3, assuming management estimates the useful life of Bellagio to be:

a. 25 years.   b. 15 years.   c. 10 years.   d. 1 year.

PROBLEM 4–10
Analyzing Self-Constructed Assets

Jay Manufacturing, Inc., began operations five years ago producing probos, a new medical instrument it hoped to sell to doctors and hospitals. The demand for probos far exceeded initial expectations, and the company was unable to produce enough probos to meet demand. The company was manufacturing this product using self-constructed equipment at the start of operations. To meet demand, it needed more efficient equipment. The company decided to design and self-construct this new, more efficient equipment. A section of the plant was devoted to development of the new equipment and a special staff was hired. Within six months, a machine was developed at a cost of $170,000 that successfully increased production and reduced labor costs substantially. Sparked by the success of this new machine, the company built three more machines of the same type at a cost of $80,000 each.

Required:

a. In addition to satisfying a need that outsiders could not meet within the desired time, why might a company self-construct fixed assets for its own use?

b. Generally, what costs should a company capitalize for a self-constructed fixed asset?

c. Discuss the propriety of including in the capitalized cost of self-constructed assets:
   (1) The increase in overhead caused by the self-construction of fixed assets.
   (2) A proportionate share of overhead on the same basis as that applied to goods manufactured for sale.

d. Discuss the accounting treatment for the $90,000 amount ($170,000 − $80,000) by which the cost of the first machine exceeded the cost of subsequent machines.

(AICPA Adapted)

PROBLEM 4–11
Analyzing Intangible Assets (Patents)

On June 30, Year 1, your client, the Vandiver Corp., is granted two patents covering plastic cartons that it has been producing and marketing profitably for the past three years. One patent covers the manufacturing process, and the other covers related products. Vandiver executives tell you that these patents represent the most significant breakthrough in the industry in three decades. The products have been marketed under the registered trademarks Safetainer, Duratainer, and Sealrite. Your client has already granted licenses under the patents to other manufacturers in the U.S. and abroad and is receiving substantial royalties. On July 1, Year 1, Vandiver commenced patent infringement actions against several companies whose names you recognize as those of substantial and prominent competitors. Vandiver's management is optimistic that these suits will result in a permanent injunction against the manufacture and sale of the infringing products and collection of damages for loss of profits caused by the alleged infringement. The financial vice president has suggested that the patents be recorded at the discounted value of expected net royalty receipts.

Required:

a. Explain what an intangible asset is.

b. (1) Explain what is meant by "discounted value of expected net royalty receipts."
   (2) How would such a value be calculated for net royalty receipts?

c. What basis of valuation for Vandiver's patents is generally accepted in accounting? Give supporting reasons for this basis.

d. (1) Assuming no problems of implementation and ignoring generally accepted accounting principles, what is the preferable basis of evaluation for patents? Explain.
   (2) Explain what would be the preferable conceptual basis of amortization.

e. What recognition or disclosure, if any, is Vandiver likely to make for the infringement litigation in its financial statements for the year ending September 30, Year 1? Explain.

(AICPA Adapted)

CASES

CASE 4-1
Inventory Valuation in the Film Industry

Financial statements of **Columbia Pictures** include the following note:

Columbia Pictures

> **Inventories.** The costs of feature films and television programs, including production advances to independent producers, interest on production loans, and distribution advances to film licensors, are amortized on bases designed to write off costs in proportion to the expected flow of income.
>
> The cost of general release feature productions is divided between theatrical ion and television ion, based on the proportion of net revenues expected to be derived from each source. The portion of the cost of feature productions allocated to theatrical ion is amortized generally by the application of tables which write off approximately 62% in 26 weeks, 85% in 52 weeks, and 100% in 104 weeks after release. Costs of two theatrical productions first released on a reserved-seat basis are amortized in the proportion that rentals earned bear to the estimated final theatrical and television rentals. Because of the depressed market for the licensing of feature films to television and poor acceptance by the public of a number of theatrical films released late in the year, the company made a special provision for additional amortization of recent releases and those not yet licensed for television to reduce such films to their currently estimated net realizable values.

Required:

a. Identify the main determinants for valuation of feature films, television programs, and general release feature productions by Columbia Pictures.

b. Are the bases of valuation reasonable? Explain.

c. Indicate additional information on inventory valuation that an unsecured lender to Columbia Pictures would wish to obtain and any analyses the lender would wish to conduct.

CASE 4-2
Financial Statement Consequences of LIFO and FIFO

Falcon.Com purchases its merchandise at current market costs and resells the product at a price 20 cents higher. Its inventory costs are constant throughout the current year. Data on the number of units in inventory at the beginning of the year, unit purchases, and unit sales are shown here:

Number of units in inventory—beginning of year (@ $1 per unit cost)	1,000 units
Number of units purchased during year @ $1.50 per unit cost	1,000 units
Number of units sold during year @ $1.70 per unit selling price	1,000 units

The beginning-of-year balance sheet for Falcon.Com reports the following:

Inventory (1,000 units @ $1).......	$1,000
Total equity.................................	$1,000

Required:

a. Compute the after-tax profit of Falcon.Com separately for both the (1) FIFO and (2) LIFO methods of inventory valuation assuming the company has no expenses other than cost of goods sold and its income tax rate is 50%. Taxes are accrued currently and paid the following year.

b. If all sales and purchases are for cash, construct the balance sheet at the end of this year separately for both the (1) FIFO and (2) LIFO methods of inventory valuation.

c. Describe the significance of each of these methods of inventory valuation for income determination and financial position in a period of increasing costs.

d. What problem does the LIFO method pose in constructing and analyzing interim financial statements?

(CFA Adapted)

CHECK
(*b*) Total assets, FIFO: $1,700, LIFO: $1,200

CASE 4–3

Financial Statement Effects of Alternative Inventory Methods

Droog Co. is a retailer dealing in a single product. Beginning inventory at January 1 of this year is zero, operating expenses for this same year are $5,000, and there are 2,000 common shares outstanding. The following purchases are made this year:

	Units	Per Unit	Cost
January	100	$10	$ 1,000
March	300	11	3,300
June	600	12	7,200
October	300	14	4,200
December	500	15	7,500
Total	1,800		$23,200

Ending inventory at December 31 is 800 units. End-of-year assets, excluding inventories, amount to $75,000, of which $50,000 of the $75,000 are current. Current liabilities amount to $25,000, and long-term liabilities equal $10,000.

Required:

CHECK

(*a*) Income, FIFO: $8,500,
LIFO: $5,900,
AC: $7,112

a. Determine net income for this year under each of the following inventory methods. Assume a sales price of $25 per unit and ignore income taxes.
   (1) FIFO
   (2) LIFO
   (3) Average cost

b. Compute the following ratios under each of the inventory methods of FIFO, LIFO, and average cost.
   (1) Current ratio
   (2) Debt-to-equity ratio
   (3) Inventory turnover
   (4) Return on total assets
   (5) Gross margin as a percent of sales
   (6) Net profit as a percent of sales

c. Discuss the effects of inventory accounting methods for financial statement analysis given the results from parts *a* and *b*.

CASE 4–4

Analysis of Investing Activities

Refer to the annual report of **Campbell Soup** in Appendix A.   **Campbell Soup**

a. Compute Campbell Soup's working capital at the end of Year 11.

b. Campbell Soup reports net receivables totaling over $527 million. To whom has it extended credit and how much bad debt reserve is provided against these receivables? What percentage of total receivables is considered uncollectible?

c. What cost flow assumption does Campbell Soup use for inventories? What is its inventory write-down policy?

CHECK

(*d*) Inventory turnover, 5.37

d. The inventory turnover ratio (cost of goods sold/average inventory) is a measure of inventory management efficiency and effectiveness. Compute the inventory turnover ratio for Campbell Soup and comment on ways that it might improve the ratio.

e. How much is the LIFO reserve for Campbell Soup? What are the total tax benefits realized by Campbell Soup as of the end of fiscal Year 11 because it chose the LIFO inventory cost flow assumption (assume a 35% tax rate)?

(*f*) $672.4 mil.

f. What would Campbell Soup's pretax income have been in Year 11 if it had chosen FIFO?

g. What percentage of total assets is Campbell Soup's investment in plant assets? What depreciation method does it use for fixed assets? What percentage of historical cost is the accumulated depreciation amount associated with these assets? What can the percentage depreciated calculation reveal to an analyst about fixed assets?

h. Campbell Soup reports intangible assets totaling about $436 million at the end of Year 11. What major transaction(s) gave rise to this amount?

Toro Manufacturing is organized on January 1, Year 5. During Year 5, financial reports to management use the straight-line method of depreciating plant assets. On November 8, you (as consultant) hold a conference with Toro's officers to discuss the depreciation method for both tax and financial reporting. Toro's president suggests the use of a new method he feels is more suitable than straight line during this period of predicted rapid expansion of production and capacity. He shows an example of his proposed method as applied to a fixed asset with an original cost of $32,000, estimated useful life of five years, and a salvage value of $2,000, as follows:

CASE 4–5
Analyzing Depreciation

End of Year	Years of Life Used	Fraction Rate	Depreciation Expense	Accumulated Depreciation at Year-End	Book Value at Year-End
1	1	$\frac{1}{15}$	$ 2,000	$ 2,000	$30,000
2	2	$\frac{2}{15}$	4,000	6,000	26,000
3	3	$\frac{3}{15}$	6,000	12,000	20,000
4	4	$\frac{4}{15}$	8,000	20,000	12,000
5	5	$\frac{5}{15}$	10,000	30,000	2,000

Toro's president favors this new method because he asserts it:

1. Increases funds recovered in years near the end of the assets' useful lives when maintenance and replacement costs are high.

2. Increases write-offs in later years and thereby reduce taxes.

Required:

a. What are the purpose of and the principle behind accounting for depreciation?

b. Is the president's proposal within the scope of GAAP? Discuss the circumstances, if any, where this method is reasonable and those, if any, where it is not.

c. The president requests your advice on the following additional questions:
  (1) Do depreciation charges recover or create cash? Explain.
  (2) Assuming the IRS accepts the proposed depreciation method, and it is used for both financial reporting and tax purposes, how does it affect availability of cash generated by operations?

5

ANALYZING INVESTING ACTIVITIES: INTERCORPORATE INVESTMENTS

■ ■ ■ ■ ■ ■ ■

A LOOK BACK `<`

Chapters 3 and 4 focused on accounting analysis of financing and investing activities. We explained and analyzed these activities as reflected in financial statements and interpreted them in terms of expectations for company performance.

A LOOK AT THIS CHAPTER `●`

This chapter extends our analysis to intercorporate investments. We analyze both intercorporate investments and business combinations from the perspective of the investor company. We show the importance of interpreting disclosures on intercompany activities for analysis of financial statements. We conclude with a discussion of the accounting for investments in derivative securities.

A LOOK AHEAD `>`

Chapter 6 extends our analysis to operating activities. We analyze the income statement as a means to understand and predict future company performance. We also introduce and explain important concepts and measures of income.

ANALYSIS OBJECTIVES

- Analyze financial reporting for intercorporate investments.

- Analyze financial statement disclosures for investment securities.

- Interpret consolidated financial statements.

- Analyze implications of the purchase (and pooling) method of accounting for business combinations.

- Interpret goodwill arising from business combinations.

- Describe derivative securities and their implications for analysis.

- Analyze the fair value option for financial assets and liabilities.

- Explain consolidation of foreign subsidiaries and foreign currency translation (Appendix 5A).

- Describe investment return analysis (Appendix 5B).

The Goodwill Plunge

NEW YORK–Viacom reported a loss of $17.5 billion in 2004 (28% of its equity) primarily due to its write-off of $18 billion of goodwill relating to its Radio and Outdoor segments that was previously recorded in its balance sheet as an asset. The company describes its rationale for the write-off as follows: "Competition from other advertising media, including Internet advertising and cable and broadcast television has reduced Radio and Outdoor growth rates." In short, forecasted cash flows from these investments were less than had been anticipated when the investments were purchased, thus slashing their value.

These goodwill write-offs follow from an accounting standard passed in 2001 relating to business combinations. Previously, goodwill was amortized over a period of up to 40 years, resulting in an earnings drag that compa-

nies complained had compromised their ability to compete globally. Under the current accounting standard, instead of being amortized, goodwill is tested annually for impairment. It was during such an annual test

> mistakes show up . . . as sporadic write-offs of unprecedented proportions.

that Viacom determined its goodwill had become impaired.

How should we interpret these write-offs? While companies and Wall Street analysts generally stress that goodwill write-offs are one-time, noncash charges that have no impact on underlying operations or cash flow, many accounting experts disagree. These experts argue that write-offs represent an admission by management that the

companies' investments are no longer worth what they were recorded at. "We are going to get confirmation that hundreds of billions of dollars in shareholder capital has been wasted or destroyed," says David Tice, manager of the Prudent Bear fund.

Believing their own growth stories and enjoying high stock valuations that gave them pricey stock to swap for acquisitions, companies engaged in an unprecedented number of acquisitions. Many of the prices paid, in hindsight, look excessive. "The serial acquisitions many companies made are not going to generate the revenues they anticipated. That suggests management made some bad deals," says Lehman Bros. accounting expert Robert Willens. These mistakes show up, not as orderly amortization of goodwill, but as sporadic write-offs of unprecedented proportions.

PREVIEW OF CHAPTER 5

Intercompany investments play an increasing role in business activities. Companies purchase intercompany investments for many reasons, such as diversification, expansion, and competitive opportunities and returns. This chapter considers the analysis and interpretation of these business activities as reflected in financial statements and analyzes financial statement disclosures for investment securities. We consider current reporting requirements from an analysis perspective–both for what they do and do not tell us. We describe how current disclosures are relevant for analysis, and how we might usefully apply analytical adjustments to these disclosures. We direct special attention to the unrecorded assets and liabilities relating to intercompany investments. We describe derivative securities and their implications for analysis.

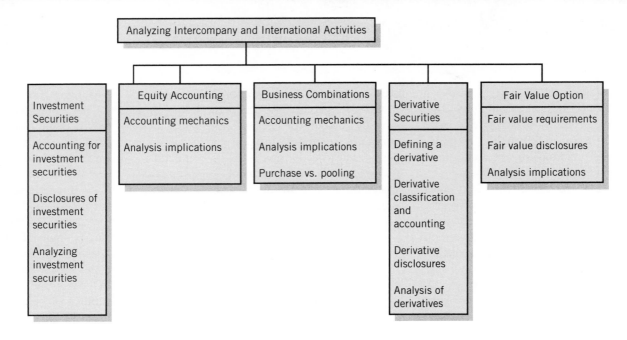

·······INVESTMENT SECURITIES

Companies invest assets in **investment securities** (also called *marketable securities*). Investment securities vary widely in terms of the type of securities that a company invests in and the purpose of such investment. Some investments are temporary repositories of excess cash held as marketable securities. They also can include funds awaiting investment in plant, equipment, and other operating assets, or can serve as funds for payment of liabilities. The purpose of these temporary repositories is to deploy idle cash in a productive manner. Other investments, for example equity participation in an affiliate, are often an integral part of the company's core activities.

Investment securities can be in the form of either debt or equity. **Debt securities** are securities representing a creditor relationship with another entity—examples are corporate bonds, government bonds, notes, and municipal securities. **Equity securities** are securities representing ownership interest in another entity—examples are common stock and nonredeemable preferred stock. Companies classify investment securities among their current and/or noncurrent assets, depending on the investment horizon of the particular security.

For most companies, investment securities constitute a relatively minor share of total assets and, with the exception of investments in affiliates, these investments are in financial, rather than operating, assets. This means these investments usually are *not* an integral part of the operating activities of the company. However, for financial institutions and insurance companies, investment securities constitute important operating assets.

In this section we first explain the classification and accounting for investment securities. We then examine disclosure requirements for investment securities, using pertinent disclosures from Microsoft's annual report. We conclude the section by discussing analysis of investment securities.

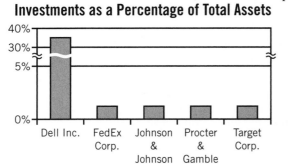

Accounting for Investment Securities

The accounting for investment securities is prescribed under *SFAS 115*. This standard departs from the traditional lower-of-cost-or-market principle by prescribing that investment securities be reported on the balance sheet at cost or fair (market) value, depending on the type of security and the degree of influence or control that the investor company has over the investee company. This means that, unlike other assets, investment securities can be valued at market even when market value exceeds the acquisition cost.

Fair value of an asset is the amount the asset can be exchanged for in a current, normal transaction between willing parties. When an asset is regularly traded, its fair value is *readily determinable* from its published market price. If no published market price exists for an asset, fair value is determined using historical cost. See Chapter 2 for a detailed discussion of fair value.

Accounting for an investment security is determined by its classification. Exhibit 5.1 presents the classification possibilities for investment securities. Investment securities are broadly classified as either debt or equity securities. Debt securities, in turn, are further classified based on the purpose of the investment. Equity securities, on the other hand, are classified on the extent of interest—that is, the extent of investor ownership in and, therefore, influence or control over, the investee. Equity securities reflecting no significant ownership interest in the investee are further classified on the purpose of the investment. Because the accounting for investments in debt and equity securities are different, we explain each separately.

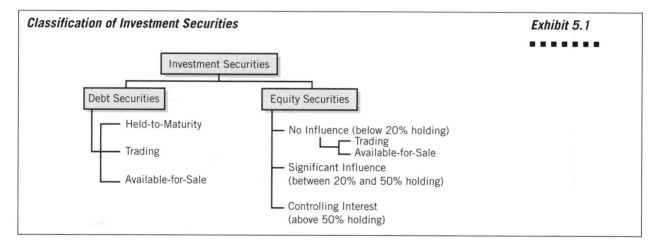

Classification of Investment Securities

Exhibit 5.1

Debt Securities

Debt securities represent creditor relationships with other entities. Examples are government and municipal bonds, company bonds and notes, and convertible debt. Debt securities are classified as trading, held to maturity, or available for sale. Accounting guidelines for debt securities differ depending on the type of security. Exhibit 5.2 describes the criteria for classification and the accounting for each class of debt securities.

Held-to-Maturity Securities. **Held-to-maturity securities** are debt securities that management has both the ability and intent to hold to maturity. They could be either short term (in which case they are classified as current assets) or long term (in which case they

Exhibit 5.2 ■ ■ ■ ■ ■ ■ ■ *Classification and Accounting for Debt Securities*

			ACCOUNTING	
			INCOME STATEMENT	
Category	Description	Balance Sheet	Unrealized Gains/Losses	Other
Held-to-maturity	Securities acquired with both the intent and ability to hold to maturity	Amortized cost	Not recognized in either net income or comprehensive income	Recognize realized gains/losses and interest income in net income
Trading	Securities acquired mainly for short-term or trading gains (usually less than three months)	Fair value	Recognize in net income	Recognize realized gains/losses and interest income in net income
Available-for-sale	Securities neither held for trading nor held-to-maturity	Fair value	Not recognized in net income, but recognized in comprehensive income	Recognize realized gains/losses and interest income in net income

are classified as noncurrent assets). Companies report short-term (long-term) held-to-maturity securities on the balance sheet at cost (amortized cost). No unrealized gains or losses from these securities are recognized in income. Interest income and realized gains and losses, including amortization of any premium or discount on long-term securities, are included in income. The held-to-maturity classification is used only for debt securities.

Trading Securities. **Trading securities** are debt (or noninfluential equity) securities purchased with the intent of actively managing them and selling them for profit in the near future. Trading securities are current assets. Companies report them at aggregate fair value at each balance sheet date. Unrealized gains or losses (changes in fair value of the securities held) and realized gains or losses (gains or losses on sales) are included in net income. Interest income from the trading securities held in the form of debt is recorded as it is earned. (Dividend income from the trading securities held in the form of equity is recorded when earned.) The trading classification is used for both debt and equity securities.

Available-for-Sale Securities. **Available-for-sale securities** are debt (or noninfluential equity) securities not classified as either trading or held-to-maturity securities. These securities are included among current or noncurrent assets, depending on their maturity and/or management's intent regarding their sale. These securities are reported at fair value on the balance sheet. However, changes in fair value are excluded from net income and, instead, are included in comprehensive income (Chapter 6 defines comprehensive income). With available-for-sale debt securities, interest income, including amortization of any premium or discount on long-term securities, is recorded when earned. (With available-for-sale equity securities, dividends are recorded in income when earned.) Realized gains and losses on available-for-sale securities are included in income. The available-for-sale classification is used for both debt and equity securities.

Transfers between Categories. When management's intent or ability to carry out the purpose of investment securities significantly changes, securities usually must be reclassified (transferred to another class). Normally, debt securities classified as held-to-maturity cannot be transferred to another class except under exceptional circumstances such as a merger, acquisition, divestiture, a major deterioration in credit rating, or some other extraordinary event. Also, transfers from available-for-sale to trading are normally not permitted. However, whenever transfers of securities between classes do occur, the securities must be adjusted to their fair value. This fair value requirement ensures that a company transferring securities immediately recognizes (in its income statement) changes in fair value. It also reduces the likelihood a company could conceal changes in fair value by transferring securities to another class that does not recognize fair value changes in income. Exhibit 5.3 summarizes the accounting for transfers between various classes.

Accounting for Transfers between Security Classes			**Exhibit 5.3**
TRANSFER			
From	**To**	**Effect on Asset Value in Balance Sheet**	**Effect on Income Statement**
Held-to-maturity	Available-for-sale	Asset reported at fair value instead of (amortized) cost	Unrealized gain or loss on date of transfer included in comprehensive income
Trading	Available-for-sale	No effect	Unrealized gain or loss on date of transfer included in net income
Available-for-sale	Trading	No effect	Unrealized gain or loss on date of transfer included in net income
Available-for-sale	Held-to-maturity	No effect at transfer; however, asset reported at (amortized) cost instead of fair value at future dates	Unrealized gain or loss on date of transfer included in comprehensive income

Equity Securities

Equity securities represent ownership interests in another entity. Examples are common and preferred stock and rights to acquire or dispose of ownership interests such as warrants, stock rights, and call and put options. Redeemable preferred stock and convertible debt securities are not considered equity securities (they are classified as debt securities). The two main motivations for a company to purchase equity securities are (1) to exert influence over the directors and management of another entity (such as suppliers, customers, subsidiaries) or (2) to receive dividend and stock price appreciation income. Companies report investments in equity securities according to their ability to influence or control the investee's activities. Evidence of this ability is typically based on the percentage of voting securities controlled by the investor company. These percentages are guidelines and can be overruled by other factors. For example, significant influence can be conferred via contact even without a significant ownership percentage. Exhibit 5.4 summarizes the classification and accounting for equity securities.

No Influence—Less than 20% Holding.   When equity securities are nonvoting preferred or when the investor owns less than 20% of an investee's voting stock, the ownership is considered noninfluential. In these cases, investors are assumed to possess minimal influence over the investee's activities. These investments are classified as either trading or available-for-sale securities, based on the intent and ability of management. Accounting for these securities is already described under debt securities that are similarly classified.

Significant Influence—Between 20% and 50% Holding.   Security holdings, even when below 50% of the voting stock, can provide an investor the ability to exercise significant

IPO NO-NO
Raising cash for new companies through initial public offerings is rife with conflicts. Investment banks push their analysts to give IPO clients sky-high ratings. And banks routinely underprice IPOs so they can use shares in a hot new stock to reward friends and woo potential banking clients.

Exhibit 5.4 ■ ■ ■ ■ ■ ■ ■   ***Classification and Accounting for Equity Securities***

| Attribute | NO INFLUENCE | | Significant Influence | Controlling Interest |
	Available-for-Sale	Trading		
Ownership	Less than 20%	Less than 20%	Between 20% and 50%	Above 50%
Purpose	Long- or intermediate-term investment	Short-term investment or trading	Considerable business influence	Full business control
Valuation basis	Fair value	Fair value	Equity method	Consolidation
Balance sheet Asset value	Fair value	Fair value	Acquisition cost adjusted for proportionate share of investee's retained earnings and appropriate amortization	Consolidated balance sheet
Income statement: Unrealized gains	In comprehensive income	In net income	Not recognized	Not recognized
Income statement: Other income effects	Recognize dividends and realized gains and losses in net income	Recognize dividends and realized gains and losses in net income	Recognize proportionate share of investee's net income less appropriate amortization in net income	Consolidated income statement

influence over an investee's business activities. Evidence of an investor's ability to exert significant influence over an investee's business activities is revealed in several ways, including management representation and participation or influence conferred as a result of contractual relationships. In the absence of evidence to the contrary, an investment (direct or indirect) of 20% or more (but less than 50%) in the voting stock of an investee is presumed to possess significant influence. The investor accounts for this investment using the equity method.

The **equity method** requires investors initially to record investments at cost and later adjust the account for the investor's proportionate share in both the investee's income (or loss) because acquisition and decreases from any dividends received from the investee. We explain the mechanics of this process in the next section of this chapter.

Controlling Interest—Holdings of More than 50%.   Holdings of more than 50% are referred to as **controlling interests**–where the investor is known as the *holding company* and the investee as the *subsidiary*. *Consolidated financial statements* are prepared for holdings of more than 50%. We explain consolidation later in the chapter.

ANALYSIS VIEWPOINT   *. . . YOU ARE THE COMPETITOR*

Toys "R" Us, a retailer in toys and games, is concerned about a recent transaction involving a competitor. Specifically, Marvel Entertainment, a comic book company, obtained 46% of equity securities in Toy Biz by granting Toy Biz an exclusive worldwide license to use all of Marvel's characters (such as Spider-Man, Incredible Hulk, Storm) for toys and games. What is the primary concern of Toys "R" Us? What is Marvel's motivation for its investment in Toy Biz's equity securities?

The Fair Value Option

A recent standard *(SFAS 159)* allows companies to selectively report held-to-maturity and available-for-sale securities at fair value. If a company chooses this option, then the accounting for all available-for-sale and held-to-maturity securities will be similar to that accorded to trading securities under *SFAS 115*. Specifically, for all investment securities (trading, available for sale, and held to maturity), (1) the carrying value on the balance sheet will be the fair value, and (2) all unrealized gains and losses will be included in net income. The fair value option can be voluntarily applied in a selective manner to any class of securities that the company chooses, but once fair value has been adopted for a class of securities, the company cannot reverse the option. We discuss the fair value option in detail in a later section of this chapter.

The fair value option is not available for equity investments that need to be consolidated. It is also not generally allowed for those securities for which the equity method of accounting applies.

Disclosures for Investment Securities

This section focuses on the disclosures required under *SFAS 115*. We use Microsoft as an example. Exhibit 5.5 provides excerpts from Microsoft Corporation's notes relating to debt and marketable equity securities (holdings below 20%). Microsoft classifies the majority of its debt and equity investment as available for sale and reports acquisition cost, fair value, and unrealized gain/loss details for each class of its investments. On June 30, 2004, the estimated fair value of Microsoft's available-for-sale securities was $72,802 million, including $10,729 million of equity and $62,073 million of fixed maturity securities (debt and cash). The cost of these securities is $71,275 million, implying a cumulative unrealized gain of $1,527 million (consisting of a $1,820 million gross unrealized gain and a $293 million gross unrealized loss), which is included in the accumulated other comprehensive income (OCI) account in stockholders' equity. In addition, Microsoft reports that it owns restricted or nonpublicly traded securities that it records at cost as prescribed by GAAP. The excess of the estimated (by Microsoft) fair market value of these securities over their reported cost is $470 million. This unrealized gain is not reflected either on the balance sheet or in OCI since the securities are reported at cost.

The company's income statement reports investment income for the recent year of $3,187 million. The notes to the financial statement reveal that this income includes dividends and interest of $1,892 million, net recognized gains in investments of $1,563 million, and net losses on derivatives of $268 million (we discuss accounting for derivative investments later in the chapter).

Analyzing Investment Securities

Analysis of investment securities has at least two main objectives: (1) to separate operating performance from investing (and financing) performance and (2) to analyze accounting distortions due to accounting rules and/or earnings management involving investment securities. We limit our analysis to debt securities and noninfluential (and marketable) equity securities. Analysis of the remaining equity securities is discussed later in this chapter.

Separating Operating from Investing Assets and Performance

The operating and investing performance of a company must be separately analyzed. This is because a company's investing performance can distort its true operating

Exhibit 5.5   *Investment Securities Disclosures—Microsoft Corporation*

■ ■ ■ ■ ■ ■ ■

INVESTMENTS

Equity and other investments include both debt and equity instruments. Debt securities and publicly traded equity securities are classified as available-for-sale and are recorded at market using the specific identification method. Unrealized gains and losses (excluding other-than-temporary impairments) are reflected in OCI. All other investments, excluding those accounted for using the equity method, are recorded at cost. The components of investments are as follows:

June 30, 2004 (in millions)	Cost Basis	Unrealized Gains	Unrealized Losses	Recorded Basis	Cash and Equivalents	Short-Term Investments	Equity and Other Investments
Fixed maturity securities							
Cash	$ 1,812	$ —	$ —	$ 1,812	$ 1,812	$ —	$ —
Money market mutual funds	3,595	—	—	3,595	3,595	—	—
Commercial paper	7,286	—	—	7,286	4,109	3,177	—
Certificates of deposit	415	—	—	415	330	85	—
U. S. government and agency securities	20,565	26	(54)	20,537	4,083	16,454	—
Foreign government bonds	4,524	41	(60)	4,505	—	4,505	—
Mortgage-backed securities	3,656	21	(42)	3,635	—	3,635	—
Corporate notes and bonds	15,048	122	(50)	15,120	1,010	12,629	1,481
Municipal securities	5,154	39	(25)	5,168	1,043	4,125	—
Fixed maturity securities	62,055	249	(231)	62,073	15,982	44,610	1,481
Equity securities							
Common stock and equivalents	7,722	1,571	(62)	9,231	—	—	9,231
Preferred stock	1,290	—	—	1,290	—	—	1,290
Other investments	208	—	—	208	—	—	208
Equity securities	9,220	1,571	(62)	10,729	—	—	10,729
Total	$71,275	$1,820	$(293)	$72,802	$15,982	$44,610	$12,210

At June 30, 2004, unrealized losses of $293 million . . . are primarily attributable to changes in interest rates . . . Management does not believe any unrealized losses represent an other-than temporary impairment based on our evaluation of available evidence as of June 30, 2004.

Common and preferred stock and other investments that are restricted for more than one year or are not publicly traded are recorded at cost. At June 30, 2003, the recorded basis of these investments was $2.15 billion, and their estimated fair value was $2.56 billion. At June 30, 2004, the recorded basis of these investments was $1.65 billion, and their estimated fair value was $2.12 billion. The estimate of fair value is based on publicly available market information or other estimates determined by management.

Investment Income (Loss)

The components of investment income (loss) are as follows:

Year Ended June 30 (in millions)	2002	2003	2004
Dividends and interest	$2,119	$1,957	$1,892
Net recognized gains(losses) on investments	(1,807)	44	1,563
Net losses on derivatives	(617)	(424)	(268)
Investment income(loss)	$ (305)	$1,577	$3,187

performance. For this purpose, it is important for an analyst to remove all gains (losses) relating to investing activities—including dividends, interest income, and realized and unrealized gains and losses—when evaluating operating performance. An analyst also needs to separate operating and nonoperating assets when determining the return on net operating assets (RNOA).

As a rule of thumb, all debt securities and marketable noninfluential equity securities, and their related income streams, are viewed as investing activities. Still, an analyst must review the nature of a company's business and the objectives behind different investments before classifying them as operating or investing. Here are two cases where the rule of thumb does not always apply:

- Financial institutions focus on financing and investing activities. This implies that all financing and investing income and assets are operating-related for financial institutions.
- Some nonfinancial institutions derive a substantial portion of their income from investing activities. For example, finance subsidiaries are sometimes the most profitable business units for companies such as General Electric and General Motors. For such companies it is important to separate the performance of the financing (and investing) units from these companies' core operations—although income from such important activities should not be considered secondary.

There are no "cookbook" solutions for determining whether investment securities (and related income streams) are investing or operating in nature. This classification must be made based on an assessment of whether each investment is a strategic part of operations or made purely for the purpose of investment.

Analyzing Accounting Distortions from Securities

SFAS 115 takes an important step towards fair value accounting for investment securities. However, this standard does not fully embrace fair value accounting. Instead, the standard is a compromise between historical cost and fair value, leaving many unresolved issues along with opportunities for earnings management. This means an analyst must examine disclosures relating to investment securities to identify potential distortions due to both accounting methods and earnings management. This analysis is especially important when analyzing financial institutions and insurance companies because investing activities constitute the core of their operations and provide the bulk of their income. We list some of the potential distortions caused by the accounting for investment securities that an analyst must watch for:

- **Opportunities for gains trading:** The standard allows opportunities for *gains trading* with available-for-sale and held-to-maturity securities. Because unrealized gains and losses on available-for-sale and held-to-maturity securities are excluded from net income, companies can increase net income by selling those securities with unrealized gains and holding those with unrealized losses. However, the standard requires unrealized gains and losses on available-for-sale securities be reported as part of comprehensive income. An analyst must therefore examine comprehensive income disclosures to ascertain unrealized losses (if any) on unsold available-for-sale securities.
- **Liabilities recognized at cost:** Accounting for investment securities is arguably one-sided. That is, if a company reports its investment securities at fair value, why not its liabilities? For many companies, especially financial institutions, asset positions are not managed independent of liability positions. As a result, accounting

....

OUT OF LUCK
Defrauded investors have
many avenues for relief—
but none that promises
much restitution. For
example, class-action
cases against solvent
companies return an
average of only 6%
of claimed losses.

can yield earnings volatility exceeding what the true underlying economics suggest. This consideration led regulators to exclude unrealized holding gains and losses on available-for-sale securities from income. Excluding holding gains and losses from income affects our analysis of the income statement, but does not affect analysis of the balance sheet. Still, unrealized holding gains and losses on available-for-sale securities are reported in comprehensive income.

- **Inconsistent definition of equity securities:** There is concern that the definition of equity securities is arbitrary and inconsistent. For instance, convertible bonds are excluded from equity securities. Yet convertible bonds often derive much of their value from the conversion feature and are more akin to equity securities than debt. This means an analyst should question the exclusion of convertible securities from equity. Redeemable preferred stocks also are excluded from equity securities and, accordingly, our analysis must review their characteristics to validate this classification.

- **Classification based on intent:** Classification of (and accounting for) investment securities depends on management intent, which refers to management's objectives regarding disposition of securities. This intent rule can result in identical debt securities being separately classified into one or any combination of all three classes of trading, held-to-maturity, and available-for-sale securities. This creates ambiguities in how changes in market values of securities are accounted for. An analyst should assess the credibility of management intent by reviewing "premature" sale of held-to-maturity securities. If premature sales occur, they undermine management's credibility.

....

CONVERTIBLES
Evidence shows that
convertible bonds earn
about 80% of the returns of
diversified stock funds but
with only 65% of the
price volatility.

Analysis Research
....
DO FAIR VALUE DISCLOSURES
EXPLAIN STOCK PRICES AND RETURNS?

Researchers have investigated whether fair value disclosures of investment securities are helpful in explaining variation in stock prices and/or stock returns. The evidence suggests that fair value disclosures do provide useful information beyond book values in explaining stock prices. This is especially apparent with financial institutions. Research also suggests that disclosures for unrealized gains and losses of marketable investment securities provide information beyond net income in explaining stock prices and stock returns.

........EQUITY METHOD ACCOUNTING

Equity method accounting is required for intercorporate investments in which the investor company can exert *significant influence* over, but does not control, the investee. In contrast with passive investments, which we discussed earlier in this chapter, equity method investments are reported on the balance sheet at adjusted cost, not at market value. If originally purchased at book value, the amount reported is equal to the percentage of the investee company's stockholders' equity which is owned by the investor. Equity method accounting is generally used for investments representing 20% to 50% of the voting stock of a company's equity securities. The criterion for the use of the equity method, however, is whether the investor company can exert significant influence over the investee company, regardless of the percentage of stock owned.

Once the investor company can exert *control* over the investee company, consolidation is required. Consolidation entails replacing the equity method investment account with the balance sheet of the investee company to which that investment relates (we cover consolidation mechanics in the next section). Accordingly, the equity method is sometimes referred to as a *one-line consolidation*. The primary difference between consolidation and equity method accounting rests in the level of detail reported in the financial statements, because the consolidation process does not affect either total stockholders' equity or the net income of the investor company.

There is wide application of equity method accounting for investments in unconsolidated affiliates, joint ventures, and partnerships. These types of investments have increased markedly as companies have sought to form corporate alliances to effectively utilize assets and to gain competitive advantage. It is important, therefore, to understand the mechanics relating to equity method accounting to appreciate what is reported *and what is not reported* in financial statements.

ANALYSIS VIEWPOINT   **. . . YOU ARE THE ANALYST**

Coca-Cola Company has three types of bottlers: (1) independently owned bottlers, in which the company has no ownership interest; (2) bottlers in which the company has invested and has noncontrolling ownership; and (3) bottlers in which the company has invested and has controlling ownership. In line with its long-term bottling strategy, the company periodically considers options for reducing ownership in its consolidated bottlers. In Note 2 of its annual report, Coca-Cola reports that it owns equity interest of 24% to 38% in some of the largest bottlers in the world. Does Coca-Cola "control" these bottlers by virtue of its ownership of the syrup formula? Should these bottlers be consolidated in its annual reports? How would the consolidation of these bottlers affect its turnover and solvency ratios?

Equity Method Mechanics

We begin with a discussion of the mechanics of equity method accounting. Assume that Global Corp. acquires for cash a 25% interest in Synergy, Inc. for $500,000, representing one-fourth of Synergy's stockholders' equity as of the acquisition date. The investment is, therefore, acquired at book value. Synergy's condensed balance sheet as of the date of the acquisition is

Current assets	$ 700,000
Property, plant, and equipment	5,600,000
Total assets	$6,300,000
Current liabilities	$ 300,000
Long-term debt	4,000,000
Stockholders' equity	2,000,000
Total liabilities and equity	$6,300,000

The initial investment is recorded on Global's books as,

Investment	500,000	
Cash		500,000

Global reports the investment account as a noncurrent asset on its balance sheet. This $500,000 investment represents a 25% interest in an investee company with total assets of $6,300,000 and liabilities of $4,300,000.

Subsequent to the date of the acquisition, Synergy reports net income of $100,000 and pays dividends of $20,000. Global records its proportionate share of Synergy's earnings and the receipt of dividends as follows,

Investment...	25,000	
Equity in earnings of investee company		25,000
To record proportionate share of investee company earnings		
Cash	5,000	
Investment		5,000
To record receipt of dividends		

Global's earnings have increased by its proportionate share of the net income of Synergy. This income will be reported in the other income section of the income statement as it is treated similarly to interest income. In contrast to the accounting for available-for-sale and trading securities described earlier in this chapter, the dividends received are not recorded as income. Instead, they are treated as a return of the capital invested in Synergy, and the investment account is reduced accordingly.

There is symmetry between Global's investment accounting and Synergy's stockholders' equity:

	Global Corp. Investment Account			Synergy, Inc. Stockholders' Equity		
Beg.	500,000				2,000,000	Beg.
	25,000	5,000		20,000	100,000	
End	520,000				2,080,000	End

Global's investment remains at 25% of Synergy's stockholders' equity.

There are a number of important points relating to equity method accounting:

- The investment account is reported at an amount equal to the proportionate share of the stockholders' equity of the investee company. Substantial assets and liabilities may, therefore, not be recorded on balance sheet unless the investee is consolidated. This can have important implications for the analysis of the investor company.
- Investment earnings (the proportionate share of the earnings of the investee company) should be distinguished from core operating earnings in the analysis of the earnings of the investor company unless the investment is deemed to be strategic in nature.
- Contrary to the reporting of available-for-sale and trading securities discussed earlier in this chapter, investments accounted for under the equity method are reported at adjusted cost, not at market value. Substantial unrealized gains may, therefore, not be reflected in assets or stockholders' equity. (Losses in value that are deemed to be other than temporary, however, must be reflected as a write-down in the carrying amount of the investment with a related loss recorded in the income statement.)
- An investor should discontinue equity method accounting when the investment is reduced to zero (such as due to investee losses) and should not provide for additional losses unless the investor has guaranteed the obligations of the investee or is otherwise committed to providing further financial support to the investee. Equity method accounting only resumes once all cumulative deficits have been recovered via investee earnings.

- If the amount of the initial investment exceeds the proportionate share of the book value of the investee company, the excess is allocated to identifiable tangible and intangible assets that are depreciated/amortized over their respective useful lives. Investment income is reduced by this additional expense. The excess not allocated in this manner is treated as goodwill and is no longer amortized.

Analysis Implications of Intercorporate Investments

Our analysis continues with several important considerations relating to intercorporate investments. This section discusses the more important implications.

Recognition of Investee Company Earnings

Equity method accounting assumes that a dollar earned by an investee company is equivalent to a dollar earned for the investor, even if not received in cash. While disregarding the parent's potential tax liability from remittance of earnings by an affiliate, the dollar-for-dollar equivalence of earnings cannot be taken for granted. Reasons include:

- A regulatory authority can sometimes intervene in a subsidiary's dividend policy.
- A subsidiary can operate in a country where restrictions exist on remittance of earnings or where the value of currency can deteriorate rapidly. Political risks can further inhibit access to earnings.
- Dividend restrictions in loan agreements can limit earnings accessibility.
- Presence of a stable or powerful minority interest can reduce a parent's discretion in setting dividend or other policies.

Our analysis must recognize these factors in assessing whether a dollar earned by the affiliate is the equivalent of a dollar earned by the investor.

Unrecognized Capital Investment

The investment account is often referred to as a one-line consolidation. This is because it represents the investor's percentage ownership in the investee company stockholders' equity. Behind this investment balance are the underlying assets and liabilities of the investee company. There can be a significant amount of unrecorded assets and liabilities of the investee company that are not reflected on the balance sheet of the investor.

Consider the case of Coca-Cola presented in the Analysis Viewpoint on page 273. Coca-Cola owns approximately 36% of Coca-Cola Enterprises (CCE), one of its bottling companies. It accounts for this investment under the equity method and reports an investment balance as of December 31, 2004, of $1,679 million, approximately its proportionate share of the $5.4 billion stockholders' equity of CCE. The balance sheet of CCE reports total assets of $26.4 billion and total liabilities of $21.0 billion. The investment balance on Coca-Cola's balance sheet, representing 5% of its reported total assets, belies a much larger investment and financial leverage.

The concern facing the analyst is how to treat this sizable off-balance-sheet investment. Should financial ratio analysis be conducted solely on the reported financial statements of Coca-Cola? Should CCE be consolidated with Coca-Cola by the analyst and financial ratios computed on the consolidated financial statements? Should only Coca-Cola's proportionate interest in the assets and liabilities of CCE be included in place of the investment account for purposes of analysis? These are important issues that must be addressed before beginning the analysis process.

Provision for Taxes on Undistributed Subsidiary Earnings

When the undistributed earnings of a subsidiary are included in the pretax accounting income of a parent company (either through consolidation or equity method accounting), it can require a concurrent provision for taxes. This provision depends on the action and intent of the parent company. Current practice assumes all undistributed earnings transfer to the parent and, thus, a provision for taxes is made by the parent in the current period. This assumption is overcome, however, if persuasive evidence exists that the subsidiary either has or will invest undistributed earnings permanently or will remit earnings through a tax-free liquidation. In analysis, we should be aware that the decision on whether taxes are provided on undistributed earnings is primarily that of management.

........BUSINESS COMBINATIONS

Business combinations refer to the merger with, or acquisition of, a business. They occur when one company acquires a substantial part of one or more other companies' equity securities. (We confine our discussion in this section to the acquisition of the stock of the investee company. Asset purchases are treated no differently than the purchase of any other asset: the assets are recorded at their purchase price.) Business combinations require that subsequent financial statements report on the combined activities of this new entity. Accounting for a business combination requires a decision on how to value the assets and liabilities of the new entity. This decision can involve a complete revaluation to market value of all assets and liabilities acquired, with substantial effects extending to current and future financial statements. This accounting decision is different from the intercorporate investment discussion earlier in the chapter that focuses not on the accounting for the "combination" but on the valuation and accounting for the investment itself. Analysis of business combinations must recognize management's incentives, the accounting implications, and the need to evaluate and interpret financial statements of the new entity.

Companies Reporting Business Combinations

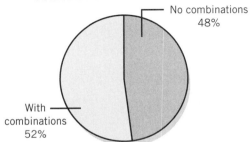

No combinations 48%

With combinations 52%

Business combinations with sound economic motivations have a long history. Among the economic reasons for business combinations are (1) acquiring valuable sources of materials, productive facilities, technology, marketing channels, or market share; (2) securing financial resources or access to them; (3) strengthening management; (4) enhancing operating efficiency; (5) encouraging diversification; (6) rapidity in market entry; (7) achieving economies of scale; and (8) acquiring tax advantages. We should also recognize certain intangible reasons for business combinations. In certain cases these intangibles are the best explanation for the high costs incurred. They include management prestige, compensation, and perquisites. Management's accounting choices in recording business combinations are often better understood when considering these motivations.

However, business combinations also can arise as a means to enhance a company's image, its perceived growth potential, or its prosperity, and it is a means of increasing reported earnings. Specifically, financial engineers can utilize methods in accounting for business combinations to deliver a picture of earnings growth that is, in large part, illusory. The means to achieve illusionary earnings growth include:

- Merging a growth company having a high price-earnings ratio with a company having lesser growth prospects, and using payment in the high-growth company's stock. This transaction can contribute to further earnings per share growth and can reinforce and even increase the acquiring company's high price-earnings ratio. Markets sometimes fail to fully account for the potential lower quality of acquired earnings. This is primarily a transitory problem inherent in the market evaluation mechanism, and it is not easily remedied by regulators.

- Using latitude in accounting for business combinations. This is distinct from genuine economic advantages arising from combinations. We consider alternative accounting methods for business combinations in the next section.

Accounting for Business Combinations

The Financial Accounting Standards Board recently enacted two significant pronouncements (*SFAS 141,* "Business Combinations," and *SFAS 142,* "Goodwill and Other Intangible Assets") relating to accounting and reporting for business combinations (effective for fiscal periods beginning December 15, 2001, and after). These standards mandate the use of the *purchase method* of accounting for the acquisition and the subsequent nonamortization of goodwill.

Under the purchase method of accounting, companies are required to recognize on their balance sheets the fair market value of the (tangible and intangible) assets acquired together with the fair market value of any liabilities assumed. Furthermore, the tangible assets are depreciated and the identifiable intangible assets amortized over their estimated useful lives. In a significant departure from prior practice, however, *SFAS 142* mandates that goodwill will no longer be amortized. This nonamortization approach is applied to both previously recognized and newly acquired goodwill. Instead, goodwill is subject to an annual test for impairment. When the carrying amount of goodwill exceeds its implied fair value, an impairment loss will be recognized equal to that excess.

Consolidated Financial Statements

Consolidated financial statements report the results of operations and financial condition of a parent corporation and its subsidiaries in one set of statements. A parent company's financial statements evidence ownership of stock in a subsidiary through an investment account. From a legal point of view, a parent company owns the stock of its subsidiary. A parent does not own the subsidiary's assets nor is it usually responsible for the subsidiary's debts, although it frequently guarantees them. Consolidated financial statements disregard the separate legal identities of the parent and its subsidiary in favor of its "economic substance." That is, consolidated financial statements reflect a business entity controlled by a single company–the parent.

Mechanics of Consolidations

Consolidation involves two steps: *aggregation* and *elimination*. First, consolidated financial statements aggregate the assets, liabilities, revenues, and expenses of subsidiaries with their corresponding items in the financial statements of the parent company. The second step is to eliminate *intercompany transactions* (or reciprocal accounts) to avoid double counting or prematurely recognizing income. For example, both a parent's account payable to its subsidiary and its subsidiary's account receivable from the parent are eliminated when preparing a consolidated balance sheet. Likewise, sales and cost of goods sold are eliminated for intercompany inventory sales.

The net effect of the consolidation on the balance sheet is to report the subsidiary acquired at its fair market value as of the date of acquisition. That is, all of the subsidiary's tangible and separately identifiable intangible assets are reported at their appraised values. Any excess of the purchase price over the fair market values of these identifiable assets is recorded as goodwill.

We now turn to a discussion of the consolidation process. Consider the following case:

On December 31, Year 1, Synergy Corp. purchases 100% of Micron Company by exchanging 10,000 shares of its common stock ($5 par value, $77 market value) for all of the common stock of Micron, which will remain in existence as a wholly owned subsidiary of Synergy. On the date of the acquisition, the book value of Micron is $620,000. Synergy is willing to pay the market price of $770,000 because it feels that Micron's property, plant, and equipment (PP&E) is undervalued by $20,000, it has an unrecorded trademark worth $30,000, and intangible benefits of the business combination (corporate synergies, market position, and the like) are valued at $100,000. The purchase price is, therefore, allocated as follows:

Purchase price $770,000
Book value of Micron 620,000
Excess $150,000

Excess allocated to		Useful Life	Annual Depreciation/Amortization
Undervalued PP&E	$ 20,000	10 years	$2,000
Trademark	30,000	5 years	6,000
Goodwill	100,000	Indefinite	0
	$150,000		$8,000

Goodwill can only be recorded following the recognition of the fair market values of all tangible (PP&E) and identifiable intangible (trademark) assets acquired. Synergy makes the following entry to record the acquisition,

Investment in Micron 770,000
Common stock .... 50,000 (at par value)
Additional paid-in-capital 720,000

During Year 2, Micron earns $150,000 and pays no dividends. The investment, accounted for under the equity method, has a balance on Synergy's books at December 31, Year 2, as follows:

Beginning balance (12/31/Y1) $770,000
Investment income 150,000
Dividends .... (0)
Amortization of excess (above) .... (8,000)
Ending balance (12/31/Y2) $912,000

Under current GAAP, goodwill is not amortized and the net investment income recognized by Synergy is $142,000, including its proportionate share (100% in this case) of Micron's earnings less $8,000 of expense relating to depreciation of the excess PP&E

($2,000) and the amortization of the trademark ($6,000). The individual company trial balances for both Synergy and Micron at the end of Year 2 are presented in the accompanying table together with the consolidation worksheet and consolidated totals.

SYNERGY CORP. AND SUBSIDIARY
Trial Balances and Consolidated Financial Statements
For Year Ended December 31, Year 2
Prepared under the Purchase Accounting Method

	Synergy	Micron	Debits	Credits	Consolidated
Revenues...................................	$ 610,000	$ 370,000			$ 980,000
Operating expenses	(270,000)	(140,000)			(410,000)
Depreciation expense........................	(115,000)	(80,000)	[4]$ 2,000		(197,000)
Amortization expense........................	0	0	[4] 6,000		(6,000)
Investment income	142,000	0	[3] 142,000		0
Net income.................................	$ 367,000	$ 150,000			$ 367,000
Retained earnings, 1/1/Y1	$ 680,000	$ 490,000	[1] 490,000		$ 680,000
Net income.......................................	367,000	150,000			367,000
Dividends paid.................................	(90,000)				(90,000)
Retained earnings, 12/31/Y2........	$ 957,000	$ 640,000			$ 957,000
Cash...	$ 105,000	$ 20,000			$ 125,000
Receivables	380,000	220,000			600,000
Inventory...	560,000	280,000			840,000
Investment in Micron........................	912,000	0		[1]$620,000	0
				[2] 150,000	
				[3] 142,000	
Plant, property, and equipment, net...	1,880,000	720,000	[2] 20,000	[4] 2,000	2,618,000
Trademark..	0	0	[2] 30,000	[4] 6,000	24,000
Goodwill..			[2] 100,000		100,000
Total assets	$3,837,000	$1,240,000			$4,307,000
Liabilities..	$ 780,000	$ 470,000			$1,250,000
Common stock.................................	800,000	100,000	[1] 100,000		800,000
Additional paid-in capital................	1,300,000	30,000	[1] 30,000		1,300,000
Retained earnings	957,000	640,000			957,000
Total liabilities and equity	$3,837,000	$1,240,000	$920,000	$920,000	$4,307,000

The original balance of the investment account on the purchase date ($770,000) represents the market value of Micron. It includes the market value of Micron's reported net assets plus fair market value of the previously unrecognized trademark and the goodwill purchased in the acquisition. The four consolidation entries are (numbers refer to those in the debit and credit columns in the table):

1. Replace $620,000 of the investment account with the book value (at the beginning of the year) of the assets acquired. If less than 100% of the subsidiary is owned, the credit to the investment account is equal to the percentage of the book value owned and the remaining credit is to a liability account, *minority interest*. The minority interest account is treated as a component of equity for

analysis purposes whether or not reported as such on the balance sheet. A recent standard *(SFAS 160)* now requires that minority interest be included as part of shareholders' equity.

2. Replace $150,000 of the investment account with the fair value adjustments required to fully record Micron's assets at fair market value.

3. Eliminate the investment income recorded by Synergy and replace that account with the income statement of Micron. If less than 100% of the subsidiary is owned, the investment income reported by the Synergy is equal to its proportionate share, and an additional expense for the balance is reported for the *minority interest* in Micron's earnings.

4. Record the depreciation of the fair value adjustment for Micron's PP&E and the amortization of the trademark. Note, there is no amortization of goodwill under current GAAP.

There are several important points to understand about the consolidation process:

- The consolidated balance sheet includes the book value of Synergy and the fair market value of Micron as of the acquisition date, less depreciation/amortization of the excess of the Micron market value over its book value. The investment account on the investor's balance sheet has been replaced by the investee company balance sheet to which it relates. Further, the additional tangible and intangible assets purchased have been recognized as an increase in the carrying amount of currently reported assets (write-up of PPE) and as additional assets (trademark and goodwill).

- The consolidated income statement includes the income statements of both Synergy and Micron. The investment income recorded by Synergy on its books is replaced by the income statement of Micron. In addition, depreciation expense includes the depreciation expense that Micron records on the book value of its depreciable assets plus the depreciation of the excess of fair market value over book value recorded upon acquisition of Micron. Second, the newly created trademark asset is amortized over its useful life, resulting in additional expense of $6,000. The goodwill recognized in the acquisition is not amortized.

- Goodwill is only recorded after recognizing the fair market values of all tangible and intangible assets acquired. Companies are required to identify any intangible assets acquired. These intangibles are deemed to have an identifiable useful life and are, therefore, subject to annual amortization.

■ ■ ■ ■ ■ ■ ■

MICKEY'S PROFITS IMPROVE

Changes in the accounting for goodwill have increased Walt Disney Company's earnings. Disney's acquisition of CapitalCities/ABC resulted in goodwill of $19.2 billion. The $480 million annual hit to Disney's earnings from goodwill amortization is no longer present under current accounting rules.

Impairment of Goodwill

Goodwill recorded in the consolidation process has an indefinite life and is, therefore, not amortized. It is, however, subject to annual review for impairment. This review is a two step process. In the first step, the fair market value of Micron is compared with the book value of its associated investment account on Synergy's books ($912,000 as of December 31, Year 2). The fair market value of Micron can be determined using a number of alternative methods, such as quoted market prices of comparable businesses, or a discounted free cash flow valuation method. If the current market value is less than the investment balance, goodwill is deemed to be impaired and an impairment loss must be recorded in the consolidated income statement.

Assume that the fair market value of Micron is estimated to be $700,000 as of December 31, Year 2, and that the fair market value of the net tangible and identifiable intangible assets is $660,000. This results in an impairment loss of $60,000 as follows:

Fair market value of Micron		$ 700,000
Current assets	$ 520,000	
PP&E...	570,000	
Trademark..	20,000	
Liabilities...	(450,000)	
Net assets.......................................		660,000
Implied goodwill...............................		40,000
Current balance goodwill		(100,000)
Impairment loss...............................		$ 60,000

The resulting entry on Synergy's books is:

Goodwill impairment loss...	60,000	
Investment in Micron		60,000

The impairment loss will be reported as a separate line item in the operating section of Synergy's consolidated income statement. In addition, a portion of the goodwill contained in Synergy's investment account is written off, and the balance of goodwill in the consolidated balance sheet is reduced accordingly. Disclosures are also required detailing the facts and circumstances resulting in the impairment, and the method by which Synergy determines the fair market value of Micron.

Issues in Business Combinations
Contingent Consideration

In some business combinations, the parties cannot agree on a price. This yields the notion of *contingent consideration,* where it is agreed that additional money will be paid by the buyer to the seller if future performance goals are met by the combined company. Under current accounting, that future *earn-out* payment is recognized as additional purchase cost when the money is paid (typically as an increase in goodwill). The FASB has proposed a revision to the business combination standard that includes new accounting for contingent consideration. In the proposed standard, the fair value of the business being acquired must be determined as of the date of the acquisition. Embedded in the arrangement would be the fair value of the buyer's obligation for contingent payments. That amount would be included in the purchase price. That is, the agreement for future payments must be fair-valued on the date of purchase *and* then continually revalued each subsequent quarter to reflect actual performance. This will result in earnings volatility as the contingent consideration is revalued.

Allocating Total Cost

Once a company determines the total cost of an acquired entity, it is necessary to allocate this cost to individual assets. All identifiable assets acquired and liabilities assumed in a business combination are assigned a portion of the total cost, normally equal to their fair value at date of acquisition. Identifiable assets include intangible as well as tangible assets. *SFAS 141* requires companies to identify and value specific categories of intangible assets. These include the following:

1. Trademarks and other marketing-related assets.
2. Noncompetition agreements.

3. Customer lists, contracts, and other customer-related assets.
4. Artistic-related intangible assets such as literary or music works, and video and audiovisual material, including television programs and music videos.
5. Intangible assets relating to contractual relationships such as licensing, royalty, advertising, and management contracts, lease or franchise agreements, broadcast rights, employment contracts, and the like.
6. Patents, computer software, databases, trade secrets or formulae, and other technology-based intangible assets.

Only after the purchase price has been allocated to the fair market value of all tangible and identifiable intangible assets, less the market value of all liabilities assumed, can any of the purchase price be assigned to goodwill. The reason is that all assets other than goodwill have an identifiable useful life, resulting in depreciation and amortization expense. Goodwill, however, is deemed to have an indefinite life and is not amortized.

It is possible that market or appraisal values of identifiable assets acquired, less liabilities assumed, exceed the cost of the acquired company (*negative goodwill*). In those rare cases, values otherwise assignable to noncurrent assets acquired (except long-term investments in marketable securities) are reduced by this excess. Then, the remainder, if any, is recorded in the income statement as an extraordinary gain net of tax.

Types of Intangible Assets Reported by Companies

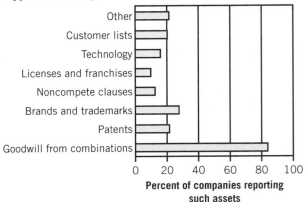

Percent of companies reporting such assets

In-Process Research and Development (IPR&D)

Some companies write off a large portion of an acquisition's costs as purchased research and development. Moreover, there has been a dramatic increase in such write-offs within the past decade, especially in the high-tech industry. Under prior GAAP, this practice was attractive as it allowed acquiring companies to reduce or even eliminate any allocation of the purchase price to goodwill and, thus, lower or avoid future earnings charges from the resulting goodwill amortization.

In the IPR&D write-off situation, companies value the IPR&D assets of the acquired companies before writing them off. However, there is no guidance on how to value IPR&D. Given the incentive to avoid recognizing IPR&D as goodwill, companies are alleged to value IPR&D as high as possible to increase the write-off and reduce or eliminate subsequent goodwill amortization. Such a write-off creates quality-of-earnings concerns if IPR&D is overstated because it would understate assets and overstate future return on equity (and assets).

The abuse of IPR&D write-offs led the SEC to investigate its use. Some acquisitions were, subsequently, challenged and the companies were required to restate historical financial statements. Recently, the FASB has proposed that IPR&D be capitalized and amortized rather than expensed.

Debt in Consolidated Financial Statements

Liabilities in consolidated financial statements do not operate as a lien upon a common pool of assets. Creditors, whether secured or unsecured, have recourse in the event of default only to assets owned by the specific corporation that incurred the liability. If a parent company guarantees a liability of a subsidiary, then the creditor has the guarantee as additional security with potential recourse provisions. The consolidated balance sheet does not help us assess the margin of safety enjoyed by creditors. To assess the security of liabilities, our analysis must examine the individual financial statements of each subsidiary. We must also remember that legal constraints are not always effective measures of liability. For example, American Express recently covered the obligations of a warehousing subsidiary not because of any legal obligation, but because of concern for its own reputation.

ANALYSIS VIEWPOINT   **. . . YOU ARE THE LAWYER**

One of your clients calls on you with a legal matter. Your client has nearly all of her savings invested in the common stock of NY Research Labs, Inc. Her concern stems from the financial statements of NY Research Labs that were released yesterday. These financial statements are, for the first time, consolidated statements involving a subsidiary, Boston Chemicals Corp. Your client is concerned her investment in NY Research Labs is now at greater risk due to several major lawsuits against Boston Chemicals—some have the potential to bankrupt Boston Chemicals. How do you advise your client? Should she be more concerned about her investment in NY Research Labs because of the consolidation?

Gains on Subsidiary IPOs

Tycom, Ltd., a wholly owned subsidiary of Tyco International, Ltd., sold previously unissued shares to outside parties in an initial public offering (IPO). As a result of the sale, Tyco International, Ltd.'s percentage ownership in Tycom, Ltd., decreased from 100% to 89% and the parent company recorded a pretax gain of $2.1 billion ($1.01 billion after tax) in its consolidated statement of income. IPOs by subsidiaries are becoming increasingly common as companies seek to capture unrecognized gains in the value of their subsidiary stock holdings while, at the same time, retaining control over their subsidiaries.

The rationale for the gain treatment can be seen from this example: assume that Synergy owns 100% of Micron with a book value of stockholders' equity of $1,000,000 and records the investment in Micron at $1,000,000. Micron sells previously unissued shares for $500,000 and, thereby, reduces Synergy's ownership to 80%. Synergy now owns 80% of a subsidiary with a book value of $1,500,000 for an investment equivalent of $1,200,000. The value of its investment account has thus risen by $200,000. The FASB formally supports the treatment of this "gain" as an increase in additional paid-in capital. The SEC, however, in *Staff Accounting Bulletin 51,* allows companies to record the credit to either additional paid-in capital or to earnings. The effect on stockholders' equity of Synergy is the same. But in the first alternative, stockholders' equity is increased by an increase in additional paid-in capital. In the second alternative, stockholders' equity is increased via the closure of net income to retained earnings and a gain is recorded in the statement of income.

Preacquisition Sales and Income

When an acquisition of a subsidiary occurs in midyear companies only report their equity in subsidiary income from the acquisition date forward. There are, however, two methods available under GAAP *(Accounting Research Bulletin 51)*, to accomplish this:

1. The company can issue a consolidated income statement with sales, expenses, and income of the subsidiary from the acquisition date forward.
2. The company can report in its consolidated income statement subsidiary sales and expenses for the entire year and back out preacquisition earnings so that only postacquisition earnings are included in consolidated net income.

The effect on consolidated net income is the same for either method, that is, only net income of the acquired company subsequent to the acquisition date is included in consolidated earnings. Top line (sales) growth, however, can be dramatically different depending on the acquisition date and magnitude of the acquired company's sales. Companies whose growth occurs primarily via acquisitions (vs. "organic," or internal, growth) can be particularly troublesome for analysts.

The amount of preacquisition income is likely to be deemed immaterial and included in other expense categories rather than reported as a separate line item. One hint into the accounting method employed is to examine the pro forma disclosures required in the acquisitions footnote. Companies are required to report pro forma sales and income as if the investees had been included for the entire year. A comparison of these pro forma sales against reported consolidated sales can provide insight into the accounting choice made by management in this area.

Push-Down Accounting

Purchase accounting requires the assets and liabilities of an acquired company to be included in the consolidated financial statements of the purchaser at their market values. A controversial issue is how the acquired company reports these assets and liabilities in its separate financial statements (if that company survives as a separate entity and is publicly traded). The SEC requires that purchase transactions resulting in an entity's becoming substantially wholly owned (as defined in Regulation S-X) establish a new basis of accounting for the purchased assets and liabilities if the acquired company issues securities in public markets. For example, if Company A acquires substantially all the common stock of Company B in one or a series of purchase transactions, Company B's financial statements must reflect the new basis of accounting arising from its acquisition by Company A. When ownership is under control of the parent, the basis of accounting for purchased assets and liabilities should be the same regardless of whether the entity continues to exist or is merged into the parent's operations. That is, Company A's cost of acquiring Company B is "pushed down" and used to establish a new accounting basis in Company B's separate financial statements. The SEC recognizes that the existence of outstanding public debt, preferred stock, or significant minority interest in a subsidiary can impact a parent's ability to control ownership. In these cases, the SEC has not insisted on push-down accounting.

Additional Limitations of Consolidated Financial Statements

Consolidated financial statements often are meaningful representations of the financial condition and results of operations of the parent-subsidiary entity. Nevertheless, there are limitations in addition to those already discussed.

- Financial statements of the individual companies composing the larger entity are not always prepared on a comparable basis. Differences in accounting principles, valuation bases, amortization rates, and other factors can inhibit homogeneity and impair the validity of ratios, trends, and other analyses.

- Consolidated financial statements do not reveal restrictions on use of cash for individual companies. Nor do they reveal intercompany cash flows or restrictions placed on those flows. These factors obscure the relation between liquidity of assets and the liabilities they aim to meet.

- Companies in poor financial condition sometimes combine with financially strong companies, thus obscuring our analysis—because assets of one member of the consolidated entity cannot necessarily be seized to pay liabilities of another.

- Extent of intercompany transactions is unknown unless the procedures underlying the consolidation process are reported—consolidated statements generally reveal only end results.

- Accounting for the consolidation of finance and insurance subsidiaries can pose several problems for analysis. Aggregation of dissimilar subsidiaries can distort ratios and other relations—for example, current assets of finance subsidiaries are not generally available to satisfy current liabilities of the parent. Assets and liabilities of separate entities are not interchangeable, and consolidated financial statements obscure the priorities of creditors' claims.

Consequences of Accounting for Goodwill

The excess of the purchase price over the market value of identifiable net assets acquired represents payment for super (abnormal) earnings. Superearnings are attributed to brand names and other items offering superior competitive position. Superior competitive position is subject to change from a myriad of economic and environmental forces. With effort and opportunity, a company can maintain a superior position. Nevertheless, goodwill is not permanent.

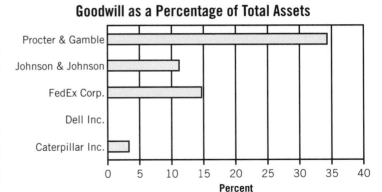

Goodwill as a Percentage of Total Assets

The residual measurement of goodwill gives rise to potential measurement problems. For example, payments resulting from errors of estimation, of intense bidding contests, or of carelessness with owner or creditor resources get swept into goodwill. These payments can even include finder's fees, legal costs, investment banker fees, and interim financing costs. Warren Buffett, chairman of Berkshire Hathaway, recognized this residual measurement of goodwill in writing to his shareholders: "When an overexcited management purchases a business at a silly price . . . silliness ends up in the goodwill account. Considering the lack of managerial discipline that created the account, under the circumstances it might better be labeled no-will." The crux of this issue is: Does goodwill represent superior earnings power and do its benefits extend to future periods? Our analysis must realize that in too many cases the answer is no.

If companies do write off goodwill in the face of substantial losses by purchased subsidiaries, the timing of the write-off seldom reflects prompt recognition of this loss in value. The following case reflects this.

ANALYSIS EXCERPT

Bangor Punta Corporation acquired Piper Aircraft for payment that included a substantial amount for goodwill. Ultimately, time revealed that this payment was for superlosses rather than superearnings. In one period, Bangor Punta earned $3.1 million on a consolidated basis, while Piper Aircraft lost $22.4 million. Only when confronting a subsequent operating loss of $38.5 million by Piper Aircraft and an overall consolidated loss did Bangor Punta write off the Piper Aircraft goodwill of $54.7 million. It also appears that Bangor Punta did so with a "big bath." That is, recognition of the write-off was delayed until its impact was diminished by Bangor Punta's own loss (it took all the hits at one time). This write-off also yielded the beneficial side effect of relieving Bangor Punta's future income of goodwill amortization charges.

To help in our analysis, we might better understand goodwill and its implications for analysis if we compare the accounting definition of goodwill to the usual analyst's definition:

> *Accounting definition of goodwill.* Goodwill is the excess of cost over fair market value of net assets acquired in a purchase transaction. No attempt is made to explicitly identify components of this asset or the economic values assigned to them. Whatever has been paid for and that cannot be separately identified is assigned to goodwill.
>
> *Analyst's definition of goodwill.* Goodwill reflects real economic value such as that due to brand names requiring costly development and maintenance. Goodwill can also reflect overpayments attributed to unrealistic expectations, undisciplined zeal, or lack of sound judgment and proper analysis. Evaluation of goodwill requires careful analysis of a company's competitive market position and superior earning power with respect to its operations. Goodwill represents a nonpermanent advantage that must manifest itself in superior earning power; if not, it does not exist.

Analysis of goodwill continues to be challenging. Billions of dollars in goodwill are on corporate balance sheets. In certain companies, it represents a substantial part of net assets or even exceeds total equity. Payment for superior earning power is warranted. Still, analysis must be aware that in many cases goodwill is nothing more than mechanical application of accounting rules giving little consideration to value received in return. The process by which billions of dollars in goodwill are placed on balance sheets is illustrated by the battle for control of RJR Nabisco:

ANALYSIS EXCERPT

Prior to the bidding battle for RJR Nabisco, the market (dominated by financial institutions holding 40 percent of its stock) valued the company at about $12 billion. A group, led by RJR Nabisco's CEO, started the bidding by offering $17 billion for the company—$5 billion more than the value assigned to it by the market. RJR Nabisco was eventually sold for $25 billion, including $13 billion in goodwill. Undoubtedly swept into this account were significant costs of financing, professional and investment banking talent, and other expenses involved in this costly bidding war. A reasonable analysis concern is the extent to which goodwill reflects, or does not reflect, the present value of future residual income (superearnings).

Finally, our analysis must also realize that goodwill on corporate balance sheets typically fails to reflect a company's entire intangible earning power (due to market position, brand names, or other proprietary advantages). That is, under generally accepted accounting principles, internally developed goodwill cannot be recorded as an asset. This is evidenced in the case of Altria Group, Inc.

ANALYSIS EXCERPT

Altria (formerly Philip Morris) acquired General Foods for $5.8 billion, of which about $2.8 billion was payment for goodwill. General Foods' brand names arguably justify this premium. On Altria's balance sheet, goodwill makes up nearly 80% of equity. Yet, it does not include the considerable value of Altria's own brand names.

Pooling Accounting for Business Combinations

Prior to the passage of the current business combination accounting standards, companies were allowed to use an alternate accounting method: pooling of interest. Although disallowed for business combinations initiated subsequent to June 30, 2001, companies may continue the use of pooling accounting for acquisitions accounted for under that method prior to the effective date of the standard. Pooling accounting was widely used and will continue to impact financial statements for many years to come. It is important, therefore, for analysts to understand the accounting for business combinations under this method. This section describes the mechanics of pooling accounting and follows with a discussion of the analysis implications.

The difference between the pooling and purchase accounting methods lies in the amount recorded as the initial investment in the acquired company. Under the purchase method, as we have seen, the investment account is debited for the purchase price, that is, the fair market value of the acquired company on the date of acquisition. Under the pooling method, this debit is in the amount of the book value of the acquired company. Assets are not written up from the historical cost balances reported on the investee company balance sheet, no new intangible assets are created in the acquisition, and no goodwill is reported. The avoidance of goodwill was the principle attraction of this method as companies would thereby avoid the subsequent earnings drag from goodwill amortization.

Mechanics of Pooling-of-Interest Accounting

Continuing with our previous example, under pooling accounting, the initial investment is recorded as follows:

Investment in Micron	620,000	
Common stock		50,000 (at par value)
Additional paid-in capital		80,000
Retained earnings		490,000

The investment account is $150,000 less than in our previous example as the assets of the acquired company are recorded at book value rather than market value. In addition, Synergy records beginning retained earnings and paid-in capital (common stock and additional paid-in capital) equal to that of Micron as of the beginning of the year.

During the year, Micron earns $150,000. The investment is accounted for under the equity method and has a balance on Synergy's books at December 31, Year 2, as follows:

Beginning balance (12/31/Y1)........ $620,000
Investment income.......................... 150,000
Dividends....................................... 0
Ending balance (12/31/Y2)............. $770,000

The consolidated balance sheet under pooling accounting is as follows:

SYNERGY CORP. AND SUBSIDIARY
Trial Balances and Consolidated Financial Statements
For Year Ended December 31, Year 2
Prepared under the Pooling Accounting Method

	Synergy	Micron	Debits	Credits	Consolidated
Revenues...	$ 610,000	$ 370,000			$ 980,000
Cost of goods sold...........................	(270,000)	(140,000)			(410,000)
Depreciation expense	(115,000)	(80,000)			(195,000)
Amortization expense	0	0			0
Investment income..........................	150,000	0	[2]$150,000		0
Net income.................................	$ 375,000	$ 150,000			$ 375,000
Retained earnings, 1/1/Y1..............	$1,170,000	$ 490,000	[1] 490,000		$1,170,000
Net income.....................................	375,000	150,000			375,000
Dividends paid	(90,000)				(90,000)
Retained earnings, 12/31/ Y2.....	$1,455,000	$ 640,000			$1,455,000
Cash...	$ 105,000	$ 20,000			$ 125,000
Receivables.....................................	380,000	220,000			600,000
Inventory	560,000	280,000			840,000
Investment in Micron.......................	770,000	0		[1]$620,000 [2] 150,000	0
Plant, property, and equipment, net..	1,880,000	720,000			2,600,000
Total assets....................................	$3,695,000	$1,240,000			$4,165,000
Liabilities	$ 780,000	$ 470,000			$1,250,000
Common stock.................................	800,000	100,000	[1] 100,000		800,000
Additional paid-in capital...............	660,000	30,000	[1] 30,000		660,000
Retained earnings...........................	1,455,000	640,000			1,455,000
Total liabilities and equity..............	$3,695,000	$1,240,000	$770,000	$770,000	$4,165,000

The original balance of the investment account on the purchase date ($620,000) represents the book value of Micron's stockholder's equity. It consists of the beginning of the year retained earnings plus Micron's paid-in capital (common stock plus additional paid-in capital). In contrast to the purchase method, however, the investment balance does not include the fair market value of the tangible assets, the previously unrecognized trademark, and the goodwill purchased in the acquisition. The two consolidation entries accomplish the following:

1. Replace $620,000 of the investment account with the book value of the assets acquired.
2. Eliminate the investment income recorded by Synergy and replace that account with the income statement of Micron.

There are several important points to understand about the consolidation process using the pooling method:

- The consolidated balance sheet includes the book value of both Synergy and Micron.
- The consolidated income statement includes the income statements of both Synergy and Micron. Depreciation is only computed on the historical book values of both companies, not the acquisition price. Net income is, therefore, higher.
- There is no recognition of the unrecorded trademark or goodwill. Consequently, prior to the passage of the current business accounting standards, this would have avoided amortization of goodwill.
- The income of Micron is included for the entire year in the year of acquisition, not subsequent to the acquisition date.

The difference in net income between purchase and pooling is due to pooling's reporting of fixed assets at $720,000 (their historical cost to Micron) and the consequent omission of the excess depreciation/amortization expense. This example emphasizes that reporting of income for the combined company at either $367,000 or $375,000 depends on how the acquisition is accounted for. Note that revaluation of assets and liabilities, or absence thereof, is the fundamental difference between pooling and purchase accounting. Pooling potentially understates assets and overstates income in current and future periods. This heightens our concern with potentially inflated earnings from pooling accounting.

For analysis, we summarize likely consequences from pooling accounting for the combined company that markedly distinguish it from purchase accounting:

- Assets are acquired and carried at book value and not the market value of the consideration given. To the extent goodwill or other identifiable intangible assets are purchased, the acquiring company does not report them on its balance sheet.
- Understatement of assets yields understatement in combined company equity.
- Understatement of assets (including inventory, property, plant, equipment, goodwill, and intangibles) yields understatement of expenses (such as cost of goods sold, depreciation, and amortization) and overstatement of income.
- Understatement of assets yields likely overstatement of gains on asset disposition.
- Understatement of equity or overstatement of income yields overstatement in return on investment ratios.
- Income statements and balance sheets of the combined entity are restated for all periods reported. (Under purchase accounting, they are combined and reported *postacquisition*–although pro forma statements showing preacquisition combined results are typically furnished.)

Restating prior periods' statements can lead to a type of double counting similar in effect to an acquirer of a pooled company reporting gains on the sale of undervalued acquired (pooled) assets. Such a case is evidenced in the following.

MURKY POOL

In one acquisition accounted for as a pooling, Applied Materials paid $1.8 billion to take over Etec Systems, a maker of laser gear. Etec's book value was $249 million—meaning that $1.5 billion of the purchase price is not recorded on the books.

ANALYSIS EXCERPT

Blockbuster Entertainment enhanced earnings by means of acquisitions accounted for as poolings. This arguably inflated its stock price—used to consummate additional poolings. Blockbuster acquired its largest franchisee, Video Superstore, for stock. Blockbuster's past sales of video tapes to Video Superstore contributed greatly to Blockbuster's profits. When Video Superstore was pooled, the revenues and profits related to the intercompany video tape sales were eliminated in comparative statements. With these prior sales and profits reported at now lower levels, Blockbuster's growth curve appeared all the more impressive.

One crude adjustment for omitted values in a pooling transaction is to estimate the difference between reported amounts and the market value of assets acquired. This difference would then be amortized against reported income on some reasonable basis to arrive at results comparable to those achieved under purchase accounting. Generally, purchase accounting is designed to recognize the acquisition to which a buyer and seller in a business acquisition agree. As such, it is more relevant for our analysis needs provided we are interested in market values at the date of a business combination rather than the original costs of the seller.

ANALYSIS VIEWPOINT   *. . . YOU ARE THE INVESTMENT BANKER*

Your client, LA Delivery, requests your services in offering common stock to potential shareholders. You are excited about this engagement for, among other reasons, you are offered a 7% fee for services. Prior to accepting the engagement, you perform an analysis of the company and its financial statements. One matter concerns you. You discover LA Delivery recently acquired Riverside Trucking. LA Delivery accounts for this acquisition using pooling accounting. Your concern stems from pooling accounting and its potential to understate assets of Riverside Trucking. This would imply a corresponding overstatement in income due to lower expenses attributed to less depreciation with the understated assets. Because Riverside Trucking's income is pooled with that of LA Delivery's income, the income number and financial ratios based on income are *inflated*. The pooling accounting used by LA Delivery is acceptable practice and is fully disclosed in the financial statements. Do you accept this engagement?

DERIVATIVE SECURITIES

Companies are exposed to different types of *market risks*. These risks arise because the profitability of business operations is sensitive to fluctuations in several areas such as commodity prices, foreign currency exchange rates, and interest rates. To lessen these market risks, companies enter into *hedging transactions*. **Hedges** are contracts that seek to insulate companies from market risks. A hedge is similar in concept to an insurance policy, where the company enters into a contract that ensures a certain payoff regardless of market forces. Financial instruments such as futures, options, and swaps are commonly used as hedges. These financial instruments are called *derivative financial instruments*. A **derivative** is a financial instrument whose value is derived from the value of another asset, class of assets, or economic variable such as a stock, bond, commodity price, interest rate, or currency exchange rate. However, a derivative contracted as a hedge can expose companies to considerable risk. This is either because it is difficult to find a derivative that entirely hedges the risk exposure, because the parties to the derivative contract fail to understand the potential risks from the instrument, or because the *counterparty* (the other entity in the hedge) is not financially strong. Companies also have been known to use derivatives to speculate.

ANALYSIS EXCERPT

We have established strict counterparty credit guidelines and enter into transactions only with financial institutions of investment grade or better. We monitor counterparty exposures daily and any downgrade in credit rating receives immediate review. If a downgrade in the credit rating of a counterparty were to occur, we have provisions requiring collateral in the form of U.S. Government securities for substantially all our transactions.
                                                                              —Coca-Cola Co.

Derivative use has exploded in the past decade. The value of derivative contracts is now in the multitrillion dollar range. This increased use of derivatives, along with their complexity and risk exposure, has led the FASB to place derivative accounting at the forefront of its agenda, yielding a number of rulings in quick succession. The SEC also has called for additional disclosures in annual reports relating to risk exposure from derivatives. The accounting and disclosure requirements for derivatives are prescribed under *SFAS 133*. This section defines and classifies derivatives, describes the accounting and disclosure requirements, and concludes with a discussion of the analysis of derivatives.

Defining a Derivative

A variety of financial instruments are used for hedging activities, including the following:

- **Futures contract**–an agreement between two or more parties to purchase or sell a certain commodity or financial asset at a future date (called *settlement date*) and at a definite price. Futures exist for most commodities and financial assets. It also is possible to buy a futures contract on indexes such as the S&P 500 stock index.
- **Swap contract**–an agreement between two or more parties to exchange future cash flows. It is common for hedging risks, especially interest rate and foreign currency risks. In its basic form, a swap hedges both balance sheet and cash flow exposures. One example is an *interest-rate swap*. A company may wish to convert fixed interest-rate debt to variable rate debt (we discuss Campbell Soup's activities in this regard later in this section). The company works with an intermediary, typically a bank, to find another company with floating rate debt that seeks fixed rate debt. The two companies *swap* interest rates and the bank takes a fee for the transaction. A *foreign currency swap* is similar to an interest-rate swap, except its purpose is to hedge foreign currency risk rather than interest-rate risk.
- **Option contract**–grants a party the right, not the obligation, to execute a transaction. To illustrate, an option to purchase a security at a specific contract price at a future date is likely to be exercised only if the security price on that future date is higher than the contract price. An option also can be either a call or a put. A *call option* is a right to buy a security (or commodity) at a specific price on or before the settlement date. A *put option* is an option to sell a security (or commodity) at a specific price on or before the settlement date.

Accounting for Derivatives

Exhibit 5.6 shows the classification of derivatives for accounting purposes. All derivatives, regardless of their nature or purpose, are recorded at market value on the balance sheet. However, unlike fair value accounting for investment securities, where

■ ■ ■ ■ ■ ■ ■
CREDIT DEFAULT SWAPS
Banks use these derivatives to insure against losses on corporate loans or bonds. The market has grown nearly 50% in recent years, to nearly $2 trillion. Yet the risk does not disappear—it is absorbed by the sellers of protection such as insurance companies (and other banks).

Exhibit 5.6

■ ■ ■ ■ ■ ■ ■

Classification of Derivatives for Accounting

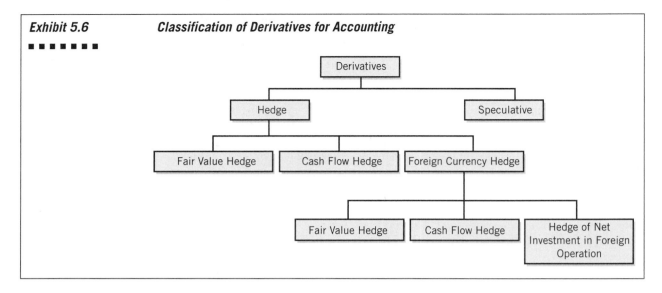

only assets and not corresponding liabilities are marked to market, the accounting for derivatives affects *both* sides of transactions (wherever applicable) by marking to market. This means if a derivative is an effective hedge, the effects of changes in fair values usually should cancel out and have a minimal effect on profits and stockholders' equity. Exhibit 5.7 summarizes the accounting for different derivatives. The accounting for derivatives is different depending on their classification by the company. Derivatives are, first, classified as fair value, cash flow, or foreign currency hedges. Then, the accounting for those derivatives, together with the asset or liability to which the derivatives relates, follows.

Unrealized gains and losses on fair value hedges as well as on the related asset or liability are recorded in income and affect current profitability. As long as the hedge is

Exhibit 5.7

■ ■ ■ ■ ■ ■ ■

Accounting for Derivatives

Derivative	Balance Sheet	Income Statement
Speculative	Derivative recorded at fair value	Unrealized gains and losses included in net income
Fair value hedge	Both derivative and hedged asset and/or liability recorded at fair value	Unrealized gains and losses on both derivative and hedged asset and/or liability included in net income
Cash flow hedge	Derivative recorded at fair value (offset by accumulated comprehensive income)	Unrealized gains and losses on effective portion of derivative are recorded in other comprehensive income until settlement date, after which transferred to net income; unrealized gains and losses on the ineffective portion of derivative are included in net income
Foreign currency fair value hedge	Same as fair value hedge	Same as fair value hedge
Foreign currency cash value hedge	Same as cash flow hedge	Same as cash flow hedge
Foreign currency hedge of net investment in foreign operation	Derivative (and cumulative unrealized gain or loss) recorded at fair value (part of cumulative translation adjustment in accumulated comprehensive income)	Unrealized gains and losses reported in other comprehensive income as part of translation adjustment

Helix Co. owns 5,000 shares of Prima as part of its available-for-sale securities. On October 1, 2005, Helix purchases 5,000 March 2006 put options (50 contracts) of Prima at an exercise price of $50 (market price of Prima on October 1, 2005, is $58) for $5 per option. On December 31, 2005, Prima's stock trades at $53 and its put option is valued at $7 per option. The balance sheet and income statement effects on Helix for the fourth quarter of 2005 follow:

ILLUSTRATION 5.1
■■■■■■■

BALANCE SHEET		
	10/1/05	12/31/05
Investment securities	$290,000	$265,000
Put option	25,000	35,000
Effect on total assets...........	$315,000	$300,000

INCOME STATEMENT	
Unrealized loss on securities............	$(25,000)
Unrealized gain on put option	10,000
Effect on net income	$(15,000)

The net effect in the fourth quarter of 2005 is a charge of $15,000 to net income, which is matched by a corresponding decrease in total asset value. Notice that this put option is not a perfect hedge.

effective, this accounting does not affect profit and stockholders' equity in a material manner because balance sheet and income statement effects are largely offsetting. Illustration 5.1 provides an example of fair value hedge accounting.

Alternatively, unrealized gains and losses arising from cash flow hedges, are reported as part of other comprehensive income (as a component of stockholders' equity and not in current income) until the effective date of the transaction, after which they are transferred to income and are offset by the effect of the transaction itself. (Note that unrealized gains and losses on speculative hedges are reported immediately in income.) Illustration 5.2 provides an example of cash flow hedge accounting.

Ace Co. took a $5 million, five-year floating-interest-rate loan from a bank on January 1, 2005 (interest payable annually on December 31). On January 1, 2006, Ace swaps its future variable interest payments on this loan for fixed 8% interest payments. On December 31, 2006, Ace pays $400,000 (8% of $5 million) on the swap instrument–its interest payment on the original loan would have been $300,000 (6% of $5 million). This means the swap results in an excess annual interest payment of $100,000 for 2006. The present value of this expected excess interest payment from the swap as of December 31, 2006, is $267,300 (computed as $100,000 per year for three additional years discounted at 6% per annum). Ace's balance sheet effects as of December 31, 2005 and 2006, related to this swap are:

ILLUSTRATION 5.2
■■■■■■■

	12/31/05	12/31/06
Fair value of swap liability.....................................	$0	$267,300
Accumulated other comprehensive income	0	(267,300)
Effect on total liabilities and equity......................	$0	$ 0

Ace's income statement effects from the swap for year 2006 are:

Net income effect (interest expense)*	$(100,000)
Other comprehensive income effect (unrealized loss on marketable securities)†	(267,300)

*Realized loss for the year—excess interest payment for 2006.

†Unrealized loss for the year—change in present value of future excess interest payments reflected in accumulated comprehensive income.

Ultimately, the gain or loss on the derivative, together with its cost, is reflected in net income under both fair value and cash flow hedge accounting. The difference in the accounting for the various hedges lies in the timing of the gain or loss recognition, that is, whether the gain or loss is recognized currently in income or deferred in OCI until the transaction is completed.

Disclosures for Derivatives

Companies are required to disclose qualitative and quantitative information about derivatives both in notes to financial statements and elsewhere (usually in the Management's Discussion and Analysis section). The purpose of these disclosures is to inform analysts about potential risks underlying derivative securities.

Qualitative Disclosures

Disclosures generally outline the types of hedging activities conducted by the company and the accounting methods employed. Many companies, for example, use derivatives to hedge interest-rate and foreign currency risks.

Quantitative Disclosures

Campbell Soup also provides quantitative information relating to its interest rate and foreign exchange hedging activities in the MD&A section of the annual report. These disclosures are provided in Exhibit 5.8.

Interest Rate Risk Exposure

Campbell Soup's hedging activities relating to interest rates employ swap agreements in order to maintain a desired relation between fixed- and floating-rate debt. The company indicates that it has entered into $875 million of fixed-to-variable swaps in order to increase the level of variable-rate debt. The fixed-to-variable interest-rate swap lowers the fixed rate debt to $1,674 million ($2,549 million − $875 million) and increases the floating-rate debt to $1,679 million ($804 million + $875 million), or 50% of the total.

Why would Campbell want to increase its percentage of floating-rate debt? Generally speaking, variable-rate debt carries a lower interest rate than fixed-rate debt. So, the company can lower its interest costs with this swap. It is also taking on interest-rate risk. However, this may not be as problematic as it may first appear. The amount of floating-rate debt the company can safely absorb depends on the covariance of EBITDA with interest rates. The higher this covariance, the greater percentage of debt the company can borrow on a floating-rate basis and not incur significant risk to reported profits should interest rates fluctuate in the future. Campbell Soup's target level of floating-rate debt referenced in the MD&A disclosure is determined on this basis.

Foreign Exchange Exposure

Campbell Soup reports that it has foreign exchange risk relating to transactions in non-$US currencies, investments in subsidiaries, and subsidiary debt denominated in foreign currencies. Campbell Soup utilizes cross-currency swaps and forward exchange contracts to hedge its risk on assets and liabilities denominated in foreign currencies, and indicates that it has outstanding $1,004 million of cross-currency swaps. As the $US strengthens (weakens) vis-à-vis foreign currencies, assets (liabilities) that are denominated in those currencies lose (gain) value. These losses (gains) on assets and liabilities are offset via gains (losses) in the foreign currency hedge, thus lessening the variability of its income.

Campbell Soup Market Risk Sensitivity Section—MD&A

Exhibit 5.8

■ ■ ■ ■ ■ ■ ■

Market Risk Sensitivity

The principal market risks to which the company is exposed are changes in commodity prices, interest rates and foreign currency exchange rates. In addition, the company is exposed to equity price changes related to certain employee compensation obligations. The company manages its exposure to changes in interest rates by optimizing the use of variable-rate and fixed-rate debt and by utilizing interest rate swaps in order to maintain its variable-to-total debt ratio within targeted guidelines. International operations, which accounted for approximately 36% of 2004 net sales, are concentrated principally in Australia, Canada, France, Germany, and the United Kingdom. The company manages its foreign currency exposures by borrowing in various foreign currencies and utilizing cross-currency swaps and forward contracts. Swaps and forward contracts are entered into for periods consistent with related underlying exposures and do not constitute positions independent of those exposures. The company does not enter into contracts for speculative purposes and does not use leveraged instruments.

The company principally uses a combination of purchase orders and various short- and long-term supply arrangements in connection with the purchase of raw materials, including certain commodities and agricultural products. The company may also enter into commodity futures contracts, as considered appropriate, to reduce the volatility of price fluctuations for commodities such as corn, cocoa, soybean meal, soybean oil, and wheat. At August 1, 2004, and August 3, 2003, the notional values and unrealized gains or losses on commodity futures contracts held by the company were not material.

The information below summarizes the company's market risks associated with debt obligations and other significant financial instruments as of August 1, 2004. Fair values included herein have been determined based on quoted market prices. The information presented below should be read in conjunction with Notes 16 and 18 to the Consolidated Financial Statements.

The table below presents principal cash flows and related interest rates by fiscal year of maturity for debt obligations. Variable interest rates disclosed represent the weighted-average rates of the portfolio at the period end. Notional amounts and related interest rates of interest rate swaps are presented by fiscal year of maturity. For the swaps, variable rates are the weighted-average forward rates for the term of each contract.

EXPECTED FISCAL YEAR OF MATURITY

(millions)	2005	2006	2007	2008	2009	Thereafter	Total	Fair Value
Debt								
Fixed rate	$ 6	$ 1	$ 606	$ 1	$ 301	$ 1,634	$ 2,549	$2,736
Weighted-average interest rate	2.87%	6.19%	6.20%	6.35%	5.88%	6.23%	6.17%	
Variable rate	$ 804						$ 804	$ 804
Weighted-average interest rate	3.30%						3.30%	
Interest Rate Swaps								
Fixed to variable			$ 200[2]		$175[3]	$ 500[4]	$ 875	$ —
Average pay rate[1]			5.11%		5.50%	5.15%	5.21%	
Average receive rate			6.20%		5.88%	4.95%	5.42%	

[1] Weighted-average pay rates estimated over life of swap by using forward LIBOR interest rates plus applicable spread.

[2] Hedges $100 million of 5.50% notes and $100 million of 6.90% notes due in 2007.

[3] Hedges $175 million of 5.875% notes due in 2009.

[4] Hedges $300 million of 5.00% notes and $200 million of 4.875% notes due in 2013 and 2014, respectively.

As of August 3, 2003, fixed-rate debt of approximately $2.6 billion with an average interest rate of 6.17% and variable-rate debt of approximately $1 billion with an average interest rate of 2.07% were outstanding. As of August 3, 2003, the company had also swapped $475 million of fixed-rate debt to variable. The average rate received on these swaps was 5.24% and the average rate paid was estimated to be 4.89% over the remaining life of the swaps. Additionally, the company had swapped $300 million of floating-rate debt to fixed. The swap matured in 2004.

The company is exposed to foreign exchange risk related to its international operations, including nonfunctional currency intercompany debt and net investments in subsidiaries.

The table below summarizes the cross-currency swaps outstanding as of August 1, 2004, which hedge such exposures. The notional amount of each currency and the related weighted-average forward interest rate are presented in the Cross-Currency Swaps table.

CROSS-CURRENCY SWAPS

(millions)	Expiration	Interest Rate	National Value	Fair Value	(millions)	Expiration	Interest Rate	National Value	Fair Value
Pay variable SEK	2005	4.01%	$ 18	$ (1)	Pay fixed CAD	2009	5.13%	$ 61	$ (5)
Receive variable USD		3.95%			Receive fixed USD		4.22%		
Pay fixed SEK	2005	5.78%	$ 47	$ (15)	Pay fixed GBP	2011	5.97%	$ 200	$ (44)
Receive fixed USD		5.25%			Receive fixed USD		6.08%		
Pay variable Euro	2005	2.71%	$ 137	$ 6	Pay fixed GBP	2011	5.97%	$ 30	$ (1)
Receive variable USD		2.38%			Receive fixed USD		5.01%		
Pay variable Euro	2006	3.06%	$ 32	$ 1	Pay fixed GBP	2011	5.97%	$ 40	$ 1
Receive variable USD		3.12%			Receive fixed USD		4.76%		
Pay variable GBP	2006	6.35%	$ 125	$ (11)	Pay fixed CAD	2014	6.24%	$ 61	$ (5)
Receive variable USD		3.80%			Receive fixed USD		5.66%		
Pay variable CAD	2007	4.89%	$ 53	$ (3)	Total			$1,004	$(154)
Receive variable USD		4.32%							
Pay fixed Euro	2007	5.46%	$ 200	$ (77)					
Receive fixed USD		5.75%							

The cross-currency swap contracts outstanding at August 3, 2003, represented two pay fixed SEK receive fixed USD swaps with national values of $31 million and $47 million, a pay fixed EURO receive fixed USD swap with a notional value of $200 million, and a pay fixed GBP receive fixed USD swap with a notional value of $200 million. The aggregate fair value of these swap contracts was $(97) million as of August 3, 2003.

The company is also exposed to foreign exchange risk as a result of transactions in currencies other than the functional currency of certain subsidiaries, including subsidiary debt. The company utilizes foreign exchange forward purchase and sale contracts to hedge these exposures.

Analysis of Derivatives
Objectives for Using Derivatives

Identifying a company's objectives for use of derivatives is important because risk associated with derivatives is much higher for speculation than for hedging. In the case of hedging, risk does not arise through strategic choice. Instead it arises from problems with the hedging instrument, either because the hedge is imperfect or because of unforeseen events. In the case of speculation, a company is making a strategic choice to bear the risk of market movements. Some companies take on such risk because they are in a position to diversify the risk (in a manner similar to that of an insurance company). More often, managers speculate because of "informed hunches" about market movements. We must realize that many companies (implicitly) speculate even when they suggest derivatives are used for hedging. One reason for this is that when a company hedges specific exposures it does not always hedge overall company risk (see the following discussion).

Risk Exposure and Effectiveness of Hedging Strategies

Once an analyst concludes a company is using derivatives for hedging, the analyst must evaluate the underlying risks for a company, the company's risk management strategy, its hedging activities, and the effectiveness of its hedging operations. Unfortunately, disclosures currently mandated under *SFAS 133* do not always provide meaningful information to conduct a thorough analysis. For example, Campbell Soup uses fixed-to-variable swaps to achieve a targeted percentage of variable-rate debt and takes on interest-rate risk in the process. The company does not, however, provide information to describe the method by which it arrives at this targeted percentage, nor does it describe the level of interest-rate risk that it is undertaking in the process. Likewise, the company does not provide information on the degree of foreign exchange exposure and the extent to which this has been mitigated by the use of cross-currency swaps and forward contracts.

    SFAS 133 was principally designed to provide readers with current values of derivative instruments and the effect of changes in these values on reported profitability. Oftentimes, however, the fair market values are immaterial and the notional amounts do not provide information necessary to evaluate the effectiveness of the company's hedging activities. Companies are not required to quantify, for example, the extent to which exposures have been mitigated via hedging activities which would, if disclosed, provide investors and creditors with a greater understanding of the effectiveness of the hedging strategy.

Transaction-Specific versus Companywide Risk Exposure

Companies hedge specific exposures to transactions, commitments, assets, and/or liabilities. While hedging specific exposures usually reduces overall risk exposure of the company to an underlying economic variable, companies rarely use derivatives with an aim to hedge overall companywide risk exposure. Moreover, accounting rules disallow hedge accounting unless the hedge is specifically linked to an identifiable asset, liability, transaction, or commitment. This raises a broader question: What is the ultimate purpose of hedging? If the purpose of hedging is to reduce overall business risk by reducing the sensitivity of a company's cash flows (or net asset values) to a specific risk factor, then does hedging individual risk exposures achieve this? It probably does, but not necessarily. To see this, Illustration 5.3 shows how hedging a specific risk exposure *increases* a company's overall exposure to this risk.

Dynamics Co. takes government contracts on a cost plus basis. This means Dynamics is allowed to add a profit margin equal to a fixed percentage of its cost. A major allowable element of its cost is interest. Dynamics finances its operations largely with variable interest rate loans. In a move to reduce volatility of its interest payments, Dynamics enters into a floating-for-fixed interest-rate swap. What is the impact of this hedge on Dynamics' overall cash flow volatility? To help answer this, recall that Dynamics' profit margin is a fixed percentage of cost, and that cost includes interest. This implies any increase in interest is automatically hedged through the cost-plus-basis contract, and that its profit margin is *positively* related to interest. Consequently, if Dynamics hedged its variable interest with a variable-for-fixed interest-rate swap, then its cash flow risk exposures to changes in interest rates *increase*.

ILLUSTRATION 5.3

■ ■ ■ ■ ■ ■ ■

The relevant analysis question is whether rational managers enter into derivative contracts that increase overall companywide risk. In some cases the answer is yes. Such actions can arise because of the size and complexity of modern businesses and the difficulty of achieving *goal congruence* across different divisions of a company. For example, the treasury department of a company might be responsible for controlling financing cash flows and then enter into interest-rate swaps to reduce volatility of interest payments even though these interest payments could be negatively correlated with the company's operating cash flows. Similarly, the American and European divisions of a company might hedge currency risk exposures with conflicting aims because each division is attempting to manage its specific risk exposure without considering overall companywide risk. An analyst must evaluate overall companywide effects of derivatives and be aware that hedging specific risk exposures does not necessarily ensure hedging of companywide risk.

Inclusion in Operating or Nonoperating Income

Another analysis issue is whether to view unrealized (and realized) gains and losses on derivative instruments as part of operating or nonoperating income. To the extent derivatives are hedging instruments, then unrealized and realized gains and losses should not be included in operating income. Also, the fair value of such derivatives should be excluded from operating assets. This classification is clear for derivative instruments that hedge interest-rate movements since the underlying exposure (usually interest expense or interest income) is itself a nonoperating item. For hedging of other types of risks, such as foreign currency and commodity price risks, classification is less clear.

■ ■ ■ ■ ■ ■ ■

GLOBAL HEDGE
By locating plants in countries where it does business, so its costs are in the same currency as its revenues, IBM reduces the impact of currency swings without hedging.

Analysis Research

■ ■ ■ ■ ■ ■ ■   **DO DERIVATIVES REDUCE RISK?**

Researchers have investigated managerial motivations for using derivatives, along with the impacts of derivative use, for company risk. While there is mixed evidence about whether derivatives are used for hedging or speculative purposes, the preponderance of evidence suggests that managers use derivatives to hedge overall companywide risk. Companies that invest in derivatives reveal a marked decline in risk as reflected in reduced stock returns' volatility. The reduction in risk exposure to the underlying risk type (such as interest-rate exposure and foreign currency exposure) is even more striking. Overall, evidence shows that, on average, managers use derivatives for hedging specific risk exposures that ultimately reduce overall companywide risk.

That is, gains and losses (and fair values) from derivatives are nonoperating when (1) hedging activities are not a central part of a company's operations and (2) including effects of hedging in operating income conceals the underlying volatility in operating income or cash flows. However, when a company offers risk management services as a central part of its operations (as many financial institutions do), we must view all speculative gains and losses (and fair values) as part of operating income (and operating assets or liabilities).

········THE FAIR VALUE OPTION

The FASB has recently made significant strides toward reporting all financial assets and liabilities on a fair value basis. *SFAS 157* provides a unified framework for fair value accounting. *SFAS 159* provides companies with the option of selectively reporting financial assets and liabilities at fair value. Both standards prescribe detailed note disclosures. We introduced the concept of fair value in Chapter 2 and provided a conceptual overview of fair value accounting. In this section we will discuss the recent fair value reporting and disclosure requirements for financial assets and liabilities.

Fair Value Reporting Requirements
Assets and Liabilities Eligible for the Fair Value Option

SFAS 159 allows companies to report a wide range of financial assets and liabilities on fair value basis. These include investments in debt and equity securities, financial instruments, derivatives, and various types of financial obligations. However, the following are not allowed to be reported on fair value basis under *SFAS 159* (even though they may appear to be in the nature of financial assets or obligations): (1) investment in subsidiaries that need to be consolidated, (2) postretirement benefit assets and obligations, (3) lease assets and obligations, (4) certain types of insurance contracts, (5) loan commitments, and (6) equity method investments under certain conditions.

Selective Application

Companies are allowed substantial flexibility to selectively apply the fair value option to individual assets or liabilities. The flexibility is allowed even within a specific asset class. For example, a company may apply the fair value option to certain available-for-sale securities but not for others. However, once the fair value option is applied to a particular asset (or liability), then it cannot be reversed.

Reporting Requirements

If a company chooses the fair value option for an asset or liability, then the following reporting rules apply:

- The carrying amount of the asset (or liability) in the balance sheet will always be at its fair value on the measurement date.
- All changes in the fair value of the asset (or liability), including unrealized gain and losses, will be included in net income. In other words, assets and liabilities subject to the fair value option will be accounted for in similar manner to trading securities.
- The manner in which the unrealized gain/loss will be included is not specified. Companies may choose to report the unrealized gain/loss portion differently from cash flow components (such as interest, dividends, or realized gain/loss) or together.

Fair Value Disclosures

Exhibit 5.9 provides details from the fair value footnote of Wells Fargo Bank's September 2007 10Q. We also report the abbreviated balance sheet as on September 30, 2007, and the income statement for the nine-month period ending September 2007. Wells Fargo reports that it elected to exercise the fair value option for (1) prime residential mortgages

---

Fair Value Disclosures—Wells Fargo Bank   **Exhibit 5.9**
■ ■ ■ ■ ■ ■ ■

Abridged Financial Statements for the Nine Months Ended September 30, 2007

BALANCE SHEET		INCOME STATEMENT	
	$ million		**$ million**
Assets		Interest income	$25,935
Cash and short-term investments	$ 16,746	Interest expense	10,449
Trading assets	7,298	Provision for credit losses	2,327
Securities available for sale	57,440	Net interest income after provision	13,159
Mortgages held for sale ($26,714 at fair value)	29,699	Noninterest income	
Loans held for sale	1,011	Fees, service charges, leases	7,872
Loans net of allowance for losses	359,093	Mortgage banking	2,302
Mortgage servicing rights ($18,223 at fair value)	18,683	Insurance	1,160
Premises and equipment	5,002	Net gains on available for sale investments	661
Goodwill	12,018	Other	1,704
Other assets	41,737		13,699
	$548,727	Administrative expenses	16,754
Liabilities and Stockholders' Equity		Income before tax	10,104
Deposits	$334,956	Tax provision	3,298
Short-term borrowing	41,729	**Net income**	**$ 6,806**
Long term debt	95,592	Other comprehensive income:	
Other liabilities	28,712	Foreign currency translation	$ 24
	500,989	Pensions adjustment	17
Stockholders' equity	47,738	Unrealized loss on available for sale securities	(226)
	$548,727	Unrealized gains on derivative securities	174
		Comprehensive income	**$ 6,795**

Note 16. Fair Value of Assets and Liabilities

Effective January 1, 2007, upon adoption of *SFAS 159*, The Fair Value Option for Financial Assets and Financial Liabilities, including an amendment of FASB Statement No. 115, we elected to measure mortgages held for sale (MHFS) at fair value prospectively for new prime residential MHFS originations for which an active secondary market and readily available market prices currently exist to reliably support fair value pricing models used for these loans. We also elected to remeasure at fair value certain of our other interests held related to residential loan sales and securitizations. We believe the election for MHFS and other interests held (which are now hedged with free-standing derivatives (economic hedges) along with our MSRs) will reduce certain timing differences and better match changes in the value of these assets with changes in the value of derivatives used as economic hedges for these assets. There was no transition adjustment required upon adoption of *SFAS 159* for MHFS because we continued to account for MHFS originated prior to 2007 at the lower of cost or market value. Upon adoption of *SFAS 159*, we were also required to adopt *SFAS 157*, Fair Value Measurements. In addition, we elected to measure mortgage servicing rights (MSRs) at fair value effective January 1, 2006, upon adoption of *SFAS 156*, Accounting for Servicing of Financial Assets.

(continued)

Fair Value Disclosures—Wells Fargo Bank (concluded) ■■■■■■■■

The following table presents the balances of assets and liabilities measured at fair value on a recurring basis.

(in millions)	SEPTEMBER 30, 2007			
	Total	Level 1	Level 2	Level 3
Trading assets	$ 7,298	$ 1,403	$ 5,385	$ 510
Securities available for sale	57,440	32,734	20,969	3,737
Mortgages held for sale	26,714	—	26,636	78
Mortgage servicing rights (residential)	18,223	—	—	18,223
Other assets	1,060	791	249	20
Total	$110,735	$ 34,928	$53,239	$22,568
Other liabilities	$ (3,079)	$(1,936)	$ (822)	$ (321)

The changes in Level 3 assets and liabilities measured at fair value on a recurring basis are summarized as follows:

(in millions)	Trading Assets (excluding derivatives)	Securities Available for Sale	Mortgages Held for Sale	Mortgage Servicing Rights (residential)	Net Derivative Assets and Liabilities	Other Liabilities (excluding derivatives)
Nine months ended September 30, 2007						
Balance, beginning of period	$360	$3,447	$—	$17,591	$(68)	$(282)
Total net losses for the period included in:						
Net income	(31)	—	(1)	(951)	(259)	(47)
Other comprehensive income	—	(8)	—	—	—	—
Purchases, sales, issuances and settlements, net	181	298	16	1,583	297	54
Net transfers into/out of Level 3	—	—	63	—	4	—
Balance, end of period	$510	$3,737	$78	$18,223	$(26)	$(275)
Net unrealized gains (losses) included in net income for the period relating to assets and liabilities held at September 30, 2007 (1)	$ 15	$ —	$ (1)	$1,341	$(22)	$ (48)

The assets accounted for under *SFAS 159* are initially measured at fair value. Gains and losses from initial measurement and subsequent changes in fair value are recognized in earnings. The changes in fair values related to initial measurement and subsequent changes in fair value that are included in current period earnings for the nine months ended September 30, 2007, are as follows: (1) for mortgages held for sale (MHFS), $477 million gain included in mortgage banking noninterest income; and (2) for other interests held, $32 million loss included in other noninterest income.

held for resale (MHFS) and (2) certain interest related to residential loan sales and securitization. In the adjacent table, Wells Fargo reports details of various assets and liabilities that have been recorded at fair value on the balance sheet. Not all of them are those for which the fair value option has been exercised. For example, residential mortgage servicing rights (MSR) are recorded at fair value under an earlier standard *(SFAS 156)* that Wells Fargo adopted in the previous year. More importantly, trading and available-for-sale investment securities are recorded at fair value on the balance sheet under *SFAS 115*. Has Wells Fargo exercised the fair value option for investment securities? The income statement shows that Wells Fargo reports an unrealized loss of $226 million on available-for-sale as part of other comprehensive income. This reveals that Wells Fargo has not adopted the fair value option for these investments; under the fair value option, the unrealized loss would be included in net income. Also, when we examine the balance sheet, we see that Wells Fargo has not adopted the fair value option for all mortgages held for resale (MHFS) and mortgage servicing rights (MSR): only $26.714 billion of the $29.699 billion MHFS and $18.233 billion of the $18.683 billion MSR are reported at fair value. Overall, this suggests that Wells Fargo has exercised considerable discretion in deciding what financial assets to report at fair value.

Wells Fargo also provides a breakup of the fair values based on the types of inputs used in determining their values: level 1 (based on quoted prices for the exact security being valued); level 2 (based on quoted prices for similar securities or from inactive markets); and level 3 (based on unobservable inputs using the company's assumptions). Such information provides an assessment of the reliability of Wells Fargo's fair value measurements. Of the total $110.735 billion of assets recorded at fair value, $34.928 billion (32%) use level 1, $53.239 billion (48%) use level 2, and $22.568 billion (20%) use level 3 inputs. The lion's share of the level 3 inputs relate to the mortgage servicing rights (MSR), which are valued using only level 3 inputs. Because level 3 inputs are unreliable, the next table provides details of changes in their fair values, including how much of this change is recorded in net income. For mortgage servicing rights, the fair value increased by $632 million (from $17,591 million to $18,223 million). This increase arises because of net purchases of $1,583 million and a $951 million loss in value that was included in net income. Further information reveals that Wells Fargo recorded an unrealized gain of $1,341 million on these securities that was included in net income.

Finally, Wells Fargo reveals that it recorded a net gain of $445 million in net income for all financial assets for which it exercised the fair value option—a gain of $477 million on mortgages held for sale (MHFS) and a $32 million loss for other interests—during the nine months ended September 2007.

Analysis Implications
Reliability of Fair Value Measurements

An important analysis task is evaluating the reliability of fair value measurements and their effect on the financial statements. We note that only 32% of Wells Fargo's fair value measures use level 1 inputs, while 20% use level 3 inputs. Additionally, we see that most of the level 1 inputs pertain to its portfolio of investment securities (for which Wells Fargo chose not to elect the fair value option). Once investment securities are excluded, less than 2% of Wells Fargo's fair value measures use level 1 inputs, and a highly significant 40% use level 3 inputs. Such a significant use of level 3 inputs casts doubts about the reliability of Wells Fargo's fair value estimates and is clearly cause for caution.

The lion's share of the level 3 inputs pertain to mortgage servicing rights (MSR). We also note that a $951 million loss pertaining to MSR was included in net income during the nine months ending September 2007. Further information (from Note 15 in Wells Fargo's 10Q, not reported in the exhibit) suggests that this loss comprises of two components: a $1,341 million unrealized gain arising from changes in assumptions used to determine fair value of the MSRs and $2,292 million loss arising from a provision for anticipated losses arising from the mortgage crisis that hit the U.S. economy during this period. Changes in fair values arising from changes in underlying assumptions must be viewed with utmost skepticism. In this case, we cannot rule out the possibility that the assumptions changes are an attempt on the part of Wells Fargo to soften the unfavorable effects of the mortgage crisis on net income.

Opportunistic Adoption of SFAS 159

SFAS 159 allows considerable discretion to companies in choosing the specific assets or liabilities for which they exercise the fair value option. An analyst needs to verify whether the fair value election has been opportunistic with an aim to window dressing the financial statements. Wells Fargo has chosen to exercise the fair value option for prime residential mortgages held for resale (MHFS) and certain interest related to residential loan sales and securitization. What is the effect of Wells Fargo's fair value choices on its financial statements? The net gain included in net income (for the nine months ending September 2007) because of the fair value election under *SFAS 159* is $445 million. However, an unrealized loss of $226 million on available-for-sale securities was not included in net income because the company chose not to elect the fair value option for investment securities, even though the fair value estimates of investment securities are more reliable, on average, than those for which the fair value option was exercised. This evidence suggests that Wells Fargo was opportunistic in its choice of assets to use the fair value option.

Additionally, a gain of $1,341 million was included in income because of changes in fair value of mortgage servicing rights (MSR) arising from assumption changes, for which Wells Fargo chose to exercise the fair value option under *SFAS 156*. (Note that the loss provision of $2,292 relating to MSR would have been made in the absence of fair value accounting.) As we note earlier, unrealized gains (or losses) arising from assumption changes are highly unreliable and should be analyzed with care.

Overall, the evidence suggests that Wells Fargo has been significantly managing its net income upward for the nine months ended September 2007 through its use of fair value accounting—both through the selective application the fair value option and through changes in measurement assumptions.

.....APPENDIX 5A INTERNATIONAL ACTIVITIES

CONSOLIDATION OF FOREIGN SUBSIDIARIES

Many non-U.S. subsidiaries conduct business activities in their local currencies. That is, sales are made, assets are purchased, and debts are created and paid in the local currency. Their financial statements, therefore, are reported in the local currency. Before a non-U.S. subsidiary can be consolidated with its U.S. parent, however, the local-currency-denominated financial statements must be converted into U.S. dollars.

Current accounting standards prescribe two translation approaches, the **current rate method** (most commonly used) and the **temporal method.** If the subsidiary is relatively independent, the current rate method is employed. If the subsidiary is closely integrated with the parent, the temporal method is employed. One final note, subsidiaries located in highly inflationary economies (cumulative three-year inflation rates in excess of 100%) are required to employ the temporal method.

There are important implications of the choice of the translation method. If the current rate method is employed, **translation adjustments** are reported in other comprehensive income (OCI) and do not affect current income. If the temporal method is employed, however, these adjustments are reported as **remeasurement** gains and losses in the income statement. The majority of multinational corporations employ the current rate method and, thereby, defer these translation gains and losses for as long as they continue to own the foreign subsidiary.

Translation of financial statements involves four exchange rates:

1. **Historical**–the exchange rate in effect when the transaction originally occurred.
2. **Current**–the exchange rate in effect at the end of the accounting period.
3. **Specific**–the exchange rate in effect when specific transactions occur.
4. **Weighted-average**–the weighted-average exchange rate in effect during the accounting period.

A comparison of the current and temporal methods is illustrated by the table below.

	EXCHANGE RATE USED FOR TRANSLATION	
Account	Current Rate Method	Temporal Method
Cash and securities	Current	Current
Inventory	Current	Historical
PP&E and intangibles	Current	Historical
Current liabilities	Current	Current
Long-term liabilities	Current	Current
Capital stock	Historical	Historical
Retained earnings	Derived	Derived
Dividends	Specific	Specific
Revenues	Average	Average
Expenses	Average	Average
COGS	Average	Historical
Depreciation/amortization	Average	Historical
Translation adjustment	Other comprehensive income	
Remeasurement gains (losses)		Income statement

Under the current method, all assets and liabilities are translated at the current rate, or spot rate, in effect as of the statement date. Stockholders' equity accounts are translated at historical rates with dividends translated at the specific rate in effect when the dividends are declared. Income statement items that are deemed to have occurred evenly throughout the period are translated at the weighted-average exchange rate, with specific exchange rates for nonrecurring items like gains or losses on the sale of assets. Finally, the cumulative translation adjustment is reported in other comprehensive income and does not affect current profitability. It is, in effect, deferred until the foreign subsidiary is sold.

The temporal method requires *monetary* assets and liabilities (cash, receivables, and short-term and long-term debt) to be translated at the current exchange rate. All other assets and stockholders' equity accounts are translated at the historical exchange rate, with dividends translated at the specific date the dividends are declared. Revenues and expenses occurring evenly throughout the period are translated at the weighted-average exchange rate, but expenses relating to assets translated at historical exchange rates are reported at those historical exchange rates. For example, depreciation is computed based on the originally capitalized cost of the fixed asset and is, therefore, a function of the exchange rate in effect when the asset was acquired. Likewise, because inventories are translated at the historical rates in effect when acquired, cost of goods sold is computed using those capitalized costs and the cost flow assumption (e.g., LIFO/FIFO) used by the company. Finally, remeasurement gains and losses as a result of the translation process are reflected in current income and, thereby, affect the current profitability of the company.

Accounting for Foreign Currency Translation

We now illustrate the mechanics of foreign currency translation under the current method as it is the most commonly used. BritCo, a wholly owned British subsidiary of DollarCo, incorporates when the exchange rate is £1 = $1.10. No capital stock changes have occurred since incorporation. The trial balance of BritCo at December 31, Year 6, expressed in units is reproduced in Step (5) as follows:

Additional Information for Translation:

1. BritCo's trial balance is adjusted to conform to DollarCo's accounting principles. The pound (£) is the functional currency of BritCo.
2. The Cumulative Foreign Exchange Translation Adjustment account at December 31, Year 5, is $30,000 (credit).
3. The dollar balance of Retained Earnings at December 31, Year 5, is $60,000.
4. Exchange rates are as follows:

> January 1, Year 6 .... £1 = $1.20
> December 31, Year 6 ...... £1 = $1.40
> Average for Year 6 .... £1 = $1.30

5. All accounts receivable, payables, and noncurrent liability amounts are denominated in the local currency. BritCo's December 31, Year 6, trial balance is:

	Debit	Credit
Cash	£ 100,000	
Accounts receivable	300,000	
Inventories, at cost	500,000	
Prepaid expenses	25,000	
Property, plant, and equipment (net)	1,000,000	
Long-term note receivable	75,000	
Accounts payable		£ 500,000
Current portion of long-term debt		100,000
Long-term debt		900,000
Capital stock		300,000
Retained earnings, January 1, Year 6		50,000
Sales		5,000,000
Cost of sales	4,000,000	
Depreciation	300,000	
Other expenses	550,000	
Totals	£6,850,000	£6,850,000

6. Sales, purchases, and all operating expenses occur evenly throughout the year. Accordingly, use of the average exchange rate produces results as if each individual

month's revenues and expenses are translated using the rate in effect during each
month. In this case, cost of goods sold is also convertible by use of the average rate.
7. Income tax consequences, if any, are ignored in this illustration.

Exhibit 5A.1 reports the translation of the trial balance into both a balance sheet and
income statement. The balance sheet highlights the reporting of translation adjustments

Exhibit 5A.1

■ ■ ■ ■ ■ ■ ■

BRITCO
Translated Balance Sheet and Income Statement
Year Ended December 31, Year 6

	£	Exchange Rate	Translation Code or Explanation*	$US
Balance Sheet				
Cash	100,000	1.4	C	140,000
Accounts receivable	300,000	1.4	C	420,000
Inventories, at cost	500,000	1.4	C	700,000
Prepaid expenses	25,000	1.4	C	35,000
Property, plant, and equipment (net)	1,000,000	1.4	C	1,400,000
Long-term note receivable	75,000	1.4	C	105,000
Total assets...	2,000,000			2,800,000
Accounts payable...................................	500,000	1.4	C	700,000
Current portion of long-term debt	100,000	1.4	C	140,000
Long-term debt	900,000	1.4	C	1,260,000
Total liabilities	1,500,000			2,100,000
Capital stock..	300,000	1.1	H	330,000
Retained earnings:				
Balance, 1/1/Year 6	50,000		B	60,000
Current year net income.........................	150,000		F	195,000
Balance, 12/31/Year 6	200,000			255,000
Cumulative foreign exchange translation adjustment:				
Balance, 1/1/Year 6			B	30,000
Current year translation adjustment.......			G	85,000
Balance, 12/31/Year 6				115,000
Total stockholders' equity.......................	500,000			700,000
Total liabilities and equity......................	2,000,000			2,800,000
Income Statement				
Sales...	5,000,000	1.3	A	6,500,000
Cost of sales	(4,000,000)	1.3	A	(5,200,000)
Depreciation...	(300,000)	1.3	A	(390,000)
Other expenses.......................................	(550,000)	1.3	A	(715,000)
Net income...	150,000			195,000

*Translation code or explanation:

C = Current rate.   B = Balance in U.S. dollars at the beginning of the period.
H = Historical rate.   F = Per income statement.
A = Average rate.   G = Amount needed to balance the financial statements.

as a separate component of shareholders' equity–usually this is simply reported in a more general component titled Accumulated Other Comprehensive Income (Loss). A review of the translated financial statements of BritCo reveals the following:

1. The company converts all income statement items using the average rate of exchange during the year.
2. All assets and liabilities are translated at the current rate of exchange as of the balance sheet date. Capital stock is translated at the historical rate. If all of a foreign entity's assets and liabilities are measured in its functional currency and are translated at the current exchange rate, then the net accounting effect of a change in the exchange rate is the effect on the entity's net assets. This accounting result is compatible with the concept of economic hedging, which is the basis of the net investment view. That is, no gains or losses arise from hedged assets and liabilities, and the dollar equivalent of the unhedged net investment increases or decreases as the functional currency strengthens or weakens.
3. Notice that after the translated net income for Year 6 of $195,000 is added to the retained earnings in the balance sheet, a translation adjustment of $85,000 must be inserted to balance the statement. When this current year translation adjustment (credit) of $85,000 is added to the $30,000 beginning credit balance of the Cumulative Foreign Exchange Translation Adjustment account, the ending balance equals a credit of $115,000. This is the beginning balance of this equity account for January 1, Year 7.

Analysis of Translation Gain or Loss

Use of the current rate translation yields a balancing figure of $85,000 in the translated balance sheet. This translation gain of $85,000 for BritCo is added to the Cumulative Foreign Exchange Translation Adjustment account in equity. Exchange rate changes do not affect accounts translated at historical rates because such accounts are assigned the dollar amount prevailing at their origination. Accordingly, exchange gains and losses arise from translation of assets and liabilities at the current rate. Because companies translate equity accounts at historical rates, it is the remaining net assets translated at current rates that are exposed to risk of changes in exchange rates. If the dollar strengthens against the foreign currency, the dollar value of foreign net assets declines and yields exchange losses. If the dollar weakens against the foreign currency, the dollar value of foreign net assets increases and yields exchange gains–this is the case with BritCo in Year 6.

The $85,000 translation gain for BritCo, that we computed indirectly, is also computable directly. We start with the beginning net asset position of £350,000 (capital stock of £300,000 + retained earnings of £50,000). Then we multiply the beginning balance of net assets by the change in exchange rate between the beginning and end of the year–in our illustration, this is a strengthening of $0.20 ($1.40 − $1.20) per pound. Because net assets increase in Year 6, the entire beginning balance is exposed to the change in exchange rate for the year, yielding a gain of $70,000 for this part of net assets (computed as £350,000 × $0.20). The second part involves the *change* in net assets during the year. Here we multiply the change by the difference between the year-end rate ($1.40) and the rate prevailing at the date or dates when change(s) occur. We know in the BritCo example that the change occurs due to income earned. Revenue and expense items are translated at the average exchange rate ($1.30). Therefore, we multiply the increase in net assets by the difference between the year-end rate and the average rate ($1.40 − $1.30) or $0.10. We can directly compute the translation gain as follows:

Translation gain on beginning net assets (£350,000 × [$1.40 − $1.20])........................	$70,000
Translation gain on increase in net assets for Year 6 (£150,000 × [$1.40 − $1.30])	15,000
Total translation gain...	$85,000

When the cause of a change in net assets for the year is due to reasons other than those related to operations, the company needs to identify the reasons along with the rate of exchange for translation. These adjustments enter the computation of translation gain or loss consistent with the above procedures.

Accounting for Foreign Investment by Parent Company

When the parent company accounts for the investment in a foreign subsidiary by using the equity method, the parent records its proportionate share of the translation adjustment. In our illustration, DollarCo makes the following entries in Year 6 (in $US):

Investment in BritCo..	195,000	
Equity in Earnings of Subsidiary...		195,000
To record equity in BritCo's earnings (£150,000 × 1.3).		
Investment in BritCo..	85,000	
Translation Adjustment..		85,000
To record current year translation adjustment.		

If DollarCo sells its investment in BritCo on January 1, Year 7, then DollarCo: (1) records a gain or loss on the difference between the proceeds of the sale and the reported (book) value of the investment and (2) transfers the Cumulative Foreign Exchange Translation Adjustment account, with a credit balance of $115,000, to income.

ANALYSIS IMPLICATIONS OF FOREIGN CURRENCY TRANSLATION

Accounting for foreign currency translation is controversial, partly due to the difficulty and complexity of translation. Our analysis requires an understanding of both the economic underpinnings and the accounting mechanics to evaluate and predict effects of currency rate changes on a company's financial position.

The temporal method of translation is most faithful to and consistent with the historical cost accounting model. Under this method, nonmonetary items like property, plant, equipment, and inventories are stated at translated dollar amounts at date of acquisition. Similarly, companies translate depreciation and cost of goods sold on the basis of these historical-dollar costs. Because fluctuations in exchange rates do not affect the reported amounts of these nonmonetary assets, exposure to balance sheet translation gains and losses is measured by the excess (or deficit) of monetary assets over monetary liabilities (which are translated at current rates). For example, under the temporal method, if a foreign subsidiary has an excess of monetary liabilities over monetary assets *(high debt position)*, then the following relations prevail:

Dollar Versus Local Currency	Balance Sheet Translation Effect
Dollar strengthens	Gain
Dollar weakens	Loss

If a foreign subsidiary has an excess of monetary assets over monetary liabilities *(high equity position)*, then the following relations ensue:

Dollar Versus Local Currency	Balance Sheet Translation Effect
Dollar strengthens	Loss
Dollar weakens	Gain

Companies generally do not like translation gains and losses subjected to variation in economic environments as with the temporal method. They dislike even more the recording of these unpredictable gains and losses in net income, yielding earnings volatility. Admittedly, company criticism is not as strong when the translation process results in gains rather than losses.

Current practice does *not* follow the temporal method *except* in two cases:

1. When a foreign entity is merely an extension of the parent.
2. When hyperinflation causes translation of nonmonetary assets to unrealistically low reported values because of using the current rate. The foreign currency thus loses its usefulness and a more stable currency is used.

Current practice generally uses the current method. This approach selectively introduces current value accounting. It also allows gains and losses to bypass the net income statement (reported, instead, in comprehensive income). This removes from current operations certain risk effects of international activities and the risks of changes in exchange rates. Yet, while insulating income from balance sheet translation gains and losses, the current rate method introduces a different translation exposure. Namely, while translation exposure for the temporal method is measured by the difference between monetary assets and monetary liabilities, the translation exposure for the functional currency approach is measured by the *size of the net investment*. This is because all balance sheet items, except equity, are translated at the current rate. We illustrate this as follows.

SwissCo, a subsidiary of AmerCo, started operations on January 1, Year 1, with a balance sheet in euros (€) as follows:

	€		€
Assets		**Liabilities and Equity**	
Cash	100	Accounts payable	90
Receivables	120	Capital stock	360
Inventory	90		
Fixed assets	140		
Total assets	450	Total liabilities and equity	450

The income statement for the year ended December 31, Year 1, is:

	€
Sales	3,000
Cost of sales (including depreciation of SF 20)	(1,600)
Other expenses	(800)
Net income	600

The December 31, Year 1, balance sheet is:

Assets	€	Liabilities and Equity	€
Cash	420	Accounts payable	180
Receivables	330	Capital stock	360
Inventory	270	Retained earnings	600
Fixed assets (net)	120		
Total assets	1,140	Total liabilities and equity	1,140

The following exchange rates are applicable:

January 1, Year 1 .... $1 = €2.0
December 31, Year 1 .... $1 = €3.0
Year 1 average .... $1 = €2.5

The beginning and ending balance sheets are translated into dollars as follows:

	JANUARY 1, YEAR 1			DECEMBER 31, YEAR 1		
	€	Conversion	$	€	Conversion	$
Assets						
Cash	100	÷2.0	50	420	÷3.0	140
Receivables	120	÷2.0	60	330	÷3.0	110
Inventory	90	÷2.0	45	270	÷3.0	90
Fixed assets (net)	140	÷2.0	70	120	÷3.0	40
Total assets	450		225	1,140		380
Liabilities and Equity						
Accounts payable	90	÷2.0	45	180	÷3.0	60
Capital stock	360	÷2.0	180	360	÷2.0	180
Retained earnings	—		—	600	*	240
Translation adjustment						(100)
Total liabilities and equity	450		225	1,140		380

*Per income statement—since each *individual income statement item is translated at the average rate, net income in dollars is* €600 ÷ 2.5 = $240.

The translation adjustment account (a component of equity as reported in comprehensive income) is independently calculated as:

	€	$
Total equity (equals net assets):		
In € at December 31, Year 1	€960	
Converted into dollars at year-end rate (÷ 3.0)		$ 320
Less:		
Capital stock at December 31, Year 1,		
per converted balance sheet (in dollars)		(180)
Retained earnings balance at December 31, Year 1,		
per converted balance sheet (in dollars)		(240)
Translation adjustment—loss		$(100)

We can derive several analysis insights from this illustration. First, the translation adjustment (loss of $100 in Year 1) is determined from the net investment in SwissCo at end of Year 1 (€960) multiplied by the change in exchange rates. The exchange rate declines from €2.0 per dollar for capital stock, and from €2.5 per dollar for retained earnings, to the year-end exchange rate of €3.0 per dollar. Consequently, the € investment expressed in dollars suffers a loss of $100. This is intuitive–when an investment is expressed in a foreign currency and that currency weakens in relation to the dollar, then the investment value (in dollars) declines. The reverse occurs if that currency strengthens.

Second, under the current rate method, currency translation affects equity (but not income). As such, this approach affects, among other ratios, the debt-to-equity ratio (potentially endangering debt covenants) and book value per share for the translated balance sheet (but not for the foreign currency balance sheet). Because equity capital represents the measure of exposure to balance sheet translation gain or loss under this approach, that exposure is potentially more substantial than under the temporal method, especially with a subsidiary financed with low debt and high equity. Our analysis can estimate the translation adjustment impact by multiplying year-end equity by the estimated change in the period-to-period rate of exchange.

Third, we can examine the effect of a change in exchange rates on the translation of the income statement. If we assume in Year 2 that SwissCo reports the same income but the € further *weakens* to €3.5 (average for year) per dollar, then the translated income totals €600 ÷ 3.5 = $171, or a decline of $69 from the Year 1 level of $240. This loss would be reflected in the translated income statement. In contrast, if the € *strengthens* to €2.0 per dollar (average for year), the translated income totals €600 ÷ 2.0 = $300, or a gain of $60 from the Year 1 level of $240. This gain is reflected in net income and recognizes that income earned in € is worth more dollars. Under the current rate method, translated income varies directly with changes in exchange rates. This makes our estimation of the income statement translation effect easier.

Our analysis must be aware that net income also includes the results of completed foreign exchange transactions. Further, any gain or loss on translation of a current payable by the subsidiary to the parent (which is not of a long-term nature) flows through net income.

A substantial drop in the dollar relative to many important currencies has the effect of increasing the reported net income of consolidated foreign subsidiaries. It also often increases equity, in certain cases by substantial amounts. This effect lowers measures such as return on equity. Should the dollar recover its value, the results are the opposite and yield lower reported net income.

While current practice yields smaller fluctuations in net income relative to the fluctuations in exchange rates, it yields substantial changes in equity because of changes in the cumulative translation adjustment (CTA) account. For companies with a large equity base, these changes are arguably insignificant. But for companies with a small equity base these changes, which further reduce equity, yield potentially serious effects on debt-to-equity and other ratios. This can put a company at risk of violating its debt covenants or other accounting-based restrictions. Exposure to changes in the CTA depends on the degree of exposure in foreign subsidiary net assets to changes in exchange rates. Companies can reduce this exposure by reducing the net assets of their foreign subsidiaries. This can be achieved by withdrawing foreign investment through dividends or by substituting foreign debt for equity. We must recognize that an increasing debit balance in the CTA is often symptomatic of a failure to manage properly the foreign exchange exposure. This can result from investments denominated in persistently weak currencies, among other reasons.

.....APPENDIX 5B INVESTMENT RETURN ANALYSIS

ADJUSTMENTS TO FINANCIAL STATEMENTS

What adjustments due to investment securities must we make when determining economic income and permanent income? Recall that economic income includes all changes to shareholder wealth. This means all components of investing income (interest, dividends, and realized and unrealized gains and losses) for all classes of investment securities must be included when determining economic income. Because comprehensive income includes unrealized gains and losses only from trading and available-for-sale securities, we must adjust comprehensive income to include unrealized gains and losses from held-to-maturity securities.[1] Unrealized gains and losses on held-to-maturity securities are disclosed in the notes.

Determining permanent income is more involved and is computed as follows:

$$\text{Permanent investment income} = \text{Expected ROI} \times (\text{Beginning fair value of investment} + \text{Ending fair value of investment})/2$$

The expected return on investment (ROI) for the portfolio of securities held by the company is computed as follows: Expected ROI = Required ROI + Historical deviation of the Realized ROI less the Required ROI. Required ROI is the weighted-average cost of capital for the company's investment portfolio given its risk and asset composition. The historical deviation component reflects the performance of the company's investments. It is important to consider a sufficiently long history to purge transitory effects from this component (we discuss the computation of realized ROI in the next section).

---

[1] Some argue that including unrealized gains and losses from held-to-maturity securities in income is incorrect because the company does not intend to sell these securities till maturity and, thus, fluctuations in market values of those securities are of no consequence. This argument is erroneous. It is true that *future realizations* from a security that is not expected to be sold will remain constant. However, the *present value* of these future realizations will change with changes in expected interest rates, which is what is reflected in the securities' current market prices.

Next, what adjustments should be made to the balance sheet? Trading and available-for-sale securities are presently reported at fair value, while held-to-maturity securities are reported at cost. For analysis purposes, we want all investment securities (including held-to-maturity) reported at fair value in the balance sheet. Accordingly, we want to adjust held-to-maturity securities to fair value. Remember that offsetting adjustments must be made to equity to reflect any adjustments to the fair value.

EVALUATING INVESTMENT PERFORMANCE

Evaluating investment performance is an important analysis task. This task is especially important for companies where investment income constitutes a large portion of their income. For example, investment performance is one of the most important factors for success with banks, insurance companies, and other financial institutions. The performance of investment securities is evaluated using a return on investment (ROI) metric, which we loosely define as the realized investment income for the period divided by the average investment base:

$$\text{Realized ROI} = \frac{\text{Investment income}}{(\text{Beginning fair value of investment} + \text{Ending fair value of investment})/2}$$

The investment income, or numerator, is made up of three parts: Interest (and dividend) income + Realized gains and losses + Unrealized gains and losses. Note that ROI for investment securities is based on fair values, both for determining investment income (by including unrealized gains and losses) and for measuring average investment base (by using fair values of investments). This means evaluation of investment performance is not limited to analysis of only realized amounts.

We compute Coca-Cola's return on investment for Year 9 in Exhibit 5B.1. First, we determine Coca-Cola's investment income as follows: interest and dividend income as

Exhibit 5B.1	*Evaluating Investment Performance—Coca-Cola*		
	Held to Maturity	**Available for Sale**	**Total**
Investment Income (Year 9)			
Interest and dividend income................................	$ 219	$ —	$ 219
Realized gains and losses.....................................	—	—	—
Unrealized gains and losses.................................	—	(70)	(70)
Total before tax..	219	(70)	149
Tax adjustment (33%)...	(72)	23	(49)
Total after tax..	$ 147	$ (47)	$ 100
Average Investment Base (Year 8)			
Year 8 Fair value	$1,591	$526	$2,117
Year 9 Fair value	1,431	422	1,853
Average	$1,511	$474	$1,985
Return on Investment (ROI)			
Before tax...	14.5%	−14.8%	7.5%
After tax	9.7%	−9.9%	5.0%

reported in the income statement *plus* realized gains and losses (reported in its notes to be immaterial) *plus* unrealized gains and losses as reported in comprehensive income.[2] We also adjust for taxes using the company's effective tax rate of 33%. Next, the average investment base is computed from the beginning and ending fair values. Finally, Coca-Cola's ROI is computed. For its total securities it is 7.5% before tax and 5% after tax. The total ROI pretax return of 7.5% is made up of a pretax return of 14.5% (negative 14.8%) on its held-to-maturity (available-for-sale) securities. The loss on its available-for-sale securities is mainly due to its equity investments in bottling companies. Also, its pretax return of 14.5% on held-to-maturity securities appears especially high, particularly when most of these securities are of extremely short maturity. This might be explained by one or both of the following: (1) interest income as reported on the income statement may include interest income from other sources, and/or (2) the fair value of held-to-maturity securities on the current balance sheet may be much lower than the daily balance. The second possibility is more likely given seasonality in Coca-Cola's business, especially because securities in this class are predominantly short term.

How do we evaluate Coca-Cola's, or any company's, investment performance? One approach is to compare the realized ROI with the required ROI (weighted-average cost of capital) based on the composition and risk of the asset classes in the portfolio. However, this approach attributes transitory market movements to investment performance. Another approach is to compare the realized ROI against a benchmark ROI—where the benchmark ROI is the realized ROI for a portfolio with a similar risk profile for the period under analysis.

GUIDANCE ANSWERS TO ANALYSIS VIEWPOINTS

COMPETITOR

Toys "R" Us is concerned about the threat of the Marvel/Toy Biz agreement for its future sales in toys and games. Financial statement disclosure of this agreement is useful not only for those interested in Marvel and Toy Biz, but also (and in some cases markedly more so) to competitors like Toys "R" Us. Because of this agreement, Marvel character-based toys are one of the leading boys' action figure lines, and Toy Biz recently introduced Marvel Interactive CD-ROM comics. Toy Biz is now arguably one of the fastest-growing toys and games companies and lists its securities on the New York Stock Exchange. The motivation for Marvel's acquisition of 46% of the equity securities in Toy Biz is to retain some influence on the business activities of Toy Biz—especially as it relates to Marvel-related products. It is also an opportunity for Marvel to expand its operations using the existing expertise of Toy Biz and, thus, to reduce its investment risk.

ANALYST

It appears the ED would require consolidation of many of the bottlers in category (2)—those in which Coca-Cola has noncontrolling ownership. It is difficult to precisely gauge the impact of consolidation on its solvency ratios. Still, it is likely that consolidation would yield solvency ratios that reflect less favorably on Coca-Cola.

LAWYER

Your client needs to be informed about a distinction between "economic substance" and "legal responsibility." Consolidated financial statements are meant to recognize the entire business entity under a centralized control.

[2] Note that comprehensive income does not include unrealized gains and losses from held-to-maturity securities. Because Coca-Cola does not report any unrealized gains and losses on its held-to-maturity securities, we use the unrealized gains and losses reported in comprehensive income. If a company reports unrealized gains and losses from held-to-maturity securities, we need to include those when determining the return on investment. The unrealized gains and losses from held-to-maturity securities can be obtained by determining the difference between the ending and beginning unrealized gains and losses from held-to-maturity securities disclosed in the notes.

Economic substance suggests that all subsidiaries under a parent's control are its responsibility and should be reported as such—yielding consolidated statements. Legal responsibility is *not* the same. Shareholders like your client (and NY Research Labs) are *not* responsible for any losses incurred by lawsuits against Boston Chemicals Corporation. Shareholders' risks generally extend only to their investment in a corporation's stock. In sum, NY Research Labs is not responsible for lawsuits of Boston Chemicals because of consolidation. But the amount of NY Research Labs' investment in common stock of Boston Chemicals is subject to the risk presented from these lawsuits.

INVESTMENT BANKER

There are two important aspects to this case. First, you require complete and accurate disclosure of your client's stock offering according to accepted practices. This includes your analysis of LA Delivery's financial statements to ensure adherence to accepted accounting

principles. On this dimension, you are entirely assured. Second, and not unrelated to the first point, you require that your client is not misrepresenting its financial position. This is important for your reputation and future business opportunities as an investment banker. Here is the dilemma. LA Delivery properly reports its financial statements using pooling accounting for its acquisition of Riverside Trucking. Yet you know from your analysis that pooling does not entirely reflect the economic substance of this transaction. More specifically, you expect its common stock will fetch a price considerably higher than what its fundamentals suggest. To accept this engagement you would like to report pro forma statements for LA Delivery assuming *purchase accounting* for Riverside Trucking. In this way you are comfortable in fairly representing the economic substance of your client's financial position. If LA Delivery refuses to disclose any additional information than that required under acceptable practices, you might be forced to decline this engagement.

QUESTIONS

5–1. Describe accounting procedures governing valuation and presentation of noncurrent investments. Distinguish between accounting for investments in equity securities of an investee when holding (*a*) less than 20% of voting shares outstanding and (*b*) 20% or more of voting shares outstanding.

5–2. *a.* Evaluate the accounting for investments when holding between 20 and 50% of equity securities of an investee from the view of an analyst of financial statements.
   b. When are losses in noncurrent security investments recognized? Evaluate the accounting governing recognition of these losses.

5–3. Describe weaknesses and inconsistencies in accounting for noncurrent security investments that are relevant for analysis purposes.

5–4. Many investors view noninfluential stock investments (stock purchased to earn return versus stock purchased to gain influence over another entity for strategic purposes) as a signal to sell a stock. Why might a noninfluential stock investment be perceived as a negative signal about the prospects of a company?

5–5. Distinguish between hedging and speculative activities with regard to derivatives.

5–6. Describe a futures contract.

5–7. Describe a swap contract. How are swaps typically used by companies?

5–8. Describe an option contract. When is an option likely to be exercised?

5–9. What is a hedge transaction?

5–10. When does a derivative security qualify for hedge accounting under *SFAS 133?*

5–11. Give an example of a cash flow hedge and an example of a fair value hedge.

5–12. Describe the accounting treatment for both fair value hedges and cash flow hedges.

5–13. Describe the accounting treatment for speculative derivatives.

5–14. Evaluate the following statement from an analysis viewpoint: "A parent company is not responsible for the liabilities of its subsidiaries nor does it own the assets of its subsidiaries. As such, consolidated financial statements distort legal realities."

5–15. Describe important information potentially disclosed in the individual parent and subsidiary companies' financial statements that is not found in their consolidated statements.

(CFA Adapted)

5–16. Identify and explain some of the important limitations of consolidated financial statements.

5–17. The following note appears in the financial statements of Best Company for the period ending December 31, Year 1:

> Event subsequent to December 31, Year 1: In January Year 2, Best Company acquired Good Products, Inc., and its affiliates by the issuance of 48,063 shares of common stock. Net assets of the combined companies amount to $1,016,198, and net income for Year 1 is $150,000. To the extent the acquired companies earn in excess of $1,000,000 over the next five years, Best Company is required to issue additional shares not to exceed 151,500, and limited to a market value of $2,000,000.

    a. Explain whether this disclosure is necessary and adequate.
    b. If Good Products, Inc., is acquired in December Year 1, at what price does Best Company record this acquisition? (*Note:* Best Company's shares traded at $22 on the acquisition date.)
    c. Explain the contingency for additional consideration.
    d. If the contingency materializes to the maximum limit, how does Best Company record this investment?

5–18. Describe how you determine the valuation of assets acquired in a purchase when:
    a. Assets are acquired by incurring liabilities.
    b. Assets are acquired in exchange of common stock.

5–19. From an analysis point of view, is pooling accounting or purchase accounting for a business combination preferable? Explain with reference to the balance sheet and income statement.

5–20. Assume a company appropriately determines the total cost of a purchased entity. Explain how the company allocates this total cost to the following assets.
    a. Goodwill.
    b. Negative goodwill (bargain purchase).
    c. Marketable securities.
    d. Receivables.
    e. Finished goods.
    f. Work in process.
    g. Raw materials.
    h. Plant and equipment.
    i. Land and mineral reserves.
    j. Payables.
    k. Goodwill recorded by acquired company.

5–21. Describe the analysis procedure available to adjust an income statement using pooling accounting so as to be comparable with an income statement using purchase accounting.

5–22. When an acquisition accounted for as a purchase is effected for stock or other equity securities, discuss what our analysis should be alert to.

5–23. Resources, Inc., is engaged in an aggressive program of acquiring competing companies through the exchange of common stock.
    a. Explain how an acquisition program might contribute to the rate of growth in earnings per share of Resources, Inc.
    b. Explain how the income statements of prior years might be adjusted to reflect the potential future earnings trend of the combined companies.

(CFA Adapted)

5–24. When a balance sheet reports a substantial dollar amount for goodwill, discuss what we should be concerned with in our analysis.

5–25. Indicate factors that can alter estimates for the benefit periods of intangible assets.

5–26^A. Identify and discuss the major provisions of accounting for foreign currency translation.

5–27^A. Discuss the major objectives of current accounting practice involving foreign currency translation.

5–28^A. Identify and discuss at least three implications for analysis of financial statements that result from the accounting for foreign currency translation.

EXERCISES

EXERCISE 5–1

Motivation for Classification of Investment Securities

An important element in accounting for investment securities concerns the distinction between its noncurrent and current classification.

Required:

a. Why do most companies maintain an investment portfolio consisting of both current and noncurrent securities?

b. What factors should an analyst consider when evaluating whether investments in marketable equity securities are properly classified as current or noncurrent? How do these factors affect the accounting treatment for unrealized losses?

EXERCISE 5–2

Analysis of Microsoft Investments

Refer to Exhibit 5.5 to answer the following questions about **Microsoft Corporation** investments.

Microsoft Corporation

a. Microsoft reports unrealized gains and unrealized losses on securities. Accordingly, the investment cost basis is marked to market. What type of account is increased or decreased as a result (asset account, liability account, other gain account, other loss account, or equity account)?

b. If Microsoft investments were trading securities, what type of account would have been increased or decreased when the investment account is marked to market?

c. Given that Microsoft designates its securities portfolio as available-for-sale, what possibilities exist for the company to manage earnings using its investments?

EXERCISE 5–3

Investment Securities

A company can have passive interest (noninfluencial) investments, significant influential investments, or controlling interests. Passive interest investments can be trading, available-for-sale, or held-to-maturity securities.

Required:

a. Describe the valuation basis at which each of these types of investments is reported on the balance sheet.

b. If the investment type is reported at fair value, indicate where any value fluctuation is reported (net income or comprehensive income).

c. What is the rationale for reporting held-to-maturity securities at cost? Does this rationale make economic sense?

(CFA Adapted)

EXERCISE 5–4

Interpreting Accounting for Business Combinations

Spellman Company acquires 90% of Moore Company in a business combination. The total consideration is agreed upon, but the exact nature of Spellman's payment is not yet fully specified. This business combination is accounted for as a purchase. It is expected that at the date of the business combination, the fair value will exceed the book value of Moore's assets minus liabilities. Spellman desires to prepare consolidated financial statements that include the financial statements of Moore.

Required:

a. Explain how the method of accounting for a business combination affects whether goodwill is reported.

b. If goodwill is recorded, explain how to determine the amount of goodwill.

c. From a conceptual standpoint, explain why consolidated financial statements should be prepared.

d. From a conceptual standpoint, identify the first necessary condition before consolidated financial statements are prepared.

The diagram below portrays Company X (the parent or investor company), its two subsidiaries C1 and C2, and its "50 percent or less owned" affiliate C3. Each of the companies has only one type of stock outstanding, and there are no other significant shareholders in either C2 or C3. All four companies engage in commercial and industrial activities.

EXERCISE 5–5

Analyzing and Interpreting Intercorporate Investments

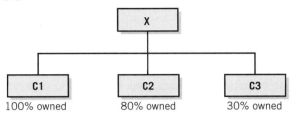

Required:

a. Explain whether or not each of the separate companies maintains distinct accounting records.

b. Identify the type of financial statements each company prepares for financial reporting.

c. Assume you have the ability to enforce your requests of management, describe the type of financial statement information about these companies (separate or consolidated) that you would request.

d. Explain what Company X reports among its assets regarding subsidiary C1.

e. In the consolidated balance sheet, explain how the 20 percent of C2 that is *not* owned by Company X is reported.

f. Identify the transaction that is necessary before C3 is included line by line in the consolidated financial statements.

g. If combined statements are reported for C1 and C2, discuss the need for any elimination entries.

Bethel Company has a foreign wholly owned subsidiary, Home Brite Company. The parent uses the current rate method to compute the cumulative translation adjustment.

EXERCISE 5–6ᴬ

Interpreting the Effects of Functional Currency

Required:

Explain how the use of the current rate method affects each of the following:

a. Reported sales and income of Home Brite.

b. Computation of translation gains and losses.

c. Reporting of translation gains and losses.

(CFA Adapted)

PROBLEMS

Munger.Com began operations on January 1, 2006. The company reports the following information about its investments at December 31, 2006:

PROBLEM 5–1

Investment Disclosures

Current assets ($ in thousands)	Cost	Market
Investments in marketable debt securities:		
Able Corp. bonds (held-to-maturity)	$ 330	$ 290 – N/C 330
Bryan Co. bonds (available-for-sale)	800	825
Caltran, Inc. bonds (trading)	550	515
Investments in marketable equity securities:		
Available-for-sale	1,110	1,600
Trading	1,500	950

Required:

a. Show how each of these investments are reported on the Munger.Com balance sheet.

b. For assets that are marked to market, indicate where the unrealized value fluctuation is reported (in net income and/or in comprehensive income).

PROBLEM 5–2

*Analyzing and
Interpreting Marketable
Equity Securities*

Cited here are four unrelated cases involving marketable equity securities:

1. A noncurrent portfolio of available-for-sale equity securities with an aggregate market value in excess of cost; includes one particular security whose market value has declined to less than one-half of the original cost.

2. The balance sheet of a company does not classify assets and liabilities as current and noncurrent. The portfolio of available-for-sale equity securities includes securities normally considered current that have a net cost in excess of market value of $2,000. The remainder of the portfolio has a net market value in excess of cost of $5,000.

3. An available-for-sale marketable equity security, whose market value is currently less than cost, is classified as noncurrent but is to be reclassified as current.

4. A company's noncurrent portfolio of marketable equity securities consists of the common stock of one company. At the end of the prior year, the market value of the security was 50% of original cost, and this effect was properly reflected in a Valuation Adjustment account. However, at the end of the current year, the market value of the security had appreciated to twice the original cost. The security is still considered noncurrent at year-end.

Required:

For each of the cases, describe how the information provided affects the classification, carrying value, and income reported for that company's investment securities.

PROBLEM 5–3

*Analyzing Investment
Securities Transactions*

The following data are taken from the December 31 annual report of Bailey Company:

($ in thousands)	2004	2005	2006
Sales........................	$50,000	$60,000	$70,000
Net income.................	2,000	2,200	2,500
Dividends paid............	1,000	1,200	1,500

Bailey had 1,000,000 common shares outstanding during this entire period and there is no public market for Bailey Company shares. Also during this period, Simpson Corp. bought Bailey shares for cash, as follows:

January 1, 2004   10,000 shares at $10 per share
January 1, 2005   290,000 shares at $11 per share, increasing ownership to 300,000 shares
January 1, 2006   700,000 shares at $15 per share, resulting in 100% ownership of Bailey Company

Simpson assumed significant influence over Bailey's management in 2005. Ignore income tax effects and the opportunity costs of making investments in Bailey for the requirements listed here.

Required:

a. Compute the effects of these investments on Simpson's reported sales, net income, and cash flows for each of the years 2004 and 2005.

b. Compute the carrying (book) value of Simpson's investment in Bailey as of December 31, 2004, and December 31, 2005.

c. Identify the U.S. GAAP-based accounting method Simpson would use to account for its intercorporate investment in Bailey for 2006. Give two reasons this accounting method must/should be used.

(CFA Adapted)

Burry Corporation acquires 80% of Bowman Company for $40 million on January 1, Year 6. At the time of acquisition, Bowman has total net assets with a fair value of $25 million. For the years ended December 31, Year 6, and December 31, Year 7, Bowman reports net income (loss) and pays dividends as shown here:

	Net Income (loss)	Dividends Paid		Net Income (loss)	Dividends Paid
Year 6	$2,000,000	$1,000,000	Year 7	$(600,000)	$800,000

The excess of the acquisition price over the fair value of net assets acquired is assigned to goodwill. Since goodwill has an indefinite life, it is not amortized.

Required:

a. Compute the value of Burry's investment in Bowman Co. as of December 31, Year 7, under the equity method.

b. Discuss the strengths and weaknesses of the income statement and balance sheet in reflecting the economic substance of this transaction and subsequent business activities using the equity method.

(CFA Adapted)

PROBLEM 5–4
Intercorporate Investments under the Equity Method

CHECK
Investment at Dec. 31,
Year 7, $39,680,000

The following data are from the annual report of Francisco Company, a specialized packaging manufacturer:

	Year 6	Year 7	Year 8
Sales..	$25,000	$30,000	$35,000
Net income...	2,000	2,200	2,500
Dividends paid....................................	1,000	1,200	1,500
Book value per share (year-end)	11	12	13

Note: Francisco had 1,000 common shares outstanding during the entire period. There is no public market for Francisco shares.

Potter Company, a manufacturer of glassware, made the following acquisitions of Francisco common shares:

January 1, Year 6	10 shares at $10 per share
January 1, Year 7	290 shares at $11 per share, increasing ownership to 300 shares
January 1, Year 8	700 shares at $15 per share, yielding 100% ownership of Francisco

Ignore income tax effects and the effect of lost income on funds used to make these investments.

Required:

a. Compute the effects of these investments on Potter Company's reported sales, net income, and cash flows for each of the Years 6 and 7.

PROBLEM 5–5
Analyzing Financial Statement Effects of Intercorporate Investments

b. Calculate the carrying value of Potter Company's investment in Francisco as of December 31, Year 6, and December 31, Year 7.

c. Discuss how Potter Company accounts for its investment in Francisco during Year 8. Describe any additional information necessary to calculate the impact of this acquisition on Potter Company's financial statements for Year 8.

(CFA Adapted)

PROBLEM 5–6

Interpreting Pro Forma Balance Sheets under Purchase and Pooling

Your supervisor asks you to analyze the potential purchase of Drew Company by your firm, Pierson, Inc. You are provided the following information (in millions):

	Pierson, Inc., Historical Cost-Based	DREW COMPANY Historical Cost-Based	Fair Value
Current assets.................................	$ 70	$ 60	$ 65
Land..	60	10	10
Buildings, net.................................	80	40	50
Equipment, net...............................	90	20	40
Total assets....................................	$300	$130	$165
Current liabilities...........................	$120	$ 20	$ 20
Shareholders' equity.......................	180	110	—
Total liabilities and equity..............	$300	$130	

Required:

a. Prepare a pro forma combined balance sheet using purchase accounting. Note that Pierson pays $180 million in cash for Drew where the cash is obtained by issuing long-term debt.

b. Discuss how differences between pooling and purchase accounting for acquisitions affect future reported earnings of the Pierson/Drew business combination.

(CFA Adapted)

PROBLEM 5–7

Analyzing Intercorporate and International Investments

Refer to the financial statements of **Campbell Soup Company** in Appendix A at the end of the book.

Campbell Soup Company

Required:

a. As of July 28, Year 11, Campbell owned 33% of Arnotts Limited. Explain where Campbell reports the amounts representing this investment.

b. Note 18 contains disclosures regarding the market value of the company's investment in Arnotts Limited. Explain whether this market value is reflected in Campbell's financial statements beyond the disclosures referred to.

c. In July of Year 11, Campbell acquired the remaining shares of Campbell Canada. This is in addition to one other acquisition during Year 11. Describe what the difference between the purchase price paid for these acquisitions and the fair market value of the acquired net assets implies for analysis purposes.

d. Prepare a composite journal entry recording the total Year 11 acquisitions.

e. Explain the likely causes of changes in the cumulative translation adjustment accounts for (1) Europe and (2) Australia.

CASES

Axel Corporation acquires 100% of the stock of Wheal Company on December 31, Year 4. The following information pertains to Wheal Company on the date of acquisition:

	Book Value	Fair Value
Cash	$ 40,000	$ 40,000
Accounts receivable	60,000	55,000
Inventory	50,000	75,000
Property, plant, and equipment (net)	100,000	200,000
Secret formula (patent)	—	30,000
Total assets	$250,000	$400,000
Accounts payable	$ 30,000	$ 30,000
Accrued employee pensions	20,000	22,000
Long-term debt	40,000	38,000
Capital stock	100,000	—
Other contributed capital	25,000	—
Retained earnings	35,000	—
Total liabilities and equity	$250,000	$ 90,000

Axel Corporation issues $110,000 par value ($350,000 market value on December 31, Year 4) of its own stock to the shareholders of Wheal Company to consummate the transaction, and Wheal Company becomes a wholly owned, consolidated subsidiary of Axel Corporation.

Required:

a. Prepare journal entries for Axel Corp. to record the acquisition of Wheal Company stock assuming (1) pooling accounting and (2) purchase accounting.

b. Prepare the worksheet entries for Axel Corp. to eliminate the investment in Wheal Company stock in preparation for a consolidated balance sheet at December 31, Year 4 assuming (1) pooling accounting and (2) purchase accounting.

c. Calculate consolidated retained earnings at December 31, Year 4 (Axel's retained earnings at this date are $150,000), assuming:
   (1) Axel Corp. uses the pooling method for this business combination.
   (2) Axel Corp. uses the purchase method for acquisition of Wheal Company.

CASE 5–1
Accounting Entries for Consolidation of Intercorporate Investments

CHECK
(b) Cr. Investment in Wheal for $110,000 in (1), and $350,000 total in (2)

TYCO International was featured in a November 1999, article in *BusinessWeek* for its accounting methods related to acquisitions. In mid-October 1999, Tyco's market value declined by 23% amid allegations by an analyst that the company was inflating its growth picture using accounting gimmicks along with rumors that Tyco's auditors would resign. Tyco has spent $30 billion on deals in the past three years alone–$23 billion paid with stock. It has focused on mundane technologies–including security systems, electronic connectors, industrial valves, and health care products. Tyco reported that its fiscal 1999 net income before special charges more than doubled to $2.6 billion, and sales jumped 83%, to $22.5 billion. Before the allegations, Tyco's market value was over $80 billion, up from just $1.7 billion in 1992.

Some analysts allege Tyco aggressively managed its earnings using acquisitions to produce eye-popping numbers. Wall Street's short-sellers have long whispered about Tyco's accounting. Tyco is known as a "rollup" company–one that uses its lofty stock price to snap up companies with lower PE multiples–whose acquisitions strategy is now at risk given its stock price decline. Tyco's problems center around aggressive merger-related accounting, including restating

TYCO International

CASE 5–2
Analyzing TYCO: Aggressive or Out of Line?

downward the results of acquired companies before the deals close to make its future results look better. Most of Tyco's biggest acquisitions are accounted for using pooling accounting. This means Tyco restates its financials, effectively pretending the acquired company was part of Tyco long before the deal closed. These restatements make it difficult to compare one period to the next. Adding to the confusion, Tyco has taken $4 billion in merger-related charges in recent years, changed the end of its fiscal year from December to September, and moved its headquarters from the United States to Bermuda for a lower tax rate. One analyst claims that Tyco is using huge charges to create "cookie jars" of reserves against future operating expenses.

Indeed, Tyco's earnings look anything but stellar once the massive charges are taken into account. With these charges, Tyco shows huge net losses in both fiscal 1996 and 1997 and an 83 percent drop in net income in the first nine months of fiscal 1999. However, Wall Street convention is to overlook such charges, figuring that pro-forma earnings provides a better picture of "normalized" earnings.

Tyco rejects all allegations. Its CEO says the SEC conducted full legal and accounting reviews of filings for Tyco's three largest deals over the past two years. The CEO also says only 6 of the 120 recent deals involved pooling, although it was applied to some of its biggest deals. Accounting questions aside, Tyco is adept at cutting costs. For example, Tyco has cut annual operating costs by $200 million at U.S. Surgical since its acquisition in 1988. However, former U.S. Surgical execs and competitors say Tyco may have lost some of the innovation needed to ensure its future in an evolving medical supply business. Said one exec, "They had a lot of interesting products in the pipeline, but [Tyco] pulled the plugs on all of that."

Required:

a. Describe how merger-related accounting inhibits a user's ability to use accounting reports to make period-to-period comparisons. Is this true for both the purchase method and the pooling method? Explain.

b. Explain why a high price-to-earnings ratio is crucial to Tyco's acquisitions strategy.

c. How do merger-related charges potentially enable a company to inflate future operating earnings? How can a user of financial statements assess whether this is occurring?

d. Many short-term gains in acquisition come from cutting costs. What potential long-term harm can cost-cutting create?

e. Tyco's controversy is arguably a quality of earnings concern, where Tyco strategically used the discretion in GAAP. Why is the market's reaction to this alleged behavior so severe?

f. Many companies report pro-forma earnings that exclude one-time acquisition costs and, increasingly, goodwill amortization. Critique the use of pro-forma earnings for financial statement analysis.

CASE 5–3

Derivatives–Hedging Strategies, Accounting, and Economic Effects

Newmont Mining is the largest gold producer in North America and second largest in the world, with mining interests

Newmont Mining

in the U.S., Mexico, Peru, Uzbekistan, and Indonesia. In 1998, Newmont produced 4.07 million ounces of gold and its proven and probable reserves total 52.6 million ounces.

The price of gold is usually inversely related to the performance of financial assets such as stocks and bonds. Gold mining shares often provide a leveraged exposure to movements in gold price and, thus, are a convenient hedge against downturns in financial markets, especially those precipitated by inflation. However, gold prices have been in a secular downtrend for the past 18 years and especially in the past 3 years–gold prices fell from around $400 an ounce in early 1996 to around $250 an ounce by mid-1998. The prolonged bear market in gold has driven many gold-mining companies out of business. Many other companies have attempted to mitigate their exposure to the decline in gold prices with a variety of derivative instruments such as forward sales, and the purchase and sale of gold options. Some large companies such as Barrick Gold, Placer Dome, and Ashanthi Gold Fields have hedged major portions (upwards of 50% in some cases) of their gold reserves. While these hedging strategies reduce downside risk, they also limit gains from a sustained rally in the price of gold.

Newmont's management has avoided hedging its production because of its philosophy of providing its shareholders with the maximum exposure to gold price movements. Until recently, the only hedging by Newmont pertained to a minor quantity of its production from an Indonesian mine. The absence of hedging combined with the steep decline in gold prices adversely affected Newmont's profitability. This decline in profitability is despite Newmont's success at cost reduction–its less than $180 an ounce cost of production is one of the lowest in the industry. As gold prices continued to fall, Newmont's stock price declined from a high of $60 in 1996 to under $20 in 1998. Its creditors became increasingly uncomfortable with the exposure of the company to falling gold prices. Accordingly, in July and August 1999 (when the gold price was near its 20-year low of $250 an ounce) Newmont decided to hedge part of its reserves, although the proportion of reserves hedged is still one of the lowest in the industry.

Newmont's hedging program is designed to protect near-term cash flows in case of any further decline in gold price but to preserve leverage for any gold price increase. Details of its hedging program and accounting treatment follows:

1. *Forward sales commitments and associated call options from Indonesian mine:* The company agreed to sell 125,000 ounces of gold per year through 2000 from an Indonesian mine at a price of $454 per ounce. According to the company, the purpose of this hedge is to accelerate income and mitigate country risk. The accounting treatment for this contract is hedge accounting—all unrealized gains and losses on the contracts are deferred until the delivery date of the associated ounces. At the time of delivery, the contract price is recognized in income. As a result, the accounting numbers should reflect the spirit of the investment, which is to lock-in the price of gold. The proceeds from sale of gold will be supplemented or offset by gains and losses on the related hedge contract. Outstanding sales commitments as of September 30, 1999, are:

	1999	2000
Ounces.................	31,250	125,000
Average price........	$454	$454

Coincident with the forward sales contracts, the company purchased call options on 50,000 ounces of gold per year for the same time period. These options give the company the right, but not the obligation, to purchase gold at $454 per ounce. The effect of these options is to allow the company, in a rising gold price environment, to realize the market price above $454 per ounce on 40% of the ounces subject to the forward sales contracts. The accounting treatment for the call options is the same as the related forward sales contracts (hedge accounting—all unrealized gains and losses on the contracts are deferred until the delivery date of the associated ounces). In combination, the forward sales and associated calls allow Newmont to create a floor price for its future production without entirely losing out on the upside potential. Outstanding call options at September 30, 1999, are:

	1999	2000
Ounces..................	12,500	50,000
Average price	$454	$454

2. *Prepaid forward sales and purchases in July 1999:* In July 1999, the company entered into a prepaid forward sale agreement covering 483,333 ounces of gold for delivery in 2005, 2006, and 2007 and received $137.2 million. The proceeds were used to pay down its debt. The initial proceeds received on this sale were based on a $300 per ounce gold price. If gold price exceeds $300 per ounce at the time of delivery, the company will receive additional proceeds subject to a ceiling of $380 per ounce. The initial proceeds were recorded as deferred revenue. As gold is delivered against this contract, a proportionate amount of the deferred revenue will be recognized as sales income. The company also agreed to deliver 35,900 ounces per year from 2000 to 2007 in a prepaid manner. To facilitate contracting for a fixed price without losing the benefit of upside potential, the company simultaneously signed forward purchase contracts for like quantities at prices increasing from $263 per ounce in 2000 to $354 per ounce in 2007. The accounting treatment for this transaction involves increasing or reducing the sales income from the forward sales contracts by the difference between the market price and forward purchase price at the scheduled future delivery dates.

3. *Purchased put and call options in August 1999:* In August 1999, with the price of gold at a 20-year low, the company sought to establish a floor price for a portion of its production with the purchase of put options. These options gave the company the right, but not the obligation, to sell 2.85 million ounces of gold at $270 per ounce. If the gold price is above $270, the options expire unexercised and the company sells gold at the higher market price. To avoid paying cash for the put options, the company sold call options on 2.35 million ounces for delivery in 2004 to 2009 at prices ranging from $350 to $392 an ounce. The sales proceeds from the call options

exactly offset the purchase cost of the put options. The call options give the purchaser the right to buy the specified amount of gold at the stated strike price. If the market price is above the strike price at the time of maturity, the company can deliver the contracted quantity of gold to the option holder or roll the contracts over to a future delivery date. If the market price is below the strike price at the time of maturity, the options expire unexercised. Alternatively, the company can buy back the calls before they become exercisable. The written calls did not involve any margin-call risk or lease rates.

The accounting treatment for the put options is hedge accounting. As such, any gains and losses on the contracts are deferred until the exercise date. If the gold price is below $270, the company exercises the put option and recognizes $270 per ounce as sales income. If the gold price is above $270 the company sells gold at the higher market price. Although no cash was paid for the put options, the fair value of the options at the time of purchase (approximately $37 million) is recorded as a prepaid asset and amortized over the term of the put options (the amortization is accounted for as an offset against revenue).

Because the call options are longer term, an interpretation of GAAP requires the call options to be marked to market at the end of each quarter. The market value of the calls reflects the approximate price for which the options could be sold on the last day of each quarter. The initial fair value of the call options (the proceeds that would have been received if sold outright) is $37 million. Depending on the gold price and other factors that affect option pricing, the fair value can vary significantly from one quarter to the next, and the change in fair value is recognized as a gain or loss each quarter. By the end of the options' term, if gold price is below the strike price on the calls, the option value will be $0 and the initial $37 million fair value would have been included in income.

Subsequent Events:

While well-conceived hedging strategies reduce risk, in retrospect, the timing of the Newmont's hedging activities was unfortunate. In late September 1999 (just after the purchase of puts and writing of calls) the Consortium of European Central Banks, whose selling had contributed largely to the decline in the price of gold during the past 3 years, announced a moratorium on gold sales for the next 5 years. As a result, gold prices shot up from around $250 per ounce to over $300 per ounce in just a few days. Newmont was forced to recognize an unrealized loss on the written calls in its financial statements for the quarter ended September 1999 because the upward spike in gold price increased the fair value of the call options.

For the quarter ended September 1999, Newmont earned $2.3 million, or 2 cents per share, before noncash, hedge-related accounting charges. The average realized gold price for the period was $271 per ounce. This compares with earnings of $6.1 million, or 4 cents per share, at an average realized gold price of $295 per ounce in the corresponding quarter of 1998. In the quarter ended September 1999, gold production rose 4% to 1,043,000 ounces, while total cash costs were reduced 6% to $174 per ounce and total production costs declined 10% to $228 per ounce. As a result of the amortization of the put options and holding loss on the written long-dated calls, an after-tax noncash charge of $41.3 million is recorded in the September 1999 quarter. Given these holding losses, the company's net loss for the quarter is $39 million, or 23 cents per share.

Newmont believes the accounting applied to the long-dated call options is inappropriate and does not reflect the economic fundamentals of the hedging transaction. First, the company believes that marking only the written calls to market is inconsistent and distorts the economic reality of the company's underlying economic position. As a largely unhedged producer, the company's cash flow per quarter is expected to increase by $1 million for each $1 increase per ounce in the price of gold. Moreover, the company cannot mark its 52.6 million ounces of gold reserves to market value. Interestingly, the company points out that if the price of gold fell precipitously near the end of the next quarter, the company's fundamental value would decline but it would get to book a gain on its written call options. Second, the company argues that it has no cash flow exposure from the written calls unless it reverses the transaction. The written calls are not subject to margin calls or lease rates. The company has the necessary gold reserves to meet the committed quantities of gold, and the strike price of the calls is well above its cost of production. The company will incur an opportunity cost to the extent the prevailing gold price on the expiration of the calls is above the strike price. The company also notes that the accounting treatment is different from the long-standing industry practice of recording gains and losses only when realized and it induces unnecessary volatility to reported income.

NEWMONT MINING CORPORATION AND SUBSIDIARIES
Statement of Consolidated Operations
For quarter ended September 30

(in $millions)	1999	1998
Sales	$340.2	$349.9
Amortization of put option	(12.2)	—
Other income	9.8	2.7
	337.8	352.6
Cost of sales	(206.5)	(206.5)
Depreciation, depletion, and amortization	(60.7)	(72.9)
Exploration and research	(14.3)	(18.9)
General administrative	(12.5)	(11.7)
Other expenses	(4.2)	1.0
Interest (net)	(14.6)	(19.5)
Unrealized loss on written call options	(51.3)	—
Tax provision	7.8	3.3
Minority interest and equity loss	(20.5)	(21.3)
Net income	$ (39.0)	$ 6.1

BALANCE SHEET
As of September 30

(in $millions)	1999	1998	Liabilities and Equity	1999	1998
Assets			**Liabilities and Equity**		
Fair value of put options	$ 23.1	$ —	Current liabilities	$ 193.1	$ 212.5
Other current assets	467.9	513.1	Long-term debt	1,073.5	1,201.1
Total current assets	491.0	513.1	Deferred revenue	137.2	—
Noncurrent assets	2,792.2	2,673.7	Fair value of written calls	88.9	—
			Other liabilities	263.5	240.9
			Minority interest	117.6	92.8
			Liabilities	1,873.8	1,747.3
			Equity	1,409.4	1,439.5
Total assets	$3,283.2	$3,186.8	Total liabilities and equity	$3,283.2	$3,186.8

Required:

a. Describe and analyze the hedging transactions of Newmont. What is Newmont's motivation for each of its hedging transactions?

b. Because *SFAS 133* is effective for fiscal years beginning June 15, 1999, Newmont's September 1999 quarterly financials are not subject to the standard. Explain how each of the hedging transactions entered into by Newmont will be classified and accounted for under *SFAS 133*.

c. Examine the underlying economics for each of its hedging transactions. Does the accounting (both under *SFAS 133* and the earlier method employed by Newmont) reflect economic reality?

d. Newmont is not allowed to use hedge accounting for the written calls. Is this appropriate?

e. Evaluate Newmont's criticisms of the accounting for its written calls. Is Newmont's criticism justified?

f. What is the underlying economic reality of the sudden increase in gold price for Newmont? Do its financial statements reflect economic reality? Would marking all assets and liabilities to fair value improve the presentation of its balance sheet and income statement?

CASE 5–4[A]

Analyzing Translated Financial Statements and Intercorporate Investments

The December 31, Year 8, trial balance of SwissCo Ltd., a Swiss company, follows (in euros, €).

	Debit	Credit
Cash..	€ 50,000	
Accounts receivable..................................	100,000	
Allowance for doubtful accounts		€ 10,000
Inventory, January 1, Year 8......................	150,000	
Property, plant, and equipment (net).......	800,000	
Accounts payable		80,000
Notes payable..		20,000
Capital stock...		100,000
Retained earnings, January 1, Year 8		190,000
Sales		2,000,000
Purchases (of inventory)...........................	1,000,000	
Depreciation expense...............................	100,000	
Other expenses (including taxes).............	200,000	
	€2,400,000	€2,400,000

Additional Information:

1. SwissCo uses the periodic inventory system along with the FIFO costing method for inventory and cost of goods sold. On December 31, Year 8, the inventory balance is €120,000—it is carried at FIFO cost.

2. SwissCo capital stock was issued six years ago when the company was established; the exchange rate at that time was €1 = $0.30. The company purchased plant and equipment five years ago when the exchange rate was €1 = $0.35; also, the note payable was made out to a local bank at the same time.

3. Revenues are earned and expenses (including cost of goods sold) are incurred uniformly throughout Year 8. Inventory available at December 31, Year 8, is purchased throughout the second half of Year 8.

4. The December 31, Year 7, balance sheet (in U.S. dollars) of SwissCo shows Retained Earnings of $61,000.

5. The spot rates for the euro in Year 8 are:

January 1, Year 8	$0.32
Average for Year 8	$0.37
Average for second half of Year 8	$0.36
December 31, Year 8..........................	$0.38

6. Management determined the functional currency of SwissCo is the euro. Therefore, use the current rate method.

Required:

a. Prepare a trial balance in U.S. dollars for SwissCo as of December 31, Year 8.

b. Prepare an income statement for the year ended December 31, Year 8, and the balance sheet at December 31, Year 8 (both in U.S. dollars) for SwissCo.

c. Assume Unisco Corporation, a U.S. firm, purchases a 75% ownership interest in SwissCo at book value on January 1, Year 8. Prepare the entry Unisco makes at December 31, Year 8, to record its equity in SwissCo's Year 8 earnings. Unisco Corp. uses the equity method in accounting for its investment in SwissCo.

CHECK
(b) Net income, $247,900; Total assets, $402,800

CASE 5–5[A]

Analyzing Translated Financial Statements

On December 31, Year 8, U.S. Dental Supplies (USDS) created a wholly owned foreign subsidiary, Funi, Inc. (FI), located in the country of Lumbaria. The condensed balance sheet of Funi as of December 31, Year 8, reported in local currency (the pont), follows:

FUNI, INC.
Balance Sheet
December 31, Year 8

Ponts (millions)

Assets		Liabilities and Equity	
Cash..................................	180	Capital stock...............	600
Fixed assets (net).............	420		
Total assets.......................	600		

Funi initially adopted the U.S. dollar as its functional currency and translated its Year 9 balance sheet and income statement in accordance with U.S. accounting practice. These statements are reproduced here:

FUNI, INC.
Balance Sheet
December 31, Year 9

	Ponts (millions)	Exchange Rate (ponts/US$)	US$ (millions)		Ponts (millions)	Exchange Rate (ponts/US$)	US$ (millions)
Assets				**Liabilities and Equity**			
Cash	82	4.0	$ 20.5	Accounts payable.................	532	4.0	$133.0
Accounts receivable.	700	4.0	175.0	Capital stock........................	600	3.0	200.0
Inventory.................	455	3.5	130.0	Retained earnings...............	465		112.5
Fixed assets (net)	360	3.0	120.0				
Total assets	1,597		$445.5	Total liabilities and equity....	1,597		$445.5

FUNI, INC.
Income Statement
For Year Ended December 31, Year 9

	Ponts (millions)	Exchange Rate (ponts/US$)	US$ (millions)
Sales...	3,500	3.5	$1,000.0
Cost of sales.............................	(2,345)	3.5	(670.0)
Depreciation expense................	(60)	3.0	(20.0)
Selling expense.........................	(630)	3.5	(180.0)
Translation gain (loss)..............	—		(17.5)
Net income................................	465		$ 112.5

USDS subsequently instructed Funi to change its functional currency to the pont. The following exchange rates (pont per U.S. dollar) are applicable:

January 1, Year 9	3.0	Average for Year 9	3.5	December 31, Year 9	4.0

Required:

a. Prepare a pro forma balance sheet as of December 31, Year 9, and an income statement for the year ending December 31, Year 9, for Funi. Both statements should be prepared in U.S. dollars, using the pont as the functional currency for Funi.

b. Analyze and describe the comparative effects of selecting the dollar versus the pont as the functional currency for Funi:
  (1) U.S. dollar balance sheet as of December 31, Year 10.
  (2) U.S. dollar income statement for year ended December 31, Year 10.
  (3) U.S. dollar financial ratios for Year 10.

(CFA Adapted)

CHECK
(a) Total assets, $399.25;
Net income, $132.86

6

ANALYZING OPERATING ACTIVITIES

ANALYSIS OBJECTIVES

- Explain the concepts of income measurement and their implications for analysis of operating activities.

- Describe and analyze the impact of nonrecurring items, including extraordinary items, discontinued segments, accounting changes, write-offs, and restructuring charges.

- Analyze revenue and expense recognition and its risks for financial statement analysis.

- Analyze deferred charges, including expenditures for research, development, and exploration.

- Explain supplementary employee benefits and analyze the disclosures for employee stock options (ESOs).

- Describe and interpret interest costs and the accounting for income taxes.

- Analyze and interpret earnings per share data (Appendix 6A).

- Discuss economics of employee stock options (Appendix 6B).

Spin City of Earnings

NEW YORK–"When do exceptional charges become so routine that they're not exceptional anymore? If the company is Eastman Kodak, apparently never. Kodak has taken one-time restructuring charges every year for the past 12, wiping out virtually half of its $11.4 billion operating earnings since 1992" (*BusinessWeek* 2004).

Of course, companies have routinely taken restructuring charges. But nervous investors fear that huge multiyear write-offs increasingly distort earnings–so much so, that some question whether the meaning of earnings numbers and their value as a measure of performance is getting trampled.

There are two issues inherent in restructuring charges. First, is the timing. Restructuring charges represent asset write-offs and the accruals of future liabilities such as severance payments. Because both are estimates, an overly conservative company can

front-load such charges. This burdens the current income statement and benefits future income statements. This practice is referred to as a "big bath." Second is the question of interpretation–should such charges be treated as normal operating expenses or as transitory charges? Kodak prefers the latter. "Kodak pegged

> ... write-offs
> increasingly
> distort earnings ...

operating earnings at $2.25 to $2.55 a share before charges. That puts its price-earnings ratio at 13, cheap compared with the 18 average for the Standard & Poor's 500 stock index. But take out up to $400 million for restructuring, and Kodak's per-share earnings nosedive to 80 cents to $1.30, while its p-e soars as high as 38."

Companies are burying all sorts of normal operating expenses in these charges. "Kodak may try to spirit the changes away in presentations, but investors should be leery. The restructuring charges aren't simply for selling old equipment and factories at a loss. Hard cash will be flying out the door–up to $200 million a year–to pay severance and other real costs."

"Should recurring restructuring charges be segregated in the income statement and eliminated from pro forma operating earnings in press releases?" Many companies appear to think so. "Somebody woke up to the fact that if you take something as a restructuring charge, investors will forgive you immediately," says Robert S. Miller, the nonexecutive chairman hired to clean up Waste Management. "We've almost lost the notion of what are earnings and what are one-time charges."

PREVIEW OF CHAPTER 6

Income is the net of revenues and gains *less* expenses and losses. Income is one measure of operating activities and it is determined using the accrual basis of accounting. The income statement reports net income for a period of time along with the income components: revenues, expenses, gains, and losses. We analyze income and its components to assess company performance and risk exposures, and to predict the amounts, timing, and uncertainty of future cash flows. While "bottom line" net income frames our analysis, income components provide the crucial pieces of a mosaic revealing the economic portrait of a company's operating activities. This chapter describes the analysis and interpretation of income components. We consider current reporting requirements and their implications for analysis of income components. We describe how we might usefully apply analytical adjustments to income components and related disclosures to enhance the analysis. We direct special attention to revenue recognition and the recording of major expenses and costs. The content and organization of this chapter are as follows:

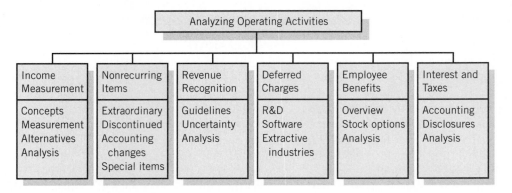

INCOME MEASUREMENT
Income Concepts—A Recap

Income summarizes the financial effects of a business's operating activities. The main purpose of the income statement is to explain how income is determined, with its important components reported as separate line items. In Chapter 2 we introduced both economic and accounting concepts of income and distinguished them from cash flows. In this section, we recap the salient points from the discussion in Chapter 2. However, it is recommended that readers browse the section in Chapter 2 before proceeding with the rest of the discussion on income measurement.

To recap, there are two alternative concepts of income: economic income and permanent income. **Economic income** measures the net change in shareholder's wealth during a period and is typically equal to a period's cash flows plus change in present value of expected future cash flows. **Permanent income** is an estimate of the stable average income that a business is expected to earn over its lifetime, given the current state of its business. Permanent income (also called sustainable income or recurring income) is conceptually similar to *sustainable earning power,* and its determination is a major quest in analysis. While economic income measures *change* in shareholder value, permanent income is *proportional* to value.

Accounting (reported) income is based on accrual accounting and is determined by recognizing revenues and matching costs to the recognized revenues. Accounting income purports to measure neither economic income nor permanent income. In addition, accounting income has measurement error, arising because of accounting distortions introduced by arbitrary rules, earnings management, and estimation error. Because of these reasons, accounting income can be visualized as comprising of three components: (1) a **permanent or recurring component,** where each dollar is equal to $1/r$ dollars of company value (r is cost of capital); (2) a **transitory component,** where each dollar is merely equal to one dollar of company value; and (3) a **value irrelevant component,** which is irrelevant for valuation.

A major quest in analysis is identifying the permanent or recurring component of reported income. Standard setters are aware of the need to separate recurring and nonrecurring components of income. Accordingly, the line items on the income statement are arranged in a manner that allows an analyst to identify nonrecurring components. As a first step toward determining permanent income, analysts determine **core income,** which is the current period's reported income after removing all nonrecurring (or value irrelevant components).

Accounting is gradually, but inexorably, adopting a model of *fair value accounting.* Under fair value accounting, reported income is conceptually similar to economic income and will include large, nonrecurring components in the form of unrealized gains/losses arising because of changes in assets' and liabilities' fair values. The importance of analyzing income and isolating its permanent component will be an even more important task as fair value accounting becomes more pervasive.

Measuring Accounting Income

Revenues (and gains) and expenses (and losses) are the two major components of accounting income. This section discusses these two components. Exhibit 6.1 shows a typical income statement with major line items along with some alternative income measures.

Revenues and Gains

Revenues are earned inflows or prospective earned inflows of cash that arise from a company's ongoing business activities. These include cash inflows such as cash sales, and

---

Income Statement

Exhibit 6.1

■■■■■■■

AMBER CORP. AND SUBSIDIARIES
Consolidated Income Statement ($ millions)

	2006	2005	2004
Revenues	$14,314	$12,716	$13,033
Cost of goods sold	(8,270)	(7,454)	(7,943)
Gross profit	6,044	5,262	5,090
Expenses			
Selling and administrative	(2,964)	(2,478)	(2,396)
Research and development	(1,234)	(899)	(855)
Restructuring charge	—	(1,016)	—
Interest expense	(725)	(715)	(654)
Income before taxes	1,121	154	1,185
Income taxes	(336)	(351)	(355)
Income from continuing operations	785	(197)	830
Gain from extinguishment of debt	38	—	—
Loss from operating discontinued segment	—	0	(23)
Gain from sale of discontinued segment	—	—	66
Net income	$ 823	$ (197)	$ 873
Foreign currency translation adjustments	82	(54)	(31)
Unrealized holding gain on available-for-sale securities	24	22	6
Post retirement benefits adjustment	0	(4)	—
Comprehensive income	$ 929	$ (233)	$ 848

prospective cash inflows such as credit sales. **Gains** are earned inflows or prospective earned inflows of cash arising from transactions and events unrelated to a company's ongoing business activities. Exhibit 6.1 provides an example of a gain–specifically, a gain on sale of a discontinued segment. The distinction between revenues and gains is based on the ongoing business activities that produce revenues. Revenues are expected to persist indefinitely for a going concern. In contrast, gains are nonrecurring. This distinction is important for analysis, especially when determining sustainable income.

Revenue recognition methods can significantly affect reported income. Revenue recognition is becoming more complex, as it is increasingly linked with e-commerce activity. It is also an area with minimal guidance from accounting standards. This permits opportunities for earnings management. Accordingly, analyzing revenue recognition practices is crucial in financial statement analysis. For this reason we devote a section to revenue recognition later in the chapter.

Expenses and Losses

Expenses are incurred outflows, prospective outflows, or allocations of past outflows of cash that arise from a company's ongoing business operations. **Losses** are decreases in a company's net assets arising from peripheral or incidental operations of a company. Accounting for expenses and losses often involves assessing the amount and timing of their allocation to reporting periods. Timing is a matter of when they are incurred, often based on matching them with revenues generated.

Another important issue is that of cost *deferral* (or multiperiod allocation). Accountants capitalize costs whose benefits are realized over many periods. These costs are systematically allocated to future periods. In contrast, many costs are incurred in the same period in which they are recognized. (It is not necessary that cash outflows for expenses and losses occur at the same time they are recognized.)

Alternative Income Classifications and Measures

Proper income classification is important in analysis. Income can be classified along two major dimensions: (1) operating versus nonoperating and (2) recurring versus nonrecurring. Many times, these two dimensions of classification are used synonymously. For example, certain analysts (and even certain companies) refer to an income measure that excludes all nonrecurring items as operating income. While it may be true that a majority of operating income components tend to be recurring, it must be understood that these two classifications are distinct, both in nature and purpose. For example, a nonrecurring item such as loss of inventory from fire is an operating loss. Similarly, a nonoperating item such as interest income may be recurring in nature. The operating versus nonoperating classification depends primarily on the source of the revenue or expense–namely, whether it arises from the ongoing operations of the company or from its securities transactions or financing activities. The recurring versus nonrecurring classification depends primarily on the behavior of the revenue or expense–namely, whether it is expected to persist or it is a one-time event. It is important for an analyst to appreciate the differences between these alternative classifications. Exhibit 6.2 stresses the distinction in these dimensions of classifying income.

Recurring and Nonrecurring Income

The importance of classifying income components as recurring or nonrecurring arises from the need to determine the permanent and transitory components of income. In

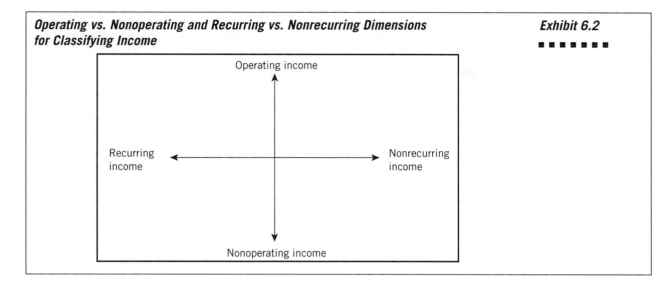

Operating vs. Nonoperating and Recurring vs. Nonrecurring Dimensions for Classifying Income

Exhibit 6.2

this section, we discuss alternative income measures reported in financial statements and their implications for analysis.

Alternative Measures of Accounting Income.   Income statements typically report three alternative income measures: (1) net income, (2) comprehensive income, and (3) continuing income. **Net income** is regarded as the bottom line measure of income. In reality, it is not. GAAP allows a number of direct adjustments to equity, called *dirty surplus* items, that bypass the income statement. *SFAS 130* attempts to remedy this problem with an alternative measure of income called *comprehensive income*. **Comprehensive income** reflects nearly all changes to equity, other than those from owner activities (such as dividends and share issuances). This implies that comprehensive income is the bottom-line measure of income, and is the accountant's proxy for economic income. Unfortunately, companies are allowed to report comprehensive income in the statement of changes in equity instead of the income statement. The income statement in Exhibit 6.1, however, does include both measures of income. Comprehensive income differs from net income in that it reflects certain unrealized holding gains and losses foreign currency translation adjustments, and minimum pension liability adjustments (not reported are derivative gains and losses which also affect comprehensive income).

Accountants also report an intermediate measure of income called *continuing income*. **Continuing income** is a measure that excludes extraordinary items, cumulative effects of accounting changes, and the effects of discontinued operations. For this reason, continuing income is often called *income before extraordinary items, income before discontinued operations,* or *income before cumulative effect of accounting change,* or any combination as appropriate. Companies without these components need not report continuing income. Exhibit 6.1 includes income from continuing operations as a separate line item.

Many analysts compute another measure of income that we refer to as *core income.* (This is because core income, which excludes all nonrecurring and unusual items, can better reflect the results of current operations. However, as we noted earlier, the distinction between operating and nonoperating income is separate from the sustainability of income components.) **Core income** is a measure that excludes all nonrecurring items that are reported as separate line items on the income statement. In Exhibit 6.1, core income equals the continuing income reported in 2006 and 2004. Yet in 2005, core income is different—it excludes the after-tax effect of the restructuring charge of $1,016 million. In this case, core income equals continuing income *plus* the restructuring charge that is multiplied by one minus the 35% marginal tax rate, or $463 [computed as $(197) plus the quantity $1,016 \times 0.65$].

Analysis Implications.   Accounting standards require alternative income measures so users can identify sustainable and nonsustainable income components. Many analysts prefer an income measure that corresponds to one of the reported measures or some variation that excludes (or includes) certain line items. Debates rage over what constitutes the "correct" measure of income. We caution against such debates for two reasons.

First, a correct measure of income is not possible without specifying analysis objectives. As already noted, income serves two important but different roles: to measure the net change in equity and to provide an estimate of sustainable earning power. It is impossible for a single income measure to satisfy both objectives at the same time.

Second, the alternative accounting income measures result from merely including, or excluding, certain line items. This means they are still *accounting measures* of income and are subject to accounting distortions. At best, these alternative accounting income measures are starting points for more detailed accounting analysis necessary to estimate sustainable income. For example, comprehensive income is a natural starting point to determine economic income.

Operating and Nonoperating Income

Operating income is a measure of company income from ongoing operating activities. There are three important aspects of operating income. First, operating income pertains only to income generated from operating activities. Therefore, any revenues (and expenses) not related to business operations are not part of operating income. Second, and related to the first, operating income focuses on income for the company as a whole rather than for debt and equity holders. This means that financing revenues and expenses (mainly interest expense) are excluded when measuring operating income. Third, operating income pertains only to ongoing business activities. This means any income or loss pertaining to discontinued operations is excluded from operating income.

Nonoperating income includes all components of income not included in operating income. It is sometimes useful when analyzing nonoperating income to separate components pertaining to financing activities from those pertaining to discontinued operations.

Analysis Implications.   The usefulness of operating income arises from an important goal in corporate finance. That is, the desire to separate investing (and operating) decisions such as capital budgeting, from those of financing decisions such as dividend policy. Because of this goal, it is necessary to determine a comprehensive measure of company income that is independent of a company's financing and securities investment decisions. Operating income is one such measure. Note that operating income before taxes is similar to earnings before interest and taxes (EBIT), while operating income after taxes is similar to net operating profit after taxes (NOPAT).

In most cases, operating income can be determined by rearranging the income statement and making proper adjustments for taxes. Still, it is sometimes necessary to draw on more detailed adjustments using information in notes. For example, when a company has operating leases, the entire lease rental is included as an operating expense even though the lease payment includes an interest component. In this case, operating income is understated unless the analyst estimates the interest component and makes the necessary adjustments using note information. It is beyond the scope of this chapter to show how to compute operating income. We return to this topic in the financial analysis part of the book.

Comprehensive Income

GAAP has long espoused the comprehensive, or all-inclusive, concept of income, where the bottom-line income number articulates with equity in successive balance sheets–that is, the bottom-line income reflects all changes in shareholders' equity arising from other than owner transactions. This articulation is called *clean surplus.* Nevertheless, standard setters have over time allowed certain components of comprehensive income to bypass the income statement as direct adjustments to equity. These adjustments, called *dirty surplus,* have increased in importance and magnitude in recent years. The motivation for these dirty surplus items comes from concerns about excessive income volatility if all changes to equity flow through the income statement. Still, many users are concerned that allowing changes to equity to bypass the income statement will reduce the reliability of accounting income. To address these concerns, companies are required to report a measure of comprehensive income in addition to net income.

Measuring Comprehensive Income.   As defined by *SFAS 130,* comprehensive income is computed by adjusting net income for dirty surplus items, collectively called *other comprehensive income.* We show the determination of comprehensive income from a typical company:

Net income		$1,205
Other comprehensive income		
+/− Unrealized holding gain (loss) on marketable securities	$305	
+/− Foreign currency translation adjustment	(12)	
+/− Postretirement benefits adjustment	(17)	
+/− Unrealized holding gain or loss on derivative instruments	945	1,221
Comprehensive income		$2,426

The other comprehensive income for this company consists of four components: (1) unrealized holding gains or losses that result from changes in the fair (market) value of available-for-sale investment securities, (2) foreign currency translation gains and losses, (3) changes in the funded status of postretirement benefits not included in net income, and (4) unrealized holding gains or losses arising from the effective portion of cash flow hedges (derivatives). These amounts are expressed on an after-tax basis. All four components are in the nature of unrealized (holding) gains or losses. The components arise from changes in the value of assets and liabilities that do not originate from arm's-length transactions. A few analysts maintain that the transaction basis of net income is an important distinction between net income and comprehensive income. We show that this distinction is neither important nor necessarily true.

Analysis Implications.   The importance of comprehensive income for financial statement analysis arises because it is the accountant's proxy for economic income. Comprehensive income is preferred to net income, where the latter measure purports to estimate neither economic nor sustainable income.

A few analysts argue the importance of net income vis-à-vis comprehensive income relates to the notion that net income is transaction-based while comprehensive income is not. However, this argument is not entirely correct. Namely, net income has many components in the nature of unrealized gains or losses that are not transaction based. For example, net income includes holding gains or losses from trading securities, from fair value hedges, and from the ineffective portion of cash flow hedges. Moreover, the fact that some income components arise through arm's-length transactions is a distinction that is irrelevant from an economic point of view since unrealized gains or losses are a legitimate part of economic income.

It is important to recognize that comprehensive income must be adjusted in determining economic income. We confine discussion in this section to evaluating the appropriateness of the four usual items included in other comprehensive income. In particular, unrealized gains and losses arising from investment and/or derivative securities are a legitimate part of economic income. However, note that unrealized holding gains on investment securities reported as part of other comprehensive income excludes holding gains on held-to-maturity securities. Similarly, foreign currency translation adjustments and postretirement benefits adjustments must be included when determining economic income.

Some analysts argue that all components of other comprehensive income are irrelevant because they do not persist. Research shows the only component of other comprehensive income that is relevant for equity valuation is the unrealized holding gain or loss on marketable securities, and even that applies only to financial institutions (Dhaliwal, Subramanyam, and Trezevant, 2000). Research also suggests that while the funded status of postretirement benefit plans is useful for valuation, unrealized gains and losses arising from changes in funded status are value irrelevant as a component of income (Hann, Heflin, and Subramanyam, 2007). This implies certain components of comprehensive income are irrelevant for determining permanent income, which is probably a more important measure for equity valuation than is economic income. Still, as we already pointed out, economic income is an important measure that has a role distinct from permanent income. The components of other comprehensive income are important in determining economic income.

......NONRECURRING ITEMS

This section describes several nonrecurring items—including extraordinary items, discontinued segments, accounting changes, restructuring charges, and special items—along with their analysis and interpretation.

Extraordinary Items

Extraordinary items are distinguished by their unusual nature and by the infrequency of their occurrence. Prior to the passage of *SFAS 145* (effective for fiscal years beginning after May 2002), the vast majority of extraordinary items were gains and losses from early retirement of debt. Others included losses from natural disasters and expropriation of assets. However, the proportion of companies reporting extraordinary items has declined markedly. This is because under current accounting standards, gains and losses relating to the extinguishment of debt must be both unusual and infrequent (see our discussion of criteria later) to be classified as an extraordinary item, and debt refinancing does not typically meet these criteria.

Extraordinary items are classified separately in the income statement. Because of the stringent criteria for classification, extraordinary items are uncommon. Exhibit 6.3 reports the frequency and magnitude of extraordinary items. The proportion of companies reporting extraordinary items is typically less than 6%, but has increased to as much as 12.4% of reporting companies. Extraordinary items, when they occur, usually constitute less than 3% of sales. The proportion of negative and positive extraordinary items is about the same.

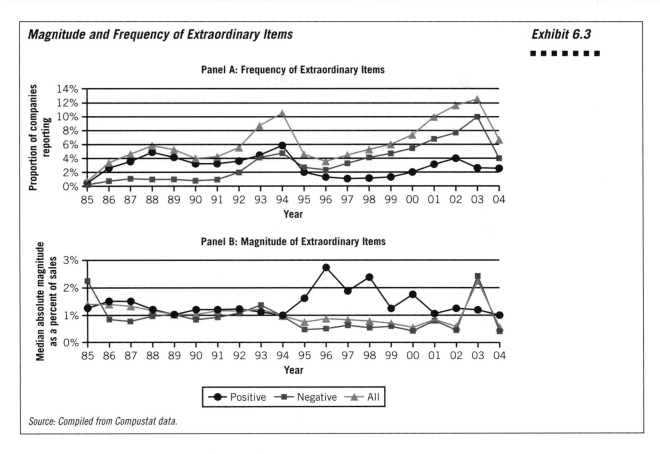

Magnitude and Frequency of Extraordinary Items   *Exhibit 6.3*

Panel A: Frequency of Extraordinary Items

Panel B: Magnitude of Extraordinary Items

Positive   Negative   All

Source: Compiled from Compustat data.

Accounting for Extraordinary Items

To qualify as extraordinary, an item must be *both* unusual in nature and infrequent in occurrence. These terms are defined as follows:

- **Unusual nature.** An event or transaction that has a high degree of abnormality and is unrelated to, or only incidentally related to, the ordinary and typical activities of the company.
- **Infrequent occurrence.** An event or transaction that is not reasonably expected to recur in the foreseeable future.

Extraordinary items are reported, net of tax, as separate line items in the income statement after continuing income. When a company reports extraordinary items, continuing income is called *income before extraordinary items.* Any item that is either unusual or infrequent (not both) cannot be classified as an extraordinary item.

Practice also requires companies to *not* report certain gains and losses as extraordinary items because they are not unusual in nature and are expected to recur as a consequence of customary and continuing business activity. Examples include:

- Write-down or write-off of receivables, inventories, equipment leased to others, deferred R&D costs, or other intangible assets.
- Gains or losses on disposal of a business segment.
- Gains or losses from sale or abandonment of property, plant, or equipment.
- Effects of a strike, including those against competitors and major suppliers.
- Adjustment of accruals on long-term contracts.

Analyzing Extraordinary Items

Extraordinary items are nonrecurring in nature. An analyst, therefore, excludes extraordinary items when computing permanent income. Extraordinary items also are excluded from income when making comparisons over time or across companies. Yet, while extraordinary items are transitory, they yield a cost (or benefit) on the company, dollar for dollar. An analyst must therefore include the entire amount of the extraordinary item when computing economic income.

Extraordinary items are often operating in nature. However, they differ from normal operating revenues or expenses because they are nonrecurring. For example, a loss of inventory from fire arises as a part of the company's operations (and reveals the nature of operating risks inherent in the company's business), but it is not expected to occur on a regular basis. Thus, extraordinary items that arise from a company's business operations are included when computing operating income but excluded when determining permanent income. Extraordinary items also reveal risk exposures of a company. While these risks may be remote, their occurrence suggests the possibility of recurrence at some future date. The large magnitude of most extraordinary losses also encourages analysis even when their occurrence is infrequent. In some cases, extraordinary items may recur, although infrequently. For example, a warehouse by the beach in an area susceptible to hurricanes may incur flood damage every few years. An analyst must consider this when evaluating sustainable earning power.

ANALYSIS VIEWPOINT   **. . . YOU ARE THE SUPPLIER**

Your company supplies raw materials to Chicago Construction Corp. Your job is to annually assess customers for credit terms and policies. Chicago Construction's net income for this year is down by 12%. Your analysis of its financial statements shows this decrease is due to an extraordinary loss attributed to a construction site fire. Absent this extraordinary loss, income is up by 23%. What is your credit assessment of Chicago Construction?

Discontinued Operations

Companies sometimes dispose of entire divisions or product lines. When these dispositions pertain to separately identifiable business segments, they are accorded special accounting treatment in the income statement. A recent standard *(SFAS 144)* has broadened such treatment to include any component of an entity (rather than a segment of a business). A component of an entity comprises operations (and cash flows) that can be clearly distinguished, operationally and for purposes of financial reporting, from the rest of the business.

Exhibit 6.4 shows the magnitude and frequency of discontinued operations over the past two decades. Through the mid-1990s, approximately 2% of publicly traded companies reported discontinued operations in their income statements. Since that time, the frequency of these items has increased markedly to about 12% in 2004. The magnitude of discontinued operations as a percentage of sales, however, has remained fairly constant at about 2% of sales, although decreases in income tend to be larger than the effect of discontinued operations, resulting in net increases. Discontinued operations, when they occur, can be a substantial component of net income.

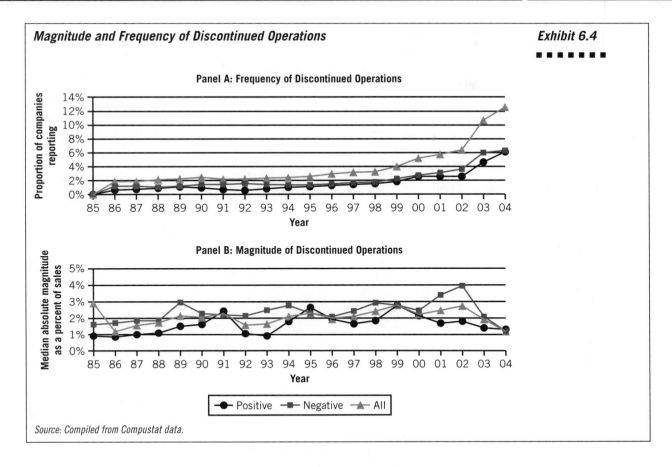

Magnitude and Frequency of Discontinued Operations   **Exhibit 6.4**

Panel A: Frequency of Discontinued Operations

Panel B: Magnitude of Discontinued Operations

Legend: Positive — Negative — All

Source: Compiled from Compustat data.

Accounting for Discontinued Operations

To qualify as discontinued operations, the assets and business activities of the divested segment must be clearly distinguishable (both physically and operationally) from the assets and business activities of the remaining entity. For example, discontinuance of an entire line of products will usually qualify as a discontinued operation, but not the discontinuance of a particular brand. Judgment is involved in deciding what constitutes a discontinued operation since it depends on the nature and scale of a company's business—what constitutes a discontinued operation for one company may not for another. Companies also record gains or losses from discontinued operations when they sell their stake (either fully or partially) in a consolidated subsidiary.

Accounting and reporting for discontinued operations is twofold. First, the income statements for the current and prior two years are restated after excluding the effects of the discontinued operations from the line items that determine continuing income. Second, gains or losses pertaining to the discontinued operations are reported separately, net of their related tax effects, and are excluded from continuing income. Continuing income is called *income before discontinued operations* when discontinued operations are reported.

A company reports gains or losses from discontinued operations (for the current and two prior years) in two categories: (1) operating income or loss from discontinued operations until the management commits to the disposal and (2) gains and losses on disposal, including operating income or loss during the phase-out period. We provide an example of the reporting for discontinued operations in Illustration 6.1.

ILLUSTRATION 6.1

■ ■ ■ ■ ■ ■ ■

Kmart agreed to sell a majority stake in its consolidated subsidiary, Builders Square. Accordingly, Kmart recorded an after-tax loss on disposal of discontinued operations of $385 million in Year 6 and restated its prior two years' income statements to reflect this discontinuance. This restatement resulted in a loss of $260 million in the prior year, which was the operating loss of Builders Square for that year. The left-side of the excerpt below shows the lower part of Kmart's income statements (from its Year 6 annual report). The right side shows the original and restated income statements for Year 5 and an explanation of the $260 million loss on discontinued operations. Note that the loss on disposal of discontinued operations includes $61 million ($446 million less $385 million) in Year 6 and $30 million in Year 5 related to discontinuances *other than* Builders Square.

LOWER PORTION OF INCOME STATEMENT

	Year 6	Year 5
Net income (loss) from continuing operations before extraordinary item	$231	$(230)
Loss from discontinued operations, net of taxes	(5)	(260)
Loss on disposal of discontinued operations, net of taxes	(446)	(30)
Extraordinary item	—	(51)
Net income (loss)	$(220)	$(571)

ORIGINAL AND RESTATED INCOME STATEMENT FOR YEAR 5

	Original	Restated (Builders)	Difference
Net income (loss) from continuing operations before extraordinary item	$(490)	$(230)	$(260)
Loss from discontinued operations, net of taxes		(260) ←	
Loss on disposal of discontinued operations, net of taxes	(30)	(30)	
Extraordinary item	(51)	(51)	
Net income (loss)	$(571)	$(571)	

Analyzing Discontinued Operations

Analysis is futuristic and decision oriented. Therefore, for purposes of analysis, all effects of discontinued operations must be removed from current and past income. This rule applies regardless of whether the objective is determining economic or permanent income or in determining operating or nonoperating income. The adjustment is straightforward for the current and past two years because companies are required to restate their income statements and report the income or loss on discontinued operations separately. Such ready information does not exist for prior years. Some companies restate summary financial information, including income, for the past 10 years, which we can then use. Also, some companies report several prior years' information about discontinued operations separately. Yet, in most cases this information is unavailable. In such situations, an analyst must be careful when conducting intertemporal analysis, such as evaluating income patterns over time.

With regard to a company's financial condition, an analyst must remove the assets and liabilities of the discontinued operations from the balance sheet (if they are not already removed). Amounts for assets and liabilities are typically provided in footnote disclosures. The cumulative gains or losses from discontinued operations should not, however, be removed from equity.

Accounting Changes

Companies can change accounting methods and assumptions underlying financial statements for certain reasons. Sometimes, accounting methods are changed because of a new accounting standard. Other times, accounting methods and/or assumptions are changed to better reflect changing business activities or conditions. Also, managers sometimes change accounting methods and/or assumptions to window-dress financial statements, particularly for managing earnings. To discourage managers from unjustified switching from one accounting method to another, accounting standards require that "in the preparation of financial statements there is a presumption that an accounting principle once adopted should not be changed in accounting for events and transactions of a similar type . . . the presumption that an entity should not change an accounting principle may be overcome only if the enterprise justifies the use of an alternative acceptable accounting principle on the basis that it is preferable."

Accounting standards distinguish among four types of accounting changes: (1) a change in accounting principle, (2) a change in accounting estimate, (3) a change in reporting entity, and (4) correction of an error. We discuss reporting requirements pertaining to each type and examine analysis implications.

Reporting of Accounting Changes

Change in Accounting Principle.   A change in accounting principle occurs when a company switches from one generally accepted accounting principle to another generally accepted accounting principle. The phrase *accounting principle* refers to both the accounting standards and practices used and the methods of applying them. An example of a change in accounting principle is a change in depreciation method from straight line to accelerated.

Under current accounting standards, when a change occurs, current period income is computed using the new principle. The cumulative effect of this change in principle (net of tax) on retained earnings as of the beginning of the period when the change occurs is computed. This cumulative effect is reported in the income statement after extraordinary items, but before net income. This computation is a "catch-up" adjustment, because previously published financial statements are not revised.

The FASB has recently issued a standard *(SFAS 154)* that replaces the cumulative effect treatment, described in the prior paragraph, with retrospective application. That is, the proposed statement will require restatement of prior period statements following the newly adopted accounting principle together with prospective application of that principle. If restatement is impracticable, companies will apply the accounting principle prospectively from the earliest feasible date.

We provide an example of an accounting principle change in Illustration 6.2 per the earlier standard. It is too early to provide an example of a retrospective application under *SFAS 154.*

Change in Accounting Estimate.   Accrual accounting requires estimates of items such as useful lives of assets, warranty costs, inventory obsolescence, pension assumptions, and uncollectible receivables. These are known as *accounting estimates*. Accounting estimates are approximations based on unknown future conditions. As such, accounting estimates can change. There exist certain accounting and disclosure requirements when changes occur in accounting estimates. These are:

- **Prospective application**–a change is accounted for in the period of change and, if applicable, future periods as and when any effects occur (there is no retroactive restatement).
- **Note disclosure**–disclose the effects of the change on both net income and income before extraordinary items (including earnings per share) for the current period only, even when a change affects future periods.

ILLUSTRATION 6.2
■ ■ ■ ■ ■ ■ ■

The following excerpt is an example of the reporting for a change in accounting principle:

SEABOARD CORPORATION—CONSOLIDATED STATEMENT OF EARNINGS

($ thousands)	Year 6	Year 5	Year 4
Earnings before cumulative effect of a change in accounting principle..............	$2,840	$20,202	$35,201
Cumulative effect of changing accounting for inventory (net of $1,922 tax)........	3,006	—	—
Net earnings..	$5,846	$20,202	$35,201

Note: Inventories
During the fourth quarter of Year 6, the company changed its method of accounting for spare parts and supplies used in poultry and pork processing operations retroactively effective January 1, Year 6. Previously these spare parts and supplies were expensed when purchased. Under the new method such purchases will be recorded as inventory and charged to operations when used. The company believes this method is preferable as it provides a better matching of revenues and expenses. The cumulative effect of this accounting change at January 1, Year 6, was to increase net income by $3,006 thousand or $2.02 per common share. The effect of this accounting change was to increase income before cumulative effect of change in accounting principle by $788,000 or $0.53 per common share for the year ended December 31, Year 6. The pro forma effect of retroactive application of this new method of accounting would not materially affect the results of operations for years ended December 31, Year 5 and Year 4.

Illustration 6.3 identifies one example of a change in accounting estimate.

ILLUSTRATION 6.3
■ ■ ■ ■ ■ ■ ■

Delta Airlines previously depreciated its flight equipment over 15 years using a salvage value of 10%. In the fourth quarter of a recent year, Delta changed its depreciation policy to one that assumes a life of 20 years with a salvage value of 5%. This change decreased Delta's depreciation expense by $36 million in that fourth quarter and, consequently, increased its fiscal year net income by $22 million.

Under the newly proposed standard, in addition to estimates of useful lives and salvage values, changes in depreciation policies (such as from straight line to declining balance) will also be treated as a change in estimate and applied prospectively.

Analyzing Accounting Changes

There are several points an analyst must consider when analyzing accounting changes. First, accounting changes are "cosmetic" and yield no cash flow consequences–either present or future. This means the financial condition of a company is not affected by a change in accounting.

Second, while an accounting change is cosmetic, it can sometimes better *reflect* economic reality. For example, a company's decision to extend the depreciable lives of its machinery might be an attempt to better match costs with actual usage patterns. In principle, a necessary condition for a change in accounting methods is that the change better reflect the underlying economics.

Third, an analyst must be alert to earnings management. Earnings management is less of an issue in the adoption of new standards—although, managers may time its adoption for a period when its effect is most favorable (or least detrimental). However, in the case of voluntary accounting changes, earnings management is a likely motivation. While managers sometimes manage earnings through changes in accounting principles, the more popular and shrewd method of earnings management is by changing accounting estimates. Unlike a change in accounting principle, where the cumulative effect is highlighted in the income statement, information about changes in estimates often are buried in the notes. To illustrate, the motive for Delta Airlines' change in depreciation policy, described in Illustration 6.3, is apparent when we examine its pattern in operating losses around that time: Year 2–$(675) million; Year 3–$(575) million; Year 4–$(447) million. This pattern depicts a marked improvement over time—a compounded decrease in losses of 13% per annum. However, when we restate reported numbers as per the original depreciation methods, we see the following pattern in operating losses: Year 2–$(675) million; Year 3–$(609) million; Year 4–$(583) million. This shows the accounting change increases income by $34 million in Year 3 and by $136 million in Year 4. The decline in operating losses using the original data is, thus, a mere 5% per annum.

Another concern with accounting changes is earnings manipulation. Unlike earnings management, which is window dressing within the confines of GAAP, earnings manipulation arises when companies stray beyond acceptable practices. When the SEC staff spots such accounting practices, the company is asked to restate its financial statements. Such restatements, reported in *Accounting Enforcement Releases* (or *AERs*), suggest that a company is adopting excessively aggressive accounting practices. While honest errors do arise, an analyst should be concerned when a company is forced by the SEC to restate its financial statements. At a minimum, this reflects poor earnings quality, and an analyst must take extra care when analyzing financial statements of such companies.

Fourth, an analyst must assess the impact of accounting changes on comparisons across time. It is important for an analyst to compare "apples with apples." This means making sure any comparisons (especially across time) are made with a consistent set of accounting rules. If the company reports the effects of accounting changes for prior years' data in its notes, the income history can be adjusted. If no such information is reported, an analyst must be aware of the potential limitations for any comparisons across time. This is important because companies sometimes change accounting estimates to window-dress earnings' history.

Finally, an analyst would want to evaluate the effect of an accounting change on both economic income and permanent income. For estimating permanent income, the analyst can use the reported numbers under the new method and ignore the cumulative effect. For estimating economic income of the current period, both the current and cumulative effect are included. More generally, an analyst must evaluate the ability of the change to better reflect economic reality. If the change is arbitrary or seems to impair the ability of the numbers to reflect economic reality, then we can undo the effects of the change using note information.

Special Items

Special items refer to transactions and events that are unusual or infrequent, but not both. These items are typically reported as separate line items on the income statement *before* continuing income. Often, special items are nonroutine items that do not meet the criteria for classification as extraordinary.

■ ■ ■ ■ ■ ■ ■
PRICEY D&O
Providers of directors and officers (D&O) liability coverage are demanding full disclosure from clients. The alternative is vastly higher premiums or no coverage at all. Companies are being rejected for dubious revenue-recognition practices, poor internal controls, and financial restatements. Last year a company might have paid a few hundred thousand dollars per year for D&O coverage that now costs more than $1 million.

Exhibit 6.5   **Frequency and Magnitude of Special Items**

■ ■ ■ ■ ■ ■ ■

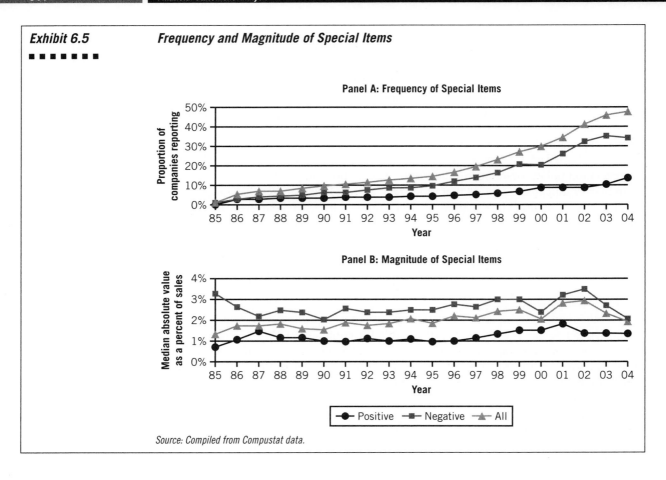

Source: Compiled from Compustat data.

Special items constitute the most common and important class of nonrecurring items. As reported in Exhibit 6.5, their frequency is increasing. The frequency of special items has increased dramatically, from 1% of reporting companies through the 1980s to nearly 48% of reporting companies. Most of this increase has been concentrated in special items that reduce income, primarily restructuring expenses. The magnitude of special items has remained fairly constant at about 2% of sales, with negative effects consistently higher in absolute value than positive effects. These items, when they occur, can have a significant impact on reported profits, often turning a profitable year into a loss. They are generally the most transitory item in income from continuing operations.

Exhibit 6.6 shows the makeup of one-time special charges both by frequency and by dollar value. Restructuring charges and asset write-offs of goodwill, inventory, and property, plant, and equipment (PP&E) form the bulk of such charges. Of these, impairment of long-lived assets and restructuring charges constitute the two major categories of special items. There are two differences between them. First, restructuring charges are associated with major reorganizations of a company as a whole or within a division. Restructuring often involves a change in business strategy, financing, or physical reorganization of the business. On the other hand, asset impairments are narrower in scope, involving the write-down or write-off of a class of assets. A second major difference is that asset impairments are mainly accrual accounting adjustments, while restructuring charges often involve substantial cash flow commitments either contemporaneously or in the future.

Special items pose challenges for analysis. First, the economic implications of special items, such as restructuring charges, are complex. Second, many special items are

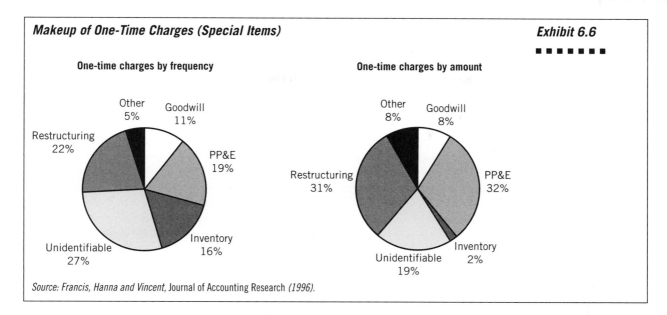

Makeup of One-Time Charges (Special Items)

Exhibit 6.6

One-time charges by frequency

Other 5%
Goodwill 11%
Restructuring 22%
PP&E 19%
Unidentifiable 27%
Inventory 16%

One-time charges by amount

Other 8%
Goodwill 8%
Restructuring 31%
PP&E 32%
Unidentifiable 19%
Inventory 2%

Source: Francis, Hanna and Vincent, Journal of Accounting Research *(1996)*.

discretionary and, hence, serve earnings management aims. The remainder of this section focuses on the two major types of special items: asset impairments and restructuring charges. We describe the accounting and reporting for these items, and discuss the analysis implications.

Asset Impairments

Impairment of Long-Lived Assets.   A long-lived asset is said to be impaired when its fair value (market value or value from use within the company) is below its carrying value (book value in the balance sheet). Asset impairments occur for many reasons, these include a decline in the asset market value, a decline in market demand for the output from the asset, technological obsolescence, and changes in the company's business strategy. Asset impairments are a byproduct of conservatism—report at the lower of cost or market. GAAP does not permit writing up asset values.

Asset impairments must be distinguished from both restructurings and disposals of segments. We have already discussed differences between a restructuring and an asset impairment. An asset impairment is also different from a disposal of a business segment, both in its accounting treatment and in its economic implications. In a disposal, a company sells one or more assets, or a business segment, and ceases to operate the disposed assets. In contrast, an impaired asset, while it can be sold or disposed of in any manner, is often retained in the company and operated at a reduced level, made idle, or abandoned. From an accounting point of view, disposal of a business segment is treated as discontinued operations that we discussed earlier, while asset impairments are recorded as special items.

SFAS 121 prescribes a two-step procedure for determining the amount of impairment[1]. First, an asset impairment is recognized when the carrying value of the asset is below the *undiscounted* value of future expected cash flows from the asset. Second, once this condition is satisfied, the amount of loss is measured as the difference between the

[1] *SFAS 121* has now been superseded by *SFAS 144*. However, *SFAS 144* has not altered provisions relating to impairments in a material manner.

asset carrying value and its fair value, which equals the *discounted* value of future expected cash flows from the asset if its fair value cannot be determined from the market.

This standard does not require disclosure about the determination of the impairment amount, nor does it require disclosure about probable asset impairments. The standard also allows flexibility in determining when and how much of an asset's value to write off and does not require a plan for disposal of the asset. Illustration 6.4 gives a typical disclosure of asset impairment.

ILLUSTRATION 6.4
■ ■ ■ ■ ■ ■ ■

Chiron Corp. reported an impairment loss of $31.3 million in its income statement pertaining to its manufacturing facility in Puerto Rico. The company discloses the following information in its notes: "The cumulative impact on the company's manufacturing needs of recent product developments prompted management to conclude that Chiron currently has excess manufacturing capacity relative to its projected needs. Specifically, management concluded that the company's need for its idle pharmaceutical fill and finishing facility in Puerto Rico (the "Puerto Rico facility"), originally outfitted as a second manufacturing site of Betaseron, was eliminated due to manufacturing process improvements and cumulative impact of the introduction of a competing product . . . [later] management determined that it could not find a suitable use for the Puerto Rico facility consistent with its previous expectations for the facility's use as a contract manufacturing plant. As a result, the company reviewed the carrying amount of the Puerto Rico facility and related machinery and equipment assets for impairment in accordance with *SFAS 121*. Consequently, . . . the Company recorded a $31.3 million impairment loss to record the Puerto Rico facility and related machinery and equipment at their individual estimated fair market values determined on the basis of independent appraisals."

Impairment of Other Assets.   In addition to impairment of long-lived assets, companies sometimes write off other types of assets such as receivables, inventories, and goodwill. While the values of inventory and receivables are determinable with reasonable accuracy, the write-off of goodwill is the result of a valuation process and is, therefore, somewhat subjective (see Chapter 5).

Restructuring Charges

Unlike asset impairments, restructuring charges are usually associated with major changes in a company's business and strategy. Restructuring usually entails extensive reorganization including divestment of business units, termination of contractual agreements, discontinuation of product lines, worker retrenchment, change in management, and writing off of assets often combined with new investments in plant, technology, and manpower. Restructuring comes at a cost. Divested business units often are sold at a loss, laid-off employees demand compensation, written-off fixed assets and inventory yield losses, lease buy-outs are costly, and new investments and improvements must be paid for. Companies usually make a provision for the cost of the restructuring program, including severance accruals and accruals for asset write-downs, among others. This provision is created through a restructuring charge, which is entirely charged to the current income statement as a special item. When the restructuring program is implemented, sometimes over many years, actual costs are charged against the provision as and when incurred. The remaining balance in the provision is shown as a restructuring reserve. Any remaining balance in the reserve at the completion of the program is reversed by recording it back to income.

To illustrate, Kodak extensively re-structured its operations in 2003 and 2004, taking cumulative charges in excess of $1.1 billion. These charges reduced income from continuing oper-ations by over 60% in 2003 and changed its 2004 profit into a loss.

As mentioned in its MD&A, Kodak's main motivation for its restructur-ing program is cost reduction. Kodak discusses its restructuring activities in its 2004 annual report: "Currently, the Company is being adversely impacted by the progressing digital substitution. As the Company continues to adjust its

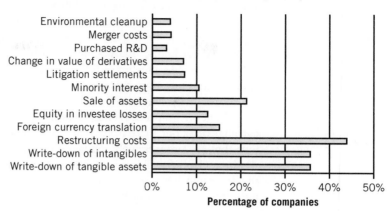

Types of Special Losses Reported by Companies

operating model in light of changing business conditions, it is probable that ongoing cost reduction activities will be required from time to time."

Analyzing Special Items

Analyzing special items is a challenging and important task in accounting analysis. The use of estimates creates opportunities for managing earnings. Also challenging is understanding the underlying economics of special items, especially restructuring charges. The importance of special items arises because of their frequency and impact on net income of past, present, and future periods. In this section, we explain why spe-cial items are a popular tool for earnings management. We then describe the implica-tions of special charges and the adjustments necessary for financial statements.

Earnings Management and Special Charges.   Exhibit 6.5 showed that a large pro-portion of special items, both in frequency and in magnitude, is income-decreasing. Further, the proportion of companies reporting income-decreasing items is increasing over time. This increase in special charges is troubling and has gained the attention of the SEC. The SEC warns that earnings management techniques such as the use of "big-bath restructuring charges" are eroding confidence in financial reporting.

What is the motivation for reporting special charges? The answer is that one-time charges are of less concern to investors under the assumption they are nonrecurring and, therefore, do not persist into the future. If classified as transitory (nonrecurring) items by analysts, their impact on stock price is considerably lessened.

To illustrate, consider a company earning $2 per share in perpetuity. Given a cost of capital of 10%, the value of this company is $20 ($2/0.10). Now, alternatively, assume this company overstates earnings by $1 per share for four consecutive periods and then reverses them with a single charge in the final year as follows:

($ per share)	Year 1	Year 2	Year 3	Year 4
Recurring earnings	$3	$3	$3	$ 3
Special charge	0	0	0	(4)
Net income	$3	$3	$3	$(1)

This pattern of net income suggests a permanent component of $3 per share and a transitory component of a negative $4 per share in Year 4. (Recall the impact of a dollar of permanent earnings to company value is equal to that dollar divided by its cost of capital, whereas the impact of a dollar of transitory earnings to company value is a dollar.) Accordingly, many analysts would naively value this company's stock at $26 [($3/0.10) − $4]. Further, if the analyst entirely ignores this one-time charge (as some analysts suggest), then this company's stock is valued at $30 ($3/0.10). These amounts are substantially different than the correct value of $20.

Exhibit 6.7 graphically illustrates this point. The recast line reflects a constant "true" earnings of $2 per share from Year −9 to Year 0. The reported line shows reported earnings that are progressively managed upward, with a massive charge taken in Year −3. At the end of Year 0, both cumulative reported and cumulative "true" earnings are, in reality, equal because all earnings management has been reversed. The dotted lines indicate forecasts of both "true" earnings and reported earnings trends beyond Year 0 based on past earnings' time series. It can be seen that an illusion of higher permanent earnings and earnings growth can be created by regularly managing earnings upward (for example, by delaying the write-down of impaired assets or other accruals) and reversing the accruals with special one-time charges.

Exhibit 6.7

■ ■ ■ ■ ■ ■ ■

Managing Earnings Level and Growth Perceptions with a One-Time Charge

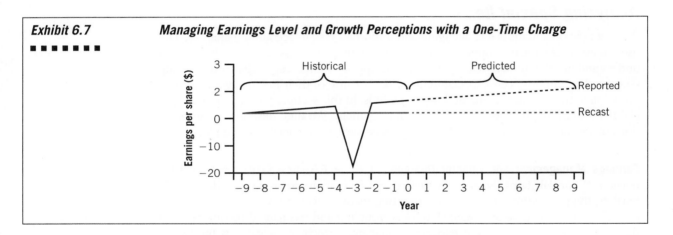

This graphical illustration shows that when analysts focus on only recurring components of earnings and ignore nonrecurring charges, managers are motivated to manage earnings in this manner. The illustration also shows we should be wary of special charges. It is important to investigate companies that repeatedly take one-time charges to determine if these charges are the result of an earnings management strategy.

Income Statement Adjustments.   As Exhibit 6.7 reveals, one-time charges can seriously distort earnings patterns and trends. It is important for an analyst to make adjustments for determining the effect of special charges, especially on permanent income. This section discusses adjustments to determine a company's permanent income and then discusses adjustments to determine economic income. Permanent income should reflect the profitability of a company under normal circumstances. Most special charges constitute operating expenses that need to be reflected in permanent income. At a basic level, special charges reflect either understatements of past expenses or "investments" for improved future profitability.

To illustrate, consider a company that invests $40 million in machinery to manufacture a drug. The company expects the drug to be sold over the remaining life of its patent, which is eight years. Accordingly, the company depreciates the machinery (on a straight-line basis with no salvage value) over an eight-year period–depreciation expense is $5 million per year. At the end of the fourth year, however, a competing, revolutionary product eliminates the market for this company's drug. Consequently, the company stops producing the drug at the end of the fourth year. Also, the machinery is scrapped and the company recognizes an asset impairment charge of $20 million (which is the machine's carrying value at the end of the fourth year). The company reports the impairment as a one-time charge that is not expected to occur again. Do we concur with this company's assessment? Well, let's begin by looking at the cause of the asset impairment. Basically, the impairment arose because the company overestimated the economic life of the drug and, hence, the machine. This led to undercharging depreciation expense over the four-year period when the machine was used. The proper analysis for this case would be to adjust depreciation expense assuming a four-year life and restate past (and current) earnings. Specifically, we would decrease current period earnings (along with each of the prior three years' earnings if we are analyzing earnings trend) by $5 million.

An actual example of such a scenario is the $31.3 million write-down of the Puerto Rico manufacturing facility by Chiron (see Illustration 6.4). This facility is idled because of process improvements and the introduction of a competing product, which led to recognizing an impairment loss. It is important to note that the costs of the Puerto Rico facility are normal operating expenses and that these costs must be allocated to the entire period during which the facility has been operational–this period often can be determined by examining past financial reports. If it cannot be determined, these costs can be distributed over an arbitrary prior period of, say, five years.

Sometimes special charges are "investments" for improving future profitability. To illustrate, consider a company that streamlines its procurement procedures. This streamlining results in reducing the workforce in the procurement department by 20%, which is expected to save the company $1.3 million per year in the future. The laid-off workers are paid $4.2 million as severance compensation. The company decides to expense this entire amount as a one-time charge. On the surface, this accounting treatment seems reasonable. However, note the worker severance is expected to reduce future expenses by $1.3 million per year. Consequently, the $4.2 million severance compensation is similar to an investment in a long-term asset that is expected to generate net revenues (or reduced costs) of $1.3 million per year in the future. This means the proper accounting is to allocate the $4.2 million over current and future periods when the benefits are expected to be realized. If this period cannot be determined, then we can use an estimate–say, a period of five years.

Most restructuring charges are, at least in part, in the form of an investment. One objective of restructuring programs is streamlining a company's operations so as to improve future profitability. A restructuring program that consists of cash outflows such as severance compensation and accrual adjustments such as asset write-offs is a type of investment for improving future profitability. Accordingly, our analysis should allocate that portion of the restructuring charge over future periods expected to reap the benefits from the restructuring program.

One caveat: because restructuring charges usually impact several different years, an analyst often needs to examine prior years' reports so as to estimate the impact of allocating past restructuring charges in determining permanent income. Also, unlike permanent income, where an analyst must determine normal profitability for a company, the determination of economic income involves measuring the effects on equity of all events that occur in the period. This means the entire amount of any special charges is included when determining economic income. Restructuring charges often include a provision for the estimated future cost of the restructuring program. This entire charge is taken in the year the program is initiated, although the actual costs are incurred over several later periods. In this situation, an alternative approach in determining economic income is to only adjust for amounts actually incurred for each year, rather than the entire charge. For example, while AT&T took a $923 million restructuring charge in 2004, only $550 million related to 2004. The remaining $373 million will be charged to future years. When such a method is adopted, it is important to remember to also include actual costs related to past restructuring programs.

Adjustments to Balance Sheet. A major focus of the asset impairment standard is the balance sheet. Consequently, unlike income that is distorted by one-time charges, these charges (especially inventory and long-term asset write-downs) improve the ability of the balance sheet to reflect business reality by reporting assets closer to net realizable values.

Still, two points demand attention. First, as already noted, a portion of most restructuring charges is often in the form of a provision. This means the effects on assets and liabilities are reflected gradually over time when the actual costs are incurred. A question that arises is should the balance sheet include the entire provision or should the remaining balance in the restructuring reserve (reflecting costs yet incurred) be netted against equity? The answer depends on the analysis objectives. If the analysis is considering a going-concern scenario, it is better to keep the provision in the balance sheet because it reflects a more realistic picture of the long-term assets and liabilities. However, if the analysis objective is to determine the liquidating value of a company, it is better to offset the restructuring provision against equity. Care must be taken to ensure that determination of economic income is consistent with the balance sheet treatment. The second main point is that asset write-offs introduce a conservative bias in the reporting of assets and liabilities. Because asset write-ups are not permitted in the United States, (they are, e.g., allowed in the United Kingdom), the balance sheet is conservatively distorted from asset impairments.

REVENUE RECOGNITION

Revenues are defined in practice as "inflows or other enhancements of assets of an entity or settlements of its liabilities" resulting from a company's "ongoing major or central operations." **Gains,** on the other hand, are increases in net assets (equity) resulting from "peripheral or incidental transactions" of a company. Distinguishing between revenues and gains depends on the usual business activities of a company. Because our analysis treats these items differently (i.e., revenues are expected to persist, while gains are not), their distinction is important. It is also important to understand when a company recognizes revenues and gains. Our analytical adjustments sometimes modify income numbers using revenue recognition information. An important question is when, or at what point, in the sequence of revenue-earning activities in which a company is engaged, is it proper to recognize revenues and gains as earned? This section addresses this question.

Guidelines for Revenue Recognition

From our analysis perspective, inappropriate accrual recognition of revenues (and gains) can have one of two undesirable consequences:

1. If a company records revenue prematurely or belatedly, then revenue is assigned to the wrong period.
2. If a company records revenue prior to reasonable certainty of realization, then revenue might be recorded in one period and later canceled or reversed in another—this overstates income in the first period and understates it in the latter period.

These two effects adversely affect income measurement. To counter this, accounting applies strict and conservative rules regarding revenue recognition. Generally, revenue is recognized when it is both realized (or realizable) and earned. Exhibit 6.8 lists criteria that must be satisfied for revenue recognition. While these criteria are seemingly straightforward, they are subject to certain exceptions and have, in practice, been interpreted in different ways. To understand these variations for analysis purposes, the next section considers the application of these criteria under special circumstances.

Revenue Recognition Criteria   **Exhibit 6.8**

- Earning activities creating revenue are substantially complete, and no significant effort is necessary to complete the transaction.
- Risk of ownership in sales is effectively passed to the buyer.
- Revenue and the associated expense are measured or estimated with reasonable accuracy.
- Revenue recognized normally yields an increase in cash, receivables, or securities. Under certain conditions it yields an increase in inventories or other assets, or a decrease in liabilities.
- Revenue transaction is at arm's length with an independent party(ies) (not with controlled parties).
- Revenue transaction is not subject to revocation (such as a right of return).

Uncertainty in Revenue Collection

Companies use a provision for doubtful (uncollectible) accounts to reflect uncertainty in the collectibility of receivables from credit sales. A company makes a judgment, based on the circumstances, when it can no longer reasonably assure the collectibility of receivables. This judgment can be conservative or it might use liberal or optimistic assumptions. When collectibility is no longer reasonably assured, practice follows a general procedure to defer recognition of revenue until cash is collected.

Revenue When Right of Return Exists

When the buyer has a right of return, revenue is recognized at the time of sale *only* if the following conditions are met:

- Price is substantially fixed or determinable at the sale date.
- Buyer pays the seller or is obligated to pay the seller (not contingent on resale).
- Buyer's obligation to seller is unchanged in event of theft or damage to product.
- Buyer has economic substance apart from the seller.

- Seller has no significant obligations for future performance related to the sale.
- Returns are reasonably estimated.

If these conditions are met, sales revenue and cost of sales are recorded but reduced to reflect estimated returns and related expenses; if not met, revenue recognition is postponed.

Franchise Revenues

Accounting standards for franchisors require that franchise fee revenue from franchise sales be recognized only when all material services or conditions relating to the sale are substantially performed or satisfied by the franchisor. This also applies to continuing franchise fees, continuing product sales, agency sales, repossessed franchises, franchising costs, commingled revenue, and relationships between a franchisor and a franchisee. A typical franchise fee arrangement follows:

ANALYSIS EXCERPT

Application, License, and Royalty Fees. All fees from licensed operation are included in revenue as earned. Management accelerated the revenue recognition for application fees from the time the site was approved or construction began to the time cash is received. Management believes this method will more accurately relate the income recognition to performance of the related service. . . . License fees are earned when the related store opens. Unearned license fees which have been collected are included in current liabilities. Royalty fees are based on licensee revenues and are recognized in the period the related revenues are earned.

—Church's Chicken

Product Financing Arrangements

A *product financing arrangement* is an agreement involving the transfer or sponsored acquisition of inventory that (although it sometimes resembles a sale of inventory) is in substance a means of financing inventory. For example, if a company transfers ("sells") inventory to another company and concurrently agrees to repurchase the inventory at a later date, this transaction is likely a product financing arrangement and not a sale and subsequent purchase of inventory. In essence, if a party bearing the risks and rewards of ownership transfers inventory to a purchaser and in a related transaction agrees to repurchase the product at a specified price over a specified time, or guarantees some specified resale price for sales of the product to outside parties, the arrangement is a product financing arrangement and is accounted for as such. In this case the inventory remains on the seller's statements and the seller recognizes no revenue.

Revenue under Contracts

Accounting for *long-term* construction contracts for items like buildings, aircraft, ships, or heavy machinery poses conceptual problems for the determination of revenue and profit. GAAP requires companies to use the **percentage-of-completion method** when reasonable estimates exist for both costs to complete a contract and progress toward completion of the contract. A common basis of profit estimation is to record part of the estimated total profit based on the ratio of costs incurred to date divided by expected total costs. Other acceptable methods of estimation are based on units completed, engineering estimates, or units delivered. Under this method, current or anticipated losses are fully recognized in the period when they are initially identified. Johnson Controls describes its revenue recognition as follows:

ANALYSIS EXCERPT

Revenue Recognition. The Company recognizes revenue from long-term systems installation contracts of the Controls Group over the contractual period under the percentage-of-completion method of accounting (see "Long-Term Contracts"). In all other cases, the Company recognizes revenue at the time products are shipped and title passes to the customer or as services are performed.

Long-Term Contracts. Under the percentage-of-completion method of accounting used for long-term contracts, sales and gross profit are recognized as work is performed based on the relationship between actual costs incurred and total estimated costs at completion. Sales and gross profit are adjusted prospectively for revisions in estimated total contract costs and contract values. Estimated losses are recorded when identified. Claims against customers are recognized as revenue upon settlement. The amount of accounts receivable due after one year is not significant.

Unearned Revenue

Under long-term performance contracts–such as product warranty contracts and software maintenance contracts–revenues are often collected in advance. Under such circumstances, revenues are recognized proportionally over the entire period of the contract. The logic for such accounting is that although revenue in this case is *realizable*, it is not *earned* until the contract's service period expires. The amount of revenues that are still unrecognized appear in the balance sheet as a liability called *unearned revenue.*

Analysis Implications of Revenue Recognition

The income statement is important to the analysis and valuation of a company. This statement is also important to management for these same reasons and others, including its role in accounting-based contractual agreements, management pressure to achieve income-based results, management compensation linked to income, and the value of stock options. Given management's incentives, we rationally expect management to select and apply accounting principles that best meet their own interests but are still within acceptable accounting practice. The objectives of income reporting do not always align with management's incentives in this area. Our analysis must be alert to management propensities in this area and the accounting discretion available.

ANALYSIS EXCERPT

Datapoint Corporation recorded a significant amount of sales that sales representatives booked by asking customers to order millions of dollars of computer equipment months in advance with payment to be made later. In many of these cases, Datapoint recorded sales when it had not even manufactured such equipment. It is reported that its sales representatives were under intense pressure to achieve unreasonable or unattainable goals. Datapoint subsequently reversed these sales and consented to an SEC order barring it from such future violations.

Recording of revenue is a critical event in income determination. Our analysis must take aim at the accounting methods to ascertain whether they properly reflect economic reality. For example, if a manufacturer records profits on sale to a dealer, our analysis must inquire about dealer inventories and market conditions—because real earnings activity consists of selling to the ultimate consumer.

Managers' propensities and incentives to manage revenue yield many pronouncements on the subject of revenue recognition by accounting regulatory agencies. In spite of these, our analysis must remain alert to accounting approaches skirting the spirit, if not the letter, of these pronouncements. The following excerpt provides an example:

ANALYSIS EXCERPT

Prime Motor Inns earns a major portion of its income, not from core operations, but rather from hotel sales, construction fees, and interest. In recording these nonrecurring revenues, Prime Motor Inns stretched recognition criteria by accepting notes and receivables of dubious value, and by guaranteeing to buyers of their hotels, and their bankers, certain levels of future income. While they recorded revenues, they did not record contingent liabilities associated with these revenues.

Aware of these revenue recognition problems, the SEC expressed its belief that significant uncertainties regarding a seller's ability to realize noncash proceeds received in transactions often arise when the purchaser is thinly capitalized, or highly leveraged, or when the purchaser's assets consist primarily of those purchased from the seller. These characteristics raise doubt as to whether revenue recognition is appropriate. Circumstances fueling questions about revenue recognition include:

- Lack of substantial equity capital in the purchasing entity other than that provided by the seller.
- Existence of contingent liabilities such as debt guarantees or agreements requiring the seller to infuse cash into the purchasing entity under certain conditions.
- Sale of assets or operations that have historically not produced operating cash flows sufficient to fund future debt service and dividend expectations.

Even when a company receives cash proceeds, any guarantees or other agreements requiring the company to infuse cash into the purchasing entity impacts the validity of revenue recognition. Revenue should not be recognized until (1) cash flows from operating activities are sufficient to fund debt service and dividend requirements (on an accrual basis), or (2) the company's investment in the purchasing entity is or can be readily converted to cash and the company has no further obligations under any debt guarantees or other agreements requiring it to make additional investments in the purchasing entity. Amounts of any deferred revenue, including deferral of interest or dividend revenue, are generally disclosed in a balance sheet as a deduction from the related asset account. Notes to the financial statements usually offer a description of such transactions including any commitments and contingencies, and the accounting methods applied.

Current practice generally does not allow for recognition of revenue in advance of sale. For example, it is not typical to recognize increases in the market value of property such as land, equipment, or buildings; the accretion of values in timber or natural resources; or increases in the value of inventories. Yet the timing of sales is an important item that is partly within the discretion of management. This gives management certain latitude in revenue recognition as evidenced in the following:

ANALYSIS EXCERPT

Thousand Trails, a membership campground operator, recorded revenue from membership fees when a new member initially signed even though these fees were nearly 90% financed and many canceled within days of signing. When their revenue recognition practices became public, Thousand Trails' stock price sharply declined.

ANALYSIS VIEWPOINT   *. . . YOU ARE THE BANKER*

Playground Equipment Company calls on you for a long-term loan to expand operations. Although you are its banker, they are a recent client with new management. In reviewing financial statements as part of its application, you notice it recognizes revenue *during production.* The statements report: "revenue is recognized during production because production activity is the critical event in the company's earning process . . . and deferring revenue substantially impairs the usefulness of the financial statements." You ask a colleague for her opinion, and she feels its revenue recognition method is too liberal. She voices a preference for revenue recognition at point of sale or, possibly, when cash is received. Do you require Playground Equipment to restate its statements? What risks do you see in acting on this loan?

DEFERRED CHARGES

Deferred charges are costs incurred that are deferred because they are expected to benefit future periods. The increasing complexities of business activities are expanding the number and types of deferred charges. Examples are research and development costs and computer software expenditures. The distinction between deferred charges and intangible assets is often vague. In most cases, costs arising from operating activities are classified as deferred charges, while those arising from investing activities are classified as intangible assets.

The motivation for deferral of costs is to better match costs with expected benefits. This motivation underlies the capitalization of all long-term assets and was discussed in Chapter 4. If a cost incurred in the current period benefits a future period by either a contribution to revenues or reduction in costs, then a company defers this cost until the future period(s). For example, if a company incurs start-up costs in operating new, better, or more efficient facilities, it can defer these costs and match (amortize) them to expected future benefit periods.

Research and Development

Companies undertake research, exploration, and development activities for many reasons. Some of these activities are directed at maintaining existing products, while others aim at developing new products and processes. Research activities aim at discovery, and development activities are a translation of research. R&D activities exclude routine or periodic alterations in ongoing operations, market research, and testing activities.

Accounting for Research and Development

Accounting for R&D expenses is problematic. Reasons for difficulties in R&D accounting include:

- High uncertainty of ultimate benefits derived from R&D activities.
- An often significant lapse of time between initiation of R&D activities and determination of their success.
- Evaluation problems due to the intangible nature of most R&D activities.

These characteristics of R&D activities cause difficulties in accounting for them. Consequently, U.S. accounting requires companies to expense R&D costs when incurred. Only costs of materials, equipment, and facilities having *alternative future uses* (in R&D projects or otherwise) are capitalized as tangible assets.

Analysis Research
VALUING R&D EXPENDITURES

Are R&D expenditures assets? Do R&D expenditures benefit periods other than the period of the outlay? Analysis research implies R&D expenditures are valued much like other long-lived assets. For expenditures benefiting the current period only, the market immediately reduces the value of the company. Examples include rent, utilities, and taxes. If an expenditure benefits future periods, and those benefits exceed its costs, the market does not reduce the value of the company— in fact, the expenditure *increases*

company value. Research indicates the market assesses R&D expenditures in a manner similar to many long-lived assets like property, plant, and equipment. In several cases, the market is found to value R&D expenditures as possessing greater future value than many long-lived assets. This market assessment accorded R&D expenditures is inconsistent with the accounting treatment for them. R&D expenditures are generally expensed as incurred. Why the discrepancy? The accounting treatment is a convenient solu-

tion to a difficult valuation problem. More research is needed to precisely estimate the net benefits of R&D expenditures before capitalization of their costs is likely. More important, we need research on a measurement system to better assess the future benefits of *specific* R&D expenditures. R&D expenditures are not all equal, and advances in accounting for R&D depend on better techniques to recognize these differences and appropriately account for them.

Costs identified with R&D activities include:

- Materials, equipment, and facilities acquired or constructed for a *specific* R&D project, or purchased intangibles having *no* alternative future uses (in R&D projects or otherwise).
- Materials consumed in R&D activities; and depreciation of equipment or facilities, and amortization of intangible assets used in R&D activities having alternative future uses.
- Salaries and other related costs of personnel engaged in R&D activities.
- Services performed by others in connection with R&D activities.
- Allocation of indirect costs, excluding general and administrative costs not directly related to R&D activities.

Analyzing Research and Development

Analysis of R&D expenditures is challenging. They are often of sufficient magnitude to warrant scrutiny in an analysis of a company's current and future income. Accounting for R&D expenditures is a simple solution to a complex phenomenon. Future benefits are undoubtedly created by many R&D activities and, conceptually, these R&D

expenditures should not be expensed as incurred. It is the uncertainty of these benefits that limits R&D capitalization. Yet expensing R&D costs impairs the usefulness of income. For example, when a company incurs a major R&D outlay in a desire for future benefits, there is a decline in income at the same time the market often revalues upward the company's stock price. Our analysis recognizes that while current accounting virtually assures no overstatement in R&D assets, it is at the loss of reasonable measures of expenditures to match with revenues arising from R&D activities. Accounting ignores the productive experience of many ongoing R&D activities. It does, however, achieve a uniformity of accounting for R&D activities and avoids difficult judgments with a policy of capitalization and deferral. Nevertheless, current "nonaccounting" for R&D activities fails to effectively serve the needs and interests of users of financial statements.

In spite of accounting problems, it is reasonable to assume companies pursue R&D projects with expectations of positive returns. Companies often have specific return expectations, and their realization or nonrealization can be monitored and estimated as R&D projects progress. A policy of deferral of R&D costs affords managements and their independent auditors, who regularly work with uncertainties and estimates, an opportunity to convey useful information of R&D outlays. Currently, R&D outlays are treated as if they have no future benefits. Consequently, our analysis does not benefit from the insights of those in the best position to provide them.

To assess the quality and potential value of R&D outlays, our analysis needs to know more than the periodic R&D expense. We desire information on the types of research performed, the R&D outlays by category, technical feasibility, commercial viability, and the potential of projects periodically assessed and reevaluated. We also desire information on a company's success/failure experience with R&D activities to date. Current accounting does not provide us this basic information. Except in cases of voluntary disclosure, or an investor or lender with sufficient influence, we are unable to obtain this information.

What our analysis can safely assume is that expensing of R&D outlays yields more conservative balance sheets. There are likely fewer "bad" news surprises from R&D activities with this accounting treatment. Still, our analysis must realize that with a lack of information about potential benefits, we are also unaware of potential disasters befalling a company tempted or forced to spend added funds in R&D projects whose promise is great but whose failure is imminent.

ANALYSIS VIEWPOINT   **. . . YOU ARE THE ANALYST**

The announcement of net income for California Technology Corporation shows an increase of 10%. Your analysis of its operating activities reveals the increase in income is due to a decrease in research and development expenditures. If R&D expenditures for California Technology equaled that for the previous year, income would be down by more than 15%. What is your assessment of the future profitability of California Technology Corporation based on its income announcement?

Computer Software Expenses

Development of computer software is a specialized activity that does not fit the usual expenditures of R&D activities. Development of software for marketing purposes is an ongoing activity leading directly to current or future revenues. At some point in the software's development cycle, its costs need to be deferred and matched against future revenues. Current practice in accounting for expenditures of computer software to be sold, leased, or otherwise marketed identifies a point referred to as *technological feasibility* where these costs are capitalized and matched against future revenues. Until the establishment of the point of technological feasibility, all expenditures are expensed as incurred (similar to R&D). Expenditures incurred after technological feasibility, and until the product is ready for general release to customers, are capitalized as an intangible asset. Additional costs to produce software from the masters and package it for distribution are inventoried and charged against revenue as a cost of the product sold.

Exploration and Development Costs in Extractive Industries

The search for new deposits of natural resources is important to companies in extractive industries. These industries include oil, natural gas, metals, coal, and nonmetallic minerals. The importance of these industries and their special accounting problems deserve our separate attention. As with R&D activities, the search for and development of natural resources is characterized by high risk. Risk involves uncertainty; and for income determination, uncertainty yields measurement and recognition problems. For extractive industries, the problem is whether exploration and development costs that are reasonably expected to be recovered from sale of natural resources are expensed as incurred or capitalized and amortized over the expected future benefit period. While many companies expense exploration and development costs as incurred, some charge off a portion and capitalize the remainder. Few companies capitalize all exploration and development costs.

Accounting for Extractive Industries

Accounting regulators have made various attempts to curtail these divergent practices. The FASB prescribed *successful efforts accounting* for oil and gas producing companies. This directs that exploration costs, except costs of drilling exploratory wells, are capitalized when incurred. These costs are later expensed if the resource is unsuccessful *or* reclassified as an amortizable asset if proved oil or gas reserves are discovered. The SEC disagreed with this approach and instead favored *reserve recognition accounting* (a current value method). This led the FASB to reconsider and, in effect, permitted the same alternatives to continue. The SEC subsequently requested the FASB to develop supplementary disclosures, including value-based disclosures. The FASB responded with the following required supplementary *disclosures* for publicly traded oil and gas producers:

- Proved oil and gas reserve quantities.
- Capitalized costs related to oil and gas producing activities.
- Costs incurred in acquisition, exploration, and development activities.
- Results of operations for oil and gas producing activities.
- Measures of discounted future net cash flows for proved reserves.

Both publicly traded and other companies are required to disclose the method of accounting for costs incurred in oil and gas producing activities and the manner of disposing of related capitalized costs.

Disclosure is one thing and accounting measurement is another. The successful efforts accounting method has not received general support. Yet, in sanctioning use of full-cost accounting, the SEC provided that costs under this method are capitalized up to a ceiling. This ceiling is determined by the present value of company reserves. Capitalized costs exceeding this ceiling are expensed. When falling oil prices lower this ceiling, companies have and likely will continue to pressure the SEC to suspend or modify the rules.

Analysis Implications for Extractive Industries

The variety of acceptable methods of treating exploration and development costs in extractive industries hampers our comparison of results across companies. Accounting in this industry continues to exhibit diversity. The two methods in common use, and the variations on these methods, can yield significantly different results. Our analysis must be aware of this. Many analysts favor successful efforts accounting over full-cost accounting because it better matches costs with related revenues and is more consistent with current accounting practices. Successful efforts accounting requires a direct relation between costs incurred and specific reserves discovered before these exploration and development costs are capitalized. In contrast, full-cost accounting permits companies to label unsuccessful exploration and development activities as assets.

·······SUPPLEMENTARY EMPLOYEE BENEFITS

This section describes the accounting, analysis, and interpretation of supplementary employee benefits, with an emphasis on employee stock options.

Overview of Supplementary Employee Benefits

Societal pressures, competition, and scarcity of employee talent have led to a proliferation of employee benefits supplementary to salaries and wages. Some fringe benefits like vacation pay, bonuses, profit sharing, and paid health or life insurance are identifiable with the period when earned or granted. These identifiable expenses do not pose problems of accounting recognition and accrual. Other supplementary benefits, due to their tentative or contingent nature, are not accorded full or timely accounting recognition. Some of these benefits and the accounting for them are described here:

- **Deferred compensation contracts** are promises to pay employees in the future, some with contingencies. A company often grants them to key executives it wishes to retain or who desire deferring income to postretirement or lower tax years. These contracts often include noncompete clauses or specify an employee's availability for consulting services. Accounting generally requires that at least the present value of deferred compensation is accrued in a systematic and rational manner over the period of active employment starting when the contract is entered into.
- **Stock appreciation rights (SARs)** are stock rights granted to an employee on a specified number of shares. SAR awards are based on the increase in market value of a company's stock since date of grant and can be awarded in cash, stock, or a combination of both. Under these plans, a company records compensation expense at each period. Expense is computed as the difference between the award price of the shares and their grant date option price. Accounting provides a method for apportioning expense over the service period–changes in market price from period to period are reflected as adjustments to compensation expense.

Employee Stock Options

Employee stock options (ESOs), also referred to as *stock-based compensation,* are arguably the most popular form of incentive compensation. There are many reasons for this popularity. First, companies contend ESOs enhance performance by giving employees a stake in the business and thereby align employee and company incentives. Second, ESOs are viewed by employees as means to riches. Thousands of managers, scientists, accountants, engineers, programmers, and secretaries have become millionaires with ESOs. Because of this, ESOs have emerged as a tool to attract talented and enterprising workers. Third, although ESOs are a form of employee compensation, they do not have direct cash flow effects. Fourth, under prior GAAP, ESOs provided employee benefits without requiring the recording of costs. The opposition of companies to the FASB's proposal in the mid-1990s to deduct the cost of ESOs from income is testimony to the importance of this factor. This section explains characteristics of ESOs and defines key terms. Our discussion includes the accounting and reporting for ESOs. We conclude with a discussion of analyzing ESOs.

Characteristics of Employee Stock Options

An employee stock option is a contractual opportunity granted by a company to an employee whereby the employee can purchase a fixed number of shares of the company at a specified price on or after a specified future date. Exhibit 6.9 illustrates an option granted to an employee. The *exercise price* is the price for which the employee has the right to purchase the shares. Exercise price often is set equal to the stock price on the *grant date*. The *vesting date* is the earliest date the employee can exercise the option–the employee can exercise the option at any date after the vesting date. Most ESOs have *vesting periods* of between 2 and 10 years. When the stock price is higher than the exercise price, the option is said to be *in-the-money*. It is *out-of-the-money* when the stock price is less than the exercise price.

Exhibit 6.9   **Illustration of an Option Granted to an Employee**

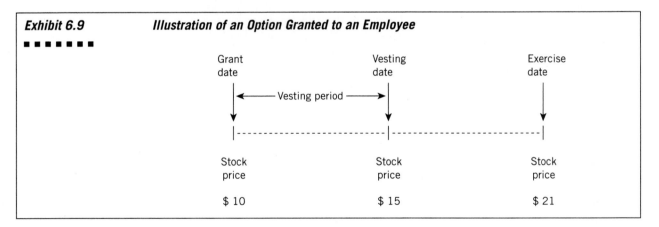

Employee stock options fit two broad categories: incentive and nonqualified. *Incentive,* or tax-favored qualified, stock options are not taxed until the stock is sold by the employee. These options must be granted at fair market value and the stock must be held for two years from the date of the grant and another one year from the date they are exercised. The difference between the exercise price and the selling price is usually taxed as ordinary income. *Nonqualified* stock options do not have the tax benefits of qualified options. These options are sometimes granted at a discount from fair market value and employees are taxed at the time of exercise on the difference between the exercise price and the stock's fair market value. In this case, the company benefits from a tax deduction equal to the amount of income recognized by the employee.

Economic Costs and Benefits of ESOs

There are both economic benefits and costs for ESOs. The main benefit of ESOs is the potential increase in company value that can arise through incentive effects on employee behavior. ESOs aim to align incentives of employees and the company by providing employees an opportunity to participate in shareholder wealth creation. Because incentives are better aligned, it is argued that ESOs will induce employees to work harder and in the best interests of the company. While strong arguments support the incentive effects of providing employee stock options, the evidence linking ESOs to improved employee performance is not definitive. U.S. evidence of the incentive effects of ESOs is mixed, and evidence from other countries suggests there may be other, more important, factors affecting employee motivation. Still, ESOs are a popular and powerful factor in attracting talented employees. ESOs also may increase the *risk propensity* of managers. That is, ESOs may motivate managers to venture into more risky projects because managers can share in the increased upside potential but have the benefit of the downside protection offered by the option. Therefore, ESOs often are granted to managers in growth and innovative industries to induce more risk-taking.

The cost of employee stock options is their potential dilutive effects. That is, when exercised, ESOs transfer wealth from shareholders to employees by diluting current shareholders' stake in the company. But does the company incur a cost when the exercise price equals the stock price on the grant date? The *intrinsic value approach* to this question implies there is no cost. This approach measures cost as the extent to which the exercise price is lower than the stock price on the grant date. It is based on the erroneous logic that granting ESOs, with exercise price equal to stock price, is similar to issuing stock at the prevailing market price. The intrinsic value approach ignores two types of costs that arise even when the exercise price is equal to current stock price. The first is *interest cost*, which arises because the ESO is exercisable at a future date but at the currently prevailing stock price. The second is *option cost*, which is the cost of providing an employee the option to purchase (or not purchase) the company's stock. These costs are considered in option pricing models that suggest that options have value even when granted at the prevailing market price.

The benefits of employee stock options–through increased employee motivation–is reflected through items that are traditionally included in income, such as increased revenues or decreased costs. Therefore, it makes sense to match the economic costs of granting ESOs with their potential benefits that are already reflected in income. This is the economic logic behind the current accounting for employee stock options that has raised storms of protest from American corporations, particularly those in the high-tech industries.

Accounting and Reporting for ESOs

There are two major accounting issues related to ESOs: (1) dilution of earnings per share (EPS) and (2) recognizing the cost of the employee stock option as an expense in current income. This section briefly discusses both issues. Appendix 6B provides details of ESO accounting.

Dilution of Earnings per Share.   *SFAS 128* recognizes the potential dilution from ESOs when determining **diluted earnings per share.** The treasury stock method determines the extent of dilution based on both the exercise price and the current stock price. ESOs in-the-money are considered *dilutive securities* and affect diluted EPS. ESOs out-of-the-money are considered *antidilutive securities* and do not affect diluted EPS. Appendix 6A gives a detailed explanation of EPS terminology and computations.

Compensation Expense.   Accounting and reporting for ESOs are prescribed under *SFAS 123* and its successor, *SFAS 123(R)*. *SFAS 123(R)* requires that companies recognize the amortized cost of the ESO grants in income as share-based compensation expense. Specifically, *SFAS 123(R)* requires companies to determine the value of the

Exhibit 6.10

Factors Affecting the Fair Value of an Option

Factor	Effect on fair value
Exercise price	−
Stock price on date of grant	+
Expected life of option	+
Risk-free rate of interest	+
Expected volatility of stock	+
Expected dividends of stock	−

ESO grant and amortize this amount over the expected exercise period, typically the options' vesting period. The value of the ESO grant is determined by multiplying the number of options granted with the fair value of each option on the date of the grant (see Exhibit 6.10). Options' fair values are determined using well-known option pricing models such as the Black-Scholes model or the bionomial lattice model, based on assumptions provided by the company. While share-based compensation expense is charged to income, it is not reported as a separate line item in the income statement.

Because of political pressure, the original standard *(SFAS 123)* did not require that companies *recognize* this cost in net income, although companies were required to disclose *pro forma* income that included ESO compensation expense in a footnote. In the post-Enron political environment, transparency in financial reporting became popular, and *SFAS 123* was revised as *SFAS 123(R),* which now requires that companies recognize compensation expense in net income. Appendix 6B details the accounting specified under *SFAS 123(R).*

Disclosures of Employee Stock Options

Exhibit 6.11 provides excerpts from the footnotes of Cisco Systems' 2007 annual report. The footnotes give details on options granted, outstanding, and exercisable, along with assumptions used for computing the fair value of options granted and their effect on income. Between July 29, 2006, and July 28, 2007, Cisco granted 206 million options to its employees at a weighted-average exercise price of $23.32. During the year, 309 million options were exercised, and 54 million were canceled (e.g., when employees left Cisco without exercising their options). On July 28, 2007, Cisco had 1,289 million outstanding options (both vested and nonvested), of which 829 million outstanding options had vested but were not yet exercised. The weighted-average exercise price on outstanding options was $26.60, which was slightly below Cisco's stock price on that day of $28.97. The aggregate intrinsic value (total in-the-money value) of the outstanding options on July 28, 2007, was approximately $9,698 million. This is the amount that the Cisco's employees stood to gain if all outstanding options were exercised on that date. Also, on July 28, 2007, Cisco had 294 million options available for grant (i.e., have been authorized by the board of directors) but not yet granted.

During fiscal year 2007, the weighted-average fair value per option granted was $7.11, which is determined assuming a dividend yield of 0%, a risk-free interest rate of 4.6%, an expected life of 6.7 years, and a stock price volatility of 26%. Cisco uses the bionomial lattice model (instead of the Black-Scholes model) for valuing its options, which requires additional assumptions regarding Cisco's stock returns' distribution such as skewness and kurtosis. Cisco's share-based compensation expense (amortized cost of granting ESOs) for fiscal 2007 was $931 million, which was almost 15% of its net income for that year.

Note that the share-based compensation expense is included in income during fiscal 2007 and 2006 [under *SFAS 123(R)*], while it is not included in income during fiscal 2005 (under the older standard, *SFAS 123*). Cisco also reports that the option compensation expense was included under various categories in the income statement including cost of sales, R&D, sales & marketing, and general administrative costs.

Finally, Exhibit 6.11 includes information from Cisco's income statement regarding the dilutive effect of ESOs on EPS. During fiscal 2007, assuming exercise of all vested options at the earliest opportunity, Cisco's outstanding shares would have been diluted by 210 million (from 6,055 million to 6,265 million), lowering its EPS from $1.21 (basic EPS) to $1.17 (diluted EPS). The EPS computation (see Appendix 6B) considers only the effect of *dilutive* options in the computation of diluted EPS. Options that are "under water" (have an exercise price greater than market price) are excluded from the EPS computation as their inclusion would increase diluted EPS (they are considered *antidilutive*).

Analyzing Employee Stock Options

Should compensation expense arising from employee stock options be charged to income? Earlier, we noted that granting options creates costs and benefits. The effects of the benefits (if any) will be recorded in income through higher revenues or lower costs arising from a motivated workforce. Therefore, it makes sense to match the costs of granting the ESOs to these benefits. This is exactly what the accounting under *SFAS 123(R)* does.

However, it must be noted that the ESOs (in the absence of incentive effects) impose no cash flow commitment on the company nor involve any resource allocation away from the shareholders in total. Specifically, ESOs do not affect either total liabilities or shareholders' equity. Any wealth transfer occurs only between current shareholders and prospective shareholders (employees). The analysis implication is that while the potential reduction in the value of *current* equity shares must be considered (such as in equity analysis), it can be ignored for evaluating solvency and liquidity (such as in credit analysis). Therefore, a credit analyst must exclude share-based compensation expense from income when evaluating profitability–for example, when determining interest coverage ratios.

On July 28, 2007, Cisco had 1,289 million outstanding ESOs at an aggregate intrinsic value of $9,698 million. We noted earlier that the aggregate intrinsic value is the employees' net gain if all outstanding ESOs were exercised on that date. Because the employees' gain comes at the expense of the current shareholders, this amount constitutes the potential transfer of wealth from current shareholders to employees through dilution arising from ESO grants; it is often referred to as the *option overhang*. Cisco's option overhang is around 5.7% of its market value of equity. Option overhang can be a considerably higher proportion of market value of equity for younger tech companies and is a significant factor that must be considered in equity analysis and valuation. While Cisco reports the exact amount of the option overhang in its footnote, most companies do not. However, an analyst can use note information provided to derive this amount using the following formula:

$$\text{Aggregate intrinsic value (option overhang)} = (\text{Stock price} - \text{Average exercise price}) \times \text{Outstanding number of options}$$

for all in-the-money options (i.e., those with exercise price below stock price). For example, for the exercise price range of $0.001 - $15.00, the option aggregate intrinsic value using the note information is ($28.97 - $11.02) × 122 million = $2,190 million, which approximately equals that reported by Cisco for that category.

Exhibit 6.11 **_Disclosures on Employee Stock Options—Cisco Systems Inc._**

■ ■ ■ ■ ■ ■ ■

Stock Incentive Plan Program Description

As of July 28, 2007, the Company had five stock incentive plans. In addition, the Company has, in connection with the acquisitions of various companies, assumed the stock incentive plans of the acquired companies or issued replacement share-based awards. Share-based awards are designed to reward employees for their long-term contributions to the Company and provide incentives for them to remain with the Company. The number and frequency of share-based awards are based on competitive practices, operating results of the Company, and government regulations. Since the inception of the stock incentive plans, the Company has granted stock options to virtually all employees, and the majority has been granted to employees below the vice president level.

General Share Based Award Information

	Share-Based Awards Available for Grant	Number Outstanding	Weighted-Average Exercise Price per Share
Balance at July 29, 2006	464	1,446	$25.08
Granted and assumed	(206)	206	23.32
Exercised		(309)	16.00
Cancelled/forfeited/expired	19	(54)	34.04
Restricted stock and other share-based awards	(7)		
Additional shares reserved	24		
Balance at July 28, 2007	294	1,289	$26.60

The following table summarizes significant ranges of outstanding and exercisable options as of July 28, 2007 (in millions except per-share amounts):

	STOCK OPTIONS OUTSTANDING				STOCK OPTIONS EXERCISABLE		
Range of Exercise Price	Number Outstanding	Remaining Life (in years)	Weighted-Average Exercise Price per Share	Aggregate Intrinsic Value	Number Exercisable	Weighted Average Exercise Price per Share	Aggregate Intrinsic Value
$0.001–$15.00	122	4.58	$11.02	$2,183	93	$11.09	$1,659
$15.01–$18.00	230	5.81	17.24	2,700	124	16.76	1,513
$18.01–$20.00	303	5.48	19.22	2,958	183	19.19	1,780
$20.01–$25.00	246	6.77	22.38	1,622	74	21.42	560
$25.01–$35.00	117	3.07	27.18	235	85	27.43	156
$35.01–$50.00	25	1.70	40.01		25	40.01	
$50.00–$72.56	246	1.87	54.89		245	54.89	
Total	1,289		$26.60	$9,698	829	$30.13	$5,668

The aggregate intrinsic value in the preceding table represents total pretax intrinsic value based on the stock price of $28.97 as of July 27, 2007, which would have been received by the option holders had those options been exercised as of that date. The total of in-the-money stock options exercisable on July 28, 2007 (July 29, 2006) was 549 (969) million.

Valuation and Expense Information under SFAS 123(R)

On July 31, 2005, the Company adopted _SFAS 123(R)_, which requires the measurement and recognition of compensation expense for all share-based payment awards made to the Company's employees and directors including employee stock options and employee stock purchase rights based on estimated fair values. Employee share-based compensation expense (after-tax) under _SFAS 123(R)_ was as follows (in millions):

	FISCAL YEAR-ENDED		
	July 28, 2007	July 29, 2006	July 30, 2005
Included in cost of sales	143	162	
Research and development	289	346	
Sales and marketing	392	427	
General and administrative	107	115	
Total employee share-based compensation expense	$931	$1,050	$1,034*

* The number for 2005 is pro forma compensation expense under _SFAS 123_ that was not included in income.

(continued)

Disclosures of Employee Stock Options—Cisco Systems Inc. *(concluded)*

■ ■ ■ ■ ■ ■ ■

Upon adoption of *SFAS 123(R)*, the Company began estimating the value of employee stock options and employee stock purchase rights on the date of grant using a lattice-binomial model. Prior to the adoption of *SFAS 123(R)*, the value of each employee stock option and employee stock purchase right was estimated on the date of grant using the Black-Scholes model for the purpose of the pro forma financial information required in accordance with *SFAS 123*.

The Company's employee stock options have various restrictions including vesting provisions and restrictions on transfer and hedging, among others, and are often exercised prior to their contractual maturity. Binomial lattice models are more capable of incorporating the features of the Company's employee stock options than closed-form models such as the Black-Scholes model. The use of a binomial lattice model requires extensive actual employee exercise behavior data and a number of complex assumptions including expected volatility, risk-free interest rate, expected dividends, kurtosis, and skewness. The weighted-average assumptions, using the binomial lattice model, the weighted-average expected life and estimated value of employee stock options and employee stock purchase rights are summarized as follows:

	FISCAL YEAR-ENDED	
	July 28, 2007	July 29, 2006
Weighted-average assumptions:		
Expected volatility	26.0%	23.7%
Risk-free interest rate	4.6%	4.3%
Expected dividend	0.0%	0.0%
Kurtosis	4.5	4.3
Skewness	(0.79)	(0.62)
Weighted-average expected life	6.7	6.6
Weighted-average estimated value	$ 7.11	$ 5.15

Earnings per-Share Information (from the income statement)

	FISCAL YEAR-ENDED		
	July 28, 2007	July 29, 2006	July 30, 2005
Net income (millions)	$7,333	$5,580	$5,741
Net income per share—basic	$ 1.21	$ 0.91	$ 0.88
Net income per share—diluted	$ 1.17	$ 0.89	$ 0.87
Shares used in per-share calculation—basic (millions)	6,055	6,158	6,487
Shares used in per-share calculation—diluted (millions)	6,265	6,272	6,612

INTEREST COSTS

Interest is compensation for use of money. It is the *excess* cash paid or collected beyond the money (principal) borrowed or loaned. Interest is determined by several factors, and one of the most important is credit (nonpayment) risk of the borrower. *Interest expense* is determined by the interest rate, principal, and time.

Interest Computation

Interest expense for a company is the nominal rate paid on debt financing including, in the case of bonds, the amortization of any discount or premium. A complication arises when companies issue convertible debt or debt with warrants. These situations yield a nominal rate below the cost of similar debt not enjoying these added features. In the case of convertible debt, accounting practice considers the debt and equity features inseparable. Therefore, no portion of the proceeds from issuance of convertible debt is accounted for as attributable to the conversion feature. In the case of debt issued with attached stock warrants, the proceeds attributable to the value of the warrants are accounted for as paid-in capital. The corresponding charge is to a debt discount account that is amortized over the life of the debt issue, increasing the effective interest cost.

Interest Capitalization

Capitalization of interest is required as part of the cost of assets constructed or otherwise produced for a company's *own use* (including assets constructed or produced for a company by others where deposits or progress payments are made). The objectives of interest capitalization are to (1) measure more accurately the acquisition cost of an asset and (2) amortize acquisition cost against revenues generated by an asset. An example follows:

> In connection with various construction projects, interest of approximately $19,118,000, $30,806,000, and $17,393,000 was capitalized as property, plant, and equipment.
>
> –New York Times Company

Analyzing Interest

Our analysis must realize that current accounting for interest on convertible debt is controversial. Many contend that ignoring the value of a conversion privilege and using the coupon rate as the measure of interest ignores the real interest cost. Somewhat contrary to this position, computation of diluted earnings per share uses the number of shares issuable *in the event of conversion of convertible debt.* This in effect creates an additional charge to the coupon rate through diluting earnings per share.

Accounting for interest capitalization is also disputable. Some analysts take the position that interest represents a period cost and is not capitalizable. Whatever one's views, our analysis must realize that accounting for interest capitalization is vague, leading to variations in practice. We must remember that capitalized interest is included in assets' costs and enters expense via depreciation and amortization. To assess the impact of interest capitalization on net income, our analysis must know the amount of capitalized interest currently charged to income via depreciation and amortization. We also need this amount to accurately compute the fixed-charge coverage ratio (see Chapter 10). Unfortunately, practice does not require disclosure of these amounts, so our analysis is often handicapped. One potential source of this information is Form 10-K disclosures.

⋯⋯INCOME TAXES

Income tax expense is a substantial cost of business. Understanding the accounting for income taxes is important to successful analysis of financial statements. The discussion here focuses on the accounting and analysis of periodic income tax expense and associated assets and liabilities, and not on tax law.

Accounting for Income Taxes
Temporary and Permanent Differences

The complexity in accounting for income taxes arises because the rules for determining taxable income (i.e., for purposes of determining taxes payable) are based on the prevailing tax laws, and these rules are different from the rules for determining reported income under GAAP, which forms the basis for the financial statements. In general, tax rules are closer to "cash basis" accounting, permitting fewer accruals than allowed under GAAP. Also, rules for calculating certain accruals, such as depreciation, are different under tax laws than under GAAP. Additionally, tax laws allow exemptions or deductions for certain items that have no real economic basis (e.g., interest income from certain types of bonds are exempt from taxes). Finally, tax authorities do not provide refunds for net operating losses; rather these losses are carried forward and offset with income arising in future periods. For these reasons, income reported in the financial statements can differ substantially from **taxable income** (i.e., income used for determining taxes payable under the tax laws). Companies, therefore, maintain two sets of accounting books, one for financial reporting (the "GAAP books") and one for tax accounting (the "tax books").

The differences between tax and GAAP income are essentially of two types: temporary and permanent. **Temporary differences,** as the name suggests, are differences that are temporary in nature and are expected to reverse in the future. Such discrepancies are mainly in the nature of timing differences between tax and GAAP accounting. For example, GAAP allows companies to take a restructuring charge for estimated costs of restructuring that may last several years, while tax laws allow deductions only when restructuring costs are actually incurred. Temporary differences are accounted for using deferred tax adjustments.

Permanent differences, as the name suggests, are differences that are permanent in nature. Such discrepancies arise because tax laws and GAAP fundamentally differ in their treatment of the item. For example, interest income from certain municipal bonds is tax exempt and therefore not included in determining taxable income, while it is included when determining GAAP income. Permanent differences are not accounted for in the financial statements; instead they are factored into the **effective tax rate,** which is the actual tax rate incurred by the business during the period. Effective tax rates can differ from the **statutory tax rate** (currently 35% for U.S. corporations) because of permanent differences. Exhibit 6.12 provides examples of common temporary and permanent differences.

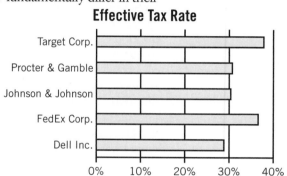

Effective Tax Rate

Temporary and Permanent Differences between GAAP Income and Taxable Income   **Exhibit 6.12**

TEMPORARY DIFFERENCES

Recognized Earlier in Tax Than in GAAP	**Recognized Later in Tax Than in GAAP**
Revenues	**Revenues**
1. Subscription revenue received in advance.	1. Installment sales—accrual method in GAAP.
2. Advance rent received.	2. Equity method of accounting for investment.
3. Prepaid service contracts.	**Expenses**
4. Royalties received in advance.	1. Product warranty expenses/liabilities.
Expenses	2. Postemployment benefits.
1. Accelerated depreciation for tax.	3. Bad debt allowances.
2. Capitalization of certain costs.	4. Write-down of assets—inventory, PPE.
	5. Restructuring charges
	6. Capital lease expenses
	7. Tax loss carryforwards

PERMANENT DIFFERENCES

1. Interest income from tax-exempt bonds not recognized by tax law.
2. Tax credits.
3. Taxes on unremitted earnings from foreign subsidiaries.
4. ESOP dividend deductions.
5. Foreign income taxed at rates different from U.S. statutory rates.
6. Medicare prescription drug benefits.

Deferred Taxes

Temporary differences can cause taxable income to deviate substantially from pretax income prepared under GAAP. Therefore, charging the actual tax payable during the year (which is computed using taxable income) against pretax GAAP income violates the basic matching principle of accounting and results in after-tax income that can be volatile and even meaningless. To avoid these problems, accountants use inter-period allocations known as **deferred tax adjustments.** The basis for deferred tax adjustments is to better match the tax expense for the period with the pretax income reported under GAAP. In the process, deferred tax accounting creates important balance sheet items called **deferred tax assets** or **deferred tax liabilities.**

We explain deferred tax accounting through the following two examples, which are detailed in Exhibit 6.13. In Case A we examine a situation where a company buys an asset for $30,000, which it fully depreciates in the GAAP books over three years. Tax laws, however, allow the asset to be depreciated over an accelerated two-year period. Also, the company earns income before depreciation and tax of $25,000 per year from use of the asset.

We first examine what happens in the tax books. Because the asset is depreciated over the first two years, the taxable income during the first two years ($10,000 per year) is much lower than that in the third year ($25,000). Accordingly, the tax payable in the first two years ($3,500 per year) is much lower than that in the third ($8,750). Under GAAP, however, pretax income is identical ($15,000) in each of the three years, which is consistent with the unchanged economic performance across these three years. What would happen if we used the tax payable under the tax laws as the tax expense in the GAAP books? The reported net income during the three years would be $11,500, $11,500, and $6,250, respectively. Obviously these numbers do not depict the underlying economic performance, which was unchanged across the three years. Accordingly, in the GAAP books we match the tax expense (tax provision) during the year to the pretax GAAP income; such matching suggests the tax provision should be $5,250 each year (35% of $15,000). Accordingly, we artificially increase the tax provision during the first two years by $1,750 each and fully reverse the entire amount during the third year. These artificial adjustments are called deferred tax adjustments. The deferred tax adjustments in this case initially reduce income and, therefore, retained earnings. To compensate (i.e., to "balance" the balance sheet) we create deferred tax liabilities of $1,750 and $3,500 during Years 1 and 2, which are completely reversed in Year 3.

We next examine a scenario which creates deferred tax assets. Specifically, we have a situation (Case B) in which a company takes a $30,000 restructuring charge in Year 1. The tax laws, however, allow this charge to be deducted only over the three years when they are actually incurred ($10,000 per year). Once again the company earns $25,000 per year before restructuring and tax. Again, we see that using tax payable (as per tax law) as the tax expense creates a situation in which the tax expense is not matched with the pretax GAAP income. Accordingly, we again create deferred tax adjustments. However, note that–unlike Case A where the adjustments initially *increased* tax provision and created deferred tax *liabilities*–the tax adjustments in Case B initially *decrease* tax provision and therefore create deferred tax *assets*.

The Nature of Deferred Tax Liabilities (or Assets)

We note that deferred tax liabilities (or assets) arise in order to compensate for the effect of the deferral on income and therefore on retained earnings. However, what is the nature of these assets or liabilities? Like all deferrals, they are not assets or liabilities in

Illustration of Deferred Tax Accounting

Exhibit 6.13

■ ■ ■ ■ ■ ■ ■

Case A: Deferred Tax Liability: GAAP depreciation straight line 3 years; Tax depreciation straight line 2 years

	TAX BOOKS				GAAP BOOKS			
	Year 1	Year 2	Year 3	Total	Year 1	Year 2	Year 3	Total
Income before depreciation and tax ..	$25,000	$25,000	$25,000	$75,000	$25,000	$25,000	$25,000	$75,000
Depreciation expense	15,000	15,000		30,000	10,000	10,000	10,000	30,000
Income before tax (a)	10,000	10,000	25,000	45,000	15,000	15,000	15,000	45,000
Tax payable (35%)	3,500	3,500	8,750	15,750	3,500	3,500	8,750	15,750
Deferred tax					1,750	1,750	(3,500)	0
Tax provision (b)	3,500	3,500	8,750	15,750	5,250	5,250	5,250	15,750
Net income (a) − (b)	$ 6,500	$ 6,500	$16,250	$29,250	$ 9,750	$ 9,750	$ 9,750	$29,250
Net income without deferred tax					$11,500	$11,500	$ 6,250	$29,250

Deferred Tax Adjustments	Year 1	Year 2	Year 3
Income before tax (GAAP books)	$15,000	$15,000	$ 15,000
Income before tax (tax books)	10,000	10,000	25,000
Difference	$ 5,000	$ 5,000	($10,000)
Deferred tax adjustment (35%)	$ 1,750	$ 1,750	($ 3,500)
Deferred tax liability	$ 1,750	$ 3,500	$ 0

Case B: Deferred Tax Asset: GAAP restructuring charge in first year; Tax restructuring expenditires spread over 3 years

	TAX BOOKS				GAAP BOOKS			
	Year 1	Year 2	Year 3	Total	Year 1	Year 2	Year 3	Total
Income before restructuring and tax ..	$25,000	$25,000	$25,000	$75,000	$ 25,000	$25,000	$25,000	$75,000
Restructuring charge (expense)	10,000	10,000	10,000	30,000	30,000			30,000
Income before tax (a)	15,000	15,000	15,000	45,000	(5,000)	25,000	25,000	45,000
Tax payable (35%)	5,250	5,250	5,250	15,750	5,250	5,250	5,250	15,750
Deferred tax					(7,000)	3,500	3,500	0
Tax provision (b)	5,250	5,250	5,250	15,750	(1,750)	8,750	8,750	15,750
Net income (a) − (b)	$ 9,750	$ 9,750	$ 9,750	$29,250	($ 3,250)	$16,250	$16,250	$29,250
Net Income without deferred tax					($10,250)	$19,750	$19,750	$29,250

Deferred Tax Adjustments	Year 1	Year 2	Year 3
Income before tax (GAAP books)	($ 5,000)	$25,000	$25,000
Income before tax (tax books)	15,000	15,000	15,000
Difference	($20,000)	$10,000	$10,000
Deferred tax adjustment (35%)	($ 7,000)	$ 3,500	$ 3,500
Deferred tax asset	$ 7,000	$ 3,500	$ 0

the "true" sense. For example, a deferred tax liability does not impose any obligation on the business to pay taxes, nor does the deferred tax asset confer any rights to claim taxes. All that a deferred tax liability (or asset) suggests is that the actual tax payments will be proportionally higher (or lower) in future because tax payments were proportionally lower (or higher) in the past. In general, a deferred tax liability or asset signifies:

- Deferred tax liability: GAAP income was greater than taxable income in the past; past tax payments were relatively (i.e., as % of GAAP income) lower, therefore future tax payments expected to be relatively (i.e., as % of GAAP income) higher.
- Deferred tax asset: GAAP income was less than taxable income in the past; past tax payments were relatively higher, therefore future tax payments expected to be relatively lower.

In this sense, deferred tax liabilities (or assets) *do* provide information about future cash flows. However, it is important to note that the ability of these liabilities or assets to forecast future cash flows is crucially dependent on the temporary differences reversing in the future. While, on average, temporary differences do reverse, there are many factors that can prevent such reversals. The most important factor preventing reversal is growth—when a company grows, new deferrals created in future will overwhelm the reversal of past deferrals. In addition, factors such as changes in tax laws and accounting rules, inflation, and future losses can also affect the reversal of deferred tax liabilities or assets.

Accounting for Deferred Taxes

Accounting for deferred taxes is specified under *SFAS 109*. Although the objective of deferred tax accounting is matching the tax expense with pretax GAAP income, the accounting for deferred taxes takes an asset-liability approach. That is, the focus is on computation of the balance sheet items, deferred tax assets and liabilities. Income tax expense (or provision) is not computed directly. Rather, it is computed as the difference between the change in deferred tax assets and liabilities, and the tax payable to taxing authorities.

Deferred taxes are determined separately for each tax-paying component (an individual entity or group of entities consolidated for tax purposes) in each tax jurisdiction. Determination includes computing total deferred tax liability (or assets) for each taxable temporary difference (and operating loss carry-forwards, if any) using the applicable tax rates.

All deferred tax assets need to be evaluated for the probability of realization. A **valuation allowance** must be created to reduce deferred tax assets to the extent to which it is deemed that the assets are more likely (more than 50% probability) to *not* be realized. Determination of the valuation allowance is subjective and thus a potent tool for earnings management.[2]

Income Tax Disclosures

Exhibit 6.14 presents the income tax footnote from the Dell 2005 annual report. Dell reports tax expense (provision) of $1,402 million. Of that amount, $1,473 million represents total tax payments (both domestic and foreign, including a nonrecurring tax repatriation charge), and $(71) million is the deferred tax adjustment. Therefore, deferrals actually reduce Dell's tax expense during fiscal 2005. Dell also provides a summary of the components of its deferred tax liabilities and assets. Its $192 million of deferred tax

---

[2] A recent ruling under *FIN 48* specifies that companies must create a contingent liability for any additional tax payments that could arise (with greater than 50% probability) under an IRS audit.

Dell Income Tax Footnote

Exhibit 6.14

The provision for income taxes consists of the following:

	FISCAL YEAR ENDED		
	January 28, 2005	January 30, 2004	January 31, 2003
	(in millions)		
Current			
Domestic	$ 984	$ 969	$702
Foreign	209	132	94
Tax repatriation charge	280	—	—
Deferred	(71)	(22)	109
Provision for income taxes	$1,402	$1,079	$905

Deferred taxes have not been provided on excess book basis in the amount of approximately $2.9 billion in the shares of certain foreign subsidiaries because these basis differences are not expected to reverse in the foreseeable future and are essentially permanent in duration. These basis differences arose primarily through the undistributed book earnings of the subsidiaries that Dell intends to reinvest indefinitely. The basis differences could reverse through a sale of the subsidiaries, the receipt of dividends from the subsidiaries as well as various other events. Net of available foreign tax credits, residual income tax of approximately $740 million would be due upon a reversal of this excess book basis.

The components of Dell's net deferred tax asset are as follows:

	FISCAL YEAR ENDED	
	January 28, 2005	January 30, 2004
	(in millions)	
Deferred tax assets		
Deferred revenue	$ 241	$ 86
Inventory and warranty provisions	232	260
Investment impairments and unrealized gains	23	39
Provisions for product returns and doubtful accounts	22	21
Capital loss	6	96
Leasing	—	69
Other	99	104
	623	675
Deferred tax liabilities		
Fixed assets	(156)	(129)
Leasing	(10)	—
Other	(26)	(74)
	(192)	(203)
Net deferred tax asset	$ 431	$ 472
Current portion (included in other current assets)	$ 425	$ 339
Noncurrent portion (included in other noncurrent assets)	6	133
Net deferred tax asset	$ 431	$ 472

(continued)

Dell Income Tax Footnote *(concluded)*

■ ■ ■ ■ ■ ■ ■

The effective tax rate differed from the statutory U.S. federal income tax rate as follows:

	FISCAL YEAR ENDED		
	January 28, 2005	January 30, 2004	January 31, 2003
U.S. federal statutory rate	35.0%	35.0%	35.0%
Foreign income taxed at different rates	(11.6)	(7.3)	(7.9)
Tax repatriation charge	6.3	—	—
Other	1.8	1.3	2.8
Effective tax rate	31.5%	29.0%	29.9%

---

liabilities arises primarily from PP&E and relates to the use of accelerated depreciation in its tax books and straight-line depreciation for financial reporting. Its $623 million of deferred tax assets arise as a result of the recognition of deferred revenue and the accrual of expenses (inventory and warranty provisions) in its income statement that have not yet been paid and are, therefore, not deductible for tax purposes. Also, Dell has not set up a valuation allowance for its deferred tax assets as it expects all of these benefits to be realized. The net deferred tax asset of $431 million is reported on its balance sheet, primarily as a current asset. Finally, Dell provides a reconciliation of the statutory corporate income tax rate of 35% with its 31.5% effective tax rate. Most of this permanent difference is due to the repatriation of earnings of foreign subsidiaries at favorable tax rates in 2004. The footnote therefore provides information regarding both temporary and permanent differences.

Analyzing Income Taxes
Financial Statement Adjustments

We noted that deferred tax assets (or liabilities) are not "true" assets (liabilities) in the sense that they do not confer any future benefits or impose any future obligations on the company. Because of this, many analysts exclude them from the balance sheet when conducting ratio analysis. For example, credit raters such as Moody's recommend that deferred tax assets or liabilities be excluded when determining solvency or liquidity ratios such as debt-to-equity ratio or current ratio. To exclude deferred tax liabilities (or assets) from the balance sheet, we need to remove them from wherever they are classified and adjust the net amount to equity. For example, for Dell's balance sheet on January 28, 2005, we need to reduce current (noncurrent) assets by $425 million ($6 million) and correspondingly reduce shareholders' equity (specifically retained earnings) by $431 million.

Present Valuing Deferred Tax Assets and Liabilities

Deferred tax assets (or liabilities) represent potential future cash flows arising from reversal of temporary differences. However, these reversals could arise many years later, in which case the present value of the cash flow effects will be much smaller than that recorded on the balance sheet. Some analysts, therefore, recommend present valuing these asset or liabilities. To do that, it is important to understand the nature of each deferred asset or liability component and estimate how many years later, on average, they would reverse. For example, Dell classifies most of its deferred assets and liabilities as current assets, which suggests that most of them are expected to reverse within a year. Therefore, it is not necessary to present value Dell's deferred tax assets or liabilities.

Forecasting Future Income and Cash Flows

Income tax disclosures are useful for forecasting future cash flows. We need to consider both permanent and temporary differences in our cash flow forecasts. First, let us consider permanent differences. Most valuation textbooks recommend using the statutory tax rate (currently 35%) when forecasting future earnings or cash flows. The statutory tax rate is a useful estimate of the *marginal* tax rate; that is, it helps us identify the tax effect for an additional dollar of income. It is less useful as an estimate of the *average* tax rate of a company. This is because companies may have permanent differences that can permanently lower (or, in rare cases, increase) its tax rates. A better estimate of a company's average tax rate is its effective tax rate. Because earnings (or cash flow) forecasts need to use average (rather than marginal) tax rates, effective tax rates may be more useful for this purpose. However, effective tax rates have to be used carefully because they can be very volatile. Thus, a company's effective tax rate during a year is unlikely to be a good estimate of its future effective tax rates. For this purpose an analyst should examine a company's effective tax rates over the past few years to determine its permanent component. It is also useful to analyze the nature of the permanent differences so as to better estimate the permanent component of the effective tax rate.

Temporary differences (measured by deferred tax assets or liabilities) are useful in forecasting cash flows (but not in forecasting income). The presence of large deferred tax liabilities (assets) suggests that the company's tax payments in the future are likely to be higher (lower) than its tax provision. However, in order to use this information in cash flow forecasting, it is necessary to estimate when the deferrals are expected to reverse. It is also important to realize that similar deferrals can be created in the future, which could offset the effects of the reversal of the current deferred tax assets or liabilities.

Analyzing Permanent and Temporary Differences

An analyst must evaluate why effective tax rates differ from statutory tax rates by examining the components that cause the divergence. In particular, it is important to identify any nonrecurring components that temporarily affect effective tax rates.

It is also important to analyze the nature of the temporary differences identified by the components of deferred tax assets and liabilities. An analyst must evaluate the "reversibility" of the deferrals and also make estimates about how quickly the reversals are expected to occur. For example, most of Dell's deferred tax assets are expected to reverse within one year. Also, since Dell has not created a valuation allowance, it appears unlikely that the deferred tax assets will not be realized. Overall, there appears little doubt about reversibility of Dell's deferred tax assets.

Earnings Management and Earnings Quality

The valuation allowance is a popular tool of earnings management. An analyst should therefore carefully examine any changes–in particular, a decrease–in the valuation allowance, because it could be an attempt to manage earnings.

In general, many analysts compare GAAP and taxable income to evaluate earnings quality. The presence of large deferred tax liabilities (assets) suggests that GAAP income in the past has been higher (lower) than taxable income. Therefore, companies with large deferred tax liabilities (assets) are likely adopting aggressive (conservative) accounting practices.

.....APPENDIX 6A EARNINGS PER SHARE: COMPUTATION AND ANALYSIS

Earnings per share (EPS) data are widely used in evaluating the operating performance and profitability of a company. This appendix describes the principles governing earnings per share computation and interpretation. A key feature in earnings per share computation is recognition of the potential impact of dilution. **Dilution** is the reduction in earnings per share (or increase in net loss per share) resulting from dilutive securities being converted into common stock, the exercise of options and warrants, or the issuance of additional shares in compliance with contracts. Because these adverse effects on earnings per share can be substantial, the earnings per share computation serves to call attention to the potentially dilutive effects of a firm's capital structure.

The computation and reporting requirements (see *SFAS 128*) for earnings per share are consistent with international accounting standards. *SFAS 128* requires dual presentation of *basic EPS* and *diluted EPS* on income statements of companies with complex capital structures and requires a reconciliation of the numerator and denominator of basic EPS to diluted EPS. To understand these computations and their interpretation, this appendix (1) explains simple and complex capital structures, (2) describes the various earnings per share measures, and (3) provides several case examples.

SIMPLE CAPITAL STRUCTURE

A **simple capital structure** consists only of common stock and nonconvertible senior securities and does not include potentially dilutive securities. For companies with simple capital structures, a single presentation of earnings per share is required and is computed as follows:

$$\text{Basic earnings per share} = \frac{\text{Net income} - \text{Preferred dividends}}{\text{Weighted-average number of common shares outstanding}}$$

In the numerator of this computation, dividends of cumulative senior equity securities, whether earned or not, are deducted from net income or added to net loss. The precise computation of weighted-average number of common shares is the sum of shares outstanding each day, divided by the number of days in the period.

COMPLEX CAPITAL STRUCTURE

A company is viewed as having a **complex capital structure** if it has outstanding potentially dilutive securities such as convertible securities, options, warrants, and other similar stock issue agreements. More than 25% of publicly traded companies have potentially dilutive securities. The relation between basic and diluted earnings per share for these companies is depicted as:

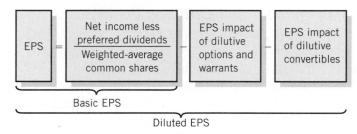

This dual presentation warns users of the potential for dilution in earnings per share. Both of these earnings per share figures are reported with equal prominence on income statements of companies with complex capital structures. These companies need not report diluted earnings per share when its potential common shares are antidilutive. **Antidilutive securities** are those that increase earnings per share when exercised or converted.

Basic Earnings per Share

The basic earnings per share computation for companies with complex capital structures is identical to that for companies with simple capital structures.

Diluted Earnings per Share

Companies with complex capital structures must report both basic and diluted EPS figures. Exhibit 6A.1 portrays the computation of

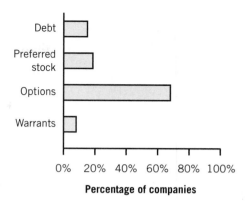

Sources of Potential Dilution

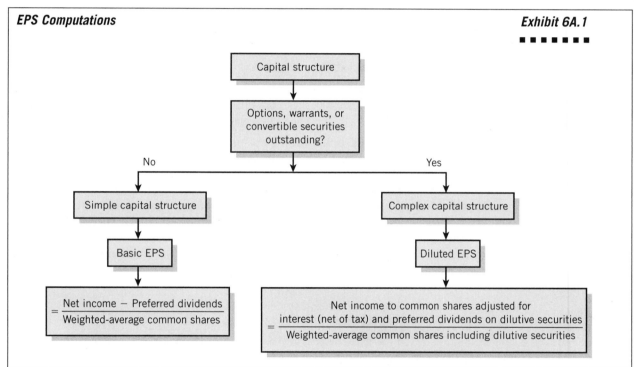

EPS Computations   *Exhibit 6A.1*

earnings per share for complex capital structures. Diluted EPS reflects *all* potential common shares that decrease earnings per share. We consider only the more familiar types of potentially dilutive securities—stock options and warrants, and convertible preferred stocks and bonds.

Diluted EPS is computed on an *as if* basis, that is, we assume that all convertible securities are converted and options exercised at the earliest possible opportunity (e.g., the beginning of the year if the securities are outstanding on that date). The numerator for diluted EPS adjusts net income for the following effects of the exercise of convertible securities or options:

1. If preferred shares have been converted into common, any preferred dividends must be removed as we are assuming that the preferred shares are no longer outstanding.
2. If bonds are converted, any interest expense must be backed out of net income. This is accomplished by adding back the after-tax amount of the interest accrued.

The denominator adds the additional shares issued as a result of conversion or exercise of options. For convertible bonds, the amount of shares to be issued upon conversion is added directly. For options, we assume that the proceeds from the exercise of the option are used to repurchase shares in the open market at the average stock price. Only the net shares issued are added to the denominator.

To illustrate the computation of EPS, consider a company with the following securities outstanding:

- *Common stock:* 1,000,000 shares outstanding for the entire year.
- *Preferred stock:* 500,000 shares outstanding for the entire year.
- *Convertible bonds:* $5,000,000 6% bonds, sold at par, convertible into 200,000 shares of common stock.
- *Employee stock options:* options to purchase 100,000 shares at $30 have been outstanding for the entire year. The average market price of the company's common stock during the year is $40.
- *Net income:* $3,000,000
- *Preferred dividends:* $50,000
- *Marginal tax rate:* 35%

$$\text{Basic EPS} = \frac{\$3,000,000 - \$50,000}{1,000,000} = \$2.95$$

$$\text{Diluted EPS} = \frac{\$3,000,000 - \$50,000 + [(\$5,000,000 \times 6\%)(1 - .35)]}{1,000,000 + 200,000 + 25,000} = \$2.57$$

Basic EPS is computed as net income less preferred shares divided by the weighted-average (by fraction of the year outstanding) number of shares outstanding during the year.

Diluted EPS assumes conversion of all convertible securities and exercise of all dilutive options at their earliest possible opportunity, in this case the beginning of the year. The third term in the numerator is the add-back of after-tax interest that would not have been paid had the bonds converted into common stock. The tax adjustment is necessary since pretax income would have increased by the amount of forgone interest expense. The additional shares assumed to be issued upon conversion of the bonds are added into the denominator. The third term in the denominator relates to the exercise of the options. This is computed as follows:

Shares purchased upon exercise of option	100,000
Exercise price	× $30
Proceeds received upon exercise	$3,000,000
Average market price of common stock............	÷ $40
Shares repurchased with option proceeds........	75,000

Net increase in shares due to exercise of options = 100,000 − 75,000 = 25,000.

ANALYSIS OF EARNINGS PER SHARE

Earnings per share requirements in accounting are often criticized because they extend to areas outside the usual realm of accountancy. Accounting for earnings per share relies on pro forma presentations influenced in large measure by market fluctuations. It also involves itself with areas of financial statement analysis. Whatever the merits of these criticisms, our analysis must welcome this initiative by the accounting profession. Factors considered in computation of earnings per share are varied and require considerable proprietary data, so it is appropriate to place this responsibility on management and its auditors. Our analysis must, however, bring a thorough understanding of the bases on which earnings per share are computed so that we can draw reliable inferences. The earnings per share disclosures require a reconciliation of the numerators and denominators of basic and diluted earnings per share computations. This entails disclosure of the individual income and common share effects of all securities that affect earnings per share. Such disclosure provides us additional insights into companies' complex capital structures.

Despite these improvements in earnings per share computations and disclosures, serious barriers to effective analysis remain:

- Computation of basic earnings per share ignores the potential effects of dilution from options and warrants. This can "boost" the earnings per share of certain companies by 10% to 20% or more, while potentially obscuring the risk from issuances of new shares. Our analysis must study diluted earnings per share to avoid this pitfall.
- There are inconsistencies in treating certain securities as the equivalent of common stock for computing earnings per share while not considering them as part of shareholders' equity. Consequently, it is difficult in analysis to effectively link reported earnings per share with the debt-leverage position pertaining to those earnings.
- The dilutive effects of options and warrants depend on the company's common stock price. This can yield a "circular effect," in that reporting of earnings per share can influence stock prices that, in turn, influence earnings per share. Hence, reported earnings per share can be affected by stock price and not solely reflect the economic fundamentals of the company. This also suggests that our projection of reported earnings per share consider not only future earnings but also future stock prices.

·····APPENDIX 6B ACCOUNTING FOR EMPLOYEE STOCK OPTIONS

Two accounting issues relate to employee stock options: (1) determination of diluted EPS under SFAS 128 and (2) determination of share-based compensation expense under SFAS 123(R) and related effects on the balance sheet. We discuss both accounting issues with illustrations in this appendix.

DETERMINING DILUTED EPS

Because ESOs potentially dilute current shareholders' equity holdings, their effects must be considered when determining diluted EPS. Only in-the-money options (i.e., those with exercise price below stock price) are considered *dilutive* securities–those that will potentially dilute current shareholders' equity holdings–and are included in diluted EPS computation. Options that are out-of-the-money–underwater options, where the exercise price exceeds stock price–are considered *antidilutive* and are not included in computing diluted EPS. For determining diluted EPS, the treasury stock approach is used. Illustration 6B.1 provides an example of the effects of ESOs on diluted EPS.

DETERMINING COMPENSATION EXPENSE

Determining the ESOs compensation expense for a period is a two-step process: (1) determining the cost of ESOs granted and (2) amortizing this cost over the vesting period of the option to determine compensation expense for each period. In addition there are balance sheet effects of recording compensation expense. We discuss each in turn.

ILLUSTRATION 6B.1

A company's net income is $100,000, and its weighted-average shares outstanding are 10,000. During the year, the company issues 2,000 ESOs at an exercise price of $20. We compute both basic and diluted EPS here under two separate scenarios: (1) average stock price during the year is $40 and (2) average stock price during the year is $10.

	Scenario 1	Scenario 2		Scenario 1	Scenario 2
Number of ESOs outstanding......................	2000 shares	2000 shares	Net income *(d)*........................	$100,000	$100,000
Exercise price...	$20	$20	Compute *(d)/(c)*.......................	$9.09	$12.50
Proceeds of ESOs issuance.........................	$40,000	$40,000	**Basic EPS**		
Average stock price.....................................	$40	$10	($100,000/10,000 shares)...	**$10.00**	**$10.00**
Treasury shares that can be purchased	1,000 shares	4,000 shares			
Number of ESOs less treasury shares *(a)*.....	1,000 shares	(2,000) shares	Dilutive or antidilutive?	Dilutive	Antidilutive
Average number of shares outstanding *(b)*....	10,000 shares	10,000 shares	**Diluted EPS**	**$9.09**	**$10.00**
Number of diluted shares *(c)* = *(a + b)*.....	11,000 shares	8,000 shares			

Determining ESO Cost

The cost of ESOs is determined at the time of the grant. ESO cost is the product of the fair value of each individual option and the number of options granted. The fair value of the ESO is determined by applying an option pricing model (usually the Black-Scholes or the Lattice model) as of the grant date. Exhibit 6.10 identified the factors affecting the fair value of an option. Note that the expected life of the option is based on the expected exercise date, not the vesting date. The number of options expected to vest is determined by adjusting the number of options granted for the expected employee turnover during the expected life of the option. As already noted, ESO cost is determined only once, at the time of the grant. No adjustments to this cost are made, even if the fair value of the ESO changes.

Amortizing ESO Cost

While companies hope ESOs motivate employees to work in the interest of shareholders, they also specify minimum vesting periods to further align employee and company incentives over the long run. This ESO benefit is expected to persist at least until the employee is free to exercise the option. Accordingly, the fair value of granted ESOs is amortized on a straight-line basis over the vesting period. Compensation expense for a period is based on the cumulative amortization of all past and current ESOs that are yet to vest.

Balance Sheet Effects

Under SFAS 123(R), cumulative compensation expense is credited to a special component of shareholder's equity called "Paid-in-Capital: Stock Compensation," which is subsequently transferred to regular paid-in share capital when options are exercised. Illustration 6B.2 provides an example of ESO accounting under *SFAS 123(R)*.

ILLUSTRATION 6B.2

Stock-Based Compensation Accounting under SFAS 123(R)—An Example

ABC Company issued 10,000 options to its CEO on January 1, 2006, at the prevailing market price of $3 per share. The options were expected to vest over a 2-year period. The

(continued)

Black-Scholes value of the option was valued at $1 per share. On December 31, 2007, the CEO exercised all options. Market price on that day was $6 per share. Assume a 35% tax rate. The accounting entries are given here.

January 1, 2006

No entry on grant date.

The total pretax "cost" to the company is $1 × 10,000 = $10,000. However, this expense is amortized over 2006 and 2007.

December 31, 2006

The amortized pretax option expense recognized in 2006 is $5,000. At a 35% tax rate, the tax saving is $1,750, which results in a $3,250 after-tax expense. The pretax expense will be charged to a special part of shareholder's equity called paid-in-capital–stock-based compensation.

The journal entry will be as follows:

	Debit	Credit
Stock-based compensation expense	3,250	
Deferred tax asset	1,750	
Paid-in-capital—stock-based compensation		5,000

December 31, 2007 (before exercise)

The journal entry will be identical to that in 2006.

Therefore, the cumulative effect on the balance sheet as of December 31, 2007 (prior to the option exercise), is as follows:

Assets		Liabilities	
Deferred tax asset	$ 3,500	Shareholder's equity:	
		• Paid-in share capital— stock-based compensation	$10,000
		• Retained earnings	(6,500)

December 31, 2007 (after exercise)

What happens when the options are exercised? First, note that $3 × 10,000 = $30,000 of cash is received from the CEO. In return, we issue 10,000 shares to the CEO. Second, because the options are no longer outstanding, we reverse the $10,000 that is in paid-in share capital–stock compensation. The sum total is charged to normal paid-in share capital (it is split between the par-value and the additional paid-in share capital as required).

The journal entry is:

	Debit	Credit
Cash	$30,000	
Paid-in-share capital— stock-based compensation		$10,000
Paid-in-share capital		40,000

Therefore as of December 31, 2007, the net effect on the balance sheet is as follows:

Assets		Liabilities	
Deferred tax asset	$3,500	Shareholder's equity:	
Cash	30,000	Paid-in-share capital	$40,000
		Paid-in share capital— stock-based compensation	—
		Retained earnings	(6,500)

GUIDANCE ANSWERS TO ANALYSIS VIEWPOINTS

SUPPLIER

Your credit assessment of Chicago Construction is likely positive. While the company's extraordinary loss is real, it is not recurring. This implies the 23% increase in net income is more representative of the ongoing business activities of Chicago Construction than the 12% decrease after the extraordinary loss. You must also assess the extent to which the fire loss is extraordinary. That is, this loss might be more than what extraordinary implies, or it might signal a new risk exposure for Chicago Construction. Nevertheless, on the information provided, the credit terms should be at least as good and perhaps better in the coming year.

BANKER

Playground Equipment's recognition of revenue during production is probably too liberal. Recognizing revenue during production is acceptable only when total revenues and expenses are estimated with reasonable certainty *and* when realization (payment) is reasonably assured. For most companies, these conditions are not met. Unless we are highly confident that Playground Equipment's earnings process meets these stringent conditions, we should require restatement (or an alternative statement) using point of sale as the basis for revenue recognition. If Playground Equipment has considerable collection risks or costs, we might require restatement using

revenue recognition when cash is received. The more conservative the statements used in our analysis, the less risky should be our loan agreement with Playground Equipment. The primary risk we are exposed to in acting on its loan is risk of nonpayment or default. Additional risks include interest rate changes, renegotiation potential, delayed payments, industry changes, and personal employment/promotion.

ANALYST

All corporations wish to minimize expenses. When net income increases due to decrease in expenditures, this is generally good news. Nevertheless, our analysis must examine the source of the expenditure decrease *and* assess its potential ramifications. In the case of California Technology, our analysis reveals a less than comfortable situation. Because most R&D outlays are expensed as incurred, we know that each dollar decrease in R&D outlays increases current net income by a dollar. But because R&D is the essence of a high technology corporation, our analysis of California Technology is troubling. Unless R&D costs have generally fallen in the industry (which is unlikely), California Technology's decrease in R&D expenditures hints at a less than optimistic future. While short-term income rises from decreases in R&D outlays, long-run income is likely to suffer.

QUESTIONS

[Superscript[A,B] denotes assignments based on Appendix 6A, 6B]

6–1. Explain why an analyst attaches great importance to evaluation of the income statement.

6–2. Define income. Distinguish income from cash flow.

6–3. What are the two basic economic concepts of income? What implications do they have for analysis?

6–4. Explain how accountants measure income.

6–5. Distinguish between net income, comprehensive income, and continuing income. Cite examples of items that create differences between these three income measures.

6–6. Although comprehensive income is the bottom line income number, it is rarely reported in the income statement. Where will you typically find details regarding comprehensive income?

6–7. Analysts often refer to the core income of a company. What is meant by the term *core income?*

6–8. Distinguish between operating and nonoperating income. Cite examples of items that are typically included in each category.

6–9. Operating vs. nonoperating and recurring vs. nonrecurring are two distinct dimensions of classifying income. Explain this statement and discuss whether or not you agree with it.

6–10. How does accounting define an *extraordinary* item? Cite three examples of such an item. What are the analysis implications of such an item?

6–11. Describe the accounting treatment for discontinued operations. How should an analyst treat discontinued operations?

6–12. What conditions are necessary for an item to qualify as a prior period adjustment?

6–13. Identify some accounting sources of income distortion.

6–14. For each of the three items, (1) depreciation, (2) inventory, and (3) installment sales, explain:
   a. Two acceptable accounting methods for reporting purposes.
   b. How each of the two acceptable accounting methods identified affect current period income.

(CFA Adapted)

6–15. Accounting practice distinguishes among different types of accounting changes. Identify three different types of accounting changes.

6–16. Explain what special items are. Give three examples of special items.

6–17. How do companies use special charges to influence investors' perceptions regarding company value?

6–18. How should an analyst treat special items?

6–19. Describe the conditions that are usually required before revenue is considered realized.

6–20. Identify the conditions that are usually required before a sale with right of return is recognized as a sale and the resulting receivable is recognized as an asset.

6–21. An ability to estimate future returns (when right of return exists) is an important consideration in revenue recognition. Identify factors impairing the ability to predict future returns.

6–22. Explain how accounting practice defines a product financing arrangement.

6–23. Distinguish between the two major methods used to account for revenue under long-term contracts.

6–24. Describe aspects of revenue recognition that an analyst must be especially alert to.

6–25. Discuss the accounting standards that govern R&D costs. What are the disclosure requirements?

6–26. What information does our analysis need regarding R&D outlays, especially in light of the limited disclosure requirements in practice?

6–27. What aspects of the valuation and the amortization of goodwill must analysts be alert to?

6–28. Contrast the computation of total interest costs of a bond issue with warrants attached to an issue of convertible debt.

6–29. a. What is the main provision of accounting for capitalization of interest, and what are its objectives?
   b. How is interest to be computed, and how is the interest rate to be ascertained?
   c. What restrictions to capitalization are imposed in practice and when does the capitalization period begin?

6–30. Distinguish between the intrinsic value and the fair value of an option.

6–31. List and discuss the factors that affect the fair value of an option.

6–32. Describe the calculation of compensation expense associated with employee stock options. Is it necessary for a company to charge option-related compensation expense to income? Where in the income statement is compensation expenses reported?

6–33. What are the economic costs to issuing employee stock options at the prevailing market price?

6–34. What is option overhang? What does it measure? How is it determined?

6–35. Net income computed on the basis of financial reporting often differs from taxable income due to permanent differences. What are permanent differences and how do they arise?

6–36. What factors cause the effective tax rate to differ from the statutory rate?

6–37. What are the main requirements of accounting for income taxes?

6–38. List four general cases giving rise to temporary differences between financial reporting and tax reporting.

6–39. What are the disclosure requirements when accounting for income taxes?

6–40. Identify and explain at least one flaw to which tax allocation procedures are subject.

6–41^A. Why is a thorough understanding of the principles governing computation of EPS important to our analysis?

6–42^A. Discuss uses of EPS and reasons or objectives for the current method of reporting EPS.

6–43^A. What is the purpose underlying the reporting of diluted EPS?

6–44^A. How does the payment of dividends on preferred stock affect the EPS computation?

6–45^A. EPS can affect a company's stock prices. Can a company's stock prices affect EPS?

6–46^A. Accounting for earnings per share has certain weaknesses that our analysis must consider for interpreting EPS data. Identify and discuss at least two weaknesses.

6–47^A. In estimating the value of common stock, the amount of EPS is considered an important element.
   a. Explain why EPS is important in the valuation of common stock.
   b. Is EPS equally important in valuing a preferred stock? Why or why not?

(CFA Adapted)

EXERCISES

EXERCISE 6–1
Analyzing Discontinued Operations

Many companies report discontinued operations in their income statements and balance sheets.

Required:

a. What is your best estimate of the summary journal entry recording the disposal of discontinued operations.

b. What is included in the income (expense) items relating to discontinued operations as reported in the income statement?

c. Discuss the importance of discontinued operations in analyzing a company's financial statements.

d. What is the rationale for separately reporting the results of discontinued operations?

EXERCISE 6–2
Analyzing Accounting Reserves

The following quote is taken from an article (by L. Bernstein) scrutinizing use of reserves to recognize future costs and losses.

> The growing use of reserves for future costs and losses impairs the significance of periodically reported income and should be viewed with skepticism by the analyst of financial statements. That is especially true when the reserves are established in years of heavy losses, when they are established in an arbitrary amount designed to offset an extraordinary gain, or when they otherwise appear to have as their main purpose the relieving of future income or expenses properly chargeable to it. The basic justification in accounting for the recognition of future losses stems from the doctrine of conservatism that, according to one popular application, means that one should anticipate no gains, but take all the losses one can clearly see as already incurred.

Required:

a. Discuss the merits of Bernstein's arguments and apprehensions regarding reserves.

b. Explain how this perspective can be factored into an analysis of past earnings trends, estimates of future earnings, and the valuation of common stock.

c. Cite examples of such reserves—you can draw on those in the chapter.

(CFA Adapted)

EXERCISE 6–3
Interpreting Disclosures of Accounting Changes

There are various types of accounting changes requiring different types of reporting treatments. Understanding the different changes is important to analysis of financial statements.

Required:

a. Under what category of accounting changes is the change from sum-of-the-years'-digits method of depreciation to the straight-line method for previously recorded assets classified? Under what circumstances does this type of accounting change occur?

b. Under what category of accounting changes is the change in expected service life of an asset (due to new information) classified? Under what circumstances does this type of accounting change occur?

c. Regarding changes in accounting principle:
   (1) How does a company compute the effect of such changes?
   (2) How does a company report the effect of these changes?

   Note: Do not discuss earnings per share requirements.

d. Why are accounting principles, once adopted, normally consistently applied over time?

e. What is the rationale for disclosure of a change from one accounting principle to another?

f. Discuss how your analysis of mandatory accounting changes might differ from that of voluntary accounting changes.

g. Discuss how companies might time the adoption of mandatory accounting changes for their own benefit.

h. Discuss how the adoption of mandatory accounting changes can create an opportunity to establish a hidden reserve. Cite examples.

(AICPA Adapted)

Harvatin Group reported net income totaling $1,000,000 for the year 2006. The following is additional information obtained from the Harvatin Group's financial reports:

EXERCISE 6–4
Computing Comprehensive Income

- The Company purchased 100,000 shares of Micron Specialists for $10 per share during the fourth quarter of 2006. The investment is accounted for as "available for sale." The value of the shares is $9 at the end of 2006.
- The Company purchased 10,000 shares of Sunswept Properties for $20 per share during the fourth quarter of 2006. The investment is accounted for as "trading" securities. The value of the shares is $22 at the end of 2006.
- The company began operations in the Baltic region of Europe during the year and reports a foreign currency translation gain at the end of 2006 totaling $50,000.
- The actual return on assets in its pension fund total $150,000. The expected return was $110,000.
- The company has substantial prior service cost associated with its employee pension plan. As a result, the company had to record an additional minimum pension liability during the year totaling $25,000.
- The company reported unrealized holding losses on derivative instruments totaling $12,000.

Required:

a. Compute comprehensive income for Harvatin Group.

b. For each item in comprehensive income, discuss balance sheet accounts affected by the item.

Revenue is usually recognized at the point of sale. Under special circumstances, dates other than the point of sale are used for timing of revenue recognition.

EXERCISE 6–5
Analysis of Revenue Recognition and Timing

Required:

a. Why is point of sale usually used as the basis for the timing of revenue recognition?

b. Disregarding special circumstances when bases other than the point of sale are used, discuss the merits of both of the following objections to the sale basis of revenue recognition:
   (1) It is too conservative because revenue is earned throughout the entire process of production.
   (2) It is too liberal because accounts receivable do not represent disposable funds, sales returns and allowances can occur, and collection and bad debt expenses can be incurred in a later period.

c. Revenue can be recognized (1) during production and (2) when cash is received. For each of these two bases of timing revenue recognition, give an example of the circumstances where it is properly used and discuss the accounting merits of its use in lieu of the sales basis.

(AICPA Adapted)

EXERCISE 6–6

Analyzing
Percentage-of-
Completion
Figures

Michael Company accounts for a long-term construction contract using the percentage-of-completion method. It is a four-year contract currently in its second year. Recent estimates of total contract costs indicate the contract will be completed at a profit to Michael Company.

Required:

a. What theoretical justification is there for Michael Company's use of the percentage-of-completion method?

b. How are progress billings accounted for? Include in your discussion the classification of progress billings in the Michael Company financial statements.

c. How is income computed in the second year of the four-year contract using the cost method of determining percentage of completion?

d. What is the effect on earnings in the second year of the four-year contract when using the percentage-of-completion method instead of the completed-contract method? Discuss.

(AICPA Adapted)

EXERCISE 6–7

Interpreting Revenue
Recognition for Leases
(book and tax effects)

Crime Control Co. accounts for a substantial part of its alarm system sales under the sales-type (capitalized) lease method. Under this method the company computes the present value of the total receipts it expects to get (over periods as long as eight years) from a lease and records this present value amount as sales in the first year of the lease. Justification for this accounting is that the 8-year lease extends over more than 75% of the 10-year useful life of the equipment. While the sales-type lease method is used for financial reporting, for tax purposes the company reports revenues only when received. Because first-year expenses of a lease are particularly large, the company reports substantial tax losses on these leases.

Required:

a. Critics maintain the sales-type lease method "front loads" income and that reported earnings may not be received in cash for several years. Comment on this criticism.

b. Will financial reporting income be improved from the company's tax benefit?

c. The company insists it can achieve earnings results similar to those achieved by the sales-type lease method by selling the lease receivables to third-party lessors or financial institutions. Comment on this assertion.

(AICPA Adapted)

EXERCISE 6–8

Revenue Recognition in
Dot.Com Companies

Lookhere.Com and StopIn.Com enter into a reciprocal agreement whereby (1) StopIn.Com is given valuable advertising space on the home page of Lookhere.Com and (2) Lookhere.Com is given valuable advertising space on the home page of StopIn.Com. The main source of revenue for both StopIn.Com and Lookhere.Com is sales of advertising on their respective websites. Both companies recognize advertising revenue received from the other company and recognize advertising expense paid to the other company. Accounting regulators express support for the accounting treatment applied by these companies.

Required:

a. Do you believe these companies should be allowed to recognize revenue in conjunction with the advertising agreements described above?

b. Why do you believe these companies want to record revenue along with its offsetting expense for these transactions?

c. How would you assess such transactions in an analysis of these companies?

An analyst must be familiar with the concepts involved in determining income. The amount of income reported for a company depends on the recognition of revenues and expenses for a given time period. In certain cases, costs are recognized as expenses at the time of product sale; in other situations, guidelines are applied in capitalizing costs and recognizing them as expenses in future periods.

EXERCISE 6–9
Expensing vs. Capitalization of Costs

Required:

a. Explain the rationale for recognizing costs as expenses at the time of product sale.

b. What is the rationale underlying the appropriateness of treating costs as expenses of a period instead of assigning the costs to an asset? Explain.

c. Under what circumstances is it appropriate to treat a cost as an asset instead of as an expense? Explain.

d. Certain expenses are assigned to specific accounting periods on the basis of systematic and rational allocation of asset cost. Explain the underlying rationale for recognizing expenses on this basis.

e. Identify the conditions necessary to treat a cost as a loss.

(AICPA Adapted)

The annual research and development costs for Frontier Biotech for years 2002 through 2006 are shown here ($ millions):

EXERCISE 6–10
Analyzing Research and Development Costs

2002	2003	2004	2005	2006
$5.1	$5.9	$6.0	$6.2	$3.3

Required:

a. Comment on the manner in which research and development costs impact net income in both the current year and in future years.

b. How would you assess the reduced research and development expenditure in year 2006?

A current exposure draft requires companies to recognize the fair value of employee stock options as an operating expense. Options pricing models are used to estimate the fair value of the options. Under current GAAP, companies have the choice to provide footnote disclosure of pro forma effects on net income of the costs of employee stock options.

EXERCISE 6–11
Analyzing Employee Stock Option Disclosures

Required:

a. Discuss whether an analyst would have a preference for recording ESO costs in the body of the income statement or disclosing the pro forma effect of ESO costs in the footnotes.

b. If you are analyzing an annual report that footnotes ESO effects on net income describe how you can use the pro forma disclosures to recast your analysis for the impact of employee stock options.

c. Identify at least four ratios in your financial analysis that are impacted by the recognition or nonrecognition (footnoting) of ESO cost.

On August 1, 2003, the board of directors of Incent.Com approved a stock option plan for its middle managers and software design professionals (100 employees). The plan awards 1,000 shares of $5 par value common stock to each employee. The grant date is January 1, 2004. The option (exercise) price of the shares is the opening stock price on January 1, 2004 ($20). The options are nontransferable and are exercisable after December 31, 2008. The options expire when the employee leaves the company or on December 31, 2015, whichever is first. Management estimates annual forfeitures will be 4% and that the expected life of the options is 6 years. The fair value of the options based on the Black-Scholes Options Pricing Model is $8 per option. On the first exercise date, 50,000 options are exercised when the stock price is $60 per share.

EXERCISE 6–12
Interpreting Employee Stock Options

Required:

a. Is this a compensatory or noncompensatory stock option plan? Explain.

b. Why would Incent.Com offer such a plan to its employees?

c. What is the grant date, vesting date, and exercise date for this ESO plan?

d. Are the stock options "in-the-money" at the grant date? Explain.

e. When should total compensation cost be measured? Explain.

f. How much compensation cost should be recognized in total in relation to this stock option plan?

g. In which periods should total compensation cost be allocated to as compensation expense?

h. Explain how this ESO plan transfers wealth from stockholders to employees.

EXERCISE 6–13

Information Disclosures and Employee Stock Options

Some research shows that the price of stock is likely to fall in the days leading up to the fixing of the exercise price for employee stock options. It is suggested that the price decreases are the result of selective news releases from managers. Specifically, managers are asserted to delay the release of good news until after the ESO grant date and, instead, selectively release bad news before the date that the stock option exercise price is fixed.

Required:

a. Why do you believe managers are willing to announce bad news but not good news in advance of the stock option grant date?

b. How might you adjust your reaction to news announcements (or lack thereof) around the date when employee stock option exercise prices are set?

EXERCISE 6–14

Interpreting Deferred Income Taxes

Primrose Co. uses the deferred method for interperiod tax allocation. Primrose reports depreciation expense for machinery purchases for the current year using the modified accelerated cost recovery system (MACRS) for income tax purposes and the straight-line basis for financial reporting. The tax deduction is the larger amount this year. Primrose also received rent revenues in advance this year. It included these revenues in this year's taxable income. For financial reporting, rent revenues are reported as unearned revenues, a current liability.

Required:

a. What is the conceptual underpinning for deferred income taxes?

b. How does Primrose determine and account for the income tax effect for both depreciation and rent? Explain.

c. How does Primrose classify the income tax effect of both depreciation and rent on its balance sheet and income statement? Explain.

EXERCISE 6–15

Earnings Management Motives

Companies sometimes use earnings management techniques to increase reported earnings per share by as little as 1 cent.

Required:

Explain why a 1 cent change in reported earnings per share would be insignificant for some companies but significant for other companies. Include in your answer references to at least two earnings targets toward which a company might be managing earnings per share.

Publicly traded companies are required to report earnings per share data on the face of the income statement.

Required:

Compare and contrast basic earnings per share with diluted earnings per share for each of the following:

a. The effect of dilutive stock options and warrants on the number of shares used in computing earnings per share.

b. The effect of dilutive convertible securities on the number of shares used in computing earnings per share data.

c. The effect of antidilutive securities in computing earnings per share.

(CFA Adapted)

EXERCISE 6–16^A

Analyzing Earnings per Share

Accounting requires presentation of earnings per share data along with the income statement.

Required:

a. Explain the meaning of basic earnings per share.

b. Explain how diluted earnings per share differs from basic earnings per share.

(CFA Adapted)

EXERCISE 6–17^A

Interpreting Earnings per Share

Champion had 2 million shares outstanding on December 31, Year 7, its year-end. On March 31, Year 8, Champion paid a 10% stock dividend. On June 30, Year 8, Champion sells $10 million of 5% convertible debentures, convertible into common shares at $5 per share. The AA bond rate on the issue date is 10%.

1. Basic earnings per share for Year 8 is computed on the following number of shares:
   a. 2,050,000   c. 3,200,000
   b. 2,150,000   d. 4,200,000

2. Assume that Champion also has outstanding warrants to purchase 1 million shares at $5 per share. The price of Champion common shares is $8 per share at December 31, Year 8, and the average share price for Year 8 is $4. For the computation of basic earnings per share, how many *additional* shares must be assumed to be outstanding because of the warrants?
   a. Zero   c. 625,000
   b. 375,000   d. 1,000,000

3. Given the same facts as in (2), how many *additional* shares must be assumed to be outstanding because of the warrants when computing diluted earnings per share?
   a. Zero   c. 625,000
   b. 375,000   d. 1,000,000

(CFA Adapted)

EXERCISE 6–18^A

Earnings per Share Computations (multiple choice)

CHECK
(1) b

PROBLEMS

The *unaudited* income statements of Disposo Corporation are reproduced below.

	Year 8	Year 7
Sales	$1,100	$900
Costs and expenses	990	860
Loss on asset disposal	10	—
Income before taxes	100	40
Tax expense	50	20
Net income	$ 50	$ 20

PROBLEM 6–1

Disclosing Discontinued Operations

Note: On August 15, Year 8, the company decided to discontinue its Metals Division. The business was sold on December 31, Year 8, at book value except for a factory building with a book value of $25 that was sold for $15. Operations of the Metals Division were:

	Sales	Income (Loss)
Year 7.....................................	$300	$8
Jan. 1 to Aug. 15, Year 8..........	250	(3)
Aug. 16 to Dec. 31, Year 8.......	75	(1)

CHECK
Year 8 Continuing
income, $59

Required:

Correct the Year 7 and Year 8 income statements to reflect the proper reporting of discontinued operations.

PROBLEM 6–2

*Revenue Recognition
(multiple choice)*

1. In preparing its Year 9 adjusting entries, the Singapore Company neglected to adjust rental fees received in advance for the amount of rental fees earned during Year 9. What is the effect of this error?
   a. Net income is understated, retained earnings are understated, and liabilities are overstated.
   b. Net income is overstated, retained earnings are overstated, and liabilities are unaffected.
   c. Net income, retained earnings, and liabilities all are understated.

2. The Sutton Construction Company entered into a contract in early Year 8 to build a tunnel for the city at a price of $11 million. The company estimated total cost of the project at $10 million and three years to complete. Actual costs incurred (on budget) and billings to the city are as follows:

	Costs Incurred	Billings to City
Year 8	$2,500,000	$2,000,000
Year 9	4,000,000	3,500,000
Year 10	3,500,000	5,500,000

40% $\widehat{T.C.}$

Using the percentage-of-completion method for revenue recognition, what does Sutton Construction report for revenues and profit for Year 9?

	Revenues	Profit		Revenues	Profit
a.	$4,000,000	$300,000	*c.*	$3,850,000	$350,000
b.	$4,400,000	$400,000	*d.*	$3,500,000	$500,000

CHECK
(2) b

3. Using the percentage-of-completion method in accounting for long-term projects, a company can increase reported earnings by:
   a. Accelerating recognition of project expenditures.   *c.* Switching to completed-contract accounting.
   b. Delaying recognition of project expenditures.   *d.* Overestimating the total cost of the project.

4. Revenue can be recognized at the time of:
   a. Production.   *c.* Collection.
   b. Sale.   *d.* All of the above.

5. In October, a company shipped a new product to retailers. Which one of the following conditions would prohibit immediate recognition of revenue?
   a. Terms of the sale require the company to provide extensive promotional materials to retailers before December 1.
   b. Retailers are not obligated to pay the purchase price until February, after their holiday sales are collected.
   c. On the basis of past performance, reliable estimates are that 20% of the product is returned.
   d. The company is unable to enforce agreements concerning discounting of the retail sales of the product.

6. In accounting for long-term contracts, how does the percentage-of-completion method of revenue recognition differ from the completed contract method? (Choose one answer from *a, b, c,* or *d* below.)
   i. Present value of income tax payments is minimized.
   ii. Revenue for each period reflects more closely the results of construction activity during the period.

iii. Current status of uncompleted contracts is reported more accurately.

iv. Percentage-of-completion method relies less on estimates for both the degree of completion and the extent of future costs to be incurred.

a. *i* and *ii.*   c. *ii* and *iii.*
b. *i* and *iii.*   d. *ii* and *iv.*

7. R. Lott Corporation, which began business on January 1, Year 7, uses the installment sales method of accounting. The following data are available for December 31, Year 7 and Year 8:

	Year 7	Year 8
Balance of deferred gross profit on sales account		
Year 7	$300,000	$120,000
Year 8	—	$440,000
Gross profit on sales	30%	40%

The installment accounts receivable balance at December 31, Year 8, is:

a. $1,000,000   c. $1,400,000
b. $1,100,000   d. $1,500,000

CHECK
(7) d

(CFA Adapted)

$$\left[(120,000 / 30\%) + (440,000 / 40\%) \right] = 400,000 + 1,100,000 = 1,500,000$$

PROBLEM 6–3
Revenue Recognition and Fraudulent Behavior

Cendant

Cendant was formed on December 18, 1997, via the merger of CUC International and HFS, Inc. The company owns the rights to franchises and brands including Avis, Century 21 Real Estate, Coldwell Banker, Days Inn, Howard Johnson, and Ramada. The consolidated entity got off to a bad start when it was revealed that CUC International executives had been committing "widespread and systemic" accounting fraud with intent to deceive investors. When the company announced that it had discovered "potential accounting irregularities" the stock dropped from $36 to $19 per share. Eventually the stock would fall to as low as $6 per share as the company struggled to convince investors about management's integrity. According to the company's own investigation, CUC executives had inflated earnings by over $650 million over a three-year period using several tactics, including: (1) failing to timely record returned credit card purchases and membership cancellations, (2) improperly capitalizing and amortizing expenses related to attracting new members, and (3) recording fictitious sales.

Required:

a. For each of three fraudulent tactics employed by CUC, identify an analysis technique that could have identified the accounting improprieties.

b. Both the investors and the management of HFS had relied on audited financial statements in making decisions regarding CUC International. What do you believe was the external auditor's culpability in not detecting these fraudulent practices?

Refer to the financial statements of **Campbell Soup Company** in Appendix A.

Campbell Soup Company

PROBLEM 6–4
Analyzing Income Tax Disclosures

Required:

a. Estimate the amount of depreciation expense reported on Campbell's tax returns for each of the Years 11, 10, and 9. Use a tax rate of 34%.

CHECK
(a) Year 11, $211.9 mil.

b. Identify the amounts and sources in each of the Years 11, 10, and 9 for the following (*note:* combine federal, foreign, and state taxes).
  (1) Earnings before income taxes.
  (2) Expected income tax at 34%.
  (3) Total income tax expense.

(4) Total income tax due.

(5) Total income tax due and not yet paid at end of Years 11, 10, and 9.

c. Why does the effective tax rate for Years 11, 10, and 9 differ from 34% of income before taxes? Answer with a reconciliation including explanations.

d. There is a small tax benefit derived from the divestiture and restructuring charges in Year 10. Can you estimate the cash outlays for these charges in Year 10?

PROBLEM 6–5

Understanding Revenue Recognition and Deferred Income Taxes

Big-Deal Construction Company specializes in building dams. During Years 3, 4, and 5, three dams were completed. The first dam was started in Year 1 and completed in Year 3 at a profit before income taxes of $120,000. The second and third dams were started in Year 2. The second dam was completed in Year 4 at a profit before income taxes of $126,000, and the third dam was completed in Year 5 at a profit before income taxes of $150,000. The company uses percentage-of-completion accounting for financial reporting and the completed-contract method of accounting for income tax purposes. The applicable income tax rate is 50% for each of the Years 1 through 5. Data relating to progress toward completion of work on each dam as reported by the company's engineers are given here:

Dam	Year 1	Year 2	Year 3	Year 4	Year 5
1	20%	60%	20%		
2		30	60	10%	
3		10	30	50	10%

Required:

For each of the five years, Year 1 through Year 5, compute:

a. Financial reporting (book) income.

b. Taxable income.

c. Change in deferred income taxes.

PROBLEM 6–6

Analyzing Preoperating Costs and Deferred Income Taxes

Stead Corporation is formed in Year 4 to take over the operations of a small business. This business proved very stable for Stead, as is evidenced here ($ in thousands):

	Year 4	Year 5	Year 6
Sales....................................	$10,000	$10,000	$10,000
Expenses (except taxes)........	9,000	9,000	9,000
Income before taxes.............	$ 1,000	$ 1,000	$ 1,000

Stead also expends $1,400,000 on preoperating costs for a new product during Year 4 (not included in the above figures). These costs are deferred for financial reporting purposes but are deducted in calculating Year 4 taxable income. During Year 5, the new product line is delayed; and in Year 6, Stead abandons the new product and charges the deferred cost of $1,400,000 to the Year 6 income statement. The applicable tax rate is 50%.

Required:

a. Prepare comparative income statements for Years 4, 5, and 6. Identify all tax amounts as either current or deferred.

b. Compute both current and deferred taxes payable for the balance sheet for each of the Years 4, 5, and 6 (assume all tax payments and refunds occur in the year following the reporting year).

Playgrounds, Inc., is granted a distribution franchise by Shady Products in Year 1. Operations are profitable until Year 4 when some of the company's inventories are confiscated and large legal expenses are incurred. Playgrounds' tax rate is 50% each year (all expenses and costs are tax deductible). Relevant income statement data are (in thousands):

PROBLEM 6–7

Accounting for Income Tax Expense

	Year 1	Year 2	Year 3	Year 4	Year 5	Year 6	Year 7	Year 8
Sales............................	$50	$80	$120	$ 100	$200	$400	$500	$600
Cost of sales	20	30	50	300	50	120	200	250
General and administrative	10	15	20	100	20	30	40	50
Pretax income..............	$20	$35	$ 50	$(300)	$130	$250	$260	$300

Required:

Compute tax expense for each of the Years 1 through 8, and present comparative income statements for these years (assume a 3-year carryback period, a 20-year carryforward period for any losses, and a 100% valuation allowance for the loss carryforward).

CHECK

Year 4 loss, $(247.5); Year 8 income, $150

The financial data below should be used to answer the following two questions.

PROBLEM 6–8ᴬ

Earnings per Share Computations (multiple choice)

WRESTLING FEDERATION OF AMERICA, INC.
Capital Structure and Earnings for Year 7

Number of common shares outstanding on December 31, Year 7	2,700,000
Number of common shares outstanding during Year 7 (weighted average)..............	2,500,000
Market price per common share on December 31, Year 7...	$ 25
Weighted-average market price per share during Year 7	$ 20
Options outstanding during Year 7:	
Number of shares issuable on exercise of options...	200,000
Exercise price	$ 15
Convertible bonds outstanding (December 31, Year 3, issue date):	
Number of convertible bonds..	10,000
Shares of common issuable on conversion (per bond)..	10
Coupon rate..	5.0%
Proceeds per bond at issue (at par value)...	$ 1,000
Net income for Year 7...	$6,500,000
Tax rate for Year 7	40.0%

1. Basic earnings per share for Year 7 is (choose one of the following):
   a. $2.41   c. $2.60
   b. $2.57   d. $2.50

2. Diluted earnings per share for Year 7 is (choose one of the following):
   a. $2.43   c. $2.54
   b. $2.55   d. $2.60

(CFA Adapted)

PROBLEM 6–9ᴬ
Computing
Earnings
per Share

Ace Company's net income for the year is $4 million and the number of common shares outstanding is 3 million (there is no change in shares outstanding during the year). Ace has options and warrants outstanding to purchase 1 million common shares at $15 per share.

Required:

a. If the average market value of the common share is $20, year-end price is $25, interest rate on borrowings is 6%, and the tax rate is 50%, then compute both basic and diluted EPS.

CHECK
(*b*) Diluted EPS, $0.95

b. Do the same computations as in *a* assuming net income for the year is only $3 million, the average market value per common share is $18, and year-end price is $20 per share.

CASES

CASE 6–1
Understanding
Revenue Recognition

BIKE Company starts with $3,000 cash to finance its business plan of producing bike helmets using a simple assembly process. During the first month of business, the company signs sales contracts for 1,300 units (sales price of $9 per unit), produces 1,200 units (production cost of $7 per unit), ships 1,100 units, and collects in full for 900 units. Production costs are paid at the time of production. The company has only two other costs: (1) sales commissions of 10% of selling price when the company collects from the customer, and (2) shipping costs of $0.20 per unit paid at time of shipment. Selling price and all costs per unit have been constant and are likely to remain the same.

Required:

a. Prepare comparative (side-by-side) balance sheets and income statements for the first month of BIKE Company for each of the following three alternatives:
   (1) Revenue is recognized at the time of shipment.
   (2) Revenue is recognized at the time of collection.
   (3) Revenue is recognized at the time of production.

   Note: Net income for each of these three alternatives is (1) $990, (2) $810, and (3) $1,080, respectively.

b. The method where revenue is recognized at time of collection, known as the *installment method,* is acceptable for financial reporting in unusual and special cases. Why is BIKE Company likely to prefer this method for tax purposes?

c. Comment on the usefulness of the installment method for a credit analyst in using both the balance sheet and income statement.

CASE 6–2
Analyzing
Operating
Activities

Refer to the annual report of **Campbell Soup** in Appendix A.   **Campbell Soup**

Required:

a. Compute all of the expense categories as a percentage of sales for each of the three years shown. Analyze and comment on the percentages computed.

b. Comment on the extent to which each component in (*a*) is expected to persist into future years.

c. The provision for income taxes makes up what percent of earnings before income taxes? What factors might cause this percentage to deviate from the statutory percentage of 35%?

d. Campbell Soup reports divestiture and restructuring programs in Years 9 and 10. What amount of expense is recorded relating to these programs? To what activities do these costs relate? How do you interpret these costs?

e. How might large liabilities such as Campbell Soup's restructuring liabilities be used to manage earnings?

On September 16, 20X8, **Toys "R" Us** [**ToysRUs.Com**], the world's largest
toy seller, announced strategic initiatives to restructure its business. The total
cost to implement these initiatives yielded a charge of $508 million, which exceeded operating
earnings from the prior year. The $508 million charge consisted of costs to close and/or downsize
stores, distribution centers, and administrative functions to streamline store formats, inventories
and supply chains; and for changes in accounting estimates and provisions for legal settlements.
These initiatives included the closing of 50 toy stores in the international division, predominantly
in continental Europe, and 9 in the U.S. that did not meet the company's return on investment
goals. It also closed 31 Kids "R" Us stores and converted 28 nearby U.S. toy stores into combination
stores. Combination stores sell toys and apparel. These initiatives were expected to save more than
$75 million in 20X9 and even more in subsequent years. At the time of the restructuring an-
nouncement, the company had 116,000 employees and 1,145 stores worldwide. Of the 1,145
stores, 697 are in the U.S. The company also ran 214 Kids "R" Us stores, 101 Babies "R" Us stores,
and 2 KidsWorld stores. It hoped to reverse a trend of losing sales to Wal-Mart and other discount
retailers. Toys "R" Us had an 18.4% U.S. toy market share in 20X7, down from 18.9% in 20X6. Wal-
Mart's share and Target's share rose from 15.3% to 16.4%, and 6.4% to 7.1%, respectively, during
that time. Toys "R" Us selected financial reports follow:

Toys "R" Us

CASE 6–3

*Analyzing Restructuring
Activities*

Letter to Stockholders

To Our Stockholders

20X8 was indeed a year of enormous challenge and change. We've spent the year intensively
reviewing every aspect of our business and making some tough calls aimed at repositioning
our worldwide business. Key elements of our strategic plan include a Total Solutions Strategy
focused on our C-3 plan, which includes the reformatting and repositioning of our toy stores;
development of a customer-driven culture; expanding product development; improving our
customer value proposition; accelerating our supply chain management program; and expanding
our channels of selling. In conjunction with these restructuring efforts, we have been proactively
rebuilding and reshaping a stronger management team which will serve to build the foundation
for repositioning your Company in the years ahead. We believe that the sum total of these efforts
will serve as the springboard toward implementing our expanded vision for the future:
to position Toys"R"Us as the worldwide authority on kids, families and fun.

20X8 Restructuring Benefits

We ended 20X8 a much healthier and vibrant company. This was attributable to some tough
strategic decisions that will shape the Company's future. We recorded restructuring and other
charges of $508 million net of taxes, which caused the Company to incur a net loss in 20X8. The
impact of making these tough calls will be evident in our future operations, growth, and financial
performance. These charges are the result of an exhaustive review of all our operations in 20X8
from both a strategic and an Economic Value Added (EVA®) perspective. These reviews
prompted the following significant actions:

- The closing and/or downsizing of approximately 50 toy stores in the International arena,
predominantly in continental Europe, and about 9 U.S. toy stores which do not meet the
Company's strategic or financial objectives. This will free our management to focus on higher
return opportunities;
- The conversion of 28 existing U.S. toy stores into "combo" stores, which will enable us
to close 31 nearby Kids "R" Us stores. In addition to reducing operating costs and releasing
working capital, this will allow us to enhance our productivity by further expanding kids'
apparel into additional Toys"R"Us stores;
- The consolidation of several distribution centers and over half a dozen administrative offices.
These actions will reduce administrative support functions in the U.S. and Europe, which will
not only generate selling, general and administrative efficiencies, but "flatten" our organization
and bring our management even closer to our stores and customers;
- The continuation of taking aggressive markdowns on clearance product to optimize inventory
levels, accommodate new product offerings and accelerate our store reformatting. In
conjunction with the initial stages of our supply chain re-engineering, we have already been

able to reduce same store inventories in all our divisions by over $560 million or 24% at year end 20X8, with roughly $480 million or 31% of this favorable swing coming from reduced inventory in the U.S. toy stores division alone. This brought us into the new year with heightened merchandise flexibility and increased "open to buy" as we begin the rollout of the initial phase of our store reformat program in 20X9.

One of our other key priorities in 20X8 was to build a strong executive team, and we are well on our way towards assembling a truly outstanding management team. Since the beginning of 20X8, more than 50 percent of our officer team has either joined the company from the outside, or has been promoted or transferred to new assignments, bringing fresh perspectives and proven skills to our business.

It is obvious our 20X8 sales and earnings were not what we wanted them to be. However, we've spent a year making tough calls and hard decisions, and we're now ready to move forward stronger and more focused than ever.

Total Solutions Strategy

Our restructuring program, in September 20X8, was the first step required to launch a winning strategy for Toys "R" Us–a strategy which will realign our assets, organization and thinking based on customer-driven priorities in a more competitive marketplace. In the "R" Us brand, we have one of the best-known brand names in the world: our challenge is to more effectively develop this strong customer franchise potential. Today's retail marketplace demands stores that are exciting, easy to shop and customer-friendly. While our selection is still superior to our competitors, that alone is not compelling enough to rebuild market share and brand loyalty. We must become more focused on developing greater everyday customer value in terms of price, service, and the total shopping experience.

Management's Discussion and Analysis

Results of Operations and Financial Condition

During 20X8 the Company announced strategic initiatives to reposition its worldwide business and other charges including the customer-focused reformatting of its toy stores into the new C-3 format, as well as the restructuring of its International operations which resulted in a charge of $353 million ($279 million net of tax benefits, or $1.05 per share). The strategic initiatives resulted in a restructuring charge of $294 million. The other charges of $59 million primarily consist of changes in accounting estimates and provisions for legal settlements. The Company is closing and/or downsizing underperforming stores and consolidating distribution centers and administrative offices. As a result, approximately 2,600 employees will be terminated worldwide. Stores expected to be closed had aggregate store sales and net operating losses of approximately $322 million and $5 million, respectively, for the year ended January 30, 20X9. The write-down of property, plant, and equipment relating to the above mentioned closures and downsizings were based on both internal and independent appraisals. Unused reserves at January 30, 20X9, should be utilized in 20X9, with the exception of long-term lease commitments, which will be utilized in 20X9 and thereafter. Details on the components of the charges are described in the Notes to the Consolidated Financial Statements and are as follows:

Description	Charge	Utilized	Reserve Balance
Closings/downsizings:			
Lease commitments	$ 81	$ —	$ 81
Severance and other closing costs	29	4	25
Write-down of property, plant & equipment	155	155	—
Other	29	5	24
Total restructuring	$294	$164	$130
Changes in accounting estimates and			
Provisions for legal settlements	$ 59	$ 20	$ 39

In 20X8 the Company also announced markdowns and other charges of $345 million ($229 million net of tax benefits, or $.86 per share). Of this charge, $253 million relates to markdowns required to clear excess inventory from stores. These markdowns should enable the Company to achieve its optimal inventory assortment and streamline systems so that it can proceed with the C-3 conversions on an accelerated basis. The Company's objective with its new C-3 concept is to provide customers with a better shopping experience leading to increased sales and higher inventory turns. In addition, the Company recorded $29 million in markdowns related to the store closings discussed previously. The Company also recorded charges to cost of sales of $63 million related to inventory system refinements and changes in accounting estimates. Unused reserves at January 30, 20X9, are expected to be utilized in 20X9. Details of the markdowns and other charges are as follows:

Description	Charge	Utilized	Reserve Balance
Markdowns			
Clear excess inventory	$253	$179	$ 74
Store closings	29	2	27
Change in accounting estimates & other	63	57	6
Total cost of sales	$345	$238	$107

The strategic initiatives, markdowns, and other charges described above are expected to improve the Company's free cash flow and increase operating earnings.

CONSOLIDATED STATEMENTS OF EARNINGS
Toys "R" Us, Inc., and Subsidiaries

(In millions except per share data)	Year Ended		
	January 30, 20X9	January 31, 20X8	February 1, 20X7
Net sales	$11,170	$11,038	$9,932
Cost of sales..	8,191	7,710	6,892
Gross profit	2,979	3,328	3,040
Selling, advertising, general, and			
administrative expenses	2,443	2,231	2,020
Depreciation, amortization, and asset write-offs	255	253	206
Restructuring and other charges.......................	294	—	60
Total operating expenses..............................	2,992	2,484	2,286
Operating income (loss)...............................	(13)	844	754
Interest expense	102	85	98
Interest and other income..................................	(9)	(13)	(17)
Interest expense, net....................................	93	72	81
Earnings (loss) before income taxes..................	(106)	772	673
Income taxes	26	282	246
Net earnings (loss)	$ (132)	$ 490	$ 427
Basic earnings (loss) per share.........................	$ (0.50)	$ 1.72	$ 1.56

CONSOLIDATED BALANCE SHEETS
Toys "R" Us, Inc., and Subsidiaries

(In millions)	January 30, 20X9	January 31, 20X8
Assets		
Current assets		
Cash and cash equivalents	$ 410	$ 214
Accounts and other receivables	204	175
Merchandise inventories	1,902	2,464
Prepaid expenses and other current assets	81	51
Total current assets	2,597	2,904
Property and equipment		
Real estate, net	2,354	2,435
Other, net	1,872	1,777
Total property and equipment	4,226	4,212
Goodwill, net	347	356
Other assets	729	491
	$7,899	$7,963
Liabilities		
Current liabilities		
Short-term borrowings	$ 156	$ 134
Accounts payable	1,415	1,280
Accrued expenses and other current liabilities	696	680
Income taxes payable	224	231
Total current liabilities	2,491	2,325
Long-term debt	1,222	851
Deferred Income taxes	333	219
Other liabilities	229	140
Stockholders' equity		
Common stock	30	30
Additional paid-in capital	459	467
Retained earnings	4,478	4,610
Foreign currency translation adjustments	(100)	(122)
Treasury shares, at cost	(1,243)	(557)
Total stockholders' equity	3,624	4,428
	$7,899	$7,963

Financial Statement Footnote

Restructuring and Other Charges

On September 16, 20X8, the Company announced strategic initiatives to reposition its worldwide business. The cost to implement these initiatives, as well as other charges resulted in a total charge of $333 ($266 net of tax benefits, or $1.00 per share). The Company determined that the strategic initiatives required a restructuring charge of $294 to close and/or downsize stores, distribution centers, and administrative functions. This worldwide plan includes the closing of 50 toy stores in the International division, predominantly in continental Europe, and 9 in the United States that do not meet the Company's return on investment objectives. The Company will also close 31 Kids "R"Us stores and convert 28 nearby U.S. toy stores into combination stores in the new C-3 format discussed below. Combination stores include toys and an apparel selling space of approximately 5,000 square feet. Other charges consist primarily of changes in accounting estimates and provisions for legal settlements of $39 recorded in selling, general, and administrative expenses. Of the total restructuring and other charges, $149 relates to domestic operations and $184 relates to International operations. Remaining reserves of $149 should be utilized in 20X9, with the exception of long-term lease commitments, which will be utilized in 20X9 and thereafter.

Also on September 16, 20X8, the Company announced mark-downs and other charges to cost of sales of $345 ($229 net of tax benefits, or $.86 per share). The Company has designed a new store format called C-3. The Company plans to convert approximately 200 U.S. toy stores to the new C-3 format in 20X9. Of this charge, $253 related to markdowns required to clear excess inventory from its stores so the Company can proceed with its new C-3 store format on an accelerated basis. Another component of the charge was inventory markdowns of $29 related to the closing and/or downsizing of stores discussed above. The Company also recorded charges to cost of sales of $63 related to inventory system refinements and changes in accounting estimates. Of these charges, $288 relate to domestic operations and $57 relate to International operations. Remaining reserves of $107 are expected to be utilized in 20X9.

Additionally, in the fourth quarter of 20X8, the Company recorded a charge of $20 ($13 net of tax benefits, or $.05 per share), related to the resolution of third party claims asserted from allegations made by the Federal Trade Commission. This charge was in addition to a $15 charge relating to the same matter, included in the charges mentioned above.

At January 30, 20X9, the Company had approximately $45 of liabilities remaining for its restructuring program announced in 20X5 primarily relating to long-term lease obligations.

The Company believes that reserves are adequate to complete the restructuring and other programs described previously.

On July 12, 20X6, an arbitrator rendered an award against the Company in connection with a dispute involving rights under a license agreement for toy store operations in the Middle East. Accordingly, the Company recorded a provision of $60 during 20X6 ($38 net of tax benefits, or $.14 cents per share), representing all costs in connection with this matter.

Required:

Refer to the Toys "R" Us financial information to answer the following questions.

1. What is the total amount that Toys "R" Us spent for its restructuring plan? Analyze the breakdown of charges and identify where the charge is reported in the income statement.

2. Recast the income statement without the restructuring charge and analyze operating performance for 20X9 by comparing with 20X8 performance.

3. Identify the major elements of its restructuring strategy and their economic effects. What will be the effect on future income and how are the savings expected to arise?

4. Discuss how the restructuring liability could be used by Toys "R" Us as a vehicle for earnings management. In your opinion is Toys "R" Us managing earnings through this charge?

5. Describe how an analyst would recast the balance sheet and income statement of Toys "R" Us to reflect the restructuring costs as an investment to create future cost savings.

6. How can the relative success of these restructuring activities be measured?

CASE 6–4ᴬ

*Analyzing
Earnings per Share
with Convertible
Debentures*

The officers of Environmental, Inc., considered themselves fortunate when the company sold a $9,000,000 subordinated convertible debenture issue on June 30, Year 1, with a 6% coupon. They had the alternative of refunding and enlarging the outstanding term loan, but the interest cost would have been one-half point above the AA bond rate. The AA bond rate was as high as 8½% until March 29, Year 1, when it was lowered to 8%, the rate that prevailed until September 21, Year 1, when it was lowered again to 7½%. As of December 31, Year 1, Environmental, Inc., had the following capital structure:

7% term loan*	$3,000,000
6% convertible subordinated debentures†	9,000,000
Common stock, $1 par, authorized 2,000,000 shares, issued and outstanding	900,000
900,000 warrants, expiring July 1, Year 6‡	—
Additional Paid-In Capital	1,800,000
Retained earnings	4,500,000

*Term loan (originally $5,000,000) is repayable in semiannual installments of $500,000.

†Convertible subordinated debentures, sold June 30, Year 1, are convertible any time at $18 until maturity. Sinking fund of $300,000 per year to start in Year 6.

‡Warrants entitle holder to purchase one share for $10 to expiration on July 1, Year 6.

Additional data for Year 1:

Interest expense	$ 500,000
Net income	1,500,000
Dividends paid	135,000
Earnings retained	900,000

Market prices December 31, Year 1 (averages for Year 1)	
Convertible debentures 6%	$107
Common Stock	$13
Stock Warrants	$4.5
Treasury bills interest rate at 12/31/Year 1	6%

Required:

CHECK
(*a*) Diluted EPS, $1.20

a. Calculate and show computations for basic and diluted earnings per share figures for common stock for the Year 1 annual report (assume a 50% tax rate).

b. What is the times-interest-earned ratio for Year 2 assuming net income before interest and taxes is the same as in Year 1 (a 50% income tax rate applies)?

(CFA Adapted)

Part I. Information concerning the capital structure of Dole Corporation is reproduced below:

CASE 6–5^A

Determining Earnings per Share

DECEMBER 31

	Year 5	Year 6
Common stock..........................	90,000 shares	90,000 shares
Convertible preferred stock	10,000 shares	10,000 shares
8% convertible bonds	$1,000,000	$1,000,000

During Year 6, Dole pays dividends of $1 per share on its common stock and $2.40 per share on its preferred stock. The preferred stock is convertible into 20,000 shares of common stock. The 8% convertible bonds are convertible into 30,000 shares of common stock. Net income for the year ended December 31, Year 6, is $285,000. The income tax rate is 50%.

Required:

a. Compute basic earnings per share for the year ended December 31, Year 6.

b. Compute diluted earnings per share for the year ended December 31, Year 6.

CHECK
(*a*) Diluted EPS, $2.32

Part II. The R. Lott Company's net income for the year ended December 31, Year 6, is $10,000. During Year 6, R. Lott declares and pays $1,000 cash dividends on preferred stock and $1,750 cash dividends on common stock. At December 31, Year 6, 12,000 shares of common stock are issued and outstanding–10,000 of which were issued and outstanding throughout the entire year and 2,000 of which were issued on July 1, Year 6. There are no other common stock transactions during the year, and there is no potential dilution of earnings per share.

Required:

Compute the Year 6 basic earnings per common share of R. Lott Company.

7

CASH FLOW ANALYSIS

A LOOK BACK <

In Chapter 6 we analyzed operating activities using accrual measures. We examined revenue and expense recognition methods for interpretation of operations. Per share figures for income were also examined.

A LOOK AT THIS CHAPTER •

In this chapter we analyze cash flow measures for insights into all business activities, with special emphasis on operations. Attention is directed at company and business conditions when interpreting cash flows. We also consider alternative measures of cash flows.

A LOOK AHEAD >

The next chapter begins our focus on a more strategic application and analysis of financial statements. We analyze return on investment, asset utilization, and other measures of performance that are relevant to a wide class of financial statement users. We describe several tools of analysis to assist in evaluation of company performance and return.

ANALYSIS OBJECTIVES

- Explain the relevance of cash flows in analyzing business activities.

- Describe the reporting of cash flows by business activities.

- Describe the preparation and analysis of the statement of cash flows.

- Interpret cash flows from operating activities.

- Analyze cash flows under alternative company and business conditions.

- Describe alternative measures of cash flows and their usefulness.

- Illustrate an analytical tool in evaluating cash flows (Appendix 7A).

Rite Aid's Bad Case of Cash Woes

HARRISBURG, PA–Rite Aid's financial problems began with an overly aggressive store construction and acquisition binge by its former CEO that drained cash. That CEO built more than 1,600 new stores, shelled out $1.4 billion for Thrifty PayLess, a 1,000-store West Coast chain that proved a drag on earnings, and paid $1.5 billion for pharmacy-benefits manager PCS Health Systems.

The fallout: for the next five years, Rite Aid's cash outflows for investing activities totaled $5 billion. At the same time, its cash inflows from operating activities totaled $800 million. This means Rite Aid financed most of its investments and working capital increases with debt–as reflected by a five-fold increase in total liabilities from $1,738 million to $9,393 million as of 2000.

The crushing debt load impacted the company's ability to obtain supplier credit for inventory purchases and strapped the company of much-needed cash for operating activities. Store sales suffered as a result of inventory shortages, reductions in advertising expenditures, and the inability to be price competitive. The consequent reduction in stock price also prohibited the company

> **Analysis of cash flows would have exposed these ills.**

from selling common stock to refinance its debt and resulted in a downgrade in its credit rating.

The company is now in turnaround mode under the leadership of its new CEO. The company has sold the PCS Health Systems investment for a net cash inflow of $480 million that it used to reduce its indebtedness. It has also convinced bondholders to accept common stock in exchange for approximately $580 million of indebtedness.

Rite-Aid also sold accounts receivable to a special purpose entity (raising $150 million), and sold and leased back 36 stores (raising $94 million). The proceeds have been used to retire indebtedness. Although the company is making progress, much work needs to be done because its indebtedness as of 2005 amounted to over $5.6 billion, as compared with $323 million of equity.

Analysis of cash flows would have exposed these potential ills early on. Adds T. D. Barrett, an analyst at Massachusetts Financial Services, "This company clearly got in way over its head." The prescription for Rite Aid's ills must include sensible checks on its excessive cash outflows for investing activities–checks that can be monitored by analysis of its statement of cash flows.

PREVIEW OF CHAPTER 7

Cash is the residual balance from cash inflows *less* cash outflows for all prior periods of a company. Net cash flows, or simply *cash flows,* refers to the current period's cash inflows less cash outflows. Cash flows are different from accrual income measures of performance. Cash flow measures recognize inflows when cash is received but not necessarily earned, and they recognize outflows when cash is paid but the expenses not necessarily incurred. The statement of cash flows reports cash flow measures for three primary business activities: operating,

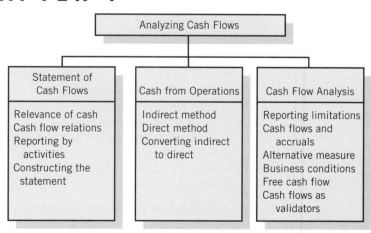

investing, and financing. Operating cash flows, or cash flows from operations, are the cash basis counterpart to accrual net income. More generally, information on cash flows helps us assess a company's ability to meet obligations, pay dividends, increase capacity, and raise financing. It also helps us assess the quality of earnings and the dependence of income on estimates and assumptions regarding future cash flows. This chapter describes cash flows and their relevance to analysis of financial statements. We describe current reporting requirements and their implications for analysis of cash flows, and we explain useful analytical adjustments to cash flows using financial data.

·······STATEMENT OF CASH FLOWS

The purpose of the statement of cash flows is to provide information on cash inflows and outflows for a period. It also distinguishes among the sources and uses of cash flows by separating them into operating, investing, and financing activities. This section discusses important cash flow relations and the layout of the cash flow statement.

Relevance of Cash

Cash is the most liquid of assets and offers a company both liquidity and flexibility. It is both the beginning and the end of a company's operating cycle. A company's operating activities involve cash conversion into various assets (such as inventories) that are used to yield receivables from credit sales. The operating cycle is complete when the collection process returns cash to the company, enabling a new operating cycle to begin.

Our analysis of financial statements recognizes that accrual accounting, where companies recognize revenue when earned and expenses when incurred, differs from cash basis accounting. Yet net cash flow is the end measure of profitability. It is cash, not income, that ultimately repays loans, replaces equipment, expands facilities, and pays dividends. Accordingly, analyzing a company's cash inflows and outflows, and their operating, financing, or investing sources, is one of the most important investigative exercises. This analysis helps in assessing liquidity, solvency, and financial flexibility. **Liquidity** is the nearness to cash of assets and liabilities. **Solvency** is the ability to pay liabilities when they mature. **Financial flexibility** is the ability to react and adjust to opportunities and adversities.

Useful but incomplete information on sources and uses of cash is available from comparative balance sheets and income statements. However, a comprehensive picture of cash flows is derived from the **statement of cash flows** (SCF). This statement is important to analysis and provides information to help users address questions such as:

- How much cash is generated from or used in operations?
- What expenditures are made with cash from operations?
- How are dividends paid when confronting an operating loss?
- What is the source of cash for debt payments?
- How is the increase in investments financed?
- What is the source of cash for new plant assets?
- Why is cash lower when income increased?
- What is the use of cash received from new financing?

Users of financial statements analyze cash flow to answer these and many similar questions. The statement of cash flows is key to the reconstruction of many transactions, which is an important part of the analysis. Analysis of this statement requires our understanding of the accounting measures underlying its preparation and presentation. This chapter focuses first on these important accounting fundamentals and then on the analytical uses for the statement of cash flows.

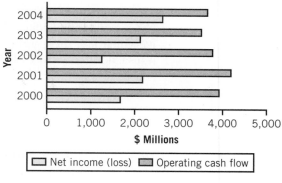

Operating Cash Flows and Net Income of Dell

Reporting by Activities

The statement of cash flows reports cash receipts and cash payments by operating, financing, and investing activities—the primary business activities of a company.

Operating activities are the earning-related activities of a company. Beyond revenue and expense activities represented in an income statement, they include the net inflows and outflows of cash resulting from related operating activities like extending credit to customers, investing in inventories, and obtaining credit from suppliers. Operating activities relate to income statement items (with minor exceptions) and to balance sheet items relating to operations—usually working capital accounts like receivables, inventories, prepayments, payables, and accrued expenses.

Investing activities are means of acquiring and disposing of noncash assets. These activities involve assets expected to generate income for a company, such as purchases and sales of PPE and investment in securities. They also include lending funds and collecting the principal on these loans.

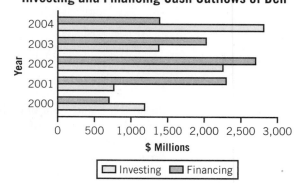

Investing and Financing Cash Outflows of Dell

Financing activities are means of contributing, withdrawing, and servicing funds to support business activities. They include borrowing and repaying funds with bonds and other loans. They also include contributions and withdrawals by owners and their return (dividends) on investment.

Constructing the Cash Flow Statement

There are two acceptable methods for reporting cash flows from operations, the indirect and direct methods. While both methods yield identical bottom-line results, their format differs. With the **indirect method,** net income is adjusted for noncash income (expense) items and accruals to yield cash flows from operations. An advantage of this method is the disclosure of a reconciliation of differences between net income and operating cash flows. This can aid some users that predict cash flows by first predicting income and then adjusting income for leads and lags between income and cash flows—that is, using the noncash accruals. The indirect method is most commonly employed in practice and we use it initially to illustrate preparation of the statement of cash flows. Computation of the statement of cash flows using the **direct method** is provided subsequently for comparison. This method adjusts each income item for its related accruals and, arguably, provides a better format to assess the amount of operating cash inflows (outflows). The format for computing net cash provided by investing and financing activities is the same for both methods. Only the preparation of net cash flows from operations differs.

Preparation of the Statement of Cash Flows

The statement of cash flows is a blend of the income statement and the balance sheet. Net income is first adjusted for noncash income and expense items to yield cash profits which are, then, further adjusted for cash generated and used by balance sheet transactions to yield cash flows from operations, as well as investing and financing activities.

Consider first the net cash from operations. Its computation is as follows:

Net income
+ Depreciation and amortization expense
± Gains (losses) on sales of assets
± Cash generated (used) by current assets and liabilities

Net cash flows from operating activities

The starting point for the statement of cash flows is net income which we first adjust for noncash depreciation and amortization expense. To better understand this add-back, consider that cash outflow occurs when tangible and intangible assets are purchased. The depreciation (amortization) process, then, allocates that cost over their useful lives to match the expense against the revenues generated by those assets with the following accounting entries,

Depreciation expense XXX
    Accumulated depreciation XXX
Amortization expense XXX
    Intangible asset... XXX

Because the statement of cash flows focuses on cash flows, we need to eliminate these noncash expenses that are recognized in the computation of net income, hence the add-back of depreciation and amortization expense. Adding depreciation and amortization expense does not increase operating cash flow, it merely zeros out the expense subtracted in the computation of net income. This can easily be seen by expanding net income as follows:

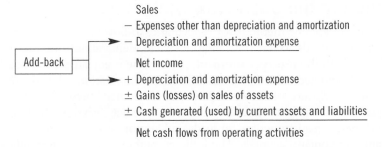

We also adjust net income for gains (losses) on the sales of assets in a similar fashion. The purpose of the adjustment, however, is not to eliminate these investment gains (losses) in their entirety, but to move them out of the operating section of the statement of cash flows. The cash inflows from the sales of these assets are reflected in net cash flows from investing activities.

The final adjustments involve analysis of cash generated and used by changes in current assets and liabilities. To see these effects, consider the simple example of a $100 sale on account:

Accounts receivable	100	
Sales..		100

In the period of sale, net income is increased by $100, but no cash has been generated as the receivable has not yet been collected. The statement of cash flows at this point reports net income of $100 and net cash from operations of $0 as follows:

Net income	$ 100
Depreciation and amortization expense.........	0
Gains (losses) on sale of assets....................	0
Change in accounts receivable	(100)
Net cash flow from operations........................	$ 0

In the following period, the receivable is collected and the statement of cash flows looks like this:

Net income	$ 0
Depreciation and amortization expense.........	0
Gains (losses) on sale of assets....................	0
Change in accounts receivable	100
Net cash flow from operations........................	$100

The reduction in accounts receivable has generated a $100 cash inflow and is, therefore, reported as a positive amount in the statement of cash flows.

The adjustments for changes in balance sheet accounts can be summarized as follows:

Account	Increase	Decrease
Assets..............	Cash Outflow	Cash Inflow
Liabilities.........	Cash Inflow	Cash Outflow

Once net income has been adjusted for depreciation and amortization expense and gains (losses) on the sales of assets, the final step in the preparation of cash flows from operations is to examine changes in current assets (liabilities) and, using the matrix presented above, to reflect these changes as cash inflows (outflows), coded as positive (negative) amounts, respectively.

We now apply these concepts in the preparation of the statement of cash flows for Gould Corporation, whose balance sheet and income statement are presented in Exhibits 7.1 and 7.2, respectively. The following additional information about Gould for Year 2 is available:

1. The company purchased a truck during the year at a cost of $30,000 that was financed in full by the manufacturer.
2. A truck with a cost of $10,000 and a net book value of $2,000 was sold during the year for $7,000. There were no other sales of depreciable assets.
3. Dividends paid during Year 2 are $51,000.

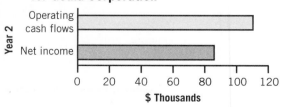

Operating Cash Flows and Net Income for Gould Corporation

Exhibit 7.1

■■■■■■■

GOULD CORPORATION
Comparative Balance Sheets
December 31, Year 2 and Year 1

	Year 2	Year 1	Absolute Value of Change
Cash	$ 75,000	$ 51,000	$ 24,000
Receivables	48,000	39,000	9,000
Inventory	54,000	60,000	6,000
Prepaid expenses	6,000	9,000	3,000
Plant assets	440,000	350,000	90,000
Accumulated depreciation	(145,000)	(125,000)	20,000
Intangible assets	51,000	58,000	7,000
Total assets	$529,000	$442,000	
Accounts payable	$ 51,000	$ 56,000	5,000
Accrued expenses	18,000	14,000	4,000
Long-term note payable	30,000	0	30,000
Mortgage payable	0	150,000	150,000
Preferred stock	175,000	0	175,000
Common stock	200,000	200,000	0
Retained earnings	55,000	22,000	33,000
Total liabilities and equity	$529,000	$442,000	

Gould's statement of cash flows is presented in Exhibit 7.3. The operating section begins with net income of $84,000, which is then adjusted for noncash depreciation and amortization expense. Next, the gain on sale of assets is subtracted to zero it out (the proceeds will be reflected in net cash flows from investing activities). Finally, changes in current

Exhibit 7.2

■■■■■■■

GOULD CORPORATION
Income Statement
For Year Ended December 31, Year 2

Sales	$660,000
Cost of sales	(363,000)
Gross profit	297,000
Operating expenses	(183,000)
Depreciation & amortization	(35,000)
Gain on sale of asset	5,000
Net income	$ 84,000

Exhibit 7.3

■ ■ ■ ■ ■ ■ ■

GOULD CORPORATION
Statement of Cash Flows
For Year Ended December 31, Year 2

Net income	$ 84,000	
Add (deduct)		
Depreciation and amortization expense	35,000	
Gain on sale of assets	(5,000)	
Accounts receivable	(9,000)	
Inventories	6,000	
Prepaid expenses	3,000	
Accounts payable	(5,000)	
Accrued expenses	4,000	
Net cash flow from operating activities		$113,000
Purchase of equipment	(70,000)	
Sale of equipment	7,000	
Net cash flows from investing activities		(63,000)
Mortgage payable	(150,000)	
Preferred stock	175,000	
Dividends	(51,000)	
Net cash flows from financing activities		(26,000)
Net increase in cash		24,000
Beginning cash		51,000
Ending cash		$ 75,000

Note: Assets costing $30,000 were purchased during Year 2 and were financed in whole by the manufacturer.

assets and liabilities are reflected as cash inflows (outflows) using the matrix presented above. Gould realized $113,000 in net cash flow from operations in Year 2.

Net cash flows from investing activities include purchases (p) and sales (s) of plant assets. Purchases can be inferred from the T-account for plant assets (PP&E):

Plant Assets

	350,000		
(p)	100,000	10,000	(s)
	440,000		

Beginning with a balance of $350,000, PP&E was reduced by the cost of the asset sold (s). Net purchases (p), then, can be inferred as the amount necessary to yield the ending balance of $440,000. Of the $100,000 increase in PP&E, only $70,000 was paid in cash as the remainder was financed by the manufacturer. Thus, the $70,000 cash payment appears as purchases in the statement of cash flows. The $30,000 equipment purchase is a noncash investing and financing activity and is not reflected in the body of the statement of cash flows. Instead, it is referenced in an explanatory footnote.

The journal entry for the sale of the asset is:

Cash..	7,000	
Accumulated depreciation..	8,000	
Asset (cost)...		10,000
Gain on sale..		5,000

The gain on sale of $5,000 is deducted from net income to zero it out of the operating section and the $7,000 cash proceeds are reported in the investing section of the statement of cash flows. Net cash flows from investing activities reflect a net cash outflow of $(63,000).

Net cash flows from financing activities reflect changes in long-term liability and equity accounts. Here, the repayment of the mortgage ($150,000), issuance of preferred stock ($175,000) and payment of dividends ($51,000) are included. The net cash flows from financing activities reflect a net outflow of $(26,000).

The net change in cash is equal to the sum of the net cash flows from operations, investing, and financing activities:

Net cash flow from operations......................	$113,000
Net cash flows from investing activities	(63,000)
Net cash flows from financing activities.......	(26,000)
Net change in cash	24,000
Beginning cash	51,000
Ending cash	$ 75,000

The statement of cash flows also provides explanatory notes detailing any noncash investing and financing activities. In our example, this includes the purchase of a truck financed by the manufacturer.

ANALYSIS VIEWPOINT   **. . . YOU ARE THE BOARD MEMBER**

You are a school board member. Your district has received contributions from a publishing company to support educational programs. New management recently took control of the publishing company and reported a $1.2 million annual loss. Net cash flows were an equally dismal $1.1 million decrease—with reported decreases in investing and financing equaling $1.9 million and $0.7 million, respectively. The new management warns you that its contributions to educational programs are ending due to the company's financial distress, including this period's $1.3 million extraordinary loss. What is your course of action?

Special Topics

This section presents several special circumstances that commonly arise in connection with the statement of cash flows and warrant discussion.

Equity Method Investments

Under equity method accounting, the investor records as income its percentage interest in the income of the investee company and records dividends received as a reduction of the investment balance (see Chapter 5). The portion of undistributed earnings, then, is noncash income and should be eliminated from the statement of cash flows, leaving only that portion of earnings that has been received in cash. This is accomplished by subtracting from net income the percentage interest in earnings of the investee company net of dividends received. For example, assume that Gould Corp. owns a 40% interest in Netcom Inc. Netcom reports net income of $100,000 and distributes $60,000 as dividends. Gould includes $40,000 ($100,000 × 40%) as equity earnings on its investment in its net income and reduces its investment balance by $24,000 (dividends received). The $16,000 of reported investment earnings not received in cash must be deducted from net income in computing net cash received from operations.

Acquisitions of Companies with Stock

When one company purchases another with stock, consolidated assets and liabilities increase together with equity accounts as discussed in Chapter 5. Only those changes in balance sheet accounts resulting from cash transactions, however, are reported in the statement of cash flows. As a result, the balance sheet adjustments reported to compute operating cash flows do not equal the changes in balance sheet accounts themselves. Instead, noncash changes in balance sheet accounts are reported in the notes to the statement of cash flows as noncash investing and financing activities, similar to the acquisition of the truck by Gould Corporation that was financed by the manufacturer in the example presented above.

Postretirement Benefit Costs

Pension and other post employment benefit plans accrue expense for service costs and interest, net of expected returns on plan assets, as discussed in Chapter 3. Cash contributions to the pension plan are recorded as a reduction of cash and an increase in the investment balance. The excess of net benefit expense over the cash contribution to the funded plans, or cash benefits paid directly out of the company's funds (in the case of unfunded postretirement benefit plans), must be added to net income in computing net cash flows from operating activities.

Securitization of Accounts Receivable

Companies are increasingly utilizing securitization of accounts receivable via special purpose entities (SPEs) as a method of improving cash flow (see Chapter 3). Securitization involves the transfer of receivables to a SPE that purchases them with the proceeds of bonds sold in the capital markets. Companies account for the reduction in receivables as an increase in cash flow from operations since that relates to a current asset. Analysts need to be cognizant of the source of receivables reductions and question whether they represent true improvement in operating performance or a disguised borrowing.

Direct Method

The **direct** (or **inflow-outflow) method** reports gross cash receipts and cash disbursements related to operations–essentially adjusting each income statement item from accrual to cash basis. A majority of respondents to the accounting *Exposure Draft* preceding current requirements for reporting cash flows, especially creditors, preferred the direct method. The direct method reports total amounts of cash flowing in and out of a company from operating activities. This offers most analysts a better format to readily assess the amount of cash inflows and outflows for which management has discretion. The risks to lenders are typically greater for fluctuations in cash flows from operations vis-à-vis fluctuations in net income. Information on the individual amounts of operating cash receipts and payments is important in assessing such fluctuations and risks. These important analytical considerations at first convinced regulators to require the direct method of reporting cash flows. But partly because preparers of information claimed this method imposes excessive implementation costs, regulators decided to only encourage the direct method and to permit the indirect method. When companies report using the direct method, they must disclose a reconciliation of net income to cash flows from operations (the indirect method) in a separate schedule.

Converting from Indirect to Direct Method

We now show how to convert cash flows from operations reported under the indirect method to the direct method. Accuracy of conversion depends on adjustments using data available from external accounting records. The method of conversion we describe is sufficiently accurate for most analytical purposes.

Conversion from the indirect to the direct format is portrayed in Exhibit 7.4 using values from Gould Corporation. We begin by disaggregating net income ($84,000) into total revenues ($660,000) and total expenses ($576,000). Next, our conversion adjustments are applied to relevant categories of revenues or expenses. From these adjustments we report the direct format of Gould Corporation's cash flows from operations. The gain from sale of equipment (transferred to investing activities) is omitted from the direct method presentation.

Exhibit 7.4

Cash Flows from Operations Section

GOULD CORPORATION
Cash Flows from Operations
For Year Ended December 31, Year 2
($ thousands)

Cash flows from operating activities

Cash receipts from customers[a]	$651,000
Cash paid for inventories[b]	(362,000)
Cash paid for operating expenses[c]	(176,000)
Net cash flows from operations	$113,000

Computations
[a] Sales of $660,000 less increase in accounts receivables of $9,000.
[b] Cost of goods sold of $363,000 less decrease in inventories of $6,000 plus decrease in accounts payable of $5,000.
[c] General, selling, and administrative expenses of $218,000 less (noncash) depreciation and amortization of $35,000, less decrease in prepaid expenses of $3,000, less increase in accrued expenses of $4,000.

ANALYSIS IMPLICATIONS OF CASH FLOWS

Cash flow information yields several implications for our financial analysis. We discuss the more significant implications in this section.

Limitations in Cash Flow Reporting

Following are some limitations of the current reporting of cash flow:

- Practice does not require separate disclosure of cash flows pertaining to either extraordinary items or discontinued operations.
- Interest and dividends received and interest paid are classified as operating cash flows. Many users consider interest paid a financing outflow, and interest and dividends received as cash inflows from investing activities.
- Income taxes are classified as operating cash flows. This classification can distort analysis of the three individual activities if significant tax benefits or costs are attributed to them in a disproportionate manner.
- Removal of pretax (rather than after-tax) gains or losses on sale of plant or investments from operating activities distorts our analysis of both operating and investing activities. This is because their related taxes are *not* removed, but left in total tax expense among operating activities.

Interpreting Cash Flows and Net Income

Our analysis of Gould Corporation focused on the two primary financial statements directed to operating activities: the statement of cash flows and the income statement. In spite of practitioners' best efforts to explain the combined usefulness of both operating statements, not all users understand the dual information roles of cash flows and accrual net income. A recurrent misunderstanding among users is the meaning of *operations* and, also, the comparative relevance of cash flows and accrual net income in providing insights into operating activities. More simply, what different insights into operating activities do these two statements provide?

To help us understand their combined usefulness, we return to our analysis of Gould Corporation. Exhibit 7.5 lists amounts side by side from both operating statements and indicates their measurement objectives. We recognize the function of an income statement is to

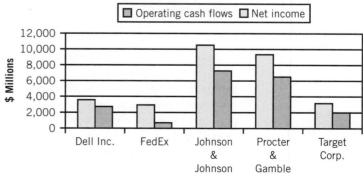

Operating Cash Flows and Net Income

Exhibit 7.5

■ ■ ■ ■ ■ ■ ■

GOULD CORPORATION

Comparison of Accrual and Cash Reporting

	Income Statement	Operating Cash Flows	
Sales	$660,000	$651,000	Cash collections from customers
Gain on sale of asset	5,000		
	665,000	651,000	Total cash collections
Cost of goods sold	(363,000)	(362,000)	Payments to suppliers
Operating expenses	(183,000)	(176,000)	Payments for expenses
Depreciation and amortization	(35,000)		
Net income	$ 84,000	$113,000	Cash from operations

measure company profitability for a period. An income statement records revenues when earned and expenses when incurred. No other statement measures profitability in this manner. Yet an income statement does *not* show us the timing of cash inflows and outflows, nor the effect of operations on liquidity and solvency. This information is available to us in the statement of cash flows, shown separately for operating, investing, and financing activities.

Cash flows from operations is a broader view of operating activities than is net income. Cash flows from operations encompass all earning-related activities of a company. This measure concerns not only revenues and expenses but also the cash demands of these activities. They include investing in customer receivables and inventories, and the financing provided by suppliers of goods and services. This difference is evident in Exhibit 7.5 where we arrive at operating cash receipts and disbursements by analyzing changes in operating assets and liabilities to adjust income statement items. Cash flow from operations focuses on the liquidity aspect of operations. It is *not* a measure of profitability because it does not include important costs like the use of long-lived assets in operations nor revenues like the noncash equity in earnings of subsidiaries or nonconsolidated affiliates.

We must bear in mind that a *net* measure, be it net income or cash flows from operations, is of limited usefulness. Whether our purpose of analysis is evaluation of prior performance or prediction of future performance, the key is information about **components** of these net measures. Our discussion in Chapter 11 emphasizes our evaluation of operating performance, and future earning power depends not on net income but on its components.

Accounting accruals determining net income rely on estimates, deferrals, allocations, and valuations. These considerations sometimes allow more subjectivity than do the factors determining cash flows. For this reason we often relate cash flows from operations to net income in assessing its quality. Some users consider earnings of higher quality when the ratio of cash flows from operations divided by net income is greater. This derives from a concern with revenue recognition or expense accrual criteria yielding high net income but low cash flows. Cash flows from operations effectively serve as a check on net income, but not a substitute for net income. Cash flows from operations

---

Analysis Research
■■■■■■■
USEFULNESS OF CASH FLOWS

Are cash flow measures useful for users of financial statements? Do cash flow measures offer any additional information beyond accrual measures? Do securities markets react to cash flow information? Analysis research provides valuable insights into these important questions. Several studies of users identify a market shift away from traditional accrual measures like net income in favor of cash flow measures. Cash flow measures are increasingly used for credit analysis, bankruptcy prediction, assigning loan terms, earnings quality assessments, solvency forecasts, and setting dividend and expansion policies. Users of these measures include investors, analysts, creditors, auditors, and management.

Capital market studies provide evidence consistent with the use of cash flow measures. Namely, cash flows from operations explain changes in stock prices beyond those explained by net income. Research also suggests the usefulness of cash flow measures depends on the company and economic conditions prevailing. Evidence indicates the *components* of cash flows, and not the aggregate figure, are what drive the usefulness of cash flow data.

---

include a financing element and are useful for evaluating and projecting both short-term liquidity and longer-term solvency.

Cash flows from operations exclude, by definition, elements of revenues and expenses not currently affecting cash. Our analysis of operations and profitability should not proceed without considering these elements. Both the income statement and the statement of cash flows are designed to meet different needs of users. The income statement uses accrual accounting in recognizing revenues earned and expenses incurred. Cash flows from operations report revenues received in cash and expenses paid. It is not an issue of which statement is superior to another—only a matter of our immediate analysis needs. Our use of these statements requires that we bear in mind the statements' objectives and limitations.

ANALYSIS EXCERPT

Coca-Cola recently marketed a large initial share offering, not on the basis of traditional measures like price-earnings ratio (which was near 100), but on the basis of operating cash flows (specifically, earnings before taxes, depreciation, interest, and goodwill amortization). This latter measure substantially exceeded net income that was depressed due to heavy noncash charges.

■■■■■■■ANALYSIS OF CASH FLOWS

Since conditions vary from company to company, it is difficult to formulate a standard analysis of cash flows. Nevertheless, certain commonalities exist. First, our analysis must establish the major past sources of cash and their uses. A common-size analysis of the statement of cash flows aids in this assessment. In estimating trends, it is useful to total the major sources and uses of cash over a period of a few years since annual or quarterly reporting periods are often too short for meaningful inferences. For example, financing of major projects often spans several years. In evaluating sources and uses of cash, the analyst should focus on questions like:

- Are asset replacements financed from internal or external funds?
- What are the financing sources of expansion and business acquisitions?

Major Sources of Cash for Campbell Soup (Years 6–11)

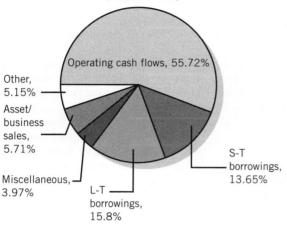

Operating cash flows, 55.72%

Other, 5.15%

Asset/business sales, 5.71%

Miscellaneous, 3.97%

L-T borrowings, 15.8%

S-T borrowings, 13.65%

Major Uses of Cash for Campbell Soup (Years 6–11)

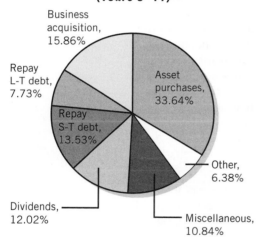

Business acquisition, 15.86%

Repay L-T debt, 7.73%

Repay S-T debt, 13.53%

Asset purchases, 33.64%

Dividends, 12.02%

Other, 6.38%

Miscellaneous, 10.84%

- Is the company dependent on external financing?
- What are the company's investing demands and opportunities?
- What are the requirements and types of financing?
- Are managerial policies (such as dividends) highly sensitive to cash flows?

Case Analysis of Cash Flows of Campbell Soup

We illustrate the analysis of prior years' statements of cash flows for Campbell Soup Company in the Comprehensive Case following Chapter 11. Our analysis covers the six-year period ending July 28, Year 11. Exhibit CC.10 presents these statements in common-size format.

Our analysis of these statements reveals several insights. During this six-year period the major sources of cash are operations ($3,010 million), long-term debt ($854 million), and short-term debt ($737 million)—see Exhibit CC.4 and Campbell's statements in Appendix A. Major uses are plant purchases (net of sales) of $1,647 million, business acquisitions (net of sales) of $718 million, and cash dividends of $649 million. During this six-year period, cash and cash equivalents increased by $24 million. Sources of cash from operations as a percentage of total sources average 55.7%, with a low of 31.3% in Year 9—see Exhibit CC.10. Year 11 is the most profitable of the six, reflecting a recovery after two years of poor performance and restructuring activities. For this six-year period, cash from operations covered net cash used in investing activities and nearly all dividends paid. Cash flows are partially insulated from the sharp declines in earnings for Years 9 and 10 because restructuring charges of $682 million involved no cash outlays.

Inferences from Analysis of Cash Flows

The Campbell Soup case illustrates the range of useful insights drawn from this analysis. An overall analysis of financial statements then either corroborates or refutes the inferences from the analysis of cash flows.

There are useful generalizations we can make about potential inferences from analysis of the statement of cash flows. First, our analysis of the statement of cash flows enables us to appraise the quality of management's decisions over time and their impact on the company's results of operations and financial position. When our analysis covers a long time period, it can yield insights into management's success in responding to changing business conditions and their ability to seize opportunities and overcome adversities.

Inferences from our analysis of cash flows include where management committed its resources, where it reduced investments, where additional cash was derived from, and where claims against the company were reduced. Inferences also pertain to the disposition of earnings and the investment of discretionary cash flows. Analysis also enables us to infer the size, composition, pattern, and stability of operating cash flows.

We previously described patterns of cash flows through a company. The operating cycle (Chapter 4) depicts the short-term investment of cash in inventories, the increase in receivables arising from their sale, and the recovery of cash as receivables are collected. The investment in long-term operating assets, such as PPE, follows a much longer cycle. Eventually, all productive uses of cash impact the sales process and are converted into receivables or cash. Profitable operations yield cash recoveries exceeding amounts invested and, consequently, increase cash inflows. Losses yield the opposite effect.

We must examine the components of operating cash flows. Components often hold important clues about the stability of cash sources. For example, increases in operating cash flows that result from the securitization of accounts receivable or the reduction in inventories are not usually a reliable source of cash. This is because cash inflows from the continued reduction of receivables is limited. Similarly, although excess inventories can be reduced without detrimental effects, at some point reductions in inventory adversely impact sales, and cash must be expended to replenish inventory.

Increases in operating cash flows that arise from increases in current liabilities also are not usually a sustainable source of cash inflow. For example, companies can lean on the trade (increase trade payables) to increase operating cash flow. At some point, however, suppliers will respond by charging higher costs or discontinuing shipments for their products (remember, they are incurring higher costs and lower operating cash flows as their level of receivables increases). Similarly, accruals represent unpaid liabilities for which an expense has been currently reported. Accrued wages must be paid, as must accrued rent, and so forth. Increases in accruals typically represent a short-term deferral of cash outflow.

Alternative Cash Flow Measures

Users sometimes compute **net income plus depreciation and amortization** as a crude proxy for operating cash flow. One variant of this measure is the popular EBITDA (earnings before interest, taxes, depreciation, and amortization). This measure suffers from several problems:

1. The add-back of depreciation is sometimes interpreted to mean that the expense is not legitimate. That is incorrect. The using up of long-term depreciable assets is a real expense that must not be ignored.
2. Some interpret the depreciation add-back to indicate that cash has been provided for the replenishment of the long-term assets. That is also incorrect. The add-back of depreciation expense does not generate cash. It merely zeros out the noncash expense from net income as discussed above. Cash is provided by operating and financing activities, not by depreciation.
3. Net income plus depreciation ignores changes in working capital accounts that comprise the remainder of net cash flows from operating activities. Yet changes in working capital accounts often comprise a large portion of cash flows from operating activities. Examination of working capital components provides insight into the persistence of operating cash flows as discussed in the previous section.

Oversimplification of operating cash flows by the use of net income plus depreciation, EBITDA, or the like, misinterprets the nature of depreciation expense and ignores valuable information that is revealed by examination of changes in working capital accounts.

Company and Economic Conditions

A balance sheet describes the assets of a company at a point in time and the manner in which those assets are financed. An income statement portrays the results of operations for a period of time. Income increases assets, including cash and noncash (both current and noncurrent) assets. Expenses are the consumption of assets (or incurrence of liabilities). Accordingly, net income is linked to cash flows through adjustments in balance sheet accounts.

It is conceivable that a profitable company can find it difficult to meet current obligations and need cash for expansion. Success through increasing sales can yield liquidity problems and restrict cash due to a growing asset base. Accordingly, there might be insufficient cash to cover maturing obligations. It is also important for us to distinguish performance across business activities. It is especially important to separate operating performance and profitability from those of investing and financing activities. All activities are essential and interconnected, but they are not identical and reflect on different aspects of a company. A statement of cash flows reveals the implications of earnings activities for cash. It reveals assets acquired and how they are financed. It describes how net income and cash flows from operations are different. The ability to generate cash flows from operations is vital to financial health. No business survives in the long run without generating cash from operations. Yet we must interpret cash flows and trends with care and an understanding of economic conditions.

While both successful and unsuccessful companies can experience problems with cash flows from operations, the reasons are markedly different. A successful company confronting increasing investments in receivables and inventories to meet expanding customer demand often finds its growing profitability useful in obtaining additional financing from both debt and equity suppliers. This profitability (positive accrual income) ultimately yields positive cash flows. An unsuccessful company experiences cash shortages from slowdowns in receivable and inventory turnovers, losses in operations, or combinations of these and other factors. The unsuccessful company can increase cash flows by reducing receivables and inventories, but usually this is done at the expense of services to customers, further depressing profits. These factors are signs of current and future crises and cash shortages, including declining trade credit. Decreasing cash flows for an unsuccessful company have entirely different implications than they do for a successful one. Even if an unsuccessful manager borrows money to offset the decline in operating cash flows, the costs and results of borrowing only magnify the ultimate loss. Profitability is our key variable; without it a company is doomed to failure.

We must also interpret changes in operating working capital items in light of economic circumstances. An increase in receivables can imply expanding consumer demand for products or it can signal an inability to collect amounts due in a timely fashion. Similarly, an increase in inventories (and particularly of raw materials) can imply anticipation of increases in production in response to consumer demand, or it can imply an inability to accurately anticipate demand or sell products (especially if finished goods inventory is increased).

Inflationary conditions add to the financial burdens and challenges of companies. The more significant challenges include replacing plant assets, increasing investments in inventories and receivables, and dividend policies based on profits that do not provide for current costs of resources used in operations. While managerial decisions are not necessarily based on financial statements, we cannot dismiss their importance and implications. We look to the statement of cash flows for information on the effects, in current dollars, of how management copes under inflationary conditions. This yields a focus on cash flows from operations after capital expenditures and dividends.

Free Cash Flow

A useful analytical derivative of the statement of cash flows is the computation of **free cash flow.** As with other analytical measures, we must pay attention to components of the computation. Ulterior motives in reporting the components used in computing free cash flow can sometimes affect its usefulness. While there is not agreement on its exact definition, one of the more useful measures of free cash flow is:

Cash flows from operations
— Net capital expenditures required to maintain productive capacity
— Dividends on preferred stock and common stock (assuming a payout policy)
Free cash flow (FCF)

Another definition that is widely used and similar in concept is: FCF = NOPAT − Change in NOA. This definition defines free cash flows to the firm as net operating profits after tax (NOPAT) less the increase in net operating assets (NOA). The increase in NOA subsumes the change in working capital for net cash flows from operations and the increase in long-term operating assets (similar to the second line in the formula presented above). The focus, however, is on the company as a whole, without regard to its financing. Consequently, dividends (a financing activity) are not considered.

Positive free cash flow reflects the amount available for business activities after allowances for financing and investing requirements to maintain productive capacity at current levels. Growth and financial flexibility depend on adequate free cash flow. We must recognize that the amount of capital expenditures needed to maintain productive capacity is generally not disclosed. Rather it is part of total capital expenditures, which are disclosed, but can include outlays for expansion of productive capacity. Separating capital expenditures between these two components is problematic. The statement of cash flows does not separate capital expenditures into maintenance and expansion components.

ANALYSIS VIEWPOINT   *. . . YOU ARE THE CREDIT ANALYST*

You are a credit analyst at a credit-rating agency for industrial companies. A company you are rating has a strong history of positive (1) net cash flows and (2) cash flows from operations. However, its free cash flow has recently turned negative and you expect it to remain negative into the foreseeable future. Do you change your credit rating of the company?

Cash Flows as Validators

The statement of cash flows is useful for prediction of operating results on the basis of acquired and planned productive capacity. It is also of use in assessment of a company's future expansion capacity, its capital requirements, and its sources of cash inflows. The statement of cash flows is an essential bridge between the income statement and the balance sheet. It reports a company's cash inflows and outflows, and a company's ability to meet current obligations. Moreover, the statement of cash flows provides us with important clues on:

- Feasibility of financing capital expenditures.
- Cash sources in financing expansion.
- Dependence on external financing (liabilities versus equity).
- Future dividend policies.
- Ability in meeting debt service requirements.
- Financial flexibility to unanticipated needs and opportunities.
- Financial practices of management.
- Quality of earnings.

The statement of cash flows is useful in identifying misleading or erroneous operating results or expectations. Further discussion of earnings quality and the usefulness of cash flows as validators appears in Chapter 11. Nevertheless, like other statements, the statement of cash flows is a reliable and credible source of a company's actions and intentions—more so than are predictions and press releases of management.

We must take care to examine relations among items in a statement of cash flows. Certain transactions are related—for example, purchasing assets by issuing debt. Yet our analysis must be careful not to infer relations among items where none exist. A change in cash, whether positive or negative, cannot be judged solely by the statement of cash flows. It must be analyzed in relation to other variables in a company's financial structure and operating results. For example, an increase in cash can arise from sacrificing a company's future earning power by selling valuable assets, or by taking on debt at high costs or unfavorable terms. Relations among financial statement items and their implications are important for the reliability of our analysis.

........SPECIALIZED CASH FLOW RATIOS

The following two ratios are often useful in analyzing a firm's flow of funds.

Cash Flow Adequacy Ratio

The **cash flow adequacy ratio** is a measure of a company's ability to generate sufficient cash from operations to cover capital expenditures, investments in inventories, and cash dividends. To remove cyclical and other random influences, a three-year total is typically used in computing this ratio. The cash flow adequacy ratio is calculated as:

$$\frac{\text{Three-year sum of cash from operations}}{\text{Three-year sum of capital expenditures, inventory additions, and cash dividends}}$$

Investment in other important working capital items like receivables is omitted because they are financed primarily by short-term credit (such as growth in accounts payable). Accordingly, only additions to inventories are included. Note in years where inventories decline, the downward change is treated as a zero change in computing the ratio.

Using the financial statement data from Campbell Soup Company in Appendix A, we compute its (three-year) cash flow adequacy ratio as:

$$\frac{\$1,610.9^{(a)}}{\$1,390.3^{(b)} + \$113.2^{(c)} + \$348.5^{(d)}} = 0.87$$

[a]Cash from operations–item 64 .
[b]Property additions–items 65 and 67 .
[c]Inventory additions–item 62 .
[d]Cash dividends–item 77 .

Proper interpretation of the cash flow adequacy ratio is important. A ratio of 1 indicates the company exactly covered these cash needs without a need for external financing. A ratio below 1 suggests internal cash sources were insufficient to maintain dividends and current operating growth levels. For Campbell Soup Company, the ratio indicates that for the three years ending in Year 11, Campbell's operating cash flows fell short of covering dividends and operating growth. While not illustrated here, if we compute a six-year ratio, a more favorable ratio emerges. The cash flow adequacy ratio also reflects on the inflationary effects for funding requirements of a company. As with other analyses, inferences drawn from this ratio should be supported with further analysis and investigation.

Cash Reinvestment Ratio

The **cash reinvestment ratio** is a measure of the percentage of investment in assets representing operating cash retained and reinvested in the company for both replacing assets and growth in operations. This ratio is computed as:

$$\frac{\text{Operating cash flow} - \text{Dividends}}{\text{Gross plant} + \text{Investment} + \text{Other assets} + \text{Working capital}}$$

A reinvestment ratio in the area of 7% to 11% is generally considered satisfactory. Using the financial statements of Campbell Soup Company, we compute the cash reinvestment ratio for Year 11:

$$\frac{\$805.2^{(e)} - \$137.5^{(f)}}{(\$2,921.9 + \$477.6)^{(g)} + 404.6^{(h)} + (\$1,518.5 - \$1,278.0)^{(i)}} = 16.5\%$$

[e]Cash from operations–item 64 .
[f]Cash dividends–item 77 .
[g]Gross plant assets–items 158 thru 161 ; plus: intangibles–items 163 and 164 .
[h]Other assets–item 39 .
[i]Total current assets–item 36 ; less: total current liabilities–item 45 .

.....APPENDIX 7A ANALYTICAL CASH FLOW WORKSHEET

This appendix provides a usable worksheet to facilitate the conversion of financial data to the direct (inflow-outflow) format for cash flows from operations. We often desire to convert a company's indirect format for cash flows from operations to an analytically more useful direct format. Exhibit 7A.1 displays a worksheet designed to simplify this conversion.

Exhibit 7A.1

■ ■ ■ ■ ■ ■ ■

WORKSHEET TO COMPUTE
CASH FLOW FROM OPERATIONS (CFO)

Direct Presentation ($ in _____)

Company: _____

Year Ended _____

		YEAR		
Cash receipts from operations				
Net sales and revenues[a]	*1	$ _____	$ _____	$ _____
Other revenue and income (see also lines 22 and 25)	*2	_____	_____	_____
(I) D in current receivables	3	_____	_____	_____
(I) D in noncurrent receivables[b]	4	_____	_____	_____
Other adjustments[c]	5	_____	_____	_____
Total cash receipts	6	_____	_____	_____
Cash disbursements for operations				
Total expenses (include interest and taxes)[a]	*7	_____	_____	_____
Less expenses and losses not using cash:				
Depreciation and amortization	8	_____	_____	_____
Noncurrent deferred income taxes	9	_____	_____	_____
Other _____	10	_____	_____	_____
Other _____	11	_____	_____	_____
Other _____	12	_____	_____	_____
Changes in current operating assets and liabilities				
I (D) in inventories	13	_____	_____	_____
I (D) in prepaid expenses	14	_____	_____	_____
(I) D in accounts payable	15	_____	_____	_____
(I) D in taxes payable	16	_____	_____	_____
(I) D in accruals	17	_____	_____	_____
I or D other _____	18	_____	_____	_____
I or D other _____	19	_____	_____	_____
I or D in noncurrent accounts[b]	20	_____	_____	_____
Total cash disbursements[d]	21	_____	_____	_____
Dividends received				
Equity in income of unconsolidated affiliates	*22	_____	_____	_____
Less undistributed equity in income of affiliates	23	_____	_____	_____
Dividends from unconsolidated affiliates	24	_____	_____	_____
Other cash receipts (disbursements) [e]	*25	_____	_____	_____
Describe _____ [a]	25	_____	_____	_____
_____ [a]	25	_____	_____	_____
Total cash flow from operations[f]	26	_____	_____	_____

Footnote all amounts that are composites or that are not self-evident. Indicate all sources for figures. I(D) refers to increases (decreases) in accounts.

* *The sum of the five lines denoted by asterisks must equal reported net income per income statement.*

[a] *Including adjustment (grossing up) of revenue and expense of discontinued operations disclosed in footnote(s). Describe computation. Include other required adjustments and explain.*

[b] *That relating to operations—describe in notes.*

[c] *Such as removal of gains included above—describe in notes.*

[d] *That include (from supplemental disclosures):*

Cash paid for interest (net of amount capitalized)	$_____		_____	_____
Cash paid for income taxes	$_____		_____	_____

[e] *These include extraordinary items, discontinued operations, and any other item not included above. The amount in line 25 is after adjustment to cash basis while the * refers to item(s) included in income before such adjustment. (Present details in notes.)*

[f] *Reconcile to amount reported by company. If not reported, reconcile to change in cash for period along with investing and financing activities.*

GUIDANCE ANSWERS TO ANALYSIS VIEWPOINTS

BOARD MEMBER
Your initial course of action is to verify management's claim of financial distress. A $1.2 million loss along with a $1.1 million decrease in net cash flows seemingly supports their claim. However, you should be suspicious of management's motives and its aversion to community activism. Consequently, you scrutinize the financial results, and your findings reveal a markedly different picture. You note cash flows from operations increased $1.5 million ($-$1.1 = CFO $-$ $1.9 $-$ $0.7). You note that net income *before* the extraordinary loss is a positive $100,000. This is sufficient and powerful information with which to confront management. A serious and directed discussion is likely to yield reconsideration of this company's support of your educational programs.

INVESTOR
Several factors can account for an increase in net cash flows when a loss is reported. Possibilities include: (1) early recognition of expenses relative to revenues generated (such as

research and development), (2) valuable long-term sales contracts not yet recognized in income, (3) issuances of debt or equity to finance expansion, (4) selling of assets, (5) delayed cash payments, and (6) prepayment on sales. Our analysis of D.C. Bionics needs to focus on the components of both net income and net cash flows, and their implications for future performance.

CREDIT ANALYST
The downward turn in free cash flow is an ominous sign. Free cash flow is the cash remaining after providing for commitments necessary to maintain operations at current levels. These commitments include a company's continuing operations, interest payments, income taxes, net capital expenditures, and dividends. A negative free cash flow implies a company must either sell assets or acquire financing (debt or equity) to maintain current operations. A significant change in free cash flow must be seriously scrutinized in assigning a new credit rating.

[Superscript[A] denotes assignments based on Appendix 7A.]

QUESTIONS

7–1. What is the meaning of the term *cash flow?* Why is this term subject to confusion and misrepresentation?

7–2. What information can a user of financial statements obtain from the statement of cash flows?

7–3. Describe the three major activities the statement of cash flows reports. Cite examples of cash flows for each activity.

7–4. Explain the three categories of adjustments in converting net income to cash flows from operations.

7–5. Describe the two methods of reporting cash flow from operations.

7–6. Contrast the purpose of the income statement with that of cash flow from operations.

7–7. Discuss the importance to analysis of the statement of cash flows. Identify factors entering into the interpretation of cash flows from operations.

7–8. Describe the computation of free cash flow. What is its relevance to financial analysis?

7–9. List insights that the statement of cash flows can provide to our analysis.

EXERCISES

Refer to the financial statements of **Campbell Soup Company** in Appendix A.

Campbell Soup Company

EXERCISE 7–1
Interpreting Differences between Income and Cash from Operations

Required:
Explain how Campbell Soup Company can have net income of $401.5 million, but generate $805.2 million in cash from operations in Year 11. Explain this in language understood by a general businessperson. Illustrate your explanation by reference to the major reconciling items.

EXERCISE 7–2

Relations in the
Statement of
Cash Flows

It is important that an analyst understand the activities that comprise the statement of cash flows, including the disclosure of their individual elements.

Required:

a. Practice requires the classification of cash inflows and outflows into three categories. Identify and describe those categories.

b. Which noncash activities are reported in the statement of cash flows and how are they reported?

c. Assume First Corporation retains you to consult with them on preparation of the statement of cash flows using the indirect method for the year ended December 31, Year 8. Advise them on how the following separate items affect the statement of cash flows and how they are shown on the statement:
   (1) Net income for the fiscal year is $950,000, including an extraordinary gain of $60,000.
   (2) Depreciation expense of $80,000 is included in the income statement.
   (3) Uncollectible accounts receivable of $50,000 are written off against the allowance for uncollectible accounts. Bad debts expense of $24,000 is included in determining earnings for the year, and the same $24,000 amount is added to the allowance for uncollectible accounts.
   (4) Accounts receivable increase by $140,000 during the year and inventories decline by $60,000.
   (5) Taxes paid to governments amount to $380,000.
   (6) A gain of $5,000 is realized on the sale of a machine; it originally cost $75,000 and $25,000 is undepreciated on the date of sale.
   (7) On June 5, Year 8, buildings and land are purchased for $600,000; First Corp. gave in payment $100,000 cash, $200,000 in market value of its unissued common stock, and a $300,000 mortgage note.
   (8) On August 8, Year 8, First Corp. converts $700,000 face value of its 6 percent convertible debentures into $140,000 par value of its common stock. The bonds are originally issued at face value.
   (9) The board of directors declares a $320,000 cash dividend on October 30, Year 8, payable on January 15, Year 9, to stockholders of record on November 15, Year 8.
   (10) On December 15, Year 8, First Corp. declares a 2-for-1 stock split payable on December 25, Year 8.

EXERCISE 7–3

Analyzing
Operating
Cash Flows

The following data are taken from the records of Saro Corporation and subsidiaries for Year 1:

Net income	$10,000
Depreciation, depletion, and amortization	8,000
Disposals of property, plant, and equipment (book value) for cash	1,000
Deferred income taxes for Year 1 (noncurrent)	400
Undistributed earnings of unconsolidated affiliates	200
Amortization of discount on bonds payable	50
Amortization of premium on bonds payable	60
Decrease in noncurrent assets	1,500
Cash proceeds from exercise of stock options	300
Increase in accounts receivable	900
Increase in accounts payable	1,200
Decrease in inventories	850
Increase in dividends payable	300
Decrease in notes payable to banks	400

Required:

CHECK
CFO, $19,340

a. Determine the amount of cash flows from operations for Year 1 (use the indirect format).

b. For the following items, explain their meaning and implications, if any, in adjusting net income to arrive at cash flows from operations.
   (1) Issuance of treasury stock as employee compensation.
   (2) Capitalization of interest incurred.
   (3) Amount charged to pension expense differing from the amount funded.

The balance sheets of Barrier Corporation as of December 31, Year 2, and Year 1, and its statement of income and retained earnings for the year ended December 31, Year 2, follow:

EXERCISE 7–4

*Deriving
Cash Flows from
Financial Statements*

BARRIER CORPORATION
Balance Sheets
December 31, Year 2 and Year 1

	Year 2	Year 1	Increase (decrease)
Assets			
Cash	$ 275,000	$ 180,000	$ 95,000
Accounts receivable	295,000	305,000	(10,000)
Inventories	549,000	431,000	118,000
Investment in Ort Inc., at equity	73,000	60,000	13,000
Land	350,000	200,000	150,000
Plant and equipment	624,000	606,000	18,000
Accumulated depreciation	(139,000)	(107,000)	(32,000)
Goodwill	16,000	20,000	(4,000)
Total assets	$2,043,000	$1,695,000	$348,000
Liabilities and Stockholders' Equity			
Accounts payable	$ 604,000	$ 563,000	$ 41,000
Accrued expenses	150,000	—	150,000
Bonds payable	160,000	210,000	(50,000)
Deferred income taxes	41,000	30,000	11,000
Common stock, par $10	430,000	400,000	30,000
Additional paid-in capital	226,000	175,000	51,000
Retained earnings	432,000	334,000	98,000
Treasury stock, at cost	—	(17,000)	17,000
Total liabilities and equity	$2,043,000	$1,695,000	$348,000

BARRIER CORPORATION
Statement of Income and Retained Earnings
For Year Ended December 31, Year 2

Net sales		$1,937,000
Undistributed income from Ort Inc.		13,000
Total net revenue		1,950,000
Cost of sales		(1,150,000)
Gross income		800,000
Depreciation expense	$ 32,000	
Amortization of goodwill	4,000	
Other expenses (including income taxes)	623,000	(659,000)
Net income		$ 141,000
Retained earnings, January 1, Year 2		334,000
		475,000
Cash dividends paid		(43,000)
Retained earnings, December 31, Year 2		$ 432,000

Additional information:

- Capital stock is issued to provide additional cash.
- All accounts receivable and payable relate to operations.
- Accounts payable relate only to items included in cost of sales.
- There are no noncash transactions.

Required:

Determine the following amounts:

a. Cash collected from sales during Year 2.

b. Cash payments on accounts payable during Year 2.

c. Cash receipts during Year 2 *not* provided by operations.

d. Cash payments for noncurrent assets purchased during Year 2.

CHECK

(*b*) $1,227,000

EXERCISE 7–5

Interpreting
Cash Flows

Indicate if each transaction and event is (1) a source of cash, (2) a use of cash, and/or (3) an adjustment leading to a source or use of cash (assume an indirect format). List also its placement in the statement of cash flows: operations (O), financing (F), investing (I), noncash significant (NCS), noncash nonsignificant (NCN), or no effect (NE).

Example

Transaction or Event	Source	Use	Adjustment	Category in Statement of Cash Flows
Cash dividend received	X			O

a. Increase in accounts receivable.

b. Pay bank note.

c. Issue common stock.

d. Sell marketable securities.

e. Retire bonds.

f. Declare stock dividend.

g. Purchase equipment.

h. Convert bonds to preferred stock.

i. Pay dividend.

j. Increase in accounts payable.

EXERCISE 7–6

Interpreting
Cash Flows

Indicate if each transaction and event is (1) a source of cash, (2) a use of cash, and/or (3) an adjustment leading to a source or use of cash (assume an indirect format). List also its placement in the statement of cash flows: operations (O), financing (F), investing (I), noncash significant (NCS), noncash nonsignificant (NCN), or no effect (NE).

Example

Transaction or Event	Source	Use	Adjustment	Category in Statement of Cash Flows
Issue bonds for cash	X			F

a. Decrease in inventory.

b. Paid current portion of long-term debt.

c. Retire treasury stock.

d. Purchase marketable securities (noncurrent).

e. Issue bonds for property.

f. Declare stock dividend.

g. Sell equipment for cash.

h. Convert bonds to preferred stock.

i. Purchase inventory on credit.

j. Decrease in accounts payable from return of merchandise.

During a meeting of the management committee of Edsel Corporation, a number of proposals are made to alleviate its weak cash position and improve income. Evaluate and comment on both the immediate *and* long-term effects of the following proposals on the measures indicated. Indicate increase (+), decrease (−), or no effect (NE).

EXERCISE 7–7

Interpreting Economic Impacts of Transactions

	EFFECT ON		
Proposal	Net Income	Cash from Operations	Cash Position
1. Substitute stock dividends for cash dividends.			
2. Delay needed capital expenditures.			
3. Reduce repair and maintenance outlays.			
4. Increase the provision for depreciation:			
a. For GAAP books only.			
b. For tax only.			
c. For both GAAP books and tax.			
5. Require earlier payment from clients.			
6. Delay payment to suppliers and pass up cash discounts.			
7. Borrow money short term.			
8. Switch from sum-of-the-years'-digits to straight-line depreciation for books only.			
9. Pressure dealers to buy more.			
10. Reduce funding of pension plan to the minimum legal level.			
11. Reduce inventories by implementing a just-in-time inventory system.			
12. Sell trading securities that have declined by $1,000 in the current period but are still valued at $3,000 above cost.			
13. Reissue treasury shares.			

CHECK

(12) −, NE, +

An economics book has the following statement: "For the business firm there are, typically, three major sources of funds. Two of these, depreciation reserves and retained earnings, are internal. The third is external, consisting of funds obtained either by borrowing, or by the sale of new equities."

EXERCISE 7–8

Depreciation as a Source of Cash

Required:

a. Is depreciation a source of cash? (Exclude all considerations pertaining to depreciation differences between taxable income and accounting income.)

b. If depreciation is not a source of cash, what might explain the belief by some that depreciation is a source of cash?

c. If depreciation is a source of cash, explain the manner in which depreciation provides cash to the business.

EXERCISE 7–9

Analyzing the Statement of Cash Flows

Refer to the financial statements of **Campbell Soup Company** in Appendix A.

Campbell Soup Company

Required:

a. How much cash does Campbell Soup collect from customers during Year 10? (*Hint:* Use the statement of cash flows to derive the beginning balance of receivables.)

CHECK
(*c*) $3,982.4 mil.

b. How much is paid in cash dividends on common stock during Year 11?

c. How much is the total cost of goods and services produced and otherwise generated in Year 11? Consider all inventories.

d. How much is the deferred tax provision for Year 11? What effect did it have on current liabilities?

e. What effect does Year 11 depreciation expense have on cash from operations?

f. Why are the "Divestitures & restructuring" provisions in the statement of cash flows for Year 10 added back to net income in arriving at cash from operations?

g. What does the adjustment "Effect of exchange rate changes on cash" represent?

h. Note 1 to the financial statements discusses the accounting for disposal of property. Where is the adjustment for any gain or loss reported in the statement of cash flows?

CHECK
(*i*) Year 11, $306.6 mil.

i. Compute free cash flows for all years shown.

j. Campbell is an established manufacturer. How would you expect the free cash flows of a start-up competitor in this industry to differ from Campbell?

k. If Campbell launched a new product line in Year 12, how would you expect the three sections of the statement of cash flows to be affected?

EXERCISE 7–10

Linking Operating Cash Flows with Earnings Quality

In reviewing the financial statements of NanoTech Co., you discover that net income increased while operating cash flows decreased for the most recent two consecutive years.

Required:

a. Explain how net income could increase for NanoTech while its operating cash flows decrease. Your answer should include three illustrative examples.

b. Describe how operating cash flows can serve as one indicator of earnings quality.

(CFA Adapted)

EXERCISE 7–11

Relation of Cash Flows to Company Life Cycle

Analysts often exploit the relation between a company's life cycle (see Exhibit 2.3) and its cash flows to better understand company performance and financial condition.

Required:

a. Explain how a company's transition from the growth stage to "cash cow" is reflected in the statement of cash flows.

b. Describe how the decline of a "cash cow" is reflected in the statement of cash flows.

PROBLEMS

Refer to **Campbell Soup Company's** statement of cash flows in Appendix A.

Campbell Soup Company

PROBLEM 7–1[A]

Converting Cash from Operations under Indirect Method to Direct

Required:

Convert Campbell's statement of cash flows for Year 11 to show cash flows from operations (CFO) using the direct method.

For purposes of this problem only, *assume* the following:

a. Net change in other current assets and current liabilities of $30.6 consists of:

Decrease in prepaid expenses	$(25.3)
Decrease in accounts payable	42.8
Increase in taxes payable	(21.3)
Increase in accruals and payrolls	(26.8)
	$(30.6)

b. Campbell disposed of a division in Year 11 reporting revenues of $7.5 million and an after-tax loss of $5.3 million. The loss is included in expenses. The CFO presentation should include revenues and expenses of the discontinued operations in Year 11.

Refer to **Campbell Soup Company's** statement of cash flows in Appendix A.

Campbell Soup Company

PROBLEM 7–2[A]

Converting the Statement of Cash Flows to Alternative Formats

Required:

Convert Campbell's statement of cash flows for Year 10 to report its cash from operations under the direct method. (For purposes of this assignment only, assume Campbell disposed of a division in Year 10 that had revenues of $7.5 million and an after-tax loss of $5.3 million. The loss is included in expenses. The CFO presentation should include revenues and expenses of discontinued operations in Year 10.)

A colleague who is aware of your understanding of financial statements asks for help in analyzing the transactions and events of Zett Corporation. The following data are provided:

PROBLEM 7–3

Preparing and Analyzing the Statement of Cash Flows (Indirect)

ZETT CORPORATION
Balance Sheets
December 31, Year 1 and Year 2

	Year 1	Year 2
Cash	$ 34,000	$ 34,500
Accounts receivable, net	12,000	17,000
Inventory	16,000	14,000
Investments (long term)	6,000	—
Fixed assets	80,000	93,000
Accumulated depreciation	(48,000)	(39,000)
Total assets	$100,000	$119,500

(continued)

PROBLEM 7–3
(concluded)

	Year 1	Year 2
Accounts payable..........................	$ 19,000	$ 12,000
Bonds payable...............................	10,000	30,000
Common stock	50,000	61,000
Retained earnings..........................	21,000	28,000
Treasury stock	—	(11,500)
Total liabilities and equity..............	$100,000	$119,500

Additional data for the period January 1, Year 2, through December 31, Year 2, are:

1. Sales on account, $70,000.
2. Purchases on account, $40,000.
3. Depreciation, $5,000.
4. Expenses paid in cash, $18,000 (including $4,000 of interest and $6,000 in taxes).
5. Decrease in inventory, $2,000.
6. Sales of fixed assets for $6,000 cash; cost $21,000 and two-thirds depreciated (loss or gain is included in income).
7. Purchase of fixed assets for cash, $4,000.
8. Fixed assets are exchanged for bonds payable of $30,000.
9. Sale of investments for $9,000 cash.
10. Purchase of treasury stock for cash, $11,500.
11. Retire bonds payable by issuing common stock, $10,000.
12. Collections on accounts receivable, $65,000.
13. Sold unissued common stock for cash, $1,000.

Required:

a. Prepare a statement of cash flows (indirect method) for the year ended December 31, Year 2.

b. Prepare a side-by-side comparative statement contrasting two bases of reporting: (1) net income and (2) cash flows from operations.

c. Which of the two financial reports in (b) better reflects profitability? Explain.

CHECK
Year 2 CFO, $0

PROBLEM 7–4
Analyzing the Statement of Cash Flows (Indirect)

Dax Corporation's genetically engineered flowers have rapidly gained market acceptance and shipments to customers have increased dramatically. The company is preparing for significant increases in production. Management notes that despite increasing profits the cash balance has declined, and it is forced to nearly double its debt financing in the current year. You are hired to advise management as to specific causes of the cash deficiency and how to remedy the situation. You are given the following balance sheets of Dax Corporation for Years 1 and 2 ($ thousands):

DAX CORPORATION
Balance Sheets
December 31, Year 2 and Year 1

($ thousands)	Year 2		Year 1	
Assets				
Cash		$ 500		$ 640
Accounts receivable, net...................		860		550
Inventories.....................................		935		790
Prepaid expenses............................		25		—
Total current assets		$2,320		$1,980
Patents	$ 140			
Less accumulated amortization........	(10)	130		—
Plant and equipment	2,650		$1,950	
Less accumulated depreciation	(600)	2,050	(510)	1,440
Other assets	200		175	
Less accumulated depreciation	(30)	170	(25)	150
Total assets		$4,670		$3,570
Liabilities and Equity				
Accounts payable............................		$ 630		$ 600
Deferred income tax.........................		57		45
Other current liabilities....................		85		78
Total current liabilities.....................		772		723
Long-term debt...............................		1,650		850
Common stock, $1 par.....................		2,000		1,800
Retained earnings		248		197
Total liabilities and equity		$4,670		$3,570

In addition, the following information is available:

1. Net income for Year 2 is $160,000 and for Year 1 it is $130,000.

2. Cash dividends paid during Year 2 are $109,000 and during Year 1 they are $100,000.

3. Depreciation expense charged to income during Year 2 is $95,000, and the provision for bad debts (expense) is $40,000. Expenses include cash payments of $28,000 in interest costs and $70,000 in income taxes.

4. During Year 2 the company purchases patents for $140,000 in cash. Amortization of patents during the year amounts to $10,000.

5. Deferred income tax for Year 2 amounts to $12,000 and for Year 1 it amounts to $15,000.

Required:

a. Prepare a statement of cash flows (indirect method) for Year 2.

b. Explain the discrepancy between net income and cash flows from operations.

c. Describe options available to management to remedy the cash deficiency.

CHECK
(*a*) Year 2 CFO, $(166,000)

PROBLEM 7–5

*Preparing the
Statement of
Cash Flows
(Direct)*

Using the income statement and balance sheets of Niagara Company below, prepare a statement of cash flows for the year ended December 31, Year 9, using the direct method.

NIAGARA COMPANY
Income Statement
For Year Ended December 31, Year 9

Sales	$1,000
Cost of goods sold	(650)
Depreciation expense	(100)
Sales and general expense	(100)
Interest expense	(50)
Income tax expense	(40)
Net income............................	$ 60

NIAGARA COMPANY
Balance Sheets
December 31, Year 9 and Year 8

	Year 8	Year 9
Assets		
Cash...	$ 50	$ 60
Accounts receivable, net...........	500	520
Inventory.................................	750	770
Current assets..........................	1,300	1,350
Fixed assets, net......................	500	550
Total assets	$1,800	$1,900
Liabilities and Equity		
Notes payable to banks	$ 100	$ 75
Accounts payable	590	615
Interest payable........................	10	20
Current liabilities	700	710
Long-term debt........................	300	350
Deferred income tax.................	300	310
Capital stock	400	400
Retained earnings	100	130
Total liabilities and equity	$1,800	$1,900

CHECK
CFO, $165

(CFA adapted)

PROBLEM 7–6

*Interpreting Cash Flow
Effects of Transactions*

An ability to visualize quickly the effect of a transaction on the cash resources of a company is a useful analytical skill. This visualization requires an understanding of the economics underlying transactions and how they are accounted for. Expressing transactions in entry form can help one understand business activities.

Required:

A schematic statement of cash flows is reproduced below. The titles of lines in the schematic are given labels (letters). Several business activities are listed below the schematic. For each of the activities listed, identify the lines affected and by what amount. Each activity is separate and unrelated to another. The company closes its books once each year on December 31. Do not consider subsequent activities. Use the labels (letters) shown below. Do not indicate the effect on any line not given a label. If a transaction has no effect, write none. In indicating effects for lines labeled *Y* and *C,* use a + to indicate an increase and a − to indicate a decrease. (*Hint:* Every activity with an effect, affects at least two lines–equal debits and credits. An analytical entry can aid in arriving at a solution.)

Schematic Statement of Cash Flows

SOURCES OF CASH

(Y)	Net income	_____ (Y)
(YA)	Additions and addbacks of expenses and losses not using cash..........	_____ (YA)
(YS)	Subtractions for revenues and gains not generating cash	_____ (YS)
	Changes in current operating assets and liabilities	
(CC)	Add credit changes..	_____ (CC)
(DC)	Deduct debit changes..	_____ (DC)
(NC)	Add (deduct) changes in noncurrent operating accounts	_____ (NC)
	Cash flow from operations Y + YA − YS + CC − DC + or − NC	_____
(DE)	Proceeds of debt and equity issues	_____ (DE)
(IL)	Increase in nonoperating current liabilities.........................	_____ (IL)
(AD)	Proceeds of long-term assets dispositions	_____ (AD)
(OS)	Other sources of cash..	_____ (OS)
	Total sources of cash	_____

USES OF CASH

(ID)	Income distributions...	_____ (ID)
(R)	Retirements of debt and equity	_____ (R)
(DL)	Decreases in nonoperating current liabilities	_____ (DL)
(AA)	Long-term assets acquisitions	_____ (AA)
(OU)	Other uses of cash...	_____ (OU)
	Total uses of cash	_____
(C)	Increase (decrease) in cash..	_____ (C)

SCHEDULE OF NONCASH INVESTING AND FINANCING ACTIVITIES

(NDE)	Issue of debt or equity	_____ (NDE)
(NCR)	Other noncash-generating credits......................................	_____ (NCR)
(NAA)	Acquisitions of assets	_____ (NAA)
(NDR)	Other noncash-requiring debts..	_____ (NDR)

Examples:

a. Sales of $10,000 are made on credit.

b. Cash dividends of $4,000 are paid.

c. Entered into long-term capital lease obligation (present value $60,000).

Answers in the Form [Line, Amount]:

a. [DC, $10,000], [+ Y, $10,000]

b. [ID, $4,000], [− C, $4,000]

c. [NAA, $60,000], [NDE, $60,000]

Business activities:

a. Provision for bad debts of $11,000 for the year is included in selling expenses.

b. Depreciation of $16,000 is charged to cost of goods sold.

c. Company acquires a building by issuance of a long-term mortgage note for $100,000.

d. Treasury stock with a cost of $7,000 is retired and canceled.

e. The company has outstanding 50,000 shares of common stock with par value of $1. The company declares a 20 percent stock dividend at the end of the year when the stock is selling for $16 a share.

f. Inventory costing $12,000 is destroyed by fire. The insurance company pays only $10,000 toward this loss, although the market value of the inventory is $15,000.

g. Inventories originally costing $25,000 are used by production departments in producing finished goods that are sold for $35,000 in cash and $5,000 in accounts receivable.

h. Accounts receivable of $8,000 are written off. There is an allowance for doubtful accounts balance of $5,000 prior to the write off.

i. Long-lived assets are acquired for $100,000 cash on January 1. The company decides to depreciate $20,000 each year.

j. A machine costing $15,000 with accumulated depreciation of $6,000 is sold for $8,000 cash.

PROBLEM 7–7

*Interpreting
Cash Flow
Effects of
Transactions*

Complete the requirements of Problem 7–6 using the business activities listed below:

Part I

a. An annual installment of $100,000 due on long-term debt is paid on its due date.

b. Equipment originally costing $12,000 with $7,000 of accumulated depreciation is sold for $4,000 cash.

c. Obsolete inventory costing $75,000 is written down to zero.

d. Treasury stock costing $30,000 is sold for $28,000 cash.

e. A plant is acquired by issuing a $300,000 mortgage payable due in equal installments over six years.

f. The company's 30 percent-owned unconsolidated subsidiary earns $100,000 and pays dividends of $20,000. The company recorded its 30 percent share of these items using the equity method.

g. A product is sold for $40,000, to be paid with $10,000 down plus $10,000 each year for three years. Interest at 10 percent of the outstanding balance is due. Consider only the effect at the time of sale (the company's operating cycle is less than one year).

h. The company uses a periodic inventory method. Certain inventory is mistakenly valued at $1,000—it should have been valued at $10,000. Show the effect of correcting the error.

i. Cash of $400,000 is used to acquire 100 percent of ZXY Manufacturing Company. At date of acquisition, ZXY has current assets of $300,000 (including $40,000 in cash); plant and equipment of $670,000; current liabilities of $160,000; and long-term debt of $410,000.

j. A provision for bad debt expense of $60,000 is made (calculated as a percent of sales for the period).

Part II

a. Cash of $120,000 is invested in a 30-percent-owned company.

b. A 30 percent-owned subsidiary earns $25,000 (in total) and pays no dividends.

c. A 30 percent-owned subsidiary earns $30,000 (in total) and pays dividends of $10,000 (in total).

d. Equipment with an original cost of $15,000 and accumulated depreciation of $12,000 is sold for $4,000 cash.

e. The company borrows $60,000 from its banks on November 30 payable on June 30 of next year.

f. Convertible bonds with a face value of $9,000 are converted into 1,000 shares of common stock with a par value of $2 per share.

g. Treasury stock with a cost of $4,000 is sold for $6,000 cash.

h. Common stock (par value $2) with a fair market value of $100,000 plus $100,000 cash are given to acquire 100 percent of ZXY Mfg. Co. At date of acquisition ZXY had current assets of $120,000 (including $40,000 cash); plant and equipment of $180,000; current liabilities of $60,000; and long-term debt of $40,000.
   (1) Identify the effect on the parent's statement.
   (2) Identify the effect on the consolidated statement.

i. The minority's share of income is $4,000.

j. Inventory with a cost of $80,000 is written down to its market value of $30,000.

k. Accounts receivable for $1,200 are written off. The company uses an allowance for doubtful accounts.

l. A noncancelable lease of equipment for 10 years with a present value of $120,000 is capitalized.

m. A 15 percent stock dividend is declared. The 60,000 shares of common stock issued to cover the dividend have a par value of $2 per share and a fair market value of $3 per share.

n. A provision of $27,000 for uncollectible accounts is made (calculated as a percent of sales for the period).

While on assignment you discover that you have misplaced the balance sheet of Bird Corporation as of January 1, Year 1. However, you do have the following data on Bird Corporation:

PROBLEM 7–8

Reconstructing a Balance Sheet from Cash Flows

BIRD CORPORATION
Postclosing Trial Balance
December 31, Year 1

Debit balances

Cash	$ 100,000
Accounts receivable	120,000
Inventory	130,000
Property, plant, and equipment	550,000
Other noncurrent investments	200,000
Total	$1,100,000

Credit balances

Accounts payable	$ 100,000
Current portion of long-term debt	80,000
Accumulated depreciation	270,000
Long-term debt	200,000
Common stock	300,000
Retained earnings	150,000
Total	$1,100,000

BIRD CORPORATION
Statement of Cash Flows
For Year Ended December 31, Year 1

Cash flows from operations

Net income..		$150,000
Add (deduct) adjustment to cash basis		
Depreciation.......................................	$ 85,000	
Loss on sale of equipment....................................	5,000	
Gain on sale of noncurrent investments..............	(50,000)	
Increase in accounts receivable..........................	(30,000)	
Increase in inventories.......................................	(20,000)	
Increase in accounts payable..............................	40,000	30,000
Cash from operations...		180,000

Cash flows from investing activities

Additions to property and equipment.......................	(150,000)	
Sale of equipment...	10,000	
Sale of investments...	95,000	
Cash used for investing activities		(45,000)

Cash flows from financing activities

Issuance of common stock......................................		10,000	
Additions to long-term debt......................................	$15,000		
Decrease in current portion of long-term debt...........	(30,000)	(15,000)	
Cash dividends..		(80,000)	
Cash used for financing activities...........................			(85,000)
Net increase in cash..			$ 50,000

CHECK

Total assets, $725,000

Required:

Using the available data and information, prepare the balance sheet of Bird Corporation as of January 1, Year 1. T-accounts can be helpful in reconstructing the individual accounts. (*Note:* Equipment sold had accumulated depreciation of $50,000.)

PROBLEM 7–9
*Analyzing
Economic Impacts of
Transactions*

Indicate whether the following independent transactions increase (+), decrease (−), or do not affect (NE) the current ratio, the amount of working capital, and cash from operations. Also indicate the amounts of any effects. The company presently has a current ratio of 2 to 1 along with current liabilities of $160,000.

	Current Ratio Effect	Working Capital Effect $___	Cash from Operations Effect $___
a. Paid accrued wages of $1,000.			
b. Purchased $20,000 worth of material on account.			
c. Received judgment notice from the court that the company must pay $70,000 damages for patent infringement within six months.			
d. Collected $8,000 of accounts receivable.			
e. Purchased land for factory for $100,000 cash.			
f. Repaid currently due bank note payable of $10,000.			
g. Received currently due note receivable of $15,000 from customer as consideration for sale of land.			
h. Received cash of $90,000 from stockholders as donated capital.			
i. Purchased machine costing $50,000; $15,000 down and the balance to be paid in seven equal annual installments.			
j. Retired bonds maturing five years hence at par of $50,000. Bonds have unamortized premium of $2,000.			
k. Declared dividends of $10,000 payable after year-end.			
l. Paid the dividends in k in cash.			
m. Declared a 5% stock dividend.			
n. Paid the stock dividend in m.			
o. Signed a long-term purchase contract of $100,000 to commence a year from now.			
p. Borrowed $40,000 cash for one year.			
q. Paid accounts payable of $20,000.			
r. Purchase a patent for $20,000.			
s. Wrote off $15,000 of current marketable securities that became worthless.			
t. $8,500 of organization expenses were written off.			
u. Recorded depreciation expense of $70,000.			
v. Sold $28,000 of merchandise on account.			
w. Sold a building for $90,000 that had a book value of $45,000.			
x. Sold a machine at cost for $5,000; received $2,500 down and the balance receivable in six months.			
y. Recorded income tax expense of $80,000, half of which is deferred (long term).			

PROBLEM 7–10

Analyzing Operating Flow Measures

Your banker confides to you after looking at a number of financial statements that she is confused about the difference between two operating measures, net income and cash from operations.

Required:

a. Explain the purpose and significance of these two operating measures.

b. Several financial transactions or events follow. For each transaction or event, indicate whether it yields an increase (+), decrease (−), or no effect (NE) on each of the two measures.

	EFFECT OF TRANSACTION/EVENT ON:	
	Net Income	Cash from Operations
1. Sales of marketable securities for cash at more than their carrying value.		
2. Sale of merchandise with deferred payments (one-half within one year and one-half after one year).		
3. Reclassify noncurrent receivable as current receivable.		
4. Payment of current portion of long-term debt.		
5. Collection of an account receivable.		
6. Recording the cost of goods sold.		
7. Purchase of inventories on account (credit terms).		
8. Accrual of sales commissions (to be paid at a later date).		
9. Payment of accounts payable (resulting from purchase of inventory).		
10. Provision for depreciation on a sales office.		
11. Borrowing cash from a bank on a 90-day note payable.		
12. Accrual of interest on a bank loan.		
13. Sale of partially depreciated equipment for cash at less than its book value.		
14. Flood damage to merchandise inventories (no insurance coverage).		
15. Declaration and payment of a cash dividend on preferred stock.		
16. Sale of merchandise on 90-day credit terms.		
17. Provision for uncollectible accounts receivable.		
18. Write-off of an uncollectible receivable.		
19. Provision for income tax expense (to be paid the following month).		
20. Provision for deferred income taxes (set up because depreciation for tax reporting exceeded depreciation for financial reporting).		
21. Purchase of a machine (fixed asset) for cash.		
22. Payment of accrued salary expense to employees.		

PROBLEM 7–11

Preparing and Interpreting the Statement of Cash Flows

Following the acquisition of **Kraft** during Year 8, the **Philip Morris Companies** released its Year 8 financial statements. The Year 8 financial statements and other data are reproduced on the next page.

Kraft
Philip Morris Companies

PHILIP MORRIS COMPANIES, INC.
Balance Sheets ($ millions)
December 31, Year 8 and Year 7

	Year 8	Year 7
Assets		
Cash and cash equivalents	$ 168	$ 90
Accounts receivable	2,222	2,065
Inventories	5,384	4,154
Current assets	7,774	6,309
Property, plant, and equipment, net	8,648	6,582
Goodwill, net	15,071	4,052
Investments	3,260	3,665
Total assets	$34,753	$20,608
Liabilities and Stockholders' Equity		
Short-term debt	$ 1,259	$ 1,440
Accounts payable	1,777	791
Accrued liabilities	3,848	2,277
Income taxes payable	1,089	727
Dividends payable	260	213
Current liabilities	8,233	5,448
Long-term debt	17,122	6,293
Deferred income taxes	1,719	2,044
Stockholders' equity	7,679	6,823
Total liabilities and stockholders' equity	$34,753	$20,608

PHILIP MORRIS COMPANIES, INC.
Income Statement ($ millions)
For Year Ending December 31, Year 8

Sales	$ 31,742
Cost of goods sold	(12,156)
Selling and administrative expenses	(14,410)
Depreciation expense	(654)
Goodwill amortization	(125)
Interest expense	(670)
Pretax income	3,727
Income tax expense	(1,390)
Net income	$ 2,337

Note: Dividends declared, $941 million.

PHILIP MORRIS PURCHASE OF KRAFT

Allocation of Purchase Price ($ millions)

Accounts receivable	$ 758
Inventories	1,232
Property, plant, and equipment	1,740
Goodwill	10,361
Short-term debt	(700)
Accounts payable	(578)
Accrued liabilities	(530)
Long-term debt	(900)
Purchase price (net of cash acquired)	$11,383

CHECK
(*a*) CFO, $5,205 mil.

CHECK
(*c*) $3,331

Required:

a. Prepare a statement of cash flows (indirect method) for Philip Morris. (*Hint:* Acquisition of Kraft requires you to remove the assets acquired and liabilities incurred as a result of that acquisition from the balance sheet before computing changes used in preparing the statement of cash flows. Philip Morris pays $11.383 billion for Kraft, net of cash acquired—see the Allocation of Purchase Price table.)

b. Calculate cash flows from operations using the direct method for Philip Morris.

c. Based on your answer to *a*, compute Philip Morris's free cash flow for Year 8. Discuss how free cash flow impacts the company's future earnings and financial condition.

(CFA Adapted)

PROBLEM 7–12
*Analyzing Cash
from Operations
(Direct)*

Refer to the financial statements of ZETA Corporation reproduced in assignment Case CC–2 of the Comprehensive Case (following Chapter 11).

CHECK
(*a*) Year 6 CFO, $6,400

Required:

a. Prepare a schedule computing cash flows from operations using the direct method. Include revenues and expenses of discontinued operations. Include a list of important assumptions and weaknesses as a note to your cash statement. Support all amounts shown. (*Hint:* Discontinued operations cannot be separated from continuing operations, but unadjusted income and expense of discontinued operations can be.)

b. ZETA's statement of cash flows reports income taxes paid in Year 6 of $2,600. Verify this amount independently.

c. Reconcile the change in "accounts payable and accruals" reported in the statement of cash flows with the number derived from the balance sheet. Explain the reason(s) for any difference. (*Hint:* Refer to notes 3 and 4.)

CASES

The statement of cash flows for **Lands' End** is reproduced here:

Lands' End

CASE 7–1
*Cash Flow and
Free Cash Flow
Analysis*

LANDS' END, INC. & SUBSIDIARIES
Consolidated Statements of Cash Flows

($ in thousands)	FOR PERIOD ENDED		
	Year 9	Year 8	Year 7
Cash flows from operating activities			
Net income	$ 31,185	$ 64,150	$ 50,952
Adjustments to reconcile net income to			
net cash flows from operating activities—			
Pretax non-recurring charge	12,600	—	—
Depreciation and amortization	18,731	15,127	13,558
Deferred compensation expense	653	323	317
Deferred income taxes	(5,948)	(1,158)	994
Pretax gain on sale of subsidiary	—	(7,805)	—
Loss on disposal of fixed assets	586	1,127	325
Changes in assets and liabilities excluding			
effects of divestitures			
Receivables	(5,640)	(7,019)	(675)
Inventory	21,468	(104,545)	22,371
Prepaid advertising	(2,844)	(7,447)	4,758
Other prepaid expenses	(2,504)	(1,366)	(145)
Accounts payable	4,179	11,616	14,205
Reserve for returns	1,065	944	629
Accrued liabilities	6,993	8,755	4,390
Accrued profit sharing	(2,030)	1,349	1,454
Income taxes payable	(5,899)	(1,047)	8,268
Other	1,665	64	394
Net cash flows from (used for) operating activities	74,260	(26,932)	121,795
Cash flows from (used for) investing activities			
Cash paid for capital additions	(46,750)	(47,659)	(18,481)
Proceeds from sale of subsidiary	—	12,350	—
Net cash flows used for investing activities	(46,750)	(35,309)	(18,481)
Cash flows from (used for) financing activities			
Proceeds from short-term debt	6,505	21,242	1,876
Purchases of treasury stock	(35,557)	(45,899)	(30,143)
Issuance of treasury stock	1,845	409	604
Net cash flows used for financing activities	(27,207)	(24,248)	(27,663)
Net increase (decrease) in cash and cash equiv.	$ 303	$ (86,489)	$ 75,651
Beginning cash and cash equivalents	6,338	92,827	17,176
Ending cash and cash equivalents	$ 6,641	$ 6,338	$ 92,827

Required:

a. Lands' End recently implemented a strategy of filling nearly all orders when the order is placed. In what year do you believe the company implemented this strategy and how is the strategy reflected in the information contained in the statement of cash flows?

b. Explain how the following items reconcile net income to net cash flows from operating activities:
   (1) Depreciation   (2) Receivables   (3) Inventory   (4) Reserve for returns

CHECK
(c) Yr 9, $27,510

c. Calculate free cash flows for each year shown.

d. How does Lands' End use its free cash flow? Do you think its use of free cash flows reflects good financial strategy?

CASE 7–2

*Analysis of
Cash Flows
for a Dot.Com*

The statement of cash flows for **Yahoo!** is reproduced here: **Yahoo!**

YAHOO! INC.
Consolidated Statements of Cash Flows

(in thousands)	YEAR ENDED DECEMBER 31,		
	Year 8	Year 7	Year 6
Cash flows from operating activities			
Net income (loss)	$ 25,588	$(25,520)	$ (6,427)
Adjustments to reconcile net income (loss) to net cash provided by (used in) operating activities:			
Depreciation and amortization	10,215	2,737	639
Tax benefits from stock options	17,827	—	—
Non-cash charges related to stock option grants and warrant issuances	926	1,676	197
Minority interests in operations of consolidated subsidiaries	(68)	(727)	(540)
Purchased in-process research and development	17,300	—	—
Other non-cash charge	—	21,245	—
Changes in assets and liabilities:			
Accounts receivable, net	$(13,616)	$ (5,963)	$ (4,269)
Prepaid expenses	2,144	(6,110)	(386)
Accounts payable	515	2,425	1,386
Accrued expenses and other current liabilities	16,688	7,404	4,393
Deferred revenue	33,210	2,983	1,665
Due to related parties	(451)	330	948
Net cash provided by (used in) operating activities	110,278	480	(2,394)
Cash flows from investing activities			
Acquisition of property and equipment	(11,911)	(6,722)	(3,442)
Cash acquired in acquisitions	199	—	—
Purchases of marketable securities	(471,135)	(58,753)	(115,247)
Proceeds from sales and maturities of marketable securities	158,350	86,678	43,240
Other investments	(5,445)	(1,649)	(729)
Net cash provided by (used in) investing activities	(329,942)	19,554	(76,178)

(continued)

(in thousands)	YEAR ENDED DECEMBER 31,		
	Year 8	Year 7	Year 6
Cash flows from financing activities			
Proceeds from issuance of Common Stock, net......................	280,679	7,516	42,484
Proceeds from issuance of Convertible Preferred Stock..........	—	—	63,750
Proceeds from minority investors...	600	999	1,050
Other...	—	1,106	(128)
Net cash provided by financing activities.................................	281,279	9,621	107,156
Effect of exchange rate changes on cash and cash equivalents..	288	(380)	(63)
Net change in cash and cash equivalents.................................	$ 61,903	$ 29,275	$ 28,521
Cash and cash equivalents at beginning of year.......................	63,571	34,296	5,775
Cash and cash equivalents at end of year................................	$125,474	$ 63,571	$ 34,296

CASE 7–2
(concluded)

Required:

a. Yahoo!'s operations did not produce significant cash flows during Year 6 and Year 7. How does Yahoo! finance its growth in the absence of sufficient operating cash flows?

b. What appears to drive the operating cash flows of Yahoo!?

c. Yahoo! engages in purchases and sales of marketable securities. Why do you believe Yahoo! pursues this activity?

d. Yahoo! reports $33.21 million of deferred revenue. Based on your understanding of Yahoo!'s operations, what do you believe this amount represents?

CHECK
(a) Equity financing

The management of Wyatt Corporation is frustrated because its parent company, SRW Corporation, repeatedly rejects Wyatt's capital spending requests. These refusals led Wyatt's management to conclude its operations play a limited role in the parent's long-range plans. Acting on this assumption, Wyatt's management approaches a merchant banking firm about the possibility of a leveraged buyout of itself. In their proposal, Wyatt management stresses the stable, predictable cash flows from Wyatt's operations as more than adequate to service the debt required to finance the proposed leveraged buyout. As a partner in the merchant banking firm, you investigate the feasibility of their proposal. You receive the following balance sheet and supplementary information for Wyatt Corporation. The management of Wyatt further discloses that, following their proposed purchase, they intend to acquire machinery costing $325,000 in each of the next three years to overcome the previous low level of capital expenditures while a subsidiary of SRW Corporation. Management argues these expenditures are needed for competitive reasons.

CASE 7–3
*Credit Analysis for a
Leveraged Buyout*

Required:

a. Using information in the balance sheet and the supplementary disclosures, prepare a statement of cash flows (indirect method) for the year ended December 31, Year 10.

b. Using the statement of cash flows from *a* and assuming that debt service is $300,000 per year after the leveraged buyout, evaluate the feasibility of management's proposal.

CHECK
(a) CFO, $269,000

WYATT CORPORATION
Balance Sheets
December 31, Year 10 and Year 9

	Year 9	Year 10
Assets		
Cash	$ 175,000	$ 192,000
Accounts receivable	248,000	359,000
Inventory	465,000	683,000
Total current assets	888,000	1,234,000
Land	126,000	138,000
Building and machinery	3,746,000	3,885,000
Less accumulated depreciation	(916,000)	(1,131,000)
Total assets	$3,844,000	$4,126,000
Liabilities and Shareholders' Equity		
Accounts payable	$ 156,000	$ 259,000
Taxes payable	149,000	124,000
Other short-term payables	325,000	417,000
Total current liabilities	630,000	800,000
Bonds payable	842,000	825,000
Total liabilities	1,472,000	1,625,000
Common stock	846,000	863,000
Retained earnings	1,526,000	1,638,000
Total shareholders' equity	2,372,000	2,501,000
Total liabilities and equity	$3,844,000	$4,126,000

Supplementary Information:

1. Dividends declared and paid in Year 10 were $74,000.
2. Depreciation expense for Year 10 was $246,000.
3. Machinery originally costing $61,000 was sold for $34,000 in Year 10.

(CFA Adapted)

CASE 7–4

Analyzing a Management Buyout Using the Statement of Cash Flows

The management of Dover Corporation claims that the securities market undervalues shares of its company. They propose to take it private by means of a leveraged buyout. Management's proposal contains the following features:

1. The leveraged buyout is expected to yield additional after-tax annual interest costs of $200,000.
2. To make Dover Corporation competitive, management plans to undertake:
   a. Annual investments in equipment of $180,000.
   b. Annual buildups in inventory of $60,000.
3. Management expects no additional financing demands beyond that listed in (1) and plans to use cash generated by operations as the primary financing source.

At the end of Year 8, management requests you to analyze the feasibility of their proposal. They provide you with the financial data listed below to assist in your analysis.

	DECEMBER 31		
	Year 8	Year 7	Net Change
Assets			
Cash..	$ 471,000	$ 307,000	$ 164,000
Marketable equity securities, at cost............	150,000	250,000	(100,000)
Allowance to adjust securities to market......	(10,000)	(25,000)	15,000
Accounts receivable, net..............................	550,000	515,000	35,000
Inventories..	810,000	890,000	(80,000)
Investment in Top Corp., at equity...............	420,000	390,000	30,000
Property, plant, and equipment....................	1,145,000	1,070,000	75,000
Less accumulated depreciation....................	(345,000)	(280,000)	(65,000)
Patents, net..	109,000	118,000	(9,000)
Total assets..	$3,300,000	$3,235,000	$ 65,000
Liabilities and Stockholders' Equity			
Accounts payable and accrued liabilities.....	$ 845,000	$ 960,000	$(115,000)
Note payable, long-term...............................	600,000	900,000	(300,000)
Deferred income taxes.................................	190,000	190,000	—
Common stock, $10 par value......................	850,000	650,000	200,000
Additional paid-in capital............................	230,000	170,000	60,000
Retained earnings.......................................	585,000	365,000	220,000
Total liabilities and equity...........................	$3,300,000	$3,235,000	$ 65,000

Additional Information:

1. On January 2, Year 8, Dover sold equipment costing $45,000, with a carrying amount of $28,000, for $18,000 cash.

2. On March 31, Year 8, Dover sold one of its marketable equity securities for $119,000 cash. There are no other transactions involving marketable equity securities.

3. On April 15, Year 8, Dover issues 20,000 shares of its common stock for cash at $13 per share.

4. On July 1, Year 8, Dover purchases equipment for $120,000 cash.

5. Dover's net income for Year 8 is $305,000. Dover pays a cash dividend of $85,000 on October 26, Year 8.

6. Dover acquires a 20 percent interest in Top Corporation's common stock during Year 5. There is no goodwill attributable to the investment, which is accounted for using the equity method. Top reports net income of $150,000 for the year ended December 31, Year 8. No dividend is paid on Top's common stock during Year 8.

CHECK
CFO, $272,000

Required:

Prepare an analysis evaluating the financial feasibility of management's plans. (*Hint:* Prepare a statement of cash flows. Use the indirect method.)

8

RETURN ON INVESTED CAPITAL AND PROFITABILITY ANALYSIS

ANALYSIS OBJECTIVES

- Describe the usefulness of return measures in financial statement analysis.

- Explain return on invested capital and variations in its computation.

- Analyze return on net operating assets and its relevance for analysis.

- Describe disaggregation of return on net operating assets and the importance of its components.

- Describe the relation between profit margin and asset turnover.

- Analyze return on common shareholders' equity and its role in analysis.

- Describe disaggregation of return on common shareholders' equity and the relevance of its components.

- Explain operating and financial leverage and how to assess a company's success in using leverage to increase returns.

A Good Fit for Gap?

SAN FRANCISCO–Gap Inc.'s return on equity reached a high of 59% in 2000; then it took a nosedive. Gap had lost touch with its customers. Its distinctive lines became uninspired and its Old Navy value-priced line of clothes cannibalized customers from the higher-margin Gap lines and cheapened the company's image. Sales growth slowed from over 30% per year to less than half that level. Inventory turnover dropped from over seven times a year to less than four as the company struggled to reduce unsold inventories.

Gap had borrowed heavily as it spent money to upgrade and expand its stores. Its financial leverage increased to more than $0.76 in debt for each $1.00 in equity, nearly double the $0.40 average for all publicly traded companies. Given its lack of profitability and high debt load, credit agencies lowered the rating on Gap bonds to just above "junk" status.

Gap desperately needed a change in strategy. It brought in Paul Pressler to run the company. Pressler had previously managed Disney's theme parks and brought a new customer focus. He began closing unprofitable stores to generate cash that he then used to pay down debt. Gap's financial leverage dropped by over half, to a more conservative level of 29%.

> ... Gap has yet to return to its glory years ...

He upgraded the company's information systems to gain better control over operations, and its gross profit margin increased from 30% to 39%; a dramatic increase for a company in the highly competitive retail clothing industry. Pressler also successfully trimmed a percentage point off Gap's SG&A expenses as a percent of sales.

The increase in gross margin and decrease in operating costs combined to increase Gap's operating profit margin from loss levels to an 8% profit, which is much higher than the 5.5% average for competitors.

In response, Gap's stock price doubled. Yet, many analysts see its increased stock price as merely reflective of a stronger balance sheet as Gap used its cash to reduce debt and to repurchase shares.

Gap's marketing side has yet to bear fruit. "The stores do not look good; the product is not great, nor is it just OK," says Jennifer Black, a retailing analyst who has her own firm. "They lost their focus ... who is their target customer?" (*Forbes,* 2005)

Downsizing and systems upgrades can only do so much. Although Pressler has been a good fit so far for Gap, he has yet to return Gap to its glory years as a premier marketer. Gap's share price will not fully take off until he does.

PREVIEW OF CHAPTER 8

Financial statement analysis involves assessing both risk and return. *Return on invested capital* refers to a company's earnings relative to both the level and source of financing. It is a measure of a company's success in using financing to generate profits. This chapter describes return on invested capital and its relevance to financial statement analysis. We explain variations in measurement of return on invested capital and their interpretation. We also disaggregate return on invested capital into important components for additional insights into company performance and future operations. The role of financial leverage and its importance for returns analysis is examined. This chapter demonstrates each of these analysis techniques using actual financial statement data, including those of Campbell Soup Company.

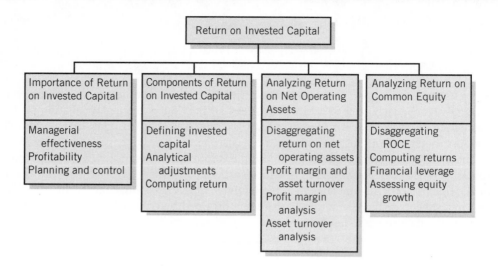

·······IMPORTANCE OF RETURN ON INVESTED CAPITAL

We can analyze company performance in several ways. Revenue, net income, and asset growth are performance measures in common use. Yet none of these measures *individually* are useful as a comprehensive measure of company performance. The reason stems from their interdependency and the interdependency of business activities. For example, increases in revenue are desirable only if they increase profits. Asset increases are desirable only if they generate additional sales volume. To assess net income we must relate it to invested capital. For example, a profit of $1 million is assessed differently if a company's invested capital is $2 million or $200 million.

Analysis of company performance demands *joint* analysis, where we assess one measure relative to another. The relation between income and invested capital, referred to as **return on invested capital (ROIC)** or *return on investment (ROI),* is probably the most widely recognized measure of company performance. It allows us to compare companies on their success with invested capital. It also allows us to assess a company's return relative to its capital investment risk, and we can compare the return on invested capital to returns of alternative investments. Government treasury bonds reflect a minimum return due to their low risk. Riskier investments are expected to yield higher returns. Analysis of return on invested capital compares a company's income, or other performance measure, to the company's level and source of financing. It determines a company's ability to succeed, attract financing, repay creditors, and reward owners. We use return on invested capital in several areas of our analysis including: (1) managerial effectiveness, (2) level of profitability, and (3) planning and control.

Measuring Managerial Effectiveness

The level of return on invested capital depends primarily on the skill, resourcefulness, ingenuity, and motivation of management. Management is responsible for a company's business activities. It makes financing, investing, and operating decisions. It selects actions, plans strategies, and executes plans. Return on invested capital, especially when computed over intervals of a year or longer, is a relevant measure of a company's managerial effectiveness.

Measuring Profitability

Return on invested capital is an important indicator of a company's long-term financial strength. It uses key summary measures from both the income statement (profits) and the balance sheet (financing) to assess profitability. This profitability measure has several advantages over other long-term measures of financial strength or solvency that rely on only balance sheet items (such as debt to equity ratio). It can effectively convey the return on invested capital from varying perspectives of different financing contributors (creditors and shareholders).

Measure for Planning and Control

Return on invested capital serves an important role in planning, budgeting, coordinating, evaluating, and controlling business activities. This return is composed of the returns (and losses) achieved by the company's segments or divisions. These segment returns are also made up of the returns achieved by individual product lines, projects, and other components. A well-managed company exercises control over returns achieved by each of its profit centers and rewards its managers on these results. In evaluating investing alternatives, management assesses performance relative to expected returns. Out of this assessment come strategic decisions and action plans for the company.

■ ■ ■ ■ ■ ■ ■
DELL HURDLE
Dell Computer has its marketing department compute return on investment for *each* equipment sale.

ANALYSIS VIEWPOINT . . . *YOU ARE THE AUDITOR*

You are the audit manager responsible for substantive audit tests of a manufacturing client. Your analytical procedures reveal a 3% increase in sales from $2 to $2.06 (millions) and a 4% decrease in total expenses from $1.9 to $1.824 (millions). Both changes are within your "reasonableness" criterion of ±5%. Accordingly, you do not expand audit tests of these accounts. The audit partner in charge questions your lack of follow-up on these deviations and expressly mentions *joint* analysis. What is the audit partner referring to?

.... COMPONENTS OF RETURN ON INVESTED CAPITAL

Analyzing company performance using return on invested capital is conceptually sound and appealing. **Return on invested capital** is computed as:

$$\frac{\text{Income}}{\text{Invested capital}}$$

There is, however, not complete agreement on the computation of either the numerator or denominator in this relation. These differences are valid and stem from the diverse perspectives of financial statement users. This section describes these differences and explains how different computations are relevant to different users or analyses. We begin with a discussion of invested capital, followed by consideration of income.

Invested Capital for a Typical Company

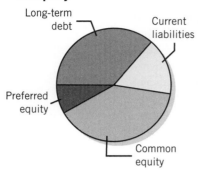

Long-term debt

Current liabilities

Preferred equity

Common equity

Defining Invested Capital

There is no universal measure of invested capital from which to compute rate of return. The different measures of invested capital used reflect users' different perspectives. In this section we describe two different measures of invested capital and explain their relevance to different users and interpretations.

Net Operating Assets

Many analysts segregate the balance sheet and income statements into operating and nonoperating components and compute a **return on net operating assets (RNOA)** as the summary measure of performance. This parsing of financial statements into operating and nonoperating components follows from the view that operating activities are the most long-lasting and relevant for the determination of stock price.

Net Operating Income after Tax to Net Operating Assets

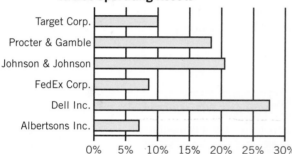

Target Corp.
Procter & Gamble
Johnson & Johnson
FedEx Corp.
Dell Inc.
Albertsons Inc.

0% 5% 10% 15% 20% 25% 30%

Operating activities are the core activities of the company. They include all the activities necessary to bring a company's product or service to market, and to service its customer needs. Operating activities are crucial, and companies must execute them well over the long run if they are to survive. In the income statement, operating activities typically include sales, cost of goods sold, and selling and general and administrative (SG&A) expenses. On the balance sheet, operating activities are represented by the assets and liabilities relating to these income statement accounts, such as accounts receivable, inventories, PPE, accounts payable, and accrued expenses.

Many firms invest excess cash in financial assets, such as marketable securities, and earn returns that are typically included in the income statement as "other" income. Likewise, firms borrow money on short-term and long-term debt, resulting in interest expense. Although effective management of an investment portfolio along with astute borrowing can benefit income, these nonoperating revenues and expenses are regarded as ancillary to the core operating activities of the business. Consequently, investment returns and borrowing expenses do not typically have a major impact on company value, unless they are extreme.

Our approach is to analyze a company along this operating/nonoperating dimension, with the return on net operating assets (RNOA) as the summary measure of performance. RNOA, which we more fully explore below, is defined as net operating income after tax (NOPAT) divided by average net operating assets (NOA).

More specifically, operating assets are comprised of total assets less financial assets such as investments in marketable securities. Operating liabilities are comprised of total liabilities less interest-bearing debt. Operating assets less operating liabilities yields *net operating assets (NOA)*. The appropriate income measure to compare with net operating assets is *net operating income after tax (NOPAT),* which equals revenues less operating expenses such as cost of goods sold, SG&A expenses, and taxes (NOPAT excludes investment income and interest expense). We discuss the composition of both NOA and NOPAT in greater depth later in the chapter. Returns on net operating assets for selected companies are provided in the margin graphic.

Common Equity Capital

Return on common equity (ROCE) is defined as net income less preferred dividends divided by average common equity. Common equity is equal to total shareholders' equity less preferred stock. Preferred stock is excluded from the computation since, from the viewpoint of common shareholders, preferred stock has a fixed claim to the net assets and cash flow of the company, just like debt.

Common equity can alternatively be defined as equal to total assets less debt and preferred stock. The proportion of debt and equity financing of assets is a capital structure decision that each company must make. The amount of equity in the capital structure, and thus the amount of equity used in the computation of return on equity, is, therefore, a function of the degree to which the company is financed with debt (that is, more debt means less equity). Likewise, the numerator (net income) is impacted by the amount of interest expense that the company must pay on its debt. As we discuss more fully below, the return on common equity captures both the returns on net operating assets discussed above and the effects of financial leverage (the use of debt versus equity in the capital structure). Net income to common equity for selected companies is provided in the margin graphic.

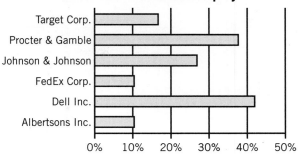

Net Income to Common Equity

Computing Invested Capital for the Period

Regardless of our *invested capital* definition, we compare the return for the period with its investment base. The invested capital for the period is typically computed using the *average* capital available to a company during the period. An average is used to reflect changes in invested capital during the period. The most common method is adding beginning and ending year invested capital and dividing by 2. We must use care in applying averaging. Companies in certain industries choose a "natural" rather than calendar business year. For example, in retailing the natural business year ends when inventories and sales are low (for example, January 31 after the holiday season). In this case, averaging year-ends yields the lowest rather than the average invested capital during the period. A more accurate method is to average interim amounts—for example, adding quarter-end invested capital amounts and dividing by 4.

Adjustments to Invested Capital and Income

Our analysis of return on invested capital uses reported financial statement numbers as a starting point. As we discussed in several prior chapters, many accounting numbers call for analytical adjustment. Also, several numbers not reported in financial statements need to be included. Some adjustments, like those relating to inventory, affect both the numerator and denominator of return on invested capital, moderating their effect. Whatever their impacts, the analysis of return on invested capital should use the appropriately adjusted financial statement numbers as described in earlier chapters.

Computing Return on Invested Capital

This section applies our discussion to an analysis of return on invested capital. We illustrate the different measures of both income and invested capital for the computations. For this purpose, we draw on the financial statements of Excell Corporation reproduced in Exhibits 8.1 and 8.2. Our return on invested capital computations are for Year 9 and use amounts rounded to the nearest million.

Exhibit 8.1

■ ■ ■ ■ ■ ■ ■

EXCELL CORPORATION
Income Statements
For Years Ended December 31, Year 8 and Year 9

($ thousands)	Year 8	Year 9
Sales	$1,636,298	$1,782,254
Cost of goods sold and operating expenses	1,473,293	1,598,679
Operating profit	163,005	183,575
Interest expense	21,825	20,843
Pretax profit	141,180	162,732
Tax expense	52,237	58,584
Net income	$ 88,943	$ 104,148

Return on Net Operating Assets

Return on net operating assets (RNOA) is computed as:

$$\text{RNOA} = \frac{\text{Net operating profits after tax (NOPAT)}}{\text{Average net operating assets (NOA)}}$$

The denominator of the equation, **net operating assets (NOA),** is equal to operating assets less operating liabilities. Operating assets and liabilities are those necessary to conduct the company's business, and include cash, accounts receivable, inventories, prepaid expenses, deferred tax assets, property, plant and equipment (PPE), and long-term investments related to strategic acquisitions (such as equity method investments, goodwill, and acquired intangible assets). Netted from these operating assets are current operating liabilities, such as accounts payable and accrued expenses, and long-term operating liabilities, such as pensions and other postretirement (OPEB) liabilities and deferred income tax liabilities.

Nonoperating assets include investments in marketable securities, nonstrategic equity investments, and investments in discontinued operations prior to sale. Nonoperating liabilities include bonds and other long-term interest-bearing liabilities, and the noncurrent portion of capitalized leases. **Net financial obligations (NFO)** is equal to nonoperating liabilities less nonoperating assets (liabilities are listed first to yield a positive sign since most companies have more financial liabilities than financial assets).

The distinction between operating and nonoperating activities is summarized in the following representation of a typical balance sheet:

BALANCE SHEET

Operating assets	OA	Financial liabilities*		FL
Less operating liabilities	(OL)	Less financial assets		(FA)
		Net financial obligations		NFO
		Stockholders' equity†		SE
Net operating assets	NOA	Net financing		NFO + SE‡

*Includes preferred stock.
†Excludes preferred stock.
‡NOA = NFO + SE.

Exhibit 8.2

■ ■ ■ ■ ■ ■ ■

EXCELL CORPORATION
Balance Sheets
At December 31, Year 8 and Year 9

($ thousands)	Year 8	Year 9
Assets		
Cash	$ 115,397	$ 71,546
Marketable securities	38,008	43,854
Accounts receivable, net	177,538	182,859
Inventories	204,362	256,838
Total current assets	535,305	555,097
Investments in unconsolidated subsidiaries	33,728	62,390
Marketable securities	5,931	56,997
Property, plant, & equipment, net	1,539,221	1,633,458
Goodwill	6,550	6,550
Total long-term assets	1,585,430	1,759,395
Total assets	$2,120,735	$2,314,492
Liabilities		
Notes payable	$ 7,850	$ 13,734
Accounts payable	138,662	155,482
Taxes payable	24,370	13,256
Current maturities of long-term debt	30,440	33,822
Total current liabilities	201,322	216,294
Long-term debt	507,329	473,507
Pension and OPEB liabilities	743,779	852,237
Total long-term liabilities	1,251,108	1,325,744
Equity		
Common stock	413,783	413,783
Additional paid-in capital	19,208	19,208
Retained earnings	436,752	540,901
Treasury stock	(201,438)	(201,438)
Total stockholders' equity	668,305	772,454
Total liabilities and equity	$2,120,735	$2,314,492

Since the accounting equation stipulates that Assets = Liabilities + Equity, we can also represent the balance sheet with the following operating- and nonoperating-based identity:

Net operating assets (NOA) = Net financial obligations (NFO) + Stockholders' equity (SE)

For Excell Corporation (Exhibit 8.2), the net operating assets (NOA) are equal to total assets less nonoperating assets, such as short-term and long-term investments in marketable securities. Operating liabilities are equal to total liabilities less nonoperating liabilities, such as notes payable to banks, long-term indebtedness payable within one year, and long-term indebtedness. Net operating assets (NOA) for Years 8 and 9 is computed as follows:

	Year 8	Year 9
Cash	$ 115,397	$ 71,546
Accounts receivable, net	177,538	182,859
Inventories	204,362	256,838
Investments in unconsolidated subsidiaries	33,728	62,390
Property, plant, & equipment, net	1,539,221	1,633,458
Goodwill	6,550	6,550
Accounts payable	(138,662)	(155,482)
Taxes payable	(24,370)	(13,256)
Pension and OPEB liabilities	(743,779)	(852,237)
Net operating assets	$1,169,985	$1,192,666

Investments in unconsolidated subsidiaries relate to equity method investments, which we discuss in Chapter 5. These are presumed to be strategic investments and, therefore, are treated as operating assets. Likewise, goodwill is treated as operating so long as the investment is strategic in nature and is presumed as such unless facts dictate otherwise. Investments in discontinued operations (not present in this example) are treated as nonoperating since the business unit no longer contributes to the operating profits of the company.

Net financial obligations are equal to financial obligations such as notes and other debt payable and dividends payable (not present in this example), less financial assets such as short-term and long-term investments in marketable securities. For Excell, NFO for Years 8 and 9 is computed as follows:

	Year 8	Year 9
Notes payable	$ 7,850	$ 13,734
Current maturities of long-term debt	30,440	33,822
Long-term debt	507,329	473,507
Marketable securities—current	(38,008)	(43,854)
Marketable securities—noncurrent	(5,931)	(56,997)
Net financial obligations	$501,680	$420,212

Finally, NOA = NFO + SE as follows:

$$
\begin{array}{llll}
 & \text{NOA} & = \text{NFO} & + \quad \text{SE} \\
\text{Year 8} & \$1,169,985 & = \$501,680 & + \$668,305 \\
\text{Year 9} & \$1,192,666 & = \$420,212 & + \$772,454
\end{array}
$$

The numerator of the RNOA equation, **net operating profit after tax (NOPAT),** is the after-tax profit earned from net operating assets. The distinction between operating and nonoperating activities is summarized in the following representation of a typical income statement:

INCOME STATEMENT

Operating revenues...		OR
Operating expenses		(OE)
Operating tax expense		
Tax provision	(TAX)	
Tax shield on interest	(SHLD)	
Operating tax expense		(TE)
Operating income		OI
Net financial expense		
Interest expense*	(INTX)	
Interest revenue	INTR	
Tax shield on interest	SHLD	
Net financial expense		(NFE)
Net income..		(NI)

Includes dividends on preferred stock.

Operating income includes sales less cost of goods sold (COGS), operating expenses (OE) such as selling, general and administrative (SG&A) expenses, and income taxes. Operating tax expense has two components: the tax provision less the tax shield. Tax shield on interest refers to the reduction of taxable income (and, thus, tax expense) arising from the deductibility of interest expense. The tax shield on interest reduces the effective tax rate (tax expense/pretax income) which is applied to both pretax operating profit and nonoperating revenue and expense. Items excluded from NOPAT include interest revenue and expense, dividend revenue, nonoperating investment gains and losses, and income or loss from discontinued operations (all computed net of tax).

Specifically, NOPAT is computed as follows[1]:

$$\text{NOPAT} = (\text{Sales} - \text{Operating expenses}) \times (1 - [\text{Tax expense}/\text{Pretax profit}])$$

For Excell, NOPAT for Years 8 and 9 is,

	Effective tax rate	NOPAT
Year 8	$52,237/$141,180 = 37%	$163,005 × (1 − 37%) = $102,693
Year 9	$58,584/$162,732 = 36%	$183,575 × (1 − 36%) = $117,488

Excell's **return on net operating assets (RNOA)** for Year 9 is equal to:

$$\begin{aligned} \text{RNOA} &= \text{NOPAT/Average NOA} \\ &= \$117,488/[(\$1,169,985 + \$1,192,666) \div 2] \\ &= 9.95\% \end{aligned}$$

Return on Common Shareholders' Equity

Return on common equity typically excludes from invested capital all but common shareholders' equity. The **return on common equity** of Excell Corporation for Year 9

---

[1] Alternatively, some analysts simply *assume* a flat marginal corporate tax rate, such as 35%. The implication is that deviations from this *assumed* rate are treated as nonoperating revenue (expense).

is computed as:

$$\frac{\text{Net income} - \text{Preferred dividends}}{\text{Average common shareholders' equity}}$$

$$\frac{\$104,148 - \$0}{(\$668,305 + \$772,454)/2} = 14.46\%$$

As we explain on page 463, ROCE consists of two components: an operating return (RNOA) and a nonoperating return (the positive or negative effects of financial leverage). Excell's higher return on common shareholders' equity as compared to its return on net operating assets reflects the favorable effects of financial leverage in this case.

•••••••ANALYZING RETURN ON NET OPERATING ASSETS

Return on invested capital is useful in management evaluation, profitability analysis, and planning and control. Our use of return on invested capital for these tasks requires a thorough understanding of this return measure. This is because the return measure includes components with the potential to contribute to an understanding of company performance. This section examines this return when invested capital is viewed from an operating standpoint, commonly referred to as **return on net operating assets (RNOA).**

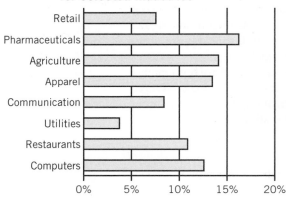

Return on Net Operating Assets for Selected Industries

Disaggregating Return on Net Operating Assets

Recall that the return on net operating assets (RNOA) is computed as:

$$\frac{\text{Net operating profit after tax (NOPAT)}}{\text{Average net operating assets (NOA)}}$$

We can disaggregate this return into meaningful components relative to sales. This disaggregation of return on net operating assets is:

**Return on net operating assets = Net operating × Net operating
profit margin   asset turnover**

$$\frac{\text{NOPAT}}{\text{Average NOA}} = \frac{\text{NOPAT}}{\text{Sales}} \times \frac{\text{Sales}}{\text{Average NOA}}$$

The NOPAT to sales relation is called **net operating profit margin** (or simply NOPAT margin) and measures a company's operating profitability relative to sales. The sales to net operating assets relation is called the **net operating asset turnover** (or simply NOA turnover) and measures a company's effectiveness in generating sales from net operating assets. This decomposition highlights the role of these components, both NOPAT margin and NOA turnover, in determining return on net operating assets (RNOA). NOPAT margin and NOA turnover are useful measures that require analysis to gain insights into a company's profitability. We describe the major components determining return on net operating assets in Exhibit 8.3. The first level of this analysis focuses on the interaction of NOPAT margin and NOA turnover. The second level of analysis highlights other important factors determining profit margin and asset turnover.

Disaggregating Return on Net Operating Assets   *Exhibit 8.3*

■ ■ ■ ■ ■ ■ ■

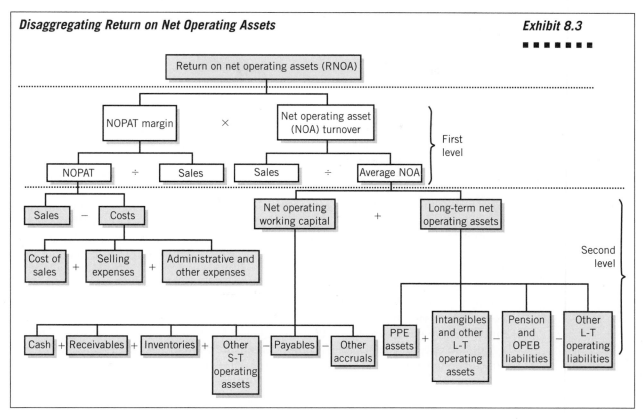

Effect of Operating Leverage

Net operating assets (NOA) are reduced by increases in operating liabilities, thus increasing net operating asset turnover. Provided that the increase in operating liabilities does not affect NOPAT, RNOA is also increased. The operating liability effect is seen in this alternate decomposition of RNOA:

$$\text{RNOA} = \frac{\text{NOPAT}}{\text{Sales}} \times \frac{\text{Sales}}{\text{Average OA}} \times (1 + \text{OLLEV})$$

where OA is Operating Assets (gross) and OLLEV **(Average Operating liabilities/ Average NOA)** is the operating liability leverage ratio. Since OLLEV is a positive number, increasing OLLEV increases RNOA.

The intuition behind the equation is this: operating liabilities generally do not entail a cost if used judiciously. For example, increasing accounts payable by delaying payment allows the company to use suppliers' capital which is at low or no cost so long as the payment is not delayed too much. (At some point, however, the supplier, realizing that the use of its capital is adding to its cost [that is, receivables, a nonearning asset, are higher] will exact a higher price for its goods or services or may decide not to sell to the company altogether.) The result is a reduction in NOA, no increase in NOPAT, and an increase in RNOA. The firm has, in effect, profited from the use of its suppliers' capital. This avoids the need to finance its operating assets with costly debt or equity capital.

Relation between Profit Margin and Asset Turnover

The relation between NOPAT margin and NOA turnover is illustrated in Exhibit 8.4. As defined, RNOA equals NOPAT margin (in percent) multiplied by NOA turnover. As Exhibit 8.4 shows, Company X achieves a 10% RNOA with a relatively high NOPAT margin and a low NOA turnover. In contrast, Company Z achieves the same RNOA

Exhibit 8.4

■■■■■■■

Analysis of Return on Net Operating Assets

	Company X	Company Y	Company Z
Sales	$5,000,000	$10,000,000	$10,000,000
NOPAT	$ 500,000	$ 500,000	$ 100,000
NOA	$5,000,000	$ 5,000,000	$ 1,000,000
NOPAT margin	10%	5%	1%
NOA turnover	1	2	10
Return on net operating assets	10%	10%	10%

but with a low NOPAT margin and high NOA turnover. Company Y's margin and turnover is between these two companies. Namely, Company Y has a 10% RNOA with a NOPAT margin one-half that of Company X and an NOA turnover double that of Company X. This exhibit indicates there are many combinations of profit margins and asset turnovers yielding a 10% RNOA.

Since RNOA is a function of both margin and turnover, it is tempting to analyze a company's ability to increase RNOA by increasing profit margin while holding turnover constant, or vice versa. Unfortunately, the answer is not that simple because the two measures are not independent. Profit margin is a function of sales (selling price × units sold) and operating expenses. Turnover is also a function of sales (sales/assets). Consequently, increasing profit margin by increasing selling prices impacts units sold. Also, reductions of marketing-related operating expenses in an effort to increase profitability usually impacts product demand. Selling prices, marketing, R&D, production, and a host of other business areas must all be managed effectively to maximize RNOA.

We can generalize the returns analysis of Exhibit 8.4 to show a continuous range of possible combinations of profit margins and asset turnovers yielding a constant return on assets (the solid line in the graph in Exhibit 8.5). Exhibit 8.5 portrays graphically this

Exhibit 8.5

■■■■■■■

Relation between NOPAT Margin, NOA Turnover, and Return on Net Operating Assets

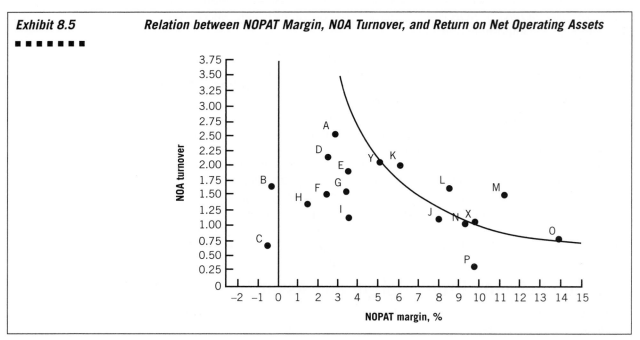

relation between NOPAT margin (horizontal axis) and NOA turnover (vertical axis). The curve drawn in this exhibit traces all combinations of NOPAT margin and NOA turnover yielding a constant return on net operating assets. This curve slopes from the upper left corner of low NOPAT margin and high NOA turnover to the lower right corner of high NOPAT margin and low NOA turnover. We plot the data from Companies X and Y (from Exhibit 8.4) in Exhibit 8.5–designated points X and Y, respectively. The remaining points A through P are combinations of NOPAT margins and NOA turnovers of other companies. Graphing returns of companies within an industry around a constant return on asset curve is a valuable method of comparing profitability. More important, such graphing reveals the relation between NOPAT margin and NOA turnover determining RNOA and is extremely useful in company analysis.

Disaggregating return on net operating assets as in Exhibit 8.5 provides insights in assessing companies' strategic actions to increase returns. For example, Companies B and C must concentrate on restoring profitability. Moreover, assuming the industry represented in Exhibit 8.5 has a representative NOPAT margin and NOA turnover, the evidence suggests Company P should focus on improving NOA turnover while Company A should focus on increasing NOPAT margin. Other companies like H and I should best concentrate on both NOPAT margin and NOA turnover.

Analysis of return on assets can reveal additional insights into strategic activity. As an example, consider two companies in the same industry with identical returns on net operating assets.

	Company AA	Company BB
Sales	$ 1,000,000	$20,000,000
Income	$ 100,000	$ 100,000
Assets	$10,000,000	$10,000,000
NOPAT margin	10%	0.5%
NOA turnover	0.1	2.0
Return on net operating assets	1%	1%

Both companies' returns on net operating assets are poor. Yet, the strategically corrective action for each is different. Our analysis of such cases must evaluate the likelihood of managerial success and other factors in improving performance. In particular, Company AA has a 10% NOPAT margin while Company BB's is considerably lower. On the other hand, a dollar invested in assets yields only $0.10 in sales for Company AA, whereas Company BB achieves $2 in sales for each dollar invested. Accordingly, one part of our analysis focuses on Company AA's assets, asking questions such as: Why is turnover so low? Are there assets yielding little or no return? Are there idle assets requiring disposal? Are assets inefficiently or ineffectively utilized? We would expect that Company AA can achieve immediate improvements by concentrating on increasing turnover (by increasing sales, reducing investment, or both). It is likely more difficult for Company AA to increase profit margin much beyond the industry norm.

Company BB confronts a much different scenario. Our analysis suggests Company BB should focus on correcting its low profit margin. Reasons for low profit margins are varied but often include inefficient production methods, unprofitable product lines, excess capacity with high fixed costs, or excessive selling and administrative expenses. Companies with low profit margins sometimes discover that changes in tastes and technology require increased investment in assets to finance sales. This implies that to maintain its return on assets, a company must increase its profit margin or else production is no longer moneymaking.

There is a tendency to view a high profit margin as a sign of good operating performance. Yet we must emphasize the importance of return on invested capital (however defined) as the ultimate test of profitability. A supermarket is content with a NOPAT margin of 1% to 2% because of its high NOA turnover owing to a relatively low asset investment. Similarly, a discount store accepts a low NOPAT margin to generate high asset turnover (primarily in inventories). In contrast, capital-intensive industries like steel, chemicals, and automobiles having large asset investments and low NOA turnovers must achieve higher NOPAT margins to be successful. Exhibit 8.6 portrays graphically the relation between NOPAT margin and NOA turnover for several industries. We graph the 10.3% return on assets curve in Exhibit 8.6 because it is the median for publicly traded companies.

Exhibit 8.6

Net Operating Asset Turnover and Net Operating Profit Combinations for a Given RNOA

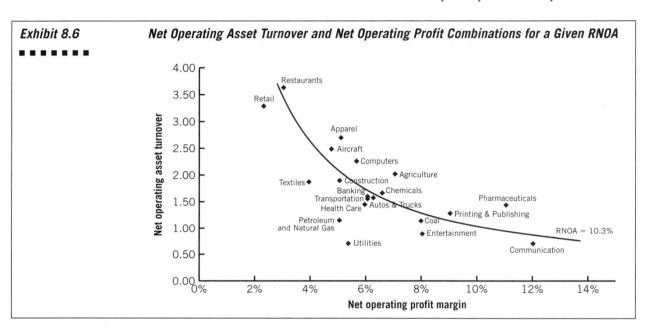

We must remember that analysis of returns for a single year is potentially misleading. The cyclical nature of many industries yields swings in profit margins where some years' profits can be excessive while others are not. Companies must be analyzed using returns computed over several years and spanning a business cycle.

Disaggregation of Profit Margin

Operating profit margin (OPM) is defined as

$$\frac{\text{Net operating profit after tax (NOPAT)}}{\text{Sales}}$$

The operating profit margin is a function of the per-unit selling price of the product or service compared with the per-unit costs of bringing that product or service to market and servicing customer needs after the sale. For analysis purposes, it is useful to disaggregate pretax profit margin (PM) into its components:

$$\text{Pretax PM} = \text{Pretax sales PM} + \text{Pretax other PM}$$

$$\text{Pretax sales PM} = \frac{\text{Gross margin}}{\text{Sales}} - \frac{\text{Selling expense}}{\text{Sales}} - \frac{\text{Administration expense}}{\text{Sales}} - \frac{\text{R\&D}}{\text{Sales}}$$

$$\text{Pretax other PM} = \frac{\text{Equity income}}{\text{Sales}} \pm \frac{\text{Special items}}{\text{Sales}} \pm \cdots$$

Following are several areas of importance in our analysis of profitability.

Gross Profit. Gross profit (or *gross margin*) is measured as revenues less cost of sales. It is frequently reported as a percent (*gross profit percent*), computed as gross profit divided by sales. The gross profit, or gross profit percent, is a key performance measure. All other costs must be covered by gross profit, and any income earned is the balance remaining after these costs. Also, gross profit must be sufficiently large to finance essential future-directed discretionary expenditures like research and development, marketing, and advertising. Gross profits vary across industries depending on factors like competition and differences in the factors of production (production wage rates, costs of raw materials, levels of capital investment, and the like).

Analyzing changes in sales and cost of sales is useful in identifying major drivers of gross profit. Changes in gross profit often derive from one or a combination of the following:

- Increase (decrease) in sales volume.
- Increase (decrease) in unit selling price.
- Increase (decrease) in cost per unit.

Interpreting the results of an analysis of changes in gross profit requires identifying the major factors responsible for these changes. Moreover, we often extend the analysis to focus on strategic activities to remedy or improve gross profit (through volume, price, or cost). For example, if we determine the reason for a decrease in gross profit is a decline in unit selling prices, and this reflects overcapacity in the industry and price cutting, then our analysis of the company is pessimistic given management's lack of potential strategic responses. However, if the reason for a decrease in gross profit is an increase in unit costs, then our analysis is more optimistic yielding a wider range of potential strategic responses for management.

When interpreting cost of sales and gross profit, especially for comparative analysis, we must direct attention to potential distortions arising from accounting methods. Even though this is applicable to all cost analysis, it is especially important with inventories and depreciation accounting (recall that depreciation expense relating to production equipment is a component of cost of goods sold). These two items merit special attention because they represent costs that are usually substantial in amount and subject to alternative accounting methods that can markedly affect their measurement.

Selling Expenses. The importance of the relation between selling expenses and revenues varies across industries and companies. In certain companies, selling expenses are primarily commissions that are highly variable, while in others they are largely fixed. Our analysis must attempt to distinguish between these variable and fixed components, which can then be usefully analyzed relative to revenues.

When selling expenses as a percentage of revenues show an increase, we should focus attention on the increase in selling expense generating the associated increase in revenues. Beyond a certain level of selling expenses, there are lower marginal increases in revenues. This can be due to market saturation, brand loyalty, or increased expense in new territories. It is important for us to distinguish between the percentage of selling expenses to revenues for new versus continuing customers. This has implications for forecasts of profitability. If a company must substantially increase selling expenses to increase sales, its profitability is limited or can decline.

Certain sales promotion expenses, particularly advertising, yield current *and* future benefits. Measuring future benefits from these expenses is extremely difficult. Expenditures for future-directed marketing activities are largely discretionary, and our analysis must consider year-to-year trends in these expenditures. Beyond the ability of these expenditures to influence future sales, they provide insights into management's tendency to "manage" reported earnings.

General and Administrative Expenses.   Most general and administrative expenses are fixed, largely because these expenses include items like salaries and rent. There is a tendency for these expenses to increase, especially in prosperous times. When analyzing these expenses, our analysis should direct attention at both the trend in these expenses and the percentage of revenues they consume.

Disaggregation of Asset Turnover

The standard measure of asset turnover in determining return on assets is:

$$\frac{\text{Sales}}{\text{Average Net Operating Assets}}$$

Further evaluation of component changes in turnover rates for individual assets can be useful in a company analysis. This section examines asset turnover for *component asset and liability accounts.*

Asset turnover measures the intensity with which companies utilize assets. The most relevant measure of asset utilization is sales, since sales are essential to profits. In special cases like start-up or development companies, our analysis of turnover must recognize that most assets are committed to *future* business activities. Also, unusual supply problems or work stoppages are conditions affecting asset utilization and require special evaluation and interpretation. This section describes various analyses using disaggregation of asset turnover.

In general, turnover rates reflect the relative productivity of assets, that is, the level of sales volume that we derive from each dollar invested in a particular asset. All things equal, we prefer higher turnover rates for assets than lower (the reverse is true for liabilities). This generalization must be viewed with caution, however. We can increase turnover rates by lowering our investment in assets, but this might be counterproductive. Consider, for example, if we choose to reduce the amount of credit we grant to our customers. At some point we will lose sales, and any benefits we derive from the lower levels of receivables will be offset by a decline in sales. The same argument holds for inventories. We need a certain level of inventories to support our current level of sales. Any less and we run the risk of stock-outs and lost sales. So, our investment in assets must be *optimized,* not necessarily minimized.

Accounts Receivable Turnover.   The accounts receivable turnover rate is defined as follows:

Accounts receivable turnover = Sales/Average accounts receivable

Receivables are an asset that must be financed at some cost of capital. In addition, receivables entail collection risk and require additional overhead in the form of credit and collection departments. From this perspective, reducing the level of receivables lessens these costs. If we reduce receivables too much with an overly restrictive credit policy, however, the reduction adversely impacts sales. Receivables must, therefore, be effectively managed.

An alternate view of accounts receivable turnover is the **average collection period,** which follows:

Average collection period = Accounts receivable/Average daily sales

This metric reflects how long accounts receivable are outstanding, on average. In general, the lower the receivables turnover rate, the higher the average collection period.

Inventory Turnover. The inventory turnover rate is computed as follows:

Inventory turnover = Cost of goods sold/Average inventory

This ratio uses cost of goods sold (COGS) as the measure of sales volume because the denominator, inventory, is reported at cost, not retail. Accordingly, both the numerator and denominator are measured at cost. A decline in the inventory turnover ratio often indicates that the firm's products are uncompetitive, perhaps because of a style that is out of fashion or noncurrent technology. In addition, inventories must be financed at some cost and they yield additional costs in the form of insurance, storage, logistics, theft, and the like. Companies want enough inventory to meet customer demand without stock-outs, and no more.

Like the average collection period, an alternate view of the inventory turnover rate follows:

Average inventory days outstanding = Inventory/Average daily cost of goods sold

The average inventory days outstanding gives us some indication of the length of time that inventories are available for sale. We want the average inventory days outstanding to be as short as possible. This can be accomplished by minimizing raw materials through production management techniques, like just-in-time deliveries, or the reduction of work-in-progress inventory from use of efficient production processes that eliminate bottlenecks. In addition, companies desire to minimize finished goods inventory by producing to order, not to estimated demand, if possible. These management tools increase inventory turnover and reduce the inventory days outstanding.

Long-Term Operating Asset Turnover. Long-term operating asset turnover is computed as follows:

Long-term operating asset turnover = Sales/Average long-term operating assets

Capital intensive industries, such as manufacturing companies, require large investments in long-term assets. Accordingly, such companies have lower long-term operating asset turnovers than do less capital intensive companies, like service businesses. Long-term operating assets must be financed at some cost of capital. In addition, they must be insured and maintained. Moreover, since investment capital is a finite resource, every dollar invested in long-term operating assets is one dollar less that can be invested in other more quickly turning earning assets. For these reasons, companies desire to minimize the investment in long-term operating assets required to generate a dollar of sales.

The long-term operating asset turnover rate can be increased by either increasing the numerator by increasing throughput (sales) or by reducing the denominator. Reducing long-term operating assets is a difficult process. Aside from outright disposal of underutilized assets, many companies have attempted to reduce their investment in long-term operating assets by acquiring them together with other companies. Corporate alliances, joint ventures, and special purpose entities (discussed in Chapter 3) are some of the techniques that are effectively used to reduce investment in long-term operating assets.

Accounts Payable Turnover.   Current operating assets like inventories are financed in large part by accounts payable. Such payables usually represent interest-free financing and are, therefore, less expensive than using borrowed money to finance inventory purchases or production. Accordingly, companies use trade credit whenever possible. This is called *leaning on the trade.* The **accounts payable turnover rate** is computed as:

$$\text{Accounts payable turnover} = \text{Cost of goods sold/Average accounts payable}$$

Like inventories, payables are reported at cost, not retail prices. Thus, for consistency with the denominator, cost of goods sold (not sales) is used in the numerator. All else equal, companies prefer to utilize this cheap source of financing as much as possible and, therefore, have a lower accounts payable turnover rate (meaning a higher level of payables). Lowering the accounts payable turnover rate is accomplished by delaying payment to suppliers, and this delay in payment can damage relations with the supplier if used excessively. Payables, therefore, must be managed carefully.

A metric analogous to accounts payable turnover is the **average payable days outstanding,** which follows:

$$\text{Average payable days outstanding} = \text{Accounts payable/Average daily}$$
$$\text{cost of goods sold}$$

A lower accounts payable turnover rate corresponds to a higher average payable days outstanding.

Net Operating Working Capital Turnover.   Net operating working capital is equal to operating current assets less operating current liabilities. Net operating working capital is an asset that must be financed just like any other asset. Consequently, companies desire to *optimize* investment in this asset. The operating working capital turnover rate is computed as follows:

$$\text{Net operating working capital turnover} = \text{Net sales/Average net operating}$$
$$\text{working capital}$$

Companies generally desire a higher net operating working capital turnover rate than a lower one, all else equal, because a higher operating working capital turnover reflects less investment in working capital for each dollar of sales. Net operating working capital turns more quickly as receivables and inventories turn more quickly, and it also turns more quickly when companies lean on the trade (when payables turn more slowly). Thus, turnover of net operating working capital improves as a result of proper management of its components.

ANALYZING RETURN ON COMMON EQUITY

Return on common shareholders' equity (ROCE), or simply return on common equity, is of great interest to the shareholders of a company. Creditors usually receive a fixed return on their financing. Preferred shareholders usually receive a fixed dividend. Yet common shareholders are provided no fixed or promised returns. These shareholders have claims on the *residual* earnings of a company only after all other financing sources are paid. Accordingly, the return on shareholders' equity is most important to common shareholders. The relation between return on shareholders' equity and return on net operating assets is also important as it bears on the analysis of a company's success with financial leverage.

Return on common shareholders' equity serves a key role in equity valuation. Recall the accounting-based stock valuation formula from Chapter 1:

$$V_t = BV_t + \frac{NI_{t+1} - (k \times BV_t)}{(1 + k)} + \frac{NI_{t+2} - (k \times BV_{t+1})}{(1 + k)^2} + \cdots$$

where V is company value, BV is book value of stockholders' equity, NI is net income, and k is cost of equity capital (the return that shareholders *expect* to earn on their investment). Through algebraic simplification, the formula can be restated in terms of future returns on common shareholders' equity (ROCE):

$$V_t = BV_t + \frac{(ROCE_{t+1} - k)BV_t}{(1 + k)} + \frac{(ROCE_{t+2} - k)BV_{t+1}}{(1 + k)^2} + \cdots$$

where ROCE is as defined above. This formula is intuitively appealing. Namely, it implies that companies with expected ROCE greater than the investors' required rate of return (k) increase value in excess of that implied by book value alone.

Disaggregating the Return on Common Equity

While ROCE in the above formula is computed using the beginning-of-period balance of common equity, in practice we use the *average* balance for the period under analysis. As with return on net operating assets, disaggregating return on common equity into components is extremely useful for analysis purposes. Recall that the return on common shareholders' equity is computed as:

$$\frac{\text{Net income} - \text{Preferred dividends}}{\text{Average common shareholders' equity}}$$

Return on Equity for Selected Industries

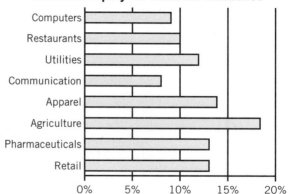

We can disaggregate return on common shareholders' equity to obtain:[2]

$$\textbf{ROCE} = \textbf{RNOA} + (\textbf{LEV} \times \textbf{Spread})$$

where **RNOA** is the return on net operating assets, as defined above, and the second term **(LEV × Spread)** is the effect of financial leverage. The first component of the financial leverage effect is the degree of financial leverage **(LEV)**, measured by the

---

[2] An alternate view of the ROCE disaggregation is provided by the following equivalent equation:

$$\text{ROCE} = \text{Adjusted profit margin} \times \text{Asset turnover} \times \text{Leverage}$$

$$\frac{\begin{array}{c}\text{Net income} - \\ \text{Preferred dividends}\\ \hline \text{Average}\\ \text{common equity}\end{array}} = \frac{\begin{array}{c}\text{Net income} - \\ \text{Preferred dividends}\\ \hline \text{Sales}\end{array}} \times \frac{\text{Sales}}{\begin{array}{c}\text{Average}\\ \text{assets}\end{array}} \times \frac{\begin{array}{c}\text{Average}\\ \text{assets}\end{array}}{\begin{array}{c}\text{Average}\\ \text{common equity}\end{array}}$$

For Excell Corporation, the ROCE for Year 9 can alternatively be computed as follows:

$$\text{ROCE} = \frac{\$104,148}{\$1,782,254} \times \frac{\$1,782,254}{([\$2,120,735 + \$2,314,492]/2)} \times \frac{(\$2,120,735 + \$2,314,492)/2}{(\$668,305 + \$772,454)/2}$$

$$14.46\% = 5.844\% \quad \times 0.804 \quad\quad\quad\quad \times 3.078$$

relative amounts of net financial obligations and stockholders' equity used by the company to finance its net operating assets. The second component is the **spread,** the return on net operating assets (RNOA) less the net financial return **(NFR)**, where NFR is the average net return on financial (nonoperating) liabilities and assets. NFR is computed as the net financial expense **(NFE)** divided by the average net financial obligations **(NFO)** outstanding during the year. Just as NFO includes interest-bearing liabilities, less marketable securities and other nonoperating assets (such as discontinued operations and other nonstrategic investments), so does NFE include interest expense, less investment returns on marketable securities. Further, just as NFO can be either positive (reflecting more nonoperating liabilities than nonoperating assets) or negative (reflecting more nonoperating assets than nonoperating liabilities), so can NFE be positive (reflecting more interest expense than investment returns) or negative (reflecting more investment returns than interest expense). Specifically, the terms used in the equation above are defined as follows:

Term	Definition
LEV (financial leverage)	Average NFO/Average equity
NFO (net financial obligations)	Interest-bearing liabilities less marketable securities and other nonoperating assets (or NOA − Equity)
Spread	RNOA–NFR
NFR (net financial rate)	NFE/Average NFO
NFE (net financial expense)	Interest expense less investment returns from nonoperating assets

The effect of financial leverage (LEV) on ROE can be summarized as follows: financial leverage increases ROE so long as the spread is positive. Simply put, if a company can earn a higher return on net operating assets than the cost of debt that finances those assets, the excess return accrues to the benefit of its shareholders. All else equal, then, its shareholders would be better off continuing to employ lower-cost debt as the company expands than to finance that expansion with higher-cost equity capital (only up to a certain level, of course, as continued issuance of debt is risky).

Return on common equity (ROCE) consists of both an operating component (RNOA) and a nonoperating component (LEV × Spread). This operating and nonoperating distinction is important for several reasons:

- The vast majority of companies provide goods and services to customers as their primary business. This is where their expertise lies. Although finance divisions in companies are staffed with highly competent personnel, we want those companies to excel in their core competencies, and not to have poor operating performance masked by good financial performance.
- Operating activities have the most pronounced and long-lasting effects on company value. Research confirms that the stock price multiple on operating earnings is many times that on financial earnings.
- Although companies can realize an increase in ROE through judicious use of financial leverage, debt payments (interest and principal) are contractual obligations that must be met in good times and in bad. Increasing debt, therefore, increases the risk of default should cash flows decline, and default can have disastrous consequences for the firm, including bankruptcy.

It is for these reasons that analysts are vitally concerned about the proportion of ROCE that accrues from operating activities and that which results from an increase in financial leverage.

For Excell Corporation, the components of ROCE disaggregation for Year 9 follow:

RNOA .... 9.95% (from page 453 above)

LEV (Average NFO/Average SE) .... 0.64 $= \dfrac{(\$501{,}680 + \$420{,}212)/2}{(\$668{,}305 + \$772{,}454)/2}$

NFR (NFE/Average NFO) .... 2.90% $= \dfrac{\$20{,}843 \times (1 - 0.36)}{(\$501{,}680 + \$420{,}212)/2}$

Spread (RNOA − NFR)................................... 7.05% = (9.95% − 2.90%)
ROCE (RNOA + [LEV × Spread]) .... 14.46% = 9.95% + (0.64 × 7.05%)

ROCE using the standard definition is 14.46%, computed as $\left[\frac{\$104{,}148 - \$0}{(\$668{,}305 + \$772{,}454)/2}\right]$ per above. For Excell Corporation, 69% (9.95%/14.46%) of its ROCE is derived from operating activities (RNOA). The average for publicly traded firms is about 84% (Nissim and Penman, 2001). Excell is, therefore, relying relatively more than usual on nonoperating activities to achieve its current level of ROCE.

Return on nonoperating activities is a function of the degree of financial leverage and the spread. The degree of financial leverage is generally under the control of the company. It can decide the relative proportions of debt and equity in its capital structure and the amount of liquidity (excess cash invested in marketable securities) that it maintains.

Spread is a function of the interest rate on debt and investment returns. Both of these can be examined separately as follows:

NFE/NFO = (Net interest rate × FL/NFO) − (Return on financial assets × FA/NFO)

where FL and FA are financial liabilities and financial assets, respectively. Most companies borrow money on fixed rates of interest (or utilize swaps and other derivative instruments to convert floating rate borrowings to fixed). The interest rate portion of NFE is, therefore, likely to be relatively fixed. The investment return portion, however, is likely to fluctuate with swings in the capital markets. An increased spread which arises from a boom market will not be sustained, and the resulting increase in ROCE should not be given as much weight in our analysis as will an increase resulting from more persistent operating returns.

ANALYSIS VIEWPOINT   **. . . YOU ARE THE CONSULTANT**

You are the management consultant to a client seeking a critical review of its performance. As part of your analysis you compute ROCE and its components (industry norms in parenthesis): asset turnover = 1.5 (1.0); leverage = 2.1 (2.2); pretax adjusted profit margin = 0.05 (0.14); and retention rate = 0.40 (0.24). What does your preliminary analysis of these figures suggest?

Computing Return on Invested Capital

This section applies our analysis of return on invested capital to the financial statements of Campbell Soup Company reproduced in Appendix A.

Return on Net Operating Assets (RNOA)

Campbell Soup's net operating assets (NOA) for years 11 and 10 are computed as follows ($ millions):

CAMPBELL SOUP NET OPERATING ASSETS (NOA)

	Year 11	Year 10
Cash	$ 178.9	$ 80.7
Accounts receivable	527.4	624.5
Inventories	706.7	819.8
Prepaid expenses	92.7	118.0
Property, plant, & equipment	1,790.4	1,717.7
Intangible assets	435.5	383.4
Other assets	404.6	349.0
Accounts payable	(482.4)	(525.2)
Accrued liabilities	(408.7)	(491.9)
Taxes payable	(67.7)	(46.4)
Other liabilities	(305.0)	(319.9)
Net operating assets	$2,872.4	$2,709.7

Its net financial obligations are computed as follows ($ millions):

CAMPBELL SOUP NET FINANCIAL OBLIGATIONS (NFO)

	Year 11	Year 10
Notes payable	$ 282.2	$ 202.3
Dividend payable	37.0	32.3
Long-term debt	772.6	805.8
Marketable securities	(12.8)	(22.5)
Net financial obligations	$1,079.0	$1,017.9

The operating accounting identity holds as follows ($ millions):

	Net operating assets (NOA)	=	Net financial obligations (NFO)	+	Stockholders' equity (SE)
Year 11	2,872.4	=	1,079.0	+	1,793.4
Year 10	2,709.7	=	1,017.9	+	1,691.8

Campbell Soup's net operating profit after tax (NOPAT) is computed as follows ($ millions):

Effective tax rate .... $39.8\% = \$265.9/\$667.4$
NOPAT .... $\$460.4 = (\$6,204.1 - \$4,095.5 - \$956.2 - \$306.7 - \$56.3 - \$0.8$
$- \$26.2 + \$2.4) \times (1 - 39.8\%)$

Campbell Soup's return on net operating assets (RNOA) for Year 11 is ($ millions),

$$\frac{\$460.4}{(\$2,872.4 + \$2,709.7)/2} = 16.5\%$$

Disaggregated Return on Net Operating Assets

We can disaggregate Campbell's Year 11 return on net operating assets (RNOA) into its operating profit margin and net operating asset turnover components:

$$\text{Return on net operating assets} = \text{Operating profit margin} \times \text{Net operating asset turnover}$$

$$= \frac{\text{NOPAT}}{\text{Sales}} \times \frac{\text{Sales}}{\text{Average net operating assets}}$$

$$16.5\% = \frac{\$460.4}{\$6,204.1} \times \frac{\$6,204.1}{(\$2,872.4 + \$2,709.7)/2} = 7.42\% \times 2.22$$

Return on Common Equity

Campbell Soup's return on common shareholders' equity for Year 11 is computed as follows ($ millions and includes reference codes to Campbell's relevant financial statement items):

$$\text{ROCE} = \frac{\text{Net income} - \text{Preferred dividends}}{\text{Average common equity}}$$

$$= \frac{\$401.5\boxed{28} - \$0}{[(\$1,793.4) + (\$1,691.8)]/2\boxed{54}} = \frac{\$401.5}{\$1,742.6} = 23\%$$

Disaggregated Return on Common Equity

Campbell Soup's ROCE, computed as a function of RNOA, financial leverage, and spread is as follows ($ millions):

RNOA   16.5% (above)
LEV   0.6% $= [(\$1,079.0 + \$1,017.9)/2]/[(\$1,793.4 + \$1,691.8)/2]$
NFR   5.6% $= (\$460.4 - \$401.5)/[(\$1,079.0 + \$1,017.9)/2]$
Spread 10.9% $= 16.5\% - 5.6\%$
ROCE   23% $= 16.5\% + (0.60 \times 10.9\%)$

Campbell Soup's RNOA is further disaggregated into its margin and turnover components as follows ($ millions):

RNOA	=	NOPAT margin (NOPAT/Sales)	×	NOA turnover (Sales/Average NOA)
16.5%	=	7.4% ($460.4/$6,204.1)	×	2.22 $6204.1/([2,872.4 + $2,709.7]/2)

The third level analysis proceeds with the computation of individual revenue and expense items as a percent of sales. For Year 11, the common size income statement follows:

Campbell Soup Company Common Size

Income Statement	Year 11
Sales	100.0%
Cost of goods sold	66.0
Gross profit	34.0
Marketing & selling expenses	15.4
Administrative expenses	4.9
Research & development expenses	0.9
Operating profit	12.8
Interest expense	1.9
Interest income	−0.4
Foreign exchange losses	0.0
Other expense	0.4
Special items	0.0
	10.9
Equity earnings in affiliates	0.0
Minority interests	−0.1
Earnings before taxes	10.8
Tax expense	4.3
Net earnings	6.5%

Turnover rates for individual assets are also computed as follows ($ millions):

Accounts receivable turnover (Sales/Average accounts receivables)	10.77[a]
Average collection period (Accounts receivable/Average daily sales)	31.03[b]
Inventory turnover (Cost of goods sold/Average inventories)	5.37[c]
Average inventory days outstanding (Inventories/Average daily cost of goods sold)	62.98[d]
Long-term operating asset turnover (Sales/Average long-term operating assets)	2.44[e]

[a]($6,204.1/([$527.4 + $624.5]/2))
[b]($527.4/([$6204.1/365]))
[c]($4,095.5/([$706.7 + $819.8])/2)
[d]($706.7/($4,095.5/365))
[e]($6,204.1/([$1,790.4 + $435.5 + $404.6] + [$1,717.7 + $383.4 + $349.0])/2)

We conduct a comparative analysis of these ratios across time in the section on analysis of return on invested capital for the Comprehensive Case chapter. An analysis of return on invested capital measures across time is often revealing of company performance. If ROCE declines, it is important for us to identify the component(s) responsible for this decline to better assess past and future company performance. We can also then better assess areas of greatest potential improvement in ROCE and the likelihood of a company successfully pursuing this strategy. For example, if leverage cannot be prudently increased our analysis focuses on operating profit margin and net operating asset turnover. An analysis of company strategies and the potential for improvements also depends on industry and economic conditions. We pursue answers to questions such as: Is operating profit margin high or low in comparison with the industry? What is the potential improvement in net operating asset turnover in this industry? Evaluating returns using the structured approach described in this chapter and interpreting them in their proper context can greatly aid our analysis.

RETURN ON COMMON SHAREHOLDERS' EQUITY

How does a company's return on common shareholders' equity (ROCE) behave across time? Do certain companies consistently have high or low ROCE? Do companies' ROCEs tend to move toward an average ROCE? Analysis research has addressed these important questions. *On average,* a company's ROCE for the current period is a good predictor of its ROCE for the next period. However, as the time horizon increases, a company's ROCE tends to converge toward the average industry ROCE. This is usually attributed to the effects of competition. Companies that are able to sustain high ROCEs typically command large premiums over book value.

A large portion of the variability in companies' ROCEs is due to changes in RNOA. This is because, on average, leverage factors do not vary significantly over time. Finally, disaggregating net income into operating and nonoperating components improves forecasts.

Assessing Growth in Common Equity
Equity Growth Rate

We can assess the common equity growth rate of a company through earnings retention. This analysis emphasizes equity growth *without* resort to external financing. To assess equity growth, we assume earnings retention *and* a constant dividend payout over time. The **equity growth rate** is computed as:

$$\text{Equity growth rate} = \frac{\text{Net income} - \text{Preferred dividends} - \text{Common dividends}}{\text{Average common equity}}$$

The equity growth rate for Year 11 of Campbell Soup, using its financial statements reproduced in Appendix A, is computed as:

$$14.9\% = \frac{\$401.5 \boxed{28} - \$0 - \$142.2 \boxed{89}}{(\$1,793.4 + \$1,691.8) \div 2 \boxed{54}}$$

This measure implies that Campbell Soup can grow 14.9% per year without increasing its current level of financing and assuming a continuation of current levels of profitability and common stock dividends.

Sustainable Equity Growth Rate

The **sustainable equity growth rate,** or simply sustainable equity growth, recognizes that internal growth for a company depends on *both* earnings retention and the return earned on the earnings retained. Specifically, the **sustainable equity growth rate** is computed as:

$$\text{Sustainable equity growth rate} = \text{ROCE} \times (1 - \text{Payout rate})$$

For Campbell Soup Company, we find the dividend payout rate for Year 11 equals 35% ($142.2/$401.5). We then compute Campbell Soup's sustainable equity growth rate for Year 11 as:

$$14.95\% = 23\% \times (1 - 0.35)$$

When estimating future equity growth rates it is often advisable to average (or otherwise recognize) sustainable growth rates for several recent years. We should also recognize potential changes in earnings retention and forecasted ROCE.

.....APPENDIX 8A CHALLENGES OF DIVERSIFIED COMPANIES

The analysis of financial statements of diversified companies must separate and interpret the impact of individual business segments on the company as a whole. This is challenging because different segments or divisions can experience varying rates of profitability, risk, and growth opportunities. Their existence is an important reason why our analysis requires considerable detailed information by business segment. Our evaluation, projection, and valuation of earnings requires this information be separated into segments sharing characteristics of variability, growth, and risk. Asset composition and financing requirements of segments often vary and demand separate analysis. A creditor is interested in knowing which segments provide cash and which use it. The makeup of investing and financing activities, the size and profitability of segments, and the performance of segment management provide important information. We show in Chapter 11 that income forecasting benefits from forecasting by segments.

REPORTING BY SEGMENTS

Information reported on operating results and financial position by segments varies. Full disclosure would provide detailed income statements, balance sheets, and statements of cash flow for each important segment. However, full disclosure by segments is rare in practice because of difficulties in separating segments and management's reluctance to release information that can harm its competitive position.

Regulatory agencies have established reporting requirements for industry segments, international activities, export sales, and major customers. Evaluating risk and return is a major objective of financial statement analysis, and practice recognizes the value of segment disclosures in this evaluation. Analysis of companies operating across industry segments or geographic areas, which often have different rates of profitability, risk, and growth, is aided by segment data. These data assist us in analyzing uncertainties affecting the timing and amount of expected cash inflows and outflows.

Practice considers a segment significant if its sales, operating income (or loss), *or* identifiable assets are 10% or more of the combined amounts of all the company's operating segments. To ensure that these segments constitute a substantial portion of a company's operations, the combined sales of all segments reported must be at least 75% of the company's combined sales. For each segment, companies must report selected annual financial information (see *SFAS 131*) including: (1) sales–both to other segments and to external customers; (2) operating income–revenues less operating expenses; (3) identifiable assets; (4) interest and tax expenses or benefits; (5) special items' gains and losses; and (6) depreciation, depletion, and amortization expense. Additionally, if a company derives 10% or more of revenues from sales to a single customer, revenues from this customer must be reported. The SEC also requires a narrative description of the company's business by operating segments such as information on competition, customer dependence, principal products and services, backlogs, sources and availability of raw materials, patents, research and development costs, number of employees, and the seasonality of its business.

ANALYSIS IMPLICATIONS OF SEGMENT REPORTS

Diversified companies, and the loss of identity for subsidiary companies in consolidated financial statements, create challenges for analysis. While segment information is available, our analysis must be careful in using this information for profitability tests. The more specific and detailed segment information is, the more dependent it is on accounting allocations of revenues and expenses. Allocation of common costs as practiced in internal accounting is often based on notions of fairness, reasonableness, and acceptability to managers. These notions are of little relevance to our profitability analysis. Allocations of joint expenses are often arbitrary and limited in their validity and precision. Examples are research and development costs, promotion expenses, advertising costs, interest, pension costs, federal and state income taxes, and general and administrative costs. There are no accepted principles in allocating or transferring costs of one segment to another. We must recognize these limitations when relying on segment reports.

Segment reports are and must be analyzed as "soft" information—information subject to manipulation and preinterpretation by management. It must be treated with uncertainty, and inferences drawn from these data must be subjected to alternative sources of verification. Nevertheless, segment data supported by alternative evidence can be extremely useful for analysis. Specifically, segment data can aid our analysis of:

- *Sales growth.* Analysis of trends in sales by segments is useful in assessing profitability. Sales growth is often the result of one or more factors including: (1) price changes, (2) volume changes, (3) acquisitions/divestitures, and (4) changes in exchange rates. A company's Management's Discussion and Analysis section usually offers insights into the causes of sales growth.
- *Asset growth.* Analysis of trends in identifiable assets by segments is relevant for our profitability analysis. Comparing capital expenditures to depreciation can reveal the segments undergoing "real" growth. When analyzing geographic segment reports, our analysis must be alert to changes in foreign currency exchange rates that can significantly affect reported values.
- *Profitability.* Measures of operating income to sales and operating income to identifiable assets by segment are useful in analyzing profitability. Due to limitations with segment income data, our analysis should focus on trends versus absolute levels.

Exhibit CC.1 in the Comprehensive Case chapter reports a summary of segment information for Campbell Soup Company. Note 2 of Campbell Soup's financial statements also reports geographic area information.

Analysis Research
■■■■■■ USEFULNESS OF SEGMENT DATA

Analysis research provides evidence that segment disclosures are useful in forecasting future profitability. We know that total sales and earnings of a company equals the sum of the sales and earnings of all segments (less any intercompany transactions). As long as different segments are subject to different economic factors, the accuracy of segment-based forecasts should exceed that of forecasts based on consolidated data.

Combining company-specific segment data with industry-specific forecasts improves the accuracy of sales and earnings forecasts. Evidence shows that the introduction of segment reporting requirements increased the accuracy and reduced the dispersion of earnings forecasts made by professional securities analysts. This implies that our profitability analysis can also benefit from segment data.

GUIDANCE ANSWERS TO ANALYSIS VIEWPOINTS

AUDITOR

Joint analysis is the assessment of one measure of company performance relative to another. In the case of our manufacturing client, both *individual* analyses yield percentage changes within the $\pm 5\%$ acceptable range. However, a joint analysis would suggest a more alarming situation. Consider a joint analysis using profit margin (net income/sales). The client's profit margin is 11.46% ($2,060,000 − $1,824,000/$2,060,000) for the current year compared with 5.0% ($2,000,000 − $1,900,000/$2,000,000) for the prior year—a 129% increase in profit margin! This is what the audit partner is concerned with, and encourages expanded audit tests including joint analysis to verify or refute the client's figures.

CONSULTANT

Your preliminary analysis highlights deviations from the norm in (1) asset turnover, (2) pretax adjusted profit margin, and (3) retention rate. Asset turnover for your client is better than the norm. Your client appears to efficiently use its assets. One note of warning: we need to be assured all assets are accounted for and properly valued, and we want to know if the company is sufficiently replacing its aging assets. Your client's pretax adjusted profit margin is 60% lower than the norm. This is alarming, especially in light of the positive asset turnover ratio. Our client has considerably greater costs than the norm, and we need to direct efforts to identify and analyze these costs. Retention rate is also considerably worse than competitors. Our client is paying a greater proportion of its income in taxes. We need to utilize tax experts to identify and appropriately plan business activities with tax considerations in mind.

QUESTIONS

8–1. How is return on invested capital used as an internal management tool?

8–2. Why is return on invested capital one of the most relevant measures of company performance? How do we use this measure in our analysis of financial statements?

8–3. Why is interest, expense ignored when computing return on net operating assets (RNOA)?

8–4. Discuss the motivation for excluding "nonproductive" assets from invested capital when computing return. What circumstances justify excluding intangible assets from invested capital?

8–5. Why must income used in computing return on invested capital be adjusted to reflect the capital base (denominator) used in the computation?

8–6. What is the relation between return on net operating assets and sales? Consider both NOPAT sales and sales to net operating assets in your response.

8–7. Company A acquires Company B because the latter has a NOPAT margin exceeding the industry norm. After acquisition, a shareholder complains that the acquisition lowered return on net operating assets. Discuss possible reasons for this occurrence.

8–8. Company X's NOPAT margin is 2% of sales. Company Y has a net operating asset turnover of 12. Both companies' RNOA are 6% and are considered unsatisfactory by industry norms. What is the net operating asset turnover of Company X? What is the NOPAT margin for Company Y? What strategic actions do you recommend to the managements of the respective companies?

8–9. What is the purpose of measuring asset turnover for different asset categories?

8–10. What factors (limitations) enter into our evaluation of return on net operating assets?

8–11. How is the equity growth rate computed? What does it measure?

8–12. *a.* How do return on net operating assets and return on common equity differ?
      b. What are the components of return on common shareholders' equity? What do the components measure?

8–13. *a.* Equity turnover is sales divided by average shareholders' equity. What does equity turnover measure? How is it related to return on common equity? (*Hint:* Look at the components of ROCE.)
      b. "Growth in earnings per share from an increase in equity turnover is unlikely to continue indefinitely." Do you agree or disagree with this assertion? Explain your answer and discuss the components of equity turnover for their impact on earnings.

8–14. What circumstances justify including convertible debt as equity capital when computing return on shareholders' equity?

(CFA Adapted)

EXERCISES

FIT Corporation's return on net operating assets (RNOA) is 10% and its tax rate is 40%. Its net operating assets ($4 million) are financed entirely by common shareholders' equity. Management is considering its options to finance an expansion costing $2 million. It expects return on net operating assets to remain unchanged. There are two alternatives to finance the expansion:

1. Issue $1 million bonds with 12% coupon, and $1 million common stock.
2. Issue $2 million bonds with 12% coupon.

Required:

a. Determine net operating income after tax (NOPAT) and net income for each alternative.

b. Compute return on common shareholders' equity for each alternative (use ending equity).

c. Calculate the assets-to-equity ratio for each alternative.

d. Compute return on net operating assets and explain how the level of leverage interacts with it in helping determine which alternative management should pursue.

EXERCISE 8–1
Analyzing Financial Leverage for Alternative Financing Strategies

Roll Corporation's return on net operating assets (RNOA) is 10% and its tax rate is 40%. Its net operating assets ($10 million) are financed entirely by common shareholders' equity. Management is considering using bonds to finance an expansion costing $6 million. It expects return on net operating assets to remain unchanged. There are two alternatives to finance the expansion:

1. Issue $2 million bonds with 5% coupon and $4 million common stock.
2. Issue $6 million bonds with 6% coupon.

Required:

a. Compute Roll's current net operating income after tax (NOPAT) and net income.

b. Determine net income and net operating income after tax for each alternative financing plan.

c. Compute return on common shareholders' equity for each alternative (use ending equity).

d. Explain any difference in the ROCE for the alternative plans computed in (*c*). Include a discussion of leverage in your response.

EXERCISE 8–2
Analyzing Returns and Strategies of Alternative Financing

Selected financial information from Syntex Corporation is reproduced below:

1. NOA turnover (average NOA equals ending NOA) is 2.
2. NOPAT margin equals 5%.
3. Leverage ratio (average NFO/average common equity) is 1.786, and the Spread is 4.4%.

Required:

a. Compute return on net operating assets (RNOA).

b. Compute return on common equity using its three major components.

c. Analyze the disaggregation of return on common equity. What is the "leverage advantage (in percent return) accruing to common equity"?

EXERCISE 8–3
Disaggregating Return Measures for Analyzing Leverage

Refer to the financial data in Case 10–5 (on page 595). In analyzing this company, you feel it is important to differentiate between operating success and financing decisions.

Required:

a. Explain the difference between ABEX's ROCE in Year 5 and in Year 9. Your analysis should include computation and discussion of the components determining return on common shareholders' equity.

b. Explain why ABEX's earnings per share nearly doubled between Year 5 and Year 9 despite the decline in its return on common shareholders' equity.

(CFA Adapted)

EXERCISE 8–4
Disaggregating and Analyzing Return on Common Equity

CHECK
(*a*) Year 9 ROCE, 9.07%

EXERCISE 8–5

Analyzing Returns and Effects of Leverage

Selected financial information for ADAM Corporation is reproduced below:

1. NOA turnover (average NOA equals ending NOA) is 3.

2. NOPAT margin is 7%.

3. Leverage ratio (average NFO to average common equity) is 1.667, and the Spread is 8.4%.

Required:

a. Compute return on net operating assets (RNOA).

b. Compute return on common equity using its three major components.

c. Prepare an analysis of the composition of return on common equity describing the advantage or disadvantage accruing to common shareholders' equity from use of leverage.

EXERCISE 8–6

Analyzing Financial Leverage for Shareholders' Returns

Rose Corporation's condensed balance sheet for Year 2 is reproduced below:

Assets

Current assets	$ 250,000
Noncurrent assets	1,750,000
Total assets	$2,000,000

Liabilities and Equity

Current liabilities	$ 200,000
Noncurrent liabilities (8% bonds)	675,000
Common stockholders' equity	1,125,000
Total liabilities and equity	$2,000,000

Additional Information:

1. Net income for Year 2 is $157,500.

2. Income tax rate is 50%.

3. Amounts for total assets and shareholders' equity are the same for Years 1 and 2.

4. All assets and current liabilities are considered to be operating.

Required:

a. Determine whether leverage (from long-term debt) benefits Rose's shareholders. (*Hint:* Examine ROCE with and without leverage.)

b. Compute Rose's NOPAT and RNOA (use ending NOA).

c. Demonstrate the favorable effect of leverage given the disaggregation of ROCE and your answer to part (b).

EXERCISE 8–7

Understanding Return Measures (multiple choice)

1. Which of the following situations best correspond with a ratio of "sales to average net tangible assets" exceeding the industry norm? (Choose one answer.)
   a. A company expanding plant and equipment during the past three years.
   b. A company inefficiently using its assets.
   c. A company with a large proportion of aged plant and equipment.
   d. A company using straight-line depreciation.

2. A measure of asset utilization (turnover) is (choose one answer):
   a. Sales divided by average long-term operating assets.
   b. Return on net operating assets.

c. Return on common equity.

d. NOPAT divided by sales.

3. Return on net operating assets depends on the (choose one answer):

a. Interest rates and pretax profits.

b. Debt to equity ratio.

c. After-tax operating profit margin and NOA turnover.

d. Sales and total assets.

Return on net operating assets is a function of both profit margin and net operating asset turnover.

Required:

How do you believe that knowledge of operating profit margin and operating asset turnover would contribute to analysis of the reported return on net operating assets for the following companies (that is, if the business reported high return on net operating assets, is it more likely that operating profit margin is especially high or that operating asset turnover is especially high or both)? Make your assessments relative to industry norms.

a. BMW

b. Ford

c. Sak's Fifth Avenue

d. Target

e. Wal-Mart

f. McDonald's

g. Amazon.com

EXERCISE 8–8

Predicting the Components of Return on Assets

Two auto dealers, Legend Auto Sales and Reliable Auto Sales, compete in the same area. Both purchase autos for $10,000 each and sell them for $12,000 each. Both maintain 10 cars on the lot at all times. A local basketball legend owns Legend Auto Sales. As a result, Legend sells 100 cars each year, while Reliable sells only 50 cars each year. The dealerships have no other revenues or expenses.

Required:

The town banker has denied Reliable Auto Sales a loan because its return on net operating assets is inferior to its rival. The owner of Reliable Auto Sales has engaged you to help explain why its return on net operating assets is inferior to that of Legend Auto Sales. Please prepare a memorandum for Reliable Auto Sales explaining the problem. Present quantitative support for your conclusions.

EXERCISE 8–9

Analyzing Return on Assets

A machine that produces hockey pucks costs $20,500 and produces 10 pucks per hour. Two similar companies purchase the machine and begin producing and selling pucks. The first company, Northern Sales is located in International Falls, Minnesota. The second company, Southern Sales is located in Huntsville, Alabama. Northern Sales operates the machine 20 hours per day to meet customer demand. Southern sales operates the machine 10 hours per day to meet customer demand. Sales data for the first month of operations are:

	Northern	Southern
Property, plant, and equipment	$20,500	$20,500
Accumulated depreciation—Property, plant, and equipment	$500	$500
Pucks sold	6,000 pucks	3,000 pucks
Sales	$12,000	$6,000

Required:

Calculate the property, plant, and equipment turnover ratio (sales divided by average PPE) for both Northern Sales and Southern Sales. Explain how this ratio impacts the return on net operating assets of each company (assume the profit margin for each company is the same and that there has been no change in PPE).

EXERCISE 8–10

Analyzing Property, Plant, and Equipment Turnover

EXERCISE 8–11

Analyzing the Relation between Revenues and Expenses

A press report carried the following news item: *General Motors, Ford, and Chrysler are expected to post losses on fourth-quarter operations despite sales gains. Automakers' revenues are based on factory output rather than retail sales by dealers, and last quarter's sales increases were from the bulging inventories at the end of the third quarter, rather than from models produced in the fourth quarter.*

Required:

Discuss likely accounting-based reasons that contribute to these expected fourth-quarter losses of automakers.

PROBLEMS

PROBLEM 8–1

Determining Return on Invested Capital (conceptual)

Quaker Oats, in its annual report discloses the following:

Quaker Oats Company

Financial Objectives: Provide total shareholder returns (dividends plus share price appreciation) that exceed both the cost of equity and the S&P 500 stock index over time. Quaker's total return to shareholders for Year 11 was 34%. That compares quite favorably to our cost of equity for the year, which was about 12%, and to the total return of the S&P 500 stock index, which was 7%. Driving this strong performance, real earnings from continuing operations grew 7.4% over the last five years, return on equity rose to 24.1%. [Quaker Oats' stock price at the beginning and end of Year 11 was $48 and $62, respectively, and the Year 11 dividends are $1.56 per share.]

The Benchmark for Investment

We use our cost of capital as a benchmark, or hurdle rate, to ensure that all projects undertaken promise a suitable rate of return. The cost of capital is used as the discount rate in determining whether a project will provide an economic return on its investment. We estimate a project's potential cash flows and discount these cash flows back to present value. This amount is compared with the initial investment costs to determine whether incremental value is created. Our cost of capital is calculated using the approximate market value weightings of debt and equity used to finance the Company.

$$\text{Cost of equity} + \text{Cost of debt} = \text{Cost of capital}$$

When Quaker is consistently able to generate and reinvest cash flows in projects whose returns exceed our cost of capital, economic value is created. As the stock market evaluates the Company's ability to generate value, this value is reflected in stock price appreciation.

The cost of equity. The cost of equity is a measure of the minimum return Quaker must earn to properly compensate investors for the risk of ownership of our stock. This cost is a combination of a "risk-free" rate and an "equity risk premium." The risk-free rate (the U.S. Treasury Bond rate) is the sum of the expected rate of inflation and a "real" return of 2 to 3%. For Year 11, the risk-free rate was approximately 8.4%. Investors in Quaker stock expect the return of a risk-free security plus a "risk premium" of about 3.6% to compensate them for assuming the risks in Quaker stock. The risk in holding Quaker stock is inherent in the fact that returns depend on the future profitability of the Company. Quaker's cost of equity was approximately 12%.

The cost of debt. The cost of debt is simply our after-tax, long-term debt rate, which was around 6.4%.

Required:

a. Quaker reports the "return to shareholders" to be 34%.
   (1) How is this return computed (provide calculations)?
   (2) How is this return different from return on common equity?

b. Explain how Quaker Oats arrives at a 3.6% "risk premium" needed by common shareholders as compensation for assuming the risks of Quaker Oats' stock.

c. Explain how Quaker Oats determines the 6.4% cost of debt.

Zear Company produces an electronic processor and sells it wholesale to manufacturing and retail outlets at $10 each. In Zear's Year 8 fiscal period, it sold 500,000 processors. Fixed costs for Year 8 total $1,500,000, including interest costs on its 7.5% debentures. Variable costs are $4 per processor for materials. Zear employs about 20 hourly paid plant employees, each earning $35,000 in Year 8.

Zear is currently confronting labor negotiations. The plant employees are requesting substantial increases in hourly wages. Zear forecasts a 6% increase in fixed costs and no change in either the processor's price or in material costs for the processors. Zear also forecasts a 10% growth in sales volume for Year 9. To meet the necessary increase in production due to sales demand, Zear recently hired two additional hourly plant employees.

The condensed balance sheet for Zear at the end of fiscal Year 8 follows (the tax rate is 50%):

PROBLEM 8–2
Analyzing Company Returns and Proposed Wage Increases

Assets		Liabilities and equity	
Current assets		Current liabilities	$2,000,000
Cash ....$	700,000	Long-term 7½% debenture...........	2,000,000
Receivables....................	1,000,000	6% preferred stock, 10,000	
Other.............................	800,000	shares, $100 par value............	1,000,000
Total current assets............	2,500,000	Common stock............................	1,800,000
Fixed assets (net)	5,500,000	Retained earnings.......................	1,200,000
Total assets ....$	$8,000,000	Total liabilities and equity...........	$8,000,000

Required:

a. Compute Zear's return on invested capital for Year 8 where invested capital is:

(1) Net operating assets at end of Year 8 (assume all assets and current liabilities are operating).

(2) Common equity capital at end of Year 8.

b. Calculate the maximum annual wage increase Zear can pay each plant employee and show a 10% return on net operating assets.

(CFA Adapted)

CHECK
(a) RNOA = 7.92%

Selected income statement and balance sheet data from **Merck & Co.** for Year 9 are reproduced below:

Merck & Co.

PROBLEM 8–3
Disaggregating and Interpreting Return on Common Equity

MERCK & COMPANY, INC.
Year 9 Selected Financial Data ($ millions)

Income Statement Data

Sales revenue $7,120	
Depreciation	230
Interest expense	10
Pretax income..	2,550
Income taxes	900
Net income	1,650

(continued)

PROBLEM 8–3
(concluded)

Balance Sheet Data

Current assets...$4,850
Fixed assets, net.. 2,400
Total assets 7,250
Current liabilities 3,290
Long-term debt.. 100
Shareholders' equity.. 3,860
Total liabilities & shareholders' equity 7,250

CHECK
(*a*) ROCE = 42.7%
(*b*) RNOA = 42.0%

Required:

a. Calculate return on common equity for Year 9 using year-end amounts and assuming no preferred dividends.

b. Disaggregate Merck's ROCE into operating (RNOA) and nonoperating components. Comment on Merck's use of leverage. (Assume all assets and current liabilities are operating and a 35% tax rate.)

PROBLEM 8–4

Disaggregating and Analyzing Return on Invested Capital

As a financial analyst at a debt-rating agency, you are asked to analyze return on invested capital and asset utilization (turnover) measures for ZETA Corporation. Selected financial information for Years 5 and 6 of ZETA Corporation are reproduced in the Comprehensive Case chapter (see Case CC–2).

CHECK
(*a*) RNOA = 18.14%

Required:

a. Compute the following return measures for Year 6 (assume a 50% tax rate):
   (1) Return on net operating assets.   (2) Return on common equity.

b. Disaggregate ROCE for Year 6. Comment on Zeta's use of financial leverage.

PROBLEM 8–5

Disaggregating and Analyzing Return on Common Equity

Selected financial statement data from Texas Telecom, Inc., for Years 5 and 9 are reproduced below ($ millions):

	Year 5	Year 9
Income Statement Data		
Revenues	$542	$979
Operating income............................	35	68
Interest expense.............................	7	0
Pretax income	28	68
Income taxes...................................	14	34
Net income......................................	14	34
Balance Sheet Data		
Long-term operating assets............	$ 52	$ 63
Working capital...............................	123	157
Total liabilities...............................	50	0
Total shareholders' equity..............	125	220

CHECK
(*a*) Yr. 5 RNOA = 10.0%

Required:

a. Calculate return on common equity and disaggregate ROCE for Years 5 and 9 using end-of-year values for computations requiring an average (assume fixed assets and working capital are operating and a 50% tax rate).

b. Comment on Texas Telecom's use of financial leverage.

Johnson Corporation sells primarily two products: (A) consumer cleaners and (B) industrial purifiers. Its gross margin and components for the past two years are:

PROBLEM 8–6
Analyzing Changes is Gross Margin

	Year 7	Year 6
Sales revenue		
Product A	$60,000	$35,000
Product B	30,000	45,000
Total	90,000	80,000
Deduct cost of goods sold		
Product A	50,000	28,000
Product B	19,500	27,000
Total	69,500	55,000
Gross margin	$20,500	$25,000

In Year 6, the selling price of A is $5 per unit, while in Year 7 it is $6 per unit. Product B sells for $50 per unit in both years. Security analysts and the business press expressed surprise at Johnson's 12.5% increase in sales and $4,500 decrease in gross margin for Year 7.

Required:

Prepare an analysis statement of the change in gross margin for Year 7 versus Year 6. Discuss and show the effects of changes in quantities, prices, costs, and product mix on gross margin.

CHECK
Net decrease, $(4,500)

Comparative income statements of Spyres Manufacturing Company for Years 9 and 8 are reproduced below:

PROBLEM 8–7
Common-Size Analysis of Comparative Income Statements

	Year 9	Year 8
Net sales	$600,000	$500,000
Cost of goods sold	490,000	430,000
Gross margin	110,000	70,000
Operating expenses	101,000	51,000
Income before taxes	9,000	19,000
Income taxes	2,400	5,000
Net income	$ 6,600	$ 14,000

Required:

a. Prepare common size statements showing the percent of each item to net sales for both Year 8 and Year 9. Include a column reporting the percentage increase or decrease for Year 9 relative to Year 8 (round numbers to the tenth of 1%).

b. Interpret the trend shown in your percentage calculations of a. What areas identified from this analysis should be a matter of managerial concern?

PROBLEM 8–8

Variations in Income and Income Components

At a meeting of your company's Investment Policy Committee the possibility of investing in ZETA Corporation (see Case CC-2 in the Comprehensive Case chapter) is considered. During discussions, a committee member asked about the major factors explaining the change in ZETA Corporation's income from Year 5 to Year 6.

Required:

Analyze variations in income and income components for ZETA Corporation that compares Year 6 to Year 5. Analyze and interpret your results. (*Hint:* ZETA's notes are useful for this purpose.)

PROBLEM 8–9

Analyzing Line-of-Business Data (extending beyond the book)

Selected data from Kemp Corporation are reproduced below:

KEMP CORPORATION Product-Line Information ($ thousands)				
	Year 1	Year 2	Year 3	Year 4
Data communications equipment				
Net sales	$4,616	$5,630	$4,847	$6,890
Income contribution	570	876	996	1,510
Inventory	2,615	2,469	2,103	1,897
Time recording devices				
Net sales	3,394	4,200	4,376	4,100
Income contribution	441	311	34	412
Inventory	1,193	2,234	2,574	2,728
Hardware for electronics industry				
Net sales	—	—	$ 1,564	$ 1,850
Income contribution	—	—	771	919
Inventory	—	—	331	287
Home sewing products				
Net sales	$1,505	$ 1,436	1,408	1,265
Income contribution	291	289	276	342
Inventory	398	534	449	526
Corporate totals				
Net sales	9,515	11,266	12,195	14,105
Income contribution	1,302	1,476	2,077	3,183
Inventory	4,206	5,237	5,457	5,438

Required:

a. For Year 4, compute the following ratios:
   (1) Inventory/Sales.
   (2) Inventory/Income contribution.

b. Compute the percentage of each product line's income contribution to the total for each year. Interpret this evidence.

c. Comment on the desirability of an investment in each product line.

CASES

CASE 8–1
*Comprehensive
Analysis of Return on
Common Equity*

While you are an analyst at Investment Counselors, Inc., the senior portfolio manager at your firm makes a decision to increase sporting goods apparel manufacturer stocks in the firm's managed funds. You are assigned to recommend one stock as an initial investment to meet this long-run objective. You diligently analyze and evaluate all communication stocks and narrow the decision to two athletic shoe manufacturing companies: Nike and Reebok.

The senior portfolio manager requests that you analyze the internal sources of earnings growth for each company. You decide to disaggregate and evaluate the internal growth components for each company to explain any trends in your variable of interest, *return on common equity*. You identify the key components driving ROCE and develop the following spreadsheet:

Nike	Year 5	Year 4	Year 3	Year 2	Year 1
Return on equity (ROCE)	21.6%	12.1%	18.1%	17.8%	18.5%
Return on net operating assets (RNOA)	19.2%	15.5%	14.2%	13.4%	13.3%
Financial leverage (LEV)	14.4%	24.8%	32.8%	41.3%	46.0%
Spread	16.6%	−13.9%	11.9%	10.6%	11.3%
Sales growth	14.55%	8.13%	4.26%	5.49%	2.49%
Gross profit margin	42.9%	41.0%	39.3%	39.0%	39.9%
SG&A expense/Sales	32.7%	31.9%	31.4%	30.6%	31.5%
NOPAT/Sales	7.8%	7.1%	7.0%	6.6%	6.8%
Tax expense/Pretax income	34.8%	34.1%	34.3%	36.0%	37.0%
NOA turnover	2.44	2.19	2.03	2.02	1.96
Receivables turnover	5.83	5.50	5.78	5.95	5.79
Average collection period	62.62	66.33	63.19	61.37	63.09
Inventory turnover	4.45	4.37	4.29	4.03	4.13
Average inventory days outstanding	82.07	83.50	85.04	90.54	88.37
Long-term operating asset turnover	6.56	5.46	4.67	4.47	4.18
Accounts payable turnover	10.48	11.72	12.83	11.86	10.62
Average payable days outstanding	34.84	31.13	28.46	30.78	34.36
Return on equity (ROCE)	15.7%	15.1%	15.0%	13.4%	1.9%
Return on net operating assets (RNOA)	12.7%	12.3%	12.1%	10.1%	7.9%
Financial leverage (LEV)	36.7%	44.5%	53.8%	78.8%	101.0%
Spread	8.2%	6.3%	5.4%	4.2%	−6.0%
Sales growth	11.43%	4.51%	4.45%	−1.19%	−10.07%
Gross profit margin	38.4%	38.3%	36.7%	37.9%	38.5%
SG&A expense/Sales	32.2%	32.4%	31.8%	33.6%	35.2%
NOPAT/Sales	5.0%	4.8%	4.3%	3.8%	3.2%
Tax expense/Pretax income	30.8%	31.0%	31.0%	36.1%	36.0%
NOA turnover	2.55	2.59	2.84	2.66	2.50
Receivables turnover	7.31	7.77	7.42	6.81	6.20

(continued)

CASE 8–1
(concluded)

Reebok	Year 5	Year 4	Year 3	Year 2	Year 1
Average collection period	49.96	46.98	49.22	53.58	58.86
Inventory turnover	5.71	5.06	5.01	4.40	3.76
Average inventory days outstanding	63.95	72.10	72.88	82.88	97.17
Long-term operating asset turnover	13.67	12.62	12.31	10.25	9.03
Accounts payable turnover	13.33	13.16	12.66	10.92	9.99
Average payable days outstanding	27.37	27.74	28.83	33.43	36.54

Required:

a. Describe and interpret how the recent five-year trend in the components of ROCE determine the ROCE for both Nike and Reebok.

b. Recommend a "buy" on one of these companies based on your analysis. Support your recommendation with reference to your analysis in *(a)*.

CASE 8–2

Analyzing Return on Invested Capital

Walt Disney Company (Disney) is a diversified international entertainment company with operations in three business segments. Revenue and operating income data for the three segments are shown below.

Walt Disney Company

BUSINESS SEGMENT DATA
Years Ending September 30

($ millions) Business Segments	YEAR 13		YEAR 9	
	Revenue	Operating Income	Revenue	Operating Income
Theme Parks and Resorts	$3,441	$ 747	$2,595	$ 785
Film Entertainment	3,673	622	1,588	256
Consumer Products	1,415	355	411	188
	$8,529	$1,724	$4,594	$1,229

The profitability of the leisure-time industry is influenced by various factors including economic conditions, the amount of available leisure time, oil and transportation prices, and weather patterns. Disney management has been very aggressive in raising theme park admission prices. For the 10-year period ending in Year 13, admission prices increased at an annual rate of 8–9% compared to less than 4% for U.S. consumer price inflation. Disney's Film Entertainment business has grown rapidly because of increasing acceptance of The Disney Channel and, importantly, management efforts to exploit the expanding distribution opportunities available for its extensive video library. Disney's Consumer Products revenue has also grown meaningfully as the company has moved its product mix aggressively toward direct publishing and direct retail and away from higher-margined licensing and royalty income sources. During the fourth quarter of fiscal Year 13 (ending September 30, Year 13), Disney wrote off the full carrying value of Euro Disney. The charge was $350 million ($218 million after tax).

WALT DISNEY COMPANY
Selected Financial Statement and Other Data
Years Ending September 30

($ millions except per share data)	Year 13	Year 9
Income Statement		
Revenue	$ 8,529	$4,594
Operating expenses	(6,968)	(3,484)
Interest expense	(158)	(24)
Investment and interest income	186	67
Income (loss) from Euro Disney	(515)	0
Pretax income	1,074	1,153
Taxes	(403)	(450)
Net income	$ 671	$ 703
Earnings per share	$ 1.23	$ 1.27
Dividends per share	$ 0.23	$ 0.11
Balance Sheet		
Cash	$ 363	$ 381
Receivables	1,390	224
Inventories	609	909
Other	1,889	662
Current assets	4,251	2,176
Property, plant, and equipment, net	5,228	3,397
Other assets	2,272	1,084
Total assets	$11,751	$6,657
Current liabilities	$ 2,821	$1,262
Borrowings	2,386	861
Other liabilities	1,514	1,490
Stockholder's equity	5,030	3,044
Total liabilities and stockholder's equity	$11,751	$6,657
Cash Flow from Operations	$ 2,145	$1,275
Other Data		
Common shares outstanding (millions)	544	552
Closing price, common stock per share	$ 37.75	$30.22

Note: Total assets except "other" current assets, current liabilities, and other liabilities are considered operating, as is the Euro Disney loss.

Required:

a. Calculate and disaggregate Disney's return on common equity for *each* of the *two* fiscal years ending September 30, Year 9, and September 30, Year 13 (use years-end figures for any ratio computations typically using averages).

b. Drawing only on your answers to part (a) and the data available, identify the *two* components that contributed most to the observed change in Disney's return on common equity between Year 9 and Year 13. State *two* reasons for the observed change in *each* of the *two* components.

(CFA Adapted)

CASE 8–3

Analysis of Common-Size Profitability Information

The following data are excerpted from the annual report of **Lands' End:**   **Lands' End**

For the period ended	Year 9	Year 8	Year 7	Year 6	Year 5
Net sales..	100%	100%	100%	100%	100%
Cost of sales......................................	55.0	53.4	54.5	57.0	57.6
Gross profit...	45.0	46.6	45.5	43.0	42.4
Selling, general, and administrative........	39.7	38.8	37.9	38.0	36.0
Other expenses	3.0	2.7	3.0	2.0	2.8
Net income...	2.3%	5.1%	4.6%	3.0%	3.6%

Required:

a. Discuss three factors that determine the level of sales and the level of gross profit as a percentage of sales in the context of the operations of Lands' End.

b. Interpret the gross profit percentage (45% in fiscal Year 9) in simple terms and in the context of Lands' Ends operations.

c. Catalog mailing costs constitute a large percentage of the selling, general, and administrative costs for Lands' End. These costs have risen steadily as a percent of sales (only 32.4% in fiscal Year 4). Discuss drivers (determinants) of total catalog mailing costs and indicate ways that Lands' End can control these costs. With each suggestion, indicate how the level of sales might be affected.

CASE 8–4

Analysing Line-of-Business Data

Selected financial data for Petersen Corporation's revenue and income (contribution) are reproduced below:

Line of Business	Year 1	Year 2	Year 3	Year 4
Revenue				
Manufactured and engineered products				
Engineered equipment...	$ 30,341	$ 29,807	$ 32,702	$ 43,870
Other equipment	5,906	5,996	6,824	7,424
Parts, supplies, and services.............................	29,801	29,878	33,623	44,223
Total manufactured & engineered products........	66,048	65,681	73,149	95,517
Engineering and erecting services.....................	—	—	12,261	36,758
Total environmental systems group	66,048	65,681	85,410	132,275
Frye Copysystems	25,597	28,099	31,214	39,270
Sinclair & Valentine..	—	53,763	57,288	60,973
A. L. Garber	16,615	15,223	20,445	24,808
Total graphics group..	42,212	97,085	108,947	125,051
Total consolidated revenue	$108,260	$162,766	$194,357	$257,326

(continued)

Line of Business	Year 1	Year 2	Year 3	Year 4
Income				
Manufactured and engineered products..................	$ 3,785	$ 3,943	$ 9,209	$ 10,762
Engineering and erecting services	—	—	1,224	3,189
International operations...	2,265	2,269	2,030	2,323
Total environmental systems group	6,050	6,212	12,463	16,274
Frye Copysystems...	1,459	2,011	2,799	3,597
Sinclair & Valentine..	—	3,723	4,628	5,142
A. L. Garber	(295)	926	1,304	1,457
Total graphics group...	1,164	6,660	8,731	10,196
Total divisional income...	7,214	12,872	21,194	26,470
Unallocated expenses and taxes	(5,047)	(8,146)	(13,179)	(16,449)
Total income from continuing operations	$ 2,167	$ 4,726	$ 8,015	$10,021

CASE 8–4
(concluded)

Required:

a. Use common-size statements to analyze every division's (1) contribution to total consolidated revenue, (2) contribution to total divisional income, and (3) ratio of income to revenue.

b. Interpret and comment on the evidence revealed from your computations in *a*.

Sears and Wal-Mart

Wal-Mart and Sears (prior to its merger with Kmart), two large retailers in the U.S., offer an interesting study in contrasts. Wal-Mart has steadily grown to become the world's largest retail company and probably the most successful story in the history of retailing, Sears, on the other hand, had a long and checkered past. In the early 1990s the company almost went out of business. It subsequently reinvented itself, made a comeback (although somewhat bumpier than its investors and creditors would have liked) and, finally, merged with Kmart. The table below provides some comparative information on the two companies for 1999 (the financial statements are available in Exhibits I and II).

CASE 8–5
Analysis of Profitability, Turnover, and Leverage

$ Billions	Market Cap	Revenue	Total Assets	Equity	Net Income	Earnings Growth*	ROE	Dividend Payout	P/E Ratio	P/B Ratio
Sears	$ 11.21	$ 41.07	$36.95	$ 6.84	$1.45	5.5%	22.5%	24%	7.73	1.64
Wal-Mart	$244.02	$166.81	$70.349	$25.83	$5.38	17.5%	22.9%	16%	45.35	9.45

*Cannot compute form data provided

The differences between the two companies are striking, especially with respect to market valuation. While Wal-Mart's assets were twice that of Sears, its market capitalization at that time was more than 20 times that of Sears! The P/E and P/B ratios shed further light on this issue: the P/E and P/B ratios for Wal-Mart are almost six times as large as those of Sears!

This differential valuation is more surprising because Wal-Mart and Sears appeared to be equally profitable: in that year their ROEs were comparable at 22.5% and 22.9%, respectively. Part of the higher market valuation of Wal-Mart could be attributable to its superior growth: Wal-Mart's earnings grew at a compounded 17.5% per annum during the 1990s compared to 5.5% for Sears over a comparable period. However, earnings growth may not be the entire story. A more detailed analysis of the profitability of the two companies is called for, and it is important to analyze how each company generates this return.

CHECK
(2) Sears RNOA = 8.76%;
    Wal-Mart
    RNOA = 15.02%

Required:

1. Rearrange the income statement and the balance sheet of the two companies for 1999 and 1998 in the operating/ nonoperating format described in the text (for example, compute NOA, NFO and SE for the balance sheet, and compute NOPAT, NFE and NI for the income statement.)

2. Provide a breakdown of the ROEs of the two companies for 1999, showing the financial and operating leverages described in the text and their effects (you may use closing balance sheet data for computation of the return ratios). What does this analysis tell you about the inherent riskiness of the two companies?

3. Analyze the profit margin and asset turnover ratios of Sears and Wal-Mart by using line item information from the financial statements.

4. Sears's low return-on-assets ratios and high leverage could be partly attributable to its credit card operations—in effect, Sears is partly a financial institution. Exhibit III provides select financial information about Sears' credit card and other businesses obtained from segment information in notes to its financial statements. Using this information, analyze the relative returns on Sears's retailing and financing businesses and its impact on the overall risk-return profile of the company.

5. Summarize your conclusions for the difference between the market capitalization for Sears and Wal-Mart using the analysis you performed in parts 1 through 4.

Sears' Financial Statements

Exhibit I
■ ■ ■ ■ ■ ■ ■

SEARS CONSOLIDATED STATEMENTS OF INCOME

($ millions)	1999	1998
Revenues		
Merchandise sales and services	$36,728	$36,957
Credit revenues...	4,343	4,618
Total revenues	41,071	41,575
Costs and expenses		
Cost of sales, buying, and		
occupancy	27,212	27,444
Selling and administrative........................	8,418	8,384
Provision for uncollectible		
accounts...	871	1,287
Depreciation and amortization.................	848	830
Interest	1,268	1,423
Restructuring and impairment costs	41	352
Total costs and expenses......................	38,658	39,720
Operating income	**2,413**	**1,855**
Other income, net......................................	6	28
Income before income taxes,		
minority interest, and		
extraordinary loss	**2,419**	**1,883**
Income taxes...	904	766
Minority interest......................................	62	45
Income before extraordinary loss...........	**1,453**	**1,072**
Extraordinary loss on early		
extinguishment of		
debt, net of tax		24
Net income...	**$ 1,453**	**$ 1,048**

SEARS CONSOLIDATED BALANCE SHEETS

($ millions)	1999	1998
Assets		
Current assets		
Cash and cash equivalents	$ 729	$ 495
Retained interest in transferred credit card		
receivables...	3,144	4,294
Credit card receivables...	18,793	18,946
Less allowance for uncollectible accounts	760	974
Net credit card receivables	18,033	17,972
Other receivables..	404	397
Merchandise inventories...	5,069	4,816
Prepaid expenses and deferred charges	579	506
Deferred income taxes	709	791
Total current assets...	28,667	29,271
Property and equipment		
Land	370	395
Buildings and improvements...	5,837	5,530
Furniture, fixtures, and equipment	5,209	4,871
Capitalized leases	496	530
Gross property and equipment	11,912	11,326
Less accumulated depreciation	5,462	4,946
Total property and equipment, net.	6,450	6,380
Deferred income taxes...	367	572
Other assets..	1,470	1,452
Total assets	**$36,954**	**$37,675**
Liabilities		
Current liabilities		
Short-term borrowings...	$ 2,989	$ 4,624
Current portion of long-term debt and		
capitalized lease obligations	2,165	1,414
Accounts payable and other liabilities	6,992	6,732
Unearned revenues	971	928
Other taxes...	584	524
Total current liabilities...	13,701	14,222
Long-term debt and capitalized lease obligations	12,884	13,631
Postretirement benefits..	2,180	2,346
Minority interest and other liabilities	1,350	1,410
Total liabilities...	30,115	31,609
Shareholders' equity		
Common shares ($0.75 par value per share,		
1,000 shares authorized, 369.1 and		
383.5 shares outstanding)	323	323
Capital in excess of par value	3,554	3,583
Retained earnings..	5,952	4,848
Treasury stock—at cost	(2,569)	(2,089)
Deferred ESOP expense	(134)	(175)
Accumulated other comprehensive income	(287)	(424)
Total shareholders' equity	6,839	6,066
Total liabilities and shareholders' equity	**$36,954**	**$37,675**

Exhibit II   Wal-Mart's Financial Statements

■ ■ ■ ■ ■ ■ ■

WAL-MART INCOME STATEMENT

($ millions)	1999	1998
Revenues		
Net sales	$165,013	$137,634
Other income—net	1,796	1,574
	166,809	139,208
Cost and expenses		
Cost of sales	129,664	108,725
Operating, selling and general and administrative expenses	27,040	22,363
Interest costs		
Debt	756	529
Capital leases	266	268
	157,726	131,885
Income before income taxes, minority interest, equity in unconsolidated subsidiaries, and cumulative effect of accounting change	9,083	7,323
Provision for income taxes		
Current	3,476	3,380
Deferred	(138)	(640)
	3,338	2,740
Income before minority interest, equity in unconsolidated subsidiaries, and cumulative effect of accounting change	5,745	4,583
Minority interest and equity in unconsolidated subsidiaries	(170)	(153)
Income before cumulative effect of accounting change	5,575	4,430
Cumulative effect of accounting change, net of tax benefit of $119	(198)	
Net income	$ 5,377	$4,430

WAL-MART CONSOLIDATED BALANCE SHEETS

($ millions)	1999	1998
Assets		
Current assets		
Cash and cash equivalents	$ 1,856	$ 1,879
Receivables	1,341	1,118
Inventories		
At replacement cost	20,171	17,549
Less LIFO reserve	378	473
Inventories at LIFO cost	19,793	17,076
Prepaid expenses and other	1,366	1,059
	24,356	21,132
Total current assets		
Property, plant, and equipment, at cost		
Land	8,785	5,219
Building and improvements	21,169	16,061
Fixtures and equipment	10,362	9,296
Transportation equipment	747	553
	41,063	31,129
Less accumulated depreciation	8,224	7,455
Net property, plant, and equipment	32,839	23,674
Property under capital lease		
Property under capital lease	4,285	3,335
Less accumulated amortization	1,155	1,036
Net property under capital leases	3,130	2,299
Other assets and deferred charges		
Net goodwill and other acquired intangible assets	9,392	2,538
Other assets and deferred charges	632	353
Total Assets	$70,349	$49,996
Liabilities and Shareholders' Equity		
Current liabilities		
Commercial paper	$ 3,323	$ —
Accounts payable	13,105	10,257
Accrued liabilities	6,161	4,998
Accrued income taxes	1,129	501
Long-term debt due within one year	1,964	900
Obligations under capital leases due within one year	121	106
Total current liabilities	25,803	16,762
Long-term debt	13,672	6,908
Long-term obligations under capital leases	3,002	2,699
Deferred income taxes and other	759	716
Minority interest	1,279	1,799
Shareholders' equity		
Preferred stock ($ .10 par value; 100 shares authorized, none issued)		
Common stock ($ .10 par value; 5,500 shares authorized, 4,457 and 4,448 issued and outstanding in 2000 and 1999, respectively)	446	445
Capital in excess of par value	714	435
Retained earnings	25,129	20,741
Other accumulated comprehensive income	(455)	(509)
Total shareholders' equity	25,834	21,112
Total liabilities and shareholders' equity	$70,349	$49,996

Select Segment Information—Sears

Exhibit III

($ millions)	1999			1998		
	Credit	Others	Total	Credit	Others	Total
Revenue	$ 4,085	$36,986	$41,071	$ 4,369	$37,206	$41,575
Depreciation	14	792	848	13	784	830
Interest revenue	0	59	59	0	59	59
Interest expense	1,116	211	1,327	1,244	238	1,482
Operating income	1,347	1,388	2,413	1,144	922	1,855
Total assets	$20,622	$14,541	$36,954	$21,605	$25,364	$37,675

Note: Columns for Others and Credit may not add up to Total because of corporate expenses.

9

PROSPECTIVE ANALYSIS

■ ■ ■ ■ ■ ■ ■

A LOOK BACK `<`

The preceding chapter dealt with analysis of company returns—both profitability and return on invested capital. Emphasis was on rate of return measures, disaggregation of returns, and accounting analysis of income components. That return-based chapter complements later chapters that focus on risk, including liquidity and solvency.

A LOOK AT THIS CHAPTER `●`

We study forecasting and pro forma analysis of financial statements in this chapter. We provide a detailed example of the forecasting process to project the income statement, the balance sheet, and the statement of cash flows. We describe the relevance of forecasting for security valuation and provide an example using forecasted financial statements to implement a valuation model. We discuss the concept of value drivers and their reversion to long-run equilibrium levels.

A LOOK AHEAD `>`

Chapter 10 expands our analysis of a company to short-term liquidity, capital structure, and long-term solvency. We explain liquidity and describe analysis tools such as accounting-based ratios, turnover, and operating activity measures of liquidity. We also analyze capital structure and interpret its implications for company performance and solvency.

LEARNING OBJECTIVES

- Describe the importance of prospective analysis.

- Explain the process of projecting the income statement, the balance sheet, and the statement of cash flows.

- Discuss and illustrate the importance of sensitivity analysis.

- Describe the implementation of the projection process for valuation of equity securities.

- Discuss the concept of value drivers and their reversion to long-run equilibrium levels.

Fundamental Analysis Is Back

NEW YORK—For years, two great armies of investors have done battle on Wall Street. In one camp stand growth investors, willing to pay dearly for companies they believe can generate big profits for years to come. In the other camp are value investors. They'll buy only into companies with real assets and solid earnings in the here and now—and at bargain prices. As yet, value investing is more a framework than a set of codified rules. It relies more on forecasting, even though Benjamin Graham and David Dodd, who laid the principles of value investing, frowned on forecasts.

BusinessWeek (2004) reports that "When you look at the Russell 1000 Value and Russell 1000 Growth indexes, which are now 25 years old, value beats growth by three percentage points a year, on average. Economists . . . using their own indexes,

show value beating growth by an average 2.6% a year over 75 years." Whether you use growth or value criteria, it's more important to pay attention to the fundamentals of a company's business than it is to set investment criteria based solely on ratios like price-to-earnings or PE to sales growth.

Value investors' descriptions of their investing styles are also

> **. . . pay attention to the fundamentals of a company's business . . .**

varied. But if you listen closely, the bottom line is the same—assessment of fundamentals. In the broadest terms, value investors are looking for companies that trade at less than their real value in the hope that the value is eventually recognized by other

market players and reflected in higher stock prices.

To identify such latent value, investors need to examine companies' fundamental business prospects. "You want a company where something is going to change, either externally, like a fundamental change in its industry, or internally, like a change in management," says the portfolio manager of the Oppenheimer Value Fund.

Prospective analysis is a central component of value investing. It relies on a sound understanding of the company's fundamentals and its economic environment. From this base, forecasts of future performance are developed that provide the basis for valuation of stock price. Whichever investing philosophy we subscribe to, the message is clear: understand where the company's business model and strategic plan are taking it.

PREVIEW OF CHAPTER 9

Prospective analysis is the final step in the financial statement analysis process. It can be undertaken only after the historical financial statements have been properly adjusted to accurately reflect the economic performance of the company. As discussed in previous chapters, these adjustments may include, for example, eliminating transitory items in the income statement or reallocating them to past or future years, capitalizing (expensing) items that have been expensed (capitalized) by management, capitalizing operating leases, equity method investments, and other forms of off-balance sheet financing, and so forth. Prospective analysis includes forecasting of the balance sheet, income statement and statement of cash flows.

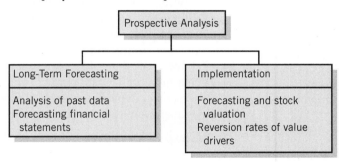

Prospective analysis is central to security valuation. Both the free cash flow and residual income valuation models described in Chapter 1 require estimates of future financial statements. The residual income model, for example, requires projections of future net profits and book values of equity in order to estimate current stock price. Prospective analysis is also useful to examine the viability of companies' strategic plans. For this, we analyze whether a company will be able to generate sufficient cash flows from operations to finance expected growth or whether it will be required to seek debt or equity financing in the future. We are also interested in analyzing whether current strategic plans will yield the benefits forecasted by company management. And finally, prospective analysis is useful to creditors to assess a company's ability to meet its debt service requirements.

Our discussion of projection mechanics centers on forecasts of the financial statements for Target Corporation. We provide a detailed explanation of the forecasting process in the next section.

·······THE PROJECTION PROCESS

We begin our discussion with a comprehensive example of the projection process using the financial statements of Target Corporation.

Projecting Financial Statements

The projection process begins with the income statement, followed by the balance sheet and the statement of cash flows.

Projected Income Statement

The income statements of Target as of 2003–2005 are provided in Exhibit 9.1 together with selected ratios. The projection process begins with an expected growth in sales. In this example we use historical trends to predict future levels. A more detailed analysis would incorporate outside information such as the following:

- **Expected level of macroeconomic activity.** Since Target customers' purchases are influenced by the level of personal disposable income, our analysis might incorporate estimates relating to the overall growth in the economy and the expected growth of retail sales in particular. For example, if the economy is in a cyclical upturn, we might be comfortable in projecting an increase in sales greater than that of the recent past.
- **The competitive landscape.** Has the number of competitors increased? Or, have weaker rivals ceased operations? Changes in the competitive landscape will influence our projections of unit sales as well as Target's ability to raise prices. Both of these will impact top line growth.
- **New versus old store mix.** New stores typically enjoy significantly greater sales increases than older stores since they may tap poorly served markets or provide a more up-to-date product mix than existing competitors. Older stores, by comparison, typically grow at the overall rate of growth in the local economy. Our analysis must consider, therefore, expansion plans announced by management.

We begin with an assumption that sales will grow at 11.455% in 2006, the same growth rate as in 2005. Once the projection has been completed, sensitivity analysis will examine the implications of higher and lower growth rates on our forecasts.

Target Corporation Income Statements

Exhibit 9.1

(in millions)	2005	2004	2003
Sales	$46,839	$42,025	$37,410
Cost of goods sold	31,445	28,389	25,498
Gross profit	15,394	13,636	11,912
Selling, general and administrative expense	10,534	9,379	8,134
Depreciation and amortization expense	1,259	1,098	967
Interest expense	570	556	584
Income before tax	3,031	2,603	2,227
Income tax expense	1,146	984	851
Income (loss) from extraordinary items and discontinued operations	1,313	190	247
Net income	$ 3,198	$ 1,809	$ 1,623
Outstanding shares	891	912	910
Selected Ratios (in percent)			
Sales growth	11.455%	12.336%	
Gross profit margin	32.866	32.447	
Selling, general and administrative expense/Sales	22.490	22.318	
Depreciation expense/Gross prior-year PP&E	6.333	5.245	
Interest expense/Prior-year long-term debt	5.173	4.982	
Income tax expense/Pretax income	37.809	37.803	

Target's gross profit margin has increased slightly to 32.866% of sales. For our purposes, we assume 32.866%, the most recent gross profit margin. In practice, our estimate of gross profit margin will be influenced, in part, by the strength of the economy and the level of competition in Target's markets. For example, in an increasingly competitive environment we might question the company's ability to increase gross profit margin as selling prices will be difficult to increase. Selling, general, and administrative (SG&A) expenses have also remained constant at about 22% of sales. Our projection of SG&A expense is 22.49% of sales, the most recent experience. In practice, we might examine individual expense items and estimate each individually, incorporating knowledge we have gained from the MD&A section of the financial statements or from outside sources. For a retailing company like Target, trends in wage and occupancy costs and advertising expenses require greater scrutiny.

Depreciation expense is a significant line item and should be projected separately. It is a fixed expense and is a function of the amount of depreciable assets. In recent years, Target has reported depreciation expense of approximately 6% of the balance of beginning-of-year gross property, plant, and equipment. Our projection assumes 6.333% of the 2005 property, plant, and equipment (PP&E) balance, the most recent experience.

Similarly, we compute the historical ratio of interest expense relative to beginning-of-year interest-bearing debt. This ratio has recently increased slightly over the past two years from 4.982% to 5.173%. Our projection assumes 5.173% of the beginning-of-year balance of interest-bearing debt. In practice, our estimates will incorporate projections of future levels of long-term interest rates. Finally, tax expense as a percentage of pretax income has been constant at the most recent level of 37.809%, used in our projection.

Exhibit 9.2

■ ■ ■ ■ ■ ■ ■

Target Corporation Projected Income Statement

(in millions)	Forecasting Step	2006 Estimate
Income statement		
Total revenues	1	$52,204
Cost of goods sold	3	35,047
Gross profit	2	17,157
Selling, general, and administrative expense	4	11,741
Depreciation and amortization expense	5	1,410
Interest expense	6	493
Income before tax	7	3,513
Income tax expense	8	1,328
Income (loss) from extraordinary items and discontinued operations	9	0
Net income	10	$ 2,185
Outstanding shares		891
Forecasting Assumptions (in percent)		
Sales growth		11.455%
Gross profit margin		32.866
Selling, general, and administrative expense/Sales		22.490
Depreciation expense/Gross prior-year PP&E		6.333
Interest expense/Prior-year long-term debt		5.173
Income tax expense/Pretax income		37.809

Given these assumptions, Target's projected income statement for 2006 is presented in Exhibit 9.2. The following are the steps in the projection of this statement:

1. Sales: $52,204 = $46,839 × 1.11455
2. Gross profit: $17,157 = $52,204 × 32.866%
3. Cost of goods sold: $35,047 = $52,204 − $17,157
4. Selling, general, and administrative: $11,741 = $52,204 × 22.49%
5. Depreciation and amortization: $1,410 = $22,272 (beginning-period PP&E gross) × 6.333%
6. Interest: $493 = $9,538 (beginning-period interest-bearing debt) × 5.173%
7. Income before tax: $3,513 = $17,157 − $11,741 − $1,410 − $493
8. Tax expense: $1,328 = $3,513 × 37.809%
9. Extraordinary and discontinued items: none
10. Net income: $2,185 = $3,513 − $1,328

Projected Balance Sheet

The balance sheets of Target for 2003–2005 are provided in Exhibit 9.3 together with selected ratios. The forecast of the 2006 balance sheet involves the following steps:

1. Project current assets other than cash, using projected sales or cost of goods sold and appropriate turnover ratios as described below.
2. Project PP&E increases with capital expenditures estimate derived from historical trends or information obtained in the MD&A section of the annual report.

Target Corporation Balance Sheets

Exhibit 9.3

■ ■ ■ ■ ■ ■ ■

(in millions)	2005	2004	2003
Cash	$ 2,245	$ 708	$ 758
Receivables	5,069	4,621	5,565
Inventories	5,384	4,531	4,760
Other current assets	1,224	3,092	852
Total current assets...	13,922	12,952	11,935
Property, plant, and equipment (PP&E)...................	22,272	19,880	20,936
Accumulated depreciation	5,412	4,727	5,629
Net property, plant, and equipment	16,860	15,153	15,307
Other assets	1,511	3,311	1,361
Total assets	$32,293	$31,416	$28,603
Accounts payable...	$ 5,779	$ 4,956	$ 4,684
Current portion of long-term debt............................	504	863	975
Accrued expenses	1,633	1,288	1,545
Income taxes & other	304	1,207	319
Total current liabilities	8,220	8,314	7,523
Deferred income taxes and other liabilities......................	2,010	1,815	1,451
Long-term debt...	9,034	10,155	10,186
Total liabilities	19,264	20,284	19,160
Common stock	74	76	76
Additional paid-in capital..	1,810	1,530	1,256
Retained earnings	11,145	9,526	8,111
Shareholders' equity..	13,029	11,132	9,443
Total liabilities and net worth	$32,293	$31,416	$28,603
Selected Ratios			
Accounts receivable turnover rate....................................	9.240	9.094	6.722
Inventory turnover rate...	5.840	6.266	5.357
Accounts payable turnover rate	5.441	5.728	5.444
Accrued expenses turnover rate	28.683	32.628	24.214
Taxes payable/Tax expense..	26.527%	122.663%	37.485%
Dividends per share	$ 0.310	$ 0.260	$ 0.240
Capital expenditures (CAPEX)—in millions......................	3,012	2,671	3,189
CAPEX/Sales	6.431%	6.356%	8.524%

3. Project current liabilities other than debt, using projected sales or cost of goods sold and appropriate turnover ratios as described below.
4. Obtain current maturities of long-term debt from the long-term debt footnote.
5. Assume other short-term indebtedness is unchanged from prior year balance unless they have exhibited noticeable trends.
6. Assume initial long-term debt balance is equal to the prior period long-term debt less current maturities from (4) above.

7. Assume other long-term obligations are equal to the prior year's balance unless they have exhibited noticeable trends.

8. Assume initial estimate of common stock is equal to the prior year's balance.

9. Assume retained earnings are equal to the prior year's balance plus (minus) net profit (loss) and less expected dividends.

10. Assume other equity accounts are equal to the prior year's balance unless they have exhibited noticeable trends.

The sum of steps (3)−(10) yields total liabilities and equity. Total assets are, then, set equal to this amount and the resulting cash figure is computed as total assets less (1) and (2). At this point, cash will either be too high or too low. Long-term debt and common stock are then adjusted for issuances (repurchases) as appropriate to yield the desired level of cash and to maintain historical financial leverage. These adjustments indicate the degree of financing required to support the company's growth.

To begin, the projection of receivables, inventories, PP&E, accounts payable, and accrued expenses uses sales and cost of goods sold projections together with turnover rates for these accounts. For example, the receivables turnover rate based on ending accounts receivable is:

$$\text{Accounts receivable turnover rate} = \frac{\text{Sales}}{\text{Accounts receivable balance}}$$

Next, the projected accounts receivables can be computed as:

$$\text{Projected accounts receivable} = \frac{\text{Projected sales}}{\text{Accounts receivable turnover rate}}$$

Our projection of accounts receivables assumes the most recent turnover rate of 9.24.

Similarly, we use the most recent inventory turnover rate (based on ending inventories) of 5.84 together with cost of goods sold to project inventories. A more refined level of analysis might examine Target's ability to sell off accounts receivable to special purpose entities. And for inventories, we might examine inventory turnover rates for seasoned versus new stores and the anticipated growth of new stores. Existing inventories might be projected to grow with the level of anticipated sales growth. Additional inventories required for new stores would be added to this amount.

Property, plant, and equipment is estimated as the prior year's gross PP&E balance plus historical capital expenditures as a percentage of sales. Historical capital expenditures are obtained from the statement of cash flows. Over the past three years, capital expenditures as a percentage of sales have remained steady at about 6.4% of sales. We use 6.43% to estimate capital expenditures for 2006. Once the projection is complete, this percentage can be subsequently adjusted to examine the financial implications of higher (lower) levels of capital expenditures.

Accounts payable estimates are based on historical payable turns and cost of goods sold. We use the most recent turnover ratio (based on ending accounts payable) of 5.441 to estimate 2006 payables. Similarly, accrued expenses as a percentage of sales are estimated with the most recent accrual turnover rate of 28.683. Finally, taxes payable are estimated based on the historical relation of payables to tax expense, and we use the most recent level of 26.527% to project 2006 taxes payable.

A schedule of current maturities of long-term debt is provided in the footnotes. We use the amount for 2006 referenced in the schedule. Long-term debt, then, is initially estimated as the previous balance of long-term debt less our estimate of its current maturities. This level of debt will be adjusted to achieve the desired balance of cash and financial leverage once the initial balance sheet is constructed. Likewise, common and treasury stock are assumed to be equal to the prior year's balances.

Target Corporation Projected Balance Sheet   *Exhibit 9.4*

■ ■ ■ ■ ■ ■ ■

(in millions)	Forecasting Step	2006 Estimate	2005
Cash	17	$ 1,402	$ 2,245
Receivables	1	5,650	5,069
Inventories	2	6,001	5,384
Other current assets	3	1,224	1,224
Total current assets		14,277	13,922
Property, plant, and equipment	4	25,629	22,272
Accumulated depreciation	5	6,822	5,412
Net property, plant, and equipment	6	18,807	16,860
Other assets	7	1,511	1,511
Total assets		$34,595	$32,293
Accounts payable	8	$ 6,441	$ 5,779
Current portion of long-term debt	9	751	504
Accrued expenses	10	1,820	1,633
Income taxes & other	11	352	304
Total current liabilities		9,364	8,220
Deferred income taxes and other liabilities	12	2,010	2,010
Long-term debt	13	8,283	9,034
Total liabilities		19,657	19,264
Common stock	14	74	74
Additional paid-in capital	15	1,810	1,810
Retained earnings	16	13,054	11,145
Shareholders' equity		14,938	13,029
Total liabilities and net worth		$34,595	$32,293

Selected Ratios

		2006 Estimate	2005
Accounts receivable turnover rate		9.240	9.240
Inventory turnover rate		5.840	5.840
Accounts payable turnover rate		5.441	5.441
Accrued expenses turnover rate		28.683	28.683
Taxes payable/Tax expense		26.527%	26.527%
Dividends per share		$ 0.310	$ 0.310
Capital expenditures (CAPEX)—in millions		3,357	3,012
CAPEX/Sales		6.431%	6.431%

Given these assumptions, Target's projected balance sheet for 2006 is presented in Exhibit 9.4. The following are the steps in the projection of this statement (data sources in parentheses):

1. Receivables: $5,650 = $52,204 (Sales)/9.24 (Receivable turnover).
2. Inventories: $6,001 = $35,047 (Cost of goods sold)/5.84 (Inventory turnover).
3. Other current assets: no change.
4. PP&E: $25,629 = $22,272 (Prior year's balance) + $3,357 (Capital expenditure estimate: estimated sales of $52,204 × 6.431% CAPEX/sales percentage).

5. Accumulated depreciation: $6,822 = $5,412 (Prior balance) + $1,410 (Depreciation estimate).
6. Net PP&E: $18,807 = $25,629 − $6,822.
7. Other long-term assets: no change.
8. Accounts payable: $6,441 = $35,047 (Cost of goods sold)/5.441 (Payable turnover).
9. Current portion of long-term debt: amount reported in long-term debt footnote as the current maturity for 2006.
10. Accrued expenses: $1,820 = $52,204 (Sales)/28.683 (Accrued expense turnover).
11. Taxes payable: $352 = $1,328 (Tax expense) × 26.527% (Tax payable/Tax expense).
12. Deferred income taxes and other liabilities: no change.
13. Long-term debt: $8,283 = $9,034 (Prior year's long-term debt) − $751 (Scheduled current maturities from step 9).
14. Common stock: no change.
15. Additional paid-in capital: no change.
16. Retained earnings: $13,054 = $11,145 (Prior year's retained earnings) + $2,185 (Projected net income) − $276 (Estimated dividends of $0.31 per share × 891 million shares).
17. Cash: amount needed to balance total liabilities and equity less steps (1)–(7).

The initial balance sheet estimate yields a cash balance of $1,402 million. This represents 4.1% of projected total assets. Although lower than the 2005 level of 7% of total assets, this cash balance is in line with prior percentages in the 2–3% range. If the estimated cash balance is much higher or lower, further adjustments can be made to (1) invest excess cash in marketable securities (projected income will need to be adjusted for the additional nonoperating investment income), or (2) reduce long-term debt and/or equity proportionately so as to keep the degree of financial leverage consistent with prior years. If the level of cash is too low, additional long-term debt and/or common stock can be increased as required, keeping the level of financial leverage constant. Our projection indicates that Target will be able to fund its growth with available funds and internally generated cash.

Projected Statement of Cash Flows

The projected statement of cash flows is computed from the projected income statement and projected balance sheet as discussed in Chapter 7. It is presented in Exhibit 9.5. The projected net cash flows from operations of $3,295 million partially finance the capital expenditures of $3,357 million, reductions of long-term debt in the amount of $504 million, and dividends of $276 million. The remaining deficit results in an $843 million reduction in cash.

Sensitivity Analysis

The projected financial statements are primarily based on expected relations between income statement and balance sheet accounts. In this example, we used the most recent ratios as Target's operations are fairly stable and we are assuming no significant changes in operating strategy.

It is often useful, however, to vary these assumptions in order to analyze their impact on financing requirements, return on assets and equity, and so on. For example, if we assume increases in capital expenditures to 7.5% of sales, capital expenditures will rise to $3.9 billion, and the cash balance will decline to $845 million, 2.4% of total assets and

<table>
<tr><td colspan="2">Target Corporation Projected Statement of Cash Flows</td><td>Exhibit 9.5</td></tr>
</table>

Target Corporation Projected Statement of Cash Flows　　　　**Exhibit 9.5**

■■■■■■■

(in millions)	2006 Estimate
Net income	$2,185
Items to adjust income to cash flows	
Depreciation and amortization	1,410
Receivables	(581)
Inventories	(617)
Accounts payable	662
Accrued expenses	187
Income taxes and other	48
Net cash flow from operations	3,294
Capital expenditures	(3,357)
Net cash flow from investing activities	(3,357)
Long-term debt	(504)
Dividends	(276)
Net cash flow from financing activities	(780)
Net change in cash	$ (843)
Beginning cash	2,245
Ending cash	$1,402

below the level of prior years. In that case, external financing in the form of debt and/or equity will be required. Similar increases in financing requirements would also result from a decrease in receivable or inventory turns. Analysts often prepare several projections to examine best (worst) case scenarios in addition to the most likely case. This sensitivity analysis highlights which assumptions have the greatest impact on financial results and, consequently, help to identify those areas requiring greater scrutiny.

Application of Prospective Analysis in the Residual Income Valuation Model

As we stated at the outset of this chapter, prospective analysis is central to security analysis. The residual income valuation model, for example, defines equity value at time t as the sum of current book value and the present value of all future expected residual income:

$$V_t = \mathrm{BV}_t + \frac{\mathrm{E}(\mathrm{RI}_{t+1})}{(1+k)^1} + \frac{\mathrm{E}(\mathrm{RI}_{t+2})}{(1+k)^2} + \frac{\mathrm{E}(\mathrm{RI}_{t+3})}{(1+k)^3} + \cdots$$

where BV_t is book value at the end of period t, RI_{t+n} is residual income in period $t+n$, and k is cost of capital (see Chapter 1). **Residual income** at time t is defined as comprehensive net income minus a charge on beginning book value, that is, $\mathrm{RI}_t = \mathrm{NI}_t - (k \times \mathrm{BV}_{t-1})$.

Exhibit 9.6   **Valuation of Syminex Common Stock**

	HISTORICAL FIGURES		FORECAST HORIZON					TERMINAL YEAR
	2004	2005	2006	2007	2008	2009	2010	2011
Sales growth..	8.50%	8.6957%	8.90%	9.10%	8.00%	7.00%	6.00%	3.50%
Net profit margin (Net income/Sales)	9.05%	9.1554%	9.20%	9.40%	9.40%	9.40%	9.40%	9.40%
Net working capital turnover (Sales/Avg. NWC)....	22.7353	11.8271	11.8271	11.8271	11.8271	11.8271	11.8271	11.8271
Fixed assets turnover (Sales/Avg. fixed assets) ...	1.8341	1.9878	1.9878	1.9878	1.9878	1.9878	1.9878	1.9878
Total operating assets/Total equity....................	2.3362	2.5186	2.5186	2.5186	2.5186	2.5186	2.5186	2.5186
Cost of equity			12.5%					
($ thousands)								
Sales	$81,324	$88,396	$96,263	$105,023	$113,425	$121,365	$128,647	$133,149
Net income	7,360	8,093	8,856	9,872	10,662	11,408	12,093	12,516
Net working capital	3,577	7,474	8,139	8,880	9,590	10,262	10,877	11,258
Fixed assets...	44,340	44,469	48,427	52,834	57,060	61,054	64,718	66,983
Total operating assets	47,917	51,943	56,566	61,713	66,651	71,316	75,595	78,241
Long-term liabilities..	27,406	31,319	34,106	37,210	40,187	43,000	45,580	47,175
Total stockholders' equity................................	20,511	20,624	22,460	24,503	26,464	28,316	30,015	31,066
Residual Income Computation								
Net income			$ 8,856	$ 9,872	$ 10,662	$ 11,408	$ 12,093	$ 12,516
Beginning equity			$20,624	$ 22,460	$ 24,503	$ 26,464	$ 28,316	$ 30,015
Required equity return.....................................			12.5%	12.5%	12.5%	12.5%	12.5%	12.5%
Expected income...			$ 2,578	$ 2,807	$ 3,063	$ 3,308	$ 3,540	$ 3,752
Residual income..			$ 6,278	$ 7,065	$ 7,599	$ 8,100	$ 8,553	$ 8,764
Discount factor...			0.8889	0.7901	0.7023	0.6243	0.5549	
Present value of residual income.......................			$ 5,581	$ 5,582	$ 5,337	$ 5,057	$ 4,746	
Cumulative present value of residual income....			$ 5,581	$ 11,163	$ 16,500	$ 21,557	$ 26,303	
Terminal value of residual income....................							$ 54,039	
Beginning book value of equity.........................							$ 20,624	
Value of equity..							$100,966	
Common shares outstanding (thousands).........							1,737	
Value of equity per share							$ 58.13	

The valuation process requires estimates of future net income and the book value of stockholder's equity. Exhibit 9.6 provides an example for the valuation of Syminex Corp. common stock as of 2005. In this relatively simple form, the valuation model requires estimates of six parameters:

- Sales growth.
- Net profit margin (Net income/Sales).
- Net working capital turnover (Sales/Net working capital).
- Fixed-asset turnover (Sales/Fixed assets).
- Financial leverage (Operating assets/Equity).
- Cost of equity capital.

Sales are expected to grow at 8.9% and 9.1% in 2006 and 2007, then trail off with growth rates of 8%, 7%, and 6% for the next three years. This five-year period is the forecast horizon, the period of time about which we have the greatest confidence in our estimates. We assume that sales will continue to grow with the long-run rate of inflation, 3.5%, thereafter.

Net profit margins are expected to increase to 9.2% and 9.4% over the next two years and to level off at that percentage thereafter. Net working capital and fixed-asset turnover rates are expected to remain at present levels of 11.8271 and 1.9878 times, respectively. Financial leverage is also expected to remain constant at the current level of 2.5186. Finally, the cost of equity capital is estimated at 12.5%.[1]

Net income is estimated using projected sales and projected net profit margin (Sales × Net profit margin). Net working capital and fixed assets are estimated using projected sales and the estimated turnover rates for net working capital and fixed assets, respectively (Sales/Turnover rate). Finally, equity is projected using the operating assets to equity ratio (Operating assets = Net working capital + Fixed assets).

Given these estimates, residual income for 2006 is estimated as projected net income less beginning of the year equity × the cost of equity capital of 12.5%,

$$\$6,278 = \$8,856 - (\$20,624 \times .125)$$

Subsequent years during the forecast horizon are computed similarly. Each year during the forecast horizon is, then, discounted at the cost of equity capital (12.5%). For example, the discount factor for the second year is computed as:

$$0.7901 = \frac{1}{1.125^2}$$

Present values for each year in the forecast horizon are summed to yield a cumulative present value through 2010 of $26,303.

The residual income projected in 2011 is assumed to grow at the rate of inflation (3.5%). The present value of this annuity, discounted to 2005 is:[2]

$$\$54,039 = \frac{\$8,764}{(.125 - .035)(1.125)^5}$$

The estimated value of Syminex common stock as of 2005 is equal to the book value of its stockholder's equity ($20,624) plus the present value of its residual income ($26,303 + $54,039) for a total of $100,966. Given outstanding shares of 1,737, per share value of Syminex common stock is $58.13.

Valuation of equity shares is critically dependent on the projection process. As discussed above, our valuation should closely examine the sensitivity of share price estimates to underlying assumptions in the projections.

---

[1] The cost of equity capital is given by the capital asset pricing model (CAPM): $r_e = r_f + \beta (r_m - r_f)$, where β is the beta of the stock (an estimate of its variability and reported by several services such as Standard and Poor's), r_f is the risk-free rate (commonly assumed as the 10-year government bond rate), and r_m is the expected return to the entire market. The expression $(r_m - r_f)$ is the "spread" of equities over the risk-free rate, often assumed to be around 5%. Given a 4% 10-year government bond rate and a β = 1.7, the cost of equity capital for Syminex is: $k = 4\% + 1.7 (5\%) = 12.5\%$.

[2] The present value (PV) of annuity (A) expected to grow at g% per year and discounted at k% is given by $PV = \dfrac{A}{k - g}$. The remaining term in the denominator (1.125^5) discounts this PV, which occurs in Year 5, back to the present at the 12.5% cost of capital.

Trends in Value Drivers

The residual income model defines stock price as the book value of stockholders' equity plus the present value of expected residual income (RI), where $RI_t = NI_t - (k \times BV_{t-1})$. Residual income can also be expressed in ratio form as,

$$RI = (ROE_t - k) \times BV_{t-1}$$

where $ROE = NI_t/BV_{t-1}$. This form highlights the fact that stock price is only impacted so long as $ROE \neq k$. In equilibrium, competitive forces will tend to drive rates of return (ROE) to cost (k) so that abnormal profits are competed away. The estimation of stock price, then, amounts to the projection of the reversion of ROE to its long-run value for a particular company and industry.

Exhibit 9.7 presents ROE performance for quintiles of all firms in the Compustat data base. For each year, portfolios of firms in each ROE quintile are formed and the ROEs for each firm in the portfolio are tracked for the subsequent 10 years. The graph presents the median value for each portfolio. Two observations are evident:

1. ROEs tend to revert to a long-run equilibrium. This reflects the forces of competition. Furthermore, the reversion rate for the least profitable firms is greater than that for the most profitable firms. And finally, reversion rates for the most extreme levels of ROE are greater than those for firms at more moderate levels of ROE.

2. The reversion is incomplete. That is, there remains a difference of about 12% between the highest and lowest ROE firms even after 10 years. This may be the result of two factors: differences in risk that are reflected in differences in their costs of capital (k); or, greater (lesser) degrees of conservatism in accounting policies.

Exhibit 9.7 reveals that most of the reversion is complete after about 5 years. This lends support to our use of a 5-year forecast horizon for Syminex as there is little impact on share price after the point at which $ROE = k$ regardless of the growth rate assumption for sales.

ROE is considered a *value driver* since it is the variable that directly affects stock price. ROA is further disaggregated into profit margin and turnover (see Chapter 8). These components are also value drivers and are two of the input items we project in

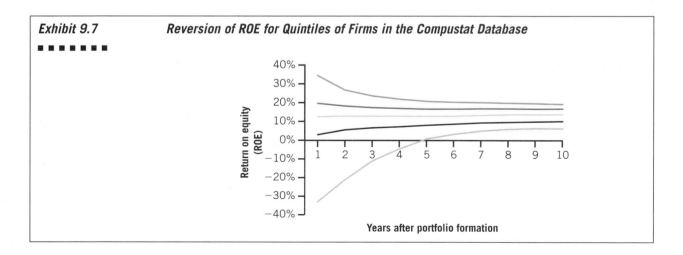

Exhibit 9.7

Reversion of ROE for Quintiles of Firms in the Compustat Database

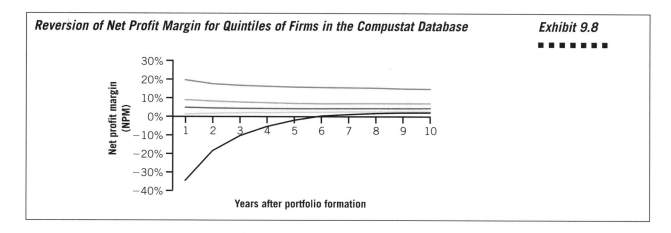

Reversion of Net Profit Margin for Quintiles of Firms in the Compustat Database   *Exhibit 9.8*

Net profit margin (NPM)

Years after portfolio formation

our valuation of Syminex. It is useful, therefore, to understand the reversion rates for these components as well.

Exhibit 9.8 presents a graph highlighting the reversion of net profit margins (NPM) for quintiles of firms in the Compustat database. It has been constructed similarly to the ROE graph in Exhibit 9.7. The marked reversion rates for the highest and lowest NPM firms are evident. In addition, the reversion rate for the lowest profit firms is greater than that for the most profitable firms and the reversion rates for both extreme groups are greater than those for less extreme profit firms. Finally, there remains a difference between the highest and lowest NPM portfolios at the end of 10 years of approximately the same spread as that for ROE. Much of the reversion in ROE, then, appears to be driven by reversion in NPM.

Total asset turnover (TAT) is the second component of ROA. In Exhibit 9.9 we present reversion rates for TAT that are constructed on the same basis as the previous graphs. Although some reversion is evident, it is much less than that of the profitability measures. In addition, there is a wide range of asset turnover rates between the highest and lowest turnover firms. This reflects varying degrees of capital intensity.

Our projection of profit margins and turnover rates needs to consider typical reversion patterns and the level of the drivers from their long-run average at the point when the estimation is made. Furthermore, we need to be mindful of industry characteristics as these exhibit marked differences along the net profit margin–total asset turnover

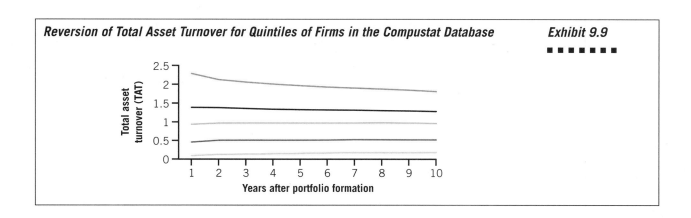

Reversion of Total Asset Turnover for Quintiles of Firms in the Compustat Database   *Exhibit 9.9*

Total asset turnover (TAT)

Years after portfolio formation

dimension as discussed in Chapter 8. And finally, our projection horizon need not be excessively long as we lose confidence in our estimates and ROE tends to revert to close to the cost of capital over a relatively short period of time.

ANALYSIS VIEWPOINT   *. . . YOU ARE THE STOCKBROKER*

You are analyzing the long-term cash forecasts of Boston Biotech, Inc., that are reported along with a scheduled initial public offering (IPO) of its common stock for next month. You notice Boston Biotech's forecasts of net cash flows are zero or negative for the next five years. During this same time period, Boston Biotech is forecasting net income at more than 10% of equity. Your co-workers at the securities firm question the reliability of these forecasts. Can you identify potential explanations for the disparity between the five-year forecasts of cash flows and income?

.....APPENDIX 9A SHORT-TERM FORECASTING

For analysis of short-term liquidity, one of the most useful tools is **short-term cash forecasting.** Short-term cash forecasting is of interest to internal users like managers and auditors in evaluating a company's current and future operating activities. It is also of interest to external users like short-term creditors who need to assess a company's ability to repay short-term loans. Our analysis stresses short-term cash forecasting when a company's ability to meet current obligations is in doubt. The accuracy of cash flow forecasting is inversely related to the *forecast horizon*–the longer the forecast period, the less reliable the forecasts. This is due to the number and complexity of factors influencing cash inflows and outflows that cannot be reliably estimated in the long term. Even in the case of short-term cash forecasting, the information required is substantial. Since cash flow forecasting often depends on publicly available information, our objective is "reasonably accurate" forecasts. By studying and preparing cash flow forecasts, our analysis should achieve greater insights into a company's cash flow patterns.

CASH FLOW PATTERNS

It is important for us to review the nature of cash flow patterns before examining models for cash flow analysis and projection. Cash and cash equivalents (hereafter simply *cash*) are the most liquid of assets. Nearly all management decisions to invest in assets or pay expenses require the immediate or eventual use of cash. This results in management's focus on cash rather than on other concepts of liquid funds. Some users (like creditors) sometimes consider assets like receivables and inventories part of liquid assets given their near-term conversion into cash.

Holding cash provides little or no return and, in times of rising prices, cash (like all monetary assets) is exposed to purchasing power loss. Nevertheless, holding cash represents the least exposure to risk. Management is responsible for the decisions to invest cash in assets or to immediately pay costs. These *cash conversions* increase risk because the ultimate recovery of cash from these activities is less than certain. Risks associated with these cash conversions are of various types and degrees. For instance, risk in converting cash into temporary investments is less than the risk in committing cash to long-term payout assets like plant and equipment. Investing cash in assets or costs aimed at developing and marketing new products often carries more serious cash-recovery risks. Both short-term liquidity and long-term solvency depend on the recovery and realizability of cash outlays.

Cash inflows and outflows are interrelated. A failure of any aspect of the company's business activities to successfully carry out its assigned task affects the entire cash flow system. A lapse in sales affects the conversion of finished goods into receivables and cash, leading to a decline in cash availability. A company's inability to replace this cash from sources like equity, loans, or accounts payable can impede production activities and produce losses in future sales. Conversely, restricting expenditures on items like advertising and marketing can slow the conversion of finished goods into receivables and cash. Long-term restrictions in either cash outflows or inflows can lead to company insolvency.

Our analysis must recognize the interrelations between cash flows, accruals, and profits. Sales is the driving source of operating flows. When finished goods representing the accumulation of many costs and expenses are sold, the company's profit margin produces an inflow of liquid funds through receivables and cash. The higher the profit margin, the greater the growth of liquid funds. Profits often primarily derive from the difference between sales and cost of sales (gross profit) and have enormous consequences to cash flows. Many costs, like those flowing from utilization of plant and equipment or deferred charges, do not require cash outlays. Similarly, items like long-term installment sales of land create noncurrent receivables limiting the relevance of accruals for cash flows. Our analysis must appropriately use these measures in assessing cash flow patterns.

Cash flows are limited in an important respect. As cash flows into a company, management has certain discretion in its disbursement. This discretion depends on commitments to outlays like dividends, inventory accumulation, capital expenditures, or debt repayment. Cash flows also depend on management's ability to draw on sources like equity and debt. With noncommitted cash inflows, referred to as free cash flows, management has considerable discretion in their use. It is this noncommitted cash component that is of special interest and importance for our analysis.

IMPORTANCE OF FORECASTING SALES

The reliability of our cash forecast depends on the *quality of the sales forecast*. With few exceptions, such as funds from financing or funds used in investing activities, most cash flows relate to and depend on sales. Our forecasting of sales includes an analysis of:

- Directions and trends in sales.
- Market share.
- Industry and economic conditions.
- Productive and financial capacity.
- Competitive factors.

These components are typically assessed along product lines potentially affected by forces peculiar to their markets. Later examples illustrate the importance of sales forecasts.

CASH FLOW FORECASTING WITH PRO FORMA ANALYSIS

The reasonableness and feasibility of short-term cash forecasts are usefully checked by means of **pro forma financial statements.** We accomplish this by using assumptions underlying cash forecasts to construct a pro forma income statement for the forecast period and a pro forma balance sheet for the end of the forecast period. Financial ratios and other relations are derived from these pro forma financial statements and checked for feasibility against historical relations. These comparisons must recognize adjustments for factors expected to affect them during the cash forecast period.

We illustrate cash flow forecasting using financial data from IT Technologies, Inc. IT Technologies recently introduced a new electronic processor that has enjoyed excellent market acceptance. IT's management estimates sales ($ thousands) for the next six months ending June 30, Year 1, as: $100, $125, $150, $175, $200, and $250 (see the bar graph). The current cash balance at January 1, Year 1, is $15,000. In light of the predicted increase in sales, IT's treasurer hopes to maintain *minimum* monthly cash balances of $20,000 for January; $25,000 for February; $27,000 for March; and $30,000 for April, May, and June. The treasurer foresees a need for additional funds to finance sales expansion. The treasurer expects that new equipment valued at $20,000 will be purchased in February by giving a note payable to the seller. The note will be repaid, beginning in February, at the rate of $1,000 per month. The new equipment is not planned to be operational until August of Year 1.

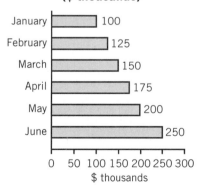

IT's Forecasted Sales ($ thousands)

January   100
February   125
March   150
April   175
May   200
June   250

0   50 100 150 200 250 300
$ thousands

The treasurer plans several further steps to fund these financing requirements. First, she obtains a financing commitment from an insurance company to acquire $110,000 of IT's long-term bonds (less $2,500 issue costs). These bond sales are planned for April ($50,000) and May ($60,000). She plans to sell real estate for additional financing, including $8,000 in May and $50,000 in June, and will sell equipment (originally costing $25,000 with a book value of zero) for $25,000 in June. The treasurer approaches IT's banker for approval of short-term financing to cover additional funding needs. The bank's loan officer requires the treasurer to prepare a *cash forecast* for the six months ending June 30, Year 1, along with *pro forma financial statements* for that period, to process her request. The loan officer also requests that IT Technologies specify its uses of cash and its sources of funds for loan repayment. The treasurer recognizes the importance of a cash forecast and proceeds to compile data necessary to comply with the loan officer's request.

As one of her first steps, the treasurer estimates the pattern of receivables collections. Prior experience suggests the following collection pattern:

Collections	Percent of Total Receivables
In month of sale	40%
In second month	30
In third month	20
In fourth month	5
Written off as bad debts	5
	100%

This collection pattern along with expected product sales allows the treasurer to construct estimates of cash collections shown in Exhibit 9A.1.

Exhibit 9A.1
■ ■ ■ ■ ■ ■ ■

Estimates of Cash Collections
for Months January Through June, Year 1

	January	February	March	April	May	June
Sales	$100,000	$125,000	$150,000	$175,000	$200,000	$250,000
Collections of sales*						
1st month—40%	$ 40,000	$ 50,000	$ 60,000	$ 70,000	$ 80,000	$100,000
2nd month—30%		30,000	37,500	45,000	52,500	60,000
3rd month—20%			20,000	25,000	30,000	35,000
4th month—5%				5,000 ←	6,250 ←	7,500 ←
Total cash collections	$ 40,000	$ 80,000	$117,500	$145,000	$168,750	$202,500
Write-offs—5%				5,000 ←	6,250 ←	7,500 ←

* For simplicity, cash collections from sales prior to January are ignored.

Analyzing expense patterns in prior periods' financial statements yields expense estimates based on either sales or time. Exhibit 9A.2 shows these expense estimates. IT Technologies pays off these expenses (excluding the $1,000 monthly depreciation) when incurred. The only exception is for purchases of materials, where 50% is paid in the month of purchase and 50% in the following month. Materials inventory on January 1, Year 1, is $57,000. The treasurer estimates materials inventory for the end of each month from January to June of Year 1 as: $67,000, $67,500, $65,500, $69,000, $67,000, and $71,000, respectively. She also estimates the pattern of payments on accounts payable for these materials. Exhibit 9A.3 shows these expected payments. Since the electronic processor is manufactured to specific order, no finished goods inventories are expected to accumulate.

The treasurer's resulting cash forecast for each of the six months ending June 30, Year 1, is shown in Exhibit 9A.4. Using these forecasts, Exhibit 9A.5 shows IT Technologies' pro forma income statement for the six months ending June 30, Year 1. Also, both actual and pro forma balance sheets of

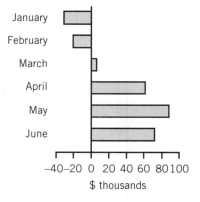

**IT's Forecasted Cash
($ thousands)
(from Exhibit 9A.4)**

Exhibit 9A.2

■ ■ ■ ■ ■ ■ ■

Expense Estimates
for Months January Through June, Year 1

Materials	30% of sales
Labor	25% of sales
Manufacturing overhead	
Variable...	10% of sales
Fixed...	$8,000 per month (includes $1,000 depreciation per month)
Selling expenses	10% of sales
General and administrative expenses	
Variable...	8% of sales
Fixed...	$7,000 per month

IT Technologies as of January 1 and June 30, respectively, of Year 1 are shown in Exhibit 9A.6.

Our prospective analysis should critically examine the pro forma statements and submit them to *feasibility tests* on both their forecasts and their assumptions. We should evaluate both ratios and relations revealed in pro forma financial statements and compare them to historical ratios to determine their reasonableness and feasibility. As an example, IT Technologies' current ratio increases from 2.6 on January 1, Year 1, to 3.5 in the pro forma balance sheet of June 30, Year 1. In addition, for the six months ended June 30, Year 1, the projected return on ending equity exceeds 9%. These and other measures such as turnover, trends, and common-size comparisons should be evaluated.

Exhibit 9A.3

■ ■ ■ ■ ■ ■ ■

Estimates of Cash Payments for Materials
for Months January Through June, Year 1

	January	February	March	April	May	June
Materials purchases*	$40,000	$38,000	$43,000	$56,000	$58,000	$79,000
Payments						
1st month—50%	$20,000	$19,000	$21,500	$28,000	$29,000	$39,500
2nd month—50%		20,000	19,000	21,500	28,000	29,000
Total payments	$20,000	$39,000	$40,500	$49,500	$57,000	$68,500

* *Material purchases reconcile with material costs and changes in inventories.*

Exhibit 9A.4

■ ■ ■ ■ ■ ■ ■

IT TECHNOLOGIES, INC.
Cash Forecast
For Months January through June, Year 1

	January	February	March	April	May	June	Six-Month Totals
Cash balance—beginning.................	$ 15,000	$ 20,000	$ 25,750	$ 27,250	$ 30,580	$ 30,895	$ 15,000
Add cash receipts for							
Cash collections (Exh. 9A.1)..........	40,000	80,000	117,500	145,000	168,750	202,500	753,750
Sale of real estate*........................	—	—	—	—	8,000	50,000	58,000
Sale of bonds*..............................	—	—	—	47,500	60,000	—	107,500
Sale of equipment*.......................	—	—	—	—	—	25,000	25,000
Total cash available......................	55,000	100,000	143,250	219,750	267,330	308,395	959,250
Less cash disbursements for							
Materials (Exh. 9A.3)....................	20,000	39,000	40,500	49,500	57,000	68,500	274,500
Labor[†].......................................	25,000	31,250	37,500	43,750	50,000	62,500	250,000
Fixed overhead[†]	7,000	7,000	7,000	7,000	7,000	7,000	42,000
Variable overhead[†]......................	10,000	12,500	15,000	17,500	20,000	25,000	100,000
Selling expenses[†].........................	10,000	12,500	15,000	17,500	20,000	25,000	100,000
General and administrative[†].........	15,000	17,000	19,000	21,000	23,000	27,000	122,000
Taxes[‡].......................................	—	—	—	—	—	19,000	19,000
Purchase of fixed assets*.............	—	1,000	1,000	1,000	1,000	1,000	5,000
Total cash disbursements.............	87,000	120,250	135,000	157,250	178,000	235,000	912,500
Tentative cash balance (deficit).........	(32,000)	(20,250)	8,250	62,500	89,330	73,395	46,750
Minimum cash required*	20,000	25,000	27,000	30,000	30,000	30,000	—
Borrowing required	52,000	46,000	19,000	—	—	—	117,000
Repayment of loan........................	—	—	—	30,000	58,000	29,000	(117,000)
Interest paid on balance[§]	—	—	—	1,920	435	145	2,500
Ending cash balance........................	$20,000	$ 25,750	$ 27,250	$ 30,580	$ 30,895	$ 44,250	$ 44,250
Loan balance.................................	$52,000	$ 98,000	$117,000	$ 87,000	$ 29,000	—	—

* *Treasurer's expectations taken from information on prior pages.*
[†] *Estimates computed using information from Exhibit 9A.2.*
[‡] *Taxes total a 40% combined state and federal rate. Taxes of $19,000 are paid in June, with the balance accrued.*
[§] *Interest is computed at the rate of ½% per month and paid at month-end. Any loan is taken out at the beginning of a month.*

Unexpected variations in important relations should be either explained or adjustments made to assumptions and expectations if errors are identified. These steps increase the reliability of pro forma statements for our analysis.

We should recognize that electronic spreadsheet programs are available to assist us in pro forma analysis. The ease of changing variables for sensitivity tests improves the usefulness of pro forma statements. Nevertheless, we should not confuse the ease and flexibility of these programs with the crucial need to develop and verify estimates and assumptions underlying their output. The reasonableness of important estimates and assumptions, and the usefulness of this analysis, depend on our critical evaluation and judgment and *not* on our technology.

Exhibit 9A.5

■■■■■■■

IT TECHNOLOGIES, INC.
Pro Forma Income Statement
For Six Months Ended June 30, Year 1

		Source of Estimate
Sales	$1,000,000	Forecasted sales
Cost of sales		
Materials	300,000	Exhibit 9A.2
Labor	250,000	Exhibit 9A.2
Overhead	148,000	Exhibit 9A.2
Total cost of sales	698,000	
Gross profit	302,000	
Selling expense	100,000	Exhibit 9A.2
Bad debts expense	18,750	Exhibit 9A.1
General and administrative expense	122,000	Exhibit 9A.2
Operating expenses	240,750	
Operating income	61,250	
Gain on sale of equipment	25,000	Treasurer
Interest expense	(2,500)	Exhibit 9A.4 note
Income before taxes	83,750	
Income taxes (40% rate)	33,500	Exhibit 9A.4 note
Net income	$ 50,250	

GUIDANCE ANSWERS TO ANALYSIS VIEWPOINTS

STOCKBROKER

The disparity in Boston Biotech's forecasts of cash flows and income is not necessarily of concern. Many growing companies experience little to no positive cash flows in the near term. Of course, these low near-term cash flows are expected to yield above-average cash flows in the future. Boston Biotech could potentially be recording substantial operating cash flows that are offset by large cash outflows in new investments, debt retirements, or dividends. Our analysis must look to the components of both cash flows and income to address our potential interest in Boston Biotech's IPO of common stock. Instead of spurning the stock of Boston Biotech, we might find it a lucrative and un- derpriced security due to our superior knowl- edge of accounting in financial statements.

LOAN OFFICER

Your first step is to corroborate or refute management's explanation for decreased sales in recent years. If their explanations are *not* validated with objective evidence, then you should reject DEC's application–hint of un- scrupulous behavior is reason enough for im- mediate nonapproval. If you are able to verify management's explanations, your next step is to assess the *level and uncertainty* of DEC's sales forecasts. Your analysis of sales forecasts should consider important economic factors, including consumer demand, industry com- petition, supplier costs, and DEC's productive

Exhibit 9A.6

■ ■ ■ ■ ■ ■ ■

IT TECHNOLOGIES, INC.
Balance Sheets

	Actual January 1, Year 1		Pro Forma June 30, Year 1	
Assets				
Current assets				
Cash..	$ 15,000		$ 44,250	
Accounts receivable (net)...............	6,500		234,000	
Inventories—materials..................	57,000		71,000	
Total current assets.......................		$ 78,500		$349,250
Real estate...	58,000		—	
Fixed assets..	206,400		201,400	
Accumulated depreciation....................	(36,400)		(17,400)	
Net fixed assets.................................		228,000		184,000
Other assets..		3,000		3,000
Deferred bond issue costs..................		—		2,500
Total assets..		$309,500		$538,750
Liabilities and Equity				
Current liabilities				
Accounts payable............................	$ 2,000		$ 41,500	
Notes payable................................	28,500		43,500	
Accrued taxes................................	—		14,500	
Total current liabilities...................		$ 30,500		$ 99,500
Long-term debt.................................	15,000		125,000	
Common stock....................................	168,000		168,000	
Retained earnings..............................	96,000	279,000	146,250	439,250
Total liabilities and equity..................		$309,500		$538,750

capacity/quality. Perhaps more important given DEC's circumstances is your assessment of uncertainty with sales. For example, sales might be objectively forecasted at $1 million, but the range of likely sales might extend anywhere from $0.5 to $1.5 million. Recent volatility in consumer demand, material costs, and supplier relations suggests substantially greater risk than normal. Your assessment of increased risk can yield a response extending from a slight increase in interest rates or increased collateral demands to ultimate loan rejection. Consequently, while DEC's sales forecasts might be unbiased, we must recognize differences in uncertainty associated with sales forecasts in practice.

[Superscript [A] denotes assignments based on Appendix 9A.]

QUESTIONS

9–1. What are some of the uses for prospective analysis?

9–2. What steps must usually take place before the forecasting process can begin?

9–3. In addition to recent trends, what other items of information might be brought to bear in the projection of sales?

9–4. What is the forecast horizon?

9–5. What assumption is usually made about sales growth at the end of the forecast horizon?

9–6. Describe the steps in forecasting the income statement.

9–7. Describe the two-step process of forecasting the balance sheet.

9–8. What are value drivers?

9–9. Describe the typical trend of value drivers over time.

9–10^A. Why are short-term cash forecasts important for the analysis of financial statements?

9–11^A. What limitations are associated with short-term cash forecasting?

9–12^A. Describe the relation between inflows of cash and outflows of cash.

9–13^A. It is often asserted: *From an operational point of view, management focuses on cash rather than working capital.* Do you agree with this statement? Why or why not?

9–14^A. Describe the primary difference between "funds flow" analysis and ratio analysis. Which analysis technique is preferred and why?

9–15^A. What is the usual first step in preparing cash forecasts, and what considerations are required in this step?

EXERCISES

EXERCISE 9–1

Forecasting Income and Income Components

Refer to the financial statements of **Quaker Oats Company** in Problem 9–6. Prepare a forecasted income statement for Year 12 using the following assumptions ($ millions):

1. Revenues are forecast to equal $6,000.

2. Cost of sales forecast uses the average percent relation between cost of sales and sales for the three-year period ending June 30, Year 11.

3. Selling, general, and administrative expenses are expected to increase by the same percent increase occurring from Year 10 to Year 11.

4. Other expenses are predicted to be 8% higher than in Year 11.

5. A $2 million loss (net of taxes) is expected from disposal of net assets from discontinued operations.

CHECK
Forecast NI, $140.1 mil.

6. Interest expense, net of interest capitalized and interest income, is expected to increase by 6% due to increased financial needs.

7. The effective tax rate is equal to that of Year 11.

EXERCISE 9–2

Forecasting Sales and Net Income

Quarterly sales and net income data for **General Electric** for Year 1 through Year 9 are shown below ($ millions).

General Electric

	Sales	Net Income		Sales	Net Income		Sales	Net Income
Dec. Y1	$17,349	$1,263	Sep. Y4	$14,442	$1,457	Jun. Y7	$21,860	$2,162
Mar. Y2	12,278	964	Dec. Y4	17,528	1,685	Sep. Y7	21,806	2,014
Jun. Y2	13,984	1,130	Mar. Y5	14,948	1,372	Dec. Y7	24,876	2,350
Sep. Y2	13,972	996	Jun. Y5	17,630	1,726	Mar. Y8	22,459	1,891
Dec. Y2	16,040	1,215	Sep. Y5	17,151	1,610	Jun. Y8	24,928	2,450
Mar. Y3	12,700	1,085	Dec. Y5	19,547	1,865	Sep. Y8	23,978	2,284
Jun. Y3	14,566	656	Mar. Y6	16,931	1,517	Dec. Y8	28,455	2,671
Sep. Y3	14,669	1,206	Jun. Y6	18,901	1,908	Mar. Y9	24,062	2,155
Dec. Y3	17,892	1,477	Sep. Y6	19,861	1,788	Jun. Y9	27,410	2,820
Mar. Y4	12,621	1,219	Dec. Y6	22,848	2,067			
Jun. Y4	14,725	1,554	Mar. Y7	19,998	1,677			

Required:

Use these data and any other historical information available to forecast sales and net income for each of the quarters ending September Year 9, December Year 9, March Year 10, and June Year 10. Explain the basis of your forecasts.

In Year 2006, Cough.com is in its second year of operations. Cough.com produces children's cough medicine. Industry sales of children's cough medicine for 2005 totaled $3 billion. For 2005, Cough.com had sales totaling $2.4 million (.08% market share).

EXERCISE 9–3
Forecasting Sales and Net Income

Required:

a. Explain how predictions of the total market and market share can be used in the forecasting process.

b. What data might you seek to enhance your sales forecast and how might such data be gathered?

c. Illustrate what-if scenarios in which market share gained by Cough.com is (1) 5% greater than and (2) 5% worse than the predicted .08% of the Year 2006 expected industry sales of $3.2 billion.

CHECK
(c) 1. $2.688 mil.

d. For *each* of these two separate scenarios, illustrate what-if analysis when total expected industry sales of $3.2 billion are (1) 10% greater than and (2) 10% worse than expected.

The Lyon Corporation is a merchandising company. Prepare a short-term cash forecast for July of Year 6 following the format of Exhibit 9A.4. Selected financial data from Lyon Corporation as of July 1 of Year 6 are reproduced below ($ thousands):

EXERCISE 9–4ᴬ
Preparing a Short-Term Cash Forecast

Cash, July 1, Year 6	$ 20
Accounts receivable, July 1, Year 6	20
Forecasted sales for July	150
Forecasted accounts receivable, July 31, Year 6	21
Inventory, July 1, Year 6	25
Desired inventory, July 31, Year 6	15
Depreciation expense for July	4
Miscellaneous outlays for July	11
Minimum cash balance desired	30
Accounts payable, July 1, Year 6	18

Additional Information:

1. Gross profit equals 20% of cost of goods sold.
2. Lyon purchases all inventory on the second day of the month and receives it the following week.
3. Lyon pays 75% of payables within the month of purchase and the balance in the following month.
4. Lyons pays all remaining expenses in cash.

CHECK
Cash bal., $54

PROBLEMS

Comparative income statements and balance sheets for **Coca-Cola** are shown below ($ millions).

Coca-Cola

PROBLEM 9–1
Preparing Pro Forma Financial Statements

	Year 2	Year 1
Income Statement		
Net sales	$20,092	$19,889
Cost of goods	6,044	6,204
Gross profit	14,048	13,685
Selling, general, and administrative expense	7,893	9,221
Depreciation and amortization expense	803	773
Interest expense (revenue)	(308)	292
Income before tax	5,660	3,399
Income tax expense	1,691	1,222
Net income	$ 3,969	$ 2,177
Outstanding shares	3,491	3,481

(continued)

PROBLEM 9–1
(concluded)

	Year 2	Year 1
Balance Sheet		
Cash	$ 1,934	$ 1,892
Receivables..	1,882	1,757
Inventories	1,055	1,066
Other current assets	2,300	1,905
Total current assets	7,171	6,620
Property, plant, and equipment...	7,105	6,614
Accumulated depreciation	2,652	2,446
Net property, plant, and equipment...	4,453	4,168
Other noncurrent assets..	10,793	10,046
Total assets..	$22,417	$20,834
Accounts payable and Accrued liabilities..................................	$ 3,679	$ 3,905
Short-term debt and current maturities of long-term debt	3,899	4,816
Income tax liabilities...	851	600
Total current liabilities..	8,429	9,321
Deferred income taxes and other liabilities..............................	1,403	1,362
Long-term debt	1,219	835
Total noncurrent liabilities	2,622	2,197
Common stock	873	870
Capital surplus	3,520	3,196
Retained earnings..	20,655	18,543
Treasury stock	13,682	13,293
Shareholders' equity	11,366	9,316
Total liabilities and equity...	$22,417	$20,834

Required:

a. Use the following ratios to prepare a projected income statement, balance sheet, and statement of cash flows for Year 3.

Sales growth	1.02%
Gross profit margin	69.92%
Selling, general, and administrative expense/Sales...............	39.28%
Depreciation expense/Prior-year PPE gross...........................	12.14%
Interest expense/Prior-year long-term debt	5.45%
Income tax expense/Pretax income	29.88%
Accounts receivable turnover	10.68
Inventory turnover...	5.73
Accounts payable turnover	1.64
Taxes payable/Tax expense	50.33%
Total assets/Stockholders' equity (financial leverage)............	2.06
Dividends per share	$1.37
Capital expenditures/Sales..	5.91%

b. Based on your initial projections, how much external financing (long-term debt and/or stockholders' equity) will Coca-Cola need to fund its growth at projected increases in sales?

Comparative income statements and balance sheets for **Best Buy** are shown below ($ millions).

Best Buy

PROBLEM 9–2

Preparing Pro Forma Financial Statements

	Year 2	Year 1
Income Statement		
Net sales	$15,326	$12,494
Cost of goods	12,267	10,101
Gross profit	3,059	2,393
Selling, general and administrative expense	2,251	1,728
Depreciation and amortization expense	167	103
Income before tax	641	562
Income tax expense	245	215
Net income	$ 396	$ 347
Outstanding shares	208	200

Balance Sheet	Year 2	Year 1
Cash	$ 746	$ 751
Receivables	313	262
Inventories	1,767	1,184
Other current assets	102	41
Total current assets	2,928	2,238
Property, plant, and equipment	1,987	1,093
Accumulated depreciation	543	395
Net property, plant, and equipment	1,444	698
Other noncurrent assets	466	59
Total assets	$ 4,838	$ 2,995
Accounts payable and accrued liabilities	$ 2,473	$ 1,704
Short-term debt and current maturities of long-term debt	114	16
Income tax liabilities	127	65
Total current liabilities	2,714	1,785
Long-term liabilities	122	100
Long-term debt	181	15
Total long-term liabilities	303	115
Common stock	20	20
Capital surplus	576	247
Retained earnings	1,225	828
Shareholders' equity	1,821	1,095
Total liabilities and equity	$ 4,838	$ 2,995

Required:

a. Use the following ratios to prepare a projected income statement, balance sheet, and statement of cash flows for Year 3.

Sales growth..	22.67%
Gross profit margin	19.96%
Selling, general, and administrative expense/Sales	14.69%
Depreciation expense/Prior-year PPE gross...	15.28%
Income tax expense/Pretax income	38.22%
Accounts receivable turnover (Sales/Accounts receivable)	48.96
Inventory turnover (Cost of goods sold/Inventory)	6.94
Accounts payable turnover (Cost of goods sold/Accounts payable)..............	4.96
Taxes payable/Tax expense	51.84%
Total assets/Stockholders' equity (financial leverage)................................	2.55
Dividends per share...	$ 0.00
Capital expenditures/Sales..	6.71%

b. Based on your initial projections, how much external financing (long-term debt and/or stockholders' equity) will Best Buy need to fund its growth at projected increases in sales?

PROBLEM 9–3

*Preparing Pro Forma
Financial Statements*

Comparative income statements and balance sheets for **Merck** ($ millions) follow:

Merck

	Year 2	Year 1
Income Statement		
Net sales	$47,716	$40,343
Cost of goods	28,977	22,444
Gross profit	18,739	17,899
Selling, general and administrative expense...........	6,531	6,469
Depreciation and amortization expense..................	1,464	1,277
Interest expense	342	329
Income before tax..	10,402	9,824
Income tax expense	3,121	3,002
Net income...	$ 7,282	$ 6,822
Outstanding shares...	2,976	2,968
Balance Sheet		
Cash	$ 3,287	$ 4,255
Receivables..	5,215	5,262
Inventories	3,579	3,022
Other current assets...	880	1,059
Total current assets	12,961	13,598
Property, plant, and equipment............................	18,956	16,707
Accumulated depreciation...................................	5,853	5,225
Net property, plant, and equipment.......................	13,103	11,482
Other noncurrent assets....................................	17,942	15,075
Total assets...	$44,006	$40,155
Accounts payable and accrued liabilities................	$ 5,904	$ 5,391
Short-term debt and current maturities of long-term debt........	4,067	3,319
Income taxes payable..	1,573	1,244
Total current liabilities	11,544	9,954

(continued)

	Year 2	Year 1
Deferred income taxes and other liabilities	11,614	11,768
Long-term debt	4,799	3,601
Total noncurrent liabilities	16,413	15,369
Common stock	30	30
Capital surplus	6,907	6,266
Retained earnings	31,500	27,395
Treasury stock	(22,387)	(18,858)
Shareholders' equity	16,050	14,833
Total liabilities and equity	$44,007	$40,154

PROBLEM 9–3
(concluded)

Required:

a. Use the following ratios to prepare a projected income statement, balance sheet, and statement of cash flows for Year 3.

Sales growth	18.27%
Gross profit margin	39.27%
Selling, general, and administrative expense/Sales	13.69%
Depreciation expense/Prior-year property, plant & equipment (gross)	8.76%
Interest expense/Prior-year long-term debt	4.94%
Income tax expense/Pretax income	30.00%
Accounts receivable turnover (Sales/Accounts receivable)	9.15
Inventory turnover (Cost of goods sold/Inventory)	8.10
Accounts payable turnover (Cost of goods sold/Accounts payable)	4.91
Taxes payable/Tax expense	50.41%
Total assets/Stockholders' equity (financial leverage)	2.35
Dividends per share	$ 1.06
Capital expenditures/Sales	9.04%

b. Based on your initial projections, how much external financing (long-term debt and/or stockholders' equity) will Merck need to fund its growth at projected increases in sales?

Following are financial statement information for Welmark Corporation as of Year 2 and Year 3.

PROBLEM 9–4
Using Prospective Analysis to Value Securities

WELMARK CORPORATION

	Year 2	Year 3
Sales growth	8.50%	10.65%
Net profit margin (Net income/Sales)	6.71%	8.22%
Net working capital turnover (Sales/Average net working capital)	8.98	9.33
Fixed asset turnover (Sales/Average fixed assets)	1.67	1.64
Total operating assets/Total equity	1.96	2.01
Number of shares outstanding	1,737	1,737
($ thousands)		
Sales	$25,423	$28,131
Net income	1,706	2,312
Net working capital	2,832	3,015
Fixed assets	15,232	17,136
Total operating assets	18,064	20,151
Long-term liabilities	8,832	10,132
Total stockholders' equity	9,232	10,019

Required:

Using the residual income model, prepare a valuation of the common stock of Welmark Corporation as of Year 3 under the following assumptions:

a. Forecast horizon of five years

b. Sales growth of 10.65% per year over the forecast horizon and 3.5% thereafter.

c. All financial ratios remain at Year 3 levels

d. Cost of equity capital is 12.5%

PROBLEM 9–5ᴬ

Preparing Pro Forma Financial Statements

Telnet Corporation is a newly formed computer manufacturer. Telnet plans to begin operations on January 1, Year 2. Selected financial information is available for the preparation of Telnet's six-month forecasted performance covering the period January 1 to June 30 of Year 2.

Forecasted *monthly* sales $250,000

Monthly operating expenses

Labor...	30,500
Rent for factory	10,000
Variable overhead	22,500
Depreciation on equipment	35,000
Amortization of patents...........................	500
Selling and administrative expenses........	47,500
Materials...	125,000

Additional Information:

1. Collection period .... 45 days
2. Purchase terms.. n/30
3. Ending finished goods inventory $100,000
4. Ending raw material inventory... $ 35,000
5. Effective tax rate 50%
6. Beginning cash balance .... $ 60,000
7. Minimum cash balance required... $ 40,000
8. Prepaid expenses on June 30, Year 2................................... $ 7,000
9. No inventory is in process on June 30, Year 2.
10. Sales are made evenly throughout the period.
11. Expenses are paid in cash (unless otherwise indicated).
12. Telnet Corporation's balance sheet data on January 1, Year 2, appears as:

Cash.................. $ 60,000		Patents........................... $ 40,000	
Equipment........ 1,200,000		Shareholders' equity........ 1,300,000	

CHECK
(*a*) NI, $8,000
(*b*) Total assets, $1,584,000
(*c*) Borrowing, $143,000

Required:

a. Prepare a pro forma income statement to portray the forecasted financial position of Telnet Corporation for the six-month period ended June 30, Year 2.

b. Prepare a pro forma balance sheet as of June 30, Year 2.

c. Prepare a cash forecast analysis as in Exhibit 9A.4 for the six-month period ended June 30, Year 2.

Refer to the following financial statements of **Quaker Oats Company.**

Quaker Oats Company

PROBLEM 9-6

Forecasting the Statement of Cash Flows

INCOME STATEMENT

Year ended June 30 ($ millions except per share data)	Year 11	Year 10	Year 9
Net sales	$5,491.2	$5,030.6	$4,879.4
Cost of goods sold	2,839.7	2,685.9	2,655.3
Gross profit	2,651.5	2,344.7	2,224.1
Selling, general and administrative expenses	2,121.2	1,844.1	1,779.0
Interest expense—net of $9.0, $11.0 and $12.4 interest income	86.2	101.8	56.4
Other expense—net	32.6	16.4	149.6
Income from continuing operations before income taxes	411.5	382.4	239.1
Provision for income taxes	175.7	153.5	90.2
Income from continuing operations	235.8	228.9	148.9
Income (loss) from discontinued operations—net of tax	(30.0)	(59.9)	54.1
Net income	205.8	169.0	203.0
Preferred dividends—net of tax	4.3	4.5	—
Net income available for common	$ 201.5	$ 164.5	$ 203.0
Per common share			
Income from continuing operations	$ 3.05	$ 2.93	$ 1.88
Income (loss) from discontinued operations	(.40)	(.78)	.68
Net income	$ 2.65	$ 2.15	$ 2.56
Dividends declared	$ 1.56	$ 1.40	$ 1.20
Average Number of common shares outstanding (in 000's)	75,904	76,537	79,307

BALANCE SHEET

June 30 ($ millions)	Year 11	Year 10	Year 9
Assets			
Current assets			
Cash and cash equivalents	$ 30.2	$ 17.7	$ 21.0
Short-term investments, at cost which approximates market	—	0.6	2.7
Receivables—net of allowances	691.1	629.9	594.4
Inventories			
Finished goods	309.1	324.1	326.0
Grain and raw materials	86.7	110.7	114.1
Packaging materials and supplies	26.5	39.1	39.0
Total inventories	422.3	473.9	479.1
Other current assets	114.5	107.0	94.2
Net current assets of discontinued operations	—	252.2	328.5
Total current assets	1,258.1	1,481.3	1,519.9
Other receivables and investments	79.1	63.5	26.4
Property, plant, and equipment	1,914.6	1,745.6	1,456.9
Less accumulated depreciation	681.9	591.5	497.3
Properties—net	1,232.7	1,154.1	959.6

(continued)

PROBLEM 9–6
(continued)

June 30 ($ millions)

Assets	Year 11	Year 10	Year 9
Intangible assets, net of amortization	446.2	466.7	484.7
Net non-current assets of discontinued operations	—	160.5	135.3
Total assets	$3,016.1	$3,326.1	$3,125.9

Liabilities and Equity

Current liabilities

	Year 11	Year 10	Year 9
Short-term debt	$ 80.6	$ 343.2	$ 102.2
Current portion of long-term debt	32.9	32.3	30.0
Trade accounts payable	350.9	354.0	333.8
Accrued payrolls, pensions, and bonuses	116.3	106.3	118.1
Accrued advertising and merchandising	105.7	92.6	67.1
Income taxes payable	45.1	36.3	8.0
Payable to Fisher-Price	29.6	—	—
Other accrued liabilities	165.8	173.8	164.9
Total current liabilities	926.9	1,138.5	824.1
Long-term debt	701.2	740.3	766.8
Other liabilities	115.5	100.3	89.5
Deferred income taxes	366.7	327.7	308.4

Preferred stock, no par value, authorized 1,750,000 shares:
issued 1,282,051 of $5.46 cumulative convertible shares in Year 9

	Year 11	Year 10	Year 9
(liquidating preference $78 per share)	100.0	100.0	100.0
Deferred compensation	(94.5)	(98.2)	(100.0)
Treasury preferred stock, at cost, 10,089 shares at June 30, Year 11	(.7)	—	—

Common shareholders' equity

Common stock, $5 par value, authorized 200,000,000 shares;

	Year 11	Year 10	Year 9
issued 83,989,396 shares	420.0	420.0	420.0
Additional paid-in capital	7.2	12.9	18.1
Reinvested earnings	1,047.5	1,164.7	1,106.2
Cumulative exchange adjustment	(52.9)	(29.3)	(56.6)
Deferred compensation	(168.0)	(164.1)	(165.8)
Treasury common stock, at cost, 7,660,675 shares; 8,402,871 shares; and 5,221,981 shares, respectively	(352.8)	(386.7)	(184.8)
Total common shareholders' equity	901.0	1,017.5	1,137.1
Total liabilities and common shareholders' equity	$3,016.1	$3,326.1	$3,125.9

Using Quaker's financial statements and the analysis guidance from the chapter, prepare a fore-casted statement of cash flows for Year 12 using the following information:

Selected Forecast Data ($ millions)	Year 12
Sources of cash	
Assets retirements	$ 20
Uses of cash	
Repayment of long-term debt	45
Capital expenditures—Property, plant, and equipment	300
Cash dividends on capital stock	135
Other cash expenditures	30
Revenue forecast	6,000

Additional assumptions for your forecasting task include:

1. Income from continuing operations in Year 12 is expected to equal the average percentage of income from continuing operations to sales for the three-year period ending June 30, Year 11.

2. The depreciation and amortization forecast for Year 12 uses the average percentage relation of depreciation and amortization to income from continuing operations for the period Year 9 through Year 11. The average is computed at 82.33%.

3. Forecasts of deferred income taxes (noncurrent portion) and other items in Year 12 reflect the past three years' relation of deferred taxes (noncurrent) and other items to total income from continuing operations of 22.9%.

4. Provisions for restructuring charges are predicted to be zero for Year 12.

5. Days' sales in receivables is expected to be 42 for Year 12.

6. Days' sales in inventory of 55 and a ratio of cost of sales to sales of 0.51 are forecasted for Year 12.

7. Changes in other current assets are predicted to be equal to the average increase/decrease over the period Year 9 through Year 11 of $25.6.

8. Days' purchases in accounts payable of 45 is forecasted for Year 12, and purchases are expected to increase in Year 12 by 12% over Year 11 purchases of $2,807.20.

9. Change in other current liabilities is predicted to be equal to the average increase/decrease over the period Year 9 through Year 11 of $24.5.

10. There are no expected discontinued operations.

11. Decreases in short-term debt are predicted at $40 million each year.

12. No cash inflows are expected from issuance of debt for spin-off and no cash effects from purchases or issuances of common and preferred stock.

13. Predicted year-end cash needs are equal to a level measured by the ratio of cash to revenues prevailing in Year 11.

14. Additions to long-term debt in Year 12 are equal to the amount needed to meet the desired year-end cash balance.

CASES

Refer to the following financial statements for **Kodak**:

Kodak

CASE 9–1

Forecasting Pro Forma Financial Statements

INCOME STATEMENT

For Year Ended December 31 (in millions)	20x6	20x5	20x4
Net sales	$13,234	$13,994	$14,089
Cost of goods sold	8,670	8,375	8,086
Gross profit	4,564	5,619	6,003
Selling, general, and administrative expenses	2,781	2,665	2,846
Research and development costs	779	784	817
Restructuring costs (credits) and other	659	(44)	350
Earnings from operations	345	2,214	1,990
Interest expense	219	178	142
Other income (charges)	(18)	96	261
Earnings before income taxes	108	2,132	2,109
Provision for income taxes	32	725	717
Net earnings	$ 76	$ 1,407	$ 1,392

BALANCE SHEET

At December 31 (in millions, except share and per share data)	20x6	20x5
Assets		
Current assets		
Cash and cash equivalents	$ 448	$ 246
Receivables, net	2,337	2,653
Inventories, net	1,137	1,718
Deferred income taxes	521	575
Other current assets	240	299
Total current assets	4,683	5,491
Property, plant, and equipment, net	5,659	5,919
Goodwill, net	948	947
Other long-term assets	2,072	1,855
Total assets	$13,362	$14,212
Liabilities and shareholders' equity		
Current liabilities		
Accounts payable and other current liabilities	$ 3,276	$ 3,403
Short-term borrowings	1,378	2,058
Current portion of long-term debt	156	148
Accrued income taxes	544	606
Total current liabilities	5,354	6,215
Long-term debt, net of current portion	1,666	1,166
Postemployment liabilities	2,728	2,722
Other long-term liabilities	720	681
Total liabilities	10,468	10,784
Shareholders' equity		
Common stock, $2.50 par value		
950,000,000 shares authorized: issued 391,292,760 shares in 20x6 and 20x5;		
290,929,701 and 290,484,266 shares outstanding in 20x6 and 20x5	978	978
Additional paid in capital	849	871
Retained earnings	7,431	7,869
Accumulated other comprehensive loss	(597)	(482)
	8,661	9,236
Treasury stock, at cost; 100,363,059 shares in 20x6 and 100,808,494 shares in 20x5	(5,767)	(5,808)
Total shareholders' equity	2,894	3,428
Total liabilities and shareholders' equity	$13,362	$14,212

Required:

Prepare forecasts of its income statement, balance sheet, and statement of cash flows for 20x7 under the following assumptions:

a. All financial ratios remain at 20x6 levels.

b. Kodak will not record restructuring costs for 20x7.

c. Taxes payable are at the 20x6 level of $544 million.

d. Depreciation expense charged to SG&A is $765 million and $738 million for 20x6 and 20x5, respectively.

e. Gross PPE is $12,982 million and $12,963 million for 20x6 and 20x5, respectively.

f. Projected current maturities of long-term debt are $13 million for 20x7.

Miller Company is planning to construct a two-unit facility for the loading of beverage barrels onto ships. On or before January 1, Year 2, stockholders will invest $100,000 in the company's capital stock to provide the initial working capital. To finance the construction program (total planned cost is $1,800,000) the company will obtain a commitment from a lending organization for a loan of $1,800,000. This loan is to be secured by a 10-year mortgage note bearing interest at 5% per year on the unpaid balance. The principal amount of the loan is to be repaid in equal semiannual installments of $100,000 beginning June 30, Year 3. Since loan proceeds will only be required as construction work progresses, the company agrees to pay a commitment fee beginning January 1, Year 2, equal to 1 percent per year on the unused portion of the loan commitment. This fee is payable when amounts are "drawn down" except for the first draw-down.

Work on the construction of the facility will commence in the fall of Year 1. The first payment to the contractors is due on January 1, Year 2, at which time the commitment and loan agreement become effective and the company will make its first draw-down for payment to the contractors in the amount of $800,000. As construction progresses, additional payments will be made to the contractors by drawing down the remaining loan proceeds as follows (payments to contractors are made on the same dates as the loan proceeds are drawn down):

| April 1, Year 2 .... $500,000 | December 31, Year 2 .... $100,000 |
| July 1, Year 2 .... 300,000 | April 1, Year 3 .... 100,000 |

Because of weather conditions, the facility operates from April 1 through November 30 of each year. The construction program will permit the completion of the first of two plant units (capable of handling 5,000,000 barrels) in time for its use during the Year 2 shipping season. The second unit (capable of handling an additional 3,000,000 barrels) will be completed in time for the Year 3 season. It is expected 5,000,000 barrels will be handled by the facility during the Year 2 season. Thereafter, barrels handled are expected to increase in each subsequent year by 300,000 barrels until a level of 6,500,000 barrels is reached. The company's revenues are derived by charging the consignees of the beverage for its services at a fixed rate per barrel loaded. All revenues are collected in the month of shipment. Based upon past experience with similar facilities, Miller Company expects operating profit to average $0.04 per barrel before charges for interest, financing fees, and depreciation. Depreciation is $0.03 per barrel.

Required:

Prepare a cash forecast for each of the three calendar years: Year 2, Year 3, and Year 4. Evaluate the sufficiency of cash obtained from the issuance of capital stock, draw-downs on the loan, and the operating facility to cover cash payments to the contractor and the creditor (principal and interest).

CASE 9–2
Preparing and Analyzing Cash Forecasts

CHECK
Ending cash:
Year 2, $1,929,000
Year 3, $254,500

CASE 9–3

*Preparing a Cash
Forecast for a Company
in Distress*

Royal Company has incurred substantial losses for several years and is insolvent. On March 31, Year 5, Royal petitions the court for protection from creditors and submits the following balance sheet:

ROYAL COMPANY
Balance Sheet
March 31, Year 5

	Book Value	Liquidation Value
Assets		
Accounts receivable	$100,000	$ 50,000
Inventories	90,000	40,000
Plant and equipment	150,000	160,000
Total assets	$340,000	$250,000
Liabilities and Stockholders' Equity		
Accounts payable—general creditors	$600,000	
Common stock	60,000	
Retained earnings	(320,000)	
Total liabilities and equity	$340,000	

Royal's management informed the court that the company developed a new product and a prospective customer is willing to sign a contract for the purchase of (at a price of $90 per unit) 10,000 units during the year ending March 31, Year 6; 12,000 units during the year ending March 31, Year 7; and 15,000 units during the year ending March 31, Year 8. The product can be manufactured using Royal's current facilities. Monthly production with immediate delivery is expected to be uniform within each year. Receivables are expected to be collected during the calendar month following sales. Production costs per unit for the new product are:

Direct materials ....$20   Direct labor.............$30   Variable overhead.........$10

Fixed costs (excluding depreciation) amount to $130,000 per year. Purchases of direct materials are paid during the calendar month following purchase. Fixed costs, direct labor, and variable overhead are paid as incurred. Inventory of direct materials are equal to 60 days' usage. After the first month of operations during which Royal will order 90 days' supply, 30 days' usage of direct materials is ordered each month.

Creditors have agreed to reduce their total claims to 60% of their March 31, Year 5, balances under two conditions:

1. Existing accounts receivable and inventories are liquidated immediately with the proceeds going to creditors.

2. The remaining balance in accounts payable is paid as cash is produced from future operations—but in no event is it to be paid later than March 31, Year 7. No interest is paid on these obligations.

Under this proposal, creditors would receive $110,000 more than the current liquidation value of Royal's assets. The court engages you to determine the feasibility of this proposal.

Required:

Prepare a cash forecast for years ending March 31, Year 6 and Year 7. Ignore any need to borrow and repay short-term funds for working capital purposes and show the cash expected to be available to pay creditors, the actual payments to creditors, and the cash remaining after payments to creditors.

CHECK
Ending cash bal.:
Year 6, $75,000
Year 7, $15,000

(AICPA Adapted)

You are a loan officer for Pacific Bank. The senior loan officer submits to you the following selected financial information as of September 30, Year 6, for Union Corporation, which has filed a loan application:

CASE 9–4
Comprehensive Analysis of Loan Request

Current assets

Cash	$ 12,000
Accounts receivable	10,000
Inventory	63,600
Plant and equipment, net	100,000
Total liabilities	0

Actual sales

September, Year 6	40,000

Forecasted sales

October, Year 6	48,000
November, Year 6	60,000
December, Year 6	80,000
January, Year 7	36,000

Sales are 75% for cash and 25% on account. Receivables are collected in full in the month following the sale. For example, the accounts receivable balance of $10,000 on September 30, Year 6, equals 25% of the sales from September, of which all $10,000 is paid in October. Gross profit averages 30% of sales *before* purchase discounts. Therefore, the gross invoice cost of goods sold is 70% of sales. Union Corp. carries $30,000 of inventory plus additional inventory sufficient to provide for the anticipated sales of the following month. Purchase terms are 2/10, n/30. Since purchases are made early in each month and all discounts are taken, payments are consistently made in the month of purchase.

Salaries and wages average 15% of sales, rent averages 5% of sales, and all other expenses (except depreciation) average 4% of sales. These expenses are paid in cash when incurred. Depreciation expense is $750 per month, computed on a straight-line basis. Equipment expenditures are forecasted at $600 in October and $400 in November. Depreciation on these new expenditures is not recorded until Year 7. Union Corp. maintains a minimum cash balance of $8,000. Any borrowings are made at the beginning of the month and any repayments are made at the end of the month, both in multiples of $1,000 (excluding interest). Interest is paid when the principal is repaid, equal to a rate of 6% per year.

Required:

a. The senior loan officer requests you prepare the following schedules for the months of October, November, and December, and for the total three months (quarter) ending in December of Year 6:
   (1) Estimated total cash receipts.
   (2) Estimated cash disbursements for purchases (purchases are 70% of sales for the following month).
   (3) Estimated cash disbursements for operating expenses.
   (4) Estimated total cash disbursements.
   (5) Estimated net cash receipts and disbursements.
   (6) Estimated financing required.

b. For the three months (quarter) ending in December of Year 6, prepare a:
   (1) Forecasted income statement (ignore taxes).
   (2) Forecasted balance sheet.

CREDIT ANALYSIS

ANALYSIS OBJECTIVES

- Explain the importance of liquidity, and describe working capital measures of liquidity and their components.

- Interpret the current ratio and cash-based measures of liquidity.

- Analyze operating cycle and turnover measures of liquidity and their interpretation.

- Illustrate what-if analysis for evaluating changes in company conditions and policies.

- Describe capital structure and its relation to solvency.

- Explain financial leverage and its implications for company performance and analysis.

- Analyze adjustments to accounting book values to assess capital structure.

- Describe analysis tools for evaluating and interpreting capital structure composition and for assessing solvency.

- Analyze asset composition and coverage for solvency analysis.

- Explain earnings-coverage analysis and its relevance in evaluating solvency.

- Describe capital structure risk and return and its relevance to financial statement analysis.

- Interpret ratings of organizations' debt obligations (Appendix 10A).

- Describe prediction models of financial distress (Appendix 10B).

Is GM a Credit Risk?

NEW YORK–During economic booms, leverage can help companies make the most of their money. But if growth evaporates, the once-manageable debt becomes a drag on earnings.

General Motors (GM) provides an example. Declining market share, coupled with higher payments on borrowed funds, pensions and health care, resulted in the 2005 downgrade of GM bonds to junk status. The effect on GM is higher interest costs and reduced borrowing sources; many investment funds are prohibited from owning bonds that are below "investment grade."

More generally, credit-rating agencies aggressively slashed corporate credit ratings as the economy slowed in the early 2000s. Downgrades soared to record levels, raising corporate borrowing costs.

Ratings agencies have today ratcheted up their oversight. "We've accelerated and heightened our credit-review process," says the executive managing director of Standard & Poor's. S&P is spending more time looking over company accounts and broadening its review to include customers and competitors. Ratings agencies are also paying more attention to equity and

> **Ratings agencies have today ratcheted up their oversight**

corporate bond prices as early warning signs of company trouble.

How much debt is too much? A good place to start is to look at capital, which is usually measured as long-term debt plus shareholders'

equity. As a rule of thumb, debt is preferably less than 50% of capital. But this rule must be adjusted to benchmark companies against their competitors. For example, in cyclical industries such as paper and chemicals, where revenues can swing wildly, the less debt the better.

For GM, Fitch Ratings offered the following comment relating to its downgrade of GM's credit rating, "GM's difficulties are augmented by its high and inflexible cost structure, unrelenting price competition, continued industry expansion and overcapacity, and increasing raw material and legacy costs. In addition, this has occurred amidst a relatively favorable economic growth environment." This chapter examines such ratings in the more general context of credit analysis.

PREVIEW OF CHAPTER 10

Liquidity refers to the availability of company resources to meet short-term cash requirements. A company's short-term liquidity risk is affected by the timing of cash inflows and outflows along with its prospects for future performance. Analysis of liquidity is aimed at companies' operating activities, their ability to generate profits from sale of products and services, and working capital requirements and measures. Section 1 of this chapter describes several financial statement analysis tools used

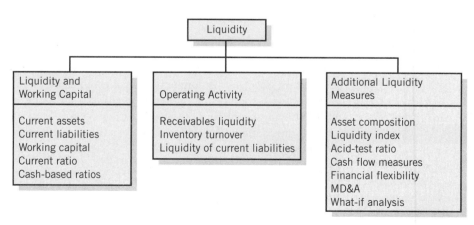

Liquidity

Liquidity and Working Capital	Operating Activity	Additional Liquidity Measures
Current assets Current liabilities Working capital Current ratio Cash-based ratios	Receivables liquidity Inventory turnover Liquidity of current liabilities	Asset composition Liquidity index Acid-test ratio Cash flow measures Financial flexibility MD&A What-if analysis

to assess liquidity risk. We begin with a discussion of the importance of liquidity and its link to working capital. We explain and interpret useful ratios of both working capital and a company's operating cycle for assessing liquidity. We also discuss potential adjustments to these analysis tools and the underlying financial statement numbers. What-if analysis of changes in a company's conditions or strategies concludes this section.

Solvency refers to a company's long-run financial viability and its ability to cover long-term obligations. All business activities of a company–financing, investing, and operating–affect a company's solvency. One of the most important components of solvency analysis is the composition of a company's capital structure. **Capital structure** refers to a company's sources of financing and its economic attributes. Section 2 of this chapter describes capital structure and explains its importance to solvency analysis. Since solvency depends on success in operating activities, we examine earnings and the ability of earnings to *cover* important and necessary company expenditures. We describe

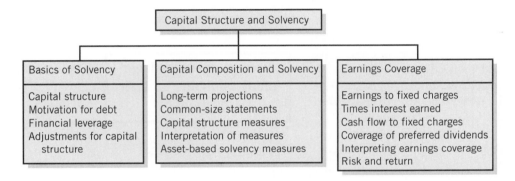

various tools of solvency analysis, including leverage measures, analytical accounting adjustments, capital structure analysis, and earnings-coverage measures. We demonstrate these analysis tools with data from financial statements. We also discuss the relation between risk and return inherent in a company's capital structure and its implications for financial statement analysis.

SECTION 1: LIQUIDITY

Section 1 focuses on liquidity. We consider solvency and capital structure in Section 2.

......LIQUIDITY AND WORKING CAPITAL

Liquidity is the ability to convert assets into cash or to obtain cash to meet short-term obligations. *Short term* is conventionally viewed as a period up to one year, though it is identified with the normal operating cycle of a company (the time period encompassing the buying-producing-selling-collecting cycle).

The importance of liquidity is best seen by considering repercussions stemming from a company's inability to meet short-term obligations. Liquidity is a matter of degree. Lack of liquidity prevents a company from taking advantage of favorable discounts or profitable opportunities. More extreme liquidity problems reflect a company's inability to cover current obligations. This can lead to forced sale of investments and other assets at reduced prices and, in its most severe form, to insolvency and bankruptcy.

For a company's shareholders, a lack of liquidity can foretell a loss of owner control or loss of capital investment. When a company's owners possess unlimited liability (proprietorships and certain partnerships), a lack of liquidity endangers their personal assets. To creditors of a company, a lack of liquidity can yield delays in collecting interest and principal payments or the loss of amounts due them. A company's customers and suppliers of products and services are also affected by short-term liquidity problems. Implications include a company's inability to execute contracts and damage to important customer and supplier relationships.

These scenarios highlight why measures of liquidity are of great importance in our analysis of a company. If a company fails to meet its current obligations, its continued existence is doubtful. Viewed in this light, all other measures of analysis are of secondary importance. While accounting measurements assume indefinite existence of the company, our analysis must always assess the validity of this assumption using liquidity and solvency measures.

Working capital is a widely used measure of liquidity. **Working capital** is defined as the excess of current assets over current liabilities. It is important as a measure of liquid assets that provide a safety cushion to creditors. It is also important in measuring the liquid reserve available to meet contingencies and the uncertainties surrounding a company's balance of cash inflows and outflows.

Current Assets and Liabilities

Current assets are cash and other assets reasonably expected to be (1) realized in cash or (2) sold or consumed within one year (or the normal operating cycle of the company if greater than one year). Balance sheet accounts typically included as current assets are cash, marketable securities maturing within the next fiscal year, accounts receivable, inventories, and prepaid expenses. **Current liabilities** are obligations expected to be satisfied within a relatively short period of time, usually one year. Current liabilities typically include accounts payable, notes payable, short-term bank loans, taxes payable, accrued expenses, and the current portion of long-term debt.

Our analysis must assess whether all current obligations with a reasonably high probability of eventual payment are reported in current liabilities. Their exclusion from current liabilities handicaps analysis of working capital. Three common concerns are:

1. Contingent liabilities associated with loan guarantees. We need to assess the likelihood of this contingency materializing when we compute working capital.
2. Future minimum rental payments under noncancelable operating lease agreements.
3. Contracts for construction or acquisition of long-term assets often call for substantial progress payments. These obligations for payments are reported in the footnotes as "commitments" and *not* as liabilities in the balance sheet. When computing working capital, our analysis should often include these commitments.

We also should recognize that current deferred tax assets (debits) are no more current assets than current deferred tax liabilities (credits) are current liabilities. Current deferred tax assets do not always represent expected cash inflows in the form of tax refunds. These assets usually serve to reduce future income tax expense. An exception is the case of net operating loss carrybacks. Similarly, current deferred tax liabilities do not always represent future cash outflows. Examples are temporary differences of a recurring nature (such as depreciation) that do not necessarily result in payment of taxes because their reversing differences are offset by equal or larger originating differences.

Working Capital Measure of Liquidity

Loan agreements and bond indentures often contain stipulations for maintenance of minimum working capital levels. Financial analysts assess the magnitude of working capital for investment decisions and recommendations. Government agencies compute aggregates of companies' working capital for regulatory and policy actions. And published financial statements distinguish between current and noncurrent assets and liabilities in response to these and other user needs.

Yet the amount of working capital is more relevant to users' decisions when related to other key financial variables like sales or total assets. It is of limited value for direct comparative purposes and for assessing the adequacy of working capital. This is seen in Illustration 10.1.

ILLUSTRATION 10.1
■ ■ ■ ■ ■ ■ ■

The following two companies have an equal amount of working capital. Yet, a quick comparison of the relation of current assets to current liabilities indicates Company A's working capital position is superior to Company B's.

	Company A	Company B
Current assets..............	$300,000	$1,200,000
Current liabilities	(100,000)	(1,000,000)
Working capital	$200,000	$ 200,000

Current Ratio Measure of Liquidity

The previous illustration highlights the need to consider *relative* working capital. That is, a $200,000 working capital excess yields a different conclusion for a company with $300,000 in current assets than one with $1,200,000 in current assets. A common relative measure in practice is the current ratio. The **current ratio** is defined as:

$$\text{Current ratio} = \frac{\text{Current assets}}{\text{Current liabilities}}$$

In Illustration 10.1, the current ratio is 3:1 ($300,000/$100,000) for Company A and 1.2:1 ($1,200,000/$1,000,000) for Company B. This ratio reveals a different picture for companies A and B. The ability to differentiate between companies on the basis of liquidity helps account for the widespread use of the current ratio.

Relevance of the Current Ratio

Reasons for the current ratio's widespread use as a measure of liquidity include its ability to measure:

- **Current liability coverage.** The higher the amount (multiple) of current assets to current liabilities, the greater assurance we have that current liabilities will be paid.

- **Buffer against losses.** The larger the buffer, the lower the risk. The current ratio shows the margin of safety available to cover shrinkage in noncash current asset values when ultimately disposing of or liquidating them.
- **Reserve of liquid funds.** The current ratio is relevant as a measure of the margin of safety against uncertainties and random shocks to a company's cash flows. Uncertainties and shocks, such as strikes and extraordinary losses, can temporarily and unexpectedly impair cash flows.

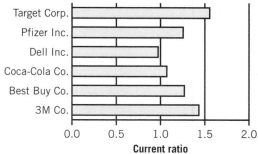

Current Ratios for Selected Companies

While the current ratio is a relevant and useful measure of liquidity and short-term solvency, it is subject to certain limitations we must be aware of. Consequently, before we describe the usefulness of the current ratio for our analysis, we discuss its limitations.

Limitations of the Current Ratio

A first step in critically evaluating the current ratio as a tool for liquidity and short-term solvency analysis is for us to examine both its numerator and denominator. If we define *liquidity* as the ability to meet cash outflows with adequate cash inflows, including an allowance for unexpected decreases in inflows or increases in outflows, then it is appropriate for us to ask: Does the current ratio capture these important factors of liquidity? Specifically, does the current ratio:

- Measure and predict the pattern of future cash inflows and outflows?
- Measure the adequacy of future cash inflows to outflows?

The answer to both these questions is generally no. The current ratio is a static measure of resources available at a point in time to meet current obligations. The current reservoir of cash resources does not have a logical or causal relation to its future cash inflows. Yet future cash inflows are the greatest indicator of liquidity. These cash inflows depend on factors excluded from the ratio, including sales, cash expenditures, profits, and changes in business conditions. To clarify these limitations, we need to examine more closely the individual components of the current ratio.

Numerator of the Current Ratio

We discuss each individual component of current assets and its implications for analysis using the current ratio.

Cash and Cash Equivalents.   Cash held by a well-managed company is primarily of a precautionary reserve intended to guard against short-term cash imbalances. For example, sales can decline more rapidly than cash outlays for purchases and expenses in a business downturn, requiring availability of excess cash. Since cash is a nonearning asset and cash equivalents are usually low-yielding securities, a company aims to minimize its investment in these assets. The cash balance has little relation to the existing level of business activity and is unlikely to convey predictive implications. Further, many companies rely on cash substitutes in the form of open lines of credit not entering into the computation of the current ratio.

Marketable Securities.   Cash in excess of the precautionary reserve is often spent on investment securities with returns exceeding those for cash equivalents. These investments are reasonably viewed as available to discharge current liabilities. Since investment securities are reported at their fair values (see Chapter 4), much of the guesswork from estimating their net realizable value is removed. Our analysis must recognize that the further removed the balance sheet date is from our analysis date, the greater likelihood for unrecorded changes in these investments' fair values.

Accounts Receivable.   A major determinant of accounts receivable is sales. The relation of accounts receivable to sales is governed by credit policies and collection methods. Changes in receivables correspond to changes in sales, though not necessarily on a directly proportional basis. Our analysis of accounts receivable as a source of cash must recognize, except in liquidation, the revolving nature of this asset. That is, the collection of one account is succeeded by a new extension of credit. Accordingly, the level of receivables is not a measure of future net cash inflows.

Inventories.   Like receivables, the major determinant of inventories is sales or expected sales—not the level of current liabilities. Since sales are a function of demand and supply, methods of inventory management (such as economic order quantities, safety stock levels, and reorder points) maintain inventory increments varying not in proportion to demand but by lesser amounts. The relation of inventories to sales is underscored by the observation that sales initiate the conversion of inventories to cash. Determination of future cash inflows from the sale of inventories depends on the profit margin that can be realized since inventories are reported at the lower of cost or market. The current ratio does not recognize sales level or profit margin, yet both are important determinants of future cash inflows.

Prepaid Expenses.   Prepaid expenses are expenditures for future benefits. Since these benefits are typically received within a year of the company's operating cycle, they preserve the outlay of current funds. Prepaid expenses are usually small relative to other current assets. However, our analysis must be aware of the tendency of companies with weak current positions to include deferred charges and other items of dubious liquidity in prepaid expenses. We should exclude such items from our computation of working capital and the current ratio.

Denominator of the Current Ratio

Current liabilities are the focus of the current ratio. They are a source of cash in the same way receivables and inventories use cash. Current liabilities are primarily determined by sales, and a company's ability to meet them when due is the object of working capital measures. For example, since purchases giving rise to accounts payable are a function of sales, payables vary with sales. As long as sales remain constant or are rising, the payment of current liabilities is a refunding activity. In this case the components of the current ratio provide little, if any, recognition to this activity or to its effects on future cash flows. Also, current liabilities entering into the computation of the current ratio do not include prospective cash outlays—examples are certain commitments under construction contracts, loans, leases, and pensions.

Using the Current Ratio for Analysis

From our discussion of the current ratio, we can draw at least three conclusions.

1.   Liquidity depends to a large extent on *prospective* cash flows and to a lesser extent on the level of cash and cash equivalents.

2. No direct relation exists between balances of working capital accounts and likely patterns of future cash flows.

3. Managerial policies regarding receivables and inventories are directed primarily at efficient and profitable asset utilization and secondarily at liquidity.

These conclusions do not bode well for the current ratio as an analysis tool and we might question why it enjoys widespread use in analysis. Reasons for using the current ratio include its understandability, its simplicity in computation, and its data availability. Its use also derives from the creditor's (especially banker's) propensity toward viewing credit situations as conditions of last resort. They ask themselves: What if there were a complete stoppage of cash inflows? Would current assets meet current liabilities? This extreme analysis is not always a useful way of assessing liquidity. Two other points are also pertinent. First, our analysis of short-term liquidity and solvency must recognize the relative superiority of cash flow projections and pro forma financial statements versus the current ratio. These analyses require information not readily available in financial statements, including product demand estimation (see Chapter 9). Second, if our analysis uses the current ratio as a static measure of the ability of current assets to satisfy current liabilities, we must recognize this is a different concept of liquidity from the one described above. In our context, liquidity is the readiness and speed that current assets are convertible to cash and the extent this conversion yields shrinkage in current asset values.

It is not our intent to reject the current ratio as an analysis tool. But it is important for us to know its relevant use. Moreover, there is no "adjustment" to rectify its limitations. Consequently, to what use can we apply the current ratio? The relevant use of the current ratio is only to measure the ability of current assets to discharge current liabilities. In addition, we can consider the excess of current assets, if any, as a liquid surplus available to meet imbalances in the flow of funds and other contingencies. These two applications are applied with our awareness that the ratio assumes company liquidation. This is in contrast to the usual going-concern situation where current assets are of a revolving nature (such as new receivables replacing collected receivables) and current liabilities are of a refunding nature (such as new payables covering payables due).

Provided we apply the current ratio in the manner described, there are two elements that we must evaluate and measure before the current ratio can usefully form a basis of analysis:

1. Quality of both current assets and current liabilities.
2. Turnover rate of both current assets and current liabilities—that is, the time necessary for converting receivables and inventories into cash and for paying current liabilities.

Several adjustments, ratios, and other analysis tools are available to make these evaluations and enhance our use of the current ratio (see subsequent pages). The remainder of this section describes relevant applications of the current ratio in practice.

Comparative Analysis

Analyzing the trend in the current ratio is often enlightening. Changes in the current ratio over time, however, must be interpreted with caution. Changes in this ratio do not necessarily imply changes in liquidity or operating performance. For example, during a recession a company might continue to pay current liabilities while inventory and receivables accumulate, yielding an increase in the current ratio. Conversely, in a successful period, increases in taxes payable can lower the current ratio. Company expansion often accompanying operating success can create larger working capital requirements. This "prosperity squeeze" in liquidity decreases the current ratio and is the result of company expansion unaccompanied by an increase in working capital—see Illustration 10.2.

ILLUSTRATION 10.2
■ ■ ■ ■ ■ ■ ■

Technology Resources, Inc., experiences a doubling of current assets and a quadrupling of current liabilities with *no change* in its working capital. This yielded a prosperity squeeze evidenced by a 50% decline in the current ratio.

	Year 1	Year 2
Current assets............	$300,000	$600,000
Current liabilities	(100,000)	(400,000)
Working capital	$200,000	$200,000
Current ratio..............	3:1	1.5:1

Ratio Management

Our analysis must look for "management" of the current ratio, also known as *window dressing*. Toward the close of a period, management will occasionally press the collection of receivables, reduce inventory below normal levels, and delay normal purchases. Proceeds from these activities are then used to pay off current liabilities. The effect of these activities is to increase the current ratio—see Illustration 10.3.

ILLUSTRATION 10.3
■ ■ ■ ■ ■ ■ ■

Technology Resources, Inc., increases its current ratio by making an earlier-than-normal payoff of $50,000 of current liabilities:

	Before Payoff	After Payoff
Current assets	$ 200,000	$150,000
Current liabilities..........	(100,000)	(50,000)
Working capital.............	$ 100,000	$100,000
Current ratio	2:1	3:1

Our analysis should also go beyond annual measures and use interim measures of the current ratio. Interim analysis makes it more difficult for management to window dress and allows us to gauge seasonal effects on the ratio. For example, a strong current ratio in December can be misleading if a company experiences a credit squeeze at its seasonal peak in July.

Rule of Thumb Analysis

A frequently applied rule of thumb is if the current ratio is 2:1 or better, then a company is financially sound, while a ratio below 2:1 suggests increasing liquidity risks. The 2:1 norm implies there are $2 of current assets available for every $1 of current liabilities or, alternatively viewed, the value of current assets can in liquidation shrink by as much as 50% and still cover current liabilities. A current ratio much higher than 2:1, while implying superior coverage of current liabilities, can signal inefficient use of resources and a reduced rate of return. Our evaluation of the current ratio with any rule of thumb is of dubious value for two reasons:

1. Quality of current assets and the composition of current liabilities are more important in evaluating the current ratio (for example, two companies with identical current ratios can present substantially different risks due to variations in the quality of working capital components).
2. Working capital requirements vary with industry conditions and the length of a company's net trade cycle.

Net Trade Cycle Analysis

A company's working capital requirements are affected by its desired inventory investment and the relation between credit terms from suppliers and those extended to customers. These considerations determine a company's **net trade cycle.** Computation of a company's net trade cycle is described in Illustration 10.4

Selected financial information from Technology Resources for the end of Year 1 is reproduced below:

ILLUSTRATION 10.4
■ ■ ■ ■ ■ ■ ■

Sales for Year 1	$360,000
Receivables	40,000
Inventories*	50,000
Accounts payable†	20,000
Cost of goods sold (including depreciation of $30,000)	320,000

*Beginning inventory is $100,000.
†These relate to purchases included in cost of goods sold.

We estimate Technology Resources' purchases per day as:

Ending inventory	$ 50,000
Cost of goods sold	320,000
	370,000
Less: Beginning inventory	(100,000)
Cost of goods purchased and manufactured	270,000
Less: Depreciation in cost of goods sold	(30,000)
Purchases	$240,000

Purchases per day = $240,000 ÷ 360 = $666.67

Then, the net trade cycle for Technology Resources is computed as (in days):

$$\text{Accounts receivable} = \frac{\$40,000}{\$360,000 \div 360} = 40.00 \text{ days}$$

$$\text{Inventories} = \frac{\$50,000}{\$320,000 \div 360} = \frac{56.24 \text{ days}}{96.24 \text{ days}}$$

$$\text{Less: Accounts payable} = \frac{\$20,000}{\$240,000 \div 360} = 30.00 \text{ days}$$

$$\text{Net trade cycle (days)} = 66.24 \text{ days}$$

The numerator and denominator in Illustration 10.4 are adjusted on a consistent basis. Specifically, accounts receivable reported in sales dollars are divided by sales per day, inventories reported at cost are divided by cost of goods sold per day, and accounts payable reported in dollars of purchases are divided by purchases per day. Consequently, while the day measures are expressed on different bases, our estimation of the net trade cycle is on a consistent basis. This analysis shows Technology Resources has 40 days of sales tied up in receivables, maintains 56 days of goods available in inventory, and receives only 30 days of purchases as credit from its suppliers. The longer the net trade cycle, the larger is the working capital requirement. Reduction in the number of days' sales in receivables or cost of sales in inventories lowers working capital requirements. An increase in the number of days' purchases as credit received from suppliers lowers working capital needed. Working capital requirements are determined by industry conditions and practices. Comparisons using industry current ratios, and analysis of working capital requirements using net trade cycle measures, are useful in analysis of the adequacy of a company's working capital.

ANALYSIS VIEWPOINT   **. . . YOU ARE THE BANKER**

International Machines Corporation (IMC) calls on you for a short-term one-year $2 million loan to finance expansion in the United Kingdom. As part of your loan analysis of IMC you compute a 4:1 current ratio on current assets of nearly $1.6 million. Analysis of industry competitors yields a 1.9:1 average current ratio. What is your decision on IMC's loan application using this limited information? Would your decision change if IMC's application is for a 10-year loan?

Cash-Based Ratio Measures of Liquidity

Cash and cash equivalents are the most liquid of current assets. In this section, we examine cash-based ratio measures of liquidity.

Cash to Current Assets Ratio

The ratio of "near-cash" assets to the total of current assets is one measure of the degree of current asset liquidity. This measure, known as the **cash to current assets ratio,** is computed as:

$$\frac{\text{Cash} + \text{Cash equivalents} + \text{Marketable securities}}{\text{Current assets}}$$

The larger this ratio, the more liquid are current assets.

Cash to Current Liabilities Ratio

Another ratio measuring cash adequacy is the **cash to current liabilities ratio.** It is computed as:

$$\frac{\text{Cash} + \text{Cash equivalents} + \text{Marketable securities}}{\text{Current liabilities}}$$

This ratio measures the cash available to pay current obligations. This is a severe test ignoring the refunding nature of current assets and current liabilities. It supplements the cash to current assets ratio in measuring cash availability from a different perspective. To view this ratio as an extension of the quick ratio (see later analysis in this chapter) is, except in extreme cases, a too severe test of short-term liquidity. Still the importance of cash as the ultimate form of liquidity should not be underestimated. The record of business failures provides many examples of insolvent companies with sizable noncash assets (both current and noncurrent) and an inability to pay liabilities or to operate.

OPERATING ACTIVITY ANALYSIS OF LIQUIDITY

Operating activity measures of liquidity are important in credit analysis. This section considers three operating activity measures based on accounts receivable, inventory, and current liabilities.

Accounts Receivable Liquidity Measures

For most companies selling on credit, accounts and notes receivable are an important part of working capital. In assessing liquidity, including the quality of working capital and the current ratio, it is necessary to measure the quality and liquidity of receivables. Both quality and liquidity of accounts receivable are affected by their turnover rate. *Quality* refers to the likelihood of collection without loss. A measure of this likelihood is the proportion of receivables within terms of payment set by the company. Experience shows that the longer receivables are outstanding beyond their due date, the lower is the likelihood of collection. Their turnover rate is an indicator of the age of receivables. This indicator is especially useful when compared with an expected turnover rate computed using the permitted credit terms. *Liquidity* refers to the speed in converting accounts receivable to cash. The receivables turnover rate is a measure of this speed.

Accounts Receivable Turnover

The **accounts receivable turnover** ratio is computed as:

$$\frac{\text{Net sales on credit}}{\text{Average accounts receivable}}$$

Notes receivable from normal sales should be included when computing accounts receivable turnover. We should also include only credit sales when computing this ratio because cash sales do not create receivables. Since financial statements rarely separately disclose cash and credit sales, our analysis often must compute this ratio using total net sales (that is, assuming cash sales are insignificant). If cash sales are not insignificant, then this ratio is less useful. However, if the proportion of cash sales to total sales is relatively stable, then year-to-year comparisons of changes in the receivables turnover ratio are reliable. The most direct way for us to determine *average* accounts receivable is to add beginning and ending accounts receivable for the period and divide by two. Using monthly or quarterly figures yields more accurate estimates. The more that sales fluctuate, the more likely this ratio is distorted. The receivables turnover ratio indicates how often, on average, receivables revolve–that is, are received and collected during the year. Illustration 10.5 provides an example.

Consumer Electronics reports sales of $1,200,000, beginning receivables of $150,000, and year-end receivables of $250,000. Its accounts receivable turnover ratio is computed as:

$$\frac{\$1,200,000}{(\$150,000 + \$250,000) \div 2} = \frac{\$1,200,000}{\$200,000} = 6$$

ILLUSTRATION 10.5

Days' Sales in Receivables for Selected Industries

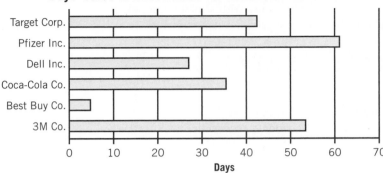

Days' Sales in Receivables

While the accounts receivable turnover ratio measures the speed of collections and is useful for comparison purposes, it is not directly comparable to the terms of trade a company extends to its customers. This latter comparison is made by converting the turnover ratio into days of sales tied up in receivables. The **days' sales in receivables** measures the number of days it takes, on average, to collect accounts receivable based on the year-end balance in accounts receivable. It is computed by dividing accounts receivable by average daily sales as follows:

$$\text{Days' sales in receivables} = \text{Accounts receivable} \div \frac{\text{Sales}}{360}$$

Using data from Consumer Electronics, the computation follows:[1]

$$\frac{\text{Accounts receivable}}{\text{Average daily sales}} = \frac{\$250,000}{(\$1,200,000/360)} = \frac{\$250,000}{\$3,333} = 75 \text{ days}$$

Interpretation of Receivables Liquidity Measures

Accounts receivable turnover rates and collection periods are usefully compared with industry averages or with the credit terms given by the company. When the collection period is compared with the terms of sale allowed by the company, we can assess the extent of customers paying on time. For example, if usual credit terms of sale are 40 days, then an average collection period of 75 days reflects one or more of the following conditions:

- Poor collection efforts.
- Delays in customer payments.
- Customers in financial distress.

The first condition demands corrective managerial action, while the other two reflect on both the quality and liquidity of accounts receivable and demand judicious managerial action. An initial step is to determine whether accounts receivable are representative of company sales activity. For example, receivables may be sold to SPEs and, if the SPEs are properly structured, the receivables are removed from the books. Intermittent sales of accounts receivable may, therefore, distort the ratio computations. It is not

---

[1] An alternative measure, the **receivables collection period,** measures the number of days it takes, on average, to collect accounts receivable based on the *average* balance in accounts receivable. It is computed by dividing the accounts receivable turnover ratio into 360 days (an approximate number of days in a year):

$$\text{Collection period} = \frac{360}{\text{Accounts receivable turnover}}$$

Using the figures from Consumer Electronics in Illustration 10.5, the receivables collection period is:

$$\frac{360}{6} = 60 \text{ days}$$

uncommon for companies to continue to service the accounts for the SPE. In this case the total amount of serviced receivables is provided in the footnotes. These can be added to those reported on the balance sheet to arrive at total outstanding receivables. The turnover ratios are then computed using total outstanding receivables.

Another complication relates to whether the receivable turnover ratios are computed based on gross or net accounts receivable. If the latter, the resulting computations are affected by the company's degree of conservatism in estimating uncollectible accounts. It is generally preferable to compute turnover ratios based on gross receivables to avoid this problem.

Certain trend analyses also merit our study. The trend in collection period over time is important in helping assess the quality and liquidity of receivables. Another trend to watch is the relation between the provision for doubtful accounts and gross accounts receivable, computed as:

$$\frac{\text{Provision for doubtful accounts}}{\text{Gross accounts receivable}}$$

Increases in this ratio over time suggest a decline in the collectibility of receivables. Conversely, decreases in this ratio suggest improved collectibility or the need to reevaluate the adequacy of the doubtful accounts provision. Overall, accounts receivable liquidity measures are important in our analysis. They are also important as measures of asset utilization, a subject we address in Chapter 8.

Inventory Turnover Measures

Inventories often constitute a substantial proportion of current assets. The reasons for this often have little to do with a company's need to maintain adequate liquid funds. Inventories are investments made for purposes of obtaining a return through sales to customers. In most companies, a certain level of inventory must be kept. If inventory is inadequate, sales volume declines below an attainable level. Conversely, excessive inventories expose a company to storage costs, insurance, taxes, obsolescence, and physical deterioration. Excessive inventories also tie up funds that can be used more profitably elsewhere. Due to risks in holding inventories, and given that inventories are further removed from cash than receivables are, they are normally considered the least liquid current asset. Our evaluation of short-term liquidity and working capital, which involves inventories, must include an evaluation of the quality and liquidity of inventories. Measures of inventory turnover are excellent tools for this analysis.

Inventory Turnover

The **inventory turnover ratio** measures the average rate of speed at which inventories move through and out of a company. Inventory turnover is computed as:

$$\frac{\text{Cost of goods sold}}{\text{Average inventory}}$$

Consistency requires we use cost of goods sold in the numerator because, like inventories, it is reported at cost. Sales, in contrast, includes a profit margin. Average inventory is computed by adding the beginning and ending inventory balances, and dividing by two. This averaging computation can be refined by averaging quarterly or monthly inventory figures. When we are interested in evaluating the *level* of inventory at a specific date, such as year-end, we compute the inventory turnover ratio using the inventory balance at that date in the denominator.

Days' Sales in Inventory for Selected Companies

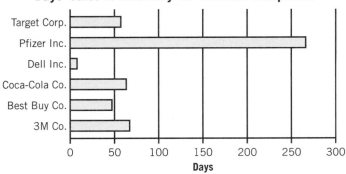

Days' Sales in Inventory

Another measure of inventory turnover useful in assessing a company's purchasing and production policy is the number of **days' sales in inventory,** computed as:[2]

$$\text{Inventories} \div \frac{\text{Cost of goods sold}}{360}$$

This ratio tells us the number of days required to sell *ending* inventory assuming a given rate of sales. Illustration 10.6 provides an example.

ILLUSTRATION 10.6   Selected financial information from Macon Resources for Year 8 is reproduced below:

Sales $1,800,000
Cost of goods sold 1,200,000
Beginning inventory........ 200,000
Ending inventory............. 400,000

$$\text{Days' sales in inventory} = \frac{\$400,000}{\$1,200,000/360} = 120 \text{ days}$$

Interpreting Inventory Turnover

The current ratio views current asset components as sources of funds to potentially pay off current liabilities. Viewed similarly, inventory turnover ratios offer measures of both the quality and liquidity of the inventory component of current assets. *Quality of inventory* refers to a company's ability to use and dispose of inventory. We should recognize, however, that a continuing company does not use inventory for paying current liabilities since any serious reduction in normal inventory levels likely cuts into sales volume.

When inventory turnover decreases over time, or is less than the industry norm, it suggests slow-moving inventory items attributed to obsolescence, weak demand, or nonsalability. These conditions question the feasibility of a company recovering inventory costs. We need further analysis in this case to see if decreasing inventory turnover is due to inventory buildup in anticipation of sales increases, contractual commitments, increasing prices, work stoppages, inventory shortages, or other legitimate reason. We also must be aware of inventory management (such as just-in-time systems) aimed at keeping inventory levels low by integrating ordering, producing, selling, and distributing. Effective inventory management increases inventory turnover.

[2] An alternative measure, the **days to sell inventory ratio,** is computed as:

$$\frac{360}{\text{Inventory turnover}}$$

This ratio tells us the number of days a company takes in selling *average* inventory for that year. Using the figures from Illustration 10.6, the days to sell inventory ratio is computed as:

$$\text{Inventory turnover ratio} = \frac{\$1,200,000}{(\$200,000 + \$400,000) \div 2} = 4$$

$$\text{Days to sell inventory ratio} = \frac{360}{4} = 90 \text{ days}$$

Another useful inventory liquidity measure is its **conversion period** or **operating cycle.** This measure combines the collection period of receivables with the days to sell inventories to obtain the time interval to convert inventories to cash. Using results computed from our two independent illustrations above, we would compute the conversion period as:

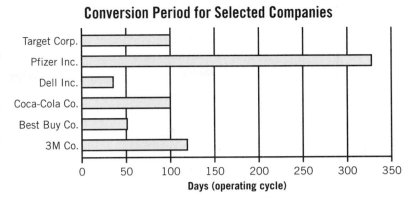

Conversion Period for Selected Companies

Days (operating cycle)

Days' sales in receivables	75
Days' sales in inventories	120
Conversion period	195

This implies it takes 195 days for a company to both sell its inventory and to collect the receivables, based on current levels of receivables and inventories.[3]

In evaluating inventory turnover, our analysis must be alert to the influence of alternative accounting principles for valuing the ratio's components. Our discussion of accounting for inventory in Chapter 4 is relevant here. Use of the LIFO method of inventory valuation can seriously impair the usefulness of both turnover and current ratios. For example, inventory valuation affects both the numerator and denominator of the current ratio—the latter through its effect on taxes payable. Information is often available in the financial statements enabling us to adjust unrealistically low LIFO inventory values in times of rising prices, making these values useful for inclusion in turnover and current ratios. Notice that even if two companies use the LIFO method for inventory valuation, their inventory-based ratios are likely *not* comparable because their LIFO inventory pools (bases) are almost certainly acquired in different years with different price levels. We also must remember that companies using a "natural year" may have at year-end an atypically low inventory level. This can increase a turnover ratio to an abnormally high level.

ANALYSIS VIEWPOINT   *. . . YOU ARE THE CONSULTANT*

King Entertainment, Inc., engages your services as a management consultant. One of your tasks is to streamline costs of inventory. After studying prior performance and inventory reports, you propose to strategically reduce inventories through improved inventory management. Your proposal expects the current inventory turnover of 20 will increase to 25. Money not invested in inventory can be used to decrease current liabilities—the costs of holding current liabilities average 10% per year. What is your estimate of cost savings if predicted sales are $150 million and predicted cost of sales is $100 million?

---

[3] Alternative computations commonly in use are (*a*) *Days to sell inventory + Collection period,* as described in footnotes 1 and 2, and (*b*) *Days' sales in receivables (days to sell inventory) + Days' sales in inventory (collection period) – Average payment period (days' purchases in accounts payable).* This latter computation recognizes that a portion of working capital is provided by a company's suppliers (the average payment period and day's purchases in accounts payable are discussed in the section Days' Purchases in Accounts Payable).

Liquidity of Current Liabilities

Current liabilities are important in computing both working capital and the current ratio for two related reasons:

1. Current liabilities are used in determining whether the excess of current assets over current liabilities affords a sufficient margin of safety.
2. Current liabilities are deducted from current assets in arriving at working capital.

In using working capital and the current ratio, the point of view is one of liquidation and *not* of continuing operations. This is because in normal operations current liabilities are not paid off but are of a refunding nature. Provided sales remain stable, both purchases and current liabilities should remain steady. Increasing sales usually yield increasing current liabilities.

Quality of Current Liabilities

The quality of current liabilities is important in analysis of working capital and the current ratio. Not all current liabilities represent equally urgent or forceful payment demands. At one extreme, we find liabilities for various taxes that must be paid promptly regardless of current financial pressures. Collection powers of federal, state, and local government authorities are formidable. At the other extreme are current liabilities to suppliers with whom a company has a long-standing relationship and who depend on and value its business. Postponement and renegotiation of these liabilities in times of financial pressures are both possible and common.

The quality of current liabilities must be judged on their degree of urgency in payment. We should recognize if fund inflows from current revenues are viewed as available for paying current liabilities, then labor and similar expenses requiring prompt payment have a first call on revenues. Trade payables and other liabilities are paid only after these outlays are met. We examined this aspect of funds flow in the prior chapter.

Our analysis also must be aware of unrecorded liabilities having a claim on current funds. Examples are purchase commitments and certain postretirement and lease obligations. When long-term loan acceleration clauses exist, a failure to meet current installments can render the entire debt due and payable.

Days' Purchases in Accounts Payable

A measure of the extent to which companies "lean on the trade" is the **average payable days outstanding.** This measure is computed as:[4]

$$\text{Average payable days outstanding} = \frac{\text{Accounts payable}}{\text{Cost of goods sold} \div 360}$$

The average payable days outstanding provides an indication of the average time the company takes in paying its obligations to suppliers. The longer the payment period, the greater the use of suppliers' capital.

A related measure is **accounts payable turnover.** It is computed as: Cost of goods sold ÷ Average accounts payable. This ratio indicates the speed at which a company pays for purchases on account.

---

[4] Purchases can be substituted for cost of goods sold in this formula, and can be estimated as:
Purchases = Cost of goods sold + Ending inventory − Beginning inventory.

........ADDITIONAL LIQUIDITY MEASURES
Current Assets Composition

The composition of current assets is an indicator of working capital liquidity. Use of common-size percentage comparisons facilitates our evaluation of comparative liquidity, regardless of the dollar amounts. Consider Illustration 10.7 as a case example.

Texas Electric's current assets along with their common-size percentages are reproduced below for Years 1 and 2:

Current assets	Year 1		Year 2	
Cash	$ 30,000	30%	$ 20,000	20%
Accounts receivable	40,000	40	30,000	30
Inventories	30,000	30	50,000	50
Total current assets	$100,000	100%	$100,000	100%

An analysis of Texas Electric's common-size percentages reveals a marked deterioration in current asset liquidity in Year 2 relative to Year 1. This is evidenced by a 10% decline for both cash and accounts receivable.

Acid-Test (Quick) Ratio

A more stringent test of liquidity uses the **acid-test (quick) ratio.** This ratio includes those assets most quickly convertible to cash and is computed as:

$$\frac{\text{Cash + Cash equivalents + Marketable securities + Accounts receivable}}{\text{Current liabilities}}$$

Inventories are often the least liquid of current assets and are not included in the acid-test ratio. Another reason for excluding inventories is that their valuation typically involves more managerial discretion than required for other current assets. Yet we must remember that inventories for some companies are more liquid than slow-paying receivables. Our analysis must assess the merits of excluding inventories in evaluating liquidity. The interpretation of the acid-test ratio is similar to that of the current ratio.

Cash Flow Measures

The static nature of the current ratio and its inability (as a measure of liquidity) to recognize the importance of cash flows in meeting maturing obligations has led to a search for a dynamic measure of liquidity. Since liabilities are paid with cash, a comparison of operating cash flow to current liabilities is important. A ratio comparing operating cash flow to current liabilities overcomes the static nature of the current ratio since its numerator reflects a flow variable. This **cash flow ratio** is computed as:

$$\frac{\text{Operating cash flow}}{\text{Current liabilities}}$$

The cash flow ratio computation for Campbell Soup in Year 11 is (data taken from financial statements reproduced in Appendix A):

$$\frac{\$805.2}{\$1,278} = 0.63$$

Financial Flexibility

There are important *qualitative* considerations bearing on short-term liquidity. These are usefully characterized as depending on the financial flexibility of a company. **Financial flexibility** is the ability of a company to take steps to counter unexpected interruptions in the flow of funds. It can mean the ability to borrow from various sources, to raise equity capital, to sell and redeploy assets, or to adjust the level and direction of operations to meet changing circumstances. A company's capacity to borrow depends on several factors and is subject to change. It depends on profitability, stability, size, industry position, asset composition, and capital structure. It also depends on credit market conditions and trends. A company's capacity to borrow is important as a source of cash and in turning over short-term debt. Prearranged financing or open lines of credit are reliable sources of cash. Additional factors bearing on an assessment of a company's financial flexibility are (1) ratings of its commercial paper, bonds, and preferred stock, (2) any restrictions on its sale of assets, (3) the extent expenses are discretionary, and (4) ability to respond quickly to changing conditions (such as strikes, demand shifts, and breaks in supply sources).

Management's Discussion and Analysis

As we discussed in Chapter 1, the Securities and Exchange Commission requires companies to include in their annual reports an expanded management discussion and analysis of financial condition and results of operations (MD&A). The financial condition section requires a discussion of liquidity–including known trends, demands, commitments, or uncertainties likely to impact the company's ability to generate adequate cash. If a material deficiency in liquidity is identified, management must discuss the course of action it has taken or proposes to take to remedy the deficiency. Internal and external sources of liquidity and any material unused sources of liquid assets must be identified and described. Our analysis benefits from management's discussion and analysis. For example, Dell includes a useful discussion titled Liquidity, Capital Commitments, and Contractual Cash Obligations in its MD&A section (see Appendix A).

What-If Analysis

What-if analysis is a useful technique to trace through the effects of changes in conditions or policies on the resources of a company. What-if analysis is illustrated in this section using the following selected financial data from Consolidated Technologies, Inc., at December 31, Year 1:

Cash	$ 70,000
Accounts receivable	150,000
Inventory	65,000
Fixed assets	200,000
Accumulated depreciation	43,000
Accounts payable	130,000
Notes payable	35,000
Accrued tax liability	18,000
Capital stock	200,000

The following additional information is reported for the year ended December 31, Year 1:

Sales	$750,000
Cost of sales	520,000
Purchases	350,000
Depreciation	25,000
Net income	20,000

Consolidated Technologies anticipates 10% growth in sales for Year 2. All revenue and expense items are expected to increase by 10%, except for depreciation, which remains the same. All expenses are paid in cash as they are incurred, and Year 2 ending inventory is projected at $150,000. By the end of Year 2, Consolidated Technologies expects to have notes payable of $50,000 and a zero balance in accrued taxes. The company maintains a minimum cash balance of $50,000 as a managerial policy.

Case 10.1 Consolidated Technologies is considering a change in credit policy where ending accounts receivable reflect 90 days of sales. What impact does this change have on the company's cash balance? Will this change affect the company's need to borrow? Our analysis of this what-if situation is as follows:

CONSOLIDATED TECHNOLOGIES
Cash Forecast
For Year Ended December 31, Year 2

Cash, January 1, Year 2			$ 70,000
Cash collections			
Accounts receivable, January 1, Year 2		$150,000	
Sales		825,000	
Total potential cash collections		975,000	
Less: Accounts receivable, December 31, Year 2		(206,250)(a)	768,750
Total cash available			838,750
Cash disbursements			
Accounts payable, January 1, Year 2	$130,000		
Purchases	657,000(b)		
Total potential cash disbursements	787,000		
Accounts payable, December 31, Year 2	(244,000)(c)	543,000	
Notes payable, January 1, Year 2	35,000		
Notes payable, December 31, Year 2	(50,000)	(15,000)	
Accrued taxes		18,000	
Cash expenses(d)		203,500	749,500
Cash, December 31, Year 2			89,250
Cash balance desired			50,000
Cash excess			$ 39,250

(continued)

(concluded)

Explanations:

(a) $825,000 \times \dfrac{90}{360} = \$206,250.$

(b)
Year 2 cost of sales*: $520,000 × 1.1 =	$572,000
Ending inventory (given)	150,000
Goods available for sale	$722,000
Beginning inventory	(65,000)
Purchases	$657,000

* *Excluding depreciation.*

(c) $\text{Purchases} \times \dfrac{\text{Beg. accounts payable}}{\text{Year 1 purchases}} = \$657,000 \times \dfrac{\$130,000}{\$350,000} = \underline{\$244,000}$

(d)
Gross profit ($825,000 − $572,000)		$253,000
Less: Net income	$24,500*	
Depreciation	25,000	(49,500)
Other cash expenses		$203,500

* *110% of $20,000 (Year 1 income) + 10% of $25,000 (Year 1 depreciation).*
Alternatively, $185,000 × 1.10 = $203,500, where $185,000 is last year's other cash expenses.

This change in credit policy would yield an excess in cash and no required borrowing.

Case 10.2 What if Consolidated Technologies worked to achieve an *average* accounts receivable turnover of 4.0 (instead of using *ending* receivables as in the previous case)? What impact does this change have on the company's cash balance? Our analysis of this what-if situation follows:

Excess cash balance as computed above		$39,250
Change from *ending* to *average* accounts receivable (A. R.)		
turnover increases year-end accounts receivable to:		

$\text{Average A. R.} = \dfrac{\$825,000}{4} = \$206,250$

Ending A. R. = [$206,250 × 2] − $150,000 = $262,500[a]

Less: Accounts receivable balance from Case 10.1	(206,250)	56,250 (cash decrease)
Cash to be borrowed		$17,000 (cash deficit)

[a] $\text{Average A. R.} = \dfrac{\text{Sales}}{\text{Average A. R. turnover}};$ Ending A. R. = [(Average A. R.) × 2] − Beginning A. R.

Consolidated Technologies would be required to borrow funds to achieve expected performance under the conditions specified.

Case 10.3 What if, in addition to the conditions prevailing in Case 10.2, the company's suppliers require payment within 60 days? What is the effect of this payment requirement on the cash balance? Our analysis of this case is as follows:

Cash required to borrow (from Case 10.2)		$ 17,000
Ending accounts payable (from Case 10.1)	$244,000	
Ending accounts payable under 60-day payment:		
$\text{Purchases} \times \dfrac{60}{360} = \$657,000 \times \dfrac{60}{360}$		(109,500)
Additional disbursements required		134,500
Cash to be borrowed		$151,500

This more demanding payment schedule from suppliers would place additional borrowing requirements on Consolidated Technologies.

SECTION 2: CAPITAL STRUCTURE AND SOLVENCY
·······BASICS OF SOLVENCY

Analyzing solvency of a company is markedly different from analyzing liquidity. In liquidity analysis, the time horizon is sufficiently short for reasonably accurate forecasts of cash flows. Long-term forecasts are less reliable and, consequently, analysis of solvency uses less precise but more encompassing analytical measures.

Analysis of solvency involves several key elements. Analysis of capital structure is one of these. *Capital structure* refers to the sources of financing for a company. Financing can range from relatively permanent equity capital to more risky or temporary short-term financing sources. Once a company obtains financing, it subsequently invests it in various assets. Assets represent secondary sources of security for lenders and range from loans secured by specific assets to assets available as general security for unsecured creditors. These and other factors yield different risks associated with different assets and financing sources.

Another key element of long-term solvency is *earnings* (or *earning power*)–implying the recurring ability to generate cash from operations. Earnings-based measures are important and reliable indicators of financial strength. Earnings is the most desirable and reliable source of cash for long-term payment of interest and debt principal. As a measure of cash inflows from operations, earnings is crucial to covering long-term interest and other fixed charges. A stable earnings stream is an important measure of a company's ability to borrow in times of cash shortage. It is also a measure of the likelihood of a company's rebounding from conditions of financial distress.

Lenders guard themselves against company insolvency and financial distress by including loan covenants in the lending agreements. Loan covenants set conditions of *default,* often based on accounting measures, at a level to allow the lender the opportunity to collect on the loan before severe financial distress. Covenants are often designed to (1) emphasize key measures of financial strength like the current ratio and debt to equity ratio, (2) prohibit the issuance of additional debt, or (3) ensure against disbursement of company resources through excessive dividends or acquisitions. Covenants cannot assure lenders against operating losses–invariably the source of financial distress. Covenants and protective provisions also cannot substitute for our alertness and monitoring of a company's results of operations and financial condition. The enormous amount of both public and private debt financing has led to some standardized approaches to its analysis and evaluation. While this chapter explains many of these approaches, Appendix 10A discusses the analysis of debt securities by rating agencies, and Appendix 10B describes the use of ratios as predictors of financial distress.

■ ■ ■ ■ ■ ■ ■
DEBT LIMIT
Each year, about 40% of small-business owners seek a loan. Banks reject about one-quarter of them.

Importance of Capital Structure

Capital structure is the equity and debt financing of a company. It is often measured in terms of the relative magnitude of the various financing sources. A company's financial stability and risk of insolvency depend on its financing sources and the types and amounts of various assets it owns. Exhibit 10.1 portrays a typical company's asset distribution and its financing sources. This exhibit highlights the potential variety in the investing and financing items that constitute a company–depicted within the accounting framework of assets equal liabilities plus equity.

Exhibit 10.1　　***A Typical Company's Asset Distribution and Capital Structure***

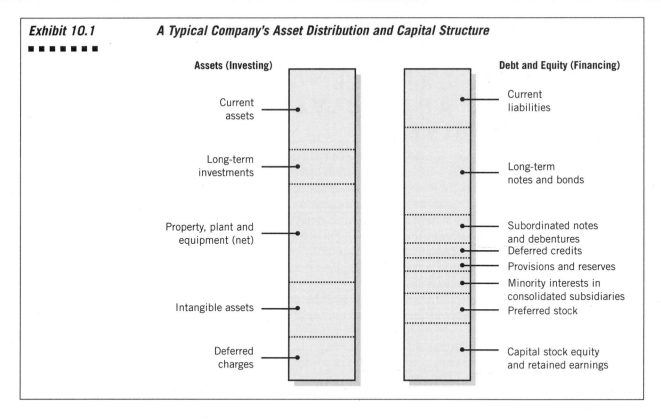

Characteristics of Debt and Equity

The importance of analyzing capital structure derives from several perspectives, not the least is the difference between debt and equity. **Equity** refers to the *risk capital* of a company. Characteristics of equity capital include its uncertain or unspecified return and its lack of any repayment pattern. Equity capital contributes to a company's stability and solvency. It is usually characterized by a degree of permanence, persistence in times of adversity, and a lack of any mandatory dividend requirement. A company can confidently invest equity financing in long-term assets and expose them to business risks without threat of recall.

Unlike equity capital, both short-term and long-term **debt** capital must be repaid. The longer the debt repayment period and the less demanding its repayment provisions, the easier it is for a company to service debt capital. Still, debt must be repaid at specified times regardless of a company's financial condition, and so too must periodic interest on most debt. Failure to pay principal and interest typically results in legal proceedings where common shareholders can lose control of the company and all or part of their investment. When the proportion of debt in the total capital structure of a company is larger, the higher are the resulting fixed charges and repayment commitments. The likelihood of a company's inability to pay interest and principal when due and potential losses for creditors also increases.

For investors in common stock, debt reflects a risk of loss of the investment, balanced by the potential of profits from financial leverage. **Financial leverage** is the use of debt to increase earnings. Leverage magnifies both managerial success (income) and failure (losses). Excessive debt limits management's initiative and flexibility for pursuing profitable opportunities. For creditors, increased equity capital is preferred as protection against losses from adversities. Lowering equity capital as a proportionate share of a company's financing decreases creditors' protection against loss and consequently increases credit risk. Our analysis task is to measure the degree of risk resulting from a company's capital structure. The remainder of this section looks at the motivation for debt capital and measuring its effects.

Motivation for Debt Capital

From a shareholder's perspective, debt is a preferred external financing source for at least two reasons:

1. Interest on most debt is fixed and, provided interest cost is less than the return on net operating assets, the excess return is to the benefit of equity investors.
2. Interest is a tax-deductible expense whereas dividends are not.

We discuss each of these factors in this section due to their importance for debt financing and risk analysis.

Concept of Financial Leverage

Companies typically carry both debt and equity financing. Creditors are generally unwilling to provide financing without protection provided by equity financing. Financial leverage refers to the amount of debt financing in a company's capital structure. Companies with financial leverage are said to be **trading on the equity.** This indicates a company is using equity capital as a borrowing base in a desire to reap excess returns.

Exhibit 10.2 illustrates trading on the equity. This exhibit computes the returns achieved for two companies referred to as Risky, Inc., and Safety, Inc.

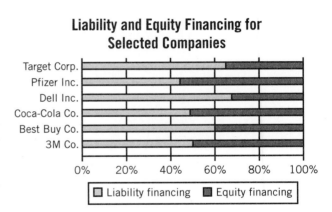

Liability and Equity Financing for Selected Companies

Trading on the Equity—Returns for Different Earnings Levels ($ millions)

Exhibit 10.2

| | | FINANCING SOURCES | | Operating Income before | 10% Debt | Taxes | Net | NOPAT [operating income | RETURN ON | |
| | | | | | | | | | Net Operating | Equity[†] |
	Assets	Debt	Equity	Taxes	Interest	(40%)	Income	× (1 − 40%)]	Assets (RNOA)[*]	(ROE)
Year 1										
Risky, Inc	$1,000	$400	$ 600	$200	$40	$64	$ 96	$120	12%	16%
Safety, Inc	1,000	0	1,000	200	0	80	120	120	12	12
Year 2										
Risky, Inc.	1,000	400	600	100	40	24	36	60	6	6
Safety, Inc.	1,000	0	1,000	100	0	40	60	60	6	6
Year 3										
Risky, Inc.	1,000	400	600	50	40	4	6	30	3	1
Safety, Inc.	1,000	0	1,000	50	0	20	30	30	3	3

[*]Return on net operating assets = NOPAT/Net Operating Assets.
[†]Return on equity = Net income/Shareholders' equity.

These two companies have identical net operating assets and operating income. Risky, Inc., derives 40% of its financing from debt while Safety, Inc., is debt-free, or *unlevered*. For Year 1, when the average return on net operating assets is 12%, the return on stockholders' equity of Risky, Inc., is 16%. This higher return to stockholders is due to the excess return on net operating assets over the *after-tax* cost of debt (12% versus 6%, the latter computed as 10% [*1 − 0.40*]). Safety, Inc.'s return on equity always equals the return on assets since there is no debt. For Year 2, the return on assets of Risky, Inc., equals the after-tax cost of debt and, consequently, the effects of leverage are neutralized. For Year 3, leverage is shown to be a double-edged sword. Specifically, when the return on net operating assets is *less* than the after-tax cost of debt, Risky, Inc.'s return on equity is lower than the return on equity for debt-free Safety, Inc. To generalize from this example: (1) a levered company is *successfully* trading on the equity when return on assets exceeds the after-tax cost of debt, (2) a levered company is *unsuccessfully* trading on the equity when return on net operating assets is less than the after-tax cost of debt, and (3) effects of leveraging are magnified in both good *and* bad years.

Tax Deductibility of Interest

One reason for the advantageous position of debt is the *tax deductibility of interest.* We illustrate this tax advantage by extending the case in Exhibit 10.2. Let us reexamine the two companies' results ($ millions) for Year 2:

Year 2	Risky, Inc.	Safety, Inc.
Income before interest and taxes	$100	$100
Interest (10% of $400)	(40)	0
Income before taxes	60	100
Taxes (40%)	(24)	(40)
Net income	36	60
Add back interest paid to bondholder	40	0
Total return to security holders (debt and equity)	$ 76	$ 60

Recall the leverage effects are neutral in Year 2. Still, notice that even when the return on net operating assets equals the after-tax cost of debt, the total amount available for distribution to debt and equity holders of Risky, Inc., is $16 higher than the amount available for the equity holders of Safety, Inc. This is due to the lower tax liability for Risky, Inc. We must remember the value of tax deductibility of interest depends on having sufficient income. To generalize from this example: (1) interest is tax deductible while cash dividends to equity holders are not, (2) because interest is tax deductible the income available to security holders can be much larger, and (3) nonpayment of interest can yield bankruptcy whereas nonpayment of dividends does not.

Other Effects of Leverage

Beyond the advantages from excess return to financial leverage and the tax deductibility of interest, a long-term debt position can yield other benefits to equity holders. For example, a growth company can avoid earnings per share dilution through issuance of debt. In addition, if interest rates are increasing, a leveraged company paying a fixed lower interest rate is more profitable than its nonleveraged competitor. However, the reverse is also true. Finally, in times of inflation, monetary liabilities (like most debt capital) yield price-level gains.

Adjustments for Capital Structure Analysis

Measurement and disclosure of liability (debt) and equity accounts in financial statements are governed by the application of accepted accounting principles. We discussed
principles governing measurement and disclosure of liability and equity accounts in
Chapter 3. Our analysis must remember these principles when analyzing capital structure and its implications for solvency.

Adjustments to Book Values of Liabilities

The relation between liabilities and equity capital, the two major sources of a company's financing, is an important factor in assessing long-term solvency. An understanding of this relation is therefore essential in our analysis. There exist liabilities not
fully reflected in balance sheets and there are financing-related items whose accounting
classification as debt or equity must not be blindly accepted in our analysis. Our identification and classification of these items depend on a thorough understanding of their
economic substance and the conditions to which they are subject. The discussion in this
section supplements the important analytical considerations in Chapter 3.

Deferred Income Taxes.   An important question is whether we treat deferred taxes as a
liability, as equity, or as part debt and part equity. Our answer depends on the nature of
the deferral, past experience of the account (such as its growth pattern), and the
likelihood of future reversals. In reaching our decision, we must recognize that, under
normal circumstances, deferred taxes reverse and become payable when a company's
size declines. To the extent future reversals are a remote possibility, as conceivable with
timing differences from accelerated depreciation, deferred taxes should be viewed like
long-term financing and treated like equity. However, if the likelihood of a drawing
down of deferred taxes in the foreseeable future is high, then deferred taxes (or part of
them) should be treated like long-term liabilities.

Operating Leases.   Current accounting practice requires that most financing long-term
noncancelable leases be shown as debt. Yet companies have certain opportunities to
structure leases in ways to avoid reporting them as debt. Operating leases should be
recognized on the balance sheet for analytical purposes, increasing both fixed assets and
liabilities as discussed in Chapter 3.

Off-Balance-Sheet Financing.   In determining the debt for a company, our analysis
must be aware that some managers attempt to understate debt, often with new and
sometimes complex means. We discuss several means for doing this in Chapter 3, including sales of receivables, off-balance-sheet financing arrangements utilizing special
purpose entities (SPEs), and equity method investments. Our critical reading of notes
and management comments, along with inquiries to management, can often shed light
on the existence of unrecorded liabilities.

Contingent Liabilities.   Contingencies such as product guarantees and warranties represent obligations to offer future services or goods that are classified as liabilities. Typically, reserves created by charges to income are also considered liabilities. Our analysis must make a judgment regarding the likelihood of commitments or contingencies becoming actual liabilities and then treat these items accordingly. For example, guarantees of indebtedness of subsidiaries or others that are likely to become liabilities should be treated as liabilities.

Minority Interests.   Minority interests in consolidated financial statements represent the book value of ownership interests of minority shareholders of subsidiaries in the consolidated group. These are *not* liabilities similar to debt because they have neither mandatory dividend payment nor principal repayment requirements. Capital structure measurements concentrate on the mandatory payment aspects of liabilities. From this point of view, minority interests are more like outsiders' claims to a portion of equity or an offset representing their proportionate ownership of assets.

Convertible Debt.   Convertible debt is usually reported among liabilities (or as an item separate from both debt and equity listings). If conversion terms imply this debt will be converted into common stock, then it can be classified as equity for purposes of capital structure analysis.

Preferred Stock.   Most preferred stock requires no obligation for payment of dividends or repayment of principal. These characteristics are similar to those of equity. However, as we discussed in Chapter 3, preferred stock with mandatory redemption requirements is similar to debt and should be considered as debt in our analysis.

ANALYSIS VIEWPOINT   *. . . YOU ARE THE ANALYST*

You are an analyst for a securities firm. Your supervisor asks you to assess the relative risk of two potential *preferred equity* investments. Your analysis indicates these two companies are identical in all aspects of both returns and risks with the exception of their financing composition. The first company is financed 20% by debt, 20% from preferred equity, and 60% from common equity. The second is financed 30% by debt, 10% from preferred equity, and 60% from common equity. Which company presents the greater preferred equity risk?

·······CAPITAL STRUCTURE COMPOSITION AND SOLVENCY

The fundamental risk with a leveraged capital structure is the risk of inadequate cash under conditions of adversity. Debt involves a commitment to pay fixed charges in the form of interest and principal repayments. While certain fixed charges can be postponed in times of cash shortages, the fixed charges related to debt cannot be postponed without adverse repercussions to a company's shareholders and creditors. This section discusses several measures commonly used to estimate the degree of financial leverage and to evaluate the risk of insolvency.

Common-Size Statements in Solvency Analysis

A common measure of financial risk for a company is its capital structure composition. **Composition analysis** is performed by constructing a **common-size statement** of the liabilities and equity section of the balance sheet. Exhibit 10.3 illustrates a common-size analysis for Tennessee Teletech, Inc. An advantage of common-size analysis of capital structure is in revealing the relative magnitude of financing sources for a company. We see Tennessee Teletech is primarily financed from common (35.6%) and preferred (17.8%) stock and liabilities (41.2%)—and a small amount of earnings is retained in the company (4.5%). Common-size analysis also lends itself to direct comparisons across different companies. A variation of common-size analysis is to perform the analysis using ratios. Another variation focuses only on long-term financing sources, excluding current liabilities.

Common-Size Analysis of Tennessee Teletech's Capital Structure

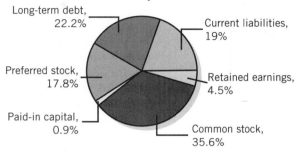

Long-term debt, 22.2%	Current liabilities, 19%
Preferred stock, 17.8%	Retained earnings, 4.5%
Paid-in capital, 0.9%	Common stock, 35.6%

Tennessee Teletech's Capital Structure: Common-Size Analysis			Exhibit 10.3
Current liabilities	$ 428,000	19.0%	
Long-term debt	500,000	22.2	
Equity capital			
Preferred stock	400,000	17.8	
Common stock	800,000	35.6	
Paid-in capital	20,000	0.9	
Retained earnings	102,000	4.5	
Total equity capital	1,322,000	58.8	
Total liabilities and equity	$2,250,000	100.0%	

Capital Structure Measures for Solvency Analysis

Capital structure ratios are another means of solvency analysis. Ratio measures of capital structure relate components of capital structure to each other or their total. In this section we describe the most common of these ratios. We must take care to understand the meaning and computation of any measure or ratio before applying it.

Total Debt to Total Capital

A comprehensive ratio is available to measure the relation between total debt (Current debt + Long-term debt + Other liabilities as determined by analysis such as deferred taxes and redeemable preferred) and total capital [Total debt + Stockholders' equity (including preferred)]. The **total debt to total capital ratio** (also called **total debt ratio**) is expressed as

$$\frac{\text{Total debt}}{\text{Total capital}}$$

Recall that total capital equals, by definition, total assets. The total debt to total capital ratio for Year 11 of Campbell Soup (financial statements are in Appendix A) is computed as:

$$\frac{\$1,278^{(a)} + \$772.6^{(b)} + \$305.0^{(c)}}{\$1,793.4^{(d)} + \$2,355.6^{(e)}} = \frac{\$2,355.6}{\$4,149.0} = 0.57$$

[a] Current liabilities
[b] Long-term debt
[c] Other liabilities
[d] Total shareholders' equity
[e] Total debt (numerator)

This measure is often expressed in ratio form, such as 0.57, or described as debt constituting 57% of Campbell Soup's capital structure.

Total Debt to Equity Capital

Another measure of the relation of debt to capital sources is the ratio of total debt (as defined above) to *equity* capital. The **total debt to equity capital ratio** is defined as:

$$\frac{\text{Total debt}}{\text{Shareholders' equity}}$$

The total debt to equity capital ratio for Year 11 of Campbell Soup is computed as:

$$\frac{\$2,355.6}{\$1,793.4} = 1.31$$

This ratio implies that Campbell Soup's total debt is 1.31 times its equity capital. Alternatively stated, Campbell Soup's credit financing equals 1.31 for every $1 of equity financing.

Long-Term Debt to Equity Capital

The **long-term debt to equity capital ratio** measures the relation of long-term debt (usually defined as all noncurrent liabilities) to equity capital. A ratio in excess of 1:1 indicates greater long-term debt financing compared to equity capital. This ratio is commonly referred to as the debt to equity ratio and it is computed as:

$$\frac{\text{Long-term debt}}{\text{Shareholders' equity}}$$

For Year 11 of Campbell Soup, the long-term debt to equity ratio equals:

$$\frac{\$2,355.6^{(a)} - \$1,278^{(b)}}{\$1,793.4^{(c)}} = 0.60$$

[a] Total debt
[b] Total current liabilities
[c] Shareholders' equity

Short-Term Debt to Total Debt

The ratio of debt maturing in the short term relative to total debt is an important indicator of the short-run cash and financing needs of a company. Short-term debt, as opposed to long-term debt or sinking fund requirements, is an indicator of enterprise reliance on short-term (primarily bank) financing. Short-term debt is usually subject to frequent changes in interest rates.

Interpretation of Capital Structure Measures

Common-size and ratio analyses of capital structure are primarily measures of the *risk* of a company's capital structure. The higher the proportion of debt, the larger the fixed charges of interest and debt repayment, and the greater the likelihood of insolvency during periods of earnings decline or hardship. Capital structure measures serve as *screening devices*. For example, when the ratio of debt to equity capital is relatively small (10% or less), there is no apparent concern with this aspect of a company's financial condition—our analysis is probably better directed elsewhere. Should our analysis reveal debt is a significant part of capitalization, then further analysis is necessary. Extended analysis should focus on several different aspects of a company's financial condition, results of operations, and future prospects.

Analysis of short-term liquidity is always important because before we assess long-term solvency we want to be satisfied about the near-term financial survival of the company. We described various analyses of short-term liquidity already in this chapter. Loan and bond indenture covenants requiring maintenance of minimum working capital levels attest to the importance of current liquidity in ensuring a company's long-term solvency. Additional analytical tests of importance include the examination of debt maturities (as to amount and timing), interest costs, and risk-bearing factors. The latter factors include a company's earnings stability or persistence, industry performance, and composition of assets.

DEFAULT
A study indicated that fewer than 1% of companies that carry the "A" rating have defaulted on their debt. This compares to 35% of companies with the "B" rating that have defaulted.

Asset-Based Measures of Solvency

This section describes two categories of asset-based analyses of a company's solvency.

Asset Composition in Solvency Analysis

The assets a company employs in its operating activities determine to some extent the sources of financing. For example, fixed and other long-term assets are typically not financed with short-term loans. These long-term assets are usually financed with equity capital. Debt capital is also a common source of long-term asset financing, especially in industries like utilities where revenue sources are stable.

Asset composition analysis is an important tool in assessing the risk exposure of a company's capital structure. Asset composition is typically evaluated using common-size statements of asset balances. Exhibit 10.4 shows a common-size analysis of Tennessee Teletech's assets (its liabilities and equity are analyzed in Exhibit 10.3). Judging by the distribution of assets and the

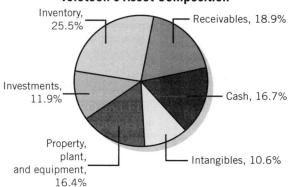

Common-Size Analysis of Tennessee Teletech's Asset Composition

Inventory, 25.5%
Receivables, 18.9%
Investments, 11.9%
Cash, 16.7%
Property, plant, and equipment, 16.4%
Intangibles, 10.6%

Exhibit 10.4 **Tennessee Teletech's Asset Composition: Common-Size Analysis**

Current assets		
Cash	$ 376,000	16.7%
Accounts receivable (net)...................	425,000	18.9
Merchandise inventory.......................	574,000	25.5
Total current assets.................................	1,375,000	61.1
Investments..	268,000	11.9
Property, plant, and equipment (net).......	368,000	16.4
Intangibles...	239,000	10.6
Total assets..	$2,250,000	100.0%

---

related capital structure, it appears that since a relatively high proportion of assets is current (61%), a 41% total liabilities position is not excessive. Further analysis and measurements might alter or reinforce this preliminary interpretation.

EARNINGS COVERAGE

Our discussion of capital structure measures recognizes their usefulness as screening devices. They are a valuable means of deciding whether risk inherent in a company's capital structure requires further analysis. One limitation of capital structure measures is their inability to focus on availability of cash flows to service a company's debt. As debt is repaid, capital structure measures typically *improve* whereas annual cash requirements for paying interest or sinking funds remain *fixed* or *increase* (examples of the latter include level payment debt with balloon repayment provisions or zero coupon bonds). This limitation highlights the important role of a company's **earnings coverage,** or *earning power,* as the source of interest and principal repayments. While highly profitable companies can in the short term face liquidity problems because of asset composition, we must remember that long-term earnings are the major source of liquidity, solvency, and borrowing capacity.

Relation of Earnings to Fixed Charges

The relation of earnings to fixed charges is part of **earnings coverage analysis.** Earnings coverage measures focus on the relation between debt-related fixed charges and a company's earnings available to meet these charges. These measures are important factors in debt ratings (see Appendix 10A). Bond indentures often specify minimum levels of earnings coverage for additional issuance of debt. Securities and Exchange Commission regulations require that the ratio of *earnings to fixed charges* be disclosed in the prospectus of all debt securities registered. The typical measure of the **earnings to fixed charges ratio** is:

$$\frac{\text{Earnings available for fixed charges}}{\text{Fixed charges}}$$

The concept underlying this measure is straightforward. Yet application of this measure is complicated by what is included in both "earnings available for fixed charges" and "fixed charges."

Computing Earnings Available for Fixed Charges

We previously discussed differences between income determined using accrual accounting and cash from operations (see Chapters 2, 6, and 7). For example, certain revenue items like undistributed subsidiary earnings and sales on extended credit terms do not generate immediate cash inflows (although a parent can determine dividends for controlled subsidiaries). Similarly, certain expenses like depreciation, amortization, depletion, and deferred tax charges do not require cash outflows. These distinctions are important since fixed debt charges are paid out of cash, not earnings. Our analysis must recognize that unadjusted net income is not necessarily a good measure of cash available for fixed charges. Using earnings as an approximation of cash from operations is sometimes appropriate while in others it can misstate the amount available for servicing fixed charges. Our approach to this problem lies not with generalizations but in careful analysis of noncash revenue and expense items that make up income. For example, in analyzing depreciation as a noncash expense, we must remember the long-run necessity of a company's replacing plant and equipment.

The income level used in computing earnings coverage ratios deserves attention. We must consider the question: What level of income is most representative of the amount actually available in future periods for paying debt-related fixed charges? Average earnings from continuing operations that span the business cycle and are adjusted for likely future changes are probably a good approximation of the average cash available from future operations to pay fixed charges. If one objective of an earnings coverage ratio is to measure a creditor's maximum exposure to risk, an appropriate earnings figure is one that occurs at the low point of the company's business cycle.

Computing Fixed Charges

The second major component in the earnings to fixed charges ratio is fixed charges. In this section we examine the fixed charges typically included in the computation. Analysis of fixed charges requires us to consider several important components.

Interest Incurred.   Interest incurred is the most direct and obvious fixed charge arising from debt. We can approximate the amount of interest incurred by referring to the mandatory disclosure of *interest paid* in the statement of cash flows. Interest incurred differs from the reported interest paid due to reasons that include (1) changes in interest payable, (2) interest capitalized being netted, and (3) discount and premium amortization. In the absence of information, interest paid is a good approximation of interest incurred.

Interest Implicit in Lease Obligations.   We discussed accounting recognition of leases as financing devices in Chapter 3. When a lease is capitalized, the interest portion of the lease payment is included in interest expense on the income statement, while most of the balance is usually considered repayment of the principal obligation. A question arises when our analysis discovers certain leases that should be capitalized but are not. This question goes beyond the accounting question of whether capitalization is appropriate or not. We must remember a long-term lease represents a fixed obligation that must be given recognition in computing the earnings to fixed charges ratio.

Preferred Stock Dividend Requirements of Majority-Owned Subsidiaries.   These are viewed as fixed charges because they have priority over the distribution of earnings to the parent. Items that would be or are eliminated in consolidation should not be viewed as fixed charges. We must remember that all fixed charges not tax deductible must be tax adjusted. This is done by increasing them by an amount equal to the income tax required to yield an after-tax income sufficient to cover these fixed charges. The preferred stock dividend requirements of majority-owned subsidiaries are an example of a non-tax-deductible fixed charge. We make an adjustment to compute the "gross" amount:

$$\frac{\text{Preferred stock dividend requirements}}{1 - \text{Effective tax rate}}$$

Principal Repayment Requirements.   Principal repayment obligations are from a cash outflow perspective as onerous as interest obligations. In the case of rental payments, a company's obligations to pay principal and interest must be met simultaneously. Several reasons are advanced as to why requirements for principal repayments are not given recognition in earnings to fixed charges ratio calculations, including:

- The earnings to fixed charges ratio is based on income. It assumes if the ratio is at a satisfactory level, a company can refinance obligations when they become due or mature. Accordingly, they need not be met by funds from earnings.
- If a company has an acceptable debt to equity ratio it should be able to reborrow amounts equal to principal repayments.
- Inclusion can result in double counting. For example, funds recovered by depreciation provide for debt repayment. If earnings reflect a deduction for depreciation, then fixed charges should not include principal repayments. There is some merit to this argument if debt is used to acquire depreciable fixed assets and if there is some correspondence between the pattern of depreciation and principal repayments. We must recognize that depreciation is recovered typically only from profitable or at least break-even operations. Therefore, this argument's validity is subject to these conditions. We must also recognize the definition of *earnings* in the earnings to fixed charges ratio emphasizes cash from operations as that available to cover fixed charges. Using this concept eliminates the double-counting problem since noncash charges like depreciation would be added back to net income in computing earnings coverage.
- A problem with including debt repayment requirements in fixed charges is that not all debt agreements provide for sinking funds or similar repayment obligations. Any arbitrary allocation of indebtedness across periods would be unrealistic and ignore differences in pressures on cash resources from actual debt repayments across periods. In the long run, maturities and balloon payments must all be met. One solution rests with our careful analysis of debt repayment requirements. This analysis serves as the basis in judging the effect of these requirements for long-term solvency. To assume debt can be refinanced, rolled over, or otherwise paid from current operations is risky. Rather, we must recognize debt repayment requirements and their timing in analysis of long-term solvency. Including sinking fund or other early repayment requirements in fixed charges is a way of recognizing these obligations. Another way is applying debt repayment requirements over a period of 5 to 10 years into the future and relating these to after-tax funds expected to be available from operations.

Guarantees to Pay Fixed Charges.   Guarantees to pay fixed charges of unconsolidated subsidiaries or of unaffiliated persons (entities) should be added to fixed charges if the requirement to honor the guarantee appears imminent.

Other Fixed Charges. While interest payments and principal repayment requirements are the fixed charges most directly related to the incurrence of debt, there is no reason to restrict our analysis of long-term solvency to these charges or commitments. A thorough analysis of fixed charges should include all long-term rental payment obligations[5] (not only the interest portion), and especially those rentals that must be met under noncancelable leases. The reason short-term leases can be excluded from consideration in fixed charges is they represent obligations of limited duration, usually less than three years. Consequently, these leases can be discontinued in a period of financial distress. Our analysis must evaluate how essential these leased items are to the continued operation of the company. Additional charges not directly related to debt, but considered long-term commitments of a fixed nature, are long-term noncancelable purchase contracts in excess of normal requirements.

Computing Earnings to Fixed Charges

The conventional formula, and one adopted by the SEC, for computing the earnings to fixed charges ratio is:

$$\frac{\begin{array}{l}(a)\text{ Pretax income from continuing operations }plus\text{ }(b)\text{ Interest expense }plus\\ (c)\text{ Amortization of debt expense and discount or premium }plus\text{ }(d)\text{ Interest portion of}\\ \text{operating rental expenses }plus\text{ }(e)\text{ Tax-adjusted preferred stock dividend requirements of}\\ \text{majority-owned subsidiaries }plus\text{ }(f)\text{ Amount of previously capitalized interest amortized in}\\ \text{the period }minus\text{ }(g)\text{ Undistributed income of less than 50\%-owned subsidiaries or affiliates}\end{array}}{\begin{array}{c}(h)\text{ Total interest incurred }plus\text{ }(c)\text{ Amortization of debt expense and discount or premium}\\ plus\text{ }(d)\text{ Interest portion of operating rental expenses }plus\text{ }(e)\text{ Tax-adjusted preferred stock}\\ \text{dividend requirements of majority-owned subsidiaries}\end{array}}$$

Individual components in this ratio are labeled *a–h* and are further explained here:

a. Pretax income before discontinued operations, extraordinary items, and cumulative effects of accounting changes.
b. Interest incurred less interest capitalized.
c. Usually included in interest expense.
d. Financing leases are capitalized so the interest implicit in these is already included in interest expense. However, the interest portion of long-term operating leases is included on the assumption many long-term operating leases narrowly miss the capital lease criteria, but have many characteristics of a financing transaction.
e. Excludes all items eliminated in consolidation. The dividend amount is increased to pretax earnings required to pay for it.[6]
f. Applies to nonutility companies. This amount is not often disclosed.
g. Minority interest in income of majority-owned subsidiaries having fixed charges can be included in income.
h. Included whether expensed or capitalized.

[5] Capitalized long-term leases affect income by the interest charge implicit in them and by the amortization of the property right. To consider the "principal" component of these leases as fixed charges (after income is reduced by amortization of the property right) can yield double counting.
[6] Computed as (Preferred stock dividend requirements)/(1 − Income tax rate). The income tax rate is computed as Actual income tax provision/Income before income taxes, extraordinary items, and cumulative effect of accounting changes.

For ease of presentation, two items (provisions) are left out of the ratio above, but they should be reflected in the ratio when they exist:

1. Losses of majority-owned subsidiaries should be considered in *full* when computing earnings.
2. Losses on investments in less than 50%-owned subsidiaries accounted for by the equity method should not be included in earnings *unless* the company guarantees subsidiaries' debts.

Finally, the SEC requires that if the earnings to fixed charges ratio is less than 1.0, the amount of earnings insufficient to cover fixed charges should be reported.

Illustration of Earnings to Fixed Charges Ratio

This section illustrates actual computation of the earnings to fixed charges ratio. Our first case focuses on CompuTech Corp., whose income statement is reproduced in Exhibit 10.5 along with selected notes. Using this information for CompuTech ($ thousands) we compute the earnings to fixed charges ratio as (letter references are to the ratio definition):

$$\frac{\$2,200\ (a) + \$700\ (b \text{ and } c) + \$300\ (d) + \$80\ (f) - \$600\ (g) + \$200^*}{\$840\ (h) + \$60\ (c) + \$300\ (d)} = 2.40$$

* *Note:* The SEC permits inclusion in income of the minority interest in the income of majority-owned subsidiaries having fixed charges. This amount is added to reverse a similar deduction from income.

Pro Forma Computation of Earnings to Fixed Charges

In situations where fixed charges not yet incurred are recognized in computing the earnings to fixed charges ratio (such as interest costs under a prospective debt issuance), it is acceptable to estimate offsetting benefits expected from these future cash inflows and include them in pro forma earnings. Benefits derived from prospective debt can be measured in several ways, including interest savings from a planned refunding activity, income from short-term investments where proceeds can be invested, or other reasonable estimates of future benefits. When the effect of a prospective refinancing plan changes the ratio by 10% or more, the SEC usually requires a pro forma computation of the ratio reflecting changes to be effected under the plan.

Times Interest Earned Analysis

Another earnings coverage measure is the **times interest earned ratio.** This ratio considers interest as the only fixed charge needing earnings coverage:

$$\frac{\text{Income} + \text{Tax expense} + \text{Interest expense}}{\text{Interest expense}}$$

The numerator in this ratio is sometimes referred to as earnings before interest and taxes, or EBIT, and then the ratio is referred to as EBIT/I. The times interest earned ratio is a simplified measure. It ignores most adjustments to both the numerator and denominator that we discussed with the earnings to fixed charges ratio. While its computation is simple, it is potentially misleading and not as effective an analysis tool as the earnings to fixed charges ratio.

Exhibit 10.5
■ ■ ■ ■ ■ ■ ■

COMPUTECH CORPORATION
Income Statement

Net sales..		$13,400,000
Income of less than 50%-owned affiliates (all undistributed)		600,000
Total revenue...		14,000,000
Cost of goods sold	$7,400,000	
Selling, general, and administrative expenses	1,900,000	
Depreciation (excluded from above costs)[1]	800,000	
Interest expense, net[2]	700,000	
Rental expense[3]	800,000	
Share of minority interests in consolidated income[4]	200,000	(11,800,000)
Income before taxes..		2,200,000
Income taxes		
Current..	800,000	
Deferred	300,000	(1,100,000)
Income before extraordinary item		1,100,000
Extraordinary gain (net of $67,000 tax)		200,000
Net income..		$ 1,300,000
Dividends		
On common stock	$ 200,000	
On preferred stock	400,000	(600,000)
Earnings retained for the year		$ 700,000

Selected notes to financial statements:

[1] *Depreciation includes amortization of previously capitalized interest of $80,000.*

[2] *Interest expense consists of:*

Interest incurred (except items below)...	*$740,000*
Amortization of bond discount..	*60,000*
Interest portion of capitalized leases...	*100,000*
Interest capitalized...	*(200,000)*
Interest expense...	*$700,000*

[3] *Interest implicit in noncapitalized leases amounts to $300,000.*

[4] *These subsidiaries have fixed charges.*

   Additional information (for the income statement period):

Increase in accounts receivable...	*$310,000*
Increase in inventories..	*180,000*
Increase in accounts payable	*140,000*
Decrease in accrued taxes	*20,000*

Relation of Cash Flow to Fixed Charges

Companies must pay fixed charges in cash while net income includes earned revenues and incurred expenses that do not necessarily generate or require immediate cash. This section describes a cash-based measure of fixed-charges coverage to address this limitation.

Cash Flow to Fixed Charges Ratio

The **cash flow to fixed charges ratio** is computed using *cash from operations* rather than earnings in the numerator of the earnings to fixed charges ratio. Cash from operations is reported in the statement of cash flows. The cash flow to fixed charges ratio is defined as:

$$\frac{\text{Pretax operating cash flow} + \text{Adjustments } (b) \text{ through } (g) \text{ defined on page 559}}{\text{Fixed charges}}$$

Using financial data of CompuTech from Exhibit 10.5 we can compute pretax cash from operations for this ratio as:

Pretax income	$2,200,000
Add (deduct) adjustments to cash basis	
Depreciation	800,000
Deferred income taxes (already added back)	—
Amortization of bond discount	60,000
Share of minority interest in income	200,000
Undistributed income of affiliates	(600,000)
Increase in receivables	(310,000)
Increase in inventories	(180,000)
Increase in accounts payable	140,000
Decrease in accrued tax	(20,000)
Pretax cash from operations	$2,290,000

Fixed charges needing to be added back to pretax cash from operations are:

Pretax cash from operations	$2,290,000
Interest expensed (less bond discount added back above)	640,000
Interest portion of operating rental expense	300,000
Amount of previously capitalized interest amortized during period*	—
Total numerator	$3,230,000

* Assume included in depreciation (already added back).

The numerator does not reflect a deduction of $600,000 (undistributed income of affiliates) because it, being a noncash source, is already deducted in arriving at pretax cash from operations. Also the "share of minority interests in consolidated income" is already added back in arriving at pretax cash from operations. Fixed charges for the ratio's denominator are:

Interest incurred	$ 900,000
Interest portion of operating rentals	300,000
Fixed charges	$1,200,000

CompuTech's cash flow to fixed charges ratio is computed as:

$$\frac{\$3,230,000}{\$1,200,000} = 2.69$$

Permanence of Cash from Operations

The relation of a company's cash flows from operations to fixed charges is important to an analysis of long-term solvency. Because of this relation's importance, we assess the "permanence" of operating cash flows. We typically do this in evaluating the components constituting operating cash flows. For example, the depreciation add-back to net income is more permanent than net income because recovery of depreciation from sales precedes receipt of any income. For all businesses, selling prices must (in the long run) reflect the cost of plant and equipment used in production. The depreciation add-back assumes cash flow benefits from recovery of depreciation are available to service debt. This assumption is true only in the short run. In the long run, this cash recovery must be dedicated to replacing plant and equipment. An exception can occur with add-backs of items like amortization of goodwill that are not necessarily replaced or depleted. Permanence of changes in the operating working capital (operating current assets less operating current liabilities) component of operating cash flows is often difficult to assess. Operating working capital is linked more with sales than with pretax income and therefore is often more stable than operating cash flows.

Earnings Coverage of Preferred Dividends

Our analysis of preferred stock often benefits from measuring the earnings coverage of preferred dividends. This analysis is similar to our analysis of how earnings cover debt-related fixed charges. The SEC requires disclosure of the ratio of combined fixed charges and preferred dividends in the prospectus of all preferred stock offerings. Computing the earnings coverage of preferred dividends must include in fixed charges all expenditures taking precedence over preferred dividends. Since preferred dividends are not tax deductible, after-tax income must be used to cover them. Accordingly, the **earnings coverage of preferred dividends ratio** is computed as:

$$\frac{\text{Pretax income} + \text{Adjustments } (b) \text{ through } (g) \text{ defined on page 559}}{\text{Fixed charges} + \left(\dfrac{\text{Preferred dividends}}{1 - \text{Tax rate}}\right)}$$

Using the financial data from CompuTech Corp. in Exhibit 10.5, we can compute its earnings coverage of preferred dividends ratio. This is identical to using CompuTech's ratio of earnings to fixed charges (computed earlier) and adding the tax-adjusted preferred dividend requirement. Computation of the earnings coverage to preferred dividends ratio is ($ thousands):

$$\frac{\$2,200 \ (a) + \$700 \ (b \text{ and } c) + \$300 \ (d) + \$80 \ (f) - \$600 \ (g) + \$200^*}{\$840 \ (h) + \$60 \ (c) + \$300 \ (d) + \left(\dfrac{\$400^\dagger}{1 - 0.50}\right)} = 1.44$$

Note: Letters refer to components in the earnings to fixed charges ratio (see page 559).

* Minority interest in income of majority-owned subsidiaries (see prior discussion).

† Tax-adjusted preferred dividend requirement.

If there are two or more preferred issues outstanding, the coverage ratio is usually computed for each issue by omitting dividend requirements of junior issues and including all prior fixed charges and senior issues of preferred dividends.

Interpreting Earnings Coverage Measures

Earnings coverage measures provide us insight into the ability of a company to meet its fixed charges out of current earnings. There exists a high correlation between earnings coverage measures and the default rate on debt–that is, the higher the coverage, the lower the default rate. A study of creditor experience with debt revealed the following default and yield rates for debt classified according to times interest earned ratios:

Times Interest Earned	Default Rate	Promised Yield	Realized Yield	Loss Rate
3.0 and over	2.1%	4.0%	4.9%	−0.9%
2.0–2.9	4.0	4.3	5.1	−0.8
1.5–1.9	17.9	4.7	5.0	−0.3
1.0–1.4	34.1	6.8	6.4	0.4
Under 1.0	35.0	6.2	6.0	0.2

Our attention on earnings coverage measures is sensible since creditors place considerable reliance on the ability of a company to meet its obligations and continue operating. An increased yield rate on debt seldom compensates creditors for the risk of losing principal. If the likelihood of a company meeting its obligations through continuing operations is not high, creditors' risk is substantial.

Importance of Earnings Variability and Persistence for Earnings Coverage

An important factor in evaluating earnings coverage measures is the behavior of earnings and cash flows across time. The more stable the earnings pattern of a company or industry, the lower is the acceptable earnings coverage measure. For example, a utility experiences little in the way of economic downturns or upswings and therefore we accept a lower earnings coverage ratio. In contrast, cyclical companies like machinery manufacturers can experience both sharp declines and increases in performance. This uncertainty leads us to impose a higher earnings coverage ratio on these companies. Both *earnings variability* and *earnings persistence* are common measures of this uncertainty across time. Our analysis can use one or both of these measures in determining the accepted standard for earnings coverage. Earnings persistence often is measured as the (auto) correlation of earnings across time.

Importance of Measurements and Assumptions for Earnings Coverage

Determining an acceptable level for earnings coverage depends on the method of computing an earnings coverage measure. We described several earnings coverage measures in this chapter. Many of these measures assume different definitions of *earnings* and *fixed charges*. We expect lower levels for earnings coverage measures employing the most demanding and stringent definitions. Both the SEC and our computation of the earnings to fixed charges coverage ratio use earnings *before* discontinued operations, extraordinary items, and cumulative effects of accounting changes. While excluding these three items yields a less variable earnings stream, it also excludes important components that are part of a company's business activities. Accordingly, we suggest these components be included in computing the *average* coverage ratio over several years. The acceptable level also varies with the measure of earnings—for example, earnings measured as the average, worst, best, or median performance. The quality of earnings is another important factor. We should not compute earnings coverage ratios using shortcuts or purposefully conservative means. For example, using after-tax income in computing coverage ratios where fixed charges are tax deductible is incorrect and uses conservatism improperly. Our acceptable level of coverage must ultimately reflect our willingness and ability to incur risk (relative to our expected return). Appendix 10A refers to acceptable levels of coverage ratios used by rating agencies in analyzing debt securities.

Capital Structure Risk and Return

It is useful for us to consider recent developments in financial innovations for assessing the risk inherent in a company's capital structure. A company can increase risks (and potential returns) of equity holders by increasing leverage. For example, a *leveraged buyout* uses debt to take a company private by buying out equity holders. The acquirors rely on future cash flows to service the increased debt and on anticipated asset sales to reduce debt. Another potential benefit of leverage is the tax deductibility of interest while dividends paid to equity holders are not tax deductible. Still, substitution of debt for equity yields a riskier capital structure. This is why bonds used to finance certain leveraged buyouts are called *junk bonds*. A junk bond, unlike its high-quality counterpart, is part of a high-risk capital structure where its interest payments are minimally covered by earnings. Economic adversities rapidly jeopardize interest payments and principal of junk bonds. Junk bonds possess the risk of equity more so than the safety of debt.

Financial experience continually reminds us of those who forget the relation between risk and return. It is no surprise that highly speculative financial periods spawn risky securities. Our surprise is the refusal by some to appreciate the adjective *junk* when applied to bonds. Similarly, zero coupon bonds defer all payment of interest to maturity and offer several advantages over standard debt issues. However, when issued by companies with less than outstanding credit credentials, the risk with zero coupon bonds is substantially higher than with standard debt—due to the uncertainty of receiving interest and principal many years into the future. Another financial innovation called *payment in kind (PIK) securities* pay interest by issuing additional debt. The assumption is a debtor, possibly too weak to pay interest currently, will subsequently be successful enough to pay it later. While innovations in financing companies' business activities continue, and novel terms are coined, our analysis must focus on substance over form. The basic truth about the relation between risk and return in a capital structure remains.

Factors contributing to risk and our available tools of analysis discussed in this and preceding chapters point to our need for thorough and sound financial analysis. Relying on credit ratings or others' rankings is a delegation of our analysis and evaluation responsibilities. It is risky for us to place partial or exclusive reliance on these sources of analysis. No matter how reputable, these sources *cannot* capture our unique risk and return expectations.

.....APPENDIX 10A RATING DEBT

10-Year Treasury and Corporate Bond Yields

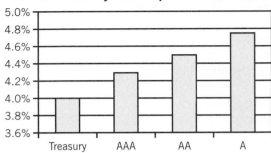

A comprehensive and complex system for rating debt securities is established in the world economy. Ratings are available from several highly regarded investment research firms: Moody's, Standard & Poor's (S&P), Duff and Phelps, and Fitch Ratings. Many financial institutions also develop their own in-house ratings.

BOND CREDIT RATINGS

The bond credit rating is a composite expression of judgment about the *creditworthiness* of the bond issuer and the quality of the specific security being rated. A rating measures credit risk where *credit risk* is the probability of developments unfavorable to the interests of creditors. This judgment of creditworthiness is expressed in a series of symbols reflecting degrees of credit risk. Specifically, the top four rating grades from Standard & Poor's are:

AAA　Bonds rated AAA are highest-grade obligations. They possess the highest degree of protection as to principal and interest. Marketwise, they move with interest rates and provide maximum safety.

AA　Bonds rated AA also qualify as high-grade obligations and in the majority of instances differ little from AAA issues. Here, too, prices move with the long-term money market.

A　Bonds rated A are regarded as upper-medium grade. They have considerable investment strength but are not free from adverse effects of changes in economic and trade conditions. Interest and principal are regarded as safe. They predominantly reflect money rates in their price behavior, and to some extent economic conditions.

BBB　Bonds rated BBB, or medium-grade category, are borderline between sound obligations and those where the speculative element begins to predominate. These bonds have adequate asset coverage and normally are protected by satisfactory earnings. Their susceptibility to changing conditions, particularly economic downturns, necessitates constant monitoring. Marketwise, these bonds are more responsive to business and trade conditions than to interest rates. This grade is the lowest that typically qualifies for commercial bank investment.

BOND QUALITY RATINGS

Rating Grades	Standard & Poor's	Moody's
Highest grade	AAA	Aaa
High grade	AA	Aa
Upper medium	A	A
Lower medium	BBB	Baa
Marginally speculative	BB	Ba
Highly speculative	B	B, Caa
Default	D	Ca, C

There is a lower selection of ratings, including **BB,** lower-medium grade to marginally speculative; **B,** very speculative; and **D,** bonds in default.

A major reason why debt securities are widely rated while equity securities are not is because there is far greater uniformity of approach and homogeneity of analytical measures in analyzing creditworthiness than in analyzing future market performance of equity securities. This wider agreement on what is being measured in credit risk analysis has resulted in acceptance of and reliance on published credit ratings for several purposes.

Criteria determining a specific rating are never precisely defined. They involve both *quantitative* (ratio and comparative analyses) and *qualitative* (market position and management quality) factors. Major rating agencies refuse to disclose their precise mix of factors determining ratings (which is usually a committee decision). They wish to avoid arguments about the validity of qualitative factors in ratings. These rating agencies use the analysis techniques discussed throughout this book. The following description of factors determining ratings is based on published sources and from discussions with officials of rating agencies.

RATING COMPANY BONDS

In rating an industrial bond issue, the rating agency focuses on the issuing company's asset protection, financial resources, earning power, management, and specific provisions of the debt. Also important are company size, market share, industry position, cyclical influences, and general economic conditions.

Asset protection refers to the extent a company's debt is covered by its assets. One measure is net tangible assets to long-term debt. One rating agency uses a rule of thumb where a bond needs a net tangible asset to long-term debt value of 5:1 for a AAA rating; 4:1 for a AA rating; 3 to 3.5:1 for an A rating; and 2.5:1 for a BBB rating. Concern with undervalued assets, especially with companies in the natural resources or real estate industries, leads to adjustments to these rating levels. Another rule of thumb suggests the long-term debt to total capital ratio be under 25% for a AAA, near 30% for a AA, near 35% for an A, and near 40% for a BBB rating. Additional factors entering rating agencies' consideration of asset protection include book value; composition of working capital; the quality and age of property, plant, and equipment; off-balance-sheet financing; and unrecorded liabilities.

Financial resources refer to liquid resources like cash and working capital accounts. Analysis measures include the collection period of receivables and inventory turnover. Their values are assessed relative to industry and absolute standards. Raters also analyze the issuer's use of both short-term and long-term debt, and their mix.

Future earning power, and the issuer's cash-generating ability, is an important factor in rating debt securities because the level and quality of future earnings determine a company's ability to meet its obligations, especially those of a long-term nature. Earning power is usually a more reliable source of protection than assets. One common measure of protection due to earning power is the earnings to fixed charges coverage ratio. A rule of thumb suggests an acceptable earnings to fixed charges ratio is 5:1 to 7:1 for a AAA rating, over 4:1 for a AA rating, over 3:1 for an A rating, and over 2:1 for a BBB rating. Another measure of debt servicing potential is cash flow from operations to long-term debt. A rule of thumb suggests this ratio be over 65% for a AAA, 45 to 60% for a AA, 35 to 45% for an A, and 25 to 30% for a BBB rating.

Management's abilities, foresight, philosophy, knowledge, experience, and integrity are important considerations in rating debt. Through interviews, site visits, and other analyses, the raters probe management's goals, strategies, plans, and tactics in areas like research and development, product promotion, product planning, and acquisitions.

Debt provisions are usually written in the bond indenture. Raters analyze the specific provisions in the indenture designed to protect interests of bondholders under a variety of conditions. These include analysis of stipulations (if any) for future debt issuances, security provisions like mortgaging, sinking funds, redemption provisions, and restrictive covenants.

▪ ▪ ▪ ▪ ▪ ▪ ▪

IS DEBT TOO HIGH?

To get a sense for whether a company has too much debt, compare its debt level with the average for companies with different ratings. The following table gives ratios (code: [1] is the long-term debt to equity ratio and [2] is the total debt to equity ratio) for different credit ratings:

	[1]	[2]
AAA	4.4%	4.5%
AA	23.0	34.1
A	33.3	42.9
BBB	41.5	47.9
BB	56.4	59.8
B	73.6	76.0

LIMITATIONS IN THE RATINGS GAME

Debt ratings are useful to a large proportion of debt issuances. Yet we must understand the inherent limitations of the standardized procedures of rating agencies. As with equity security analysis, our analysis can improve on these ratings. Debt issuances reflect a wide range of characteristics. Consequently, they present us with opportunities to identify differences within rating classes and assess their favorable or unfavorable impact within their ratings class. Also, there is evidence that rating changes lag the market. This lag effect presents us with additional opportunities to identify important changes prior to their being reported by rating agencies.

.....APPENDIX 10B PREDICTING FINANCIAL DISTRESS

A common use of financial statement analysis is identifying areas needing further investigation and analysis. One of these applications is **predicting financial distress.** Research has made substantial advances in suggesting various ratios as predictors of distress. This research is valuable in providing additional tools for analyzing long-term solvency. Models of financial distress, commonly referred to as **bankruptcy prediction models,** examine the trend and behavior of selected ratios. Characteristics of these ratios are used in identifying the likelihood of future financial distress. Models presume that evidence of distress appears in financial ratios and that we can detect it sufficiently early for us to take actions to either avoid risk of loss or to capitalize on this information.

ALTMAN Z-SCORE

Probably the most well-known model of financial distress is **Altman's Z-score.** Altman's Z-score uses multiple ratios to generate a predictor of distress.[7] Altman's Z-score uses a statistical technique (multiple discriminant analysis) to produce a predictor that is a linear function of several explanatory variables. This predictor classifies or predicts the likelihood of bankruptcy or nonbankruptcy. Five financial ratios are included in the Z-score: X_1 = Working capital/Total assets, X_2 = Retained earnings/Total assets, X_3 = Earnings before interest and taxes/Total assets, X_4 = Shareholders' equity/Total liabilities, and X_5 = Sales/Total assets. We can view X_1, X_2, X_3, X_4, and X_5 as reflecting (1) liquidity, (2) age of firm and cumulative profitability, (3) profitability, (4) financial structure, and (5) capital turnover rate, respectively. The Altman Z-score is computed as:

$$Z = 0.717\ X_1 + 0.847\ X_2 + 3.107\ X_3 + 0.420\ X_4 + 0.998\ X_5$$

A Z-score of less than 1.20 suggests a high probability of bankruptcy, while Z-scores above 2.90 imply a low probability of bankruptcy. Scores between 1.20 and 2.90 are in the gray or ambiguous area.[8]

---

[7] See E. Altman, "Financial Ratios, Discriminant Analysis, and the Prediction of Corporate Bankruptcy," *Journal of Finance* 22 (September 1968), pp. 589–609. Also see J. Begley, J. Ming, and S. Watts, "Bankruptcy Classification Errors in the 1980s: An Empirical Analysis of Altman's and Ohlson's Models," *Review of Accounting Studies* (1997).

[8] The model shown here is from Altman, *Corporate Financial Distress* (New York: John Wiley, 1983), pp. 120–124. This model is more generalizable than his earlier 1968 model which can only be applied to publicly traded companies. The earlier model is: $Z = 1.2\ X_1 + 1.4\ X_2 + 3.3\ X_3 + 0.6\ X_4 + 1.0\ X_5$. But X_4 in the earlier model requires the market value of preferred and common equity be available. The new model can be applied to *both* publicly traded and nonpublicly traded companies with no measurable effect on prediction performance. Use of the earlier model is fine provided it is only applied to publicly traded companies.

DISTRESS MODELS AND FINANCIAL STATEMENT ANALYSIS

Research efforts identify a useful role for ratios in predicting financial distress. However, we must *not* blindly apply this or any other model without informed and critical analysis of a company's fundamentals. There is no evidence to suggest computation of a Z-score is a better means of analyzing long-term solvency than is the integrated use of the analysis tools described in this book. Rather, we assert the use of ratios as predictors of distress is best in complementing our rigorous analysis of financial statements. Evidence does suggest the Z-score is a useful screening, monitoring, and attention-directing device.

GUIDANCE ANSWERS TO ANALYSIS VIEWPOINTS

BANKER

Your decision on IMC's one-year loan application is positive for at least two reasons. First, your analysis of IMC's short-term liquidity is reassuring. IMC's current ratio of 4:1 suggests a considerable margin of safety in its ability to meet short-term obligations. Second, IMC's current assets of $1.6 million and current ratio of 4:1 implies current liabilities of $400,000 and a working capital excess of $1.2 million. This working capital excess totals 60 percent of the loan amount. The evidence supports approval of IMC's loan application. However, if IMC's application is for a 10-year loan, our decision is less optimistic. While the current ratio and working capital suggest a good safety margin, there are indications of inefficiency in operations. First, a 4:1 current ratio is in most cases too excessive and characteristic of inefficient asset use. Second, IMC's current ratio is more than double that of its competitors. Our decision regarding a long-term loan is likely positive, *but* substantially less optimistic than a short-term loan.

CONSULTANT

Cost savings are assumed to derive from paying off current liabilities with money not invested in inventory. Accordingly, cost savings equal (Inventory reduction × 10%). Under the old system, inventory equaled $5 million. This is obtained using the inventory turnover ratio: 20 = $100 million/ Average inventory. With the new system, inventory equals $4 million; computed using the new inventory turnover: 25 = $100 million/Average inventory. The cost savings are $100,000—computed from ($5 million − $4 million) × 10%.

ENTREPRENEUR

The main criterion in your analysis is to compare the restaurant's return on assets to the after-tax cost of debt. If your restaurant can continue to earn 9% on assets, then the *after-tax* cost of debt must be less than 9% for you to successfully trade on the equity. Since the tax rate is 40%, you could successfully trade on the equity by adding new debt with an interest rate of 15% or less [9% (1 − 0.40)]. The lower the interest rate is from 15%, the more successful is your trading on the equity. You must recognize that taking on debt increases the riskiness of your business (due to the risk of unsuccessfully trading on the equity). This is because if your restaurant's earnings decline to where return on assets falls below the after-tax cost of debt, then return on equity declines even further. Accordingly, your assessment of earnings stability, or *persistence,* is a crucial part of the decision to add debt.

ANALYST

The preferred equity risk is greater for the second company. For the first company, senior securities (to preferred equity) constitute 20% of financing. However, for the second company, senior securities constitute 30% of financing. In a situation of bankruptcy, 30% of residual value must be paid to debtors prior to payments to preferred equity holders. In addition, financial leverage for the second company is potentially greater, although precise assessment of leverage risk depends on the features of preferred stock (features such as fixed return, cumulative, nonparticipating, redeemable, and nonvoting make preferred stock more like debt).

QUESTIONS

10–1. Why is liquidity important in analysis of financial statements? Explain its importance from the viewpoint of more than one type of user.

10–2. Working capital equals current assets less current liabilities. Identify and describe factors impairing the usefulness of working capital as an analysis measure.

10–3. Are fixed assets potentially includable in current assets? Explain. If your answer is yes, describe situations where inclusion is possible.

10–4. Certain installment receivables are not collectible within one year. Why are these receivables sometimes included in current assets?

10–5. Are all inventories included in current assets? Why or why not?

10–6. What is the justification for including prepaid expenses in current assets?

10–7. Assume a company under analysis has few current liabilities but substantial long-term liabilities. Notes to the financial statements report the company has a "revolving loan agreement" with a bank. Is this disclosure relevant to your analysis?

10–8. Certain industries are subject to peculiar financing and operating conditions calling for special consideration in drawing distinctions between *current* and *noncurrent*. How should analysis recognize this in evaluating short-term liquidity?

10–9. Your analysis of two companies reveals identical levels of working capital. Are you confident in concluding their liquidity positions are equivalent?

10–10. What is the current ratio? What does the current ratio measure? What are reasons for using the current ratio for analysis?

10–11. Since cash generally does not yield a return, why does a company hold cash?

10–12. Is there a relation between level of inventories and sales? Are inventories a function of sales? If there is a relation between inventories and sales, is it proportional?

10–13. What are management's objectives in determining a company's investment in inventories and receivables?

10–14. What are the limitations of the current ratio as a measure of liquidity?

10–15. What is the appropriate use of the current ratio as a measure of liquidity?

10–16. What are cash-based ratios of liquidity? What do they measure?

10–17. How can we measure "quality" of current assets?

10–18. What does accounts receivable turnover measure?

10–19. What is the days' sales in receivables? What does it measure?

10–20. Assume a company's days' sales in receivables is 60 days in comparison to 40 days for the prior period. Identify at least three possible reasons for this change.

10–21. What are the repercussions to a company of (*a*) overinvestment and (*b*) underinvestment in inventories?

10–22. What problems are expected in an analysis of a company using the LIFO inventory method when costs are increasing? What effects do price changes have on the (*a*) inventory turnover ratio and (*b*) current ratio?

10–23. Why is the composition of current liabilities relevant to our analysis of the quality of the current ratio?

10–24. A seemingly successful company can have a poor current ratio. Identify possible reasons for this result.

10–25. What is window-dressing of current assets and liabilities? How can we recognize whether financial statements are window-dressed?

10–26. What is the rule of thumb governing the expected level of the current ratio? What risks are there in using this rule of thumb for analysis?

10–27. Describe the importance of sales in assessing a company's current financial condition and the liquidity of its current assets.

10–28. Identify important qualitative considerations in the analysis of a company's liquidity. What SEC disclosures help our analysis in this area?

10–29. What is the importance of what-if analysis on the effects of changes in conditions or policies for a company's cash resources?

10–30. Identify several key elements in the evaluation of solvency.

10–31. Why is analysis of a company's capital structure important?

10–32. What is meant by *financial leverage?* Identify one or more cases where leverage is advantageous.

10–33. Dynamic Electronics, Inc., a successful and high-growth company, consistently experiences a favorable difference between the rate of return on its assets and the interest rate paid on borrowed funds. Explain why this company should not increase its debt to the 90% level of total capitalization and thereby minimize any need for equity financing.

(CFA Adapted)

10–34. How should we treat deferred income taxes in an analysis of capital structure?

10–35. In analysis of capital structure, how should lease obligations not capitalized be treated? Under what conditions should they be considered equivalent to debt?

10–36. What is off-balance-sheet financing? Provide one or more examples.

10–37. What are liabilities for pensions? What factors should our analysis of a company's pension obligations take into consideration?

10–38. When is information on unconsolidated subsidiaries important to solvency analysis?

10–39. Would you classify the items below as equity or liabilities? State your reason(s) and any assumptions.
   a. Minority interest in consolidated financial statements.
   b. Appropriated retained earnings.
   c. Guarantee for product performance on sale.
   d. Convertible debt.
   e. Preferred stock.

10–40. *a.* Why might an analysis of financial statements need to adjust the book value of assets?
   b. Give three examples of the need for possible adjustments to book value.

10–41. In evaluating solvency, why are long-term projections necessary in addition to a short-term analysis? What are some limitations of long-term projections?

10–42. What is the difference between common-size analysis and capital structure ratio analysis? Explain how capital structure ratio analysis is useful to financial statement analysis.

10–43. Equity capital on the balance sheet is reported using historical cost accounting and at times differs considerably from market value. How should our analysis allow for this, if at all, in analyzing capital structure?

10–44. Why is the evaluation of asset composition useful for capital structure analysis?

10–45. What does the earnings to fixed charges ratio measure? What does this ratio add to the other tools of credit analysis?

10–46. In computing the earnings to fixed charges ratio, what broad categories of items are included in fixed charges? What tax adjustments must be considered for these items?

10–47. A company you are analyzing has a purchase commitment of raw materials under a noncancelable contract that is substantial in amount. Under what conditions do you include this purchase commitment in computing fixed charges?

10–48. Is net income a reliable measure of cash available to meet fixed charges?

10–49. Company B is a wholly owned subsidiary of Company A. Company A is also Company B's principal customer. As a potential lender to Company B, what particular facets of this relationship concern you most? What safeguards, if any, do you require in any loan contract?

10–50. Comment on the assertion: *"Debt is a supplement to, not a substitute for, equity financing."*

10–51. A company in need of additional equity financing sells convertible debt. This action postpones equity dilution and the company ultimately sells its shares at an effectively higher price. What are the advantages and disadvantages of this action?

10–52. *a.* What is the reason for restrictive covenants in long-term debt indentures?
        b. What is the reason for provisions regarding:
            (1) Maintenance of minimum working capital (or current ratio)?
            (2) Maintenance of minimum shareholders' equity?
            (3) Restrictions on dividend payments?
            (4) Power of creditors to elect a majority of the board of directors of the debtor company in the event of default under terms of the loan agreement?

10–53. Why are debt securities regularly rated while equity securities are not?

10–54. What factors do rating agencies emphasize in rating an industrial bond? Describe these factors.

10–55. Can an analysis of financial statements improve on published bond ratings? Explain.

10–56. What is the reason(s) why companies hire bond rating agencies to rate their debt?

EXERCISES

EXERCISE 10–1

Interpreting Effects of Transactions on Liquidity Measures

The Lux Company experiences the following unrelated events and transactions during Year 1. The company's existing current ratio is 2:1 and its quick ratio is 1.2:1.

1. Lux wrote off $5,000 of accounts receivable as uncollectible.
2. A bank notifies Lux that a customer's check for $411 is returned marked insufficient funds. The customer is bankrupt.
3. The owners of Lux Company make an additional cash investment of $7,500.
4. Inventory costing $600 is judged obsolete when a physical inventory is taken.
5. Lux declares a $5,000 cash dividend to be paid during the first week of the next reporting period.
6. Lux purchases long-term investments for $10,000.
7. Accounts payable of $9,000 are paid.
8. Lux borrows $1,200 from a bank and gives a 90-day, 6% promissory note in exchange.
9. Lux sells a vacant lot for $20,000 that had been used in its operations.
10. A three-year insurance policy is purchased for $1,500.

Required:

Separately evaluate the immediate effect of each transaction on the company's:

a. Current ratio

b. Quick (acid-test) ratio

c. Working capital

EXERCISE 10–2

Interpreting Effects of Transactions on Liquidity Measures

Interpret the effect of the following six *independent* events and transactions for the:

a. Accounts receivable turnover (currently equals 3.0).

b. Days' sales in receivables.

c. Inventory turnover (currently equals 3.0).

The three columns to the right of each event and transaction are identified as (*a*), (*b*), and (*c*) corresponding to the three liquidity measures. For each event and transaction indicate the effect as an increase (I); decrease (D); or no effect (NE).

Events and Transactions	(a)	(b)	(c)
1. Beginning inventory understatement of $500 is corrected this period.	_____	_____	_____
2. Sales on account are underreported by $10,000.	_____	_____	_____
3. $10,000 of accounts receivable are written off by a charge to the allowance for doubtful accounts.	_____	_____	_____
4. $10,000 of accounts receivable are written off by a charge to bad debts expense (direct method).	_____	_____	_____
5. Under the lower-of-cost-or-market method, inventory is reduced to market by $1,000.	_____	_____	_____
6. Beginning inventory overstatement of $500 is corrected this period.	_____	_____	_____

Interpret the effect of the following six *independent* events and transactions for the:

a. Accounts receivable turnover (equals 4.0 prior to the event).

b. Days' sales in receivables.

c. Inventory turnover (equals 4.0 prior to the event).

The three columns to the right of each event and transaction are identified as (a), (b), and (c) corresponding to the three liquidity measures. For each event and transaction indicate the effect as an increase (I); decrease (D); or no effect (NE).

EXERCISE 10–3
Interpreting Effects of Transactions on Liquidity Measures

Events and Transactions	(a)	(b)	(c)
1. $5,000 of accounts receivable are written off by a charge to allowance for doubtful accounts.	_____	_____	_____
2. Beginning inventory understatement of $1,000 is corrected this period.	_____	_____	_____
3. Under the lower-of-cost-or-market method, inventory is reduced to market by $2,000.	_____	_____	_____
4. Obsolete inventory of $3,000 is identified and written off.	_____	_____	_____
5. Beginning inventory overstatement of $2,000 is corrected this period.	_____	_____	_____
6. Sales on account are overstated by $10,000 and corrected this period.	_____	_____	_____

The management of a corporation wishes to improve the appearance of its current financial position as reflected in the current and quick ratios.

Required:

a. Describe four ways in which management can window-dress the financial statements to accomplish this objective.

b. For each technique you identify in (a), describe the procedures, if any, you can use in your analysis to detect the window-dressing.

(CFA Adapted)

EXERCISE 10–4 ✓
Identifying Window-Dressing

EXERCISE 10–5

*Determining the Effect of
Transactions on
Solvency Ratios*

Financial data ($ thousands) for Wisconsin Wilderness, Inc., are reproduced below:

Short-term liabilities	$ 500
Long-term liabilities	800
Equity capital	1,200
Cash from operations	300
Pretax income..................	200
Interest expense	40

Indicate the effect that each of the Wisconsin Wilderness transactions and events (1 through 10) on the next page has on each of the four ratios below. (Each transaction or event is independent of others—consider only the immediate effect.) Use I for increase, D for decrease, and NE for no effect.

a. Total debt to equity.

b. Long-term debt to equity.

c. Earnings to fixed charges (exceeds 1.0 before transactions and events).

d. Cash flow to fixed charges (exceeds 1.0 before transactions and events).

	a	b	c	d
1. Increase in tax rate.				
2. Retire bonds—paid in cash.				
3. Issue bonds to finance expansion.				
4. Issue preferred stock to finance expansion.				
5. Depreciation expense increases.				
6. Collect accounts receivable.				
7. Refinance debt resulting in higher interest cost.				
8. Capitalize higher proportion of interest expense.				
9. Convert convertible debt into common stock.				
10. Acquire inventory on credit.				

EXERCISE 10–6

*What-If Analysis of
Capital Structure
(multiple choice)*

The following information is relevant for Questions 1 and 2:
Austin Corporation's Year 8 financial statement notes include the following information:

a. Austin recently entered into operating leases with total future payments of $40 million that equal a discounted present value of $20 million.

b. Long-term assets include held-to-maturity debt securities carried at their amortized cost of $10 million. Fair market value of these securities is $12 million.

c. Austin guarantees a $5 million bond issue, due in Year 13. The bonds are issued by Healey, a nonconsolidated 30%-owned affiliate.

After analysis, you decide to adjust Austin's balance sheet for each of the above three items.

1. Among the effects of these adjustments for the times interest earned coverage ratio is (choose one of the following):
   a. Lease capitalization increases this ratio.
   b. Lease capitalization decreases this ratio.
   c. Recognizing the debt guarantee decreases this ratio.
   d. Held-to-maturity debt securities adjustment increases this ratio.

2. Among the effects of these adjustments for the long-term debt to equity ratio is (choose one of the following):
   a. Only the held-to-maturity debt securities adjustment decreases this ratio.
   b. Only lease capitalization decreases this ratio.
   c. All three adjustments decrease this ratio.
   d. All three adjustments increase this ratio.

3. What is the effect of a cash dividend payment on the following ratios (all else equal)?

	Times Interest Earned	Long-Term Debt to Equity
a.	Increase	Increase
b.	No effect	Increase
c.	No effect	No effect
d.	Decrease	Decrease

4. What is the effect of selling inventory for profit on the following ratios (all else equal)?

	Times Interest Earned	Long-Term Debt to Equity
a.	Increase	Increase
b.	Increase	Decrease
c.	Decrease	Increase
d.	Decrease	Decrease

5. The existence of uncapitalized operating leases is to (choose one of the following):
   a. Overstate the earnings to fixed charges coverage ratio.
   b. Overstate fixed charges.
   c. Overstate working capital.
   d. Understate the long-term debt to equity ratio.

(CFA Adapted)

PROBLEMS

Refer to the financial statements of **Campbell Soup Company** in Appendix A.

Campbell Soup Company

PROBLEM 10–1

Analyzing Measures of Short-Term Liquidity

Required:

a. Compute the following liquidity measures for Year 10:
   (1) Current ratio.
   (2) Acid-test ratio.
   (3) Accounts receivable turnover (accounts receivable balance at end of Year 9 is $564.1).
   (4) Inventory turnover (inventory balance at end of Year 9 is $816.0).
   (5) Days' sales in receivables.
   (6) Days' sales in inventory.
   (7) Conversion period (operating cycle).
   (8) Cash and cash equivalents to current assets.
   (9) Cash and cash equivalents to current liabilities.
   (10) Days' purchases in accounts payable.
   (11) Net trade cycle.
   (12) Cash flow ratio.

Check
(a) 7. 105.54
10. 46.36
11. 59.18

b. Assess Campbell's liquidity position using results from (a).

c. For Year 10, compute ratios 1, 4, 5, 6, and 7 using inventories valued on a FIFO basis (FIFO inventory at the end of Year 9 is $904).

d. What are the limitations of the current ratio as a measure of liquidity?

e. How can analysis and use of other related measures (other than the current ratio) enhance the evaluation of liquidity?

PROBLEM 10–2

What-If Analysis of Cash Requirements

Selected financial data of Future Technologies, Inc., at December 31, Year 1, are shown below:

Cash	$ 42,000	Accounts payable	$ 78,000
Accounts receivable	90,000	Notes payable	21,000
Inventory	39,000	Accrued taxes	10,800
Fixed assets	120,000	Capital stock	120,000
Accumulated depreciation	25,800	Retained earnings	35,400

The following additional information is available for the year ended December 31, Year 1:

Sales	$450,000	Depreciation	$15,000
Cost of goods sold (excluding depreciation)	312,000	Net income	12,000
Purchases	210,000		

For Year 2, Future Technologies anticipates a 5% sales growth. To counterbalance this lower than expected growth rate, the company implements cost-cutting strategies to reduce cost of goods sold by 2% from the Year 1 level. All other expenses are expected to increase by 5%. Expected net income for Year 2 is $20,000. Ending Year 2 inventory is estimated at $90,000 and there is no expected balance in accrued taxes. The company requires $175,000 to buy new equipment in Year 2. The minimum desired cash balance is $30,000. The company offers a discount of 2% of sales if payment is received in 10 days. It is expected that 10% of sales take advantage of this discount, while the remaining 90% are collected (on average) in 60 days.

CHECK

Predicted borrowing, $103,232

Required:

Prepare a what-if analysis of cash needs (cash forecast) for Year 2. Will Future Technologies need to borrow money?

PROBLEM 10–3

What-If Analysis of Changes in Credit Policy

Shown below are selected financial accounts of RAM Corp. as of December 31, Year 1:

Cash	$ 80,000	Accounts payable	$130,000
Accounts receivable	150,000	Notes payable	35,000
Inventory	65,000	Accrued taxes	20,000
Fixed assets	200,000	Capital stock	200,000
Accumulated depreciation	45,000		

The following additional information is available for Year 1:

Sales	$800,000	Depreciation	$25,000
Cost of sales (excludes depreciation)	520,000	Net income	20,000
Purchases	350,000		

RAM Corp. anticipates growth of 10% in sales for the coming year. All corresponding revenue and expense items are expected to increase by 10%, except for depreciation, which remains the same. All expenses are paid in cash as incurred during the year. Year 2 ending inventory is predicted at $150,000. By the end of Year 2, the company expects a notes payable balance of $50,000 and no accrued taxes. The company maintains a minimum cash balance of $50,000 as a managerial policy.

Required:

Consider each of the following circumstances separately and independently of each other and focus only on changes described. (*Hint:* Prepare an analysis of cash needs (cash forecast) for Year 2, and then calculate the effect of each of these three separate alternative scenarios.)

a. RAM is considering changing its credit policy. This change implies ending accounts receivable would represent 90 days of sales. What is the impact of this policy change on RAM's current cash position? Will the company be required to borrow?

b. RAM is considering a change to a 120-day collection period based on ending accounts receivable. What is the effect(s) of this change on its cash position?

c. Suppliers are considering changing their policy of extending credit to RAM to require payment on purchases within 60 days; there would be no change in RAM's collection period. What is the effect(s) of this change on its cash position?

CHECK
(a) Cash excess, $33,500
(c) Cash needed, $46,000

Reproduced below are selected financial data at the end of Year 5 and *forecasts* for the end of Year 6 for Top Corporation:

PROBLEM 10–4 ✓
What-If Analysis of Cash Demands

Account	Year 5	Year 6 (Forecast)	Account	Year 5	Year 6 (Forecast)
Cash	$ 35,000	?	Accounts payable	$ 65,000	$122,000
Accounts receivable	75,000	?	Notes payable	17,500	15,000
Inventory	32,000	$ 75,000	Accrued taxes	9,000	0
Fixed assets	100,000	100,000	Capital stock	100,000	100,000
Accumulated depreciation	21,500	25,000			

Additional forecast estimates for Year 6:

Sales................... $412,500   Net income............................ $10,000
Cost of sales........ 70% of sales forecast   Days' sales in receivables....... 90 days

Required:

Assuming all expenses are paid in cash when incurred and that cost of sales is exclusive of depreciation, forecast the ending cash balance for Year 6. If Top Corp. wishes to maintain a minimum cash balance of $50,000, must it borrow?

CHECK
Cash needed, $27,125

You are an investment analyst at Valley Insurance. Robert Jollie, a CFA and your superior, recently asked you to prepare a report on Gant Corporation's liquidity. Gant is a manufacturer of heavy equipment for the agricultural, forestry, and mining industries. Most of its plant capacity is located in the United States and a majority of its sales are international. Gant's investment bankers are offering Valley Insurance a participation in a private placement debenture issue. Beyond the traditional ratio analysis, your memo to Jollie stresses the following:

PROBLEM 10–5
Qualitative Assessment of Liquidity

1. Gant's current ratio is 2:1.

2. During the prior fiscal year, Gant's working capital increased substantially.

3. While Gant's earnings are below record levels, rigorous cost controls yield an acceptable level of profitability and provide a basis for continued liquidity.

After reviewing your memo, Jollie dismisses it as "totally inadequate"–not because it did not include a quantitative analysis of financial ratios, but because it did not effectively address liquidity. Jollie writes:

> Liquidity is a cash issue, and liquidity analysis is a process of evaluating the risk of whether a company can pay its debts as they come due. The vagaries and inconsistencies of working capital definitions do not adequately address this issue. Working capital analysis simply accounts for the change in a company's working capital position and adds little to an assessment of liquidity.

Required:

a. Identify five key information items directly reflecting on Gant's liquidity that you should attempt to derive from this company's financial statements and management interviews.

b. Identify five *qualitative* financial and economic assessments specific to Gant and its industry that you should consider in further analyzing Gant's liquidity.

(CFA Adapted)

PROBLEM 10–6

Interpreting Measures of Short-Term Liquidity

As lending officer for Prudent Bank you are analyzing the financial statements of ZETA Corporation (see Case CC–2 in the Comprehensive Case Chapter for data) as part of ZETA's loan application. Your superior requests you evaluate ZETA's liquidity using the two-year financial information available. The following additional information is acquired (in $ thousands): Inventory at January 1, Year 5, $32,000.

Required:

a. Compute the following measures for both Years 5 and 6:
   (1) Current ratio.
   (2) Days' sales in receivables.
   (3) Inventory turnover.

CHECK
(5) Year 5, 79
   Year 6, 76

   (4) Days' sales in inventory.
   (5) Days' purchases in accounts payable (assume all cost of sales items are purchased).
   (6) Cash flow ratio.

b. Comment on any significant year-to-year changes identified from the analysis in (*a*).

PROBLEM 10–7

Calculating Solvency Ratios

Refer to the financial statements of **Campbell Soup Company** in Appendix A.

Campbell Soup Company

Required:

a. Compute the following measures for Year 10. (Assume 50% of deferred income taxes will reverse in the foreseeable future—the remainder should be considered equity.)
   (1) Total debt to equity.
   (2) Total debt to total assets.
   (3) Long-term liabilities to equity.
   (4) Total equity to total liabilities.
   (5) Fixed assets to equity.
   (6) Short-term liabilities to total debt.
   (7) Earnings to fixed charges.
   (8) Cash flow to fixed charges.
   (9) Working capital to total debt.

CHECK
(1) 1.21
(7) 2.14
(8) 5.27

b. Under the heading "Balance Sheets" in its Management's Discussion and Analysis section, Campbell refers to the ratio of total debt to capitalization (33.7%). Verify Campbell's computation for Year 10.

The income statement of Kimberly Corporation for the year ended December 31, Year 1, is reproduced below:

PROBLEM 10–8

Computing and Analyzing Earnings Coverage Ratios

KIMBERLY CORPORATION
Consolidated Income Statement ($ thousands)
For Year Ended December 31, Year 1

Sales...		$14,000
Undistributed income of less than 50%-owned affiliates........		300
Total revenue..		14,300
Cost of goods sold..	$6,000	
Selling and administrative expenses.......................................	2,000	
Depreciation..	600	
Rental expense...	500	
Share of minority interest in consolidated income...................	200	
Interest expense	400	(9,700)
Income before taxes		4,600
Income taxes		
Current	900	
Deferred..	400	(1,300)
Net income		$ 3,300
Less dividends..		
Common stock..	300	
Preferred stock...	400	(700)
Earnings retained for the year...		$ 2,600

Additional Information:

1. The following changes occurred in current assets and current liabilities for Year 1:

Current accounts	Increase (decrease)		Current accounts	Increase (decrease)
Accounts receivable..................	$900		Notes payable to bank	$(200)
Inventories.................................	(800)		Accounts payable	700
Dividend payable	(100)			

2. The effective tax rate is 40%.

3. Shares of minority interests in consolidated income do not have fixed charges.

4. Interest expense includes:

Interest incurred (except items below)...................	$600
Amortization of bond premium..............................	(300)
Interest on capitalized leases	140
Interest incurred	440
Less interest capitalized	(40)
Interest expense...	$400

5. Amortization of previously capitalized interest (included in depreciation) is $60.

6. Interest implicit in operating lease rental payment (included in rental expense) is $120.

Required:

a. Compute the following earnings coverage ratios:
    (1) Earnings to fixed charges.
    (2) Cash flow to fixed charges.
    (3) Earnings coverage of preferred dividends.

b. Analyze and interpret the earnings coverage ratios in (*a*).

PROBLEM 10–9

*Computing and
Analyzing Earnings
Coverage Ratios*

The income statement of Lot Corp. for the year ended December 31, Year 1, follows:

LOT CORPORATION
Income Statement ($ thousands)
For Year Ended December 31, Year 1

Sales		$27,400
Undistributed income of less than 50%-owned affiliates		400
Total revenue		27,800
Less: Cost of goods sold		(14,000)
Gross profit		13,800
Selling and administrative expenses	$3,600	
Depreciation[a]	1,200	
Rental expense[b]	1,400	
Share of minority interest in consolidated income[c]	600	
Interest expense[d]	1,200	(8,000)
Income before taxes		5,800
Income taxes		
Current	2,000	
Deferred	1,000	(3,000)
Net income		$ 2,800
Dividends		
Preferred stock	400	
Common stock	1,000	(1,400)
Earnings retained for the year		$ 1,400

[a] Represents depreciation excluded from all other expense categories and includes $100 amortization of previously capitalized interest.

[b] Includes $400 of interest implicit in operating lease rental payments that should be considered as having financing characteristics.

[c] These subsidiaries have fixed charges.

[d] Interest expense includes:

Interest incurred (except items below)	$ 880
Amortization of bond discount	100
Interest portion of capitalized leases	340
Interest capitalized	(120)
	$1,200

Additional Information:

1. The following changes occurred in current assets and liabilities for Year 1:

Current accounts	Increase (decrease)		Current accounts	Increase (decrease)
Accounts receivable	$(1,600)		Notes payable	$ (400)
Inventories	2,000		Accounts payable	2,000
Dividend payable	240			

2. Tax rate is 40%.

Required:

a. Compute the following earnings coverage ratios:
   (1) Earnings to fixed charges.
   (2) Cash flow to fixed charges.
   (3) Earnings coverage of preferred dividends.

b. Analyze and interpret the earnings coverage ratios in (*a*).

CHECK
(1) 4.48
(2) 6.04

Your supervisor is considering purchasing the bonds and preferred shares of ARC Corp. She furnishes you the following ARC income statement and expresses concern about the coverage of fixed charges.

PROBLEM 10–10
Analyzing Coverage Ratios

ARC CORPORATION
Consolidated Income Statement
For Year Ended December 31, Year 5

Sales		$27,400
Income of less than 50%-owned affiliates (note 1)		800
Total revenue		28,200
Cost of goods sold		(14,000)
Gross profit		14,200
Selling and administrative expenses	$3,600	
Depreciation (note 2)	1,200	
Rental expenses (note 3)	1,400	
Share of minority interests in consolidated income (note 4)	600	
Interest expense (note 5)	1,200	(8,000)
Income before income taxes		6,200
Income taxes		
Current	$2,000	
Deferred	1,000	$(3,000)
Net income		$ 3,200
Dividends		
Preferred stock	400	
Common stock	1,000	(1,400)
Increase in retained earnings		$ 1,800

(continued)

PROBLEM 10–10
(concluded)

Notes:
1. For the income from affiliates, $600 is undistributed.
2. Includes $80 amortization of previously capitalized interest.
3. Includes $400 of interest implicit in operating lease rental payments.
4. These subsidiaries do not have fixed charges.
5. Interest expense includes:

Interest incurred (except items below)	$ 880
Amortization of bond discount.....................	100
Interest portion of capitalized leases	340
Interest capitalized	(120)
	$1,200

6. The following changes occurred in current year balance sheet accounts:

Accounts receivable	$(600)
Inventories	160
Payables and accrued expenses..................	120
Dividends payable.....................................	(80)
Current portion of long-term debt	(100)

7. Tax rate is 40 percent.

Required:

a. Compute the following earnings coverage ratios:
   (1) Earnings to fixed charges.   (3) Earnings coverage of preferred dividends.
   (2) Cash flow to fixed charges.

b. Analyze and interpret the earnings coverage ratios in (a).

PROBLEM 10–11

Calculating Financial Ratios on Debt and Equity Securities

Refer to the following financial data of Fox Industries Ltd.:

FOX INDUSTRIES LIMITED
Condensed Income Statement ($ thousands)

	FISCAL YEAR ENDED				
	Year 7	Year 6	Year 5	Year 4	Year 3
Earnings before depreciation, interest on long-term debt, and taxes	$8,750	$8,250	$8,000	$7,750	$7,250
Less: Depreciation...	(4,000)	(3,750)	(3,500)	(3,500)	(3,250)
Earnings before interest on long-term debt and taxes	$4,750	$4,500	$4,500	$4,250	$4,000

FOX INDUSTRIES LIMITED
Capitalization at December 31, Year 7 ($ thousands)

Long-term debt
  First mortgage bonds
    5.00% serial bonds due Year 8 to Year 10 .... $ 7,500
    6.00% sinking fund bonds due Year 15 (note 1)............... 17,500
  Debentures
    6.50% sinking fund debentures due Year 16 (note 1)........ 10,000
  Total long-term debt... $35,000

(continued)

Capital stock

$1.10 cumulative redeemable preferred, stated value $5.00 per share (redeemable at $20.00 share).................	$ 1,500
400,000 Class A shares, no-par value (note 2)	14,000
1,000,000 common shares, no par value...............................	6,000
Total capital stock	21,500
Paid-in capital...	7,000
Retained earnings..	18,500
Total long-term debt and equity..	$82,000

Notes:
1. *Combined annual sinking fund payments are $500.*
2. *Subject to the rights of the preferred shares, the Class A shares are entitled to fixed cumulative dividends at the rate of $2.50 per share per annum, and are convertible at the holder's option, at any time, into common shares on the basis of two common shares for one Class A share.*

Required:

a. Compute the (1) earnings coverage ratio for Year 7, and (2) average earnings coverage ratio for the five-year period Year 3 through Year 7 (inclusive), separately on the first mortgage bonds and on the sinking fund debentures at the end of Year 7.

b. Compute the long-term debt to equity ratio as of December 31, Year 7, and identify the proportion of equity represented by shares senior to common shares.

c. Assuming a 50% income tax rate, calculate the (1) earnings coverage ratio for Year 7, and (2) average earnings coverage ratio for the five-year period Year 3 through Year 7 (inclusive), on the $1.10 cumulative redeemable preferred shares at the end of Year 7.

d. Assuming a 50% income tax rate and full conversion of the Class A shares, calculate earnings per common share for the end of Year 7.

CHECK
(c) 1. 1.7
    2. 1.6
(d) $0.56

(CFA Adapted)

TOPP Company is planning to invest $20,000,000 in an expansion program expected to increase income before interest and taxes by $4,000,000. TOPP currently is earning $5 per share on 2,000,000 shares of common stock outstanding. TOPP's capital structure prior to the investment is:

Total debt	$20,000,000
Shareholders' equity........	50,000,000
Total capitalization..........	$70,000,000

Expansion can be financed by the sale of 400,000 shares at $50 each or by issuing long-term debt at 6%. TOPP's most recent income statement follows:

Sales		$100,000,000
Variable costs.......................................	$60,000,000	
Fixed costs..	20,000,000	
Total costs...		(80,000,000)
Income before interest and taxes		20,000,000
Interest expense (6% rate)....................		(1,000,000)
Income before taxes		19,000,000
Income taxes (40% rate)........................		(7,600,000)
Net income		$ 11,400,000

Required:

a. Assuming TOPP maintains its current income level and achieves the expected income from expansion, what will be TOPP's earnings per share:
   (1) If expansion is financed by debt?   (2) If expansion is financed by equity?

b. At what level of income before interest and taxes will earnings per share be equal under both alternatives?

PROBLEM 10–13

*Analytical Adjustment
of the Debt to
Capitalization Ratio*

You are a senior portfolio manager with Reilly Investment Management reviewing the biweekly printout of equity value screens prepared by a brokerage firm. One of the screens used to identify companies is a "low long-term debt/total long-term capital ratio." The printout indicates this ratio for Lubbock Corporation is 23.9%. Your reaction is that Lubbock might be a potential takeover target and you proceed to analyze Lubbock's balance sheet reproduced below:

LUBBOCK CORPORATION
Condensed Balance Sheet, ($ millions)
December 31, Year 7

Assets

Cash and equivalents	$ 100
Receivables	350
Marketable securities	150
Inventory	800
Other current assets	400
Total current assets	1,800
Plant and equipment, net	1,800
Total assets	$3,600

Liabilities and Equity

Note payable	$ 125
Accounts payable	175
Taxes payable	150
Other current liabilities	75
Total current liabilities	525
Long-term debt	675
Deferred taxes (noncurrent)	175
Other noncurrent liabilities	75
Minority interest	100
Common stock	400
Retained earnings	1,650
Total liabilities and equity	$3,600

Further analysis of Lubbock's financial statements reveals the following notes:

1. A subsidiary, Lubbock Property Corp., holds, as joint venture partner, a 50% interest in its head office building in Chicago, and 10 regional shopping centers in the United States. The parent company has guaranteed the indebtedness of these properties, which total $250,000,000 at December 31, Year 7.

2. The LIFO cost basis was used in the valuation of inventories at December 31, Year 7. If the FIFO method of inventory was used in place of LIFO, inventories would have exceeded reported amounts by $200,000,000.

3. The company leases most of its facilities under long-term contracts. These leases are categorized as operating leases for accounting purposes. Future minimum rental payments as of December 31, Year 7 are: $90,000,000 per year for Year 8 through Year 27. These leases carry an implicit interest rate factor of 10%, which translates to a present value of approximately $750,000,000.

Required:

a. Explain how the information in each note is used to adjust items on Lubbock's balance sheet.

b. Calculate an adjusted *long-term debt to total long-term capitalization* ratio applying the proposed adjustments from (*a*). Ignore potential income tax effects.

c. As a potential investor, you consider other accounting factors in evaluating Lubbock's balance sheet including:
   (1) Valuation of marketable securities.   (2) Treatment of deferred taxes.

   Discuss how each of these accounting factors can impact Lubbock's *long-term debt to total long-term capitalization* ratio.

(CFA Adapted)

You are analyzing the bonds of ZETA Company (see Case CC–2 in the Comprehensive Case Chapter for data) as a potential long-term investment. As part of your decision-making process, you compute various ratios for Years 5 and 6. Additional data and information to be considered only for purposes of this problem follow ($ thousands):

PROBLEM 10–14

Analyzing and Interpreting Financial Ratios

1. Interest consists of:

	Year 6	Year 5
Interest incurred (except items below)........	$ 9,200	$5,000
Amortization of bond discount....................	2,500	2,000
Interest portion of capitalized leases..........	80	—
Interest capitalized.....................................	(1,780)	(1,000)
	$10,000	$6,000

2. Depreciation includes amortization of previously capitalized interest of $1,200 for Year 6 and $1,000 for Year 5.
3. Interest portion of operating rental expense considered a fixed charge: $20 in Year 6 and $16 in Year 5.
4. The associated company is less than 50% owned.
5. Deferred taxes constitute a long-term liability.
6. Present value of noncapitalized financing leases is $200 for both years.
7. Excess of the projected pension benefit obligation over the accumulated pension benefit obligation is $2,800 for both years.
8. End of Year 4 total assets and equity capital are $94,500 and $42,000, respectively.
9. Average market price per share of ZETA's common stock is $40 and $45 for Year 6 and Year 5, respectively.

Required:

a. Compute the following analytical measures for both Year 6 and Year 5:
   (1) Total debt to total assets.   (4) Earnings to fixed charges.
   (2) Total debt to equity.   (5) Cash flow to fixed charges.
   (3) Long-term debt to equity.

b. Analyze and interpret both the level and year-to-year trend in these measures.

CHECK
Year 6
(4) 2.61
(5) 2.25

As a new employee of Clayton Asset Management, you are assigned to evaluate the credit quality of BRT Corp. bonds. Clayton holds the bonds in its high-yield bond portfolio. The following information is provided to assist in the analysis.

PROBLEM 10–15

Analysis of Creditworthiness with Merger Activity

1. BRT Corporation is a rapidly growing company in the broadcast industry. It has grown primarily through a series of aggressive acquisitions.

2. Early in Year 6, BRT announced it was acquiring a competitor in a hostile takeover that would double its assets but also increase debt. The credit rating of BRT debt fell from BBB to BB. The acquisition reduced the financial flexibility of BRT but increased its presence in the broadcasting industry.

3. In the middle of Year 7, BRT announced it is merging with another large entertainment company. The merger will alter BRT's capital structure and also make it the leader in the broadcast industry. The Year 6 acquisition combined with this merger will increase the total assets of BRT by a factor of four. A large portion of the total assets are intangible, representing franchise and distribution rights.

4. While the outlook for the broadcasting industry remains strong, large telecommunication companies attempting to enter the broadcasting industry are keeping competitive pressures high. Laws and regulations also promote the competitiveness of the environment, but initial start-up costs make it difficult for new companies to enter the industry. Large capital expenditures are required to maintain and improve existing systems as well as to expand current business.

5. For your analysis, you are provided with the financial data shown here:

BRT CORPORATION
Balance Sheet Data (in millions)
At December 31

	Year 3	Year 4	Year 5	Year 6	Projected Year 7
Current assets	$ 654	$ 718	$2,686	$ 2,241	$ 5,255
Fixed assets, net	391	379	554	1,567	2,583
Other assets (intangibles)	2,982	3,090	3,176	8,946	20,435
Total assets	$4,027	$4,187	$6,416	$12,754	$28,273
Current liabilities	$ 799	$ 876	$ 966	$ 1,476	$ 3,731
Long-term debt	2,537	2,321	2,378	7,142	15,701
Other liabilities	326	292	354	976	349
Total equity	365	698	2,718	3,160	8,492
Total liabilities and equity	$4,027	$4,187	$6,416	$12,754	$28,273

BRT CORPORATION
Income Statement Data
(In Millions Except per Share Data)
For Year Ended December 31

	Year 3	Year 4	Year 5	Year 6	Projected Year 7
Net sales	$1,600	$1,712	$2,005	$4,103	$9,436
Operating expenses	(1,376)	(1,400)	(1,620)	(3,683)	(8,603)
Operating income	224	312	385	420	833
Interest expense	(296)	(299)	(155)	(270)	(825)
Income taxes	(20)	(42)	(130)	(131)	(4)
Net income	$ (92)	$ (29)	$ 100	$ 19	$ 4
Earnings per share	$ (0.86)	$ (0.24)	$ 0.83	$ 0.09	$ 0.01
Average price per share	$26.30	$34.10	$44.90	$40.10	$40.80
Average shares outstanding	107	120	121	198	359

BRT CORPORATION
Selected Ratios

	Year 3	Year 4	Year 5	Year 6	Projected Year 7
Operating income to sales.............	14.0%	18.2%	19.2%	10.2%	*
Sales to total assets......................	0.39	0.41	0.31	0.32	0.33
Earnings before interest and					
taxes to total assets.................	5.5%	7.4%	6.0%	3.3%	*
Times interest earned....................	0.76	1.04	2.48	1.55	*
Long-term debt to total assets......	63.0%	55.4%	37.0%	55.9%	*

CLAYTON ASSET MANAGEMENT
Credit Rating Standards

	AVERAGE RATIOS BY RATING CATEGORY						
Financial Ratios	**AA**	**A**	**BBB**	**BB**	**B**	**CCC**	**CC**
Operating income to sales (%)..........	16.2	13.4	12.1	10.3	8.5	6.4	5.2
Sales to total assets.........................	2.50	2.00	1.50	1.00	0.75	0.50	0.25
Earnings before interest and taxes							
to total assets..............................	15.0%	10.0%	8.0%	6.0%	4.0%	3.0%	2.0%
Times interest earned.......................	5.54	3.62	2.29	1.56	1.04	0.79	0.75
Long-term debt to total assets..........	19.5%	30.4%	40.2%	51.8%	71.8%	81.0%	85.4%
Bond Credit Spread Information							
Current yield spread in basis points							
over 10-year Treasuries.................	45	55	85	155	225	275	350

Required:

a. Calculate the following ratios using the projected Year 7 financial information:
   (1) Operating income to sales.   (3) Times interest earned.
   (2) Earnings before interest and taxes to total assets.   (4) Long-term debt to total assets.

b. Discuss the effect of the Year 7 merger on the creditworthiness of BRT through an analysis of each of the ratios in (*a*).

c. BRT Corporation 10-year bonds are currently rated BB and are trading at a yield to maturity of 7.70%. The current 10-year Treasury note is yielding 6.15%. Based on your work in (*a*) and (*b*), the background information, and information on Selected Ratios and Credit Rating Standards, state and justify whether Clayton should hold or sell the BRT Corporation bonds in its portfolio. Include qualitative factors in your discussion.

(CFA adapted)

PROBLEM 10–16
Comparative Credit Analysis of Companies

Assume you are a fixed-income analyst at an investment management firm. You are following the developments at two companies, Sturdy Machines and Patriot Manufacturing, which are both U.S.-based industrial companies that sell their products worldwide. Both companies operate in cyclical industries. Sturdy Machines' profits have suffered from a rising dollar and a slump in its business. The company has said that major cuts in its operating expenses are likely to be necessary if it is to make a profit next year. On the other hand, Patriot Manufacturing has been able to maintain its profitability and enhance its balance sheet. Selected data for both companies follow:

Ratio	Year 5	Year 6	Year 7
Sturdy Machines			
Cash flow/total debt (%)	37.3	31.0	33.0
Total debt/capital (%)	38.2	40.1	41.3
Pretax interest coverage (times)	4.2	2.3	1.1
Patriot Manufacturing			
Cash flow/total debt (%)	34.6	38.0	43.1
Total debt/capital (%)	40.0	37.3	34.9
Pretax interest coverage (times)	2.7	4.5	6.1

You are monitoring the bonds of these companies for possible purchase. You notice that a rating agency recently downgraded the senior debt of Sturdy Machines from AA to A and upgraded the senior debt of Patriot Manufacturing from AA to AAA. You received the following yield quotes from a broker:

- Sturdy Machines 7.50% due June 1, 2008, quoted at 7.10%.
- Patriot Manufacturing 7.50% due June 1, 2008, quoted at 7.10%.

Required:

Recommend which of the above bonds you should buy. Justify your choice with reference to at least two ratios and two qualitative factors from the information provided.

(CFA adapted)

CASES

CASE 10–1

Preparing and Interpreting Cash Flow Forecasts

Fax Corporation's income statement and balance sheet for the year ended December 31, Year 1, are reproduced below:

FAX CORPORATION
Income Statement
For Year Ended December 31, Year 1

Net sales		$960,000
Cost of goods sold (excluding depreciation)		(550,000)
Gross profit		410,000
Depreciation expense	$ 30,000	
Selling and administrative expenses	160,000	(190,000)
Income before taxes		220,000
Income taxes (state and federal)		(105,600)
Net income		$114,400

FAX CORPORATION
Balance Sheet
December 31, Year 1

Assets

Current assets

Cash	$ 30,000	
Marketable securities	5,500	
Accounts receivable	52,000	
Inventory	112,500	
Total current assets		$200,000
Plant and equipment	630,000	
Less: Accumulated depreciation	(130,000)	500,000
Total assets		$700,000

Liabilities and Equity

Current liabilities

Accounts payable	$ 60,000	
Notes payable	50,000	
Total current liabilities		$110,000
Long-term debt		150,000
Equity		
Capital stock	250,000	
Retained earnings	190,000	440,000
Total liabilities and equity		$700,000

Additional Information:

1. Purchases in Year 1 are $480,000.

2. In Year 2, management expects 15% sales growth and a 10% increase in all expenses except for depreciation, which increases by 5%.

3. Management expects an inventory turnover ratio of 5.5 for Year 2.

4. A receivable collection period of 90 days, based on *year-end* accounts receivable, is planned for Year 2.

5. Year 2 income taxes, at the same rate of pretax income for Year 1, will be paid in cash.

6. Notes payable at the end of Year 2 will be $30,000.

7. Long-term debt of $25,000 will be paid in Year 2.

8. FAX desires a minimum cash balance of $20,000 in Year 2.

9. The ratio of accounts payable to purchases for Year 2 is the same as in Year 1.

10. All selling and administrative expenses will be paid in cash in Year 2.

11. Marketable securities and equity accounts at the end of Year 2 are the same as in Year 1.

Required:

a. Prepare a statement of forecasted cash inflows and outflows (what-if analysis) for the year ended December 31, Year 2.

b. Will FAX Corporation have to borrow money in Year 2?

CHECK
Forecast cash needed,
$55,920

CASE 10–2

*Preparing and
Interpreting Cash Flow
Forecasts*

Kopp Corporation's income statement and balance sheet for the year ending December 31, Year 1, are reproduced below:

KOPP CORPORATION
Income Statement
For Year Ended December 31, Year 1

Net sales		$ 960,000
Cost of goods sold		(550,000)
Gross profit		410,000
Depreciation expense	$ 30,000	
Selling and administrative expenses	160,000	(190,000)
Income before taxes		220,000
Income taxes (48%)		(105,600)
Net income		$ 114,400

KOPP CORPORATION
Balance Sheet
December 31, Year 1

Assets

Current assets

Cash	$ 30,000	
Marketable securities	5,500	
Accounts receivable	52,500	
Inventory	112,000	
Total current assets		$200,000
Plant and equipment	630,000	
Less: Accumulated depreciation	(130,000)	500,000
Total assets		$700,000

Liabilities and Equity

Current liabilities

Accounts payable	$ 60,000	
Notes payable	50,000	
Total current liabilities		$110,000
Long-term debt		150,000
Equity		
Capital stock	250,000	
Retained earnings	190,000	440,000
Total liabilities and equity		$700,000

Additional Information:

1. Purchases in Year 1 are $450,000.

2. In Year 2, management expects 15% sales growth and a 10% increase in all expenses except for depreciation, which increases by 5%.

3. Inventory turnover for Year 1 is 5.0, and management expects an inventory turnover ratio of 6.0 for Year 2.

4. A receivable collection period of 90 days, based on *year-end* accounts receivable, is planned for Year 2.

5. Year 2 income taxes, at the same rate on pretax income in Year 1, will be paid in cash.

6. Notes payable of $20,000 will be paid in Year 2.

7. Long-term debt of $25,000 will be repaid in Year 2.

8. Kopp desires a minimum cash balance of $20,000 in Year 2.

9. The ratio of accounts payable to purchases will remain the same in Year 2 as in Year 1.

Required:

a. Prepare a statement of forecasted cash inflows and outflows (what-if analysis) for the year ending December 31, Year 2.

b. Will Kopp Corporation have to borrow money in Year 2?

CHECK
Forecasted cash need,
$35,898

Ian Manufacturing Company was organized five years ago and manufactures toys. Its most recent three years' balance sheets and income statements are reproduced below:

CASE 10–3
*Making a
Lending Decision*

IAN MANUFACTURING COMPANY
Balance Sheets
June 30, Year 5, Year 4, and Year 3

	Year 5	Year 4	Year 3
Assets			
Cash	$ 12,000	$ 15,000	$ 16,000
Accounts receivable, net	183,000	80,000	60,000
Inventory	142,000	97,000	52,000
Other current assets	5,000	6,000	4,000
Plant and equipment, net	160,000	110,000	70,000
Total assets	$502,000	$308,000	$202,000
Liabilities and Equity			
Accounts payable	$147,800	$ 50,400	$ 22,000
Federal income tax payable	30,000	14,400	28,000
Long-term liabilities	120,000	73,000	22,400
Common stock, $5 par value	110,000	110,000	80,000
Retained earnings	94,200	60,200	49,600
Total liabilities and equity	$502,000	$308,000	$202,000

IAN MANUFACTURING COMPANY
Condensed Income Statements
For Years Ended June 30, Year 5, Year 4, Year 3

	Year 5	Year 4	Year 3
Net sales	$1,684,000	$1,250,000	$1,050,000
Cost of goods sold	(927,000)	(810,000)	(512,000)
Gross profit	757,000	440,000	538,000
Marketing and administrative costs	(670,000)	(396,700)	(467,760)
Operating income	87,000	43,300	70,240
Interest cost	(12,000)	(7,300)	(2,240)
Income before income tax	75,000	36,000	68,000
Income tax	(30,000)	(14,400)	(28,000)
Net income	$ 45,000	$ 21,600	$ 40,000

A reconciliation of retained earnings for years ended June 30, Year 4, and Year 5, follows:

IAN MANUFACTURING COMPANY
Statement of Retained Earnings
For Years Ended June 30, Year 5 and Year 4

	Year 5	Year 4
Balance, beginning	$ 60,200	$49,600
Add: Net income	45,000	21,600
Subtotal	105,200	71,200
Deduct: Dividends paid	(11,000)	(11,000)
Balance, ending	$ 94,200	$60,200

Additional Information:

1. All sales are on account.
2. Long-term liabilities are owed to the company's bank.
3. Terms of sale are net 30 days.

Required:

a. Compute the following measures for both Years 4 and 5:
  (1) Working capital.
  (2) Current ratio.
  (3) Acid-test ratio.
  (4) Accounts receivable turnover.
  (5) Collection period of receivables.
  (6) Inventory turnover.
  (7) Days to sell inventory.
  (8) Debt-to-equity ratio.
  (9) Times interest earned.

CHECK
(a) (5) Year 5, 28.10
    (8) Year 5, 1.46

b. Using Year 3 as the base year, compute an index-number trend series for:
   (1) Sales.
   (2) Cost of goods sold.
   (3) Gross profit.
   (4) Marketing and administrative costs.
   (5) Net income.

c. Based on your analysis in (a) and (b), prepare a one-page report yielding a recommendation on whether to grant a loan to Ian Manufacturing. Support your recommendation with relevant analysis.

Altria Group, formerly known as Philip Morris Companies, is a major manufacturer and distributor of consumer products. It has a history of steady growth in sales, earnings, and cash flows. In recent years Altria has diversified with acquisitions of Miller Brewing and General Foods. In Year 8, Altria acted to further diversify by announcing an unsolicited cash tender offer for all the 124 million outstanding shares of Kraft at $90 per share. After negotiation, Kraft accepts a $106 per share all-cash offer from Altria. Assume you are an analyst with Investment Services, and that soon after the cash tender offer you are requested by your supervisor to review the potential acquisition of Kraft and assess its impact on Altria's credit standing. You assemble various information using the following projected Year 8 and Year 9 financial data:

Altria Group Inc.

CASE 10–4[A]

Determining Bond Rating

ALTRIA GROUP, INC.
Projected Financial Data ($ millions)

	Year 8 Estimate Excluding Kraft	YEAR 9 ESTIMATE			
		Before Kraft	Kraft Only	Adjustments	Consolidated
Selected Income Statement Data					
Sales					
Domestic tobacco..............................	$ 8,300	$ 8,930			$ 8,930
International tobacco.........................	8,000	8,800			8,800
General Foods	10,750	11,600			11,600
Kraft...			$11,610		11,610
Beer	3,400	3,750			3,750
Total sales	30,450	33,080	11,610		44,690
Operating income					
Domestic tobacco..............................	$ 3,080	$ 3,520		$ 35	$ 3,555
International tobacco.........................	800	940			940
General Foods	810	870			870
Kraft...			$ 1,050	50	1,100
Beer	190	205			205
Other...	105	125			125
Goodwill amortization	(110)	(110)		(295)	(405)
Total operating income......................	4,875	5,550	1,050	(210)	6,390
Percent of sales	16.0%	16.8%	9.0%		14.3%
Interest expense	(575)	(500)	(75)	(1,025)	(1,600)
Corporate expense.............................	(200)	(225)	(100)	(40)	(365)
Other expense....................................	(5)	(5)			(5)

(continued)

CASE 10–4[A]
(concluded)

	Year 8 Estimate Excluding Kraft	YEAR 9 ESTIMATE			
		Before Kraft	Kraft Only	Adjustments	Consolidated
Pretax income..	4,095	4,820	875	(1,275)	4,420
Percent of sales.......................................	13.4%	14.6%	7.5%		9.9%
Income taxes	(1,740)	(2,000)	(349)	493	(1,856)
Tax rate...	42.5%	41.5%	40.0%		42.0%
Net income	$ 2,355	$ 2,820	$ 526	$ (782)	$ 2,564
Selected Year-End Balance Sheet Data					
Short-term debt..	$ 1,125	$ 1,100	$ 683		$ 1,783
Long-term debt..	4,757	3,883	895	$11,000	15,778
Stockholders' equity	8,141	9,931	2,150	(2,406)	9,675
Other Selected Financial Data					
Depreciation and amortization	720	750	190	295	1,235
Deferred taxes	100	100	10	280	390
Equity in undistributed earnings of unconsolidated subsidiaries...............	110	125			125

Required:

a. You arrange a visit with Altria management. Given the information you have assembled above, identify and discuss five major industry considerations you should pursue when questioning management.

b. Additional information is collected showing median ratio values along with their bond rating category for three financial ratios. Using this information reported in the excerpt below along with the projections above:
   (1) Calculate these same three ratios for Altria for Year 9 using:
       (a) Amounts *before* accounting for the Kraft acquisition.
       (b) Consolidated amounts *after* the Kraft acquisition.
   (2) Discuss and interpret the two sets of ratios from 1 compared to the median values for each bond rating category. Determine and support your recommendation on a rating category for Altria *after* the Kraft acquisition.

(CFA Adapted)

CHECK
(1b) 3 ratios:
   3.76, .619, .231

Additional Information:

MEDIAN RATIO VALUES ACCORDING TO BOND RATING CATEGORIES

Ratio	AAA	AA	A	BBB	BB	B	CCC
Pretax interest coverage...........................	14.10	9.67	5.40	3.63	2.25	1.58	(0.42)
Long-term debt as a percent of L-T Debt + Equity..............	11.5%	18.7%	28.3%	34.3%	48.4%	57.2%	73.2%
Cash flow* as a percent of total debt	111.8%	86.0%	50.9%	34.2%	22.8%	14.1%	6.2%

For the purpose of calculating this ratio, Standard & Poor's defines cash flow as net income plus depreciation, amortization, and deferred taxes, less equity in undistributed earnings of unconsolidated subsidiaries.
Source: Standard & Poor's.

Assume you are an analyst at a brokerage firm. One of the companies you follow is ABEX Chemicals, Inc., which is rapidly growing into a major producer of petrochemicals (principally polyethylene). You are uneasy about competitors in the petrochemical business, their aggressive expansion, and the possibility of a recession in the next year or two. In response, you compile a summary of relevant industry statistics. Your analysis suggests prices of petrochemicals produced by ABEX will likely decline over the next 12 to 18 months. Primarily for this reason, you consider ABEX's credit standing as risky. You also note that ABEX common stock recently declined from $15 to $9 per share. Because of this price decline and subsequent instability, you further extend your credit analysis of ABEX. You focus on the external environment, company fundamentals, and stock price behavior. A description of your findings follows:

External environment. While uncertainty about the economy persists, you conclude the key issue for the petrochemical industry is not demand but overcapacity. As revealed in Exhibit I, polyethylene production is expected to remain flat in Year 10 and capacity to increase, causing operating rates to fall. The result is increased competition and lower product prices. In the long run you expect use of polyethylene to grow 4% per annum and prices to rise 5% per annum, beginning in Year 12.

Company fundamentals. ABEX's operating income depends primarily on two businesses: pipeline distribution of natural gas (gas transmission) and petrochemical production. The gas transmission business is declining due to lower gas production and price constraints, but your outlook is for modest increases in volume and transmission rates. Your summary of key statistics for pipeline operations is included in Exhibit I. The more unpredictable component of ABEX's operating income is the petrochemical operation. Operating income from petrochemicals are sensitive to selling price, production costs, and volume of polyethylene sales. A key to estimating operating income is estimation of future prices and costs, and ABEX's market share. ABEX's management is confident their lower cost structure makes them price competitive and permits a higher capacity operating rate than their competitors. Exhibit I includes a summary of key statistics for polyethylene operations.

CASE 10–5

Comprehensive Analysis of Creditworthiness

Exhibit I

■ ■ ■ ■ ■ ■ ■

TOTAL U.S. POLYETHYLENE CAPACITY, PRODUCTION, AND PRICES

	Year 5	Year 6	Year 7	Year 8	Year 9	Projected Year 10	Projected Year 11	Compound Annual Growth
Total production (lbs. millions)	15,600	16,100	17,600	18,900	19,700	19,700	19,800	
Growth rate	7.6%	3.2%	9.3%	7.4%	4.2%	0.0%	0.5%	4.1%
Total capacity (lbs. millions)	17,600	17,700	18,600	20,100	21,200	23,400	24,300	
Growth rate	2.9%	0.6%	5.1%	8.1%	5.5%	10.4%	3.8%	5.5%
Capacity operating rate	88.6%	91.0%	94.6%	94.0%	92.9%	84.2%	81.5%	
Average price per pound	$ 0.41	$0.37	$0.36	$0.51	$0.52	$0.47	$0.57	
Percent change	−9.8%	−10.8%	−2.7%	24.4%	2.0%	−9.6%	21.3%	5.6%

(continued)

Exhibit I
(concluded)

■ ■ ■ ■ ■ ■ ■

ABEX CHEMICALS, INC.
Selected Key Statistics

	Year 5	Year 6	Year 7	Year 8	Year 9	Projected Year 10
Polyethylene operations						
Production (lbs. millions)	1,840	1,975	2,870	4,835	5,000	4,950
Approximate capacity (lbs. millions)	1,900	2,100	2,950	5,000	5,500	5,500
Capacity operating rate..............................	97%	94%	97%	97%	91%	90%
Average price received	$0.411	$0.367	$0.356	$0.511	$0.515	$0.470
Average cost/pound produced	$0.338	$0.307	$0.285	$0.350	$0.394	$0.370
Pipeline transportation operations						
$/1,000 cubic feet (price)..........................	$0.286	$0.253	$0.248	$0.221	$0.192	$0.187
Gas transported (trillion cubic feet)	4.64	4.88	4.67	5.00	5.85	6.29
Operating profit margin	25.6%	27.2%	27.3%	25.9%	26.8%	27.0%

Stock price evaluation. Some investors value companies using discounted cash flows, but you are increasingly emphasizing the quality of cash flow, earning power, yield, book value, and earnings components. You also assemble financial statements and key financial ratios for ABEX (see Exhibits II–IV).

Required:

Your firm's fixed income portfolio manager asks you to further extend your investigation of ABEX. The manager wants your assessment of whether the credit quality (risk) of ABEX's debt has changed during the most recent three years–Year 7 through Year 9. You decide to analyze key financial ratios for ABEX, focusing on areas of (1) asset protection, (2) liquidity, and (3) earning power.

a. Identify *five ratios* from Exhibit IV relevant to at least one of these three areas of analysis. Discuss and interpret both levels and trends in these five key ratios from Year 7 through Year 9.

b. Compare and analyze the pipeline and petrochemical divisions using three *qualitative* measures relevant to ABEX's credit quality for the period Year 7 through Year 9.

c. Using your analysis from (a) and (b), discuss whether ABEX's credit quality has changed from Year 7 through Year 9.

(CFA Adapted)

Exhibit II

ABEX CHEMICALS, INC.
Consolidated Income Statements ($ millions)

	Year 5	Year 6	Year 7	Year 8	Year 9
Revenues					
Petrochemicals	$ 757	$ 725	$ 1,021	$ 2,472	$ 2,575
Pipelines	1,328	1,235	1,156	1,106	1,123
Total revenues	2,085	1,960	2,177	3,578	3,698
Operating costs*					
Petrochemicals	(622)	(607)	(818)	(1,691)	(1,970)
Pipelines	(988)	(899)	(840)	(820)	(822)
Total operating costs	(1,610)	(1,506)	(1,658)	(2,511)	(2,792)
Operating income					
Petrochemicals	135	118	203	781	605
Pipelines	340	336	316	286	301
Total operating income	475	454	519	1,067	906
Interest on long-term debt					
Petrochemicals	(60)	(84)	(78)	(211)	(266)
Pipelines	(169)	(166)	(166)	(172)	(178)
Total interest expense	(229)	(250)	(244)	(383)	(444)
Administrative expenses	(22)	(24)	(23)	(28)	(40)
Rental expenses	(15)	(17)	(17)	(20)	(22)
Income from investments	25	8	4	7	4
Income before taxes	234	171	239	643	404
Income taxes					
Current	(78)	(30)	(45)	(40)	(44)
Deferred	(23)	(35)	(67)	(201)	(136)
Total taxes	(101)	(65)	(112)	(241)	(180)
Net income	133	106	127	402	224
Preferred dividends	(77)	(74)	(26)	(17)	(17)
Net available for common	$ 56	$ 32	$ 101	$ 385	$ 207
Average shares outstanding[†] (millions)	128	135	185	231	253
Basic earnings per common share	$0.44	$0.24	$0.54	$1.67	$0.82
Common dividends per share	0.40	0.40	0.40	0.40	0.50
Cash flow per common share	2.52	2.44	2.26	3.85	2.85

Operating costs include costs of goods sold and depreciation, where depreciation equals ($ millions):

Petrochemicals	$ 48	$ 60	$ 62	$135	$233
Pipelines	96	95	97	98	102
Total depreciation	$144	$155	$159	$233	$335

[†]Year 10 estimate is 305 million shares outstanding.

Exhibit III

■ ■ ■ ■ ■ ■ ■

ABEX CHEMICALS, INC.
Consolidated Balance Sheets ($ millions)

	Year 5	Year 6	Year 7	Year 8	Year 9
Assets					
Current assets					
Cash and short-term investments...............	$ 45	$ 48	$ 74	$ 102	$ 133
Accounts receivable	279	300	414	868	923
Inventories	125	121	128	501	535
Total current assets....................................	449	469	616	1,471	1,591
Investments and other assets..........................	631	380	167	252	400
Goodwill...	35	90	105	330	560
Property, plant, and equipment (net)					
Petrochemicals...	1,184	1,245	1,323	2,670	3,275
Pipelines	2,282	2,484	2,547	2,540	2,530
Total assets	$4,581	$4,668	$4,758	$7,263	$8,356
Liabilities and Shareholders' Equity					
Current liabilities					
Bank indebtedness.......................................	$ 226	$ 77	$ 72	$ 215	$ 245
Accounts payable and accrued liabilities.....	333	312	377	768	787
Current portion of long-term debt	99	70	76	86	136
Other current payables................................	35	33	32	34	54
Total current liabilities	693	492	557	1,103	1,222
Long-term debt					
Petrochemicals...	553	743	721	2,017	2,176
Pipelines	1,686	1,648	1,638	1,702	1,725
Advances—gas contracts	115	135	186	290	210
Deferred income taxes	125	160	227	428	564
Total liabilities...	3,172	3,178	3,329	5,540	5,897
Preferred stock..	861	826	329	216	216
Common stock and retained earnings	548	664	1,100	1,507	2,243
Total shareholders' equity...............................	1,409	1,490	1,429	1,723	2,459
Total liabilities and shareholders' equity..........	$4,581	$4,668	$4,758	$7,263	$8,356
Average shares outstanding (millions)*...........	128	135	185	231	253

*Year 10 estimate is 305 million shares outstanding.

Exhibit IV

■ ■ ■ ■ ■ ■ ■

ABEX CHEMICALS, INC.
Selected Financial Ratios

	Year 5	Year 6	Year 7	Year 8	Year 9
Petrochemicals operating margin	17.8%	16.3%	19.9%	31.6%	23.5%
Pipeline operating margin	25.6%	27.2%	27.3%	25.9%	26.8%
Return on assets (EBIT/total assets)	10.1%	9.0%	10.2%	14.1%	10.2%
Pretax profit margin	11.2%	8.7%	11.0%	18.0%	10.9%
Tax rate	43.2%	38.0%	46.9%	37.5%	44.4%
Petrochemicals asset turnover					
(sales/fixed assets)	0.64	0.58	0.77	0.93	0.79
Pipelines asset turnover (sales/fixed assets)	0.58	0.50	0.45	0.44	0.44
Turnover (sales/total assets)	0.46	0.42	0.46	0.49	0.44
Debt to common equity	4.30	3.80	2.31	2.66	1.83
Net tangible assets to long-term debt	58.4%	55.4%	52.0%	34.7%	46.2%
Long-term debt to total capitalization	62.6%	62.9%	64.0%	70.0%	62.6%
Total assets to total shareholders' equity	3.25	3.13	3.33	4.22	3.40
Pretax interest coverage	1.63	1.46	1.80	2.54	1.84
Operating cash flow to long-term debt	20.2%	18.0%	20.4%	26.6%	22.1%
Collection period	48 days	55 days	68 days	87 days	90 days
Inventory turnover	11.0	11.0	12.0	7.2	4.7
Short-term debt to total debt	12.1%	5.5%	5.8%	7.5%	9.3%
Petrochemicals average cost of long-term debt	10.9%	11.3%	10.8%	10.5%	12.2%
Pipeline average cost of long-term debt	10.0%	10.1%	10.1%	10.1%	10.3%
Average cost of preferreds	8.9%	9.0%	7.9%	7.9%	7.9%

11

EQUITY ANALYSIS AND VALUATION

A LOOK BACK `<`

Prior chapters on financial analysis dealt with analysis of company returns, both profitability and return on invested capital, along with prospective and credit analysis.

A LOOK AT THIS CHAPTER `·`

This chapter emphasizes equity analysis and valuation. Our earnings-based analysis focuses on assessing earnings persistence and earning power. Attention is directed at techniques to aid us in measuring and applying these analysis concepts. Our discussion of equity valuation focuses on issues in estimating company values and forecasting earnings.

A LOOK AHEAD `>`

The Comprehensive Case applies many of the financial statement analysis tools and insights described in the book. These are illustrated using financial information from Campbell Soup Company. Explanation and interpretation accompany all analyses.

ANALYSIS OBJECTIVES

- Analyze earnings persistence, its determinants, and its relevance for earnings forecasting.

- Explain recasting and adjusting of earnings and earnings components for analysis.

- Describe equity valuation and its relevance for financial analysis.

- Analyze earning power and its usefulness for forecasting and valuation.

- Explain earnings forecasting, its mechanics, and its effectiveness in assessing company performance.

- Analyze interim reports and consider their value in monitoring and revising earnings estimates.

Oracle of Omaha Dispenses Wisdom

OMAHA, NE–Warren Buffett, chairman of Berkshire Hathaway, recently commented, "Bad terminology is the enemy of good thinking. When companies or investment professionals use terms such as *EBITDA* and *pro forma*, they want you to unthinkingly accept concepts that are dangerously flawed." Buffett offered an example: "In golf, my score is frequently below par on a *pro forma* basis: I have firm plans to 'restructure' my putting stroke and therefore only count the swings I take before reaching the green."

Unfortunately, pro forma earnings measures gained in popularity in the 1990s as companies sought to redefine the benchmark against which they would be evaluated by the market. Any expense that might be deemed unfavorable was quickly excluded while transitory revenues, such as gains on asset sales and pension income, remained. Pro forma earnings quickly became known as EBUI, or earnings before unpleasant items.

Pro forma earnings are not GAAP, companies use them to portray a rosy earnings picture,

and informed investors expect that these numbers are biased.

But what about GAAP earnings? *BusinessWeek* (2001) reported the following case in point: "Construction giant and military contractor Halliburton . . . reported earnings of $339 million, even though it spent $775 million more than it took in from customers. The company did nothing illegal. Halliburton made big outlays in 2003 on contracts with the U.S. Army

> **The onus is on the investor . . .**

for work on Iraq–contracts for which it expected to be paid later. Still, it counted some of these expected revenues immediately because they related to work done last year." Only a thorough reading of the financial statement footnotes would have revealed the company's accounting practice.

"The problem with today's fuzzy earnings numbers is not accrual accounting itself. It's that investors, analysts, and money managers are having an increasingly hard time figuring out what

judgments companies make to come up with those accruals, or estimates. The scandals at Enron, WorldCom, Adelphia Communications, and other companies are forceful reminders that investors could lose billions by not paying attention to how companies arrive at their earnings." (*Business Week*, 2004)

Companies' desire to redefine earnings and to employ aggressive interpretations of accounting standards stems from the mechanics of valuing stock prices. This process involves projecting earnings or cash flows into the future and then discounting them to the present to arrive at price. To be meaningful, projections must focus only on the portion of earnings that is likely to persist into the future. The higher those earnings are, the higher the resulting stock price. That's why companies offer a myriad of definitions of pro forma earnings, and manage GAAP earnings, to portray their business in the most favorable light. The onus is on the investor to ferret out the "true" persistent level of earnings.

PREVIEW OF CHAPTER 11

Equity analysis and valuation is the focus of this chapter. Previous chapters examined return and profitability analyses of financial statements. This chapter extends these analyses to consider earnings persistence, valuation, and forecasting. *Earnings*

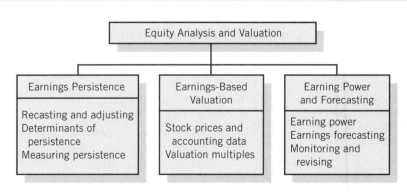

Equity Analysis and Valuation		
Earnings Persistence	Earnings-Based Valuation	Earning Power and Forecasting
Recasting and adjusting Determinants of persistence Measuring persistence	Stock prices and accounting data Valuation multiples	Earning power Earnings forecasting Monitoring and revising

21

persistence is broadly defined to include the stability, predictability, variability, and trend in earnings. We consider earnings management as a determinant of persistence. Our *equity valuation* analysis emphasizes earnings and other accounting measures for computing company value. *Earnings forecasting* considers earning power, estimation techniques, and monitoring mechanisms. This chapter also describes several useful tools for earnings-based equity analysis. Specifically, we describe recasting and adjustment of financial statements. We also distinguish between recurring and nonrecurring, operating and non-operating, and extraordinary and nonextraordinary earnings components. Throughout the chapter we emphasize the application of earnings-based analysis with several illustrations.

▪▪▪▪▪▪▪▪ EARNINGS PERSISTENCE

A good financial analysis identifies components in earnings that exhibit stability and pre-dictability—that is, *persistent* components. We separate these persistent components from random or nonrecurring components. This analysis aids us in producing reliable forecasts of earning power for valuation. Analysis also must be alert to earnings management and income smoothing. Earnings management and income smoothing can imply more stability and predictability than present in the underlying characteris-tics. Company management often asserts that such activities remove dis-tortions or peculiarities from operat-

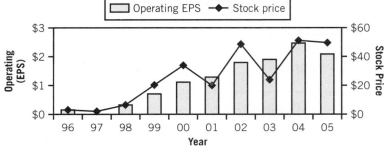

ing results. Yet these activities can mask natural and cyclical irregularities that are part of a company's environment and experience. Identifying these influences is important for us in assessing a company's risk. This section considers elements bearing on analysis of earnings persistence, including earnings level, trend, and components.

Recasting and Adjusting Earnings

One task in equity analysis is to recast earnings and earnings components so that stable, normal, and continuing elements that constitute earnings are separated and distin-guished from random, erratic, unusual, and nonrecurring elements. The latter elements require separate analytical treatment or investigation. Recasting also aims to identify elements included in current earnings that should more properly be included in the operating results of one or more prior periods.

Information on Earnings Persistence

Analysis of operating results for the recasting and adjusting of earnings requires reliable and relevant information. Major sources of this information include the:

- Income statement, including its components:
  - Income from continuing operations.
  - Income from discontinued operations.
  - Extraordinary gains and losses.
  - Cumulative effect of changes in accounting principles.
- Other financial statements and notes.
- Management discussion and analysis.

We often find "unusual" items separated within the income statement (typically on a pretax basis), but their disclosure is optional and does not always include sufficient information to assess their significance or persistence. We access all available information sources and management, if possible, to obtain this information. Relevant information includes that affecting earnings comparability and interpretation. Examples are product-mix changes, technological innovations, work stoppages, and raw material constraints.

Recasting Earnings and Earnings Components

Once we secure all available information, we recast and adjust the income statements of several years (typically at least five) to assess earnings persistence. Recasting and adjusting earnings aids in determining the earning power of a company. We explain recasting in this section and adjusting in the next, although both can be performed in one statement.

Recasting aims at rearranging earnings components to provide a meaningful classification and relevant format for analysis. Components can be rearranged, subdivided, or tax effected, but the total must reconcile to net income of each period. Discretionary expenses should be segregated. The same applies to components like equity in income (loss) of unconsolidated subsidiaries or affiliates, often reported net of tax. Components reported pretax must be removed along with their tax effects if reclassified apart from income from continuing operations.

Income tax disclosures enable us to separate factors that either reduce or increase taxes. This separation permits us to analyze the recurring nature of these factors. All permanent tax differences and credits are included. This analytical procedure involves computing taxes at the statutory rate and deducting tax benefits arising from various items such as tax credits, capital gains rates, tax-free income, or lower foreign tax rates. We also must add factors such as additional foreign taxes, nontax-deductible expenses, and state and local taxes (net of federal tax benefit). Immaterial items can be considered in a lump sum labeled *other*.

Analytically recast income statements contain as much detail as necessary for our analysis objectives and are supplemented by notes. Exhibit 11.1 shows the analytically recast income statements for Campbell Soup Company. These statements are annotated with key numbers referencing Campbell's financial statements in Appendix A. Financial data preceding Year 10 are taken from company reports summarized in the Comprehensive Case chapter, which also contains a discussion and an integration of Exhibit 11.1.

HINT

"Adjusting" aims to assign earnings components to the periods in which they best belong.

Adjusting Earnings and Earnings Components

The adjusting process uses data from recast income statements and other available information to assign earnings components to periods where they most properly belong. We must be especially careful in assigning extraordinary or unusual items (net of tax) to periods. Also, the income tax benefit of a carryforward of operating losses should normally be moved to the year of the loss occurrence. Costs or benefits from settlements of lawsuits can relate to one or more preceding periods. Similarly, gains or losses from disposal of discontinued operations usually relate to operating results of several years. For changes in accounting principles or estimates, all years under analysis should be adjusted to a comparable basis. If the new principle is the desirable one, prior years should be restated to this new method. This restatement redistributes the "cumulative effect of change in accounting principle" to the relevant prior years. Changes in estimates are accounted for prospectively in practice with few exceptions. Our ability to adjust all periods to a comparable basis depends on information availability.

Exhibit 11.1   **Recast Income Statements**

CAMPBELL SOUP COMPANY
Recast Income Statements for Year 6 through Year 11 ($ millions)

Reference Item		Year 11	Year 10	Year 9	Year 8	Year 7	Year 6
13	Net sales	$6,204.1	$6,205.8	$5,672.1	$4,868.9	$4,490.4	$4,286.8
19	Interest income	26.0	17.6	38.3	33.2	29.5	27.4
	Total revenues	6,230.1	6,223.4	5,710.4	4,902.1	4,519.9	4,314.2
	Costs and expenses						
145	Cost of products sold (see Note 1 below)	3,727.1	3,893.5	3,651.8	3,077.8	2,897.8	2,820.5
144	Marketing and selling expenses (see Note 2 below)	760.8	760.1	605.9	514.2	422.7	363.0
16	Advertising (see Note 2 below)	195.4	220.4	212.9	219.1	203.5	181.4
17	Repairs and maintenance (see Note 1 below)	173.9	180.6	173.9	155.6	148.8	144.0
102	Administrative expenses	306.7	290.7	252.1	232.6	213.9	195.9
20	Research and development expenses	56.3	53.7	47.7	46.9	44.8	42.2
104	Stock price-related incentive programs (see Note 3 below)	15.4	(0.1)	17.4	(2.7)	—	8.5
162A	Foreign exchange adjustment	0.8	3.3	19.3	16.6	4.8	0.7
103	Other, net (see Note 3 below)	(3.3)	(2.0)	(1.4)	(4.7)	(0.4)	(9.0)
18	Depreciation (see Note 1 below)	194.5	184.1	175.9	162.0	139.0	120.8
	Amortization of intangible and other assets (see Note 3 below)	14.1	16.8	16.4	8.9	5.6	6.0
	Interest expense	116.2	111.6	94.1	53.9	51.7	56.0
	Total costs and expenses	5,557.9	5,712.7	5,266.0	4,480.2	4,132.2	3,930.0
23	Earnings before equity in earnings of affiliates and minority interests	672.2	510.7	444.4	421.9	387.7	384.2
24	Equity in earnings of affiliates	2.4	13.5	10.4	6.3	15.1	4.3
25	Minority interests	(7.2)	(5.7)	(5.3)	(6.3)	(4.7)	(3.9)
26	Income before taxes	667.4	518.5	449.5	421.9	398.1	384.6
	Income taxes at statutory rate*	(226.9)	(176.3)	(152.8)	(143.5)	(179.1)	(176.9)
	Income from continuing operations	440.5	342.2	296.7	278.4	219.0	207.7
135	State taxes (net of federal tax benefit)	(20.0)	(6.6)	(3.8)	(11.8)	(8.6)	(8.0)
	Investment tax credit	—	—	—	—	4.4	11.6
137	Nondeductible amortization of intangibles	(4.0)	(1.6)	(1.2)	(2.6)	(1.4)	—†
138	Foreign earnings not taxed or taxed at other than statutory rate	2.0	(2.2)	(0.2)	3.2	11.1	15.2
139	Other: Tax effects	(17.0)	(2.2)	(0.1)	(3.7)	7.5	(4.7)

(continued)

Recast Income Statements *(concluded)*

Reference Item		Year 11	Year 10	Year 9	Year 8	Year 7	Year 6
[22]	Divestitures, restructuring, and unusual charges	—	(339.1)	(343.0)	(40.6)	4.5	—
	Tax effect of divestitures, restructuring, and unusual charges (Note 4)	—	13.9	64.7	13.9	—	—
	Gain on sale of businesses in Year 8 and subsidiary in Year 7	—	—	—	3.1	9.7	—
	Loss on sale of exercise equipment subsidiary, net of tax	—	—	—	—	(1.7)	1.4
[153A]	LIFO liquidation gain (see Note 1 below)	401.5	4.4	13.1	1.7	2.8	223.2
	Income before cumulative effect of accounting change	401.5	4.4	13.1	241.6	247.3	223.2
	Cumulative effect of accounting change for income taxes	—	—	—	32.5	—	—
[28]	Net income as reported	$ 401.5	$ 4.4	$ 13.1	$ 274.1	$ 247.3	$ 223.2
[14]	**Note 1:** Cost of products sold	$4,095.5	$4,258.2	$4,001.6	$3,392.8	$3,180.5	$3,082.8
[144]	Less: Repair and maintenance expenses	(173.9)	(180.6)	(173.9)	(155.6)	(148.8)	(144.0)
[162A]	Less: Depreciation(a)	(194.5)	(184.1)	(175.9)	(162.0)	(139.0)	(120.8)
[153A]	Plus: LIFO liquidation gain(b)				2.6	5.1	2.5
		$3,727.1	$3,893.5	$3,651.8	$3,077.8	$2,897.8	$2,820.5
[15]	**Note 2:** Marketing and selling expenses	$ 956.2	$ 980.5	$ 818.8	$ 733.3	$ 626.2	$ 544.4
[145]	Less: Advertising	(195.4)	(220.4)	(212.9)	(219.1)	(203.5)	(181.4)
		$ 760.8	$ 760.1	$ 605.9	$ 514.2	$ 422.7	$ 363.0
[21]	**Note 3:** Other expenses (income)	$ 26.2	$ 14.7	$ 32.4	$ (3.2)	$ (9.5)	$ 5.5
[102]	Less: Stock price-related incentive programs	(15.4)	0.1	(17.4)	2.7	(8.5)	(8.5)
[103]	Less: Amortization of intangible and other assets	(14.1)	(16.8)	(16.4)	(8.9)	(5.6)	(6.0)
	Less: Gain on sale of businesses (Year 8) and subsidiary (Year 7)				4.7	14.7	
[104]	Other net	$ (3.3)	$ (2.0)	$ (1.4)	$ (4.7)	$ (0.4)	$ (9.0)
[136]	**Note 4:** Tax effect of divestitures, restructuring, and unusual charges at statutory rate	—	115.3(c)	116.6(d)	13.9	—	—
	Nondeductible divestitures, restructuring, and unusual charges	—	(101.4)(e)	(51.9)(f)	—	—	—
		—	13.9	64.7	13.9	—	—

* The statutory federal tax rate is 34% in Year 8 through Year 11, 45% in Year 7, and 46% in Year 6.

† This amount is not reported for Year 6.

(a) We assume most depreciation is included in cost of products sold.

(b) LIFO liquidation gain before tax—for example, for Year 8 this is $2.5 million, computed as $1.7/(1 − 0.34).

(c) $339.1 [22] × 0.34 = $115.3.

(d) $343.0 [22] × 0.34 = $116.6.

(e) $179.4 [26] × 0.565 [136] = $101.4.

(f) $106.5 [26] × 0.487 [136] = $51.9.

Before we assess earnings persistence it is necessary to obtain the best possible income statement numbers with our adjustments. Exhibit 11.2 shows the adjusted income statements of Campbell Soup Company. All earnings components must be considered. If we decide a component should be excluded from the period it is reported, we can either (1) shift it (net of tax) to the operating results of one or more prior periods or (2) spread (average) it over earnings for the period under analysis. We should only spread it over prior periods' earnings when it cannot be identified with a specific period. While spreading (averaging) helps us in determining earning power, it is not helpful in determining earnings trends. We also must realize that moving gains or losses to other periods does not remedy the misstatements of prior years' results. For example, a damage award for patent infringement in one period implies prior periods suffered from lost sales or other impairments. Further details and analyses of Exhibit 11.2 are identified and discussed in the Comprehensive Case.

Exhibit 11.2   **Adjusted Income Statements**
■ ■ ■ ■ ■ ■ ■

CAMPBELL SOUP COMPANY
Adjusted Income Statements for Year 6 through Year 11

($ millions)	Year 11	Year 10	Year 9	Year 8	Year 7	Year 6	Total
Net income as reported	$401.5	$ 4.4	$ 13.1	$274.1	$247.3	$223.2	$1,163.6
Divestitures, restructuring & unusual charges		339.1	343.0	40.6			
Tax effect of divestitures, restructuring, etc.		(13.9)	(64.7)	(13.9)			
Gain on sale of businesses (Year 8) and sale of subsidiary (Year 7), net of tax				(3.1)	(9.7)		
Loss on sale of exercise equipment subsidiary					1.7		
Alaska Native Corporation transaction					(4.5)		
LIFO liquidation gain				(1.7)	(2.8)	(1.4)	
Cumulative effect of change in accounting for income taxes				(32.5)			
Adjusted net income	$401.5	$329.6	$291.4	$263.5	$232.0	$221.8	
Total net income for the period							$1,739.80
Average net income for the period							$ 289.97*

* One measure of average earning power.

■

Analysis must also recognize that certain management characterizations of revenue or expense items as unusual, nonrecurring, infrequent, or extraordinary are attempts to reduce earnings volatility or minimize selected earnings components. These characterizations also extend to the inclusion in equity of transactions such as gains and losses on available-for-sale securities and foreign currency translation adjustments. We often exclude equity effects from our adjustment process. Yet these items are part of a company's lifetime earnings. These items increase or decrease equity and affect earning power. Accordingly, even if we omit these items from the adjustment process, they belong in the analysis of average earning power.

Determinants of Earnings Persistence

After recasting and adjusting earnings, our analysis next focuses on determining earnings persistence. Earnings management, variability, trends, and incentives are all potential determinants of earnings persistence. We also should assess earnings persistence over both the business cycle and the long run.

Earnings Trend and Persistence

Earnings that reflect a steady growth trend are desirable. We can assess earnings trends by statistical methods or with **trend statements.** Examples of trend statements using selected financial data of Campbell Soup are reported in Exhibits CC.8 and CC.9 in the Comprehensive Case chapter. Trend analysis uses earnings numbers taken from the recasting and adjusting procedures illustrated in Exhibit 11.2. Earnings trends often reveal important clues to a company's current and future performance (cyclical, growth, defensive) and bear on the quality of management. We must be alert to accounting distortions affecting trends. Especially important are changes in accounting principles and the effect of business combinations, particularly purchases. We must make adjustments for these changes. Probably one major motivation of earnings management is to effect earnings trends. Earnings management practices assume earnings trends are important for valuation. They also reflect a belief that retroactive revisions of earnings previously reported have little impact on security prices. For example, once a company incurs and reports a loss, this perspective suggests its existence is often as important as its magnitude for valuation purposes. These assumptions and the propensities of some managers to use accounting as a means of improving earnings trend has led to sophisticated earnings management techniques, including income smoothing.

Earnings Management and Persistence

There are several requirements to meet the definition of *earnings management.* These requirements are important as they distinguish earnings management from misrepresentations and distortions. Earnings management uses acceptable accounting reporting principles for purposes of reporting specific results. It uses the available discretion in selecting and applying accounting principles to achieve its goals, and it is arguably performed within the framework of accepted practice. It is a matter of form rather than of substance. It does not affect actual transactions (such as postponing outlays to later periods) but, instead, does affect a redistribution of credits or charges across periods. A main goal is to moderate earnings variability across periods by shifting earnings between good and bad years, between future and current years, or various combinations. Actual earnings management takes many forms. Some forms of earnings management that we should be especially alert to include:

- *Changes in accounting methods or assumptions.* Examples of companies that changed methods or assumptions include Chrysler, who revised upward the assumed rate of return on its pension portfolio and substantially increased earnings when sales were slumping, and Continental Airlines who lengthened depreciable lives and increased residual values of aircraft, thereby boosting subsequent earnings.
- *Offsetting extraordinary (and unusual) gains and losses.* This practice removes unusual or unexpected earnings effects that can adversely impact earnings trend.
- *Big baths.* This technique recognizes future periods' costs in the current period, when the current period is unavoidably badly performing. This practice relieves future periods' earnings of these costs.

- *Write-downs.* Write-downs of operating assets such as plant and equipment or intangibles such as goodwill when operating results are poor is another earnings management tool. Companies often justify write-downs by arguing that current economics do not support reported asset values. An example is Cisco Systems that wrote off $2.25 billion of inventories as part of a restructuring program.
- *Timing revenue and expense recognition.* This technique times revenue and expense recognition to manage earnings, including trend. Examples are the timing of revenue recognition, asset sales, research expenditures, advertising, maintenance, and repairs. Unlike most earnings management techniques, these decisions can involve the timing of actual transactions. An example is General Electric which offset gains with restructuring expenses to smooth earnings fluctuations.

Management Incentives and Persistence

We previously described the impact of management incentives on both the accounting and the analysis of financial statements (see Chapters 1–6). This is especially evident in assessing earning persistence and in performing credit analysis. Experience shows that some managers, owners, and employees manipulate and distort reported earnings for personal benefits. Companies in financial distress are particularly vulnerable to these pressures. Such practices are too often justified by these individuals as a battle for survival. Prosperous companies also sometimes try to preserve hard-earned reputations as earnings growth companies through earnings management. Compensation plans and other accounting-based incentives or constraints provide added motivation for managers to manage earnings. The impacts of management incentives reveal themselves in the following cases:

Analysts must recognize the incentives confronting managers with regard to earnings. Earnings management is often initially achieved by understating reported earnings. This creates a "reserve" to call on in any future low earnings periods. For example, Sears boosted its allowance for uncollectible accounts and used the reserve to inflate earnings for many years. While this point is arguable, this is not the purpose of financial reporting. We are better served by full disclosure of earnings components along with management's explanation. We can then average, smooth, or adjust reported earnings in accordance with our analysis objectives. Another probable instance of earnings management is that of General Motors—see Illustration 11.1.

ILLUSTRATION 11.1

■ ■ ■ ■ ■ ■ ■

GM reported a revision in useful lives of its plant and equipment—reducing depreciation and amortization charges by $1.2 billion. GM's chairperson reported *"GM earned $3.6 billion for the year, up 21% . . . despite a 9% reduction in worldwide unit sales."* Yet without the $1.2 billion decline in depreciation and amortization, earnings would have decreased. This accounting change followed a year earlier provision of $1.3 billion for plant closings and restructurings. However, only $0.5 billion had been charged against this provision four years later, leaving the rest to absorb still future years' costs. After yet another change in leadership at GM, there was an additional $2.1 billion charge to earnings to cover costs of closing several more plants, including closings planned several years into the future. This sequence of events impairs confidence in both financial statements and management. Accordingly, we must work to reliably estimate earning power using techniques like averaging, recasting, and adjusting of earnings.

Given the performance incentives of managers, and the use of accounting numbers to control and monitor their performance, analysis must recognize the potential for earnings management and even misstatements. Analysis must identify companies with strong incentives to manage earnings, and then scrutinize these companies' accounting practices to ensure the integrity of financial statements.

Persistent and Transitory Items in Earnings

Recasting and adjusting earnings for equity valuation rely on separating stable, persistent earnings components from random, transitory components. Assessing persistence is important in determining earning power. Earnings forecasting also relies on persistence. A crucial part of analysis is to assess the persistence of the gain and loss components of earnings. This section describes how we can determine the persistence of nonrecurring, unusual, or extraordinary items. We also discuss how they should be handled in evaluating earnings level, management performance, and earnings forecasting.

Analyzing and Interpreting Transitory Items

The purpose of analyzing and interpreting extraordinary items is twofold:

1. Determine whether an item is transitory (less persistent). This involves assessing whether an item is unusual, nonoperating, or nonrecurring.
2. Determine adjustments that are necessary given assessment of persistence. Special adjustments are sometimes necessary for both evaluating and forecasting earnings.

We describe both of these analyses in this section.

Determining Persistence (Transitory Nature) of Items.   Given the incentives confronting managers in reporting transitory items, we must render independent evaluation of whether a gain or loss is transitory. We also must determine how to adjust for them. For this purpose we arrange items into two broad categories: nonrecurring operating and nonrecurring nonoperating.

1. *Nonrecurring operating gains and losses.* These gains and losses relate to operating activities but recur infrequently or unpredictably. Operating items relate to a company's *normal business activities.* The concept of normal operations is far less clear than many realize. A plant's operating revenues and expenses are those associated with the workings of the plant. In contrast, proceeds from selling available-for-sale marketable securities are nonoperating gains or losses. The other important concept, that of *recurrence,* is one of frequency. There are no predetermined generally accepted boundaries separating a recurring event from a nonrecurring one. For example, a regular event generating a gain or loss is classified as recurring. An unpredictable event, which occurs infrequently, is classified as nonrecurring. Yet an event occurring infrequently but whose occurrence is predictable raises questions as to its classification. An example is the relining of blast furnaces—they endure for many years and their replacement is infrequent, but the need for it is predictable. Some companies provide for these types of replacements with a reserve.

Analysis of nonrecurring operating gains and losses must recognize their inherent infrequencies and lack of recurring patterns. We treat them as belonging to the reporting period. We must also address the question of normal operations. For example, it is a bakery's purpose to bake bread, rolls, and cakes, but it is presumably outside normal activities to buy and sell marketable securities for gains and losses, or even to sell baking machinery that is replaced with more efficient machinery. This limited interpretation of operating activities can be challenged. Some argue the objective is not baking but for management to increase equity or stock values. This is accomplished through strategic classification of financing, investing, and operating activities. It is not limited to a narrow view of normal operations. We can usefully evaluate a much wider range of gains and losses as being derived from operating activities. This view results in many nonrecurring operating gains and losses considered as part of operating activities in the period when they occur.

Analysis of nonrecurring operating items does not readily fit a mechanical rule. We must review the information and will doubtless find some items more likely to be recurring than others and some more operating than others. This review affects our recasting, adjusting, and forecasting of earnings. We should also recognize the magnitude of an item as an important factor. Once we complete the analysis of recurring earnings, we often need to focus on average earnings experience over a few years rather than the result of a single year. A focus on average earnings is especially important for companies with fluctuating amounts of nonrecurring and other extraordinary items. A single year is too short and too arbitrary a period to evaluate the earning power of a company or for forecasting earnings. Illustration 11.2 sheds more light on this point.

ILLUSTRATION 11.2 ■ ■ ■ ■ ■ ■ ■	The past few years have seen several large charges to earnings for reorganization, redeployment, or regrouping. Companies taking substantial write-offs include ($ billions) Viacom $18 and AT&T $13. Information supplied with these events is often limited, but there is no denying these companies' enormous "revisions" of previously reported results. In one stroke, these write-offs *correct* prior years' overreporting of earnings. Analysis must be alert to aggressive write-offs to relieve future periods of charges properly attributable to them.

2. *Nonrecurring nonoperating gains and losses.* These items are nonrepeating and unpredictable and fall outside normal operations. Events driving these items are typically extraneous, unintended, and unplanned, yet they are rarely entirely unexpected. Business is subject to risks of adverse events and random shocks, be they natural or manmade. Business transactions are subject to the same. An example is damage to plant facilities due to the crash of an aircraft when your plant is not located near an airport. Other examples might include: (1) substantial uninsured casualty losses not within the usual risks of the company, (2) expropriation by a foreign government of assets owned by the company, and (3) seizure or destruction of property from war, insurrection, or civil disorders when not expected. These occurrences are typically nonrecurring but their relation to operating activities varies. All are occurrences in the regular course of business. Even assets destroyed by acts of nature reflect the risks of business. Unique events are rare. What often appears unique is frequently symptomatic of new risks affecting earning power and future operations. Analysis must consider this possibility. But barring evidence to the contrary, these items are regarded as extraordinary and omitted from operating results of a single year. They are, nevertheless, part of the long-term performance of a company.

Adjustments to Extraordinary Items Reflecting Persistence.   The second step in analyzing transitory items is to consider their effects on both the resources of the company and the evaluation of management.

- *Effects of transitory items on company resources.* Every transitory gain and loss has a dual effect. For example, when recording a gain, a company also records an increase in resources. Similarly, a loss results in a decrease in resources. Since return on invested capital measures the relations of net income to resources, transitory gains and losses affect this measure. The larger the transitory item, the larger its effect on return. If we use earnings and current events in forecasting, then transitory items convey more than past performance. That is, if a transitory loss decreases capital for expected returns, then future returns are lost. Conversely, a transitory gain increases capital and future expected returns. In forecasting profitability and return on investment, analysis must take account of the effects of recorded transitory items and the likelihood of future events causing transitory items.

- *Effect of transitory items on evaluation of management.* One implication frequently associated with transitory gains and losses is their lack of association with normal or planned business activities. Because of this they are often not used when evaluating management performance. Analysis should question their exclusion from management performance evaluation. What are the normal or planned activities that relate to management's decisions? Whether we consider securities transactions, plant asset transactions, or activities of divisions and subsidiaries, these all reflect on actions taken by management with specific purposes. These actions typically require more consideration or deliberation than ordinary operating decisions because they are often unusual in nature and involve substantial amounts. All of these actions reflect on management's ability as evidenced in the following:

ANALYSIS EXCERPT

Viacom reported a transitory charge of $1.5 billion in writing down its ill-fated investment in Blockbuster. This loss implies prior years' earnings were overstated *and* it also raises questions about management's investment decisions.

Management should be aware of the risks of natural or manmade disasters and impediments. Business decisions are managers' responsibility. For example, a decision to pursue international activities is made with the knowledge of the risks involved. A decision to insure or not is a normal operating decision. Essentially, nothing is entirely unexpected or unforeseeable. Management does not engage in, or is at least not expected to engage in, business activities unknowingly. Decision making is within the expected activities of a business. Every company is subject to inherent risks, and management should not blindly pursue activities without weighing these risks.

In an assessment of operating results, distinguishing between normal and transitory items is sometimes meaningless. Management's beliefs about the quality of its decisions are nearly always related to the normalcy, or lack thereof, of business conditions. This is evident in the Management Discussion and Analysis. Yet the best managers anticipate the unexpected. When failures or shortcomings occur, poor managers typically take time to "explain" these in a way to avoid responsibility. While success rarely requires explanation, failure evokes long explanations and blame to unusual or unforeseeable events. In a competitive economy, normal conditions rarely prevail for any length of time. Management is paid to anticipate and expect the unusual. Explanations are not a substitute for performance.

ANALYSIS VIEWPOINT   *. . . YOU ARE THE ANALYST/FORECASTER*

You are analyzing a company's earnings persistence in preparing its earnings forecasts for publication in your company's online forecasting service. Its earnings and earnings components ("net income" and "income from continuing operations") are stable and exhibit a steady growth trend. However, you find "unusual gains" relating to litigation comprising 40% of current earnings. You also find "extraordinary losses" from environmental costs. How do these disclosures affect your earnings persistence estimate?

EARNINGS-BASED EQUITY VALUATION

Company valuation is an important objective for many users of financial statements. Reliable estimates of value enable us to make buy/sell/hold decisions regarding securities, assess the value of a company for credit decisions, estimate values for business combinations, determine prices for public offerings of a company's securities, and pursue many other useful applications. This section continues our discussion of accounting-based equity valuation and incorporates it within the analysis of financial statements.

Traditional descriptions of company equity valuation rely on the *discounted cash flow (DCF) method*. Under the DCF method, the value of a company's equity is computed based on forecasts of cash flows available to equity investors. These forecasts are then discounted using the company's cost of equity capital.[1] It is important to emphasize that the accounting-based equity valuation model introduced earlier in this book and discussed in this section is theoretically consistent with the DCF method.

Relation between Stock Prices and Accounting Data

Recall the accounting-based equity valuation model introduced in Chapter 1:

$$V_t = BV_t + \frac{E(RI_{t+1})}{(1 + k)^1} + \frac{E(RI_{t+2})}{(1 + k)^2} + \frac{E(RI_{t+3})}{(1 + k)^3} + \cdots$$

where BV_t is book value at the end of period t, RI_{t+n} is residual income in period $t + n$, and k is cost of capital. **Residual income** at time t is defined as comprehensive net income minus a charge on beginning book value, that is, $RI_t = NI_t - (k \times BV_{t-1})$. The model directly shows the importance of future profitability in estimating company value—that is, by using estimates of future net income and book values. Accurate estimates of these measures can be made only after consideration of the quality and persistence of a company's earnings and earning power.

A common criticism of accounting-based valuation methods is that earnings are subject to manipulation and distortion at the hands of management whose personal objectives and interests depend on reported accounting numbers. Indeed, a good portion of the book focuses on the need for our analysis to go "beyond the numbers." A reasonable question, therefore, is: Does the potential manipulation of accounting data influence the accuracy of accounting-based estimates, or forecasts, of company value? The answer is both yes *and* no.

The numerical example in Illustration 11.3 confirms the "no" part of the answer. We demonstrate that while accounting choices necessarily affect both earnings and book value, valuation is unaffected. Although conservative (aggressive) accounting results in lower (higher) book values of stockholders' equity, this is exactly offset by higher (lower) expected residual income.

The "yes" part of the answer is based on the reality that analysis uses reported accounting data (and other information) as a basis for projecting future profitability. To the extent accounting choices mask the true economic performance of the company, a less experienced analyst can be misled regarding the company's current and future performance. Consequently, the analysis techniques described in this book are important for equity analysis even though the accounting-based valuation model is mathematically immune from accounting manipulations.

---

[1] A common alternative is to discount expected cash flows available to both debt and equity holders using the company's weighted-average cost of debt and equity capital. This yields an estimate of the total value of the company. The value of a company's equity is obtained by subtracting the value of its debt.

Consider two identical companies. These companies use the same accounting methods and are expected to report income of $20 million before depreciation in all future years. At the beginning of Year 0, each company has a book value of $40 million; and during the year, each incurs a cash expenditure of $10 million. Company A decides to capitalize the expenditure and depreciate it over the next two years under the straight-line method. Company B chooses to expense the expenditure immediately. Each company has a cost of equity capital of 15% and does not intend to pay dividends in the foreseeable future. Since earnings for both companies are identical after Year 2, the difference in valuation of the two companies will be affected only by differences in earnings through Year 2. Accordingly, we assume that residual income for Year 3 and beyond equals zero. Ignoring income taxes, the companies report the following results:

ILLUSTRATION 11.3

■ ■ ■ ■ ■ ■ ■

Company A:	Year 0	Year 1	Year 2
Income before effect of expenditure.......... $20	$20	$20
Depreciation of $10 expenditure 0	5	5
Net income $20	$15	$15
Book value at year-end $60	$75	$90

Company B:	Year 0	Year 1	Year 2
Income before effect of expenditure.......... $20	$20	$20
Depreciation of $10 expenditure 10	0	0
Net income $10	$20	$20
Book value at year-end $50	$70	$90

The valuations of Company A and Company B, computed at the end of Year 0, follow:

Company A valuation = $60 + [$15 − (15% × $60)]/1.15 + [$15 − (15% × $75)]/1.15² = $68.05

Company B valuation = $50 + [$20 − (15% × $50)]/1.15 + [$20 − (15% × $70)]/1.15² = $68.05

Generally, the phrase *conservative accounting* is applied to methods that result in lower income and lower book values in early years. Accordingly, by immediately expensing the $10 expenditure, Company B is using more conservative accounting. Despite the use of different accounting treatments for the $10 expenditure, the estimated values for Companies A and B are equal. Mathematically, the accounting-based equity valuation model yields the same valuation estimates for any accounting system that follows the clean surplus relation.

Fundamental Valuation Multiples

Two widely cited valuation measures are the price-to-book (PB) and price-to-earnings (PE) ratios. Users often base investment decisions on the observed values of these ratios. We describe how an analysis can arrive at "fundamental" PB and PE ratios without referring to the trading price of a company's shares. By comparing our fundamental ratios to those implicit in current stock prices, we can evaluate the investment merits of a publicly traded company. For those companies whose shares are not traded in active markets, the fundamental ratios serve as a means for estimating equity value.

Price-to-Book (PB) Ratio

The **price-to-book (PB) ratio** is expressed as:

$$\frac{\text{Market value of equity}}{\text{Book value of equity}}$$

Analysis Research
■ ■ ■ ■ ■ ■ ■

EARNINGS PERSISTENCE

Earnings persistence plays an important role in company valuation. Analysis research indicates nonrecurring earnings increase company value on a dollar-for-dollar basis, while the stock price reaction to persistent sources of earnings is higher and positively associated with the degree of persistence.

An analyst cannot rely solely on income statement classifications in assessing the persistence of a company's earnings. Research indicates that many types of nonrecurring items often are included in income from continuing operations. Examples are gains and losses from asset disposals, changes in accounting estimates, asset writedowns, and provisions for future losses. Analysis must carefully examine the financial statement notes, MD&A, and other disclosures for the existence of these items. Evidence also shows that extraordinary items and discontinued operations (special items) may be partly predictable and can provide information regarding future profitability.

Recent analysis research indicates that companies currently reporting negative income along with special items are more likely to report special items in the following year. These subsequent years' special items are likely to be of the same sign. Profitable companies with discontinued operations are more likely to report higher earnings in subsequent years.

By substituting the accounting-based expression for equity value in the numerator, the PB ratio can be expressed in terms of accounting data as follows:

$$\frac{V_t}{BV_t} = 1 + \left[\frac{(ROCE_{t+1} - k)}{(1 + k)}\right] + \left[\frac{(ROCE_{t+2} - k)}{(1 + k)^2} \times \frac{BV_{t+1}}{BV_t}\right]$$
$$+ \left[\frac{(ROCE_{t+3} - k)}{(1 + k)^3} \times \frac{BV_{t+2}}{BV_t}\right] + \cdots$$

This expression yields several important insights. As future ROCE and/or growth in book value increase, the PB ratio increases. Also, as the cost (risk) of equity capital, k, increases, the PB ratio decreases. Recognize that PB ratios deviate from 1.0 when the market expects residual earnings (both positive and negative) in the future. If the present value of future residual earnings is positive (negative), the PB ratio is greater (less) than 1.0.

Price-to-Earnings (PE) Ratio

The **price-to-earnings (PE) ratio** is expressed as:

$$\frac{\text{Market value of equity}}{\text{Net income}}$$

Ohlson and Juettner-Nauroth (2000) show that the PE ratio can be written as a function of short-term (STG) and long-term growth (LTG) of earning per share (eps) as follows:

$$\frac{P_0}{eps_1} = \frac{1}{k} \times \frac{STG - LTG}{k - LTG}$$

where k is the cost of equity capital, STG (LTG) is the expected short-term (long-term) percentage change in eps relative to expected "normal" growth, STG > LTG and LTG < k.[2] STG can be thought of as analysts' consensus five-year growth rate in eps and LTG as the long-run rate of inflation beyond the forecast horizon.

This equation yields two important insights: (1) The PE ratio is inversely related to the cost of capital, that is, it will be lower (higher) the higher (lower) the cost of equity

---

[2] Expected normal growth is at the rate of the cost of capital, that is, $eps_1 = eps_0 \times (1 + k)$ and eps includes the normal return on any dividends paid during the year (e.g., $k \times$ dividends).

capital, and (2) the PE ratio is positively related to the expected growth in eps relative to normal growth.

The PE ratio does not say anything about the absolute level of earnings (whether eps is high or low), only the rate at which eps is expected to increase relative to normal expected growth.

An interesting case is one in which the long-term expected growth in eps relative to normal eps is expected to remain at a constant level (for example, when LTG = 0). In this case, the ratio reduces to

$$\frac{P}{eps} = \frac{STG}{k^2}$$

In this form, the PE ratio is related to the short-term growth in eps relative to expected normal growth. This provides the rationale for the **PEG ratio,** a popular stock-screening metric. As an example, assume that a stock's PE ratio is 20 and the cost of capital is 10%. Proponents of this method classify a stock as fairly priced if the expected growth in eps is 20%, underpriced if the expected growth in eps is greater than 20% and overpriced if the expected growth in eps is less than 20%.

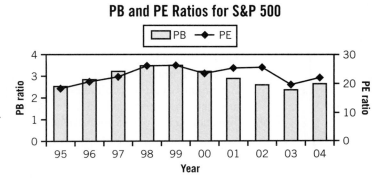

PB and PE Ratios for S&P 500

While the validity of the PEG ratio has yet to be demonstrated empirically, its widespread use highlights investors' appreciation of the relation between PE and eps growth.

Illustration of Earnings-Based Valuation

We illustrate earnings-based valuation using financial information from Christy Company. The book value of equity for Christy Company at January 1, Year 1, is $50,000. The company has a 15% cost of equity capital (k). After careful study of the company and its prospects using analysis techniques described in this book, we obtain the following predictions of accounting data:

	Year 1	Year 2	Year 3	Year 4	Year 5*
Sales	$100,000	$113,000	$127,690	$144,290	$144,290
Operating expenses	77,500	90,000	103,500	118,000	119,040
Depreciation	10,000	11,300	12,770	14,430	14,430
Net income	$ 12,500	$ 11,700	$ 11,420	$ 11,860	$ 10,820
Dividends	$ 6,000	$ 4,355	$ 3,120	$ 11,860	$ 10,820

    * Note: For Year 6 and beyond, both accounting data and dividends are expected to approximate Year 5 levels.

To apply the accounting-based valuation model, we compute expected future book values and ROCEs using the accounting predictions above. For example, expected book value at January 1, Year 2, is computed as $56,500 ($50,000 beginning book value + $12,500 net income − $6,000 dividends). Expected book values at January 1, Years 3 through 5, are $63,845, $72,145, and $72,145, respectively.

Recall that the accounting-based valuation model uses ROCEs computed using *beginning-of-period* book value. Therefore, expected ROCE for Year 1 is 25%

($12,500 ÷ $50,000). Expected ROCEs for Years 2 through 5 are 20.71%, 17.89%, 16.44%, and 15%, respectively.

The value of Christy Company's equity at January 1, Year 1, is computed using the accounting-based valuation model as follows:

$$\$58,594 = \$50,000 + \frac{(0.25 - 0.15) \times \$50,000}{1.15} + \frac{(0.2071 - 0.15) \times \$56,500}{1.15^2}$$

$$+ \frac{(0.1789 - 0.15) \times \$63,845}{1.15^3} + \frac{(0.1644 - 0.15) \times \$72,145}{1.15^4}$$

$$+ \frac{(0.15 - 0.15) \times \$72,145}{1.15^5} + 0 + \cdots$$

This accounting-based valuation implies that Christy's stock should sell at a PB ratio of 1.17 ($58,594 ÷ $50,000) at January 1, Year 1. To the extent that expectations of stock market participants differ from those implied by the valuation model, the PB ratio using actual stock price will differ from 1.17. In this case, we must consider two possibilities: (1) estimates of future profitability are too optimistic or pessimistic, and/or (2) the company's stock is mispriced. This determination is a major part of fundamental analysis. Three additional observations regarding this illustration are important.

1. Expected ROCE equals 15% for Year 5 and beyond. This 15% return is equal to Christy Company's cost of capital for those years. Since ROCE equals the cost of capital for Year 5 and beyond, these years' results do not change the value of Christy Company (that is, residual earnings equal zero for those years). Our assumption that ROCE gradually nears the cost of capital arises from basic economics. That is, if companies in an industry are able to earn ROCEs in excess of the cost of capital, other companies will enter the industry and drive residual earnings to zero.[3] The anticipated effects of competition are implicit in estimates of future profitability. For example, net income as a percentage of sales steadily decreases from 12.5% ($12,500 ÷ $100,000) in Year 1 to 7.5% ($10,820 ÷ $144,290) in Year 5 and beyond.

2. Since PE ratios are based on both *current* and *future* earnings, a PE ratio for Christy Company as of January 1, Year 1, cannot be calculated since prior years' data are unavailable. We can compute the PE ratio at January 1, Year 2. It is calculated as follows (we calculate Christy's residual income earnings in Problem 11–5):

$$\underline{\underline{4.91}} = \frac{1.15}{0.15} + \frac{\left(\frac{1.15}{0.15}\right)}{12,500}\left[\frac{3,225 - 5,000}{1.15} + \frac{1,844 - 3,226}{1.15^2} + \frac{1,039 - 1,845}{1.15^3} + \frac{0 - 1,039}{1.15^4}\right] - \frac{6,000}{12,500}$$

3. Valuation estimates assume dividend payments occur at the end of each year. A more realistic assumption is that, on average, these cash outflows occur midway through the year. To adjust valuation estimates for midyear discounting, we multiply the present value of future residual earnings by $(1 + k/2)$. For Christy Company the adjusted valuation estimate equals $59,239. This is computed as $50,000 plus $[1 + (.15⁄2)] \times \$8,594$.

---

[3] We must be alert to the possibility that even when residual earnings are zero, conservatism in accounting principles can create the *appearance* of residual profitability. While this issue is not pursued here, our analysis must consider the effects of conservative accounting principles on future ROCEs. For example, due to mandated expensing of most research and development costs, firms in the pharmaceutical industry are characterized by relatively high ROCEs.

........EARNING POWER AND FORECASTING FOR VALUATION

This section expands on the role of earning power and earnings forecasts for valuation. We also discuss the use of interim reports to monitor and revise these valuation inputs.

Earning Power

Earning power refers to the earnings level for a company that is expected to persist into the foreseeable future. With few exceptions, earning power is recognized as a primary factor in company valuation. Accounting-based valuation models include the capitalization of earning power, where capitalization involves using a factor or multiplier reflecting the cost of capital and its future expected risks and returns. Many analyses of earnings and financial statements are aimed at determining earning power.

Measuring Earning Power

Earning power is a concept derived from financial analysis, not accounting. It focuses on the stability and persistence of earnings and earnings components. Financial statements are used in computing earning power. This computation requires knowledge, judgment, experience, and perspective. Earnings are the most reliable and relevant measure for valuation purposes. While valuation is future oriented, we must recognize the relevance of current and prior company performance for estimating future performance. Recent periods' earnings extending over a business cycle represent actual operating performance and provide us a perspective on operating activities from which we can estimate future performance. Valuation is extremely important for many decisions (such as investing, lending, tax planning, adjudication of valuation disputes). Accordingly, valuation estimates must be credible and defensible, and we must scrutinize departures from the norm.

Time Horizon for Earning Power

A one-year period is often too short a period to reliably measure earnings. This is because of the long-term nature of many investing and financing activities, the effects of business cycles, and the existence of various nonrecurring factors. We can usually best measure a company's earning power by using average (or cumulative) earnings over several years. The preferred time horizon in measuring earning power varies across industries and other factors. A typical horizon is 5 years (and sometimes up to 10 years) in computing average earnings. This extended period is less subject to distortions, irregularities, and other transitory effects impairing the relevance of a single year's results. A five-year earnings computation often retains an emphasis on recent experience while avoiding less relevant performance.

Our discussion of both earnings quality and persistence emphasizes the importance of several earnings attributes including trend. Earnings trend is an important factor in measuring earning power. If earnings exhibit a sustainable trend, we can adjust the averaging process to weigh recent earnings more heavily. As an example, in a five-year earnings computation, the most recent earnings might be given a weight of 5/15, the next most recent earnings a weight of 4/15, and so on until earnings from five years ago receives a weight of 1/15. The more a company's recent experience is representative of future activities, the more relevant it is in the earnings forecast computation. If recent performance is unlike a company's future plans, then less emphasis is placed on prior earnings and more on earnings forecasts.

Adjusting Earnings per Share

Earning power is measured using *all* earnings components. Every item of revenue and expense is part of a company's operating experience. The issue is to what year we assign these items when computing earning power. In certain cases our earnings analysis might be limited to a short time horizon. As described earlier in this chapter, we adjust short time series of earnings for items that better relate to other periods. If this is done on a per share basis, every item must be adjusted for its tax effect using the company's effective tax rate unless the applicable tax rate is specified. All items must also be divided by the number of shares used in computing earnings per share (see Appendix 6A). An example of analytical adjustments for A. H. Robins Company appears in Illustration 11.4.

ILLUSTRATION 11.4

■ ■ ■ ■ ■ ■ ■

An Example of per Share Earnings Adjustments

Item	Year 2	Year 1
Effective tax rate change...	+$0.02	
Settlement of litigation...	+0.07	+$0.57
Change to straight-line depreciation.......................	+0.02	
Reserves for losses on foreign assets......................	+0.02	−0.15
Loss on sale of divisions...	−0.19	
Change to LIFO	−0.07	
Litigation settlements and expense...........................	−0.09	−0.12
Foreign exchange translation	−0.03	−0.04
R&D expenditures exceeding prior levels.................	−0.11	
Higher percent allowance for doubtful accounts	−0.02	
± Per share earnings impact...................................	−$0.38	+$0.26
Per share earnings as reported	$1.01	$1.71
Add back negative (−) impact to Year 2	0.38	
Subtract positive (+) impact from Year 1...........		(0.26)
Adjusted earnings per share	$1.39	$1.45

Earnings Forecasting

A major part of financial statement analysis and valuation is earnings forecasting. From an analytical perspective, evaluating earnings level is closely related to forecasting earnings. This is because a relevant forecast of earnings involves an analysis of earnings components and an assessment of their future levels. Accordingly, much of this chapter's previous discussion is applicable to earnings forecasting. Earnings forecasting follows an analysis of earnings components and involves generating estimates of their future levels. We should consider interactions among components and future business conditions. We should also consider persistence and stability of earnings components. This includes analysis of permanent (recurring) and transitory (nonrecurring) elements.

Mechanics of Earnings Forecasting

Forecasting requires us to effectively use all available information, including prior periods' earnings. Forecasting also benefits from disaggregation. Disaggregation involves using data by product lines or segments and is especially useful when these segments differ by risk, profitability, or growth. Divisional earnings for TechCom, Inc., reveal how strikingly different divisional performance can be masked by aggregate results:

TECHCOM EARNINGS ($ MILLIONS)

	2003	2004	2005	2006
Electronic products........	$1,800	$1,700	$1,500	$1,200
Customer services	600	800	1,100	1,400
Total net income	$2,400	$2,500	$2,600	$2,600

We must also differentiate forecasting from extrapolation. *Extrapolation* typically assumes the continuation of a trend and mechanically projects that trend into the future.

Analysis research reveals various statistical properties in earnings. Annual earnings growth often behaves in a random fashion. Some users interpret this as implying earnings growth cannot be forecasted. We must remember these studies reflect aggregate behavior and not individual company behavior. Furthermore, reliable earnings forecasting is not done by naive extrapolation of past earnings growth or trends. It is done by analyzing earnings components and considering all available information, both quantitative and qualitative. It involves forecasting these components and speculating about future business conditions.

An often useful source of relevant information for earnings forecasting is the Management Discussion and Analysis. It contains information on management's views and attitudes about the future, along with a discussion of factors influencing company performance. While companies have been slow to respond to the market demand for numerical forecasts of financial position and performance, they are encouraged to report forward-looking information in the MD&A.

Elements in Earnings Forecasting

While earnings forecasting depends on future prospects, the forecasting process must rely on current and past evidence. We forecast expected future conditions in light of this evidence. Analysis must assess continuity and momentum of company performance, including its industry, but it should be put in perspective. We should not confuse a company's past with its future and the uncertainty of forecasting. We must also remember that earnings is total revenues less total expenses, and that earnings forecasts reflect these components. A relatively minor change in a component can cause a large change in earnings.

Another element in earnings forecasting is checking on a forecast's reasonableness. We often use return on invested capital for this purpose. If the earnings forecast yields returns substantially different from returns realized in the past or from industry returns, we should reassess the forecasts and the process. Differences in forecast returns from what is reasonable must be explained. Return on invested capital depends on earnings—where earnings are a product of management quality and asset management.

- *Management quality.* It takes resourceful management to "breathe life" into assets by profitably and efficiently using them. To assume stability of relations and trends implies there is no major change in the skill, depth, and continuity of management. It also implies no major changes in the type of business where management's skills are proven.
- *Asset management.* A second element of profitable operations is asset management and success in financing those assets. Companies require assets to expand operations. Continuity of success and forecasts of growth depend on financing sources and their effects on earnings.

A company's financial condition is another element to earnings forecasting. Lack of liquidity can constrain successful management, and risky capital structure can limit management's actions. These and other economic, industry, and competitive factors are relevant to earnings forecasting. In forecasting earnings we must add expectations about the future to our knowledge of the past. We should also evaluate earnings trends with special emphasis on indicators of future performance like capital expenditures, order backlogs, and demand trends for products and services. It is important for us to realize that earnings forecasting is accompanied by considerable uncertainty. Forecasts may prove quite different from realizations because of unpredictable events or circumstances. We counter uncertainty by continual monitoring of performance relative to forecasts and revising forecasts as appropriate.

Reporting Earnings Forecasts

Recent years have witnessed increased interest in disclosures of earnings forecasts by companies. We should recognize that management (insider) forecasting is different from forecasts made by financial analysts (outsiders). The reliability of forecasts depends on information access and assumptions made. Use of management or analyst forecasts in our analysis depends on an assessment of the assumptions underlying them. The SEC encourages forecasts made in *good faith* that have a reasonable basis. It recommends they be reported in financial statement format and accompanied by information adequate for investors to assess reliability. To encourage forecast disclosures, the SEC has "safe harbor" rules protecting companies from lawsuits in case their predictions do not come true. These rules protect companies provided their forecasts are reasonably based and made in good faith. Because of practical legal considerations, few companies avail themselves of these safe harbor rules and publish forecasts. The following caveat from The Limited is typical of companies' reluctance to report forecasts:

ANALYSIS EXCERPT

The Company cautions that any forward-looking statements . . . involve risks and uncertainties, and are subject to . . . changes in consumer spending patterns, consumer preferences and overall economic conditions, the impact of competition and pricing, changes in weather patterns, political stability, currency and exchange risks and changes in existing or potential duties, tariffs, quotas, postal rate increases and charges; paper and printing costs, availability of suitable store locations at appropriate terms, ability to develop new merchandise and ability to hire and train associates.

Interim Reports for Monitoring and Revising Earnings Estimates

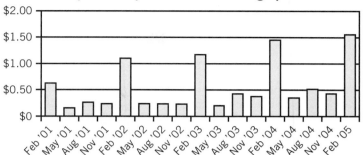

Best Buy Quarterly EPS from Continuing Operations

Assessing the earning power or earnings forecasts of a company relies on estimates of future conditions not amenable to verification. Our analysis must continually monitor company performance and compare it with the most recent forecasts and assumptions. We should regularly revise forecasts to incorporate current business conditions. Interim (less than one year) financial statements are a valuable source of information for monitoring performance. Interim statements are usually issued quarterly and are designed to meet users' needs. They are useful in revising estimates of earning power and earnings forecasts. Yet we must recognize certain limitations in interim reporting related to difficulties in assigning earnings components to periods of under one year in length. The remainder of this chapter describes these limitations and their effects on interim reports.

Period-End Accounting Adjustments

Determining operating results for a one-year period requires many accrual adjustments and estimates. These year-end adjustments are often complex, time-consuming, and costly. Examples include revenue recognition, determining inventory costs, allocating overhead, obtaining market values of securities, and estimating bad debts. Adjustments for interim periods are often less complete and use less reliable information than their year-end counterparts. This likely yields a less accurate earnings measure for interim periods.

Seasonality in Business Activities

Many companies experience seasonality in their business activities. Sales, production, and other operating activities are often unevenly distributed across interim periods. This can distort comparisons of interim earnings. It also creates problems in allocating certain discretionary costs like advertising, research, development, repairs, and maintenance. If these expenses vary with sales, they are usually accrued on the basis of expected sales for the entire year. Reporting problems also extend to allocating fixed costs across interim periods.

Integral Reporting Method

Interim reports are generally reported in a manner consistent with annual reporting requirements. Adopting the view that quarterly reports are integral to the entire year rather than a discrete period, practice requires accrual of revenues and expenses across interim periods. This includes accruals for inventory shrinkages, quantity discounts, and uncollectible accounts. Losses are not usually deferred beyond the interim period when they occur, and extraordinary items are reported in the interim period when they occur. But accrual of advertising costs is not acceptable on the basis that their benefits cannot be anticipated. Similarly, LIFO inventory liquidations are not considered for interim periods and only permanent declines in inventory values are recorded for interim reports. In contrast, income taxes are accrued using the effective tax rate expected for the annual period.

SEC Interim Reporting Requirements

The SEC is keenly interested in interim reporting. It requires quarterly reports (Form 10-Q), reports on current developments (Form 8-K), disclosure of separate fourth-quarter results, and details of year-end adjustments. Several reporting requirements exist for interim reports filed with the SEC. Principal requirements include:

- Comparative interim and year-to-date income statement data–can be labeled *unaudited* but must be included in annual reports (small companies are exempt).
- Comparative balance sheets.
- Year-to-date statement of cash flows.
- Pro forma information on business combinations accounted for as purchases.
- Conformity with accepted accounting principles and disclosure of accounting changes, including a letter from the auditor reporting whether the changes are preferable.
- Management's narrative analysis of operating results, with explanations of changes in revenues and expenses across interim periods.
- Disclosure as to whether a Form 8-K is filed during the period–reporting either unusual earnings adjustments or change of auditor.

These disclosures are believed to assist users in better understanding a company's business activities. They also are believed to assist users in estimating the trend in business activities across periods in a timely manner.

Analysis Implications of Interim Reports

Our analysis must be aware of estimation errors and the discretion inherent in interim reports. The limited involvement of auditors with interim reports reduces their reliability relative to annual audited financial statements. Exchange regulations offer some, albeit limited, assurance. Yet not all reporting requirements for interim reports are necessarily best for our analysis. For example, including extraordinary items in the interim period when they occur requires adjustment for use in analysis. Similarly, while accruing expenses across interim periods is reasonable, our analysis must remember there are no precise rules governing these accruals. Shifting expenses across interim periods is often easier than shifting revenues. Therefore, analysis often emphasizes interim revenues as a measure of interim performance. Further, certain seasonality problems with interim reports are overcome by computing *year-to-date cumulative numbers,* including the results of the most recent quarter.

GUIDANCE ANSWERS TO ANALYSIS VIEWPOINTS

ANALYST/FORECASTER
More persistent earnings reflect recurring, stable, and predictable operating elements. Your estimate of earnings persistence should consider these elements. More persistent earnings comprise recurring operating elements. Finding 40% of earnings from unusual gains implies less persistence because its source is nonoperating. You can also question classification of litigation gains as unusual–they are sometimes better viewed as extraordinary.

The extraordinary loss component also implies less persistence. In this case you need to assess whether environmental costs are truly extraordinary for this company's business. Together, these components suggest less persistence than suggested by the stable and steady growth trend in aggregate earnings. This lower persistence should be reflected in both the level and uncertainty of your earnings forecast.

QUESTIONS

11–1. Why is analysis of research and development expenses important in assessing and forecasting earnings? What are some concerns in analyzing research and development expenses?

11–2. What is the relation between the reported values of assets and reported earnings? What is the relation between the reported values of liabilities, including provisions, and reported earnings?

11–3. What is the purpose in recasting the income statement for analysis?

11–4. Where do we find the data necessary for analysis of operating results and for their recasting and adjustment?

11–5. Describe the recasting process. What is the aim of the recasting process in analysis?

11–6. Describe the adjustment of the income statement for financial statement analysis.

11–7. Explain earnings management. How is earnings management distinguished from fraudulent reporting?

11–8. Identify and explain at least three types of earnings management.

11–9. What factors and incentives motivate companies (management) to engage in earnings management? What are the implications of these incentives for financial statement analysis?

11–10. Why is management interested in the reporting of extraordinary gains and losses?

11–11. What are the analysis objectives in evaluating extraordinary items?

11–12. What three categories can unusual or extraordinary items be usefully subdivided into for purposes of analysis? Provide examples for each category. How should an analysis treat items in each of these categories? Is a certain treatment implied under all circumstances? Explain.

11–13. Describe the effects of extraordinary items on:

   a. Company resources.

   b. Management evaluation.

11–14. Comment on the following statement: "Extraordinary gains or losses do not result from 'normal' or 'planned' business activities and, consequently, they should not be used in evaluating managerial performance." Do you agree?

11–15. Can accounting manipulations influence earnings-based estimates of company valuation? Explain.

11–16. a. Identify major determinants of PB and PE ratios.

   b. How can the analyst use jointly the values of PB and PE ratios in assessing the merits of a particular stock investment?

11–17. What is the difference between forecasting and extrapolation of earnings?

11–18. How do MD&A disclosure requirements aid in earnings forecasting?

11–19. What is earning power? Why is earning power important for financial statement analysis?

11–20. How are interim financial statements used in analysis? What accounting problems with interim statements must we be alert to in an analysis?

11–21. Interim financial reports are subject to limitations and distortions. Identify and discuss at least two reasons for this.

11–22. What are major disclosure requirements for interim reports? What are the objectives of these requirements?

11–23. What are the implications of interim reports for financial analysis?

EXERCISES

Refer to the financial statements of **Quaker Oats Company** in Problem 9-6 along with the following footnote.

Quaker Oats Company

EXERCISE 11–1

Analyzing and Interpreting Maintenance and Repairs Expense

SUPPLEMENTARY EXPENSE DATA

($ millions)	Year 11	Year 10	Year 9
Advertising, media, and production	$ 277.5	$ 282.8	$ 256.5
Merchandising	1,129.9	912.5	886.2
Total advertising and merchandising..........	$1,407.4	$1,195.3	$1,142.7
Maintenance and repairs	$ 96.1	$ 96.6	$ 93.8
Depreciation expense	$ 125.2	$ 103.5	$ 94.5
Research and development	$ 44.3	$ 43.3	$ 39.3

Required:

a. Prepare a schedule where maintenance and repairs expense is shown (i) as a percent of revenues and (ii) as a percent of property, plant, and equipment (net) for:
   (1) Year 9 and Year 10, separately.
   (2) Total of Years 9 and 10.
   (3) Average of Years 9 and 10.
   (4) Year 11.

b. Interpret the comparison of the spending level for maintenance and repairs in Year 11 with the average level of spending for Years 9 and 10.

CHECK
(4) (i) 1.75%
    (ii) 7.80%

EXERCISE 11–2

*Interpreting
Extraordinary Items*

The president of Vancouver Viacom made the following comments to shareholders:

> Regarding management attitudes, Vancouver Viacom has resisted joining an increasing number of companies who along with earnings announcements make extraordinary or nonrecurring loss announcements. Many of these cases read like regular operating problems. When we close plants, we charge earnings for the costs involved or reserved as we approach the event. These costs, in my judgment, are usually a normal operating expense and something that good management should expect or anticipate. That, of course, raises the question of what earnings figure should be used in assessing a price-earnings ratio and the quality of earnings.

Required:

a. Discuss your reactions to these comments.

b. What factors determine whether a gain or loss is extraordinary?

CHECK
(1) No
(5) No
(10) No

c. Explain whether you would classify the following items as extraordinary and why.
   (1) Loss suffered by foreign subsidiaries due to a change in the foreign exchange rate.
   (2) Write-down of inventory from cost to market.
   (3) Loss attributable to an improved product developed by a competitor.
   (4) Decrease in net income from higher tax rates.
   (5) Increase in income from liquidation of low-cost LIFO inventories due to a strike.
   (6) Expenses incurred in relocating plant facilities.
   (7) Expenses incurred in liquidating unprofitable product lines.
   (8) Research and development costs written off from a product failure (non-marketed).
   (9) Software costs written off because demand for a product was weaker than expected.
   (10) Financial distress of a major customer yielding a bad debts provision.
   (11) Loss on sale of rental cars by a car rental company.
   (12) Gains on sales of fixed assets.
   (13) Rents received from employees who occupy company-owned houses.
   (14) Uninsured casualty losses.
   (15) Expropriation by a foreign government of an entire division of the company.
   (16) Seizure or destruction of property from an act of war.

A financial analyst's comments on income statement classifications follow:

> We should drop the word extraordinary and leave it to users to decide whether items like a strike will recur next year or not, and to decide whether a lease abandonment will recur or not. We need an all-inclusive statement with no extraordinary items. Let users apply the income statement for predictive purposes by eliminating items that will not recur. But let the record show all events that have an impact–there are really no values that "don't count." The current operating performance approach to reporting has no merit. I argue that everything is relevant and needs to be included. By omitting items from current operating performance we are relegating them to a lesser role. I do not believe this is conceptually correct. We include everything to better evaluate management and forecast earnings. Users can individually decide on the merits of an inventory write-off or the planned sale or abandonment of a plant. Both items deserve to adversely affect income because they reflect management performance. Both items can be excluded by the user in forecasting earnings. The current system yields abuses. Even an earthquake is part of the picture. A lease abandonment recurs in the oil industry. No man is wise enough to cut the Gordian knot on this issue by picking and choosing what is extraordinary, recurring, typical, or customary.

EXERCISE 11–3
Extraordinary Items in Financial Statement Analysis

Required:

a. Describe your views on this statement. What is your opinion on how extraordinary items should be reported?

b. Discuss how extraordinary items should be treated in financial analysis.

Interim accounting statements comprise a major part of financial reporting. There is ongoing discussion considering the relevance of reporting on business activities for interim periods.

EXERCISE 11–4
Interpreting Disclosures in Interim Financial Statements

Required:

a. Discuss how revenues are recognized for interim periods. Comment on differences in revenue recognition for companies (1) subject to large seasonal fluctuations in revenue, and (2) having long-term contracts accounted for using percentage of completion for annual periods.

b. Explain how product and period costs are recognized for interim periods.

c. Discuss how inventory and cost of goods sold can be given special accounting treatment for interim periods.

d. Describe how the provision for income taxes is computed and reported in interim reports.

(AICPA Adapted)

An analyst needs to understand the sources and implications of variability in financial statement data.

EXERCISE 11–5
Identifying Sources of Variability in Financial Data

Required:

Identify factors affecting variability in earnings per share, dividends per share, and market price per share that derive from

a. The company

b. The economy

(CFA Adapted)

PROBLEMS

PROBLEM 11–1

Recasting of the Income Statement

Refer to the financial statements of **Quaker Oats Company** in Problem 9-6 along with the following footnotes.

Quaker Oats Company

SUPPLEMENTARY EXPENSE DATA

($ millions)	Year 11	Year 10	Year 9
Advertising, media and production	$ 277.5	$ 282.8	$ 256.5
Merchandising	1,129.9	912.5	886.2
Total advertising and merchandising	$1,407.4	$1,195.3	$1,142.7
Maintenance and repairs	$ 96.1	$ 96.6	$ 93.8
Depreciation expense	$ 125.2	$ 103.5	$ 94.5
Research and development	$ 44.3	$ 43.3	$ 39.3

INTEREST (INCOME) EXPENSE

($ millions)	Year 11	Year 10	Year 9
Total interest expense	$101.9	$120.2	$ 75.9
Total interest income	(9.0)	(11.0)	(12.4)
Net interest allocated to discontinued operations	(6.7)	(7.4)	(7.1)

($ millions)	Year 11 Amount	Year 11 % of Pretax Income	Year 10 Amount	Year 10 % of Pretax Income	Year 9 Amount	Year 9 % of Pretax Income
Tax provision based on the federal statutory rate	$139.9	34.0%	$130.0	34.0%	$81.3	34.0%
State and local income taxes, net of federal income tax benefit	16.7	4.1	11.9	3.1	7.7	3.2
ANC benefit	—	—	—	—	(1.7)	(.7)
Repatriation of foreign earnings	4.3	1.0	4.8	1.3	(2.1)	(.9)
Non-U.S. tax rate differential	8.2	2.0	9.8	2.5	8.8	3.7
U.S. tax credits	(.2)	—	(.1)	—	(.7)	(.3)
Miscellaneous items—net	6.8	1.6	(2.9)	(.8)	(3.1)	(1.3)
Actual tax provision	$175.7	42.7%	$153.5	40.1%	$90.2	37.7%

OTHER (INCOME) EXPENSE

($ millions)	Year 11	Year 10	Year 9
Foreign exchange (gains) losses—net	$ (5.1)	$ 25.7	$ 14.8
Amortization of intangibles	22.4	22.2	18.2
Losses (gains) from plant closings and operations sold or to be sold—net	8.8	(23.1)	119.4
Miscellaneous—net	6.5	(8.4)	(2.8)
Net other expense	$32.6	$ 16.4	$149.6

CHECK

Recast cont. income Years 11–9, $252.7, $224.5, $126.8

Required:

a. Recast Quaker Oats' income statements through Income from Continuing Operations for Years 11, 10, and 9 (estimate federal income tax at 34%).

b. Interpret trends revealed by the recasted income statements.

You are considering the purchase of all outstanding preferred and common stock of Finex, Inc., for $700,000 on January 2, Year 2. Finex's financial statements for Year 1 are reproduced below.

PROBLEM 11–2

Analyzing Pre- and Post-acquisition Financial Statements

FINEX, INC.
Balance Sheet
As of December 31, Year 1

Cash	$ 55,000
U.S. government bonds	25,000
Accounts receivable, net	150,000
Merchandise inventory	230,000
Land	40,000
Buildings, net[a]	360,000
Equipment, net[b]	130,000
Total assets	$990,000
Accounts payable	$170,000
Notes payable, current	50,000
Bonds payable, due Year 12[c]	200,000
Preferred stock, 6%, $100 par	100,000
Common stock, $100 par	400,000
Paid-in capital in excess of par	43,000
Retained earnings[d]	27,000
Total liabilities and equity	$990,000

Income Statement
For Year Ended December 31, Year 1

Net sales	$860,000
Cost of good sold	546,000
Gross profit	314,000
Selling and administrative expenses	240,000
Net operating income	74,000
Income tax expense	34,000
Net income	$ 40,000

[a] Accumulated depreciation on buildings, $35,000.
    Depreciation expense in Year 1, $7,900.
[b] Accumulated depreciation on equipment, $20,000.
    Depreciation expense in Year 1, $9,000.
[c] Bonds are sold at par.
[d] Dividends paid in Year 1: preferred, $6,000;
    common, $20,000.

You need to adjust net income to estimate the earnings potential of an acquisition. The company uses the FIFO method of inventory valuation and all inventories can be sold without loss. With the change in ownership you expect an additional 5% of net accounts receivable to be uncollectible. You assume sales and all remaining financial relations are constant.

Required:

a. What reported value would be individually assigned to Land, Buildings, and Equipment after the proposed purchase assuming that we allocate the excess purchase price to these three assets in proportion to their respective book values on the Year 1 balance sheet? (implicitly assumes that these assets are undervalued by this amount)

b. Prepare a balance sheet for Finex, Inc., immediately after your proposed purchase.

c. Estimate Finex, Inc.'s net operating income for Year 2 under your ownership. (*Hint:* Use the same ratio of depreciation expense to assets; and one-third of depreciation is charged to cost of goods sold.)

d. Assuming your minimum required ratio of net operating income to net sales is 8%, should you purchase Finex, Inc.?

CHECK

(*b*) Total assets, $1,120,000

(*c*) Net oper. inc., $72,008

PROBLEM 11–3

Analyzing Credit Constraints for a Bank Loan

Aspero, Inc., has sales of approximately $500,000 per year. Aspero requires a short-term loan of $100,000 to finance its working capital requirements. Two banks are considering Aspero's loan request but each bank requires certain minimum conditions be satisfied. Bank America requires at least a 25% gross margin on sales, and Bank Boston requires a 2:1 current ratio. The following information is available for Aspero for the current year:

- Sales returns and allowances are 10% of sales.
- Purchases returns and allowances are 2% of purchases.
- Sales discounts are 2% of sales.
- Purchase discounts are 1% of purchases.
- Ending inventory is $138,000.
- Cash is 10% of accounts receivable.
- Credit terms to Aspero's customers are 45 days.
- Credit terms Aspero receives from its suppliers are 90 days.
- Purchases for the year are $400,000.
- Ending inventory is 38% greater than beginning inventory.
- Accounts payable are the only current liability.

CHECK

Bank America rejects loan.

Required:

Assess whether Aspero, Inc., meets the credit constraint for a loan from either or both banks. Show computations.

PROBLEM 11–4

Accounting-Based Equity Valuation

CHECK

1/1/Year 2

(*b*) $60,747

(*c*) $61,066

(*e*) 1.09

Use the data from Christy Company in the chapter to answer the following.

a. Calculate Christy Company's residual income for each of Year 1 through Year 5.

b. Use the accounting-based equity valuation model to estimate the value of Christy's equity at January 1 of each of Year 2 through Year 5.

c. The chapter's discussion of Christy Company assumes that accounting for book value is not conservative. How does the use of conservative accounting principles affect the accounting-based valuation task?

d. Use the PB formula to determine the PB ratio at January 1 of each of Year 2 through Year 5.

e. Use the PE formula to determine the PE ratio at January 1 of each of Year 3 through Year 5.

CASES

Income statements of **Ferro Corporation,** along with its note 7 on income taxes and selected information from its Form 10-K, are reproduced below:

Ferro Corporation

CASE 11–1

Analyzing and Interpreting Trends in Earnings and Earnings Components

CONSOLIDATED STATEMENT OF INCOME
Years Ended December 31, Year 6 and Year 5

($ thousands)	Year 6	Year 5
Net sales	$376,485	$328,005
Cost of sales	266,846	237,333
Selling and administrative expenses	58,216	54,140
Research and development	9,972	8,205
Operating expenses	335,034	299,678
Operating income	41,451	28,327
Other income		
Equity in net earnings of affiliated companies	1,394	504
Royalties	710	854
Interest earned	1,346	1,086
Miscellaneous	1,490	1,761
Total other income	4,940	4,205
Other charges		
Interest expense	4,055	4,474
Unrealized foreign currency translation loss	4,037	1,851
Miscellaneous	1,480	1,448
Total other charges	9,572	7,773
Income before taxes	36,819	24,759
U.S. and foreign income taxes (note 7)	16,765	11,133
Net income	$ 20,054	$ 13,626

Notes to Financial Statements

Income tax expense is comprised of the following components ($ thousands):

Year 6	U.S. Federal	Foreign	Total	Year 5	U.S. Federal	Foreign	Total
Current	$5,147	$11,125	$16,272	Current	$2,974	$ 8,095	$11,069
Deferred	353	140	493	Deferred	180	(116)	64
Total	$5,500	$11,265	$16,765	Total	$3,154	$ 7,979	$11,133

Deferred income taxes were mainly the result of using accelerated depreciation for income tax purposes and straight-line depreciation in the consolidated financial statements. State and local income taxes totaling approximately $750,000 and $698,000 in Year 6 and Year 5, respectively, are included in other

(continued)

CASE 11–1
(concluded)

expense categories. A reconciliation between the U.S. federal income tax rate and the effective tax rate for Year 6 and Year 5 follows:

	Year 6	Year 5
U.S. federal income tax rate	48.0%	48.0%
Earnings of consolidated subsidiaries taxed at rates less than		
the U.S. federal income tax rate	(5.3)	(5.3)
Equity in after-tax earnings of affiliated companies	(1.4)	(0.8)
Unrealized foreign exchange translation loss	5.3	3.6
Additional U.S. taxes on dividends from subsidiaries and affiliates	0.8	1.0
Investment tax credit	(1.5)	(0.9)
Miscellaneous	(0.4)	(0.6)
Effective tax rate	45.5%	45.0%

The following information from Ferro Corporation's Form 10-K is available:

	Year 6	Year 5
Cost of sales includes ($ thousands)		
Repairs and maintenance	$15,000	$20,000
Loss on disposal of chemicals division	—	7,000
Selling and administrative expenses include ($ thousands)		
Advertising	$ 6,000	$ 7,000
Employee training program	4,000	5,000

Recast oper. income,
Year 6 = $20,520;
Year 5 = $17,215

Required:

a. Recast Ferro's income statements for Years 5 and 6. Show computations.

b. Identify factors causing income tax expense to differ from 48% of pretax income. Identify any random or unstable factors.

c. What significant changes can you identify in Ferro's operating policies for Year 6? (*Hint:* Limit your analysis to outlays for repairs and maintenance, advertising, and employee training programs.)

CHECK

CASE 11–2

*Assessing Earnings
Quality and Proposed
Accounting Changes*

Canada Steel, Ltd., produces steel castings and metal fabrications for sale to manufacturers of heavy construction machinery and agricultural equipment. Early in Year 3 the company's president sent the following memorandum to the financial vice president:

TO: Robert Kinkaid, Financial Vice President

FROM: Richard Johnson, President

SUBJECT: Accounting and Financial Policies

Fiscal Year 2 was a difficult year, and the recession is likely to continue into Year 3. While the entire industry is suffering, we might be hurting our performance unnecessarily with accounting and business policies that are not appropriate. Specifically:

(1) We depreciate most fixed assets over their estimated useful lives on a "tonnage-of-production" method. Accelerated methods and shorter lives are used for tax purposes. A switch to straight-line for financial reporting purposes could: (a) eliminate the deferred tax liability on our balance sheet, and (b) leverage our profits if business picks up.

(2) Several years ago you convinced me to change from the FIFO to LIFO inventory method. Since inflation is now down to a 4% annual rate, and balance sheet strength is important in our current environment, I estimate we can increase shareholders' equity by about $2.0 million, working capital by $4.0 million, and Year 3 earnings by $0.5 million if we return to FIFO in Year 3. This adjustment is real–these profits were earned by us over the past several years and should be recognized.

(3) If we make the inventory change, our stock repurchase program can be continued. The same shareholder who sold us 50,000 shares last year at $100 per share would like to sell another 20,000 shares at the same price. However, to obtain additional bank financing, we must maintain the current ratio at 3:1 or better. It seems prudent to decrease our capitalization if return on assets is unsatisfactory. Also, interest rates are lower (11% prime) and we can save $60,000 after taxes annually once our $3.00 per share dividend is resumed.

These actions would favorably affect our profitability and liquidity ratios as shown in the pro forma income statement and balance sheet data for Year 3 ($ millions):

	Year 1	Year 2	Year 3 Estimate
Net sales	$50.6	$42.3	$29.0
Net income (loss)	$ 2.0	$ (5.7)	$ 0.1
Net profit margin	4.0%	—	0.3%
Dividends	$ 0.7	$ 0.6	$ 0.0
Return on assets	7.2%	—	0.4%
Return on equity	11.3%	—	0.9%
Current assets	$17.6	$14.8	$14.5
Current liabilities	$ 6.6	$ 4.9	$ 4.5
Long-term debt	$ 2.0	$ 6.1	$ 8.1
Shareholders' equity	$17.7	$11.4	$11.5
Shares outstanding (000s)	226.8	170.5	150.5
Per common share			
Book value	$78.05	$66.70	$76.41
Market price range	$42–34	$65–45	$62–55*

* Year to date.

Required:

Assume you are Robert Kinkaid, the financial vice president. Appraise the president's rationale for each of the proposals. You should place special emphasis on how each accounting or business decision affects earnings quality. Support your response with ratio analysis.

(CFA Adapted)

CASE 11–3

Accounting-Based Equity Valuation

After careful financial statement analysis, we obtain these predictions for Colin Technology:

Year	Net Income	Beginning Book Value	Year	Net Income	Beginning Book Value
1	$1,034	$5,308	5	$1,278	$6,728
2	1,130	5,292	6	1,404	7,266
3	1,218	5,834	7	1,546	7,856
4	1,256	6,338			

Colin Technology's cost of equity capital is estimated at 13 percent.

CHECK

(a) $7,205
(d) $8,644

Required:

a. Abnormal earnings are expected to be $0 per year after Year 7. Use the accounting-based equity valuation model to estimate Colin's value at the beginning of Year 1.

b. Determine Colin's PB ratio using the results in (a). Colin's actual market-based PB ratio is 1.95. What do you conclude from this PB comparison?

c. Determine Colin's PE ratio using the results in (a). Colin's actual market-based PE ratio is 10. What do you conclude from this PE comparison?

d. If we expect Colin's sales and profit margin to remain unchanged after Year 7 with a stable book value of $8,506, use the accounting-based equity valuation model to estimate Colin's value at the beginning of Year 1.

CASE 11–4

IT Professional Service Company Valuations– Revenue Multiples

IT service companies develop Web storefronts that are integrated with back-end implementation systems. Only a small number of companies offer such extensive e-business integration. The industry continues to grow because of customer demand. Unlike traditional valuation, companies in the IT services sector are valued based on revenue multiples. Following are two tables that summarize comparable valuation multiples and operating metrics as of November 22, 2005–a leading Wall Street investment bank, using its own estimates and company data, compiled these tables.

Valuation Multiples

Company	Price at 11/22/05	Shares (millions)	Market Value	REVENUE ESTIMATES 2005	2006	Growth	Latest Quarter Revenue	Growth	REVENUE MULTIPLE 2005	2006
Breakaway Solutions	$ 62.63	23.9	$1,497	25	43	72%	7	38%	59.9	34.8
Rare Medium	31.25	78.0	2,438	50	100	100	5	100	48.8	24.4
Scient	129.38	38.9	5,033	95	222	134	31	88	53.0	22.7
Viant	87.00	26.0	2,262	59	110	86	19	71	38.3	20.6
Proxicom	73.50	29.2	2,146	79	122	54	24	45	27.2	17.6
US Interactive	41.25	22.1	912	34	55	62	10	29	26.8	16.6
Razorfish	73.50	46.5	3,420	148	230	55	41	20	23.1	14.9
AppNet	48.63	31.3	1,522	109	150	38	30	20	14.0	10.1
iXL Enterprises	37.00	64.5	2,388	200	370	85	64	39	11.9	6.5
Modem Media	54.00	11.7	632	71	102	44	21	32	8.9	6.2
Luminant Worldwide	38.38	23.7	909	94	149	58	25	—	9.6	6.1
USWeb/CKS	42.50	89.1	3,787	506	925	83	138	22	7.5	4.1
Selected averages	—	—	—	—	—	73%	—	46%	27.4	15.4
Selected medians	—	—	—	—	—	67%	—	38%	25.0	15.7

Operating Metrics

Company	Gross Margin	Revenue/ Headcount	Billable Headcount	Billing Rates	Annual Turnover	Average Utilization
Breakaway Solutions.................	52.4%	$214,000	140	$138	20%	73%
Rare Medium	51.0	188,000	327	200	—	70
Scient	53.8	303,000	484	—	12	71
Viant..	55.0	324,000	254	—	28	67
Proxicom	48.8	214,000	492	149	17	79
US Interactive	44.2	187,000	212	160	24	68
Razorfish	57.8	197,000	868	153	18	62
AppNet.......................................	45.1	175,000	715	115	16	73
iXL Enterprises..........................	44.0	217,000	1,260	152	30	73
Modem Media	44.7	209,000	455	132	8	78
Luminant Worldwide..................	—	180,000	—	—	24	73
USWeb/CKS...............................	40.0	223,000	3,190	155	21	69
Selected averages......................	48.8%	$219,283	—	$150	20%	71%
Selected medians	48.8%	$211,500	—	$152	20%	72%

Required:

a. Considering that the IT services sector is still in its infancy, explain why analysts employ a revenue multiple model when valuing these companies. How do the "nonfinancial" operating metrics supplement this model?

b. Can you explain why the distribution of revenue multiples appears to have such a wide variance? Notice that billing rates do not appear to be as varied.

c. Most operating metrics are based on headcount. This can be a problem for an industry enjoying such rapid growth. Can you explain how this can be a problem? (*Hint:* Average utilization is the percentage of the 2,080 normal work year that is billed to clients beginning on the day that the employee is hired.)

d. Explain why the revenue multiples for year 2006 are all lower than the comparable revenue multiples for 2005.

e. With such rapid industry expansion comes consolidation through business combinations. Shortly after the above tables were compiled, Razorfish completed a merger with International Integration (I-Cube), another company in the IT services sector. Razorfish offered I-Cube shareholders 0.875 share of Razorfish for each one I-Cube share. The deal was valued at $24.72 per share, nearly 18% above what I-Cube was trading for prior to the announcement. At the time of the acquisition announcement, I-Cube was trading at a price-to-revenue multiple of seven. What is your assessment of the price that Razorfish paid to acquire I-Cube?

CC

APPLYING FINANCIAL STATEMENT ANALYSIS

■■■■■■■

A LOOK BACK <

Chapters 1 and 2 provided us a broad overview of financial statement analysis using Dell as a primary example. Chapters 3–6 described the accounting analysis of financing, investing, and operating activities, and offered us insights into company performance and financial condition. Chapters 7–11 emphasized the application and interpretation of key financial analysis tools and techniques.

A LOOK AT THIS CASE •

This case is a comprehensive analysis of financial statements and related notes. We use Campbell Soup Company as a focus. We describe the steps in analyzing financial statements, the building blocks of analysis, and essential attributes of an analysis report. We support our analysis using many of the tools and techniques described throughout the book. Explanation and interpretation accompany all of our analyses.

ANALYSIS OBJECTIVES

• Describe the steps in analyzing financial statements.

• Review the building blocks of financial statement analysis.

• Explain important attributes of reporting on financial statement analysis.

• Describe implications for financial statement analysis of evaluating companies in specialized industries or with unique characteristics.

• Analyze in a comprehensive manner the financial statements and notes of Campbell Soup Company.

CAMDEN, NJ–Campbell Soup has used several slogans over the years, many of which are all too familiar given the company's ubiquitous advertising campaigns. The latest is, "It's not enough to be a legend." And that's the problem. The company is the world's largest maker and marketer of soup, and a leading producer of juice beverages, sauces, biscuits, and confectionery products. Its industry, however, remains a competitive, slow-growth environment.

Campbell has resisted change, and consequently, missed several opportunities. Its slavish devotion to condensed soup relegated many growth products lacking for research and development funds and marketing support. In response, company management orchestrated several restructurings, including cost cutting and asset efficiency programs.

Analysis of a company such as Campbell Soup must recognize that cost cutting and improvement in asset productivity, while essential to high performance, does not deliver growth. Growth of a consumer products company results from a strong presence in vibrant markets, wealth-creating acquisitions, and creative new product development. All of these have been historically lacking for Campbell Soup.

Stock prices are a function of both profitability and growth. Consequently, until its management discovers a profitable growth market to invest shareholder capital, Campbell Soup's market value can only moderately increase. This fact is painfully evident in its stock price (CPB),

> **It's not enough to be a legend.**

which remains at 1996 levels despite a recent run-up. Further, until the recent year, Campbell Soup had markedly increased its financial leverage. The added risk to creditors resulted in a downgrade of its debt, falling from the highest credit level of AAA to A. Although still financially strong, the credit markets recognize some deterioration as the company increased debt during its restructuring programs.

"It's not enough to be a legend" is not only self-evident, but is also the constraint to Campbell's future success. The company must reinvent itself, and that may mean forgetting its legendary heritage.

In its BUY recommendation, PiperJaffray renders the following somewhat optimistic conclusion: "We raised our multiple assumption from 18.5x to 19x reflecting sustainable margin improvements. Similar to other large-cap packaged goods companies, we are looking for low single-digit organic sales growth, mid-single-digit operating profit growth based on margin expansion and operational efficiency, and 5%–7% EPS growth from cash reinvestment activity benefits. After three years into the transformation plan, we remain encouraged by what we see at CPB. We believe cold-blend technology, easy-open tops, new convenient soup offerings, and new retail shelving systems will grow the U.S. soup business. CPB is focused on innovation, brand building, and executing its sales strategy, leading to better sales growth and cash flow generation." Time will tell if that prediction proves accurate.

PREVIEW OF COMPREHENSIVE CASE

A comprehensive case analysis of the financial statements and notes of Campbell Soup Company is our focus. This book has prepared us to tackle all facets of financial statement analysis. This comprehensive case analysis provides us the opportunity to illustrate and apply these analysis tools and techniques. This case also gives us the opportunity to show how we draw conclusions and inferences from detailed analysis. We review the basic steps of analysis, the building blocks, and key attributes of an expert analysis report. Throughout the case we emphasize applications and inferences associated with financial statement analysis.

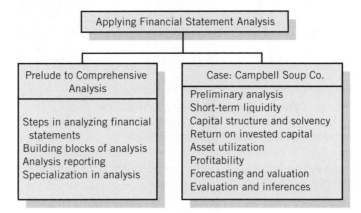

.......STEPS IN ANALYZING FINANCIAL STATEMENTS

Our task in analyzing financial statements can be usefully summarized for consistency and organizational efficiency. There are generalizations and guidelines that help us conduct financial statement analysis. Still, we must remember that analysis depends on judgments and thus should be flexible. This flexibility is necessary because of the diversity of situations and circumstances in practice and the need for us to aggressively apply ideas, experience, and knowledge.

Financial statement analysis is oriented toward achieving specific objectives. *The first step is to explicitly define the analysis objectives.* Our evaluation of the issues and concerns leading up to specification of objectives is an important part of analysis. This evaluation helps us develop an understanding of pertinent and relevant objectives. It also helps eliminate extraneous objectives and avoid unnecessary analysis. Identifying objectives is important to an effective and efficient analysis. Effectiveness in analysis implies a focus on the important and relevant elements of financial statements. Efficiency in analysis implies economy of time and effort–see Illustration CC.1a.

ILLUSTRATION CC.1a
■ ■ ■ ■ ■ ■

Assume you are a bank loan officer handling a request for a short-term loan to finance inventory. A reasonable objective is for you to *assess the intent and ability of the borrower to repay the loan in a timely manner.* Your analysis concentrates on what information is necessary to assess the borrower's intent and ability. You need not focus on extraneous issues like long-term industry conditions affecting the borrower's long-run performance.

The second step in analysis is to formulate specific questions and criteria consistent with the analysis objectives. Answers to these questions should be both relevant to achieving the analysis objectives and reliable for making business decisions. Criteria for answers must be consistent with our risk and return requirements–see Illustration CC.1b.

ILLUSTRATION CC.1b
■ ■ ■ ■ ■ ■

In your role as bank loan officer you need to specify relevant questions and criteria for making the loan decision in Illustration CC.1a. Criteria for the borrower include:

- Willingness to repay the short-term loan.
- Ability to repay the short-term loan (liquidity).
- Identification of future sources and uses of cash during the loan period.

Addressing analysis questions and defining criteria depend on a variety of information sources, including those bearing on the borrower's character. Financial statement analysis can answer many of these questions, but not all. Tools other than financial statement analysis (such as strategy analysis) must be used to answer some of these questions.

The third step in analysis is identifying the most effective and efficient tools of analysis. These tools must be relevant in answering the questions posed and the criteria established, and must be appropriate for the business decision at hand. These tools include many of the procedures and techniques discussed throughout the book—see Illustration CC.1c.

Your role as loan officer requires decisions regarding what financial statement analysis tools to use for the short-term loan request in Illustration CC.1a. You will probably choose one or more of the following analysis tools:

ILLUSTRATION CC.1c
■ ■ ■ ■ ■ ■ ■

- Short-term liquidity measures.
- Inventory turnover measures.
- Cash flow and earnings forecasts.
- Pro forma analysis.

Many of these analysis tools include estimates and projections of future conditions. This future orientation is a common thread of all analysis tools.

The fourth step in analysis is interpreting the evidence. Interpretation of financial data and measures is the basis of our decision and subsequent action. This is a crucial and difficult step in analysis, and requires us to apply our skills and knowledge of business and nonbusiness factors. It is a step demanding study and evaluation. It requires us to picture the business reality and environment behind the numbers. There is no mechanical substitute for this step. Yet the quality of our interpretation depends on properly identifying the objectives of analysis, defining the questions and their decision criteria, and selecting efficient and effective analysis tools—see Illustration CC.1d.

Your loan decision requires you to integrate and evaluate the evidence, and then interpret it for purposes of reaching a decision on whether to make the loan or not. It can also include various loan parameters: amount, interest rate, term, payment pattern, and loan restrictions. It also requires an analysis of the client's business strategy and an assessment of the business environment.

ILLUSTRATION CC.1d
■ ■ ■ ■ ■ ■ ■

This step is similar to the skill requirements of several professions. For example, weather forecasting offers an abundance of analytical data demanding interpretation. Most of us exposed to weather information could not reliably interpret barometric pressure, relative humidity, or wind velocity. We only need to know the weather forecast resulting from the professional interpretation of weather data. Medicine, law, engineering, biology, and genetics provide similar examples.

Our analysis and interpretation of financial statements must remember that the data depict a richer reality. Analysis of financial data result in further levels of abstraction. As an example, no map or picture of the Rocky Mountains conveys their magnificence. One must visit these mountains to fully appreciate them because maps or pictures, like financial statements, are abstractions. This is why it is often advantageous for us to go beyond financial statements and "visit" companies—that is, use their products, buy services, visit stores, talk with customers, and immerse oneself in companies' business activities. The static reality portrayed by abstractions in financial statements is unnatural. Reality is dynamic and evolving. Recognizing the limitations of financial statements is necessary in analysis. This does not detract from their importance. Financial statements are the means by which a company's financial realities are reduced to a common denominator. This common denominator is quantifiable, can be statistically evaluated, and is amenable to prediction.

.... BUILDING BLOCKS OF FINANCIAL STATEMENT ANALYSIS

Financial statement analysis focuses on one or more elements of a company's financial condition or operating results. Our analysis emphasizes six areas of inquiry–with varying degrees of importance. We described these six areas of inquiry and illustrated them throughout the book. They are considered "building blocks" of financial statement analysis.

1. **Short-term liquidity.** Ability to meet short-term obligations.
2. **Capital structure and solvency.** Ability to generate future revenues and meet long-term obligations.
3. **Return on invested capital.** Ability to provide financial rewards sufficient to attract and retain financing.
4. **Asset turnover.** Asset intensity in generating revenues to reach a sufficient profitability level.
5. **Operating performance and profitability.** Success at maximizing revenues and minimizing expenses from operating activities over the long run.
6. **Forecasting and valuation.** Projection of operating performance, ability to generate sufficient cash flows to fund investment needs, and valuation.

Applying the building blocks to financial statement analysis involves determining:

- Objectives of the analysis.
- Relative emphasis among the building blocks.

To illustrate, an equity investor when evaluating the investment merit of a common stock often emphasizes earnings- and returns-based analyses. This involves assessing operating performance and return on invested capital. A thorough analysis requires an equity investor to assess other building blocks although with perhaps lesser emphasis. Attention to these other areas is necessary to assess risk exposure. This usually involves some analysis of liquidity, solvency, and financing. Further analysis can reveal important risks that outweigh earning power and lead to major changes in the financial statement analysis of a company.

We distinguish among these six building blocks to emphasize important aspects of a company's financial condition and performance. Yet we must remember these areas of analysis are interrelated. For example, a company's operating performance is affected by availability of financing and short-term liquidity conditions. Similarly, a company's credit standing is not limited to satisfactory short-term liquidity, but also depends on its operating performance and asset turnover. Early in the analysis, we must tentatively determine the relative emphasis of each building block and the order of analysis. Order of emphasis and analysis can subsequently change due to evidence collected and/or changes in the business environment.

REPORTING ON FINANCIAL STATEMENT ANALYSIS

The foundation of a reliable analysis is an understanding of its objectives. This understanding leads to efficiency of effort, effectiveness in application, and relevance in focus. Most analyses face constraints on availability of information. Decisions must be made using incomplete or inadequate information. One goal of financial statement analysis is reducing uncertainty through a rigorous and sound evaluation. A **financial statement analysis report** helps on each of these points by addressing all the building blocks of analysis. It helps identify weaknesses in inference by requiring explanation, and it forces us to organize our reasoning and to verify the flow and logic of analysis. The report also serves as a communication device with readers. The writing process reinforces judgments and vice versa, and it helps refine inferences from evidence bearing on key building blocks.

A good report separates interpretations and conclusions of analysis from the information underlying them. This separation enables readers to see the process and rationale of analysis. It also enables the reader to draw personal conclusions and make modifications as appropriate. A good analysis report typically contains at least six sections devoted to:

1. **Executive summary.** Brief summary focused on important analysis results; it launches the analysis report.
2. **Analysis overview.** Background material on the company, its industry, and its economic environment.
3. **Evidential matter.** Financial statements and information used in the analysis. This includes ratios, trends, statistics, and all analytical measures assembled.
4. **Assumptions.** Identification of important assumptions regarding a company's industry and business environment, and other important assumptions for estimates and forecasts, including its business strategy.
5. **Crucial factors.** Listing of important favorable and unfavorable factors, both quantitative and qualitative, for company performance—usually listed by areas of analysis.
6. **Inferences.** Includes forecasts, estimates, interpretations, and conclusions drawing on all prior sections of the report.

We must remember that *importance* is defined by the user. The analysis report should include a brief table of contents to help readers focus on those areas most relevant to their decisions. All irrelevant matter must be eliminated. For example, decades-old details of the beginnings of a company and a detailing of the miscues of analysis are irrelevant. Ambiguities and qualifications to avoid responsibility or hedge inferences should also be eliminated. Finally, writing is important. Mistakes in grammar and errors of fact compromise the credibility of analysis.

SPECIALIZATION IN FINANCIAL STATEMENT ANALYSIS

Analysis of financial statements is usually viewed from the perspective of a "typical" company. Yet we must recognize the existence of several distinct factors (such as unique accounting methods and business environments). These factors arise from several influences including special industry conditions, government regulations, social concerns, and political visibility. Analysis of financial statements for these companies requires we understand their accounting peculiarities. We must prepare for this by learning the specialized areas of accounting relevant to the company under analysis. For example, analysis of an oil and gas company would require knowledge of accounting concepts peculiar to that industry, including determining cost centers, pre-discovery costs, discovery costs, and disposing of capitalized costs. In addition, analysis of an oil and gas company would confront special problems in analyzing exploratory, development, and related expenditures, and in amortization and depletion practices. Another example is insurance accounting. This analysis would require knowledge of the industry and its regulations. Challenges arise in understanding recognition of premium revenues, accounting for acquisition costs of new business, and determination of policy reserves. Another example is public utilities. Regulation results in specialized accounting concepts and problems for analysis. There are questions related to the adequacy of provisions for depreciation, and problems concerning the utility's "rate base" and the method used in determining it. Like any profession, specialized areas of inquiry require specialized knowledge. Financial statement analysis is no exception.

·······COMPREHENSIVE CASE: CAMPBELL SOUP COMPANY

We illustrate many of the major components of financial statement analysis using information and data from Campbell Soup Company.

Preliminary Financial Analysis

Campbell Soup Company is one of the world's largest food companies focusing on convenience foods for human consumption. The company's operations are organized within three divisions: Campbell North America, Campbell Biscuit and Bakery, and Campbell International. Within each division there are groups and business units. Major groups within the Campbell North America division are Soups, Convenience Meals, Grocery, Condiments, and Canadian operations.

The company's products are primarily for home use, but various items are also manufactured for restaurants, vending machines, and institutions. The company distributes its products through direct customer sales. These include chain stores, wholesalers, distributors (with central warehouses), institutional and industrial customers, convenience stores, club stores, and government agencies. In the United States, sales solicitation activities are conducted by subsidiaries, independent brokers, and contract distributors. No major part of Campbell's business depends on a single customer. Shipments are made promptly after receipt and acceptance of orders as reflected in no significant backlog of unfilled orders.

Sales Analysis by Source

Campbell's sales by division from Year 6 through Year 11 are shown in Exhibit CC.1. Its North American and International divisions are the largest contributors of sales, accounting for 68.7% and 19.7%, respectively, in Year 11.

Soup is the primary business of Campbell U.S., capturing about 60% of the entire soup market. This includes dry, ramen noodle, and microwavable soups. Other

Exhibit CC.1

CAMPBELL SOUP COMPANY
Sales Contribution and Percentage of Sales by Division

($ millions)	Year 11	Year 10	Year 9	Year 8	Year 7	Year 6
Sales Contribution						
Campbell North America						
Campbell USA	$3,911.8	$3,932.7	$3,666.9	$3,094.1	$2,881.4	$2,910.1
Campbell Canada	352.0	384.0	313.4	313.1	312.8	255.1
	4,263.8	4,316.7	3,980.3	3,407.2	3,194.2	3,165.2
Campbell Biscuit and Bakery						
Pepperidge Farm	569.0	582.0	548.4	495.0	458.5	420.1
International Biscuit	219.4	195.3	178.0	—	—	—
	788.4	777.3	726.4	495.0	458.5	420.1
Campbell International	1,222.9	1,189.8	1,030.3	1,036.5	897.8	766.2
Interdivision	(71.0)	(78.0)	(64.9)	(69.8)	(60.1)	(64.7)
Total sales	$6,204.1	$6,205.8	$5,672.1	$4,868.9	$4,490.4	$4,286.8
Percentage of Sales						
Campbell North America						
Campbell USA	63.0%	63.4%	64.7%	63.5%	64.2%	67.9%
Campbell Canada	5.7	6.2	5.5	6.4	6.9	5.9
	68.7	69.6	70.2	69.9	71.1	73.8
Campbell Biscuit and Bakery						
Pepperidge Farm	9.2	9.4	9.7	10.2	10.2	9.8
International Biscuit	3.5	3.1	3.1	—	—	—
	12.7	12.5	12.8	10.2	10.2	9.8
Campbell International	19.7	19.2	18.2	21.3	20.0	17.9
Interdivision	(1.1)	(1.3)	(1.2)	(1.4)	(1.3)	(1.5)
Total sales	100.0%	100.0%	100.0%	100.0%	100.0%	100.0%

Campbell Soup brands include ready-to-serve soups: Home Cooking, Chunky, and Healthy Request. An integral part of its soup business is Swanson's canned chicken broth. Americans purchase more than 2.5 billion cans of Campbell's soups each year, and on average have nine cans in their pantry at any time during the year.

Fiscal Year 11 is a successful transition year for Campbell. It completed major divestitures and accomplished significant restructuring and reorganization projects. Corporate goals concerning earnings, returns, and cash flows are being met. The North American and International divisions produced strong earnings results. The company enters Year 12 with a reconfigured product portfolio, positioned to support continued solid financial performance. This performance gives Campbell an opportunity to increase consumer advertising and to further the introduction of new product lines and continue support for flagship products.

Campbell's Sales by Divisions

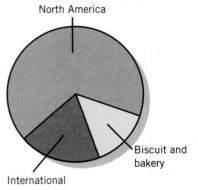

North America

International

Biscuit and bakery

Comparative Financial Statements

Comparative financial statements for Campbell for Years 6 through 11 are presented in Exhibits CC.2, CC.3, and CC.4 (financial statements and related information for Campbell Soup are in Appendix A). The auditor's opinions on its financial statements for the past six years are unqualified.

Exhibit CC.2
■ ■ ■ ■ ■ ■ ■

CAMPBELL SOUP COMPANY
Income Statements
For Year 6 through Year 11

(in millions, except per share data)	Year 11	Year 10	Year 9	Year 8	Year 7	Year 6
Net sales	$6,204.1	$6,205.8	$5,672.1	$4,868.9	$4,490.4	$4,286.8
Costs and expenses						
Cost of products sold	4,095.5	4,258.2	4,001.6	3,392.8	3,180.5	3,082.7
Marketing and selling expenses	956.2	980.5	818.8	733.3	626.2	544.4
Administrative expenses	306.7	290.7	252.1	232.6	213.9	195.9
Research and development expenses	56.3	53.7	47.7	46.9	44.8	42.2
Interest expense	116.2	111.6	94.1	53.9	51.7	56.0
Interest income	(26.0)	(17.6)	(38.3)	(33.2)	(29.5)	(27.4)
Foreign exchange losses, net	0.8	3.3	19.3	16.6	4.8	0.7
Other expense (income)	26.2	14.7	32.4	(3.2)	(9.5)	5.5
Divestitures, restructuring, and unusual charges	0.0	339.1	343.0	40.6	0.0	0.0
Total costs and expenses	5,531.9	6,034.2	5,570.7	4,480.3	4,082.9	3,900.0
Earnings before equity in earnings of affiliates and minority interests	672.2	171.6	101.4	388.6	407.5	386.8
Equity in earnings of affiliates	2.4	13.5	10.4	6.3	15.1	4.3
Minority interests	(7.2)	(5.7)	(5.3)	(6.3)	(4.7)	(3.9)
Earnings before taxes	667.4	179.4	106.5	388.6	417.9	387.2
Taxes on earnings	265.9	175.0	93.4	147.0	170.6	164.0
Earnings before cumulative effect of accounting change	401.5	4.4	13.1	241.6	247.3	223.2
Cumulative effect of change in accounting for income taxes	0	0	0	32.5	0	0
Net earnings	$ 401.5	$ 4.4	$ 13.1	$ 274.1	$ 247.3	$ 223.2
Earnings per share	$3.16	$0.03	$0.10	$2.12*	$1.90	$1.72
Weighted-average shares outstanding	127.00	126.60	129.30	129.30	129.90	129.50

* Including $0.25 per share cumulative effect of change in accounting for income taxes.

Exhibit CC.3

■ ■ ■ ■ ■ ■ ■

CAMPBELL SOUP COMPANY
Balance Sheets
At End of Year 6 through Year 11

($ millions)	Year 11	Year 10	Year 9	Year 8	Year 7	Year 6
Assets						
Current assets						
Cash and cash equivalents	$ 178.90	$ 80.70	$ 120.90	$ 85.80	$ 145.00	$ 155.10
Other temporary investments	12.80	22.50	26.20	35.00	280.30	238.70
Accounts receivable	527.40	624.50	538.00	486.90	338.90	299.00
Inventories	706.70	819.80	816.00	664.70	623.60	610.50
Prepaid expenses	92.70	118.00	100.40	90.50	50.10	31.50
Total current assets	1,518.50	1,665.50	1,601.50	1,362.90	1,437.90	1,334.80
Plant assets, net of depreciation	1,790.40	1,717.70	1,540.60	1,508.90	1,349.00	1,168.10
Intangible assets, net of amortization	435.50	383.40	466.90	496.60	—	—
Other assets	404.60	349.00	323.10	241.20	310.50	259.90
Total assets	$4,149.00	$4,115.60	$3,932.10	$3,609.60	$3,097.40	$2,762.80
Liabilities and Shareowners' Equity						
Current liabilities						
Notes payable	$ 282.20	$ 202.30	$ 271.50	$ 138.00	$ 93.50	$ 88.90
Payable to suppliers and others	482.40	525.20	508.20	446.70	374.80	321.70
Accrued liabilities	408.70	491.90	392.60	236.90	182.10	165.90
Dividend payable	37.00	32.30	29.70	—	—	—
Accrued income taxes	67.70	46.40	30.10	41.70	43.40	49.60
Total current liabilities	1,278.00	1,298.10	1,232.10	863.30	693.80	626.10
Long-term debt	772.60	805.80	629.20	525.80	380.20	362.30
Other liabilities, mainly deferred income tax	305.00	319.90	292.50	325.50	287.30	235.50
Shareowners' equity						
Preferred stock; authorized 40,000,000 sh.; none issued	—	—	—	—	—	—
Capital stock, $0.15 par value; authorized 140,000,000 sh.; issued 135,622,676 sh.	20.30	20.30	20.30	20.30	20.30	20.30
Capital surplus	107.30	61.90	50.80	42.30	41.10	38.10
Earnings retained in the business	1,912.60	1,653.30	1,775.80	1,879.10	1,709.60	1,554.00
Capital stock in treasury, at cost	(270.40)	(107.20)	(70.70)	(75.20)	(46.80)	(48.40)
Cumulative translation adjustments	23.60	63.50	2.10	28.50	11.90	(25.10)
Total shareowners' equity	1,793.40	1,691.80	1,778.30	1,895.00	1,736.10	1,538.90
Total liabilities and shareowners' equity	$4,149.00	$4,115.60	$3,932.10	$3,609.60	$3,097.40	$2,762.80

Further Analysis of Financial Statements

Growth rates for important financial measures, annually compounded, are reported in Exhibit CC.5. These rates are computed using four different periods and are based on per share data (see Exhibit CC.9). Most impressive is the growth in net income per share over the past five years (12.93%). Growth in sales per share over the same recent five-year period is at a rate less than that of net income. Equity per share growth in the recent 5-year period declined compared to the 10-year period. This

Exhibit CC.4

■ ■ ■ ■ ■ ■ ■

CAMPBELL SOUP COMPANY
Statements of Cash Flows
For Year 6 through Year 11

($ millions)	Year 11	Year 10	Year 9	Year 8	Year 7	Year 6	Total
Cash flows from operating activities							
Net earnings..	$ 401.5	$ 4.4	$ 13.1	$ 274.1	$ 247.3	$ 223.2	$1,163.6
To reconcile net earnings to net cash provided by operating activities:							
Depreciation and amortization	208.6	200.9	192.3	170.9	144.6	126.8	1,044.1
Divestitures and restructuring	—	339.1	343.0	17.6	—	—	699.7
Deferred taxes	35.5	3.9	(67.8)	13.4	45.7	29.0	59.7
Other, net	63.2	18.6	37.3	43.0	28.0	16.6	206.7
Cumulative effect of accounting change....................	—	—	—	(32.5)	—	—	(32.5)
(Increase) decrease in accounts receivable................	17.1	(60.4)	(46.8)	(104.3)	(36.3)	(3.6)	(234.3)
(Increase) decrease in inventories............................	48.7	10.7	(113.2)	54.2	(3.9)	23.1	19.6
Net change in other current assets and liabilities.......	30.6	(68.8)	(0.6)	30.2	42.9	48.7	83.0
Net cash from operating activities	805.2	448.4	357.3	466.6	468.3	463.8	3,009.6
Cash flows from investing activities							
Purchases of plant assets...	(361.1)	(387.6)	(284.1)	(245.3)	(303.7)	(235.3)	(1,817.1)
Sale of plant assets	43.2	34.9	39.8	22.6	—	29.8	170.3
Businesses acquired	(180.1)	(41.6)	(135.8)	(471.9)	(7.3)	(20.0)	(856.7)
Sale of businesses	67.4	21.7	4.9	23.5	20.8	—	138.3
Increase in other assets	(57.8)	(18.6)	(107.0)	(40.3)	(50.1)	(18.0)	(291.8)
Net change in other temporary investments...............	9.7	3.7	9.0	249.2	(60.7)	(144.1)	66.8
Net cash used in investing activities	(478.7)	(387.5)	(473.2)	(462.2)	(401.0)	(387.6)	(2,590.2)
Cash flows from financing activities							
Long-term borrowings	402.8	12.6	126.5	103.0	4.8	203.9	853.6
Repayments of long-term borrowings.........................	(129.9)	(22.5)	(53.6)	(22.9)	(23.9)	(164.7)	(417.5)
Increase (decrease) in short-term borrowings*...........	(137.9)	(2.7)	108.2	8.4	(20.7)	4.6	(40.1)
Other short-term borrowings	117.3	153.7	227.1	77.0	89.3	72.9	737.3
Repayments of other short-term borrowings	(206.4)	(89.8)	(192.3)	(87.6)	(66.3)	(88.5)	(730.9)
Dividends paid	(137.5)	(124.3)	(86.7)	(104.6)	(91.7)	(104.6)	(649.4)
Treasury stock purchases	(175.6)	(41.1)	(8.1)	(29.3)	—	—	(254.1)
Treasury stock issued	47.7	12.4	18.5	0.9	1.6	4.0†	85.1
Other, net	(0.1)	(0.1)	23.5	2.3	18.6	17.9	62.1
Net cash from (used in) financing activities	(219.6)	(101.8)	163.1	(52.8)	(88.3)	(54.5)	(353.9)
Effect of exchange rate change on cash	(8.7)	0.7	(12.1)	(10.8)	(7.1)	(3.7)	(41.7)
Net increase (decrease) in cash and cash equivalents	$ 98.2	$ (40.2)	$ 35.1	$ (59.2)	$ (28.1)	$ 18.0	$ 23.8
Cash and cash equivalents at beginning of year............	80.7	120.9	85.8	145.0	173.1	155.1	155.1
Cash and cash equivalents at end of year......................	$ 178.9	$ 80.7	$ 120.9	$ 85.8	$ 145.0	$ 173.1	$ 178.9

* With less than three-month maturities.
† Stock of $2.8 issued for a pooling of interest.

Exhibit CC.5

■ ■ ■ ■ ■ ■ ■

CAMPBELL SOUP COMPANY
Five-Year Growth Rates*

Per share	Years 6 to 11	Average for Years 6 to 8 to Average for Years 9 to 11
Sales................	8.09%	5.95%
Net income..........	12.93	−10.53
Dividends...........	11.50	6.69
Equity................	3.55	0.53

Ten-Year Growth Rates*

Per share	Years 1 to 11	Average for Years 1 to 3 to Average for Years 9 to 11
Sales................	8.51%	7.22%
Net income..........	12.19	−0.44
Dividends...........	8.18	6.62
Equity................	6.22	5.13

* Growth rates (annually compounded) are computed using the compound interest method (where n = compounding period, and r = Rate of growth):

$$\text{Future value (FV)} = \text{Present value (PV)} \times \left(1 + \frac{r}{100}\right)^{n}$$

For example, net sales per share during Years 6 to 11 grew at a rate of:

$$FV = PV\left(1 + \frac{r}{100}\right)^{n} \Leftrightarrow \$48.85 = \$33.10\left(1 + \frac{r}{100}\right)^{5}$$

$$r = 8.09\%$$

finding, including the two negative growth rates in the exhibit, is due to divestitures and restructurings in Years 9 and 10. We also compute common-size income statements and balance sheets in Exhibits CC.6 and CC.7. Exhibit CC.8 presents the trend indexes of selected accounts for Campbell Soup. Exhibit CC.9 shows Campbell Soup's per share results.

Analysis of Exhibit CC.4 reveals operating cash flows are a steady and growing source of cash, with a substantial increase in Year 11 net operating cash flows ($805 million). The slight cash downturn in Year 9 is due primarily to an increase in inventories ($113 million) and a decrease (negative) in deferred taxes ($68 million). The increase in inventories is tied to management's desire to improve customer service, and the decrease in deferred taxes relates to restructuring and unusual charges that are not tax deductible, resulting in

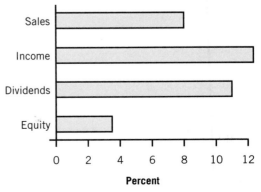

Campbell's Five-Year Growth Rates

Exhibit CC.6

■ ■ ■ ■ ■ ■ ■

CAMPBELL SOUP COMPANY
Common-Size Income Statements
For Year 6 through Year 11

	Year 11	Year 10	Year 9	Year 8	Year 7	Year 6
Net sales	100.00%	100.00%	100.00%	100.00%	100.00%	100.00%
Costs and expenses						
Cost of products sold	66.01%	68.62%	70.55%	69.68%	70.83%	71.91%
Marketing and selling expenses	15.41	15.80	14.44	15.06	13.95	12.70
Administrative expenses	4.94	4.68	4.44	4.78	4.76	4.57
Research and development expenses	0.91	0.87	0.84	0.96	1.00	0.98
Interest expense	1.87	1.80	1.66	1.11	1.15	1.31
Interest income	(0.42)	(0.28)	(0.68)	(0.68)	(0.66)	(0.64)
Foreign exchange losses, net	0.01	0.05	0.34	0.34	0.11	0.02
Other expense (income)	0.42	0.24	0.57	(0.07)	(0.21)	0.13
Divestitures, restructuring, and unusual charges	—	5.46	6.05	0.83	—	—
Total costs and expenses	89.17%	97.23%	98.21%	92.02%	90.93%	90.98%
Earnings before equity in earnings of affiliates						
and minority interests	10.83%	2.77%	1.79%	7.98%	9.07%	9.02%
Equity in earnings of affiliates	0.04	0.22	0.18	0.13	0.34	0.10
Minority interests	(0.12)	(0.09)	(0.09)	(0.13)	(0.10)	(0.09)
Earnings before taxes	10.76%	2.89%	1.88%	7.98%	9.31%	9.03%
Taxes on earnings	4.29	2.82	1.65	3.02	3.80	3.83
Earnings before cumulative effect of accounting change	6.47%	0.07%	0.23%	4.96%	5.51%	5.21%
Cumulative effect of accounting change for income taxes	—	—	—	0.67	—	—
Net earnings	6.47%	0.07%	0.23%	5.63%	5.51%	5.21%

Campbell's Operating Cash Flow

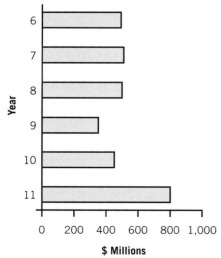

$78 million of credits to tax expense but higher current tax liabilities. We also see that the declines in net income for Years 9 and 10 are not reflected in operating cash flows. This is because these declines are from restructuring and divestiture charges having no immediate cash flow effects.

Campbell's common-size statements of cash flows for the six years ending with Year 11 are shown in Exhibit CC.10. This exhibit reveals several patterns in the company's cash flows over these six years. Transitory fluctuations in cash, such as those due to the high usage of cash for investing activities in Year 7 (62%), are put in perspective by including aggregate figures in a total column. Total operating cash flows constitute more than one-half of all cash inflows. This finding along with evidence that financing activities (using 7% of cash inflows) are mostly refinancing is indicative of Campbell's financial strength and financing practices. The total column reveals that cash used for acquiring assets and businesses consumes nearly 50% of cash inflows, and about 12% of cash inflows are used for dividends.

Exhibit CC.7
■ ■ ■ ■ ■ ■ ■

CAMPBELL SOUP COMPANY
Common-Size Balance Sheets
At End of Year 6 through Year 11

	Year 11	Year 10	Year 9	Year 8	Year 7	Year 6	Year 11 Industry Composite*
Current assets							
Cash and cash equivalents	4.31%	1.96%	3.07%	2.38%	4.69%	5.61%	3.4%
Other temporary investments	0.31	0.55	0.67	0.97	9.05	8.64	
Accounts receivable	12.71	15.17	13.68	13.49	10.94	10.82	16.5
Inventories	17.03	19.92	20.75	18.41	20.13	22.10	38.6
Prepaid expenses	2.23	2.87	2.55	2.51	1.62	1.14	2.2
Total current assets	36.60%	40.47%	40.73%	37.76%	46.43%	48.31%	60.7%
Plant assets, net of depreciation	43.15	41.74	39.18	41.80	43.55	42.28	21.0
Intangible assets, net of amortization	10.50	9.32	11.87	13.76	—	—	
Other assets	9.75	8.48	8.22	6.68	10.02	9.41	18.3
Total assets	100.00%	100.00%	100.00%	100.00%	100.00%	100.00%	100.0%
Current liabilities							
Notes payable	6.80%	4.92%	6.90%	3.82%	3.02%	3.22%	6.7%
Payable to suppliers and others	11.63	12.76	12.92	12.38	12.10	11.64	10.2
Accrued liabilities	9.85	11.95	9.98	6.56	5.88	6.00	15.8
Dividend payable	0.89	0.78	0.76	—	—	—	
Accrued income taxes	1.63	1.13	0.77	1.16	1.40	1.80	
Total current liabilities	30.80%	31.54%	31.33%	23.92%	22.40%	22.66%	32.7%
Long-term debt	18.62	19.58	16.00	14.57	12.27	13.11	19.7
Other liabilities, mainly deferred taxes	7.35	7.77	7.44	9.02	9.28	8.52	1.5
Shareowners' equity							
Preferred stock; authorized 40,000,000 sh.; none issued	—	—	—	—	—	—	
Capital stock, $0.15 par value; authorized 140,000,000 sh.; issued 135,622,676 sh.	0.49	0.49	0.52	0.56	0.66	0.73	
Capital surplus	2.59	1.50	1.29	1.17	1.33	1.38	
Earnings retained in the business	46.10	40.17	45.16	52.06	55.19	56.25	
Capital stock in treasury, at cost	(6.52)	(2.60)	(1.80)	(2.08)	(1.51)	(1.75)	
Cumulative translation adjustments	0.57	1.54	0.05	0.79	0.38	(0.91)	
Total shareowners' equity	43.22%	41.11%	45.23%	52.50%	56.05%	55.70%	46.1%
Total liabilities and equity	100.00%	100.00%	100.00%	100.00%	100.00%	100.00%	100.0%

* Reported for accounts where data are available.

Exhibit CC.8
■ ■ ■ ■ ■ ■ ■

CAMPBELL SOUP COMPANY
Trend Index of Selected Accounts (Year 6 = 100%)

	Year 11	Year 10	Year 9	Year 8	Year 7	Year 6
Cash and cash equivalents	115%	52%	78%	55%	93%	$ 155.1
Accounts receivable	176	209	180	163	113	299.0
Temporary investments	5	9	11	15	117	238.7
Inventory	116	134	134	109	102	610.5
Total current assets	114	125	120	102	108	1,334.8
Total current liabilities	204	207	197	138	111	626.1
Working capital	34	52	52	70	105	708.7
Plant assets, net	153	147	132	129	115	1,168.1
Other assets	156	134	124	93	119	259.9
Long-term debt	213	222	174	145	105	362.3
Total liabilities	192	198	176	140	111	1,223.9
Shareowners' equity	117	110	116	123	113	1,538.9
Net sales	145	145	132	114	105	4,286.8
Cost of products sold	133	138	130	110	103	3,082.7
Administrative expenses	157	148	129	119	109	195.9
Marketing and sales expenses	176	180	150	135	115	544.4
Interest expense	208	199	168	96	92	56.0
Total costs and expenses	142	155	143	115	105	3,900.0
Earnings before taxes	172	46	28	100	108	387.2
Net income	180	2*	6*	123	111	223.2

* Excluding the effect (net of statutory tax) of divestitures, restructuring, and unusual charges would change these amounts to: Year 10—102% and Year 9—104%.

Overall, cash inflows from operations (56%) are used for both financing (7%) and investing (48%) activities. Campbell's net cash position over these six years is stable, never deviating more than 7% from the prior year. Its growth for the entire six-year period is less than 1%.

Exhibit CC.9
■ ■ ■ ■ ■ ■ ■

CAMPBELL SOUP COMPANY
Per Share Results

	Year 11	Year 10	Year 9	Year 8	Year 7	Year 6
Sales	$ 48.85	$ 49.02	$ 43.87	$ 37.66	$ 34.57	$ 33.10
Net income	3.16	0.03	0.10	2.12	1.90	1.72
Dividends	1.12	1.00	0.90	0.81	0.71	0.81
Book value	14.12	13.36	13.76	14.66	13.36	11.86
Average shares outstanding (mil.)	127.0	126.6	129.3	129.3	129.9	129.5

649

Exhibit CC.10
■ ■ ■ ■ ■ ■ ■

CAMPBELL SOUP COMPANY
Common-Size Statements of Cash Flows*
For Year 6 through Year 11

	Year 11	Year 10	Year 9	Year 8	Year 7	Year 6	Total
Cash flows from operating activities							
Net earnings	26.89%	0.54%	1.15%	25.14%	38.42%	27.88%	21.54%
To reconcile net earnings to net cash provided by operating activities:							
Depreciation and amortization	13.97	24.58	16.82	15.67	22.47	15.84	19.33
Divestitures and restructuring provisions	—	41.49	30.00	1.61	—	—	12.95
Deferred taxes	2.38	0.48	(5.93)	1.23	7.10	3.62	1.11
Other, net	4.23	2.28	3.26	3.94	4.35	2.07	3.83
Cumulative effect of accounting change	—	—	—	(2.98)	—	—	(0.60)
(Increase) decrease in accounts receivable	1.15	(7.39)	(4.09)	(9.57)	(5.64)	(0.45)	(4.34)
(Increase) decrease in inventories	3.26	1.31	(9.90)	4.97	(0.61)	2.89	0.36
Net change in other current assets and liabilities	2.05	(8.42)	(0.05)	2.77	6.67	6.08	1.54
Net cash provided by operating activities	53.92%	54.86%	31.25%	42.80%	72.76%	57.94%	55.72%
Cash flows from investing activities							
Purchase of plant assets	(24.18)%	(47.42)%	(24.85)%	(22.50)%	(47.19)%	(29.39)%	(33.64)%
Sale of plant assets	2.89	4.27	3.48	2.07	—	3.72	3.15
Businesses acquired	(12.06)	(5.09)	(11.88)	(43.28)	(1.13)	(2.50)	(15.86)
Sale of businesses	4.51	2.66	0.43	2.16	3.23	—	2.56
Increase in other assets	(3.87)	(2.28)	(9.36)	(3.70)	(7.78)	(2.25)	(5.40)
Net change in other temporary investments	0.65	0.45	0.79	22.86	(9.43)	(18.00)	1.24
Net cash used in investing activities	(32.06)%	(47.41)%	(41.39)%	(42.39)%	(62.31)%	(48.42)%	(47.95)%
Cash flows from financing activities							
Long-term borrowings	26.97%	1.54%	11.07%	9.45%	0.75%	25.47%	15.80%
Repayments of long-term borrowings	(8.70)	(2.75)	(4.69)	(2.10)	(3.71)	(20.57)	(7.73)
Increase (decrease) in short-term borrowings	(9.23)	(0.33)	9.46	0.77	(3.22)	0.57	(0.74)
Other short-term borrowings	7.86	18.81	19.87	7.06	13.88	9.11	13.65
Repayments of other short-term borrowings	(13.82)	(10.99)	(16.82)	(8.03)	(10.30)	(11.06)	(13.53)
Dividends paid	(9.21)	(15.21)	(7.58)	(9.59)	(14.25)	(13.07)	(12.02)
Treasury stock purchases	(11.76)	(5.03)	(0.71)	(2.69)	—	—	(4.70)
Treasury stock issued	3.19	1.52	1.62	0.08	0.25	0.50	1.58
Other, net	(0.01)	(0.01)	2.06	0.21	2.89	2.24	1.15
Net cash from (used in) financing activities	(14.71)%	(12.46)%	14.27%	(4.84)%	(13.72)%	(6.81)%	(6.55)%
Effect of exchange rate change on cash	(0.58)	0.09	(1.06)	(0.99)	(1.10)	(0.46)	(0.77)
Net increase (decrease) in cash and equivalents	6.58%	(4.92)%	3.07%	(5.43)%	(4.37)%	2.25%	0.44%

* Common-size percentages are based on total cash inflows = 100%. For Year 11, the 100 percent consists of CFO (26.89 + 13.97 + 2.38 + 4.23 + 1.15 + 3.26 + 2.05) + Sale of plant assets (2.89) + Sale of bus. (4.51) + Decrease in temp. invest. (0.65) + LT borrowings (26.97) + ST borrowings (7.86) + Treas. st. issued (3.19).

It is often useful to construct a summary of cash inflows and cash outflows by major categories of activities. Using Exhibit CC.4, we prepare the following chart of summary cash inflows and cash outflows:

($ millions)	Year 11	Year 10	Year 9	Year 8	Year 7	Year 6	Total
Operating activities	$805.2	$448.4	$357.3	$466.6	$468.3	$463.8	$3,009.6
Investing activities	(478.7)	(387.5)	(473.2)	(462.2)	(401.0)	(387.6)	(2,590.2)
Financing activities	(219.6)	(101.8)	163.1	(52.8)	(88.3)	(54.5)	(353.9)
Increase (decrease) in cash	98.2	(40.2)	35.1	(59.2)	(28.1)	18.0	23.8

The picture emerging from this summary is that Campbell has major outlays for (1) investing–$2,590.2 million–and (2) financing (including dividends)–$353.9 million. Despite these outlays, Campbell experienced a slight cumulative increase of $23.8 million in cash. Notably, these activities are funded by Campbell's net operating cash inflows of $3,009.6 million. Notice that in Years 7, 8, and 10 the cash balances are drawn down to fund investing and financing activities. Still, operating cash flows for this six-year period are sufficient to fund *all* of Campbell's investing and financing needs and still leave excess cash of $23.8 million.

Two additional measures of Campbell's cash flows are reported in Exhibit CC.11. The cash flow adequacy ratio provides insight into whether Campbell generates sufficient

Exhibit CC.11

■ ■ ■ ■ ■ ■ ■

CAMPBELL SOUP COMPANY
Analysis of Cash Flow Ratios ($ millions)

(1) Cash flow adequacy ratio* $= \dfrac{\text{6-year sum of sources of cash from operations}}{\text{6-year sum of capital expenditures, inventory additions, and cash dividends}}$

$$= \frac{\$3,009.6}{(\$1,817.1 + \$856.7) + (\$113.2 + \$3.9) + \$649.4} = 0.875$$

(2) Cash reinvestment ratio† $= \dfrac{\text{Cash provided by operations} - \text{Dividends}}{\text{Gross PPE} + \text{Investments} + \text{Other assets} + \text{Working capital}}$

Year 6 to Year 11 average $= \dfrac{\$3,009.6 - \$649.4}{\$15,183.7 + \$1,888.3 + \$2,929.7} = 11.8\%$

Year 11 $= \dfrac{\$805.2 - \$137.5}{\$2,921.9 + \$404.6 + \$240.5} = 18.7\%$

Year 10 $= \dfrac{\$448.4 - \$124.3}{\$2,734.9 + \$349.0 + \$367.4} = 9.4\%$

Year 9 $= \dfrac{\$357.3 - \$86.7}{\$2,543.0 + \$323.1 + \$369.4} = 8.4\%$

Year 8 $= \dfrac{\$466.6 - \$104.6}{\$2,539.7 + \$241.2 + \$499.6} = 11.0\%$

Year 7 $= \dfrac{\$468.3 - \$91.7}{\$2,355.1 + \$310.5 + \$744.1} = 11.0\%$

Year 6 $= \dfrac{\$463.8 - \$104.6}{\$2,089.1 + \$259.9 + \$708.7} = 11.7\%$

* All amounts are from the statement of cash flows.
† Numerator amounts are from the statement of cash flows and denominator amounts are from the balance sheet.

cash from operations to cover capital expenditures, investments in inventories, and cash dividends. Campbell's cash flow adequacy ratio for the six-year period is 0.875, implying that funds generated from operations are insufficient to cover these items (see denominator) and that there is a need for external financing. We must remember this is an aggregate (six-year sum) ratio. When we look at individual years, including Year 11, the cash flow adequacy ratio suggests sufficient cash resources. The exceptions are Years 7 and 9. A second measure, the cash reinvestment ratio, provides insight into the amount of cash retained and reinvested into the company for both asset replacement and growth. Campbell's cash reinvestment ratio is 11.8% for the six-year period. This reinvestment rate is satisfactory for the industry. The Year 11 reinvestment ratio is much higher (18.7%) than normal. Years 9 and 10 show a lower ratio due to decreases in operating cash flows.

Short-Term Liquidity

Various measures of short-term liquidity for the most recent six years are reported in Exhibit CC.12. This exhibit also includes industry composite data for Year 11. Several findings should be noted. The current ratio in Year 11 is at its lowest level for the past six years. Its value of 1.19 is measurably lower than the industry composite of 1.86. This is due in part to growth in current liabilities over recent years. Current liabilities are double what they were in Year 6, while current assets in Year 11 are but 114% of its Year 6 level. A substantial amount of notes payable are reclassified as long-term debt in Year 10. This helps improve the current ratio. Also, Exhibit CC.13 reveals that cash and cash equivalents in Year 11 represent a larger proportion of current assets (11.78%) compared with the industry (5.60%).

Campbell's acid-test ratio for the past three years (0.56) is slightly below the Year 11 industry composite (0.61)—see Exhibit CC.12. The assets and liabilities composing the acid-test ratio can be compared with the industry composite using Exhibit CC.7. This exhibit along with Exhibit CC.13 reveals that inventories constitute a lower proportion of total assets (17%) and total current assets (47%) than they do for the industry (39% and 64%, respectively). Also, inventory turnover for Campbell in Year 11 is 5.37 versus 2.53 for the industry. These measures indicate Campbell has less funds invested in inventory relative to the industry. This conclusion is supported with evidence from Exhibit CC.8 where inventory growth is less than sales growth (116% versus 145%). These improvements in inventory management are concurrent with Campbell's launching of the just-in-time inventory system. This improvement is especially evident with raw materials. Exhibit CC.14 reports inventory data showing a decline in the proportion of raw materials to total inventories consistent with this inference.

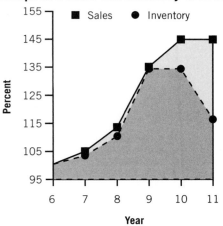

Campbell's Sales and Inventory Growth

The LIFO inventory method is used in accounting for approximately 70% of its inventories in Year 11 and 64% in Year 10 (see annual report note 14 in Appendix A). Exhibit CC.15 compares income and cost of goods sold using the LIFO and FIFO inventory methods. When prices are rising, LIFO income is typically lower than FIFO. In Campbell's case LIFO yielded income less than FIFO in Years 7, 9, and 11. During other years the reverse occurs. This might be due to declining costs or inventory liquidation.

Campbell's accounts receivable turnover has been declining over the past six years, but it is still above the industry level in Year 11 (see Exhibit CC.12). We also see from Exhibit CC.8 that accounts receivable are growing faster than sales, reaching a peak in

Exhibit CC.12

■ ■ ■ ■ ■ ■ ■

CAMPBELL SOUP COMPANY
Short-Term Liquidity Analysis

Units	Measure	Year 11	Year 10	Year 9	Year 8	Year 7	Year 6	Year 11 Industry Composite
1. Ratio	Current ratio	1.19	1.28	1.30	1.58	2.07	2.13	1.86
2. Ratio	Acid-test ratio	0.56	0.56	0.56	0.70	1.10	1.11	0.61
3. Times	Accounts receivable turnover	10.77	10.68	11.07	11.79	14.08	14.42	8.37
4. Times	Inventory turnover	5.37	5.21	5.41	5.27	5.15	4.96	2.53
5. Days	Days' sales in receivables	30.60	36.23	34.15	36.00	27.17	25.11	43.01
6. Days	Days' sales in inventory	62.12	69.31	73.41	70.53	70.59	71.29	142.03
7. Days	Approximate conversion period	92.72	105.54	107.56	106.53	97.76	96.40	185.32
8. Percent	Cash to current assets	11.78%	4.84%	7.55%	6.30%	10.08%	11.62%	5.60%
9. Percent	Cash to current liabilities	14.00%	6.22%	9.81%	9.94%	20.90%	24.77%	10.40%
10. $ mil.	Working capital	240.50	367.40	369.40	499.60	744.10	708.70	54.33
11. Days	Days' purchases in accounts payable	42.39	44.40	45.72	47.40	42.42	37.57	—
12. Days	Average net trade cycle	50.33	61.14	61.84	59.13	55.34	58.83	—
13. Percent	Cash provided by operations to average current liabilities	62.51%	35.44%	34.10%	59.93%	70.96%	77.34%	—

Notes:

For Year 11, the computations are as follows ($ in millions):

$$(3) \quad \frac{\text{Net sales } \boxed{13}}{\text{Average accounts receivable } \boxed{33}} = \frac{\$6,204.1}{(\$527.4 + \$624.5)/2} = 10.77$$

$$(4) \quad \frac{\text{Cost of products sold } \boxed{14}}{\text{Average inventory } \boxed{34}} = \frac{\$4,095.5}{(\$706.7 + \$819.8)/2} = 5.37$$

$$(5) \quad \frac{\text{Ending accounts receivable } \boxed{33}}{\text{Sales } \boxed{13}/360} = \frac{\$527.4}{\$6,204.1/360} = 30.60$$

$$(6) \quad \frac{\text{Ending inventory } \boxed{34}}{\text{Cost of products sold } \boxed{14}/360} = \frac{\$706.7}{\$4,095.5/360} = 62.12$$

(7) Approximate conversion period = (5) Days' sales in receivables + (6) Days' sales in inventory

$$(11) \quad \frac{\text{Accounts payable } \boxed{41}}{\text{Cost of goods sold}/360} = \frac{\$482.4}{\$11.38} = 42.39$$

(12) Number of days' sales in:

Accounts receivable	30.60
Inventories	62.12
Subtotal	92.72
Less: accounts payable	42.39
Total	50.33

$$(13) \quad \frac{\text{Cash from operations } \boxed{64}}{(\text{Beginning current liabilities} + \text{Ending current liabilities } \boxed{45}) \div 2} = \frac{\$805.2}{\$1,288} = 62.51$$

Exhibit CC.13

■ ■ ■ ■ ■ ■ ■

CAMPBELL SOUP COMPANY
Common-Size Analysis of Current Assets and Current Liabilities

	Year 11	Year 10	Year 9	Year 8	Year 7	Year 6	Year 11 Industry Composite
Current assets							
Cash and cash equivalents	11.78%	4.85%	7.55%	6.30%	10.09%	11.62%	5.60%
Other temporary investments	0.84	1.35	1.64	2.57	19.49	17.88	—
Accounts receivable	34.73	37.50	33.59	35.72	23.57	22.40	27.18
Inventories	46.54	49.22	50.95	48.77	43.37	45.74	63.60
Prepaid expenses	6.11	7.08	6.27	6.64	3.48	2.36	3.62
Total current assets	100.00%	100.00%	100.00%	100.00%	100.00%	100.00%	100.00%
Current liabilities							
Notes payable	22.08%	15.58%	22.04%	15.99%	13.48%	14.20%	20.49%
Payable to suppliers and others	37.75	40.46	41.25	51.74	54.02	51.38	31.19
Accrued liabilities	31.98	37.89	31.86	27.44	26.25	26.50 ⎫	
Dividend payable	2.89	2.49	2.41	—	—	— ⎬ =	48.32
Accrued income taxes	5.30	3.58	2.44	4.83	6.25	7.92 ⎭	
Total current liabilities	100.00%	100.00%	100.00%	100.00%	100.00%	100.00%	100.00%

Year 10 (209%) with a decline in Year 11 (176%). This is suggestive of a more aggressive credit policy. The days' sales in accounts receivable (see Exhibit CC.12) worsened between Years 6 and 10, but improved slightly in Year 11. Similar behavior is evidenced with the days' sales in inventory, with a general worsening from Years 6 through 9. Yet the days' sales in inventory in Year 11 returns to 62.12 days versus the 71.29 days for

Exhibit CC.14

■ ■ ■ ■ ■ ■ ■

CAMPBELL SOUP COMPANY
Inventory Data ($ millions)

Ending inventories	Year 11	Year 10	Year 9	Year 8	Year 7	Year 6
Raw materials, containers, and supplies	$342.3	$384.4	$385.0	$ 333.4	$333.6	$340.4
Finished products	454.0	520.0	519.0	412.5	372.4	348.1
Subtotal	796.3	904.4	904.0	745.9	706.0	688.5
Less: Adjustment of inventories to LIFO	89.6	84.6	88.0	81.2	82.4	78.5
Total ending inventories	$706.7	$819.8	$816.0	$ 664.7	$623.6	$610.0
Raw materials, containers, and supplies	43.0%	42.5%	42.6%	44.7%	47.3%	49.4%
Finished products	57.0	57.5	57.4	55.3	52.7	50.6
	100.0%	100.0%	100.0%	100.0%	100.0%	100.0%

Exhibit CC.15

■ ■ ■ ■ ■ ■ ■

CAMPBELL SOUP COMPANY
Inventory Data Using FIFO versus LIFO

($ millions)	Year 11	Year 10	Year 9	Year 8	Year 7	Year 6
Beginning inventory	$ 904.4	$ 904.0	$ 745.9	$ 706.0	$ 688.5	$ 707.0
Production inputs (same as LIFO)	3,982.4	4,262.0	4,152.9	3,433.9	3,193.6	3,070.1
Goods available for sale	4,886.8	5,166.0	4,898.8	4,139.9	3,882.1	3,777.1
Less: Ending inventory	796.3	904.4	904.0	745.9	706.0	688.5
Cost of products sold (FIFO)	$4,090.5	$4,261.6	$3,994.8	$3,394.0	$3,176.1	$3,088.6
Cost of products sold (LIFO)	$4,095.5	$4,258.2	$4,001.6	$3,392.8	$3,180.5	$3,082.7
Effect of restatement to FIFO increases (decreases) cost of products sold by:	$ (5.0)	$ 3.4	$ (6.8)	$ 1.2	$ (4.4)	$ 5.9
Net of tax* effect of restatement to FIFO decreases (increases) net income by:	$ (3.3)	$ 2.2	$ (4.5)	$ 0.8	$ (2.4)	$ 3.2

* Tax rate is 34% for Years 8 through 11, 45% for Year 7, and 46% for Year 6.

Year 6. This is mainly due to improved inventory turnover, which helps Campbell in comparison to industry norms.

Campbell's success in managing current liabilities is varied. While the days' purchases in accounts payable increased from Year 6 through Year 9, the recent two years' results have leveled off (see Exhibit CC.12). Similarly, its average net trade cycle fluctuates over the past six years. But by Year 11, this period (about 50 days) is below the Year 6 level of roughly 59 days. This finding is consistent with the company's improving liquidity.

Capital Structure and Solvency

We next analyze Campbell's capital structure and solvency (the analysis above related to cash forecasting is relevant to solvency). Changes in the company's capital structure are measured using various analyses and comparisons. Campbell's capital structure for the six years ending in Year 11 is depicted in Exhibit CC.16. For analytical purposes, one-half of deferred taxes is considered a long-term liability and the other half as equity. Exhibit CC.17 shows a common-size analysis of capital structure. For Year 11, liabilities constitute 53% and equity 47% of Campbell's financing.

Selected capital structure and long-term solvency ratios are reported in Exhibit CC.18. The total debt to equity ratio increases markedly in the past three years, yet remains at or below the industry norm (1.17). The source of this increase is attributed to long-term debt, see Exhibit CC.8. In particular, Exhibit CC.8 shows the trend index of long-term debt (213) exceeds that for current liabilities (204), total liabilities (192), and shareowners' equity (117). This is also evident in Campbell's long-term debt to equity ratio, where in Year 11 the ratio for Campbell (48%)

Campbell's Financing Sources

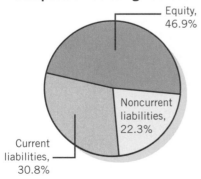

Exhibit CC.16

■ ■ ■ ■ ■ ■ ■

CAMPBELL SOUP COMPANY
Analysis of Capital Structure

($ millions)	Year 11	Year 10	Year 9	Year 8	Year 7	Year 6
Long-term liabilities						
Notes payable....................	$ 757.8	$ 792.9	$ 610.3	$ 507.1	$ 358.8	$ 346.7
Capital lease obligation..................	14.8	12.9	18.9	18.7	21.4	15.6
Total long-term debt...................	772.6	805.8	629.2	525.8	380.2	362.3
Deferred income taxes*..................	129.3	117.6	109.0	140.3	124.0	99.6
Other long-term liabilities................	23.0	28.5	19.6	15.6	15.8	16.3
Total long-term liabilities................	924.9	951.9	757.8	681.7	520.0	478.2
Current liabilities†..............................	1,278.0	1,298.1	1,232.1	863.3	693.8	626.1
Total liabilities......................................	$2,202.9	$2,250.0	$1,989.9	$1,545.0	$1,213.8	$1,104.3
Equity capital						
Common shareholders' equity............	$1,793.4	$1,691.8	$1,778.3	$1,895.0	$1,736.1	$1,538.9
Minority interests..............................	23.5	56.3	54.9	29.3	23.5	20.1
Deferred income taxes*....................	129.2	117.5	109.0	140.3	124.0	99.5
Total equity capital.............................	1,946.1	1,865.6	1,942.2	2,064.6	1,883.6	1,658.5
Total liabilities and equity....................	$4,149.0	$4,115.6	$3,932.1	$3,609.6	$3,097.4	$2,762.8

* For analytical purposes, 50% of deferred income taxes are considered debt and the remainder equity.
† Including the current portion of notes payable.

exceeds the industry composite of 43%. Campbell is moving away from its historically conservative capital structure toward a more aggressive one. This is evidenced by a lower level of fixed charge coverage ratios using both earnings and operating cash flows compared with Years 6 through 8. Consistent with our analysis, Campbell's long-term debt is rated A by the major rating agencies—down from the AAA rating the company enjoyed previously, but still an excellent rating. The company's creditors enjoy sound asset protection and superior earning power.

Return on Invested Capital

The return on invested capital ratios for Campbell are reported in Exhibit CC.19. These ratios reveal several insights. The return on net operating assets is stable for Years 7 and 8, declines sharply for Years 9 and 10, and then rebounds strongly to 16.77% in Year 11. Analysis of Years 9 and 10 shows these years' low returns are due to divestitures and restructuring charges. Yet we must keep in mind the marked increase in return for Year 11 is probably due in part to the two prior years' write-offs.

Further analysis of return on net operating assets for Year 11 shows it is comprised of a 8.01% NOPAT margin and a net operating asset turnover of 2.09. Both these components show improvement over their values from Year 8 (comparisons with Year 10 and Year 9 ratios are less relevant due to accounting charges). Campbell's management hopes these improvements for Year 11 are reflective of its major restructuring, closings,

Exhibit CC.17

■ ■ ■ ■ ■ ■ ■

CAMPBELL SOUP COMPANY
Common-Size Analysis of Capital Structure

	Year 11	Year 10	Year 9	Year 8	Year 7	Year 6
Long-term liabilities						
Notes payable	18.26%	19.27%	15.52%	14.05%	11.59%	12.55%
Capital lease obligation	0.36	0.31	0.48	0.52	0.69	0.56
Total long-term debt	18.62%	19.58%	16.00%	14.57%	12.28%	13.11%
Deferred income taxes*	3.12	2.86	2.77	3.88	4.00	3.61
Other long-term liabilities	0.55	0.69	0.50	0.43	0.51	0.59
Total long-term liabilities	22.29%	23.13%	19.27%	18.88%	16.79%	17.31%
Current liabilities†	30.80	31.54	31.34	23.92	22.40	22.66
Total liabilities	53.09%	54.67%	50.61%	42.80%	39.19%	39.97%
Equity capital						
Common shareholders' equity	43.22%	41.11%	45.22%	52.50%	56.05%	55.70%
Minority interests	0.57	1.37	1.40	0.81	0.76	0.73
Deferred income taxes*	3.12	2.85	2.77	3.89	4.00	3.60
Total equity capital	46.91%	45.33%	49.39%	57.20%	60.81%	60.03%
Total liabilities and equity	100.00%	100.00%	100.00%	100.00%	100.00%	100.00%

* For analytical purposes, 50% of deferred income taxes are considered debt and the remainder equity.
† Including the current portion of notes payable.

and business reorganizations during Years 9 and 10. Because of those restructuring programs and cost-cutting efforts, profit margins are higher. Prior years' returns are depressed by several poorly performing or ill-fitting businesses. Those businesses are now divested and Campbell has streamlined and modernized its manufacturing.

Campbell's return on common equity (21.52%) exceeds its most recent performance. The source of improvement is due to a solid improvement in RNOA and, to a lesser extent, an increase in financial leverage coupled with a positive spread. Like the profit component in return on net operating assets, the improved net income margin likely benefits from write-offs in Years 10 and 9. Disaggregation of Campbell's return on common equity (item 5 in Exhibit CC.19) shows that changes in the NOPAT margin are primarily responsible for fluctuations in return on equity during recent years. NOPAT margin is as low as 1.92 percent in Year 9 from the divestitures and restructurings, and it is as high as 8.01 percent in Year 11 partly due to the rebound from prior year changes and potential cost overprovisions. The other two components have also shown improvement. Net operating asset turnover has increased since Year 7. The leverage ratio has also increased since Year 9, with a consequent increase in ROCE, albeit with an increase in risk. The increase in financial leverage has resulted in the downgrade of Campbell Soup's debt rating to A from AAA.

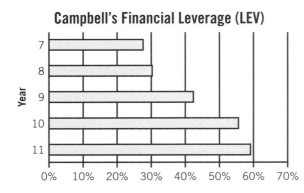

Campbell's Financial Leverage (LEV)

Exhibit CC.18

■ ■ ■ ■ ■ ■ ■

CAMPBELL SOUP COMPANY
Capital Structure and Solvency Ratios

	Year 11	Year 10	Year 9	Year 8	Year 7	Year 6	Year 11 Industry Composite
1. Total debt to equity	1.13	1.21	1.02	0.75	0.64	0.67	1.17
2. Total debt ratio	0.53	0.55	0.51	0.43	0.39	0.40	0.54
3. Long-term debt to equity	0.48	0.51	0.39	0.33	0.28	0.29	0.43
4. Equity to total debt	0.88	0.83	0.98	1.34	1.56	1.50	0.86
5. Fixed assets to equity	0.92	0.92	0.79	0.73	0.72	0.70	0.46
6. Current liabilities to total liabilities	0.58	0.58	0.62	0.56	0.58	0.57	0.61
7. Earnings to fixed charges	5.16	2.14	1.84	6.06	6.41	6.28	—
8. Cash flow to fixed charges	7.47	5.27	5.38	8.94	8.69	9.26	—

The computations for Year 11 are shown here:

$$(1) \quad \frac{\text{Total debt*}}{\text{Equity capital*}} = \frac{2,202.9}{1,946.1} = 1.13$$

$$(2) \quad \frac{\text{Total debt*}}{\text{Total debt and equity}\boxed{55}} = \frac{2,202.9}{4,149.0} = 0.53$$

$$(3) \quad \frac{\text{Long-term debt*}}{\text{Equity capital*}} = \frac{924.9}{1,946.1} = 0.48$$

$$(4) \quad \frac{\text{Equity capital*}}{\text{Total debt*}} = \frac{1,946.1}{2,202.9} = 0.88$$

$$(5) \quad \frac{\text{Plant assets}\,\boxed{37}}{\text{Equity capital*}} = \frac{1,790.4}{1,946.1} = 0.92$$

$$(6) \quad \frac{\text{Current liabilities}\,\boxed{45}}{\text{Total liabilities*}} = \frac{1,278.0}{2,202.9} = 0.58$$

$$(7) \quad \frac{\substack{\text{Pretax income}\,\boxed{26}\,+\,\text{Interest expense}\,\boxed{18}\,+ \\ \text{Interest portion of rent expense}^\dagger\,-\,\text{Undistributed equity in earnings in affiliates}\,\boxed{24},\,\boxed{169A}}}{\text{Interest incurred}\,\boxed{98}\,+\,\text{Interest portion of rent expense}^*\,\boxed{143}} = \frac{667.4 + 116.2 + 20 - (2.4 - 8.2)}{136.9 + 20} = 5.16$$

$$(8) \quad \frac{\substack{\text{Cash flows from operations}\,\boxed{64}\,+\,\text{Current tax expense}\,\boxed{124A}\,+ \\ \text{Interest expense}\,\boxed{18}\,+\,\text{Interest portion of rent expense}^\dagger\,\boxed{143}}}{\text{Interest incurred}\,\boxed{98}\,+\,\text{Interest portion of rent expense}^\dagger\,\boxed{143}} = \frac{805.2 + 230.4 + 116.2 + 20}{136.9 + 20} = 7.47$$

* From Exhibit CC.16.
† One-third of rent expense under operating leases. For Year 11: ⅓ of $59.7 $\boxed{143}$.

The leverage ratio for Year 11 implies that Campbell is borrowing $0.589 on each dollar of equity. The total $1.589 in funds are then able to generate $3.32 in sales because assets are turning over at a rate of 2.09 times. This $3.32 in sales earns $0.27 or 8.01% in net operating income after tax.

Notice that Campbell's Year 11 equity growth rate (13.85%) markedly improved relative to prior years. Even if we exclude Years 9 and 10, this rate is nearly double the level for Years 6 through 8. The negative ratios for Years 9 and 10 are because Campbell maintained its dividend payout with its divestitures and restructuring. The strong

Exhibit CC.19

■ ■ ■ ■ ■ ■ ■

CAMPBELL SOUP COMPANY
Return on Invested Capital Ratios*

	Year 11	Year 10	Year 9	Year 8	Year 7	Year 6
1. Return on net operating assets-(RNOA)	16.77%	6.31%	3.91%	10.65%	12.96%	
2. Return on common equity-(ROCE)	21.52%	0.24%	0.67%	14.07%	14.14%	
3. Return on long-term debt and equity	17.02%	3.04%	2.96%	12.27%	12.35%	
4. Equity growth rate	13.85%	−6.30%	−3.67%	8.59%	8.79%	
5. Disaggregation of ROCE						
RNOA	16.77%	6.31%	3.91%	10.65%	12.96%	
LEV	58.90%	55.47%	42.16%	30.28%	27.52%	
Spread	8.07%	−10.95%	−7.68%	11.32%	4.27%	
ROE (RNOA + [LEV × Spread])	21.52%	0.24%	0.67%	14.07%	14.14%	
where:						
NOA	$3,037.70	$2,892.15	$2,854.95	$2,721.55	$2,353.45	$2,107.85
NFO (NOA − SE)	1,115.09	1,082.85	967.65	686.25	493.35	469.45
SE	1,922.61	1,809.30	1,887.30	2,035.30	1,860.10	1,638.40
NOPAT	497.12	181.42	108.94	270.14	289.12	272.81
NFE (NOPAT − NI)	95.62	177.02	95.84	(3.96)	41.82	49.61
NI	401.50	4.40	13.10	274.10	247.30	223.20
6. Disaggregation of RNOA						
NOPAT margin	8.01%	2.92%	1.92%	5.55%	6.44%	
NOA turnover	2.09	2.16	2.03	1.92	2.01	
RNOA (margin × turnover)	16.77%	6.31%	3.91%	10.65%	12.96%	

*Legend:
NOA	Net operating assets
SE	Stockholders' equity (CC.16)
NFO (NOA − SE)	Net financial obligations (calculations do not assume 50% of deferred taxes as equity as in CC.16)
NOPAT	Net operating profit after tax
NI	Net income
NFE (NOPAT − NI)	Net financial expense
RNOA	NOPAT/Average NOA
LEV	Financial leverage (Average NFO/Average SE)
NBC	Net borrowing costs (NFE/Average NFO)
Spread	RNOA − NBC
ROE (computed)	RNOA + (LEV × Spread)
NOPAT margin	NOPAT/Sales
NOA turnover	Sales/Average NOA

Computations for Year 11 follow:

(1) Net operating assets for Year 11 is computed as follows:
　　$4,149.0　(total assets; all considered operating)
　　−958.8　(operating current liabilities; $1,278 − $282.2 − $37.0)
　　−152.5　(one-half of deferred income tax liability considered operating)
　　$3,037.7　(net operating assets for Year 11)

NOPAT for Year 11 is equal to $497.12 ($6,204.1 − $4,095.5 − $956.2 − $306.7 − $56.3 − $0.8 − $26.2 + 2.4) × (1 − 0.35); assuming other income (expense) and equity earnings of affiliates are operating, and interest income (expense) and minority interest expense are nonoperating. Also, using the statutory income tax rate of 35%, RNOA is computed as:

$$RNOA = \frac{\$497.12}{(\$3,037.7 + \$2,892.15/2)} = 16.77\%$$

(continued)

(concluded)
■ ■ ■ ■ ■ ■ ■

(2) ROCE $= \dfrac{\text{Net income} - \text{Preferred dividend}}{\text{Average common equity}^\dagger} = \dfrac{401.5}{[(1{,}946.1 - 23.5) + (1{,}865.6 - 56.3)]/2} = 21.52\%$

(3) Return on LTD and equity $= \dfrac{\text{Net income} + \text{Interest expense } (1 - \text{Tax rate}) + \text{MI}}{\text{Average long-term liabilities}^\ddagger + \text{Average equity}^\dagger} = \dfrac{401.5 + 116.2\,(1 - 0.35) + 7.2}{(924.9 + 951.9)/2 + (1{,}946.1 + 1{,}865.6)/2} = \underline{\underline{17.02\%}}$

(4) Equity growth rate $= \dfrac{\text{Net income} - \text{Dividends paid}}{\text{Average common equity}^\dagger} = \dfrac{401.5 - 137.5}{(1{,}946.1 + 1{,}865.6)/2} = 13.85\%$

† Including 50% of deferred taxes assumed as equity, and excluding minority interests (MI). See Exhibit CC.16.
‡ Including 50% of deferred taxes. See Exhibit CC.16.

rebound in this ratio for Year 11 bodes well for future growth in sales and earnings. A higher level of reinvestment frees Campbell from reliance on outside financing sources to fund its growth. The Year 11 net income of $401.5 million and dividends of $142.2 million leave sufficient funds for reinvestment and internally financed growth.

Analysis of Asset Utilization

Campbell's asset utilization measures are reported in Exhibit CC.20. Campbell's asset turnover (2.09 for Year 11 of Exhibit CC.19) has increased slightly since Year 8, but declined in the most recent year. Contributing to this overall increase in asset turnover are marked changes in turnover for individual asset components. Cash and cash equivalents evidence the most variability during this period. Variability in cash and cash equivalents is also evidenced in both the sales to working capital turnover ratio and in

Exhibit CC.20
■ ■ ■ ■ ■ ■ ■

CAMPBELL SOUP COMPANY
Asset Utilization Ratios

(Based on year-end amounts)	Year 11	Year 10	Year 9	Year 8	Year 7	Year 6	Year 11 Industry Composite
1. Sales to cash and equivalents......	34.7	76.9	46.9	56.8	31.0	27.6	40.6
2. Sales to receivables.....................	11.8	9.9	10.5	10.0	13.2	14.3	8.4
3. Sales to inventories	8.8	7.6	7.0	7.3	7.2	7.0	3.6
4. Sales to working capital	25.8	16.9	15.4	9.8	6.0	6.1	4.9
5. Sales to fixed assets....................	3.5	3.6	3.7	3.2	3.3	3.7	6.6
6. Sales to other assets*	7.4	8.5	7.2	6.6	14.5	16.5	7.5
7. Sales to total assets	1.5	1.5	1.4	1.4	1.5	1.6	1.4
8. Sales to short-term liabilities	4.9	4.8	4.6	5.6	6.5	6.9	4.2

* Including intangible assets.

the common-size balance sheet in Exhibit CC.7. Exhibit CC.7 reveals a gradual disposal of temporary investments. The sizeable $98.2 million increase in Year 11 cash and cash equivalents is primarily due to improvements in operating performance (see Exhibit CC.4).

Campbell's accounts receivable turnover shows a slight improvement in Years 8 through 11 relative to earlier years. The continued improvement in Year 11 is helped by this year's decrease of $97.1 million in receivables. Regarding inventory turnover, Campbell's expressed desire to decrease inventories at every stage of its manufacturing process is revealing itself through an improved inventory turnover ratio (8.8). It is important to see that Campbell's asset and asset component turnover ratios often compare favorably to industry norms. In several key areas like receivables (11.8 versus 8.4), inventories (8.8 versus 3.6), and working capital (25.8 versus 4.9), its turnover ratio is better than the industry composite.

Campbell's Sales and Cost of Sales Growth

Analysis of Operating Performance and Profitability

Selected profit margin ratios for Campbell are reported in Exhibit CC.21. We see that Campbell's gross profit margin for Year 11 is better than the industry norm (34.0% versus 29.3%). However its net profit margin is at or slightly below the industry level (6.47% versus 6.60%). After the divestitures and restructuring of Years 9 and 10, Campbell's net profit margin is better than it was in Years 6 through 8. These moves included eliminating administrative personnel and unsuccessful divisions. Results in Year 11 already show indications of tighter control over several areas of operating expenses. Continued cost control should allow Campbell to further improve its profitability and exceed industry norms.

Exhibit CC.21

■ ■ ■ ■ ■ ■ ■

CAMPBELL SOUP COMPANY
Analysis of Profit Margin Ratios

Profit margins	Year 11	Year 10	Year 9	Year 8	Year 7	Year 6	Year 11 Industry Composite
1. Gross profit margin	34.00%	31.38%	29.45%	30.32%	29.17%	28.09%	29.30%
2. Operating profit margin	12.63%	4.69%	3.54%	9.09%	10.46%	10.34%	—
3. Net profit margin	6.47%	0.07%	0.23%	5.63%	5.51%	5.21%	6.60%

Computations for Year 11 are shown here:

$$(1) \ \text{Gross profit margin} = \frac{\text{Net sales} - \text{Cost of products sold}}{\text{Net sales}} = \frac{6{,}204.1 - 4{,}095.5}{6{,}204.1} = 34\%$$

$$(2) \ \text{Operating profit margin} = \frac{\text{Income before taxes and interest expense}}{\text{Net sales}} = \frac{667.4 + 116.2}{6{,}204.1} = 12.63\%$$

We link these profitability measures with evidence in earlier analyses. Improvement evidenced in the gross profit margin confirms earlier results in Exhibit CC.6 showing a gradual decline in cost of products sold (66.01% in Year 11 versus 71.91% in Year 6). While continued improvement in gross profit margin is possible, it will be difficult to achieve. The key for a profit ratio to benefit from improved gross profit margin is continued control over administrative and marketing expenses. This analysis is corroborated by our earlier trend index analysis. Exhibit CC.8 shows sales in Year 11 are 145% higher than for Year 6. Yet cost of products sold is only 133% greater, and the total of costs and expenses is 142% greater. This combination yields a net income that is 180% larger than the Year 6 level. The general inference from these trend indexes is that sales, gross margin, and net income are growing at a relatively faster rate than costs and expenses.

Exhibit CC.8 reveals that interest expense grew throughout the six-year period but at a relatively lower rate than did total liabilities, except for Year 11. This reflects a lower cost of borrowing resulting primarily from lower interest rates. We also see that Campbell is probably a more risky borrower compared to three to five years earlier as reflected in its increasing debt to equity ratio.

The Supplemental Schedule of Sales and Earnings in Campbell's annual report (item ①) shows the contributions of international operations to Year 11. International earnings total $92.3 million, including $35.3 million from Campbell Canada, $17.6 million from International Biscuit, and $39.4 million from Campbell International. International earnings represents about 11.6% of total operating earnings. In Years 10 and 9, international operations contribute negatively to total earnings. This is due to the restructuring in those years, reducing total operating earnings by $134.1 million in Year 10 and by $82.3 million in Year 9. These negative contributions are in addition to losses from foreign currency translation of $3.8 million and $20.0 million in Years 10 and 9, respectively. Foreign currency translation is not significant in Year 11. Nevertheless, international operations for the past six years comprise nearly 20% of total sales (see Exhibit CC.1). International operations are expected to continue to exert a significant impact on Campbell's profitability.

Campbell's effective tax rate (note 9) is 39.8% in Year 11, 97.5% in Year 10, and 87.7% in Year 9. The extraordinarily high rates for the latter two years are due mainly to the large amounts of nondeductible divestiture, restructuring, and unusual charges, representing 56.5 and 48.7% of earnings before taxes, respectively (note 9). If we exclude these divestitures, the effective tax rate declines to about 40%. Campbell is also taking advantage of tax loss carryforward benefits from international subsidiaries. At the end of Year 11 the company has $77.4 million remaining in unused tax loss carryforward benefits. About one-half of these expire by Year 16 and the remainder are available indefinitely. Most deferred taxes result from pensions, depreciation timing differences, divestiture, restructuring, and unusual charges. Deferred taxes due to depreciation differences are relatively large through Year 10, then decline to a low of $5.9 million in Year 11.

Analysis of depreciation data for Campbell is reported in Exhibit CC.22. This evidence shows that accumulated depreciation as a percentage of gross plant assets remains stable (44.6% in Year 11). Stability in depreciation expense, as a percentage of either plant assets or sales, is also evident in Exhibit CC.22. Accordingly, there is no evidence that earnings quality is affected due to changes in depreciation.

Analysis of discretionary expenditures in Exhibit CC.23 shows spending in all major categories during Year 11 declines compared to most prior years. This potentially results from more controlled spending and enhanced efficiencies. Recall our common-size analysis of factors affecting net earnings in Exhibit CC.6. This analysis is corroborative of

Exhibit CC.22

■ ■ ■ ■ ■ ■ ■

CAMPBELL SOUP COMPANY
Analysis of Depreciation

	Year 11	Year 10	Year 9	Year 8	Year 7	Year 6
1. Accumulated depreciation as a percent of gross plant assets*........	44.6%	42.3%	43.1%	43.7%	46.6%	48.6%
2. Annual depreciation expenses as a percent of gross plant	7.7%	7.7%	7.6%	6.9%	6.4%	6.4%
3. Annual depreciation expenses as a percent of sales......................................	3.1%	3.0%	3.1%	3.3%	3.1%	2.8%

Computations for Year 11 are shown here:

$$(1) \quad \frac{1,131.5 \ \boxed{162}}{758.7 \ \boxed{159} + 1,779.3 \ \boxed{160}} = 44.6\%$$

$$(2) \quad \frac{194.5 \ \boxed{162A}}{758.7 \ \boxed{159} + 1,779.3 \ \boxed{160}} = 7.7\%$$

$$(3) \quad \frac{194.5 \ \boxed{162A}}{6,204.1 \ \boxed{13}} = 3.1\%$$

*Exclusive of land and projects in progress.

some of the factors evidenced in Exhibit CC.23. For example, gross margin is increasing while (on a relative basis) increases in marketing, selling, interest, and "other" expenses outpace increases in sales. Administrative expenses and research and development expenses are not increasing with sales. Statutory tax rates decline over this period, thereby holding down growth in tax expenses. Profitability increases because the growth in gross margin is not offset with increases in expenses.

Recast income statements of Campbell for the most recent six years were reported in Exhibit 11.1. These recast statements support many of the observations recognized in this section. Campbell's adjusted income statements for this same period are shown

Exhibit CC.23

■ ■ ■ ■ ■ ■ ■

CAMPBELL SOUP COMPANY
Analysis of Discretionary Expenditures

($ millions)	Year 11	Year 10	Year 9	Year 8	Year 7	Year 6
Net sales	$6,204.1	$6,205.8	$5,672.1	$4,868.9	$4,490.4	$4,286.8
Plant assets (net)*....................................	1,406.5	1,386.9	1,322.6	1,329.1	1,152.0	974.1
Maintenance and repairs.........................	173.9	180.6	173.9	155.6	148.8	144.0
Advertising	195.4	220.4	212.9	219.1	203.5	181.4
Research & development (R&D)	56.3	53.7	47.7	46.9	44.8	42.2
Maintenance and repairs ÷ sales...........	2.8%	2.9%	3.1%	3.2%	3.3%	3.4%
Maintenance and repairs ÷ plant...........	12.4	13.0	13.1	11.7	12.9	14.8
Advertising ÷ sales	3.1	3.6	3.8	4.5	4.5	4.2
R&D ÷ sales..	0.9	0.9	0.8	1.0	1.0	1.0

* Exclusive of land and projects in process.

in Exhibit 11.2. The adjusted statements reveal an increasing trend in net income from Year 9 to Year 10–this contrasts with reported income.

Forecasting and Valuation

The final step in the analysis process is forecasting future financial performance. The inferences we expect to draw from this analysis depend on the analyst's perspective. For example, if our perspective is that of the company's creditor we are interested in forecasts of future cash flows, either short term or long term depending on the length of our credit arrangement. These cash flow forecasts are derived from our projection of the company's income statement and balance sheet as illustrated in Chapter 9. If the perspective of the analysis is that of an equity investor, we are interested in the company's ability to realize the benefits of its strategic plan. Specifically, our focus is on whether the company can generate positive residual profits in the future. Again, forecasts of the income statement and balance sheet are required.

Exhibit CC.24 reproduces the reported income statements for Campbell Soup's Years 6–11 together with a forecast for Year 12. Also included are selected historical ratios and our assumptions for the Year 12 forecast. The forecasting process begins with our expectations for the level of sales. Campbell Soup's sales growth had been strong (4.75% to 16.5% per year) until Year 11 when sales declined slightly. As the company discussed in its MD&A section (see Appendix A), the sales decline is primarily attributable

---

Exhibit CC.24

■ ■ ■ ■ ■ ■ ■

CAMPBELL SOUP COMPANY
Forecasted Income Statement

($ millions)	Year 12 Forecast	Reported Year 11	Year 10	Year 9	Year 8	Year 7	Year 6
Net sales	$6,514.3	$6,204.1	$6,205.8	$5,672.1	$4,868.9	$4,490.4	$4,286.8
Cost of products sold	4,494.9	4,095.5	4,258.2	4,001.6	3,392.8	3,180.5	3,082.7
Gross profit	2,019.4	2,108.6	1,947.6	1,670.5	1,476.1	1,309.9	1,204.1
Marketing, selling, administrative, and R&D expenses	1,385.2	1,319.2	1,324.9	1,118.6	1,012.8	884.9	782.5
Interest & other expenses	128.1	122.0	443.3	445.4	74.7	7.1	34.4
Earnings before taxes	506.2	667.4	179.4	106.5	388.6	417.9	387.2
Taxes on earnings	201.5	265.9	175.0	93.4	147.0	170.6	164.0
Cumulative loss (gain) from accounting change	0.0	0.0	0.0	0.0	(32.5)	0	0
Net earnings	$ 304.7	$ 401.5	$ 4.4	$ 13.1	$ 274.1	$ 247.3	$ 223.2
Shares outstanding	127.0	127.0	126.6	129.3	129.3	129.9	129.5
Selected ratios							
Sales growth	5.00%	−0.03%	9.41%	16.50%	8.43%	4.75%	
Gross profit margin	31.00%	33.99%	31.38%	29.45%	30.32%	29.17%	
Selling, general, and administrative expenses/Sales	21.26%	21.26%	21.35%	19.72%	20.80%	19.71%	
Depreciation expense/Prior year plant assets (net)	12.14%	12.14%	13.04%	12.74%	12.67%	12.38%	
Interest and other expenses/Sales	1.97%	1.97%	7.14%	7.85%	1.53%	0.16%	
Taxes on earnings/Earnings before taxes	39.84%	39.84%	97.55%	87.70%	37.83%	40.82%	

to the divestiture (discontinuation) of several businesses (product lines). Absent these effects, the company reveals that sales would have increased by 4% for the year. Our forecast of Year 12 sales is based on an expected increase of 5%.

Campbell Soup's gross profit margin has been steadily increasing from 29% to 31% in Year 10. Year 11's gross profit margin increased significantly to 34%. The MD&A section does not provide an explanation for this increase and 30–31% is more in line with recent history. As a result, we use 31% for the gross profit margin in our forecast. Cost of goods sold, then, is computed as the difference between sales and gross profit.

Selling, general, and administrative (SG&A) expenses have remained fairly constant at 20–21% of sales. We use 21.26%, the most recent percentage, in our forecast. Interest and other expenses have fluctuated widely over the period under review, from 0.16% to 7.14% and, most recently, 1.97% of sales. This category includes interest expense (revenue), foreign exchange gains (losses) and transitory items like restructuring charges and expenses resulting from divestitures. This last category was particularly large in Years 9 and 10, amounting to 6.0% and 5.4% of sales, respectively. Absent these transitory items, interest and other expenses would have been in the 2% range. Since we have no knowledge of planned restructuring expenses or divestitures in Year 12, we use 1.97% in our projection, the most recent percentage of sales.

Projected sales less projected expenses yield our forecast of pretax profits. We then subtract income tax expense to arrive at our projected net profit. Tax expense as a percentage of pretax profit has fluctuated widely for the period under review, from 37.8% to 97.6% in Year 10. The higher percentages of tax expense are typically due to nondeductible expenses in reported earnings. These include restructuring expenses that are accrued for financial reporting purposes, but are not deductible for tax purposes until paid. As a result, the higher percentages are probably not realistic for our projections and we use 39.8%, the most recent experience, to project Year 12 net profit.

Exhibit CC.25 reproduces the historical balance sheets of Campbell Soup for Years 6–11 together with our initial forecast for Year 12. Receivables, inventories, accounts payable, and accruals are all projected using their most recent turnover rates (and year-end balances) and our projections for sales and cost of goods sold. Receivable turnover rates, for example, have fluctuated between 9.94 and 14.34 times with 11.76 the most recent turnover rate. We use the recent turnover in our forecast and forecast receivables using projected sales as follows:

$$\text{Projected accounts receivable} = \frac{\text{Projected sales}}{\text{Turnover rate}} = \frac{\$6,514.3}{11.76} = \$553.8$$

Other working capital accounts are forecasted similarly. Accrued expenses are projected using sales and the accrued expense turnover rate of 15.18 for Year 11. Inventories and accounts payable are likewise projected using cost of goods sold and their respective turnover rates. Other current assets and liabilities are assumed equal to the Year 11 balance.

Short-term debt is assumed equal to the Year 11 balance. Current maturities of long-term debt are projected using amounts provided in the long-term debt footnote 19. Campbell Soup reports that scheduled maturities of long-term debt are $227.7 million for Year 12. This amount is included in current liabilities for Year 11. Projected maturities of long-term debt in Year 13 are reported at $118.9 million, a reduction of $108.8 million. As a result, assuming other short-term debt remains constant at Year 12 levels, the short-term and current maturities of long-term debt account is projected to decline by $108.8 million from $282.2 million in Year 11 to a projected level of $173.4 million for Year 12.

Exhibit CC.25

CAMPBELL SOUP COMPANY
Forecasted Balance Sheet

($ millions)	Year 12 Initial Forecast	Reported					
		Year 11	Year 10	Year 9	Year 8	Year 7	Year 6
Cash and cash equivalents	$ (99.4)	$ 178.9	$ 80.7	$ 120.9	$ 85.8	$ 145.0	$ 155.1
Accounts receivable	553.8	527.4	624.5	538.0	486.9	338.9	299.0
Inventories	775.6	706.7	819.8	816.0	664.7	623.6	610.5
Other current assets	105.5	105.5	140.5	126.6	125.5	330.4	270.2
Total current assets	1,335.5	1,518.5	1,665.5	1,601.5	1,362.9	1,437.9	1,334.8
Plant assets, net of depreciation	1,963.8	1,790.4	1,717.7	1,540.6	1,508.9	1,349.0	1,168.1
Other long-term assets	840.1	840.1	732.4	790.0	737.8	310.5	259.9
Total assets	$4,139.4	$4,149.0	$4,115.6	$3,932.1	$3,609.6	$3,097.4	$2,762.8
Payable to suppliers and others	$ 529.4	$ 482.4	$ 525.2	$ 508.2	$ 446.7	$ 374.8	$ 321.7
Notes payable	173.4	282.2	202.3	271.5	138.0	93.5	88.9
Accrued liabilities	429.1	408.7	491.9	392.6	236.9	182.1	165.9
Accrued income taxes	51.3	67.7	46.4	30.1	41.7	43.4	49.6
Dividend payable	37.0	37.0	32.3	29.7	0	0	0
Total current liabilities	1,220.3	1,278.0	1,298.1	1,232.1	863.3	693.8	626.1
Long-term debt	653.7	772.6	805.8	629.2	525.8	380.2	362.3
Deferred income tax and other liabilities	305.0	305.0	319.9	292.5	325.5	287.3	235.5
Total liabilities	2,179.0	2,355.6	2,423.8	2,153.8	1,714.6	1,361.3	1,223.9
Preferred stock	0.0	0.0	0.0	0.0	0.0	0.0	0.0
Capital stock	20.3	20.3	20.3	20.3	20.3	20.3	20.3
Capital surplus	107.3	107.3	61.9	50.8	42.3	41.1	38.1
Earnings retained and cumulative translation adjustments	2,103.2	1,936.2	1,716.8	1,777.9	1,907.6	1,721.5	1,528.9
Capital stock in treasury	(270.4)	(270.4)	(107.2)	(70.7)	(75.2)	(46.8)	(48.4)
Total shareowners' equity	1,960.4	1,793.4	1,691.8	1,778.3	1,895.0	1,736.1	1,538.9
Total liabilities and shareholders' equity	$4,139.4	$4,149.0	$4,115.6	$3,932.1	$3,609.6	$3,097.4	$2,762.8
Accounts receivable turnover*	11.76	11.76	9.94	10.54	10.00	13.25	14.34
Inventory turnover*	5.80	5.80	5.19	4.90	5.10	5.10	5.05
Accounts payable turnover*	8.49	8.49	8.11	7.87	7.60	8.49	9.58
Accruals turnover	15.18	15.18	12.62	14.45	20.55	24.66	25.84
Taxes payable/Tax expense	25.46%	25.46%	26.51%	32.23%	28.37%	25.44%	30.24%
Financial leverage (Total assets/Stockholders' equity)	2.11	2.31	2.43	2.21	1.90	1.78	1.80
Dividends paid per share	$ 1.083	$ 1.083	$ 0.982	$ 0.671	$ 0.81	$ 0.71	$ 0.81
Capital expenditures	390.9	361.1	387.6	284.1	245.3	303.7	235.3
Capital expenditures/Sales	6.00%	5.82%	6.25%	5.01%	5.04%	6.76%	5.49%
Depreciation expense	217.4	208.6	200.9	192.3	170.9	144.6	126.8

*Computed using ending balances only.

Property, plant, and equipment is projected at the prior year's balance plus projected capital expenditures and less depreciation. Capital expenditures as a percentage of sales have remained fairly constant at 5–6% of sales. We use 6% in our forecast. Likewise, depreciation expense as a percentage of the prior year's balance of PP&E has ranged from 12.14% (most recently) to 13.04% (see Exhibit CC.24). We use 12.14% as this reflects the most recent depreciation policies of the company.

Other long-term assets are projected at the Year 11 balance. These consist of intangible assets, such as goodwill, and miscellaneous other long-term assets. Since goodwill is no longer amortized, we use the prior year's balance as we have no knowledge of expected changes in other long-term assets.

Long-term debt is initially projected at the balance of long-term debt in Year 11 less the portion now recognized as current maturities of long-term debt in current liabilities ($118.9 million). Once the initial cash balance is computed, we will adjust this for any new financing required. Other long-term debt is assumed to remain at Year 1 levels.

Common stock, capital surplus, and treasury stock are assumed to remain at Year 11 levels. Projected retained earnings are equal to the Year 11 retained earnings balance plus the projected profit of $304.5 million less projected dividends of $137.5 million (Year 11's payout of $1.083 per share for 127 million outstanding shares).

Setting total assets equal to total liabilities and subtracting forecasted current assets (other than cash) and long-term assets yields an initial negative estimate for cash of $(99.4 million). We, then, add $350 million to long-term debt, representing the financing that Campbell Soup will require based on our projections. This yields a forecasted cash balance of $250.6 million, in line with previous year's levels of cash. In addition, the leverage ratio (total assets / total equity) is projected at 2.29, about the same as the Year 11 level. The revised balance sheet forecast is provided in Exhibit CC.26.

We conclude this section by valuing the Campbell Soup common stock as of Year 11 and using forecasts for Year 12 and beyond. The valuation analysis is provided in Exhibit CC.27. We use a five-year forecast horizon, beginning with Year 12 forecasted above and continuing through Year 16. Year 17 is the assumed terminal year and we project sales growth at the rate of inflation from that period forward. To simplify the analysis, we project only the five parameters we utilized in our valuation example in Chapter 9:

1. Sales growth.
2. Net profit margin (Net income/Sales).
3. Net working capital turnover (Sales/Net working capital).
4. Fixed asset turnover (Sales/Fixed assets).
5. Financial leverage (Operating assets/Equity).

The summary balance sheet and income statement begin with our estimate for Year 12. Years 13–17 are computed using the same sales growth, net profit margin, working capital, and fixed asset turnover rates and leverage used for Year 12. These could, of course, be modified if we had information indicating an expected change in one or more of the forecast parameters. Finally, we assume a cost of equity capital of 7%.[1]

The expected level of profits, based on beginning stockholders' equity of $1,793 million and a 7% yield, is $126 million. The forecasted net income for Year 12 is $305 million. Residual profits are, therefore, projected at $179 million. These are discounted to the present with a factor of .89 (1/1.12) as discussed in Chapter 9. We forecast residual

---

[1] Under CAPM, with long-term government bond yields of 5%, a beta for Campbell Soup stock of 0.394, and an equity risk premium of 5%, the cost of equity capital is 5% + (0.394 × 5%) = 6.97, or approximately 7%.

Exhibit CC.26

■ ■ ■ ■ ■ ■ ■

CAMPBELL SOUP COMPANY

Final Forecasted Balance Sheet

($ millions)	Year 12 Final Forecast	Year 12 Initial Forecast
Cash and cash equivalents	$ 250.6	$ (99.4)
Accounts receivable	553.8	553.8
Inventories	775.6	775.6
Other current assets	105.5	105.5
Total current assets	1,685.5	1,335.5
Plant assets, net of depreciation	1,963.8	1,963.8
Other long-term assets	840.1	840.1
Total assets	$4,489.4	$4,139.4
Payable to suppliers and others	$ 529.4	$ 529.4
Notes payable	173.4	173.4
Accrued liabilities	429.1	429.1
Accrued income taxes	51.3	51.3
Dividend payable	37.0	37.0
Total current liabilities	1,220.3	1,220.3
Long-term debt	1,003.7	653.7
Deferred income tax and other liabilities	305.0	305.0
Total liabilities	2,529.0	2,179.0
Preferred stock	0.0	0.0
Capital stock	20.3	20.3
Capital surplus	107.3	107.3
Earnings retained and cumulative translation adjustments	2,103.2	2,103.2
Capital stock in treasury	(270.4)	(270.4)
Total shareowners' equity	1,960.4	1,960.4
Total liabilities and shareowners' equity	$4,489.4	$4,139.4

income for each additional year and also discount these to the present. The terminal year residual income is treated as a perpetuity beginning in Year 17. The present value of this perpetuity is also discounted. The cumulative present value of the projected residual income is $5,193 million ($787 million + $4,406 million) which, when added to the beginning book value of $1,793 million, yields a value for the common equity of $6,987 million, or $55.01 per share based on 127 million outstanding common shares.

Our estimate of $55.01 is considerably lower than the market price range of $72.38–$84.88 for Campbell Soup in the fourth quarter of Year 11 as reported in note 24. Clearly, the market is expecting stronger performance than we have assumed. One possibility is the company's gross profit margin. We have assumed that the reported gross profit margin of nearly 34% in Year 11 is an aberration and that it will revert to historical levels of 31%. If the market is, in fact, expecting gross profit margins to remain at 34%, the net profit margin will increase by 1.8% after tax to 6.47%. The resulting stock price estimate is $82.76 per share. Similarly, the market may be forecasting higher growth rates in sales or increasing improvement in asset turnover ratios.

Exhibit CC.27

■ ■ ■ ■ ■ ■ ■

CAMPBELL SOUP COMPANY
Valuation of Common Stock

	REPORTED		FORECAST HORIZON					TERMINAL
	Year 10	Year 11	Year 12	Year 13	Year 14	Year 15	Year 16	Year 17
Sales growth	9.43%	−0.03%	5.00%	5.00%	5.00%	5.00%	5.00%	3.50%
Net profit margin (Net income/Sales)	0.07%	6.47%	4.67%	4.67%	4.67%	4.67%	4.67%	4.67%
Net working capital (NWC) turnover								
Sales/Average NWC	16.89	25.80	14.00	14.00	14.00	14.00	14.00	14.00
Fixed assets turnover								
Sales/Average fixed assets	2.53	2.36	2.32	2.32	2.32	2.32	2.32	2.32
Total operating assets/Total equity	1.67	1.60	1.67	1.67	1.67	1.67	1.67	1.67
Cost of equity			7.0%					
($ millions)								
Net sales	$6,206	$6,204	$6,514	$6,840	$7,182	$7,541	$7,918	$8,195
Net earnings	4	402	305	320	336	353	370	383
Net working capital	367	241	465	488	513	539	565	585
Long-term assets	2,450	2,631	2,804	2,944	3,091	3,246	3,408	3,527
Total operating assets	2,818	2,871	3,269	3,433	3,604	3,784	3,974	4,113
Long-term liabilities	1,126	1,078	1,309	1,374	1,443	1,515	1,591	1,646
Total shareowners' equity	1,692	1,793	1,960	2,058	2,161	2,269	2,383	2,466
Residual Income Computation								
Net income			$ 305	$ 320	$ 336	$ 353	$ 370	$ 383
Beginning-year equity			$1,793	$1,960	$2,058	$2,161	$2,269	$2,383
Required equity return			7.0%	7.0%	7.0%	7.0%	7.0%	7.0%
Expected earnings			$ 126	$ 137	$ 144	$ 151	$ 159	$ 167
Residual income			$ 179	$ 183	$ 192	$ 201	$ 211	$ 216
Discount factor			0.93	0.87	0.82	0.76	0.71	
Present value of horizon residual income			$ 167	$ 159	$ 156	$ 154	$ 151	
Cumulative present value of horizon residual income		$ 787						
Present value of terminal residual income		4,406						
Beginning book value of equity		1,793						
Value of equity		$6,987						
Common shares outstanding (millions)		127						
Value of equity per share		$55.01						

Summary Evaluation and Inferences

This case analysis considered all facets of Campbell Soup Company's operating results and financial position. We also forecasted the company's income statement, balance sheet, and statement of cash flows. This type of analysis, modified for the analysis perspective, is valuable for informed business decisions. While these data and information from our analysis are indispensable, they are not sufficient in arriving at final decisions. This is because other qualitative and quantitative factors from outside of the financial statements should be brought to bear on these decisions.

Since lending, investing, or other business analysis decisions require more information than provided in accounting and financial analysis, we often summarize the analysis and its inferences in a financial analysis report. This report (see the discussion earlier in this chapter) lists the most relevant and salient findings from the analysis, which depend on the analysis perspective. The remainder of this section provides a brief listing of the main findings of our analysis of Campbell Soup Company.

Short-Term Liquidity

The assessment of Campbell's short-term liquidity is a mixed one. Both current and acid-test ratios do not compare favorably with industry norms. Yet Campbell's cash position compares favorably with its industry, and its accounts receivable and inventory turnover ratios are better than industry norms. Moreover, Campbell's conversion period is better (less) than that of the industry, and its cash position is strong, allowing for cash to be used for nonoperating activities like acquisitions and retirement of debt.

Capital Structure and Solvency

Campbell has aggressively transformed its capital structure in recent years to a less conservative one. This inference is drawn from absolute and industry comparative measures. Total liabilities make up about 53% of total financing, and long-term liabilities equal about one-half of equity. On the positive side, both earnings to fixed charges and cash flow to fixed charges ratios are strong, the exception being earnings coverage ratios for Years 9 and 10 (due to restructuring). These strong ratios imply good protection for Campbell's creditors. The company also has the strength to take on additional debt, and the market continues to assign Campbell a superior credit rating (A).

Return on Invested Capital

Campbell's return on net operating assets varies. In Years 7 and 8 it is stable at around 11%–13%, but in Years 9 and 10 it declines to a low of around 4% due primarily to divestiture, restructuring, and unusual charges. In Year 11, return on net operating assets rebounds to a strong 16.77%, composed of an 8.01% NOPAT margin and a net operating asset turnover of 2.09. Campbell's return on common equity is 21.52% for Year 11. This return also evidences setbacks in Years 9 and 10 for the same reasons as the return on net operating assets. An important factor affecting return on common equity (beyond the same components comprising return on net operating assets) is financial leverage. The leverage ratio equals 0.589 in Year 11 and is higher than in prior years mainly due to a more risky capital structure. A favorable finding is Campbell's increased equity growth rate for Year 11, due in large part to strong earnings and a higher rate of earnings retention.

Asset Turnover (Utilization)

Campbell's net operating asset turnover is increasing. While its turnover of cash and cash equivalents fluctuates from year to year, Campbell's accounts receivable and inventory turnovers are improving and exceed industry norms. These improvements are due mainly to Campbell's efforts to reduce working capital through, among other activities, less receivables and inventories. Nevertheless, asset turnover compares favorably to the industry despite the relatively low cash turnover and fixed assets turnover.

Operating Performance and Profitability

Campbell's gross profit margin is steadily improving and above the industry average. Yet its net profit margin is not as solid. This is due primarily to increased operating expenses, and the inability of Campbell's management in controlling these expenses. Recent activities suggest that Campbell is attempting to gain greater control over these expenses.

Campbell's Price-to-Earnings Ratio

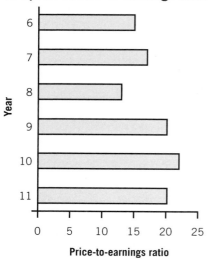

Source: Exhibit CC.28.

Financial Market Measures

Selected financial market measures for Campbell are shown in Exhibit CC.28. The first four measures reflect the market's valuation of Campbell's equity securities, while the fifth (dividend payout) reflects management discretion. Earnings per share figures for Years 9 and 10 are adjusted to exclude the effect of divestitures, restructuring, and unusual charges. While earnings per share increases from $1.72 in Year 6 to $3.16 in Year 11 (see Exhibit CC.2), the earnings yield declines over the same period because of steadily increasing price-to-earnings and price-to-book ratios. This is mainly due to a strong equity market. Similarly, while dividends per share increase from $0.65 in Year 6 to $1.12 in Year 11, the dividend yield declines from 2.5% to 1.74% over the same period. Declines in earnings yield and dividend yield are attributable mainly to steady increases in price-to-earnings and price-to-book ratios. Both ratios reflect the market's appreciation and confidence in Campbell's prior and expected performance. This analysis shows Campbell's operating performance is strong despite temporary declines in Years 9 and 10.

Higher price-to-earnings and price-to-book ratios benefit a company in several ways. These include the ability to raise a given amount of equity capital by issuing fewer shares and the ability to use common stock as a means of payment for acquisitions. Yet, increasing stock valuations expose existing and especially new common shareholders to increasing risks, including the risk of stagnating or reversing stock valuations. This occurs because, unlike in early stages of a bull market, prices can potentially deviate from company fundamentals in reflecting upward price momentum. Consider, for example, the difference between the current market price for Campbell Soup and our estimate in the case analysis. When stock valuations reflect this price momentum, experience shows it is promptly erased once information on the fundamentals fails to support the high stock price. Assessing price momentum, as important and crucial as it is for equity investing, cannot be gauged by means of the analysis tools here. They involve the study of market expectations and

---

Exhibit CC.28

■ ■ ■ ■ ■ ■ ■

CAMPBELL SOUP COMPANY
Market Measures

	Year 11	Year 10*	Year 9*	Year 8	Year 7	Year 6
1. Price-to-earnings (range)	27–14	26–18	29–12	16–11	19–14	20–10
2. Price-to-book (range)	6.0–3.1	4.7–3.2	4.5–1.8	2.3–1.6	2.7–2.0	2.9–1.5
3. Earnings yield	4.91%	4.53%	4.91%	7.45%	6.20%	6.61%
4. Dividend yield	1.74%	1.88%	2.08%	2.85%	2.32%	2.50%
5. Dividend payout ratio...............	35.44%	41.53%	42.45%	38.21%	37.37%	37.79%

Computations for Year 11 are shown here:
(1) High and Low for the year: High—84.88/3.16 = 27; Low—43.75/3.16 = 14 [see item 184].
(2) High and Low for the year: High—84.88/14.12 = 6.0; Low—43.75/14.12 = 3.1 [see item 185].
(3) Earnings per share/Average market price = 3.16/[(84.88 + 43.75)/2] = 4.91%.
(4) Dividend per share/Average market price = 1.12/64.32 = 1.74%.
(5) Dividend per share/Earnings per share = 1.12/3.16 = 35.44%.
* Year 10 and Year 9 results are shown for EPS before effects of divestitures, restructuring, and unusual charges of $2.33 and $2.02 per share, respectively.

cycles. The difference between Campbell's return on its invested capital and an equity investor's return on investment is discussed in Chapter 8.

Using Financial Statement Analysis

Our analysis of the financial statements of Campbell Soup Company consisted of two major parts: (1) detailed analysis and (2) summary and inferences. In our *analysis report,* the summary and inferences (executive summary) often precede detailed analysis. The detailed analysis section is usually directed at a specific user. For example, our bank loan officer who must decide on a short-term loan application typically directs attention to short-term liquidity and cash flow analysis and forecasting. A secondary objective of the loan officer is to assess capital structure and operating performance. Regarding the investment committee of our insurance company scenario, it would take a more long-term perspective. This implies more attention needs to be directed at capital structure and long-term solvency. Its secondary focus is on operating performance, return on invested capital, asset utilization, and short-term liquidity (in order of emphasis). Finally, the potential investor in Campbell shares has varying interest in all aspects of our analysis. The emphasis across areas is different for this user, and the likely order of priority is operating performance, return on invested capital, capital structure, long-term solvency, and short-term liquidity. A competent financial statement analysis contains sufficient detailed evaluation along with enough information and inferences to permit its use by different users with varying perspectives.

QUESTIONS

CC–1. Identify and describe the six major building blocks of financial statement analysis. What is the initial step in applying the building blocks to an analysis of financial statements?

CC–2. What type of investigation should precede analysis of financial statements?

CC–3. What are the analytical implications of recognizing that financial statements are an abstraction of a company's underlying business transactions and events?

CC–4. What additional knowledge and analytical skills must an analysis of financial statements bring to bear on companies operating in specialized or regulated industries?

CC–5. What are the attributes of a good financial analysis report? What distinct sections constitute a complete financial analysis report?

EXERCISES

The following financial data are available for each of two manufacturers of mountain bikes.

EXERCISE CC–1

Evaluating Financial Ratios in Determining Price-to-Earnings (PE)

	AXEL	BIKE
Capital structure		
5%, 20-year notes	$10,000,000	—
Common equity	$20,000,000	$30,000,000
Number of common shares	500,000	750,000
Earnings per share		
Year 6	$ 4.25	$ 3.00
Year 5	3.50	2.50
Year 4	2.25	1.67
Year 3	2.75	2.00
Year 2	1.70	1.95
Sales (Year 6)	30,000,000	30,000,000
Net income (Year 6)	2,125,000	2,250,000

(continued)

(concluded)

	AXEL	BIKE
Selected balance sheet data at end of Year 6		
Cash and cash equivalents..................................	$ 3,000,000	$ 5,850,000
Accounts receivable	5,000,000	3,750,000
Inventories	12,000,000	10,000,000
Total current assets	20,000,000	19,600,000
Accounts payable...	4,000,000	3,500,000
Accrued expenses...	2,000,000	2,000,000
Taxes payable..	1,000,000	1,100,000
Total current liabilities.....................................	7,000,000	6,600,000
Plant and equipment, net	13,000,000	15,900,000
Patents, net	4,000,000	100,000

CHECK
Axel
(a) 21%
(b) 33%
(g) 16.5%

Required:

Compute and analyze each of the following seven factors and ratios. For each factor and ratio, does the evidence imply a higher or lower PE for Axel or Bike?

a. Growth in earnings per share.

b. Financial leverage ratio.

c. Return on common equity.

d. Net income as % of sales.

e. Current ratio, receivables turnover, and sales to plant and equipment.

f. Patent position.

g. Return on long-term assets.

(CFA Adapted)

EXERCISE CC–2

Identifying Industry Classification by Company Financial Statements

Reproduced below are condensed common-size financial statements of companies operating in nine different industries. The nine industries represented are:

a. Tobacco manufacturing   d. Utilities   g. Grocery stores

b. Pharmaceuticals   e. Investment advising h. Computer equipment

c. Health care   f. Breweries   i. Public opinion surveys

Required:

Examine the relations in these balance sheets and income statements and match the (1) through (9) companies with the (a) through (i) industries. It might be helpful to consult published industry ratios.

COMPANY BALANCE SHEETS*

Account	(1)	(2)	(3)	(4)	(5)	(6)	(7)	(8)	(9)
Current receivables...............	9.77%	19.20%	3.35%	25.96%	0.55%	8.10%	26.34%	17.38%	15.33%
Inventories	6.22	14.87	5.18	0.00	7.91	20.11	31.69	0.00	0.00
Plant and equipment, net......	224.39	28.20	51.20	24.52	6.94	26.25	31.36	88.97	3.19
Other assets.........................	46.56	29.15	5.48	26.65	3.71	18.50	16.91	24.35	219.59
Total assets..........................	286.94%	91.42%	65.21%	77.13%	19.11%	72.96%	106.30%	130.70%	238.11%
Cost of P&E (gross)...............	279.83%	39.06%	70.33%	35.78%	9.64%	39.31%	45.91%	106.64%	6.29%
Current liabilities..................	18.78%	22.70%	11.19%	29.92%	7.31%	13.31%	19.30%	19.33%	76.89%
Long-term liabilities..............	158.69	9.22	26.65	10.19	6.06	16.40	4.11	73.32	72.18
Shareholders' equity..............	109.47	59.50	27.37	37.02	5.74	43.25	82.89	38.05	89.04
Total liabilities and equity.....	286.94%	91.42%	65.21%	77.13%	19.11%	72.96%	106.30%	130.70%	238.11%

*All numbers expressed as a percentage of total revenues.

Company Income Statements

Account	(1)	(2)	(3)	(4)	(5)	(6)	(7)	(8)	(9)
Revenues	100.00%	100.00%	100.00%	100.00%	100.00%	100.00%	100.00%	100.00%	100.00%
Cost of sales	49.50	31.11	67.48	63.29*	77.20	68.16	56.24	81.06*	16.55*
Depreciation expense	8.36	2.26	2.47	3.51	1.14	3.50	4.76	4.33	0.81
Interest expense	8.81	1.14	2.03	0.47	0.59	1.26	0.31	4.04	10.75
Advertising expense	0.00	2.39	4.82	0.12	3.89	6.97	3.86	0.00	6.24
R&D expense	0.76	7.95	0.24	0.00	0.00	0.00	11.06	0.00	0.00
Income taxes	11.47	8.11	2.44	6.80	0.77	4.71	2.98	4.44	33.01
All other items (net)	6.63	29.08	15.59	18.54	15.50	8.89	14.15	(0.46)	0.73
Total expenses	85.53%	82.04%	95.07%	92.73%	99.09%	93.49%	93.36%	93.41%	68.09%
Net income	14.47%	17.96%	4.93%	7.27%	0.91%	6.51%	6.64%	6.59%	31.91%

* Companies (4), (8), and (9) carry zero inventory, meaning that cost of sales is primarily operating expenses.

PROBLEMS

Selected financial ratios from the (i) S&P 400, (ii) the brewing industry, and (iii) **Anheuser-Busch Companies** (BUD), for Years 2 through 6 are reproduced below.

Anheuser-Busch Companies

PROBLEM CC–1

Analysis of Credit Quality

Required:

a. Using these financial ratios, analyze the relative credit position of:
   (1) Brewing industry compared with the S&P 400.
   (2) Anheuser-Busch compared with the brewing industry.
   (3) Anheuser-Busch compared with the S&P 400.

b. Using these financial ratios and your analysis from (a), describe the current position of Anheuser-Busch and discuss whether you feel there has been a change in the credit quality of Anheuser-Busch during this five-year period.

	YEAR 2			YEAR 3			YEAR 4			YEAR 5			YEAR 6		
	S&P 400	Brewing Industry	BUD	S&P 400	Brewing Industry	BUD	S&P 400	Brewing Industry	BUD	S&P 400	Brewing Industry	BUD	S&P 400	Brewing Industry	BUD
Current ratio	1.5	1.3	1.1	1.5	1.4	1.2	1.5	1.3	1.1	1.4	1.5	1.2	1.4	1.4	1.0
Quick ratio	0.9	0.7	0.4	0.9	0.8	0.7	0.8	0.7	0.05	0.8	1.0	0.6	0.7	0.8	0.4
Long-term debt/Total assets (%)	24	21	25	23	18	22	25	15	18	26	15	17	27	17	19
Total debt ratio (%)*	43	37	41	42	36	39	44	31	34	48	32	33	48	34	37
Times interest earned	4.0	7.2	12.2	4.6	7.5	12.7	4.8	7.6	13.3	4.2	10.1	14.9	3.6	11.0	9.8
Cash flow/Long-term debt (%)	54	52	43	61	70	55	65	84	71	57	88	79	51	80	73
Cash flow/Total debt (%)*	23	29	26	25	35	32	25	39	38	20	40	40	20	38	38
Total asset turnover	1.2	1.2	1.2	1.2	1.4	1.4	1.2	1.5	1.6	1.2	1.3	1.5	1.1	1.3	1.4
Net profit margin (%)	3.95	5.36	6.3	4.42	5.58	5.8	4.77	5.12	6.0	3.84	5.73	6.3	3.75	6.16	6.17
Return on assets (%)	4.64	6.46	7.4	5.10	7.98	8.0	5.80	7.47	8.7	4.41	7.66	8.7	3.97	7.90	8.89

*Total debt is defined as long-term debt plus current liabilities.

PROBLEM CC–2

Forecasting Future Income, and What-If Analysis

CHECK
(a) Oper. inc., $812.58
(c) 1. $0.34/sh. incr.

Refer to the financial statement data of ABEX Chemicals, Inc., reproduced in Case 10–5.

Required:

a. Prepare a forecast of ABEX's total operating income for Year 10. (*Hint:* Refer to forecast data for volume, price, and cost.)

b. Identify additional information necessary to prepare a forecast of earnings per share (EPS) for Year 10, and identify five primary sources where you can obtain this information (you should identify *primary* sources and not necessarily external sources for the information needed).

c. Forecast and explain incremental changes in ABEX's earnings per share based on each of the following two independent scenarios for the petrochemical division only.
   (1) Price of polyethylene in Year 10 is 8% higher than shown in the selected key statistics.
   (2) Volume of production and sales of polyethylene is 8% higher than shown in the selected key statistics.

(CFA Adapted)

PROBLEM CC–3

Analysis of Bond Investment, Ratio Analysis, and Financial Distress

You are the portfolio manager of a high-yield bond portfolio at Solomon Group.

Florida Gypsum Corporation

You are concerned about the financial stability of **Florida Gypsum Corporation** (FGC), whose bonds represent one of the holdings in your portfolio at the *middle of Year 6*. The bonds you hold, 13.25% senior subordinated debentures due in Year 16, were issued at par in Year 5, and are currently priced in your portfolio at 53. Your high-yield bond sales staff is not optimistic they can even develop a bid at that level. FGC is a large producer of gypsum products, accounting for approximately one-third of total gypsum sales. The company also manufactures ceiling tile, caulks, sealants, floor and wall adhesives, and other specialty building products.

In Year 5, FGC did a leveraged recapitalization of its balance sheet. This involved paying a large dividend to common shareholders financed with several new subordinated debt financings, including the 13.25% debentures that you hold. The company's primary competitor, American Gypsum, is highly leveraged, following its acquisition by a large Canadian company. Due to a downturn in residential and commercial construction activity beginning in Year 4, demand for gypsum wallboard fell off through the middle of Year 6. However, capacity continues to expand at a rate of nearly 2% per year. As a result, capacity utilization has declined to 85% currently, from 87% in Year 4 and a peak of 95% in Years 1 and 2. The price of wallboard, which peaked in Year 2, has subsequently declined by more than 30%.

To help you in analyzing FGC's prospects, you assemble various financial data that follow. The director of fixed income research at Solomon Group suggests that you look carefully at ratios of short-term liquidity and operating performance, specifically the quick ratio, accounts receivable turnover ratio, inventory turnover ratio, and operating profit margin. You prepare the table below and schedule a meeting with the director to discuss what the firm should do with FGC.

FLORIDA GYPSUM CORPORATION
Selected Liquidity and Operating Performance Ratios

	YEAR ENDED		Six Months Ended
	Year 4	Year 5	Mid-Year 6
Quick (acid-test) ratio..............	0.73	0.78	0.77
Accounts receivable turnover.......	8.9	8.1	7.4
Inventory turnover.......................	11.4	12.4	13.3
Operating profit margin*.............	16.6%	13.3%	14.9%

*Computed before interest and taxes.

Financial statement data for Florida Gypsum Corporation include the following:

FLORIDA GYPSUM CORPORATION
Balance Sheets

($ millions)	End of Year 4	End of Year 5	At middle of Year 6
Assets			
Current assets			
Cash & cash equivalents	$ 31.3	$ 250.0	$ 95.6
Accounts receivable	274.1	278.3	320.4
Inventories	144.1	124.6	128.4
Net assets of discontinued operations	415.1	20.4	—
Total current assets	864.6	673.3	544.4
Property, plant & equipment, net	909.0	906.4	878.4
Purchased goodwill	148.9	146.5	144.5
Other assets	35.0	95.0	90.0
Total assets	$1,957.5	$1,821.2	$1,657.3
Liabilities and shareholders' equity			
Current liabilities			
Commercial paper & notes payable	$ 38.3	$ 1.3	$ 1.6
Accounts payable	141.6	125.4	125.2
Accrued expenses	188.2	256.9	244.0
Other current liabilities	14.8	38.7	13.7
Current portion of long-term debt	33.0	259.3	154.5
Total current liabilities	415.9	681.6	539.0
Long-term debt	724.9	2,384.3	2,344.0
Deferred income tax	194.1	206.2	212.6
Minority interest	12.8	20.0	22.0
Shareholders' equity	609.8	(1,470.9)	(1,460.3)
Total liabilities and shareholders' equity	$1,957.5	$1,821.2	$1,657.3

FLORIDA GYPSUM CORPORATION
Income Statements

($ millions)	YEAR ENDED Year 4	YEAR ENDED Year 5	Six Months Ended Mid-year 6
Net sales	$2,254.4	$2,248.0	$1,107.7
Cost of goods sold	(1,598.6)	(1,671.9)	(841.4)
Gross profit	655.8	576.1	266.3
Selling and administrative expenses	(268.7)	(253.7)	(122.9)
Interest expense	(69.2)	(178.3)	(148.9)
Interest income	5.3	12.7	4.8
Recapitalization & restructuring expenses	(53.4)	(20.0)	—
Other expenses, net	34.3	(15.9)	17.0
Pretax earnings from continuing operations	304.1	120.9	16.3
Income taxes	(130.9)	(48.2)	(5.9)
Earnings from continuing operations	$ 173.2	$ 72.7	$ 10.4

FLORIDA GYPSUM CORPORATION
Selected Cash Flow Data

($ millions)	YEAR ENDED		Six Months Ended
	Year 4	Year 5	Mid-year 6
Cash Flow from Operations			
Earnings from continuing operations	$173.2	$ 72.7	$ 10.4
Depreciation, depletion & amortization	76.6	83.0	42.5
Noncash interest expense.....................................	—	19.1	22.3
Minority interest	13.2	9.1	4.0
Deferred income taxes	1.5	12.6	6.4
Other noncash items relating to operations..........	15.2	(6.1)	(11.7)
(Increase) decrease in noncash working capital...	43.8	91.8	(84.1)
Other cash flows from operations.........................	(24.0)	(62.0)	3.9
Total net cash flow from operations.....................	$299.5	$220.2	$ (6.3)
Net Liquid Balance			
Cash and cash equivalents	$ 31.3	$250.0	$ 95.6
Less current notes payable..................................	(38.3)	(1.3)	(1.6)
Less current portion of long-term debt	(33.0)	(259.3)	(154.5)
Net liquid balance	$ (40.0)	$ (10.6)	$ (60.5)
Net liquid balance as percent of total assets	(2.0)%	(0.6)%	(3.7)%

Required:

CHECK

(*b*) Examine CFO,
Net liquid bal.,
Times int. earned,
ROA, ROCE

a. The director of fixed income research subsequently argues that the four ratios computed do not reveal important changes in the financial condition of FGC. Discuss limitations of these ratios in assessing the liquidity and operating performance of a company like FGC.

b. Identify at least two better measures of short-term liquidity and operating performance for FGC. Calculate their values and discuss their trend over the period Year 4 through middle of Year 6. Explain why these measures better reflect FGC's liquidity and operating performance.

c. Based on the analysis performed in (*b*) and on the background information provided, recommend and justify whether you should attempt to sell the FGC bonds, retain them, or buy more FGC bonds.

(CFA Adapted)

CASES

CASE CC–1

*Comprehensive
Financial Analysis*

Select a company from a nonregulated industry for which you can obtain complete financial statements for at least the most recent six years.

Required:

Based on these financial statements, the company's background, industry statistics, and other market and company information, prepare a financial statement analysis report covering the following points:

a. Executive summary of the company and its industry.

b. Detailed evaluation of:
   (1) Short-term liquidity (current debt-paying ability).
   (2) Cash forecasting and pro forma analysis.
   (3) Capital structure and solvency.
   (4) Return on invested capital.
   (5) Asset turnover (utilization).

   (6) Profitability and equity analysis.
   Note: You are expected to use a variety of financial analysis tools in answering (*b*). Your analysis should yield inferences for each of these six areas.

c. Comment on the usefulness of the financial statements of this company for your analysis.

d. How did accounting principles used in the financial statements affect your analytical measures?

e. Prepare a forecast of the income statement, balance sheet, and statement of cash flows for a five-year horizon and a terminal year in Year 6.

f. Estimate the value of your company's common stock per share using the valuation analysis and procedures described in the Comprehensive Case.

The financial statements and notes of ZETA Corporation are reproduced over the next several pages.

CASE CC–2
Comprehensive Financial Analysis

Required:

Answer the following questions and provide supporting calculations. Explain the accounts and amounts used in each analysis.

a. What transactions and events explain the $7,000 increase in stockholders' equity for Year 6?

b. Note 6 discloses "capitalized lease obligations" of $1,000. What accounts are increased in Year 6, and by what amounts, to reflect these leases? Explain. How are these leases reflected in the statement of cash flows?

CHECK
(c) Repaid $2,500

c. Use T-account analysis to determine how much long-term debt is paid in Year 6. Does your answer agree with the amount reported by ZETA?

d. Note 1 describes a change in accounting principle.
  (1) What effect did this change in accounting have on the Year 6 balance sheet and income statement?
  (2) Describe the necessary adjustments in the Year 5 balance sheet and income statement for an effective comparison of Year 5 with Year 6.
  (3) How would the $1,000 "cumulative effect" for Year 6 be reported in a statement of cash flows (direct method). (*Hint:* Reconstruct the accounts and amounts affected to record the $1,000 effect.)

e. Note 3 describes ZETA's acquisition of TRO Company.
  (1) Is TRO a separate legal entity at December 31, Year 6, or is it dissolved into ZETA?
  (2) What effect did the acquisition of TRO Company have at December 31, Year 6 (date of acquisition), on the:
     i. ZETA balance sheet?
     ii. Consolidated balance sheet?
  (3) What are TRO's revenues for Year 6?

CHECK
(e) 3. $19,000

ZETA CORPORATION
Consolidated Balance Sheets
As of December 31, Year 6 and Year 5

($ thousands)	Year 6	Year 5
Assets		
Current assets		
Cash	$ 2,000	$ 2,000
Receivables	25,000	20,000
Inventories (notes 1 and 2)	56,000	38,000
Prepaid expenses	1,000	1,000
Total current assets	84,000	61,000
Investment in associated companies	14,000	11,000
Property, plant, and equipment	61,000	52,000
Less: accumulated depreciation	(23,000)	(19,000)
Net property, plant, and equipment	38,000	33,000
Goodwill	2,000	—
Total assets	$138,000	$105,000

(continued)

(concluded)

($ thousands)	Year 6	Year 5
Liabilities and Stockholders' Equity		
Current liabilities		
Notes payable to banks	$ 16,000	$ 14,000
Accounts payable and accruals	29,000	23,000
Income taxes payable	7,000	2,000
Current portion of long-term debt (note 6)	2,000	1,000
Total current liabilities	54,000	40,000
Long-term debt (note 6)	25,000	15,200
Deferred income taxes (note 5)	3,600	2,000
Minority interest	1,400	800
Stockholders' equity (note 7)		
Common stock, $5 par value	5,500	5,000
Paid-in capital	24,500	15,000
Retained earnings	24,000	27,000
Total stockholders' equity	54,000	47,000
Total liabilities and stockholders' equity	$138,000	$105,000

ZETA CORPORATION
Consolidated Income Statement
For Years Ended December 31, Year 6 and Year 5

($ thousands)	Year 6	Year 5
Net sales	$186,000	$155,000
Equity in income (loss) of associated companies	2,000	(1,000)
Expenses		
Cost of sales	120,000	99,000
Selling and administrative expenses	37,000	33,000
Interest expense	10,000	6,000
Total costs and expenses	167,000	138,000
Income before taxes and minority interest	21,000	16,000
Income tax expense (note 5)	10,000	7,800
Income before minority interest	11,000	8,200
Minority interest	200	—
Income from continuing operations	10,800	8,200
Discontinued operations (note 4)		
Operations, net of tax	(1,100)	(1,200)
Loss on disposal, net of tax	(700)	—
Total gain (loss) from discontinued operations	(1,800)	(1,200)
Income before cumulative effect of accounting change	9,000	7,000
Cumulative effect of change in accounting, net of tax (note 1)	1,000	—
Net income	$ 10,000	$ 7,000
Pro forma income (change in accounting is applied retroactively):		
Income from continuing operations	$ 10,800	$ 8,500
Discontinued operations	(1,800)	(1,200)
Total pro forma net income	$ 9,000	$ 7,300

f. For the asset "Investment in associated companies":
   (1) Explain all changes during Year 6.
   (2) Identify all effects in the statement of cash flows relating to this investment.

g. For the "Minority interest" reported in the balance sheet:
   (1) Explain all changes during Year 6.
   (2) Show how this account relates to the asset "Investment in associated companies."

CHECK
(h) $750 incr.

h. If the FIFO method of inventory valuation is used (instead of LIFO), how much would Year 6 net income be increased or decreased?

i. Note 4 describes "discontinued operations":
   (1) What accounts (and amounts) are effected on October 31, Year 6, to record the loss on disposal?
   (2) What effect did the loss on disposal of $700 have on the statement of cash flows? (Identify specific items and amounts.)
   (3) How should the discontinued operation and $1,100 operating loss be reported in a statement of cash flows using the direct format, assuming we desire to include these operations among cash inflows and outflows?

j. How is goodwill reflected in the Year 7 (next year) statement of cash flows?

k. Explain all changes during Year 6 in the Net Property, Plant, and Equipment account.

ZETA CORPORATION
Consolidated Statement of Cash Flows
For Years Ended December 31, Year 6 and Year 5

($ thousands)		Year 6	Year 5
Cash provided from (used for) operations			
Net income		$ 10,000	$ 7,000
Add (deduct) adjustments to cash basis:			
Depreciation		6,000	4,000
Deferred income taxes		1,600	1,000
Minority interest		200	—
Undistributed income of associated companies		(1,400)	1,300
Loss on discontinued operations		700	—
Increase in accounts receivable (5,000 − 2,000†)		(3,000)	(2,400)
Increase in inventories (18,000 + 100* − 2,200†)		(15,900)	(6,000)
Increase in prepaid expenses		—	(200)
Increase in accounts payable and accruals			
(6,000 − 300* − 3,200†)		2,500	2,000
Increase in income taxes payable (5,000 + 700)*		5,700	1,000
Net cash provided from (used for) operations		6,400	7,700
Cash provided from (used for) investing activities			
Additions to property, plant, and equipment		(6,500)	(5,800)
Acquisition of TRO Company (excluding cash of $4,200):			
Property, plant, and equipment	$(6,000)		
Goodwill	(2,000)		
Long-term debt	4,800		
Minority interest	400		
Current assets (receivables and inventories)	(4,200)		
Current liabilities	3,200	(3,800)	—
Investment in associated companies		(1,600)	—
Proceeds from disposal of equipment		500	—
Net cash used for investing activities		(11,400)	(5,800)

(continued)

(concluded)

($ thousands)	Year 6	Year 5
Cash provided from (used for) financing		
Issuance of long-term debt	7,500	5,000
Reduction in long-term debt	(1,500)	(1,000)
Dividends paid	(3,000)	(2,000)
Increase (decrease) in notes payable to bank	2,000	(3,500)
Net cash provided from (used for) financing activities	5,000	(1,500)
Net increase (decrease) in cash‡	$ 0	$ 400

* Adjustments of noncash transactions arising from discontinued operations (see note 4).
† Adjustments relating to acquisition of TRO Co (note 3).
‡ Supplemental disclosures of cash flow information:

	Year 6	Year 5
Cash paid for interest	10,000	6,000
Cash paid for income taxes	2,600	4,800

  Schedule of noncash activities:
    Capital lease of $1,000 incurred on the lease of equipment

ZETA CORPORATION
Notes to Consolidated Financial Statements ($ thousands)

Note 1: Change in accounting principle
During Year 6, the company broadened its definition of overhead costs to be included in the determination of inventories to more properly match costs with revenues. The effect of the change in Year 6 is to increase income from continuing operations by $400. The adjustment of $1,000 (after reduction for income taxes of $1,000) for the cumulative effect for prior years is shown in the net income for Year 6. The pro forma amounts show the effect of retroactive application of the revised inventory costing assuming that the new method had been in effect for all prior years.

Note 2: Inventories
Inventories are priced at cost (principally last-in, first-out [LIFO] method of determination) not in excess of replacement market. If the first-in, first-out (FIFO) method of inventory accounting had been used, inventories would have been $6,000 and $4,500 higher than reported at December 31, Year 6, and December 31, Year 5, respectively.

Note 3: Acquisition of TRO Company
Effective December 31, Year 6, the company purchased most of the outstanding common stock of TRO Company for $8,000 in cash. The excess of the acquisition cost over fair value of the net assets acquired, $2,000, will be recorded as goodwill and not amortized. The following unaudited supplemental pro forma information shows the condensed results of operations as though TRO Company had been acquired as of January 1, Year 5.

	Year 6	Year 5
Revenues	$205,000	$172,000
Net income	10,700	7,400

Details of acquisition (resources and obligations assumed):

Cash	$4,200
Accounts Receivable	2,000
Inventories	2,200
Property, Plant & Equipment	6,000
Long-Term Debt	4,800
Accounts Payable & Accruals	3,200

Note 4: Discontinued operations

As of October 31, Year 6, the board of directors adopted a plan authorizing the disposition of the assets and business of its wholly owned subsidiary, Zachary Corporation. The "Loss on Disposal" is $700 (net of income tax credits of $700) and is based upon the estimated realizable value of the assets to be sold plus a provision for costs of $300 for operating the business until its expected disposition in early Year 7. Property, plant, and equipment is reduced by $1,000 and inventories are reduced by $100 to net realizable value. The provision for costs of $300 is included in "Accounts payable and accruals" and is reduced to $200 at year-end. Net sales of the operations to be discontinued are $18,000 in Year 6 and $23,000 in Year 5.

Note 5: Income taxes

The income tax expense consists of the following:

	Year 6	Year 5
Current	$ 8,400	$6,800
Deferred	1,600	1,000
Total	$10,000	$7,800

The effective tax rates of 47.6% and 48.8% for Year 6 and Year 5, respectively, differ from the statutory federal income tax rate of 50% due to research and development tax credits of $500 in Year 6 and $200 in Year 5. Deferred taxes result from the use of accelerated depreciation methods for income tax reporting and the straight-line method for financial reporting.

Note 6: Long-term debt

	Year 6	Year 5
10% promissory notes to institutional investors payable in annual installments of $900 through Year 10	$13,000	$13,900
Unsecured notes to banks—interest 1% over prime	4,000	—
Capitalized lease obligations—payable to Year 9 with an average interest rate of 8%	1,000	—
11% subordinated note payable in annual installments of $500 from Year 7 through Year 16	5,000	—
Other mortgages and notes	4,000	2,300
	27,000	16,200
Less current maturities	2,000	1,000
Total long-term debt	$25,000	$15,200

The various loan agreements place certain restrictions on the corporation including the payment of cash dividends on common stock and require the maintenance of working capital, as defined, of not less than $18,000. Approximately $10,000 of retained earnings is available for payment of cash dividends on common stock at December 31, Year 6. The corporation entered into several long-term noncancelable leases of equipment during Year 6 which have been capitalized for financial reporting. There are no other significant lease arrangements.

Note 7: Stockholders' equity

The corporation has 5 million shares of authorized common stock, par value $5. There are 1 million shares outstanding at December 31, Year 5, and this is increased by a 10% dividend payable in common stock during Year 6. The changes in retained earnings are as follows:

	Year 6	Year 5
Beginning balance	$ 27,000	$22,000
Add net income.......................	10,000	7,000
Less cash dividends	(3,000)	(2,000)
Less 10% stock dividend........	(10,000)	—
Ending balance	$ 24,000	$27,000

CASE CC–3

Comprehensive Analysis of Equity Investments

Coca-Cola Company
Coca-Cola Enterprises

The Policy Committee of your company decides to change investment strategies. This change entails an increase in exposure to the stocks of large companies producing consumer products dominated by leading brands. The committee decides the soft drink industry, specifically **Coca-Cola Company** (KO) and **Coca-Cola Enterprises** (CCE) qualify as potential purchases for your company's portfolio. As the company's beverage industry expert, you must prepare a financial analysis of these two soft drink producers.

KO owns the brands included in its broad product line. Its marketing efforts center on worldwide advertising promoting these soft drinks. KO manufactures primarily soft drink extract. The production process requires only low-cost raw materials and relatively limited fixed asset investment. Extract is inexpensive to ship and requires limited numbers of production facilities throughout the world. KO's position as a leading soft drink extract producer is protected by the technical nature of its manufacturing process, the restricted formula for its product, and strong brand names established from over a century of operations. Competition is limited essentially to one competitor, PepsiCo. KO plays almost no direct role in domestic manufacturing and distribution beyond the output of soft drink extract.

CCE's business is also dominated by soft drinks. CCE purchases extract from KO and transforms it into completed products sold in a wide variety of retail outlets throughout the United States. This costly, complex production and distribution system requires hundreds of plants and warehouses, and thousands of vehicles. Marketing efforts emphasize local promotion. Competition consists of a large number of highly automated, similarly organized companies also manufacturing soft drinks from extract. Selected financial statements and notes for these two companies follow:

Consolidated Balance Sheets
December 31, Year 8

($ millions)	Coca-Cola Company (KO)	Coca-Cola Enterprises (CCE)
Assets		
Current assets		
Cash and cash equivalents	$1,231	$ —
Trade accounts receivable	627	294
Inventories...	779	125
Other current assets	608	69
Total current assets	3,245	488
Other investments		
Investments in affiliates.......................	1,912	—
Other..	478	66
Total other investments	2,390	66
Fixed assets		
Land	117	135
Plant and equipment	2,500	1,561
Other..	293	42
Total fixed assets.................................	2,910	1,738
Less: accumulated depreciation	(1,150)	(558)
Total fixed assets, net..........................	1,760	1,180
Goodwill..	56	2,935
Total assets..	$7,451	$4,669
Liabilities & shareholders' equity		
Current liabilities		
Short-term debt	$1,363	$ 148
Accounts payable..................................	1,081	402
Other current liabilities.........................	425	—
Total current liabilities..........................	2,869	550
Long-term debt	761	2,062
Deferred income taxes...........................	270	222
Other long-term liabilities......................	206	27
Shareholders' equity		
Preferred stock.....................................	300	250
Common stock	3,045	1,558
Total shareholders' equity.....................	3,345	1,808
Total liabilities & shareholders' equity	$7,451	$4,669

Year 8 Consolidated Statements of Income

($ millions except per share data)	Coca-Cola Company (KO)	Coca-Cola Enterprises (CCE)
Revenues..	$8,338	$3,874
Cost of goods sold....................................	(3,702)	(2,268)
Gross profit..	4,636	1,606
Selling & administrative expenses............	(3,038)	(1,225)
Provision for restructuring.......................	—	(27)
Operating profit.......................................	1,598	354
Interest expense......................................	(231)	(211)
Gain on sale of operations.......................	—	104
Equity in income of affiliates..................	48	—
Other income...	167	21
Pretax income...	1,582	268
Income taxes...	(538)	(115)
Net income..	$1,044	$ 153
Preferred cash dividends.........................	(6)	(10)
Income available for common..................	$1,038	$ 143
Earnings per share..................................	$ 2.85	$ 1.03

Data Extracted from Financial Statement Footnotes

Coca-Cola Company (KO)

1. Certain soft drink and citrus inventories are valued on the last-in first-out (LIFO) method. The excess of current costs over LIFO stated values amount to approximately $30 million at December 31, Year 8.
2. The market value of the company's investments in publicly traded equity investees exceed the company's carrying value at December 31, Year 8, by approximately $291 million.
3. The company is contingently liable for guarantees of indebtedness owed by some of its licensees and others, totaling approximately $133 million at December 31, Year 8.
4. Pension plan assets total $496 million. The projected benefit obligation for all plans totals $413 million.

Coca-Cola Enterprises (CCE)

1. Inventory cost is computed principally on the last-in first-out (LIFO) method. At December 31, Year 8, the LIFO reserve is $2,077,000.
2. In December Year 8, the company repurchases for cash various outstanding bond issues. These transactions result in a pretax gain of approximately $8.5 million.
3. The company leases office and warehouse space, and machinery and equipment under lease agreements. At December 31, Year 8, future minimum lease payments under noncancellable operating leases are as follows ($ thousands):

Year 9...............	$11,749
Year 10.............	8,436
Year 11.............	6,881
Year 12.............	4,972
Year 13.............	3,485
Later years	11,181
Total	$46,704

4. Pension plan assets total $197 million. Total projected benefit obligation for all plans is $151 million.

Selected Financial Ratios*
For Year 8

	Coca-Cola Company (KO)	Coca-Cola Enterprises (CCE)
Return on assets	0.16	0.06
Total debt ratio	0.55	0.61
Net profit margin	0.13	0.04
Receivables turnover	13.30	13.18
Property, plant & equipment turnover	4.74	3.28
Return on common equity	0.34	0.09
Current ratio	1.13	0.89
Inventory turnover	4.75	18.14
Long-term debt to equity	0.23	1.14
Gross profit margin	0.56	0.41
Acid-test ratio	0.65	0.53
Asset turnover	1.12	0.83
Times interest earned	7.85	2.27

*For simplicity, ratios are computed using year-end data rather than on Year 8 average data when applicable.

Required:

Use *only* the financial information reproduced here in answering requirements (*a*) and (*b*).

a. Your comparative analysis of these two soft drink companies requires using the ratios reported. You identify four key areas of comparison in your analysis:
   (1) Short-term liquidity.
   (2) Capital structure and solvency.
   (3) Asset utilization.
   (4) Profitability.
   Discuss differences between KO and CCE in each of these four areas.

b. Using the financial statement information, identify *five* adjustments to the financial statements you feel would enhance their comparability and usefulness for financial analysis. For each of your five adjustments, discuss the effects of these adjustments on your answer to (*a*).

(CFA Adapted)

FINANCIAL STATEMENTS

Appendix A contains selections and adaptations from the Form 10-K filings (annual reports) for two companies: Colgate Palmolive and Campbell Soup. Numerous chapter illustrations and assignment materials refer to this information.

Coltage Palmolive Co.   A1–A35

Campbell Soup   A36–A56

- Form 10-K (Annual Report)
- Selected items are number coded from
  1 through 187 for ease in referencing.

Financial Statement

Colgate Palmolive Co.

Management's Discussion and Analysis of Financial Condition and Results of Operations

Executive Overview

Colgate-Palmolive Company seeks to deliver strong, consistent business results and superior shareholder returns by providing consumers, on a global basis, with products that make their lives healthier and more enjoyable.

To this end, the Company is tightly focused on two product segments: Oral, Personal and Home Care; and Pet Nutrition. Within these segments, the Company follows a closely defined business strategy to develop and increase market leadership positions in key product categories. These product categories are prioritized based on their capacity to maximize the use of the organization's core competencies and strong global equities and to deliver sustainable long-term growth.

Operationally, the Company is organized along geographic lines with specific regional management teams having responsibility for the financial results in each region. The Company competes in more than 200 countries and territories worldwide, with established businesses in all regions contributing to the Company's sales and profitability. This geographic diversity and balance helps to reduce the Company's exposure to business and other risks in any one country or part of the world.

The Oral, Personal and Home Care segment is operated through four reportable operating segments, North America, Latin America, Europe/South Pacific and Greater Asia/Africa, which sell to a variety of retail and wholesale customers and distributors. In the Pet Nutrition segment, Hill's also competes on a worldwide basis selling its products principally through the veterinary profession and specialty pet retailers.

On an ongoing basis, management focuses on a variety of key indicators to monitor business health and performance. These indicators include market share, sales (including volume, pricing and foreign exchange components), gross profit margin, operating profit, net income and earnings per share; and measures to optimize the management of working capital, capital expenditures, cash flow and return on capital. The monitoring of these indicators, as well as the Company's corporate governance practices (including the Company's Code of Conduct), are used to ensure that business health and strong internal controls are maintained.

To achieve its financial objectives, the Company focuses the organization on initiatives to drive growth and to fund growth. The Company seeks to capture significant opportunities for growth by identifying and meeting consumer needs within its core categories, in particular by deploying valuable consumer and shopper insights in the development of successful new products regionally which are then rolled out on a global basis. Growth opportunities are enhanced in those areas of the world in which economic development and rising consumer incomes expand the size and number of markets for the Company's products.

The investments needed to fund this growth are developed through continuous, corporate-wide initiatives to lower costs and increase effective asset utilization. The Company also continues to prioritize its investments toward its higher-margin businesses, specifically Oral Care, Personal Care and Pet Nutrition. The Company purchased Tom's of Maine, Inc. in the second quarter of 2006. This acquisition allowed the Company to enter the fast growing health and specialty trade channel where Tom's of Maine toothpaste and deodorant are market leaders. In 2004, the Company completed its acquisition of GABA Holding AG (GABA), a privately owned European oral care company headquartered in Switzerland.

Consistent with the Company's strategy to prioritize higher-margin businesses, in the fourth quarter of 2006 the Company announced its agreement to sell its Latin American and Canadian bleach brands. The transaction closed in Canada during the fourth quarter of 2006. The Latin American transaction is expected to close during the first half of 2007. Also, consistent with this strategy the Company divested its North American and Southeast Asian heavy-duty laundry detergent brands during 2005.

In December 2004, the Company commenced a four-year restructuring and business-building program (the 2004 Restructuring Program) to enhance the Company's global leadership position in its core businesses. As part of this program the Company anticipates the rationalization of approximately one-third of the Company's manufacturing facilities, closure of certain warehousing facilities and an estimated 12% workforce reduction. The cost of implementing the 2004 Restructuring Program is estimated to result in cumulative pretax charges, once all the phases are approved and implemented, totaling between $750 and $900 ($550 and $650 aftertax). Savings are projected to be in the range of $325 and $400 ($250 and $300 aftertax) annually by 2008.

Looking forward into 2007, while the Company expects market conditions to remain highly competitive, the Company believes it is well positioned for continued growth. As further explained in the Outlook section on page 29 of this report, over the long-term, the Company's continued focus on its consumer products business and the strength of its global brand names, its broad international presence in both developed and developing markets, and its strong capital base all position it to take advantage of growth opportunities and to increase profitability and shareholder value.

Results of Operations

Net Sales

Worldwide sales were $12,237.7 in 2006, up 7.5% from 2005 driven by unit volume gains of 5.5%, net selling price increases of 1.5% and a positive foreign exchange impact of 0.5%. Excluding the impact of the 2005 divestment of the Company's heavy-duty laundry detergent business in North America and Southeast Asia, sales increased 9.0% in 2006 on volume growth of 7.0%.

Sales in the Oral, Personal and Home Care segment were $10,568.6 in 2006, up 7.0% from 2005 driven by volume growth of 5.0%, net selling price increases of 1.0% and a positive foreign exchange impact of 1.0%. Excluding the impact of the 2005 divestments of the Company's heavy-duty laundry detergent business in North America and Southeast Asia, sales increased 9.0% on volume growth of 7.0%. The May 2006 acquisition of Tom's of Maine, Inc. did not have a material impact on reported sales, net income and earnings per share for the year ended December 31, 2006.

Sales in Pet Nutrition were $1,669.1 in 2006, up 10.0% from 2005 driven by volume growth of 6.0% and net selling price increases of 4.5%, offset by a 0.5% negative impact of foreign exchange.

In 2005, worldwide sales were $11,396.9. Sales increased 7.5% from 2004 driven by volume gains of 5.5%, an increase in net selling prices of 0.5% and a positive foreign exchange impact of 1.5%.

Gross Profit

Gross profit margin was 54.8% in 2006, 54.4% in 2005 and 55.1% in 2004. In 2006, Gross profit benefited from higher pricing, a continued focus on cost-savings programs and the shift toward higher margin products, which more than offset the impact of higher raw and packaging material costs and increased restructuring charges. Restructuring charges of $196.2 for the year ended December 31, 2006, which related to accelerated depreciation and certain employee termination benefits under the 2004 Restructuring Program, were included in Cost of sales. Cost of sales for the year ended December 31, 2005 included restructuring charges of $100.2. These charges lowered the reported gross profit margin by 160 basis points (bps) and 90 bps in 2006 and 2005, respectively.

The reduction in gross profit margin in 2005 from 2004 was driven by costs associated with the Company's ongoing 2004 Restructuring Program. In 2005, the benefits from higher pricing, the Company's shift towards higher margin oral care products

and cost-savings programs more than offset the impact of higher raw and packaging material costs.

For additional information regarding the Company's 2004 Restructuring Program, refer to "Restructuring Activities" below and Note 4 to the Consolidated Financial Statements.

Selling, General and Administrative Expenses

Selling, general and administrative expenses as a percentage of sales were 35.6% in 2006, 34.4% in 2005, and 34.2% in 2004. The 120 bps increase in 2006 was driven by higher levels of advertising (30 bps), charges related to the Company's 2004 Restructuring Program (40 bps) and incremental stock-based compensation expense recognized as a result of adopting Statement of Financial Accounting Standards (SFAS) No. 123 (Revised 2004), "Share-Based Payment" (SFAS 123R) (60 bps). During 2006, the increase in gross profit margin and other savings programs funded an increase in advertising of 11% to $1,320.3, on top of a 12% increase in 2005, to $1,193.6, supporting new product launches and helping increase market shares throughout the world. Selling, general and administrative expenses as a percentage of sales in 2005 only increased by a net 20 bps despite a 40 bps increase in advertising as ongoing cost-savings programs more than offset increases in shipping and handling costs (30 bps) and selling and marketing costs (10 bps).

Other (Income) Expense, Net

Other (income) expense, net was $185.9, $69.2, and $90.3 in 2006, 2005 and 2004, respectively. The components of Other (income) expense, net are presented below:

	2006	2005	2004
Minority interest	$ 57.5	$ 55.3	$ 47.9
Amortization of intangible assets	16.3	15.6	14.3
Equity (income)	(3.4)	(2.0)	(8.5)
Gains on sales of non-core product lines, net	(46.5)	(147.9)	(26.7)
2004 Restructuring Program	153.1	80.8	65.3
2003 restructuring activities	—	—	2.8
Pension and other retiree benefits	—	34.0	—
Investment losses (income)	(5.7)	19.7	(8.7)
Other, net	14.6	13.7	3.9
Total Other (income) expense, net	$185.9	$ 69.2	$ 90.3

As noted in the preceding table, Other (income) expense, net in 2006 included a gain on the sale of the Company's household bleach business in Canada, which was more than offset by increased restructuring charges related to the Company's 2004 Restructuring Program of $153.1.

Investment losses (income) consisted of gains and losses on foreign currency contracts, principally due to declines and increases in the fair value of foreign denominated deposits which are economic hedges of certain foreign currency debt but do not qualify for hedge accounting.

Other (income) expense, net in 2005 included a gain on the sale of heavy-duty laundry detergent businesses in North America and Southeast Asia, which was partially offset by charges related to the Company's 2004 Restructuring Program and pension and other retiree benefits. The charges associated with certain pension and other retiree benefits were primarily a result of the con-

20

version of one of the Company's international pension plans to a defined contribution plan for all eligible participants and a lump sum payment of normal retirement benefits associated with a retirement plan in the U.S. as required by Statement of Financial Accounting Standard (SFAS) No. 88, "Employers' Accounting for Settlements and Curtailments of Defined Benefit Pension Plans and for Termination Benefits" (SFAS 88).

Other (income) expense, net in 2004 included charges of $65.3 related to the Company's 2004 Restructuring Program and a gain of $26.7 on the sale of certain detergent businesses in Latin America.

Operating Profit

In 2006, Operating profit decreased 2% to $2,160.5 as compared with an increase of 4% in 2005 to $2,215.0 from $2,122.1 in 2004. All years presented benefited from sales growth and cost-saving initiatives. The decrease in 2006 was primarily due to an increase in restructuring charges of $212.6, lower gains on sale of non-core brands of $101.4 and incremental stock-based compensation expense of $69.8 recognized as a result of adopting SFAS 123R, partially offset by a higher gross profit margin.

Gains on sale of non-core product lines of $46.5, $147.9 and $26.7 recognized in 2006, 2005 and 2004, respectively, were more than offset by restructuring charges related to the Company's 2004 Restructuring Program of $395.4, $182.8 and $68.7 in 2006, 2005 and 2004, respectively. In addition, Operating profit included $34.0 of charges related to the remeasurement of certain pension obligations in 2005 and $19.7 of business realignment cost in 2004.

For additional information regarding the Company's 2004 Restructuring Program, refer to "Restructuring Activities" below and Note 4 to the Consolidated Financial Statements.

Interest Expense, Net

Interest expense, net was $158.7 in 2006, compared with $136.0 in 2005 and $119.7 in 2004. Interest expense, net was higher in 2006 due to an increase in average interest rates to approximately 5.0% from approximately 4.0% in 2005. Higher interest rates and higher average debt levels primarily to finance the GABA acquisition resulted in increased interest expense in 2005. In 2004, low interest rates allowed the Company to lower interest expense despite increased debt levels resulting from the GABA acquisition.

Income Taxes

The effective income tax rate was 32.4% in 2006, versus 35.0% in 2005 and 33.7% in 2004. The 2006 effective tax rate was increased as a result of the lower effective tax rate on restructuring charges (80 bps) and decreased by a lower effective tax rate on the sale of the household bleach business in Canada (30 bps).

The 2005 effective tax rate was impacted by $40.9 of income taxes (200 bps) for the incremental repatriation of $780 of foreign earnings related to the American Jobs Creation Act of 2004 (the AJCA) as well as the lower effective tax rate on charges incurred in connection with the Company's 2004 Restructuring Program (130 bps), which in total increased the reported effective tax rate by 330 bps.

Both years benefited from the Company's global tax planning strategies which are reflected principally in overseas earnings being taxed at lower rates.

The impact of the 2004 Restructuring Program on the effective income tax rate for an individual period will depend upon the projects and the related tax jurisdictions involved. The tax benefit derived from the charges incurred in 2006, 2005 and 2004 for the 2004 Restructuring Program was at a rate of 27.6%, 20.6% and 30.1%, respectively. Over its duration, charges associated with the 2004 Restructuring Program are projected to generate tax benefits at a rate between 25% and 30%.

For additional information regarding the Company's income taxes refer to Note 11 to the Consolidated Financial Statements.

Net Income

Net income was $1,353.4 in 2006 or $2.46 per share on a diluted basis compared with $1,351.4 in 2005 or $2.43 per share and $1,327.1 in 2004 or $2.33 per share. Net income in 2006 included $38.2 ($0.07 per share) of gains on the sale of the household bleach business in Canada which was more than offset by $286.3 ($0.52 per share) of charges related to the Company's 2004 Restructuring Program and $48.1 ($0.09 per share) of incremental stock-based compensation charges due to the adoption of SFAS 123R. In 2005, Net income was impacted by a net aftertax charge of $115.2 ($0.21 per share) resulting from restructuring charges, gains on sales of certain non-core brands, income tax expense for the incremental repatriation of foreign earnings related to the AJCA and certain pension charges. Net income in 2004 includes an aftertax charge of $48.0 ($0.09 per share) associated with the initial phase of the 2004 Restructuring Program.

Segment Results

Effective January 1, 2006, the Company modified the geographic reporting structure of its Oral, Personal and Home Care segment in order to address evolving markets and more closely align countries with similar consumer needs and retail trade structures. Management responsibility for Eastern European operations, including Russia, Turkey, Ukraine and Belarus, was transferred to Greater Asia management and responsibility for operations in the South Pacific, including Australia, was transferred to European management. The financial information for 2005 and 2004 has been reclassified to conform to the new reporting structure.

The Company markets its products in over 200 countries and territories throughout the world in two distinct business segments: Oral, Personal and Home Care; and Pet Nutrition. Management evaluates segment performance based on several factors, including Operating profit. The Company uses Operating profit as a measure of operating segment performance because it excludes the impact of corporate-driven decisions related to interest expense and income taxes.

Worldwide Net Sales by Business Segment and Geographic Region

	2006	2005	2004
Oral, Personal and Home Care			
North America[1]	$ 2,590.8	$ 2,509.8	$ 2,378.7
Latin America	3,019.5	2,623.8	2,266.0
Europe/South Pacific	2,952.3	2,845.9	2,759.4
Greater Asia/Africa	2,006.0	1,897.2	1,747.0
Total Oral, Personal and Home Care	10,568.6	9,876.7	9,151.1
Pet Nutrition[2]	1,669.1	1,520.2	1,433.1
Total Net sales	$12,237.7	$11,396.9	$10,584.2

(1) Net sales in the U.S. for Oral, Personal and Home Care were $2,211.2, $2,124.2 and $2,000.3 in 2006, 2005 and 2004, respectively.

(2) Net sales in the U.S. for Pet Nutrition were $897.9, $818.1 and $781.0 in 2006, 2005 and 2004, respectively.

Worldwide Operating Profit by Business Segment and Geographic Region

	2006	2005	2004
Oral, Personal and Home Care			
North America	$ 550.1	$ 545.7	$ 530.1
Latin America	872.9	698.0	627.7
Europe/South Pacific	681.2	619.8	611.5
Greater Asia/Africa	278.7	245.5	237.6
Total Oral, Personal and Home Care	2,382.9	2,109.0	2,006.9
Pet Nutrition	447.9	412.8	389.7
Corporate	(670.3)	(306.8)	(274.5)
Total Operating profit	$2,160.5	$2,215.0	$2,122.1

North America

Net sales in North America increased 3.0% in 2006 to $2,590.8 on 3.5% volume growth and a 0.5% positive impact of foreign exchange, offset by a 1.0% reduction in net selling prices. Net sales, excluding the divested heavy-duty laundry detergent business increased 6.5% on volume gains of 7.0%. The May 2006 acquisition of Tom's of Maine, Inc. contributed 1.0% to North American sales and volume growth. In the U.S., new product activity contributed to growth across categories. Successful new products included Colgate Luminous Mint Twist toothpaste, Colgate 360° manual toothbrush, Softsoap Brand Decorative Collection liquid hand soap, Irish Spring MoistureBlast bar soap, Softsoap Brand Pure Cashmere moisturizing body wash and liquid hand soap, Fabuloso multi-purpose spray cleaner and Palmolive Oxy Plus Odor Eliminator dish liquid. In 2005, Net sales in North America increased 5.5% to $2,509.8 on volume gains of 4.0%, positive foreign exchange of 1.0% and increases in net selling prices of 0.5%. Net sales in 2005, excluding the divested heavy-duty laundry detergent business, increased 8.0% on volume gains of 6.5%.

Operating profit in North America increased 1% in 2006 to $550.1, even after the negative profit impact of the 2005 detergent divestment and increased commercial investment. In 2005, Operating profit in North America increased 3% to $545.7 as increased sales were partially offset by declines in gross profit margin reflecting increased raw and packaging material costs.

Latin America

Net sales in Latin America increased 15.0% in 2006 to $3,019.5 as a result of 10.0% volume growth, 4.0% higher pricing and 1.0% positive impact of foreign exchange. Every country in the region contributed to the very strong volume gains, led by Brazil, Mexico, Venezuela, Central America, Colombia, Argentina and Ecuador. Growth was driven by strong sales of Colgate Total, Colgate Sensitive, Colgate Max Fresh and Colgate Anti-Cavity toothpastes and the recent launch of Colgate 360° manual toothbrush. In other categories, Palmolive Nutri-Milk and Protex Oats bar soaps, Lady Speed Stick Double Defense deodorant, Palmolive Hydra Natura ActiFirm and Extra Dry body lotions and Palmolive Naturals expanded line of hair care products contributed to gains in the region. In 2005, Net sales in Latin America increased 16.0% to $2,623.8 as a result of 7.0% volume growth, increases in net selling prices of 4.0% and a positive foreign exchange impact of 5.0%. Net sales in 2005, excluding divested detergent businesses in Ecuador and Peru, increased 16.5% on volume gains of 7.5%.

Operating profit in Latin America increased 25% to $872.9 in 2006 and increased 11% to $698.0 in 2005. Both years benefited from increased sales and higher gross profit margins, which more than offset the increased level of advertising.

Europe/South Pacific

Net sales in Europe/South Pacific increased 3.5% in 2006 to $2,952.3 as a result of 4.0% volume growth and 0.5% positive impact of foreign exchange, offset by a 1.0% reduction in net selling prices. Net sales in 2006, excluding the 2005 divestments, increased 4.5% on volume gains of 5.0%. Volume gains in Australia, the United Kingdom, Denmark, Spain, Italy, Switzerland, Greece, Ireland, Poland, Hungary, Romania and the GABA business more than offset volume declines in Germany and France due to challenging economic conditions. Successful new products driving these gains included Colgate Time Control, Colgate Max Fresh and Colgate Sensitive Multi-Protection toothpastes. Recent innovations contributing to gains in other categories included Colgate 360° manual toothbrush, Colgate Plax Whitening mouth rinse, Palmolive Pure Cashmere, Palmolive BodYogurt and Palmolive Naturals with Olive Milk shower gels, and Ajax Professional Degreaser and Ajax Professional Double Power spray cleaners. In 2005, Net sales in Europe/South Pacific increased 3.0% to $2,845.9 on 4.5% volume growth, a 0.5% positive impact of foreign exchange and a 2.0% decline in net selling prices. Excluding divestments, Net sales in 2005 increased 3.5% on volume gains of 5.0%. The June 2004 acquisition of GABA contributed 4.0% to European/South Pacific sales and volume growth in 2005.

Operating profit in Europe/South Pacific increased 10% to $681.2 in 2006, as a result of volume growth and ongoing cost-control initiatives partially offset by an increased level of advertising. Operating profit in Europe/South Pacific increased 1% to $619.8 in 2005 reflecting volume growth and increased gross profit margins partially offset by an increased level of advertising.

Greater Asia/Africa

Net sales in Greater Asia/Africa increased 5.5% in 2006 to $2,006.0 on volume gains of 2.5%, an increase in net selling prices of 2.0% and 1.0% positive impact of foreign exchange. Net sales, excluding the divested detergent business in Southeast Asia, increased 10.5% on volume gains of 7.5%. Strong volume gains were achieved in nearly every country in the region led by Malaysia, Thailand, Philippines, Vietnam, India, the Gulf States, South Africa, and Russia and the rest of the countries in the Commonwealth of Independent States. Successful new products driving the oral care growth included Colgate Max Fresh, Colgate Sensitive Multi-Protection, Colgate Anti-Cavity and Darlie Tea Care Mint toothpastes, and Colgate 360° manual toothbrush. New products contributing to growth in other categories in the region included Palmolive Nutri-Milk bar soap, Palmolive Naturals shampoo and conditioner, Protex Deo 12 bar soap and shower gel, and Lady Speed Stick Aloe deodorant. In 2005, Net sales in Greater Asia/Africa increased 8.5% to $1,897.2 on 8.0% volume growth, a 1.0% positive impact of foreign exchange and a 0.5% decline in net selling prices.

Operating profit in Greater Asia/Africa increased 14% in 2006 to $278.7 reflecting increased sales and gross profit margins, partially offset by an increased level of advertising. Operating profit grew 3% in Greater Asia/Africa to $245.5 in 2005 as a result of volume growth, which more than offset an increased level of advertising and higher shipping and handling costs.

Pet Nutrition

Net sales for Hill's Pet Nutrition increased 10.0% in 2006 to $1,669.1 on volume gains of 6.0% and an increase in net selling prices of 4.5%, offset by a 0.5% negative impact of foreign exchange. Strong sales of Science Diet Lamb Meal & Rice Recipe Large Breed dog food, Science Diet Lamb Meal & Rice Recipe Small Bites dog food and Science Diet Indoor Cat food continued to drive growth in the U.S. specialty retail channel. In the U.S. veterinary channel, Prescription Diet j/d Canine, the relaunch of Prescription Diet d/d Canine and Feline foods and a new chicken variety for Prescription Diet Feline r/d and w/d foods contributed to growth. Internationally, growth was strong led by Belgium, Germany, Denmark, Italy, the United Kingdom, Australia, Brazil, Taiwan and Russia. New pet food products contributing to the international growth included Prescription Diet j/d Canine, Prescription Diet Feline Chunks in Gravy pouches and Science Plan Neutered Cat, a new veterinary exclusive product. In 2005, Net sales for Hill's Pet Nutrition increased 6.0% to $1,520.2, driven by volume growth of 4.0%, an increase in net selling prices of 1.5% and positive foreign exchange of 0.5%.

Operating profit grew 9% in 2006 to $447.9 due to increased sales, partially offset by higher advertising spending. Operating profit in Pet Nutrition grew 6% to $412.8 in 2005 as a result of increased sales and gross profit margins, partially offset by higher advertising and increased shipping and handling costs.

Corporate

Operating profit (loss) for the Corporate segment was ($670.3), ($306.8) and ($274.5) for 2006, 2005 and 2004, respectively. Corporate operations include research and development costs, unallocated overhead costs, stock-based compensation related to stock options and restricted stock awards, restructuring and related implementation costs, and gains and losses on sales of non-core brands and assets. The components of Operating profit (loss) for the Corporate segment are presented below:

	2006	2005	2004
Gains on sales of non-core product lines, net	$ 46.5	$ 147.9	$ 26.7
2004 Restructuring Program	(395.4)	(182.8)	(68.7)
Pension and other retiree benefits	—	(24.8)	—
Adoption impact of SFAS 123R	(69.8)	—	—
Unallocated overhead cost and other, net	(251.6)	(247.1)	(232.5)
Total Corporate Operating profit (loss)	$(670.3)	$(306.8)	$(274.5)

The increase in Corporate Operating profit (loss) in 2006 as compared to 2005 was primarily driven by restructuring charges and incremental stock-based compensation, offset by lower gains on the sale of certain non-core brands. In 2005, Corporate operating expenses increased due to restructuring charges and the remeasurement of certain pension obligations as required by SFAS 88, offset by gains on the sale of heavy-duty laundry detergent brands in North America and Southeast Asia.

Restructuring Activities

2004 Restructuring Program

In December 2004, the Company commenced a four-year restructuring and business-building program (the 2004 Restructuring Program) to enhance the Company's global leadership position in its core businesses. As part of this program, the Company anticipates streamlining its global supply chain through the rationalization of approximately one-third of its manufacturing facilities and the closure of certain warehousing facilities and also plans to centralize its purchasing and other business support functions. Business-building initiatives include enhancing and reallocating resources with an increase and upgrade in the sales, marketing and new product organizations in high-potential developing and other key markets, and the consolidation of these organizations in certain mature markets. The 2004 Restructuring Program is expected to result in approximately a 12% workforce reduction.

The cost of implementing the 2004 Restructuring Program is estimated to result in cumulative pretax charges, once all phases are approved and implemented, totaling between $750 and $900 ($550 and $650 aftertax). Savings are projected to be in the range of $325 and $400 ($250 and $300 aftertax) annually by 2008. Over the course of the four-year 2004 Restructuring Program, it is estimated that approximately 50%-60% of the charges will result in cash expenditures. The estimated cost in 2007 is between $175 and $250 ($125 and $175 aftertax). While the Company believes the overall program will be completed within existing estimates, charges and savings may vary in a given year.

During 2004, in connection with the initial phase of the program, the Company announced the closing or reconfiguration of eight manufacturing facilities in North America, Greater Asia/Africa, Europe and Latin America and the realignment of marketing and sales organizations in Europe/South Pacific and Greater Asia/Africa. During 2005, the Company commenced additional projects, the more significant of which related to changes being implemented in its European and North American manufacturing networks. These changes will allow the Company to more cost effectively manufacture toothpaste, taking advantage of state-of-the-art technologies, and obtain cost-savings through the transfer of bar soap manufacturing to an established U.S. third party.

The Company plans to consolidate toothpaste production in Europe, which is currently located at five company sites, into a new state-of-the-art manufacturing facility in Poland. Upon completion of the consolidation project within the next year, toothpaste manufacturing is expected to cease at the Company's facilities in Salford, United Kingdom; Anzio, Italy; Brasov, Romania; Gebze, Turkey; and Halinow, Poland. Other manufacturing activities will continue at these sites, except the Salford facility, which is expected to be closed. In North America, the Company plans to phase down production at its Jeffersonville, Indiana plant with all production expected to cease by January 2008. The plan calls for transferring production of the Company's market leading Colgate Total toothpaste to a new state-of-the-art facility to be built in Morristown, Tennessee, and the relocation of other production and administrative services currently performed at Jeffersonville to other facilities. The Company's Kansas City, Kansas facility, formally the site of U.S. bar soap production, was closed in late 2006 and all production was transitioned to an established U.S. third-party manufacturer.

In 2006, the Company continued with the implementation of previously announced projects, most notably the changes being implemented in its European and North American manufacturing networks. In addition, the Company implemented several new projects including a voluntary early retirement program in the United States, enabling the Company to continue to re-align organizational resources consistent with its business-building goals. Also consistent with it global manufacturing strategy, the Company initiated the closure of its toothbrush facility in Puerto Rico.

For the years ended December 31, 2006, 2005 and 2004 restructuring and implementation related charges are reflected in the following income statement categories:

	2006	2005	2004
Cost of sales	$196.2	$100.2	$ 3.4
Selling, general and administrative expense	46.1	1.8	—
Other (income) expense, net	153.1	80.8	65.3
Total 2004 Restructuring Program charges pretax	$395.4	$182.8	$68.7
Total 2004 Restructuring Program charges aftertax	$286.3	$145.1	$48.0

Restructuring charges, in the preceding table, are recorded in the Corporate segment as these decisions are corporate-driven and are not included in internal measures of segment operating performance.

Total 2006 charges relate to restructuring activities in North America (45%), Europe/South Pacific (19%), Latin America (4%), Greater Asia/Africa (7%), Pet Nutrition (1%) and Corporate (24%). Total program-to-date accumulated charges relate to restructuring activities in North America (39%), Europe/South Pacific (32%), Latin America (4%), Greater Asia/Africa (7%), Pet Nutrition (1%) and Corporate (17%). Since the inception of the 2004 Restructuring Program in December 2004, the Company has incurred total charges of $646.9 ($479.4 aftertax) in connection with the implementation of various projects.

The majority of costs incurred since inception relate to the following significant projects: the voluntary early retirement program in the U.S.; the announced closing of the Jeffersonville, Indiana oral care facility; the consolidation of toothpaste production in Europe; and exiting certain manufacturing activities in other categories in Portugal, Belgium, Denmark, Canada and Kansas City, Kansas.

The following table summarizes the activity for the restructuring charges discussed above and related accrual:

	Termination Benefits	Incremental Depreciation	Asset Impairments	Other	Total
Year Ended December 31, 2006					
Charges	$ 41.6	$ 3.3	$ 22.0	$ 1.8	$ 68.7
Cash payments	(1.4)	—	—	(1.4)	(2.8)
Charges against assets	—	(3.3)	(22.0)	—	(25.3)
Foreign exchange	1.5	—	—	—	1.5
Balance at December 31, 2004	$ 41.7	$ —	$ —	$ 0.4	$ 42.1
Charges	58.6	65.3	30.2	28.7	182.8
Cash payments	(47.8)	—	—	(23.4)	(71.2)
Charges against assets	(11.4)	(65.3)	(30.2)	(6.4)	(113.3)
Other	(1.4)	—	—	4.2	2.8
Foreign exchange	(4.4)	—	—	(0.1)	(4.5)
Balance at December 31, 2005	$ 35.3	$ —	$ —	$ 3.4	$ 38.7
Charges	212.7	91.5	6.6	84.6	395.4
Cash payments	(89.7)	—	—	(75.3)	(165.0)
Charges against assets	(98.4)	(91.5)	(6.6)	(6.7)	(203.2)
Other	(10.0)	—	—	5.2	(4.8)
Foreign exchange	3.5	—	—	0.1	3.6
Balance at December 31, 2006	$ 53.4	$ —	$ —	$ 11.3	$ 64.7

24

Termination benefits are calculated based on long-standing benefit practices, local statutory requirements and, in certain cases, voluntary termination arrangements. Termination benefits incurred pursuant to the 2004 Restructuring Program include pension and other retiree benefit enhancements of $108.4 and $12.8 as of December 31, 2006 and 2005, respectively, and are reflected as Charges against assets and Other charges within Termination Benefits in the preceding table, as the corresponding balance sheet amounts are reflected as a reduction of pension assets and an increase to other retiree benefit liabilities, respectively. During 2006 the Company made an $85.0 voluntary contribution to partially fund this obligation. The Company anticipates that it will make incremental cash contributions to its plans in order to fund these pension obligations over the duration of the 2004 Restructuring Program.

Incremental depreciation was recorded to reflect changes in useful lives and estimated residual values for long-lived assets that will be taken out of service prior to the end of their normal service period. Asset impairments have been recorded to write down assets held for sale or disposal to their fair value based on amounts expected to be realized.

Liquidity and Capital Resources

The Company expects cash flow from operations and existing credit facilities will be sufficient to meet foreseeable business operating and recurring cash needs (including dividends, capital expenditures, planned stock repurchases and restructuring payments). The Company's strong cash-generating capability and financial condition also allow it to access financial markets worldwide.

Cash Flow

Net cash provided by operations in 2006 was $1,821.5 as compared with $1,784.4 in 2005 and $1,754.3 in 2004. The increase in 2006 reflects the Company's improved profitability partially offset by changes in working capital, higher tax payments and increased spending related to the 2004 Restructuring Program.

The Company's working capital as a percentage of sales increased to 2.3% of sales in 2006 as compared with 1.7% of sales in 2005. The Company defines working capital as the difference between current assets (excluding cash and marketable securities, the latter of which is reported in other current assets) and current liabilities (excluding short-term debt). The Company's working capital changes were driven in part by increased inventory levels, higher accounts receivable balances and higher tax payments, offset by higher levels of payables and accruals. Inventory days coverage ratio increased to 69 in 2006 as compared to 61 in 2005, largely as a result of efforts to ensure continued product supply during factory closings related to the 2004 Restructuring Program. Higher balances in accounts receivables were due primarily to higher sales in the fourth quarter of 2006 and a slight increase in days sales outstanding over the prior year, partly due to timing. Higher tax payments were the result of improved profitability as well as the timing of payments. A portion of tax payments for calendar year 2005 were made in 2006, including tax payments of approximately $20 relating to the sale of the Company's Southeast Asian detergent brands in the fourth quarter of 2005.

Investing activities used $620.4 of cash during 2006 compared with uses of $220.7 and $1,090.4 during 2005 and 2004, respectively. The change over 2005 is primarily due to higher payments in 2006 associated with acquisitions versus higher proceeds in 2005 associated with divestitures, along with increased capital spending in 2006.

In 2006, the Company purchased 84% of the outstanding shares of Tom's of Maine, Inc. for approximately $100 plus transaction costs. Additionally, the Company increased its ownership interests in its Poland and Romania subsidiaries to 100% at a cost of approximately $95. In 2005, the Company increased its ownership interests in certain subsidiaries to 100% at a cost of $38.5, primarily related to its Malaysia subsidiary. In 2004, payments for acquisitions pertained to the purchase of 100% of the outstanding shares of GABA.

Consistent with the Company's strategy to prioritize higher margin businesses, investing activities include proceeds from the sale of certain non-core product lines. Investing activities reflect $55.0 of proceeds from the sale of the Company's Canadian bleach brands in 2006 and $215.6 of proceeds from the sale of the Company's Southeast Asian and North American heavy-duty detergent brands in 2005. Investing activities for 2004 include the Company's sale of certain non-core detergent brands in Latin America for an aggregate sales price of $37.0.

Capital expenditures were $476.4, $389.2 and $348.1 for 2006, 2005 and 2004, respectively. Capital spending is trending upwards as a result of the Company's multi-year restructuring and business-building program and continues to focus primarily on projects that yield high aftertax returns. Overall capital expenditures for 2007 are expected to increase to a rate of approximately 5% of Net sales.

Financing activities used $1,059.0 of cash during 2006 compared to $1,524.4 and $611.1 during 2005 and 2004, respectively. Financing activities in 2006 reflect higher proceeds from exercise of stock options, which more than offset an increase in common and preference stock dividend payments as well as higher share repurchases associated with the share repurchase programs authorized by the Board of Directors in 2006 and 2004. Additionally, debt increased $139.1, net of payments, in 2006 versus a decrease of $78.4, net of proceeds, in 2005.

In 2005, financing activities reflect a cash payment of $89.7 to an outside investor as a result of the discontinuation of a financing subsidiary of the Company. The Company previously had a financing subsidiary with outside equity investors, the purpose of which was to purchase some of the Company's receivables thereby giving the Company access to additional sources of capital. The subsidiary, including such receivables, was consolidated and the amounts invested by outside investors were reported as a minority interest.

Dividend payments in 2006 were $677.8, up from $607.2 in 2005 and $536.2 in 2004. Common stock dividend payments increased to $1.25 per share in 2006 from $1.11 per share in 2005 and $0.96 per share in 2004. The Series B Preference Stock dividend payments increased to $10.00 per share in 2006 from $8.88 per share in 2005 and $7.68 per share in 2004. Management currently intends to continue to pay dividends at increasing annual amounts per share from cash provided by operations.

25

The Company repurchases common shares in the open market and in private transactions to maintain its targeted capital structure and to fulfill the requirements of its compensation and benefit plans. In October 2004, the Board of Directors authorized the Company to purchase up to 20 million shares of the Company's common stock through December 31, 2005 (the 2004 Program) and, in December 2005, the Board of Directors extended this authorization through March 31, 2006. The Company completed this program in the first quarter of 2006. In March 2006, the Board of Directors approved a new stock repurchase program (the 2006 Program), under which the Company may purchase up to 30 million common shares. Aggregate repurchases in 2006, including repurchases under the 2004 and 2006 Programs as well as other Board authorizations, were 15.0 million common shares for a total purchase price of $884.7. Aggregate repurchases for 2005 were 15.1 million common shares for a total purchase price of $796.2. Aggregate repurchases for 2004 were 12.4 million common shares for a total purchase price of $637.9.

Long-term debt increased to $3,497.1 as of December 31, 2006 as compared to $3,274.7 as of December 31, 2005 and total debt increased to $3,671.2 as of December 31, 2006 as compared to $3,446.2 as of December 31, 2005. The Company's long-term debt is rated AA– by Standard & Poor's and Aa3 by Moody's Investors Service. During 2005, the Company issued 250 million of Swiss franc-denominated five-year bonds (approximately $205 at the December 31, 2006 exchange rate) at a fixed rate of 1.9%.

Domestic and foreign commercial paper outstanding was $651.6 and $621.8 as of December 31, 2006 and 2005, respectively, and is denominated in U.S. dollars, Swiss francs and Canadian dollars. The maximum commercial paper outstanding during 2006 and 2005 was $1,400 and $1,715, respectively. These borrowings carry a Standard & Poor's rating of A-1+ and a Moody's Investors Service rating of P-1. At December 31, 2006 and 2005, commercial paper and certain current maturities of notes payable totaling $674.0 and $641.9, respectively, are classified as long-term debt, as the Company has the intent and ability to refinance such obligations on a long-term basis, including, if necessary, by utilizing its lines of credit that expire in 2011.

At December 31, 2006, the Company had access to unused domestic and foreign lines of credit of approximately $2,500 and also had $1,417.2 of medium-term notes available for issuance pursuant to an effective shelf registration statement. The Company's domestic lines of credit include a five-year revolving credit facility of $1,500.0 which was extended an additional year in the fourth quarter of 2006 and now expires in November 2011. These domestic lines are available for general corporate purposes and to support commercial paper issuance.

The ESOP notes guaranteed by the Company and certain credit facilities contain cross-default provisions. Noncompliance with these requirements could ultimately result in the acceleration of amounts owed. The Company is in full compliance with all such requirements and believes the likelihood of noncompliance is remote.

The following represents the scheduled maturities of the Company's contractual obligations as of December 31, 2006:

	Payments Due by Period						
	Total	2007	2008	2009	2010	2011	Thereafter
Long-term debt including current portion[1]	$3,463.8	$1,424.5	$163.0	$231.2	$295.4	$ 25.5	$1,324.2
Net cash interest payments on long-term debt[2]	1,615.9	210.9	107.4	95.6	85.5	75.8	1,040.7
Capitalized leases	33.3	26.2	1.1	1.1	1.0	1.0	2.9
Operating leases	529.8	117.0	104.1	87.7	66.7	51.2	103.1
Purchase obligations[3]	864.0	568.8	246.6	38.7	9.6	0.3	—
Total[4]	$6,506.8	$2,347.4	$622.2	$454.3	$458.2	$153.8	$2,470.9

(1) Long-term debt due in 2007 includes $674.0 of commercial paper and certain current maturities of notes payable that have been classified as long-term debt as of December 31, 2006, as the Company has the intent and ability to refinance such obligations on a long-term basis, including, if necessary, by utilizing its unused lines of credit that expire in 2011.

(2) Includes the net interest payments on fixed and variable rate debt and associated interest rate swaps. Interest payments associated with floating rate instruments are based on management's best estimate of projected interest rates for the remaining term of variable rate debt.

(3) The Company has outstanding purchase obligations with suppliers at the end of 2006 for raw, packaging and other materials in the normal course of business. These purchase obligation amounts represent only those items which are based on agreements that are enforceable and legally binding and that specify minimum quantity, price and term and do not represent total anticipated purchases.

(4) Long-term liabilities associated with the Company's postretirement plans are excluded from the table above due to the uncertainty of the timing of these cash disbursements. The amount and timing of cash funding related to these benefit plans will generally depend on local regulatory requirements, various economic assumptions (the most significant of which are detailed in "Critical Accounting Policies and Use of Estimates" below) and voluntary Company contributions. Based on current information, the Company does not anticipate having to make any mandatory contributions to its qualified U.S. pension plan until 2008. Management's best estimate of cash required to be paid directly from the Company's assets for its postretirement plans for the year ending December 31, 2007 is approximately $57. In addition, the Company currently plans to make approximately $50 of voluntary contributions to the U.S. pension plans.

As more fully described in Note 13 to the Consolidated Financial Statements, the Company is contingently liable with respect to lawsuits, environmental matters, taxes and other matters arising in the ordinary course of business. While it is possible that the Company's cash flows and results of operations in a particular period could be materially affected by the one-time impact of the resolution of such contingencies, it is the opinion of management that the ultimate disposition of these matters will not have a material impact on the Company's financial position, or ongoing results of operations and cash flows.

Off-Balance Sheet Arrangements

The Company does not have off-balance sheet financing or unconsolidated special purpose entities.

Managing Foreign Currency, Interest Rate and Commodity Price Exposure

The Company is exposed to market risk from foreign currency exchange rates, interest rates and commodity price fluctuations. Volatility relating to these exposures is managed on a global basis by utilizing a number of techniques, including working capital management, selective borrowings in local currencies and entering into selective derivative instrument transactions, issued with standard features, in accordance with the Company's treasury and risk management policies. The Company's treasury and risk management policies prohibit the use of leveraged derivatives or derivatives for trading purposes.

As the Company markets its products in over 200 countries and territories, it is exposed to currency fluctuations related to manufacturing and selling its products in currencies other than the U.S. dollar. The Company's major foreign currency exposures involve the markets in Europe and certain Latin American countries, although all regions of the world are subject to foreign currency changes versus the U.S. dollar. The Company monitors its foreign currency exposures in these markets through a combination of cost-containment measures, selling price increases and foreign currency hedging of certain costs in an effort to minimize the impact on earnings of foreign currency rate movements.

The Company primarily utilizes currency forward contracts, cross-currency interest rate swaps, local currency deposits and local currency borrowings to hedge portions of its exposures relating to foreign currency purchases and assets and liabilities created in the normal course of business. From time to time, the Company hedges certain of its forecasted foreign currency transactions using forward contracts with durations no greater than 18 months.

Interest rate swaps and debt issuances are utilized to manage the Company's targeted mix of fixed and floating rate debt and to minimize significant fluctuations in earnings and cash flows that may result from interest rate volatility.

The Company is exposed to price volatility related to raw materials used in production. Futures contracts are used on a limited basis to manage volatility related to anticipated raw material inventory purchases. In 2006, the results of the Company's commodity hedging activities were not material.

The Company is exposed to credit loss in the event of nonperformance by counterparties to the financial instrument contracts held by the Company; however, nonperformance by these counterparties is considered remote as it is the Company's policy to contract with diversified counterparties that have a long-term debt rating of AA–/Aa3 or higher.

Value at Risk

The Company's risk management procedures include the monitoring of interest rate and foreign exchange exposures and hedge positions utilizing statistical analyses of cash flows, market value and sensitivity analysis. However, the use of these techniques to quantify the market risk of such instruments should not be construed as an endorsement of their accuracy or the accuracy of the related assumptions. Market exposures are evaluated using a value-at-risk (VAR) model and an earnings-at-risk (EAR) model that are intended to measure the maximum potential loss in interest rate and foreign exchange financial instruments, assuming adverse market conditions occur, given a 95% confidence level. Historical interest rates and foreign exchange rates are used to estimate the volatility and correlation of future rates.

The estimated maximum potential one-day loss in fair value of interest rate or foreign exchange rate instruments, calculated using the VAR model, is not material to the consolidated financial position, results of operations or cash flows of the Company in 2006 and 2005. The estimated maximum yearly loss in earnings due to interest rate or foreign exchange rate instruments, calculated utilizing the EAR model, is not material to the Company's results of operations in 2006 and 2005. Actual results in the future may differ materially from these projected results due to actual developments in the global financial markets.

For information regarding the Company's accounting policies for financial instruments and description of financial instrument activities, refer to Notes 2 and 7 to the Consolidated Financial Statements.

Recent Accounting Pronouncements

In June 2006, the Financial Accounting Standards Board (FASB) issued FASB Interpretation No. 48, "Accounting for Uncertainty in Income Taxes — an interpretation of FASB Statement No. 109" (FIN 48), which prescribes accounting for and disclosure of uncertainty in tax positions. This interpretation defines the criteria that must be met for the benefits of a tax position to be recognized in the financial statements and the measurement of tax benefits recognized. The provisions of FIN 48 are effective as of the beginning of the Company's 2007 fiscal year, with the cumulative effect of the change in accounting principle recorded as an adjustment to opening retained earnings. The Company is currently finalizing its analysis of the impact on the Consolidated Financial Statements of adopting FIN 48 and believes that the impact, if any, will not be material.

Refer to Note 2 to the Consolidated Financial Statements for further discussion of recent accounting pronouncements.

Critical Accounting Policies and Use of Estimates

The preparation of financial statements requires management to use judgment and make estimates. The level of uncertainty in estimates and assumptions increases with the length of time until the underlying transactions are completed. Actual results could ultimately differ from those estimates. The accounting policies that are most critical in the preparation of the Company's Consolidated Financial Statements are those that are both important to the presentation of the Company's financial condition and results of operations and require significant or complex judgments and estimates on the part of management. The Company's critical accounting policies are reviewed periodically with the Audit Committee of the Board of Directors.

In certain instances, accounting principles generally accepted in the United States of America allow for the selection of alternative accounting methods. The Company's significant policies that involve the selection of alternative methods are accounting for shipping and handling costs and inventories.

■ Shipping and handling costs may be reported as either a component of cost of sales or selling, general and administrative expenses. The Company reports such costs, primarily related to warehousing and outbound freight, in the Consolidated Statements of Income as a component of Selling, general and administrative expenses. Accordingly, the Company's gross profit margin is not comparable with the gross profit margin of those companies that include shipping and handling charges in cost of sales. If such costs had been included in cost of sales, gross profit margin as a percent of sales would have decreased by 770 bps from 54.8% to 47.1% in 2006 and decreased by 750 bps and 720 bps in 2005 and 2004, respectively, with no impact on reported earnings.

■ The Company accounts for inventories using both the first-in, first-out (FIFO) method (approximately 80% of inventories) and the last-in, first-out (LIFO) method (approximately 20% of inventories). There would have been no impact on reported earnings for 2006, 2005 and 2004 had all inventories been accounted for under the FIFO method.

The areas of accounting that involve significant or complex judgments and estimates are pensions and other postretirement benefits, stock options, asset impairment, tax valuation allowances, and legal and other contingencies.

■ In pension accounting, the most significant actuarial assumptions are the discount rate and the long-term rate of return on plan assets. The discount rate for U.S. plans was 5.80%, 5.50% and 5.75% as of December 31, 2006, 2005 and 2004, respectively. Discount rates used for the U.S. defined benefit and other postretirement plans are based on a yield curve constructed from a portfolio of high-quality bonds for which the timing and amount of cash outflows approximate the estimated payouts of the U.S. plans. For the Company's international plans, the discount rates are set by benchmarking against investment-grade corporate bonds rated AA or better. The assumed long-term rate of return on plan assets for U.S. plans was 8.0% as of December 31, 2006, 2005 and 2004. In determining the long-term rate of return, the Company considers the nature of the plans' investments, an expectation for the plans' investment strategies and the historical rate of return. The historical rate of return for the U.S. plans for the most recent 15-year period was 9%. In addition, the current rate of return assumption for the U.S. plans is based upon a targeted asset allocation of approximately 33% in fixed income securities (which are expected to earn approximately 6% in the long-term), 63% in equity securities (which are expected to earn approximately 9.25% in the long-term) and 4% in real estate and other (which are expected to earn approximately 6% in the long-term).

A 1% change in either the discount rate or the assumed rate of return on plan assets of the U.S. pension plans would cumulatively impact future Net income by approximately $10. A third assumption is the long-term rate of compensation, a change in which would partially offset the impact of a change in either the discount rate or the long-term rate of return. This rate was 4.0% as of December 31, 2006, 2005 and 2004. (Refer to Note 10 to the Consolidated Financial Statements for further discussion of the Company's pension and other postretirement plans.)

■ The most judgmental assumption in accounting for other postretirement benefits is the medical cost trend rate. The Company reviews external data and its own historical trends for health care costs to determine the medical cost trend rate. The assumed rate of increase is 10% for 2007, declining 1% per year until reaching the ultimate assumed rate of increase of 5% per year. The effect of a 1% increase in the assumed long-term medical cost trend rate would reduce Net income by approximately $4.

■ Effective January 1, 2006, the Company adopted SFAS 123R, "Share-Based Payment," (SFAS 123R) using the modified prospective method. SFAS 123R requires companies to recognize the cost of employee services received in exchange for awards of equity instruments, such as stock options and restricted stock, based on the fair value of those awards at the date of grant. The Company uses the Black-Scholes-Merton (Black-Scholes) option pricing model to determine the fair value of stock-option awards under SFAS 123R. The weighted average estimated fair value of each stock option granted for the year ended December 31, 2006 was $10.30. The Black-Scholes model uses various assumptions to determine the fair value of options. These assumptions include expected term of options, expected volatility, risk-free interest rate and expected dividend yield. While these assumptions do not require significant judgment, as the significant inputs are determined from independent third-party sources, changes in these inputs however, could result in significant changes in fair value. A one year change in term would result in a 15% change in fair value. A one percent change in volatility would change fair value by 4%.

■ Asset impairment analysis performed for goodwill and intangible assets requires several estimates including future cash flows, growth rates and the selection of a discount rate. Since the estimated fair value of the Company's intangible assets substantially exceeds the recorded book value, significant changes in these estimates would have to occur to result in an impairment charge related to these assets. Asset impairment analysis related to certain fixed assets in connection with the 2004 Restructuring Program requires management's best estimate of net realizable value.

■ Tax valuation allowances are established to reduce tax assets such as tax loss carryforwards, to net realizable value. Factors considered in estimating net realizable value include historical results by tax jurisdiction, carryforward periods, income tax strategies and forecasted taxable income.

■ Legal and other contingency reserves are based on management's assessment of the risk of potential loss, which includes consultation with outside legal counsel and advisors. Such assessments are reviewed each period and revised, based on current facts and circumstances, if necessary. While it is possible that the Company's cash flows and results of operations in a particular quarter or year could be materially affected by the one-time impacts of the resolution of such contingencies, it is the opinion of management that the ultimate disposition of these matters will not have a material impact on the Company's financial position, or ongoing results of operations and cash flows. (Refer to Note 13 to the Consolidated Financial Statements for further discussion of the Company's contingencies.)

The Company generates revenue through the sale of well-known consumer products to trade customers under established trading terms. While the recognition of revenue and receivables requires the use of estimates, there is a short time frame (typically less than 60 days) between the shipment of product and cash receipt, thereby reducing the level of uncertainty in these estimates. (Refer to Note 2 to the Consolidated Financial Statements for further description of the Company's significant accounting policies.)

Outlook

Looking forward into 2007, while the Company expects market conditions to remain highly competitive, it believes it is well positioned for continued growth. It anticipates continuing to prioritize its investments in key categories and markets in order to further strengthen its competitive position and build market share. The 2004 Restructuring Program is designed to enhance the Company's global leadership position in its core businesses. As part of the 2004 Restructuring Program, the Company is in the process of streamlining its global supply chain, reallocating resources with an increase and upgrade in the sales, marketing and new product organizations in high-potential developing and other key markets and the consolidation of these organizations in certain mature markets. The savings and benefits from the 2004 Restructuring Program, along with the Company's other ongoing cost-savings and growth initiatives, are anticipated to provide additional funds for investment in support of key categories and new product development while also supporting an increased level of profitability.

However, as noted above, the Company operates in a highly competitive global marketplace that is experiencing increased trade concentration and industry consolidation. In addition, changes in economic conditions, movements in commodity prices and foreign currency exchange rates can impact future operating results as measured in U.S. dollars. In particular, economic and political uncertainty in some countries in Latin America and changes in the value of Latin American and European currencies may impact the overall results of these regions. Historically, the consumer products industry has been less susceptible to changes in economic growth than many other industries. Over the long-term, the Company's continued focus on its consumer products business and the strength of its global brand names, its broad international presence in both developed and developing markets, and its strong capital base all position it to take advantage of growth opportunities and to increase profitability and shareholder value.

Cautionary Statement on Forward-Looking Statements

In this report we may make statements that constitute or contain "forward-looking" information as that term is defined in the Private Securities Litigation Reform Act of 1995 or by the Securities and Exchange Commission (SEC) in its rules, regulations and releases. Such statements may relate, for example, to sales or volume growth, earnings growth, financial goals, cost-reduction plans, estimated charges and savings associated with the 2004 Restructuring Program, and new product introductions among other matters. These statements are made on the basis of our views and assumptions as of the time the statements are made and we undertake no obligation to update these statements. We caution investors that any such forward-looking statements we make are not guarantees of future performance and that actual results may differ materially from anticipated results or expectations expressed in our forward-looking statements. For some of the factors that could impact our business and cause actual results to differ materially from forward-looking statements see Item 1A–Risk Factors of our Annual Report on Form 10-K for the year ended December 31, 2006 filed with the SEC on February 23, 2007.

Report of Independent Registered Public Accounting Firm

To the Board of Directors and Shareholders of
Colgate-Palmolive Company:

We have completed integrated audits of Colgate-Palmolive
Company's consolidated financial statements and of its internal
control over financial reporting as of December 31, 2006, in
accordance with the standards of the Public Company Accounting Oversight Board (United States). Our opinions, based on our
audits, are presented below.

Consolidated financial statements

In our opinion, the accompanying consolidated balance sheets
and the related consolidated statements of income, retained
earnings, comprehensive income and changes in capital
accounts and cash flows present fairly, in all material respects, the
financial position of Colgate-Palmolive Company and its subsidiaries at December 31, 2006 and 2005, and the results of their
operations and their cash flows for each of the three years in the
period ended December 31, 2006 in conformity with accounting
principles generally accepted in the United States of America.
These financial statements are the responsibility of the Company's
management. Our responsibility is to express an opinion on these
financial statements based on our audits. We conducted our
audits of these statements in accordance with the standards of
the Public Company Accounting Oversight Board (United States).
Those standards require that we plan and perform the audit to
obtain reasonable assurance about whether the financial statements are free of material misstatement. An audit of financial
statements includes examining, on a test basis, evidence supporting the amounts and disclosures in the financial statements,
assessing the accounting principles used and significant estimates
made by management, and evaluating the overall financial
statement presentation. We believe that our audits provide a
reasonable basis for our opinion.

As disclosed in Note 2, the Company changed the manner
in which it accounts for share-based payment upon adoption of
the accounting guidance of Statement of Financial Accounting
Standards No. 123(R) on January 1, 2006. In addition, as disclosed
in Note 2, the Company changed the manner in which it
accounts for defined benefit pension and other post retirement
plans upon adoption of the accounting guidance of Statement of
Financial Accounting Standards No. 158 on December 31, 2006.

Internal control over financial reporting

Also, in our opinion, management's assessment, included in the
accompanying Management's Report on Internal Control over
Financial Reporting, that the Company maintained effective internal control over financial reporting as of December 31, 2006
based on criteria established in *Internal Control—Integrated
Framework* issued by the Committee of Sponsoring Organizations of the Treadway Commission (COSO), is fairly stated, in
all material respects, based on those criteria. Furthermore, in
our opinion, the Company maintained, in all material respects,

effective internal control over financial reporting as of December
31, 2006, based on criteria established in *Internal Control—
Integrated Framework* issued by the COSO. The Company's management is responsible for maintaining effective internal control
over financial reporting and for its assessment of the effectiveness
of internal control over financial reporting. Our responsibility is to
express opinions on management's assessment and on the effectiveness of the Company's internal control over financial reporting
based on our audit. We conducted our audit of internal control
over financial reporting in accordance with the standards of the
Public Company Accounting Oversight Board (United States).
Those standards require that we plan and perform the audit to
obtain reasonable assurance about whether effective internal
control over financial reporting was maintained in all material
respects. An audit of internal control over financial reporting
includes obtaining an understanding of internal control over
financial reporting, evaluating management's assessment, testing
and evaluating the design and operating effectiveness of internal
control, and performing such other procedures as we consider
necessary in the circumstances. We believe that our audit
provides a reasonable basis for our opinions.

A company's internal control over financial reporting is a
process designed to provide reasonable assurance regarding the
reliability of financial reporting and the preparation of financial
statements for external purposes in accordance with generally
accepted accounting principles. A company's internal control over
financial reporting includes those policies and procedures that
(i) pertain to the maintenance of records that, in reasonable
detail, accurately and fairly reflect the transactions and dispositions of the assets of the company; (ii) provide reasonable assurance that transactions are recorded as necessary to permit
preparation of financial statements in accordance with generally
accepted accounting principles, and that receipts and expenditures of the company are being made only in accordance with
authorizations of management and directors of the company;
and (iii) provide reasonable assurance regarding prevention or
timely detection of unauthorized acquisition, use, or disposition
of the company's assets that could have a material effect on the
financial statements.

Because of its inherent limitations, internal control over financial reporting may not prevent or detect misstatements. Also, projections of any evaluation of effectiveness to future periods are
subject to the risk that controls may become inadequate because
of changes in conditions, or that the degree of compliance with
the policies or procedures may deteriorate.

PricewaterhouseCoopers LLP

New York,
New York
February 22, 2007

30

Report of Management

Management's Report on Internal Control over Financial Reporting

The Company's management is responsible for establishing and maintaining adequate internal control over financial reporting. The Company's internal control over financial reporting is a process designed under the supervision of its Chief Executive Officer and Chief Financial Officer to provide reasonable assurance regarding the reliability of financial reporting and the preparation of the Company's financial statements for external reporting in accordance with accounting principles generally accepted in the United States of America. Management evaluates the effectiveness of the Company's internal control over financial reporting using the criteria set forth by the Committee of Sponsoring Organizations of the Treadway Commission (COSO) in Internal Control — Integrated Framework. Management, under the supervision and with the participation of the Company's Chief Executive Officer and Chief Financial Officer, assessed the effectiveness of the Company's internal control over financial reporting as of December 31, 2006 and concluded that it is effective.

The Company's independent registered public accounting firm, PricewaterhouseCoopers LLP, has audited the effectiveness of the Company's internal control over financial reporting and management's assessment of the effectiveness of the Company's internal control over financial reporting as of December 31, 2006, and has expressed unqualified opinions in their report which appears on page 30.

Management's Responsibility for Consolidated Financial Statements

The management of Colgate-Palmolive Company is also responsible for the preparation and content of the accompanying consolidated financial statements as well as all other related information contained in this annual report. These financial statements have been prepared in accordance with accounting principles generally accepted in the United States of America and necessarily include amounts which are based on management's best estimates and judgments.

The consolidated financial statements included in this annual report have been audited by PricewaterhouseCoopers LLP and their report, in which they express their unqualified opinion on such financial statements, appears on page 30.

Audits

The Board of Directors engaged PricewaterhouseCoopers LLP to audit the effectiveness of the Company's internal control over financial reporting, management's assessment of the effectiveness of such internal controls over financial reporting as of December 31, 2006 and the consolidated financial statements for each of the three years ended December 31, 2006. Their report was based on an audit conducted in accordance with standards of the Public Company Accounting Oversight Board (United States of America) and included tests of accounting records and system of internal control and such other procedures to enable them to render opinions on the effectiveness of the Company's internal control over financial reporting and management's assessment of the effectiveness of the Company's such internal control over financial reporting as of December 31, 2006 and on the Company's consolidated financial statements.

The Board of Directors has an Audit Committee comprised entirely of independent directors. The Committee meets periodically and independently throughout the year with management, internal auditors and the independent public accountants to discuss the Company's internal controls, auditing and financial reporting matters. The internal auditors and independent public accountants have unrestricted access to the Audit Committee.

Reuben Mark
Chairman and
Chief Executive Officer

Stephen C. Patrick
Chief Financial Officer

Consolidated Statements of Income

For the years ended December 31,	2006	2005	2004
Net sales	$12,237.7	$11,396.9	$10,584.2
Cost of sales	5,536.1	5,191.9	4,747.2
Gross profit	6,701.6	6,205.0	5,837.0
Selling, general and administrative expenses	4,355.2	3,920.8	3,624.6
Other (income) expense, net	185.9	69.2	90.3
Operating profit	2,160.5	2,215.0	2,122.1
Interest expense, net	158.7	136.0	119.7
Income before income taxes	2,001.8	2,079.0	2,002.4
Provision for income taxes	648.4	727.6	675.3
Net income	$ 1,353.4	$ 1,351.4	$ 1,327.1
Earnings per common share, basic	$ 2.57	$ 2.54	$ 2.45
Earnings per common share, diluted	$ 2.46	$ 2.43	$ 2.33

COLGATE PALMOLIVE CO.

See Notes to Consolidated Financial Statements.

Consolidated Balance Sheets

As of December 31,	2006	2005
Assets		
Current Assets		
Cash and cash equivalents	$ 489.5	$ 340.7
Receivables (net of allowances of $46.4 and $41.7, respectively)	1,523.2	1,309.4
Inventories	1,008.4	855.8
Other current assets	279.9	251.2
Total current assets	3,301.0	2,757.1
Property, plant and equipment, net	2,696.1	2,544.1
Goodwill, net	2,081.8	1,845.7
Other intangible assets, net	831.1	783.2
Other assets	228.0	577.0
Total assets	$ 9,138.0	$ 8,507.1
Liabilities and Shareholders' Equity		
Current Liabilities		
Notes and loans payable	$ 174.1	$ 171.5
Current portion of long-term debt	776.7	356.7
Accounts payable	1,039.7	876.1
Accrued income taxes	161.5	215.5
Other accruals	1,317.1	1,123.2
Total current liabilities	3,469.1	2,743.0
Long-term debt	2,720.4	2,918.0
Deferred income taxes	309.9	554.7
Other liabilities	1,227.7	941.3
Total liabilities	7,727.1	7,157.0
Commitments and contingent liabilities	—	—
Shareholders' Equity		
Preference stock	222.7	253.7
Common stock, $1 par value (1,000,000,000 shares authorized, 732,853,180 shares issued)	732.9	732.9
Additional paid-in capital	1,218.1	1,064.4
Retained earnings	9,643.7	8,968.1
Accumulated other comprehensive income	(2,081.2)	(1,804.7)
	9,736.2	9,214.4
Unearned compensation	(251.4)	(283.3)
Treasury stock, at cost	(8,073.9)	(7,581.0)
Total shareholders' equity	1,410.9	1,350.1
Total liabilities and shareholders' equity	$ 9,138.0	$ 8,507.1

See Notes to Consolidated Financial Statements.

Consolidated Statements of Retained Earnings, Comprehensive Income and Changes in Capital Accounts

	Common Shares		Additional Paid-in Capital	Treasury Shares		Retained Earnings	Accumulated Other Comprehensive Income	Comprehensive Income
	Shares	Amount	Capital	Shares	Amount	Earnings	hensive Income	Income
Balance, January 1, 2004	533,697,177	$732.9	$1,126.2	199,156,003	$(6,499.9)	$7,433.0	$(1,866.8)	
Net income						1,327.1		$1,327.1
Other comprehensive income:								
Cumulative translation adjustment							75.4	75.4
Minimum Pension liability adjustment, net of tax							(21.0)	(21.0)
Other							6.2	6.2
Total comprehensive income								$1,387.7
Dividends declared:								
Series B Convertible Preference Stock, net of taxes						(25.9)		
Common stock						(510.3)		
Shares issued for stock options	2,142,895		2.1	(2,142,895)	60.5			
Treasury stock acquired	(12,383,273)			12,383,273	(637.9)			
Other	3,168,259		(34.5)	(3,168,259)	111.9			
Balance, December 31, 2004	526,625,058	$732.9	$1,093.8	206,228,122	$(6,965.4)	$8,223.9	$(1,806.2)	
Net income						1,351.4		$1,351.4
Other comprehensive income:								
Cumulative translation adjustment							17.7	17.7
Minimum Pension liability adjustment, net of tax							(18.5)	(18.5)
Other							2.3	2.3
Total comprehensive income								$1,352.9
Dividends declared:								
Series B Convertible Preference Stock, net of taxes						(28.2)		
Common stock						(579.0)		
Shares issued for stock options	1,533,768		(4.8)	(1,533,768)	61.2			
Treasury stock acquired	(15,126,263)			15,126,263	(796.2)			
Other	3,1 38,394		(24.6)	(3,138,394)	119.4			
Balance, December 31, 2005	516,170,957	$732.9	$1,064.4	216,682,223	$(7,581.0)	$8,968.1	$(1,804.7)	
Net income						1,353.4		$1,353.4
Other comprehensive income:								
Cumulative translation adjustment							89.1	89.1
Adjustment to initially apply SFAS 158, net of taxes							(380.7)	
Minimum Pension liability adjustment, net of tax							19.2	19.2
Other							(4.1)	(4.1)
Total comprehensive income								$1,457.6
Dividends declared:								
Series B Convertible Preference Stock, net of taxes						(28.7)		
Common stock						(649.1)		
Stock-based compensation expense			116.9					
Shares issued for stock options	7,095,538		107.7	(7,095,538)	227.7			
Treasury stock acquired	(14,982,242)			14,982,242	(884.7)			
Other	4,374,334		(70.9)	(4,374,334)	164.1			
Balance, December 31, 2006	512 ,658,587	$732.9	$1,218.1	220,194,593	$(8,073.9)	$9,643.7	$(2,081.2)	

See Notes to Consolidated Financial Statements.

Consolidated Statements of Cash Flows

For the years ended December 31,	2006	2005	2004
Operating Activities			
Net income	$ 1,353.4	$ 1,351.4	$ 1,327.1
Adjustments to reconcile net income to net cash provided by operations:			
Restructuring, net of cash	145.4	111.6	38.3
Depreciation and amortization	328.7	329.3	327.8
Gain before tax on sale of non-core product lines	(46.5)	(147.9)	(26.7)
Stock-based compensation expense	116.9	41.1	29.3
Cash effects of changes in:			
Receivables	(116.0)	(24.1)	(5.6)
Inventories	(118.5)	(46.8)	(76.1)
Accounts payable and other accruals	149.9	152.7	80.1
Other non-current assets and liabilities	8.2	17.1	60.1
Net cash provided by operations	1,821.5	1,784.4	1,754.3
Investing Activities			
Capital expenditures	(476.4)	(389.2)	(348.1)
Payment for acquisitions, net of cash acquired	(200.0)	(38.5)	(800.7)
Sale of non-core product lines	55.0	215.6	37.0
Purchases of marketable securities and investments	(1.2)	(20.0)	(127.7)
Proceeds from sales of marketable securities and investments	—	10.0	147.3
Other	2.2	1.4	1.8
Net cash used in investing activities	(620.4)	(220.7)	(1,090.4)
Financing Activities			
Principal payments on debt	(1,332.0)	(2,100.3)	(753.9)
Proceeds from issuance of debt	1,471.1	2,021.9	1,246.5
Payments to outside investors	—	(89.7)	—
Dividends paid	(677.8)	(607.2)	(536.2)
Purchases of treasury shares	(884.7)	(796.2)	(637.9)
Proceeds from exercise of stock options and excess tax benefits	364.4	47.1	70.4
Net cash used in financing activities	(1,059.0)	(1,524.4)	(611.1)
Effect of exchange rate changes on Cash and cash equivalents	6.7	(18.2)	1.5
Net increase in Cash and cash equivalents	148.8	21.1	54.3
Cash and cash equivalents at beginning of year	340.7	319.6	265.3
Cash and cash equivalents at end of year	$ 489.5	$ 340.7	$ 319.6
Supplemental Cash Flow Information			
Income taxes paid	$ 647.9	$ 584.3	$ 593.8
Interest paid	168.3	149.9	123.2
Principal payments on ESOP debt, guaranteed by the Company	45.0	37.0	29.8

See Notes to Consolidated Financial Statements.

35

A18

Notes to Consolidated Financial Statements

1. Nature of Operations

The Company manufactures and markets a wide variety of products in the U.S. and around the world in two distinct business segments: Oral, Personal and Home Care; and Pet Nutrition. Oral, Personal and Home Care products include toothpaste, oral rinses and toothbrushes, bar and liquid hand soaps, shower gels, shampoos, conditioners, deodorants and antiperspirants, shave products, laundry and dishwashing detergents, fabric conditioners, cleansers and cleaners, bleaches and other similar items. These products are sold primarily to wholesale and retail distributors worldwide. Pet Nutrition products include pet food products manufactured and marketed by Hill's Pet Nutrition. The principal customers for Pet Nutrition products are veterinarians and specialty pet retailers. Principal global and regional trademarks include Colgate, Palmolive, Mennen, Softsoap, Irish Spring, Protex, Sorriso, Kolynos, Elmex, Tom's of Maine, Ajax, Axion, Fabuloso, Soupline, Suavitel, Hill's Science Diet and Hill's Prescription Diet.

The Company's principal classes of products accounted for the following percentages of worldwide sales for the past three years:

	2006	2005	2004
Oral Care	38%	38%	35%
Home Care	25	26	28
Personal Care	23	23	23
Pet Nutrition	14	13	14
Total	100%	100%	100%

2. Summary of Significant Accounting Policies

Principles of Consolidation

The Consolidated Financial Statements include the accounts of Colgate-Palmolive Company and its majority-owned subsidiaries. Intercompany transactions and balances have been eliminated. The Company's investments in consumer products companies with interests ranging between 20% and 50% are accounted for using the equity method. As of December 31, 2006 and 2005, equity method investments included in Other assets were $6.8 and $5.1, respectively. Investments with less than a 20% interest are accounted for using the cost method. Unrelated third parties hold the remaining ownership interest in these investments. Net income (loss) from such investments is recorded in Other (income) expense, net in the Consolidated Statements of Income.

Use of Estimates

The preparation of financial statements in accordance with accounting principles generally accepted in the United States of America requires management to use judgment and make estimates that affect the reported amounts of assets and liabilities and disclosure of contingent gains and losses at the date of the financial statements and the reported amounts of revenues and expenses during the reporting period. The level of uncertainty in estimates and assumptions increases with the length of time until the underlying transactions are completed. As such, the most significant uncertainty in the Company's assumptions and estimates involved in preparing the financial statements includes pension and other retiree benefit cost assumptions, stock-based compensation, asset impairment, tax valuation allowances, and legal and other contingency reserves. Additionally, the Company uses available market information and other valuation methodologies in assessing the fair value of financial instruments. Judgment is required in interpreting market data to develop the estimates of fair value, and accordingly, changes in assumptions or the estimation methodologies may affect the fair value estimates. Actual results could ultimately differ from those estimates.

Revenue Recognition

Sales are recorded at the time products are shipped to trade customers and when risk of ownership transfers. Net sales reflect units shipped at selling list prices reduced by sales returns and the cost of current and continuing promotional programs. Current promotional programs, such as product listing allowances and co-operative advertising arrangements, are recorded in the period incurred. Continuing promotional programs are predominantly consumer coupons and volume-based sales incentive arrangements with trade customers. The redemption cost of consumer coupons is based on historical redemption experience and is recorded when coupons are distributed. Volume-based incentives offered to trade customers are based on the estimated cost of the program and are recorded as products are sold.

Shipping and Handling Costs

Shipping and handling costs are classified as Selling, general and administrative expenses and were $942.7, $860.2 and $767.4 for the years ended December 31, 2006, 2005 and 2004, respectively.

Marketing Costs

The Company markets its products through advertising and other promotional activities. Advertising costs are included in Selling, general and administrative expenses and are expensed as incurred. Certain consumer and trade promotional programs, such as consumer coupons, are recorded as a reduction of sales.

Cash and Cash Equivalents

The Company considers all highly liquid investments with original maturities of three months or less to be cash equivalents.

Inventories

Inventories are stated at the lower of cost or market. The cost of approximately 80% of inventories is determined using the first-in, first-out (FIFO) method. The cost of all other inventories, predominantly in the U.S. and Mexico, is determined using the last-in, first-out (LIFO) method.

Property, Plant and Equipment

Land, buildings, and machinery and equipment are stated at cost. Depreciation is provided, primarily using the straight-line method, over estimated useful lives, ranging from 3 to 15 years for machinery and equipment and up to 40 years for buildings.

Goodwill and Other Intangibles

Goodwill and indefinite life intangible assets, such as the Company's global brands, are subject to annual impairment tests. These tests were performed and did not result in an impairment charge. Other intangible assets with finite lives, such as trademarks, local brands and non-compete agreements, are amortized over their useful lives, ranging from 5 to 40 years.

Income Taxes

The provision for income taxes is determined using the asset and liability method. Under this method, deferred tax assets and liabilities are recognized based upon the differences between the financial statements and tax bases of assets and liabilities using enacted tax rates that will be in effect at the time such differences are expected to reverse. Deferred tax assets are reduced by a valuation allowance when, in the opinion of management, it is more likely than not that some portion or all of the deferred tax assets will not be realized. Provision is made currently for taxes payable on remittances of overseas earnings; no provision is made for taxes on overseas retained earnings that are deemed to be permanently reinvested.

Financial Instruments

Derivative instruments are recorded as assets and liabilities at estimated fair value based on available market information. The Company's derivative instruments that qualify for hedge accounting are primarily designated as either fair value hedges or cash flow hedges. For fair value hedges, changes in fair value of the derivative, as well as the offsetting changes in fair value of the hedged item, are recognized in earnings each period. For cash flow hedges, changes in fair value of the derivative are recorded in other comprehensive income and are recognized in earnings when the offsetting effect of the hedged item is also recognized in earnings. Cash flows related to fair value hedges and cash flow hedges are classified in the same category as the cash flows from the hedged item in the Consolidated Statements of Cash Flows.

The Company may also enter into certain foreign currency and interest rate instruments that economically hedge certain of its risks but do not qualify for hedge accounting. Changes in fair value of these derivative instruments, based on quoted market prices, are recognized in earnings each period.

Stock-Based Compensation

Effective January 1, 2006, the Company adopted Statement of Financial Accounting Standards (SFAS) No. 123 (Revised 2004), "Share-Based Payment" (SFAS 123R) using the modified prospective method and, as such, results for prior periods have not been restated. Prior to the adoption of SFAS 123R, stock option grants were accounted for in accordance with Accounting Principles Board Opinion No. 25, "Accounting for Stock Issued to Employees" (APB 25) and the Company adhered to the pro forma disclosure provisions of SFAS No. 123, "Accounting for Stock-Based Compensation" (SFAS 123). SFAS 123R requires companies to recognize the cost of employee services received in exchange for awards of equity instruments, such as stock options and restricted stock, based on the fair value of those awards at the date of grant over the requisite service period. Prior to January 1, 2006, the value of restricted stock awards, based on market prices, was expensed by the Company over the restriction period, and no compensation expense was recognized for stock option grants as all such grants had an exercise price not less than fair market value on the date of grant.

The Company uses the Black-Scholes-Merton (Black-Scholes) option pricing model to determine the fair value of stock-option awards under SFAS 123R, which is consistent with the model used for the previous pro forma disclosure under SFAS 123.

Stock-based compensation plans, related expenses and assumptions used in the Black-Scholes option pricing model are more fully described in Note 8.

Translation of Overseas Currencies

The assets and liabilities of foreign subsidiaries, other than those operating in highly inflationary environments, are translated into U.S. dollars at year-end exchange rates, with resulting translation gains and losses accumulated in a separate component of shareholders' equity. Income and expense items are translated into U.S. dollars at average rates of exchange prevailing during the year.

For subsidiaries operating in highly inflationary environments, inventories, goodwill and property, plant and equipment are translated at the rate of exchange on the date the assets were acquired, while other assets and liabilities are translated at year-end exchange rates. Translation adjustments for these operations are included in Net income.

Recent Accounting Pronouncements

In June 2006, the Financial Accounting Standards Board (FASB) issued FASB Interpretation No. 48, "Accounting for Uncertainty in Income Taxes—an interpretation of FASB Statement No. 109" (FIN 48), which prescribes accounting for and disclosure of uncertainty in tax positions. This interpretation defines the criteria that must be met for the benefits of a tax position to be recognized in the financial statements and the measurement of tax benefits recognized. The provisions of FIN 48 are effective as of the beginning of the Company's 2007 fiscal year, with the cumulative effect of the change in accounting principle recorded as an adjustment to opening retained earnings. The Company is currently finalizing its analysis of the impact on the Consolidated Financial Statements of adopting FIN 48 and believes that the impact, if any, will not be material.

In December 2006, the Company adopted SFAS No. 158, "Employers' Accounting for Defined Benefit Pension and Other Postretirement Plans, an amendment of FASB Statements No. 87, 88, 106, and 132(R)" (SFAS 158). SFAS 158 requires company plan sponsors to display the net over- or under-funded position of a defined benefit postretirement plan as an asset or liability, with any unrecognized prior service costs, transition obligations or actuarial gains/losses reported as a component of accumulated other comprehensive income in shareholders' equity. Retirement plans, other retiree benefits and the impact of adopting SFAS 158 are more fully described in Note 10.

Reclassifications

Certain prior year amounts have been reclassified to conform to the current year presentation.

37

3. Acquisitions and Divestitures

Acquisitions

On May 1, 2006, the Company completed the purchase of 84% of the outstanding shares of Tom's of Maine, Inc., for approximately $100 plus transaction costs. Tom's of Maine gives Colgate the opportunity to enter the fast growing health and specialty trade channel where Tom's of Maine toothpaste and deodorant are market leaders.

The cost to acquire Tom's of Maine, Inc. has been allocated on a preliminary basis to the assets acquired and the liabilities assumed at the date of acquisition based on estimated fair values as determined using an independent valuation.

The results of Tom's of Maine operations have been included in Colgate's North American operating segment in the Consolidated Financial Statements from the date of acquisition. The inclusion of pro forma financial data for Tom's of Maine prior to the date of acquisition would not have had a material impact on reported sales, net income and earnings per share for the years ended December 31, 2006, 2005 and 2004.

During 2006, the Company increased its ownership interests in its Poland and Romania subsidiaries to 100% at a cost of approximately $95. During 2005, the Company increased its ownership interests in certain subsidiaries to 100% at a cost of $38.5, primarily related to its Malaysia subsidiary.

On June 1, 2004, the Company purchased 100% of the outstanding shares of GABA Holding AG (GABA), a privately owned European oral care company headquartered in Switzerland. The cost of GABA, net of cash acquired, was approximately $729 plus acquisition costs. The results of GABA's operations have been included in the Company's Europe/South Pacific segment in the Consolidated Financial Statements since the date of acquisition. The aggregate purchase price for all other acquisitions in 2004 was approximately $60.

Divestitures

Consistent with the Company's strategy to prioritize higher margin businesses, during 2006 the Company announced its agreement to sell its Latin American and Canadian bleach brands for approximately $126 plus inventory at cost. The transaction includes the sale of the bleach brands Javex, Agua Jane and Nevex in Canada, Uruguay and Venezuela, respectively, and the license of the Ajax brand for bleach during a transition period in Colombia, the Dominican Republic and Ecuador.

The transaction closed in Canada during the fourth quarter of 2006, with proceeds of $55.0 and a pretax gain of $46.5 ($38.2 aftertax) included in Other (income) expense, net. These operations were not material to the Company's annual Net sales. In the Latin American countries, the transaction is expected to close during the first quarter of 2007 with the exception of the Colombian business, which is subject to regulatory approval and therefore expected to close during the second quarter of 2007.

During 2005, the Company sold its North American and Southeast Asian heavy-duty laundry detergent businesses. These operations accounted for less than 2% of the Company's annual Net sales. The aggregate proceeds from these sales were $215.6, resulting in a pretax gain of $147.9 ($93.5 aftertax) included in Other (income) expense, net.

During 2004, the Company sold its detergent businesses in Ecuador and Peru resulting in a pretax gain of $26.7 included in Other (income) expense, net for the year ended December 31, 2004.

4. Restructuring Activities

In December 2004, the Company commenced a four-year restructuring and business-building program (the 2004 Restructuring Program) to enhance the Company's global leadership position in its core businesses. As part of this program the Company anticipates the rationalization of approximately one-third of the Company's manufacturing facilities, closure of certain warehousing facilities and an estimated 12% workforce reduction. The cost of implementing the 2004 Restructuring Program is estimated to result in cumulative pretax charges, once all the phases are approved and implemented, totaling between $750 and $900 ($550 and $650 aftertax).

For the years ended December 31, 2006, 2005 and 2004 restructuring and implementation related charges are reflected in the following income statement categories:

	2006	2005	2004
Cost of sales	$196.2	$100.2	$ 3.4
Selling, general and administrative expense	46.1	1.8	—
Other (income) expense, net	153.1	80.8	65.3
Total 2004 Restructuring Program charges pretax	$395.4	$182.8	$68.7
Total 2004 Restructuring Program charges aftertax	$286.3	$145.1	$48.0

Restructuring charges, in the preceding table, are recorded in the Corporate segment as these decisions are corporate-driven and are not included in internal measures of segment operating performance.

Total 2006 charges relate to restructuring activities in North America (45%), Europe/South Pacific (19%), Latin America (4%), Greater Asia/Africa (7%), Pet Nutrition (1%) and Corporate (24%). Total program-to-date accumulated charges relate to restructuring activities in North America (39%), Europe/South Pacific (32%), Latin America (4%), Greater Asia/Africa (7%), Pet Nutrition (1%) and Corporate (17%). Since the inception of the 2004 Restructuring Program in December 2004, the Company has incurred total charges of $646.9 ($479.4 aftertax) in connection with the implementation of various projects.

The majority of costs incurred since inception relate to the following significant projects: the voluntary early retirement program in the U.S.; the announced closing of the Jeffersonville, Indiana oral care facility; the consolidation of toothpaste production in Europe; and exiting certain manufacturing activities in other categories in Portugal, Belgium, Denmark, Canada and Kansas City, Kansas.

The following table summarizes the activity for the restructuring charges discussed above and related accrual:

	Termination Benefits	Incremental Depreciation	Asset Impairments	Other	Total
Charges	$ 41.6	$ 3.3	$ 22.0	$ 1.8	$ 68.7
Cash payments	(1.4)	—	—	(1.4)	(2.8)
Charges against assets	—	(3.3)	(22.0)	—	(25.3)
Foreign exchange	1.5	—	—	—	1.5
Balance at December 31, 2004	$ 41.7	$ —	$ —	$ 0.4	$ 42.1
Charges	58.6	65.3	30.2	28.7	182.8
Cash payments	(47.8)	—	—	(23.4)	(71.2)
Charges against assets	(11.4)	(65.3)	(30.2)	(6.4)	(113.3)
Other	(1.4)	—	—	4.2	2.8
Foreign exchange	(4.4)	—	—	(0.1)	(4.5)
Balance at December 31, 2005	$ 35.3	$ —	$ —	$ 3.4	$ 38.7
Charges	212.7	91.5	6.6	84.6	395.4
Cash payments	(89.7)	—	—	(75.3)	(165.0)
Charges against assets	(98.4)	(91.5)	(6.6)	(6.7)	(203.2)
Other	(10.0)	—	—	5.2	(4.8)
Foreign exchange	3.5	—	—	0.1	3.6
Balance at December 31, 2006	$ 53.4	$ —	$ —	$ 11.3	$ 64.7

Termination benefits are calculated based on long-standing benefit practices, local statutory requirements and, in certain cases, voluntary termination arrangements. Termination benefits incurred pursuant to the 2004 Restructuring Program include pension and other retiree benefit enhancements of $108.4 and $12.8 as of December 31, 2006 and 2005, respectively, and are reflected as Charges against assets and Other charges within Termination Benefits in the preceding table, as the corresponding balance sheet amounts are reflected as a reduction of pension assets and an increase to other retiree benefit liabilities, respectively. During 2006 the Company made an $85.0 voluntary contribution to partially fund this obligation. The Company anticipates that it will make incremental cash contributions to its plans in order to fund these pension obligations over the duration of the 2004 Restructuring Program.

Incremental depreciation was recorded to reflect changes in useful lives and estimated residual values for long-lived assets that will be taken out of service prior to the end of their normal service period. Asset impairments have been recorded to write down assets held for sale or disposal to their fair value based on amounts expected to be realized.

5. Goodwill and Other Intangible Assets
The net carrying value of Goodwill as of December 31, 2006 and 2005 by segment is as follows:

	2006	2005
Oral, Personal and Home Care		
North America	$ 345.8	$ 276.6
Latin America	568.1	539.1
Europe/South Pacific	980.2	847.4
Greater Asia/Africa	172.7	167.6
Total Oral, Personal and Home Care	2,066.8	1,830.7
Pet Nutrition	15.0	15.0
Total Goodwill	$2,081.8	$1,845.7

Other intangible assets as of December 31, 2006 and 2005 are comprised of the following:

	2006			2005		
	Gross Carrying Amount	Accumulated Amortization	Net	Gross Carrying Amount	Accumulated Amortization	Net
Trademarks	$435.3	$(155.8)	$279.5	$418.5	$(158.2)	$260.3
Other finite life intangible assets	26.6	(8.1)	18.5	11.9	(10.6)	1.3
Indefinite life intangible assets	533.1	—	533.1	521.6	—	521.6
Total Other intangible assets	$995.0	$(163.9)	$831.1	$952.0	$(168.8)	$783.2

The changes in the net carrying amounts of Goodwill and Other intangible assets during 2006 are mainly due to the acquisition of Tom's of Maine, the increased ownership in the Company's Poland and Romania subsidiaries to 100% and the impact of foreign currency translation adjustments.

Amortization expense of the above trademarks and other finite life intangible assets was $16.3 for the year ended December 31, 2006. Annual estimated amortization expense for each of the next five years is expected to approximate $17.

6. Long-Term Debt and Credit Facilities

Long-term debt consists of the following at December 31:

	Weighted Average Interest Rate	Maturities	2006	2005
Notes	6.0%	2007–2078	$1,931.4	$1,824.5
Payable to banks	4.7%	2007–2009	688.7	555.7
ESOP notes, guaranteed by the Company	8.8%	2007–2009	192.1	237.1
Commercial paper	4.2%	2007	651.6	621.8
Capitalized leases			33.3	35.6
			3,497.1	3,274.7
Less: Current portion of long-term debt			776.7	356.7
Total			$2,720.4	$2,918.0

Commercial paper and certain current maturities of notes payable totaling $674.0 and $641.9 as of December 31, 2006 and 2005, respectively, are classified as long-term debt as the Company has the intent and ability to refinance such obligations on a long-term basis. Excluding commercial paper and certain current maturities of notes payable reclassified as long-term debt, scheduled maturities of long-term debt and capitalized leases outstanding as of December 31, 2006, are as follows:

Years Ended December 31,

2007	$ 776.7
2008	164.1
2009	232.2
2010	296.4
2011	26.6
Thereafter	1,327.1

The Company has entered into interest rate swap agreements and foreign exchange contracts related to certain of these debt instruments (see Note 7).

At December 31, 2006, the Company had unused credit facilities amounting to approximately $2,500 and also had $1,417.2 of medium-term notes available for issuance pursuant to effective shelf registration statements. The Company's domestic lines of credit include a five-year revolving credit facility of $1,500.0 with a syndicate of banks, which was extended an additional year in the fourth quarter of 2006 and now expires in November 2011. Commitment fees related to credit facilities are not material. The weighted average interest rate on short-term borrowings, included in Notes and loans payable in the Consolidated Balance Sheets, as of December 31, 2006 and 2005, was 5.2% and 4.0%, respectively.

The ESOP notes guaranteed by the Company and certain credit facilities contain cross-default provisions. Noncompliance with these requirements could ultimately result in the acceleration of amounts owed. The Company is in full compliance with all such requirements and believes the likelihood of noncompliance is remote.

7. Fair Value of Financial Instruments

The Company uses available market information and other valuation methodologies in assessing the fair value of financial instruments. Judgment is required in interpreting market data to develop the estimates of fair value, and accordingly, changes in assumptions or the estimation methodologies may affect the fair value estimates.

Derivative Instruments

Following are the notional amounts and net recorded fair values of the Company's derivative instruments:

	2006		2005	
	Notional Amount	Fair Value	Notional Amount	Fair Value
Interest rate swap contracts	$ 239.1	$ 2.2	$138.0	$4.8
Foreign currency contracts	1,269.3	(14.5)	875.0	3.6

The Company utilizes interest rate swap contracts to manage its targeted mix of fixed and floating rate debt. Forward and swap contracts are utilized to hedge a portion of the Company's foreign currency purchases and assets and liabilities created in the normal course of business. Forward contracts used in hedging forecasted foreign currency purchases have durations no greater than 18 months. It is the Company's policy to enter into derivative instruments with terms that match the underlying exposure being hedged. As such, the Company's derivative instruments are considered highly effective and the net gain or loss from hedge ineffectiveness was not material.

Cumulative losses related to foreign currency contracts designated as cash flow hedges which are expected to be recognized in earnings over the next 12 months, when the offsetting effects of the hedged item are also recorded in earnings, are not material.

Other Financial Instruments

The carrying amount of cash and cash equivalents, accounts receivables, marketable securities, long-term investments and short-term debt approximated fair value as of December 31, 2006 and 2005. The estimated fair value of the Company's long-term debt, including current portion, as of December 31, 2006 and 2005, was $3,584.5 and $3,161.1, respectively, and the related carrying value was $3,497.1 and $3,274.7, respectively.

Credit Risk

The Company is exposed to credit loss in the event of nonperformance by counterparties to the financial instrument contracts held by the Company; however, nonperformance by these counterparties is considered remote as it is the Company's policy to contract with diversified counterparties that have a long-term debt rating of AA–/Aa3 or higher.

8. Capital Stock and Stock-Based Compensation Plans

Preference Stock

In 1988, the Company authorized the issuance of 50,000,000 shares of Series B Convertible Preference Stock (the Preference Stock), without par value. Each share of Preference Stock is convertible into eight shares of common stock. As of December 31, 2006 and 2005, there were 3,426,737 and 3,902,988 shares of Preference Stock, respectively, outstanding and issued to the Company's Employee Stock Ownership Plan.

Stock Repurchases

The Company repurchased stock at a cost of $884.7 during 2006. The Company repurchases its common stock under a share repurchase program that was approved by the Board of Directors and publicly announced in March 2006 (the 2006 Program). Under the 2006 Program, the Company is authorized to purchase up to 30 million shares of the Company's common stock. The shares will be repurchased from time to time in open market transactions or privately negotiated transactions at the Company's discretion, subject to market conditions, customary blackout periods and other factors. The Board's authorization also authorizes share repurchases on an ongoing basis associated with certain employee elections under the Company's compensation and benefit programs.

The Company may use either authorized and unissued shares or treasury shares to meet share requirements resulting from the exercise of stock options and vesting of restricted stock awards.

Prior to the Board's approval of the 2006 Program, the Company purchased its shares under a program that was approved by the Board of Directors and publicly announced in October 2004 (the 2004 Program). Under the 2004 Program, the Company was authorized to purchase up to 20 million shares of the Company's common stock.

Stock-Based Compensation

Effective January 1, 2006, the Company adopted SFAS 123R using the modified prospective method and, as such, results for prior periods have not been restated. Prior to the adoption of SFAS 123R, stock option grants were accounted for in accordance with APB 25 and the Company adhered to the pro forma disclosure provisions of SFAS 123. Prior to January 1, 2006, the value of restricted stock awards, based on market prices, was expensed by the Company over the restriction period, and no compensation expense was recognized for stock option grants as all such grants had an exercise price not less than fair market value on the date of grant.

SFAS 123R requires companies to recognize the cost of employee services received in exchange for awards of equity instruments, such as stock options and restricted stock, based on the fair value of those awards at the date of grant. The value of restricted stock awards, based on market prices, is amortized on a straight-line basis over the requisite service period. The estimated fair value of stock options on the date of grant is amortized on a straight-line basis over the requisite service period for each separately vesting portion of the award.

SFAS 123R also requires that new awards to employees eligible for retirement prior to the award becoming fully vested be recognized as compensation cost over the period through the date that the employee first becomes eligible to retire and is no longer required to provide service to earn the award. The Company's stock options and restricted stock awards granted to eligible participants prior to the adoption of SFAS 123R that had an accelerated vesting feature associated with employee retirement continue to be recognized, as required, as compensation cost over the vesting period except in the instance of the participants' actual retirement.

The Company has two stock-based compensation plans, which are described below. The total stock-based compensation expense charged against pretax income for these plans was $116.9, $41.1 and $29.3 for the years ended December, 31, 2006, 2005 and 2004, respectively. As a result of adopting SFAS 123R on January 1, 2006, incremental stock-based compensation expense recognized for the year ended December 31, 2006 was $69.8 ($48.1 aftertax), which impacted diluted earnings per share by approximately $0.09.

Stock-based compensation expense is recorded within Selling, general and administrative expense in the Corporate segment as these amounts are not included in internal measures of segment operating performance.

The following illustrates the effect on Net income and Earnings per share if the Company had applied the fair value method of SFAS 123 prior to January 1, 2006:

	2005	2004
Net income, as reported	$1,351.4	$1,327.1
Less: pro forma stock option compensation expense, net of tax	42.9	42.3
Pro forma net income	$1,308.5	$1,284.8
Earnings per share:		
Basic – as reported	$ 2.54	$ 2.45
Basic – pro forma	2.46	2.37
Diluted – as reported	2.43	2.33
Diluted – pro forma	2.35	2.26

The Company uses the Black-Scholes option pricing model to determine the fair value of stock-option awards under SFAS 123R, which is consistent with the model used for the previous pro forma disclosure under SFAS 123. The weighted average estimated fair value of stock options granted in the year ended December 31, 2006, 2005 and 2004 was $10.30, $9.59 and $12.48, respectively. Fair value is estimated using the Black-Scholes option pricing model with the assumptions summarized in the following table:

	2006	2005	2004
Expected term of options	4 years	4 years	5 years
Expected Volatility Rate	17%	20%	26%
Risk-Free Rate	4.8%	4.0%	3.3%
Expected Dividend Yield	2.1%	2.0%	2.0%

The weighted average expected option term reflects the application of the simplified method set out in Staff Accounting Bulletin No. 107 issued by the Securities and Exchange Commission, which defines the term as the average of the contractual term of the options and the weighted average vesting period for all option tranches. Similarly, expected volatility incorporates implied share-price volatility derived from exchange traded options on the Company's common stock. Prior to 2006, such assumptions were determined based on historical data. The risk-free rate for periods within the contractual life of the option is based on the U.S. Treasury implied yield at the time of grant.

The Company elected to use the transition guidance for calculating the opening pool of windfall tax benefits as prescribed in SFAS 123R effective January, 1, 2006 instead of the alternative transition method as prescribed in FAS 123(R)-3, "Transition Election to Accounting for the Tax Effects of Share-Based Payments Awards".

Incentive Stock Plan

The Company has a plan that provides for grants of restricted stock awards for officers and other employees of the Company and its major subsidiaries. A committee of independent members of the Board of Directors administers the plan. The awarded shares are made in common stock and vest at the end of the restriction period, which is generally three years.

Restricted stock award activity for the year ended December 31, 2006 is summarized below:

	Shares (in thousands)	Weighted Average Grant Date Fair Value Per Award
Restricted stock awards as of January 1	2,949	$53
Activity:		
Granted	779	59
Vested	(538)	53
Forfeited	(74)	53
Restricted stock awards as of December 31	3,116	$55

As of December 31, 2006, there was $59.7 of total unrecognized compensation expense related to nonvested restricted stock awards, which will be recognized over a weighted-average period of 1.9 years. The total fair value of shares vested during the years ended December 31, 2006, 2005 and 2004 was $28.2, $28.3 and $41.6, respectively.

Stock Option Plans

The Company's Stock Option Plans provide for the issuance of non-qualified stock options to officers and other employees that have a contractual term of six years and generally vest over three years. As of December 31, 2006, approximately 31,551,000 shares of common stock were available for future stock option grants.

A summary of stock option plan activity as of December 31, 2006 is presented below:

	Shares (in thousands)	Weighted Average Exercise Price	Weighted Average Remaining Contractual Life (in years)	Value of Unexercised In-The-Money Options
Options outstanding, January 1	41,775	$52		
Granted	4,331	61		
Exercised	(7,413)	50		
Forfeited or expired	(741)	57		
Options outstanding, December 31	37,952	54	3	$430
Options exercisable, December 31	28,905	$53	3	$358

As of December 31, 2006, there was $41.3 of total unrecognized compensation expense related to options, which will be recognized over a weighted-average period of 1.3 years. The total value of options exercised during the years ended December 31, 2006, 2005 and 2004 was $78.2, $34.2 and $48.6, respectively.

Prior to the adoption of SFAS 123R, the Company presented the benefit of all tax deductions resulting from the exercise of stock options and vesting of restricted stock awards as operating cash flows in the Consolidated Statements of Cash Flows. As a result of adopting SFAS 123R, the benefits of tax deductions in excess of grant-date fair value of $10.4 were reported as a financing cash flow rather than as an operating cash flow in 2006. Cash proceeds received from options exercised for the year ended December 31, 2006 and 2005 were $354.0 and $47.1, respectively. The total income tax benefit recognized was approximately $38.2, $14.4 and $10.3 for the years ended December 31, 2006, 2005 and 2004, respectively.

9. Employee Stock Ownership Plan

In 1989, the Company expanded its Employee Stock Ownership Plan (ESOP) through the introduction of a leveraged ESOP that funds certain benefits for employees who have met eligibility requirements. The ESOP issued $410.0 of long-term notes due through 2009 bearing an average interest rate of 8.7%. The remaining balance of the long-term notes, which are guaranteed by the Company, is reflected in the accompanying Consolidated Balance Sheets. The ESOP used the proceeds of the notes to purchase 6.3 million shares of Preference Stock from the Company. The Preference Stock, which is convertible into eight shares of common stock, has a minimum redemption price of $65 per share and pays semiannual dividends equal to the higher of $2.44 or the current dividend paid on eight common shares for the comparable six-month period. During 2000, the ESOP entered into a loan agreement with the Company under which the benefits of the ESOP may be extended through 2035.

Dividends on the Preference Stock, as well as on the common shares also held by the ESOP, are paid to the ESOP trust and, together with cash contributions and advances from the Company, are used by the ESOP to repay principal and interest on the outstanding notes. Preference Stock is released for allocation to participants based upon the ratio of the current year's debt service to the sum of total principal and interest payments over the life of the loans. As of December 31, 2006, 1,452,030 shares were released and allocated to participant accounts and 1,974,707 shares were available for future allocation.

Dividends on the Preference Stock are deductible for income tax purposes and, accordingly, are reflected net of their tax benefit in the Consolidated Statements of Retained Earnings, Comprehensive Income and Changes in Capital Accounts.

Annual expense related to the leveraged ESOP, determined as interest incurred on the original notes, plus the higher of either principal payments or the historical cost of Preference Stock allocated, less dividends received on the shares held by the ESOP and advances from the Company, was $14.1 in 2006, $11.9 in 2005 and $14.9 in 2004. Unearned compensation, which is shown as a reduction in shareholders' equity, represents the amount of ESOP debt outstanding reduced by the difference between the cumulative cost of Preference Stock allocated and the cumulative principal payments.

Interest incurred on the ESOP's notes was $17.9 in 2006, $21.7 in 2005 and $24.7 in 2004. The Company paid dividends on the shares held by the ESOP of $37.0 in 2006, $36.9 in 2005 and $34.4 in 2004. Company contributions to the ESOP were $14.1 in 2006, $11.9 in 2005 and $14.5 in 2004.

COLGATE PALMOLIVE CO.

10. Retirement Plans and Other Retiree Benefits

In September 2006, the FASB issued Statement of Financial Accounting Standards No. 158, "Employers' Accounting for Defined Benefit Pension and Other Postretirement Plans, an amendment of FASB Statements No. 87, 88, 106, and 132(R)" (SFAS 158). SFAS 158 requires company plan sponsors to record the net over- or under-funded position of a defined benefit postretirement plan as an asset or liability, with any unrecognized prior service costs, transition obligations or actuarial gains/losses reported as a component of Accumulated other comprehensive income in shareholders' equity. The provisions of SFAS 158 are effective for fiscal years ending after December 15, 2006. Summarized information for the Company's December 31, 2006 implementation of SFAS 158 for defined benefit and other retiree benefit plans are as follows:

	Balance, Pre-SFAS 158 & without AML adjustment	2006 AML adjustment	SFAS 158 adoption adjustment	Ending Balance
Amounts Recognized in Balance Sheet				
Noncurrent assets	$ 388.0	$ —	$(316.9)	$ 71.1
Current liabilities	—	—	(44.3)	(44.3)
Noncurrent liabilities	(739.2)	27.9	(257.1)	(968.4)
Accumulated other comprehensive income adjustment, net of tax*	116.1	(19.2)	380.7	477.6
Deferred tax assets	62.4	(8.7)	237.6	291.3

*The SFAS 158 adoption adjustment of $380.7, net of tax includes a cumulative translation adjustment of $10.3.

Retirement Plans

The Company, its U.S. subsidiaries and some of its overseas subsidiaries maintain defined benefit retirement plans covering substantially all of their employees. Benefits are based primarily on years of service and employees' career earnings. In the Company's principal U.S. plans, funds are contributed to the trusts in accordance with regulatory limits to provide for current service and for any unfunded projected benefit obligation over a reasonable period. Assets of the plans consist principally of common stocks, guaranteed investment contracts with insurance companies, U.S. government and corporate obligations and investments in real estate funds. The asset allocation for the Company's defined benefit plans at the end of 2006 and 2005 and the target allocation by asset category are as follows:

	United States			International		
	Target	2006 Actual	2005 Actual	Target	2006 Actual	2005 Actual
Asset Category						
Equity securities	63%	66%	63%	50%	52%	50%
Debt securities	33	30	33	45	43	43
Real estate and other	4	4	4	5	5	7
Total	100%	100%	100%	100%	100%	100%

Equity securities in the U.S. plans include investments in the Company's common stock representing 8% of U.S. plan assets at December 31, 2006 and 7% of plan assets at December 31, 2005. Such plans purchased approximately 59,200 shares in 2006 using the proceeds from dividends on previously purchased Company stock. No shares were sold in 2006. Such plans sold approximately 9,500 shares in 2005. No shares were purchased in 2005. The plans received dividends on the Company's common stock of approximately $2 in both 2006 and 2005.

The overall investment objective is to balance risk and return so that obligations to employees are met. The Company evaluates its long-term rate of return on plan assets on an annual basis. In determining the long-term rate of return, the Company considers the nature of the plans' investments, an expectation for the plans' investment strategies and the historical rates of return. The assumed rate of return for 2006 for the U.S. plans was 8%. Histor-ical rates of return for the U.S. plans for the most recent 15-year period were 9%. Similar assessments were performed in determining rates of returns on international pension plan assets to arrive at the Company's current weighted average rate of return of 6.9%.

Other Retiree Benefits

The Company and certain of its subsidiaries provide health care and life insurance benefits for retired employees to the extent not provided by government-sponsored plans. The Company utilizes a portion of its leveraged ESOP to reduce its obligation to provide these other retiree benefits and to offset its current service cost. Additionally, during 2006 and 2005 the Company made contributions of $7.6 and $5.6, respectively, to fund the payment of future postretirement medical benefits, the maximum permitted under U.S. tax regulations.

The Company uses a December 31 measurement date for its defined benefit and other retiree benefit plans. Summarized information for the Company's defined benefit and other retiree benefit plans are as follows:

	Pension Benefits				Other Retiree Benefits	
	2006	2005	2006	2005	2006	2005
	United States		International			
Change in Benefit Obligations						
Benefit obligations at beginning of year	$1,462.4	$1,368.3	$ 658.8	$ 675.8	$ 413.0	$ 332.9
Service cost (income)	45.2	47.4	21.1	20.0	(1.9)	(3.6)
Interest cost	83.4	76.1	32.1	33.3	28.7	26.4
Participants' contributions	2.3	2.6	3.1	3.6	—	—
Acquisitions/plan amendments	36.7	2.6	(2.3)	—	—	10.2
Actuarial loss (gain)	(36.7)	83.4	(7.1)	49.4	30.9	63.7
Foreign exchange impact	—	—	60.6	(62.5)	(0.9)	(0.8)
Termination benefits	100.9	11.4	0.2	—	6.5	1.4
Curtailments and settlements	—	(34.0)	(13.8)	(27.7)	—	(0.1)
Benefit payments	(112.2)	(95.4)	(32.3)	(33.1)	(16.3)	(17.1)
Benefit obligations at end of year	$1,582.0	$1,462.4	$ 720.4	$ 658.8	$ 460.0	$ 413.0
Change in Plan Assets						
Fair value of plan assets at beginning of year	$1,236.8	$1,148.2	$ 355.8	$ 360.0	$ 12.2	$ 5.5
Actual return on plan assets	153.2	92.4	25.1	41.8	2.8	1.1
Company contributions	113.6	123.0	36.4	41.6	23.9	22.7
Participants' contributions	2.3	2.6	3.1	3.6	—	—
Foreign exchange impact	—	—	28.8	(33.0)	—	—
Settlements	—	(34.0)	(12.4)	(25.1)	—	—
Benefit payments	(112.2)	(95.4)	(32.3)	(33.1)	(16.3)	(17.1)
Fair value of plan assets at end of year	$1,393.7	$1,236.8	$ 404.5	$ 355.8	$ 22.6	$ 12.2
Funded Status						
Funded status at end of year	$ (188.3)	$ (225.6)	$(315.9)	$(303.0)	$(437.4)	$(400.8)
Unrecognized net actuarial loss	—	470.8	—	150.8	—	198.8
Unrecognized transition/prior service costs	—	9.7	—	10.0	—	1.5
Net amount recognized	$ (188.3)	$ 254.9	$(315.9)	$(142.2)	$(437.4)	$(200.5)
Amounts Recognized in Balance Sheet						
Noncurrent assets	$ 65.6	$ 400.0	$ 5.5	$ 14.4	$ —	$ —
Current liabilities	(14.2)	—	(11.5)	—	(18.6)	—
Noncurrent liabilities	(239.7)	(224.7)	(309.9)	(245.2)	(418.8)	(200.5)
Accumulated other comprehensive income	—	79.6	—	88.6	—	—
Net amount recognized	$ (188.3)	$ 254.9	$(315.9)	$(142.2)	$(437.4)	$(200.5)
Amounts recognized in accumulated other comprehensive income consist of						
Actuarial loss	$ 355.4	$ —	$ 145.5	$ —	$ 216.4	$ —
Transition/prior service cost	41.5	—	8.8	—	1.3	—
Additional minimum pension liability	—	79.6	—	88.6	—	—
	$ 396.9	$ 79.6	$ 154.3	$ 88.6	$ 217.7	$ —
Accumulated benefit obligation	$1,502.0	$1,381.1	$ 625.2	$ 572.5	$ —	$ —
Weighted Average Assumptions Used to Determine Benefit Obligations						
Discount rate	5.80%	5.50%	4.82%	4.83%	5.80%	5.50%
Long-term rate of return on plan assets	8.00%	8.00%	6.70%	6.92%	8.00%	8.00%
Long-term rate of compensation increase	4.00%	4.00%	3.41%	3.42%	—	—
ESOP growth rate	—	—	—	—	10.00%	10.00%

Plans with projected benefit obligations in excess of plan assets and plans with accumulated benefit obligations in excess of plan assets as of December 31 consist of the following:

	Years Ended December 31,	
	2006	2005
Benefit Obligation Exceeds Fair Value of Plan Assets		
Projected benefit obligation	$1,045.4	$958.0
Fair value of plan assets	470.0	387.4
Accumulated benefit obligation	757.1	696.2
Fair value of plan assets	281.7	236.0

These amounts represent non-qualified U.S. plans and certain plans at foreign locations that are primarily unfunded.

The medical cost trend rate of increase assumed in measuring the expected cost of benefits is projected to decrease ratably from 10% in 2007 to 5% in 2012 and will remain at 5% for the years thereafter. Changes in this rate can have a significant effect on amounts reported. The effect of a 1% change in the assumed medical cost trend rate would have the following effect:

	One percentage point	
	Increase	Decrease
Accumulated postretirement benefit obligation	$80	$(65)
Annual expense	7	(6)

Summarized information regarding the net periodic benefit costs for the Company's defined benefit and other retiree benefit plans are as follows:

	Pension Benefits						Other Retiree Benefits		
	2006	2005	2004	2006	2005	2004	2006	2005	2004
	United States			International					
Components of Net Periodic Benefit Cost									
Service cost	$ 45.2	$ 47.4	$ 43.8	$ 21.1	$ 20.0	$ 18.0	$ 11.9	$ 10.3	$ 8.7
Interest cost	83.4	76.1	75.7	32.1	33.3	31.5	28.7	26.4	22.7
Annual ESOP allocation	—	—	—	—	—	—	(13.8)	(13.9)	(13.0)
Expected return on plan assets	(98.9)	(90.0)	(83.4)	(25.0)	(23.7)	(21.3)	(1.3)	(0.8)	—
Amortization of transition & prior service costs (credits)	4.1	4.8	3.3	1.5	1.3	1.3	—	(0.4)	(1.0)
Amortization of actuarial loss	24.4	26.6	24.2	7.9	6.6	5.2	12.3	9.5	4.5
Net periodic benefit cost	$ 58.2	$ 64.9	$ 63.6	$ 37.6	$ 37.5	$ 34.7	$ 37.8	$ 31.1	$ 21.9
Other postretirement charges	101.7	25.6	—	1.1	12.6	—	6.5	10.7	—
Total pension cost	$159.9	$ 90.5	$ 63.6	$ 38.7	$ 50.1	$ 34.7	$ 44.3	$ 41.8	$ 21.9
Weighted Average Assumptions Used to Determine Net Periodic Benefit Cost									
Discount rate	5.50%	5.75%	6.25%	4.83%	5.53%	6.03%	5.50%	5.75%	6.25%
Long-term rate of return on plan assets	8.00%	8.00%	8.00%	6.92%	7.50%	8.10%	8.00%	8.00%	—
Long-term rate of compensation increase	4.00%	4.00%	4.25%	3.42%	3.63%	3.79%	—	—	—
ESOP growth rate	—	—	—	—	—	—	10.00%	10.00%	10.00%

Other postretirement charges amounted to $109.3 and $48.9 for the years ended December 31, 2006 and 2005, respectively. Charges in 2006 relating to certain one-time termination benefits incurred pursuant to the 2004 Restructuring Program amounted to $107.6. During 2006, the Company made voluntary contributions of $111.0 (including $85.0 related to restructuring) to its U.S. postretirement plans. Other 2006 charges required by SFAS No. 88, "Employers' Accounting for Settlement and Curtailments of Defined Benefit Pension Plans and for Termination Benefits" (SFAS 88) amounted to $1.7, including $0.8 pertaining to a curtailment resulting from the 2004 Restructuring Program.

Charges in 2005 relating to certain one-time termination benefits incurred pursuant to the 2004 Restructuring Program amounted to $12.8. Additionally, other postretirement charges in 2005 included a non-cash charge of $9.2 associated with an international postretirement obligation and other 2005 charges required by SFAS 88 amounted to $26.9. Other SFAS 88 charges included the conversion of one of the Company's international pension plans to a defined contribution plan for all eligible partici-

pants for $10.6 and a lump sum payment of normal retirement benefits associated with a retirement plan in the U.S. for $14.2.

Termination benefits incurred pursuant to the 2004 Restructuring Program in 2006 and 2005 are reflected as a restructuring charge however the related accrual resides in pension and other retiree benefit liabilities at December 31, 2006 and 2005, respectively.

The estimated actuarial loss and the estimated transition/prior service cost for defined benefit and other retiree benefit plans that will be amortized from accumulated other comprehensive income into net periodic benefit cost over the next fiscal year is as follows:

	Pension Benefits	Other Retiree Benefits
Actuarial loss	$24.5	$11.5
Transition & prior service cost	$ 6.8	—

45

Expected Contributions & Benefit Payments

Management's best estimate of cash requirements to be paid directly from the Company's assets for its postretirement plans for the year ending December 31, 2007 is approximately $107, including approximately $18 for other retiree benefit plans. These estimated cash requirements include approximately $50 of projected contributions to the Company's postretirement plans and approximately $57 of projected benefit payments made directly to participants of unfunded plans. Expected contributions are dependent on many variables, including the variability of the market value of the assets as compared to the obligation and other market or regulatory conditions. Accordingly, actual funding may differ from current estimates.

Total benefit payments expected to be paid to participants, which include payments directly from the Company's assets to participants of unfunded plans, as discussed above, as well as payments paid from the plans are as follows:

Years Ended December 31,	Pension Benefits		Other Retiree Benefits
	United States	International	
2007	$139.3	$ 34.5	$ 18.2
2008	113.7	35.1	21.3
2009	112.3	35.8	27.2
2010	113.2	51.4	27.2
2011	114.4	44.6	28.8
2012–2016	631.5	218.3	149.6

11. Income Taxes

The components of income before income taxes are as follows for the three years ended December 31:

	2006	2005	2004
United States	$ 584.9	$ 893.2	$ 846.6
International	1,416.9	1,185.8	1,155.8
Total	$2,001.8	$2,079.0	$2,002.4

The provision for income taxes consists of the following for the three years ended December 31:

	2006	2005	2004
United States	$202.7	$333.2	$271.8
International	445.7	394.4	403.5
Total	$648.4	$727.6	$675.3

Temporary differences between accounting for financial statement purposes and accounting for tax purposes result in the current provision for taxes being higher (lower) than the total provision for income taxes as follows:

	2006	2005	2004
Intangible assets	$(42.8)	$(60.2)	$(46.9)
Property, plant and equipment	18.4	34.2	(9.8)
Pension and other retiree benefits	30.5	(19.8)	4.8
Stock-based compensation	28.7	2.7	—
Other, net	(2.5)	5.6	(8.4)
Total	$ 32.3	$(37.5)	$(60.3)

The difference between the statutory U.S. federal income tax rate and the Company's global effective tax rate as reflected in the Consolidated Statements of Income is as follows:

Percentage of Income Before Tax	2006	2005	2004
Tax at United States statutory rate	35.0%	35.0%	35.0%
State income taxes, net of federal benefit	0.8	0.9	1.0
Effect of American Jobs Creation Act	—	2.0	—
Earnings taxed at other than United States statutory rate	(2.1)	(1.5)	(1.1)
Other, net	(1.3)	(1.4)	(1.2)
Effective tax rate	32.4%	35.0%	33.7%

The American Jobs Creation Act of 2004 (the AJCA), which was enacted in October 2004, created a temporary incentive for U.S. corporations to repatriate accumulated income earned abroad by providing an 85% dividends received deduction for certain qualifying dividends. The Company repatriated $780 in incremental foreign earnings in the second half of 2005 at a full year tax cost of approximately $40.9.

The components of deferred tax assets (liabilities) are as follows at December 31:

	2006	2005
Deferred Taxes – Current:		
Accrued liabilities	$ 55.3	$ 62.4
Stock-based compensation	16.5	12.8
Other, net	25.1	17.9
Total deferred taxes, current	96.9	93.1
Deferred Taxes – Long-term:		
Intangible assets	(380.9)	(338.1)
Pension and other retiree benefits	223.5	(9.7)
Stock-based compensation	40.6	17.8
Property, plant and equipment	(233.4)	(257.8)
Tax loss and tax credit carryforwards	189.4	193.3
Other, net	(23.7)	(26.4)
Valuation allowance	(125.4)	(133.8)
Total deferred taxes, long-term	(309.9)	(554.7)
Net deferred taxes	$(213.0)	$(461.6)

The major component of the valuation allowance as of December 31, 2006 and 2005 relates to tax benefits in certain jurisdictions arising from net operating losses. On an ongoing basis, the Company reassesses the need for such valuation allowance based on recent operating results, its assessment of the likelihood of future taxable income and developments in the relevant tax jurisdictions. Based on management's current assessment, it is possible that the Company will be able to reduce its valuation allowance in the near-term as the realization of deferred tax assets becomes probable.

Applicable U.S. income and foreign withholding taxes have not been provided on approximately $1,600 of undistributed earnings of foreign subsidiaries at December 31, 2006. These earnings have been and are currently considered to be permanently invested and are currently not subject to such taxes. Determining the tax liability that would arise if these earnings were remitted is not practicable.

In addition, net tax benefits of $258.0 in 2006, $12.0 in 2005 and $27.1 in 2004 recorded directly through equity predominantly include tax benefits related to employee equity compensation plans. In addition, 2006 includes $237.6 related to the implementation of SFAS 158.

In June 2006, the FASB issued Interpretation No. 48, "Accounting for Uncertainty in Income Taxes—an interpretation of FASB Statement No. 109" (FIN 48), which prescribes accounting for and disclosure of uncertainty in tax positions. This interpretation defines the criteria that must be met for the benefits of a tax position to be recognized in the financial statements and the measurement of tax benefits recognized. The provisions of FIN 48 are effective as of the beginning of the Company's 2007 fiscal year, with the cumulative effect of the change in accounting principle recorded as an adjustment to opening retained earnings. The Company is currently finalizing its analysis of the impact on the Consolidated Financial Statements of adopting FIN 48 and believes that the impact, if any, will not be material.

12. Earnings Per Share

	For the Year Ended 2006			For the Year Ended 2005			For the Year Ended 2004		
	Income	Shares (millions)	Per Share	Income	Shares (millions)	Per Share	Income	Shares (millions)	Per Share
Net income	$1,353.4			$1,351.4			$1,327.1		
Preferred dividends	(28.7)			(28.2)			(25.9)		
Basic EPS	1,324.7	515.2	$2.57	1,323.2	520.5	$2.54	1,301.2	530.9	$2.45
Stock options and restricted stock		6.1			3.8			3.9	
Convertible preference stock	28.7	29.2		28.2	32.2		25.9	34.5	
Diluted EPS	$1,353.4	550.5	$2.46	$1,351.4	556.5	$2.43	$1,327.1	569.3	$2.33

Diluted earnings per share is computed on the basis of the weighted average number of shares of common stock plus the effect of dilutive potential common shares outstanding during the period using the treasury stock method. Dilutive potential common shares include outstanding stock options and restricted stock awards.

13. Commitments and Contingencies

Minimum rental commitments under noncancellable operating leases, primarily for office and warehouse facilities, are $117.0 in 2007, $104.1 in 2008, $87.7 in 2009, $66.7 in 2010, $51.2 in 2011 and $103.1 thereafter. Rental expense amounted to $142.6 in 2006, $130.6 in 2005 and $124.5 in 2004. Capital leases included in fixed assets, contingent rentals and sublease income are not significant. The Company has various contractual commitments to purchase raw, packaging and other materials totaling $864.0.

The Company is contingently liable with respect to lawsuits, environmental matters, taxes and other matters arising out of the normal course of business.

Management proactively reviews and monitors its exposure to, and the impact of, environmental matters. The Company is a potentially responsible party to various environmental matters and as such may be responsible for all or a portion of the cleanup, restoration and post-closure monitoring of several sites. Substantially all of the Company's potential liability for these matters relates to a single superfund site associated with a prior acquisition. Substantially all of the Company's potential liability that may arise in connection with this site has been acknowledged in writing as being covered by the Company's insurance carriers which are presently making all their required payments and are expected to continue to do so in the future. While it is possible that the nonperformance of other potentially responsible parties or the Company's insurance carriers could affect the cash flows and results of operations in any particular quarter or year, it is the opinion of management that the ultimate disposition of these matters, to the extent not previously provided for, will not have a material impact on the financial position, or ongoing results of operations and cash flows of the Company.

As a matter of course, the Company is regularly audited by the Internal Revenue Service (IRS) and other tax authorities around the world in countries where it conducts business. In this regard, the IRS has completed its examination of the Company's federal income tax returns for 1996 through 2003 and has proposed an assessment that challenges the Company's tax deduc-

tions for compensation in connection with expatriate executives. During 2005, the Company and the IRS reached agreement with respect to the compensation tax deduction for 1996 through 1998, and the amount of additional tax involved did not have a material impact on the financial position, results of operations or ongoing cash flows of the Company. For the remaining years under audit, 1999 through 2003, the tax in connection with the challenged deductions is $62. Estimated incremental tax payments related to the potential disallowances for subsequent periods could be an additional $18. While the Company believes that its tax position complies with applicable tax law and intends to continue to defend its position, potential settlement discussions with the IRS for the later years are underway.

In May 2006, one of the Company's subsidiaries received an assessment from the Mexican tax authorities totaling approximately $590, at the current exchange rate, including interest and penalties, challenging Value Added Tax (VAT) credits claimed in its 2000 and 2001 VAT returns. In December 2006 another subsidiary of the Company received an income tax assessment from the Mexican tax authorities totaling approximately $175, at the current exchange rate, including interest and penalties, challenging the transfer pricing on transactions between that subsidiary and another of the Company's subsidiaries located in the United States. The Company, through its subsidiary, requested and received in 1999 a written advance ruling from the Mexican tax authorities for both VAT and income tax on which the Company relied in subsequently claiming the VAT credits and income tax treatment to which these assessments relate. The Company believes based on the advice of outside counsel that its tax filings are in full compliance with the written advance ruling and applicable tax law and regulations. The Company has entered into settlement discussions with the Mexican tax authorities regarding these matters. If such discussions are not resolved to the Company's satisfaction, it intends to vigorously challenge the assessments in the Mexican court system and through discussions between Mexican and U.S. government authorities pursuant to the income tax treaty between the countries. Although there can be no assurances, the Company believes based on the advice of outside counsel that these tax assessments are without merit, and that the Company will ultimately prevail in these matters.

In 1995, the Company acquired the Kolynos oral care business from Wyeth (formerly American Home Products) (the Seller), as described in the Company's Form 8-K dated January 10, 1995. On September 8, 1998, the Company's Brazilian subsidiary received notice of an administrative proceeding from the Central Bank of Brazil primarily taking issue with certain foreign exchange filings made with the Central Bank in connection with the financing of this strategic transaction, but in no way challenging or seeking to unwind the acquisition. The Central Bank of Brazil in January 2001 notified the Company of its decision in this administrative proceeding to impose a fine, which, at the current exchange rate, approximates $120. The Company appealed the imposition of the fine to the Brazilian Monetary System Appeals Council (the Council), and on January 30, 2007, the Council decided the appeal in the Company's favor, dismissing the fine entirely.

In addition, the Brazilian internal revenue authority has disallowed interest deductions and foreign exchange losses taken by the Company's Brazilian subsidiary for certain years in connection with the financing of the Kolynos acquisition. The tax assessments with interest, at the current exchange rate, approximate $100. The Company has been disputing the disallowances by appealing the assessments within the internal revenue authority's appellate process, with the following results to date:

- In June 2005, the First Board of Taxpayers ruled in the Company's favor and allowed all of the previously claimed deductions for 1996 through 1998, which represent more than half of the total exposure. The tax authorities have appealed this decision to the next administrative level.

- For the remaining exposure related to subsequent years, the assessment is still outstanding, and the Company is also appealing this assessment to the First Board of Taxpayers.

In the event of an adverse decision within the internal revenue authority's appellate process, further appeals are available within the Brazilian federal courts. Although there can be no assurances, management believes, based on the opinion of its Brazilian legal counsel and other experts, that the disallowances are without merit and that the Company should prevail on appeal either at the administrative level or if necessary, in the Brazilian federal courts. The Company intends to challenge these assessments vigorously.

In addition, Brazilian prosecutors reviewed the foregoing transactions as part of an overall examination of all international transfers of Reais through non-resident current accounts during the 1992 to 1998 time frame, a review which the Company understands involved hundreds and possibly thousands of other individuals and companies unrelated to the Company. At the request of these prosecutors, in February 2004, a federal judge agreed to authorize criminal charges against certain current and former officers of the Company's Brazilian subsidiary based on the same allegations made in the Central Bank and tax proceedings discussed above. Management believes, based on the opinion of its Brazilian legal counsel, that these officers behaved in all respects properly and in accordance with the law in connection with the financing of the Kolynos acquisition. Management intends to support and defend these officers vigorously.

In 2002, the Brazilian Federal Public Attorney filed a civil action against the federal government of Brazil, Laboratorios Wyeth-Whitehall Ltda., the Brazilian subsidiary of the Seller, and the Company, as represented by its Brazilian subsidiary, seeking to annul an April 2000 decision by the Brazilian Board of Tax Appeals that found in favor of the Seller's subsidiary on the issue of whether it had incurred taxable capital gains as a result of the divestiture of Kolynos. The action seeks to make the Company's Brazilian subsidiary jointly and severally liable for any tax due from the Seller's subsidiary. Although there can be no assurances, management believes, based on the opinion of its Brazilian legal counsel, that the Company should ultimately prevail in this action. The Company intends to challenge this action vigorously.

In December 2005, the Brazilian internal revenue authority issued to the Company's Brazilian subsidiary a tax assessment with interest and penalties of approximately $50 at the current exchange rate, based on a claim that certain purchases of U.S. Treasury bills by the subsidiary and their subsequent sale during the period 2000 to 2001 were subject to a tax on foreign exchange transactions. The Company is disputing the assessment within the internal revenue authority's administrative appeals process. Although there can be no assurances, management believes, based on the opinion of its Brazilian legal counsel, that the tax assessment is without merit and that the Company should prevail either through administrative appeal or if necessary through further appeal in the Brazilian federal courts. The Company intends to challenge this assessment vigorously.

In February 2006, the Company learned that French competition authorities initiated an inquiry into potential competition law violations in France involving exchanges of competitive information and agreements on selling terms and conditions among a number of consumer goods companies in France, including the Company's French subsidiary. In February 2007, the Company learned that the Swiss competition authorities will open an investigation against the Company's GABA subsidiary regarding distribution policies, retail pricing and parallel trade. At this time, no formal claim for a fine or penalty has been made in either matter. The Company's policy is to comply with antitrust and competition laws and, if a violation of any such laws is found, to take appropriate remedial action and to cooperate fully with any related governmental inquiry. The Company has undertaken a comprehensive review of its selling practices and related competition law compliance in Europe and elsewhere and, where the Company has identified a lack of compliance, it is undertaking remedial action. While the Company cannot predict the final financial impact of these competition law issues as these matters are still under review and may change, the Company has taken and will, if necessary, take additional reserves as appropriate.

While it is possible that the Company's cash flows and results of operations in a particular quarter or year could be materially affected by the impact of the above noted contingencies, it is the opinion of management that these matters will not have a material impact on the Company's financial position, or ongoing results of operations and cash flows.

14. Segment Information

Effective January 1, 2006, the Company modified the geographic reporting structure of its Oral, Personal and Home Care segment in order to address evolving markets and more closely align countries with similar consumer needs and retail trade structures. Management responsibility for Eastern European operations, including Russia, Turkey, Ukraine and Belarus, was transferred to Greater Asia management and responsibility for operations in the South Pacific, including Australia, was transferred to European management. The financial information for 2005 and 2004 has been reclassified to conform to the new reporting structure.

The Company operates in two product segments: Oral, Personal and Home Care; and Pet Nutrition. The operations of the Oral, Personal and Home Care segment are managed geographically in four reportable operating segments: North America, Latin America, Europe/South Pacific and Greater Asia/Africa. Management evaluates segment performance based on several factors, including Operating profit. The Company uses Operating profit as a measure of the operating segment performance because it excludes the impact of corporate-driven decisions related to interest expense and income taxes.

The accounting policies of the operating segments are generally the same as those described in Note 2. Intercompany sales have been eliminated. Corporate operations include restructuring and implementation related costs, stock-based compensation related to stock options and restricted stock awards, research and development costs, unallocated overhead costs, and gains and losses on sales of non-core brands and assets. Segment information regarding Net sales, Operating profit, Capital expenditures, Depreciation and amortization and Identifiable assets is detailed below:

Net sales	2006	2005	2004
Oral, Personal and Home Care			
North America[1]	$ 2,590.8	$ 2,509.8	$ 2,378.7
Latin America	3,019.5	2,623.8	2,266.0
Europe/South Pacific	2,952.3	2,845.9	2,759.4
Greater Asia/Africa	2,006.0	1,897.2	1,747.0
Total Oral, Personal and Home Care	10,568.6	9,876.7	9,151.1
Pet Nutrition[2]	1,669.1	1,520.2	1,433.1
Total Net sales	$12,237.7	$11,396.9	$10,584.2

(1) Net sales in the U.S. for Oral, Personal and Home Care were $2,211.2, $2,124.2 and $2,000.3 in 2006, 2005 and 2004, respectively.
(2) Net sales in the U.S. for Pet Nutrition were $897.9, $818.1 and $781.0 in 2006, 2005 and 2004, respectively.

Operating profit	2006	2005	2004
Oral, Personal and Home Care			
North America	$ 550.1	$ 545.7	$ 530.1
Latin America	872.9	698.0	627.7
Europe/South Pacific	681.2	619.8	611.5
Greater Asia/Africa	278.7	245.5	237.6
Total Oral, Personal and Home Care	2,382.9	2,109.0	2,006.9
Pet Nutrition	447.9	412.8	389.7
Corporate	(670.3)	(306.8)	(274.5)
Total Operating profit	$2,160.5	$2,215.0	$2,122.1

Capital expenditures	2006	2005	2004
Oral, Personal and Home Care			
North America	$ 82.4	$ 39.3	$ 55.4
Latin America	108.9	104.1	75.4
Europe/South Pacific	129.9	63.1	71.5
Greater Asia/Africa	83.8	117.9	79.6
Total Oral, Personal and Home Care	405.0	324.4	281.9
Pet Nutrition	26.8	28.5	30.4
Corporate	44.6	36.3	35.8
Total Capital expenditures	$476.4	$389.2	$348.1

Depreciation and amortization	2006	2005	2004
Oral, Personal and Home Care			
North America	$ 69.9	$ 71.2	$ 74.9
Latin America	73.4	67.1	58.8
Europe/South Pacific	69.9	76.6	82.4
Greater Asia/Africa	51.6	49.5	48.1
Total Oral, Personal and Home Care	264.8	264.4	264.2
Pet Nutrition	29.9	30.1	31.1
Corporate	34.0	34.8	32.5
Total Depreciation and amortization	$328.7	$329.3	$327.8

Identifiable assets	2006	2005	2004
Oral, Personal and Home Care			
North America	$2,006.3	$1,918.0	$2,001.4
Latin America	2,343.7	2,084.3	1,825.1
Europe/South Pacific	2,484.4	2,120.3	2,575.6
Greater Asia/Africa	1,504.8	1,336.5	1,298.6
Total Oral, Personal and Home Care	8,339.2	7,459.1	7,700.7
Pet Nutrition	646.9	614.3	614.0
Corporate[3]	151.9	433.7	358.2
Total Identifiable assets[4]	$9,138.0	$8,507.1	$8,672.9

(3) Corporate assets, which include benefit plan assets decreased as a result of the adoption of SFAS 158. SFAS 158 resulted in a decrease in Total assets with a corresponding decrease to Total liabilities and shareholders' equity in the Consolidated Balance Sheet.
(4) Long-lived assets in the U.S., primarily property, plant and equipment and goodwill and other intangibles represented approximately one-third of total long-lived assets of $5,719.6, $5,629.3 and $5,792.1 in 2006, 2005 and 2004, respectively.

15. Supplemental Income Statement Information

Other (income) expense, net	2006	2005	2004
Minority interest	$ 57.5	$ 55.3	$ 47.9
Amortization of intangible assets	16.3	15.6	14.3
Equity (income)	(3.4)	(2.0)	(8.5)
Gains on sales of non-core product lines, net	(46.5)	(147.9)	(26.7)
2004 Restructuring Program	153.1	80.8	65.3
2003 restructuring activities	—	—	2.8
Pension and other retiree benefit	—	34.0	—
Investment losses (income)	(5.7)	19.7	(8.7)
Other, net	14.6	13.7	3.9
Total Other (income) expense, net	$185.9	$ 69.2	$ 90.3

Interest expense, net	2006	2005	2004
Interest incurred	$ 170.0	$ 145.0	$ 126.0
Interest capitalized	(3.4)	(2.5)	(2.3)
Interest income	(7.9)	(6.5)	(4.0)
Total Interest expense, net	$ 158.7	$ 136.0	$ 119.7

	2006	2005	2004
Research and development	$ 241.5	$ 238.5	$ 223.4
Advertising	$1,320.3	$1,193.6	$1,063.0

16. Supplemental Balance Sheet Information

Inventories	2006	2005
Raw materials and supplies	$ 248.3	$208.1
Work-in-process	45.4	37.5
Finished goods	714.7	610.2
Total Inventories	$1,008.4	$855.8

A32

Inventories valued under LIFO amounted to $238.2 and $191.7 at December 31, 2006 and 2005, respectively. The excess of current cost over LIFO cost at the end of each year was $46.9 and $29.5, respectively. The liquidations of LIFO inventory quantities had no effect on income in 2006, 2005 and 2004.

Property, plant and equipment, net	2006	2005
Land	$ 145.9	$ 134.5
Buildings	962.3	896.5
Manufacturing machinery and equipment	3,794.8	3,540.9
Other equipment	792.0	775.2
	5,695.0	5,347.1
Accumulated depreciation	(2,998.9)	(2,803.0)
Total Property, plant and equipment, net	$ 2,696.1	$ 2,544.1

Other accruals	2006	2005
Accrued advertising	$ 438.4	$ 344.9
Accrued payroll and employee benefits	322.5	305.6
Accrued taxes other than income taxes	49.2	72.3
Restructuring accrual	64.7	38.7
Pension and other retiree benefits	44.3	—
Accrued interest	19.1	17.5
Other	378.9	344.2
Total Other accruals	$1,317.1	$1,123.2

Other liabilities	2006	2005
Minority interest	$ 111.8	$103.3
Pension and other retiree benefits	968.4	670.4
Other	147.5	167.6
Total Other liabilities	$1,227.7	$941.3

Accumulated Other Comprehensive Income

Accumulated other comprehensive income is comprised of cumulative foreign currency translation gains and losses, the SFAS 158 and minimum pension liability adjustments, unrealized gains and losses from derivative instruments designated as cash flow hedges, and unrealized gains and losses from available-for-sale securities. As of December 31, 2006 and 2005, accumulated other comprehensive income primarily consisted of cumulative foreign currency translation adjustments. In addition, in 2006 accumulated other comprehensive income includes, $477.6 of unrecognized prior service costs, transition obligations and actuarial losses related to the implementation of SFAS 158.

Other comprehensive income in 2006 primarily reflects foreign currency translation gains largely due to the strengthening of the Brazilian real and the Swiss franc. The 2005 cumulative translation adjustment reflects a weakening Euro and its effect primarily on euro-denominated long-term debt, similar effects from a weakening Swiss franc, together with a strengthening Brazilian real and Mexican peso.

17. Quarterly Financial Data   (Unaudited)

	First Quarter	Second Quarter	Third Quarter	Fourth Quarter
2006				
Net sales	$2,870.6	$3,014.3	$3,143.7	$3,209.1
Gross profit	1,563.5	1,633.1	1,728.4	1,776.6
Net income	324.5 [1]	283.6 [2]	344.1 [3]	401.2 [4]
Earnings per common share:				
Basic	0.62	0.54	0.65	0.77
Diluted	0.59 [1]	0.51 [2]	0.63 [3]	0.73 [4]
2005				
Net sales	$2,743.0	$2,837.5	$2,911.8	$2,904.6
Gross profit	1,503.6	1,539.1	1,577.6	1,584.7
Net income	300.1 [5]	342.9 [6]	347.2 [7]	361.2 [8]
Earnings per common share:				
Basic	0.56	0.64	0.66	0.68
Diluted	0.53 [5]	0.62 [6]	0.63 [7]	0.65 [8]

Note: Basic and diluted earnings per share are computed independently for each quarter presented. Accordingly, the sum of the quarterly earnings per share may not agree with the calculated full year earnings per share.

(1) Net income and diluted earnings per share for the first quarter of 2006 were reduced by a net aftertax charge of $58.9 and $0.11, respectively, reflecting the net impact of charges related to the 2004 Restructuring Program and incremental stock-based compensation charges due to the adoption of SFAS 123R.

(2) Net income and diluted earnings per share for the second quarter of 2006 were reduced by a net aftertax charge of $124.2 and $0.23, respectively, reflecting the net impact of charges related to the 2004 Restructuring Program and incremental stock-based compensation charges due to the adoption of SFAS 123R.

(3) Net income and diluted earnings per share for the third quarter of 2006 were reduced by a net aftertax charge of $77.4 and $0.14, respectively, reflecting the net impact of charges related to the 2004 Restructuring Program and incremental stock-based compensation charges due to the adoption of SFAS 123R.

(4) Net income and diluted earnings per share for the fourth quarter of 2006 were reduced by a net aftertax charge of $35.7 and $0.07, respectively, reflecting the net impact of a gain on the sale of the Company's household bleach brand in Canada, charges related to the 2004 Restructuring Program and incremental stock-based compensation charges due to the adoption of SFAS 123R.

(5) Net income and diluted earnings per share for the first quarter of 2005 were reduced by a net aftertax charge of $44.6 and $0.08 respectively, reflecting charges related to the 2004 Restructuring Program.

(6) Net income and diluted earnings per share for the second quarter of 2005 were reduced by a net aftertax charge of $28.7 and $0.05, respectively, reflecting charges related to the 2004 Restructuring Program.

(7) Net income and diluted earnings per share for the third quarter of 2005 were reduced by a net aftertax charge of $22.5 and $0.04, respectively, reflecting the net impact of a gain on the sale of the Company's heavy-duty laundry detergent brands in North America, charges related to the 2004 Restructuring Program, income taxes for incremental repatriation of foreign earnings related to the American Jobs Creation Act and charges related to certain pension obligations as required by SFAS 88.

(8) Net income and diluted earnings per share for the fourth quarter of 2005 were reduced by a net aftertax charge of $194 and $0.04, respectively, reflecting the net impact of charges related to the 2004 Restructuring Program, a gain on the sale of the Company's heavy-duty laundry detergent brands in Southeast Asia, income taxes for the incremental repatriation of foreign earnings related to the American Jobs Creation Act and a non-cash charge related to an international postretirement obligation.

Market and Dividend Information

The Company's common stock is listed on the New York Stock Exchange. The trading symbol for the common stock is CL. Dividends on the common stock have been paid every year since 1895 and the Company's regular common stock dividend payments have increased for 44 consecutive years.

Market Price of Common Stock

Quarter Ended	2006		2005	
	High	Low	High	Low
March 31	$58.28	$53.70	$55.20	$48.55
June 30	61.51	56.26	53.95	48.60
September 30	62.57	58.22	54.06	49.55
December 31	66.83	59.79	56.39	51.78
Year-end Closing Price	$65.24		$54.85	

Dividends Paid Per Common Share

Quarter Ended	2006	2005
March 31	$0.29	$0.24
June 30	0.32	0.29
September 30	0.32	0.29
December 31	0.32	0.29
Total	$1.25	$1.11

Eleven-Year Financial Summary[1]

For the years ended December 31,	2006	2005	2004	2003	2002	2001	2000	1999	1998	1997	1996
Continuing Operations											
Net sales[2]	$12,237.7	$11,396.9	$10,584.2	$9,903.4	$9,294.3	$9,084.3	$9,004.4	$8,801.5	$8,660.8	$8,786.8	$8,493.1
Results of operations:											
Net income	1,353.4 [3]	1,351.4 [4]	1,327.1 [5]	1,421.3	1,288.3	1,146.6	1,063.8	937.3	848.6	740.4	635.0
Per share, basic	2.57 [3]	2.54 [4]	2.45 [5]	2.60	2.33	2.02	1.81	1.57	1.40	1.22	1.05
Per share, diluted	2.46 [3]	2.43 [4]	2.33 [5]	2.46	2.19	1.89	1.70	1.47	1.30	1.13	0.98
Depreciation and amortization expense	328.7	329.3	327.8	315.5	296.5	336.2	337.8	340.2	330.3	319.9	316.3
Financial Position											
Current ratio	1.0	1.0	1.0	1.0	1.0	1.0	1.0	1.0	1.1	1.1	1.2
Property, plant and equipment, net	2,696.1	2,544.1	2,647.7	2,542.2	2,491.3	2,513.5	2,528.3	2,551.1	2,589.2	2,441.0	2,428.9
Capital expenditures	476.4	389.2	348.1	302.1	343.7	340.2	366.6	372.8	389.6	478.5	459.0
Total assets	9,138.0	8,507.1	8,672.9	7,478.8	7,087.2	6,984.8	7,252.3	7,423.1	7,685.2	7,538.7	7,901.5
Long-term debt	2,720.4	2,918.0	3,089.5	2,684.9	3,210.8	2,812.0	2,536.9	2,243.3	2,300.6	2,340.3	2,786.8
Shareholders' equity	1,410.9	1,350.1	1,245.4	887.1	350.3	846.4	1,468.1	1,833.7	2,085.6	2,178.6	2,034.1
Share and Other											
Book value per common share	2.81	2.67	2.43	1.71	0.69	1.54	2.57	3.14	3.53	3.65	3.42
Cash dividends declared and paid per common share	1.25	1.11	0.96	0.90	0.72	0.675	0.63	0.59	0.55	0.53	0.47
Closing price	65.24	54.85	51.16	50.05	52.43	57.75	64.55	65.00	46.44	36.75	23.06
Number of common shares outstanding (in millions)	512.7	516.2	526.6	533.7	536.0	550.7	566.7	578.9	585.4	590.8	588.6
Number of common shareholders of record	33,400	35,000	36,500	37,700	38,800	40,900	42,300	44,600	45,800	46,800	45,500
Average number of employees	34,700	35,800	36,000	36,600	37,700	38,500	38,300	37,200	38,300	37,800	37,900

(1) All share and per share amounts have been restated to reflect the 1999 and 1997 two-for-one stock splits.

(2) Net sales amounts for 2001 and prior have been revised to reflect the reclassification of certain sales incentives and promotional expenses from selling, general and administrative expenses to a reduction of net sales and cost of sales in accordance with new accounting standards.

(3) Net income and earnings per share in 2006 include a gain for the sale of the Company's household bleach business in Canada of $38.2 aftertax. This gain was more than offset by $286.3 of aftertax charges associated with the 2004 Restructuring Program and $48.1 of aftertax charges related to the adoption of SFAS 123R.

(4) Net income and earnings per share in 2005 include a gain for the sale of heavy-duty laundry detergent brands in North America and Southeast Asia of $93.5 aftertax. This gain was more than offset by $145.1 of aftertax charges associated with the 2004 Restructuring Program, $40.9 of income taxes for incremental repatriation of foreign earnings related to the American Jobs Creation Act and $22.7 aftertax of non-cash pension and other retiree benefit charges.

(5) Net income and earnings per share in 2004 include a provision for the 2004 Restructuring Program of $48.0 aftertax.

COLGATE PALMOLIVE CO.

52

A35

Campbell Soup

Supplemental Schedule of Sales and Earnings

(million dollars)	Year 11		Year 10		Year 9	
	Sales	Earnings	Sales	Earnings	Sales	Earnings
1 **Contributions by division**						
Campbell North America						
Campbell U.S.A.	$3,911.8	$632.7	$3,932.7	$370.8	$3,666.9	$242.3
Campbell Canada	352.0	35.3	384.0	25.6	313.4	23.8
	4,263.8	668.0	4,316.7	396.4	3,980.3	266.1
Campbell Biscuit and Bakery						
Pepperidge Farm	569.0	73.6	582.0	57.0	548.4	53.6
International Biscuit	219.4	17.6	195.3	8.9	178.0	11.7
	788.4	91.2	777.3	65.9	726.4	65.3
Campbell International	1,222.9	39.4	1,189.8	(168.6)	1,030.3	(117.8)
Interdivision	(71.0)		(78.0)		(64.9)	
Total sales	$6,204.1		$6,205.8		$5,672.1	
Total operating earnings		798.6		293.7		213.6
Unallocated corporate expenses		(41.1)		(16.5)		(31.3)
Interest, net		(90.2)		(94.0)		(55.8)
Foreign currency translation adjustments		.1		(3.8)		(20.0)
Taxes on earnings		(265.9)		(175.0)		(93.4)
Net earnings		$401.5		$4.4		$13.1
Net earnings per share		$3.16		$.03		$.10

Contributions by division in Year 10 include the effects of divestitures, restructuring and unusual charges of $339.1 million as follows: Campbell U.S.A. $121.8 million, Campbell Canada $6.6 million, Pepperidge Farm $11.0 million, International Biscuit $14.3 million, and Campbell International $185.4 million. Contributions by division in Year 9 include the effects of restructuring and unusual charges of $343.0 million as follows: Campbell U.S.A. $183.1 million, Campbell Canada $6.0 million, Pepperidge Farm $7.1 million, International Biscuit $9.5 million, and Campbell International $137.3 million.

CAMPBELL SOUP

2 **Results of Operations**

Overview

Campbell had record net earnings in Year 11 of $401.5 million, or $3.16 per share, compared to net earnings of $4.4 million, or 3 cents per share, in Year 10. Excluding Year 10's divestiture and restructuring charges, earnings per share increased 34% in Year 11. In Year 11, the Company sold five non-strategic businesses, sold or closed several manufacturing plants, and discontinued certain unprofitable product lines. Net sales of $6.2 billion in Year 11 were even with Year 10. Sales were up 4% excluding businesses that were divested and product lines that were discontinued in Year 11.

In Year 10 the Company incurred charges for divestitures and restructuring of $2.33 per share, reducing net earnings to 3 cents per share. In Year 9 restructuring charges of $2.02 per share reduced earnings to 10 cents per share. Excluding these charges from both years, earnings per share rose 11% in Year 10. Sales increased 9%. In Year 10 the company's domestic divisions had strong earnings performances, excluding the divestiture and restructuring charges, but the International Division's performance was disappointing principally due to the poor performance of United Kingdom frozen food and Italian biscuit operations. The Italian biscuit operations were divested in Year 11.

The divestiture and restructuring programs were designed to strengthen the Company's core businesses and improve long-term profitability. The Year 10 divestiture program involved the sale of several low-return or non-strategic businesses. The Year 10 restructuring charges provided for the elimination of underperforming assets and unnecessary facilities and included a write-off of goodwill. The restructuring charges in Year 9 involved plant consolidations, work force reductions, and goodwill write-offs.

Year 11 Compared to Year 10

3 Results by Division

Campbell North America. Operating earnings of Campbell North America, the Company's largest division, were $668.0 million in Year 11 compared to $396.4 million in Year 10 after restructuring charges of $128.4 million. Operating earnings increased 27% in Year 11 over Year 10, excluding the restructuring charges from Year 10. All of the division's core businesses had very strong earnings growth. Continued benefits of restructuring drove significant improvements in operating margins.

Sales were $4.26 billion in Year 11. Excluding divested businesses and discontinued product lines, sales increased 2% with overall volume down 2%. Soup volume was off 1.5% as a result of reduced year-end trade promotional activities. Significant volume increases were achieved in the cooking soup, ramen noodle and family-size soup categories and "Healthy Request" soup. Exceptionally strong volume performances were turned in by "Swanson" frozen dinners, "Franco-American" gravies and "Prego" spaghetti sauces with positive volume results for "LeMenu Healthy" entrees, Food Service frozen soups and entrees, and Casera Foods in Puerto Rico.

Campbell Biscuit and Bakery. Operating earnings of the Biscuit and Bakery division, which includes Pepperidge Farm in the United States, Delacre in Europe and an equity interest in Arnotts Limited in Australia, were $91.2 million in Year 11 compared with $65.9 million in Year 10 after restructuring charges of $25.3 million. Operating earnings were flat in Year 11 excluding the restructuring charges from Year 10. Sales increased 1%, however, volume declined 3%.

Pepperidge Farm operating earnings in Year 11 increased despite a drop in sales, which reflects the adverse effect of the recession on premium cookies. Several new varieties of "Hearty Slices" bread performed well. Delacre, benefiting from new management and integration into the worldwide biscuit and bakery organization, turned in significant improvement in Year 11 sales and operating earnings. Arnotts' performance in Year 11 was disappointing and included restructuring charges. Its restructuring program should have a positive impact on fiscal Year 12 results. The Year 11 comparison with Year 10 was also adversely impacted by gains of $4.0 million realized in Year 10 on the sales of businesses by Arnotts.

Campbell International. Operating earnings of the International division were $39.4 million in Year 11 compared to an operating loss of $168.6 million in Year 10 after restructuring charges of $185.4 million.

In Year 11, Campbell International achieved a significant turnaround. Operating earnings for the year more than doubled above the pre-restructuring results of the prior year. There were margin improvements throughout the system. Europe led the division's positive results. A key component was the United Kingdom's move from a loss position to profitability, driven by the benefits of restructuring and product line reconfiguration.

European Food and Confectionery units turned in another year of solid earnings growth. Mexican operations, strengthened by a new management team, also turned around from a loss to a profit position. Sales were $1.22 billion in Year 11, an increase of 6%, excluding divested businesses and discontinued product lines, and the effects of foreign currency rates. Volume was approximately the same as in Year 10.

> 4 Statements of Earnings

Sales in Year 11 were even with Year 10. Excluding divested businesses and unprofitable product lines discontinued during Year 11, sales increased 4% while volume declined approximately 2%. The decline in volume was caused by reduced year-end trade promotional activities and the adverse effect of the recession on certain premium products.

Gross margins improved 2.6 percentage points to 34.0% in Year 11 from 31.4% in Year 10. All divisions improved due to the significant benefits from restructuring and the divestitures and product-pruning activities. Productivity improvements worldwide and declining commodity prices also contributed to the higher margins.

Marketing and selling expenses, as a percentage of net sales, were 15.4% in Year 11 compared to 15.8% in Year 10. The decrease in Year 11 is due to more focused marketing efforts and controlled new product introductions. For each of the prior 10 fiscal years, these expenses had increased significantly. Advertising was down 11% in Year 11. Management expects advertising expenditures to increase in Year 12 in order to drive volume growth of core products and to support the introduction of new products.

Administrative expenses, as a percentage of net sales, were 4.9% in Year 11 compared to 4.7% in Year 10. The increase in Year 11 results principally from annual executive incentive plan accruals due to outstanding financial performance and foreign currency rates.

Interest expense increased in Year 11 due to timing of fourth quarter borrowings in order to obtain favorable long-term interest rates. Interest income was also higher in Year 11 as the proceeds from these borrowings were invested temporarily until needed. Interest expense, net of interest income, decreased from $94.0 million in Year 10 to $90.2 million in Year 11 as the increased cash flow from operations exceeded cash used for share repurchases and acquisitions.

Foreign exchange losses declined principally due to reduced effects of currency devaluations in Argentina.

Other expense was $26.2 million in Year 11 compared to $14.7 million in Year 10. The increase results principally from accruals for long-term incentive compensation plans reflecting changes in Campbell's stock price.

As discussed in the "Overview" section above, Year 10 results include divestiture, restructuring, and unusual charges of $339.1 million ($301.6 million or $2.33 per share after taxes).

Equity in earnings of affiliates declined in Year 11 principally due to the disappointing performance at Arnotts and to a $4.0 million gain on sales of businesses realized by Arnotts in Year 10.

Year 10 Compared to Year 9

> 5 Results by Division

Campbell North America. In Year 10, Campbell North America had operating earnings of $396.4 million after restructuring charges of $128.4 million. In Year 9 the division had operating earnings of $266.1 million, after restructuring charges of $189.1 million. Excluding restructuring charges from both Year 10 and Year 9 operating earnings increased 15% in Year 10, led by strong performances by the soup, grocery, "Mrs. Paul's" frozen seafood, and Canadian sectors. The olives business performed poorly in Year 10.

Sales increased 8% in Year 10 to $4.32 billion on a 3% increase in volume. There were solid volume increases in ready-to-serve soups, "Great Starts" frozen breakfasts, and "Prego" spaghetti sauces. Overall soup volume was up 1%. "Mrs. Paul's" regained the number one share position in frozen prepared seafood.

Campbell Biscuit and Bakery. In Year 10, Campbell Biscuit and Bakery had operating earnings of $65.9 million after restructuring charges of $25.3 million. In Year 9, the division's operating earnings were $65.3 million after restructuring charges of $16.6 million. Excluding restructuring charges from both Year 10 and Year 9, operating earnings of the division increased 11% in Year 10. The increase in operating earnings was driven by Pepperidge Farm's biscuit and bakery units along with Arnott's gain on sales of businesses. Pepperidge Farm's frozen unit and Delacre performed poorly. Sales increased 7% to $777.3 million. Volume increased 1%, with Pepperidge Farm's biscuit, bakery and food service units and Delacre the main contributors to the growth.

Campbell International. In Year 10, Campbell International had an operating loss of $168.6 million after restructuring charges of $185.4 million. In Year 9, the division sustained an operating loss of $117.8 million after restructuring charges of $137.3 million. Excluding restructuring charges from both Year 10 and Year 9, operating earnings declined 14% in Year 10, as strong performances in the European Food and Confectionery and Argentine operations were more than offset by poor performances in the United Kingdom frozen food and Italian biscuit operations. Sales in Year 10 were $1.19 billion, an increase of 15%. Volume was up 14% of which 11% came from acquisitions.

[6] Statements of Earnings

In Year 10 sales increased 9% on a 5% increase in volume, about half of which came from established businesses.

Gross margins improved by 1.9 percentage points to 31.4% in Year 10 from 29.5% in Year 9. All divisions had improved margins in Year 10, with Campbell North America operations posting substantial improvements.

Marketing and selling expenses, as a percentage of net sales, were 15.8% in Year 10 compared to 14.4% in Year 9. The Year 10 increase was due to heavy marketing expenditures by Campbell U.S.A. at both the national and regional levels.

Administrative expenses, as a percentage of net sales, were 4.7% in Year 10 compared to 4.4% in Year 9. The increase in Year 10 was driven by some unusual one-time expenditures, employee benefits, the weakening dollar and acquisitions.

Interest expense increased in Year 10 due to higher debt levels resulting from funding of acquisitions, higher inventory levels during the year, purchases of Campbell's stock for the treasury and restructuring program expenditures. Interest income declined in Year 10 because of a shift from local currency to lower-yielding dollar denominated temporary investments in Latin America to minimize foreign exchange losses.

Foreign exchange losses resulted principally from currency devaluations in Argentina. There was a large devaluation in Argentina in Year 9. Also, Year 10 losses were lower due to the shift in temporary investments described in the previous paragraph.

Other expense was $14.7 million in Year 10 compared to $32.4 million in Year 9. This decline results principally from reduced accruals for long-term incentive compensation plans reflecting changes in Campbell's stock price.

As discussed in the "Overview" section above, results include divestiture, restructuring and unusual charges of $339.1 million ($301.6 million or $2.33 per share after taxes) in Year 10 and $343.0 million ($260.8 million or $2.02 per share after taxes) in Year 9.

Equity in earnings of affiliates increased in Year 10 principally due to a $4.0 million gain on sales of businesses realized by Arnotts in Year 10.

[7] **Income Taxes**

The effective income tax rate was 39.8% in Year 11, 97.5% in Year 10 an 87.7% in Year 9. The principal reason for the high tax rates in Year 10 and Year 9 is that certain of the divestiture, restructuring and unusual charges are not tax deductible. Excluding the effect of these charges, the rate would be 41.0% in Year 10 and 38.9% in Year 9. The variances in all years are principally due to the level of certain foreign losses for which no tax benefit is currently available.

[8] **Inflation**

The Company attempts to mitigate the effects of inflation on sales and earnings by appropriately increasing selling prices and aggressively pursuing an ongoing cost improvement effort which includes capital investments in more efficient plants and equipment. Also, the divestiture and restructuring programs enacted in Year 9 and Year 10 have made the Company a more cost-effective producer, as previously discussed with reference to cost of products sold.

[10] **Liquidity and Capital Resources**

The Consolidated Statements of Cash Flows and Balance Sheets demonstrate the Company's continued superior financial strength.

11 Statements of Cash Flows

Operating Activities. Cash provided by operations was $805.2 million in Year 11, an 80% increase from $448.4 million in Year 10. This increased cash flow was driven by the Company's record earnings level and reduced working capital resulting from improved asset management and the restructuring program.

Investing Activities. The majority of the Company's investing activities involve the purchase of new plant assets to maintain modern manufacturing processes and increase productivity. Capital expenditures for plant assets amounted to $371.1 million in Year 11, including $10.0 million of capital lease activity, down slightly from Year 10. The Company expects capital expenditures in Year 12 to be about $400 million.

Another key investing activity of the Company is acquisitions. The total cost of acquisitions in Year 11 was $180.1 million, most of which was spent to acquire the publicly held shares of the Company's 71% owned subsidiary, Campbell Soup Company Ltd. in Canada. This will allow Campbell North America to more efficiently integrate its U.S. and Canadian operations to provide Campbell with competitive advantage in North America.

One of the Company's strategies has been to prune low-return assets and businesses from its portfolio. In Year 11 the Company realized over $100 million in cash from these activities, with $67.4 million coming from sales of businesses and $43.2 million realized from asset sales.

Also, during Year 11 the Company made contributions to its pension plans substantially in excess of the amounts expensed. This was the principal reason for the increase in other assets.

Financing Activities. During Year 11, the Company issued debt in the public markets for a total of $400 million: $100 million of 9% Notes due Year 18. $100 million of Medium-Term Notes due Year 21 at interest rates from 8.58% to 8.75%, and $200 million of 8.875%. Debentures due Year 41. The proceeds were used to reduce short-term debt by $227 million, pay off long-term debt maturing in Year 11 of $129.9 million, and to fund the purchase of the minority interest of Campbell Canada.

During Year 11, the Company repurchased approximately 3.4 million shares of its capital stock at a cost of $175.6 million. Cash received from the issuance of approximately 1.1 million treasury shares pursuant to the stock option and long-term incentive plans amounted to $47.7 million in Year 11.

Dividends of $137.5 million represent the dividends paid in Year 11. Dividends declared in Year 11 were $142.2 million or $1.12 per share, an increase of 14% over Year 10.

12 Balance Sheets

Total borrowings at the end of fiscal Year 11 were $1.055 billion compared to $1.008 billion at the end of Year 10. Even after the effects of the borrowing and treasury stock activity previously discussed, total debt as a percentage of total capitalization was 33.7%—the same as a year ago. The Company has ample sources of funds. It has access to the commercial paper markets with the highest rating. The Company's long-term debt is rated double A by the major rating agencies. It has filed a shelf registration with the Securities and Exchange Commission for the issuance from time to time of up to $100 million of debt securities. Also, the Company has unused lines of credit of approximately $635 million.

Debt-related activity is discussed in the Statements of Cash Flows section above. In addition to that, the debt balances on the Balance Sheets were affected by current maturities of long-term debt and by the classification of commercial paper to be refinanced as long-term debt in Year 10.

Aggressive management of working capital and the effect of divested businesses are evidenced by a $235.5 million decrease in current assets exclusive of changes in cash and temporary investments. Receivables are down $97.1 million and inventories declined $113.1 million from Year 10. Accounts payable are down $42.8 million because of the reduced inventory levels and divestitures. Accrued liabilities and accrued income taxes declined $61.9 million as increases due to higher earnings levels and the timing of certain payments were offset by payments and charges resulting from the divestitures and restructuring programs.

Plant assets increased $72.7 million due to capital expenditures of $371.1 million offset by the annual provision for depreciation of $194.5 million, asset sales and divestitures. Intangible assets increased $52.1 million as the acquisitions resulted in $132.3 million of additional goodwill. Amortization and divestitures accounted for the remainder of the change. Other assets increased principally as the result of the pension contribution.

Other liabilities decreased $14.9 million as the reduction of minority interest resulting from the purchase of the publicly-held shares of Campbell Canada and changes in foreign currency rates of other liabilities offset the annual deferred tax provision.

. . . .

Consolidated Statements of Earnings

. . . .

(millions)	Year 11	Year 10	Year 9
13 **NET SALES**	**$6,204.1**	$6,205.8	$5,672.1
Costs and expenses			
14 Cost of products sold	**4,095.5**	4,258.2	4,001.6
15 Marketing and selling expenses	**956.2**	980.5	818.8
16 Administrative expenses	**306.7**	290.7	252.1
17 Research and development expenses	**56.3**	53.7	47.7
18 Interest expense (Note 3)	**116.2**	111.6	94.1
19 Interest income	**(26.0)**	(17.6)	(38.3)
20 Foreign exchange losses, net (Note 4)	**.8**	3.3	19.3
21 Other expense (Note 5)	**26.2**	14.7	32.4
22 Divestitures, restructuring and unusual charges (Note 6)	**—**	339.1	343.0
22A Total costs and expenses	**$5,531.9**	$6,034.2	$5,570.7
23 Earnings before equity in earnings of affiliates and minority interests	**$ 672.2**	$ 171.6	$ 101.4
24 Equity in earnings of affiliates	**2.4**	13.5	10.4
25 Minority interests	**(7.2)**	(5.7)	(5.3)
26 Earnings before taxes	**667.4**	179.4	106.5
27 Taxes on earnings (Note 9)	**265.9**	175.0	93.4
28 **Net earnings**	**$ 401.5**	$ 4.4	$ 13.1
29 **Net earnings per share (Note 22)**	**$ 3.16**	$ .03	$ .10
30 Weighted average shares outstanding	**127.0**	129.6	129.3

CAMPBELL SOUP

CONSOLIDATED BALANCE SHEETS

(million dollars)

	July 28, Year 11	July 29, Year 10
Current Assets		
31 Cash and cash equivalents (Note 12)	$178.9	$80.7
32 Other temporary investments, at cost which approximates market	12.8	22.5
33 Accounts receivable (Note 13)	527.4	624.5
34 Inventories (Note 14)	706.7	819.8
35 Prepaid expenses (Note 15)	92.7	118.0
36 Total current assets	1,518.5	1,665.5
37 **Plant assets, net of depreciation (Note 16)**	1,790.4	1,717.7
38 **Intangible assets, net of amortization (Note 17)**	435.5	383.4
39 **Other assets (Note 18)**	404.6	349.0
Total assets	$4,149.0	$4,115.6
Current Liabilities		
40 Notes payable (Note 19)	$282.2	$202.3
41 Payable to suppliers and others	482.4	525.2
42 Accrued liabilities (Note 20)	408.7	491.9
43 Dividend payable	37.0	32.3
44 Accrued income taxes	67.7	46.4
45 Total current liabilities	1,278.0	1,298.1
46 **Long-term debt (Note 19)**	772.6	805.8
47 **Other liabilities, principally deferred income taxes (Note 21)**	305.0	319.9
Shareowners' Equity (Note 22)		
48 Preferred stock; authorized 40,000,000 shares; none issued	—	—
49 Capital stock, $.15 par value; authorized 140,000,000 shares; issued 135,622,676 shares	20.3	20.3
50 Capital surplus	107.3	61.9
51 Earnings retained in the business	1,912.6	1,653.3
52 Capital stock in treasury, 8,618,911 shares in Year 11 and 6,353,697 shares in Year 10, at cost	(270.4)	(107.2)
53 Cumulative translation adjustments (Note 4)	23.6	63.5
54 Total shareowners' equity	1,793.4	1,691.8
55 Total liabilities and shareowners' equity	$4,149.0	$4,115.6

CAMPBELL SOUP

CONSOLIDATED STATEMENTS OF CASH FLOWS

(million dollars)

		Year 11	Year 10	Year 9
	Cash Flows from Operating Activities			
56	Net earnings	**$401.5**	$4.4	$13.1
	To reconcile net earnings to net cash provided by operating activities:			
57	Depreciation and amortization	**208.6**	200.9	192.3
58	Divestitures and restructuring provisions		339.1	343.0
59	Deferred taxes	**35.5**	3.9	(67.8)
60	Other, net	**63.2**	18.6	37.3
61	(Increase) decrease in accounts receivable	**17.1**	(60.4)	(46.8)
62	(Increase) decrease in inventories	**48.7**	10.7	(113.2)
63	Net change in other current assets and liabilities	**30.6**	(68.8)	(.6)
64	Net cash provided by operating activities	**805.2**	448.4	357.3
	Cash Flows from Investing Activities			
65	Purchases of plant assets	**(361.1)**	(387.6)	(284.1)
66	Sales of plant assets	**43.2**	34.9	39.8
67	Businesses acquired	**(180.1)**	(41.6)	(135.8)
68	Sales of businesses	**67.4**	21.7	4.9
69	Increase in other assets	**(57.8)**	(18.6)	(107.0)
70	Net change in other temporary investments	**9.7**	3.7	9.0
71	Net cash used in investing activities	**(478.7)**	(387.5)	(473.2)
	Cash Flows from Financing Activities			
72	Long-term borrowings	**402.8**	12.6	126.5
73	Repayments of long-term borrowings	**(129.9)**	(22.5)	(53.6)
74	Increase (decrease) in borrowings with less than three month maturities	**(137.9)**	(2.7)	108.2
75	Other short-term borrowings	**117.3**	153.7	227.1
76	Repayments of other short-term borrowings	**(206.4)**	(89.8)	(192.3)
77	Dividends paid	**(137.5)**	(124.3)	(86.7)
78	Treasury stock purchases	**(175.6)**	(41.1)	(8.1)
79	Treasury stock issued	**47.7**	12.4	18.5
80	Other, net	**(.1)**	(.1)	23.5
81	Net cash provided by (used in) financing activities	**(219.6)**	(101.8)	163.1
82	Effect of exchange rate changes on cash	**(8.7)**	.7	(12.1)
83	**Net increase (decrease) in cash and cash equivalents**	**98.2**	(40.2)	35.1
84	Cash and cash equivalents at beginning of year	**80.7**	120.9	85.8
85	**Cash and cash equivalents at end of year**	**$178.9**	$80.7	$120.9

CONSOLIDATED STATEMENTS OF SHAREOWNERS' EQUITY

(million dollars)

	Preferred Stock	Capital Stock	Capital Surplus	Earnings Retained in the Business	Capital Stock in Treasury	Cumulative Translation Adjustments	Total Shareowners' Equity
86 Balance at July 31, Year 8	—	$20.3	$42.3	$1,879.1	$(75.2)	$28.5	$1,895.0
Net earnings				13.1			13.1
Cash dividends ($.90 per share)				(116.4)			(116.4)
Treasury stock purchased					(8.1)		(8.1)
Treasury stock issued under Management incentive and Stock option plans			8.5		12.6		21.1
Translation adjustments						(26.4)	(26.4)
87 Balance at July 30, Year 9	—	20.3	50.8	1,775.8	(70.7)	2.1	1,778.3
Net earnings				4.4			4.4
Cash dividends ($.98 per share)				(126.9)			(126.9)
Treasury stock purchased					(41.1)		(41.1)
Treasury stock issued under Management incentive and Stock option plans			11.1		4.6		15.7
Translation adjustments						61.4	61.4
Balance at July 29, Year 10	—	20.3	61.9	1,653.3	(107.2)	63.5	1,691.8
88 **Net earnings**				**401.5**			**401.5**
89 **Cash dividends ($1.12 per share)**				**(142.2)**			**(142.2)**
90 **Treasury stock purchased**					**(175.6)**		**(175.6)**
91 **Treasury stock issued under Management incentive and Stock option plans**			**45.4**		**12.4**		**57.8**
92 **Translation adjustments**						**(29.9)**	**(29.9)**
93 **Sale of foreign operations**						**(10.0)**	**(10.0)**
94 **Balance at July 28, Year 11**	—	**$20.3**	**$107.3**	**$1,912.6**	**$(270.4)**	**$23.6**	**$1,793.4**

95 **Changes in Number of Shares**

(thousands of shares)

	Issued	Out-standing	In Treasury
Balance at July 31, Year 8	135,622.7	129,038.6	6,584.1
Treasury stock purchased		(250.6)	250.6
Treasury stock issued under Management incentive and Stock option plans		790.6	(790.6)
Balance at July 30, Year 9	135,622.7	129,578.6	6,044.1
Treasury stock purchased		(833.0)	833.0
Treasury stock issued under Management incentive and Stock option plans		523.4	(523.4)
Balance at July 29, Year 10	135,622.7	129,269.0	6,353.7
Treasury stock purchased		**(3,395.4)**	**3,395.4**
Treasury stock issued under Management incentive and Stock option plans		**1,130.2**	**(1,130.2)**
Balance at July 28, Year 11	**135,622.7**	**127,003.8**	**8,618.9**

CAMPBELL SOUP

96 **❶ Summary of Significant Accounting Policies**

Consolidation. The consolidated financial statements include the accounts of the Company and its majority-owned subsidiaries. Significant intercompany transactions are eliminated in consolidation. Investments in affiliated owned 20% or more are accounted for by the equity method.

Inventories. Substantially all domestic inventories are priced at the lower of cost or market, with cost determined by the last-in, first-out (LIFO) method. Other inventories are priced at the lower of average cost or market.

Intangibles. The excess of cost of investments over net assets of purchased companies is amortized on a straight-line basis over periods not exceeding forty years.

Plant Assets. Alterations and major overhauls which substantially extend the lives of properties or materially increase their capacity are capitalized. The amounts for property disposals are removed from plant asset and accumulated depreciation accounts and any resultant gain or loss is included in earnings. Ordinary repairs and maintenance are charged to operating costs.

Depreciation. Depreciation provided in costs and expenses is on the straight-line method. The United States, Canadian and certain other foreign companies use accelerated methods of depreciation for income tax purposes.

Pension Plans. Pension costs are accrued over employees' careers based on plan benefit formulas.

Cash and Cash Equivalents. All highly liquid debt instruments purchased with a maturity of three months or less are classified as Cash Equivalents.

Financial Instruments. In managing interest rate exposure, the Company at times enters into interest rate swap agreements. When interest rates change, the difference to be paid or received is accrued and recognized as interest expense over the life of the agreement. In order to hedge foreign currency exposures on firm commitments, the Company at times enters into forward foreign exchange contracts. Gains and losses resulting from these instruments are recognized in the same period as the underlying hedged transaction. The Company also at times enters into foreign currency swap agreements which are effective as hedges of net investments in foreign subsidiaries. Realized and unrealized gains and losses on these currency swaps are recognized in the Cumulative Translation Adjustments account in Shareowners' Equity.

97 **❷ Geographic Area Information**

The Company is predominantly engaged in the prepared convenience foods industry. The following presents information about operations in different geographic areas:

	Year 11	Year 10	Year 9
Net sales			
United States	**$4,495.6**	$4,527.2	$4,233.4
Europe	**1,149.1**	1,101.4	983.7
Other foreign countries	**656.0**	673.6	542.9
Adjustment and elimination	**(96.6)**	(96.4)	(87.9)
Consolidated	**$6,204.1**	$6,205.8	$5,672.1
Earnings (loss) before taxes			
United States	**$694.8**	$427.8	$294.5
Europe	**48.8**	(178.7)	(21.3)
Other foreign countries	**55.0**	44.6	(59.6)
	798.6	293.7	213.6
Unallocated corporate expenses	**(41.1)**	(16.5)	(31.3)
Interest, net	**(90.2)**	(94.0)	(55.8)
Foreign currency translation adjustment	**.1**	(3.8)	(20.0)
Consolidated	**$667.4**	$179.4	$106.5
Identifiable assets			
United States	**$2,693.4**	$2,535.0	$2,460.5
Europe	**711.3**	942.2	886.9
Other foreign countries	**744.3**	638.4	584.7
Consolidated	**$4,149.0**	$4,115.6	$3,932.1

Transfers between geographic areas are recorded at cost plus markup or at market. Identifiable assets are all assets identified with operations in each geographic area.

. . . .

❸ Interest Expense

	Year 11	Year 10	Year 9
98 Interest expense	**$136.9**	$121.9	$97.6
99 Less interest expense capitalized	**20.7**	10.3	3.5
100	**$116.2**	$111.6	$94.1

CAMPBELL SOUP COMPANY

(million dollars)

101 **4** **Foreign Currency Translation**

Fluctuations in foreign exchange rates resulted in decreases in net earnings of $.3 in Year 11, $3.2 in Year 10 and $19.1 in Year 9.

The balances in the Cumulative translation adjustments account are the following:

	Year 11	Year 10	Year 9
Europe	$ 5.6	$43.2	$(3.5)
Canada	3.8	3.6	(2.5)
Australia	13.4	16.1	7.3
Other	.8	.6	.8
	$23.6	$63.5	$ 2.1

5 **Other Expense**

Included in other expense are the following:

	Year 11	Year 10	Year 9
102 Stock price related incentive programs	$15.4	$ (.1)	$17.4
103 Amortization of intangible and other assets	14.1	16.8	16.4
104 Other, net	(3.3)	(2.0)	(1.4)
	$26.2	$14.7	$32.4

105 **6** **Divestitures, Restructuring and Unusual Charges**

In Year 10, charges for divestiture and restructuring programs, designed to strengthen the Company's core businesses and improve long-term profitability, reduced operating earnings by $339.1; $301.6 after taxes, or $2.33 per share. The divestiture program involves the sale of several low-return or non-strategic businesses. The restructuring charges provide for the elimination of underperforming assets and unnecessary facilities and include a charge of $113 to write off goodwill in the United Kingdom.

In Year 9, charges for a worldwide restructuring program reduced operating earnings by $343.0; $260.8 after taxes, or $2.02 per share. The restructuring program involved plant consolidations, work force reductions, and goodwill write-offs.

106 **7** **Acquisitions**

Prior to July Year 11, the Company owned approximately 71% of the capital stock of Campbell Soup Company Ltd. ("Campbell Canada"), which processes, packages and distributes a wide range of prepared foods exclusively in Canada under many of the Company's brand names. The financial position and results of operations of Campbell Canada are consolidated with those of the Company. In July Year 11, the Company acquired the remaining shares (29%) of Campbell Canada which it did not already own at a cost of $159.7. In addition, the Company made one other acquisition at a cost of $20.4. The total cost of Year 11 acquisitions of $180.1 was allocated as follows:

107

Working capital	$ 5.1
Fixed assets	4.7
Intangibles, principally goodwill	132.3
Other assets	1.5
Elimination of minority interest	36.5
	$180.1

During Year 10 the Company made several small acquisitions at a cost of $43.1 which was allocated as follows:

108

Working capital	$ 7.8
Fixed assets	24.7
Intangibles, principally goodwill	18.5
Long-term liabilities and other	(7.9)
	$43.1

During Year 9, the Company made several acquisitions at a cost of $137.9, including a soup and pickle manufacturing business in Canada. The cost of the acquisitions was allocated as follows:

109

Working capital	$ 39.9
Fixed assets	34.6
Intangibles, principally goodwill	65.5
Long-term liabilities and other	(2.1)
	$137.9

These acquisition were accounted for as purchase transactions, and operations of the acquired companies are included in the financial statements from the dates the acquisitions were recorded. Proforma results

(million dollars)

of operations have not been presented as they would not vary materially from the reported amounts and would not be indicative of results anticipated following acquisition due to significant changes made to acquired companies' operations.

. . . .

110 **8** **Pension Plans and Retirement Benefits**

Pension Plans. Substantially all of the employees of the Company and its domestic and Canadian subsidiaries are covered by noncontributory defined benefit pension plans. Plan benefits are generally based on years of service and employees' compensation during the last years of employment. Benefits are paid from funds previously provided to trustees and insurance companies or are paid directly by the Company or its subsidiaries. Actuarial assumptions and plan provisions are reviewed regularly by the Company and its independent actuaries to ensure that plan assets will be adequate to provide pension and survivor benefits. Plan assets consist primarily of shares of or units in common stock, fixed income, real estate and money market funds.

Pension expense included the following:

For Domestic and Canadian trusteed plans:	Year 11	Year 10	Year 9
111 Service cost-benefits earned during the year	$ 22.1	$ 19.3	$ 17.2
112 Interest cost on projected benefit obligation	69.0	63.3	58.8
113 Actual return on plan assets	(73.4)	(27.1)	(113.8)
114 Net amortization and deferral	6.3	(38.2)	57.8
	24.0	17.3	20.0
115 Other pension expense	7.4	6.4	6.8
116 Consolidated pension expense	$ 31.4	$ 23.7	$ 26.8

Principal actuarial assumptions used in the United States were:

Measurements of projected benefit obligation—			
117 Discount rate	8.75%	9.00%	9.00%
118 Long-term rate of compensation increase	5.75%	5.50%	5.00%
119 Long-term rate of return on plan assets	9.00%	9.00%	9.00%

The funded status of the plans was as follows:

120	**July 28, Year 11**	July 29, Year 10
Actuarial present value of benefit obligations:		
Vested	$(679.6)	$(624.4)
Non-vested	(34.8)	(35.0)
Accumulated benefit obligation	(714.4)	(659.4)
Effect of projected future salary increases	(113.3)	(101.0)
Projected benefit obligation	(827.7)	(760.4)
Plan assets at market value	857.7	773.9
Plan assets in excess of projected benefit obligation	30.0	13.5
Unrecognized net loss	122.9	86.3
Unrecognized prior service cost	54.9	55.9
Unrecognized net assets at transition	(35.3)	(39.5)
Prepaid pension expense	$ 172.5	$ 116.2

Pension coverage for employees of the Company's foreign subsidiaries, other than Canada, and other supplemental pension benefits of the Company are provided to the extent determined appropriate through their respective plans. Obligations under such plans are systematically provided for by depositing funds with trusts or under insurance contracts. The assets and obligations of these plans are not material.

Savings Plans. The Company sponsors employee savings plans which cover substantially all domestic employees. After one year of continuous service the Company matches 50% of employee contributions up to five percent of compensation within certain limits. In fiscal Year 12, the Company will increase its contribution by up to 20% if certain earnings' goals are achieved. Amounts charged to costs and expenses were $10.0 in Year 11, $10.6 in Year 10, and $10.7 in Year 9.

Retiree Benefits. The Company and its domestic subsidiaries provide certain health care and life insurance benefits to substantially all retired employees and their dependents. The cost of these retiree health and life insurance benefits are expensed as claims are paid and amounted to $15.3 in Year 11, $12.6 in Year 10, and $11.0 in Year 9. Substantially all retirees of foreign subsidiaries are provided health care benefits by government sponsored plans. The cost of life insurance provided to retirees of certain foreign subsidiaries is not significant.

CAMPBELL SOUP COMPANY

. . . .

(million dollars)

The deferred income taxes result from temporary differences between financial statement earnings and taxable earnings as follows:

	Year 11	Year 10	Year 9
128 Depreciation	$ 5.9	$ 18.6	$ 11.9
129 Pensions	13.6	11.7	8.3
130 Prefunded employee benefits	(3.3)	(4.8)	(3.4)
131 Accruals not currently deductible for tax purposes	(11.4)	(5.8)	(5.3)
132 Divestitures, restructuring and unusual charges	29.3	(11.1)	(78.2)
133 Other	1.4	(4.7)	(1.1)
	$35.5	$ 3.9	$(67.8)

The following is a reconciliation of effective income tax rates with the statutory Federal income tax rate:

	Year 11	Year 10	Year 9
134 Statutory Federal income tax rate	34.0%	34.0%	34.0%
135 State income taxes (net of Federal tax benefit)	3.0	3.7	3.6
136 Nondeductible divestitures, restructuring and unusual charges		56.5	48.7
137 Nondeductible amortization of intangibles	.6	.9	1.1
138 Foreign earnings not taxed or taxed at other than statutory Federal rate	(.3)	1.2	.2
139 Other	2.5	1.2	.1
140 Effective income tax rate	39.8%	97.5%	87.7%

121 **9 Taxes on Earnings**

The provision for income taxes consists of the following:

	Year 11	Year 10	Year 9
Currently payable			
122 Federal	$185.8	$132.4	$118.8
123 State	23.4	20.8	20.9
124 Foreign	21.2	17.9	21.5
124A	230.4	171.1	161.2
Deferred			
125 Federal	21.9	1.2	(49.3)
126 State	7.5	2.6	(8.0)
127 Foreign	6.1	.1	(10.5)
127A	35.5	3.9	(67.8)
127B	$265.9	$175.0	$ 93.4

The provision for income taxes was reduced by $3.2 in Year 11, $5.2 in Year 10 and $3.5 in Year 9 due to the utilization of loss carryforwards by certain foreign subsidiaries.

Certain foreign subsidiaries of the Company have tax loss carryforwards of approximately $103.4 ($77.4 for financial purposes), of which $10.5 relate to periods prior to acquisition of the subsidiaries by the Company. Of these carryforwards, $54.8 expire through Year 16 and $48.6 may be carried forward indefinitely. The current statutory tax rates in these foreign countries range from 20% to 51%.

CAMPBELL SOUP

A49

NOTES TO CONSOLIDATED FINANCIAL STATEMENTS

. . . .

(million dollars)

Income taxes have not been accrued on undistributed earnings of foreign subsidiaries of $219.7 which are invested in operating assets and are not expected to be remitted. If remitted, tax credits are available to substantially reduce any resultant additional taxes.

The following are earnings before taxes of United States and foreign companies.

	Year 11	Year 10	Year 9
[141] United States	$570.9	$277.0	$201.5
[142] Foreign	96.5	(97.6)	(95.0)
	$667.4	$179.4	$106.5

. . . .

[143] **10 Leases**

Rent expense was $59.7 in Year 11, $62.4 in Year 10 and $60.2 in Year 9 and generally relates to leases of machinery and equipment. Future minimum lease payments under operating leases are $71.9.

. . . .

11 Supplementary Statements of Earnings Information

	Year 11	Year 10	Year 9
[144] Maintenance and repairs	$173.9	$180.6	$173.9
[145] Advertising	$195.4	$220.4	$212.9

. . . .

[146] **12 Cash and Cash Equivalents**

Cash and Cash Equivalents includes cash equivalents of $140.7 at July 28, Year 11, and $44.1 at July 29, Year 10.

. . . .

13 Accounts Receivable

	Year 11	Year 10
[147] Customers	$478.0	$554.0
[148] Allowances for cash discounts and bad debts	(16.3)	(19.9)
	461.7	534.1
[149] Other	65.7	90.4
[150]	$527.4	$624.5

. . . .

14 Inventories

	Year 11	Year 10
[151] Raw materials, containers and supplies	$342.3	$384.4
[152] Finished products	454.0	520.0
	796.3	904.4
[153] Less—adjustments of inventories to LIFO basis	89.6	84.6
	$706.7	$819.8

Liquidation of LIFO inventory quantities had no significant effect on net earnings in Year 11, Year 10, or Year 9. Inventories for which the LIFO method of determining cost is used represented approximately 70% of consolidated inventories in Year 11 and 64% in Year 10.

. . . .

15 Prepaid Expenses

	Year 11	Year 10
[154] Pensions	$19.8	$ 22.3
[155] Deferred taxes	36.6	37.7
[156] Prefunded employee benefits	1.2	13.9
[157] Other	35.1	44.1
	$92.7	$118.0

. . . .

16 Plant Assets

	Year 11	Year 10
[158] Land	$ 56.3	$ 63.8
[159] Buildings	758.7	746.5
[160] Machinery and equipment	1,779.3	1,657.6
[161] Projects in progress	327.6	267.0
[161A]	2,921.9	2,734.9
[162] Accumulated depreciation	(1,131.5)	(1,017.2)
	$1,790.4	$1,717.7

Depreciation provided in costs and expenses was $194.5 in Year 11, $184.1 in Year 10 and $175.9 in Year 9. Approximately $158.2 of capital expenditures is required to complete projects in progress at July 28, Year 11.

. . . .

(million dollars)

. . . .

17 Intangible Assets

	Year 11	Year 10
163 Cost of investments in excess of net assets of purchased companies (goodwill)	$347.8	$281.1
164 Other intangibles	129.8	134.0
	477.6	415.1
165 Accumulated amortization	(42.1)	(31.7)
	$435.5	$383.4

. . . .

18 Other Assets

	Year 11	Year 10
166 Investment in affiliates	$155.8	$169.4
167 Noncurrent prepaid pension expense	152.7	93.9
168 Other noncurrent investments	44.2	52.0
169 Other	51.9	33.7
169A	$404.6	$349.0

Investment in affiliates consists principally of the Company's ownership of 33% of the outstanding capital stock of Arnotts Limited, an Australian biscuit manufacturer. This investment is being accounted for by the equity method. Included in this investment is goodwill of $28.3 which is being amortized over 40 years. At July 28, Year 11, the market value of the investment based on quoted market prices was $213.8. The Company's equity in the earnings of Arnotts Limited was $1.5 in Year 11, $13.0 in Year 10 and $8.7 in Year 9. The Year 10 amount includes a $4.0 gain realized by Arnotts on the sales of businesses. Dividends received were $8.2 in Year 11, $7.4 in Year 10 and $6.6 in Year 9. The Company's equity in the undistributed earnings of Arnotts was $15.4 at July 28, Year 11 and $22.1 at July 29, Year 10.

170 19 Notes Payable and Long-term Debt

Notes payable consists of the following:

	Year 11	Year 10
Commercial paper	$ 24.7	$191.8
8.25% Notes due Year 11		100.3
13.99% Notes due Year 12	182.0*	
Banks	23.6	91.1
Other	51.9	69.4
Amounts reclassified to long-term debt		(250.3)
	$282.2	$202.3

Present value of $200.0 zero coupon notes, net of unamortized discount of $18.0.

At July 29, Year 10, $150 of outstanding commercial paper and $100.3 of currently maturing notes were reclassified to long-term debt and were refinanced in Year 11. Information on notes payable follows:

171	Year 11	Year 10	Year 9
Maximum amount payable at end of any monthly accounting period during the year	$603.3	$518.7	$347.1
Approximate average amount outstanding during the year	$332.5	$429.7	$273.5
Weighted average interest rate at year-end	10.1%	10.7%	12.1%
Approximate weighted average interest rate during the year	9.8%	10.8%	10.6%

The amount of unused lines of credit at July 28, Year 11 approximates $635. The lines of credit are unconditional and generally cover loans for a period of a year at prime commercial interest rates.

CAMPBELL SOUP

A51

NOTES TO CONSOLIDATED FINANCIAL STATEMENTS
. . . .

(million dollars)

Long-term debt consists of the following:

172

Fiscal year maturities	Year 11	Year 10
13.99% Notes due Year 12	$	$159.7***
9.125% Notes due Year 14	100.6	100.9
10.5% Notes due Year 16*	100.0	100.0
7.5% Notes due Year 18*	99.6	99.5
9.0% Notes due Year 18	99.8	
8.58%–8.75% Medium-Term Notes due Year 21**	100.0	
8.875% Debentures due Year 41	199.6	
Other Notes due Year 12–24 (interest 4.7%–14.4%)	58.2	82.5
Notes payable, reclassified		250.3
Capital lease obligations	14.8	12.9
	$772.6	$805.8

*Redeemable in Year 13.

**$50 redeemable in Year 18.

***Present value of $200.0 zero coupon notes, net of unamortized discount of $40.3.

173 Future minimum lease payments under capital leases are $28.0 and the present value of such payments, after deducting implicit interest of $6.5, is $21.5 of which $6.7 is included in current liabilities.

Principle amounts of long-term debt mature as follows: Year 12-$227.7 (in current liabilities); Year 13-$118.9; Year 14-$17.8; Year 15-$15.9; Year 16-$108.3 and beyond-$511.7.

The Company has filed a shelf registration statement with the Securities and Exchange Commission for the issuance from time to time of up to $300 of debt securities, of which $100 remains unissued.

Information on financial instruments follows:

At July 28, Year 11, the Company had an interest rate swap agreement with financial institutions having a notional principal amount of $100, which is intended to reduce the impact of changes in interest rates on floating rate commercial paper. In addition, at July 28, Year 11, the Company had two swap agreements with financial institutions which covered both interest rates and foreign currencies. These agreements

have a total notional principal amount of $103, and are intended to reduce exposure to higher foreign interest rates and to hedge the Company's net investments in the United Kingdom and Australia. The Company is exposed to credit loss in the event of nonperformance by the other parties to the interest rate swap agreements; however, the Company does not anticipate nonperformance by the counterparties.

At July 28, Year 11, the Company had contracts to purchase approximately $109 in foreign currency. The contracts are mostly for European currencies and have maturities through Year 12.

. . . .

20 Accrued Liabilities

	Year 11	Year 10
174 Divestiture and restructuring charges	$ 88.4	$238.8
175 Other	320.3	253.1
	$408.7	$491.9

. . . .

21 Other Liabilities

	Year 11	Year 10
176 Deferred income taxes	$258.5	$235.1
177 Other liabilities	23.0	28.5
178 Minority interests	23.5	56.3
	$305.0	$319.9

(million dollars)

179 ㉒ Shareowners' Equity

The Company has authorized 140 million shares of Capital Stock of $.15 par value and 40 million shares of Preferred Stock issuable in one or more classes, with or without par as may be authorized by the Board of Directors. No Preferred Stock has been issued.

The following summarizes the activity in option shares under the Company's employee stock option plans:

(thousands of shares)	Year 11	Year 10	Year 9
Beginning of year	4,301.1	3,767.9	3,257.0
Granted under the Year 4 long-term incentive plan at average price of $63.64 in Year 11; $47.27 in Year 10; $30.37 in Year 9	2,136.3	1,196.0	1,495.5
Exercised at average price of $29.82 in Year 11; $24.78 in Year 10; $20.65 in Year 9 in form of:			
Stock appreciation rights	(14.9)	(110.2)	(137.3)
Shares	(1,063.7)	(367.2)	(615.1)
Terminated	(216.9)	(185.4)	(232.2)
End of year	5,141.9	4,301.1	3,767.9
Exercisable at end of year	2,897.0	2,654.4	2,104.1
Shares under option-price per share:			
Range of prices: Low	$14.68	$ 6.98	$ 6.98
High	$83.31	$57.61	$34.31
Average	$46.73	$33.63	$28.21

In addition to options granted under the Year 4 long-term incentive plan, 233,200 restricted shares of capital stock were granted to certain key management employees in Year 11; 168,850 in Year 10; and 162,000 in Year 9.

There are 4,229,111 shares available for grant under the long-term incentive plan.

Net earnings per share are based on the weighted average shares outstanding during the applicable periods. The potential dilution from the exercise of stock options is not material.

㉓ Statements of Cash Flows

	Year 11	Year 10	Year 9
180 Interest paid, net of amounts capitalized	$101.3	$116.3	$ 88.9
181 Interest received	$ 27.9	$ 17.1	$ 35.5
182 Income taxes paid	$199.3	$152.8	$168.6
183 Capital lease obligations incurred	$ 10.0	$ 9.7	$ 18.0

184 ㉔ Quarterly Data (unaudited)

Year 11	First	Second	Third	Fourth
Net sales	$1,594.3	$1,770.9	$1,490.8	$1,348.1
Cost of products sold	1,082.7	1,152.6	981.6	878.6
Net earnings	105.1	135.3	76.4	84.7
Per share				
Net earnings	.82	1.07	.60	.67
Dividends	.25	.29	.29	.29
Market price				
High	54.00	60.38	87.13	84.88
Low	43.75	48.50	58.75	72.38

Year 10	First	Second	Third	Fourth
Net sales	$1,523.5	$1,722.5	$1,519.6	$1,440.2
Cost of products sold	1,057.2	1,173.0	1,049.3	978.7
Net earnings (loss)	83.0	105.2	54.6	(238.4)
Per share				
Net earnings (loss)	.64	.81	.42	(1.84)
Dividends	.23	.25	.25	.25
Market price				
High	58.50	59.63	54.13	62.00
Low	42.13	42.50	45.00	50.13

The fourth quarter of Year 10 includes divestitures, restructuring and unusual charges of $301.6 after taxes, or $2.33 per share.

CAMPBELL SOUP

A53

CAMPBELL SOUP COMPANY

Eleven Year Review—Consolidated

(millions except per share amounts)

Fiscal Year	Year 11	Year 10[a]	Year 9[b]
[185] Summary of Operations			
Net sales	$6,204.1	$6,205.8	$5,672.1
Earnings before taxes	667.4	179.4	106.5
Earnings before cumulative effect of accounting change	401.5	4.4	13.1
Net earnings	401.5	4.4	13.1
Percent of sales	6.5%	.1%	.2%
Return on average shareowners' equity	23.0%	.3%	.7%
Financial Position			
Working capital	$ 240.5	$ 367.4	$ 369.4
Plant assets–net	1,790.4	1,717.7	1,540.6
Total assets	4,149.0	4,115.6	3,932.1
Long-term debt	772.6	805.8	629.2
Shareowners' equity	1,793.4	1,691.8	1,778.3
Per Share Data			
Earnings before cumulative effect of accounting change	$ 3.16	$ .03	$ .10
Net earnings	3.16	.03	.10
Dividends declared	1.12	.98	.90
Shareowners' equity	14.12	13.09	13.76
Other Statistics			
Salaries, wages, pensions, etc.	$1,401.0	$1,422.5	$1,333.9
Capital expenditures	371.1	397.3	302.0
Number of shareowners (in thousands)	37.7	43.0	43.7
Weighted average shares outstanding	127.0	129.6	129.3

(a) Year 10 includes pre-tax divestiture and restructuring charges of $339.1 million; 301.6 million or $2.33 per share after taxes.
(b) Year 9 includes pre-tax restructuring charges of $343.0 million; $260.8 million or $2.02 per share after taxes.
(c) Year 8 includes pre-tax restructuring charges of $49.3 million; $29.4 million or 23 cents per share after taxes. Year 8 also includes cumulative effect of change in accounting for income taxes of $32.5 million or 25 cents per share.
(d) Includes employees under the Employee Stock Ownership Plan terminated in Year 7.

CAMPBELL SOUP

Year 8[c]	Year 7	Year 6	Year 5	Year 4	Year 3	Year 2	Year 1
$4,868.9	$4,490.4	$4,286.8	$3,916.6	$3,636.9	$3,292.4	$2,955.6	$2,797.7
388.6	417.9	387.2	333.7	332.4	306.0	276.9	244.4
241.6	247.3	223.2	197.8	191.2	165.0	149.6	129.7
274.1	247.3	223.2	197.8	191.2	165.0	149.6	129.7
5.6%	5.5%	5.2%	5.1%	5.3%	5.0%	5.1%	4.6%
15.1%	15.1%	15.3%	15.0%	15.9%	15.0%	14.6%	13.2%

Year 8[c]	Year 7	Year 6	Year 5	Year 4	Year 3	Year 2	Year 1
$ 499.6	$ 744.1	$ 708.7	$ 579.4	$ 541.5	$ 478.9	$ 434.6	$ 368.2
1,508.9	1,349.0	1,168.1	1,027.5	970.9	889.1	815.4	755.1
3,609.6	3,097.4	2,762.8	2,437.5	2,210.1	1,991.5	1,865.5	1,722.9
525.8	380.2	362.3	297.1	283.0	267.5	236.2	150.6
1,895.0	1,736.1	1,538.9	1,382.5	1,259.9	1,149.4	1,055.8	1,000.5

Year 8[c]	Year 7	Year 6	Year 5	Year 4	Year 3	Year 2	Year 1
$ 1.87	$ 1.90	$ 1.72	$ 1.53	$ 1.48	$ 1.28	$ 1.16	$ 1.00
2.12	1.90	1.72	1.53	1.48	1.28	1.16	1.00
.81	.71	.65	.61	.57	.54	.53	.51
14.69	13.35	11.86	10.69	9.76	8.92	8.19	7.72

Year 8[c]	Year 7	Year 6	Year 5	Year 4	Year 3	Year 2	Year 1
$1,222.9	$1,137.3	$1,061.0	$ 950.1	$ 889.5	$ 755.1	$ 700.9	$ 680.9
261.9	328.0	251.3	212.9	183.1	154.1	147.6	135.4
43.0	41.0	50.9[d]	49.5[d]	49.4[d]	40.1	39.7	41.6
129.4	129.9	129.5	129.1	129.0	129.0	129.0	129.6

CAMPBELL SOUP

A55

186

CAMPBELL SOUP COMPANY AND CONSOLIDATED SUBSIDIARIES
Property, Plant, and Equipment at Cost

(million dollars)	Land	Buildings	Machinery and Equipment	Projects in Progress	Total
Balance at July 31, Year 8	$53.2	$735.5	$1,624.4	$126.6	$2,539.7
Additions	2.8	47.6	216.4	35.2	302.0
Acquired assets*	4.8	13.6	22.6	—	41.0
Retirements and sales	(4.5)	(88.4)	(238.3)	—	(331.2)
Translation adjustments	(.5)	(2.5)	(5.9)	.4	(8.5)
Balance at July 30, Year 9	55.8	705.8	1,619.2	162.2	2,543.0
Additions	3.2	69.2	219.6	105.3	397.3
Acquired assets*	3.8	14.1	6.8	—	24.7
Retirements and sales	(2.8)	(64.0)	(222.9)	(1.1)	(290.8)
Translation adjustments	3.8	21.4	34.9	.6	60.7
Balance at July 29, Year 10	63.8	746.5	1,657.6	267.0	2,734.9
Additions	1.5	70.2	239.5	59.9	371.1
Acquired assets*	.5	3.3	.9	—	4.7
Retirements and sales	(7.5)	(49.3)	(99.9)	—	(156.7)
Rate variance	(2.0)	(12.0)	(18.8)	.7	(32.1)
Balance at July 28, Year 11	$56.3	$758.7	$1,779.3	$327.6	$2,921.9

*See "Acquisitions" in Notes to Consolidated Financial Statements.

187

Form 10-K

CAMPBELL SOUP COMPANY AND CONSOLIDATED SUBSIDIARIES
Accumulated Depreciation and Amortization of Property, Plant and Equipment

(million dollars)	Buildings	Machinery and Equipment	Total
Balance at July 31, Year 8	$285.4	$745.4	$1,030.8
Additions charged to income	31.5	144.4	175.9
Retirements and sales	(57.8)	(143.5)	(201.3)
Translations adjustments	(.8)	(2.2)	(3.0)
Balance at July 30, Year 9	258.3	744.1	1,002.4
Additions charged to income	34.2	149.9	184.1
Retirements and sales	(32.5)	(154.7)	(187.2)
Translations adjustments	5.2	12.7	17.9
Balance at July 29, Year 10	265.2	752.0	1,017.2
Additions charged to income	35.3	159.2	194.5
Retirements and sales	(17.4)	(52.1)	(69.5)
Translations adjustments	(2.8)	(7.9)	(10.7)
Balance at July 28, Year 11	$280.3	$851.2	$1,131.5

INTEREST TABLES

Table 1: Future Value of 1, $f = (1 + i)^n$

■ ■ ■ ■ ■ ■ ■

Periods	2%	2½%	3%	4%	5%	6%	7%	8%	9%	10%
1	1.02000	1.02500	1.03000	1.04000	1.05000	1.06000	1.07000	1.08000	1.09000	1.10000
2	1.04040	1.05063	1.06090	1.08160	1.10250	1.12360	1.14490	1.16640	1.18810	1.21000
3	1.06121	1.07689	1.09273	1.12486	1.15763	1.19102	1.22504	1.25971	1.29503	1.33100
4	1.08243	1.10381	1.12551	1.16986	1.21551	1.26248	1.31080	1.36049	1.41158	1.46410
5	1.10408	1.13141	1.15927	1.21665	1.27628	1.33823	1.40255	1.46933	1.53862	1.61051
6	1.12616	1.15969	1.19405	1.26532	1.34010	1.41852	1.50073	1.58687	1.67710	1.77156
7	1.14869	1.18869	1.22987	1.31593	1.40710	1.50363	1.60578	1.71382	1.82804	1.94872
8	1.17166	1.21840	1.26677	1.36857	1.47746	1.59385	1.71819	1.85093	1.99256	2.14359
9	1.19509	1.24886	1.30477	1.42331	1.55133	1.68948	1.83846	1.99900	2.17189	2.35795
10	1.21899	1.28008	1.34392	1.48024	1.62889	1.79085	1.96715	2.15892	2.36736	2.59374
11	1.24337	1.31209	1.38423	1.53945	1.71034	1.89830	2.10485	2.33164	2.58043	2.85312
12	1.26824	1.34489	1.42576	1.60103	1.79586	2.01220	2.25219	2.51817	2.81266	3.13843
13	1.29361	1.37851	1.46853	1.66507	1.88565	2.13293	2.40985	2.71962	3.06580	3.45227
14	1.31948	1.41297	1.51259	1.73168	1.97993	2.26090	2.57853	2.93719	3.34173	3.79750
15	1.34587	1.44830	1.55797	1.80094	2.07893	2.39656	2.75903	3.17217	3.64248	4.17725
16	1.37279	1.48451	1.60471	1.87298	2.18287	2.54035	2.95216	3.42594	3.97031	4.59497
17	1.40024	1.52162	1.65285	1.94790	2.29202	2.69277	3.15882	3.70002	4.32763	5.05447
18	1.42825	1.55966	1.70243	2.02582	2.40662	2.85434	3.37993	3.99602	4.71712	5.55992
19	1.45681	1.59865	1.75351	2.10685	2.52695	3.02560	3.61653	4.31570	5.14166	6.11591
20	1.48595	1.63862	1.80611	2.19112	2.65330	3.20714	3.86968	4.66096	5.60441	6.72750
21	1.51567	1.67958	1.86029	2.27877	2.78596	3.39956	4.14056	5.03383	6.10881	7.40025
22	1.54598	1.72157	1.91610	2.36992	2.92526	3.60354	4.43040	5.43654	6.65860	8.14027
23	1.57690	1.76461	1.97359	2.46472	3.07152	3.81975	4.74053	5.87146	7.25787	8.95430
24	1.60844	1.80873	2.03279	2.56330	3.22510	4.04893	5.07237	6.34118	7.91108	9.84973
25	1.64061	1.85394	2.09378	2.66584	3.38635	4.29187	5.42743	6.84848	8.62308	10.83471

Periods	11%	12%	14%	15%	16%	18%	20%	22%	24%	25%
1	1.11000	1.12000	1.14000	1.15000	1.16000	1.18000	1.20000	1.22000	1.24000	1.25000
2	1.23210	1.25440	1.29960	1.32250	1.34560	1.39240	1.44000	1.48840	1.53760	1.56250
3	1.36763	1.40493	1.48154	1.52088	1.56090	1.64303	1.72800	1.81585	1.90662	1.95313
4	1.51807	1.57352	1.68896	1.74901	1.81064	1.93878	2.07360	2.21533	2.36421	2.44141
5	1.68506	1.76234	1.92541	2.01136	2.10034	2.28776	2.48832	2.70271	2.93163	3.05176
6	1.87041	1.97382	2.19497	2.31306	2.43640	2.69955	2.98598	3.29730	3.63522	3.81470
7	2.07616	2.21068	2.50227	2.66002	2.82622	3.18547	3.58318	4.02271	4.50767	4.76837
8	2.30454	2.47596	2.85259	3.05902	3.27841	3.75886	4.29982	4.90771	5.58951	5.96046
9	2.55804	2.77308	3.25195	3.51788	3.80296	4.43545	5.15978	5.98740	6.93099	7.45058
10	2.83942	3.10585	3.70722	4.04556	4.41144	5.23384	6.19174	7.30463	8.59443	9.31323
11	3.15176	3.47855	4.22623	4.65239	5.11726	6.17593	7.43008	8.91165	10.65709	11.64153
12	3.49845	3.89598	4.81790	5.35025	5.93603	7.28759	8.91610	10.87221	13.21479	14.55192
13	3.88328	4.36349	5.49241	6.15279	6.88579	8.59936	10.69932	13.26410	16.38634	18.18989
14	4.31044	4.88711	6.26135	7.07571	7.98752	10.14724	12.83918	16.18220	20.31906	22.73737
15	4.78459	5.47357	7.13794	8.13706	9.26552	11.97375	15.40702	19.74229	25.19563	28.42171
16	5.31089	6.13039	8.13725	9.35762	10.74800	14.12902	18.48843	24.08559	31.24259	35.52714
17	5.89509	6.86604	9.27646	10.76126	12.46768	16.67225	22.18611	29.38442	38.74081	44.40892
18	6.54355	7.68997	10.57517	12.37545	14.46251	19.67325	26.62333	35.84899	48.03860	55.51115
19	7.26334	8.61276	12.05569	14.23177	16.77652	23.21444	31.94800	43.73577	59.56786	69.38894
20	8.06231	9.64629	13.74349	16.36654	19.46076	27.39303	38.33760	53.35764	73.86415	86.73617
21	8.94917	10.80385	15.66758	18.82152	22.57448	32.32378	46.00512	65.09632	91.59155	108.42022
22	9.93357	12.10031	17.86104	21.64475	26.18640	38.14206	55.20614	79.41751	113.57352	135.52527
23	11.02627	13.55235	20.36158	24.89146	30.37622	45.00763	66.24737	96.88936	140.83116	169.40659
24	12.23916	15.17863	23.21221	28.62518	35.23642	53.10901	79.49685	118.20502	174.63064	211.75824
25	13.58546	17.00006	26.46192	32.91895	40.87424	62.66863	95.39622	144.21013	216.54199	264.69780

Table 2: Present Value of 1, $p = \dfrac{1}{(1+i)^n}$

Periods	2%	2½%	3%	4%	5%	6%	7%	8%	9%	10%
1	.98039	.97561	.97087	.96154	.95238	.94340	.93458	.92593	.91743	.90909
2	.96177	.95181	.94260	.92456	.90703	.89000	.87344	.85734	.84168	.82645
3	.94232	.92860	.91514	.88900	.86384	.83962	.81630	.79383	.77218	.75131
4	.92385	.90595	.88849	.85480	.82270	.79209	.76290	.73503	.70843	.68301
5	.90573	.88385	.86261	.82193	.78353	.74726	.71299	.68058	.64993	.62092
6	.88797	.86230	.83748	.79031	.74622	.70496	.66634	.63017	.59627	.56447
7	.87056	.84127	.81309	.75992	.71068	.66506	.62275	.58349	.54703	.51316
8	.85349	.82075	.78941	.73069	.67684	.62741	.58201	.54027	.50187	.46651
9	.83676	.80073	.76642	.70259	.64461	.59190	.54393	.50025	.46043	.42410
10	.82035	.78120	.74409	.67556	.61391	.55839	.50835	.46319	.42241	.38554
11	.80426	.76214	.72242	.64958	.58468	.52679	.47509	.42888	.38753	.35049
12	.78849	.74356	.70138	.62460	.55684	.49697	.44401	.39711	.35553	.31863
13	.77303	.72542	.68095	.60057	.53032	.46884	.41496	.36770	.32618	.28966
14	.75788	.70773	.66112	.57748	.50507	.44230	.38782	.34046	.29925	.26333
15	.74301	.69047	.64186	.55526	.48102	.41727	.36245	.31524	.27454	.23939
16	.72845	.67362	.62317	.53391	.45811	.39365	.33873	.29189	.25187	.21763
17	.71416	.65720	.60502	.51337	.43630	.37136	.31657	.27027	.23107	.19784
18	.70016	.64117	.58739	.49363	.41552	.35034	.29586	.25025	.21199	.17986
19	.68643	.62553	.57029	.47464	.39573	.33051	.27651	.23171	.19449	.16351
20	.67297	.61027	.55368	.45639	.37689	.31180	.25842	.21455	.17843	.14864
21	.65978	.59539	.53755	.43883	.35894	.29416	.24151	.19866	.16370	.13513
22	.64684	.58086	.52189	.42196	.34185	.27751	.22571	.18394	.15018	.12285
23	.63416	.56670	.50669	.40573	.32557	.26180	.21095	.17032	.13778	.11168
24	.62172	.55288	.49193	.39012	.31007	.24698	.19715	.15770	.12640	.10153
25	.60953	.53939	.47761	.37512	.29530	.23300	.18425	.14602	.11597	.09230

Periods	11%	12%	14%	15%	16%	18%	20%	22%	24%	25%
1	.90090	.89286	.87719	.86957	.86207	.84746	.83333	.81967	.80645	.80000
2	.81162	.79719	.76947	.75614	.74316	.71818	.69444	.67186	.65036	.64000
3	.73119	.71178	.67497	.65752	.64066	.60863	.57870	.55071	.52449	.51200
4	.65873	.63552	.59208	.57175	.55229	.51579	.48225	.45140	.42297	.40960
5	.59345	.56743	.51937	.49718	.47611	.43711	.40188	.37000	.34111	.32768
6	.53464	.50663	.45559	.43233	.41044	.37043	.33490	.30328	.27509	.26214
7	.48166	.45235	.39964	.37594	.35383	.31393	.27908	.24859	.22184	.20972
8	.43393	.40388	.35056	.32690	.30503	.26604	.23257	.20376	.17891	.16777
9	.39092	.36061	.30751	.28426	.26295	.22546	.19381	.16702	.14428	.13422
10	.35218	.32197	.26974	.24718	.22668	.19106	.16151	.13690	.11635	.10737
11	.31728	.28748	.23662	.21494	.19542	.16192	.13459	.11221	.09383	.08590
12	.28584	.25668	.20756	.18691	.16846	.13722	.11216	.09198	.07567	.06872
13	.25751	.22917	.18207	.16253	.14523	.11629	.09346	.07539	.06103	.05498
14	.23199	.20462	.15971	.14133	.12520	.09855	.07789	.06180	.04921	.04398
15	.20900	.18270	.14010	.12289	.10793	.08352	.06491	.05065	.03969	.03518
16	.18829	.16312	.12289	.10686	.09304	.07078	.05409	.04152	.03201	.02815
17	.16963	.14564	.10780	.09293	.08021	.05998	.04507	.03403	.02581	.02252
18	.15282	.13004	.09456	.08081	.06914	.05083	.03756	.02789	.02082	.01801
19	.13768	.11611	.08295	.07027	.05961	.04308	.03130	.02286	.01679	.01441
20	.12403	.10367	.07276	.06110	.05139	.03651	.02608	.01874	.01354	.01153
21	.11174	.09256	.06383	.05313	.04430	.03094	.02174	.01536	.01092	.00922
22	.10067	.08264	.05599	.04620	.03819	.02622	.01811	.01259	.00880	.00738
23	.09069	.07379	.04911	.04017	.03292	.02222	.01509	.01032	.00710	.00590
24	.08170	.06588	.04308	.03493	.02838	.01883	.01258	.00846	.00573	.00472
25	.07361	.05882	.03779	.03038	.02447	.01596	.01048	.00693	.00462	.00378

Table 3: Future Value of an Ordinary Annuity of n Payments of 1 Each, $F_0 = \dfrac{(1+i)^n - 1}{i}$

■ ■ ■ ■ ■ ■ ■

Periods (n)	2%	2½%	3%	4%	5%	6%	7%	8%	9%	10%
1	1.00000	1.00000	1.00000	1.00000	1.00000	1.00000	1.00000	1.00000	1.00000	1.00000
2	2.02000	2.02500	2.03000	2.04000	2.05000	2.06000	2.07000	2.08000	2.09000	2.10000
3	3.06040	3.07563	3.09090	3.12160	3.15250	3.18360	3.21490	3.24640	3.27810	3.31000
4	4.12161	4.15252	4.18363	4.24646	4.31013	4.37462	4.43994	4.50611	4.57313	4.64100
5	5.20404	5.25633	5.30914	5.41632	5.52563	5.63709	5.75074	5.86660	5.98471	6.10510
6	6.30812	6.38774	6.46841	6.63298	6.80191	6.97532	7.15329	7.33593	7.52333	7.71561
7	7.43428	7.54753	7.66246	7.89829	8.14201	8.39384	8.65402	8.92280	9.20043	9.48717
8	8.58297	8.73612	8.89234	9.21423	9.54911	9.89747	10.25980	10.63663	11.02847	11.43589
9	9.75463	9.95452	10.15911	10.58280	11.02656	11.49132	11.97799	12.48756	13.02104	13.57948
10	10.94972	11.20338	11.46388	12.00611	12.57789	13.18079	13.81645	14.48656	15.19293	15.93742
11	12.16872	12.48347	12.80780	13.48635	14.20679	14.97164	15.78360	16.64549	17.56029	18.53117
12	13.41209	13.79555	14.19203	15.02581	15.91713	16.86994	17.88845	18.97713	20.14072	21.38428
13	14.68033	15.14044	15.61779	16.62684	17.71298	18.88214	20.14064	21.49530	22.95338	24.52271
14	15.97394	16.51895	17.08632	18.29191	19.59863	21.01507	22.55049	24.21492	26.01919	27.97498
15	17.29342	17.93193	18.59891	20.02359	21.57856	23.27597	25.12902	27.15211	29.36092	31.77248
16	18.63929	19.38022	20.15688	21.82453	23.65749	25.67253	27.88805	30.32428	33.00340	35.94973
17	20.01207	20.86473	21.76159	23.69751	25.84037	28.21288	30.84022	33.75023	36.97370	40.54470
18	21.41231	22.38635	23.41444	25.64541	28.13238	30.90565	33.99903	37.45024	41.30134	45.59917
19	22.84056	23.94601	25.11687	27.67123	30.53900	33.75999	37.37896	41.44626	46.01846	51.15909
20	24.29737	25.54466	26.87037	29.77808	33.06595	36.78559	40.99549	45.76196	51.16012	57.27500
21	25.78332	27.18327	28.67649	31.96920	35.71925	39.99273	44.86518	50.42292	56.76453	64.00250
22	27.29898	28.86286	30.53678	34.24797	38.50521	43.39229	49.00574	55.45676	62.87334	71.40275
23	28.84496	30.58443	32.45288	36.61789	41.43048	46.99583	53.43614	60.89330	69.53194	79.54302
24	30.42186	32.34904	34.42647	39.08260	44.50200	50.81558	58.17667	66.76476	76.78981	88.49733
25	32.03030	34.15776	36.45926	41.64591	47.72710	54.86451	63.24904	73.10594	84.70090	98.34706

Periods (n)	11%	12%	14%	15%	16%	18%	20%	22%	24%	25%
1	1.00000	1.00000	1.00000	1.00000	1.00000	1.00000	1.00000	1.00000	1.00000	1.00000
2	2.11000	2.12000	2.14000	2.15000	2.16000	2.18000	2.20000	2.22000	2.24000	2.25000
3	3.34210	3.37440	3.43960	3.47250	3.50560	3.57240	3.64000	3.70840	3.77760	3.81250
4	4.70973	4.77933	4.92114	4.99338	5.06650	5.21543	5.36800	5.52425	5.68422	5.76563
5	6.22780	6.35285	6.61010	6.74238	6.87714	7.15421	7.44160	7.73958	8.04844	8.20703
6	7.91286	8.11519	8.53552	8.75374	8.97748	9.44197	9.92992	10.44229	10.98006	11.25879
7	9.78327	10.08901	10.73049	11.06680	11.41387	12.14152	12.91590	13.73959	14.61528	15.07349
8	11.85943	12.29969	13.23276	13.72682	14.24009	15.32700	16.49908	17.76231	19.12294	19.84186
9	14.16397	14.77566	16.08535	16.78584	17.51851	19.08585	20.79890	22.67001	24.71245	25.80232
10	16.72201	17.54874	19.33730	20.30372	21.32147	23.52131	25.95868	28.65742	31.64344	33.25290
11	19.56143	20.65458	23.04452	24.34928	25.73290	28.75514	32.15042	35.96205	40.23787	42.56613
12	22.71319	24.13313	27.27075	29.00167	30.85017	34.93107	39.58050	44.87370	50.89495	54.20766
13	26.21164	28.02911	32.08865	34.35192	36.78620	42.21866	48.49660	55.74591	64.10974	68.75958
14	30.09492	32.39260	37.58107	40.50471	43.67199	50.81802	59.19592	69.01001	80.49608	86.94947
15	34.40536	37.27971	43.84241	47.58041	51.65951	60.96527	72.03511	85.19221	100.81514	109.68684
16	39.18995	42.75328	50.98035	55.71747	60.92503	72.93901	87.44213	104.93450	126.01077	138.10855
17	44.50084	48.88367	59.11760	65.07509	71.67303	87.06804	105.93056	129.02009	157.25336	173.63568
18	50.39594	55.74971	68.39407	75.83636	84.14072	103.74028	128.11667	158.40451	195.99416	218.04460
19	56.93949	63.43968	78.96923	88.21181	98.60323	123.41353	154.74000	194.25350	244.03276	273.55576
20	64.20283	72.05244	91.02493	102.44358	115.37975	146.62797	186.68800	237.98927	303.60062	342.94470
21	72.26514	81.69874	104.76842	118.81012	134.84051	174.02100	225.02560	291.34691	377.46477	429.68087
22	81.21431	92.50258	120.43600	137.63164	157.41499	206.34479	271.03072	356.44323	469.05632	538.10109
23	91.14788	104.60289	138.29704	159.27638	183.60138	244.48685	326.23686	435.86075	582.62984	673.62636
24	102.17415	118.15524	158.65862	184.16784	213.97761	289.49448	392.48424	532.75011	723.46100	843.03295
25	114.41331	133.33387	181.87083	212.79302	249.21402	342.60349	471.98108	650.95513	898.09164	1054.79118

Table 4: Present Value of an Ordinary Annuity of n Payments of 1 Each,

■ ■ ■ ■ ■ ■ ■

$$P_0 = \frac{1 - \dfrac{1}{(1 + i)^n}}{i}$$

Periods (n)	2%	2½%	3%	4%	5%	6%	7%	8%	9%	10%
1	.98039	.97561	.97087	.96154	.95238	.94340	.93458	.92593	.91743	.90909
2	1.94156	1.92742	1.91347	1.88609	1.85941	1.83339	1.80802	1.78326	1.75911	1.73554
3	2.88388	2.85602	2.82861	2.77509	2.72325	2.67301	2.62432	2.57710	2.53129	2.48685
4	3.80773	3.76197	3.71710	3.62990	3.54595	3.46511	3.38721	3.31213	3.23972	3.16987
5	4.71346	4.64583	4.57971	4.45182	4.32948	4.21236	4.10020	3.99271	3.88965	3.79079
6	5.60143	5.50813	5.41719	5.24214	5.07569	4.91732	4.76654	4.62288	4.48592	4.35526
7	6.47199	6.34939	6.23028	6.00205	5.78637	5.58238	5.38929	5.20637	5.03295	4.86842
8	7.32548	7.17014	7.01969	6.73274	6.46321	6.20979	5.97130	5.74664	5.53482	5.33493
9	8.16224	7.97087	7.78611	7.43533	7.10782	6.80169	6.51523	6.24689	5.99525	5.75902
10	8.98259	8.75206	8.53020	8.11090	7.72173	7.36009	7.02358	6.71008	6.41766	6.14457
11	9.78685	9.51421	9.25262	8.76048	8.30641	7.88687	7.49867	7.13896	6.80519	6.49506
12	10.57534	10.25776	9.95400	9.38507	8.86325	8.38384	7.94269	7.53608	7.16073	6.81369
13	11.34837	10.98318	10.63496	9.98565	9.39357	8.85268	8.35765	7.90378	7.48690	7.10336
14	12.10625	11.69091	11.29607	10.56312	9.89864	9.29498	8.74547	8.24424	7.78615	7.36669
15	12.84926	12.38138	11.93794	11.11839	10.37966	9.71225	9.10791	8.55948	8.06069	7.60608
16	13.57771	13.05500	12.56110	11.65230	10.83777	10.10590	9.44665	8.85137	8.31256	7.82371
17	14.29187	13.71220	13.16612	12.16567	11.27407	10.47726	9.76322	9.12164	8.54363	8.01255
18	14.99203	14.35336	13.75351	12.65930	11.68959	10.82760	10.05909	9.37189	8.75563	8.20141
19	15.67846	14.97889	14.32380	13.13394	12.08532	11.15812	10.33560	9.60360	8.95011	8.36492
20	16.35143	15.58916	14.87747	13.59033	12.46221	11.46992	10.59401	9.81815	9.12855	8.51356
21	17.01121	16.18455	15.41502	14.02916	12.82115	11.76408	10.83553	10.01680	9.29224	8.64869
22	17.65805	16.76541	15.93692	14.45112	13.16300	12.04158	11.06124	10.20074	9.44243	8.77154
23	18.29220	17.33211	16.44361	14.85684	13.48857	12.30338	11.27219	10.37106	9.58021	8.88322
24	18.91393	17.88499	16.93554	15.24696	13.79864	12.55036	11.46933	10.52876	9.70661	8.98474
25	19.52346	18.42438	17.41315	15.62208	14.09394	12.78336	11.65358	10.67478	9.82258	9.07704

Periods (n)	11%	12%	14%	15%	16%	18%	20%	22%	24%	25%
1	.90090	.89286	.87719	.86957	.86207	.84746	.83333	.81967	.80645	.80000
2	1.71252	1.69005	1.64666	1.62571	1.60523	1.56564	1.52778	1.49153	1.45682	1.44000
3	2.44371	2.40183	2.32163	2.28323	2.24589	2.17427	2.10648	2.04224	1.98130	1.95200
4	3.10245	3.03735	2.91371	2.85498	2.79818	2.69006	2.58873	2.49364	2.40428	2.36160
5	3.69590	3.60478	3.43308	3.35216	3.27429	3.12717	2.99061	2.86364	2.74538	2.68928
6	4.23054	4.11141	3.88867	3.78448	3.68474	3.49760	3.32551	3.16692	3.02047	2.95142
7	4.71220	4.56376	4.28830	4.16042	4.03857	3.81153	3.60459	3.41551	3.24232	3.16114
8	5.14612	4.96764	4.63886	4.48732	4.34359	4.07757	3.83716	3.61927	3.42122	3.32891
9	5.53705	5.32825	4.94647	4.77158	4.60654	4.30302	4.03097	3.78628	3.56550	3.46313
10	5.88923	5.65022	5.21612	5.01877	4.83323	4.49409	4.19247	3.92318	3.68186	3.57050
11	6.20652	5.93770	5.45273	5.23371	5.02864	4.65601	4.32706	4.03540	3.77569	3.65640
12	6.49236	6.19437	5.66029	5.42062	5.19711	4.79322	4.43922	4.12737	3.85136	3.72512
13	6.74987	6.42355	5.84236	5.58315	5.34233	4.90951	4.53268	4.20277	3.91239	3.78010
14	6.98187	6.62817	6.00207	5.72448	5.46753	5.00806	4.61057	4.26456	3.96160	3.82408
15	7.19087	6.81086	6.14217	5.84737	5.57546	5.09158	4.67547	4.31522	4.00129	3.85926
16	7.37916	6.97399	6.26506	5.95423	5.66850	5.16235	4.72956	4.35673	4.03330	3.88741
17	7.54879	7.11963	6.37286	6.04716	5.74870	5.22233	4.77463	4.39077	4.05911	3.90993
18	7.70162	7.24967	6.46742	6.12797	5.81785	5.27316	4.81219	4.41866	4.07993	3.92794
19	7.83929	7.36578	6.55037	6.19823	5.87746	5.31624	4.84350	4.44152	4.09672	3.94235
20	7.96333	7.46944	6.62313	6.25933	5.92884	5.35275	4.86958	4.46027	4.11026	3.95388
21	8.07507	7.56200	6.68696	6.31246	5.97314	5.38368	4.89132	4.47563	4.12117	3.96311
22	8.17574	7.64465	6.74294	6.35866	6.01133	5.40990	4.90943	4.48822	4.12998	3.97049
23	8.26643	7.71843	6.79206	6.39884	6.04425	5.43212	4.92453	4.49854	4.13708	3.97639
24	8.34814	7.78432	6.83514	6.43377	6.07263	5.45095	4.93710	4.50700	4.14281	3.98111
25	8.42174	7.84314	6.87293	6.46415	6.09709	5.46691	4.94759	4.51393	4.14742	3.98489

REFERENCES

Chapter Opening Source Notes

Chapter 1: Colgate Annual Reports.

Chapter 2: Target Website, October 2005; Wal-Mart Web site, October 2005.

Chapter 3: Powers report to Enron Board of Directors, February 2002; Sarbanes-Oxley Act.

Chapter 4: Hewlett Packard 2005 10-K Report; IBM 2005 10-K Report; *Fortune,* March 7, 2005.

Chapter 5: Viacom 2004 and 2005 10-K Reports; "Buying Binge Could Cost Corporate America $1 Trillion; Accounting Change Forces Goodwill Write-Downs," *USA Today,* April 5, 2002.

Chapter 6: Kodak 2005 10-K Report; *BusinessWeek,* February 2004, July 2002, May and November 2001, and April 2000.

Chapter 7: Rite Aid Website and 2005 10-K Report; *BusinessWeek,* November 1999 and January 2000.

Chapter 8: Robin Goldwyn Blumenthal, "Review & Preview Follow-up–A Return Visit to Earlier Stories–Out of Fashion: Has GAP Lost Its Way?" *Forbes* April 18, 2005; GAP Inc. 2005 10-K Report.

Chapter 9: *BusinessWeek,* October 2004, April 2002, and July 2001.

Chapter 10: *Barron's,* May 2005; *Business Wire,* 2005; *BusinessWeek,* February, April, and July 2002; General Motors 2005 10-K Report.

Chapter 11: Berkshire Hathaway 2001 Annual Report and 2005 Website; *BusinessWeek,* October 2004.

Comprehensive Case: *Wall Street Journal,* September 2004; Campbell Soup 2004 Annual Report and 2005 Website; PiperJaffray Investment Report, 2005.

Abarbanell, J.; and B. Bushee. "Fundamental Analysis, Future Earnings, and Stock Prices." *Journal of Accounting Research* 35, 1997, pp. 1–24.

Abarbanell, J. S. "Do Analysts' Earnings Forecasts Incorporate Information in Prior Stock Price Changes?" *Journal of Accounting and Economics,* June 1991, pp. 147–66.

Abdel-khalik, R. A. *Economic Effects on Leases of FASB Statement No. 13, Accounting for Leases.* Stamford, CT: Financial Accounting Standards Board, 1981.

Aboody, D. "Market Valuation of Employee Stock Options." *Journal of Accounting and Economics* 22, 1996, pp. 357–91.

Aboody, D.; and B. Lev. "The Value Relevance of Intangibles: The Case of Software Capitalization." *Journal of Accounting Research* 36, 1998, pp. 161–91.

"Accounting by Creditors for Impairment of a Loan." *Statement of Financial Accounting Standards No. 114.* Norwalk, CT: 1993.

"Accounting by Creditors for Impairment of a Loan–Income Recognition and Disclosures." *Statement of Financial Accounting Standards No. 118.* Norwalk, CT: Financial Accounting Standards Board, 1994.

"Accounting for Leases: A New Approach." *FASB Special Report.* Norwalk, CT: Financial Accounting Standards Board, 1996.

"Accounting for the Costs of Computer Software Developed or Obtained for Internal Use." *AICPA Proposed Statement of Position.* New York: American Institute of Certified Public Accountants, 1997.

"Accounting for the Impairment of Long-Lived Assets to Be Disposed Of." *Statement of Financial Accounting Standards No. 121.* Norwalk, CT: Financial Accounting Standards Board, 1995.

"Accounting for Transfers and Servicing of Financial Assets and Extinguishments of Liabilities. *Statement of Financial Accounting Standards No. 125.* Norwalk, CT: Financial Accounting Standards Board, 1996.

Ahmed, A. "Accounting Earnings and Future Economic Rents: An Empirical Analysis." *Journal of Accounting and Economics* 17, 1994, pp. 377–400.

Ajinkya, B.; and M. Gift. "Corporate Managers' Earnings Forecasts and Symmetrical Adjustments of Market Expectations." *Journal of Accounting Research* 22, Autumn 1984, pp. 425–44.

Albrecht, W.; L. Lookabill; and J. McKeown. "The Time Series Properties of Annual Earnings." *Journal of Accounting Research* 15, 1977, pp. 226–44.

Ali, A.; A. Klein; and J. Rosenfeld. "Analysts' Use of Information About Permanent and Transitory Earnings Components in Forecasting Annual EPS." *Accounting Review* 67, 1992, pp. 183–98.

Ali, A.; L. Hwang; and M. Trombley. "Accruals and Future Returns: Tests of the Naive Investor Hypothesis." working paper, 1999, University of Arizona.

Altman, Edward I. "Financial Ratios, Discriminant Analysis and the Prediction of Corporate Bankruptcy." *Journal of Finance,* September 1968, pp. 589–609.

Amir, E. "The Effect of Accounting Aggregation on the Value-Relevance of Financial Disclosures: The Case of SFAS No. 106." *Accounting Review* 71, 1996, pp. 573–90.

Amir, E. "The Market Valuation of Accounting Information: The Case of Postretirement Benefits Other than Pensions." *Accounting Review* 68, 1993, pp. 703–24.

Amir, E.; T. S. Harris; and E. K. Venuti. "A Comparison of Value-Relevance of U.S. versus Non-U.S. GAAP Accounting Measures Using Form 20-F Reconciliations." *Journal of Accounting Research Supplement* 31, 1993, pp. 230–64.

Amir, E.; M. Kirschenheiler; and K. Willard. "The Valuation of Deferred Taxes." *Contemporary Accounting Research* 14, 1997, pp. 597–622.

Anthony, J.; and K. Ramesh. "Association between Accounting Performance Measures and Stock Prices: A Test of the Life Cycle Hypothesis." *Journal of Accounting and Economics* 15, 1992, pp. 203–27.

Atiase, R. K. "Predisclosure Information, Firm Capitalization and Security Price Behavior Around Earnings Announcements." *Journal of Accounting Research*, Spring 1985, pp. 21–36.

Atiase, R. K.; L. S. Bamber; and R. N. Freeman. "Accounting Disclosures Based on Company Size: Regulations and Capital Markets Evidence." *Accounting Horizons* 2, no. 1, March 1988, pp. 18–26.

Ayers, B. C. "Deferred Tax Accounting under SFAS No. 109: An Empirical Investigation of Its Incremental Value-Relevance Relative to APB No. 11." *Accounting Review* 73, 1998, pp. 195–212.

Backer, M.; and M. L. Gosman. *Financial Reporting and Business Liquidity.* New York: National Association of Accountants, 1978.

Bahnson, P.; P. Miller; and B. Budge. "Nonarticulation in Cash Flow Statements and Implications for Education, Research, and Practice." *Accounting Horizons* 10, 1996, pp. 1–15.

Baldwin, B. A. "Segment Earnings Disclosure and the Ability of Security Analysts to Forecast Earnings per Share." *The Accounting Review,* July 1984, pp. 376–89.

Ball, B. "The Mysterious Disappearance of Retained Earnings." *Harvard Business Review,* July–August 1987.

Ball, R.; and P. Brown. "An Empirical Evaluation of Accounting Income Numbers." *Journal of Accounting Research,* Autumn 1968, pp. 159–78.

Ball, R.; and R. Watts. "Some Time Series Properties of Accounting Income." *Journal of Finance* 27, 1972, pp. 663–82.

Balsam, S.; and R. Lipka. "Share Prices and Alternative Measures of Earnings per Share." *Accounting Review* 12, 1998, pp. 234–49.

Banz, R. W. "The Relation between Return and Market Value of Common Stocks." *Journal of Financial Economics* 9, 1981, pp. 3–18.

Barclay, M.; D. Gode; and S. Kothari. "Measuring Delivered Performance." working paper, 1999, Massachusetts Institute of Technology.

Barth, M.; W. Beaver; and W. Landsman. "Relative Valuation Roles of Equity Book Value and Net Income as a Function of Financial Health." *Journal of Accounting and Economics* 25, 1998, pp. 1–34.

Barth, M. E. "Fair Value Accounting: Evidence from Investment Securities and the Market Valuation of Banks." *Accounting Review* 69, 1994, pp. 1–25.

Barth, M. E. "Relative Measurement Errors among Alternative Pension Asset and Liability Measures." *The Accounting Review* 66, 1991, pp. 433–63.

Barth, M. E.; W. H. Beaver; and W. Landsman. "Value-Relevance of Banks' Fair Value Disclosures under SFAS No. 107." *The Accounting Review* 71, 1996, pp. 513–37.

Barth, M. E.; W. H. Beaver; and W. Landsman. "The Market Valuation Implications of Net Periodic Pension Cost Components." *Journal of Accounting and Economics* 15, 1992, pp. 27–62.

Barth, M. E.; M. Clement; G. Foster; and R. Kasznik; "Brand Values and Capital Market Valuation." *Review of Accounting Studies* 3, 1998, pp. 41–68.

Barth, M. E.; and G. Clinch. "Revalued Financial Tangible, and Intangible Assets: Associations with Share Prices and Non Market-Based Value Estimates." *Journal of Accounting Research* 36, 1998, pp. 199–233.

Barth, M. E.; D. P. Cram; and K. K. Nelson. "Accruals and the Prediction of Future Cash Flows." working paper, 1999, Stanford University.

Barth M. E.; and M. F. McNichols. "Estimation and Valuation of Environmental Liabilities." *Journal of Accounting Research,* Supplement 1994, pp. 177–209.

Bartov, E. "Foreign Currency Exposure of Multinational Firms: Accounting Measures and Market Valuation." *Contemporary Accounting Research* 14, 1997, pp. 623–52.

Bartov, Eli. "The Timing of Asset Sales and Earnings Manipulation." *The Accounting Review,* October 1993, pp. 840–55.

Basu, S. "The Conservatism Principle and the Asymmetric Timeliness of Earnings." *Journal of Accounting and Economics* 24, 1997, pp. 3–37.

Basu, S. "The Relationship between Earnings Yield, Market Value and Return for NYSE Common Stocks: Further Evidence." *Journal of Financial Economics* 12, 1983, pp. 129–56.

Bauman, C. C; M P. Bauman; and R. F. Halsey. "Do Firms Use the Deferred Tax Asset Valuation Allowance to Manage Earnings?" University of Wisconsin–Milwaukee, August 2000.

Bauman, M. P. "A Review of Fundamental Analysis Research in Accounting." *Journal of Accounting Literature,* 1996, pp. 1–33.

Bauman, M. P. "A Summary of Fundamental Analysis Research in Accounting." *Journal of Accounting Literature,* 1996.

Beaver, W.; and D. Morse. "What Determines Price-Earnings Ratios?" *Financial Analysts' Journal* 34, 1978, pp. 65–76.

Beaver, W. H. *Financial Reporting: An Accounting Revolution.* 2nd edition. Prentice-Hall, Englewood Cliffs, NJ, 1998.

Beaver, William H.; Paul Kettler; and Myron Scholes. "The Association between Market-Determined and Accounting Determined Risk Measures." *The Accounting Review,* October 1970, pp. 654–82.

Beneish, M.; and E. Press. "The Resolution of Technical Default." *The Accounting Review,* April 1995, pp. 337–53.

Bernard, V. "The Feltham-Ohlson Framework: Implications for Empiricists." *Contemporary Accounting Research,* Spring 1995, pp. 733–47.

Bernard, V.; and J. Noel. "Do Inventory Disclosures Predict Sales and Earnings?" *Journal of Accounting, Auditing and Finance,* Spring 1991, pp. 145–81.

Bernard, V.; and T. Stober. "The Nature and Amount of Information in Cash Flows and Accruals." *The Accounting Review* 64, October 1989, pp. 624–52.

Bernard, V.; and J. Thomas. "Post Earnings Announcement Drift: Delayed Price Response or Risk Premium?" *Journal of Accounting Research* (Supplement) 1989, pp. 1–48.

Bernard, V. L. "Accounting-Based Valuation Methods, Determinants of Market-to-Book Ratios and Implications for Financial Statements Analysis." University of Michigan (December 1994).

Biddle, G. C.; R. M. Bowen; and J. S. Wallace. "Does EVA Beat Earnings? Evidence on Associations with Stock Returns and Firm Values." *Journal of Accounting and Economics* 24, 1997, pp. 301–36.

Biddle, G. C.; and W. E. Ricks. "Analyst Forecast Errors and Stock Price Behavior Near the Earnings Announcement

Dates of LIFO Adopters." *Journal of Accounting Research,* Autumn 1988, pp. 169–94.

Biddle, Gary C.; and Frederick W. Lindahl. "Stock Price Reactions to LIFO Adoptions: The Association Between Excess Returns and LIFO Tax Savings." *Journal of Accounting Research,* Autumn 1982, Part II, pp. 551–88.

Biggs, Stanley F.; and John J. Wild. "An Investigation of Auditor Judgment in Analytical Review." *The Accounting Review* LX, no. 4, October 1985, pp. 607–33.

Black, E. "Which Is More Value Relevant: Earnings or Cash Flows?" working paper, 1999, University of Arkansas.

Blankley, Alan I.; and Edward P. Swanson. "A Longitudinal Study of SFAS 87 Pension Rate Assumptions." *Accounting Horizons,* December 1995, pp. 1–21.

Boblitz, B.; and M. Ettredge. "The Information in Discretionary Outlays: Advertising, Research and Development." *The Accounting Review,* January 1989, pp. 108–24.

Botosan, C. "Disclosure Level and the Cost of Equity Capital." *The Accounting Review* 72, 1997, pp. 323–50.

Bowen, R.; L. DuCharme; and D. Shores. "Stakeholders' Implicit Claims and Accounting Method Choice. *Journal of Accounting and Economics* 20, no. 3, 1995.

Bowen, R. M.; D. Burgstahler; and L. A. Daley. "The Incremental Information Content of Accruals versus Cash Flows." *The Accounting Review* 62, October 1987, pp. 723–47.

Bowen, R. M.; D. Burgstahler; and L. A. Daley. "Evidence of the Relationships between Earnings and Various Measures of Cash Flow." *The Accounting Review* 61, 1986, pp. 713–25.

Bowman, R. G. "The Theoretical Relationship between Systematic Risk and Financial Variables." *Journal of Finance,* June 1979, pp. 617–30.

Brealey, R.; and S. Myers. *Principles of Corporate Finance,* 5th edition, McGraw-Hill, NY, 1996.

Brown, L.; and J. Han. "Do Stock Prices Reflect the Implications of Current Earnings for Future Earnings for ARI Firms?" *Journal of Accounting Research.*

Bulow, Jeremy. "What Are Corporate Pension Liabilities?" *Quarterly Journal of Economics,* August 1982, pp. 435–42.

Burgstahler, D.; and I. Dichev. "Earnings Management to Avoid Earnings Decreases and Losses." *Journal of Accounting and Economics* 24, 1997, pp. 99–126.

Burgstahler; D.; and I. Dichev. "Earnings, Adaptation, and Equity Value." *The Accounting Review* 72, 1997, pp. 187–215.

Burgstahler, D.; J. Jiambalvo; and Y. Pyo. "The Informativeness of Cash Flows for Future Cash Flows." working paper, 1998, University of Washington.

"Business Combinations Prior to an Initial Public Offering and Determination of the Acquiring Corporation," *SEC Staff Accounting Bulletin 97.* Washington DC: SEC, 1996.

Callen, J. L.; J. Livnat; and S. Ryan. "Capital Expenditures: Value Relevance and Fourth Quarter Effects." *The Journal of Financial Statement Analysis,* Spring 1996, pp. 13–24.

Carhart, M. "On the Persistence of Mutual Fund Performance." *Journal of Finance* 52, 1997, pp. 57–73.

Chaney, P.; C. Hogan; and D. Jeter. "The Effect of Reporting Restructuring Charges on Analysts' Forecast Revisions and Errors." *Journal of Accounting and Economics* 27, 1999, pp. 261–84.

Chaney, P. K.; and D. C. Jeter. "The Effect of Deferred Taxes on Security Prices." *Journal of Accounting, Auditing and Finance* 9, 1994, pp. 91–116.

Chen, K.; and J. Wei. "Creditors' Decisions to Waive Violations of Accounting-Based Debt Covenants." *The Accounting Review,* April 1993, pp. 218–32.

Chen, Kung H.; and Thomas A. Shimerda. "An Empirical Analysis of Useful Financial Ratios." *Financial Management,* Spring 1981, pp. 51–60.

Cheng, C. S. A.; C. Lui; and T. F. Schaefer. "The Value-Relevance of SFAS No. 95 Cash Flows from Operations as Assessed by Security Market Effects." *Accounting Horizons* 11, 1997, pp. 1–15.

Choi, B.; D. W. Collins; and W. B. Johnson. "Valuation Implications of Reliability Differences: The Case of Nonpension Postretirement Obligations." *Accounting Review* 72, 1997, pp. 351–83.

Coller, M.; and J. L. Higgs. "Firm Valuation and Accounting for Employee Stock Options." *Financial Analyst Journal* 53, 1997, pp. 26–34.

Collins, D. W. "Predicting Earnings with Subentity Data: Some Further Evidence." *Journal of Accounting Research,* Spring 1976, pp. 163–77.

Collins, D. W.; and S. P. Kothari. "An Analysis of Intertemporal and Cross-Sectional Determinants of Earnings Response Coefficients." *Journal of Accounting and Economics* 11, 1989, pp. 143–81.

Collins, D. W.; S. P. Kothari; and J. Rayburn. "Firm Size and the Information Content of Prices with Respect to Earnings." *Journal of Accounting and Economics,* March 1987.

Collins, D. W.; E. L. Maydew; and I. S. Weiss. "Changes in the Value-Relevance of Earnings and Book Values over the Past Forty Years." *Journal of Accounting and Economics* 24, 1997, pp. 39–67.

Collis, David J.; and Cynthia Montgomery. *Corporate Strategy: Resources and the Scope of the Firm.* Burr Ridge, IL: Irwin/McGraw-Hill, 1997.

"Consolidated Financial Statements: Policy and Procedures," *FASB Exposure Draft.* Norwalk, CT: Financial Accounting Standards Board, 1996.

"Consolidation of Special-Purpose Entities under FAS 125." *EITF Report 96-20.* Norwalk, CT: Financial Accounting Standards Board, 1996.

Copeland, R. M.; and M. L. Moore. "The Financial Bath: Is It Common?" *MSU Business Topics,* Autumn 1972, pp. 63–69.

Copeland, T.; T. Koller; and J. Murrin. *Valuation: Measuring and Managing the Value of Companies,* 2nd ed. New York: John Wiley and Sons, 1996.

Cushing, B. E.; and M. J. LeClere. "Evidence on the Determinants of Inventory Accounting Policy Choice." *The Accounting Review,* April 1992, pp. 355–66.

Davis, H. Z.; and Y. C. Peles. "Measuring Equilibrating Forces of Financial Ratios." *The Accounting Review,* October 1993, pp. 725–47.

Davis, Harry Z.; Nathan Kahn; and Etzmun Rosen. "LIFO Inventory Liquidations: An Empirical Study." *Journal of Accounting Research,* Autumn 1984, pp. 480–96.

Davis, M. L. "Differential Market Reaction to Pooling and Purchase Methods." *The Accounting Review,* July 1990, pp. 696–709.

DeBondt, W.; and R. Thaler. "Further Evidence of Investor Overreaction and Stock Market Seasonality." *Journal of Finance* 42, 1987, pp. 557–81.

Dechow, P. M. "Accounting Earnings and Cash Flows as Measures of Firm Performance: The Role of Accounting Accruals." *Journal of Accounting and Economics* 18, 1994, pp. 3–42.

Dechow, P. M.; S. P. Kothari; and R. L. Watts. "The Relation between Earnings and Cash Flows." *Journal of Accounting and Economics* 25, 1998, pp. 133–68.

"Derivatives and Hedging: Questions, Answers, and Illustrative Examples." *FASB Staff Paper.* Norwalk, CT: Financial Accounting Standards Board, 1996.

Dhaliwal, D.; D. Guenther; and M. Trombley. "Inventory Accounting Method and Earnings-Price Ratios." *Contemporary Accounting Research.*

Dhaliwal, D.; K. R. Subramanyam; and R. Trezevant. "Is Comprehensive Income Superior to Net Income as a Measure of Firm Performance?" *Journal of Accounting and Economics* 26, 2000, pp. 43–67.

Dhaliwal, Dan S. "Measurement of Financial Leverage in the Presence of Unfunded Pension Liabilities." *The Accounting Review,* October 1986, pp. 651–61.

Dharan, B.; and B. Lev. "The Valuation Consequences of Accounting Changes: A Multiyear Examination." *Journal of Accounting, Auditing, and Finance* 8, 1993, pp. 475–94.

"Disclosure of Accounting Policies for Derivative Financial Instruments and Derivative Commodity Instruments and Disclosure of Quantitative and Qualitative Information about Market Risk Inherent in Derivative Financial Instruments." *SEC Release 33-7386.* Washington, DC: SEC, 1997.

"Disclosure of Information about Capital Structure." *Statement of Financial Accounting Standards No. 129.* Norwalk, CT: 1997.

Dopuch, N.; and M. Pincus. "Evidence of the Choice of Inventory Accounting Methods: LIFO versus FIFO." *Journal of Accounting Research,* Spring 1988, pp. 28–59.

Duke, J. C., and H. G. Hunt. "An Empirical Examination of Debt Covenant Restrictions and Accounting-Related Debt Proxies." *Journal of Accounting and Economics,* January 1990, pp. 45–63.

Dukes, R. E. "An Investigation of the Effects of Expensing Research and Development Costs on Security Prices." In *Proceedings of the Conference on Topical Research in Accounting,* ed. M. Schiff and G. Sorter, New York: Ross Institute of Accounting Research, New York University, 1976.

Dunne, K. M. "An Empirical Analysis of Management's Choice of Accounting Treatment for Business Combinations." *Journal of Accounting and Public Policy,* July 1990, pp. 111–33.

Durkee, D. A.; J. E. Groff; and J. R. Boatsman. "The Effect of Costly vs. Costless Pension Disclosure on Common Share Prices: The Case of SFAS 36." *Journal of Accounting Literature* 7, 1988, pp. 180–96.

"Earnings per Share." *Statement of Financial Accounting Standards No. 128.* Norwalk, CT: 1997.

Easton, P. D.; and T. S. Harris. "Earnings as an Explanatory Variable for Returns." *Journal of Accounting Research,* Spring 1991, pp. 19–36.

Easton, P. D.; T. S. Harris; and J. A. Ohlson. "Accounting Earnings Can Explain Most of Security Returns: The Case of Long Event Windows." *Journal of Accounting and Economics,* June/September 1992, pp. 119–42.

Easton, Peter D.; Trevor Harris; and James Ohlson. "Aggregate Accounting Earnings Can Explain Most of Security Returns: The Case of Long Run Intervals." *Journal of Accounting and Economics,* June/September 1992, pp. 119–42.

Eccher, E. A.; K. Ramesh; and S. R. Thiagarajan. "Fair Value Disclosures by Bank Holding Companies." *Journal of Accounting and Economics* 22, 1996, pp. 79–117.

Elam, Rick. "The Effect of Lease Data on the Predictive Ability of Financial Ratios." *The Accounting Review,* January 1975, pp. 25–53.

El-Gazzar, S. M.; S. Lilien; and V. Pastena. "Accounting for Leases by Lessees." *Journal of Accounting and Economics,* October 1986, pp. 217–37.

Elliott, J.; and D. Hanna. "Repeated Accounting Write-Offs and the Information Content of Earnings." *Journal of Accounting Research Supplement* 34, 1996, pp. 135–55.

Elliott, J. A; and W. H. Shaw. "Write-Offs as Accounting Procedures to Manage Perceptions." *Journal of Accounting Research,* Supplement 1988, pp. 91–119.

Elliott, John A.; and Donna R. Philbrick. "Accounting Changes and Earnings Predictability." *The Accounting Review,* January 1990, pp. 157–74.

Ely, K.; and G. Waymire. "Accounting Standard-Setting Organizations and Earnings Relevance: Longitudinal Evidence from NYSE Common Stocks 1927–93." *Journal of Accounting Research* 37, 1999, pp. 293–317.

Emery, G. W.; and K. O. Cogger. "The Measurement of Liquidity." *Journal of Accounting Research,* Autumn 1982, pp. 290–303.

"Employers' Accounting for Postemployment Benefits." *Statement of Financial Accounting Standards No. 112.* Norwalk, CT: Financial Accounting Standards Board, 1992.

Fairfield, P. "P/E, P/B and the Present Value of Future Dividends." *Financial Analysts Journal,* July/August 1994, pp. 23–31.

Fairfield, P. M.; R. J. Sweeney; and T. L. Yohn. "Accounting Classification and the Predictive Content of Earnings." *The Accounting Review,* July 1996, pp. 337–56.

Fairfield, P. M.; R. J. Sweeney; and T. L. Yohn. "Non-Recurring Items and Earnings Predictions." *The Journal of Financial Statement Analysis,* Summer 1996, pp. 30–40.

Fama, E. "Efficient Markets: II." *Journal of Finance* 46, 1991, pp. 1575–617.

Fama, E. "Efficient Capital Markets: A Review of Theory and Empirical Work." *Journal of Finance,* 1970.

Fama, E.; and K. French. "Forecasting Profitability and Earnings." *Journal of Business,* 2000.

Fama, E.; and K. French. "Size and Book-to-Market Factors in Earnings and Returns." *Journal of Finance* 50, 1995, pp. 131–56.

Fama, E.; and K. French. "Common Risk Factors in the Returns on Stocks and Bonds." *Journal of Financial Economics* 33, 1993, pp. 3–56.

Fama, E.; and K. French. "The Cross-Section of Expected Stock Returns." *Journal of Finance* 47, 1992, pp. 427–65.

Feltham, J.; and J. A. Ohlson. "Valuation and Clean Surplus Accounting for Operating and Financial Activities." *Contemporary Accounting Research,* Spring 1995, pp. 689–731.

Fesler, R. D. "Disclosure of Litigation Contingencies." *Journal of Accountancy,* July 1990, p. 15.

Finger, C. "The Ability of Earnings to Predict Future Earnings and Cash Flow." *Journal of Accounting Research* 32, 1994, pp. 210–23.

Francis, J.; D. Hanna; and L. Vincent, "Causes and Consequences of Discretionary Asset Write-Offs." *Journal of Accounting Research,* Supplement, 1996, pp. 117–34.

Francis, J.; P. Olsson; and D. Oswald. "Comparing the Accuracy and Explainability of Dividends, Cash Flows, and Abnormal Earnings Equity Valuation Models." working paper, 1997, University of Chicago.

Francis, J.; and K. Schipper. "Have Financial Statements Lost Their Relevance?" *Journal of Accounting Research* 37, 1999, pp. 319–52.

Freeman, R.; J. Ohlson; and S. Penman. "Book Rate-of-Return and Prediction of Earnings Changes: An Empirical Investigation." *Journal of Accounting Research* 20, 1982, pp. 639–53.

Freeman, R. N. "The Association between Accounting Earnings and Security Returns for Large and Small Firms." *Journal of Accounting and Economics,* July 1987, pp. 195–228.

Fried, D.; and D. Givoly. "Financial Analysts' Forecasts of Earnings: A Better Surrogate for Market Expectations." *Journal of Accounting and Economics,* October 1982, pp. 85–108.

Fried, D.; M. Schiff; and A. C. Sondhi. *Impairments and Writeoffs of Long-Lived Assets.* Montvale, NJ: National Association of Accountants, 1989.

Gaver, J. J.; K. M. Gaver; and J. R. Austin. "Additional Evidence on the Association between Income Management and Earnings-Based Bonus Plans." *Journal of Accounting and Economics,* February 1995, pp. 3–28.

Gentry, J. A.; P. Newbold; and D. Whitford. "Classifying Bankrupt Firms with Funds Flow Components." *Journal of Accounting Research,* Spring 1985, pp. 146–60.

Gibbons. M. R.; and P. Hess. "Day of the Week Effects and Asset Returns." *Journal of Business* 54, 1981, pp. 579–96.

Gill, S.; R. Gore; and L. Rees. "An Investigation of Asset Writedowns and Concurrent Abnormal Accruals." *Journal of Accounting Research,* Supplement 1997.

Ginay, W. "The Impact of Derivatives on Form Risk: An Examination of New Derivative Users." *Journal of Accounting and Economics* 26, 1999.

Givoly, D.; and C. Hayn. "The Valuation of the Deferred Tax Liability: Evidence from the Stock Market." *The Accounting Review,* April 1992, pp. 394–410.

Givoly, D.; and C. Hayn. "Transitory Accounting Items: Information Content and Earnings Management." Tel Aviv University and Northwestern University, 1993.

Gombola, M. F.; M. E. Haskins; J. E. Katz; and D. D. Williams. "Cash Flow in Bankrupt Prediction." *Financial Management,* Winter 1987.

Gopalakrishnan, V. "The Effect of Cognition vs. Disclosure on Investor Valuation: The Case of Pension Accounting." *Review of Quantitative Finance and Accounting* 4, 1994, pp. 383–96.

Gopalakrishnan, V.; and T. F. Sugrue. "An Empirical Investigation of Stock Market Valuation of Corporate Projected Pension Liabilities." *Journal of Business Finance and Accounting* 20, September 1993, pp. 711–24.

Greenstein, M. M.; and H. Sami. "The Impact of the SEC's Segment Disclosure Requirement on Bid-Ask Spreads." *The Accounting Review,* January 1994, pp. 179–99.

Guenther, D. A.; E. L. Maydew; and S. E. Nutter. "Financial Reporting, Tax Costs, and Book-Tax Conformity." *Journal of Accounting and Economics* 23, 1997, pp. 225–48.

Guenther, D. A.; and M. A. Trombley. "The 'LIFO Reserve' and the Value of the Firm: Theory and Empirical Evidence." *Contemporary Accounting Research,* Spring 1994, pp. 433–52.

Hackel, K. S.; and J. Livnat. *Cash Flow and Security Analysis,* 2nd ed. Homewood, IL: Business One-Irwin, 1995.

Hagerman, R. L.; M. E. Zmijewski; and P. Shah. "The Association Between the Magnitude of Quarterly Earnings Forecast Errors and Risk-Adjusted Stock Returns." *Journal of Accounting Research,* Autumn 1984, pp. 526–40.

Han, Jerry C. Y.; and John J. Wild. "Timeliness of Reporting and Earnings Information Transfers." *Journal of Business Finance and Accounting* 24, nos. 3–4, April 1997, pp. 527–40.

Han, Jerry C. Y.; and John J. Wild. "Stock Price Behavior Associated with Managers' Earnings and Revenue Forecasts." *Journal of Accounting Research* 29, no. 1, Spring 1991, pp. 79–95.

Han, Jerry C. Y.; and John J. Wild. "Unexpected Earnings and Intra-Industry Information Transfers: Further Evidence." *Journal of Accounting Research* 28, no. 1, Spring 1990, pp. 211–19.

Han, Jerry C. Y.; John J. Wild; and K. Ramesh. "Managers' Earnings Forecasts and Intra-Industry Information Transfers." *Journal of Accounting and Economics* 11, no. 1, February 1989, pp. 3–33.

Hand, J. "Resolving LIFO Uncertainty–A Theoretical and Empirical Reexamination of 1974–1975 LIFO Adoptions and Non-adoptions." *Journal of Accounting Research,* Spring 1993, pp. 21–49.

Harris, T. S.; and J. A. Ohlson. "Accounting Disclosures and the Market's Valuation of Oil and Gas Properties." *Accounting Review* 62, 1987, pp. 651–70.

Hawkins, D. F.; and W. J. Campbell. *Equity Valuation: Models, Analysis and Implications.* New York: Financial Executives Research Foundation, 1978.

Hayn, C. "The Information Content of Losses." *Journal of Accounting and Economics* 20, 1995, pp. 125–53.

Healy, P. "The Effect of Bonus Schemes on Accounting Decisions." *Journal of Accounting and Economics* 7, 1985, pp. 85–107.

Healy, P.; S. Myers; and C. Howe. "R&D Accounting and the Tradeoff between Relevance and Objectivity." working paper, 1999, Massachusetts Institute of Technology.

Heian, J. B.; and B. Thies. "Consolidation of Finance Subsidiaries: $230 Billion in Off-Balance-Sheet Financing Comes Home to Roost." *Accounting Horizons,* March 1989, pp. 1–9.

Henning, S. L.; and T. Stock. "The Value-Relevance of Goodwill Write-Offs." Unpublished working paper, 1997, Southern Methodist University.

Hickman, W. B. *Corporate Bond Quality and Investor Experience.* Princeton, NJ: Princeton University Press, 1958.

Hicks, J. R. *Value and Capital,* 2nd ed. Oxford: Chaundon Press, 1946.

Holthausen, R. W. "Evidence on the Effect of Bond Covenants and Management Compensation Contracts on the Choice of Accounting Techniques: The Case of the Depreciation Switch-Back." *Journal of Accounting and Economics* 3, 1981, pp. 73–79.

Holthausen, R. W.; D. F. Larcker; and R. G. Sloan. "Annual Bonus Schemes and the Manipulation of Earnings." *Journal of Accounting and Economics* 19, 1995, pp. 29–74.

Holthausen, R. W.; and K. Palepu. "Research Investigating the Economic Consequences of Accounting Standards." Unpublished working paper, 1995, University of Pennsylvania.

Hong, H.; R. S. Kaplan; and G. Mandelker. "Pooling vs. Purchase: The Effects of Accounting for Mergers on Stock Prices." *The Accounting Review,* January 1978, pp. 31–47.

Hopwood, W.; P. Newbold; and P. A. Silhan. "The Potential for Gains in Predictive Ability Through Disaggregation: Segmented Annual Earnings." *Journal of Accounting Research,* Autumn 1982, pp. 724–32.

Imhoff, E. A., Jr.; and J. K. Thomas. "Economic Consequences of Accounting Changes: The Lease Disclosure Rule Change." *Journal of Accounting and Economics,* December 1988, pp. 277–310.

"Impact of FASB Statement No. 125, 'Accounting for Transfers and Servicing of Financial Assets and Extinguishments of Liabilities,' on EITF Issues." *FASB Staff Paper.* Norwalk, CT: Financial Accounting Standards Board, 1996.

Jennings, R.; D. Mest; and R. B. Thompson. "Investor Reaction to Disclosures of 1974–75 LIFO Adoption Decisions." *The Accounting Review,* April 1992, pp. 337–54.

Jennings, R.; J. Robinson; R. B. Thompson II; and L. Duvall. "The Relation between Accounting Goodwill Numbers and Equity Values." *Journal of Business, Finance and Accounting,* June 1996, pp. 513–34.

Jennings, R.; P. Simko; and R. Thompson. "Does LIFO Inventory Accounting Improve the Income Statement at the Expense of the Balance Sheet?" *Journal of Accounting Research* 34, no. 1, 1996.

Johnson, W. B.; and D. S. Dhaliwal. "LIFO Abandonment." *Journal of Accounting Research,* Autumn 1988, pp. 236–72.

Kang, S. "A Conceptual Framework for the Stock Price Effect of LIFO Tax Benefits." *Journal of Accounting Research,* Spring 1993, pp. 50–61.

Kang, S.; and K. Sivaramakrishnan. "Issues in Testing Earnings Management and an Instrumental Variable Approach." *Journal of Accounting Research* 33, 1995, pp. 353–67.

Kim, M.; and G. Moore. "Economic vs. Accounting Depreciation." *Journal Accounting and Economics,* April 1988, pp. 111–25.

Kimmel, P.; and T. D. Warfield. "The Usefulness of Hybrid Security Classifications–Evidence from Redeemable Preferred Stock." *The Accounting Review,* January 1995, pp. 151–67.

Kimmel, P.; and T. D. Warfield. "Variation in Attributes of Redeemable Preferred Stock: Implications for Accounting Standards." *Accounting Horizons,* June 1993, pp. 30–40.

Kinney, M.; and R. H. Trezevant. "Taxes and the Timing of Corporate Capital Expenditures." *The Journal of the American Taxation Association,* 1993, pp. 40–62.

Klammer, T. P.; and S. A. Reed. "Operating Cash Flow Formats: Does Format Influence Decisions?" *Journal of Accounting and Public Policy,* 1990, pp. 217–35.

Kleim, D. B. "Size Related Anomalies and Return Seasonality: Further Empirical Evidence." *Journal of Financial Economics* 12, 1983, pp. 13–32.

Kormendi, R.; and R. Lipe. "Earnings Innovations, Earnings Persistence, and Stock Returns." *Journal of Business* 60, July 1987, pp. 323–45.

Kothari, S.; and J. Zimmerman. "Price and Return Models." *Journal of Accounting and Economics* 20, 1995, pp. 155–92.

Kothari, S. P. "Capital Markets Research in Accounting." Unpublished working paper. Massachusetts Institute of Technology.

Kross, W.; and D. Schroeder. "Firm Prominence and the Differential Information Content of Quarterly Earnings Announcements." *Journal of Business, Finance and Accounting,* Spring 1989, pp. 55–74.

Kwon, Sung S.; and John J. Wild. "The Informativeness of Annual Reports for Firms in Financial Distress." *Contemporary Accounting Research* 11, no. 1–II, Fall 1994, pp. 331–51.

Lakonishok, J.; A. Shleifer; and R. W. Vishny. "Contrarian Investment, Extrapolation and Risk." *Journal of Finance* 49, pp. 1541–578.

Lakonishok, J.; and S. Smidt. "Are Seasonal Anomalies Real? A Ninety Year Perspective." *Review of Financial Studies* 1, 1988, pp. 435–55.

Landsman, W. "An Empirical Investigation of Pension and Property Rights." *The Accounting Review,* October 1986, pp. 662–91.

Lasman, D. A.; and R. L. Weil. "Adjusting the Debt-Equity Ratio." *Financial Analysts Journal,* September/October 1978, pp. 49–58.

Lee, C. "Accounting-Based Valuation: A Commentary." *Accounting Horizons* 13, 1999, pp. 413–25.

Lee, C. "Inventory Accounting and Earnings/Price Ratios: A Puzzle." *Contemporary Accounting Research* 26, 1988, pp. 371–88.

Lee, C.; J. Myers; and B. Swaminathan. "What Is the Intrinsic Value of the Dow?" *Journal of Finance* 54, 1999, pp. 1693–742.

Lee, C.; A. Shleifer; and R. Thaler. "Investor Sentiment and the Closed-End Fund Puzzle." *Journal of Finance* 14, 1991, pp. 75–109.

Leftwich, R. W. "Accounting Information in Private Markets: Evidence from Private Lending Agreements." *The Accounting Review* 63, January 1983, pp. 23–42.

Lev, B. "On the Association between Operating Leverage and Risk." *Journal of Financial and Quantitative Analysis,* 1974, pp. 627–41.

Lev, B.; and T. Sougiannis. "The Capitalization, Amortization, and Value-Relevance of R&D." *Journal of Accounting and Economics,* February 1996, pp. 107–38.

Lev, B.; and S. R. Thiagarajan. "Fundamental Information Analysis." *Journal of Accounting Research* 31, Autumn 1993, pp. 190–215.

Lev, B.; and P. Zarowin. "The Boundaries of Financial Reporting and How to Extend Them." *Journal of Accounting Research* 37, 1999, pp. 353–86.

"Liability Recognition for Certain Employee Termination Benefits and Other Costs to Exit an Activity (Including Certain Costs Incurred in a Restructuring)." *EITF 94-3.* Norwalk, CT: Financial Accounting Standards Board, 1994.

Lin, H.; and M. McNichols. "Underwriting Relationships and Analysts' Earnings Forecasts and Investment Recommendations." *Journal of Accounting and Economics* 25, 1998, pp. 101–27.

Lipe, R. C. "The Information Contained in the Components of Earnings." *Journal of Accounting Research,* Supplement 1986, pp. 37–64.

Liu, C.; J. Livnat; and S. G. Ryan. "Forward-Looking Financial Information: The Order Backlog as a Predictor of Future Sales." *The Journal of Financial Statement Analysis,* Fall 1996, pp. 89–99.

Livnat, J.; and P. Zarowin. "The Incremental Information Content of Cash-Flow Components." *Journal of Accounting and Economics* 25, 1990, pp. 133–68.

Lys, T.; and L. Vincent. "An Analysis of Value Destruction at AT&T's Acquisition of NCR." *Journal of Financial Economics* 39, 1995, pp. 353–78.

Lys, T. Z. "Abandoning the Transactions-Based Accounting Model: Weighing the Evidence." *Journal of Accounting and Economics* 22, 1996, pp. 155–75.

Malkiel, B. *A Random Walk Down Wall Street.* J. B. Norton and Co., 1999.

Mandelker, G. M.; and S. G. Rhee. "The Impact of the Degrees of Operating and Financial Leverage on Systematic Risk of Common Stock." *Journal of Financial and Quantitative Analysis,* March 1984, pp. 45–57.

Martin, L. G.; and G. V. Henderson. "On Bond Ratings and Pension Obligations: A Note." *Journal of Financial and Quantitative Analysis,* December 1983, pp. 463–70.

McConnell, J. J.; and C. J. Muscarella. "Corporate Capital Expenditure Decisions and the Market Value of the Firm." *Journal of Financial Economics,* 1985, pp. 399–422.

McNichols, L.; and P. Wilson. "Evidence of Earnings Management from the Provision of Bad Debts." *Journal of Accounting Research Supplement* 26, 1988, pp. 1–31.

Mellman, M.; and L. A. Bernstein. "Lease Capitalization under APB Opinion No. 5." *The New York Certified Public Accountant,* February 1966, pp. 115–22.

Mendenhall, R. "Evidence on the Possible Underweighting of Earnings Related Information." *Journal of Accounting Research,* Spring 1991, pp. 170–79.

Mikhail, M.; B. Walther; and R. Willis. "Does Forecast Accuracy Matter to Security Analysts?" *The Accounting Review* 74, 1999, pp. 185–200.

Mittelstaedt, H. F.; W. D. Nichols; and P. R. Regier. "SFAS No. 106 and Benefit Reduction in Employer-Sponsored Retiree Health Care Plans." *The Accounting Review,* October 1995, pp. 535–56.

Mittelstaedt, H. F.; and M. J. Warshawski. "The Impact of Liabilities for Retiree Health Benefits on Share Prices." *Journal of Risk and Insurance* 60, 1993, pp. 13–35.

Mohrman, M. B. "The Use of Fixed GAAP Provisions in Debt Contracts." *Accounting Horizons,* September 1996, pp. 78–91.

Morck, R.; A. Shleifer; and R. W. Vishny. "Do Managerial Objectives Drive Bad Acquisitions?" *Journal of Finance,* March 1990, pp. 31–48.

Moses, D. "Income Smoothing and Incentives: Empirical Tests Using Accounting Changes." *The Accounting Review,* April 1987, pp. 358–77.

Mulford, C. W. "The Importance of a Market Value Measurement of Debt in Leverage Ratios: Replications and Extensions." *Journal of Accounting Research,* Autumn 1985, pp. 897–906.

Murdoch, B. "The Information Content of FAS 33 Returns on Equity." *The Accounting Review,* April 1986, pp. 273–87.

Nakayama, M.; S. Lilien; and M. Benis. "Due Process and FAS No. 13." *Management Accounting,* April 1981, pp. 49–53.

Nathan, K. "Do Firms Pay to Pool? Some Empirical Evidence." *Journal of Accounting and Public Policy* 7, 1988, pp. 185–200.

Nissim, D.; and S. Penman, unpublished manuscript, March 2001.

Noe, C. "Voluntary Disclosures and Insider Transactions." *Journal of Accounting and Economics* 27, 1999, pp. 305–26.

Ohlson, J. A. "Earnings, Book Values, and Dividends in Equity Valuation." *Contemporary Accounting Research,* Spring 1995, pp. 661–87.

Ohlson, J. A.; and B. E. Juettuer-Nauroth. "Expected EPS and EPS Growth as Determinants of Value." Working paper, September 2000.

Ou, J. A.; and S. H. Penman. "Accounting Measurement, Price-Earnings Ratio, and the Information Content of Security Prices." *Journal of Accounting Research,* Supplement 1989, pp. 111–44.

Ou, J. A.; and S. H. Penman. "Financial Statement Analysis and the Prediction of Stock Returns." *Journal of Accounting and Economics,* November 1989, pp. 295–329.

Penman, S. "The Articulation of Price-Earnings Ratios and Market-to-Book Ratios and the Evaluation of Growth." *Journal of Accounting Research,* Autumn 1996, pp. 235–59.

Penman, S.; and T. Sougiannis. "A Comparison of Dividend, Cash Flow, and Earnings Approaches to Equity Valuation." working paper, 1995, University of California at Berkeley.

Penman, S. H. "Return to Fundamentals." *Journal of Accounting, Auditing and Finance,* Fall 1992, pp. 465–83.

Penman, S. H. "An Evaluation of Accounting Rate-of-Return." *Journal of Accounting, Auditing and Finance,* Spring 1991, pp. 233–55.

Pfeiffer, R. J.; P. T. Elgers; M. H. Lo; and L. L. Rees. "Additional Evidence on the Incremental Information Content of Cash Flows and Accruals: The Impact of Errors in Measuring Market Expectations." *The Accounting Review* 73, July 1998, pp. 373–86.

Philbrick, D.; and W. Ricks. "Using Value Line and IBES Analyst Forecasts in Accounting Research." *Journal of Accounting Research* 29, 1991, pp. 397–417.

Porter, Michael E. *Competitive Advantage: Creating and Sustaining Superior Performance.* New York: The Free Press, 1985.

Porter, Michael E. *Competitive Strategy.* New York: The Free Press, 1980.

Pourciau, S. "Earnings Management and Nonroutine Executive Changes." *Journal of Accounting and Economics* 16, 1993, pp. 317–36.

Pownall, G.; C. Wasley; and G. Waymire. "The Stock Price Effects of Alternative Types of Management Earnings Forecasts." *The Accounting Review* 68, 1993, pp. 896–912.

Press, E. G.; and J. B. Weintrop. "Accounting-Based Constraints in Public and Private Debt Agreements." *Journal of Accounting and Economics,* January 1990, pp. 65–95.

Ramakrishnan, R.; and R. Thomas. "Valuation of Permanent, Transitory, and Price-Irrelevant Components of Reported Earnings." *Journal of Accounting and Finance* 13, 1998.

Ramakrishnan, R.; and R. Thomas. "What Matters from the Past: Market Value, Book Value, or Earnings? Earnings Valuation and Sufficient Statistics for Prior Information." *Journal of Accounting and Finance* 7, 1992, pp. 423–64.

Rayburn, J. "The Association of Operating Cash Flow and Accruals with Security Returns." *Journal of Accounting Research* 24, Supplement 1986, pp. 112–33.

"Recognition of Liabilities in Connection with a Purchase Business Combination." *EITF 95-3.* Norwalk, CT: Financial Accounting Standards Board, 1994.

Rees, L.; and P. Elgers. "The Market's Valuation of Nonreported Accounting Measures: Retrospective Reconciliations of non-U.S. and U.S. GAAP." *Journal of Accounting Research* 35, 1997, pp. 115–27.

Reeve, J. H.; and K. G. Stanga. "The LIFO Pooling Decision: Some Empirical Results from Accounting Practices." *Accounting Horizons,* March 1987, pp. 25–34.

Reilly, F. K. "Using Cash Flows and Financial Ratios to Predict Bankruptcies." *Analyzing Investment Opportunities in Distressed and Bankrupt Companies.* Charlottesville, VA: The Institute of Chartered Financial Analysts, 1991.

Reinganum, M. R. "Misspecification of Capital Asset Pricing: Empirical Anomalies Based on Earnings Yields and Market Values." *Journal of Financial Economics* 9, 1981, pp. 19–46.

Robinson, J. R., and P. B. Shane. "Acquisition Accounting Method and Bid Premia for Target Firms." *The Accounting Review,* January 1990, pp. 25–48.

Schipper, K. "Commentary on Earnings Management." *Accounting Horizons* 3, 1989, pp. 91–102.

Schrand, C. M. "The Association between Stock-Price Interest Rate Sensitivity and Disclosures about Derivative Instruments." *Accounting Review* 72, 1997, pp. 87–109.

Selling, T. I.; and C. P. Stickney. "Disaggregating the Rate of Return on Common Shareholders' Equity: A New Approach." *Accounting Horizons,* December 1990, pp. 9–17.

Shevlin, T. "The Valuation of R&D Firms with R&D Limited Partnerships." *The Accounting Review* 66, January 1991, pp. 1–21.

Shevlin, T. J. "Taxes and Off-Balance-Sheet Financing: Research and Development Limited Partnerships." *The Accounting Review,* July 1987, pp. 480–509.

Shiller, R. J. *Market Volatility.* Cambridge, Massachusetts: The MIT Press, 1989.

Skinner, D. J. "How Well Does Net Income Measure Firm Performance? A Discussion of Two Studies." *Journal of Accounting and Economics* 26, 1999, pp. 105–11.

Skinner, D. J. "Are Disclosures about Bank Derivatives and Employee Stock Options 'Value-Relevant'?" *Journal of Accounting and Economics* 22, 1996, pp. 393–405.

Skinner, R. C. "Fixed Asset Lives and Replacement Cost Accounting." *Journal of Accounting Research*, Spring 1982, pp. 210–26.

Sloan, R. "Do Stock Prices Fully Reflect Information in Accruals and Cash Flows about Future Earnings?" *The Accounting Review* 71, July 1996, pp. 289–315.

Smith, C.; and L. M. Wakeman. "Determinants of Corporate Leasing Policy." *Journal of Finance*, July 1985, pp. 895–908.

Smith, C.; and J. B. Warner. "On Financial Contracting: An Analysis of Bond Covenants." *Journal of Financial Economics*, June 1979, 117–61.

Soffer, L.; and T. Lys. "Post-Earnings Announcement Drift and the Dissemination of Predictable Information." *Contemporary Accounting Research* 16, 1999, pp. 305–31.

Sougiannis, T. "The Accounting Based Valuation of Corporate R&D." *The Accounting Review* (January 1994): pp. 44–68.

Stewart, G., III. *The Quest for Value.* New York: Harper Business, 1991.

Stickel, S. E. "The Effect of Value Line Investment Survey Rank Changes on Common Stock Prices." *Journal of Financial Economics* 14, 1985, pp. 121–44.

Stober, T. L. "The Incremental Information Content of Financial Statement Disclosures: The Case of LIFO Liquidations." *Journal of Accounting Research*, Supplement 1986, pp. 138–60.

"Streamlining Disclosure Requirements Relating to Significant Business Acquisitions," *SEC Release 33-7355.* Washington, DC: SEC, 1996.

Subramanyam, K. "The Pricing of Discretionary Accruals." *Journal of Accounting and Economics* 22, 1996, pp. 249–81.

Subramanyam, K. "Uncertain Precision and Price Reaction to Information." *The Accounting Review* 71, 1996, pp. 207–20.

Subramanyam, K. R.; and J. J. Wild. "Going Concern Status, Earnings Persistence, and Informativeness of Earnings." *Contemporary Accounting Research* 13, no. 1 (Spring 1996), pp. 251–73.

Swaminathan, S. "The Impact of SEC Mandated Segment Data on Price Variability and Divergence of Beliefs." *The Accounting Review*, January 1991, pp. 23–41.

Sweeney, A. P. "Debt-Covenant Violations and Managers' Accounting Responses." *Journal of Accounting and Economics* 17, 1994, pp. 281–308.

Teoh, S.; I. Welch; and T. Wong. "Earnings Management and the Long-Run Underperformance of Seasoned Equity Offerings." *Journal of Financial Economics* 50, 1998, pp. 63–100.

Teoh, S. H.; I. Welch; and T. J. Wong. "Earnings Management and the Long-Run Performance of IPOs." *Journal of Finance* 53, 1998, pp. 1935–974.

"The Valuation of R&D Firms with R&D Limited Partnerships." *The Accounting Review*, January 1991, pp. 1–22.

Thomas, J. K. "Why Do Firms Terminate Their Overfunded Pension Plans?" *Journal of Accounting and Economics*, November 1989, pp. 361–98.

Trombley, M. A.; and D. A. Guenther. "Should Earnings and Book Values Be Adjusted for LIFO?" *The Journal of Financial Statement Analysis*, Fall 1995, pp. 26–32.

Tse, S. "LIFO Liquidations." *Journal of Accounting Research*, Spring 1990, pp. 229–38.

Venkatachalam, M. "Value-Relevance of Banks' Derivatives Disclosures." *Journal of Accounting and Economics* 22, 1996, pp. 327–55.

Vigeland, R. L. "The Market Reaction to Statement of Financial Accounting Standards No. 2." *The Accounting Review*, April 1981, pp. 309–25.

Vincent, L. "Equity Valuation Implications of Purchase versus Pooling Accounting." *Journal of Financial Statement Analysis* 2, 1997, pp. 5–20.

Warfield, T.; J. J. Wild; and K. L. Wild. "Managerial Ownership, Accounting Choices, and Informativeness of Earnings." *Journal of Accounting and Economics* 20, July 1995, pp. 61–91.

Warfield, T. D.; and J. J. Wild. "Accounting Recognition and the Relevance of Earnings as an Explanatory Variable for Returns." *The Accounting Review* 67, October 1992, pp. 821–42.

Whisenant, J. S. "Does Fundamental Analysis Produce More Value-Relevant Summary Measures?" Unpublished working paper, 1998, Georgetown University.

Wild, J. J. "The Prediction Performance of a Structural Model of Accounting Numbers." *Journal of Accounting Research* 25, no. 1, Spring 1987, pp. 139–60.

Wild, J. J.; and S. S. Kwon. "Earnings Expectations, Firm Size, and the Informativeness of Stock Prices." *Journal of Business Finance and Accounting* 21, no. 7 (October 1994), pp. 975–96.

Wild, John J. "The Audit Committee and Earnings Quality." *Journal of Accounting, Auditing and Finance* 11, no. 2, Winter 1996.

Wild, John J. "Stock Price Informativeness of Accounting Numbers: Evidence on Earnings, Book Values, and Their Components." *Journal of Accounting and Public Policy* 11, no. 2, Summer 1992, pp. 119–54.

Williamson, R. W. "Evidence on the Selective Reporting of Financial Ratios." *The Accounting Review*, April 1984, pp. 296–99.

Wilson, P. G. "The Relative Information Content of Accruals and Cash Flows: Combined Evidence at the Earnings Announcement and Annual Report Release Date." *Journal of Accounting Research*, Supplement 1986, pp. 165–200.

Xie, H. "Are Discretionary Accruals Mispriced? A Reexamination." working paper, 1997, University of Iowa.

Zarowin, P. "What Determines Earnings-Price Ratios: Revisited." *Journal of Accounting Auditing and Finance*, Summer 1990, pp. 439–54.

Ziebart, D. A.; and D. H. Kim. "An Examination of the Market Reactions Associated with SFAS No. 8 and SFAS No. 52." *The Accounting Review*, April 1987, pp. 343–57.

INDEX

Page numbers followed by n indicate material found in footnotes.

```
┌─────────────────────────────┐      ┌─────────────────────────────┐      ┌─────────────────────────────┐
│ Return on invested capital  │      │ Profitability               │      │ Asset utilization and       │
│                             │      │                             │      │ efficiency                  │
│ Return on net operating     │      │ Gross profit margin         │      │ Net operating assets        │
│   assets (RNOA)             │      │ Net operating profit margin │      │   turnover                  │
│ Return on common equity     │      │ Earnings per share          │      │ Accounts receivable turnover│
│   (ROCE)                    │      │ Book value per share        │      │ Days' sales in receivables  │
│ Equity growth rate          │      │ Effective interest rate     │      │ Inventory turnover          │
│ Sustainable equity growth   │      │ Operating cash flow to      │      │ Days' sales in inventory    │
│ Dividend payout rate        │      │   income                    │      │ Net operating working capital│
│ Effective tax rate          │      │                             │      │   turnover                  │
│                             │      │                             │      │ Long-term operating asset   │
│                             │      │                             │      │   turnover                  │
│                             │      │                             │      │ Accounts payable turnover   │
└─────────────────────────────┘      └─────────────────────────────┘      └─────────────────────────────┘
```

† Certain measures can be c

Definitions

Return on invested capital
Return on net operating assets (RNOA) = Net operating profit after tax/Average net operating assets
Return on common equity (ROCE) = (Net income − Preferred dividend)/Average common shareholders' equity
Equity growth rate = (Net income − Preferred dividend − Dividend payout)/Average common equity
Sustainable equity growth = ROCE × (1 − Dividend payout rate)
Dividend payout rate = Cash dividends paid/Net income
Effective tax rate = Tax expense/Income before income tax

Profitability
Gross profit margin = (Sales − Cost of sales)/Sales
Net operating profit margin = Net operating profit after tax/Sales
Earnings per share (basic) = (Net income − Preferred dividend)/Weighted average of shares outstanding
Book value per share = (Shareholders' equity − Preferred equity)/Number of shares outstanding
Effective interest rate = Total interest incurred/Average interest-bearing indebtedness
Operating cash flow to income = Operating cash flow/Net income

Asset utilization and efficiency
Net operating assets turnover = Sales/Average net operating assets
Accounts receivable turnover = Sales/Average accounts receivable
Days' sales in receivables = (Accounts receivable × 360)/Sales
Inventory turnover = Cost of sales/Average inventory
Days' sales in inventory = (Inventory × 360)/Cost of sales
Net operating working capital turnover = Sales/Average net operating working capital
Long-term operating asset turnover = Sales/Average long-term operating assets
Accounts payable turnover = Cost of sales/Average accounts payable

Liquidity
Current ratio = Current assets/Current liabilities
Working capital = Current assets − Current liabilities
Acid-test (quick) ratio = (Cash + Cash equivalents + Marketable securities + Accounts receivable)/Current liabilities
Accounts receivable turnover = Sales/Average accounts receivable
Days' sales in receivables = (Accounts receivable × 360)/Sales
Inventory turnover = Cost of sales/Average inventory
Days' sales in inventory = (Inventory × 360)/Cost of sales

‡ Number of days in a year is 360 for ratio